The SAGE Handbook of

Human Resource Management

Edited by

Adrian Wilkinson, Nicolas Bacon, Tom Redman and Scott Snell

Los Angeles | London | New Delhi
Singapore | Washington DC

SAGE Publications Ltd
1 Oliver's Yard
55 City Road
London EC1Y 1SP

SAGE Publications Inc.
2455 Teller Road
Thousand Oaks, California 91320

SAGE Publications India Pvt Ltd
B 1/I 1 Mohan Cooperative Industrial Area
Mathura Road
New Delhi 110 044

SAGE Publications Asia-Pacific Pte Ltd
33 Pekin Street #02-01
Far East Square
Singapore 048763

Library of Congress Control Number: 2009920727

British Library Cataloguing in Publication data
A catalogue record for this book is available from the British Library

ISBN 978-1-4129-2829-8

Typeset by CEPHA Imaging Pvt. Ltd., Bangalore, India
Printed in Great Britain by MPG Books Group, Bodmin, Cornwall
Printed on paper from sustainable resources

Mixed Sources
Product group from well-managed
forests and other controlled sources
www.fsc.org Cert no. SA-COC-1565
© 1996 Forest Stewardship Council

Contents

Acknowledgements

As with any book, the list of acknowledgements could be extensive, but what follows are the most important. Thanks to our editor and, as usual, our family and friends, who make the major contribution. We are grateful to the contributors' families for their support while the book was being written.

Notes on Contributors

Stephen Bach is Professor of Employment Relations at the Department of Management, King's College, University of London. His research focuses on public service HRM and changing workforce roles. His research interests include: international migration of health professionals; assistant roles in the public services; human resource management in the health sector and the future of public service trade unions. He is author of *Employment Relations and the Health Service: The Management of Reforms*, London: Routledge, 2004 and editor of *Managing Human Resources: Personnel Management in Transition*, 4th edition, Blackwell, 2005. He is a member of the Editorial Board of *Personnel Review* and *Human Resources for Health*. Stephen has acted as an advisor to the International Labour Organisation; Organisation of Economic Cooperation and Development; World Health Organisation and the UN University.

Nicolas Bacon is Professor of Human Resource Management, Nottingham University Business School, UK. His current research on trade unions includes partnership agreements, negotiations to change working practices and union learning representatives: the employment effects of buyouts and shareholder value management; and employment practices in small and medium-sized enterprises. He was editor of the *Industrial Relations Journal for several years.*

Greg Bamber is a Professor and Director of Research, Department of Management, Monash University, Melbourne, Australia. His (joint) publications include, *Up in the Air* (Cornell); *International and Comparative Employment Relations* (Sage/Allen & Unwin): *Employment Relations in the Asia Pacific* (Thomson), *Managing Managers* (Blackwell); *Organisational Change Strategies* (Longman). He has published many articles and is on the editorial board of several journals. He is conducting research on notions of high-performance human resource management in hospitals and other sectors. He has served as: an arbitrator for the British Advisory, Conciliation and Arbitration Service; President: Australian & New Zealand Academy of Management, and of the International Federation of Scholarly Associations of Management. He is also a Fellow of the British Academy of Management; an Adjunct Professor, Griffith University, Australia; and Visiting Professor, Newcastle University, England. He has been a visitor at a range of universities in other countries

Michael Barry is Associate Professor in employment relations at Griffith University. His major research interests are comparative employment relations, worker representation and employee voice, and employer associations. Michael has published on employment relations in various industries, including mining, maritime, meat, and low cost airlines. He is also an elected academic staff representative on the Council of Griffith University.

Brian E. Becker received his Ph.D. from the University of Wisconsin-Madison in 1977. He is currently Professor of Human Resources in the School of Management at the State University of

New York at Buffalo. Professor Becker has held several leadership positions in the School, serving as department chair for 13 years and currently as Senior Associate Dean. He has published widely on the financial effects of employment systems, in both union and non-union organizations. His current research and consulting interests focus on the relationship between human resources systems, strategy implementation and firm performance. In addition to a wide range of articles on these topics, Professor Becker is co-author of *The HR Scorecard: Linking People, Strategy and Performance* (Harvard Business School Press, 2001) and *The Workforce Scorecard: Managing Human Capital to Execute Strategy* (Harvard Business School Press, 2005). His most recent book (co-authored with Mark A. Huselid and Richard Beatty) is *The Differentiated Workforce*, published by HBS Press in 2009.

Devasheesh Bhave is an assistant professor at Concordia University's John Molson School of Business. He received his PhD at the Carlson School of Management, University of Minnesota. His research spans issues related to the employment relationship, electronic performance monitoring, and emotional regulation in the workplace.

Paul Boselie is an Associate Professor in Human Resource Studies in the Faculty of Social and Behavioral Sciences at Tilburg University. His research traverses HRM and performance, new institutionalism, HRM and compliance, HR roles and competencies, and people management in health care. He is the European Editor of *Personnel Review*. Paul's research has been published in *Applied Psychology, Human Relations, Human Resource Management Journal, International Journal of HRM, International Journal of Manpower, Journal of Management Studies, Management Revue* and *Personnel Review*. In 2010 his book on *Strategic Human Resource Management* (McGraw-Hill) will be published focused on a European continental HR approach.

Michelle Brown is an Associate Professor in the Department of Management & Marketing, University of Melbourne, Australia. Her research interests are in the areas of pay and performance management systems, employee involvement and organisational cynicism. Her research seeks to understand the unintended consequences of human resource management policies and practices. Recent papers have been published in *Human Resource Management, Industrial and Labor Relations Review, Journal of Labor Research* and *Asia Pacific Journal of Human Resources*.

John W. Budd is the Industrial Relations Land Grant Chair at the University of Minnesota's Carlson School of Management. His current research interests include theorizing work, unionism over the life course, and other industrial relations topics. His books include *Employment with a Human Face: Balancing Efficiency, Equity, and Voice* (Cornell University Press), *Labor Relations: Striking a Balance* (McGraw-Hill/Irwin), and *Invisible Hands, Invisible Objectives: Bringing Workplace Law and Public Policy Into Focus* (with Stephen Befort, Stanford University Press).

Pawan S. Budhwar is a Professor of International Human Resource Management and Head of Work and Organisational Psychology Group at Aston Business School. He is also the Director of the Aston India Foundation for Applied Business Research and Aston Centre for Human Resources. He received his doctorate from Manchester Business School. Pawan has published a large number of articles on People Management related topics for the Indian context in leading journals such as Organizational Behavior and Human Decision Processes, Journal of World Business, Organization Studies, Journal of International Business Studies, Journal of Organizational Behaviour, Journal of Labor Research, International Journal of HRM and British

Journal of Management. He has also written and co-edited books on HRM in the Asia-Pacific, HRM in the Middle-East, HRM in Developing Countries, Performance Management Around the Globe, the Changing Face of People Management in India and Major Works in International HRM. He is the Senior Associate Editor of British Journal of Management and Associate Editor of International Journal of Cross Cultural Management. Pawan is also an advisor to the Commonwealth Commission on Scholarships and Fellowships and a Fellow of the Higher Education Academy.

Wayne F. Cascio received his Ph.D. in industrial and organizational psychology from the University of Rochester. Currently he holds the Robert H. Reynolds Chair in Global Leadership at the University of Colorado Denver. He has served as president of the Society for Industrial and Organizational Psychology, Chair of the SHRM Foundation, the HR Division of the Academy of Management, and as a member of the Academy of Management's Board of Governors. He has authored or edited 22 books on human resource management, including *Investing in People* (with John Boudreau, 2008), *Managing Human Resources* (8th ed., 2010), and *Applied Psychology in Human Resource Management* (7th ed., with Herman Aguinis, forthcoming). He is a two-time winner of the best-paper award from the *Academy of Management Executive* for his research on downsizing and responsible restructuring. In 1999 he received the Distinguished Career award from the HR Division of the Academy of Management. He received an honorary doctorate from the University of Geneva (Switzerland) in 2004, and in 2008 he was named by the *Journal of Management* as one of the most influential scholars in management in the past 25 years. Dr. Cascio is an elected Fellow of the National Academy of Human Resources, the Academy of Management, and the American Psychological Association.

Derek Chapman is an Associate Professor in the Department of Psychology at the University of Calgary, in Alberta, Canada. He earned his Ph.D. in Industrial and Organizational Psychology from the University of Waterloo in 2000. His current research interests focus on recruiting, person-organization fit, selection interviews, and technology use in recruiting and selection. His work has appeared in a variety of publications including the *Journal of Applied Psychology, Personnel Psychology, Journal of Vocational Behavior, Journal of Occupational and Organizational Psychology* and *the International Journal of Selection and Assessment*.

Saba Colakoglu received her Ph.D in Industrial Relations and Human Resources from the School of Management and Labor Relations at Rutgers University. She is currently an Assistant Professor of Management at Berry College, Campbell School of Business in Rome, GA. Her research focuses on knowledge management, strategic human resource management, and expatriate assignment management in multinational corporations. Saba has presented her work at the annual conferences of the Academy of Management and her research on these topics appeared in the *International Journal of Human Resource Management, Human Resource Management Review, and Human Resource Management Journal*.

Fang Lee Cooke is Professor of Human Resource Management and Chinese Studies at Manchester Business School, the University of Manchester. She received her PhD from the University of Manchester, UK. Her research interests are in the area of employment relations, trade unions, gender and employment, strategic HRM, knowledge management and innovation, outsourcing, Chinese outward FDI and Chinese diaspora. Fang is the author of *HRM, Work and Employment in China* (2005) and *Competition, Strategy and Management in China* (2008). She has published over 80 academic journal articles and book chapters, in addition to numerous refereed international conference papers.

Yaw A. Debrah is Professor of Human Resource and International Management at the Swansea University (University of Wales, Swansea), UK. He earned his Ph.D from Warwick Business School, Warwick University, UK. He has held academic positions at Brunel University, Cardiff University (University of Wales, Cardiff, UK), and Nanyang Technological University, Singapore). In addition he has worked in Africa, Canada and USA. He has published numerous articles on HRM in Asia and HRM and International Business/Management in Africa. In addition, he has edited five books including *Migrant Workers in Asia, Globalization, Work, and Employment, Managing Human Resources in Africa and Human Resource Management in Developing Countries. His scholarly work has appeared in journals such as Human Relations, Journal of Applied Psychology, Organizational Behaviour, International Journal of Human Resource Management, Asia Pacific Journal of Management; Asia-Pacific Journal of Human Resources, Asia- Pacific Business Review, Australian Journal of Management, and Thunderbird International Business Review*. He is on the editorial board of International Journal of Human Resource Management, Ghana Policy Review, African Journal of Economic and Management Studies and Scientific Journal of Administrative Development.

Graham Dietz is a Lecturer in HRM and Organisational Behavior at Durham Business School, Durham University. He is also the Director of the school's four MA programmes. He completed his doctorate on workplace partnership at the London School of Economics in 2002. His research revolves around trust in the workplace: how it is built, maintained and enhanced, but also how it can be repaired again after it is destroyed. He has published in several leading international journals, including *Academy of Management Review, International Journal of Human Resource Management* and *Human Resource Management Journal*. He is currently working on research into the influence of trust dynamics on the formation of new joint consultative committees.

Lee Dyer is professor of Human Resource Management and Chair of the Department of Human Resource Studies at the ILR School, Cornell University. He holds BBA, MBA, and Ph.D. degrees from the University of Wisconsin-Madison. His research and teaching interests focus on organizational agility and complexity and human resource strategy. He has consulted and lectured on these and related topics world-wide. He has published several dozen journal articles and book chapters and over a dozen books and monographs. His editorial board assignments include *People and Strategy, International Journal of Human Resource Management, and Asia Pacific Journal of Human Resources*. He served as founding director of Cornell's Center for Advanced Human Resource Studies (CAHRS) for eight years and currently sits on the Center's Advisory Board. Professor Dyer was elected a Fellow of the National Academy of Human Resources in 1994 and received the Academy of Management's Herbert G. Heneman Jr. Career Achievement Award in 2003 and the Society of Human Resource Management's Michael R. Losey Human Resource Research Award in 2004.

Paul Edwards is Professor of Industrial Relations at Warwick Business School. His research interests include new forms of work organization, comparative workplace employee relations and employee relations in small firms. He was formerly deputy director and director of IRRU, editor of *Work, Employment and Society* and associate editor of *Human Relations*. He was elected a Fellow of the British Academy in 1998.

Jeff Ericksen is an Assistant Professor in the School of Labor and Employment Relations at the University of Illinois at Urbana-Champaign. His research interests include human resource scalability, strategic HRM, emerging organizational forms and work systems, and project team mobilization, development, and performance. His work has been published in *Administrative*

Science Quarterly, *Human Resource Management*, and the *International Journal of Human Resource Management*.

Anthony Ferner has been Professor of International Human Resource Management in Leicester Business School, De Montfort University, since 1998. Since the early 1990s his main area of research has been on employment practices and human resources in multinational companies. His particular interests are in the impact of national business system characteristics on the behaviour of multinationals. He has published widely in academic journals, including the *British Journal of Industrial Relations*, *Journal of International Business Studies*, and *Organization Studies*. His books include (co-edited with Phil Almond) *American Multinationals in Europe: Managing Employment Relations Across National Borders*, Oxford, Oxford University Press, 2006, and (co-edited with Javier Quintanilla and Carlos Sánchez-Runde), *Multinationals, Institutions and the Construction of Transnational Practices. Convergence and Diversity in the Global Economy*. Basingstoke, Palgrave 2006. Current projects include a comparative study of the relationship between multinationals and regional 'governance' actors.

Tim Finch-Lees has spent the bulk of his managerial career with Diageo PLC, occupying a variety of senior positions in the UK, France and South America. Before this, he worked for Allied-Signal in France and the USA and for Booz Allen and Hamilton in London. Currently, he is on a break from his doctoral research at Birkbeck, University of London looking after his 15 month old son, Archie.

Barry Gerhart is Professor of Management and Human Resources and the Bruce R. Ellig Distinguished Chair in Pay and Organizational Effectiveness, School of Business, University of Wisconsin-Madison. His research interests include compensation, human resource strategy, international human resources, and employee movement. Professor Gerhart received his B.S. in Psychology from Bowling Green State University and his Ph.D. in Industrial Relations from the University of Wisconsin-Madison. He serves on the editorial boards of the *Academy of Management Journal*, *Human Relations*, *Industrial and Labor Relations Review*, *International Journal of Human Resource Management*, *Journal of Applied Psychology*, *Management Revue*, and *Personnel Psychology*. Professor Gerhart is a past recipient of the Scholarly Achievement Award and of the International Human Resource Management Scholarly Research Award, both from the Human Resources Division, Academy of Management. He is also a Fellow of the American Psychological Association and of the Society for Industrial and Organizational Psychology.

Jody Hoffer Gittell is Associate Professor of Management and MBA Program Director at Brandeis University's Heller School for Social Policy and Management. Gittell's research explores how relational coordination by front-line workers contributes to quality and efficiency outcomes in high-pressure service settings. Her book *The Southwest Airlines Way: Using the Power of Relationships to Achieve High Performance* won the 2005 Sloan Industry Studies Best Book Award. Her paper titled "A Relational Model of How High Performance Work Systems Work" won a 2008 Best Paper Award in the HR Division of the Academy of Management. Recent books include *Up in the Air: How Airlines Can Improve Performance by Engaging Their Employees* and *High Performance Healthcare: Using the Power of Relationships to Achieve Quality, Efficiency and Resilience*. Gittell received her PhD from the MIT Sloan School of Management, her MA from The New School for Social Research and her BA from Reed College.

Howard Gospel is Professor of Management and Senior Research Fellow at King's College University of London. He is also an Associate Fellow of the Said Business School, University of Oxford, and of the Centre for Economic Performance, London School of Economics. His research interests are employer labour policy, corporate governance and labour management, employee voice systems, and skill formation and training. He studies these in historical and comparative perspective, with a particular interest in the UK, US, Germany, France, and Japan.

Francis Green is Professor of Economics at the University of Kent. After graduating in Physics at Oxford University, he studied Economics at the LSE, before writing his PhD thesis at Birkbeck College. His research focuses on labour economics, with special interests in skills, training, work quality and employment relations. He has published nine books and many papers in journals in book collections. He regularly provides consultancy advice for government departments, the European Commission and the OECD. His most recent book, "Demanding Work. The Paradox of Job Quality in the Affluent Economy", was published in 2006 by Princeton University Press.

Anne-Marie Greene is Associate Professor (Reader) in Industrial Relations at the University of Warwick Business School. She is a member of the editorial boards of Gender, Work and Organization and Equal Opportunities International. Her research interests include the theory and practice of diversity and equality; equality and diversity issues within trade unions; and e-collectivism, particularly the use of ICTs by trade unions. She has published widely on these subjects in journals including Work, Employment and Society; European Journal of Industrial Relations; Gender, Work and Organization; Industrial Relations Journal; International Journal of Human Resource Management; and Economic and Industrial Democracy. She is co-author of Diversity Management in the UK:Organizational and Stakeholder Approaches (Routledge, 2009) and The Dynamics of Managing Diversity: A Critical Approach (Elsevier, 2005); and author of Voices from the Shop floor: Dramas of the Employment Relationship (Ashgate, 2001).

John J. Haggerty is a Doctoral candidate at the Cornell University ILR School in Ithaca, New York where he studies with Patrick M. Wright. He is also the managing director of ILR Executive Education. John's research interests are primarily in macro HR with an emphasis on the impact of the HR function on firm performance. John has his BS in Industrial and Labor relations from Cornell, and an MBA from Case Western Reserve University. Prior to returning to Cornell for his PhD, John had a 27 year career as an HR practitioner, including 21 years at General Electric where he was the Vice President of Human Resources for their Industrial Systems business.

Richard Hall is Associate Professor of Work and Organisational Studies at the University of Sydney. His current research concerns the effects of MNC HR policies on host country practices and policies, the impact of HR Information Systems on HR strategy, and the dynamics of new technology and organizational change. With a high degree of critical scepticism, he teaches in the areas of international HRM, leadership and organizational change. He is an Associate Editor of the *Journal of Industrial Relations*. His most recent book, *New Technology @ Work*, was co-authored with Paul Boreham, Rachel Parker and Paul Thompson and was published by Routledge in 2008.

Gail Hebson is a Lecturer in Employment Studies in the Manchester Business School, University of Manchester. Her research interests include gender and class divisions in employment, the changing nature of work and careers and the experience of work in low-skilled occupations. She has published on changing gender relations in the context of organizational change (in Marchington et al (2005) *Fragmenting Work: Blurring Organisational Boundaries and Disordering Hierarchies*) and published journal articles on renewing class analysis in studies of paid work, critically analyzing industrial relations research from a gendered perspective and the changing nature of emotional labour in the teaching profession.

Ying Hong is a PhD candidate in the Department of Human Resource Management in the School of Management and Labor Relations at Rutgers University. Her research interests include strategic HRM and service linkage research, and she has published in journals such as the *Journal of Applied Psychology* and *Human Resource Management Review*.

Mark A. Huselid is Professor of HR Strategy in the School of Management and Labor Relations (SMLR) at Rutgers University. His research is focused on the linkages between HR management systems, corporate strategy, and firm performance. In addition, he also has an active research and consulting program focused on the development of balanced measurement systems to reflect the contribution of the workforce, workforce management systems, and the HR management function to business success. Dr. Huselid was the Editor of the *Human Resource Management Journal* from 2000-2004, and is a current or former member of numerous professional and academic boards. Dr. Huselid is the author of *The HR Scorecard: Linking People, Strategy & Performance* (with Brian Becker and Dave Ulrich), *The Workforce Scorecard: Managing Human Capital to Execute Strategy* (with Brian Becker and Dick Beatty), and *The Differentiated Workforce: Transforming Talent Into Strategic Impact* (with Brian Becker and Dick Beatty).

Katy Huxley is a research assistant at Cardiff Business School. Her research interests are based around industrial/employment relations and the experiences of women in work. Notable publications include an edited volume with Keith Whitfield, *Innovations in the 2004 Workplace Employment Relations Survey* (2007), and a paper published in *Industrial Relations Journal* 'Does partnership at work increase trust?' (Co-authored with David Guest, William Brown and Riccardo Peccei, 2008). Having completed an MA at Nottingham Trent and an MSc at Cardiff University, she is currently undertaking a PhD investigating the impact of union learning representatives in the workplace.

Richard Johnstone is a Professor and Director of the Socio-Legal Research Centre in the Griffith Law School, Griffith University, Queensland. Richard was the founding Director of the National Research Centre for Occupational Health and Safety Regulation at the Australian National University and is currently co-Director of the Centre. Richard's research interests are in labour law, regulation (particularly OHS regulation) and legal education. He has researched OHS standard setting, OHS enforcement, worker participation in OHS, and the regulation of OHS in relation to precarious and contingent workers. His books include *Occupational Health and Safety Law and Policy* (Thompson Law Book, 1997 and 2 ed 2004), *Occupational Health and Safety, Courts and Crime: The Legal Construction of Occupational Health and Safety Offences in Victoria*, (Federation Press, 2003); and *Regulating Workplace Safety: Systems and Sanctions*, Oxford Socio-legal Series, Oxford University Press, Oxford (OUP, 1999, with N Gunningham).

Brian S. Klaas is a Professor of Management and Chair of the Management Department at the Moore School of Business, University of South Carolina. He received his Ph.D. from the Industrial Relations Research Institute at University of Wisconsin-Madison. Professor Klaas teaches, conducts research, and consults in such areas as workplace dispute resolution, HR in the small and medium enterprise, and compensation. He has published in such journals as *Personnel Psychology, Industrial Relations, Academy of Management Journal, Academy of Management Review, Industrial and Labor Relations Review, Journal of Management*,

Journal of Labor Research, Journal of Applied Psychology, and *Human Resource Management*. His research has been funded by grants from the Upjohn Institute for Employment Research, the Riegel & Emory HR Center, and the Society of Human Resource Management.

Thomas A. Kochan is the George M. Bunker Professor at MIT's Sloan School of Management and Co-Director of the MIT Institute for Work and Employment Research. He received his Ph.D. in Industrial Relations from the University of Wisconsin. His most recent books are *Restoring the American Dream: A Working Families' Agenda for America*, 2005, *Up in the Air: How Airlines can Improve Performance by Engaging their Employees*, 2009, and *Healing Together: The Kaiser Permanente Labor Management Partnership*, 2009. He is a Past President of the International Industrial Relations Association and the Industrial Relations Research Association and was elected to the National Academy of Human Resources in 1997.

David P. Lepak is Professor and Chairperson of the HRM department in the School of Management and Labor Relations at Rutgers University. His research interests focus on the strategic management of human capital. He has published numerous articles on this topic in leading academy journals and has presented on this topic to many domestic and international audiences. He is associate editor of *Academy of Management Review* and currently serves on the editorial boards of *Academy of Management Journal, Human Resource Management, Journal of Management Studies, Human Resource Management Journal*, and *Journal of Business and Psychology*.

Filip Lievens is Professor at the Department of Personnel Management and Work and Organizational Psychology at Ghent University, Belgium. In 1999, he earned his Ph.D. from the same university. His current research interests focus on selection procedures (e.g., assessment centers, situational judgment tests) and organizational attractiveness. He has published among others in the *Annual Review of Psychology, Journal of Applied Psychology, Personnel Psychology, Human Resource Management, Intelligence, Journal of Organizational Behavior,* and *Journal of Occupational and Organizational Psychology*. He has received several awards including the Best Paper Award from the International Personnel Management Association (2001), the Distinguished Early Career Award from the Society of Industrial and Organizational Psychology (2006), and the Douglas W. Bray – Ann Howard Award from the Society of Industrial and Organizational Psychology (2007).

Victoria Lim is a PhD candidate at the University of Melbourne. Her doctoral thesis focuses on the tactics managers use when communicating negative as part of the performance management process and their rationale for the choice of tactics. She tests the effectiveness of a managers' negative feedback tactics by examining employee reactions to those tactics. Victoria holds a Bachelor of Commerce (Honours) degree. During her honours year, Victoria's research focused on performance related pay in Australian organisations. She is currently working in the public sector as a survey consultant.

Rebecca Loudoun, Ph.D. is a Lecturer in the Department of Employment Relations at Griffith University and a member of the Socio-Legal Research Centre. Since 2002, Rebecca has worked at the University teaching undergraduate and postgraduate courses in occupational health and safety, negotiation and employment relations. She has also worked on a range of research projects focussing on broad organisational, social and economic issues that influence health and safety performance. She has a particular interest in the ill-effects of shiftwork and other work systems and the nexus between workplace bargaining and occupational health and safety (OHS), including the role of unions in influencing health and safety outcomes

Christopher Mabey is Professor of HRM at Birmingham University Business School. He directs the Centre for Leadership at the University of Birmingham (CLUB) and is Director of the DBA. Since his days as an Occupational Psychologist for British Telecom and Head of Management Training for Rank Xerox (UK), Chris has been intrigued by the possibilities, the pitfalls and the paradoxes that accompany management and leadership development. He has researched and written about it from many angles, most recently in a book co-written with Tim Finch-Lees and published by Sage in 2008 called *Management and Leadership Development*. For more on this, current research and other publications see: www.business.bham.ac.uk/staff/mabeyc

Mick Marchington is Professor of Human Resource Management at Manchester Business School, University of Manchester. He has also held visiting posts at the Universities of Sydney, Auckland and Paris, and is currently the 40th Anniversary Visiting Fellow at the Institute for Employment Studies. He has published widely on HRM, including about twenty books and monographs and nearly 150 book chapters and papers in refereed journals. He is best known for his work on employee involvement and participation, and on the link between line managers and HR professionals, as well as more recent research examining HRM across organisational boundaries. He is Co-Editor of the HRMJ and is Joint Chair of the HRM Study Group of the International Industrial Relations Association, and has occupied a range of chief examiner roles at the Chartered Institute of Personnel and Development. He is a Chartered Companion of the CIPD.

Jonathan Michie holds a Chair at the University of Oxford where he is Director of the Department for Continuing Education and President of Kellogg College. Previously he was Professor of Management at the University of Birmingham where he was the Director of Birmingham Business School. Before that he held the Sainsbury Chair of Management at Birkbeck, University of London, where he was Head of the School of Management & Organizational Psychology, and prior to that was at the Judge Business School, University of Cambridge. Before moving into academia he worked in Brussels as an Expert to the European Commission on the employment, skills and training implications of technological and regulatory developments in the Information Technology & Telecommunications sector. Professor Michie is a Council Member of Acas, and a member of the Department for Business, Enterprise, and Regulatory Reform's Advisory Forum on the effects of employment legislation.

Shad S. Morris (Ph.D. Cornell University) is Assistant Professor of Management at the Fisher College of Business, The Ohio State University. Professor Morris teaches and conducts research in the areas of international business and strategic human resource management, particularly focusing on how global firms create value through people and knowledge. Professor Morris has also consulted with a variety of multinational firms and multilateral organizations.

Sandra Ohly is currently assistant professor in industrial and organizational psychology at the Goethe University of Frankfurt. She received her PhD from the Technical University of Braunschweig. Her research focuses on creativity at work, proactive behavior and suggestion making. She is also interested in the effects of time pressure on motivation and organizational behavior and in emotions, organizational change and resistance to change. Her research has been published in *Journal of Organizational Behavior, Journal of Occupational and Organisational Psychology, Journal of Applied Psychology and European Journal of Work and Organizational Psychology*

Jaap Paauwe (1953, PhD Erasmus University Rotterdam) is Professor of Human Resource Studies at Tilburg University and also affiliated to Erasmus University Rotterdam, School of

Economics. His main research interests are in the area of HRM and Performance, corporate strategy and change, industrial relations and institutional theory. In 1991 he was Academic Visitor at the London School of Economics. In 1996 he was Visiting Professor at Templeton College, Oxford University (UK) and in 2005 he joined Cornell University (Ithaca, USA) as a visiting fellow. His latest book is on *HRM and Performance: achieving long term viability* (Oxford University Press, June 2004), for which he received the Dutch HRM network Award in 2005. Together with Cambridge, INSEAD and Cornell University he is involved in a large scale international research project on improving the excellence of the HR function within multinational companies. Recently the research group at Tilburg has initiated an international research project focused on the topic of HR governance and risk management.

Sharon K. Parker is a Professor of Organizational Psychology and Director at the Institute of Work Psychology, University of Sheffield. Her research interests are focused on proactive behavior, work design, self-efficacy, and employee perspective taking. She has published 5 books, over thirty internationally refereed journal articles (including publications in top tier journals such as the *Journal of Applied Psychology* and *Academy of Management Journal),* over 30 book chapters and encyclopedia entries, numerous articles in practitioner outlets, and more than 60 technical reports. Professor Parker is an Associate Editor for the Journal of Applied Psychology.

Chris Provis is an Associate Professor in the School of Management at the University of South Australia. He originally studied and taught philosophy, then worked for some years in industrial relations, and has published papers in both areas. His present research interests lie especially in areas of business ethics, and his book *Ethics and Organisational Politics* was published by Edward Elgar in 2004. He is a past president of the Australian Association of Professional and Applied Ethics, and an active member of the Ethics Centre of South Australia.

Monder Ram is Professor of Small Business at De Montfort University and Director of the Centre for Research in Ethnic Minority Entrepreneurship. He is a leading researcher on ethnic minority entrepreneurship and has published widely on the subject. He is a fellow of the Royal Society of Arts and a director of the Institute of Small Business Affairs. Monder is also a member of the Department of Trade and Industry's Ethnic Minority Business Forum and Small Business Council.

Tom Redman is Professor of Human Resource Management and Director of Research at University of Durham Business School. His books include Managing *Managers* (1993) and *Managing through TQM: Theory and Practice* (1998). He is a Fellow of the Chartered Institute of Personnel and Development.

Rob Seidner is a PhD student in the Graduate Program in Public Administration at the University of Illinois–Chicago. He earned his MBA from Brandeis University's Heller School for Social Policy and Management, as well his BA from Brandeis. He completed a Presidential Management Fellow appointment as a human resource specialist in the U.S. Office of Personnel Management. His primary research interests involve Federal human capital practices, including recruitment, pay for performance, accountability and high performance human resource work systems. He is the co-author of "Federated Human Resource Management in the Federal Government: The Intelligence Community Model," published by the IBM Center for the Business of Government. Seidner has also published chapters in *Innovations in Human Resource Management: Getting the Public's Work Done in the 21st Century* and *Public Human Resource Management: Problems* *and Prospects* (5th Edition). With Dr. Gittell, Seidner has coauthored an award-winning article in *Organization Science*.

Scott A Snell is Professor of Business Administration, Scott teaches in the Leadership and Organization area in Darden. He is author of over fifty publications in professional journals and edited texts and has co-authored three books: *Management: Leading and Collaborating in a Competitive World, Managing Human Resources*, and *Managing People and Knowledge in Professional Service Firms.* Professor Snell has worked with companies such as American Express, AstraZeneca, CIGNA, Deutsche Telekom, Shell and the World Bank to address the alignment of human resource issues and strategic management.

Prior to joining the Darden faculty in 2007 Scott was Professor and Director of Executive Education at Cornell University's Center for Advanced Human Resource Studies (CAHRS) and Professor of Management in the Smeal College of Business at Pennsylvania State University

Phyllis Tharenou is a Professor of Organizational Behavior in the Division of Business at the University of South Australia, currently on leave of absence working in the Australian Research Council, a grants funding agency of the Australian Federal Government, as the Executive Director of Social, Behavioral and Economic Sciences. She received her PhD in organizational psychology from the University of Queensland. Her current research interests are in receptivity to international work, self-initiated international careers and repatriation, and gender differences in receptivity to international careers and career advancement. She has published in the areas of managerial career advancement, gender differences in career advancement, training and development, international careers, absenteeism, and employee self-esteem, including in the *Academy of Management Journal, Journal of Applied Psychology, Journal of Occupational and Organizational Psychology, Journal of Organizational Behavior, Journal of Vocational Behavior, Organizational Behavior and Human Decision Processes,* and *International Review of Industrial and Organizational Psychology.*

Nick Wailes is an associate professor in Work and Organisational Studies at the University of Sydney. He teaches comparative employment relations and strategic management. His current research focuses on the spillover effects of the HR practices of MNCs in host countries. His research has been published in leading international journals including the *International Journal of Human Resource Management*, the *British Journal of Industrial Relations* and the *Journal of Business Ethics*. Nick is the chair of the scientific committee for the International Industrial Relations Association 15th World Congress.

Janet Walsh is a Professor of Human Resource Management and Employment Relations in the Department of Management, King's College London. Prior to her appointment at King's College London, she has held positions at the Universities of Cambridge, Leeds, Melbourne and Royal Holloway, University of London. She has published widely in the areas of customer service work, employment flexibility and non-standard work arrangements, particularly part-time work. She is currently conducting research with the British Law Society's Association of Women Solicitors on women solicitors' careers, work-life balance and use of flexible work arrangements.

Keith Whitfield is Professor of Human Resource Management and Economics and Associate Dean for Postgraduate Studies at Cardiff Business School, and Director of Cardiff University's Research and Graduate School in the Social Sciences. His research centres on the impact of human resource management policies on the performance of organisations and on the work experience of employees. Recent papers have focused on financial participation, employee involvement and the employee experience of work. He was the ESRC's Senior Academic Consultant for the fifth Workplace Employment Relations Survey and a member of its Steering Group. Along with William Brown, Alex Bryson and John Forth, he has just completed an analysis of the evolution of employment relations of the modern British workplace, using all five of the WIRS/WERS surveys (published by Cambridge University Press in May 2009). He has also recently undertaken research for the Organisation of Economic Cooperation and Development on the imapct of labour market structures and skills development systems on innovation and entrepreneurship, and for the Economic and Scoial Research Council and UK Health and Safety Exectuive on Employee Well-Being.

Adrian Wilkinson is Professor of Employment Relations at Griffith University and Director of the Centre for Work, Organisation and Wellbeing. He is also Visiting Professor at Loughborough University Business School. His books include *Making Quality Critical* (1995), *Managing Quality and Human Resource* (1997) *Managing through TQM: Theory and Practice* (1998), *Understanding Work and Employment: Industrial Relations in Transition* (2003) and *Human Resource Management at Work* (2008). He is a Fellow and Accredited Examiner of the Chartered Institute of Personnel and Development. He is Chief Editor of the *International Journal of Management Reviews* and Associate Editor of the *Human Resource Management Journal*.

PART I

The Framing of Human Resource Management

Field of Human Resource Management

Adrian Wilkinson, Tom Redman, Scott A. Snell
and Nicolas Bacon

The purpose of this chapter is to outline some of the key elements of human resource management (HRM), and to introduce our framework for this volume. The field of HRM continues to evolve in today's organizations, in part due to the economic, technological, and social realities that influence the nature of business. In a global economy, a wide range of factors—that vary from global sourcing and labor arbitrage to regional trade agreements and labor standards to cultural differences and sustainability to strategic alliances and innovation—all point to the vital nature of HRM. In large part this is because from a strategic standpoint, observers have noted that traditional sources of advantage such as access to capital, protected markets, or proprietary technologies are rapidly eroding, and that survival depends more often on the ability to innovate, adapt, and learn, and transfer that learning globally. As one might guess, these capabilities rest squarely on the management of people.

But while few will argue against the premise that HRM issues are critical in today's organizations, the mantra of 'people are our most valuable asset' has largely been a rhetorical one in most organizations; and the research evidence has often not backed it up (cf., Snell, Shadur, and Wright, 2002). Historically, organizations have not rested their fortunes on human resources. The HR function remains among the least influential in most organizations, and competitive strategies have not typically been based on the skills, capabilities, and behaviors of employees. In fact, the harsh reality is that labor is still often viewed merely as a cost to be minimized, particularly in tough times. Executives have more often tried to minimize the impact of employees on performance by substituting capital for labor where possible, and designing bureaucratic organizations that separate those who think from those who actually do the work (Snell, Youndt, and Wright, 1996).

But there are some encouraging signs that much of this is changing. As Quinn (1992: 241) noted, 'with rare exceptions, the economic and producing power of the firm lies more in its intellectual and service capabilities than in its hard assets.' And again, this clearly highlights the importance of human resource management.

To explore how HRM is changing, and to examine best practice across its array of activities, we organize this chapter as follows. First, we present a 2×3 matrix that summarizes both micro- and macro-perspectives on elements of HRM across: (a) a human focus, (b) a resource focus, and (c) a management focus. Second, we describe the structure of the book and how the individual chapters deal with the issues raised by this matrix of HRM perspectives.

A HUMAN FOCUS

The history and evolution of HRM (Chapter 2) emphasizes its longstanding concern with a human focus. Historically, this focus placed a strong emphasis on employee rights and needs and employee wellbeing in general. This focus was much in evidence in early developments in the areas of occupational health and safety (Chapter 17) and grievance management (Chapter 19) in particular. More recently we can see this focus reflected in broad debates about work design (Chapter 16), the work-life balance (Chapter 29), and equality and diversity (Chapter 14).

At its root, HRM focuses on managing the employment relationships and the implicit, as well as explicit agreements that are established between individuals and organizations. In many instances, HR plays the role of employee advocate or 'champion' in ensuring the equitable treatment of employees in order to ensure that the interests of employees as well as the organization are protected.

A micro perspective

From a micro standpoint, HRM includes managing the nature of employment (Chapter 4). It also includes issues of employee involvement and participation (Chapter 15) that characterize the attachment of individuals

to the organization. This raises the importance of the employee's experience at work and outcomes (Chapter 22) as well as their work-life balance (Chapter 29).

A macro perspective

From a more macro perspective, the human element of HRM addresses collective agreements between employees and organizations that characterize industrial relations and collective bargaining (Chapter 18) as well as formal policies and procedures that ensure rights of redress for discipline and grievances (Chapter 19). From a broad perspective, the human focus of HRM concerns issues related to ethics (Chapter 28), equal opportunity (Chapter 14), health and safety (Chapter 17), as well as fairness and workplace justice during downsizing and redundancy (Chapter 20).

A RESOURCE FOCUS

Balancing the needs and interests of employees against the needs and interests of the organization is often a difficult task in HRM. The contradictions and tensions between different models of HRM, such as that between an 'employee champion' and a 'business partner' role in the organization have received considerable attention in the literature (Ulrich, 1997; Francis and Keegan, 2006). Although HRM by its very nature has a decidedly human focus, it also focuses on employees as a resource in driving performance. Many of the practices that are typically associated with HRM focus on increasing productivity and enhancing the competitiveness of the firm.

A micro perspective

From a micro perspective, HRM focuses on individual practices that ensure employee ability and motivation to perform effectively. Recruitment and selection (Chapter 9), for example, constitute important organizational investments to ensure that the best and the brightest talent is brought into the organization to fulfill its particular needs. Training and development (Chapter 10), in turn, augment the staffing process to build the talent base of the organization and close the gap on required skills, abilities, and other factors. Management development programs (Chapter 11) help to ensure a strong cadre of executives is available to succeed current leaders, and to provide a succession of experiences that develops this talent over time. Performance appraisal (Chapter 12) involves both the administrative and developmental requirements of performance management. It addresses ability-related factors, and seeks to motivate employees to improve individual and organizational performance. Given these aims it ties directly to the management of rewards (Chapter 13) and the various methods organizations use such as pay for performance, incentives, and the like. Finally, job design (Chapter 16) addresses the motivational basis of work and the micro-structural requirements of the organization.

A macro perspective

From a more macro perspective, a resource focus of HRM addresses the set of practices for managing the aggregate of human capital in organizations and nation states (Chapter 24). Much of this literature is informed by the resource-based view of organizations as it applies to HRM (Chapter 25). From a competitive standpoint, executives recognize that their talent base is a source of advantage, and as a consequence, they take care to develop strategies that build and deploy their work forces in ways that enhance firm performance (Chapter 21). Different models of macro HRM (Chapter 3) capture the universalistic 'best practice' approach to HRM, the contingency approaches, and the configurational approaches which emphasize the combination of practices that reinforce and support one another. Just as individual talents combine to create a collective capability in organizations, multiple HR practices also combine to create an overall strategy of HRM within a regulatory context that

affects the employer's choice of specific practices (see Chapter 5). The evolution of HR strategy (Chapter 6) has taken organizations from a fairly static view focused on person-job fit, to one focused on organizational and cultural fit, to managing a global workforce where practices differ across regions and cultures (Chapter 8). In cases of hyper-competition and rapid change, HR strategies help to create and leverage an agile workforce that can adapt to change and drive innovation. This often includes the use of contingency workers, strategic partnerships, and alliances that span organizational boundaries (Chapters 26 and 27). At the extreme, these approaches have an aggregate impact on industry innovation and national economic performance (Chapter 24).

A MANAGEMENT FOCUS

While much of the literature on HRM has focused on the needs and concerns of employees (as humans) in organizations, as well as their potential contribution as resources contributing to organizational performance, an important subset of concerns relate to the management of the HR function itself. In many ways, the evolution of the HR function, its organization, and the professionalization of HR managers, represent some of the biggest changes occurring over the last decades.

A micro perspective

Although the earliest roles and responsibilities of HR managers emerged from the administrative and transactional requirements of employment and personnel issues, the contemporary setting requires HR managers to adopt a more strategic set of roles that focus on managing change, building organizational culture, and becoming a partner in the business (Chapter 7). The skills, knowledge, and behaviors of HR managers and leaders in this context are substantially different, and many companies are challenged with identifying and developing the next generation of HR professionals.

A macro perspective

From a macro perspective the HR function has undergone a significant amount of change as well. Many firms have restructured to establish a cadre of HR generalists (business partners), complemented by centers of excellence (specialists), and supported by a shared services organization for administrative/transactional activities. In part, these changes have taken place to create economies of scale in multinational companies (Chapter 32) but some of the change is occurring in small and medium sized firms as well (Chapter 31) where strategic partnerships give smaller firms access to specialized HR talent. In both settings, the trend toward outsourcing transactional activities has also continued.

The issues related to HRM in developing countries are no less significant (Chapter 23) and related to both micro issues of HR managers as well as macro issues of organizing the HR function within the firm. Similarly, the special issues in the service sector, both private sector service (Chapter 30) and the public sector (Chapter 33) create HR challenges as well.

THE STRUCTURE OF THE HANDBOOK

The themes and developments outlined above are reflected in the chapters that follow. In the first part, the contributors provide an overview of the history and different perspectives underpinning the field. In Chapter 2, Howard Gospel outlines the historical development of human resource management, defining the field broadly to cover three interconnected areas—work relations, employment relations, and industrial relations. The chapter examines major patterns in these three areas as they have emerged over time, showing how the changing technological, market, political/legal, social, and business environments have shaped basic aspects of labor management. He classifies the history of human resource

management into three broad 'stages': from the first industrial revolution and the growth of bureaucratic personnel management from the late nineteenth century onwards; to the second industrial revolution in the mid-twentieth century involving union-based systems of industrial relations management; and the third industrial revolution of more flexible systems of human resource management.

The theme of current models of strategic human resource management is developed by Saba Colakoglu, Ying Hong and David Lepak in Chapter 3. Concentrating on the link between human resource management and the competitive advantage of firms they review the underlying theoretical approaches for universalistic, contingency and configurational perspectives in the field. The established resource-based view and behavioral perspectives are reviewed before considering emerging approaches concentrating on employee cognitive and social dimensions. The international aspects of HRM are also considered.

In Chapter 4, John Budd and Devasheesh Bhave explore the contrasting views of the employment relationship associated with four different schools of thought. Distinctions are drawn between egoist, unitarist, pluralist and critical models of the employment relationship. The underlying values, ideologies and frames of reference held by those studying and practicing human resource management are associated with different views of the purpose of employment practices and the preferred approaches to dealing with labor management issues.

In Chapter 5, Michael Barry explains how the regulatory context affects employer choices of human resource management practices. Over the last twenty years employers have reasserted their rights to manage employees free from regulations to protect employee interests and correct market failures. He argues that rather than shifting to a deregulated labor market over the last two decades, new regulatory actors have emerged to influence employers' choices of human resource management practices. In addition, the state continues to define the overarching regulatory system and employers' choices are still conditioned by this and product markets, along with the history of the firm.

In Chapter 6, Scott Snell and Shad Morris summarize the evolution of the field of HR strategy. This has involved a change from concentrating on person-job fit under scientific management, to systemic fit from the 1980s, to value creation in the differentiated work systems currently used by firms in hyper-competitive global markets. A convergence is described between the fields of HR and strategy on the issues of human capital, social capital and capabilities. Future challenges include understanding how to manage knowledge and innovation across globally dispersed and differentiated workforces, and how to effectively manage outsourcing and offshoring from a HR perspective. Despite these challenges HR concerns are now considered central to corporate strategy.

In Chapter 7, John Haggerty and Patrick Wright focus on the value added by the HR function. Moving beyond debates about implementing high-performance work practices and operating as business partners, they adopt a micro organizational approach and argue that the skills of HR professionals must improve to establish and maintain the proper climate for simple rules to signal appropriate behaviors to employees required to drive business performance. This involves translating corporate value statements into meaningful HR practices, building effective links with line managers and creating a positive organizational climate.

In the final chapter in Part One, Richard Hall and Nick Wailes broaden the theme of the influences on human resource management by considering differing practices across countries. They argue international human resource management needs to incorporate insights developed from comparative HRM and international political economy and move beyond a traditional focus on expatriate management and culture as the main explanation of differences between countries.

Part Two focuses on the fundamental areas of human resource management practice. In Chapter 9, Filip Lievens and Derek Chapman argue that an effective approach to recruitment and selection requires combining a macro level recruitment strategy and micro processes such as understanding the decision making of selectors and applicants. The chapter focuses on new research on recruitment, covering the impact of technology, the quality of applicants attracted, the important role of the recruiter, organizational image, attracting older and temporary workers, and applicant reactions to selection procedures. Recent work on personnel selection reviewed covers technological developments, selecting employees in international firms, new selection procedures, and improvements in existing selection procedures. Demonstrating the value of recruiting and selecting to organizations remains an important challenge for research in this area.

In the first of two chapters on developing employees, Phyliss Tharenou, in Chapter 10, considers the main developments in employee training and development. Four major approaches to training and development are outlined from the fields of human resource management, industrial/organizational psychology, labor economics, and industrial relations. Tharenou argues that principles and different levels of analysis from these different areas should be combined to increase training effectiveness. Research is then reviewed across three stages of the training and development process covering what occurs prior to, during, and after training. She argues that managers fail to act on many of the lessons from this research and changing managers' attitudes towards the training and development process is an important priority for future research.

The call for greater dialogue between different approaches to management and leadership development is also emphasized by Christopher Mabey and Tim Finch-Lees in Chapter 11. Identifying shortcomings in the causal links between management and leadership development and organizational performance, Mabey and Finch-Lees review existing evidence on the links to strategic intent, enhanced skill and competence, and between enhanced competence and performance. They argue that work based on functionalist assumptions overlooks a range of important issues, including the multiple meanings attributed to management and leadership development by different stakeholders, the effects on management identities, and the coercive aspects of such training programs.

In the first of two chapters on assessment and rewards, Michelle Brown and Victoria Lim, in Chapter 12, focus on the motivations and tactics that supervisors and employees use in formal evaluations of employee performance. They review the situational and personal factors that influence the supervisor's appraisal of employees, and employee reactions to performance appraisals, the effect of perceived fairness on participation, impression management, feedback on assessments and resistance to assessment. The conclusion drawn is that more research is required focusing on the interactions between supervisors and employees in the appraisal process.

In Chapter 13, Barry Gerhart concentrates on factors affecting the degree to which employers use pay for performance plans, reviewing reinforcement, expectancy, equity, agency and efficiency wage theories of motivation. He reviews evidence on the effects of pay level and pay for performance, considering the potential pitfalls and the impact of a series of alignment and contextual factors that might affect the success of pay for performance plans.

In Chapter 14, Anne-Marie Greene describes the move from liberal approaches to equal opportunities based on 'sameness' to diversity approaches founded on 'difference'. This involved a shift from a social justice case to a business case for equality, and the sharing of responsibility for equality among a wider group of stakeholders. Confusion among academics and practitioners concerning the purpose and implementation of equality practices has resulted in policies appearing similar to those under equal opportunity approaches. Legal compliance remains a major motivator, equality remains a low status management issue with limited expenditure, and equality

in most firms remains the responsibility of the HR function.

In Chapter 15, Graeme Dietz, Adrian Wilkinson and Tom Redman focus on the main factors that influence the effectiveness of schemes to increase employee involvement and participation. Adopting a life-cycle perspective, the chapter reviews these factors as they affect schemes from their initial stages, to operation and potential survival. Several important factors are highlighted, including managerial motives, the mismatch between motives and the design of schemes, and organizational- and individual-level obstacles. These factors contribute towards what are at best described as the modest outcomes of such schemes.

In Chapter 16, Sharon Parker and Sandra Ohly review classic work design theories and research, and concentrate on the relationship between work characteristics and outcomes. They consider recent work to further understand the relationship between job characteristics and outcomes, including extending beyond the big five work characteristics, expanding the outcomes associated with job characteristics, further understanding the mechanisms and moderators, and the organizational factors shaping work characteristics. They point to future work to assess the impact of collective and contextualized processes of organizing work and the design of complex professional and knowledge based jobs. The gap between work design theory and bad work design choices in practice remains of concern.

Employee wellbeing is further explored in Chapter 17 by Rebecca Loudoun and Richard Johnstone. Traditional views of health and safety at work have embraced a broader view of the factors affecting workers' physical and psychological health, and regulators require employers to take systematic approaches to manage occupational health and safety. However, they identify difficulties in firms engaging in risk management processes, reactive minimal compliance and unsatisfactory occupational health and safety regulation.

In Chapter 18, Thomas Kochan and Greg Bamber focus on industrial relations and collective bargaining with trade unions and other employee representatives. The chapter emphasizes the normative purpose of designing institutions that promote fairness alongside efficiency. The purposes of collective bargaining are outlined along with its rise and decline in the twentieth century. The key challenges looking forward concern the design of institutions to regulate employment given the globalization of markets and firms, and to balance work and family life.

In Chapter 19, questions of fairness and workplace justice are also to the fore as Brian Klaas reviews the research on discipline and grievance procedures designed to deal with problematic employee behavior. Klaas shows whether the use of formal disciplinary procedures produces benefits that outweigh the costs depends on factors in the organizational setting and the disciplinary system that affect employee perceptions. A range of questions that need to be addressed in research on grievance systems for employees are identified and the moderating role of contextual factors remains critical for research in this area.

In the final chapter of Part Two, Wayne Cascio argues that the anticipated increases in earnings and share prices from downsizing and redundancies are more likely to arise from disposing of unprofitable or technologically redundant parts of a business, but not as part of an indiscriminate management approach to reducing costs. The advantages and disadvantages of four methods to reduce the workforce are reviewed and the limited research on alternatives to downsizing considered. The negative impact of downsizing on employee attitudes and behaviors are explored among other issues, and the effects on firm performance and communities assessed. Finally, more work is called for exploring the effects of downsizing according to the different practices used and contexts in which it occurs.

Part Three of the Handbook focuses on contemporary issues in human resource management. In Chapter 21, Brian Becker and Mark Huselid outline a way forward for research into strategic human resource management and firm performance

by further applying concepts from strategic management. In arguing for an emphasis on implementing HR strategy as a source of competitive advantage, they highlight the importance of an HR architecture that embeds capabilities for concrete business processes that are firm-specific and strategically important. The practical implications for HR managers include an emphasis on workforce strategy, an increased emphasis on differentiation, measuring the HR function's performance and HR professionals developing new competencies.

In Chapter 22, Francis Green, Katy Huxley and Keith Whitfield broaden the discussion to examine the employee experience of work during a period in which many firms have revised their approach to human resource management. Although wages have increased for many workers, other aspects of the employees' experience such as the intensity of work and job stress may have become worse. However, these changes appear to vary for different groups of workers according to factors including gender, whether workers have a disability or health problems, hours worked and firm size. The authors conclude that high commitment management approaches have had little impact on employee experiences of work.

In Chapter 23, Pawan Budhwar and Yaw Debrah change the focus to consider human resource management in developing countries. This topic has attracted more attention recently as local firms in developing countries seek to compete in global markets and China and India have emerged as major economies. Most work so far has assessed the impact of national factors on HRM, including religion, traditional cultural beliefs, western colonial and modern influences, institutions, the political and legal framework, the business environment, and national history. Eleven issues are highlighted to help guide future research in this area and many of these issues insist that sensitivity to context is essential.

In Chapter 24, Jonathan Michie explores the relationship between HRM and national economic performance. National economic performance is influenced by both the aggregate of corporate performance and the ability of national economies to innovate. Politicians may however encourage numerical flexibility in the labor market at the cost of encouraging functional flexibility and high skills in firms. Developing employees and organizing work to increase the absorptive capacity of firms are also considered important HRM issues if firms are to benefit from knowledge generated in the science and university sectors.

In Chapter 25, Paul Boselie and Jaap Paauwe provide an overview of the resource based view (RBV) and its impact on human resource management. Several empirical studies are reviewed that seek to apply the RBV and a set of problems with RBV theory are considered. In order to overcome the narrow focus of the RBV on the internal resources of firms, the authors propose complementing the theory with recognition of the impact of external institutions on the firm, and a strategic balance approach recognizing the importance of the capabilities and administrative heritage of the firm.

In Chapter 26, Lee Dyer and Jeff Ericksen use concepts derived from complexity science to consider the HR challenges for firms operating under conditions of hyper competition and creative destruction. In such firms, innovation, dynamism, and the ability to adapt are required to recreate short-lived temporary competitive advantages. Although the most appropriate HR practices in such circumstances are not well understood, the authors highlight several, including: a potential role for recruiting agile performers; employees equipped to take on different assignments and tasks; a requirement for continuous development; person-based pay decided by project teams that is high relative to the market; and systems to prevent overwork and burn-out.

In Chapter 27, Mick Marchington, Fang Lee Cooke and Gail Hebson consider human resource management across organizational boundaries that arise in the employment of subcontracted, outsourced and agency workers. Although generating employee commitment to more than a single employing

organization is possible, this appears to require conditions rarely offered to workers in these circumstances, such as attempts to provide better working conditions. Furthermore, employees in multi-employer networks rarely benefit from reward, training or employee participation practices that will enhance employee commitment.

In Chapter 28, Chris Provis outlines a range of traditional and new human resource management issues that require careful ethical consideration. Managers may ignore attempts to apply ethics to employment issues because some recent management approaches may be ethically suspect, but such neglect may also have occurred because different approaches to ethics sometimes appear to produce conflicting advice on human resource management issues. Nevertheless, ethical theories help identify the issues managers should consider and discuss in human resource management, although it is considered misguided to hope for unequivocal solutions to ethical dilemmas.

In the final chapter of Part Three, Janet Walsh discusses key developments in working time and work-life balance. She examines the potential causes, national, occupational and gender variations in the time demands and pressures of paid employment and the links to work-life conflict. Assessing policies for work-life balance, Walsh highlights the important role of state legislation in employers enhancing family-friendly work practices. The organizational characteristics of family-friendly employers are assessed as well as evidence of the organizational benefits of these policies, and the reasons employers do not adopt such policies.

The contributors to Part Four consider human resource management issues from different sectoral perspectives. In Chapter 30, Jody Hoffer Gittell and Rob Seidner consider human resource management in the service industry. They argue against the view that the labor intensive nature of much service work and low cost competition makes an investment approach to HR unlikely. Instead they note that direct customer/provider interface in service work makes service quality important even in low cost segments of the market, and require HR investments. Such investments are thought to drive service sector performance through increasing employee commitment, raising skills levels and building more effective relationships.

In Chapter 31, Paul Edwards and Monder Ram focus on the relatively non-formalised human resource management practices used in small firms. The authors argue that these practices reflect a wide range of factors, including the personal choices of the founders and owners of small firms, family relationships, and some of the benefits workers find in informality. Arguing against the view that small firms require greater formality, a case is made that in a highly diverse sector, small firms seek to tie together HR practices in idiosyncratic ways to operate flexibly and develop the firm.

In Chapter 32, Anthony Ferner considers the management of human resources across borders within multi-national companies (MNCs). The field has been enriched as the initial emphasis on cross-cultural differences in values has been challenged by a comparative institutionalist approach, and a narrow substantive focus on expatriates is gradually broadening to consider non-managerial staff. Although much has been learned, Ferner calls for more conceptual sophistication and an expansion of the substantive focus of international human resource management.

In the final chapter, Stephen Bach notes the main debates in human resource management traditionally overlook the public sector. Although new public management practices became widespread and sought to introduce some private sector HR practices into the public sector, Bach notes the detrimental effects in fragmented services and uncoordinated planning. The tide in the public sector appears to be turning towards organizational reintegration, citizen involvement and partnership with the workforce.

The chapters in the Handbook attest to the continued importance of human resource management for *both* organizational performance and employee well-being. They also identify the broad and increasing scope of academic disciplines generating evidence and developing theories to understand existing practices and help guide managers in the future. The extent to which academics and managers can meet the challenges posed in these chapters will have an impact on our future working lives.

ACKNOWLEDGEMENTS

We would like to thank Kiren Shoman and Alan Moloney from Sage for their help in putting together this volume.

REFERENCES

Francis, H. and Keegan, A. (2006) 'The changing face of human resource management', *Human Resource Management Journal*, 16 (3): 231–49.

Quinn, J. B. (1992) *Intelligent Enterprise: A Knowledge and Service Based Paradigm for Industry*. NY: Free Press.

Snell, S. A., Shadur, M. A. and Wright, P. M. (2002) 'Human resources strategy: The era of our ways', Michael A. Hitt, R. Edward Freeman and Jeffrey S. Harrison (eds) *Blackwell Handbook of Strategic Management*. Oxford: Blackwell, pp. 627–49.

Snell, S. A., Youndt, M. A. and Wright, P. M. (1996) 'Establishing a framework for research in strategic human resource management: Merging resource theory and organizational learning', in G. R. Ferris (ed.), *Research in Personnel and Human Resources Management*, Vol 14. Greenwich: JAI Press, pp. 61–90.

Ulrich, D. (1997) *Human Resource Champions*. US: Harvard Business School Press.

2

Human Resources Management: A Historical Perspective

Howard Gospel

INTRODUCTION

In this chapter, the management of human resources is broadly defined to cover three broad interconnected areas – work relations, employment relations, and industrial relations. Work relations are taken to cover the way work is organised and the deployment of workers around technologies and production systems. Employment relations deal with the arrangements governing such aspects of employment as recruitment, training, job tenure, and reward systems. Industrial relations are taken to cover the voiced aspirations of workers and institutional arrangements which may arise to address them, such as joint consultation, works councils, trade unions, and collective bargaining. The focus is therefore on human resources management (lower case), which has been an eternal phenomenon in all organisations over time, and not on Human Resources Management (upper case), which is a term which has

developed over the last two decades. In addition, in this chapter, the term the management of human resources and the management of labour are used generically and interchangeably.

The focus throughout this chapter is on major patterns in these three areas as they have emerged over time, especially in large private-sector firms, over a long period from the nineteenth century onwards. It draws mainly on the core economies of the twentieth century, especially the US, the UK, Germany, France, and Japan. The focus is primarily on the management of lower and intermediate classes of labour, which have constituted the majority of employees and which are best covered in the literature.

The next section provides a broad overview of the contexts within which labour has been managed, including market, technological, political, and business contexts. There then follow sections which present broad 'stages' in the history of human resource management, taking examples from leading sectors of the economy. However, throughout, the aim is to stress continuities over time between stages, the coexistence of systems, and how older sectors adapt over time. The final section raises some caveats and areas for further research and draws broad conclusions.

THE HISTORICAL CONTEXTS OF HUMAN RESOURCE MANAGEMENT

A number of major contexts are outlined schematically here and used further in each section. These include the changing technological, market, political/legal, social, and business environments. Though these contexts shape the activities of employers, managers, and workers, the chapter also shows how the actors themselves have shaped the situations within which they operate (Dunlop, 1958).

The technological context has historically shaped basic aspects of labour management. Some writers have suggested a broad movement over time from artisan or craft production (with skilled workers having significant control over work), to mass production (often associated with Ford-type assembly-line systems in industries such as automobiles), and to more flexible production systems (sometimes referred to as post-Fordist) (Tolliday, 1998). In practice, changes have been complex, with overlaps in types of production regimes over time and with older sectors adopting aspects of new arrangements. Thus, skilled, small-batch production was never superseded in many areas often typified as mass production, such as metalworking and light assembly industries. Similarly, many aspects of work in modern retail stores, fast-food restaurants, and call centres are very much of a mass-production kind. A constant theme in the history of labour management has been employers' introduction of new technologies, workers' counter-attempts to exert some control over these, and managers' further attempts to develop and refine management systems (Nelson, 1975; Hounshell, 1984; Piore and

Sabel, 1984; Lazonick, 1990; Tolliday 1998; Scranton, 1997).

The market context comprises labour, product, and financial markets. In the labour market, there are both longer- and shorter-term influences. For example, longer-term factors include demographic change, the broad balance of labour supply and demand, and the changing composition of the labour force. Thus, in various periods in different countries, labour shortages have induced firms to substitute capital for labour and to introduce new production systems, as was the case in the United States in the early/mid-nineteenth century (Lewis, 1952; Habbakuk, 1962). Shortages also induced firms to introduce systems to attract and retain labour and these have often become embedded and left continuing inheritances, as for example with skilled labour shortages in Japan in the early twentieth century (Jacoby, 1979; Gordon, 1985, 1998). Shorter-term labour market influences include the fluctuating level of unemployment which has immediate direct effects on the balance of power between management and labour. In this respect, for example, sharp rises in unemployment in the UK in the early 1920s and early 1980s significantly affected the bargaining power of management and unions, strengthened managerial prerogatives, and led to major changes in labour management and industrial relations (Gospel, 1992).

In the case of product markets, the boundaries of markets and the degree of competition in them have an effect on labour management, both directly and indirectly. For example, Smith (1776), in his celebrated examination of a pin factory, pointed out that the extent of the market shaped the division of labour. Similarly, Commons (1909) used the extension of markets to explain the organisation of production, the emergence of distinct classes of masters and men, and the subsequent growth and organisation of trade unions. In like manner, a large and relatively homogeneous market in the US facilitated mass production in that country compared to the smaller and more fragmented markets of Europe (Habbakuk, 1962; Rosenberg, 1969;

Hounshell, 1984). The degree of competition within the product market also influences the constraints on management. Thus, over a long period from the interwar years onwards, high levels of product market protection and collusive behaviour underpinned the position of trade unions and the development of internal labour market-type arrangements in many countries. Subsequently, the progressive opening-up of markets and the growth of international competition, especially since the 1970s, have reshaped the international division of labour and the extent to which labour can extract rents from management (Gospel, 2005).

Financial markets, ownership, and corporate governance have also historically shaped human resource systems. Owner-financed and controlled firms historically often had a personal form of paternalism and such firms tended to oppose dealings with trade unions. From the early twentieth century onwards, the growth of equity financing and the separation of ownership and control in countries such as the US and the UK allowed for a more bureaucratic approach to labour and lay behind the development of what some have described as 'welfare capitalism', with strong internal labour market-type arrangements (Brandes, 1976; Jacoby, 1985, 1997). In recent years, new financial pressures from institutional owners and private equity capital have put pressures on firms to adjust employment more directly to market forces. By contrast, up until recently, the continuation of private and more concentrated ownership and greater reliance on insider finance has meant that such pressures have been less strong in Germany and Japan (Gospel and Pendleton, 2004).

The history of labour management systems has been profoundly shaped by political and legal contexts. In countries such as the US and the UK, liberal states have overall been less interventionist in labour management than in some other countries, with so-called 'voluntarism' being a strong tradition. Even in these countries, however, there have been major exceptions, especially during two world wars, the New Deal in the US, and in the 1980s under the Reagan and Thatcher administrations. By contrast, in more coordinated economies, such as Germany, Japan, and France, there has long been a tradition of state intervention in labour matters (Crouch, 1993; Friedman, 1999; Hall and Soskice, 2001; Yamamura and Streeck, 2003). Nevertheless, it is probably true to say that over time, in most countries, there has been a gradual build-up in intervention in terms of rights off-the-job (state welfare and pension systems), rights on-the-job (workmen's compensation, health and safety, racial and sexual equality legislation), and regulation of collective employment matters (the law on trade unions, collective bargaining, and information and consultation at work). In Europe, the European Union (EU) has in recent decades taken these tendencies further (Supiot, 2001).

The social context is in many ways the most difficult to categorise and summarise. Over the decades, the position of children and women at work has changed profoundly, at least in advanced market economies. The starting age of employment has slowly risen, the proportion of women in paid employment has increased, and the numbers of people who can retire from paid employment have risen. Major changes have also come with rising living standards and a greater awareness of social and human rights. Over time, social identities have also changed, with notions of 'class' playing a significant part in worker mentalities through much of the twentieth century, but becoming less powerful in more recent decades. Other social identities at work which have long existed, on the basis of gender, race, religion, and immigrant status have been successively reshaped and added to with new identities in terms of age, sexual orientation, and disability (Noiriel, 1989; Magraw, 1992; Piore and Safford, 2005). On the other hand, traditional divides between works and staff or between hourly/weekly and monthly-paid, have slowly eroded. Managements have had to take account of these changing social contexts. The so-called 'management of diversity' in the workplace is now stressed in modern management discourse; however, history shows that this has always been a concern of management (Kossek and Lobel, 1996).

A number of final points may be made about the business context of the organisation in historical perspective. First, most firms have been small and medium-sized – though in practice least is known about human resource management in such firms. Over time, big firms have come to constitute a larger proportion of total output and of total employment, though this is larger in the US and the UK than countries such as Germany, Italy, and Japan, which have more employment in medium-sized firms. Second, there have been major compositional shifts. Generalising, the typical large employer in the early- to mid-nineteenth century was a textile company; by the mid- to late-nineteenth century, the biggest single group of major firms in most economies were railway companies; by the mid-twentieth century, the main groupings were manufacturers (steel, chemicals, automobiles, electrical); and by the end of the twentieth century, the biggest single group of large firms was to be found in retailing and financial services (Gospel and Fiedler, 2008). This predominance of certain industries played an important part in laying down patterns of labour management. Third, over time, big firms in particular have developed more sophisticated hierarchies, not least in the labour area, with the growth of 'welfare' or 'labour' managers, later 'personnel' managers, and now 'human resource' managers (Niven, 1967; Jacoby, 1985; Morikawa and Kobayashi, 1986; Kocha, 1991; Tsutsui, 1998; Fombonne, 2003). However, it should be remembered that in some countries, especially those of northern continental Europe, firms still rely significantly on outside employers' organisations and their staff for the management of industrial relations. Also, in recent years, there has been some growth in the outsourcing of the human resource function (Gospel and Sako, 2008). Fourth, big firms have also changed in structure from being historically either loosely organised holding companies or centralised, functionally organised firms at the beginning

of the twentieth century, to being more coordinated multidivisional structures and sometimes decentralised networks of firms by the end of the century (Chandler, 1962, 1977; 1990; Cassis, 1997; Whittington and Mayer, 2000). As will be shown below, this has also had implications for labour management. Finally, as already suggested, ownership and governance has changed, though differentially between countries, with personal and family ownership declining over the course of the twentieth century and outsider ownership increasing in the big firm sector, especially in the US and the UK (Gospel and Pendleton, 2004).

THE EMERGENCE OF LABOUR MANAGEMENT IN THE FIRST INDUSTRIAL REVOLUTION

Here we provide a perspective on two key industries of the first industrial revolution, viz. over the period of time roughly from the late-eighteenth century to the late-nineteenth century. The two industries are very different, textiles and railways, but they provide us with a set of insights into how labour was managed during a key period of economic transformation.

Textile industries have been at the forefront of industrialisation in many countries. Classic problems for employers emerged in these industries – in terms of work relations (how to organise production and the division of labour), employment relations (how to attract, retain, and motivate labour), and industrial relations (how authority was to be maintained and whether or not to concede employees a voice at work).

In practice, nineteenth century textile and allied industries in Europe and the US always had elements of both older artisan and newer factory production. In artisanal sectors, production was on a small scale, work was often organised on the basis of putting-out to households or small workshops, and family involvement was important. In these circumstances, masters relied on key (usually male) workers to organise their own work and controlled and paid them by piece-work where this was possible. Problems for the masters were uncertainties about the quality of production and the wage-effort relationship (Mendels, 1972; Berg, 1985). As technologies developed and markets expanded, masters increasingly built their own factories and installed machinery. In turn, this meant they had the problem of attracting larger labour forces, especially where factories were located in less populated areas near water power sources. In cotton spinning, large numbers of women and children were employed, usually under tight and often coercive systems of direct control and often paid by time. However, even within the new factories, there persisted forms of inside contracting to key workers and the possibility of drawing on pools of specialised craft labour from local industrial districts (Lazonick, 1990; Rose, 2000). The motivation to develop the factory system came from market and technological opportunities, but it also gave employers a means for better control over their labour forces (Marglin, 1974; Landes, 1986).

The emergence of this system in the UK has been classically described by Pollard (1965), who emphasised its heavy reliance on child and female labour, extensive use of piece-work, and devices such as factory housing. At the same time, there was, in most textile districts, a reliance on external economies of scale, for example in terms of apprentice-type training and piece-work price lists. In the US, the more vertically integrated cotton industry moved more quickly to introduce new technologies, to build larger factories, and to develop a greater internal division of labour within the workplace under management control. Later, in Japan, during industrialisation in the late-nineteenth and early-twentieth centuries, some similar problems for management and some similar responses are discernible. For example, in that country, factory and artisan production also coexisted, though the latter was much smaller; in the large factory sector, employers used predominantly female workforces; they built factory dormitories and provided various

forms of paternalistic benefits; and used tight supervision and simple pay and benefit systems to control workers (Nakagawa, 1979; Hunter, 2003). Today, many of these forms of work organisation and employment relations have later appeared and are still to be found in textile industries in India, China, Brazil and other rapidly developing countries today.

Under early forms of labour management, industrial relations systems were diverse. As suggested, the management of labour was often a mixture of both hard, direct control and also of paternalistic oversight of a personal ad hoc kind (Joyce, 1980). Nevertheless, some key male workers could exert control over their work and employers depended on them to organise production. In the UK, by the final half of the twentieth century, unions of male textile workers had grown to become the largest in the country, along with unions for other artisan and craft trades, engineering workers, and coalminers. Those with skills or a strong position in the production process were able to force recognition from employers of their trade societies and to establish regional or national collective bargaining where firms joined together in employers' organisations had to deal with trade unions (Jowitt and McIvor, 1989; McIvor, 1996). In the United States and continental Europe, by the First World War, collective bargaining had also developed in certain craft sectors, such as small metalworking, printing, and footwear, but on the whole it was less extensive than in the UK (Mommsen and Husung, 1985; Montgomery, 1987).

From the mid-nineteenth century onwards, the railways represented a further stage in the growth of the modern business enterprises in most countries (Chandler, 1977, 1990). In terms of labour management, railway companies encountered both a traditional and a new set of problems. Traditional problems were in terms of recruiting, training, and controlling staff, albeit on a much larger scale. New problems included the complexity of scheduling, the safety of goods and passengers, and the geographical dispersion of work. Under managements from various backgrounds (technical, governmental, military, and accounting), the railway companies were the first to put in place some of the first and largest bureaucratic systems of employment. These included more systematic recruitment, the creation of job and promotion hierarchies, and related pay systems based on fixed rates of pay. They also introduced welfare arrangements, of a less personal and more bureaucratic kind, such as housing, basic sick care, and later pension benefits for some workers, usually dependent on length of service with the firm.

Talking industrial relations, the large railway companies of the US, UK, and continental Europe were run according to a 'unitarist' rather than a 'pluralist' model of management (Fox, 1985). Management was the sole source of authority, issued commands, and expected workers to obey. A plurality of sources of authority, with legitimate worker voice and checks and balances, was not permitted. Discipline was based on the notion of a 'uniformed' service. In keeping with this and in contrast with the sectors described above, trade unions were not recognised and collective bargaining was rare, until just before or after the First World War.

This pattern of bureaucratic management later grew in other sectors, such as the gas, electricity, and water utilities (Melling, 1979; Berlanstein, 1991). It also provided something of a model for areas of industry such as steel, chemicals, and, later, oil refining. Developed in the late nineteenth and early twentieth centuries, the model has in many respects persisted up to the present day in both state and private railways and utility systems, albeit since the Second World War, with extensive unionisation and collective bargaining.

This account of bureaucratic employment on the railways prompts three further points. First, the railways were some of the first companies to develop extensive hierarchies of managerial and white-collar staff. These were necessary to organise and coordinate diverse and dispersed operations. Such employees were offered something like 'careers' within the company and moved up wage

and benefit hierarchies. Though they learnt on-the-job, there were books, magazines, and courses which they could attend. Second, and by contrast, the railways were constructed and to some extent maintained in more traditional ways, by gangs of labourers, who were apart from this bureaucratic system and did not partake of the benefits of others who worked on the railways. Third, the workshops owned by the railway companies, where engines and rolling stock were built and maintained, were also different. Here workers had more control over production, belonged to occupational craft communities, were paid wages which related more to those in craft labour markets, and were more likely to belong to trade unions. Within them, craft forms of production and management existed and unions were more likely to be recognised. However, it should also be noted that the railway workshops included some of the more sophisticated engineering shops of their days, especially in terms of work organisation (Coleman, 1981; Drummond, 1995).

THE DEVELOPMENT OF PERSONNEL MANAGEMENT IN THE SECOND INDUSTRIAL REVOLUTION: THE NEW HEAVY PROCESS AND ASSEMBLY-LINE INDUSTRIES

In the late-nineteenth and early-twentieth centuries, major industries were transformed or created entirely anew with the advent of the new general purpose technology of electricity and with new production processes (steel, chemicals, and later electrical products and automobiles). Employers in these sectors used some old methods and developed other newer forms of what came to be called personnel management.

For example, in steel and chemicals, systems of internal contracting under skilled workers and gang masters continued to exist, at least for a time. Much of the work involved these arrangements and some more skilled and strategically placed workers had considerable control over work organisation. Employment was often short-term and wage and benefit systems simple. Slowly, however, different arrangements developed. Large firms, such as Carnegie and US Steel in the United States, Krupp in Germany, and Schneider in France, substituted their own foremen for internal contractors, began to recruit more systematically, trained workers internally on the job and not usually through apprenticeship systems, and developed employment hierarchies and some of the welfare arrangements described above (notably housing, workmen's compensation, sick pay and pensions) (McCreary, 1968; Stone, 1975; Jacoby, 1985; Fitzgerald, 1988; Vishniac, 1990; Gospel, 1992; Welskopp, 1994).

In these sectors and in large-scale metalworking, there was a desire on the part of employers to gain information on worker effort and to organise work more systematically under managerial control. This developed rapidly in the US, where fast-growing and large national markets and a shortage of skilled labour gave managers an incentive to invest in the development of skill-displacing technologies. In metalworking and engineering, as early as the mid- to late-nineteenth century, there emerged a distinctive 'American system of manufactures', based on standardised and interchangeable parts. This in turn came more and more to use semi-skilled or unskilled workers, who tended high throughput machinery or worked on what came to be assembly lines (Rosenberg, 1969; Hounshell, 1984).

By the early twentieth century onwards, in various forms, this led to the development of so-called 'systematic' and 'scientific' management (Litterer, 1963; Nelson, 1975; Littler, 1982; Merkle, 1980; Fridenson, 1986; Tsutsui, 1998). The latter is usually associated with Frederick Taylor (Taylor, 1911; Nelson, 1980), but there were other writers and practitioners at the time advocating new systems of labour management. Usually some combination of the following were used: a study of the organisation of work by specialist 'time' and 'work' study experts; the reorganisation of work, often leading to a greater subdivision of jobs; and the

fixing of wages by new types of bonus systems related to performance. In practice, such arrangements developed only slowly, but with some acceleration after the First World War, especially in lighter areas of manufacturing (Nelson, 1992). The most significant technological and organisational development was the spread of the assembly line and mass production from the early-twentieth century onwards (Ford, 1926; Fridenson, 1978; Hounshell, 1984; Nelson, 1975; Meyer, 1981; Schatz, 1983; Lewchuk, 1987).

Especially where unions had a presence, these developments often met with worker resistance. In part to counter unions, there was some development of new welfare and personnel policies, though these grew as much in sectors of light industry such as food and light assembly work. There was also some interest in so-called 'human relations' techniques as a less collectivist approach to the management of labour (Nelson, 1970; Nelson and Campbell, 1972; Jacoby, 1985; Gillespie, 1991; Gospel, 1992).

THE MANAGEMENT OF INDUSTRIAL RELATIONS: THE CLASSIC CASE OF THE AUTOMOBILE INDUSTRY

Up to the First World War, in all countries, employer recognition of trade unions and collective bargaining was a minority phenomenon (Bain and Price, 1980). Union membership and recognition by employers was most extensive in the UK, followed by Germany and the US. Membership was much lower in countries such as France, Italy, and Japan, in part reflecting larger agricultural sectors and smaller scale industry in those countries. Even where unions were recognised in the UK in craft industries such as metalworking and printing, in parts of cotton spinning, and in coalmining, collective bargaining was underdeveloped and often informal, spasmodic, and subject to recurrent employer counteroffensives.

The position of trade unions was significantly strengthened during the First World War: labour markets were tight, product market competition was curtailed, and both employers and the state were dependent on workers to achieve production. In these circumstances, employers were constrained to recognise unions, not least at government prompting, and collective bargaining developed, in many cases on a multi-employer basis, covering a whole industry either regionally or nationally. After the war and especially where there was economic depression in the 1920s, employers launched counter-offensives and curtailed the scope of, or withdrew entirely from, collective bargaining. The depression which affected all countries from 1929 onwards further reduced union presence and collective bargaining declined in coverage and content (Brody, 1980; Clegg, 1985; Schneider, 1991).

From the mid-1930s onwards, however, this situation changed, especially in the automobile, electrical, and other growing industries. In the UK, unions slowly increased their membership and managements had increasingly to deal with them (Tolliday and Zeitlin, 1986; Lewchuk, 1987). For the most part they chose to do this on a multi-employer basis. In France, in the late 1930s, a combination of economic and political factors led French employers to enter into new dealings with unions, albeit temporarily (Vinen, 1991; Chapman, 1991). Employer opposition was particularly strong in the United States. But, even there, the large automobile firms recognised unions, in significant part in the context of a change in the stance of government and legal requirements introduced in the New Deal from the mid-1930s onwards and during the Second World War and its aftermath (Dubofsky, 1994). Thus, General Motors recognised the United Auto Workers in 1937 and Ford followed suit in 1941. In the United States, in contrast to Britain, employers chose to deal with unions more at a company level and negotiated formal legally binding contracts which regulated wide aspects of wages, employment, and work organisation. There were elements of pattern-setting and following within industries, but, for the most part, dealings were at the level of the firm (Slichter et al., 1960; Brody, 1980; Harris, 1985; Jefferys, 1986; Tolliday and Zeitlin, 1986). By contrast, in the UK, bargaining was often at multiple levels, including informal bargaining with shop stewards at the workplace (Edwards and Terry, 1988).

In Germany, France, Italy, and Japan, the settlement with organised labour came after the war. Under Fascist and military regimes and foreign occupation, independent unions were outlawed, state- and employer-dominated labour bodies were imposed, and most aspects of work and employment were unilaterally determined by management or government. After the war, in Germany, in a situation of turmoil, unions were recognised by employers and a system of regional and industry-wide collective bargaining emerged which has largely persisted up to the present day. Reverting to an earlier German tradition, with origins in the nineteenth century mining industry and in legislation after the First World War, there was also established by law a system of works councils at company and workplace level and worker representation on the boards of German companies. In part this was at the prompting of the British occupation authorities and met with some resistance from German business. However, over time, German employers came to accept these arrangements and accommodated them into their systems of labour management (Teuteberg, 1961; Streeck, 1992; Dartmann, 1996). It should be noted that works councils and board-level representation are to be found in other continental European countries, but not usually on the scale or with the powers of those in Germany (Rogers and Streeck, 1995).

Also after the war, Japanese employers came to terms with unions, though along different lines. At first, they confronted demands from militant general and industrial unions. With support from the American occupation authorities and the Japanese government, in the late 1940s and early 1950s, employers confronted and defeated these unions in major lockouts and strikes and replaced them with a system of enterprise-based unions.

Collective bargaining was subsequently conducted mainly at enterprise level, with some industry coordination by employers' organisations and federations of unions. This settlement with enterprise unions interacted with traditional and emerging Japanese management practices and led, during the subsequent years of economic growth in the 1950s and 1960s, to key aspects of the Japanese employment system: the provision of job security for core male workers, the use of complex wage and benefit hierarchies often related to seniority, systems of management-led consultation within the firm, and a strong ideological encouragement of the notion of the company as a community. By the mid- to late-1950s, such a system was in place in firms such as Toyota, Nissan, Toshiba, Hitachi, and other large manufacturing companies. In the 1970s, this came to be recognised as the 'Japanese system of management' and attracted considerable foreign attention (Dore, 1973; Taira, 1970; Gordon, 1985; 1998; Koike, 1988; Cusomano, 1985; Shiomi and Wada, 1995; Hazama, 1997; Inagami and Whittaker, 2005). However, as will be seen below, in the slowdown in the 1990s, the system has come under growing pressure, with some reduction of 'lifetime employment', an increase in pay based more on merit and performance, and less of a role for enterprise unions, especially in bargaining about work organisation and wage levels.

The post-war industrial relations settlements in France and Italy were rather less clear and in some ways more akin to the British situation. After the war, employers increasingly had to recognise unions and enter into collective bargaining. However, they were less able to contain a system of multi-unionism (including in these two continental countries Communist-dominated unionism) and multi-level collective bargaining. Large firms such as Renault, Citroen, Peugeot, and Fiat made varying compromises, depending on the economic and political contexts at particular times (Fridenson, 1986; Durand and Hatzfeld, 2003; Musso, 2008). In some respects, it was only in the 1980s and 1990s,

when union power was on the wane, that French and Italian companies reached a settlement of their industrial relations more acceptable to management.

In big firms in most of these countries, over the first three decades after the war, with full employment and union bargaining, there developed systems of relative job security, possibilities for internal promotion to higher paying jobs, and wages based on seniority and hierarchical grading systems. However, there were differences between countries. In Japan, the US, and Germany, management maintained more control over the production system than, say, in the UK or Italy. In Germany and Japan, workers received more training than in most of the other countries and were more involved in improvements in processes and products. This was to lead to what in Germany has been called the 'diversified quality production' system and in Japan to what came to be called the Toyota or 'lean production' system, with more consultation and discretion given to better trained workers (Ohno, 1982; Dohse et al., 1985: Streeck, 1992; Shimokawa, 1993; Wada, 1995; Tolliday, 1998).

The union-based system of personnel and industrial relations management has declined differentially across these countries. In the US, union membership fell from the mid-1960s onwards, and the coverage of collective bargaining contracted (Kochan et al., 1986; Jacoby, 1997). It is now restricted to a few areas of the private sector, such as parts of the steel, automobile, engineering, and transportation industries. In France, union membership never attained very high levels; it has fallen since the 1970s, and collective bargaining is much constrained (Howell, 1992). In the UK, a change in the economic and political climate in the 1980s led to a hollowing out of the collective bargaining-based system of labour management and the development of new forms of human resource management such as will be discussed below. Along with this, union membership has fallen (Millward et al., 2000; Gospel, 2005). In Germany and Japan, changes have been slower, but in recent years employers have come to have less recourse to collective bargaining with trade unions and more to consultation with their workers, either via work councils in Germany or more informal joint committees in Japan (Thelen, 2001; Inagami and Whittaker, 2005).

THE DEVELOPMENT OF HUMAN RESOURCE MANAGEMENT: CHALLENGES OF DIVERSITY AND FLEXIBILITY IN THE 'THIRD' INDUSTRIAL REVOLUTION

Alongside the developments described above, other trends may be distinguished from the 1970s onwards. In the post-war years, sectors which grew rapidly included electrical goods, food and drink, and household and personal consumer products. In the US and the UK, large firms, which had often grown by merger and acquisition and which had increasingly diversified into new lines of business, developed multidivisional forms of organisation to manage their diverse activities (Chandler, 1962, 1977, 1990; Whittington and Mayer, 2000). Increasingly, such firms faced 'new' labour forces, enjoying higher standards of living, with less commitment to trade unions, and more heterogeneous in terms of interests.

Increasingly firms had to develop new policies to deal with growing product market competition and changes in labour market composition. Here we give the example of the fast-moving consumer goods sector where firms came to adapt and transform a set of centralised and often paternalistic policies which they had first developed in the late-nineteenth and early-twentieth centuries. Some of these approaches have since come to be collectively described as Human Resource Management (Foulkes, 1980; Jacoby, 1997; Gospel, 1992).

In the US, for example, Procter & Gamble (P&G) had organised its labour management centrally, though with some plants unionised and others remaining non-unionised. Employment systems were rather bureaucratic;

use was made of scientific management, and dealings with the labour force had elements of paternalism. As the company grew, in part organically and in part through merger and acquisition and diversified into new areas such as food and drink, paper goods, and personal care products, so it faced new problems and challenges. These it came to manage with central direction in some key areas (the development of managerial staff and the non-recognition of unions in new plants). Through the 1970s, in most other areas, human resource management was increasingly left to the level of the constituent divisions or companies, where a degree of differentiation and controlled experimentation was allowed. On the basis of this, the company introduced new forms of job flexibility, management-directed team working, and pay for skills and performance, wherever possible maintaining a non-union environment and often with the use of contingent labour.

A similar flexible and decentralised trajectory can also be seen in Unilever in the UK, though with a time lag of a decade or more. Unilever had had a tradition of rather centralised, somewhat paternalistic employment practices which it had developed in the interwar years. In the UK context, it was less able or inclined to escape from a collective bargaining based system than P&G. Nevertheless, through the 1970s and 1980s, it transformed its practices into a more differentiated and flexible set of arrangements, based on its divisions and subsidiaries (Jones, 2005a). In France, a comparable example is Danone, that country's largest food company. Over the 1970s, BSN-Danone moved from being a glass producer to a glass bottle, drinks, and diversified food producer and then later restructured around a range of food products. It developed a rhetoric and practice of human resources and social partnership with its employees, including unions, but essentially ran its various parts in a decentralised, flexible manner. This enabled experimentation and facilitated the acquisition and disposal of companies. In many instances, these and similar firms increased their flexibility by employing a core labour force, supplemented by part-time and temporary workers (Dyer et al., 2004).

Some contrast may be drawn with the German and Japanese equivalents of these companies. Henkel and Kao both had a rather centralised and paternalistic system of labour management through to the 1970s. More slowly than their counterparts referred to above, they nevertheless introduced different arrangements – less reliance on union bargaining, more reliance on joint consultation and direct employee involvement, greater use of flexible pay and conditions, and more resort to contingent employment for different parts of their companies (Feldenkirchen and Hilger, 2001; Gospel, 1992). However, to date, they have not proceeded as far as their US, UK, and French counterparts in terms of developing variegated and flexible human resource systems. In part this reflects the fact that they have grown organically and are less diversified and divisionalised companies – a broader characteristic of both countries. In part, it also reflects the fact that they have been subject to rather more legal and union constraints (in Germany) and ideological and customary constraints (in Japan).

Up to this point we have described the development of decentralised and flexible systems of human resources management which have spread across the large firm sector. However, we also stress continuities and diversities. We have already noted national differences. In addition, some firms still remain relatively centralised (automobiles) and bureaucratic (utilities). Also, in the medium and small firm sectors, firms have not had to confront the issues of diversity of operations in the same way. Here human resource management is usually less purposely decentralized and less professionalised. In some localities, medium and small firms have also maintained external economies of scale in terms of skills training and innovative working in industrial districts such as have been identified, especially in Germany and Italy (Crouch et al., 2001). There is also a considerable spread, with

some firms pursuing 'high road' practices of good pay and conditions, high training, and employee involvement, while others pursue 'low road' practices of minimal benefits and cost minimisation (Foulkes, 1980; Guest and Hoque, 1996; Osterman, 1999).

The most marked change in employment composition in the final quarter of the twentieth century has been the decline of manufacturing and blue collar jobs and the rise of services and white collar jobs. Service companies and service work cover a wide spread. They cover the financial sector, information and communications services, hotels and catering, health and personal care, and retailing. They also cover a spread in terms of company size, from small start-up firms to some of the largest companies in the world. They also cover a wide spread of occupational levels from graduate managerial, technical, and professional employees to low-level mundane work in call centres, fast food restaurants, and retail stores. Recent changes in this sector have been very much driven by the application of new technologies of information and communications.

In financial services, there are some patterns which have long existed, as in banks and insurance companies – relative job security, gendered and educationally segmented hierarchies, and salaries and benefits which rise with age. In recent years, some of these have been subject to change, especially the notion of lifetime careers and incremental salary scales. There are also new aspects, within both old and new firms in these sectors – the reliance on self-investment in training and development, greater mobility and more flexible careers, more project working, and, especially for higher-level employees, the spread of share- and stock-based pay. However, in many telephone call centres, connected with the new service economy, work is organised along different lines – with elements of mass production, tight computer monitoring, and limited pay and benefit systems. In recent years, in these areas, there has been a growth in so-called 'outsourcing' and 'offshoring' of jobs (Marchington et al., 2005).

By the end of the twentieth century the biggest single grouping of large employers were retailers such as Wal-Mart, Target, and Home Depot in the United States, Carrefour and Auchan in France, Tesco and Kingfisher in the UK, and Metro and Karstadt in Germany. Such firms have developed further some aspects of systematic and scientific management. They make extensive use of information and communication technology to match the flow of goods, customer demand, and the deployment of labour. In turn, extensive use is made of part-time employment, often young, female, and immigrant workers, to facilitate flexible scheduling. Jobs are narrowly defined, with little scope for training and development, but employees may be expected to work flexibly across jobs, such as unloading, stacking, and checkout. Wage hierarchies are short and non-wage benefits limited. In the United States, Wal-Mart and other large retailers make efforts to promote individual identification with the company and are strongly anti-union (Lichtenstein, 2006). In Europe, unions have a limited presence and play little part in management calculations.

Human resource management systems such as operate in call centres and supermarkets, have elements of mass production such as have existed from the early twentieth century onwards. However, there are a number of important differences with earlier systems. First, computer control facilitates a more exact synchronisation of production and work. Second, there would seem to be more mixed identities on the part of workers and less solidarity and opposition to management. Third, union membership shows little sign of developing as it once did in earlier mass-production systems and more sophisticated managements seem more likely to prevent its growth.

Some commentators have recently referred to a growing diversity within national systems; this may in turn maintain diversities between national systems (Katz and Darbishire, 2000). A historical perspective suggests there has always been diversity. Certainly many arrangements described above are to be found side by side within national systems, such as the provision of discretion for more skilled and higher-level employees versus mass-production-type systems for many workers as well as elements of bureaucratic forms of management versus more differentiated and flexible systems. This same diversity may increasingly be found in manufacturing where, among other factors, unions are less able to impose uniformity. Hence, in manufacturing, some firms are pursuing so-called 'high-performance' and 'high-involvement' policies while many others have not developed sophisticated human resource strategies and provide little employee voice (Foulkes, 1980; Guest and Hoque, 1996; Osterman, 1999).

CONCLUSIONS

This chapter has concentrated on major stages in the development of human resources management in advanced capitalist economies, while stressing continuities and diversities across stages. However, we register a number of gaps. The chapter has concentrated on the history of labour management in the United States, Western Europe, and Japan. It has left out other countries: smaller countries of the developed world; Russia and the Soviet Union, China, and other former Communist states; and labour management in developing countries. In addition, the chapter has focused mainly on large firms at particular stages of history. There has been some coverage of smaller firms, especially with reference to textiles at the beginning of the period and start-up high-tech companies at the end. On the whole, however, less is known about labour management in the medium and small firm sector.

The chapter has largely left out the public sector, in central and local government and in organisations such as national post offices, utility companies, and public health service organisations. Such public sector organisations are important, not only because of their size, but also because they were often considered to be 'good' employers and historically at times acted as trend-setters for the private sector. Studies of such firms show the extensive use of bureaucratic management methods, the presence of a certain paternalism, and the strength of trade unions and collective relations with the labour force, especially through the post-Second World War period (Frost, 1983; Hannah, 1979; 1982; Berlanstein, 1991). More recently, in these sectors there are new political and market pressures which are leading to management practices emphasising more flexibility and decentralisation of operations, not least as parts of the public sector have been privatised and opened to more outside market competition.

A further caveat might be that the chapter has tended to treat labour as a rather homogeneous entity. For example, little has been said specifically about the management of female labour. However, there are some excellent historical studies of women's employment, in both manufacturing and service industries which might be used to look at the management of female labour (Glucksmann, 1990; Fourcaut, 1982; Hunter, 2003; Milkman, 1987; Cobble, 1991; Omnes, 1997; Wightman, 1999). These pose questions as to whether historically the management of female labour has been largely the same as that of men or to what extent there are different patterns of gender segregation. The chapter has concentrated mainly on lower- and middle-level, especially blue-collar-type, workers, on the basis that these have been the main group of employees over most of the time period under consideration. However, in most national economies, these are now a declining part of employment. We have touched on white-collar and managerial labour forces in several of the industry sectors, for example in discussing railways in the nineteenth century and financial services in the late twentieth century. A wide literature exists on white-collar, professional, technical, supervisory, and managerial workers which might be used for studies of white collar labour

management (Lockwood, 1958; Kocha, 1977; 1991; Melling, 1980; Hyman and Price, 1983; Morikawa and Kobayashi, 1986; Morikawa, 1991; Prendergast, 1999).

The chapter has also dealt with employment within the firm largely within one country, namely the country of origin. Since the early twentieth century, a growing number of large firms have had multinational activities and this has accelerated in the post-Second World War period. Further work needs to be done on the historical development of human resource management in such multinationals, where some of the essential decisions concern whether firms take practices from their home country, adopt those of the host country, or develop distinct global patterns of labour management (Perlmutter, 1969; Enderwick, 1985; Knox and McKinlay, 1999, 2002; Ferner and Varul, 2000; Rosenweig and Nohria, 1994; Kristensen and Zeitlin, 2005; Jones 2005b).

Bearing in mind the caveats referred to above and the emphasis throughout on both change *and* continuities, a number of conclusions may be drawn from the above survey.

First, broad stages in the development of labour management can be discerned. Thus, from the early nineteenth century, there coexisted artisanal and factory models in sectors such as textiles. The railways, heavy industry, and assembly-type industries brought the development of newer more bureaucratic systems of personnel management, especially from the late nineteenth century onwards. Subsequently, in the mid-twentieth century, in the golden age of manufacturing, union-based systems of industrial relations management were strong, especially in the big firm sector. More recently there has been a growth of more differentiated and flexible systems of human resource management within firms, in both manufacturing and services. However, it was also stressed that much work in the modern service sector and in retailing still has elements of mass-production-type systems. Thus, different stages have coexisted side-by-side and older industries have adapted to new developments. Overall, the tendency may be towards growing diversity within firms and within countries.

Second, some movement may be discerned over time from direct systems of management (based on personal supervision, simple piecework systems, and traditional paternalism), to technical or mechanical systems of management (based on scientific management principles with an attempt to build control into production processes), to bureaucratic forms of working and employment, with internal labour markets and complicated administrative hierarchies (Edwards, 1979). However, in recent years, there has been some reconfiguration of bureaucratic employment systems and of internal labour markets and there have been complex backward and forward movements between direct control and more autonomy and responsibility on the job. The examples of modern retailing and work in call centres show how direct systems of supervision and computer control continue. Thus, motivation and control based on mixes of coercive, remunerative, and normative policies have always existed. There is no linear movement in the management of human resources.

Third, in terms of industrial relations, there have been significant shifts over time. In the nineteenth and early-twentieth centuries, most employers were what might be termed 'unitarist' and believed that they had a right unilaterally to dictate aspects of work and employment. The period after the Second World War saw a shift in a more 'pluralist' direction and a greater preparedness to admit employee representation in the form of trade unions and collective bargaining. Such systems grew and even predominated through the early post-Second World War years in many industries, especially in manufacturing. However, beginning in the 1970s, there has been a shift away from such managerial ideologies and their replacement by new forms of joint consultation, direct voice, and employee involvement of various kinds, such as participation in small groups and team working. To date, these shifts have been greater in countries such as the United States, France, and the UK, where union membership in the private sector is weakest, and least in countries such as Germany and the Scandinavian countries, where union membership remains stronger.

Finally, some of the changes analysed above can be captured by the notion of externalising and internalising decisions (Coase, 1937). Firms can externalise decisions in the following ways: they can make use of external subcontracting forms of production; recruit as much as possible from the external labour market and lay off workers into the market; fix wages and benefits according to market signals; and, where they have to recognise trade unions, deal with them through outside employers' organisations. By contrast, firms can internalise decisions in various ways: they can bring production in-house and develop more elaborate internal divisions of labour; rely less on the external labour market and institute stronger internal labour markets, with more in-house training and greater job security; fix wages and benefits by internal administrative rules such as seniority or job rank; and provide employee voice via company-based consultation and bargaining (Gospel, 1992). In practice, different firms in different countries have pursued mixed strategies. However, in a long-term perspective, the following might be argued. In the nineteenth century much use was made of externalising strategies, subject to paternalistic constraints and with exceptions such as the railways where companies internalised. Over the course of the twentieth century, there was some tendency towards greater internalisation of work and employment relations, with Fordist mass production and internal labour markets, but not necessarily internalisation of industrial relations, since in Europe considerable reliance was placed on outside employers' organisations. The tendency to internalise employment relations was particularly strong in continental European countries and in Japan. Over the last quarter century, there may be some movement towards an externalization of work and employment relations, but with a greater internalisation of industrial relations within the firm. However, strategies depend not only on their relative cost, but also on the capacity of the firm to pursue them and the micro- and macro-political context within which they are implemented.

REFERENCES

Bain, G.S. and Price, R. (1980) *Profiles of Union Growth.* Oxford: Blackwell.

Berg, M. (1985) *The Age of Manufactures.* Oxford: Oxford University Press.

Berlanstein, L. (1991) *Big Business and Industrial Conflict in Nineteenth Century France: A Social History of the Parisian Gas Company.* Berkeley: University of California Press.

Brandes, S.D. (1976) *American Welfare Capitalism, 1880–1940.* Chicago: Chicago University Press.

Brody, D. (1980) *Workers in Industrial America: Essays on the Twentieth Century Struggle.* Oxford: Oxford University Press.

Cassis, Y. (1997) *Big Business: The European Experience in the Twentieth Century.* Oxford: Oxford University Press.

Chandler, A. (1962) *Strategy and Structure: Chapters in the History of the American Industrial Enterprise.* Cambridge, Mass.: MIT Press.

Chandler, A. (1977) *The Visible Hand: The Managerial Revolution in American Business.* Cambridge, Mass.: Harvard University Press.

Chandler, A. (1990) *Scale and Scope: The Dynamics of Industrial Capitalism.* Cambridge, Mass.: Harvard University Press.

Chapman, H. (1991) *State Capitalism and Working Class Radicalism in the French Aircraft Industry.* Berkeley: University of California Press.

Clegg, H. (1985) *A History of British Trade Unions since 1889: Volume 2, 1910–1933.* Oxford: Clarendon Press.

Coase, R. (1937) 'The nature of the firm', *Economica,* 4 (13): 386–405.

Cobble, D. (1991) *Dishing It Out: Utilities and their Unions in the Twentieth Century.* Urbana, Ill.: University of Illinois.

Coleman, T. (1981) *The Railway Navvies.* Ebury: Vintage.

Commons, J. (1909) 'American Shoemakers 1648–1895: A sketch of industrial evolution', *Quarterly Journal of Economics,* 24 (1): 39–84.

Crouch, C. (1993) *Industrial Relations and European State Traditions.* Oxford: Oxford University Press.

Crouch, C., Le Gales, P., Trigillia, C. and Voelzkow, H. (eds) (2001) *Local Production Systems in Europe: Rise or Demise?* Oxford: Oxford University Press.

Cusomano, M. (1985) *The Japanese Automobile Industry: Technology and Management in Nissan and Toyota.* Cambridge, Mass.: Harvard University Press.

Dartmann, C. (1996) *Redistribution of Power: Joint Consultation or Productivity Coalitions? Labour and Postwar Reconstruction in Germany and Britain 1945–1953.* Bochum: Brockmeyer.

Dohse, K., Jürgens, U. and Malsh, T. (1985) 'From "Fordism" to "Toyotaism"? The social organization of the labour process in the Japanese automobile industry', *Politics and Society,* 14 (2): 115–46.

Dore, R. (1973) *British Factory – Japanese Factory.* Berkeley: University of California Press.

Drummond, D.K. (1995) *Crewe: Railway Town, Company, and People, 1840–1914.* Aldershot: Scolar Press.

Dubofsky, M. (1994) *State and Labor in Modern America.* Chapel Hill, NC: University of North Carolina Press.

Dunlop, J. (1958) *Industrial Relations Systems.* New York: Henry Holt.

Durand, J.P. and Hatzfeld, N. (2003) *Living Labour: Life on the Line at Peugeot France.* London: Palgrave Macmillan.

Dyer, D., Dazell, F. and Olegario, R. (2004) *Rising Tide.* Cambridge, Mass.: Harvard Business School Press.

Edwards, R. (1979) *Contested Terrain.* New York: Basic Books.

Edwards, P. and Terry, M. (1988) *Shopfloor Politics and Job Control.* Oxford: Blackwells.

Enderwick, P. (1985) *Multinational Business and Labour.* London: Macmillan.

Feldenkirchen, W. and Hilger, S. (2001) *Menschen und Marken.* Dusseldorf: Henkel.

Ferner, A. and Varul, M. (2000) 'Internationalisation and personnel management in German multinationals', *Human Resource Management Journal,* 10 (3): 79–96.

Fitzgerald, R. (1988) *British Labour Management and Industrial Welfare 1846–1939.* London: Croom Helm.

Fombonne, J. (2003) *Personnel et DRH.* Paris: Vuibert.

Ford, H. (1926) 'Mass production', in *Encyclopaedia Britannica,* 23rd edn suppl. vol. 2. London and New York: Encyclopaedia Britannica, pp. 821–3.

Foulkes, F.K. (1980) *Personnel Policies in Large Nonunion Companies,* Englewood Cliffs, NJ: Prentice Hall.

Fox, A. (1985) *History and Heritage.* London: Allen & Unwin.

Fourcaut, A. (1982) *Femmes a l'usine en France dans l'entre-deux-guerres.* Paris: Maspero.

Friedman, G. (1999) *State-Making and Labor Movements: France and the United States, 1876–1914.* Ithaca, NY: Cornell University Press.

Fridenson, P. (1978) 'The coming of the assembly line in Europe', in W. Krohn (ed.), *The Dynamics of Science and Technology*. Dordrecht: W. Krohn, pp. 159–75.

Fridenson, P. (1986) 'Automobile workers in France and their work, 1914–1983', in S.L. Kaplan and C.J. Koepp (eds.), *Work in France: Representation, Meaning, Organization, and Practice*. Ithaca, NY: Cornell University Press, pp. 514–47.

Frost, R. (1983) *Alternating Current*. Ithaca, NY: Cornell University Press.

Gillespie, R. (1991) *Manufacturing Knowledge*. Cambridge: Cambridge University Press.

Glucksmann, M. (1990) *Women Assemble: Women Workers in the New Industries in Interwar Britain*. London: Routledge.

Gordon, A. (1985) *The Evolution of Labor Relations in Japan: Heavy Industry 1853–1955*. Cambridge, Mass.: Harvard University Press.

Gordon, A. (1998) *The Wages of Affluence: Labor and Management in Postwar Japan*. Cambridge, Mass.: Harvard University Press.

Gospel, H. (1992) *Markets, Firms, and the Management of Labour in Modern Britain*. Cambridge: Cambridge University Press.

Gospel, H. (2005) 'Markets, firms, and unions: historical and institutionalist perspectives on the future of unions', in S. Fernie and D. Metcalf (eds), *Unions and Performance*. London: Routledge, pp. 19–44.

Gospel, H. and Fiedler, M. (2008) 'The long-run dynamics of big firms: The 100 largest employers in global perspective'. Mimeo, London, King's College.

Gospel, H. and Pendleton, A. (2004) 'Corporate governance and labour management: an international comparison', in H. Gospel and A. Pendleton, *Corporate Governance and Labour Management: An International Comparison*. Oxford: Oxford University Press, pp. 1–32.

Gospel, H. and Sako, M. (2008) 'The unbundling of corporate functions: the evolution of shared services and outsourcing in human resource management', Mimeo, Said Business School, University of Oxford.

Guest, D. and Hoque, K. (1996) 'The good, the bad, and the ugly: employment relations in new non-union workplaces', *Human Resource Management*, 5 (1): 1–14.

Habbakuk, J. (1962) *American and British Technology in the Nineteenth Century: The Search for Labor-Saving Inventions*. Cambridge: Cambridge University Press.

Hall, P. and Soskice, D. (2001) *Varieties of Capitalism*. Oxford: Oxford University Press.

Hannah, L. (1979) *Electricity before Nationalisation*. Baltimore: John Hopkins University Press.

Hannah, L. (1982) *Engineers, Managers, and Politicians*. Baltimore: John Hopkins University Press.

Harris, H. (1985) *The Right to Manage: Industrial Relations Policies of American Business in the 1940s*. Madison: University of Wisconsin Press.

Hazama, H. (1997). *History of Labor Management in Japan*. London: Macmillan.

Hounshell, D.A. (1984) *From the American System to Mass Production, 1800–1932: The Development of Manufacturing Technology in the United States*. Baltimore: John Hopkins University Press.

Howell, C. (1992) *Regulating Labor*. Princeton, NJ: Princeton University Press.

Hunter, J. (2003) *Women and the Labour Market in Japan's Industrialising Economy*. London: Routledge.

Hyman, R., and Price, R. (eds) (1983) *The New Working Class? White Collar Workers and their Organisations*. London: Macmillan.

Inagami, T. and Whittaker, D.H. (2005) *The New Community Firm: Employment, Governance and Management Reform in Japan*. Cambridge: Cambridge University Press.

Jacoby, S. (1979) 'The origins of internal labor markets in Japan'. *Industrial Relations*, 18 (2): 184–96.

Jacoby, S. (1985) *Employing Bureaucracy: Managers, Unions and the Transformation of Work in American Industry 1900–1945*. New York: Columbia University Press.

Jacoby S. (1997) *Modern Manors: Welfare Capitalism since the New Deal*. Princeton, NJ: Princeton University Press.

Jefferys, S. (1986) *Management and Managed*. Cambridge: Cambridge University Press.

Jones, G. (2005a) *Multinationals and Global Capitalism: From the Nineteenth Century to the Twenty-First Century*. Oxford: Oxford University Press.

Jones, G. (2005b) *Renewing Unilever: Transformation and Tradition*. Oxford: Oxford University Press.

Jowitt, J.A. and McIvor, A.J. (eds) (1989) *Employers and Labour in the English Textile Industries, 1850–1939*. London: Routledge.

Joyce, P. (1980) *The Culture of the Factory in Later Victorian England*. London: Methuen.

Katz, H. and Darbishire, O. (2000) *Converging Divergencies: World-Wide Changes in Employment Systems*. Ithaca, NY: Cornell University Press.

Knox, W. and McKinlay, A. (1999) 'Working for the Yankee Dollar', *Historical Studies in Industrial Relations*, 7 (1): 1–26.

Knox, W. and McKinlay, A. (2002) 'Organising the unorganised: union recruitment strategies in American transnationals', in G. Gall (ed.), *Union Organising*. London: Routledge, pp. 389–404.

Kocha, J. (1977) *White-Collar Workers in America 1900–1940*. London: Sage.

Kocha, J. (1991) *Industrial Change and Bourgeois Society: Business, Labor, and Bureaucracy in Modern Germany*. New York: Berghahn.

Kochan, T., Katz, H. and McKersie, R. (1986) *The Transformation of American Industrial Relations*. New York: Basic Books.

Koike, K. (1988) *Understanding Industrial Relations in Modern Japan*. London: Macmillan.

Kossek, E. and Lobel, S. (1996) *Managing Diversity*. Oxford: Blackwell.

Kristensen, P.H. and Zeitlin, J. (2005) *Local Players in Global Games: Strategic Constitution of a Multinational Corporation*. Oxford: Oxford University Press.

Landes, D. (1986) 'What do bosses really do?', *Journal of Economic History*, 46 (3): 585–623.

Lazonick, W. (1990) *Competitive Advantage on the Shopfloor*. Cambridge, Mass.: Harvard University Press.

Lewchuk, W. (1987) *American Technology and the British Vehicle Industry*. Cambridge: Cambridge University Press.

Lewis, W.A. (1952) 'Economic development with unlimited supplies of labour', *The Manchester School*, 22 (2): 139–91.

Lichtenstein, N. (ed.) (2006) *Wal-Mart: Template for 21st Century Capitalism*. New Press: New Press.

Litterer, J.A. (1963) 'Systematic management: design for organizational recoupling in American manufacturing firms', *Business History Review*, 27 (4): 369–91.

Littler, C. (1982) *The Development of the Labour Process in Capitalist Societies*. London: Ashgate.

Lockwood, D. (1958) *The Black Coated Worker*. London: Allen & Unwin.

McCreary, E.C. (1968) 'Social welfare and business: the Krupp welfare programme, 1860–1914', *Business History Review*, 42, Spring: 24–49.

McIvor, A.J. (1996) *Organised Capital: Employers' Associations and Industrial Relations in Northern England, c. 1880–1939*. Cambridge: Cambridge University Press.

Magraw, R. (1992) *A History of the French Working Class*, vols. 1 and 2. Oxford: Blackwell.

Marchington, M., Grimshaw, D., Rubery, G. and Willmott, H. (2005) *Fragmenting Work, Blurring Organisational Boundaries, and Disordering Hierarchies*. Oxford: Oxford University Press.

Marglin, S. (1974) 'What do bosses do? The origins and functions of hierarchy in capitalist production', *Review of Radical Political Economics*, 6 (2), Summer: 60–112.

Melling, J. (1979) 'Industrial strife and business welfare philosophy: the South Metropolitan Gas Company from the 1880s to the first world war', *Business History*, 21 (2): 183–221.

Melling, J. (1980) '"Non-commissioned officers": British employers and their supervisory workers, 1880–1920', *Business History*, 5 (2): 183–221.

Mendels, F. (1972) 'Proto-industrialisation: the first phase of the industrialisation process', *Journal of Economic History*, 32 (1): 241–61.

Meyer, S. (1981) *The Five Dollar Day: Labor Management and Social Control in the Ford Motor Company, 1908–1921*. New York: Charles Scribner.

Merkle, J. (1980) *Management and Ideology: The International Scientific Management Movement*. Berkeley: University of California Press.

Milkman, R. (1987) *The Dynamics of Job Segregation by Sex during World War II*. Urbana, Ill.: University of Illinois Press.

Millward, A., Bryson, A. and Forth, J. (2000) *All Change at Work*. London: Routledge.

Mommsen, W.J. and Husung, H.G. (eds) (1985) *The Development of Trade Unionism in Great Britain and Germany, 1880–1914*. London: Allen and Unwin.

Montgomery, D. (1987) *The Fall of the House of Labor*. New York and Cambridge: Cambridge University Press.

Morikawa, H. (1991) 'The education of engineers in modern Japan: an historical perspective', in H.F. Gospel (ed.), *Industrial Training and Technological Innovation: a Comparative and Historical Study*. London: Macmillan, pp. 136–47.

Morikawa, H. and Kobayashi, K. (eds) (1986) *Development of Managerial Enterprise*. Tokyo: Tokyo University Press.

Musso, S. (2008) 'Labour in the third industrial revolution', Mimeo, University of Turin.

Nakagawa, K. (1979) *Labour and Management*. Tokyo: Tokyo University Press.

Nelson, D. (1970) '"A newly appreciated art": the development of personnel work at Leeds and Northrup, 1915–23', *Business History Review*, 44, Winter: 520–35.

Nelson, D. (1975) *Managers and Workers: Origins of the New Factory System in the United States, 1880–1920*. Madison: University of Wisconsin Press, pp. 5–39.

Nelson, D. (1980) *Frederick W. Taylor and the Rise of Scientific Management*. Madison: University of Wisconsin.

Nelson, D. (1992) 'Scientific management in retrospect', in Daniel Nelson (ed.), *A Mental Revolution*. Columbus: Ohio State University Press, pp. 5–39.

Nelson, D. and Campbell, S. (1972) 'Taylorism versus welfare work in American industry: H. L. Gantt and the Bancrofts', *Business History Review*, 56, Spring: 1–16.

Niven, M. (1967) *Personnel Management 1913–63*. London: Institute for Personnel Management.

Noiriel, G. (1989) *Workers in French Society in the Nineteenth and Twentieth Centuries*. London: Berg.

Ohno, T. (1982) 'How the Toyota production system was created', *Japanese Economic Studies*, 10/4, Summer: 83–101.

Omnes, C. (1997) *Ouvrières Parisiennes*. Paris: École des Hautes Études en Sciences Sociales.

Osterman, P. (1999) *Securing Prosperity: How the American Labor Market has Changed and What to do about It*. Princeton, NJ: Princeton University Press.

Perlmutter, H. (1969) 'The tortuous evolution of the multinational enterprise', *The Columbia Journal of World Business*, 4 (1): 9–18.

Piore, M. and Sabel, C. (1984) *The Second Industrial Divide: Possibilities for Prosperity*. New York: Basic Books.

Piore, M. and Safford, S. (2005) 'Changing regimes of workplace governance: shifting axes of social mobilisation', Mimeo, Cambridge, Mass.: MIT Press.

Pollard, S. (1965) *The Genesis of Modern Management*. London: Edward Arnold.

Prendergast, C. (1999) 'The provision of incentives in firms', *Journal of Economic Literature*, 37 (1): 7–63.

Rogers, J. and Streeck, W. (eds) (1995) *Works Councils: Consultation, Representation, and Participation*. Chicago: Chicago University Press.

Rose, M. (2000) *Firms, Networks, and Business Values: The British and American Cotton Industries*. Cambridge: Cambridge University Press.

Rosenberg, N. (ed) (1969) *The American System of Manufactures*. Edinburgh: Edinburgh University Press.

Rosenzweig, P. and Nohria, N. (1994) 'Influences on human resource management practices in multinational companies', *Journal of International Business Studies*, 25 (2): 229–51.

Schatz, R.W. (1983) *The Electrical Workers: a History of Labor at General Electric and Westinghouse 1923–1960*. Urbana, Ill.: University of Illinois Press.

Schneider, M. (1991) *A Brief History of the German Trade Unions*. Bonn: Dietz.

Scranton, P. (1997) *Endless Novelty: Speciality Production and American Industrialisation 1865–1925*. Princeton, NJ: Princeton University Press.

Shimokawa, K. (1993) 'From the Ford system to the just-in-time production system: a historical study of international shifts in automobile production systems', *Japanese Yearbook of Business History*, 10: 83–105.

Shiomi, H. and Wada, K. (eds.) (1995) *Fordism Transformed*. Oxford: Oxford University Press.

Slichter, S.H., Healy, J.L. and Livernash, R.E. (1960) *The Impact of Collective Bargaining on Management*. Washington, DC: Brookings.

Smith, A. (1776) *An Enquiry into the Nature and Causes of the Wealth of Nations*, 1904 edn. London: Methuen.

Stone, K. (1975) 'The origins of job structures in the steel industry', in R.C. Edwards, M. Reich and D.M. Gordon (eds), *Labor Market Segmentation*. Lexington, Mass.: D.C. Heath & Co, pp. 27–84.

Streeck, W. (1992) *Social Institutions and Economic Performance: Studies of Industrial Relations in Advanced Capitalist Economies*. London: Sage.

Supiot, A. (2001) *Beyond Employment: Changes in Work and the Future of Labour Law in Europe*. Oxford: Oxford University Press.

Taira, K. (1970) *Economic Development and the Labor Market in Japan*. New York: Columbia University Press.

Taylor, F.W. (1911) *The Principles of Scientific Management*. New York: Harper.

Teuteberg, H.J. (1961) *Geschichte der industriellen Mitbestimmung in Deutschland*. Tübingen: J.C.B. Mohr.

Thelen, K. (2001) 'Varieties of labor politics in the developed democracies', in P. Hall and D. Soskice, *Varieties of Capitalism*, Oxford: Oxford University Press, pp. 71–103.

Tolliday, S. (ed) (1998) *The Rise and Fall of Mass Production*, vols. 1 and 2. Elgar Reference Collection: International library of critical writings in business history. Cheltenham: Edward Elgar.

Tolliday, S. and Zeitlin, J. (eds) (1986) *The Automobile Industry and its Workers: Between Fordism and Flexibility*. Cambridge: Polity Press.

Tsutsui, W. (1998) *Manufacturing Ideology: Scientific Management in Twentieth-Century Japan*. Princeton: Princeton University Press.

Vinen, R. (1991) *The Politics of French Business 1936–45*. Cambridge: Cambridge University Press.

Vishniac, J.E. (1990) *The Management of Labor: The British and French Iron and Steel Industries, 1860–1918*. Greenwich, Conn.: JAI Press.

Wada, K. (1995) 'The emergence of the 'flow production' method in Japan', in H. Shiomi, and K. Wada, (eds.) *Fordism Transformed*. Oxford: Oxford University Press, pp. 11–27.

Welskopp, T. (1994) *Arbeit und Macht im Hüttenwerk: Arbeits- und indust rielle Beziehungen in der*

*deutschen und amerikanischen Eisen- und Stahlin-
dustrie von den 1860er bis den 1930er Jahren.* Bonn:
Dietz.

Whittington, R. and Mayer, M. (2000) *The European
Corporation: Strategy, Structure, and Social Science.*
Oxford: Oxford University Press.

Wightman, C. (1999) *More than Munitions: Women,
Work, and the Engineering Industries 1900–1950.*
London: Longmans.

Yamamura, K. and Streeck, W. (eds) (2003) *The End
of Diversity? Prospects of German and Japanese
Capitalism.* Ithaca, NY: Cornell University Press.

3

Models of Strategic Human Resource Management

Saba Colakoglu, Ying Hong and
David P. Lepak

INTRODUCTION

The field of strategic human resource management (HRM) has been defined as 'the pattern of planned human resource deployments and activities intended to enable an organization achieve its goals' (Wright and McMahan, 1992: 298), or 'organizational systems designed to achieve competitive advantage through people' (Snell et al., 1996: 62). Both definitions reinforce the notion that HRM practices create valuable resources within the firm that are capable of producing competitive advantage through people. Indeed, more than two decades of research has accumulated a vast body of knowledge which suggests that HRM practices that impact the motivation, knowledge, skills, and behaviors of employees lead to better employee, organizational, and financial outcomes (e.g., Arthur, 1994; Batt, 2002; Boselie et al., 2005; Collins and Clark, 2003; Dyer and Reeves,

1995; Datta et al., 2005; Huselid, 1995; Youndt et al., 1996).

In order to explain such linkages between HRM practices and various dimensions of organizational effectiveness, strategic HRM researchers have drawn on theories that originated in fields as diverse as strategy, sociology, psychology, and economics, reflecting, in part, the multi-disciplinary nature of this field (Schuler and Jackson, 2005; Wright and McMahan, 1992). In this chapter, we first review an organizing logic of theoretical perspectives related to the universalistic, contingency, and configurational perspectives. Second, we briefly review two of the dominant theoretical frameworks used to inform the HRM – firm performance linkage: the resource-based view and the behavioral perspective. Third, we highlight emerging perspectives in strategic HRM research, zooming in to the employee cognitive and social dimensions. Finally, we examine the burgeoning research models focusing on international aspects of strategic HRM.

MODES OF THEORIZING IN STRATEGIC HRM RESEARCH

Conceptually, one of the pervasive questions in strategic HRM literature focuses on understanding the ways and conditions under which HRM practices contribute to firm performance. A 'taxonomy' approach, first proposed by Delery and Doty (1996), has been widely taken to categorize and organize strategic HRM research into universalistic, contingency, and configurational perspectives (Delery and Doty, 1996; McMahan et al., 1999). These three alternate perspectives guide most thinking and research in this field up to this day.

Universalistic perspective

The universalistic perspective suggests that there is a set of practices which are regarded as 'best practices in HRM' and work in all organizations regardless of context. Essentially, this perspective suggests that some HR practices are simply good practices and all firms should use them. Practices such as selectivity in recruiting and selection, employee involvement, teams, flexible work assignments, job security, training and development, and incentive programs are argued to be beneficial for any organization that uses them. Selective recruiting, for example, conveys the message that the company values outstanding employees and contributes to the attraction and retention of strategic talent in firms (Koch and McGrath, 1996; Pfeffer, 1995). According to the universalistic perspective, such intermediary outcomes benefit all organizations, despite differences in strategy, technology, industry, and the like.

In line with this thinking, empirical research that examines the universal effects of HRM practices study their individual and direct linkages with organizational outcomes. Researchers have shown that certain staffing practices such as conducting validation studies, structured interviews and intelligence

tests are positively related to company profit (Terpstra and Rozell, 1993). Similarly, certain practices associated with training (Russell et al., 1985) and compensation (Gerhart and Milkovich, 1990) are associated with important organizational outcomes across different contexts.

Contingency perspective

The contingency perspective holds that the impact of HRM practices on firm performance depends on their fit, congruence, or alignment with firms' respective internal (i.e., business strategy, life cycle/developmental stages, culture, technology, structure) and external (i.e., industry) contingencies (Baird and Meshoulam, 1988; Jackson and Schuler, 1995; Jackson et al., 1989; Lado and Wilson, 1994; Lepak et al., 2002). The guiding logic in this perspective is that HRM practices can elicit needed role behaviors for given organizational contingencies (Jackson et al., 1989; Schuler and Jackson, 1987) and affect firm performance through manipulating employees' attitudes and behaviors (Jackson and Schuler, 1995). Organizations therefore need to focus on designing HRM systems that develop employee skills, knowledge, and motivation such that employees behave in ways that are aligned with such contingencies.

Strategy

Within the field of strategic HRM, it is proposed that a firm's strategy has important implications for its HRM practices. To find support for this proposition, strategic HRM scholars have typically drawn from generic strategy typologies such as that of Miles and Snow (1984) who differentiate between prospector, defender, and analyzer companies and that of Porter (1990) who differentiates between a cost leadership and a differentiation strategy. These different types of strategies are often matched with varying degrees of emphasis on HRM practices that foster either reliable or creative employee behavior and competencies (Jackson et al., 1989; Lado and Wilson, 1994; Tsui et al., 1995). For instance, Arthur (1992) reported the matching of a 'control' or 'cost reduction'

RM system with cost leadership strategy and the linkage of a 'commitment' HRM system with differentiation/flexibility strategy in steel minimills. Jackson et al. (1989) examined the pursuing of a differentiation strategy through an HRM system that supports employee innovation. They found that in order to encourage innovation, companies tend to provide less incentive compensation and more job security so that failures will not be punished and tend to provide more training to meet both current and future needs. Similarly, Osterman (1994) found that companies undertaking a 'high road' strategy are more likely to implement innovative work practices such as quality circles, job rotation schemes, and team-based production, compared to companies with a 'low road' strategy.

However, empirical support for the performance benefits relating to the contingency perspective – that the alignment between strategy and HRM practices result in enhanced organizational performance – remains mixed (e.g, Huselid, 1995; Rodriguez and Ventura, 2003, Youndt et al., 1996). Yet, several researchers found support for the crux of the strategic contingency argument. For example, MacDuffie (1995) showed that flexible HRM systems contribute to productivity and quality when coupled with a flexible production strategy. Youndt et al. (1996) reported that the use of administrative HRM systems for a standardized production strategy reduces cost and controls behavior while the use of human-capital-enhancing HRM systems for a quality manufacturing strategy results in higher operational performance. Delery and Doty (1996) found that companies using a prospector strategy received greater financial performance from using results-oriented appraisals and providing internal career opportunities, while companies adopting a defender strategy performed better with more employee participation in decision making. At the same time, however, Huselid (1995) failed to find support for a contingency perspective. Nevertheless, the alignment between HR practices and business strategy retains a considerable spot in much of strategic HRM theorizing.

Industry sector

Significant distinctions between manufacturing and service industries have been noted by researchers and practitioners – with service industries being characterized by their intangible nature, involvement of customers in the production of services, as well as the simultaneity of their production and consumption (Bowen and Schneider, 1988). Such industry characteristics have substantial implications for managing service employees (Jackson et al., 1989). For example, employees should be self-committed to quality, attend closely to customer needs, and possess appropriate discretion to deal with customer problems. Indeed, Jackson et al. (1989) found that service sector companies were more likely to utilize customer input as part of the performance appraisal process and use the results to determine employee compensation, compared to companies in the manufacturing industry. In relation, Baron et al. (1988) examined the divisions between mass-production, service, and other sectors and found that mass-production industries tend to follow scientific management procedures and use centralized personnel functions with formal job analysis and employee record keeping.

Industry characteristics, such as capital intensity, industry growth, industry product differentiation, and industry dynamism were also shown to impact the relationships between HRM practices and firm outcomes (Datta et al., 2005). Datta et al. (2005) suggested that industries that are capital-intensive, have a high demand growth, and have more differentiated products, tend to require highly-skilled employees and reported that the impact of high-performance HRM systems on labor productivity is especially salient in these types of industries.

Technology

Technology may be defined as 'a system's processes for transforming inputs into usable outputs' (Jackson and Schuler, 1995: 244). Corresponding to the standardization and customization product typologies, the technology used for manufacturing those products can be categorized into mass production (i.e., for standardized products) and flexible specialization (i.e., for customized products). Research shows that organizations using flexible specialization or advanced manufacturing technologies require highly-skilled employees, more diverse employee skills, tend to link performance appraisal results with compensation and training needs, and use innovative work practices such as teams, job rotation, and quality circles. Possibly due to the complexity involved in managing flexible specialization technology, companies that utilize such technologies were also found to be more willing to pay managerial employees premiums in order to attract and retain them (Jackson et al., 1989; Osterman, 1994; Snell and Dean, 1992).

Organizational structure

Organizational structure refers to 'the allocation of tasks and responsibilities among individuals and departments' (Jackson and Schuler, 1995: 244). One categorization of organizational structure is to differentiate between centralized (i.e., decisions made by upper management) and decentralized (i.e., decisions made by lower levels) organizations (Tsui et al., 1995). Tsui et al. (1995) argue that centralized organizations tend to use job-focused employment relationships – defined as having explicit tasks and requirements – whereas decentralized organizations are more likely to use organization-focused relationships that are geared towards broadly-defined tasks and employee involvement. In relation, Jackson et al. (1989) noted the inferences for HRM that are derived from an organization's structure of departmentalizing by product or departmentalizing by function. They reason that compared to functional departmentalization, product-based departmentalization requires more emphasis on result-orientation, external-orientation, and integration-orientation. Their findings confirm that companies that are structured along product lines are more likely to provide stock options and bonuses based on firm-level productivity.

Configurational perspective

It is not sufficient, however, to address the vertical fit of HRM practices with contingencies internal and external to the organization. The congruence of HRM practices within the system is equally important (Baird and Meshoulam, 1988; Delery and Doty, 1996; Wright and McMahan, 1992). Such an inter-practice alignment is also referred to as 'horizontal fit', 'internal fit', 'complementarity', or 'bundling'. This perspective suggests that it is the overall configuration of a set of internally aligned HRM practices that impact organizational outcomes rather than single HRM practices taken in isolation (Delery, 1998). The guiding logic in this approach is that complementary clusters of HRM practices create multiple paths and opportunities that impact the skills, abilities, behaviors, and motivation of employees, which in turn results in increased firm performance (McDuffie, 1995; Ichniowski et al., 1997).

Conceptually, there are two forms of configurational approaches. First is the traditional configurational approach. This configurational approach extends the universalistic perspective and suggests that the combination of HRM practices, rather than any single practice, is what drives organizational performance. The central tenet of the configurational perspective is that a bundle of HRM practices must be adopted that complement each other to achieve greater performance. The degree of this internal or horizontal alignment among HRM practices influences whether or not companies realize a synergistic effect on firm effectiveness (Baird and Meshoulam, 1988).

For example, Huselid (1995) found that high-performance work systems were related with turnover rate and labor productivity, which in turn, were related to two financial indicators of firm performance. Way (2002) and Batt (2002) found significant relationships between high performance work systems and labor productivity and turnover rate for small companies and service companies, respectively. Similarly, Ichniowski et al. (1997) found a positive relationship between innovative work practices and labor productivity for steel-finishing lines. Similarly, McDuffie's (1995) results support the synergistic effects of HRM practices on organizational outcomes.

Second, some researchers adhere to a contingent configurational approach. Essentially, researchers may extend the configurational perspective and examine whether or not the benefits of internally aligned systems or bundles of HRM practices depend on some contextual factor (Lepak et al., 2006). For example, in one of the earliest strategic HRM studies, Miles and Snow (1984) proposed three different HRM systems that are internally aligned: building, acquiring, and allocating. Moreover, these three distinct HRM systems were argued to be used within companies pursuing different strategies. Essentially, within each system, HRM practices tend to have a coherent pattern corresponding to the major theme or objective of the organizational system (McMahan et al., 1999). Baird and Meshoulam (1988) proposed six major components of the HRM system: management awareness, management of the function, portfolio of programs, personnel skills, information technology, and awareness of the environment. They posit that the six components should be consistent with each other and aligned with developmental stage in order to reach maximal effectiveness and efficiency (Baird and Meshoulam, 1988). Lepak and Snell (1999; 2002) identify four configurations of HRM practices: commitment-, productivity-, compliance-, and collaborative-based HR systems corresponding to four different employment modes. Lepak and Snell (2002) found support for the matching of employee modes and HR configurations. In their study, a commitment-based HR configuration was matched with knowledge-based employees; a productivity based HR configuration was used for job-based employees; and a compliance-based HR configuration was used for contract employees.

Despite differences in the terms used to denote which practices comprise an HRM system, a consistently positive relationship between high performance work systems (Becker and Huselid, 1998; Huselid, 1995), high involvement (Guthrie, 2001), human capital enhancing (Youndt et al., 1996), commitment-based HRM systems (Arthur, 1994), or innovative employment practices (Ichniowski et al., 1997) and aggregate performance measures such as plant (e.g., Arthur, 1994; Ichniowski et al., 1997; Youndt et al., 1996), business-unit (e.g., Delery and Doty, 1996; Koch and McGrath, 1996) and corporate performance (e.g., Becker and Huselid, 1998; Huselid, 1995) has been found.

Summary

To date, these distinct modes of theorizing have and continue to dominate strategic HRM research. Our review shows that there is empirical support for all the three perspectives, albeit at varying degrees. While the universalistic perspective tends to have gained considerable empirical support, the support for the contingency perspective can be described as mixed at best. The configurational perspective remains widely accepted and adopted in strategic HRM research in which researchers tend to examine systems of HRM practices rather than single and isolated ones.

One final note on the mixed support for the contingency perspective is warranted. This perspective continues to keep its conceptual allure for strategic HRM scholars. Thus, some researchers have shifted their attention to finding alternative conceptualization of, especially, the strategy – HRM fit. For example, it is suggested that HRM systems that researchers study should be targeted toward more specific strategic objectives such as service, innovation, or safety rather than generic strategy typologies (Bowen and Ostroff, 2004; Lepak et al., 2006). That is, these scholars argue, the focus and content of HRM practices researchers study can be derived from more concrete strategic objectives that firms might have rather than the generic strategy typologies that are readily available. Thus, we expect a trend in this direction in future studies.

THEORETICAL FRAMEWORKS IN STRATEGIC HRM RESEARCH

While the previous discussion highlights different modes of theorizing researchers have emphasized in the study of the HRM – firm performance relationship, Figure 3.1 reflects a review by Wright and colleagues of various theories that have been used to provide greater insights into the different theories and their focus and assumptions of how HRM systems operate. Because there have been numerous reviews of the traditional theories that are available to strategic HRM scholars (e.g., McMahan et al., 1999; Jackson and Schuler, 1995; Schuler and Jackson, 2005), in this section we will only be covering two of the more established or at least most widely used theories that have been highly influential in this field of research: 1) the resource-based view of the firm that equips strategic HRM research with a strategic orientation; and 2) the behavioral perspective which offers a more psychological insight to understanding the impact of HRM on firm performance. These perspectives have also been categorized under strategic theories (Wright and McMahan, 1992) or proactive theories of strategic HRM (McMahan et al., 1999) which we believe are better aligned with the *raison d'être* for this line of research (Becker and Huselid, 1998). A detailed description of other theories of strategic HRM can be found in Schuler and Jackson (2005), Wright and McMahan (1992) and McMahan et al. (1999).

Resource-based view

The resource-based view (RBV) of the firm has undoubtedly dominated strategic HRM research in recent years as the main theoretical foundation that explains the linkage between HRM and firm performance. Two main assumptions underlying this view are that first, firms are heterogeneous with respect

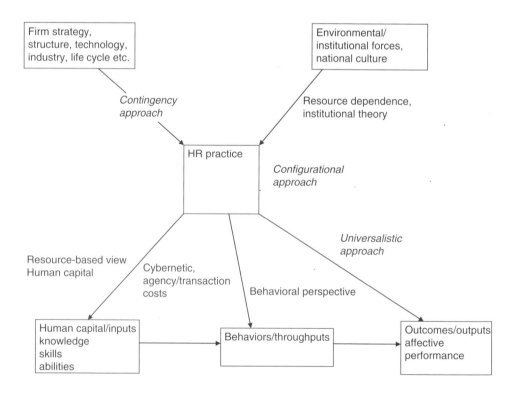

Figure 3.1   Sources: McMahan et al. (1999); Wright and McMahan (1992); Wright and Snell

to the strategic resources (i.e., physical, organizational, or human) that they control and second, that these resources are imperfectly mobile within factor markets (Barney, 1991). Based on these assumptions, companies that control valuable, rare, imperfectly imitable, and non-substitutable resources are able to generate sustained competitive advantage (Barney, 1991).

In strategic HRM research, the RBV has mainly been used to establish the rationale for empirical research rather than directly testing the theory (Boselie et al., 2005; Wright et al., 2001). Strategic HRM researchers have based their research on arguments derived from RBV, that the knowledge, skills, and abilities of a firm's workforce are instrumental in creating strategic value. Assuming that human resources are normally distributed in the labor market, this theory suggests that firms which possess rare human resources are more advantaged competitively compared to other firms. Such rare and valuable human resources can be developed through, for example, selective hiring and extensive training practices, that serve as key foundations for high investment HRM systems.

Another path by which human resources can contribute to competitive advantage is their inimitability (Lado and Wilson, 1994; Wright and McMahan, 1992). Inimitable human resources often arise from unique historical conditions, where the events that shape a firm's culture and norms do not happen in other firms. Also, causal ambiguity – that the causal relationship pertaining to the firm's competencies is intangible – can render human resources inimitable. Related, human resources can be inimitable because of their *social* complexity/interconnectedness – the idiosyncratic social relations among human resources or among the tacitness, complexity, and specificity of assets (Dierickx and Cool, 1989; Reed and DeFillipi, 1990). Finally, for human resources to create sustained competitive advantage, they should be non-substitutable by other strategic assets (Barney, 1991). This may be more applicable in knowledge-intensive industries than labor-intensive industries, where it is very hard

to replace the innovative nature of human resources by other assets (Jackson and Schuler, 1995; Wright et al., 1994).

Empirical research drawing from RBV has typically placed emphasis on examining the impact of a configuration of internally and externally aligned HRM practices, assuming that it is the complexity of alignments that makes human resources a source of competitive advantage. Based on this logic, researchers have demonstrated that high performance work systems (Huselid, 1995), innovative employment practices (Ichniowski et al., 1997), commitment HRM systems (Arthur, 1994), or high involvement HRM practices (Batt, 2002) have direct effects on market based performance (Huselid, 1995), productivity (Ichniowski et al., 1997), lower scrap rates (Arthur, 1994), lower quit rates (Arthur, 1994; Batt, 2002), and higher sales growth (Batt, 2002).

While these findings provide strong evidence for the HRM-firm performance relationship within the RBV framework, we would argue that it is not the system of HRM practices that have the qualities of a resource capable of generating sustained competitive advantage. Rather, it is the human and social capital that they create which may be valuable, inimitable, rare, and non-substitutable (Boselie et al., 2005; Wright et al., 2001). For example, Hitt et al. (2001) found a positive, curvilinear relation between the quality of education and tenure of a firm's workforce and financial performance as measured by return on sales. Similarly, Hatch and Dyer (2004) found that investments in firm-specific human capital (education requirements and screening) increased learning-by-doing performance as measured by the lowering of manufacturing costs as manufacturing experience increases.

Yet, research that explicitly examines whether or not certain HRM systems are associated with valuable, rare, inimitable, or non-substitutable resources is lacking. Rather, researchers often invoke this logic but limit their empirical examinations to a direct relationship between HRM systems and relevant outcomes. Moving forward, we would argue that strategic HRM research grounded in RBV needs to shift its focus from testing the linkages between a set of HRM practices and performance to testing its core concepts as well as contributing factors associated with time compression diseconomies, causal ambiguity, and social complexity (Wright et al., 2001).

Behavioral perspective

Complementing the previous theory, the behavioral perspective argues that although human capital is essential, employees need to exhibit appropriate role behaviors in order to contribute to the achievement of organizational goals. The central tenet of behavioral perspective, therefore, is that HRM practices affect firm outcomes through managing employees' displayed behavior (Jackson and Schuler, 1995; Schuler and Jackson, 1987). There are, in fact, different types of behaviors that are more appropriate depending on organizational strategy and other relevant contingencies. For instance, behaviors vary along repetitive versus innovative, risk taking versus risk averse, flexible versus inflexible, or competitive versus cooperative. The role for organizations is therefore to determine which behaviors are appropriate for their strategy, and which HRM practices are effective in eliciting these behaviors (Schuler and Jackson, 1987; Wright and McMahan, 1992). For instance, different types of rent sharing practices (organizational-, group-, and individual-level) that correspond to different strategic focus can elicit fundamentally different employee behaviors (Coff, 1997).

By placing emphasis on needed role behaviors, the behavioral perspective complements the human capital theory by recognizing that employee behaviors are also instrumental in organizational effectiveness in addition to employee knowledge and skills. However, despite the obvious importance of how employees actually act while at work, direct empirical tests are limited that examine the role of behaviors in the HRM-performance relationship.

EMERGING PERSPECTIVES

Having reviewed the theoretical underpinnings of the HRM-performance relationship and the dominant theories and their empirical evidence, we now explore more recent attempts to uncover the mediating mechanisms through which HRM practices impact performance. We believe that the current developments around the cognitive and social domains take the field one step closer to developing strategic HRM-specific models.

A cognitive perspective in strategic HRM

While the traditional perspectives summarized above have focused on the rationales and different paths through which HRM can influence organizational performance, one limitation they have in common is that they implicitly assume universality and predictability of employee behaviors and attitudes that stem from exposure to HRM practices. In other words, they do not explicitly recognize subjective and natural human processes such as cognitions – mental processes of perceiving, recognizing, conceiving, judging, and reasoning – as processes that employees go through before reacting to those practices. Thus, the cognitive paradigm, which focuses on how people structure their experiences and how they make sense of them (Cacioppo et al., 1981), may inform strategic HRM research further.

Taking a cognitive strategic HRM perspective suggests that employees are not merely passive responders to events but make active judgments regarding the causes of events which they observe or are exposed to (Heider, 1958). For example, Bowen and Ostroff (2004) pointed out that the effect of HRM practices depends on the ways in which employees interpret and respond to them. They suggest that the HRM-firm performance linkage can be best understood by analyzing the psychological and collective climates that HRM systems create as the mediating mechanisms in this relationship.

Accordingly, when employees share a common interpretation of what behaviors are important, expected, and rewarded, such a strong organizational climate collectively guides the behaviors of individuals towards the objectives of the firm resulting in firm performance. These scholars also propose that the 'strength' of the HRM system is what creates such shared interpretations. That is, unless the HRM system stands out in the organizational context, sends consistent massages, and results in agreement among employees about its meaning, employees will go though different cognitive cycles, inhibiting the intended effects of the HRM system.

Closely related to the psychological and collective climate view (Bowen and Ostroff, 2004), other researchers examined the role of attributions in the HR-employee outcome relationship. For example, Koys (1988; 1991) distinguished between internal attributions of HRM practices made by employees (i.e., viewed as within the control of the company) and external attributions of HR practices (i.e., viewed as out of control of the company). Internal attributions were argued to be more strongly related to employee attitudes and behaviors than external attributions. Extending this argument, Nishii (2003) distinguished between positive and negative internal attributions. Positive internal attributions – that is employee beliefs that their company uses HR practices because employees are viewed as an asset or because their company cares about their well-being – were argued to be related to positive attitudes and behaviors such as satisfaction, commitment, and organizational citizenship behaviors.

Other theories and constructs such as social exchange theory, perceived organizational support, and psychological contracts can also be categorized under a cognitive perspective since they deal with subjective and idiosyncratic perceptions or interpretive processes that employees go through to make sense of their relationship with their organizations. For example, social exchange theorists (e.g., Gouldner, 1960) examine the exchanges

that take place between employers and employees regarding perceptions of reciprocity. According to the norms of reciprocity, employees feel obliged to respond equitably to organizational inducements. These feelings of obligation, in turn, are associated with positive attitudes and more productive behaviors (Eisenberger et al., 1986; Shore and Wayne, 1993).

Closely related to social exchange theory and perceived organizational support, psychological contracts are expressed or implied promises made by the organization – i.e., job security, benefits, and pay – and the subjective perceptions of these promises by employees that lead to feelings of either their fulfillment or breach (Rousseau, 1995). Consistent with this perspective, Takeuchi et al. (2007) found that the relationship between high-performance work systems and establishment performance was mediated by both the level of human capital among employees as well as the quality of the organization's social exchange relationships with employees.

Based on these emerging developments in the cognitive domain, at least from a strategic HRM standpoint, we argue that this perspective is necessary to contour the strategic HRM picture. In fact, recent research has started to integrate the macro HRM research with the more micro perspectives such as industrial/organizational psychology and organizational behavior literature (Wright and Boswell, 2002). Thus, we encourage additional and multi-level research that examines the role of various cognitive processes in the HRM-performance relationship.

The role of social capital

Our previous discussion centered on how HRM affects human capital, cognitive processes, and behaviors of individuals as isolated entities in an organization. However, employees do not exist in isolation; instead, they are embedded in social relationships with supervisors, coworkers, subordinates, clients, and the like (Brass, 1995). The growing field of social capital research, in turn, centers on how these relationships among individuals affect employee and work outcomes and has recently started to receive attention from strategic HRM scholars (e.g., Youndt et al., 2004; Collins and Clark, 2003).

Social capital is a perspective that targets the linkages between actors, rather than the actors themselves (Brass, 1995). As opposed to human capital which resides in individuals, social capital is defined as 'the sum of the actual and potential resources embedded within, available through, and derived from the network of relationships possessed by an individual or social unit' (Nahapiet and Ghoshal, 1998: 243). There are three pivotal dimensions of social capital in the literature. The structural dimension concerns the patterns or configurations of relationships among a group of individuals (Nahapiet and Ghoshal, 1998). Two types of social structures, strong ties and weak ties, for example, have been noted to contribute to different types of knowledge transfer and learning. Strong ties among individuals enable the transfer of fine-grained and tacit knowledge; whereas weak ties are more amenable for gathering non-redundant information and stimulating novel knowledge creation (Hansen, 1999). The relational/affective dimension of social capital addresses the motives, expectations, and norms of the actors in the network (Coleman, 1988; Kang et al., 2007; Nahapiet and Ghoshal, 1998). Trust, for example, is a key element in the affective relations among networking parties. Trust embedded in social relationships is essential for interaction efficiency because it not only saves times from decision-making processes but also provides access to otherwise unattainable information and resource (Uzzi, 1997). Finally, the cognitive dimension of social capital refers to the shared understanding, language, culture, and norms among individuals (Nahapiet and Ghoshal, 1998). The common understanding of norms and sanctions are particularly useful for groups to motivate members to act for the interests of the collective entity instead of private interests (Coleman, 1988).

A switch of focus from the actors to their relations has meaningful implications for strategic HRM research. Burt (1997), for example, posits that the value of human capital is meaningless without social capital. He states that '(w)hile human capital refers to individual ability, social capital refers to opportunity' (p. 339). In other words, social capital acts as a 'catalyzer' of human capital. As noted by Subramaniam and Youndt (2005: 459), 'unless individual knowledge is networked, shared, and channeled through relationships; it provides little benefit to organizations in terms of innovative capabilities. Thus, it may be appropriate to move beyond traditional definitions of human capital that revolve primarily around educational and functional skills to include competencies surrounding interpersonal skills and networking' and examine the ways in which HRM practices can build those competencies (Collins and Clark, 2003).

Indeed, attributes of social capital have significant implications for facilitating individual, group, and organizational performance. As mentioned above, social capital is a critical facilitator of the development and utilization of human capital – the benefits of human capital can not be unleashed without the opportunities provided by social capital (Coleman, 1988). Besides, there are numerous benefits that could be brought in by social capital. The most immediate benefits are facilitating fast and fluid information and resource exchange (Uzzi, 1997), encouraging exploitative and exploratory learning and innovation (Kang et al., 2007, Subramian and Youndt, 2005, Lepak et al., 2007), and cultivating individual members' attitudes and behavior (Leana and Van Buren, 1999).

Cultivating social capital

Given the potential benefits of social capital, it is important to understand how social capital emerges within organizations. As Leana and Van Buren (1999) noted, three major ways that organizational practices can develop social capital are building stable relationships among organizational members; developing organizational reciprocity norms; and defining specified roles and establishing bureaucracy to a certain extent. Stable relationships in organizations are usually established through a long-term orientation. Time within the organization is important because it creates stable relationships among members that market transactions could not have created. HRM practices such as job security, internal labor markets, training, and collaborative work are all contributive to the development of such stable relationships that are essential for social capital. Second, various motivating mechanisms can be used to establish organizational reciprocity norms, including the use of selection, promotion, and reward mechanisms to encourage reciprocity behavior, and the employment of socializing to foster such an atmosphere.

Employing the framework of development of human capital, Adler and Kwon (2002) propose that social capital is actualized by employees' abilities, motivation, and opportunities to build social capital. Therefore, HRM practices can be geared towards a specific function to develop social capital. For instance, recruitment and selection are often used to select diverse or similar employees according to strategic needs (Brass, 1995). Training and socialization are useful ways to not only build social connections among employees (Brass, 1995), but also to prepare individuals (such as TMTs) with relationship-building skills (Collins and Clark, 2003). Performance appraisals and incentive compensation tied to the development of social capital are useful for motivating them to display such effort (Collins and Clark, 2003). Indeed, it is shown that network-building HRM practices affects firm performance through the development of TMT's social capital (Collins and Clark, 2003), and that HRM investments are associated with higher general human and social capital of organizations (Youndt et al., 2004).

Finally, related to the aforementioned organizational structure, bureaucracy and specified roles are related to the structural aspect of social capital, where the collective norms are developed through the positions of members (Leana and Van Buren, 1999). Interdependence among members through embedded relationships in the organization

may be beneficial for the development of social capital. Moreover, as opposed to markets, organizations establish network closure where explicit boundaries separate within-organization members from external entities. Such network closure may enable social capital to develop (Coleman, 1988; Nahapiet and Ghoshal, 1998).

The actual structure of the organization may also play an important role. Two types of position arrangement, vertical differentiation (positions are differentiated by administrative hierarchy) and horizontal differentiation (positions are differentiated by work flow, job design, technology etc.), are essential in determining the work relationships of employees (Brass, 1995). The former is often the characteristic of 'mechanistic organizations', where rigid structures and rules are set. The later, in contrast, often exists in 'organic organizations', where rules and procedures are flexible and the structure is decentralized (Brass, 1995). Brass argues that social networks often overlap in mechanistic organizations but are often denser and more connected in organic organizations. In addition, the physical proximity and on-going interactions between members in the organization further reinforce the relationships established. Given this, choices organizations make regarding the organizational structure will influence the likelihood that they are able to cultivate and capitalize on the benefits of social capital.

Organizations, consisting of interrelated actors, are conducive to the creation of social capital in the organization (Nahapiet and Ghoshal, 1998). At the same time, actors make conscious decisions regarding how to use their social capital in organizations. As a result, we would encourage research that focuses not only on the creation of social capital, but how it operates and how employees use their relationships to facilitate (or hinder) individual and organizational performance.

So far we have elaborated the evolution of the field from those covered in Wright and colleagues' comprehensive model, to the recognition of the unique effect of social relationship beyond traditional understanding of individual human capital and behavior in isolation, which shines much light on the field of strategic HRM as it was, is, and will be. These perspectives, however, were positioned in a general context, vastly based on the US experience. Yet, there is increasing attention to the global context and its implication for strategic HRM. In what follows, we will extend our vision to a global context and review the development of strategic HRM in other countries.

STRATEGIC HRM IN THE GLOBAL CONTEXT

We focus on two aspects of strategic HRM within the global context. First, we review some of the studies that were conducted outside the US to look for external validity evidence for the HRM-firm performance linkage. Second, we review strategic HRM models pertaining to organizations that are operating globally.

Strategic HRM outside the US

Since the mid-1990s, the majority of the high-impact developments and research in the field of strategic HRM have come from North America – and in particular, the US (Arthur, 1994, Batt, 2002; Bowen and Ostroff, 2004; Collins and Clark, 2003; Datta et al., 2005; Huselid, 1995; Lepak and Snell, 1999). As a result, some researchers have questioned whether theories of strategic HRM developed in the US generalize to other regional and cultural contexts that are significantly different from that of the US (Brewster, 2007; Wright et al., 2005). Although there has been a considerable amount of strategic HRM related research in other parts of the world (Bae and Lawler, 2000; Fey and Bjorkman, 2001; Guthrie, 2001; Li, 2003), these studies have not been reviewed collectively to increase our understanding of the generalizability of strategic HRM theories to other national and cultural contexts. Thus, one of the major issues facing the strategic HRM field remains to be the external validity and the

generalizability of these models (Wright et al., 2005). Our purpose in this section is to focus on research conducted outside the North American context to shed some light on this gap.

In order to come up with a preliminary observation on the external validity of strategic HRM theories, we reviewed 17 studies.[1] Out of the 17 studies we reviewed, three were conducted in Russia, three in Singapore, three in Korea, two in China, two in Spain, one in Belgium, one in Netherlands, one in New Zealand, one in Taiwan, one in Thailand, one in Australia, one in India, and one in Hong Kong. According to this distribution, the regional clusters that were represented in these studies were Southern Asia (India, Thailand), Confucian Asia (China, Hong Kong, Korea, Singapore, Taiwan), Latin Europe (Spain, Belgium), Germanic Europe (Netherlands), Eastern Europe (Russia), and the Anglo cluster (New Zealand and Australia) (House et al., 2004). Thus, while the number of studies conducted in a single country is low, the empirical evidence that has accumulated on a regional cluster level is considerable; thus enabling generalizability inferences for strategic HRM models.

In line with the mainstream strategic HRM studies, studies outside the North American context have relied primarily on RBV (Barney, 1991) to explain the linkages between HRM practices and firm performance (e.g., Fey and Bjorkman, 2001; Park et al., 2003). While all these studies discuss the idiosyncrasies of the national or institutional contexts in which the studies were conducted, few have explicitly incorporated cultural theories and cultural values that may impede or enhance the impact of HRM practices that were mainly developed in the US. For example, Bae and Lawler (2000) questioned whether being high on the cultural dimensions of collectivism and power distance would limit the ability of firms to implement high-involvement work systems in Korea. They suggested that in hierarchical cultures, the empowerment aspects of high-involvement HRM strategies may not be readily accepted by managers or subordinates.

Further, they argued that employees may be more fatalistic in collectivist cultures and be less prone to have the self-efficacy requisite for independent action. Similarly, Ngo et al. (1998) adopted a cultural values framework and argued that some HRM practices could be more acceptable in some countries due to differences in cultural values such as uncertainty avoidance and power distance (Hofstede, 1980). Given that cultural values are significant determinants of whether certain organizational practices are accepted and effective in a given society (Hofstede, 1980; House et al., 2004), we suggest that future studies further elaborate on the cultural context.

Despite the importance of unique cultural and institutional forces that may dictate whether HRM-performance relationship holds in different countries, the empirical studies we reviewed reveal that such practices may indeed be effective regardless of the national context. For example, Guthrie (2001) found high performance work systems to be positively related to productivity for firms in New Zealand, De Saa Perez and Garcia-Falcon (2002) found a positive relation between HRM practices and managerial, input-based, output-based, and transformational capabilities and overall firm performance in the Spanish banking industry, and Bae and Lawler (2000) found a positive relation between high-involvement HRM practices and subjective measures of organizational performance in Korea. Collectively, these findings may provide initial support for the external validity of US born strategic HRM theories and models.

While the main effects seem to be similar across countries, interesting contingency effects emerge when both local companies and subsidiaries of foreign multinational enterprises are included in the same study (Bae and Lawler, 2000; Bae et al., 2003; Ngo et al., 1998). For example, Ngo et al. (1998) argued and found some support that the relation between HRM practices and firm performance would be stronger for local firms in Hong Kong compared to the subsidiaries of American, British,

and Japanese multinationals. Their findings indicated that training and development practices and retention-oriented practices were more strongly related to employee retention and satisfaction levels despite the lower availability of such practices in local firms. Similarly, Bae et al. (2003) found that the relation between high-involvement work practices and subjective measures of performance were stronger for local firms compared to subsidiaries of foreign firms in a sample of companies in Thailand, Taiwan, Singapore, and Korea. Although such findings are preliminary at best, they may suggest that local firms are better able to align the delivery of HRM practices with the cultural values and norms of the local workforce. They may further indicate the 'liability of foreignness' costs (Zaheer, 1995; Miller and Eden, 2006) related to managing HRM in the subsidiaries of multinational enterprises; costs that are incurred due to unfamiliarity with the foreign environment.

Although there is some evidence that multinational companies respond to pressures for local isomorphism by tailoring some of their HRM practices to the local context (Myloni et al., 2004; Rosenzweig and Nohria, 1994), these practices are mostly those that are in contrast to local employee regulations – such as pay and benefit practices. More strategic practices such as selection methods, performance appraisals, training and development practices, or participation in decision-making may more closely resemble the headquarters orientation that may not be perfectly aligned with the cultural context. Therefore, future studies may try to uncover the subtle differences between the ways in which certain HRM practices are delivered by local and multinational companies to understand this contingency effect.

Models of strategic international HRM

Understanding strategic HRM within the context of multinational enterprises (MNEs) continues to grow in importance (Schuler and Jackson, 2005; Schuler et al.,

2002; Sparrow and Braun, 2007). Due to the complexity and heterogeneity of the context in which MNEs operate, unique strategic HRM issues emerge in such organizations; the most salient one being the opposing pressures for global integration on one hand, and local responsiveness on the other (Rosenzweig and Nohria, 1994; Schuler et al., 1993; Stroh and Caligiuri, 1998). As such, a common influence in these models has been Perlmutter's (1969) work that identifies three distinct attitudes of top managers in MNEs towards building their worldwide operations. The distinction between ethnocentric, polycentric, and geocentric international orientations that differ on the extent to which global integration and local sensitivity is desired or achieved is a recurrent theme in most of the strategic international HRM models.

Besides these similarities among the models, they can be categorized under two major themes: 1) 'Evolutionary models' that were typically introduced during the early years of the field's development (e.g. Adler and Ghadar, 1990; Edstrom and Lorange, 1984; Perlmutter, 1969) and 2) 'integrative models' (e.g. Schuler et al., 1993; Taylor et al., 1996) that are more intricate and that recognize the simultaneous need to integrate and differentiate international HRM practices (Sparrow and Braun, 2007).

Evolutionary models of strategic international HRM

Evolutionary models of strategic international HRM are based on the notion that HRM practices of an MNE depend on the various ways of classifying the evolution of the MNE – such as organizational or product life cycles (Adler and Ghadar, 1990; Milliman et al., 1991) or the evolution of the strategic management process from local to global (Edstrom and Lorange, 1984). For example, Adler and Ghadar (1990) examined the stages in a product's life cycle as the firm advances in to an increasingly global mode of operation. Their model predominantly focuses on the link between four stages of internationalization – domestic,

internationalization, multinationalization, globalization – and expatriate management practices, such as who will be assigned to expatriate positions (i.e. parent country nationals and third country nationals), what impact will international assignments have on individuals' careers, and how they will be rewarded and compensated based on these four stages. Milliman et al. (1991) extended the Adler and Ghadar (1990) model based on an argument that product life cycles are too short and that many MNEs have multiple products that go through different stages in their life cycles. Their model, which represents the transition from evolutionary models to more intricate integrative models, focused on four organizational life cycle stages based on Baird and Meshoulam (1988) – organizational initiation, functional growth, controlled growth, and strategic integration. These researchers further argue that, different from purely domestic organizations, there are essentially two levels of analysis in an MNE – within subsidiary/headquarters level of analysis and between subsidiaries and headquarters – and that both need to be paid attention to in strategic international HRM models.

The evolutionary models of strategic international HRM may be criticized on the grounds that they focus only on one variable that the HRM system needs to be aligned with – i.e., product life cycle – and do not take into consideration other possible variables (Sparrow and Braun, 2007). They also fall short of explaining how an MNE can implement different international policies and practices while accounting for different contingencies in multiple host countries (Sparrow and Braun, 2007). The complexity of the context and the integration-differentiation issues are addressed in-depth in the integrative models of strategic international HRM.

Integrative models of strategic international HRM

These models can be distinguished from the evolutionary models by their focus on a complex set of contingency relationships among the various components of an MNE's structure, environment, and its HRM practices (Schuler et al., 1993; 2002; Taylor et al., 1996). Such a focus on the organizational structure and strategy of the MNE in these models reflects the developments in the field of ideal-type MNEs such as the 'transnational' organization of Bartlett and Ghoshal (1988) and the 'heterarchy' of Hedlund (1986). These ideal-type structures are presented as a solution to the global integration-local responsiveness dilemma faced by MNEs. Integrative models in international HRM posit that HRM practices can simultaneously integrate the various units of the MNE together based on informal control mechanisms and also differentiate these different units by tailoring HRM practices according to local needs.

A significant feature of the integrative frameworks has been an explicit recognition that the multiple alignments between people practices, MNE's structure, and strategy result in better organizational outcomes such as performance (Carpenter et al., 2001; Peterson et al., 1996; Schuler et al., 1993; Stroh and Caligiuri, 1998). Schuler et al. (1993), for example, identified strategic components of an MNE as inter-unit linkages and internal operations, which have an impact on strategic international HRM issues, policies, and practices. In their model, exogenous (i.e. type of global industry, nature of competitors, political, legal, socio-cultural and economic conditions) and endogenous (i.e. MNE structure, international orientation, experience in running international operations) factors moderate the relation between strategic MNE components and HRM issues, functions, policies, and practices having an impact on the goals and concerns of the MNE such as global competitiveness, efficiency, and organizational learning.

Taylor et al. (1996) extend the previous models by drawing from RBV and the resource dependence theory. These scholars view MNE's home HRM system as a resource for building the global HRM system and explicitly explore how the global strategic HRM system evolves over time. Accordingly, resources may be found at the national, firm, or the subsidiary level dictating what kind of strengths the resulting HRM system will have and also which HRM competencies will be context-specific or context-generalizable. In the Taylor et al., (1996) model, parent's international strategy and top management beliefs determine the orientation of the HRM system. The orientation of the HRM system thus can be exportive, adaptive, or integrative, having an impact on the degree of similarity of the subsidiary's HRM system to the parent's HRM system.

These models have carried the international strategic HRM models to a more advanced level and the frameworks developed in these models had major impact on future strategic international HRM studies (Park et al., 2003; Peterson et al., 1996; Stroh and Caligiuri, 1998). Yet, these models may be criticized on several grounds (Edwards and Kuruvilla, 2005; Kiessling and Harvey, 2005; Schuler et al., 2002; Sparrow and Braun, 2007). First, it is suggested that the accumulation of independent variables makes these integrative frameworks almost untestable (Sparrow and Braun, 2007). Indeed, studies of strategic international HRM test only parts of the developed models and use a variety of measures, limiting our capability to develop consistent and coherent empirical evidence in this area. Second, the independence of a number of variables in these models can be questioned (Sparrow and Braun, 2007). The abundance of conceptual categorizations that refer to the global integration-local responsiveness framework (Perlmutter, 1969; Bartlett and Ghoshal, 1989; Porter, 1986) makes some of the propositions in these frameworks and studies tautological. Moreover, the same conceptualizations are used differentially in different studies to refer to strategy, industry, or international orientation, contributing to the limitation of developing a coherent body of knowledge. Finally, some argue that the conceptualization of national effects is inadequate – culture being an unsatisfactory catch-all phrase for national differences (Edwards and Kuruvilla, 2005). In sum, there is still much room for conceptual and empirical development in the study of strategic HRM in MNEs.

CONCLUSION

Strategic HRM is a dynamic field, evolving quickly from its early focus on understanding the patterns of impact of HRM practices and systems on performance to embracing the mediating mechanisms associated with individuals and the social context in which HR systems operate. We can view the theoretical models in strategic HRM as adhering to one of several dominant perspectives – the universalistic, contingency, or configurational perspectives. At the same time, researchers in this area continue to push the boundaries of what we know and are engaging in exciting research that delves deeper into the mediating mechanisms of how HRM systems work. And while most of the dominant strategic HRM theories have been developed and tested in North America, outstanding research is conducted internationally. Given the increasing globalization of companies, customers, labor, and stakeholders, we encourage more research into understanding how different facets of the internationalization of business impact on how people are managed within different cultures, as well as how companies balance the simultaneous management of a globally diverse workforce and customer base.

NOTE

1 Mainly, we gathered these studies from *Academy of Management Journal*, *Journal of International Business Studies*, and *International Journal of Human Resource Management*, for the period of 1995–2006.

REFERENCES

Adler, N.J. and Ghadar, F. (1990) 'International strategy from the perspective of people and culture: The North American context', in A.M. Rugman (ed.), *Research in Global Strategic Management*. Greenwich, CT: JAI Press, pp. 179–206.

Adler, P. and Kwon, S. (2002) 'Social capital: Prospects for a new concept', *Academy of Management Review*, 27 (1): 17–40.

Arthur, J.B. (1992) 'The link between business strategy and industrial relations systems in American steel minimills', *Industrial and Labor Relations Review*, 45: 488–506.

Arthur, J.B. (1994) 'Effects of human resource systems on manufacturing performance and turnover', *Academy of Management Journal*, 37 (3): 670–87.

Bae, J. and Lawler, J.J. (2000) 'Organizational performance and HRM strategies in Korea: Impact on firm performance in an emerging economy', *Academy of Management Journal*, 43: 502–17.

Bae, J., Chen, S., Wan, T.W.D., Lawler, J.J. and Walumba, F.O. (2003) 'Human resource strategy and firm performance in Pacific Rim countries', *International Journal of Human Resource Management*, 14: 1308–32.

Baird, L. and Meshoulam, I. (1988) 'Managing two fits of strategic human resource management', *Academy of Management Review*, 13 (1): 116–28.

Barney, J. (1991) 'Firm resources and sustainable competitive advantage', *Journal of Management*, 17: 99–129.

Baron, J.N., Devereaux-Jennings, P. and Dobbin, F.R. (1988) 'Mission control? The development of personnel systems in U.S. industry', *American Sociological Review*, 53: 497–514.

Bartlett, C.A. and Ghoshal, S. (1988) 'Organizing for worldwide effectiveness: The transnational solution', *California Management Review*, 31: 54–74.

Batt, R. (2002) 'Managing customer services: Human resources practices, quit rates, and sales growth', *Academy of Management Journal*, 45 (3): 587–97.

Becker, B.E. and Huselid, M.A. (1998) 'High performance work systems and firm performance: A synthesis of research and managerial implications', in G.R. Ferris (ed.), *Research in personnel and human resources management*, Vol. 16. Greenwich, CT: JAI Press, pp. 53–101.

Boselie, P., Dietz, G. and Boon, C. (2005) 'Commonalities and contradictions in HRM and performance research', *Human Resource Management Journal*, 15: 67–92.

Bowen, D.E. and Schneider, B. (1988) 'Services marketing and management: Implications for organizational behavior', *Research in Organizational Behavior*, 10: 43–80.

Bowen, D.E. and Ostroff, C. (2004) 'Understanding HRM-firm performance linkages: The role of "strength" of the HRM system', *Academy of Management Review*, 29: 203–21.

Brass, D.J. (1995) 'A social network perspective on human resources management', in G.R. Ferris (ed.), *Research in personnel and human resources management*, Vol. 13. Greenwich, CT: JAI Press, pp. 39–79.

Brewster, C. (2007) 'Comparative HRM: European views and perspectives', *International Journal of Human Resource Management*, 18 (5): 769–87.

Burt, R.S. (1997) 'The contingent value of social capital', *Administrative Science Quarterly*, 42 (2): 339–65.

Carpenter, M.A., Sanders, W.G. and Gregersen, H.B. (2001) 'Bundling human capital with organizational context: The importance of international assignment experience on multinational firm performance and CEO Pay', *Academy of Management Journal*, 44: 493–512.

Cacioppo, J.T., Harkins, S.G. and Petty, R.E. (1981) 'The nature of attitudes and cognitive responses and their relationships to behavior', in R.E. Petty, T.M. Ostrom and T.C. Brock (eds), *Cognitive responses in persuasion*. Hillsdale, NJ: Erlbaum, pp. 31–54.

Coff, R. (1997) 'Human assets and management dilemmas: Coping with hazard on the road to resource-based theory', *Academy of Management Review*, 22 (2): 374–402.

Coleman, J.S. (1988) 'Social capital in the creation of human capital', *American Journal of Sociology*, 94: 95–120.

Collins, C.J. and Clark, K.D. (2003) 'Strategic human practices, top management team social networks, and firm performance: The role of human resource practices in creating organizational competitive advantage', *Academy of Management Journal*, 46: 740–51.

Datta, D.K., Guthrie, J.P. and Wright, P.M. (2005) 'Human resource management and labor productivity: Does industry matter?', *Academy of Management Journal*, 48: 135–45.

De Saa-Perez, P. and Garcia-Falcon, J.M. (2002) 'A resource-based view of human resource management and organizational capabilities development', *The International Journal of Human Resource Management*, 13 (1): 123–40.

Delery, J.E. (1998) 'Issues of fit in strategic human resource management: Implications for research', *Human Resource Management Review*, 8: 289–309.

Delery, J.E. and Doty, D.H. (1996) 'Modes of theorizing in strategic human resource management: Tests of universalistic, contingency, and configurational performance predictions', *Academy of Management Journal*, 39 (4): 802–35.

Dierickx, I. and Cool, K. (1989) 'Asset stock accumulation and sustainability of competitive advantage', *Management Science*, 35: 1504–11.

Dyer, L. and Reeves, T. (1995) 'Human resource strategies and firm performance: What do we know, where do we want to go?', *International Journal of Human Resource Management*, 6: 657–67.

Edstrom, A. and Lorange, P. (1984) 'Matching strategy and human resources in multinational corporations', *Journal of International Business Studies*, 15: 2125–137.

Edwards, T. and Kuruvilla, S. (2005) 'International HRM: National business systems, organizational politics, and the international division of labour in MNCs', *International Journal of Human Resource Management*, 16 (1): 1–21.

Eisenberger, R., Huntington, R., Hutchinson, R. and Sowa, D. (1986) 'Perceived organizational support', *Journal of Applied Psychology*, 71: 500–7.

Fey, C. and Bjorkman, I. (2001) 'The effect of human resource management practices on MNC subsidiary performance in Russia', *Journal of International Business Studies*, 32: 59–75.

Gerhart, B. and Milkovich, G.T. (1990) 'Organizational differences in managerial compensation and financial performance', *Academy of Management Journal*, 33: 663–91.

Gouldner, A.W. (1960) 'The norm of reciprocity', *American Sociological Review*, 25: 161–78.

Guthrie, J.P. (2001) 'High-involvement work practices, turnovers, and productivity: Evidence from New Zealand', *Academy of Management Journal*, 44 (1): 180–90.

Hansen, M.T. (1999) 'The search-transfer problem: The role of weak ties in sharing knowledge across organization subunits', *Administrative Science Quarterly*, 44: 82–111.

Hatch, N.W. and Dyer, J.H. (2004) 'Human capital and learning as a source of sustained competitive advantage', *Strategic Management Journal*, 25: 1155–78.

Hedlund, G. (1994) 'A model of knowledge management and the N-Form corporation', *Strategic Management Journal*, 15: 73–90.

Heider, F. (1958) *The psychology of interpersonal relations*. New York: Wiley.

Hitt, M.A., Bierman, L., Shimizu, K. and Kochhar, R. (2001) 'Direct and moderating effects of human capital on strategy and performance in professional service firms: A resource-based perspective', *Academy of Management Journal*, 44: 13–28.

Hofstede, G. (1980) *Culture's consequence: International differences in work-related values*. London, UK: Sage.

House, R.J., Hanges, P.J., Javidan, M., Dorfman, P.W. and Gupta, V. (2004) *Culture, leadership, and organizations: The GLOBE study of 60 societies*. London, UK: Sage.

Huselid, M.A. (1995) 'The impact of human resource management practices on turnover, productivity, and corporate financial performance', *Academy of Management Journal*, 38 (3): 635–72.

Ichniowski, C., Shaw, K. and Prennushi, G. (1997) 'The effects of human resource management practices on productivity: A study of steel finishing lines', *The American Economic Review*, 87 (3): 219–313.

Jackson, S.E., Schuler, R.S. and Rivero, J.C. (1989) 'Organizational characteristics as predictors of personnel practices', *Personnel Psychology*, 42: 727–86.

Jackson, S.E. and Schuler, R.S. (1995) 'Understanding human resource management in the context of organizations and their environments', *Annual Review of Psychology*, 46: 237–64.

Kang, S.-C., Morris, S.S. and Snell, S.A. (2007) 'Relational archetypes, organizational learning, and value creation: Extending the human resource architecture', *Academy of Management Review*, 32: 236–57.

Kiessling, T. and Harvey, M. (2005) 'Strategic global human resource management in the twenty-first century: An endorsement of the mixed-method research methodology', *International Journal of Human Resource Management*, 16: 22–45.

Koch, M.J. and McGrath, R.G. (1996) 'Improving labor productivity: Human resource management policies do matter', *Strategic Management Journal*, 17: 335–54.

Koys, D.J. (1988) 'Values underlying personnel/human resource management. Implications of the Bishop's pastoral economic letter', *Journal of Business Ethics*, 7: 459–76.

Koys, D.J. (1991) 'Fairness, legal compliance, and organizational commitment', *Employee Responsibilities and Rights Journal*, 1: 57–68.

Lado, A.A. and Wilson, M.C. (1994) 'Human resource systems and sustained competitive advantage: A competency-based perspective', *Academy of Management Review*, 19 (4): 699–727.

Leana, C.R. and Van Buren, H.J.I. (1999) 'Organizational social capital and employment practices', *Academy of Management Review*, 24 (3): 538–55.

Lepak, D.P. and Snell, S.A. (1999) 'The human resource architecture: Toward a theory of human capital allocation and development', *Academy of Management Review*, 24 (1): 31–48.

Lepak, D.P. and Snell, S.A. (2002) 'Examining the human resource architecture: The relationships among human capital, employment, and human resource configurations', *Journal of Management*, 28: 517–43.

Lepak, D.P., Takeuchi, R. and Snell, S.A. (2002) 'Employment flexibility and firm performance: Examining the interaction effects of employment mode, environmental dynamism, and technological intensity', *Journal of Management*, 29: 681–703.

Lepak, D.P., Liao, H., Chung, Y. and Harden, E. (2006) 'A conceptual review of HR systems in strategic HRM research', in J. Martocchio (ed.), *Research in Personnel and Human Resource Management*, 25. Greenwich, CT: JAI Press, pp. 217–72.

Lepak, D.P., Takeuchi, R., Erhardt, N.L. and Colakoglu, S. (2006) 'Emerging perspectives on the relationship between HRM and performance', in R.J. Burke and C.L. Cooper (eds), *The Human Resources Revolution: Why putting People First Matters*. Oxford, UK: Elsevier, pp. 31–54.

Lepak, D.P., Smith, K.G. and Taylor, S. (2007) 'Value creation and value capture: A multi-level perspective', *Academy of Management Review*, 32: 180–95.

Li, J. (2003) 'Strategic human resource management and MNE's performance in China', *International Journal of Human Resource Management*, 14: 157–73.

MacDuffie, J.P. (1995) 'Human resource bundles and manufacturing performance: Organizational logic and flexible production systems in the world auto industry', *Industrial and Labor Relations Review*, 48: 197–221.

McMahan, G.C., Virick, M. and Wright, P.M. (1999) 'Alternative theoretical perspectives for strategic human resource management revised: Progress, problems, and prospects', in P. Wright, L. Dyer, J. Boudreau, and G. Milkovich, (eds.), *Research in Personnel and Human Resource Management*. Supplement A. Greenwich, CT: JAI Press.

Miles, R.E. and Snow, C.C. (1984) 'Designing strategic human resources systems', *Organizational Dynamics* (Summer): 36–52.

Miller, S.R. and Eden, L. (2006) 'Local density and foreign subsidiary performance', *Academy of Management Journal*, 49: 341–57.

Milliman, J., Von Glinow, M.A. and Nathan, M. (1991) 'Organizational life cycles and strategic international human resource management in multinational companies: Implications for congruence theory', *Academy of Management Review*, 16: 318–39.

Myloni, B., Harzing, A.W. and Mirza, H. (2004) 'Human Resource Management in Greece: Have the Colors of Culture Faded Away?', *International Journal of Cross Cultural Management*, 4 (1): 59–76.

Nahapiet, J. and Ghoshal, S. (1998) 'Social capital, intellectual capital, and the organizational advantage', *Academy of Management Review*, 23 (2): 242–66.

Ngo, H-Y, Turban, D., Lau, C-M. and Lui, S-Y. (1998) 'Human practices and firm performance of multinational corporations: Influences of country of origin', *International Journal of Human Resource Management*, 9: 632–52.

Nishii, L.H. (2003) *Exploring the SHRM black box: The relation between employee attributions for HR practices and unit effectiveness.* Unpublished doctoral dissertation, University of Maryland, College Park.

Osterman, P. (1994) 'How common is workplace transformation and who adopts it?', *Industrial and Labor Relations Review*, 47: 173–88.

Park, H.J., Mitsuhashi, H., Fey, C.F. and Bjorkman, I. (2003) 'The effect of human resource management practices on Japanese MNC subsidiary performance: A partial mediating model', *International Journal of Human Resource Management*, 14: 1391–406.

Perlmutter, H.V. (1969) 'The tortuous evolution of the multinational corporation', *Columbia Journal of World Business*, 4: 9–18.

Peterson, R.B., Sargent, J.D., Napier, N.K. and Shim, W.S. (1996) 'Corporate expatriate HRM policies, internationalization, and performance in the world's largest MNCs', *Management International Review*, 36: 215–31.

Pfeffer, J. (1995) 'Producing sustainable competitive advantage through the effective management of people', *Academy of Management Executive*, 9 (1): 55–72.

Porter, M.E. (1986) 'Changing patterns of international competition', *California Management Review*, 17: 9–40.

Porter, M.E. (1990) 'The Competitive Advantage of Nations', *Harvard Business Review*: 73–93.

Reed, R. and DeFillipi, R.J. (1990) 'Causal ambiguity, barriers to imitation, and sustainable competitive advantage', *Academy of Management Review*, 15 (1): 88–102.

Rodrigez, J.M. and Ventura, J. (2003) 'Human resource management systems and organizational performance : An analysis of the Spanish manufacturing industry', *International Journal of Human Resource Management*, 14: 1206–26.

Rosenzweig, P.M. and Nohria, N. (1994) 'Influences on human resource management practices in multinational corporations', *Journal of International Business Studies*, 25: 229–51.

Rousseau, D.M. (1995) *Psychological contracts in organizations: Understanding written and unwritten Agreements*. Thousand Oaks, CA: Sage.

Russell, J.S., Terborg, J.R. and Powers, M.L. (1985) 'Organizational performance and organizational level training and support', *Personnel Psychology*, 38: 849–63.

Schuler, R.S. and Jackson, S.E. (1987) 'Linking competitive strategies with human resource management practices', *Academy of Management Executive*, 1: 207–19.

Schuler, R.S. and Jackson, S.E. (2005) 'A quarter century review of human resource management in the U.S.: The growth in importance of the international perspective', *Management Revue*, 16: 1–25.

Schuler, R.S., Dowling, P.J. and De Cieri, H. (1993) 'An integrative framework of strategic international human resource management', *International Journal of Human Resource Management*, 4: 717–64.

Schuler, R.S., Budhwar, P. and Florkowski, G.W. (2002) 'International human resource management: Review and critique', *International Journal of Management Reviews*, 4: 41–70.

Shore, L.M. and Wayne, S.J. (1993) 'Commitment and employee behavior: Comparison of affective commitment and continuance commitment with perceived organizational support', *Journal of Applied Psychology*, 78: 774–80.

Snell, S.A. and Dean, J.J. (1992) 'Integrated manufacturing and human resource management: A human capital perspective', *Academy of Management Journal*, 35 (3): 467–504.

Snell, S.A., Youndt, M.A. and Wright, P.M. (1996) 'Establishing a framework for research in strategic human resource management: Merging resource theory and organizational learning', in G.R. Ferris (ed.), *Research in Personnel and Human Resources Management*. Greenwich, CT: JAI Press, pp. 61–90.

Sparrow, P.R. and Braun, W. (2007) 'HR strategy theory in international context', in M. Harris (ed.), *Handbook of Research in International Human Resource Management*. New Jersey: Lawrence Erlbaum Associates.

Stroh, L.K. and Caligiuri, P.M. (1998) 'Strategic human resources: A new source for competitive advantage in the global arena', *International Journal of Human Resource Management*, 9: 1–17.

Subramaniam, M. and Youndt, M. (2005) 'The influence of intellectual capital on the types of innovative capabilities', *Academy of Management Journal*, 48: 450–63.

Takeuchi, R., Lepak, D.P., Wang, H. and Takeuchi, K. (2007) 'An empirical examination of the mechanisms mediating between high performance work systems and the performance of Japanese organizations', *Journal of Applied Psychology*, 92: 1069–83.

Taylor, S., Beechler, S. and Napier, N. (1996) 'Toward an integrative model of strategic international human resource management', *Academy of Management Review*, 21: 959–85.

Terpstra, D.E. and Rozell, E.J. (1993) 'The relationship of staffing practices to organizational level measures of performance', *Personnel Psychology*, 46: 27–48.

Tsui, A.S., Pearce, J.L., Porter, L.W. and Hite, J.P. (1995) 'Choice of employee-organization relationship: Influence of external and internal organizational factors', in G.R. Ferris (ed.), *Research in personnel and human resources management.* Greenwich, CT: JAI Press, pp. 117–51.

Uzzi, B. (1997) 'Social structure and competition in interfirm networks: The paradox of embeddedness', *Administrative Science Quarterly*, 42: 35–67.

Way, S.A. (2002) 'High performance work systems and intermediate indicators of firm performance within the US small business sector', *Journal of Management*, 28: 765–85.

Wright, P.M. and McMahan, G.C. (1992) 'Theoretical perspectives for strategic human resource management', *Journal of Management*, 18: 295–320.

Wright, P.M., McMahan, G.C. and McWilliams, A. (1994) 'Human resources and sustained competitive advantage: A resource-based perspective', *International Journal of Human Resource Management*, 5 (2): 301–26.

Wright, P., Dunford, B. and Snell, S. (2001) 'Contributions of the resource based view of the firm to the field of strategic HRM: Convergence of two fields', *Journal of Management*, 27, 701–21.

Wright, P.M. and Boswell, W.R. (2002) 'Desegrating HRM: A review and synthesis of micro and macro human resource management research', *Journal of Management*, 24: 247–76.

Wright, P.M., Snell, S.A. and Dyer, L. (2005) 'New models of strategic HRM in a global context', *International Journal of Human Resource Management*, 16 (6): 875–81.

Youndt, M.A., Snell, S.A., Dean, J.W.J. and Lepak, D.P. (1996) 'Human resource management, manufacturing strategy, and firm performance', *Academy of Management Journal*, 39 (4): 836–66.

Youndt, M.A., Subramaniam, O. and Snell, S.A. (2004) 'Intellectual capital profiles: An examination of investments and returns', *Journal of Management Studies*, 41: 335–61.

Zaheer, S. (1995) 'Overcoming the liability of foreignness', *Academy of Management Journal*, 38: 341–63.

4

The Employment Relationship

John W. Budd and Devasheesh Bhave

The employment relationship is the connection between employees and employers through which individuals sell their labor. This might consist of an immigrant day laborer paid by the bushel to pick fruit in the hot sun, a salaried manager who has been working in an air-conditioned office for the same company for 40 years, or innumerable other situations. Irrespective of situation, all employees and employers have fundamental interests they pursue through the employment relationship, all forms of this relationship are mediated by labor markets and states, and each instance of this relationship is governed by some form of a contract, ranging from explicit union contracts and civil service rules to implicit expectations and understandings. These common building blocks of the employment relationship—employees, employers, states, markets, and contracts—are the first topic of this chapter.

These common denominators make it possible to craft a singular conceptual basis for analyzing the employment relationship that applies to the otherwise diverse forms of this relationship across occupations, industries, countries, and time. This is not to say that there is universal agreement on the nature

of this common model of the employment relationship. In fact, scholars and practitioners from different schools of thought see the employment relationship quite differently—as a mutually-advantageous trade among self-interested agents in a free market, a long-term partnership between employees and employers with common interests, a bargain between stakeholders with some competing economic interests, or an unequal power relation embedded in complex social hierarchies. The second part of this chapter therefore develops four models of the employment relationship based on different conceptualizations of the common building blocks.

The third and final major section of this chapter demonstrates that these four models of the employment relationship, in turn, provide very different perspectives on key issues in human resource management. Depending on one's frame of reference, human resource management practices, for example, can be seen as administrative mechanisms for implementing the dictates of the free market, essential strategies for creating productive employment relationships by aligning the interests of employees and employers, employer-driven initiatives that inadequately represent workers' interests when they clash with employers' interests, or manipulative managerial tools for shaping the ideology and structure of the workplace to favor employers over employees. Similarly powerful contrasts can be developed for other issues in human resource management, such as equality and diversity, labor unions, and the globalizing employment relationship. In sum, a deep understanding of the field and practice of human resource management is impossible without fully appreciating the elements of the employment relationship, their conceptualizations, and the resulting four frames of reference for human resource management.

ELEMENTS OF THE EMPLOYMENT RELATIONSHIP

In this section we sketch the major conceptualizations of the elements of the employment relationship. Each subsection starts with a description of the relevant dimension, but of central importance are the alternative conceptualizations of each dimension embraced by individuals with differing perspectives. The objective is to provide a foundation for understanding the employment relationship generally; readers interested in specific forms of this relationship in practice are encouraged to also consult other chapters in this Handbook. A more extensive discussion of the interests of employees, employers, and states can be found in Budd and Bhave (2008).

Employees

The legal landscape is littered with cases that seek to define who exactly is an 'employee' as employment relationships change and as the definition of employee can vary from law to law. An ongoing controversy, for example, is whether temporary and contingent employees are legally considered employees. For the purposes of this chapter, however, it is sufficient to define an employee as anyone who sells their labor. Executive, managerial, and supervisory employees might also have

roles as agents of their employers, but when they sell their labor, conceptually they are employees.

Employees are frequently conceptualized as an economic or a behavioral being (Kaufman, 1999). An economic or purely rational person ('homo economicus') is seen as making self-interested, utility-maximizing decisions in well-defined situations by optimally choosing actions from the entire set of possible alternatives. In this perspective, the central objective of homo economicus employees is defined as maximizing utility which increases with both income and leisure. As such, there is a labor-leisure trade-off in which work is desirable only to the extent that it produces income, at least on the margin, when deciding whether or not to work a little bit harder (Lazear and Oyer, forthcoming). This approach further sees employees as factors of production, or 'instruments' (March and Simon, 1958: 29), to be optimally allocated by employers to maximize profits.

However, the 'homo economicus' assumptions pertaining to rationality, self-interest, and information are extremely strict (Kaufman, 1999; March and Simon, 1958). As such, the socio-behavioral alternative to 'homo economicus' sees individuals as making satisfactory rather than optimal decisions that reflect a variety of intrinsic and social goals beyond selfish desires for income and leisure—such as equity and voice (Budd, 2004), dignity (Hodson, 2001), justice (Folger and Cropanzano, 1998), purposeful activity (Marx, 1844/1988, 1867/1936), power (Kelly, 1998), individual fulfillment (Donovan, 2001; Latham and Pinder, 2005; Maslow, 1943), status (Lin, 1999), identity (Leidner, 2006; Tajfel, 1978; Turner, 1982), full citizenship rights and self-determination (MacLean, 2006), pursuit of a 'calling' (Weber, 1904/1976), social exchange (Emerson, 1976; Kirchler et al., 1996), and altruism (Piliavin and Charng, 1990). Seeing employees as behavioral rather than economic entities also means seeing labor as more than just a commodity or a factor of production (Kaufman, 2005); rather, employees are seen as complex human beings motivated by intrinsic rewards and social concerns, and, by some accounts, entitled to fairness and justice.

Employers

An employer is a purchaser of labor. At its core, an employer is comprised of the owners of a private, for-profit organization, or those who control a non-profit or public sector organization. Executive, managerial, and supervisory employees are also often considered part of an 'employer' as they frequently act as an agent of their employer in managing other employees. Employers are typically modeled as maximizing profits (Manning, 2003; Wachter, 2004), or optimizing an analogous objective function for non-profit and governmental employers. The Anglo-American shareholder model of corporate governance reflects this importance of profit maximization. In this system, shareholders are residual claimants; all other stakeholders are seen as receiving fixed payments such as wages and salaries for their services. As such, shareholders are viewed as single-handedly bearing the risk of making a profit or loss and economic performance will consequently be optimized when corporate decisions maximize shareholder value (Blair, 1995). Maximizing profits and maximizing shareholder value are therefore equivalent.

Alternatively, stakeholder theory asserts that all stakeholders—not only shareholders and owners, but also employees, customers, suppliers, local communities, and others—are sufficiently affected by corporate actions to deserve the right to be considered in corporate decision-making (Donaldson and Preston, 1995). Within the context of the employment relationship, then, an employer as a collection of stakeholders rather than shareholders seeks to balance employee interests with the interests of shareholders and other stakeholders. A third conceptualization of employers sees them as complex social institutions with their own norms, cultures, and bureaucracies (Perrow, 1986;

Weber, 1919/1946). Ospina (1996: 5), for example, models employers as 'stratified social system[s] embedded in a broader system of stratification.' Along similar lines, Marxist and other critical perspectives conceptualize employers as controllers of the means of production. In this perspective, employers are not simply black boxes of production technologies seeking to maximize profits; rather, corporations are seen as bundles of power relations in which employers use their power in the workplace to control the labor process (Braverman, 1974; Edwards, 1979; Edwards, 1986; Thompson and Newsome, 2004), and in the broader socio-political arena to maintain their dominance over the working class (Burawoy and Wright, 2002).

States

The state is the third important actor in the employment relationship, and has four roles beyond that of an employer in its own right (Godard, 2005). The role that receives the most attention is the regulative role—that is, in regulating the employment relationship through employment law (in North American terms) or individual labor law (in European terms) that specifies individual employment rights and standards such as minimum wages and nondiscrimination, and through labor law (in North American terms) or collective labor law (in European terms) that regulates employees, works councils, unions, employers, and employers' associations as they interact with each other collectively. The state is a major actor in the employment relationship as the creator and enforcer of these laws. Not to be overlooked, however, are a facilitative role in which the state establishes social norms, a structural role consisting of economic policies that influence the economic environment, and a constitutive role which determines the fundamental nature of the employment relationship by the type of socio-politico-economic system embraced by the state, such as a market-based capitalist economy or a state socialist economy.

Within these roles, the state has fundamental interests in the employment relationship. The state assures freedom and the rule of law by protecting property rights and instituting legal systems for establishing and enforcing contracts (Posner, 1986). Pluralist political theory sees the state as also balancing competing power groups such as employers and employees to promote equitable outcomes (Dunleavy and O'Leary, 1987; Faulks, 1999). A critical perspective views the state as a mechanism for maintaining the power of the ruling class or other elite segment of society (Faulks, 1999; Pierson, 1996). Based on how state interests are conceptualized, therefore, the state's role in the employment relationship and labor markets can be considered to be those of laissez-faire promoter, an interventionist regulator, or even as an instrument that engenders domination by one group.

Markets

Buyers and sellers of labor are brought together by the labor market in capitalist societies. For some jobs, this might be a spot market in which employees bid for work and employers look for workers on a daily basis. For a long-term employee, the employee–employer labor market match might have been made many years ago, but the contemporary labor market nevertheless likely continues to influence the terms of this match by establishing the parameters for compensation and working conditions that will sustain the relationship.

In theory, and practice, a key issue is whether labor markets are perfectly competitive (Manning, 2003). Perfectly competitive labor markets exist when both employees and employers are price takers such that labor demand and supply completely determines wages and working conditions. In mainstream neoclassical economic thought, the invisible hand of perfectly competitive markets guides self-interested employees and employers to optimal outcomes that maximize aggregate welfare and allocate scarce resources to their most productive uses. In layperson's terms,

nearly all markets appear 'competitive,' but perfect competition requires solely private transactions, perfect information, and no transactions costs. Some therefore argue that externalities, information asymmetries, mobility costs, liquidity constraints, and transactions costs render labor markets imperfectly competitive (Kaufman, 1997; Manning, 2003). If employers have monopsony power in imperfect labor markets, employees and employers are bargainers rather than price takers, and labor market outcomes are not necessarily socially optimal. Debates between neoclassical economists and others over whether labor markets are perfectly competitive are longstanding (Kaufman, 1988) and continue to attract supporters to each side of the debate.

Contracts

The terms, conditions, and expectations under which an employee sells his or her labor to an employer are captured in a contract. This contract might be an explicit written document. CEOs, professional athletes, and unionized workers are examples of employees that are frequently covered by written contracts. An employee handbook can be another form of a contract. Employment contracts may or may not be legally enforceable depending on a country's legal doctrine, but whether legally enforceable or not, written contracts are incomplete as all of the tasks and performance expectations of employees are not specified in advance. As such, it is common to think of the employment relationship as also governed by implicit contracts of informal, legally unenforceable promises that are economic, psychological, or social in nature.

In economic theorizing, implicit contracts are rooted in uncertainty such as unknown future labor market conditions (Rosen, 1985). Rather than receiving wages that vary over time with changes in labor market conditions as in a spot market for labor, risk averse employees prefer an implicit arrangement in which the employer and employee agree to a predictable, fixed wage over time (Beaudry and DiNardo, 1991). The use of corporate pay policies rather than pure market forces to set wages is seen as consistent with this type of implicit arrangement, which is not explicitly written down and is not legally enforceable (Bertrand, 2004). The agreements are seen as self-enforcing because of transactions costs (it's costly to find a new employee or job) and the importance of maintaining one's reputation (Bull, 1987).

In psychological theorizing, the key implicit contract in the employment relationship is seen largely from the perspective of the employee and is labeled a 'psychological contract'—the employee's perception of the employer's and employee's mutual obligations in the employment relationship (Rousseau, 1995). When an employee's perceptions are fulfilled, positive work outcomes such as job satisfaction and trust are expected to result (Robinson, 1996). If an organization violates what an employee believes to be the terms of the psychological contract, counterproductive work behaviors are expected (Greenberg, 1990).

Economic and psychological perspectives on the employment relationship therefore both view implicit contracts as a tacit agreement between the employer and the employee about the terms and conditions of employment. The economic perspective focuses on the role of implicit contracts in establishing expectations for the economic exchange of work effort and pay. In contrast, the literature on psychological contracts focuses on perceived mutual obligations regarding the broad manner in which employees are treated and encompass dimensions such as fairness and respect (Robinson and Rousseau, 1994). Another difference is that psychological contracts are continually adapted during the tenure of the employee with a particular organization (Rousseau and Parks, 1993), but economic contracts are mainly revised at discrete time points, particularly in response to changes in the economic environment.

While implicit economic and psychological contracts focus on individual employee-employer interactions, a social contract is more of a macro-level perspective in which social values shape the expectations of the employment relationship. Kochan (1999: 138), for example, argues that the postwar social contract embodied the norm that 'hard work and good performance, and loyalty would be rewarded with security, fair treatment, dignity, and status.' Others argue that, in today's global economy, the liberal market value system has created a new social contract of personal responsibility and short-term economic opportunism in which lay-offs, job-hopping, contingent employment, and variable compensation are the norm (Cappelli, 1999).

FOUR MODELS OF THE EMPLOYMENT RELATIONSHIP

The discussion to this point shows that the key elements of the employment relationship can be conceptualized in very different ways. Employees can be seen as commodities, or as human beings. Employers might be black boxes of profit-maximizing technologies, or complex webs of power relations set within a broad socio-politico-economic system of class conflict. States play at least five different roles in the employment relationship. Markets are seen by some as perfectly competitive and imperfectly competitive by others. Contracts can be explicit or implicit, economic, psychological, or social. Moreover, these different conceptualizations of individuals, employers, states, markets, and contracts can be bundled together into four key models of the employment relationship—the egoist, unitarist, pluralist, and critical employment relationships (see Table 4.1). Appreciating the roots and implications of these four models is essential for understanding all aspects of work, including human resource management.

The egoist employment relationship

The egoist employment relationship focuses on rational agents pursuing individual self-interest in economic markets, and is most closely associated with mainstream neoclassical economic thought (Boyer and

Table 4.1   Four models of the employment relationship

View of employees	View of employers	View of markets	The employment relationship
The egoist employment relationship			
Rational, utility-maximizing agents optimizing the labor-leisure trade-off; factors of production	Black boxes of profit-maximizing technologies that optimize the use of factors of production	Key driver of the employment relationship to match self-interested employees and employers; ideally, perfectly competitive	A mutually-advantageous trade in a free market by self-interested economic agents
The unitarist employment relationship			
Psychological beings motivated by intrinsic rewards	Profit-maximizing organizations with a self-interest to align its interests with those of its employees	Important for establishing broad parameters for terms and conditions of employment, but not completely deterministic	A long-term partnership between employees and employers who share a unity of interests
The pluralist employment relationship			
More than a commodity; economic and psychological beings with moral worth and democratic rights	Profit-maximizing organizations that have some economic conflicts of interests with employees	Imperfectly competitive so that there are imbalances in bargaining power between employees and employers	A bargain between stakeholders with pluralistic economic interests and unequal bargaining power
The critical employment relationship			
More than a commodity; economic and psychological beings with moral worth, democratic rights, and class interests	Owners of the means of production with systemic inherent conflicts of interests with employees	But one part of a broader socio-political system that perpetuates structural inequalities between employees and employers	An unequal power relation embedded in complex socio-politico-economic inequalities

Smith, 2001). Employees' objectives are assumed to be income and leisure; the objective of employers is profit maximization. Labor is seen as a commodity no different from other productive resources, except in its tendency to shirk and therefore in its need to be monitored or motivated with economic incentives. The state's role is to protect property rights and enforce contracts in order to foster free economic transactions. Labor markets are generally seen as perfectly competitive and therefore as the primary driver of the employment relationship—wages and salaries, benefits, and other terms and conditions of employment are not set by individual employees, employers, or states, but by the invisible hand of the labor market. Under these assumptions, the egoist employment relationship is one in which employees and employers engage in voluntary, mutually-beneficial transactions to buy and sell units of productive labor based on what the market will bear.

It should be noted that the egoist label used here is not intended as a pejorative term with negative connotations; rather, it is intended to highlight the centrality of self-interest rather than conflict and power. In fact, power and conflict in the egoist model are generally sterile constructs that are treated in market-based terms. Conflicts are resolved by the marketplace such that employees and employers agree to terms that are mutually beneficial, or look for other employers or employees when the terms are not mutually beneficial. Similarly, power is market-driven and is seen as what someone can command in the marketplace. But this is largely determined through supply and demand. Self-interested trades, not power and conflict, are central to the egoist employment relationship.

Employment-at-will—the right to hire and fire, or take a job and quit, at anytime for any reason—is a key element of the egoist model of the employment relationship.

Employers and employees should be able to enter into any explicit or implicit contract involving any mutually-agreeable terms and conditions of employment, including compensation, hours, duration of employment, job duties, and the like. In the interests of both economic optimization and individual freedom, employers and employees should likewise be able to end these arrangements when conditions or preferences change, or if a better deal comes along (Epstein, 1984). Note carefully that the egoist employment relationship critically depends on embracing a value system in which efficiency is the primary objective of the employment relationship and whatever the market bears is best. Moreover, if employees and employers are equal in terms of economic power, legal expertise and protections, and political influence, then neoclassical economic theory shows that abuses and exploitation are prevented by perfect competition in the labor market. Wages are never too low or too high, they simply reflect each employee's economic value and the impersonal forces of supply and demand.

The unitarist employment relationship

The second model of the employment relationship tends to see employees as psychological rather than economic beings, and is most closely associated with scholars in industrial/organizational psychology and human resource management (Coyle-Shapiro et al., 2004; Roehling et al., 2000). Coldly rational decision-making is de-emphasized in favor of behavioral elements such as fairness, social pressure, and cognitive limitations. Narrow economic interests are de-emphasized in favor of psychological interests. Perhaps most famously, Maslow (1943) hypothesized that employees seek love, esteem, and self-actualization after their physiological and security needs are met. The literature in psychology on work motivation therefore stresses intrinsic work rewards over pay and other extrinsic rewards (Donovan, 2001; Latham and Pinder, 2005). Markets are seen as imperfectly competitive, and are therefore not completely deterministic. As such, profit-maximizing employers have a range of strategies for pursuing their organizational goals. Moreover, a key assumption is that employees and employers share a unity of all of their interests—hence, the 'unitarist' employment relationship (Bacon, 2003; Fox, 1974; Lewin, 2001)—which means that the optimal employer strategies are those that align the interests of employers and employees.

The unitarist employment relationship, therefore, is seen as a long-term partnership between employees and employers with common interests. Profitability and other organizational goals go hand-in-hand with fulfilling work, fair treatment, and the satisfaction of employees' other intrinsic desires. This model of the employment relationship is therefore the foundation for contemporary human resource management and its focus on creating policies that simultaneously benefit employees and employers (Pfeffer, 1998; Ulrich and Brockbank, 2005).

It is important to note that the unitarist employment relationship assumes away issues of power and conflict. Because employees and employers are assumed to share unified interests, power is unimportant and conflict is seen as a suboptimal state of affairs. Scholars in this tradition certainly recognize that diverse forms of conflict are an organizational reality (De Dreu and Gelfand, 2008), but this literature frequently focuses on conflict between employees, and the presence of such conflict in a particular organization is largely perceived as an opportunity for improved human resource management practices to reduce this conflict. If employer-employee conflict exists in a particular employment relationship, it is seen as stemming from poor human resource management practices that need fixing. Sustained conflict is an anathema in the unitarist model, and contemporary human resource management therefore tries to manage conflict away rather than embrace it as an inherent part of the employment relationship.

The pluralist employment relationship

The pluralist model of the employment relationship rejects the egoist perspective that employees are simply commodities (Kaufman, 2005); rather, employees are seen as complex economic and psychological agents that, as human beings, are entitled to key rights such as equity and voice (Budd, 2004). This perspective also rejects the unitarist view and instead believes that there is a plurality of interests in the employment relationship (Clegg, 1975; Fox, 1974). In other words, employees and employers are seen as having a mixture of common and conflicting interests. Both parties to the employment relationship want profitable organizations and productive workers, but conflicts are also seen as inherent such as those between wages and profits, flexibility and security, or speed and safety. Imperfect labor markets are also a key element of the pluralist model dating back to Sidney and Beatrice Webb, John R. Commons, and other founders of industrial relations (Kaufman, 1997). Today, pluralist academic views of the employment relationship are most likely to be found in industrial relations (Budd et al., 2004; Kaufman, 2004) and institutionalist labor economics (Champlin and Knoedler, 2004).

Putting the above assumptions together means that the pluralist employment relationship is a bargained exchange between stakeholders with some competing interests in which the terms of this exchange are influenced by the varied elements of the environment—including states and markets—that shape each stakeholder's bargaining power (Budd et al., 2004). The egoist model's complete determinacy of competitive markets is replaced by the indeterminacy of monopsonistic labor markets; the unitarist reliance on employer policies to simultaneously satisfy employers' and employees' interests is replaced by a concern for ways to balance interests such as efficiency, equity, and voice, such as through government regulations or labor unions (Budd, 2004).

Economic incentives and markets are seen as important mechanisms for allocating and effectively using scarce resources as in the egoist model, but pluralist thought also includes more of a role for institutions to help overcome market imperfections and serve non-economic goals.

In contrast to the unitarist model, the pluralist model sees some conflict as a natural, healthy feature of the employment relationship. As such, conflict is to be managed, not eradicated and avoided. Conflict is often managed through bargaining, and power is therefore seen as bargaining power—the leverage one has to win economic gains in the employment relationship within some range of market indeterminacy.

The critical employment relationship

The fourth and final model of the employment relationship is labeled the critical employment relationship, and is most closely associated with radical, heterodox, and feminist scholarship in sociology, economics, and industrial relations (Bowles and Gintis, 1990; Edwards, 1986; Kelly 1998; Thompson and Newsome, 2004). This model shares the labor-as-more-than-a-commodity and labor-markets-as-imperfectly-competitive assumptions of the unitarist and pluralist models. But this perspective emphasizes sharp conflicts of interests and unequal power dynamics. In Marxist and related perspectives, employers are seen as the owners and controllers of the means of production which provides both the incentive and the means to continually push for greater profits at the expense of workers. This is not seen as simply an economic issue because laws and other social constructions bestow ownership and control rights on certain groups. A Marxist perspective further assumes that employer-employee conflict is one element of unequal power relations between the capitalist and working classes throughout society (Hyman, 1975), but a class element is not necessary for critical scholarship and much research focuses on conflict (and consent) in the workplace (Edwards, 1986; Thompson and Newsome, 2004). Furthermore, feminist perspectives focus on unequal power relations between men and women; critical race perspectives focus on segregation and control along racial lines (Amott and Matthaei, 1996; Delgado and Stefancic, 2001; Gottfried, 2006; Greene, 2003; Lustig, 2004). In all of these perspectives, the labor market, the employment relationship, and the state can be seen as elements of an integrated socio-politico-economic system throughout which elites are able to perpetuate or reproduce their dominance.

Compared to the other models of the employment relationship, power and conflict are given the greatest importance in critical scholarship. For example, Marx's (1844/1988) view that workers are alienated under capitalism is rooted in powerlessness—the product of their labor does not belong to them, they have no control over what is produced, and no power over how it is produced. Marx (1867/1936: 363) further believed that 'the directing motive, the end and aim of capitalist production, is to extract the greatest possible amount of surplus-value, and consequently to exploit labor-power to the greatest possible extent.' More generally, then, the critical employment relationship is conceptualized as a struggle for power and control between competing groups, albeit with necessary amounts of accommodation and consent (Edwards, 1986; Gall, 2003; Hyman, 1975; 2006). The employment relationship is not seen as a voluntary or bargained exchange, but as a contested exchange (Bowles and Gintis, 1990). Unlike the pluralist model in which employer-employee conflict is largely economic in nature and confined to the employment relationship, the critical perspective emphasizes the social-embeddedness of power differentials and conflict in the employment relationship. Kelly's (1998) application of mobilization theory to industrial relations is another example of critical scholarship in which power and conflict are key, and contrasts sharply with Budd's (2004) emphasis on balancing employer and employee interests.

IMPLICATIONS FOR UNDERSTANDING HUMAN RESOURCE MANAGEMENT

As we can now see, the employment relationship can be modeled as a mutually-advantageous transaction in a free market, a long-term partnership of employees and employers with common interests, a bargain between stakeholders with some competing economic interests in imperfect markets, or an unequal power relation embedded in complex socio-politico-economic inequalities. Each of these four models provides very different perspectives on the fundamental aspects of human resource management, such as human resource management practices, equality and diversity, labor unions and work-related public policies, and globalization. As such, these four models, which we illustrate through the examples below, are essential for understanding the scholarship and practice of human resource management.

Human resource management practices

Human resource management practices are the policies and procedures used by employers to manage their employees—including key functions such as selecting, evaluating, rewarding, training, promoting, and terminating employees. Such practices, however, are seen very differently through the lenses of the four models of the employment relationship (see Table 4.2). In the egoist employment relationship, such practices are seen as essentially dictated by the labor market—fall behind the market, and employees will quit; get too generous relative to the market, and the employer will be unable to sell products and services at a competitive price. And by assuming a homo economicus approach, the economic aspects of such policies are emphasized, such as pay-for-performance plans, while intrinsic rewards are overlooked or assigned monetary values (Lazear, 1995). So-called low road human resources strategies that include low wages and managerial control are perhaps

Table 4.2   Views of human resource management practices

Model of the employment relationship	Human resource management practices are
Egoist	Of **secondary importance** because they are administrative or institutional mechanisms for implementing implicit contracts, incentives, and other manifestations of self-interested economic actors interacting in competitive labor markets
Unitarist	**Essential** because they are the key method for creating productive employment relationships by aligning the interests of employees and employers
Pluralist	**Useful** for aligning those employee-employer interests that are shared, **but insufficient** for balancing competing interests because of problems of unilateral employer authority and power
Critical	**Manipulative** managerial tools for shaping the ideology and structure of the workplace to strengthen capital's control and power over labor

also most consistent with the egoist theory because such strategies are rooted in a narrow conception of employee interests and in an emphasis on what the labor market will bear. In the egoist model, then, human resource management practices are largely administrative mechanisms for implementing the dictates of the labor market.

The other perspectives see human resource management practices as rules and procedures that govern the employment relationship within a particular firm through an internal labor market. But the origins and consequences of these practices are interpreted quite differently in each of these perspectives. In the unitarist model, well-designed human resource management practices are seen as the key managerial mechanism for creating profitable organizations because these practices are the way to align the extrinsic and intrinsic interests of employees and employers. Human resource management practices such as valid and reliable selection measures to hire and promote employees; training and development opportunities; respectful methods of supervision; compensation that

provides more than a living wage while also rewarding performance; benefits that foster personal growth, security, and work-life balance; and open channels of communication to prevent conflict therefore directly embody the central unitarist belief in the commonality of employee and employer interests. As a result, a plethora of management consulting programs now focus on employee engagement and alignment.

In the pluralist employment relationship, in contrast, job ladders and other elements of the internal labor market result from a mixture of pressures, such as economic efficiency, relative bargaining power, and customs (Doeringer and Piore, 1971; Osterman and Burton, 2005). But compared to egoist theorizing, limited ports of entry from the external labor market into the internal labor market are seen as shielding some human resource practices from competitive pressures (Kerr, 1954). From this pluralist perspective, then, the determination of human resource management practices occupies a conceptual middle ground between the complete determinism of competitive (external) labor markets in the egoist model and the unilateral managerial control of the unitarist model. Moreover, whereas the unitarist perspective is generally comfortable, relying on employer self-interest to promote both employee and employer objectives (since by assumption these can be aligned), the pluralist perspective rejects a sole reliance on employer goodwill (since by assumption there are some interests that clash). As will be described below, the pluralist school of thought therefore sees a productive role for government regulation and labor unions to complement human resource management practices.

In the critical employment relationship, human resource management practices are also seen as rules for governing the workplace, but through a different interpretive lens. Because of the socially-rooted, ongoing conflict between employers and employees assumed in this model, human resource management practices are not seen as methods for aligning the interests of employee and employer, but rather as disguised rhetoric that quietly undermines labor power and perpetuates capital's control (Legge, 1995). The design of routine low-skill jobs (Braverman, 1974; Montgomery, 1979) and organizational structures such as bureaucracies that create management routines through rules and procedures (Edwards, 1979) are seen as examples of employer strategies to obtain power and control over the employment relationship through the manipulation of human resource management practices. Above-market compensation policies and informal dispute resolution procedures are viewed as union substitution strategies to prevent employees from gaining more power by unionizing. Organizational behavior becomes organizational misbehavior—the study of worker resistance rather than obedience (Ackroyd and Thompson, 1999). Some critical scholars further contend that human resource management practices and the manipulation of organizational or corporate culture seek to redefine how individuals relate to employers and to employment itself, and aim to gain employees' adherence to a value system in which the values of business trump all other social values (Keenoy and Anthony, 1992).

As a specific example, consider employee monitoring. Psychological research sees monitoring as an activity to collect performance data on individuals, teams, and other organizational units (Larson and Callahan, 1990). Consistent with the unitarist view, monitoring is hypothesized to influence productivity only when it is used in conjunction with mechanisms such as providing feedback and removing barriers to effective work performance. In contrast, agency theory in economics sees monitoring as a mechanism to curb the opportunistic behavior of self-interested workers ('agents'), especially when worker effort is reasonably easy to observe (otherwise, economic incentives are needed to solve these principal-agent problems) (Fama, 1980; Jensen and Meckling, 1976). This theory is squarely within the egoist approach to theorizing about the employment relationship. In the critical model of the employment relationship, in contrast, monitoring is seen as a strategy to enhance managerial control over labor, and further augment the power of capital (Braverman, 1974).

These differences are further reflected in the fact that scholars from the various perspectives differ considerably about how they think about jobs and promotions. In the egoist model, work is pursued to earn income so self-interested workers will only exert the minimum level of effort required. Jobs, then, are seen as bundles of tasks designed to allow monitoring of effort, or when effort is difficult to observe, as bundles of tasks designed to reveal information about effort. Similarly, promotions are seen as incentive mechanisms for eliciting effort. Economics research therefore devotes a lot of attention to the incentive effects of jobs and promotions (Dewatripont et al., 1999; Itoh, 1994; Lazear and Oyer, forthcoming). In the unitarist perspective, employers and employees are seen as having common interests so jobs are instead seen as bundles of tasks designed to promote the most efficient and effective completion of these tasks, and promotions allocate workers to these tasks based on skills. Psychology research therefore analyzes task complexity, autonomy, the worker's immediate social context, and other factors that may promote or inhibit task completion (Hackman and Oldham, 1980; Salancik and Pfeffer, 1978). In the critical perspective, jobs are seen as bundles of tasks designed to reinforce managerial control. Task specialization is therefore seen as a way of deskilling work to reduce the knowledge and therefore power of workers (Braverman, 1974).

Lastly, one of the hottest areas of contemporary human resources—specifically, high-performance work practices such as flexible work arrangements, performance-based pay, and employee empowerment (Huselid, 1995; Becker and Huselid, 1998)—further reveals the importance of using the models of the employment relationship as a foundation for a deeper understanding of human resource management practices. Within the egoist and unitarist visions, questions about the effects of these practices largely reduce to questions about efficiency and organizational performance. The effects on employees beyond efficiency-related issues are frequently ignored because, in the egoist employment relationship, dissatisfied employees are free to quit, and in the unitarist employment relationship, common interests mean that what's good for employers is good for employees. But by seeing the employment relationship as including competing interests, the effects of high performance work practices on workers' stress, injury rates, pay, and job security are of equal importance to the effects on organizational performance in the pluralist employment relationship (Budd et al., 2004). In the critical employment relationship, such high performance work practices are further seen as 'management by stress'—new employer tools for increasing the pace and effort of work while increasing the uncertainty of rewards and security (Parker and Slaughter, 1995; Barker, 1993).

Equality and diversity

Beyond human resource management practices, the four models of the employment relationship generate contrasting perspectives on policy issues related to human resources (see Table 4.3). First consider equality and diversity. In the egoist employment relationship with perfectly-competitive markets and self-interested agents, discrimination on any basis except economic value should not exist. Suppose an employer discriminates by paying white men a higher wage than women and minorities in similar jobs. In a perfectly competitive market, profit-maximizing behavior will drive down the wages of white men and bid up the wages of the other groups until they all equal the value to the organization (Becker, 1957). If there is imperfect information about worker quality, then it might be profit-maximizing to generalize on the basis of demographic characteristics (for example, by assuming that parents of young children will be absent more frequently); this is called statistical discrimination (Aigner and

Cain, 1977). The unitarist perspective is similar in that discrimination is rooted in ignorance (Guion, 1998).

In any case, the existence of employment-related discrimination in the egoist and unitarist employment relationship is then seen as a type of market failure (Figart and Mutari, 2004) or managerial failure stemming from imperfect competition or information. The favored public policies are therefore skill enhancement—so that disadvantaged workers can compete better and add more value to their organizations—and non-discrimination laws that promote formal equality—that is, laws that promote colorblind or gender-blind equal opportunities for everyone, not just the traditionally-disadvantaged (Heneman and Judge, 2003). In the corporate sphere, the drive for equality has turned into a corporate-led diversity movement in which diversity is embraced not as a route toward social justice, but as a potential source of competitive advantage in which diverse employees will better serve a diverse customer base (MacLean, 2006). Managing diversity is therefore an important component of contemporary human resource management (Cleveland et al., 2000; Herriot and Pemberton, 1995), and starkly reveals the unitarist assumption that the right human resource management policies can align employee and employer interests—in this case, diversity and profitability.

In the pluralist employment relationship, segmented labor markets and occupational segregation are rooted in the core tenet of this model—unequal bargaining power. Women and minorities, for example, might be crowded into certain occupations because they lack the bargaining power to break into other better-paying occupations. Integration, not just diversity or non-discrimination, is important (Estlund, 2003). The resulting policy solutions involve institutional changes to break down barriers between segments of the labor market (Woodbury, 1987) and the promotion of labor union representation to enhance workers' power. One could further argue that the need to study gender and race in the egoist, unitarist, and pluralist schools of thought results from a failure of these models

Table 4.3 Perspectives on public policy issues in human resource management

Model of the employment relationship	Public policy issue		
	Equality and diversity	Labor unions	Globalization
Egoist	Competitive markets prevent discrimination; formal equality of opportunity is key	Unions are labor market monopolies that reduce economic welfare by impeding the operation of competitive markets	Free trade is optimal; international labor standards are harmful trade barriers
Unitarist	Discrimination stems from short-sighted managerial practices; diversity is justified as a source of competitive advantage	Unions are unnecessary third parties; their presence signals failing human resource management practices	Voluntary, self-monitored codes of conduct can effectively promote international labor standards by aligning employer-employee interests
Pluralist	Discrimination is rooted in unequal bargaining power; equality is a human right that requires institutional intervention	Unions are essential institutions for balancing bargaining power between employers and employees	Fair trade (via enforceable international labor standards) and transnational unions are necessary for redressing global imbalances in bargaining power
Critical	Discrimination and inequalities across race, gender, and class are pervasive; equality is a human right that requires structural changes	Unions are important working class advocates that counter exploitation, but are disadvantaged by structural inequalities embedded in the socio-politico-economic system	International working class solidarity and deep structural reforms are needed to prevent labor exploitation by globally-mobile capital

to eradicate discrimination in practice; ideally, gender and race should be a non-issue. The concept of class is similarly assumed away in the egoist, unitarist, and pluralist models as the employment relationship is seen as a largely an individual or an economic affair.

In the critical employment relationship, however, gender, race, and class are key constructs inseparable from culture and markets. Whether in terms of gender, race, or class, the dominant elite is seen as controlling access to good-paying jobs and therefore as restricting economic prosperity to members of this elite group whether they be men, whites, or the upper class. Gender, race, and class are further seen as integral for defining the very definition of labor. Feminist thought, for example, emphasizes that a male-dominated society equates valued work to that which occurs for pay outside the home on a full-time basis—that is, work typically done by breadwinning men (Figart and Mutari, 2004; Williams, 2000). Redressing inequalities rooted in gender, race, and class therefore require deep structural reforms that move beyond formal equality or corporate diversity programs; from this perspective,

genuine equality and inclusion requires re-defining society's values and aggressively opening up good-paying jobs to traditionally disadvantaged workers (MacLean, 2006; Marable et al., 2006; Williams, 2000).

In critical scholarship, gender, race, and class are furthermore seen not only as sources of conflict and oppression, but also of identity and mobilization. It is out of this scholarship that comes important work on working class studies (Zweig, 2000), working class agency and social history (Thompson, 1963), working class consciousness (Aronowitz, 1973; Mann, 1973), whiteness (Roediger, 1991), race-conscious union organizing (Crain, 2002), and labor feminism (Cobble, 2004).

Labor unions and public policies on work

The four models of the employment relationship yield starkly different perspectives on labor unions (Budd, 2008; Budd et al., 2004) and work-related public policies (Befort and Budd, 2009). In the egoist model, labor unions are seen as labor market monopolies that reduce economic welfare by impeding the operation of competitive markets and violating the liberties of individuals to freely enter into economic relationships (Epstein 1983; Troy 1999). Work-related public policies such as those mandating a minimum wage or paid family leave are similarly seen as negative interferences with the operation of free markets.

Labor unions and government-mandated labor standards are viewed as unnecessary in the unitarist employment relationship. When employers successfully align their interests with their employees' interests through effective human resource management practices, employees will be satisfied and will not support a labor union or need mandated employment standards. The presence of a union or employment law is taken as a signal of failed human resource management practices. Unions are further seen as outside third parties that add conflict to what should be a conflict-free employment relationship. The unitarist emphasis on individual, not collective, fulfillment and intrinsic rewards further reduces the need for these labor market institutions. Ironically, however, human resource managers in practice have greater influence in their organizations when there is a threat of unionization or new work-related government legislation, even though one of their important objectives is to prevent such developments (Jacoby, 2005).

Labor unions and mandated labor standards through work-related public policies are embraced to the greatest extent in the pluralist employment relationship (Budd et al., 2004). A core pluralist value is the rejection that labor is simply a commodity (Kaufman, 2005). Therefore, labor is entitled to equity and voice in the employment relationship (Budd, 2004). In fact, basic labor standards are increasingly argued to be human rights (Adams, 2001; Gross, 2003; Wheeler, 1994). But, in contrast to the egoist and unitarist perspectives, the twin assumptions of imperfect labor markets and some inherent conflicts of interest render markets and human resources managers unreliable for guaranteeing employee rights. Rather, labor unions and government laws are seen as

essential instruments for leveling the otherwise unequal playing field between employers and employees and thereby promoting, rather than interfering with, the optimal operation of markets (Kaufman, 1997). As argued by the Webbs (1897) over 100 years ago, 'by the Method of Collective Bargaining, the foreman is prevented from taking advantage of the competition [between workers] to beat down the earnings of the other workmen' (174). This view of unions is very different from the egoist and unitarist views because of the different conceptualizations of the employment relationship embodied within these different perspectives.

In the critical employment relationship, strong, militant labor unions are seen as important advocates for employees' interests that can counter their exploitation under capitalism by mobilizing and raising the consciousness of the working class, and by fighting for improved compensation, better working conditions, and greater control over workplace decision-making. The anarcho-syndicalist perspective within the critical school of thought also sees radical unions as the key revolutionary vehicle for overthrowing capitalism and creating a society managed by workers. But, ultimately, the pluralist reliance on collective bargaining to promote employees' interests is seen as inadequate in critical thought because structural employee-employer inequalities are modeled as embedded in the entire socio-politico-economic system. Critical scholars and activists therefore criticize conservative unions in particular for not doing enough to challenge employer power and raise working class consciousness (Eisenscher, 1999; Moody, 1999). As the state is further seen as largely promoting elite interests, work-related public policies under capitalism are also viewed as insufficient. For example, Lafer (2002) argues that government-funded job training programs for disadvantaged workers have largely been reduced to training positive attitudes such as a strong work ethic and submission to authority. As such, in the absence of good-paying jobs, these government-funded programs reinforce the power of employers by teaching workers to accept lousy working conditions and to not question the authority of employers.

Globalization and international labor standards

Globalization places great pressures on the employment relationship. Some fear that globalization creates a race to the bottom as international trade, foreign direct investment, and offshoring undermine wages, benefits, and job security in locations where these terms and conditions of employment are more generous. The four key models of the employment relationship provide key insights into the major perspectives on debates over globalization and employment issues. Moreover, by now it should be apparent that the four models contain analytical as well as a normative implications—analytical in that they provide alternative methods for understanding *how* the employment relationship works; normative in that they provide alternative perspectives on how the employment relationship *should* work. As applied to globalization, a key normative issue is how the global workplace should be governed (Budd, 2004).

In mainstream economic thought, globalization is seen as a good thing as it expands consumer choices, lowers costs, and spreads economic development (Irwin, 2002). The egoist model therefore embraces free trade and the reduction of barriers to global trade and investment. Legislated international labor standards are seen as disguised protectionism, and the global workplace should be governed by free trade. In the unitarist model, international labor standards are best achieved through educating corporations as to how to align the interests of employees and employers, and to rely on self-monitoring—this is exactly what campaigns for corporate codes of conduct seek to create (Paine et al., 2005; Tsogas, 2001). Corporate codes of conduct will be successful only if the global employment relationship is best characterized by the unitarist model.

The model of the pluralist employment relationship instead indicates a need for global institutions to help balance conflicting employer-employee interests in imperfect labor markets. Calls for fair trade, enforceable labor standards attached to global trading agreements, and transnational labor solidarity and collective bargaining (Alexander and Gilmore, 1999; Nissen, 1999) are all rooted intellectually in a pluralist perspective. This parallels traditional pluralist calls for labor standards and protections for labor unions in the domestic workplace (Budd, 2004). The critical perspective sees globalization as another example of employer domination of markets and institutions such as the World Trade Organization, and therefore sees the need not only for checks and balances in the labor market, but for deeper institutional reform, too (Coates, 2000; Cox 2002).

CONCLUSION

The employment relationship is the exchange of labor for compensation via a contract as conditioned by states and markets. The elements of this relationship—employees, employers, states, markets, and contracts—are conceptualized by scholars and practitioners in very different ways which results in four key models. In the egoist employment relationship, employment is seen as a mutually-advantageous transaction in a free market between self-interested legal and economic equals. The unitarist employment relationship consists of a long-term partnership of employees and employers with common interests. The pluralist employment relationship emphasizes bargaining between stakeholders with some common and some competing economic interests and unequal bargaining power due to imperfect markets. The critical employment relationship is an unequal power relation between competing groups that is embedded in and inseparable from systemic inequalities throughout the socio-politico-economic system. Admittedly, contemporary scholarship within these four perspectives is more sophisticated than the models we have outlined here, but our portrayal reveals the core premises of the major approaches to thinking about the employment relationship; more nuanced portrayals of these models would not change the fundamental implications of this chapter.

A difficult issue, however, is whether these four perspectives are complements or substitutes. The models are complementary to the extent that they help us understand different aspects of the employment relationship such as the importance of economic incentives (egoist), human resource management practices (unitarist), institutional interventions (pluralist), and power (critical). Moreover, these different perspectives might reasonably characterize variation across the employment relationship in practice—terms and conditions of employment might be primarily determined by the labor market for mobile, uniquely-skilled employees or low-skilled temporary workers, by sophisticated human resource management practices for core employees in large corporations, and by formal bargaining for unionized employees. On the other hand, these four perspectives can compete with each other. Intellectually, the four models force us to think about human resource management practices, equality and diversity, labor unions, and work-related public policies in very different and largely mutually-exclusive ways. These conflicts are heightened when one's attention turns to normative questions, such as the extent to which public policy should support labor unions. In such episodes, the egoist and unitarist passions can be quite hostile to the pluralist and critical passions, and vice versa.

Whether as complements or substitutes, though, these four models provide the key frames of reference and ideologies for scholars and practitioners in human resource management and other areas related to the employment relationship (Budd and Bhave, 2008). When used to analyze employment relationship issues and to guide one's actions, the four models become the four key frames of reference; when used as a platform for advocacy, they become the central ideological alternatives. Unfortunately, these frames of reference and ideologies are frequently implicit rather than explicit in scholarship and practice. A greater shared understanding of all aspects of work can result if these models are more frequently made explicit. As illustrated in this chapter, these four models have very different implications for employment practices and policies. These implications similarly underlie the typical research focus of different scholars—economists frequently focus on utility-maximizing behavior and markets, human resource management scholars on organizational performance, pluralist industrial relations scholars on labor unions, and critical scholars on race, gender, and class.

As either a field of study or a business function, human resource management is fundamentally about the employment relationship. Understanding human resource management, therefore, starts with appreciating different conceptualizations of the elements of the employment relationship, and requires understanding how these conceptualizations form four distinct models of this relationship. All too often, this intellectual grounding is implicit at best, or absent at worst. Hopefully this chapter will foster the greater level of explicitness that is sorely needed.

REFERENCES

Ackroyd, Stephen and Thompson, Paul (1999) *Organizational Misbehavior.* London: Sage.

Adams, Roy J. (2001) 'Choice or voice? rethinking American labor policy in light of the international human rights consensus,' *Employee Rights and Employment Policy Journal*, 5 (2): 521–48.

Aigner, Dennis J. and Cain, Glen G. (1977) 'Statistical theories of discrimination in labor markets,' *Industrial and Labor Relations Review*, 30 (2): 175–87.

Alexander, Robin and Gilmore, Peter (1999) 'A strategic organizing alliance across borders,' in Ray M. Tillman and Michael S. Cummings (eds), *The Transformation of U.S. Unions.* London: Boulder, pp. 255–66.

Amott, Teresa and Matthaei, Julie (eds) (1996) *Race, Gender, and Work: A Multicultural Economic History of Women in the United States.* Rev. ed. Boston: South End Press.

Aronowitz, Stanley (1973) *False Promises: The Shaping of American Working Class Consciousness.* New York: McGraw-Hill.

Bacon, Nick (2003) 'Human Resource Management and Industrial Relations,' in Peter Ackers and Adrian Wilkinson, (eds), *Understanding Work and Employment: Industrial Relations in Transition.* Oxford: Oxford University Press, pp. 71–88.

Barker, James R. (1993) 'Tightening the iron cage: concertive control in self-managing teams,' *Administrative Science Quarterly*, 38 (3): 408–37.

Beaudry, Paul and DiNardo, John (1991) 'The effect of implicit contracts on the movement of wages over the business cycle,' *Journal of Political Economy*, 99 (4): 665–88.

Becker, Brian E. and Huselid, Mark A. (1998) 'High performance work systems and firm performance: a synthesis of research and managerial implications,' *Research in Personnel and Human Resources Management*, 16: 53–101.

Becker, Gary S. (1957) *The Economics of Discrimination.* Chicago: University of Chicago Press.

Befort, Stephen F. and Budd, John W. (2009) *Invisible Hands, Invisible Objectives: Bringing Workplace Law and Public Policy Into Focus.* Stanford, CA: Stanford University Press.

Bertrand, Marianne (2004) 'From the invisible handshake to the invisible hand? How import competition changes the employment relationship,' *Journal of Labor Economics*, 22 (4): 723–65.

Blair, Margaret M. (1995) *Ownership and Control: Rethinking Corporate Governance for the Twenty-First Century.* Washington, DC: Brookings.

Bowles, Samuel and Gintis, Herbert (1990) 'Contested exchange: new microfoundations for the political economy of capitalism,' *Politics and Society*, 18 (2): 165–222.

Boyer, George R. and Smith, Robert S. (2001) 'The development of the neoclassical tradition in labor economics,' *Industrial and Labor Relations Review*, 54 (2): 199–223.

Braverman, Harry (1974) *Labor and Monopoly Capital: The Degradation of Work in the Twentieth Century.* New York: Monthly Review Press.

Budd, John W. (2004) *Employment with a Human Face: Balancing Efficiency, Equity, and Voice*, Ithaca, NY: Cornell University Press.

Budd, John W. (2008) *Labor Relations: Striking a Balance*, 2nd ed. Boston: McGraw-Hill/Irwin.

Budd, John W. and Bhave, Devasheesh (2008) 'Values, ideologies, and frames of reference in industrial relations,' in Paul Blyton, Nicolas Bacon, Jack Fiorito, and Edmund Heery (eds), *Sage Handbook of Industrial Relations.* London: Sage, pp. 92–112.

Budd, John W., Gomez, Rafael and Meltz, Noah M. (2004) 'Why a balance is best: the pluralist industrial relations paradigm of balancing competing interests,' in Bruce E. Kaufman (ed.), *Theoretical Perspectives on Work and the Employment Relationship.* Champaign, IL: Industrial Relations Research Association, pp. 195–227.

Bull, Clive (1987) 'The existence of self-enforcing implicit contracts,' *Quarterly Journal of Economics*, 102 (1): 147–60.

Burawoy, Michael and Wright, Erik Olin (2002) 'Sociological Marxism,' in Jonathan H. Turner (ed.), *Handbook of Sociological Theory.* New York: Plenum, pp. 459–86.

Cappelli, Peter (1999) *The New Deal at Work: Managing the Market-Driven Workforce.* Boston: Harvard Business School Press.

Champlin, Dell P. and Knoedler, Janet T. (eds) (2004) *The Institutionalist Tradition in Labor Economics.* Armonk, NY: M.E. Sharpe.

Clegg, H.A. (1975) 'Pluralism in industrial relations,' *British Journal of Industrial Relations*, 13 (3): 309–16.

Cleveland, Jeanette N., Stockdale, Margaret and Murphy, Kevin R. (2000) *Women and Men in Organizations.* Mahwah, NJ: Lawrence Erlbaum Associates.

Coates, David (2000) *Models of Capitalism.* Malden, MA: Polity Press.

Cobble, Dorothy S. (2004) *The Other Women's Movement.* Princeton, NJ: Princeton University Press.

Cox, Robert W. (2002) *The Political Economy of a Plural World.* New York: Routledge.

Coyle-Shapiro, Jacqueline A-M., Shore, Lynn M., Taylor, M. Susan, and Tetrick, Lois E. (eds) (2004) *The Employment Relationship: Examining Psychological and Contextual Perspectives.* New York: Oxford University Press.

Crain, Marion (2002) 'Critical race studies: colorblind unionism,' *UCLA Law Review*, 49 (5): 1313–41.

De Dreu, Carsten K.W. and Gelfand, Michele J. (eds) (2008) *The Psychology of Conflict and Conflict Management in Organizations.* New York: Lawrence Erlbaum Associates.

Delgado, Richard and Stefancic, Jean (2001) *Critical Race Theory: An Introduction.* New York: New York University Press.

Dewatripont, Mathias, Jewitt, Ian and Tirole, Jean (1999) 'The economics of career concerns, part i: comparing information structures,' *Review of Economic Studies*, 66 (226): 183–98.

Donaldson, Thomas and Preston, Lee E. (1995) 'The stakeholder theory of the corporation: concepts, evidence, and implications,' *Academy of Management Review*, 20 (1): 65–91.

Donovan, John J. (2001) 'Work motivation,' in Neil Anderson, Deniz S. Ones, Handan Kepir Sinangil, and Chockalingam Viswesvaran (eds), *Handbook of Industrial, Work, and Organizational Psychology, Volume 2*. London: Sage, pp. 53–76.

Doeringer, Peter B. and Piore, Michael J. (1971) *Internal Labor Markets and Manpower Analysis*. Lexington, MA: D.C. Heath and Company.

Dunleavy, Patrick and O'Leary, Brendan (1987) *Theories of the State: The Politics of Liberal Democracy*. London: Macmillian Education.

Edwards, P.K. (1986) *Conflict at Work: A Materialist Analysis of Workplace Relations*. Oxford: Basil Blackwell.

Edwards, Richard (1979) *Contested Terrain*. New York: Basic Books.

Eisenscher, Michael (1999) 'Labor: turning the corner will take more than mobilization,' in Ray M. Tillman and Michael S. Cummings (eds), *The Transformation of U.S. Unions*. London: Boulder, pp. 61–85.

Emerson, Richard M. (1976) 'Social exchange theory,' *Annual Review of Sociology*, 2: 335–62.

Epstein, Richard A. (1983) 'A common law for labor relations: a critique of the new deal labor legislation,' *Yale Law Journal*, 92 (8): 1357–408.

Epstein, Richard A. (1984) 'In defense of the contract at will,' *University of Chicago Law Review*, 51 (4): 947–82.

Estlund, Cynthia (2003) *Working Together: How Workplace Bonds Strengthen a Diverse Democracy*. Oxford: Oxford University Press.

Fama, Eugene (1980) 'Agency problems and the theory of the firm,' *Journal of Political Economy*, 88 (2): 288–307.

Faulks, Keith (1999) *Political Sociology: A Critical Introduction*. Edinburgh: Edinburgh University Press.

Figart, Deborah M. and Mutari, Ellen (2004) 'Wage discrimination in context: enlarging the field of view,' in Dell P.Champlin and Janet T. Knoedler (eds), *The Institutionalist Tradition in Labor Economics*. Armonk, NY: M.E. Sharpe, pp. 179–89.

Folger, Robert and Cropanzano, Russell (1998) *Organizational Justice and Human Resource Management*. Thousand Oaks, CA: Sage.

Fox, Alan (1974) *Beyond Contract: Work, Power and Trust Relations*. London: Farber and Farber.

Gall, Gregor (2003) 'Marxism and industrial relations,' in Peter Ackers and Adrian Wilkinson (eds), *Understanding Work and Employment: Industrial Relations in Transition*. Oxford: Oxford University Press, pp. 316–24.

Godard, John (2005) *Industrial Relations, the Economy, and Society*, 3rd ed. Concord, Ontario: Captus Press.

Gottfried, Heidi (2006) 'Feminist theories of work,' in Marek Korczynski, Randy Hodson, and Paul Edwards (eds), *Social Theory at Work*. Oxford: Oxford University Press, pp. 121–54.

Greenberg, Jerald (1990) 'Employee theft as a reaction to underpayment inequity: The hidden costs of pay cuts,' *Journal of Applied Psychology*, 75 (5): 561–68.

Greene, Anne-Marie (2003) 'Women and industrial relations,' in Peter Ackers and Adrian Wilkinson (eds.), *Understanding Work and Employment: Industrial Relations in Transition*. Oxford: Oxford University Press, pp. 305–15.

Gross, James A., (ed.) (2003) *Workers Rights as Human Rights*. Ithaca, NY: Cornell University Press.

Guion, Robert M. (1998) *Assessment, Measurement, and Prediction for Personnel Decisions*. Mahwah, NJ: Lawrence Erlbaum Associates.

Hackman, Richard J. and Oldham, Greg R. (1980) *Work Redesign*. Addison-Wesley: Reading, MA.

Heneman, Herbert G. and Judge, Timothy A. (2003) *Staffing Organizations*, 4th ed. Middleton, WI: McGraw-Hill/Irwin.

Herriot, Peter and Pemberton, Carole (1995) *Competitive Advantage through Diversity: Organizational Learning from Difference*. London: Sage.

Hodson, Randy (2001) *Dignity at Work*. Cambridge: Cambridge University Press.

Huselid, Mark (1995) 'The impact of human resource management practices of turnover, productivity, and corporate financial performance,' *Academy of Management Journal*, 38 (3): 635–72.

Hyman, Richard (1975) *Industrial Relations: A Marxist Introduction*. London: Macmillan.

Hyman, Richard (2006) 'Marxist thought and the analysis of work,' in Marek Korczynski, Randy Hodson, and Paul Edwards (eds), *Social Theory at Work*. Oxford: Oxford University Press, pp. 26–55.

Irwin, Douglas A. (2002) *Free Trade Under Fire*. Princeton, NJ: Princeton University Press.

Itoh, Hideshi (1994) 'Job design, delegation and cooperation: a principal-agent analysis,' *European Economic Review*, 38 (3–4): 691–700.

Jacoby, Sanford M. (2005) *The Embedded Corporation: Corporate Governance and Employment Relations in Japan and the United States*. Princeton, NJ: Princeton University Press.

Jensen, Michael C. and Meckling, William H. (1976) 'Theory of the firm: managerial behavior, agency costs, and ownership structure,' *Journal of Financial Economics*, 3 (4): 305–60.

Kaufman, Bruce E. (ed.) (1988) *How Labor Markets Work: Reflections on Theory and Practice by John Dunlop, Clark Kerr, Richard Lester, and Lloyd Reynolds*. Lexington, MA: Lexington Books.

Kaufman, Bruce E. (1997) 'Labor markets and employment regulation: the view of the 'old' institutionalists,' in Bruce E. Kaufman (ed.), *Government Regulation of the Employment Relationship*. Madison, WI: Industrial Relations Research Association, pp. 11–55.

Kaufman, Bruce E. (1999) 'Expanding the behavioral foundations of labor economics,' *Industrial and Labor Relations Review*, 52 (3): 361–92.

Kaufman, Bruce E. (2004) *The Global Evolution of Industrial Relations: Events, Ideas, and the IIRA*. Geneva: International Labour Office.

Kaufman, Bruce E. (2005) 'The social welfare objectives and ethical principles of industrial relations,' in John W. Budd and James G. Scoville (eds), *The Ethics of Human Resources and Industrial Relations*. Champaign, IL: Labor and Employment Relations Association, pp. 23–59.

Keenoy, Tom and Anthony, Peter (1992) 'HRM: metaphor, meaning, and morality,' in Paul Blyton and Peter Turnbull (eds), *Reassessing Human Resource Management*. London: Sage, pp. 233–55.

Kelly, John (1998) *Rethinking Industrial Relations: Mobilization, Collectivism and Long Waves*. London: Routledge.

Kerr, Clark (1954) 'The balkanization of labor markets,' in E. Wight Bakke, Philip M. Hauser, Gladys L. Palmer, Charles A. Myers, Dale Yoder and Clark Kerr (eds), *Labor Mobility and Economic Opportunity*. Cambridge, MA: Technology Press of MIT.

Kirchler, Erich, Fehr, Ernst, and Evans, Robert (1996) 'Social exchange in the labor market: reciprocity and trust versus egoistic money maximization,' *Journal of Economic Psychology*, 17 (3): 313–41.

Kochan, Thomas A. (1999) 'Reconstructing America's social contract in employment: the role of policy, institutions, and practices,' *Chicago-Kent Law Review*, 75 (1): 137–48.

Lafer, Gordon (2002) *The Job Training Charade*. Ithaca, NY: Cornell University Press.

Larson, James R. and Callahan, Christine (1990) 'Performance monitoring: how it affects work productivity,' *Journal of Applied Psychology*, 75 (5): 530–38.

Latham, Gary P. and Pinder, Craig C. (2005) 'Work motivation theory and research at the dawn of the twenty-first century,' *Annual Review of Psychology*, 56: 485–516.

Lazear, Edward P. (1995) *Personnel Economics*. Cambridge, MA: MIT Press.

Lazear, Edward P. and Oyer, Paul (forthcoming) 'Personnel economics,' in Robert Gibbons and D. John Roberts (eds), *Handbook of Organizational Economics*. Princeton, NJ: Princeton University Press.

Legge, Karen (1995) *Human Resource Management: Rhetorics and Realities*. Basingstoke: Macmillan Press.

Leidner, Robin (2006) 'Identity and work,' in Marek Korczynski, Randy Hodson, and Paul Edwards (eds), *Social Theory at Work*. Oxford: Oxford University Press, pp. 424–63.

Lewin, David (2001) 'IR and HR perspectives on workplace conflict: what can each learn from the other?,' *Human Resource Management Review*, 11 (4): 453–85.

Lin, Nan (1999) 'Social networks and status attainment,' *Annual Review of Sociology*, 25: 467–87.

Lustig, Jeffrey R. (2004) 'The tangled knot of race and class in America,' in Michael Zweig (ed.), *What's Class Got To Do With It? American Society in the Twenty-First Century*. Ithaca: Cornell University Press, pp. 45–60.

MacLean, Nancy (2006) *Freedom Is Not Enough: The Opening of the American Workplace*. Cambridge, MA: Harvard University Press.

Mann, Michael (1973) *Consciousness and Action Among the Western Working Class*. London: Macmillan Press.

Manning, Alan (2003) *Monopsony in Motion: Imperfect Competition in Labor Markets*. Princeton, NJ: Princeton University Press.

Marable, Manning, Ness, Immanuel and Wilson, Joseph (eds) (2006) *Race and Labor Matters in the New U.S. Economy*. Lanham, MD: Rowman and Littlefield Publishers.

March, James G. and Simon, Herbert A. (1958) *Organizations*. New York: John Wiley and Sons.

Marx, Karl (1844/1988) *Economic and Philosophic Manuscripts of 1844*. Tr. Martin Milligan. Amherst, NY: Prometheus Books.

Marx, Karl (1867/1936) *Capital: A Critique of Political Economy*. Tr. Samuel Moore and Edward Aveling. New York: The Modern Library.

Maslow, Abraham H. (1943) 'A theory of human motivation,' *Psychological Review*, 50 (4): 370–96.

Montgomery, David (1979) *Workers' Control in America: Studies in the History of Work, Technology, and Labor Struggles*. Cambridge: Cambridge University Press.

Moody, Kim (1999) 'The dynamics of change,' in Ray M. Tillman and Michael S. Cummings (eds.), *The Transformation of U.S. Unions*. London: Boulder, pp. 97–115.

Nissen, Bruce (1999) 'Cross-border alliances in the era of globalization,' in Ray M. Tillman and Michael S. Cummings (eds), *The Transformation of U.S. Unions*. London: Boulder, pp. 239–53.

Ospina, Sonia (1996) *Illusions of Opportunity: Employee Expectations and Workplace Inequality*. Ithaca, NY: Cornell University Press.

Osterman, Paul, and Burton, M. Diane (2005) 'Ports and ladders: the nature and relevance of internal labor markets in a changing world,' in Stephen Ackroyd, Rosemary Batt, Paul Thompson, and Pamela S. Tolbert (eds) *The Oxford Handbook of Work and Organization*. Oxford: Oxford University Press. pp. 425–45.

Paine, Lynn, Deshpandé, Rohit, Margolis, Joshua D., and Bettcher, Kim Eric (2005) 'Up to code: does your company's conduct meet world-class standards?' *Harvard Business Review*, 83 (12): 122–33.

Parker, Mike, and Slaughter, Jane (1995) 'Unions and management by stress,' in Steve Babson (ed) *Lean Work: Empowerment and Exploitation in the Global Auto Industry*. Detroit: Wayne State University Press, pp. 41–54.

Perrow, Charles (1986) *Complex Organizations: A Critical Essay*, 3rd ed. New York: Random House.

Pfeffer, Jeffrey (1998) *The Human Equation: Building Profits by Putting People First*. Boston: Harvard Business School Press.

Pierson, C. (1996) *The Modern State*. New York: Routledge.

Piliavin, Jane A. and Charng Hong-Wen (1990) 'Altruism: a review of recent theory and research,' *Annual Review of Sociology*, 16: 27–65.

Posner, Richard A. (1986) *Economic Analysis of Law*, 3rd ed. Boston: Little, Brown.

Robinson, Sandra L. (1996) 'Trust and breach of the psychological contract,' *Administrative Science Quarterly*, 41 (4): 574–99.

Robinson, Sandra L. and Rousseau, Denise M. (1994) 'Violating the psychological contract: not the exception but the norm', *Journal of Organizational Behavior*, 15 (3): 245–59.

Roediger, David R. (1991) *The Wages of Whiteness*. New York: Verso.

Roehling, Mark V., Cavanaugh, Marcie A., Moynihan, Lisa M., and Boswell, Wendy R. (2000) 'The nature of the new employment relationship: a content analysis of the academic and practitioner literatures,' *Human Resource Management*, 39 (4): 305–20.

Rosen, Sherwin (1985) 'Implicit contracts: a survey,' *Journal of Economic Literature*, 23 (3): 1144–75.

Rousseau, Denise M. (1995) *Psychological Contracts in Organizations*. Thousand Oaks, CA: Sage.

Rousseau, Denise M. and Parks, Judi M. (1993) 'The contracts of individuals and organizations,' *Research in Organizational Behavior*, 15: 1–43.

Salancik, Gerald R. and Pfeffer, Jeffrey (1978) 'A social information processing approach to job attitudes and task design,' *Administrative Science Quarterly*, 23 (2): 224–53.

Tajfel, H. (1978) 'Social categorization, social identity, and social comparison,' in Henri Tajfel (ed.), *Differentiation Between Social Groups*. London: Academic Press, pp. 61–76.

Thompson, E.P. (1963) *The Making of the English Working Class*. New York: Pantheon.

Thompson, Paul, and Newsome, Kirsty (2004) 'Labor process theory, work, and the employment relation,' in Bruce E. Kaufman (ed.), *Theoretical Perspectives on Work and the Employment Relationship*. Champaign, IL: Industrial Relations Research Association, pp. 133–62.

Troy, Leo. (1999) *Beyond Unions and Collective Bargaining*. Armonk, N.Y.: M.E. Sharpe.

Tsogas, George (2001) *Labor Regulation in a Global Economy*. Armonk, NY: M.E. Sharpe.

Turner, J.C. (1982) 'Towards a cognitive redefinition of the social group,' in Henri Tajfel (ed.), *Social Identity and Intergroup Relations*. New York: Cambridge University Press, pp. 15–40.

Ulrich, Dave and Brockbank, Wayne (2005) *The HR Value Proposition*. Boston: Harvard Business School Press.

Wachter, Michael L. (2004) 'Theories of the employment relationship: choosing between norms and contracts,' in Bruce E. Kaufman (ed.), *Theoretical Perspectives on Work and the Employment Relationship*. Champaign, IL: Industrial Relations Research Association. pp. 163–93.

Webb, Sidney, and Webb, Beatrice (1897) *Industrial Democracy*. London: Longmans, Green, and Co.

Weber, Max (1904/1976) *Protestant Work Ethic and the Spirit of Capitalism*. Tr. Talcott Parsons. London: Allen and Unwin.

Weber, Max (1919/1946) *From Max Weber: Essays in Sociology*. Tr. H.H. Gerth and C. Wright Mills. New York: Oxford University Press.

Wheeler, Hoyt N. (1994) 'Employee rights as human rights,' in Jacques Rojot and Hoyt Wheeler (eds), *Employee Rights and Industrial Justice*, special issue of *Bulletin of Comparative Labour Relations*, 28: 9–18.

Williams, Joan (2000) *Unbending Gender: Why Family and Work Conflict and What to Do About It*. New York: Oxford University Press.

Woodbury, Stephen A. (1987) 'Power in the labor market: institutionalist approaches to labor problems,' *Journal of Economic Issues*, 21 (4): 1781–807.

Zweig, Michael (2000) *The Working Class Majority*. Ithaca, NY: Cornell University Press.

5

The Regulative Framework for HRM

Michael Barry

INTRODUCTION

This chapter draws on insights from different fields of study to explain how the regulatory context informs the development and application of employer human resource management (HRM) choices within organisations. In considering the contribution of fields such as organisational studies, industrial relations, comparative politics, economics and legal regulation, we note that in most developed countries in the last 10–20 years, the regulation of employment has shifted from a predominantly institutional to organisational setting. Despite this change, which brings the role of HRM and 'the firm' into closer scrutiny, we nevertheless maintain that changes in regulatory structures and methods do not equate to a shift from regulation to deregulation, as is often asserted. While the management of the employment relationship now often involves organisational actors such as employees, supervisors and managers rather than institutional actors such as unions and employer associations, the regulatory context nevertheless underwrites and constrains the space in which these actors are able to shape HRM policies and practices. In developing this line of argument, the chapter draws on insights from 'new institutionalism' and contributions from regulatory studies that highlight how history, labour market institutions, and a variety of regulatory techniques set a regulatory framework within which HRM guides the management of the employment relationship.

The chapter begins by identifying the scope of the regulatory framework of HRM before discussing why the regulatory context is important for HRM. The chapter then explains how the purpose of labour market regulation, which informs the make up of the regulatory framework, has been reinterpreted to provide a reassertion of the rights of employers to manage labour free from traditional regulatory constraints. The following section conceptualises this change as part of a re-regulation rather than deregulation of work and employment, with new actors, agencies and regulatory techniques attempting to influence HRM practices. The chapter then outlines contributions from different strands of institutionalist thought that demonstrate that institutional structures remain resilient to labour market reforms and continue to provide, around the role played by HRM, a framework for labour market regulation.

WHAT IS THE REGULATIVE FRAMEWORK FOR HRM?

Regulation may be defined in very different terms. In the broadest view, 'regulation means influencing the flow of events' (Parker and Braithwaite, 2003: 119). For some, regulation is defined more narrowly as being about rules. Rules have been an important focus for those in the field of legal regulation (Black, 1997) and for those interested in the world of work, particularly in the field of industrial relations. As it developed as an academic field, mainstream industrial relations (IR) saw work and employment regulation as the study of a 'web of rules' (Dunlop, 1958; Flanders, 1975). By focusing on rules, there developed a tendency to view formal institutions operating outside the workplace – state agencies, unions and employer associations – as the dominant regulatory bodies. High union density rates and the wide coverage of industry and sectoral collective bargaining agreements in most industrialised nations reinforced a tendency to make these formal institutions the central focus of the study of the world of work. To mainstream IR, a critic could say it mattered little that this view understated the importance of the role of the direct parties to the employment relationship and the informal regulatory techniques, including customs and practices, they applied to make sense of the formal rules to which they were bound through interest representation and collective bargaining.

The limitations of this approach have been made apparent by the dramatic changes to the structure of the labour market and the traditional institutions of employment relations regulation over the last 10–20 years, including a dramatic decline of unionisation and collective bargaining in many OECD countries. These changes highlight a need to broaden the narrow conception of employment relations regulation to include organisational as well as institutional actors, and informal as well as formal regulatory techniques (Heery and Frege, 2006). Here then, the regulative framework for HRM is defined as any action, institution, or phenomenon that constrains or guides the management of the employment relationship within organisations. Included within this regulatory framework are third parties such as unions, employer associations, as well as government agencies and tribunals. Along with these macro level actors, product and labour markets play an important role in the regulative context because they affect the capacity of firms to attract, maintain and develop their human resources.

At the micro or firm level, other regulatory actors include works councils, 'in-house' staff associations, work groups and joint consultation or grievance handling committees. These 'institutions', together with their macro counterparts, set limits on the degree to which the organisation may use HRM practices to enable 'flexibility' in the allocation of labour, to control the production process, and to set and adjust terms and conditions of employment. The regulatory influence of these actors varies considerably in different jurisdictions, with work councils for example playing a limited role with basic information and consultation rights in some European countries, while in others they have extensive co-determination rights, including the ability to veto important HRM initiatives.

HRM choices are necessarily constrained by these and other regulatory actors through such regulatory tools as relevant collective bargaining or arbitrated agreements and awards, minimum wage provisions, anti-discrimination, equal opportunity and health and safety legislation as well as informal workplace customs and practices. As it is well understood that the employment relationship involves vague or implicit obligations as well as specific duties, features of the regulatory context such as custom are essential because they are the means by which 'loosely defined aspects of the labor contract are rendered into understood traditions and assumptions.' (Edwards, 1990: 45). As Edwards further points out, custom can be invoked as a regulatory tool where it gives rise to rights that are enforced through practice. Finally, all of these regulatory mechanisms orbit around the employment relationship itself, which acts as a regulatory device in that it restricts forms of opportunistic behaviour that are more common under different contracting arrangements, and it also sets limits on managerial authority (Marsden, 1999).

Taken together then, these regulatory instruments may be considered the 'rules of the game' that impact the scope and authority of available HRM choices. As Rubery and Grimshaw (2003) point out, these rules and institutions are an essential means by which labour market actors respond to pressures and challenges within diverse national systems. Rather than being viewed, as they often are, as a source of rigidity, rules and institutions 'are necessary for management and labour each to formulate decisions in a context of stable expectations about how the other acts' (Rubery and Grimshaw, 2003: 148).

The definition of a regulative context proposed here also acknowledges that HRM is an organisational function, and that the firm is itself both an organisation, and an institution of regulation (Scott, 1995; Adams. 1992). Firms are organisations in the sense that they are collective actors with an internal structure who are subject to institutional constraint. They are institutions in the sense that they are themselves a set of rules that structure interactions among actors (Knight, 1992: 3). Within organisational studies the conception of firms as institutions goes back to the work of Selznick, who argued that organisations follow a process of 'institutionalisation' over time. Institutionalisation is a form of regulation in that it limits available actions and can produce a pattern of conformity to established rules or behaviours.

Organisations can be viewed as being comprised of various stakeholders, and, along with market imperatives, stakeholder interests, may order and constrain HRM strategies and choices. From this viewpoint it follows that the culture and strategic direction of an organisation will be shaped to some degree by the prevailing balance of stakeholder interests. Stakeholders in some countries and firms may force employers to adopt mainly 'soft' HRM practices to develop employee commitment, whereas in other countries and firms employers may be able to adopt mainly 'hard' HRM practices to control employee behaviours (Legge, 1995). Moreover, organisations have their own institutional histories, and historical choices that have shaped past patterns of action may constrain future options and possible directions (Eisner et al., 2006: 2). Thus, decision-makers act within the boundaries set by an organisation's own institutional context as much as their actions are shaped by their external regulatory environment.

If organisations are to be viewed as regulatory institutions, large firms in particular can be seen as centres of regulation and regulatory innovation (Black et al., 2005: 20). As Hancher and Moran (1989) caution, we should not view regulation simply through a public (regulating agency)/ private (regulated interest) lens. For these authors, large firms acquire attributes of public status and 'the corporate strategy of individual firms is a major determinant of the direction of the regulatory process' (Hancher and Moran, 1989: 275). In economic regulation, the relationship between the regulating agency and the regulated parties is one of interdependence, rather than a traditional relationship characterised by command and control.

WHY IS THE REGULATIVE FRAMEWORK IMPORTANT FOR HRM?

It is argued that firms are increasingly individualising the employment relationship and that many of the traditional structures of labour market regulation have diminished in significance in recent years. Why then should we examine the ways in which the wider regulatory context interacts with the choices employers make that appear to reflect their immediate interests? To answer this question we could simply pose the following question: Why in some firms/sectors/industries/nations, do the direct parties make fundamentally different choices about how to regulate the employment relationship when faced with what appear to be the same organisational imperatives? If differences in regulatory contexts produce a variety of HR responses to common employment imperatives (see for example Marchington and Parker, 1990), differences in HRM styles among firms in the same industries or sectors may also reflect fundamentally divergent management ideologies and cultures, which might also be argued to be regulatory constraints. Taking a more holistic view, we could view management cultures and contextual imperatives as overlapping regulatory contexts. For example, early US experiments with welfare capitalism were not purely benevolent gestures by enlightened industrialists, heralding a new type of management culture. High wages and progressive terms and conditions were also a strategic response to the threat of union organising drives, and a means by which employers could prevent unionisation by competitively matching union wages and conditions, and sponsoring alternative forms of employee representation, (Lawrence, 1985: 26; Piore and Safford, 2006: 301, 303).

Understanding the regulatory context of HRM also helps us make sense of what the major changes to the world of work mean for workers, managers, organisations and society. The broad changes to work and employment are well known and include; increased female participation, an ageing workforce, increased casualisation and greater employment insecurity. There has been a proliferation of different guises of employment, bringing into sharp focus the growth of new corporate arrangements and work practices, such as subcontracting, franchising, home-working and the use of illegal labour. These arrangements place increasing numbers of workers outside the reach of traditional regulatory institutions that provide core protections such as minimum wages, OHS standards, workers' compensation, etc. (Quinlan, 2006).

Where employees remain within the standard employment relationship, changes to the way that relationship is constituted may similarly place them beyond the reach of traditional protections afforded by the regulatory context. The growth in individual contracting, which is associated with the continuing decline in unionisation, places increasing numbers of employees in a position where they are unable to utilise the type of (collective) bargaining instrument that might countervail the inherent bargaining power of employers and, if necessary, through interest representation, enable them to invoke industrial action to secure their bargaining claims. Given these changes, it becomes increasingly important to determine the extent to which alternative channels of employee voice and interest representation, and associated HRM employee involvement initiatives, are available to the majority of workers unable to access the traditional mechanisms of collective employment regulation.

Thus, HRM practice cannot be isolated from ongoing changes to the composition of employment, the nature of the production process and structure of the labour market. Governments have introduced labour market 'reforms' to facilitate these changes fundamentally, believing that innovation in the regulation of employment is a necessary precondition for national economic competitiveness. However, as Black et al. (2005) point out, notions of regulatory innovation have been poorly developed. Those who proclaim innovation tend to be optimistic, and often fail to recognise the context within which the change is taking place or the historical significance of the change. What are labelled innovations are often repetitions of past regulatory practice, or at best incremental changes to existing arrangements.

In the labour market, state interventions have ushered in new regulatory agencies and techniques, and different types of bargaining instruments. According to Piore and Safford (2006) there has been an evolutionary change in US employment relations regulation from a traditional framework based on extensive coverage of collective bargaining to a new regime of regulation based on limited collective bargaining but expanded employee rights protection. This change (which amounts to a re-regulation rather than deregulations of employment relations) is evidenced by such developments as the expansion of legislation to protect the rights of a range of minority and disadvantaged labour market groups as well as the emergence of new actors and regulatory methods such as private dispute resolution. In order to understand the significance of such changes for HRM we need to ask a series of questions. In what ways, if any, do changes to the structure of the regulatory framework fundamentally re-shape the balance of power between the competing parties in this regulatory arena? Thus, for example, where one regulatory agency or technique replaces another, yet performs a similar regulatory function, can we say that there has been an innovative change to the regulatory context? Similarly, when discussing new regulatory instruments we should ask whether these have changed the underlying pattern of relations between the parties, or just shifted the locus of bargaining by devolving negotiations to a different set of actors. The answers to these questions should be tested empirically rather than being informed by *a priori* assumptions. In order to make judgements about these types of questions, we need to determine how changes to the regulatory framework, and outcomes that follow those changes, affect the fundamental purposes of labour market regulation.

PURPOSES OF LABOUR MARKET REGULATION

It may be taken for granted that labour market regulation serves the purpose of promoting productivity and efficiency in the allocation of labour to achieve desired levels of production and distribution. In addition, with the development of the welfare state in the 20th century, labour market regulation also took on a protective function (Mitchell and Johnstone, 2004). The purpose of labour

law was then, in no small measure, to ensure that workers enjoyed some reprieve from the inherent tendency of the market to commodify labour. The view that employers will use an unfettered market to commodify labour – and that because of this regulation and institutions are a necessary corrective to the dominant power or employers – has been strongly held in fields such as institutional economics, industrial relations, social policy and labour law.

The basic premise of the 'old' institutional economists was that labour could not be commodified (Kaufman, 1998). For example, Polanyi (1944) saw labour as a fictitious commodity. Thus, labour was not produced to be traded on markets, and the simple act of subjecting labour to the unrestrained market would produce disastrous results. Institutions were necessary to bring the market back to society. For this reason institutions needed to be embedded in market relations. In the long run, the structure of institutions and the pattern of intervention may change, but the need for regulation – rather than the invisible hand of the market – would not.

In the labour market then, as in other areas, regulation served the purpose of correcting 'market failure' (Baldwin and Cave, 1999: 9). Stemming from the writings of social reformers (such as Sidney and Beatrice Webb) in the UK and institutional economists (such as John R. Commons) in the US, market failure could be corrected by the provision of minimum labour standards by government, as well as a regulatory framework that supported employees' ability to organise and to bargain collectively.

Although this view captures the importance of regulation from the point of view of the employee, it is incomplete in that it does not allow for a range of employer strategies that support various regulatory preferences (Barry et al., 2006). A revisionist literature has sought to correct this imbalance by highlighting a variety of employer labour market regulatory preferences. Swenson (2004), for example, has shown that under certain labour and product market conditions, groups of employers form cross-class alliances with organised labour to reach accommodations that de-commodify labour. Similarly, Mares (2003) has analysed firm preferences in relation to social security to demonstrate the conditions under which employers support policies of de-commodification. The burgeoning 'varieties of capitalism' literature (see below) also provides an analytical framework to com-pare labour market structures across distinct national systems that are supported by firm preferences based on either flexibility or close coordination.

These examples suggest that while much of the literature in the fields of labour law, industrial relations, and social policy has explained and justified the notion of labour market regulation as a form of employee protection to correct market failure and redress an imbalance in power in the employment relationship, a fuller view of the purpose of labour market regulation would also consider regulation as a form of employer protection. In many jurisdictions in the last few decades, state interventions have specifically limited the market and organisational power of labour, by such measures as limiting the right to engage in industrial action and increasing the penalties against labour activism. These interventions are often viewed by commentators as part of a neo-liberal agenda to secure a deregulated market. In fact, these labour market 'reforms' are often accomplished by implementing a greater raft of regulatory provisions, as well as new regulatory institutions. Howe (2006), for example, has challenged the application of the term deregulation to the sweeping labour market changes that have taken place in Australia under the rhetoric of deregulation in recent years. In this case, the political rhetoric of deregulation has not been matched by the sustained intervention of the Federal Government in this regulatory arena.

This type of systematic employment rela-tions reform amounts to a *re-regulation*, in which individual employee rights are strengthened while collective employee rights are systematically weakened (Rhodes, 1989: 257–8). The significance of this change is that legal rules governed by the contract of employment may mean little to employees if they are not able to be 'backed up by social sanctions as well, that is by the countervailing power of trade unions and negotiations with the employers and ultimately, if this fails, through withholding their labour'. (Kahn-Freund, cited in Rhodes, 1989: 230).

What is also significant about this re-regulation is that promoting substantive individual rights threatens the basis of estab-lished norms within the workplace, which are fundamental regulatory systems and are fundamentally collective in their nature. As Scott (1995) has pointed out, the importance of norms, as a pillar of institutional regulation, like rules, is that they structure choices and legitimize or constrain certain types of actions. HRM initiatives such as individual performance pay can prove incompatible with employees' perceptions of internal relativity (an important workplace norm expressing pay differentials within and between work groups) in the many types of work where it is difficult to determine one individual's contribution to the production process against another. Introducing individual performance rewards also introduces addition transaction costs to the HR process in terms of administering and negotiating contracts and monitoring compli-ance with performance standards (Marsden, 1999). It is for these reasons that the introduction of individual contracting has not altered substantive conditions of employment for many workers: instead, individualisation has often occurred through the use of standard (take it or leave it) contracts, and in some instances has served the alternative purpose of de-recognising unions (Deery and Mitchell, 1999).

The above highlights a broad feature of changes to the interplay between rules established by bargaining instruments and the legal regulation of the employment relationship through statute and common law (Rhodes, 1989). Labour law statutes, originally established to provide a protective function for employees by guaranteeing fun-damental rights such as to bargain collectively, organise and strike (and even to limit the scope of managerial prerogatives) have been re-interpreted by law makers in light of a perceived need to provide incentives to employers to boost jobs growth and enhance productivity and economic competitiveness. Under the rhetoric of flexibility and competitiveness we see, through state intervention, a strong preference for negotiations between the 'direct parties' that provide an assertion of the fundamental contractual basis of the employment relationship that has long been recognised to skew bargaining power in favour of the employer. Under the guise of protecting the national economy statutory provisions define large segments of the economy as 'essential', and in so doing firmly place the right to produce ahead of the right to withdraw labour. Other areas of statutory regulation limit labour activism by increasing penalties against it, and by extending the reach of the law into internal union government. The law has also provided a strong reassertion of managerial prerogative. Thus, in a strange twist of logic, employers are encouraged to hire labour by the provision of statutory measures that limit the ability of employees to obtain appropriate remedies for (or even challenge the basis of) unfair dismissals. These important changes to the regulation of the employment relationship suggest a reassessment on the part of the state of the fundamental purpose of labour market regulation such that now 'many of the things that matter to managers and workers are left to state and employer [rather than joint] regulation' (Ackers and Wilkinson, 2007).

ANALYTICAL APPROACHES TO LABOUR MARKET REGULATION

With the rise to prominence in many countries of governments espousing the need for major labour market reforms, it has been convenient to speak of a transition to a deregulated labour market. This view is certainly plausible inasmuch as many features of the traditional regulatory context of HRM – such as trade unions, collective bargaining, strikes, etc. – have either diminished in significance, or all

but disappeared from the industrial landscape in the last 10–20 years. Yet, much of the literature on work and employment has been unable to explain how institutional change has affected the dynamics of the employment relationship and the fundamental purpose of labour market regulation because it has been caught up in normative expressions of support for (uncritical HRM) or opposition to (IR) the notion of deregulation.

Regulation studies: Command and control versus decentered regulation

If it is popular to pronounce the emergence of a deregulated labour market, this view is not supported by those in the field of regulatory studies who have an interest in labour market regulation. Contributors to this field have argued the need to re-conceptualise regulation (rather than pronounce its demise) in the light of contemporary labour market changes that have reduced the role of traditional regulatory agencies and given rise to new institutions and actors (Arup et al., 2006).

One way to reconceptualise regulation has been to suggest that regulatory systems based on traditional 'command and control' – that is state sponsored rules backed by legal sanctions – have been replaced or augmented by more 'decentered' forms of regulation (Black, 2002). Looking beyond command and control recognises that in many areas a mix of regulatory tools and actors provides a more optimum regulatory outcome. So far as the employment relationship is concerned, the regulation of occupational health and safety (OHS) provides a good example of this approach. In OHS there has been a strong push since the influential 'Robens' recommendations of the 1970s for the direct parties to become more involved in the management of OHS risk in many countries. While this approach acknowledges that employers and employees have the greatest stake in devising safe work practices, and are often best placed to asses immediate risks (that vary between workplaces and industry sectors), this does not mean the adoption of a system of workplace OHS self-regulation: rather, the development of workplace structures of OHS risk management (with appointed and elected employer and employee representatives) is backed by appropriate industry codes of practice, as well as a government agency providing advice, education, inspections, compliance directions, and finally prosecutions for wilful non-compliance and repeat offenders.

If labour market regulation is becoming more 'de-centred', what impact does this have on the patterns of employment relations which shape and are shaped by employer HRM choices? One way to answer this question is to conceptualise the labour market as a regulatory arena which affords certain actors the capacity to occupy and utilise 'regulatory space' (Hancher and Moran, 1989; Scott, 2001). According to this analytical framework, regulatory actors compete for space within defined regulatory arenas. Space may be modified to suit the interests of one or more of the parties, reflecting the prevailing balance of power between the regulatory parties. In other words, the greater the space occupied by an actor, the more that actor has the capacity to shape regulatory outcomes to suit its regulatory preferences. Regulatory space may also be modified by the use of different regulatory instruments and different types of regulatory methods, such as command and control, joint regulation, self regulation.

Regulatory space is a useful analytical tool because it presents change as an ongoing part of the regulatory process rather than as a tool of transition from regulation to de-regulation. Thus, traditional actors may acquire more space (or indeed lose space) while new actors and institutions emerge to occupy and expand their regulatory space. For example, in recent years alternative forms of employee representation have emerged at that same time as unionisation has declined in most developed nations. These alternatives range from formal structures, such as staff associations and joint consultation committees, to informal mechanisms that promote employee voice through direct involvement (Bryson, 2004).

There is considerable debate among IR and HRM specialists as to whether these alternative forms have emerged to fill the 'representation gap' left over by declining unionisation, or are themselves a cause of union decline (the so called substitution versus suppression effect). Despite this conjecture, there is a growing perception that employee 'voice' arrangements are of benefit to firms, as well as being vital for employees (Freeman and Rogers, 1999), in that enhanced employee voice and involvement may lead to greater levels of employee discretionary effort which boost efficiency and productivity (Wilkinson et al., 2004). To the extent that management seeks to incorporate formal voice arrangements into a broad suite of HRM initiatives to promote direct employee involvement, it is likely that unions will face pressure on this front, as well as others, in their attempt to retain the space they have occupied as a central labour market regulator (Fiorito et al., 1987).

Employing regulatory space as an analytical device also allows us to conceptualise the state as having a role in setting the boundaries of the regulatory environment and also as an actor occupying space and exercising regulatory capacity *within* the regulatory environment. Rather than 'deregulating' the regulatory environment, the state can be seen to be directly intervening or re-regulating so as to change the composition of the regulatory arena by allocating regulatory space to some parties and taking it away from others. By such common statutory measures as enabling individual contracting or limiting the capacity of unions to engage in industrial action, the state is drawing a tighter boundary around the scope of one of the direct parties to the employment relationship to exercise its regulatory capacity (i.e. its market and organisational power) over the other. Governments may also change regulatory agencies to suit the interests of one or more of the regulated parties, or compel existing regulatory agencies to act in ways that promote the interests of one or more of the regulated parties. In effect, by 'regulating the regulator', the state may reconfigure the regulatory space to achieve its own regulatory preferences and outcomes.

Institutionalism and organisation studies

The preceding discussion suggests that research emerging from the field of regulatory studies views regulation as occurring through a variety of tools and instruments, both formal and informal. Thus, in many regulatory arenas, command and control has given way to decentred forms of regulation and new regulatory techniques. What might have been traditionally accomplished by rules backed by sanctions can perhaps be more effectively achieved through a range of less visible but not less powerful regulatory tools such as embarrassment, shaming and moral suasion. These informal tools shape behaviours according to what is defined externally as acceptable and legitimate and, at least from a regulator's point of view, the essential coercive nature of regulation may appear softened by the use of a mix of regulatory techniques rather than by a regime of force alone (Scott, 1995: 36).

This approach to regulation bears a strong resemblance to the literature in the field of organisation studies that contends that organisations are legitimised by an external normative context that both shapes the values of individuals within the organisation and regulates the operations of the organisation so as to reinforce its values. If organisations are legitimised by social and community attitudes, it stands to reason that changes in those norms may extend the scope of organisational matters that are subject to external regulation. Thus, for example, societal expectations that corporations behave in a socially responsible manner might translate into a preconscious desire by organisations to behave in such a way rather than the appearance of ethical behaviour masking rational choices organisations make, such as seeking to avoid the costs associated with non-compliance with regulations (Oliver, 1991: 148–9).

In the arena of employment relations, there is a growing awareness that OHS regulation now extends managerial responsibility for safety into areas such as bullying, harassment and employee stress with large penalties having been awarded against managerial neglect and failure to act on complaints in these areas. Public policy initiatives introduced under the banner of 'work and family' may also limit managerial discretion in work organisation by requiring organisations to pay greater attention to the development of HRM policies that promote family friendly work practices. The extent to which organisations develop policies, and change existing practices in these types of areas, as a response to changes in societal norms may determine that their long terms costs of compliance will be reduced when state intervention and judicial enactment mandate these requirements on all corporations.

According to DiMaggio and Powell (1983) the institutionalisation of organisations is best characterised as a process of 'isomorphism', in which innovators find their initiatives replicated by competitors to the point where organisational forms and behaviours appear homogeneous. Isomorphism occurs through coercive pressures stemming from societal expectations such as those mentioned above. Once organisations begin to adopt new behaviours reflecting changes in the external environment, replication (or 'modelling') occurs. Examples of HRM modelling have included well known experiments with high commitment, high performance and semi-autonomous work systems, total quality management and quality circles becoming institutionalised practices (DiMaggio and Powell, 1983: 151). For these authors, institutionalisation also occurs because organisational learning spreads through the professions. Like-minded professionals, who share insights derived from common educational and organisational experiences, adopt similar approaches to organisational strategising and problem solving, again producing institutionalisation and convergence rather than differentiation.

Before proceeding any further, it should be pointed out that the institutional perspective is not the only approach to organisation studies that recognises the importance of the link between organisational strategy and behaviour and the external environment. Indeed, the institutional perspective has been criticised for casting the organisation as necessarily passive in its relationship to the external environment. Comparing the institutional perspective to the 'resource dependence' view of the firm, Oliver (1991) argued that the institutional view offered little assessment of how organisations might resist, modify or in some way seek to shape external pressures where these diverge with the organisation's articulated self interests. Having acknowledged this, the focus here is on institutional approaches because these clearly view the external environment as a regulatory framework rather than as a series of competing pressures arising from stakeholders with divergent interests (Oliver, 1991: 147).

Other 'neo-institutional' contributions

There are a number of strands of new institutionalism with contributions coming from fields including economics and law, politics, sociology, history, as well as organisation studies. Neoinstitutional contributions have in common the view that the rational actor model does not adequately explain the dynamics of institutional and organisational behaviour. Put simply 'institutions matter' because they shape and constrain rational choices (DiMaggio and Powell, 1983). Rather than actions being the aggregation of rational individual preferences, organisations and institutions legitimise and order preferences, and they also invoke sanctions against non-compliance. They are the machinery of the regulatory framework.

The founding work in new institutionalism was undertaken by Coase who argued that firms themselves were created as institutions to minimise transactions. Later, transaction costs economics became popularised through the work of Williamson. According to Coase (1988: 38–39):

The main reason why it is profitable to establish a firm would seem to be that there is a cost of using the price mechanism ... It is true that contracts are not eliminated when there is a firm, but they are greatly reduced. A factor of production (or the owner thereof) does not have to make a series of contracts with the factors with whom he [sic] is co-operating within the firm, as would be necessary, of course, if this co-operation were a direct result of the working of the price mechanism. For this series of contracts is substituted one.

If firms are themselves constructions designed to avoid transaction costs, one of the most important regulatory devices firms use to achieve this goal is the employment relationship. For Marsden (1999) the open-ended employment relationship is the instrument of regulation that has proven the most efficient means by which organisations can engage and retain labour. This type of employment relationship offers employers access to available labour despite fluctuations in demand and supply. Because the relationship contains general rather than specific duties and obligations it is capable of delivering employers the type of flexibility they require to cope with changes in product demand and the introduction of new technology. Similarly, the employment relationship, rather than other forms of contracting, is efficient for employees because it regulates employers by placing limits on their managerial authority.

In employment relations, new institutionalism has come as a corrective to a body of literature that postulated that globalisation was promoting a convergence of regulatory systems and patterns of employment relations. Against the globalisation thesis, the contribution of new institutionalism has been to demonstrate instead that both history and institutions matter. In the long run, firms are constrained by external institutions which, in turn, may only change gradually because the force of history guides their continuity. As Godard (2004: 243) has argued in a review of new institutionalism, 'Institutional arrangements and the paradigms that underpin them tend to reflect economic, political, and social traditions that have become embedded in established rules, norms, and expectations'. By 'understanding state policies and traditions and, ultimately, the economic, political, and social foundations of these policies and the institutions they support' (Godard, 2004: 244), institutional studies can illustrate how employment relations systems in some jurisdictions make available HRM policies and practices that are simply not possible or feasible in different political and economic settings.

An important contribution of new institutionalism to our understanding the basis of the regulatory framework for HRM has been the development of the 'varieties of capitalism' literature (VOC) (Hall and Soskice, 2001). VOC contends that there are two types of capitalist models – the liberal market economy (LME) and the coordinated market economy (CME). Countries such as the US and Britain, that epitomise the LME model, have very different regulatory structures and underpinnings than countries, such as Germany, that are most closely aligned to the CME model. In LME countries, a combination of shareholder interests and stock market value shape the nature of the firm's HRM imperative. Changes to employment practices are closely aligned to the firm's current profitability, which makes flexibility a key prerequisite of employer HRM choices. Thus, British firms can sustain losses in market share because, through numerical flexibility, they can readily lay off workers.

In CME countries, non-market relationships determine a different pattern of employment relations. In CMEs, firms can access capital independent of current profitability which makes labour market flexibility a less important imperative. Moreover, strong inter-firm relationships and industry-wide systems of collective bargaining and vocational training work together to 'take wages out of competition', and in so doing limit in CMEs the attractiveness of HRM strategies that in LME countries are implemented as incentives to poach and retain labour by rewarding individual performance (Hall and Soskice, 2001: 25–27). Because CME firms have less need for labour flexibility – and because employees in these nations often enjoy greater protections against arbitrary

layoffs – there is also greater incentive for employees to invest in firm-specific skills and provide additional discretionary effort (see also Mares, 2003: 237).

The original VOC model proposed by Hall and Soskice has been the subject of considerable debate, with shortcomings highlighted by a number of authors. The limitations of VOC as an analytical tool include that it is based on an ideal-typical dualism of LME–CME divergence that does not adequately account for transitions between such polar extremes, and that it is limited mainly to North American and European developed countries, leaving aside other regional and developing nations (e.g. Hay, 2005). Despite its limitations, VOC advances our understanding of the regulatory context for HRM because it seeks to explain the preferences of firms for employment relations practices by locating them within the framework of national systems of corporate governance, industrial relations and training and education that produce strong incentives for divergence along the LME–CME spectrum. This literature remains an important corrective to that which postulates that globalisation has produced common pressures that are forcing once diverse nation states to radically change regulatory systems to enable firms to pursue common HRM practices to achieve greater labour market flexibility.

CONCLUSION

This chapter has noted that the fundamental changes that have been occurring to work and employment need to be understood within the framework of a regulatory context that both facilitates and constrains those changes. Rather than witnessing a transition to a deregulated labour market, important changes to employment structures and work practices have been accomplished with the involvement of new regulatory actors and experiments with different regulatory techniques to suit the new employment relations environment. Clearly labour market regulation has devolved so that much of this regulation now takes place directly between organisational actors rather than through interest representation by once dominant institutional actors. This transition clearly underscores the growing importance of HRM policies and practices to the management of employment relations. However, as has been pointed out, the capacity of firm-level actors to shape their own organisational outcomes remains conditioned by a number of institutional factors which include: the institutional history of the organisation and its culture and style of management; the location of the firm in industry which determines factors such as the type of bargaining structure and bargaining instruments, including forms of custom and practice, that shape employment relations; and the national context which defines the overarching regulatory system that gives expression to the capacity of HRM to play either an expansive or limited role in the regulation of the employment relationship.

REFERENCES

Ackers, P. and Wilkinson, A. (2007) 'Industrial relations and the social sciences', in P. Blyton, N. Bacon, J. Firito, and E. Heery (eds) *Sage Handbook of Industrial and Employment Relations* (forthcoming).

Adams, J. (1992) 'The corporation versus the market', *Journal of Economic Issues*, 26 (2): 397–405.

Arup, P., Gahan, J., Howe, R., Johnstone, R., Mitchell, R. and O'Donnell, A. (2006) (eds) *Labour Law and Labour Market Regulation*. NSW: The Federation Press.

Baldwin, R. and Cave, M. (1999) *Understanding Regulation: Theory, Strategy and Practice*. Oxford: Oxford University Press.

Barry, M. Michelotti, M. and Nyland, C. (2006) 'Protectionism, common advocacy and employer interests: Business contribution to labour market regulation in Australia', in C. Arup, P. Gahan, J. Howe, R. Johnstone, R. Mitchell and A. O'Donnell (eds) *Labour Law and Labour Market Regulation*. NSW: The Federation Press, pp. 43–66.

Black, J. (1997) *Rules and Regulators*. Oxford: Clarendon Press.

Black, J. (2002) 'Critical reflections on legal regulation', *Australian Journal of Legal Philosophy*, 27 (1): 1–35.

Black, J., Lodge, M. and Thatcher, M. (2005) *Regulatory Innovation: A Comparative Analysis*. Cheltenham, UK: Edward Elgar.

Bryson, A. (2004) 'Managerial responsiveness to union and nonunion worker voice in Britain', *Industrial Relations*, 43 (1): 213–41.

Coase, R. (1988) *The Firm, the Market and the Law*. Chicago: The University of Chicago Press.

Deery, S. and Mitchell, R. (eds) (1999) *Employment Relations: Individualisation and Union Exclusion*. Sydney: Federation Press.

DiMaggio, P. and Powell, W. (1983) 'The iron cage revisited: Institutional isomorphism and collective rationality in organizational fields', *American Sociological Review*, 48 (2): 147–60.

Dunlop, J. (1958) *Industrial Relations Systems*. Holt: New York.

Edwards, P. (1990) 'The politics of conflict and consent: How the labor contract really works', *Journal of Economic Behavior and Organization*, 13 (1): 41–61.

Eisner, M., Worsham, J. and Ringquist, E. (2006) *Contemporary Regulatory Policy*, 2nd edn. Colorado: Lynne Rienner.

Fiorito, J., Lowman, C. and Nelson, F. (1987) 'The impact of human resource policies on union organizing', *Industrial Relations*, 26 (2): 113–26.

Flanders, A. (1975) 'Industrial relations: What is wrong with the system?', in A. Flanders (ed.) *Management and Unions*. London: Faber and Faber, pp. 83–128.

Freeman, R. and Rogers, J. (1999) *What Workers Want*. Ithaca: Cornell University Press.

Godard, J. (2004) 'The new institutionalism, capital diversity, and industrial relations', in B. Kaufman (ed.) *Theoretical Perspectives on Work and the Employment Relationship*. Cornell University: IRL Press. pp. 229–64.

Hall, P. and Soskice, D. (2001) 'An introduction to varieties of capitalism' in P. Hall and D. Soskice (eds) *Varieties of Capitalism: The Institutional Foundations of Comparative Advantage*. Oxford: Oxford University Press.

Hancher, L. and Moran, M. (1989) 'Organising regulatory space', in L. Hancher and M. Moran (eds) *Capitalism, Culture, and Economic Regulation*. Oxford: Clarendon Press.

Hay, C. (2005) 'Two can play at that game … or can they? Varieties of capitalism, varieties of institutionalism', in D. Coates (ed.) *Varieties of Capitalism, Varieties of Approaches*. Hampshire: Palgrave Macmillan.

Heery, E. and Frege, C. (2006) 'New actors in industrial relations', *British Journal of Industrial Relations*, 44 (4): 601–04.

Howe, J. (2006) ' "Deregulation" of labour relations in Australia: Towards a more "centred" command and control model', in C. Arup, P. Gahan, J. Howe, R. Johnstone, R. Mitchell and A. O'Donnell (eds) *Labour Law and Labour Market Regulation*. Sydney: The Federation Press, pp. 147–66.

Kaufman, B. (1998) 'Regulation of the employment relationship: The "old" institutional perspective', *Journal of Economic Behavior and Organization*, 34 (3): 349–85.

Lawrence, P. (1985) 'The history of human resource management in American industry', in R. Walton and P. Lawrence (eds) *HRM: Trends and Challenges*. Boston: Harvard Business School Press, pp. 15–34.

Legge, K. (1995) *Human Resource Management: Rhetorics and Realities*. London: Macmillan.

Knight, J. (1992) *Institutions and Social Conflict*. Cambridge: Cambridge University Press.

Marchington, M. and Parker, P. (1990) *Changing Patterns of Employee Relations*. Brighton: Harvester Wheatsheaf.

Mares, I. (2003) 'The sources of business interest in social insurance: Sectoral versus national differences', *World Politics*, 55 (2): 229–58.

Marsden, D. (1999) *A Theory of Employment Systems: Micro Foundations of Societal Diversity*. Oxford: Oxford University Press.

Mitchell, R. and Johnstone, R. (2004) 'Regulating work', in C. Parker, C. Scott, N. Lacey and J. Braithwaite (eds) *Regulating Law*. Oxford: Oxford University Press, pp. 101–21.

Oliver, C. (1991) 'Strategic responses to institutional processes', *Academy of Management Review*, 16 (1): 145–79.

Parker, C. and Braithwaite, J. (2003) 'Regulation', in P. Cane and M. Tushnet (eds) *The Oxford Handbook of Legal Studies*. Oxford: Oxford University Press, pp. 119–45.

Piore, M. and Safford, S. (2006) 'Changing regimes of workplace governance, shifting axes of social mobilization, and the challenge to industrial relations theory', *Industrial Relations*, 45 (3): 299–325.

Polanyi, K. (1944) *The Great Transformation*. New York: Octagon Books.

Quinlan, M. (2006) 'Contextual factors shaping the purpose of labour law: A comparative historical perspective', in C. Arup, P. Gahan, J. Howe, R. Johnstone, R. Mitchell and A. O'Donnell (eds) *Labour Law and Labour Market Regulation*. NSW: The Federation Press, pp. 43–66.

Rhodes, M. (1989) 'Whither regulation? 'disorganised capitalism' and the West European labour market', in L. Hancher, M. Moran (eds) *Capitalism, Culture, and Economic Regulation*. Oxford: Clarendon Press, pp. 227–67.

Rubery, J. and Grimshaw, D. (2003) *The Organization of Employment: An International Perspective*. Houndmills: Palgrave Macmillan.

Scott, C. (2001) 'Analysing regulatory space: Fragmented resources and institutional design' *Public Law*, Summer: 329–53.

Scott, W.R. (1995) *Institutions and Organizations*. California: Sage.

Swenson, P. (2004) 'Varieties of capitalist interests: Power, institutions, and the regulatory welfare state in the United States and Sweden', *Studies in American Political Development*, 18 (Spring): 1–29.

Wilkinson, A., Dundon, T., Marchington, M. and Ackers, P. (2004) 'Changing patterns of employee voice: Case studies from the UK and the Republic of Ireland', *Journal of Industrial Relations*, 46 (3): 298–322.

6

The Evolution of HR Strategy: Adaptations to Increasing Global Complexity

Shad S. Morris and Scott A. Snell

INTRODUCTION

Discussions regarding the link between HR and strategy have long been evolving. From as far back as the industrial revolution, managing human resources was seen as the most costly and uncontrollable activity of the firm. The focus was on driving these costs down through person-job fit. Later, with the complexities of global competition, diversification, and total quality management, HR management was seen as something that needed to be consistent across the firm and aligned with the firm's strategy. More recently, with the increase of highly dispersed and diversified workforces, scholars have tried to understand how HR is coterminous and even formative to a firm's strategy. The implications of which are pushing scholars to venture into areas that neither HR nor strategy scholars have gone before.

The key objective of HR strategy is to guide the process by which firms develop and deploy people, relationships, and capabilities to enhance their competitiveness (Snell et al., 2001). Interestingly, this objective has not changed much over time, rather the context and environment in which firms are operating has changed. While our purpose here is not to discuss the evolution of markets and work environments, a discussion void of these considerations would be detrimental in understanding how HR strategy has and continues to evolve. Such an evolution, as we see it, has been beneficial to the overall productivity of firms as well as the overall value of the individual inside the firm.

Two things have changed over time that defines where we are today. First, the distinctions between HR strategy and competitive strategy have begun to blur (Snell et al., 2001). No longer are SHR scholars the only ones calling for a stronger focus on the people and processes inside the firm and how they are managed, but now strategy scholars realize that for their theories to be more complete and robust they must also focus on these 'micro-level' factors (e.g., Felin and Hesterly, 2007; Teece, 2007). As the value proposition of a firm rests more and more in its knowledge and service activities, strategic management depends largely on what people know and how they behave. A firm's strategy rests largely on how it is implemented by individuals, but also how it is formulated by individuals—leaving difficulty in separating how people are managed from organizational strategy.

The second change to define where we are today is in how valuable people are seen to the firm. Snell et al. (2001) pointed out that when people are no longer viewed as merely 'hands and feet' in a production function, but as key sources of strategic capability, the focus on organization and governance changes as well. Because no other resource possessed by a firm has free will or heterogeneity of ideas, products and services often originate in individuals, making human resources and how they are managed a potentially unique source of strategic leverage (Chadwick and Dabu, 2008). Further, managing the exchanges among geographically dispersed employees and between employees and external actors is difficult (i.e., the Barnard/Simon notion of partial inclusion). Many who define the firm as a knowledge community (e.g., Kogut and Zander, 1992), realize the difficulty involved in creating firm advantage. For one, the increase in differentiated workforces possess added cultural, geographical, and competency gaps (Becker and Huselid, this volume). So, in addition to managing the collective knowledge of individuals within a firm, advantage comes in being able to manage the relationships of those individuals as well (Kang et al., 2007).

While each of these issues does not change the definition of HR strategy, they certainly make it more important and at the same time more difficult. Such complexities draw closer attention to how a firm might manage its people and their knowledge in a way that is co-specialized with the relationships, capabilities, and systems in place. For example, developing and deploying people and knowledge through systems, capabilities, and relationships in a differentiated and globally dispersed environment presents extreme difficulty and coordination challenges, but is paramount to offering on-time products and services to a global client. As we delve into these issues throughout the chapter, we will summarize several of the key frameworks that have allowed HR strategy to adapt to changes in the environment. In addition, we will examine what adaptations are likely needed in the future.

To organize this discussion, we start from the industrial revolution, where cost-cutting and speed were emphasized. To strategically manage people, standardized jobs were developed and lengths were taken to make sure firms fit the job with the person. Next, we move to the diversified multinational companies of the 1970s and 1980s, discussing how internal and external fit came into play. Finally, we discuss the differentiated and globally dispersed workforces of today, where hyper-efficiency and electronic connectivity influence how human resources are viewed. We examine the extant literature on strategic management and HR management to identify how much HR strategy has evolved and where future adaptations are needed.

INDUSTRIAL REVOLUTION AND PERSON-JOB FIT

While some scholars go back to England in the guild era to understand the evolution of HR, its clear link to strategy is manifested in the early 1900s. Out of the industrial revolution came the birth of scientific management and industrial psychology. This led to the establishment of the first personnel departments in the 1920s. Here we see the underlying logic of HR strategy take shape (Snow and Snell, 1993). During the 1930s, 1940s, 1950s, and 1960s the logic underlying HR strategy was strengthened through the human relations movement as well as the academic and applied discipline of behavioral science and systems theory. However, it wasn't until the late 1970s and 1980s that we began to see real changes in the way HR strategy was being conceptualized and researched (Jamrog and Overholt, 2004). The significance of people and their alignment within the firm began to take shape. And finally, in the 1990s to date, experts noting the importance of knowledge embedded in people and their relationships began to call for an HR strategy that was not only complementary to firm strategy but indicative of it. As summarized in Table 6.1, each phase in this evolution shows how HR has been seen from a strategic perspective, but how it has adapted to meet changing needs of the environment.

The industrial revolution traded steam power and machinery for time-consuming hand labor. This led to factories where large numbers of people were employed. The result was an increase in job-specialization as well as efficiency of a typical worker (Cascio, 1993). As a result, corporate strategies focused on volume expansion and vertical integration. The main challenge focused on efficiency. Labor was considered a commodity that was bought and sold. Not only that, labor was seen as the most costly and troublesome commodity (Chandler, 1962). As a result, firms and work systems were influenced by the administrative principles of Weber, Fayol, and Taylor. These principles emphasized that individuals selected to do the work should be as perfectly matched, physically and mentally, to the demands of the job as possible. Second, employees should be trained to perform the work exactly as specified and they should not work at a pace that would be detrimental to their health. And finally, incentives should be used to ensure that employees do their jobs as instructed (Taylor, 1911).

Table 6.1   Evolution of HR strategy

HR strategy adaptation	Person-job fit	Systemic fit	Value creation
Environmental drivers	• Industrialization of work	• Global trade and competition	• Internet • Knowledge-based competition • Differentiated workforces
Strategic drivers	• Vertical Integration • Economics of Scale • Efficiency/Productivity	• TQM • Diversification	• Innovation and Change • Outsourcing and Alliances
Focus of HR strategy	• Administrative • Job-centric • Tasks	• Strategy implementation • System (e.g., team) • Behaviors/roles	• Strategy formation • Capabilities • Learning
Prevailing logic	• Analysis (job analysis) • Deductive	• Synthesis (integration) • Deductive	• Generative • Inductive
Locus of value	• Organizational Efficiency	• Organizational Knowledge	• Individual knowledge and relationships
Key design parameters	• Division of labor • Work standardization • Employment stability • Efficiency • Minimum investment	• Internal (horizontal) fit • External (vertical) fit • Bundling • High performance work systems • Configurations • Contingency models	• Strategic value of people and relationships • Uniqueness • Knowledge creation, transfer, and integration • Agile • Architectures of HR
Measurement issues	• Efficiency (cost per hire) • Validity/utility • Turnover • Department size	• Synergy among practices • Rater agreement • Strategy • Firm performance	• Knowledge • Relationships • Processes and systems • Capabilities

This required that a functional specialty be created to manage the hiring, work design, training, compensation, and relations with employees.

Adaptive advantages of person-job fit

While there was no explicit strategy for managing people in such firms, the goal of this function was to make sure people fit the job. This employment model was oriented toward employment stability, efficiency, and productivity through division of labor, specialization, and work standardization (Becker, 1976; Capelli, 1995; Hirschhorn, 1984). Jobs were designed to ensure that minimum investment in the employee was needed and that if the workers left or could no longer perform required duties, they could be replaced quickly and at little cost. Because of its strong tie to scientific management, HR-related activities were heavily analyzed. For example, job analysis—consisting of the breakdown of tasks, duties and responsibilities, as well as the alignment of these tasks and duties to the employees' knowledge, skills, and abilities—was heavily used to strategically determine who to hire and where to place them once they were hired.

These adaptations were notable in that they did two things for the field of HR. First, through an emphasis on rigorous measurement and costs, HR became a logical and precise function that could actually bring about greater efficiency for the firm. Measurement systems helped firms calculate exactly how much output they were getting from people and to reconfigure the work environment in such a way as to meet business goals (e.g., costs per new hire, validity of selection systems, turnover, and absenteeism). But even more important, these adaptations put HR on the map as a viable function that could be strategically used to ensure that the needs of the business were being met. Later on, this sole focus on the business from an HR perspective received some push back, as employee needs became a rallying cry in the later part of the industrial revolution.

Shift in the environment

With HR now in the spotlight and employee needs being a major factor in the environment, the human relations and sociotechnical schools came about, emphasizing the 'human factors' underlying productivity issues (Herzberg, 1957; McGregor, 1960; Trist, 1963). For example, the Hawthorne Studies of the Western Electric Company in Chicago provided evidence that productivity gains could be made when there was a lack of coercive approaches to productivity improvement and that workers were given opportunity to participate in the changes of their work environment (Roethlisberger and Dickson, 1939). For a few decades researchers offered argument and support in favor of a more humanistic approach to HR policy. Such arguments stood in contrast to the old approach of scientific management. The new approach, in particular sociotechnical systems, emphasized the rallying cry of many employees—that human systems need to be factored into work systems. This was quite a contrast from a purely analytical model of HR strategy.

Nonetheless, HR strategy adapted only slightly to these demands. The focus on person-job fit remained dominant—albeit slightly modified to improve working conditions—for much of the 20th century (Snell et al., 2001). Nonetheless, the tensions between labor and management throughout much of the 1950s, 1960s and 1970s made it abundantly clear that the old ways of HR strategy would not survive.

During the 1970s and 1980s the playing field for firms changed dramatically as competition moved from domestic to global. This was largely due to the increased elimination of state-enforced restrictions on exchanges across borders and decreased protectionism among nation states. Indicative of this era were the many trade agreements or 'codes' between countries that improved the global free-trade system (e.g., Tokyo and Uruguay rounds of GATT agreements in the 1970s and 1980s) (Fergusson, 2007). As a result, an increasingly integrated and complex global system of production and exchange emerged.

DIVERSIFIED MULTINATIONAL COMPANIES AND SYSTEMIC FIT

To help deal with the complexity of a changing global economy, firms developed diversification strategies and aspects of TQM. As Mason and Mitroff (1981: 15) pointed out, during this time companies adapted themselves to deal with these issues 'in a holistic or synthetic way as well as in an analytic way.' So, instead of dividing HR into its basic analytic elements, researchers began to examine how these pieces fit together to be able to integrate people and practices across various boundaries. This is about the time that the concept of HR strategy came about (Walker, 1980; Tichy et al., 1982; Miles and Snow, 1984). It was described by Wright and McMahan (1992: 298) as 'the pattern of planned HR deployments and activities.' Baird and Meshoulam (1988) noted two key issues in studying HR deployment activities: internal and external fit. Internal fit is how the components of HR support and complement one another. For example, if the firm wants to obtain and develop global leaders regardless of what unit or division they are in, they need to make sure their progression plans, training, promotions systems, and hiring systems are consistent with one another across the firm in terms of leadership development. External fit represents how the HR practices and policies are aligned with the strategic direction and stage of the firm. As firms operate domestically HR practices need to align with the local strategies, but as they diversify and internationalize, the HR practices must adapt to meet the changing demands of operating in multiple countries and environments (Sparrow et al., 2004).

Adaptive advantages of internal fit

Internal fit from a HR strategy perspective is concerned with how HR practices are aligned and mutually reinforcing. If they are aligned

correctly, they can reinforce one another and create a stronger impact on the goals of the firm. However, if they are not aligned, then disaster could strike (Boxall and Purcell, 2000). This became especially apparent as firms increased in complexity and people in the compensation unit, for example, didn't know what people in the training unit were doing. Not only were these divides difficult across sub-disciplines, but also across geographical and divisional boundaries. Hence, hiring for people who are team players and compensating on individual performance could potentially prove disastrous. In this case, managing the system rather than the individual practice may be the key element of HR strategy (Snell et al., 2001). One of the first to propose a systems-based approach to HR strategy that focused on internal fit was Beer et al. (1984). Later, scholars such as Arthur (1994) and MacDuffie (1995) showed how 'bundles' of HR practices were more important for understanding HR strategy than the practices themselves.

The research in HR strategy started to move closer to configurational models of strategy (Doty and Glick, 1994; Lado and Wilson, 1994). Scholars developed ideal types of HR practice bundles and identified them as behavior and output control (Snell, 1992), commitment-based HR (Arthur, 1994; MacDuffie, 1995), high performance work systems (Huselid, 1995), human capital enhancing systems (Youndt et al., 1996), and the transformed workplace (Kochan et al., 1986). This entire shift made HR practices more strategic in a globally complex work environment as the mechanics of individual HR practices were no longer useful, but the overarching employment relationship that companies established with their employees (cf., Baron and Kreps, 1999; Delery and Doty, 1996; Dyer and Holder, 1988; Osterman, 1987; Schuler and Jackson, 1987).

Adaptive advantages of external fit

During this time, many scholars also turned to an external (vertical) fit approach. No longer was HR only interested in improving employee commitment, but it was also directly linked to the firm's strategy (Boxall, 1996; Delery and Doty, 1996; Jackson et al., 1989; Olian and Rynes, 1984; Wright and Snell, 1991). This called for a contingency approach as firms developed different strategies depending upon the industry and environment in which they operated. One of the more noted papers was by Miles and Snow (1984). They presented a typology of competitive strategies, and then matched those strategies with specific HR strategies.

Because these competitive strategies depended upon the diversification of the firm, stage of growth, and cultural complexities, in response many of the HR strategies supported a contingency perspective (cf., Delery and Doty, 1996; Gomez-Mejia, 1992; Wright et al., 1995; Schuler and Jackson, 1987; Youndt et al., 1996). At the same time, researchers during this time were also arguing for a universal approach to HR strategy. This approach focused on creating high-commitment work systems as a strategy to improve firm performance (cf. Huselid, 1995; MacDuffie, 1995). This created some tension within the HR strategy world in terms of whether companies should pursue 'best fit' or 'best practice' (Boxall and Purcell, 2000). In other words, are there a set of global best practices out there make companies more effective if they use them, regardless of the context? Or, do work systems differ depending upon the firm strategy and environmental context?

While debates regarding this issue continue even today, they have helped us develop a broader understanding of how strategy can be implemented through administrative systems. Such developments have changed the way researchers look at the design of HR systems. Instead of only focusing on the technical characteristics of an individual HR practice, we began to examine how sets of practices worked as a system to elicit, reinforce, and support patterns of behavior that benefit the firm. As researchers have expanded how we look at HR strategy, they have developed a more integrated way to understand HR

and its link to the strategic intent of the firm. This is when HR took its place as a relevant organizational system to be compared to structure, culture, and technology.

The proliferation of strategic frameworks during this time created fervor among scholars in the formalization of the field of strategic management. It created a platform for the discussion and debate of ideas such as contingency, synergy, integration, and best practice that paved the way for the co-formalization of HR strategy. For example, while Miles and Snow (1978) and Porter (1980) have their critics, the typologies they presented during the 1980s stressed the importance of aligning the inner workings of the firm with the external environment. From this era, we see that staff managers were being asked to step up as business partners who knew where and how to fit HR systems in with the firm's strategy. Such people were not only required to know the inner workings of the personnel management, but they were also required to know how the business runs and how HR could align with or implement the firm's strategic intent.

Shift in the environment

As with the person-job fit adaptation, there were exceptions in the literature that became more and more prevalent over time. These shifts came largely as the environment in which firms operated changed. For example, Dyer (1983) and Buller (1988) found that HR and strategy had a reciprocal relationship rather than just strategy being used to inform how HR systems should look. Lengnick-Hall and Lengnick-Hall (1988) also noted that 'rarely are human resources seen as a strategic capacity from which competitive choices should be derived.' In this context, HR is seen as an enabling support function at best, and at worst a drain on resources.

By the end of the 20th century, however, the environment started changing. Traditional assets of financial capital, location, and technology began to commoditize. Global capital markets opened up and became much less of a barrier for firms; business could be done online, reducing the need for face-to-face interactions; and the rapid pace of innovation and the ability to reverse engineer reduced the time a firm had to capitalize on new technology. This decreased the number of ways a firm could differentiate itself from competition. As a result, heads turned quickly to human capital and potential as a catalyst for strategic advantage (Pfeffer, 1994).

This, in turn, created a world where people did not need to be co-located to work together on a project, where arbitrage or the differences in location actually became an advantage to many firms. Firms could rely on a much larger talent pool in order to learn from challenges addressed from all over the globe. For example, Infosys, as well as many other professional service firms, have capitalized on the fact that consultants can diagnose a Western client's problem on location in one day, send the diagnosis to a project team in India overnight, have them work on it throughout the night (daytime in India) and send it back the next morning to be implemented.

Complicating matters more, because of these shifts, the entire concept of a company has been put into question (Prahalad and Krishnan, 2008). Now, instead of a company being seen as a single outfit with full-time employees and a recognizable hierarchy, it is an ever-shifting network of suppliers, partners, outsourcers, and contingent workers who come together when necessity dictates (Lepak and Snell, 1999).

DIFFERENTIATED WORK FORCES AND VALUE CREATION

Just as the industrial revolution and global diversification of the 1900s had pushed HR strategy to evolve, the competitive challenges of today's differentiated workforces and hyper competition have called for another adaptation. The new hyper-competitive equation places a premium on knowledge-based assets such as human capital and relationships that underlie learning and innovation (cf. Leonard-Barton, 1992). In some ways, this reorientation stands in contrast to previous approaches to HR strategy. Rather than managing human resources around the firm's strategy, the strategy becomes contingent on the relationships and potential available through the firm's human resources.

Knowledge, skills, and abilities (KSAs), the primary components of a firm's human capital, are among the most valuable and distinctive resources upon which a company can draw (Barney and Wright, 1998). However, as the pace of competition increases and the geographical distance and difference in workforces widens, not only is it important to understand how to appropriately manage individual knowledge but also how to manage the coordination and integration of that knowledge. As a result, firms are often seen as networks of individual knowledge that need to be integrated and shared to deliver value (Kogut and Zander, 1993; Grant, 1996).

Adaptive advantages of talent management

In the past, HR strategy has focused on requisite behaviors required by individuals to implement a given strategy (cf. Snell et al., 2001). For example, if a firm used a low-cost strategy, as defined by Porter (1980), their HR strategy would need to focus on efficient behaviors, which meant applying routinized job design, output-based incentives, and relatively low levels of training. If the firm strategy was differentiated, as we see more of today, an emphasis would need to be placed on creativity and innovation, which suggested attracting and retaining high-skilled employees, high employee participation, and extensive training (Beatty and Schneider, 1997; Schuler and Jackson, 1987). However, even if the firm had a differentiated strategy, earlier strategy models did not incorporate HR or even view it as an important dimension. Adaptations were made as strategy scholars turned inward (using the resource-based view of the firm) to examine how internal resources could be valuable, immobile, and heterogeneous (Barney, 1991). As a result, HR strategy turned to the notion that some aspect of HR or a firm's KSAs could generate a sustained competitive advantage (e.g., Lado and Wilson, 1994; Wright et al., 1994; Coff, 1997; Boxall, 1998). Hence, the earlier separation of strategy implementation and formulation was reduced, as how people were managed and their human capital was seen as a vital source of value, immobility, and heterogeneity.

Underlying individual heterogeneity and the differentiated work environment, HR strategy started to focus on an architectural approach to managing talent. The architectural perspective takes into account that people have different knowledge, skills, and abilities and that these people need to be managed differently (e.g., Lepak and Snell, 1999). Until this point, HR scholars tended to aggregate—both conceptually and empirically—all employees into one comprehensive workforce as if it were managed with a single HR configuration. Though parsimonious and focused on macro-level phenomena, this approach takes for granted the variation that exists within the firm in terms of workforce differences. Part of these differences is seen as heterogeneity and some may even be valuable to the firm. However, with firm or aggregate level understanding of HR workforces, this internal heterogeneity is lost.

Though not taking a strategy perspective, earlier work informed HR researchers of the notable differences emerging between workforces in a single firm. For example, Baron et al. (1986) found that multiple internal labor markets exist within firms in response to firm-specific skills, occupational differentiation, and technology. Likewise, Osterman (1987) argued that industrial, salaried, craft, and secondary workforce systems were becoming more prevalent in the same firm. Matusik and Hill (1998), Rousseau (1995), and Tsui et al. (1995) have pointed to a variety of employment relationships co-existing within firms. Such relationships range from long-term with core employees to short-term exchanges with external guest workers and other forms of contract labor. Finally, Lepak and Snell (1999) showed how these differentiated workforces

can be strategically managed by deciding how valuable and how unique (heterogeneous) the KSAs of the people are. By doing this firms will be able to more accurately invest in specific employment relationships, recruiting strategies, training programs, and the like to more effectively manage today's differentiated workforce.

Building on these early beginnings, scholars are trying to better identify, measure, and manage differentiated workforces. For example, Becker and Huselid (2006) argued that research should continue to examine the role of 'best practices' that might improve firm performance. However, their main conclusion is that strategic opportunities for most firms now and in the future require a greater emphasis on contingencies within the firm based on the differentiated workforces of today. Though seemingly paradoxical, they argue that best practices still exist, but that what is best for one strategic business process in a firm may not be good for another in that same firm. Hence, future research should examine business processes within a firm (e.g., Collins and Smith, 2006). Furthermore, in this book Huselid and Becker also discuss the importance of better measures for workforce differentiation.

Focused on scientific measurement, Boudreau and Ramstad (2005a) have argued that HR needs to broaden their focus beyond HR practices and toward a 'decision science' that improves decisions about human capital throughout the firm. This requires that the HR function no longer focuses solely on itself (e.g., cost per hire, ROI on it programs, HR performance, and how its practices affect skills and performance). HR should be involved in improving the decisions about key or 'pivotal talent pools' throughout the firm. This means that HR needs to adopt a role similar to finance or marketing. Finance or marketing focus on how to acquire, allocate, and make strategic decisions about money or clients, respectively. Likewise, the role of HR should be to acquire, allocate, and make strategic decisions about talent. To do this, HR must apply the tools of segmentation—the approach used to improve decisions about customers and financial markets (Boudreau and Ramstad, 2005b). In many ways, segmentation is related to an architectural or differentiated approach to HR. The main premise is that when it comes to making decisions about talent, a firm should not apply the same processes and programs to everyone. In fact, different talent pools require different investments and attention. Such pools are linked, not around people, *per se*, but around their knowledge, skills, and abilities and how those KSAs are vital to the firm's strategy at the moment.

While investing in, paying attention to, and measuring these differentiated talent pools has become a strategic focus of HR, it is also important to understand how these different pools work together (Huselid et al., 2005). In other words, it is necessary but not sufficient to manage people from a portfolio approach. Like financial assets or clients, talent can be segmented based on value and uniqueness to the firm. However, unlike money and clients, people from different talent pools must interact and coordinate their efforts in order to achieve success. As a result, research not only focused on talent pools, but it also began to focus on relationships across these pools.

Adaptive advantages of relationship management

In an attempt to understand the link between HR practices and performance, Bowen and Ostroff (2004) argued that not only do we need to understand how knowledge, skills, and abilities are strategically important, but we must also look to 'higher order' social interactive constructs as important strategic factors leading to competitive advantage. In other words, the relationships and social context of various talent pools in an organization can be managed through HR systems and have a positive effect on a firm's performance. Such collective attitudes come from perceptions of the work climate or culture. Perceptions can be influenced or at least maintained by HR systems. In fact, Bowen and Ostroff (2004)

argue that it is not so much the practices themselves that make the difference, but the characteristics of the HR system—such as visibility, understandability, legitimacy, and relevance—that influence strong relationships and collective meaning among employees. Such relationships and shared mindsets facilitate greater sharing of knowledge that can then help an organization gain an advantage over its competitors.

Focused on relationships as well, Leana and Van Buren (1999) emphasized the potential role that HR strategy can play in getting people to work together through organizational social capital; that is, the knowledge embedded in or available through relationships. Likewise, Collins and Clark (2003) showed an empirical connection supporting network-building HR practices among top management teams and firm performance. More recently, Collins and Smith (2006) found that HR practices influence the firm's social climate, which facilitates knowledge exchange and as a result, the firm's performance.

Drawing from knowledge-based views of the firm, Kang et al. (2007) developed a framework to argue that not only is it important to focus on social capital and relationships within the firm, but that these relationships must be considered in the context of differentiated work groups or talent pools within the firm. In many regards, they argued that not only is it important for firms to understand their differentiated human capital needs, but they must also understand their differentiated social capital needs—How do you facilitate learning and exchange of ideas between contracted, spot-market labor and core workers? How do you ensure that innovations being generated in a vendor partnership across the world will benefit the rest of the firm? To answer some of these questions they examined specific relational archetypes that are vital for both knowledge exploration and knowledge exploitation. Based on business process strategy or strategic intent, a firm must be able to not only manage the talent pools, but also help to facilitate the appropriate relationships and interactions between those pools.

Furthering this discussion, Lepak et al. (2007) found that while talent pools in a support role may not be direct contributors to new knowledge within a firm, their role is vital to indirectly facilitating innovation. For example, support talent pools perform work that frees up knowledge workers for more innovation and they help to identify efficiencies within the innovation process. As a result, they found that investments in different talent pools may help or hinder knowledge sharing across employee groups. This research pointed to the importance of people working together and understanding one another, regardless of their differences.

The importance of relationships and learning has brought HR strategy even more into the strategy mix as knowledge that exists within the firm is considered not only 'a' source but 'the' source of firm advantage (Grant, 1996; Kogut and Zander, 1992). By default, this means that people and how they were managed becomes center stage for strategy formation. Not only is it important to strategically manage differentiated pools of talent, but it is important to manage the relationships within and between those pools of talent.

IN THE FUTURE

Recent trends in strategy research (e.g., Hatch and Dyer, 2004; Coff and Coff, 2006; Coff, 2002; Wang and Barney, 2006; Hitt et al., 2006; 2001) point to the key role of human capital and how it is coordinated as a primary factor leading to value added activities. This implies that the shift HR strategy has recently taken is co-evolving with the strategy literature. For the first time, we are seeing signs of the field of strategy taking cue from HR research (or at least HR related issues).

Yet, there is considerable evidence to show that HR managers are still ill-equipped to deal with issues of knowledge and innovation in today's globally dispersed and differentiated workforces. Part of the reason is that much of HR literature is still often based in one domestic location—failing to account for cross-boundary complexities. We highlight two of these complexities below as areas in which we hope to see further research. The first complexity comes from managing a globally differentiated and dispersed workforce. This presents us with issues of how HR should address issues of local adaptation and global integration. The final and related issue is seen in our lack of understanding outsourcing and offshoring from an HR perspective. Too little is known about how an organization might manage people who are not considered part of the official organization.

Globalized workforce

While significant research has been done on international issues relating to HR strategy, much of this research still takes an external fit argument. For example, focus is either on comparative HR systems (cf., Takeuchi et al., 2003) or the global/local distinctions in HR practice (cf., Bae and Lawler, 2000; Fey and Bjorkman, 2001; Rosenzweig and Nohria, 1994; Sparrow et al., 1994; Taylor et al., 1996). These discussions are valuable, but do not address issues of how firms might manage the increasing heterogeneity and uniqueness found across geographically dispersed workforces within a firm. Only recently, scholars have begun to consider the HR function to answer questions about a firm's capacity to adapt to changes in a global environment (cf., De Cieri et al., 2005).

This specifically highlights the issue of capabilities, and focuses on the importance of researchers looking inside the HR function to understand how companies develop the capacity to constantly renew HR systems in a way that allows for local adaptation and global integration. Few researchers have studied the underlying elements of capabilities within global firms (cf., Augier and Teece, 2007; Pitelis and Verbeke, 2007). But doing so would help address two potentially important questions for HR managers. First, what capabilities are most important for HR to develop? And second, what are the underlying mechanisms that allow HR to develop such capabilities?

By focusing on the HR function itself, we shift gears from traditional HR practices to better understand how HR can more effectively manage and coordinate globally dispersed talent throughout the organization. Doing so requires more than rote implementation of a specific set of standardized practices. Instead, HR must develop capabilities that improve their ability to adapt to local talent pool needs but at the same time to be able to coordinate and integrate these talent pools in ways that lead to economies of scale and scope.

For example, McWilliams et al. (2001) argued that firms can benefit from a globally differentiated workforce in two ways: capitalizing on the global labor pools, and exploiting the cultural synergies of a diverse workforce. First, global (heterogeneous) labor pools potentially provide superior human capital. This is because firms can draw from different labor pools to match the different needs of the firm (Bartlett and Ghoshal, 1989). Second, the use of heterogeneous labor pools potentially increases the quality of business decision making. When a firm draws from its multiple labor pools it has the potential to a build diverse and flexible cadre of people who are better able to bring different perspectives to a decision than a management group based solely from the parent country (Watson et al., 1993).

While McWilliams et al. (2001) highlighted the benefits of human resource heterogeneity and immobility, they also point out the difficulty in transferring and integrating these resources within the MNC. Drawing on Szulanski's (1996) concept of stickiness, they note that international exchanges are made more difficult by 'the lack of absorptive capacity of the recipient, causal ambiguity, and an arduous relationship between the source and the recipient' (Szulanski, 1996: 36). Yet, little research exists discussing how internal stickiness can be overcome in order to maximize the benefits of a global workforce while overcoming the challenges of integration and coordination (Morris et al., 2006).

Outsourcing and offshoring

Related to issues of integration and coordination, one specific area that has been underserved in the HR strategy literature is the role of HR in outsourcing and offshoring activities. Outsourcing consists of any labor activities outside of a formal or informal contract with the organization. Offshoring can consist of both captive and outsourced labor that is conducted outside of the firm's home country. Firms outsource work to offshore service providers in order to decrease costs or increase opportunities (Lewin and Peeters, 2006). In the past decade, more and more firms are outsourcing in offshore locations to increase their opportunities by developing global value creation and innovation strategies. In this regard, leading companies will be able to differentiate themselves by developing dynamic capabilities necessary for exploring and exploiting higher value-adding offshoring opportunities (Teece et al., 1997).

These value-add opportunities have received very little attention from HR scholars, but have become a major source of advantages for global organizations. Research has typically focused on strategic and financial issues dealing with a firm's decision to and management of offshoring and outsourcing activities. For example, this research discusses what outsourcing opportunities create the most strategic value and the associated costs from a net-present value perspective. These discussions tend to leave out a vital aspect of this decision—how do we coordinate and manage these offshored and/or outsourced workers?

To examine this question more thoroughly, scholars must begin to identify what it is that is unique about the changes that come from these workforce relationships. For example, Fisher et al. (2008) have argued that 'the performance of the outsourced work on the client site creates particular complexities in supervisory, reporting, and other interpersonal relationships that may lead to problems including turnover, lack of loyalty, service discontinuities, and poor service quality.' (502). In other words, outsourced and offshored work both create specific complexities in not only how the service provider workers are managed, but also in how the client workers are managed.

The relationships between outsourced and offshored workers and other talent pools within the firm create strong issues for knowledge sharing as well. As discussed by Matusik and Hill (1998), here we see issues of how to coordinate firm-specific knowledge and knowledge created by outsourced work. Part of the concern is that both talent pools (client firm workers, and service firm workers) have motivation to hoard knowledge. Client workers will withhold core knowledge that can easily spread to competitors if service providers get a hold of it. On the other hand, service workers are motivated to withhold knowledge to ensure that the knowledge they've developed isn't taken by the client and used to hire a cheaper service provider (Connelly and Gallagher, 2006). The client may also want to retain any intellectual property they've developed in process of solving the client's problem (Renn et al., 2001). The other problem is simply that when the terms of the contract end, both parties take with them their own specific knowledge and leave gaps for the other talent pool (Gallagher and McLean Parks, 2001).

The above issues provide ample room to discuss the strategic role of HR in managing knowledge across and within offshoring and outsourcing relationships. Are different HR strategies needed to facilitate sharing and integration of knowledge across the various talent pools in such situations? Future research should examine the HR strategy implications.

CONCLUSION

Our purpose in writing this chapter was to summarize the evolution of the field of HR strategy. HR strategy has moved along a path that started with humble beginnings barely recognized on the shop floor by low level supervisors during the industrial revolution to a widely debated and discussed topic in

board rooms among top-management teams today. We identified three evolutionary stages starting from the industrial revolution around the turn of the 20th century, the global diversification of the 1970s and 1980s, to the differentiated work systems and hyper-competition of today. In each of these stages we defined the environmental factors present at the time, particular assumptions, parallel strategy literature, and perspectives about managing people for firm advantage.

As firms adapted to the industrial revolution and a call for efficiency and productivity, they took on an extremely administrative role where the prevailing logic was focused on job analysis and making sure the person's knowledge and skills directly matched the job. Here workers were seen as commodities that needed to be replaced as quickly as possible if they proved not to be well suited for the job. Labor was seen as a cost that needed to be kept down in order for the firm to meet its strategy.

The focus on HR lasted many decades and did not adapt until the advent of trade liberalization and greater global competition. This was the age of large, diversified firms. Hence, HR adapted to these changes by taking a more systemic approach where HR practices and activities needed to align with one another in order to be consistent in the behaviors they were trying to produce. At the same time, external fit became a strong issue as many scholars debated 'best fit' approaches, where HR aligned with the firm strategy, versus 'best practice' approaches where many scholars argued for universal work systems that improved firm performance regardless of the strategy. Both issues focused on strategy implementation and alignment as firms started experiencing differences within.

These differences became even stronger in the 1990s and thereafter. Due to hyper-competition, the internet, and differentiated workforces, knowledge became the basic currency of all business. No longer were firms looking to people to implement their strategy, firms were looking to people to also formulate their strategy. As the key strategic drivers were innovation and change, firms had to rely on their people to create new knowledge and integrate that knowledge on a continual basis. This also led to a movement toward capabilities rather than practices as the key source of sustainable competitive advantage.

Another objective of this chapter was to show how the fields of strategy and HR are converging. No longer is there only a cry for HR to be more strategic, but the cry is starting to come back that strategy needs to include more HR. This evolution has pushed people issues at the forefront in developing today's strategic management models. These models are focusing more and more on the value of human capital, social capital, capabilities, and their underlying mechanisms to developing competitive advantage.

We believe that this co-evolution of HR and strategy will benefit both fields by providing greater understanding of the vital intersection between people and firms as they try to co-exist. For better or for worse, this co-evolution will also blend the two fields of strategy and HR strategy to the point where distinctions will be hard to make. Regardless of the effects on scholarly fields, such blending will have a positive effect for managers as we will be able to offer more comprehensive models and approaches to managing firms.

REFERENCES

Arthur, J.B. (1994) 'Effects of human resource systems on manufacturing performance and turnover', *Academy of Management Journal*, 37 (3): 670–87.

Augier, M. and Teece, D. (2007) 'Dynamic capabilities and multinational enterprise: Penrosean insights and omissions', *Management International Review*, 47 (2): 175–92.

Bae, J. and, Lawler, J.J. (2002) 'Organizational and HRM strategies in Korea: Impact on firm performance in an emerging economy', *Academy of Management Journal*, 43: 502–17.

Baird, L. and Meshoulam, L. (1988) 'Managing two fits of strategic human resources management', *Academy of Management Review*, 13 (1): 116–28.

Barney, J.B. (1991) 'Firm resources and sustained competitive advantage', *Journal of Management*, 17 (1): 99–120.

Barney, J.B. and Wright, P.M. (1998) 'On becoming a strategic partner: The role of human resources in gaining a competitive advantage', *Human Resource Management*, 37 (1): 31–47.

Baron, J.N. and Kreps, D.M. (1999) 'Consistent human resource practices', *California Management Review*, 41 (3): 29–53.

Baron, J.N., Davis-Blake, A. and Bielby, W.T. (1986) 'The structure of opportunity: How promotion ladders vary within and among organizations', *Administrative Science Quarterly*, 31: 248–73.

Bartlett, C. and Ghoshal, S. (1989) *Managing Across Borders: The Transnational Solution*. HBS Press.

Beatty R. and Schneier, C. (1997) 'New HR roles to impact organizational performance: From "partners" to "players"', *Human Resource Management*, 36 (1): 29–37.

Becker, G.S. (1976) *The economic approach to human behavior*. Chicago: University of Chicago Press.

Becker, B. and Huselid, M. (2006) 'Strategic human resources management: Where do we go from here?', *Journal of Management*, 32 (6): 898–925.

Beer, M., Spector, B., Lawrence, P.R., Mills, D.Q. and Walton, R.E. (1985) *Human Resource Management*. New York: Free Press.

Boudreau, J.W. and Ramsad, P.M. (2005a) 'Talentship and the evolution of the human resource management: From "professional practices" to "strategic talent decision science"', *Human Resource Planning Journal*, 28 (2): 17–26.

Boudreau, J.W. and Ramsad, P.M. (2005b) 'Talentship, talent segmentation, and sustainability: A new HR decision science paradigm for a new strategy definition', in M. Losey, S. Meisinger, and D. Ulrich (eds), *The Future of Human Resources Management*. Washington, DC: Society for Human Resource Management.

Boxall, P. (1998) 'Achieving competitive advantage through human resource strategy: Towards a theory of industry dynamics', *Human Resource Management Review*, 8 (3): 265–88.

Boxall, P. and Purcell, J. (2000) 'Strategic human resources management: Where have we come from and where should we be going?', *International Journal of Management Reviews*, 2 (2): 183–203.

Bowen, D. and Ostroff, C. (2004) *Academy of Management Review*.

Buller, P.F. (1998) 'Successful partnerships: HR and strategic planning at eight top firms', *Organizational Dynamics*, 17 (2): 27–44.

Cappelli, P. (1995) 'Rethinking employment', *British Journal of Industrial Relations*, 334: 563–602.

Cascio, W.F. (1993) 'Downsizing: What do we know? What have we learned?', *Academy of Management Executive*, 7 (1): 95–104.

Chadwick, C. and Dabu, A. (2008) 'Human resources, human resource management, and the competitive advantage of firms: Toward a more comprehensive model of causal linkages', *Organizational Science*, forthcoming.

Chandler, A.D. (1962) *Strategy and Structure*. Cambridge, MA: MIT Press.

Coff, R.W. (1997) 'Human assets and management dilemmas: Coping with hazards on the road to resource-based theory', *Academy of Management Review*, 22 (2): 374–402.

Coff, R.W. (2002) 'Human capital, shared expertise, and the likelihood of impasse in corporate acquisitions', *Journal of Management*, 28 (1): 107–28.

Coff, R.W., Coff, D.C. and Eastvold, R. (2006) 'The knowledge leveraging paradox: How to achieve scale without making knowledge imitable', *Academy of Management Review*, 31 (2): 452–65.

Collins, C.J. and Clark, K.D. (2003) 'Strategic human resource practice, top management team social networks, and firm performance: The role of human resource practices in creative organizational competitive advantage', *Academy of Management Journal*, 46: 720–31.

Collins, C.J. and Smith, K.G. (2006) 'Knowledge exchange and combination: The role of human resource practices in the performance of high-technology firms', *Academy of Management Journal*, 49 (3): 544–60.

Connelly, C.E. and Gallagher, D.G. (2006) 'Independent and dependent contracting: Meaning and implications', *Human Resources Management Review*, 16: 95–106.

De Cieri, H., Fenwick, M. and Hutchings, K. (2005) 'The challenge of international human resource management: Balancing the duality of strategy and practice', *The International Journal of Human Resource Management*, 16 (4): 584–98.

Delery, J. and Doty, D.H. (1996) 'Modes of theorizing in strategic human resource management: Test of universalistic, contingency and configurational performance predictions',

Doty, H.D. and Glick, W.H. (1994) 'Typologies as a unique form of theory building: Toward imploved understanding and modeling', *Academy of Management Review*, 19: 230–51.

Dryer, I. (1983) 'Bringing human resources into the strategy formulation process', *Human Resource Management*, 22: 257–71.

Dryer, L. and Holder, G.W. (1988) 'A strategic perspective of human resources management', in I. Dryer and G.W. Holder (eds) *Human Resources Management: Evolving Rules and Responsibilities*.

Washington, DC: American Society for Personnel Administration.

Felin, T. and Hesterly, W. (2007) 'The knowledge-based view, nested heterogeneity, and new value creation', *Academy of Management Review*, 32: 172–202.

Fergusson, I.F. (2007) *The World Trade Organization: Background and Issues*. Code #: 98–928.

Fey, C.F. and Bjorkman, I. (2001) 'The effect of human resource management practices on MNC subsidiary performance in Russia', *Journal of International Business Studies*, 32 (1): 59–76.

Fisher, S.L., Wasserman, M.E., Wolf, P.P. and Wears, K.H. (2008) 'Human resource issues in outsourcing: Integrating research and practice', *Human Resource Management*, 47 (3): 501–23.

Gallagher, D.G. and McLean Parks, J. (2001) 'I pledge thee my troth ... contingently: Commitment and the contingent work relationship', *Human Resource Management Review*, 11: 181–208.

Gomez-Mehia, L.R. (1992) 'Structure and process of diversification, compensation strategy, and firm performance', *Strategic Management Journal*, 13: 381–97.

Grant, R.M. (1996) 'Toward a knowledge-based theory of the firm', *Strategic Management Journal*, 17 (S2): 109–22.

Hatch, N.W. and Dyer, J.H. (2004) 'Human capital and learning as a source of sustainable competitive advantage', *Strategic Management Journal*, 25 (12): 1155–78.

Herzberg, F. (1957) *Job Attitudes: Review of research and opinion*. Pittsburgh: Psychological Service of Pittsburgh.

Hirschhorn, L. (1984) *Beyond mechanization: Work and technology in a postindustrial age*. Cambridge, MA: MTT Press.

Hitt, M.A., Bierman, L., Shimizu, K. and Kochhar, R. (2001) 'Direct and moderating effects of human capital on the strategy and performance in professional service firms: A resource-based perspective', *Academy of Management Journal*, 44: 13–28.

Hitt, M.A., Bierman, L., Uhlenbruck, K. and Shimizu, K. (2006) 'The importance of resources in the internationalization of professional service firms: the good, the bad and the ugly', *Academy of Management Journal*, in press.

Hueslid, M.A. (1995) 'The impact of human resource management practices on turnover, productivity and corporate financial performance', *Academy of Management Journal*, 38: 635–70.

Huselid, M.A., Beatty, R.W. and Becker, B.E. (2005) '"A players" or "A positions?" The strategic logic of workforce management', *Harvard Business Review*, December, 110–17.

Jackson, S.E., Schuler, R. and Rivero, J.C. (1989) 'Orgainizational characteristics as predictors of personal practices', *Personnel Psychology*, 42: 727–86.

Jamrog, J.J. and Overholt, M.H. (2004) 'Building a strategic HR Function: Continuing the evolution', *Human Resource Planning*, 27 (1): 51–62.

Kang, S-C., Morris, S.S. and Snell, S.A. (2007) 'Relational arctypes, organizational learning, and value creation: Extending the human resource architecture', *Academy of Management Review*, 32 (1): 236–56.

Kochan, T.A., Katz, H. and McKersie, R. (1986) *The Transformationof American Industrial Relations*. New York: Basic Books.

Kougut, B. and Zander, U. (1992) 'Knowledge of the firm, combinative capabalities, and the replication of technology', *Organizational Science*, 3: 383–97.

Kogut, B. and Zander, U. (1993) 'Knowledge of the firm and the evolutionary theory of the multinational enterprise', *Journal of International Business Studies*, 24 (4): 625–45.

Lado, A.A. and Wilson, M.C. (1994) 'Human resource systems and substained competitive advantage: A competency-based perspective', *Academy of Management Review*, 19 (4): 699–727.

Leanna, C.R. and VanBuren, H.J. III. (1999) 'Organizational social capital and employment practices', *Academy of Management Review*, 24 (3): 538–55.

Lengnick-Hall, C.A. and Lengnick-Hall, M.L. (1998) 'Stategic human resources management: A review of the literature and a proposed typology', *Academic Management Review*, 13 (3): 454–70.

Leonard-Barton, D. (1992) 'The factory as a learning laboratory', *Sloan Management Review*, Fall: 23–38.

Lepak, D.P. and Snell, S.A. (1999) 'The human resource architecture: Toward a theory of human capital allocation and development', *Academy of Management Review*, 38: 599–612.

Lepak, D.P., Taylor, M.S., Tekleab, A., Marrone, J. and Cohen, D.J. (2007) 'Examining variability in high investment human resource system use across employee groups, establishments, and industries', *Human Resource Management*, 46: 223–46.

Lewin, A.Y. and Peeters, C. (2006) 'The Top-Line Allure of Offshoring', *Harvard Business Review*, March, 22–24.

Mason, R.O. and Miroff, I.I. (1981) *Creating a Dialectieal Social Science: Concepts, Methods and Models*. Boston, MA: D. Reidel.

Matusik, S.F. and Hill, C.W.I. (1998) 'The utilization of contingent work, knowledge creation, and competitive advantage', *Academy of Management Review*, 23: 680–97.

McDuffie, J.P. (1995) 'Human resource bundles and manufacturing performance: Organizational logic and flexible production systems in the world auto industry', *Industrial and Labor Relations Review*, 48 (2): 197–221.

McGregor. H. (1960) *The Human Side of Enterprise*. New York: McGraw-Hill.

McWilliams, A., Van Fleet, D.D. and Wright, P.M. (2001) 'Strategic management of human resources for global competitive advantage', *Journal of Business Strategies*, 18: 1–23.

Miles, R.E. and Snow, C.C. (1984) 'Designing strategic human resources systems', *Organizational Dynamic*, Summer, 36–52.

Morris, S.S., Snell, S.A. and Wright, P.M. (2006) 'A Resource-based View of International Human Resources: Toward a Framework of Integrative and Creative Capabilities', in G. Stahl and I. Björkman (eds), *Handbook of Research in International Human Resource Management*. Cheltenham: Edward Elgar Ltd, in press, pp. 433–48.

Olian, J.D. and Rynes, S.I., (1984) 'Organizational staffing: Integrating practice with strategy', *Industrial Relations*, 23: 170–81.

Osterman, P. (1987) 'Choice of employment systems in internal labor markets', *Industrial Relation*, 26 (1): 48–63.

Pfeffer, J. (1994) *Competitive Advantage through People: Unleashing the Power of the Workforce*. Boston: Harvard Business School Press.

Pitelis, C. and Verbeke, A. (2007) 'Edith Penrose and the future of the multinational enterprise: new research directions', *MIR: Management International Review*, 47 (2): 139–49.

Porter, M.E. (1980) *Comparative Strategy: Techniques for Analyzing Industries and Competitors*. New York: Free Press.

Prahalad, C.K. and Krishnan, M.S. (2008) The *New age of innovation: Driving co-created value through global networks*. New York: The McGraw Hill Companies.

Renn, M., Hall, K. and Younger, C. (2001) 'Client confidentiality and intellectual property: Key challenges in outsourcing', *Pharmaceutical Technology*, 62–66.

Roethlisberger. F.J. and Dickson, W.J. (1939) *Management and the Worker: An Account of a Research Program Conducted by the Western Electric Company, Hawthorne Works, Chicago*. Cambridge, MA: Harvard University Press.

Rosenzweig, P. and Nohria, N. (1994) 'Influences of human resource management practices in multinational corporations', *Journal of International Business*, 25 (2): 229–51.

Rousseau, D.M. (1995) *Psychological Contractsin Organizations: Understanding Written and Unwritten Agreements.* Thousand Oaks. CA: Sage Publications.

Schuler, R.S. and Jackson, S.E. (1987) 'Linking competitive advantage through human resource practices', *Academy of Management Executive*, 1: 207–19.

Sparrow, P., Brewster, C. and Harris, H. (2004) *Globalizing Human Resource Management.* Routledge, London.

Sparrow, P., Schuler, R. and Jackson, S. (1994) 'Convergence or divergence: Human resource practices and policies for competitive advantage worldwide', *International Journal of Human Resource Management*, 5: 268–99.

Snell, S.A. (1992) 'Control theory in strategic human resource management: The mediating effect of administrative information', *Academy of Management Journal*, 35: 292–327.

Snell, S.A., Shadur, M. and Wright, P.M. (2001) 'Human resources strategy: The era of our ways', in M. A. Hitt, R.E. Freeman, and J.S. Harrison (eds), *Handbook of strategic management.* Blackwell Publishing, forthcoming.

Snow, C.C. and Snell, S.A. (1993) 'Staffing as strategy', in N. Schmitt, W.C. Borman, and Associates (eds), *Personnel Selection in Organization.* San Francisco: Jossey-Bass.

Szulanski, G. (1996) 'Exploring internal stickiness: Impediments to the transfer of best practice within the firm', *Strategic Management Journal*, 17: 27–43.

Takeuchit, N., Wakabayashi, M. and Chen, Z. (2003) 'The strategic HRM configuration for competitive advantage: Evidence from Japanese firms in China and Taiwan', *Asia Pacific Journal of Management*, 20 (4): 447–80.

Taylor, F.W. (1911) *The principles of scientific management.* NY: Harper & Row.

Taylor, S., Beechler, S. and Napier, N. (1996) 'Toward an integrative model of strategic international human resource management', *Academy of Management Review*, 21 (4): 959–85.

Teece, D.J. (2007) 'Explicating dynamic capabilities: The nature and microfoundations of (sustainable) enterprise performance', *Strategic Management Journal*, 28 (13): 1319–50.

Teece, D.J., Pisano, G. and Shuen, A. (1997) 'Dynamic capabilities and strategic management', *Strategic Management Journal*, 18 (7): 509–33.

Trichy, N.M., Fombrun, C.J. and DeVanna, M.A. (1982) 'Strategic human resource management', *Sloan Management Review*, 23: 47–61.

Trist, E.L. (1963) *Organizational Choice: Capabilities of Groups at the coal Face under Changing Technologies: The loss, Re–discovery and Transformation of a Work Tradition.* London: Tavistock Publications.

Tsui, A.S., Pearce, J.L., Porter, L.W. and Hite, J.P. (1995) 'Choice of employee–organization relationship: Influence of external and internal organization factors', in G. R. Ferris (ed.), *Research in Personnel and Human Resource Management.* Greenwich, CT: JAI Press, pp. 117–51.

Walker, J.W. (1980) *Human Resource Planning.* New York: McGraw-Hill.

Wang, H. and Barney, J.B. (2006) 'Employee Incentives to Make Firm-Specific Investments: Implications for Resource-Based Theories of Corporate Diversification', *Academy of Management Review*, 31 (2): 466–76.

Watson, W.E., Kumar, K. and Michaelson, L.K. (1993) 'Cultural diversity's impact on interaction process and performance: Comparing homogenous and diverse task groups', *Academy of Management Journal*, 36: 590–602.

Wright, P.M. and McHahan, G.C. (1992) 'Theoretical perspectives for strategic human resource management', *Journal of Management*, 18 (2): 295–320.

Wright, P.M., McMahan, G.C. and McWilliams. (1994) 'Human resource and sustained competitive advantage: A resource-based perspective', *International Journal of Human Resource Management*, 5: 301–26.

Wright, P.M., Smart, D.L. and McMahan, G.C. (1995) 'Matches between human resources and strategy among NCAA basketball teams', *Academy of Management Journal*, 38 (4): 1052–74.

Wright, P.M. and Snell, S.A. (1991) 'Toward an integrative view of strategic human resource management', *Human Resource Management Review*, 1: 203–25.

Wright, P.M. and Snell, S.A. (1998) 'Towards a unifying framework for exploring fit and flexibility in strategic human resource management', *Academy of Management Review*, 23: 756–72.

Youndt, M.A., Snell, S.A., Dean, J.W., Jr. and Lepak, D.P. (1996) 'Human resource management, manufacturing strategy, and firm performance', *Academy of Management Journal*, 39 (4): 836–66.

7

Strong Situations and Firm Performance: A Proposed Re-Conceptualization of the Role of the HR Function

John J. Haggerty and Patrick M. Wright

Facilitator: Imagine yourself in a world where all of the administrivia, the lowest value added work you do, is suddenly gone. What is it that you will now do with that available time?

　　HR Practitioner: (After a long pause) I don't honestly know, but I'm fairly certain I won't have the skills to do it.

In a recent series of global HR working group sessions, we consistently heard that somewhere between 30 and 70 per cent of the time worked by relatively high-level HR professionals is, by their own admission, low-value added, and thus only remotely connected to firm performance. While most would admit that outsourcing, automation, self-service and devolution (to line managers) are beginning to help, there is still a fairly high administrative component to their daily tasks. While this in and of itself is noteworthy, it is the sentiment above which is most worrisome.

What exactly is contemporary HR expected to be doing, and do they have the skills to meet those expectations? Candidly, many practitioners will answer, 'I don't know'.

A review of the extant literature on strategic HRM will provide a wealth of information about individual practices (performance feedback, incentive pay, participation in goal setting, job design, etc.), or bundles of practices (high performance work systems), and their relationship with firm performance, but will do little to answer the question, 'what are the people responsible for HRM within firms supposed to be doing?' That is, if the essence of strategic human resource management is the effect it has on important business outcomes, what are the activities that functional HR needs to be engaging in? How (exactly) does HRM help drive business performance?

Scholars have repeatedly referred to the practice-performance relationship as the 'black box' of HRM. The evidence suggests a relationship, but the independent variables (practices and/or bundles) are distal from the outcomes (profitability/market value), and the effects sizes are small. And this body of practice/performance literature does little to suggest what those involved in HRM as a profession should be doing, aside perhaps from adopting proven practices and bundles. This approach ignores the entire issue of organizational context.

In this chapter we suggest that conceptualizing HRM as a practice or a set of practices not only ignores important aspects of context, it may in fact lead to the development of HR functions that base their contribution to the business on practices or bundles (benchmarking), not on business results. As the field of business process outsourcing continues to mature and improve, HR functions focused on HR practices (largely administrative in nature) are finding less and less left for them to do.

We suggest a re-conceptualization of HRM not as practices and bundles, but as signals from management to employee groups and individuals. We will explore how the level of human capital in the HR function, HR systems, structure, and line management expectations of the HR function can come together to build and maintain *legitimate* HR functions. Legitimate HR functions will be better positioned to create strong situations. We believe that it is those strong situations which then allow HRM to impact firm performance through the individual interpretation of management signals and the discretionary behavior of employees.

Our argument is that the emerging role (if not the historical but rarely achieved role) of HRM, is the creation of those strong situations which allow for the development of a shared climate in which the intended signals from leaders are correctly interpreted by the target audience(s), and drive the appropriate individual (discretionary) behaviors which aggregate to generate competitive advantage. That is, amid all the complexity that is the modern competitive organization, local actors, applying simple rules, are the root of sustained competitive advantage. And the most vital role of HRM is to help the organization establish and maintain the proper climate and the decision heuristics behind those simple rules.

We will first review some of the current criticisms of HR, many of which focus on the inability of HR to achieve 'business partner' status. We will then turn our attention to the research on the HRM Performance link, and the continuing discussion of the 'black box'. We will then examine the concept of strong situations, in particular Bowen and Ostroff's (2004) HR system strength concept. We will use this new concept to go inside the black box and explore the role of the HR function in driving performance through building the strength of the HR system.

CRITIQUES OF HR

Recently, a number of established scholars and several commentators began to pay attention to the notion of HR functional excellence. In one of the most infamous passages in *Why We Hate HR*, Hammonds (2005) takes dead aim at the people of HR with the following now well-known paragraph:

> Most HR organizations have ghettoized themselves literally to the brink of obsolescence. ...They are competent at administrivia ... but companies are increasingly farming those activities out to contractors ... What's left is the more important strategic role of raising the reputational and intellectual capital of the company—but HR is, it turns out, uniquely unsuited for that. (p. 43)

While somewhat more scholarly in his approach, Lawler (2005) reaches a very similar conclusion:

> It is nearly unanimous that HR can and should add more value to corporations. The best way to do this is by being a business partner—by directly improving the performance of the business. This can be accomplished by effective talent management, helping with change management, influencing strategy, and a host of other value added activities that impact effectiveness. But HR does not seem

able to position itself as a business partner in many cases. (p. 165)

Both authors seem to be implying that the strategic role now identified as most likely to impact firm performance, turns more on the people in HR than the practices of HR. And finally, in reviewing the general inability of the HR function to operate at the desired strategic level, Becker and Hueslid (2006) suggest: 'Whether this market failure is due to a lack of knowledge, a lack of managerial competence, or an inability to execute (or more likely some combination) is open for conjecture, and it is hoped, future research.' (p. 905)

The degree of convergence on the importance of execution (not the selection of practices), and the need for improved skills among those responsible (HR professionals), is remarkable. Yet to date, little of the suggested work has been done, and the predominant focus of strategic HR research remains on practices and bundles.

HRM AND FIRM PERFORMANCE

While questions have been raised about the value added by the HR function, efforts to prove the positive impact of human resource management on the market capitalization or financial performance of firms have a well-established history (Becker and Huselid, 1998; Wright et al., 2003). Burdened by an administrative heritage, human resources practitioners have long been interested in empirical proof that their work is as valuable to firm success as the work of other support professionals such as accountants and lawyers (Boudreau and Ramstad, 2002). Theoretical work done in the early 1990s led to a flurry of academic research aimed at proving a macro or organizational level link (Wright and McMahan, 1992; Huselid, 1995; MacDuffie, 1995) between HRM and firm performance.

By the mid 1990s, a relationship between HRM and organizational level outcomes had been demonstrated empirically (Huselid, 1995; 2000). Research claimed that firms that used certain human resource practices had better performance than firms that did not. Firms that bundled practices into high-performance work systems (HPWS) had better performance than firms that did not (MacDuffie, 1995). These findings were replicated across multiple industries and sectors (Youndt et al., 1996), and eventually, in multiple countries as well. The results seemed consistent whether one used market or accounting based measures of performance (Huselid, 1995). Meta-analysis (Combs et al., 2006) of 92 individual studies confirmed a correlation of 0.20, with stronger effects for HPWS bundles than for individual HPWS practices. While methodological challenges remain (Wright et al., 2005), it is now widely accepted that how the workforce is managed has an effect on the performance of firms.

Interestingly, however, while the research said that HR practices, bundles and systems mattered, the actual role of the HR function has been largely left out (for exceptions see Lado and Wilson, 1994; Ulrich, 1997; Huselid et al., 1997). Presumably, the HR function must select the practices to implement or bundle, but little if anything was researched or written about the ability of those in HR to do that, or the processes through which that is done. While the 'fit' of HRM to strategy has been analyzed, the mechanics of how that fit is determined, and how practices are selected and implemented has not been addressed. And virtually no attention has been paid to the range of potential success (or failure) that those in HR might have when attempting to implement the best-practices or bundles. Practice selection, implementation and execution, the intellectual activity of HR professionals, has been largely ignored in the empirical literature.

While research continues on practices and bundles as the essence of HRM systems, some researchers have adopted or called for a more micro organizational approach to identify intermediate links in the causal HRM-performance chain (Collins and Clark, 2003; Bowen and Ostroff, 2004; Ostroff and Bowen, 2000). There is also a growing acknowledgement that more qualitative and contextual methodology, rooted in institutional theory, might be needed during this transition to better identify the constructs and variables that should ultimately be tested quantitatively (for a review see Paauwe, 2004). Still others are suggesting that the inherent complexity of the HRM performance relationship should be acknowledged, and efforts to understand them should not be reductionist, but should look to biological systems and complexity theory as analogs and move more deliberately to a systems level of analysis (Colbert, 2004). In a recent review of the literature and the state of the art of HRM research, Becker and Huselid (2006) acknowledge progress, but also recognize the lack of context and the need for greater attention to implementation. In fact, they quote Barney (2001) who earlier recognized, 'the ability to implement strategies is, by itself, a resource that can be a source of competitive advantage.' (p. 901)

STRONG SITUATIONS

Few organizations today maintain strict command and control hierarchies. In many contemporary organizations, layers of management have been removed, spans of control have greatly increased, and leaders and supervisors are often unable to 'meddle' in the day to day activity of their reports, some of whom may not even be in the same physical location. Policy manuals and detailed employee handbooks have largely disappeared, and employees are expected to exercise greater amounts of discretion and judgment in their day to day activities, which should be in support of the organization's strategic goals. But how does the average employee make such decisions? We suggest that organizations guide employee behavior by establishing a high level set of principles, and constantly adjust behavior by sending 'signals' through the formal and informal networks of the firm. HRM is the primary channel through which such signals are sent.

But signals, even when carefully constructed and sent, are subject to interpretation. To be effective, all recipients should hear, understand and accept the message, and should be guided to behave in similar ways to support the organization's objectives. That is, despite differences in personality, interest, focus, etc., individuals will react to messages and behave in similar (and predictable) ways. When signals are correctly interpreted and individuals behave in ways that favor desired organizational outcomes, the situation is said to be strong.

Mischel (1973; 2004) building on the earlier work of Lewin et al. (1939) in the field of psychology, introduced the concept of situational strength. Years of research into personality traits revealed substantial differences in the level of trait measured in individuals as situational characteristics varied (the 'person versus situation' debate). That is, individual conscientiousness measures varied as situational factors changed. Mischel (1973) in essence reversed this finding and suggested that strong situations could induce consistent behaviors across individuals, despite underlying differences in personality, while weak situations would allow for greater variance in interpretation and response. Thus, it is imperative to create strong situations when the desired outcome is consistency of behavior or action across employee groups. For example, if customer service is important, all employees who interact (or could interact) with customers should display courtesy and a caring attitude, regardless of their mood or affect at the point of interaction.

Human resource practices are one important way that leaders send signals to individuals in organizations. Incentive pay plans, for example, are intended to drive behavior consistent with strategic organizational goals. But, is a single HRM practice, or even a cluster of practices enough to create the strong situation Mischel envisioned? We do not believe this to be true.

We contend that the 'black box' of the HRM-firm performance link, or the ability of HRM to produce desired organizational outcomes (growth, profit, market value), is more likely to be a result of the strength of the total HR system than it is the result of individual HR practices or high-performance work systems.

HUMAN CAPITAL IN THE HR FUNCTION

Many organizations today have sets of high level principles (basic truths, laws or assumptions) that are intended to guide the decision making of employees at all levels. These may be formalized in a corporate 'values statement', or an employee code of conduct. It is here that one would find statements about the value of individual integrity, the need to be respectful of differences, and the importance of meeting or exceeding customer expectations. For example, a corporate value statement (principle) may contain the words 'employees are our most important asset', which may or may not be fully reflected and supported across a spectrum of HR practices such as pay and benefits, development, and flexible work arrangements to promote work-family balance. Similarly, a statement about ethical behavior at the principle level should translate into practices that promote the open discussion of differences, the ability to report questionable behavior anonymously and some guarantee of aggressive investigation and follow-up.

To be effective in guiding decisions, principles must be made real in ways that are meaningful to employees at all levels. Consistent with our earlier argument about the role of HR and strong situations, the degree to which there is a clear linkage between these high level principles and the individual practices employees interact with is an important determinant of HR legitimacy and system strength. But, given the myriad of employee groups and the complex architecture (Lepak and Snell, 1999) of modern organizations, how can a few principles translate into the requisite complexity of practices needed to efficiently manage a modern organization?

Our argument is that one important role of the professional employees in the HR function is to manage this complex translation function well. Employees must be able to see clearly the link between a corporation's lofty aspirational statements, and the impact (on them as individuals and groups) of individual business and human resource practices. To do this effectively, HR must be comfortable operating at both the conceptual (principles or systems) level, and the more concrete practices level. Effective translation also requires deep esoteric knowledge of the existing culture of the organization, of the best ways to present messages designed to change behavior at the individual and group level, and a realistic feel for the current frame of mind in the effected employee groups.

This suggests the need for a strong foundation upon which to build and leverage the skills implied by the translation activity above. The deep analytical capability, intuitive capacity, data input and processing speeds required to do this well favor HR professionals and functions with focused and tacit academic and functional training and professional development. HR functions that stress high level academic achievement, including specific functional knowledge and quantitative analytical training (MBAs or research oriented Masters degrees) will be better able to build and maintain the competencies necessary to create strong situations.

MANAGEMENT EXPECTATIONS

Bowen and Ostroff (2004) suggested that creating a strong HR situation should help employees understand what is expected and better enable them to determine the appropriate expected behaviors. They incorporate communication theory and push the research agenda into new territory. Can this micro approach be reconciled with the resource-based view (RBV) theoretical implication that sustained competitive advantage derives from relationships that may be socially complex and deeply embedded, thus unobservable (Wright et al., 2001)? We suggest that the relationship between line managers and human resource professionals is just such a relationship—generally unobserved, and certainly important in the development of the strong situations which translate to competitive advantage.

In order for human resources professionals to fully leverage their high-level skills, there must be a consistently high level of expectation emanating from operating management at all levels. In order to have high expectations, management must have a reasonable amount of knowledge about the state of the art in human resource capability, and must constantly measure output and demand more from the investment they make in the function. Management teams with high levels of HR domain knowledge are more likely to select highly skilled and high performing functional leaders, who in turn will build and maintain high performing HR functional organizations.

High levels of management expectation will also promote frequent interaction between line management and human resource leaders at all levels, further reinforcing the perceived legitimacy of the HR function. HR functions high in organizational legitimacy will be better able to establish and maintain strong situations, leading to a shared organizational climate.

STRONG SITUATIONS AND THEIR CRITERIA IN HRM

A strong situation is thus one in which the variability of responses to a stimuli normally associated with fundamental differences in personality are reduced. Translating this concept to the field of human resources, Bowen and Ostroff (2004) propose that 'HRM practices, as a system … contribute to firm performance by motivating employees to adopt desired attitudes and behaviors that, in the collective, help achieve the organization's strategic goals' (p. 204). They propose that organizational climate mediates the HRM-performance relationship, and they suggest that: 'strong climates … allow employees to understand the desired and appropriate responses and form a collective sense of what is expected' (p. 204). They view the HRM system as a key determinant of climate, and

begin to suggest that researchers differentiate between strong and weak HRM systems.

HRM system strength is based on 'metafeatures' (Bowen and Ostroff, 2004: pp. 208–213), described as distinctiveness, consistency and consensus. Under distinctiveness, they list:

- understandability
- visibility
- legitimacy of authority
- relevance.

Consistency is made up of:

- instrumentality
- consistent HRM messages.

While consensus refers to:

- agreement among principal HRM decision makers
- fairness.

When these metafeatures are present, and the HRM system is strong, 'the sense making process will be most likely to result in the intended organizational climate. If the HRM system is weak, the HRM practices will send messages that are ambiguous and subject to individual interpretation. Given ambiguity, one of two things may happen: variability, or unintended sense making' (Bowen and Ostroff, 2004: 213).

In the next section we will focus more directly on how strong situations and climate mediate the relationship between HRM and firm performance, and we begin to identify how the HR function can create and maintain the required conditions for a strong situation.

STRONG SITUATIONS AND THE ROLE OF HR

At the macro level, the resource-based view has emerged as the primary theoretical explanation for the relationship between HRM and firm performance (Wright et al., 2003). But theory building at lower levels of analysis has lagged (Bowen and Ostroff, 2004). Exactly how HRM effects firm performance, and through what mechanisms these effects manifest themselves is still largely unknown. The framework proposed by Bowen and Ostroff suggests that the strength of the HR system (based on the work of Michels' 'strong situations' from the sociology literature) 'can contribute to firm performance by motivating employees to adopt desired attitudes and behaviors that in the collective help achieve the organization's strategic goals.' Their analysis is multi-level, looking at the organization, the group and the individual simultaneously, and seeking to explore how the levels are linked (House et al., 1995).

While acknowledging the role of the resource-based view at the macro level, Bowen and Ostroff turn to climate as a mediating construct in their proposed multilevel analysis of the relationships between HRM and performance. What individual employees see, and how they make sense of their environment (in this case within the organizational context) forms their psychological climate (Schneider, 1990, 2000). Organizational climate is a shared perception of what the organization is like in terms of practices, policies, procedures, routines and rewards—what is important and what behaviors are expected and rewarded (Bowen and Ostroff, 2004). HRM practices and the HRM system will play a critical role in determining climate perceptions, which is in turn empirically linked to higher level behaviors and organizational performance indicators (Bowen and Ostroff, 2004). But the actual mechanisms through which these variables interrelate are still poorly understood.

They base their conception of a strong situation in the work of Lewin et al. (1939) on climate, and Mischels' work on the strength of social situations (Mischel, 1973). Strong situations 'lead all persons to construe the particular events the same way, induce uniform expectancies regarding the most appropriate response pattern, provide adequate incentives for the performance of that response pattern, and instill the skills

necessary for its satisfactory construction and execution' (Mischel, 1973, in Bowen and Ostroff, 2004: 207).

This distinction between HRM content and HRM process is important in a number of ways. Bowen and Ostroff view HRM practices as communications from the employer to the employee. Using theories from communication they discuss the need for accurate reception and yielding, or acceptance of the message (Chaiken et al., 1996). For the message to have its desired effect, both are necessary (Bowen and Ostroff, 2004).

For a situation to be considered strong, employees must hear the message, as it was intended, and must accept it prior to choosing an appropriate response. This event-effect relationship is cemented by distinctiveness (the event effect is highly observable), consistency (the event effect presents itself the same across modalities and time) and consensus (there is agreement among individuals views of the event effect relationship) (Kelley, 1967). When all are present together, the situation is strong, and employees are highly likely to interpret messages in a similar fashion and behave in ways appropriate to the organization's objectives (Bowen and Ostroff, 2004).

While Bowen and Ostroff identify the separation between HRM practices and HRM process, their analysis tends to place them back together in the form of the HRM system. They then analyze the various ways that distinctiveness, consistency, and consensus can be made palpable, leading to strong HRM situations.

It is here that we begin to depart from the Bowen and Ostroff analysis and suggest that the strength of the HRM system is leveraged more on the process and less on the content of HRM. That is, individual practices, taken in the aggregate, may not lend themselves to creation of a strong situation, but the overall HRM process does.

Bowen and Ostroff identify four characteristics of HRM that can foster distinctiveness: visibility, understandability, legitimacy of authority, and relevance. For visibility, they talk about the need for an HRM practice to be salient and readily observable. They conclude:

> The creation of a strong organizational situation requires that situational characteristics be salient and visible throughout much of the employees' daily work routines and activities. When the HRM system includes a wide spectrum of HRM practices—for example, selection, training, diversity programs, employee assistance programs, and so forth—that affect a large number of employees, visibility is likely to be higher. Expanding the number and range of practices should enhance salience and visibility, because it increases complexity and allows for the set of practices to be more figural relative to other stimuli—both of which are principle of salience (Fiske and Taylor, 1991). Additionally, shared meaning cannot be developed unless most or all employees are subjected to and can perceive the same **practices**. (Bowen and Ostroff, 2004: 208).

While we believe that the Bowen and Ostroff analysis is correct, and that visibility does in fact help create and maintain a strong organizational situation, it is not practical to think in terms of every practice being visible (or for that matter relevant) to all employees, or even at times a large sub-set of all employees. Practices vary across employee segments (hourly, non-exempt, supervisory, executive, full-time/part-time, contractor, partner, consultant), and vary considerably across industry and country. Practices are, and should be, visible to those most directly affected. Attempts to broadly disseminate information about practices that are not relevant will most likely result in significantly less attention to the chosen medium over time, weakening the organizational situation. The complexity of most organizations today, and the segmentation of employees along multiple lines, makes visibility at the practices level impractical. Efforts to make all practices visible to all employees are likely to result in white noise, effortlessly ignored by those exposed.

Similar concerns can be stated with respect to the Bowen and Ostroff (2004) notion of understandability and relevance. While it is intuitively obvious that to have an effect on an individual a practice must be understandable, and that clear communication is critical to success, the interplay between understandability and relevance cannot be overlooked. Employees are subject to an ever-increasing amount of information from traditional and new (more invasive) sources, and attention cannot be paid to all simultaneously. The signals must be clear and in some way personalized to signal a particular employee to be attentive to a message that has relevance, yet allow others to ignore the message as noise. Perhaps the best way to maximize attention to critical input is to provide it face to face (and one on one) in a quiet setting, but the reality of today's workplace makes such a communication choice unrealistic. Again, time demands and the complexity of communications in the workplace make creating a strong situation by communicating to everyone the same messages difficult if not unrealistic.

Further, attempting to achieve consistency and consensus at the dynamic and changing level of practices is also problematic. There is little apparent consistency between the CEO's pay scheme and the pay plan of the part time call-center associate. Any attempt to articulate a basis for such consistency would be widely attended to, but is unlikely to produce motivation among those at the lower end of the pay continuum. And while agreement among HRM's is important, it does not mean that they must compromise and seek practices that do not acknowledge the differences inherent across employee populations. Fairness has a contextual component to it … fair as compared to what? The notions of consistency and consensus make more sense at the less dynamic, more abstract level of process and principle.

One way, however, that visibility, understandability and relevance can be brought together to produce a coherent message that employees are likely to attend to is if the HR function and the HRM system have what Bowen and Ostroff (2004) call legitimacy of authority. It is here that the recent suggestions of Lawler begin to make sense, the organization or structure of HR matters. When properly positioned in the organization (for example directly reporting to the CEO, not through an Administrative VP or other staff position), and properly resourced with high caliber professionals, HR appears in the eyes of the organization to be legitimate. It is the perception in the minds of individual employees, all of whom hear a large number of messages every day, that certain messages, from certain sources, deserve more attention than others. Companies that have established and maintained an HR function and a system of HR processes that are viewed as important and meaningful by employees are more likely to create strong situations around HRM, and therefore have greater influence on employee behavior, leading to desired business outcomes. It is the strength of the HRM system that creates adequate and appropriate visibility, which leads to quick analysis of relevance, which leads the right employees to look intently for meaning or understanding. That is, a strong HRM system aids employees in sense making and decision-making. And since such sense making activity is continuous and in some cases unconscious, it aids in the creation of agility by promoting employee judgment on a continuous basis. Behaviors, determined in the moment by well informed employees, will support the general principles of the organization, even when established practices (rules) do not.

Thus, although Bowen and Ostroff (2004) seem to argue that visibility, understandability, relevance and legitimacy of authority are equal in their importance and impact, we would argue that the legitimacy of authority of the HRM function is a condition precedent to the other three. A legitimate HRM system also encourages consistency, and promotes consensus among groups of employees who are comparing interpretations of messages. Bowen and Ostroff leave it to others to determine and develop appropriate measures of HRM system strength. We would encourage effort be invested to first dimensionalize HRM legitimacy of authority.

Legitimacy of authority, we suggest, is not a function of HR practices, which has been the focus of much if not most of the HRM performance literature. We see the reverse relationship, that effective HR practices are a function of HRM legitimacy of authority. That is, HR functions are more able to produce and implement HR practices that have the desired impact on employee behavior if they are perceived as legitimate authority broadly in the organization. The relationship of the HR function to the top management team is a critical ingredient in its legitimacy of authority. This relationship is often visible to employees, and signals them whether to pay close attention to HR as a 'partner' in the business, or pay less attention to HR as a largely administrative function. The relative status of HR to other business functions and disciplines (e.g. accounting and finance, legal, marketing, etc.) is also often signaled to employees in a variety of ways, including office proximity, attendance at meetings and who travels with the boss. Therefore, when HR is broadly perceived to be a legitimate authority within the organization, it is more likely to be able to create and maintain strong situations, leading to enhanced performance

While these are important antecedents, they alone do not create the strong situation described by Bowen and Ostroff. We would argue that given clear evidence of legitimacy of authority, strong situations are created and maintained in the processes used to develop, implement and evaluate HRM itself, quite distinct from the practices that make up the work product, or the individuals that hold the positions within HR.

At several points in their analysis, Bowen and Ostroff (2004) draw a distinction between HR practices, and HR processes. But the bulk of their detailed review deals with practices alone as the manifestation of HR, in keeping with earlier research. Colbert (2004) is more explicit in his review, suggesting that the inherent complexity of HRM at the micro level is a natural and expected reflection of a complex adaptive system. As such, rather than work harder to reduce that complexity (and eliminate potentially valuable variance), he suggests that HRM scholars move up the 'levels of abstraction' and deal more directly at the level of policy and principle, incorporating theory from the field of complexity. His work bridges a gap in the literature from our understanding of micro level relationships to the more recent work on organizational agility (Shafer et al., 2001), and the work of Teese et al. (1997) on dynamic capabilities. The key to understanding, in contradiction to Bowen and Ostroff (2004), is not in reducing the level of abstraction, but increasing it by focusing on processes. Consistent with complexity theory, and with the work of Mintzberg (1978), Colbert (2004) suggests that the answer may lie not in the discreet contributions of traditional reductionist research, but in identifying the critical patterns in the stream of evolving HRM stategy.

Colbert's (2004) argument is that, in accordance with the RBV of the firm, many of the most critical contributions of HRM are captured not in individuals or in individual practices, but in the complex interactions and relationships among many individuals and practices (Colbert 2004). This systems level view is not new, but the addition of theory from other fields (complexity) helps provide an 'analogical bridge' (Colbert, 2004: 353) linking HRM and performance. It also fits well with Mintzberg's earlier suggestion that we should look for patterns in a stream of decisions to determine strategy.

But Colbert's model, although strong, is not complete. There is, in our experience, an additional level of abstraction that is not principle, not policy, not practice and not product. It is the process through which principles, policies and practices are created, modified, implemented and evaluated on a continuing basis. It is the device that signals employees to be attentive – the content of this process will have a significant effect on their growth and development in the firm, it will signal the behaviors that are expected, and the rewards or sanctions they will receive for compliance or non-compliance. It is in itself a complex process, but it reduces the complexity of the individual HR policies and practices by packaging them in a way that has legitimacy of authority and conveys a clear and consistent message appropriate for the audience.

For example, GE, widely regarded as a successful company, has for over 50 years utilized its 'Session C' process to manage its HRM system. The rhythms of employee participation in the process are clear and well established. The agenda for each year's Session C process is approximately 80 per cent fixed. It contains the building blocks of employee self evaluation and career interest identification, leadership and 360 performance appraisals, employee training and development interests and leadership recommendations, and a review of compensation and benefit practices and turnover. The other 20 per cent of the review agenda reflects current cares and concerns, and may involve a very 'deep dive' on a particular function (e.g. accounting or sourcing or technology), a review of the results of a recent change effort (e.g. moving six sigma from an internal efficiency program to a program to build customer relationships by sharing the results), and/or a discussion about specific industry or demographic trends that impact the management of people (e.g. movement of administrative activity to shared services centers, and/or the need to promote more innovation and creativity across the board.) If a specific HR practice has recently been changed (e.g. the 'forced distribution of employee performance'), it most likely grew out of a prior Session C (or many), and will be evaluated through the lens of future Session C's. That is, the growth and development of the HRM system is not ad hoc or situational, it is contained within a vessel that gives it context, meaning and importance to all levels of leadership and to employees through the vast commitment of leadership time (not just HR time) to the process, which is highly visible to all.

It is in this process domain that we believe the work of Bowen and Ostroff and Colbert can be reconciled. If one were to look across GE or other large complex organizations from the bottom of the chain, from the domain of HR practices, one would find the complexity and variety nearly incomprehensible. If one looks from the top, from the principle level, one would find simplicity ('we want to be the world's most competitive enterprise'), but little meaning. The policy level exists, but it is viewed as either administratively required (reporting rules), or deeply esoteric (stock option cancellation policy upon involuntary cessation of employment); policy generally does not inform action in the broad sense. The real power is at the process level, where the goal to be the world's most competitive enterprise is given form, communicated broadly through well established rhythmic occurrences (we do not say events, because they are not), routinely and frequently measured, and adapted as needed. There is no mystery as to when Session C occurs, and no doubt to its meaning and importance. The strong situation was carefully created, and is well maintained. Complexity is reduced, but variance is not eliminated.

Thus the process level of abstraction allows us to utilize Colbert's (2004) explication of the resource-based view and its irreducible complexity, yet still look for the mediating mechanisms identified by Bowen and Ostroff (2004). If we focus on HRM legitimacy of authority, and use organizational structure, frequency and quality of interaction with line management, and the existence and importance of a comprehensive HRM process as a proxy to measure legitimacy, these measures should give multi-level HR System strength data that we would hypothesize would correlate with desired employee behaviors and firm performance.

In simplest terms, our argument is that the strength of the HRM system, and the process through which it is enacted, will explain more firm performance variance than individual practices or bundles of practices. The strength of the HRM system and process will determine how well employees attend to HRM messages, how well they understand, individually and collectively what behaviors are expected, and what the outcomes will be for so behaving. With clear understanding of the expectations, and the consequences, employees can be expected to exercise judgment and display motivation. A coherent HRM process allows for any change of an HR practice to be interpreted

in an overall context that remains largely unchanged.

In fact, a strong HR process may mitigate against the potential damaging effects of an inappropriate or out of date practice … employees will know to ignore it and behave in a way that is consistent with the higher level principles as represented through the process. Strong HRM process creates the strong situations identified by Bowen and Ostroff (2004), yet operates at a higher level of abstraction than practices (but still meaningful to employees), as suggested by Colbert.

Research into the prevalence of HRM systems, and the relative strength of HRM processes should be given priority among HRM scholars. Some dimensions to consider, as explained above, include the relative value of HR and other functions, the amount of management time spent on HRM across the board, the HR skills and business understanding of those engaged in HR work, and the state of maturity of the HR organizational capital, the HRM process itself.

THE IMPORTANCE OF IMPLEMENTATION

This notion of the importance of execution, not just formulation, has a corollary in the strategy literature. In the early 1970s, Henry Mintzberg began to challenge 'conventional' notions of strategy as static plans by suggesting that strategy could be thought of as 'a pattern in a stream of decisions' (Mintzberg, 1978). This gave a more emergent feel to what had become thought of as complicated and exhaustive cookbook. It also meant that what happened after the recipe was created was also part of strategy, that is, implementation was as much a part of a strategy as formulation. Within his conceptualization of strategy he allowed for the constant tug of war between managers as a process in which many decision makers with conflicting goals bargain among themselves to produce a stream of incremental, disjointed decisions (Mintzberg 1978). Any one decision analyzed on its own may seem insignificant or inconsequential, but it may be the most important decision in determining the general direction or pattern being followed. Thus, strategy is not just what was planned, but what actually happened, regardless of the plan. This same general discussion of strategy applies to strategic HR as well.

HR practices, the deliberative product of planning and design, may or may not produce the desired business outcomes. The practitioner press is full of stories about companies that have attempted to implement 'best practices' only to discover very little or even negative impact on the outcomes desired.

While our goal is not to challenge the growing base of 'proof' that HR practices matter when it comes to business outcomes, it is our intent to suggest strongly that practices are not the full story. Our argument is that practices and implementation must be looked at together and preferably over time and as part of a complete and dynamic system. We say dynamic to make it clear that effective HRM is not fixed or static, any more than a currently enacted or emerging strategy is fixed and static. The growing body of literature on organizational agility as the root of iterative competitive advantage (Shafer et al., 2001), strongly suggests that scaleable or adaptive HR configurations are critical to maintaining the system. Agile organizations generally vest decision making at the lowest possible level (Lepak and Snell, 1999), and utilize shared values as the basis for such decisions. In such an environment an elaborate and rigid HR architecture would be viewed as obsolete and unnecessary.

Becker and Huselid (2006), while discussing 'where do we go from here' in research on the HRM performance link, speculate that there is a robust HR-firm performance effect because there is wide variation in how firms manage 'even the HR basics' (p. 905). They further suggest that the variance may be due to 'lack of knowledge, lack of managerial competence, or an inability to execute (or more likely some combination)' (p. 905). This suggestion, coupled with the criticism of the HR function from Lawler and Hammonds (above), points to the need

for more fine grained and contextual research which provides some measure of the ability of HR professionals to do the prescriptive work of a full business partner.

Lawler (2005: 167) suggests that few HR organizations have reached the desired status of the role because of the way that they are organized. Hammonds and others maintain that it is the people (Hammonds, 2005). But while this debate, structure versus people gets started, we suggest that neither position is likely to be universally supported. A great person in a bad structure is probably as bad as bad people in a great structure. The key, we suggest, is to look at the total HR system, in the context of the total business system. Unfortunately, very little in the existing research approaches HRM at this level.

Thus, in the overall context of HR functional excellence, it is helpful to connect the dots. Practices by themselves, as noted by Lado and Wilson (1994), can both create and destroy value. People by themselves (the HR function) can probably be seen to have the same potential impact. How then, do practices and people add up to strong, value added HRM? The answer may be found in looking beyond practices and people to the principles of the organization and the processes through which HRM is enacted. Our argument is that when the HR function has the right human capital ingredients, and it is broadly seen as a legitimate authority within the organization, and the line management knows the value that good HRM can deliver (and demands results), the conditions are right for HR to create and maintain the strong situations needed to effect business results.

THE HR FUNCTION AND STRONG HR SYSTEMS—PUTTING IT ALL TOGETHER

The question to ask any CEO in a discussion of what may be wrong with HRM in the company is simple and direct: 'Do you have your very best people in HR?' Most will readily say no. When asked by Jack Welch (to a group of CEOs) 'how many of you pay your HR person the same as you pay your CFO', very few hands went up in the room. How then is HR to understand (and influence) the business strategy, be seen widely in the organization as credible and important, and have the skills necessary to weave a complex web of practices into a coherent and well understood philosophy through a highly visible and recognized process? The fact is, they can not. Highly capable practitioners, trapped in organizations that do not properly build HR's legitimacy, often talk about 'pushing on a rope,' the frustrating exercise of trying to get the leadership (not the employee population!) to pay attention to critical human capital dimensions. Demanding line managers, saddled with HR practitioners drawn from the administrative heritage of the function, are frustrated as well. Only when capable practitioners and demanding line managers are paired can we expect HRM to have maximum impact on firm performance.

There are, therefore, several important pieces to building and maintaining an HRM system that creates the clear signals envisioned by Bowen and Ostroff, and provides for the higher level sense making (patterns in a stream of decisions) discussed by Colbert. At the floor is to staff HR with only the highest caliber talent—the intellectual and leadership equals to the best in any other function. They must know their craft, practice it well, and receive the highest levels of continuing education along with any other talent pool in the company. The HR function cannot be a stepchild.

But to be effective in the role of business partner or business leader, HR must also know a lot about business in general, and about the current business they support specifically. HR must not only be at the table, they must articulately and convincingly speak the language spoken by everyone else. The need for keen analytical skills and financial savvy cannot be overstated. To be in any position to leverage their core competency in HRM, HR professionals must be masters of the business as well.

Given high-level core competency in HRM, and well honed general business skills and tacit organizational knowledge, HR must also be positioned in the organization in a way that is seen as legitimate. HR cannot be expected to 'push' its agenda; managers must demand that HR not only be world class, but that it produce consistent world class outcomes measurable in the business results. Leaders at all levels in the organization need to demand more from their HR partners, and never be complacent with the simple enactment of popular best practices. HR should be measured on the basis of its ability to produce and maintain the talent the organization needs to compete and win, consistently, year after year. Only then will they deserve to be paid what CFO's are paid.

But perhaps most importantly, though rarely talked about, HR must adopt a more complete systems orientation, and develop a perpetual process through which individual HR practices are given context and meaning. Such a process must be closely linked to the aspirational principle that people are an important (if not the most important) asset in the organization. It must be a process that is not held in secret by those in the fraternity, but a process that touches every employee, in some meaningful way, on a very regular basis. So the end game of HR functional excellence has very humble beginnings. Hire the best possible people, people equally talented in their field as the best people in any other important function in the company. Teach them the business, at the detailed level. Position them properly, and demand that they perform better every year. And most importantly, build a process through which individual HR practices are tied together in a living, perpetual system that is highly visible to all. Only then will an organization have true HR functional excellence.

REFERENCES

Barney, J.B. (2001) 'Resource-based theories of competitive advantage: a ten-year retrospective on the resource-based view', *Journal of Management*, 27 (6): 643.

Becker, B. and Gerhart, B. (1996) 'The impact of human resource management on organizational performance: progress and prospects', *Academy of Management Journal*, 39 (4): 779–801.

Becker, B.E. and Huselid, M.A. (1998) 'High performance work systems and firm performance: A synthesis of research and managerial implications', in G.R. Ferris (ed.), *Research in Personnel and Human Resource Management*, Vol. 16. Greenwich, CT: JAI Press, pp. 53–101.

Becker, B.E. and Huselid, M.A. (2006) 'Strategic human resources management: where do we go from here?', *Journal of Management*, 32 (6): 898–925.

Boudreau, J.W. and Ramstad, P.M. (2002) *'What's next for human resource management'*. Working Paper 02–10, Center for Advanced Human Resource Studies, Cornell University.

Bowen, D.E. and Ostroff, C. (2004) 'Understanding the HRM-firm performance linkages: The role of the "strength" of the HRM system', *Academy of Management Review*, 29 (2): 203–21.

Chaiken, S., Wood, W. and Eagley, A.H. (1996) 'Principles of Persuasion', in E.T. Higgins and A.W. Krulanski (eds), *Social Psychology: Handbook of Basic Principles*. New York: Guilford Press, pp. 702–44.

Colbert, B.A. (2004) 'The complex resource-based view: Implications for theory and practice in strategic human resource management', *Academy of Management Review*, 29 (3): 341–58.

Collins, C. and Clark, K. (2003) 'Strategic human resource practices, top management team social networks, and firm performance: The role of human resource practices in creating organizational competitive advantage', *Academy of Management Journal*, 46 (6): 740–51.

Combs, J., Liu, Y., Hall, A. and Ketchen, D. (2006) 'How much do high-performance work practices matter? A meta-analysis of their effects on organizational performance', *Personnel Psychology*, 59 (3): 501–28.

Hammonds, K.H. (2005) *Why we hate HR*. Boston: Fast Company, pp. 40.

House, R., Rousseau, D.M. and Thomas-Hunt, M. (1995) "The meso-paradigm: A framework for the integration of micro and macro organizational behavior", in L.L. Cummings, B.M. Straw, (eds), *Research in Organizational Behavior*. 17: 41–114.

Huselid, M.A. (1995) 'The impact of human resource management practices on turnover, productivity, corporate financial performance', *Academy of Management Journal*, 39 (4): 635–72.

Huselid, M.A., Jackson, S.E. and Schuler, R.S. (1997) 'Technical and strategic human resources management effectiveness as determinants of firm performance', *Academy of Management Journal*, 40 (1): 171–88.

Kelley, H.H. (1967) 'Attribution theory in social psychology', in D. Levine (ed.), *Nebraska symposium on motivation*. Lincoln: University of Nebraska Press, pp. 192–240.

Lado, A.A. and Wilson, M.C. (1994) 'Human resource systems and sustained competitive advantage: A competency-based perspective', *Academy of Management Review*, 19 (4): 699–727.

Lawler III, E. (2005) 'From Human Resource Management to Organization Effectiveness', *Human Resource Management*, 44 (2): 165–69.

Lepak, D. and Snell, S. (1999) 'The Human Resource Architecture: Toward a Theory of Human Capital Allocation and Development', *Academy of Management Review*, 24 (1): 31–48

Lewin, K., Lippit, R. and White, R. (1939) "Patterns of aggressive behavior in experimentally created 'social climates' ", *Journal of Social Psychology*, 10: 301–21.

MacDuffie, J.P. (1995) 'Human resource bundles and manufacturing performance: Organizational logic and flexible production systems in the world auto industry', *Industrial and Labor Relations Review*, 48 (2): 197–221.

Huselid, M.A. and Becker, B.E. (2000) 'Measurement error in research on human resources and firm performance : How much errors is there and how does it influence effectsize estimates?', by Gerhart, Wright, McMahan and Snell, *Personnel Psychology*, 53 (4): 835–54.

Mintzberg, H. (1978) 'Patterns in Strategy Formation', *Management Science*, 24 (9): 934.

Mischel, W. (2004) 'Toward an Integrative Science of the Person', *Annual Review of Psychology*, 55: 1–22.

Mischel, W. (1973) 'Toward a cognitive social learning conceptualization of personality', *Psychological Review*, 80: 252–83.

Ostroff, C. and Bowen, D.E. (2000) 'Moving HR to a higher level: HR practices and organizational effectiveness', in K.J. Klein and S.W.J. Kozlowski (eds), *Multilevel theory, research, and methods in organizations: Foundations, extensions, and new directions*. San Francisco: Jossey-Bass Inc, pp. 211–66.

Paauwe, J. (2004) *HRM and performance, achieving long term viability*. Oxford: Oxford University Press.

Shafer, R.A., Dyer, L., Kilty, J., Amos, J. and Ericksen, J. (2001) 'Crafting a human resource strategy to foster organizational agility: A case study', *Human Resource Management*, 40 (3): 197–211.

Schneider, B. (1990) 'The climate for service: an application of the climate construct', in B. Schneider (ed.), *Organizational Climate and Culture*. San Francisco: Jossey-Bass, pp. 383–412.

Schneider, B. (2000) 'The psychological life of organizations', in N.M. Ashkanasy, C.P.M. Wilderom and M.F. Peterson (eds), *Handbook of organizational culture and climate*. Thousand Oaks, CA: Sage, pp. xvii–xxii.

Schuler, R.S. and Jackson, S.E. (1987) 'Linking competitive strategy and human resource management practices', *Academy of Management Executive*, 1 (3): 207–19.

Teese, D.J., Pisano, G. and Shuen, A. (1997) 'Dynamic capabilities and strategic management', *Strategic Management Journal*, 18 (7): 509–33.

Ulrich, D. (1997) *Human Resource Champions*. Boston MA: Harvard Business School Press.

Wright, P., Dunford, B. and Snell, S. (2003) 'Human resources and the resource-based view of the firm', *Journal of Management*, 6: 701–21.

Wright, P., Gardner, T., Moynihan, L. and Allen, M. (2005) 'The HR – performance relationship: Examining causal direction', *Personnel Psychology*, 58 (2): 409–46.

Wright, P.M. and McMahan, G. (1992) 'Theoretical perspectives for strategic human resources management', *Journal of Management*, 18 (2): 295–320.

Youndt, M.A., Snell, S.A., Dean, J.W. and Lepak, D.P. (1996) 'Human Resource management, manufacturing strategy, and firm performance', *Academy of Management Journal*, 39 (4): 836–66.

8

International and Comparative Human Resource Management

Richard Hall and Nick Wailes

International and comparative human resource management (HRM) are related but distinct areas of enquiry. Comparative HRM is largely concerned with questions about why and to what extent there are differences in HR practices across countries. International HRM is more focused on issues associated with the management of employees across national borders in multinational corporations (MNCs). IHRM has therefore been interested in questions about the extent to which multinational companies reproduce similar sets of HR practices across their subsidiaries. Do they, for example, try to reproduce similar practices across all of their subsidiaries or do they adjust their HR practices to host country patterns? By contrast comparative HRM has been traditionally concerned with the description of, and (more recently) the explanation of, the differences and similarities between the HR practices thought to be distinctive of different national contexts. While each tradition has reasonably distinctive origins – in the study of MNCs and their management of expatriates in one case, and in the study of comparative industrial relations in the other – we argue that the distinction is becoming increasingly artificial and unhelpful. In particular we argue that International HRM needs to incorporate the insights of comparative HRM and international political economy so that it can move beyond its traditional focus on expatriate management.

The traditional narrowness and lack of theoretical sophistication in comparative and international HRM scholarship is well documented in the literature (see Kochan et al., 1992; Clarke et al., 1999; Schuler et al., 2002; Ferner, this volume). As Clarke et al. (1999) note to the extent that comparative studies have traditionally sought to go beyond describing HR practices across countries, and explain similarities and differences, they have tended to attribute differences to national culture. The IHRM literature, on the other hand, has traditionally focused on the management of expatriate managers within multinationals (Schuler et al., 2002). Again IHRM studies have often sought to explain differences in HR practices within MNCs with reference to Hofstede's widely critiqued model of national culture (Hofstede, 1984).[1]

While mainstream international and comparative HR scholarship has increasingly focused on the links between business strategy and HRM (see De Cieri et al., 2007), a growing body of work informed by institutionalist theory has emerged over the last decade. This institutionalist literature has transformed both comparative and international human resource scholarship. Not only has institutionalism provided a theoretical basis for explaining why HR practices might differ from one country to another but it has also contributed to the study of HRM in MNCs. Macro-institutional theories have provided the basis for a reconceptualisation of the home and host country effects that shape MNCs' HR policies and practices (Edwards and Kurivilla, 2005). More recently, scholars working in this tradition have supplemented macro-institutionalism with micro-institutionalism in organisational theory to explore how differences in power relationships between corporate headquarters and subsidiaries shape the diffusion of HR policies and practices within MNCs (see, for example, Ferner and Tempel, 2006).

This chapter critically assesses the institutionalist turn in comparative and international human resource scholarship. While the institutionalist literature provides a theoretical foundation for both comparative and international HRM scholarship and has produced some important insights, there are a number of criticisms of institutionalism which suggest that the institutionalist turn may be limited. In particular, the macro institutional theories which inform much contemporary comparative and international human resource management scholarship have been criticised as static, deterministic, and prone to exaggerate the homogeneity

of outcomes within institutional fields and to have difficulty accounting for change in institutional arrangements. These features can, in turn, be attributed to the tendency of institutionalist arguments to downplay the significance of non-institutional variables in shaping political and economic outcomes. While these criticisms relate to institutionalism in general, we argue that they are particularly significant when the objects of study are corporations that operate across national borders.

In light of this criticism, we explore two alternative future directions for comparative and international human resource scholarship. First, we focus on the prospects for a synthesis between the institutionalist and strategic approaches that have emerged in the IHRM literature since the mid 1990s. There have been few attempts to draw these literatures together. However, each has the potential to address weaknesses in the other. On the one hand, institutionalism promises to overcome the excessive voluntarism of strategic IHRM and its tendency to ignore the importance of context. On the other hand, insights from strategic HRM suggest a theory of agency and make it possible to identify some of the non-institutional factors which shape the HR decisions of managers. The final section of the chapter briefly sketches a second alternative direction for comparative and international human resource management, one which draws more heavily on insights associated with political economy. We use the example of the contributions that labour process theory can make to IHRM to illustrate the potential benefits of a political economy approach to comparative and international HRM.

THE INSTITUTIONALIST TURN IN COMPARATIVE AND INTERNATIONAL HRM

The last decade has seen the emergence of an increasing body of scholarship which draws on institutional theory to explain similarities and differences in HR practices across countries and to explain the extent to which MNCs reproduce the HR policies and practices they adopt in their home countries in their subsidiaries. In particular, an increasing number of studies have been informed by Richard Whitley's (1992, 1998, 1999) national business systems (NBS) approach. Rejecting abstract and universalist explanations of economic action, Whitley attributes persistent national differences in the behaviour of managers and firms to differences in national business systems. For Whitley (1999: 33) business systems are 'distinctive patterns of economic organisation that vary in their degree and mode of authoritative coordination of economic activities, and in the organization of, and interconnections between, owners, managers, experts, and their employees'. He argues that national business systems can be distinguished along three principal dimensions: ownership relations; non-ownership relations; and employment relations and work management. On this basis he identifies six business system types: fragmented; coordinated, compartmentalised; state organised; collaborative; and highly coordinated. For Whitley (1998: 457) differences in ownership relations, non-ownership relations and employment relations and work management, are a product of differences in the institutional arrangements which:

concern the organisation and conditions governing the availability of capital and labour power, the governance of economic exchanges and the organisation of competing interests. In particular variations in the nature and policies of the state, the financial system, the education and training systems and prevalent norms and values have helped to structure qualitative differences between business systems.

While Whitley admits the possibility that national business systems may change, his key point is that, because the characteristics of national business systems are so deeply embedded in institutional arrangements, their impact on economic behaviour is likely to be persistent and enduring. Notably he suggests that differences in national business systems are likely to continue to play a profound role in structuring the behaviour of managers and firms, even in an era of internationalization, because:

significant changes in national business systems imply substantial shifts in ownership relations, the division of organisational labour, the level and/or type of non-ownership coordination processes and/or employment and labour relations. Such changes are, then, large scale and far reaching, requiring considerable institutional restructuring and realignment of major societal interests. They are unlikely to develop simply as a consequence of internationalization, or to occur within one or two decades (Whitley 1998: 476).

This view that the embeddedness of firms in a particular national business system will continue to shape the behaviour of managers and firms, even when firms expand beyond particular national boundaries, has helped inform a growing body of international and comparative HRM research. The NBS approach has helped to provide a theoretical basis for explaining not only cross national similarities and differences in HR but also home and host country effects in IHRM. In this section we selectively review some of this literature to illustrate how it has used the NBS approach to provide insights into key issues in IHRM (for reviews of this literature see Edwards and Kurivilla 2005; Tempel et al., 2006; Ferner, this volume. See also Edwards and Rees 2006 for an excellent textbook treatment of IHRM that draws on the national business systems approach).

Ferner (1997) articulates the case for the application of Whitley's approach to the study of HR in MNCs. He argues that while there is evidence to show that the country of origin has a significant impact on the HR policies and practices MNCs adopt in their subsidiaries, there is a need for a more systematic analytical framework for examining country of origin effects. He rejects the view that this effect is simply a consequence of inherent and immutable cultural differences, noting, in particular, that 'Hofstede's implication that the variables he studied are in some ways inherent properties of national psyches ... deserves to be treated with caution' (1997: 24).

Rather, he argues that many of the explanations for country of origin effects, including timing of development, organisational size and cultural differences, can be seen as consequences of more significant differences in national business systems. On this basis Ferner (1997: 26–31) calls for studies which examine how home country patterns of corporate governance and corporate control affected the international management of HR, management careers and their development, the structuring and coordination of work and development of the personnel function in MNCs. Ferner (1997: 31–33) also considered the methodological implications of the NBS approach for comparative and international HRM. Notably, while he suggested (1997: 31) that there was a need for 'systematic survey evidence to establish the prevalence in MNCs of typical national characteristics', in his view this work needs to be supplemented with 'careful qualitative case study research to follow through the complex linkages' between NBS and MNCs IR and HR. In effect he argues for a shift away from the cross-sectional survey-based research which traditionally dominated comparative and international HRM research, towards the type of research more common in comparative industrial relations scholarship.

Ferner and Quintanilla (1998) use a NBS approach to examine the HR practices of German MNCs. In a sophisticated analysis, they note that while there is evidence to suggest that in the process of internationalising German firms have adopted some Anglo-Saxon management practices, 'the consensual thrust of German employment relations … has strongly coloured the internationalisation process' (Ferner and Quintanilla 1998: 726). Thus, they find that German MNCs encourage employee co-operation, make relatively high investments in training and are less likely to use widespread downsizing than MNCs from other countries. In a subsequent article, Ferner et al. (2001) explore the impact that the NBS of host countries play in shaping the diffusion of this distinctively German pattern of HR to subsidiaries of two German MNCs in the UK and Spain. While these two countries were selected as examples of highly regulated (Spain) and highly deregulated (UK) host countries, Ferner et al. argue that (2001: 124) 'the lack of strong management traditions' in Spain meant that German MNCs had a 'greater degree of managerial choice in their subsidiaries' than was the case in the UK.

Edwards et al. (2005) use a NBS approach to explore the phenomenon of reverse diffusion in MNCs. Reverse diffusion refers the transfer of practices by MNCs from foreign subsidiaries to their operations in their country of origin and is an issue of particular strategic importance because it relates to the ability of MNCs to learn from their operations. While Edwards et al. argue that there are a number of *a priori* reasons to suggest that there will be substantial reverse diffusion by US MNCs from their operations in the UK, drawing on five case studies, they find only very limited evidence of reverse diffusion. They argue that this reflects the constraints that key features of the US NBS place on diffusion. Thus, for example, they (2005: 1277) attribute the failure of one of their cases to adopt a system of broadbanding involving teamwork to established practices of union avoidance in the parent company. Indeed, one of the few examples of reverse diffusion took place in a parent company located in a 'right to work' state, where union avoidance was less of an issue. Here, again, is an example of a sophisticated and nuanced use of the NBS approach to explain both national differences in HRM and IR in MNCs.

Edwards et al. (2005) is just one of a large number of publications drawn from a large ESRC project focusing on the HR policies and practices of US multinationals in Europe. This project recently culminated in the publication in 2006 of *American Multinationals in Europe: Managing Across National Borders* (Almond, Ferner and Tempel, 2006). In our view, this book is a very important contribution to the literature and illustrates the extent to which the institutionalist turn has transformed comparative and international HRM scholarship. While the model outlined by Ferner and Tempel (2006) illustrates the extent to which this institutionalist literature has moved away from simply relying on Whitley's NBS approach (see below for further discussion of this point), it also illustrates the important intellectual debt that the institutionalist literature owes to Whitley's NBS approach.

Given the centrality of macro-institutionalist arguments to a growing body of comparative and international HRM research, it seems appropriate to review some of the criticisms of these approaches and to assess the implications of these criticisms for the future development of the field. While the proximate origins of the institutionalist turn in comparative and international HRM lie in a rejection of culturalist arguments and the search for what Ferner (1997) described as a more 'systematic analytical framework', Whitley's NBS approach and its application to comparative and international HRM needs to be understood in the broader context of interrelated debates about the different forms that capitalism can take and the impact of globalisation. Whitley's NBS approach is one of a number of theories of capitalist diversity that have emerged since the early 1990s and which stress the importance that national level institutions play in shaping outcomes in capitalist economies (other prominent examples include Hall and Soskice, 2001; Amable 2003; for a review of these theories see Deeg and Jackson, 2007). While arguments about the diversity of capitalism can be traced back to at least as far as Shonfeld (1965), the contemporary impetus for these theories were predictions that international political (the collapse of the Soviet bloc) and economic changes (globalisation) would produce a convergence of national economic systems on an neo-liberal Anglo-saxon model (see, for example, Ohmae, 1990). These arguments are of direct relevance to comparative and international HRM, both because of considerable national diversity in patterns of HRM and the principal role attributed to MNCs in the convergence process.

In rejecting the view that there was only one way to organise capitalism (and by extension of managing human resources), theories of capitalist diversity draw on the rediscovery of the role of institutions that has taken place across many of the social sciences. Crouch (2005: 10) defines institutions broadly as 'patterns of human action and relationships that persist and reproduce themselves over time, independently of the identity of the biological individuals performing within them'. While there is considerable diversity in the new institutionalism, all of these arguments share the view that institutional arrangements, which are the product of past decisions, play an independent role in shaping social, economic and political outcomes. Viewed in this way, institutions establish the rules of the game and act as a constraint on agency. As a result, it is argued that even though capitalist societies may be faced with common pressures associated with globalisation, differences in national level institutions arrangements refract these pressures in different ways (see Wailes et al., 2003 for further discussion).

While the early 'new institutionalism' tended to focus on the impact of a single institutional arrangement (for example, constitutional arrangement, collective bargaining systems and training and skill development systems), what distinguishes theories of capitalist diversity is their emphasis on the interconnections between institutional arrangements. This is spelt out most clearly in Hall and Soskice's (2001) *Varieties of Capitalism* (VoC) approach. Hall and Soskice argue that it is possible to identify two institutionally distinct equilibria associated with the coordination problems faced by firms in a market economy: Liberal market economies (LMEs) and coordinated market economies (CMEs). For Hall and Soskice the superior economic outcomes associated with LMEs and CMEs are a product of institutional complementarities. That is, the presence of one set of institutional arrangements enhances the efficiency of others. Thus, for example, the existence of well-developed capital markets in LMEs is likely to enhance the effectiveness of financial participation schemes for managers and employees. However, Hall and Soskice

(2001: 18) also argue that 'nations with a particular type of coordination in one sphere in the economy should tend to develop complementary practices in other spheres as well'.

Theories of capitalist diversity, like the VoC and NBS approaches, have had a profound influence on a range of disciplines, and, as the preceding discussion on the NBS approach in IHRM demonstrates, have produced some important insights which discredit the simplistic claims that globalisation will produce complete or simple convergence in HRM practices. Nonetheless, these theories have also been subject to considerable criticism. Many of these criticisms are elegantly captured by Crouch (2005). While sympathetic to this approach, Crouch argues that in the process of demonstrating that economic behaviour takes place within constraints, institutionalist analyses have tended to become determinist, ignoring diversity within business systems and providing limited scope for agency. As a result he argues many of these models have trouble accounting for why institutional arrangements change.

These criticisms can be applied directly to Whitley's NBS model. Because firm behaviour is so embedded in a national business system, Whitley's model implies that all firms from a particular business system will tend to behave in a similar way. As Crouch notes this ignores the possibility that there may a range of competing 'institutional logics' within any one business system or that individual organisations may develop distinct resources and competencies (see also Morgan, 2005: 3). This raises the possibility that different firms from the same national business system may, for example, adopt distinctively different patterns of operation.

Casson and Lundan (1999) directly question the usefulness of the NBS as an analytical tool. They argue that Whitley's framework is a typology rather than a theory and that he fails to adequately explain 'how and why a particular type of NBS develops at a particular time' (Casson and Lundan, 1999). It would perhaps be fairer to argue that Whitley is inconsistent in his views about the origins

of NBS and their prospects for change. That is, at times, he appears to argue the origins of NBS lay in particular historical circumstances but at other times he uses economic efficiency arguments to explain the origins and persistence of NBS. Morgan (2007) legitimately claims that criticisms of the NBS as a static framework reflect a misunderstanding of ideal-type analysis. However he also acknowledges the 'creative tension' between 'ideal types of national systems and specific empirical studies which were more actor centred and concerned with change and process in institutions and organisations'. In effect Morgan is admitting that the NBS framework is unable by itself to account for change in institutional arrangements. The difficulty that institutionalist arguments have in explaining institutional change has been widely acknowledged in the literature (see Streeck and Thelen, 2005).

The problems that have been associated with theories of capitalist diversity in general, and Whitley's model in particular, can in turn be attributed to the underlying views about the role that institutions play in shaping social action. Whitley's NBS approach is underpinned by what Hall and Taylor (1996) describe as a culturalist view of institutions. That is, institutional arrangements not only play a role in directing social action but also determine the preferences of social actors. This view that preference formation is endogenous to institutions downplays the possibility that non-institutional factors may play a role in shaping how social actors behave. To paraphrase Pontusson (1995) by stressing the primacy of institutions, institutionalist analysis has shifted from claiming that institutions matter to arguing that only institutions matter.

As Tempel et al. (2006: 20) note 'the argument ... that business systems characteristics and national institutions are tightly linked, accords national business systems with a timelessness and provides no clear mechanisms for recognising how they change and how actors within business systems adopt deviant practices'. It is this feature of the NBS approach which makes its application to the study of HR in MNCs particularly problematic. This is not to argue that the institutionalist literature in international and comparative HRM is unaware of these problems or that it reproduces all of the flaws that have been identified in Whitley's model. Rather, we would argue that the strong empirical grounding of much of this research means that the findings of this literature highlight the limitations of the NBS approach. Thus, for example, the paper by Ferner and Quintanilla (1998) actually provides evidence that the process of internationalisation dramatically affects the managerial practices of German multinationals and concludes with comments about prospects for change in business systems, and the role of MNCs in this change process, which stand in stark contrast to Whitley's (1999) views on this subject. As Tempel et al. (2006: 21) put it 'by focusing on the interaction between MNCs and home and host country business systems, empirical studies of HRM in MNCs … portray the links between business system characteristics and institutions as being looser [than Whitley's original model]'.

This literature also goes beyond Whitley's model in other important respects. Perhaps most significantly, recent work in this tradition has begun to explore the role that interests play in shaping HRM practices in multinationals. Thus, Ferner and Tempel (2006) argue that there is a need to supplement comparative institutionalism with an understanding of the role that the internal power dynamics within MNCs play in shaping how HR practices are diffused. In particular, their 'power and institutions' approach focuses on differences in the relationship between corporate headquarters and local management in MNCs to explain observed variations in HR practices in MNCs from the same country of origin and operating in the same national environments.

While we support the greater focus on interests and the increasingly sophisticated view of MNCs that has appeared in this literature, we would argue that this literature has not gone far enough in moving beyond the limitations of Whitley's NBS framework.

Specifically, introducing an assessment of internal power dynamics in MNCs does not address two major, and related, flaws in Whitley's framework. It does not challenge the view that NBs are homogenous nor does it address the extent to which material interests may shape the HR practices in firms. The remainder of this chapter examines ways in which the institutionalist literature in international and comparative HRM can be developed to overcome these problems.

THE STRATEGIC TURN IN COMPARATIVE AND INTERNATIONAL HRM AND THE PROSPECTS OF A SYNTHESIS

In the previous section we argued that if the institutionalist comparative and international HRM literature is to develop further, it needs to provide a theory of agency and to model interests in a more compelling fashion. One means of achieving this is to explore the prospects for a synthesis between the institutionalist tradition and the other major intellectual development in IHRM during the 1990s: the renewed focus on strategy. Under the twin influences of studies in international business and the growing interest in strategic HRM, the field of international HRM started to develop a more sophisticated appreciation of the role of strategy in understanding the dynamics of HRM in MNCs and internationalising business more generally.

Prior to the highly influential work of Bartlett and Ghoshal (1989, 1990, 2000) the concept of strategy had an uncertain and underdeveloped status in early international HRM research. For example, Perlmutter's (1969) identification of distinct 'managerial mindsets' ('ethnocentric', 'polycentric' and 'geocentric') as a means of characterising the different approaches of MNCs towards international staffing was one of the few models prior to the 1990s from which some account of international HR strategy might be derived. The potential for linking typologies of HRM to international business forms, however, required a compelling account of international organisational forms. Stopford and Wells (1972) had identified a number of organisational forms characteristic of businesses as they moved through stages of internationalisation: an international divisional structure, worldwide product or area divisional structures, and global matrix structures appropriate to highly internationalised businesses that enjoyed high product diversity and high levels of international sales. Bartlett and Ghoshal's more sophisticated analysis of stages of international development presented a more highly integrated account of the various forces and features that defined four types of MNC: multidomestic, international, global and transnational.

Bartlett and Ghoshal's four-fold typology invited consideration of the HRM approaches that might be seen to be consistent with these strategies and structures (Harzing, 2004). The relatively high levels of subsidiary autonomy implied by the multi-domestic strategy can be matched with Taylor et al.'s (1996) 'adaptive' HRM system, in which HR policies at subsidiaries reflect local conditions and with Perlmutter's 'polycentric' mindset. The international and global strategies appear consistent with Taylor et al.'s 'exportive' approach to HRM, where central HR policies are exported to subsidiaries. To the extent that the flow of expertise and systems from the centre to the subsidiaries is facilitated by senior managers from HQ, the appropriate mindset might be defined as 'enthnocentric'. Lastly, the transnational strategy can be seen to imply an 'integrative' HR approach (Taylor et al., 1996) in which best practice HR policies and practices from around the globe are integrated, while recognising the need for a degree of local variation in different markets. This strategy appears consistent with Perlmutter's 'geocentric' mindset.

Bartlett and Ghoshal's typology of internationalising businesses highlighted the central strategic problem for MNCs: finding the right balance between integration and centralisation, on the one hand, and responsiveness and decentralisation, on the other. Bartlett and Ghoshal's typology might be taken to

suggest, however, that this key decision is largely a matter of recognising the stage of internationalisation and thus the strategic imperatives of the MNC. From this perspective, organisational structure and the appropriate HR policy orientation flow fairly unproblematically from this international business strategic orientation. Little scope is therefore provided for HR in MNCs to exercise much strategic influence.

Harzing (2004) has been one of the few to open up the space for a more strategic role for HR in MNCs. One of the strengths of Harzing's approach is that she has highlighted the integration-responsiveness dynamic as fundamentally a question of *control* and empirically investigated the extent to which different control mechanisms are utilised by different MNC organisational types. Focussing on multidomestic, global and transnational forms Harzing's (1999, 2004) survey of MNCs revealed that global companies relied on control strategies she terms 'personal centralised control' and 'bureaucratic formalised control'. In global MNCs decision making is centralised and policies and practices are implemented at subsidiary level through a combination of direct managerial intervention and the imposition of rules, processes and policies. On the other hand, multidomestic firms exercised relatively little control, relying on a modest degree of indirect forms of control: output control and some control through socialisation and networks. Transnational companies, concerned, as they are, with ensuring a flow of knowledge, expertise and process between multiple units tended to rely on more complex socialisation and network controls: socialisation through the transmission of corporate values and culture, information sharing and informal communication, and the use of cross-functional teams and task forces. Although Harzing does not explicitly take the next step of aligning these control strategies to specific HR practices (cf: Evans and Lorange, 1989), it seems obvious that each of these control orientations implies an important role for HR in implementing, enabling and sustaining these controls through HR policies and practices relating to staffing, performance management, knowledge management, learning and organisation development, leadership and HR planning.

In addition to the impetus for understanding the strategic role of HR in MNCs provided by the international business model of Bartlett and Ghoshal, a second force also emerged in the late 1980s and early 1990s – strategic HRM. Since the early 1980s an extensive body of research has examined the ways in which the management of human resources contributes to the achievement of the firm's strategic objectives (Devanna et al., 1981; Huselid, 1995; MacDuffie, 1995; Becker and Gerhart, 1996). By the late 1980s the strategic role of HRM in international business was supported by arguments that the effective management of human resources was critical to the success of MNCs (Stroh and Caligiuri, 1998). Indeed it has since been argued that HRM has an especially important role to play in international business (Scullion and Starkey, 2000). The main challenge for MNCs is not so much in determining what strategy to pursue as in ensuring that the strategy can be implemented across diverse and disparate international settings. HR is critical to the implementation of those strategies, often being charged with the responsibility for leading processes of cultural change and transformation (Bartlett and Ghoshal, 1989).

For all the talk of the strategic importance of HRM to international business the field of international HRM has continued to struggle to move beyond (or to 'get behind') the traditional dichotomy of integration/ centralisation – responsiveness/ decentralisation. Harzing has suggested the role of HR in implementing and managing particular control strategies, as discussed above. The study of the relative diffusion of HR policies and practices from centre to subsidiaries has been a closely related concern (Taylor et al., 1996; Edwards and Kurivilla, 2005). And a concern with the role of HR in managing strategically appropriate staffing policies and effectively managing expatriates has been the key focus for IHRM since its inception (Dowling et al.,

1999). Beyond these established research traditions, however, the contributions of strategic HRM to international HRM have been relatively modest.

Scullion and Starkey (2000) set out to uncover the role of the corporate HR function in international businesses, noting that this question had been traditionally neglected. In their study of the role of corporate HR in 30 MNCs Scullion and Starkey identify three types of organisation: 'centralised' HR companies, 'decentralised' HR companies and 'transition' HR companies. In centralised HR companies a powerful HR function in headquarters drives strategic staffing (especially the management of expatriates), group-wide appraisal and performance management systems, and remuneration (at least for the 'top' managers around the world). In decentralised HR companies the influence of corporate HR was reported to be declining for non-senior management levels, but increasing for top management. The main differences between the centralised and decentralised companies in fact seems to boil down to the extent of reach of HR policies down managerial hierarchies (corporate HR in decentralised companies is restricted to senior management), the use of inpatriation (used in centralised companies) and the existence of formal repatriation programs (present in centralised companies). The transition companies in the sample were characterised by more centralisation over the management of senior managers than in the case of decentralised companies, but other distinctions are far from clear in the case study evidence presented by Scullion and Starkey. The authors conclude on a rather different note by highlighting emerging HR trends evident across all MNCs in their sample: an increasing concern with senior management development, succession planning and the development of a senior cadre of international managers. Whatever else this might tell us, it represents a very traditional range of international HRM concerns focussed squarely on staffing and expatriate management.

One of the most influential attempts to integrate an understanding of strategic HRM into models of international business has been made by Schuler and colleagues (Schuler et al., 1993; De Cieri and Dowling, 1999; Schuler and Tarique, 2007). Since 1993 these authors have been developing an 'integrative framework' for international HRM in MNCs. While the model has changed over the years, the central features of the model remain the specification of 'exogenous factors', 'endogenous factors' and 'strategic MNC components' influencing HR policies, functions and practices, which in turn influence MNC effectiveness. The original 1993 version of the model placed 'strategic international HRM' (SIHRM) at the centre and defined SIHRM in terms of the 'human resource management issues, functions, and policies and practices that result from the strategic activities of multinational enterprises and that impact the international concerns and goals of those enterprises' (Schuler et al., 1993: 422).

The model was subsequently revised by De Cieri and Dowling (1999). In addition to moving the strategic MNC components into the 'endogenous factors' in the model, De Cieri and Dowling simplified the SIHRM part of the model to two components: 'HR function strategy' and 'HR practices' and retitled it: 'strategic HRM'. The other notable elaboration introduced by De Cieri and Dowling was the recognition that the relationships between the components of the model were reciprocal, such that strategic HRM was not simply determined by endogenous and exogenous factors (including MNC strategy) but could also affect endogenous and exogenous factors.

The model was again revised by Schuler and Tarique (2007). Their latest elaboration seeks to update the model in light of IHRM research of the past 15 years. The revised model has a stronger foundation in systems thinking and HR is given a more prominent strategic role: reversing De Cieri and Dowling's innovations, Schuler and Tarique again separate out 'strategic MNC components', define them as including 'strategic HRM systems' and 'international HRM systems' (as well as 'cross-border alliances') and give them a more powerful causal role in the model. At first inspection this appears to grant HRM

a more strategic role, however the detail of their explanation of the model still tends to portray HRM as relatively reactive and operational. Thus, when Schuler and Tarique map out 20 research topics for IHRM derived from their revised model, IHRM tends to be cast in its familiar role as the servant of organisational strategy and structure: HR is urged to consider 'how IHRM practices can help the organisation achieve economies of scale ... yet also stay sensitive to ... local conditions' (2007: 732); how it can 'analyse a country's culture more closely' (2007: 733); how it can develop 'global mindsets', separate 'global', 'regional' and 'local' workforces, and 'transnational teams' (2007: 734); and how it can use expatriates and repatriation most effectively (2007: 735) – again, this represents a very traditional list of IHRM concerns.

There are two key problems with the current approach as exemplified by the Schuler and Tarique model: firstly, while IHRM is given a more prominent place in strategy according to the theoretical model, it is by no means clear how this is reflected in empirical reality – we still lack much empirical evidence that strategic HRM is actually happening and others have noted the lack of correspondence between HR policy and HR practice in MNCs (Sparrow, 2007); in one sense, the strategic turn has tended to leave HR practice behind – the strategic potential of IHRM has been repeatedly emphasised, but the actual HR practices that constitute strategic IHRM are still relatively vague. Secondly, the context of IHRM and MNC behaviour is far from fully integrated. The Schuler model has always included reference to exogenous factors, however these factors, so central to the institutionalist approaches, are only roughly sketched in the model.

The recent proposal of a model of 'globalising HRM' (Sparrow et al., 2004; Brewster et al., 2005; Sparrow, 2007) has addressed some aspects of the two problems noted above. These researchers have attempted to move beyond the traditional focus of international HRM on expatriate management to global HRM and a focus on the management of all HRM activities by MNCs 'through the application of global rule sets' (Brewster et al., 2005: 966). While a weakness of this approach has been a failure to date to clearly distinguish 'global HRM' from the study of the diffusion of HR practices and policies across MNC units (central to many studies within an IHRM tradition), a clear strength has been the grounding of a model of globalising HRM in empirical studies of MNC HR strategies, policies and practices. Based on a survey of 64 large UK MNCs, 732 HR professionals and seven case studies, the Brewster, Sparrow and Harris model (see Brewster et al., 2005: 961) identifies particular organisational drivers and HR enablers being delivered through three key HR processes: 1) talent management and employer branding; 2) global leadership through international assignments; and 3) managing an international workforce. While the studies add useful empirical content in the form of defining specific combinations of organisational drivers and HR enablers ('strategic recipes'), the account of how these are delivered and managed through the four HR processes remains unclear. The first and second of the identified HR processes appear little different from traditional IHRM concerns. Although the third process promises to extend analysis beyond the management of expatriate assignments, the accounts of these processes make little if any reference to key issues surrounding the management of local employees in MNC subsidiaries (eg: see Sparrow et al. 2004: Ch. 7).

The studies published to date utilising the model of globalising HRM have helped identify the 'strategic recipes' used by different MNCs, however they have sacrificed some of the opportunities for integrating contextual factors when compared to the systems models associated with Schuler and colleagues. Further, the promise of the model to fully integrate detailed accounts of actual HR practices and processes implemented by MNCs has not been realised. In this sense, then, despite the volume and intensity of IHRM research in the past few years, robust models and compelling empirical accounts that integrate both the HR strategies and HR practices of contemporary MNCs in the context of different sectoral, national and regional institutional contexts remain elusive.

At first glance it would appear that a synthesis of institutionalist and strategic elements of the contemporary literature has much to recommend it. The institutionalist literature appears to address two key weaknesses in the strategic literature. The institutionalist literature provides a framework in which a better understanding of context can be integrated into the strategic IHRM literature (see, for example, Osland and Osland, 2005). In doing so the institutionalist literature promises to provide an antidote to what, in many ways, appears to be the excessive abstraction and voluntarism that underpins much of the strategic literature. While the need for greater understanding of context is well canvassed in the existing mainstream strategic literature (see, for example, Schuler et al., 2002), there has been rather less consideration of the contributions that the strategic literature can make to the institutionalist tradition. However, we would argue that consideration of the strategic dimensions of HR in MNCs has the potential to address key weaknesses in the institutionalist literature. In particular the strategic literature implies that the interests of MNCs, in particular HR policies and practices, and the extent to which they attempt to diffuse these practices across their subsidiaries, relate not just to home and host country institutional context but are also shaped by a range of firm-specific factors. A synthesis between these two bodies of work may therefore provide the basis for a more robust theory of agency and lead to the development of the type of actor-centred institutionalism that has recently begun to emerge in the comparative corporate governance literature (see Aguilera and Jackson, 2003; Fiss and Zajac, 2004).

However, despite this potential, there are a number of reasons to suggest that the existing strategic IHRM is poorly suited to provide the basis for understanding agency and interests in an institutionalist framework. In particular, strategy is not satisfactory theorised. In most of the models of IHRM reviewed above HR strategy is largely determined by broader corporate strategy. In the Schuler models, for example, strategic MNC components (including functionalist IHRM and SHRM systems) determine IHRM issues, functions, policies and practices, albeit mediated by generally-specified exogenous and endogenous factors. In the Brewster et al. models of globalising HRM, HR strategies appear to be represented by the 'strategic recipes' – combinations of various organisational drivers and HR drivers. Furthermore, HR practices are typically seen to flow unproblematically from HR strategy. Once HR strategy is set, the task for HR is the implementation of HR practices that 'fit' with that strategy.

Somewhat ironically, these models of IHRM provide little space for agency in the development and implementation of HR strategies and practices within MNCs. To the extent that agency is granted to actors in formulating HR strategy and practices, the actors are presumed to be the senior management elites responsible for determining overall business strategy, which for Schuler et al. might include the capacity to influence or determine the design of IHRM and SHRM systems, or for Brewster et al., the selection of an appropriate 'strategic recipe'. In any event, we suggest that this is a naïve and underdeveloped account of HR strategy, policy and practice.

Rather than HR policies and practices flowing unproblematically from a rational, pre-determined HR strategy, we seek to emphasise that HR strategy, policy and practice is more likely to be contested by a range of actors in the context of an array of global, national, organisational and workplace forces which shape, condition and afford ongoing processes of conflict and contestation. These forces are multiple and complex and include supra-national institutions, forms of capital accumulation prevailing in different sectors and regions, patterns of capital, labour and technological mobility, national institutional settings and policies (industrial relations, finance, fiscal, industry and skills policies and institutions), product market conditions, sectoral supply chain arrangements, as well as a wide array of organisational-level variables (such as organisational structure and business strategy) and workplace-level variables (such as the power of labour and capital and the organisation of work). We also contend that these forces are not given or fixed, but are also the subject of contestation and construction by actors. For example, a host country's industrial relations laws and regulations are not essentially fixed and immutable; they are subject to processes of social construction by, for example, unions who promote their interpretation of these laws and their implications in ways that might promote the interests of workers in a particular subsidiary. Similarly, different groups of managers (headquarters and subsidiary managers, for example) will also be engaged in constructing and influencing these laws and their implementation in ways that promote their own interests. In other words, not only should these forces be considered constraints on the agency of actors, but they might also be usefully considered as resources that can be deployed and exploited by actors.

We advocate a similarly political approach to the understanding of HR strategy, policy and practice. These are determined neither by the political, economic and institutional forces (exogenous factors) noted above, nor by the free hand of senior management. Rather, in addition to being shaped and conditioned by both (political-economic) structure and (managerial) agency, they are contested by organisational and workplace actors. For example, even in circumstances where a MNC sets a centralised HR policy and prescribed set of practices, IHRM studies have routinely discovered that central policies are implemented and translated very differently in different subsidiaries (Tayeb, 1998). Often this has been explained in terms of the national cultural conditions of the host country that require local adaptation and differentiation. However, we contend that this culturalist argument forecloses the possibility that political contests between various management factions (in both subsidiary and HQ) and groups of workers and their representatives (unions) may be decisive.

Ultimately, then, overcoming the deficiencies of IHRM's traditional treatment of strategy and institutional context implies the need to recognise that: a) exogenous factors, and institutional conditions in particular, are not static and pre-given but are actively contested in political processes; b) the actors that engage in these contests and that seek to make or influence decisions include a range of management and labour actors; and, c) the factors and conditions under which strategic, policy and practice decisions are made and contested are not simply (immovable) constraints, but can also be appropriated by actors as political resources. In other words we see considerable scope for a more political interpretation of both the formulation and implementation of HR strategies, policies and practices within MNCs (a micro-political perspective) and the global and national-institutional context which also conditions those processes of contestation, decision-making and implementation (a macro-political perspective). Recent contributions to the IHRM literature have suggested how these ideas might be used to inform a more compelling account of international HRM. We see in this work the emergence of a 'political economy of IHRM' (Edwards et al., 2007).

TOWARDS A POLITICAL ECONOMY OF IHRM

Edwards et al. (2007) contrast three approaches to the analysis of MNC's transfer of HR practices across national borders. 'Market-based approaches' emphasise the imperatives for particular HR practices generated by product, financial and labour markets and suggest that MNCs will seek to transfer best practice HR to their subsidiaries as a rational strategy exploiting the corporation's organisational competencies. 'Cross-national' approaches can be culturalist or institutionalist in orientation. Culturalist variants – the mainstay of traditional IHRM approaches to diffusion – seek to explain the transfer and translation of HR practices in terms of the cultural conditions that characterise home country and host country environments. Thus, particular HR practices (eg: performance based pay) will be seen as typical of MNCs from particular home countries (such as the US) and their transfer to subsidiaries will also be shaped by the receptivity of host country cultural conditions. Institutionalist approaches, as discussed earlier, explain the uptake, translation or rejection of corporate HR practices by reference to the institutional conditions of home and host countries. Lastly, 'micro-political' approaches emphasise how the processes of transfer are shaped by the actions of organisational actors seeking to promote their interests and those of their constituents or principals.

The integration of all three approaches allows Edwards et al. (2007) to provide space for the agency of various HQ and subsidiary managers, workers and unions, while recognising that any freedom to act is constrained or conditioned by the institutional and cultural characteristics of different national environments and market realities. While we strongly support Edwards et al.'s 'political economy' approach we elaborate their model in two ways. First, we see the comprehension and interpretation of market realities and national conditions to be subject to processes of social construction actively undertaken by various organisational actors (Gergen, 1999; Burr, 2003) – actors promote specific interpretations of national, environmental conditions and market 'realities'. Second, we contend that micro-political struggles between actors are structured by the interests of those actors. In particular, we reject the unitarist assumptions that underlie most IHRM perspectives on the workplace and organisation, and argue for an understanding of micro-political struggles that recognises the antagonistic interests that characterise relations at the workplace. Those interests are, again, constructed by actors, but the structural antagonisms between, for example, capital and labour, shape those processes of social construction.

The Edwards et al. political economy approach is closely related to the 'system, societal and dominance effects' (SSD) model associated with Smith and Meiksins (1995). This model suggests a 'triple determination' of the HR practices of MNCs (Smith, 2005): system effects, such as the political economy of a particular mode of capital accumulation, represent an underlying dynamic; societal effects include 'unique national institutions, cultures and histories'; and dominance effects highlight the force and impact of ideas and practices that are popular in 'dominant societies' – e.g. the US and Japan in post-war capitalism (Smith, 2005). While we strongly endorse the SSD model, and advocate it as a compelling elaboration of comparative HRM, it does not explicitly incorporate the micro-political struggles at the workplace level foregrounded by Edwards et al. (2007). Nevertheless, Smith clearly accepts the role played by processes of workplace and organisational politics when he notes that: '...it is only though the social interaction that groups and individuals negotiate which of these different (and perhaps competing) ways of working, standards of quality, authority relations and methods of employment will actually shape particular work situations' (Smith, 2005: 620).

A stronger focus on the nature of these micro-political struggles at the workplace level is clearly possible and, in this respect, labour process theory (LPT) approaches might provide some useful analytical categories and insights. The potential for LPT perspectives to provide a more politically-infused account of the workplace and organisational impact of IHRM has only rarely been recognised (for a recent example see, Mir and Sharpe (2004)). The core theory of the labour process can be summarised by reference to four key claims (Thompson, 1989; Smith and Thompson, 1998): 1) the centrality of the labour process – the way in which work is organised is a significant site of contestation between labour and capital; 2) the deskilling imperative – the organisation of work and the skills required to be deployed by workers are constantly being changed and renewed by management, often, though by no means always, with adverse

consequences for the skills of workers; 3) the control imperative – management typically seeks to secure and extend control over the labour process; and 4) the structured antagonism/ relative autonomy imperative – relations between labour and capital at the workplace level are characterised by 'structured antagonism' although these structural interests do not determine action and actors therefore have a degree of autonomy. Thus, while control commonly generates resistance, a wide range of relations are always possible – accommodation, compliance, consent as well as various forms of resistance.

Reconsidering the HR strategies, policies and practices of MNCs through this lens suggests a number of illustrative lines of enquiry and analysis for a new political economy of IHRM.

1) The introduction of new HR policies and practices will typically impact on, and be shaped by, forms of work organisation. For example, the introduction of teamwork will affect the range of tasks undertaken by workers, the relations between workers and between workers and managers, the skills required of workers, the autonomy and creativity of workers, the role of management, and so on. The diffusion and development of teamwork in MNCs and across borders more generally will be shaped by: the nature of competition in particular service/product markets (market-based variables), national-cultural and national-institutional factors such as traditions of collectivism and IR system regulation of employee involvement and participation (cross-national variables) and the power and influence of MNC HQ, MNC subsidiary and domestic corporate management elites and unions (micro-political variables).

2) HR policies and practices will have diverse but distinctive implications for the skills of workers. The introduction of detailed standard operating procedures for work tasks, for example, may reduce the problem-solving and tacit skills required of workers, but may enhance some of their technical skills. Training, HR development and organisation development programs which affect skill formation will be shaped by the corporate policies of MNCs, the autonomy of subsidiaries, the skill shortages and demands relevant to particular national, regional and global

service/ product markets, cultural conditions and national skills and training policies as well as by the power of unions, sectoral bodies and employer associations to influence patterns of skill development.

3) HR policies and practices will tend to enhance management control over the labour process and the organisation of work. In the context of international HRM, the control imperative is especially instructive. It was noted earlier that Harzing (2004) has been one of the few IHRM scholars who has emphasised the relation between headquarters and subsidiaries as one of control; MNCs will often use HR policies and practices in an attempt to enhance their control over subsidiary operations or performance. LPT suggests that the relations within MNC workplaces will also be characterised by control. The control-resistance dynamic, perhaps the most important LPT metaphor, when applied to IHRM sets up the possibility of analysing the various relations between four sets of actors: HQ management, HQ workers, local management and local workers. This also suggests the need to consider the extent to which the prevalence of HR practices promoted by prominent MNCs in host countries compels domestic organisations to 'follow suit' (isomorphism) or pursue distinct strategies (differentiation).

4) The notion of a degree of autonomy being exercised by actors within a framework of structurally antagonistic interests also has direct and immediate application to IHRM. This is the stuff of organisational and workplace level micro-politics which IHRM needs to comprehend and interpret. For example, where a MNC introduces a new corporate performance management system with a new range of detailed common performance metrics for company-wide appraisals, various interests may well be threatened while others might be enhanced. First, the system may impact on the interests of subsidiary workers whose autonomy and discretion might be attenuated by the new more exacting measurement of their task performance. Second, the interests of local management might be threatened by centrally-defined performance metrics sidelining local control and management techniques. Third, the interests of HQ workers might also be threatened (or advanced) by the exposure of their performance to benchmarks set by high-performing subsidiaries, now that universal metrics facilitate direct comparison across geographically dispersed units. Finally, the

interests of HQ management might be advanced as their capacity to monitor and evaluate the performance of subsidiary management teams and workers alike is enhanced through the new system. Of course, the principle of relative autonomy implies that different scenarios are always possible. New performance measures might equip local management with the data to argue the case for more resources to the benefit of local management and workers alike. Strategic micro-political alliances between workers and managers in the one subsidiary might therefore emerge. The categories of labour process theory – control, resistance, skills, autonomy and structurally antagonistic interests – can be used to extend our analysis of the nature and impact of particular HR strategies, policies and practices.

CONCLUSION

In this chapter we have reviewed the institutionalist turn in comparative and international HRM. This literature has transformed the field to the extent that we do not believe that it is possible to address issues of national differences in HRM or the transfer of HR practices in MNCs without attention to the institutional context. While this literature has provided some important insights into key issues in comparative and international HRM, it is now straining at the limits of the national business system approach from which it was originally derived. If this field is to continue to advance, we have argued, it needs to go beyond establishing that institutions and context matter and examine the interaction between interests and institutions. One way that this might be achieved is through a synthesis of the institutionalist literature with the large body of work that links IHRM to business strategy. In our view there are too many problems with the strategic literature as it currently stands for this to be a possibility. Rather, we argued here for a more avowedly political approach to comparative and international HRM. HR policies and practices in the multinational firm are not simply the result of processes of rational decision-making, institutional isomorphism or national-cultural determination. If IHRM is to prosper and reach its critical potential then it needs to recognise a wider range of relevant actors, including managers and workers in various MNC HQ, MNC subsidiary and domestic organisational contexts. It also needs to recognise that the actions of those actors are shaped by contested constructions of a dynamic macro political economy, and a series of market realities, as well as by an organisational and workplace environment that is being continually reproduced through ongoing political struggles.

NOTE

1 For a critique of Hofstede's model see McSweeny (2002). See also Gerhart and Fang (2005) for a critique of its application to human resource management.

REFERENCES

Aguilera, R. and Jackson, G. (2003) 'The cross national diversity of corporate governance: Dimensions and determinants', *Academy of Management Review*, 28 (3): 447–65.

Almond, P., Ferner, A. and Tempel, A. (eds) (2006) *American Multinationals in Europe: Managing Employment Relations Across National Borders*. Oxford: Oxford University Press, pp. 10–36.

Amable, B. (2003) *The Diversity of Modern Capitalism*. New York: Oxford University Press.

Bartlett, C. and Ghoshal, S. (1988) 'Organizing for Worldwide Effectiveness: The Transnational Solution', *California Management Review*, Fall: 54–74.

Bartlett, C. and Ghoshal, S. (1989) *Managing Across Borders: The Transnational Solution*. Cambridge: Harvard Business School Press.

Bartlett, C. and Ghoshal, S. (1990) 'Matrix management: Not a structure, a frame of mind', *Harvard Business Review*, July–August: 138–45.

Bartlett, C. and Ghoshal, S. (2000) *Transnational Management: Text, Cases and Readings in Cross-Border Management*. 3rd ed. Boston: Irwin McGraw Hill.

Becker, B. and Gerhart, G. (1996) 'The impact of human resource management on organizational performance: Progress and prospects', *Academy of Management Journal*, 39 (4): 779–801.

Brewster, C., Sparrow, P. and Harris, H. (2005) 'Towards a new model of globalizing HRM', *International Journal of Human Resource Management*, 16 (6): 949–70.

Burr, V. (2003) *Social Constructionism*. 2nd ed. London: Routledge.

Casson, M. and Lundan, S. (1999) 'Explaining international differences in economic institutions: A critique of the "National Business System" as an analytical tool', *International Studies in Management and Organisation*, 29 (2): 25–42.

Clark, T., Gospel, H. and Montgomery, J. (1999) 'Running on the sopt? A review of twenty years of research on the management of human resources in comparative and international perspective', *International Journal of Human Resource Management*, 10 (3): 520–44.

Crouch, C. (2005) *Capitalist Diversity and Change: Recombinant governance and institutional entrepreneurs*. Oxford: Oxford University Press.

De Cieri, H. and Dowling, P.J. (1999) 'Strategic human resource management in multinational enterprises: Theoretical and empirical developments', in P.M. Wright, L.D. Dyer, J.W. Boudreau, and G.T. Milkovich (eds), *Research in Personnel and Human Resources Management: Strategic Human Resources Management in the Twenty-first Century*. Stamford Connecticut: JAI Press, pp. 305–27.

De Cieri, H., Cox, J.W., Fenwick, M. (2007) 'Review of international human resource management: Integration, interrogation, imitation', *International Journal of Management Reviews*, 9 (4): 281–302.

Deeg, R. and Jackson, G. (2007) 'Towards a more dynamic theory of capitalist diversity', *Socio-Economic Review*, 5 (1): 149–79.

Devanna, M., Fombrum, C. and Tichy, N. (1981) 'Human resource management: A strategic perspective', *Organizational Dynamics*, Winter: 51–67.

Dowling, P., Welch, D. and Schuler, R. (1999) *International Human Resource Management: Managing People in a Multinational Context*. 3rd ed. Cincinnati: South-Western College Publishing.

Edwards, T. and Kuruvilla, S. (2005) 'International HRM: National business systems, organisational politics and the international division of labour in global value chains', *International Journal of Human Resource Management*, 16 (1): 1–21.

Edwards, T. and Rees, C. (2006) *International Human Resource Management: Globalisation, National Systems and Multinational Companies*. London: Prentice Hall.

Edwards, T., Almond, P., Clark, I., Colling, T. and Ferner, A. (2005) 'Reverse diffusion in US multinationals: Barriers from the American business system', *Journal of Management Studies*, 42 (6): 1261–86.

Edwards, T., Colling, T. and Ferner, A. (2007) 'Conceptual approaches to the transfer of employment practices in multinational companies: An integrated approach', *Human Resource Management Journal*, 17 (3): 201–17.

Evans, P. and Lorange, P. (1989) 'The two logics behind human resource management', in P. Evans, Y. Doz and A. Laurent (eds), *Human Resource Management in International Firms*. New York: St. Martin's Press, pp. 169–90.

Ferner, A. (1997) 'Country of origin effects and HRM in multinational companies', *Human Resource Management Journal*, 7 (1): 19–37.

Ferner, A. and Quintanilla, J. (1998) 'Multinationals, national business systems and HRM: The enduring influence of national identity or a process of "Anglo-saxionisation"?', *International Journal of Human Resource Management*, 9 (4): 710–31.

Ferner, A., Quintanilla, J. and Varul, M. (2001) 'Country of origin effects, host country effects and the management of HR in multinationals: German companies in Britain and Spain', *Journal of World Business*, 36 (2): 107–27.

Ferner, A. and Tempel, A. (2006) 'Multinationals and national buiness systems: A "Power and Institutions Perspective" ', in P. Almond and A. Ferner (eds), *American Multinationals in Europe: Managing Employment Relations Across National Borders*. Oxford: Oxford University Press, pp. 10–36.

Fiss, P. and Zajac, E. (2004) 'The diffusion of ideas over contested terrain: The (non)adoption of a shareholder value orientation among German firms', *Administrative Science Quarterly*, 49 (4): 501–34.

Gergen, K. (1999) *An invitation to social construction*. London: Sage.

Gerhart, B. and Meiyu Fang (2005) 'National culture and human resource management: Assumptions and evidence', *International Journal of Human Resource Management*, 16 (6): 971–86.

Hall, P. and Soskice, D. (2001) 'An introduction to varieties of capitalism', in P. Hall and D. Soskice (eds), *Varieties of capitalism: The institutional foundations of comparative advantage*. New York: Oxford University Press, pp. 1–69.

Hall, P. and Taylor, R. (1996) 'Political science and the three new institutionalisms', *Political Studies*, 44 (5): 936–57.

Harzing, A.W. (1999) *Managing the Multinationals: An International Study of Control Mechanisms*. Cheltenham: Edward Elgar, pp. 33–64.

Harzing, A.W. (2004) 'Strategy and structure of multinational companies', in A.W. Harzing and J. Van Ruysseveldt (eds), *International Human Resource Management*. Second Edition, London: Sage Publications. pp. 33–64.

Hofstede, G. (1984) *Culture's Consequences: International Differences in Work-Related Values*. Abridged Edition. Thousand Oaks, California: Sage.

Huselid, M. (1995) 'The impact of human resource management practices on turnover, productivity and corporate financial performance', *Academy of Management Journal*, 38 (3): 635–72.

Kochan, T., Batt, R. and Dyer, L. (1992) 'International human resource studies: A framework for future research', in D. Lewin, O. Mitchell and P. Sherer (eds), *Research Frontiers in Industrial Relations and Human Resources*. Madison WI: Industrial Relations Research Association, pp. 309–37.

MacDuffie, J.P. (1995) 'Human resource bundles and manufacturing performance: Organizational logic and flexible production systems in the world auto industry', *Industrial and Labor Relations Review*, 48 (2): 197.

McSweeny, B. (2002) 'Hofstede's model of national culture and their consequences: a triumph of faith – a failure of reason', *Human Relations*, 55 (1): 89–119.

Mir, R. and Sharpe, D.R. (2004) 'Transferring managerial practices within multinationals: Control, resistance and *empowerment*', *Academy of Management Proceedings*, 2004, E1–E6.

Morgan, G. (2005) 'Changing capitalisms? Internationalization, institutionalization, and systems of economic organization', in G. Morgan, R. Whitley, and E. Moen, (eds), *Changing Capitalisms? Internationalization, institutional change and systems of economic organization*. Oxford: Oxford University Press, pp. 1–20.

Morgan, G. (2007) 'National business systems research: Progress and prospects', *Scandinavian Journal of Management*, 23 (2): 127–45.

Ohmae, K. (1990) *The Borderless World. Power and Strategy in the Interlinked Economy*. New York: Harper Business.

Osland, A. and Osland, J. (2005) 'Contextualisation and strategic international human resource management approaches: the case of Central America and Panama', *International Journal of Human Resource Management*, 16 (12): 2218–36.

Perlmutter, H. (1969) 'The tortuous evolution of the multinational firm', *Columbia Journal of World Business*, January–February: 9–18.

Pontusson, J. (1995) 'From comparative public policy to political economy: Putting political institutions in their place and taking interests seriously', *Comparative Political Studies*, 28 (1): 117–48.

Schuler, R. and Tarique, I. (2007) 'International human resource management: A North American perspective, a thematic update and suggestions for future research', *International Journal of Human Resource Management*, 18 (5): 717–44.

Schuler, R., Budhwar, P. and Florkowski, G. (2002) 'International human resource management: Review and critique', *International Journal of Management Reviews* 4 (1): 41–70.

Schuler, R., Dowling, P. and De Cieri, H. (1993) 'An integrative framework of strategic international human resource management' *Journal of Management*, 19 (2): 419–59.

Scullion, H. and Starkey, K. (2000) 'In search of the changing role of the corporate human resource function in the international firm', *International Journal of Human Resource Management*, 11 (6): 1061–81.

Shonfield, A. (1965) *Modern Capitalism*. Oxford: Oxford University Press.

Smith, C. (2005) 'Beyond convergence and divergence: Explaining variations in organizational practices and forms', in S. Ackroyd, R. Batt, P. Thompson and P. Tolbert (eds), *The Oxford Handbook of Work and Organization*. Oxford: Oxford University Press, pp. 602–25.

Smith, C. and Meiskins, P. (1995) 'System, society and dominance effects in cross-national organisational analysis', *Work, Employment and Society*, 9 (2): 241–67.

Smith, C. and Thompson, P. (1998), 'Re-evaluating the labour process debate', *Economic and Industrial Democracy*, 19 (4): 551–77.

Sparrow, P. (2007) 'Globalisation of HR at functional level: Four UK-based case studies of the international recruitment and selection process', *International Journal of Human Resource Management*, 18 (5): 845–67.

Sparrow, P., Brewster, C. and Harris, H. (2004) *Globalizing Human Resource Management*. London: Routledge.

Stopford, J.M. and Wells, L.T. (1972) *Managing the Multinational Enterprise: Organisation of the Firm and Ownership of the Subsidiaries*. London: Longman.

Streeck, W. and Thelen, K. (2005) 'Introduction: Institutional change in advanced political economies', in W. Streeck, and K. Thelen, (eds), *Beyond Continuity: Institutional Change in Advanced Political Economies*. Oxford: Oxford University Press, pp. 1–39.

Stroh, L.K. and Caliguiri, P.M. (1998) 'Increasing global competitiveness through the effective people management', *Journal of World Business*, 33 (1): 1–16.

Tayeb, M. (1998) 'Transfer of HRM practices across cultures: An American company in Scotland', *International Journal of Human Resource Management*, 9 (2): 332–58.

Tayeb, M. (2005) *International Human Resource Management: A Multinational Company Perspective*. Oxford: Oxford University Press.

Taylor, S., Beechler, S. and Napier, N. (1996) 'Toward an integrative model of strategic international human resource management', *Academy of Management Review*, 21 (4): 959–85.

Tempel, A., Wachter, H. and Walgenbach, P. (2006) 'The comparative institutional approach to human resource management in multinational companies', in M. Geppert, and M. Mayer, (eds), *Global, National and Local Practices in Multinational* Companies. London: Palgrave MacMillan, pp. 17–37.

Thompson, P. (1989) *The Nature of Work*. 2nd ed. London: Macmillan.

Wailes, N., Ramia, G. and Lansbury, R. (2003) 'Interests, institutions and industrial relations', *British Journal of Industrial Relations*, 41 (4): 617–37.

Whitley, R. (1992) *Business Systems in East Asia: Firms, Markets and Societies*. London: Sage.

Whitley, R. (1998) 'Internationalisation and varieties of capitalism: The limited effects of cross-national coordination of economic activities on the nature of business systems', *Review of International Political Economy*, 5 (3): 445–81.

Whitley, R. (1999) *Divergent Capitalisms: The social structuring and change of national business systems*. Oxford: Oxford University Press.

PART II

Fundamentals of Human Resource Management

9

Recruitment and Selection

Filip Lievens and Derek Chapman

RECRUITMENT AND SELECTION

Few people question that recruitment and selection are key strategic domains in HRM. At the same time, recruitment and selection also have an image problem. First, recruitment and selection are often viewed as 'old' ingrained HRM domains. It seems like the traditional recruitment and selection procedures have been around for decades, which is at odds with the ever changing internal and external environment of organizations. Hence, practitioners often wonder whether there are any new research-based ways for recruiting and selecting personnel. Another image problem for recruitment and selection is that a false dichotomy is often created between so-called macro HR (examining HR systems more broadly) and micro HR (examining individual differences). It is further sometimes argued that organizations should value macro approaches and write off micro approaches as not being relevant to the business world. We posit that these image problems and debates only serve to distract and fracture the field and hide the fact that excellent HR research and practice needs to take both macro and micro issues

into consideration. For example, creating an effective recruiting strategy (some would describe this as a macro process) requires considerable understanding of the decision making processes of potential applicants (viewed as micro processes). The same can be said with respect to designing effective selection systems, etc.

The challenge for many researchers then has been to demonstrate how scientifically derived recruiting and selection practices add value to organizations. Unfortunately, when the quality and impact of recruitment and selection procedures for business outcomes are investigated, they are often described in rather simplistic terms. For example, in large-scale HR surveys (e.g., Becker and Huselid, 1998; Huselid, 1995; Wright et al., 2001, 2005) 'sound' selection practice is often equated with whether or not formal tests were administered or whether or not structured interviews were used. Similarly, effective recruitment is associated with the number of qualified applicants for positions most frequently hired by the firm. Although such questions tackle important aspects of recruitment and selection we also feel that such descriptions do not capture the sophisticated level that recruitment and selection research and practice has attained in recent years. This oversimplification in large-scale HR surveys is understandable due to the difficulty of getting usable survey data across a diverse set of companies. However, the goal of demonstrating the utility of recruiting and selection systems may be undermined by this practice and risks setting the field back if the results are interpreted out of context.

In light of these issues, the aim of this chapter is to highlight key new research developments in recruitment and selection. The general theme of this chapter is: 'Which new research developments in recruitment and selection have occurred that advance recruitment and selection practice?' In terms of time period, our review primarily focuses on developments between 2000 and 2007. Given the huge volume of work published during this time frame we do not aim to be exhaustive. Instead, we aim to cover broad themes and trends that in our opinion have changed the field.

OVERVIEW OF KEY RESEARCH FINDINGS IN PERSONNEL RECRUITMENT

In this section, we review recent developments in the field of recruiting since 2000. For an excellent and comprehensive review of earlier recruiting research, we recommend Barber (1998) or Breaugh and Starke (2000). Tight labor markets in North America have helped fuel interest in recruiting research and considerable progress has been made in the recruiting field over the past seven years. As noted above, we especially focus on research that has practical implications for organizations.

The impact of technology on recruiting

Organizations have had to adjust to the new reality of online recruiting. These technologies have created both problems and opportunities for organizations. Organizations can significantly reduce costs to advertise positions by using third party job boards (e.g., Monster.com) or through company websites. The inexpensive nature of online recruiting permits the conveyance of large amounts of information to potential applicants at a minimal cost relative to traditional advertising venues such as newspapers. Media content can be substantially richer, including graphics, photos, interactive text, and video (Allen et al., 2004). The potential also exists for the immediate tailoring of recruiting information to target the needs of prospective applicants (e.g., Dineen et al., 2002, 2007). For example, after completing a needs questionnaire online, a prospective applicant could conceivably be provided with targeted information about the organization, its benefit programs, and opportunities that addresses their individual needs. Along these lines, Dineen et al. (2007) discovered that customized information about likely fit (combined with good web aesthetics) decreased viewing time and recall of low-fitting individuals, suggesting a means to avoid these individuals of being attracted to the organization. Clearly, customized real-time recruiting approaches are within the realm of existing technologies.

Despite the benefits and efficiencies of online recruiting, a downside is that many employers complain about the flood of unqualified applicants that can result from online advertising (Chapman and Webster, 2003). This deluge of applicants can inflict considerable costs on the organization if the online recruiting process is not accompanied by an effective and efficient screening technology. The importance of integrating efficient screening tools and online recruitment needs to be emphasized to a greater extent in HR practice.

Researchers have also begun to focus more specifically on what makes an effective company website for recruiting purposes (e.g., Cober et al., 2004, 2003; Lee, 2005). Specifically, these authors suggest that web site content (e.g. cultural information), appearance (e.g., use of colors and pictures) and navigability (e.g. links to job applications and useable layout) are all important for recruiting purposes. Cober et al. (2003) found that perceptions of the website aesthetics and usability accounted for 33 per cent of the variance in pursuit intentions and 31 per cent of the variance in recommendation intentions. Clearly, investing resources in web site aesthetics such as the use of pleasing colors, pictures of smiling employees, and easy to navigate functions such as direct links to application forms can have appreciable benefits for recruiting. A study of Williamson et al. (2003) provided another practically important finding. They discovered that setting up a recruiting-oriented web site (instead of a screening-oriented web site) was associated with significantly higher attraction by prospective applicants.

Applicant quality as recruiting outcome

Traditional recruiting outcomes have been categorized into four major constructs: Job pursuit intentions, organizational attraction, acceptance intentions, and job choice (Chapman et al., 2005). Breaugh and Starke (2000) presented a large number of potential organizational goals that recruiters, could strive to reach from shortening recruiting processing to reducing turnover. More research is emerging on these additional outcomes. For example, although recruiters have always been concerned about the quality of applicants attracted, few researchers have focused on this area. This area has perhaps become more popular recently due to the concerns about online applicant quality noted in the technology section. Specifically, Carlson et al. (2002) argued that assessing the quality of the applicants attracted is a useful tool in assessing the overall utility of the recruiting/selection system. To this end, they provided a useful assessment framework. This outcome has become an important focus of recruiting research (e.g., Collins and Han, 2004; Turban and Cable, 2003).

The renewed importance of the recruiter

A longstanding debate in the recruitment field has examined the role that recruiters play in influencing applicant decisions. Earlier work suggested that recruiters play either no role or a minor one in determining applicant decisions. However, research since 2000 has confirmed that recruiters, in fact, do play a significant role in applicant job choice (Chapman et al., 2005). In their meta-analytic review, Chapman et al. tested several models to account for how recruiters influence job choice. Their best fitting model involved job and organizational characteristics as mediators of recruiter influence on attraction and job choice. In other words, recruiters appear to influence job choices by changing applicant perceptions of job and organizational characteristics. Even more importantly, this influence was most pronounced for the best candidates – those with multiple job offers (Chapman and Webster, 2006).

Ironically, there is little guidance in the selection literature regarding how to identify and select individuals well suited for recruiting. Early studies showed that applicants pay attention to and are positively influenced by recruiter behaviors such as being informative and expressing warmth (Chapman et al., 2005) but we know little about individual differences that may be associated with recruiting success. A recent meta analysis demonstrated that simple demographic factors (e.g., recruiter sex or race) are not good predictors (Chapman et al., 2005). However, there are potentially many more individual differences such as personality traits and cognitive ability that may predict recruiting outcomes. We believe that more work on individual differences in recruiting success is critical.

Despite the growing role of technology in the recruiting process, most employers and applicants continue to value an opportunity for face-to-face interaction at some point in the recruitment process. Employers who implement effective technology-based screening practices find that their recruiters are freed up from the manual sorting of resumes in order to spend more 'face time' with qualified candidates. Interestingly, this is the opposite of what most employers fear when they consider implementing online recruiting and screening processes. Rather than becoming cold, sterile places, they actually have more time to interact with their top prospects to connote empathy and warmth; exactly the recruiter traits most associated with applicant attraction (Chapman et al., 2005).

Organizational image and employer branding

It is clear that applicants consider the image of an organization as an important factor for evaluating employers. Chapman et al.'s (2005) meta-analysis on organizational image in recruiting found a corrected mean correlation of 0.50 between image and job pursuit intentions, 0.40 for attraction, and 0.41 for acceptance intentions.

In recent years, a lot of work has emerged on how applicants form images of organizations. One simple mechanism appears to be familiarity. Applicants are generally more attracted to companies that have name or brand recognition (Cable and Graham, 2000; Cable and Turban, 2001; Collins and Stevens, 2002; Turban, 2001), although it should be acknowledged that being familiar and having initially negative views of the organization can have deleterious effects on recruiting outcomes (Brooks et al., 2003). Efforts then to invest in becoming more recognized within a targeted applicant population are generally likely to prove useful for organizations. For example, for organizations who recruit primarily on university campuses, sponsoring events attended by students and advertising broadly within the campus community should increase both familiarity and attraction.

Beyond brand recognition, Lievens and Highhouse (2003) suggest that in forming images of organization individuals draw symbolic associations between the organization and themselves. This anthropomorphic approach to conceptualizing organizational

image demonstrated that applicants ascribe human personality traits such as sincerity, excitement, competence, sophistication, and ruggedness to organizations (Aaker, 1997; Lievens and Highhouse, 2003). In general, people seem to be more attracted to organizations whose traits and characteristics are perceived to be similar to their own (e.g., Slaughter et al., 2004).

Another approach to organizational image has focused on the issue of corporate social responsibility (CSR), also termed corporate social performance (CSP). Applicants have been shown to take note of CSR information such as an organization's environmental practices, community relations, sponsorship activities, and treatment of women and minorities (e.g., Aiman-Smith et al., 2001; Backhaus et al., 2002; Turban and Greening, 1997). For instance, Greening and Turban (2000) found that organizational CSP appears to influence the attractiveness of a company to applicants, such that all four of the CSP dimensions were significantly related to job pursuit intentions and the probability of accepting both an interview and a job. Aiman-Smith et al. (2001) conducted a policy-capturing study and found that a company's ecological rating was the strongest predictor of organizational attraction, over and above pay and promotional opportunities. These authors and others (see Greening and Turban, 2000; Turban and Cable, 2003; Turban and Greening, 1997) suggest that attraction stems from interpreting company image information as a signal of working conditions – a proxy of 'organizational values' – and applicants develop an affective reaction to these signals which may manifest in being attracted to that organization.

At a practical level, this increased research interest in organizational image is paralleled by the approach of employer branding (Avery and McKay, 2006; Backhaus and Tikoo, 2004; Cable and Aiman-Smith, 2000; Cable and Turban, 2003; Lievens, 2007). Employer branding or employer brand management involves promoting, both within and outside the firm, a clear view of what makes a firm different and desirable as an employer.

According to Backhaus and Tikoo (2004), employer branding is essentially a three-step process. First, a firm develops a concept of what particular value ('brand equity') it offers to prospective and current employees. The second step consists of externally marketing this value proposition to attract the targeted applicant population. To this end, early recruitment practices have been found to be particularly useful (Collins and Stevens, 2002). The third step of employer branding involves carrying the brand 'promise' made to recruits into the firm and incorporating it as part of the organizational culture. Recent evidence has shown that a strong employer brand positively affected the pride that individuals expected from organizational membership (Cable and Turban, 2003), applicant pool quantity and quality (Collins and Han, 2004), and firm performance advantages over the broad market (Fulmer et al., 2003).

Addressing aging populations

Whereas traditional recruiting research has predominantly examined attracting young employees from universities and colleges, looming demographic realities involving a major shift in the age of employees are forcing employers and researchers to learn more about attracting and retaining older workers. Information about attracting older workers has just recently begun to emerge. For example, Rau and Adams (2004) examined the growing area of 'bridge employment' whereby older workers seek out a semi-retirement opportunity. This typically involves part-time employment that can serve to supplement retirement income as well as serve to fill a variety of social and esteem needs in older workers. Emphasizing equal opportunity for older workers, flexible schedules, and pro older worker policies have been shown to interact to improve attraction of older workers (Rau and Adams, 2005). Other suggestions for appealing to older workers include flexible compensation and benefits programs, and job redesign to accommodate and appeal

to older workers (Hedge et al., 2006). Clearly, more empirical data are needed to test many of the ideas posited for attracting older workers.

Attracting temporary workers

One response to staffing highly volatile work demands has been to rely more heavily on temporary workers, interns, and employment agency employees. This approach represents a significant recruiting challenge as employers often offer lower pay, few benefits, and little training to these temporary workers as compared to core employees. There has been little empirical work examining the attraction of temporary employees, however, research conducted on cooperative education programs shows that temporary employees tend to be attracted to many of the same organizational and job characteristics as full time employees. Therefore, employers offering better pay, prestige, locations, and opportunities for advancement are likely to be more successful in attracting temporary employees. As many of these employees use internships and temporary work as a stepping stone to full-time employment, employers would benefit considerably from considering their temporary hires as a potential full-time talent pool and treat them accordingly.

Applicant reactions to selection procedures

Although recruitment and selection are often viewed as separate processes, recent studies are increasingly showing that the two processes have considerable interactive effects. Negative reactions to selection procedures have been shown to correlate with attraction, intent to pursue, job recommendations, and intentions to accept a job offer (see meta-analysis of Hausknecht et al., 2004). Applicant reactions are a complex phenomenon. For instance, many researchers have emphasized the perceptions of injustice as the primary outcome of applicant reactions (e.g., Gilliland, 1993; Bauer et al., 2001), whereas others have called for more behavioral outcomes such as effects on attraction and job choice (e.g., Chapman and Webster, 2006; Ryan and Ployhart, 2000). What is well established is that applicants make inferences about organizations based on how they are treated during the selection process. In turn, these inferences might influence how attracted they are to the organization. In designing selection procedures, HR managers should balance their recruiting and selection needs and pay attention to the potential effects that their selection practices can have on applicant attraction and job choice.

DIRECTIONS FOR FUTURE RESEARCH ON PERSONNEL RECRUITMENT

Emphasizing proactive approaches

Unlike selection research, which has a rich history of exploring very practical approaches to personnel selection, recruiting research has tended to focus on more distal predictor-attraction relationships. For example, we still lack simple descriptive information on the specific recruiting tactics used by employers. As a result, there is a dearth of research examining the effectiveness of particular recruiting tactics and strategies. The growing body of research on decision processes should help recruiting researchers make informed predictions about the likely success of these specific tactics and provide potential moderators of these approaches. Likewise, incorporating and refining theories of persuasion from social psychology in the recruiting context should provide a rich source of predictions about the crafting of recruitment messages. For instance, studies incorporating the Elaboration Likelihood Model (ELM) can tell us how to craft recruitment messages that are effective for busy job fairs or for quiet deliberation of information from a web page (e.g., Jones et al., 2006; Larsen and Philips, 2002).

Another example of such a proactive recruiting approach might consist of organizations seeking to maximize fit perceptions in order to enhance attraction. For example,

through online assessments it may be possible to identify that an applicant has higher potential person-job fit than person-organization fit. As a result, a proactive recruiting approach would be to emphasize the benefits for person-job fit for that individual throughout the recruiting process. This might involve presenting more detailed information to that individual on job characteristics, tasks, roles, etc. The aforementioned studies of Dineen and colleagues exemplify how such a proactive and customized fit approach might be accomplished in early (web-based) recruitment stages. These studies also go beyond the notion of fit as being a natural process whereby applicants self-select into organizations.

Demonstrating value to organizations

To date, recruiting researchers have largely had to rely on logical arguments to demonstrate the value of recruiting to organizations. For example, utility analyses can demonstrate the theoretical return to the company of employing an effective recruiting system over a weak recruiting system (e.g., Boudreau and Rynes, 1985). We can also argue that effective recruiting is necessary in order to generate the types of selection ratios needed to make our selection systems more effective (Murphy, 1986). However, we believe that the time has come for recruiting researchers to capture organizational level outcomes such as firm performance, organizational training costs, and turnover expenditures to more directly demonstrate the utility of recruiting practice in organizations. Along these lines, Breaugh and Starke (2000) provided a comprehensive framework for examining the types of recruiting goals that organizations can align with their overall corporate strategies. For example, as a cost-reduction strategy HR departments could design recruiting practices aimed at attracting experienced employees who need little training, thereby saving training costs. Alternatively, a company emphasizing success through teamwork would benefit from recruiting practices that attracted individuals who are comfortable and motivated in team environments. Recruiting materials then would display photos of employees engaged in team-based tasks, advertising outlets could include publications that attract a team focused audience, and benefits and rewards should emphasize rewards for team performance. Other demonstrations of value to organizations can be seen in an exemplar paper by Highhouse et al. (1999) which showed how recruiting image information (i.e., an image audit) can be applied to real world recruiting issues (in this case, the fast food industry). Understanding how your organization is viewed by potential employees is a first and necessary step toward determining recruiting strategy. Generating effective strategies to address these images (such as hiring popular students to work in your fast food restaurant in order to attract more students), can flow from studying these issues empirically.

Disentangling content from method

In order to better determine recruiting effects, researchers are urged to design multiple manipulations for various recruiting tactics. Too frequently, recruiting researchers have single manipulations of information which makes it difficult to determine whether the approach to recruiting is driving any observed differences or whether the content of the single manipulation is causing the effects. For example, in designing a study examining the role of a recruiting tactic, such as comparing the job opening to a competitor's offering versus a tactic involving simply providing additional information about the company, researchers should endeavor to provide several examples of each manipulation so that the content of the manipulation is not confounded with the tactic. Accordingly, we can gauge the relative effects of the recruiting tactics independent of the job and organizational content used in the manipulation.

Focusing on job choice

We know a lot less about behavioral outcomes such as actual job choice than we do about attitudinal outcomes such as attraction, job pursuit intentions, and job acceptance intentions. What is clear from the few studies examining actual job choice is that our traditional recruiting predictors are much weaker in their predictions of behaviors then they are of their predictions of attitudes. We need to pay more attention to multiple outcomes, longitudinal outcomes and behavioral outcomes if we are to provide organizations with information that will be practical.

OVERVIEW OF KEY RESEARCH FINDINGS IN PERSONNEL SELECTION

In this section, we review recent developments with regard to personnel selection. Due to space constraints, we refer readers to Schmidt and Hunter (1998) and Hough and Oswald (2000) for excellent overviews of the state-of-the art of personnel selection until 2000. Note too that this section deals only with developments with respect to predictors (although we acknowledge there have also been substantial developments in the criterion domain).

Rapid technological developments in personnel selection

In the last decade, the face of personnel selection has changed substantially due to the increased use of information technology (the internet) for administering, delivering, and scoring tests (Chapman and Webster, 2003). Actually, use of the internet in selection is nowadays a necessity for firms to stay competitive. The efficiency and consistency of test delivery are some of the key benefits of internet-based selection over computerized selection. Extra cost and time savings occur because neither the employer nor the applicants have to be present at the same location.

The good news is that research generally lends support to the use of the internet as a way of delivering tests. Both between-subjects (Ployhart et al., 2003) and within-subjects studies (Potosky and Bobko, 2004) have provided evidence for the equivalence of internet-based testing vis-à-vis paper-and-pencil testing. For example, Potosky and Bobko (2004) found acceptable cross-mode correlations for noncognitive tests. Timed tests, however, were an exception. For instance, cross-mode equivalence of a timed spatial reasoning test was as low as 0.44 (although there were only 30 minutes between the two administrations). As a main explanation, the loading speed inherent in internet based testing seems to make the test different from its paper-and-pencil counter-part (Potosky and Bobko, 2004; Richman et al., 1999).

Research with regard to transforming face-to-face interviews to videoconferencing interviews reveals a more mixed picture. While considerable cost savings are real-ized from using these technologies, ratings have been shown to be affected by the media used (e.g., Chapman and Rowe, 2001; Chapman and Webster, 2001). The increased efficiency of technology mediated interviews (e.g., videoconferencing interviews, tele-phone interviews, interactive voice response telephone interviews) seems also to lead to potential downsides (e.g., less favorable reactions, loss of potential applicants) as compared to face-to-face interviews, although it should be mentioned that actual job pursuit behavior was not examined (Chapman et al., 2003).

One of the more controversial techno-logical developments relates to unproctored internet testing. In this type of testing, a test administrator is absent. Accordingly, unproctored internet testing might lead to candidate authentication, cheating, and test security concerns. To date, there seems to be relative consensus that unproctored testing is best suited for low-stakes selection (Tippins et al., 2006). As a possible solution, some organizations have moved toward a two-tiered approach whereby unproctored internet-based tests are administered for screening purposes only, followed by on site proctored admin-istration of a parallel test for those passing the online version. Sophisticated verification procedures are then used to examine whether

the same person completed both tests, or alternatively, only the proctorered test is used for final hiring decisions. Other organizations combine this two-tiered approach with item response and item generation techniques so that candidates seldom receive the same test items. This requires considerable sophisti-cation as large databases of questions must be generated and the difficulty level of each item must be determined to ensure parallel tests are generated each time. Once constructed, however, the organization can reap the benefits of unproctored testing and extend the life of the system by making fraudulent activity less damaging.

The growing international face of personnel selection

The face of personnel selection has changed not only due to rapid technological develop-ments. The globalization of the economy has also considerably affected personnel selection practice and research. This internationaliza-tion causes organizations to move beyond national borders, as reflected in interna-tional collaborations, joint ventures, strategic alliances, mergers, and acquisitions. One well-known HR consequence of this rapid internationalization is the need to develop selection procedures that can be validly used to predict expatriate success. Research has a long history here (going back to the Peace Corps studies). One of the problems is that the selection of people for foreign assign-ments has traditionally been based solely on job knowledge and technical competence (Schmitt and Chan, 1998; Sinangil and Ones, 2001). However, a recent meta-analysis of predictors of expatriate success (Mol et al., 2005) revealed that there are many more possibilities. In this meta-analysis, four of the Big Five personality factors (extraver-sion, emotional stability, agreeableness, and conscientiousness), cultural sensitivity, and local language ability were predictive of expatriate job performance. A problem with the large body of research on predictors of expatriate success is that research has mainly tried to determine a list of (inter)personal factors responsible for expatriate adjustment versus failure (e.g., Mendenhall and Oddou, 1985; Ones and Viswesvaran, 1997; Ronen 1989). Unfortunately, there is little research on designing a comprehensive selection system to predict expatriate success in overseas assignments.

Another consequence of the increasing internationalization is the need for selection systems that can be used across multiple countries while at the same time recognizing local particularities (Schuler et al., 1993). This is not straightforward as differences across countries in selection procedure usage are substantial. This was confirmed by a 20-country study of Ryan et al. (1999). Apart from country differences, differences grounded in cultural values (uncertainty avoidance and power distance) also explained some of the variability in selection usage. Another large-scale study showed that countries differed considerably in how they valued specific characteristics to be used in selection (Huo et al., 2002; Von Glinow et al., 2002). Countries such as Australia, Canada, Germany, and the US assigned great importance to proven work experience in a similar job and technical skills for deciding whether someone should have the job. Conversely, companies in Japan, South Korea, and Taiwan placed a relatively low weight on job-related skills. In these countries, people's innate potential and teamwork skills were much more important. We need more studies to unravel factors that might explain differential use of selection practices across countries. In addition, we need to know how one can gain acceptance for specific selection procedures among HR decision makers and candidates. Clearly, this is complicated due to tensions between corporate requirements of streamlined selection practices and local desires of customized ones.

A final pressing issue for organizations that use selection procedures in other cultures deals with knowing whether a specific selection procedure is transportable to another culture and whether the criterion-related validity of the selection procedure is generalizable. So far, there is empirical evidence for validity generalization for cognitive ability

tests (Salgado et al., 2003a, b) and personality inventories (Salgado, 1997) as the criterion-related validity of these two predictors generalized across countries. Research dealing with the criterion-related validity of other selection procedures in an international context is scarce. One exception is a study of Ployhart et al. (2004) who examined whether the criterion-related validity of various predictors (measures of team skills, work ethic, commitment, customer focus, and cognitive ability) differed across 10 countries. They found that criterion-related validity was largely constant across countries and unaffected by culture.

Unfortunately, no studies have examined conditions that predict when the criterion-related validity of selection procedures will generalize across countries. Along these lines, Lievens (2008) highlighted among others the importance of matching predictor and criteria in an international context. The importance of predictor-criteria matching can be illustrated with assessment center exercises. The dimensions and exercises that are typically used in assessment centers in North America and Europe might be less relevant in other countries. Perhaps, in a high power distance culture, candidates are extremely uncomfortable engaging in role-plays. This does not imply that such exercises will be invalid in these cultures. The question is: Are these exercises indeed relevant for the criterion domain that one tries to predict in these cultures? Empirical research supports this logic. Lievens et al. (2003) examined whether two assessment center exercises were valid predictors of European executives' training performance in Japan. They found that a group discussion exercise was a powerful predictor of future performance as rated by Japanese supervisors later on. The presentation exercise, however, was not a valid predictor. According to Lievens et al. (2003), one explanation is that the group discussion exercise reflected the Japanese team-based decision making culture.

Another hypothesis put forth by Lievens (2008) is that the predictor constructs (especially cognitive ability) will often be very similar across cultures, but that the behavioral content and measurement of these predictors will vary across cultures. For example, Schmit et al. (2000) developed a global personality inventory with input from a panel of 70 experts around the world. Although all experts wrote items in their own language for the constructs as defined in their own language, construct validity studies provided support for the same underlying structure of the global personality inventory across countries. This might also mean that ratings in non-personality situations such as assessment centers or interviews might be prone to cultural sensitivity because there is ample evidence that the behavioral expressions and interpretations for common constructs measured might differ from one culture to another. Future research should test these hypotheses about possible moderators of the cross-cultural generalizability of the validity of selection procedures.

Development and validation of new selection procedures

One of the questions at the start of this chapter was whether in recent years new selection predictors have been developed. We believe that three 'relatively' new selection procedures have gained increased interest from researchers and practitioners alike. First, emotional intelligence measures have come under scrutiny in personnel selection. Although the concept of emotional intelligence has fuelled a lot of criticism (Matthews et al., 2004; Landy, 2005), a breakthrough is the division of emotional intelligence measures into either ability or mixed models (Zeidner et al., 2004). The mixed (self-report) model assumes emotional intelligence is akin to a personality trait. A recent meta-analysis showed that emotional intelligence measures based on this mixed model overlapped considerably with personality trait scores but not with cognitive ability (Van Rooy et al., 2005). Conversely, emotional intelligence measures developed according to the ability (emotional intelligence as an ability to perceive emotions

of oneself and of others) model correlated more with cognitive ability and less with personality.

Second, situational judgment tests (SJTs) are another emerging selection procedure. SJTs present applicants with (written or video-based) work-related situations and possible responses to these situations. Applicants have to indicate which response alternative they would choose. Granted, SJTs are not new selection procedures (the first situational judgment tests were already used in the 1930s). Yet, they have recently become increasingly popular in North-America. SJTs are somewhat of a misnomer because they do not measure 'situational judgment.' Instead, SJTs are measurement methods that can measure a variety of constructs. For example, SJTs were recently developed to capture domains as diverse as teamwork knowledge (McClough and Rogelberg, 2003; Morgeson et al., 2005; Stevens and Campion, 1999), aviation pilot judgment (Hunter, 2003), employee integrity (Becker, 2005), call center performance (Konradt et al., 2003), or academic performance (Lievens et al., 2005; Oswald et al., 2004).

One reason for the growing popularity of SJTs is that they enable to broaden the constructs being measured. Research has shown that SJTs had incremental validity over cognitive ability, experience, and personality (Chan and Schmitt, 2002; Clevenger et al., 2001). McDaniel et al. (2001) meta-analyzed 102 validity coefficients (albeit only 6 predictive validity coefficients) and found a mean corrected validity of .34. Another reason is that SJTs can be used to test large groups of applicants at once and over the internet. Finally, research on applicant reactions to SJTs showed that SJTs were perceived as favorable and that video-based interactive SJT formats even resulted in more positive perceptions than written SJT formats (e.g., Chan and Schmitt, 1997; Kanning et al., 2006; Richman-Hirsch et al., 2000). Given these advantages, SJTs constitute an attractive alternative to more expensive predictors such as assessment center exercises or structured interviews because SJTs can be used in early selection stages as an inexpensive screen for measuring interpersonally-oriented competencies. A possible downside of SJTs is that they might be prone to faking. Along these lines, recent research has shown that the type of response instructions affects the cognitive loading and amount of response distortion in situational judgment tests (Nguyen et al., 2005). Behavioral tendency instructions (e.g., 'What are you most likely to do?') exhibited lower correlations with cognitive ability, lower adverse impact but higher faking than knowledge-based instructions (e.g., 'What is the best answer?'). In addition, a recent meta-analysis of McDaniel et al. (2007) reported that SJTs with knowledge instructions correlated more highly with cognitive ability measures (0.35) than SJTs with behavioral tendency instructions did (0.19). Conversely, SJTs with behavioral tendency instructions correlated more highly with Agreeableness (0.37), Conscientiousness (0.34), and Emotional Stability (0.35) than SJTs with knowledge instructions did (0.19, 0.24, and 0.12, respectively). These results confirm that SJTs with knowledge instructions should be considered maximal performance measures, whereas SJTs with behavioral tendency instructions should be considered typical performance measures.

Third, implicit measures of personality have been developed as a possible alternative to explicit measures of personality (e.g., the typical personality scales). One example of this is Motowidlo et al.'s (2006) measure of implicit trait theories. They theorize, and then offer evidence, that individual personality shapes individual judgments of the effectiveness of behaviors reflecting high to low levels of the trait in question. Thus, it may prove possible to make inferences about personality from individual's judgments of the effectiveness of various behaviors. Another approach to implicit measurement of personality is conditional reasoning (James et al., 2005) based on the notion that people use various justification mechanisms to explain their behavior, and that people with varying dispositional tendencies will employ differing justification mechanisms. The basic paradigm is to present what appear to be logical reasoning problems, in which respondents are asked to select the response that follows most logically from an initial statement. In fact, the alternatives reflect various justification mechanisms. James et al. present validity evidence for a conditional reasoning measure of aggression. Other research found that a conditional reasoning test of aggression could not be faked, provided that the real purpose of the test is not disclosed (LeBreton et al., 2007).

Improvements in existing selection procedures

In recent years, some interesting developments with respect to existing selection procedures have emerged. One development consists of increasing the *contextualization* of sign-based predictors (cognitive ability tests, aptitude tests, and personality inventories). Although contextualization has also been used in aptitude tests (Hattrup et al., 1992), this trend is best exemplified in personality inventories. Contextualized personality inventories use a specific frame-of-reference (e.g., 'I pay attention to details at work') instead of the traditional generic format (e.g., 'I pay attention to details'). Recent studies have generally found considerable support for the use of contextualized personality scales as a way of improving the criterion-related validity of personality scales (Bing et al., 2004; Hunthausen et al., 2003). Yet, some questions remain. For instance, how far does one have to go with contextualizing personality inventories. Granted, adding an at-work tag is only a start to a full contextualization of personality inventories (e.g., 'I pay attention to details when I am planning my meetings with customers.'). In light of the fidelity-bandwidth trade-off, perhaps the answer is related to what one wants to predict. Narrow contextualized scales might be better predictors of narrow criteria, whereas more generic scales might be better predictors for a more general criterion such as job performance.

Another development relates to the increased recognition that practitioners should carefully specify predictor-criterion linkages for increasing the criterion-related validity of selection procedures. As conceptualizations of job performance broaden beyond task performance to include the citizenship and counter productivity domains it is important for organizations to carefully identify the criterion constructs of interest and to choose potential predictors on the basis of hypothesized links to these criterion constructs. All of this fits in a general trend to move away from general discussions of predictors as 'valid' to consideration of 'valid for what?.' This was first exemplified by the taxonomic work on the dimensionality of performance led by Campbell et al. (1993). This project illustrated, for example, that cognitive measures were the most valid predictors of task performance, whereas personality measures were the best predictors of an effort and leadership dimension and a counterproductive behavior dimension (labeled 'maintaining personal discipline'; McHenry et al., 1990). Now, it is generally acknowledged that this mechanism might increase the validity of personality inventories (e.g., Hogan and Holland, 2003 as the best example), assessment centers (Lievens et al., 2003).

Another recent stream of research with considerable value for selection practice is that one should be aware of potential interactions among predictor constructs (competencies). For example, interactions between conscientiousness and agreeableness (Witt et al., 2002), conscientiousness and extraversion (Witt, 2002), and Conscientiousness and social skills (Witt and Ferris, 2003) have been discovered. In all of these cases, high levels of conscientiousness, coupled with either low levels of agreeableness, low levels of extraversion, or inadequate social skills were detrimental for performance. At a practical level, these results highlight, for example, that selecting people high in Conscientiousness but low in Agreeableness for jobs that require frequent collaboration reduces validities to zero.

Finally, recent research is also informative as to what interventions not to undertake to increase criterion-related validity. For example, it is often thought that social desirability corrections (e.g., lie scales) should be used when one gathers self-report ratings (e.g., in the context of personality measurement). We have now compelling evidence that social desirability corrections should not be applied. Schmitt and Oswald (2006) showed that correcting applicants' scores had minimal impact on mean criterion performance. The futility of using social desirability corrections was also demonstrated at the individual level (i.e., who gets hired on the basis of applicant rankings, Ellingson et al., 1999). Although it is interesting to know that social desirability corrections are not useful, the question remains as to what practitioners can do when applicants fake (and we know they do). In fact, isn't it awkward that we ask applicants to be honest when responding to self-reports, while we know that this will lower their chances of being selected. Therefore, various faking reduction approaches have been tried out. However, most of them (e.g., warnings, forced choice formats) had only meager effects (Dwight and Donovan, 2003; Heggestadt et al., 2006). One promising approach consists of requiring candidates to elaborate on the ratings provided, although this strategy seems useful only when the items are verifiable (Schmitt and Kunce, 2002; Schmitt et al., 2003). Last, it was discovered that faking does not seem to be a problem when personality inventories are used for selecting out candidates (i.e., a selection process with a high selection ratio, Mueller-Hanson et al., 2003).

DIRECTIONS FOR FUTURE RESEARCH ON PERSONNEL SELECTION

Disentangling content from method

In the past, selection procedures were seen as monolithic entities. Recently, there is increased recognition to make a clear distinction between predictor constructs (content) and predictor measures (methods).

Content refers to the constructs and variables (e.g., conscientiousness, cognitive ability, finger dexterity, field dependence-independence, reaction time, visual attention) that are being measured. Methods refers to the techniques or procedures (e.g., graphology, paper-and-pencil tests, computer-administered tests, video-based tests, interviews, and assessment centers, work samples, self-reports, peer reports) that we use to measure the specified content (Arthur et al., 2003; Chan and Schmitt, 1997; Schmitt and Chan, 1998; Schmitt and Mills, 2001). Crossing these two features leads to different modalities of selection procedures. For example, a specific construct such as extraversion might be measured via various methods such as interview questions, self-report items or situational judgment test items.

This division is of paramount importance because it impacts on virtually all research done on personnel selection procedures. For example, incremental validity research of predictors (e.g., assessment center exercises used in addition to structured interviews and self-report personality inventories) that fail to take this distinction into account are misleading and are conceptually difficult to interpret. Unless one either holds the content (constructs) constant and varies the method, or holds the method constant and varies the content, one does not know what (method or construct) leads to the incremental validity obtained. Another example is research on adverse impact. For example, Chan and Schmitt (1997) showed that changing the method of an SJT (video-based instead of paper-and-pencil) resulted in less adverse impact, even though the content of the test was not changed. Likewise, in applicant reactions research it is important to know whether applicants perceive a test favorably or unfavorably because of the content of the test or because of the method of measuring the substantive content (Hausknecht et al., 2004).

Going beyond validity

Prior selection research has usually taken a micro analytical perspective. That is, the effectiveness of a selection procedure was examined for predicting individual performance. Several authors (Ployhart, 2006; Schneider et al., 2000; Schmitt, 2002) have argued that future selection research should take a more macro analytical approach to exert a real impact on organizations and organizational decision makers. This implies that the consequences of using specific selection procedures should also be ascertained at levels other than the individual level. Examples are the team, job (occupational), and organizational level.

To date, only a very limited number of studies have taken such an organizational perspective. For instance, Terpstra and Rozell (1993) correlated HR managers' use of selection procedures with performance of the firm. As argued by Ployhart (2006), this is only a first step as this study was based on self-reports of firm performance. In a similar vein, the well-known study of Huselid (1995) demonstrates that use of high performance work practices (e.g., Do companies use employment tests prior to hiring?) are related to better firm performance. Yet, they do not show that selecting better employees adds strategic value to the firm.

Future research should use a truly multilevel perspective to demonstrate whether validities at the individual level also translate into differences at other levels (and especially at the organizational level). An excellent example is the recent study of Ployhart et al. (2006). They showed that individual, job, and organizational level means personality were positively associated with job performance and job satisfaction, whereas job and organizational level variances were often negatively associated with performance and satisfaction. These results highlight the importance of personality homogeneity at different levels (cf. attraction-selection-attrition framework).

'Selling' selection innovations

At the start, we mentioned that personnel selection is typically viewed as an 'old' and 'narrow' domain in HRM. In addition, it is often viewed in rather simplistic dichotomous terms. One of the aims of our review was to illustrate the various exciting developments that have taken place in this field in recent years. As demonstrated, many of these developments have substantial value for HR practitioners working in organizations. However, this is only side of the equation. An equally vital issue is to implement these developments in organizations. One stumbling block is the lack of awareness of these new trends. For example, it was telling that a recent survey revealed among HR professionals that two of the greatest misconceptions among these professionals dealt with personnel selection, namely the relative validity of general mental ability tests as compared to personality inventories (Rynes et al., 2002).

Therefore, future research is needed to uncover factors that encourage/impede organizations' use of selection procedures. For example, a recent study (Wilk and Cappelli, 2003) showed that (apart from broader legal, economic, and political factors) the type of work practices of organizations was one of the factors that might encourage/impede organizations' use of selection procedures. Specifically, organizations seem to use different types of selection methods contingent upon the nature of the work being done (skill requirements), training, and pay level.

In a similar vein, we need to find out ways to sell selection practices to practitioners and to overcome potential resistance (Muchinsky, 2004). Probably, the provision of information about the psychometric quality and legal defensibility of selection procedures to decision makers in organizations is insufficient. An alternative might consist of linking the adoption of sound selection practices not only to validity criteria but also to organizational-level measures of performance such as annual profits, sales, or turnover (see the section 'Going Beyond the Validity of Selection Procedures'). Another way might be to use more vivid information (case studies) to persuade decision makers. However, even this way of communicating

selection interventions to practitioners might fail. Along these lines, Johns (1993) posits that we have typically placed too much emphasis on selection practices as *rational technical* interventions and therefore often fail to have an impact in organizations (e.g., attempts to 'sell' utility information or structured interviews). Conversely, practitioners in organizations perceive the introduction of new selection procedures as organizational interventions that are subject to the same pressures (power games, etc.) as other organizational innovations. Although Johns' article dates from 1993, we still have largely neglected to implement its underlying recommendations.

One possible approach to improving the use of scientifically validated recruiting and selection procedures is through the increasing professionalization of the field of HR. As more organizations insist on hiring HR personnel with professional training and credentials, the greater the likelihood that research-based practices will be valued and adopted in organizations. For example, Chapman and Zweig (2005) and Lievens and De Paepe (2004) found that trained interviewers were much more likely to practice structured interviews than their untrained counterparts. We are also hopeful that ongoing learning through professional development requirements for maintaining professional credentials will further infuse and update practice in the field. Likewise, it is necessary for researchers and instructors to engage the professional community to ensure that the research we are conducting is both relevant and timely.

EPILOGUE

The central question of this chapter was: 'Which new research developments have occurred that advance recruitment and selection practice?' On the one hand our review exemplified many areas wherein both recruitment and selection research might have practical implications for organizations. A key example is the rapid increase of technology in both recruitment and selection, as showcased by the tailoring of media rich information in recruitment and the use of videoconferencing and (un)proctored web-based testing in selection. Other examples are the renewed importance of recruiter behaviors, the value of investing in employer brand audits and employer brand management, specific guidelines for increasing the validity of extant selection procedures, the development of new selection procedures, and the adaptation of selection procedures to a cross-cultural context.

On the other hand, a common thread running through our review is that we have the difficulty of bringing our message that recruitment and selection matter to the organization across. In both recruitment and selection, we need to find ways of demonstrating the value of recruiting and selecting to organizations. In recruitment, this might be done by developing frameworks for assessing the quantity and quality of the applicant pool. In selection, a macro oriented (multilevel) approach might be needed for showing the effects of selection procedures on individual, group, and organizational outcomes.

REFERENCES

Aaker, J.L. (1997) 'Dimensions of brand personality', *Journal of Marketing Research*, 34: 347–56.

Allen, D., Van Scotter, J. and Otondo, R. (2004) 'Recruitment communication media: Impact on pre-hire outcomes', *Personnel Psychology*, 57: 143–71.

Aiman-Smith, L., Bauer, T.N. and Cable, D.M. (2001) 'Are you attracted? Do you intend to pursue? A recruiting policy-capturing study', *Journal of Business and Psychology*, 16: 219–37.

Arthur, W., Day, E.A., McNelly, T.L. and Edens, P.S. (2003) 'A meta-analysis of the criterion-related validity of assessment center dimensions', *Personnel Psychology*, 56: 125–54.

Avery, D.R. and McKay, P.F. (2006) 'Target practice: An organizational impression management approach to attracting minority and female job applicants', *Personnel Psychology*, 59: 157–87.

Backhaus, K.B., Stone, B.A. and Heiner, K. (2002) 'Exploring the relationship between corporate social performance and employer attractiveness', *Business and Society*, 41: 292–318.

Backhaus, K. and Tikoo, S. (2004) 'Conceptualizing and researching employer branding', *Career Development International*, 9: 501–17.

Barber, A.E. (1998) *Recruiting Employees: Individual and Organizational Perspectives*. Thousands Oaks, CA: Sage.

Bauer, T.N, Truxillo, D.M., Sanchez, R., Craig, J., Ferrara P. and Campion, M.A. (2001) 'Development of the Selection Procedural Justice Scale', *Personnel Psychology*, 54: 387–419.

Becker, B.E. and Huselid, M.A. (1998) 'High performance work systems and firm performance: A synthesis of research and managerial implications', in G.R. Ferris (ed.), *Research in personnel and human resource management*. Greenwich, CT: JAI Press, pp. 53–101.

Becker, T.E. (2005) 'Development and validation of a situational judgment test of employee integrity', *International Journal of Selection and Assessment*, 13: 225–32.

Bing, M.N., Whanger, J.C., Davison, H.K. and VanHook, J.B. (2004) 'Incremental validity of the frame-of-reference effect in personality scale scores: A replication and extension', *Journal of Applied Psychology*, 89: 150–7.

Boudreau, J. and Rynes, S. (1985) 'Role of recruitment in staffing utility analysis', *Journal of Applied Psychology*, 70: 354–66.

Breaugh, J.A. and Starke, M. (2000) 'Research on employee recruitment: So many studies, so many remaining questions', *Journal of Management*, 26: 405–34.

Brooks, M.E., Highhouse, S., Russell, S. and Mohr, D. (2003) 'Familiarity, ambivalence, and firm reputation: Is corporate fame a double-edged sword?', *Journal of Applied Psychology*, 88: 904–14.

Cable, D.M., Aiman-Smith, L., Mulvey, P., and Edwards, J.R. (2000) 'The sources and accuracy of job applicants' beliefs about organizational culture', *Academy of Management Journal*, 43: 1076–85.

Cable, D.M. and Graham, M.E. (2000) 'The determinants of job seekers' reputation perceptions', *Journal of Organizational Behavior*, 21: 929–47.

Cable, D.M. and Turban, D.B. (2003) 'The value of organizational reputation in the recruitment context: A brand-equity perspective', *Journal of Applied Social Psychology*, 33: 2244–66.

Cable, D.M. and Turban, D.B. (2001) 'Establishing the dimensions, sources and value of job seekers' employer knowledge during recruitment', in G.R. Ferris (ed), *Research in Personnel and Human Resources Management*. New York, NY: Elsevier Science, pp. 115–63.

Campbell, J.P., McCloy, R.A., Oppler, S.H. and Sager C.E. (1993) 'A theory of performance', in N. Schmitt and W.C. Borman (eds), *Personnel Selection in Organizations*. San Francisco, CA: Jossey Bass, pp. 35–70.

Carlson, K.D., Connerly, M.L. and Mecham, R.L. (2002) 'Recruitment evaluation: The case for assessing the quality of applicants attracted', *Personnel Psychology*, 55: 461–90.

Chan, D. and Schmitt, N. (1997) 'Video-based versus paper-and-pencil method of assessment in situational judgment tests: Subgroup differences in test performance and face validity perceptions', *Journal of Applied Psychology*, 82: 143–59.

Chan, D. and Schmitt, N. (2002) 'Situational judgment and job performance', *Human Performance*, 15: 233–54.

Chapman, D.S. and Rowe, P.M. (2001) 'The impact of videoconference media, interview structure, and interviewer gender on interviewer evaluations in the employment interview: A field experiment', *Journal of Occupational and Organizational Psychology*, 74: 279–98.

Chapman, D.S., Uggerslev, K.L., Carroll, S.A., Piasentin, K.A. and Jones, D.A. (2005) 'Applicant attraction to organizations and job choice: A meta-analytic review of the correlates of recruiting outcomes', *Journal of Applied Psychology*, 90: 928–44.

Chapman, D.S., Uggerslev, K.L. and Webster, J. (2003) 'Applicant reactions to face-to-face and technology-mediated interviews: A field investigation', *Journal of Applied Psychology*, 88: 944–53.

Chapman, D.S. and Webster, J. (2001) 'Rater correction processes in applicant selection using videoconference technology: The role of attributions', *Journal of Applied Social Psychology*, 31: 2518–37.

Chapman, D.S. and Webster, J. (2003) 'The use of technologies in the recruiting, screening, and selection processes for job candidates', *International Journal of Selection and Assessment*, 11: 113–20.

Chapman, D.S. and Webster, J. (2006) 'Integrating applicant reactions into the critical contact framework of recruiting', *International Journal of Human Resource Management*, 17: 1032–57.

Chapman, D.S. and Zweig, D.I. (2005) 'Developing a nomological network for interview structure: Antecedents and consequences of the structured selection interview', *Personnel Psychology*, 58: 673–702.

Clevenger, J., Pereira, G.M., Wiechmann, D., Schmitt, N. and Harvey, V.S. (2001) 'Incremental validity of situational judgment tests', *Journal of Applied Psychology*, 86: 410–17.

Cober, R.T., Brown, D.J. and Levy, P.E. (2004) 'Form, content, and function: An evaluative methodology for corporate employment Web sites', *Human Resource Management*, 43: 201–18.

Cober, R.T., Brown, D.J., Levy, P.E., Cober, A.B. and Keeping, L.M. (2003) 'Organizational Web sites: Web site content and style as determinants of organizational attraction', *International Journal of Selection and Assessment*, 11: 158–69.

Collins, C.J. and Han, J. (2004) 'Exploring applicant pool quantity and quality: The effects of early recruitment practices, corporate advertising, and firm reputation', *Personnel Psychology*, 57: 685–717.

Collins, C.J. and Stevens, C.K. (2002) 'The relationship between early recruitment related activities and the application decisions of new labor-market entrants: A brand equity approach to recruitment', *Journal of Applied Psychology*, 87: 1121–33.

Dineen, B.R., Ash, S.R. and Noe, R.A. (2002) 'A Web of applicant attraction: Person–organization fit in the context of Web-based recruitment', *Journal of Applied Psychology*, 87: 723–34.

Dineen, B.R., Ling, J., Ash, S.R. and DelVecchio, D. (2007) 'Aesthetic properties and message customization: Navigating the dark side of Web recruitment', *Journal of Applied Psychology*, 92: 356–72.

Dwight, S.A. and Donovan, J.J. (2003) 'Do warnings not to fake reduce faking?', *Human Performance*, 16: 1–23.

Ellingson, J.E., Sackett, P.R. and Hough, L.M. (1999) 'Social desirability corrections in personality measurement: Issues of applicant comparison and construct validity', *Journal of Applied Psychology*, 84: 155–66.

Fulmer, I.S., Gerhart, B. and Scott, K.S. (2003) 'Are the 100 best better? An empirical investigation of the relationship between being a "great place to work" and firm performance', *Personnel Psychology*, 56: 965–93.

Gilliland, S.W. (1993) 'The perceived fairness of selection systems: An organizational justice perspective', *Academy of Management Review*, 18: 694–734.

Greening, D.W. and Turban, D.B. (2000) 'Corporate social performance as a competitive advantage in attracting a quality workforce', *Business and Society*, 39: 254–80.

Hattrup K., Schmitt N. and Landis R.S. (1992) 'Equivalence of constructs measured by job-specific and commercially available aptitude-tests', *Journal of Applied Psychology*, 77: 298–308.

Hausknecht, J.P., Day, D.V. and Thomas, S.C. (2004) 'Applicant reactions to selection procedures: An updated model and meta-analysis', *Personnel Psychology*, 57: 639–83.

Hedge, J.W., Borman, W.C. and Lammlein, S.E. (eds) (2006) *The Aging Workforce*. Washington, DC, American Psychological Association.

Heggestad, E.D., Morrison, M., Reeve, C.L. and McCloy, R.A. (2006) 'Forced-choice assessments of personality for selection: Evaluating issues of normative assessment and faking resistance', *Journal of Applied Psychology*, 91: 9–24.

Highhouse, S., Zickar, M.J., Thorsteinson, T.J., Stierwalt, S.L. and Slaughter, J. (1999) 'Assessing company employment image: An example in the fast food industry', *Personnel Psychology*, 52: 151–72.

Hogan, J. and Holland, B. (2003) 'Using theory to evaluate personality and job-performance relations: A socioanalytic perspective', *Journal of Applied Psychology*, 88: 100–12.

Hough, L.M. and Oswald, F.L. (2000) 'Personnel selection: Looking toward the future – Remembering the past', *Annual Review of Psychology*, 51: 631–64.

Hunter, D.R. (2003) 'Measuring general aviation pilot judgment using a situational judgment technique', *International Journal of Aviation Psychology*, 13: 373–86.

Hunthausen, J.M., Truxillo, D.M., Bauer, T.N. and Hammer, L.B. (2003) 'A field study of frame-of-reference effects on personality test validity', *Journal of Applied Psychology*, 88: 545–51.

Huo, Y.P., Huang, H.J. and Napier, N.K. (2002) 'Divergence or convergence: A cross national comparison of personnel selection practices', *Human Resource Management*, 41: 31–44.

Huselid, M.A. (1995) 'The impact of human resource management practices on turnover, productivity and corporate financial performance', *Academy of Management Journal*, 38: 635–72.

James, L.R., McIntyre, M.D., Glisson, C.A., Green, P.D., Patton, T.W. and LeBreton, J.M. (2005) 'A conditional reasoning measure for aggression', *Organizational Research Methods*, 8: 69–99.

Johns, G. (1993) 'Constraints on the adoption of psychology-based personnel practices: Lessons from organizational innovation', *Personnel Psychology*, 46: 569–92.

Jones, D.A., Shultz, J.W. and Chapman, D.S. (2006) 'Recruiting through job advertisements: The effects of cognitive elaboration on decision making', *International Journal of Selection and Assessment*, 14: 167–79.

Kanning, U.P., Grewe, K., Hollenberg, S. and Hadouch, M. (2006) 'From the subjects' point of view – Reactions to different types of situational judgment items', *European Journal of Psychological Assessment*, 22: 168–76.

Konradt, U., Hertel, G. and Joder, K. (2003) 'Web-based assessment of call center agents: Development and validation of a computerized instrument', *International Journal of Selection and Assessment*, 11: 184–93.

Landy, F.J. (2005) 'Some historical and scientific issues related to research on emotional intelligence', *Journal of Organizational Behavior*, 26: 411–24.

Larsen, D.A. and Phillips, J.I. (2002) 'Effect of recruiter on attraction to the firm: Implications of the elaboration likelihood model', *Journal of Business and Psychology*, 16: 347–64.

LeBreton, J.M., Barksdale, C.D., Robin, J.D. and James, L.R. (2007) 'Measurement issues associated with conditional reasoning tests of personality: Deception and faking', *Journal of Applied Psychology*, 92: 1–16.

Lee, I. (2005) 'The Evolution of E-Recruiting: A content analysis of Fortune 100 career web sites', *Journal of Electronic Commerce in Organizations*, 3 (3): 57.

Lievens, F. (2007) 'Employer branding in the Belgian Army: The importance of instrumental and symbolic beliefs for potential applicants, actual applicants, and military employees', *Human Resource Management*, 46: 51–69.

Lievens, F. (2008) 'Research on selection in an international context: Current status and future directions', in M.M. Harris (ed.), *Handbook of Research in International Human Resource Management*. Lawrence Erlbaum's Organizations and Management Series. London: Prentice Hall, pp. 107–124.

Lievens, F., Buyse, T. and Sackett, P.R. (2005) 'The operational validity of a video–based situational judgment test for medical college admissions: Illustrating the importance of matching predictor and criterion construct domains', *Journal of Applied Psychology*, 90: 442–52.

Lievens, F. and De Paepe, A. (2004) 'An empirical investigation of interviewer–related factors that discourage the use of high structure interviews', *Journal of Organizational Behavior*, 25: 29–46.

Lievens, F., Harris, M.M., Van Keer, E. and Bisqueret, C. (2003) 'Predicting crosscultural training performance: The validity of personality, cognitive ability, and dimensions measured by an assessment center and a behavior description interview', *Journal of Applied Psychology*, 88: 476–89.

Lievens, F. and Highhouse, S. (2003) 'The relation of instrumental and symbolic attributes to a company's attractiveness as an employer', *Personnel Psychology*, 56: 75–102.

Matthews, G., Roberts, R.D. and Zeidner, M. (2004) 'Seven myths about emotional intelligence', *Psychological Inquiry*, 15: 179–96.

McClough, A.C. and Rogelberg, S.G. (2003) 'Selection in teams: An exploration of the Teamwork Knowledge, Skills, and Ability test', *International Journal of Selection and Assessment*, 11: 56–66.

McDaniel, M.A., Hartman, N.S., Whetzel, D.L. and Grubb, W.L. (2007) 'Situational judgment tests, response instructions, and validity: A meta-analysis', *Personnel Psychology*, 60: 63–91.

McDaniel, M.A., Morgeson, F.P., Finnegan, E.B., Campion, M.A. and Braverman, E.P. (2001) 'Use of situational judgment tests to predict job performance: A clarification of the literature', *Journal of Applied Psychology*, 86: 730–40.

McHenry, J.J., Hough, L.M., Toquam, J.L., Hanson, M.A. and Ashworth, S. (1990) 'Project a validity results – the relationship between predictor and criterion domain', *Personnel Psychology*, 43: 335–54.

Mendenhall, M. and Oddou, G. (1985) 'The dimensions of expatriate acculturation: A review', *Academy of Management Review*, 10: 39–47.

Mol, S.T., Born, M., Willemsen, M.E. and Van Der Molen, H.T. (2005) 'Predicting expatriate job performance for selection purposes: A quantitative review', *Journal of Cross-Cultural Psychology*, 36: 1–31.

Morgeson, F.P., Reider, M.H. and Campion, M.A. (2005) 'Selecting individuals in team settings: The importance of social skills, personality characteristics, and teamwork knowledge', *Personnel Psychology*, 58: 583–611.

Motowidlo, S.J., Hooper, A.C. and Jackson, H.L. (2006) 'Implicit policies about relations between personality traits and behavioral effectiveness in situational judgment items', *Journal of Applied Psychology*, 91: 749–61.

Muchinsky, P.M. (2004) 'When the psychometrics of test development meets organizational realities: A conceptual framework for organizational change, examples, and recommendations', *Personnel Psychology*, 57: 175–209.

Mueller-Hanson, R., Heggestad, E.D. and Thornton, G.C. (2003) 'Faking and selection: Considering the use of personality from select-in and select-out perspectives', *Journal of Applied Psychology*, 88: 348–55.

Murphy, K.R. (1986) 'When your top choice turns you down: Effects of rejected offers on the utility of selection tests', *Psychological Bulletin*, 99: 133–38.

Nguyen, N.T., Biderman, M.D. and McDaniel, M.A. (2005) 'Effects of response instructions on faking a situational judgment test', *International Journal of Selection and Assessment*, 13: 250–60.

Ones, D.S. and Viswesvaran, C. (1997) 'Personality determinants in the prediction of aspects of expatriate job success', in D.M. Saunder and Z. Aycan (eds), *New Approaches to Employee Management: Expatriate Management: Theory and Research*. Greenwich, CT: JAI Press. pp. 63–92.

Oswald, F.L., Schmitt, N., Kim, B.H., Ramsay, L.J. and Gillespie, M.A. (2004) 'Developing a biodata measure and situational judgment inventory as predictors of college student performance', *Journal of Applied Psychology*, 89: 187–208.

Ployhart, R.E. (2006) 'Staffing in the 21st century: New challenges and strategic opportunities', *Journal of Management*, 32: 868–97.

Ployhart, R.E., Sacco, J.M., Nishii, L.H. and Rogg, K.L. (2004, April) *The influence of culture on criterion-related validity and job performance*. Poster presented at the Annual Conference of the Society for Industrial and Organizational Psychology, Chicago, IL.

Ployhart, R.E., Weekley, J.A. and Baughman, K. (2006) 'The structure and function of human capital emergence: A multilevel examination of the attraction-selection-attrition model', *Academy of Management Journal*, 49: 661–77.

Ployhart, R.E., Weekley, J.A., Holtz, B.C. and Kemp, C. (2003) 'Web-based and paper-and-pencil testing of applicants in a proctored setting: Are personality, biodata, and situational judgment tests comparable?', *Personnel Psychology*, 56: 733–52.

Potosky, D. and Bobko, P. (2004) 'Selection testing via the Internet: Practical considerations and exploratory empirical findings', *Personnel Psychology*, 57: 1003–34.

Rau, B.L. and Adams, G. (2004) 'Job seeking among retirees seeking bridge employment', *Personnel Psychology*, 57: 719–44.

Rau, B.L. and Adams, G. (2005) 'Organizational Attraction of Retirees for Bridge Employment', *Journal of Organizational Behavior*, 26: 649–60.

Richman, W.L., Kiesler, S., Weisband, S. and Drasgow, F. (1999) 'A meta-analytic study of social desirability distortion in computer-administered questionnaires, traditional questionnaires, and interviews', *Journal of Applied Psychology*, 84: 754–75.

Richman-Hirsch, W.L., Olson-Buchanan, J.B. and Drasgow, F. (2000) 'Examining the impact of administration medium on examinee perceptions and attitudes', *Journal of Applied Psychology*, 85: 880–7.

Ronen, S. (1989) 'Training the international assignee', in I.L. Goldstein (ed.), *Training and development in organizations*. San Francisco: Jossey-Bass, pp. 417–53.

Ryan, A.M., McFarland, L., Baron, H. and Page, R. (1999) 'An international look at selection practices: Nation and culture as explanations for variability in practice', *Personnel Psychology*, 52: 359–91.

Ryan, A.M. and Ployhart, R.E. (2000) 'Applicants' perceptions of selection procedures and decisions: A critical review and agenda for the future', *Journal of Management*, 26: 565–606.

Rynes, S.L., Colbert, A.E. and Brown, K.G. (2002) 'HR professionals' beliefs about effective human resource practices: Correspondence between research and practice', *Human Resource Management*, 41: 149–74.

Salgado, J.F. (1997) 'The Five-Factor model of personality and job performance in the European Community', *Journal of Applied Psychology*, 82: 30–43.

Salgado, J.F., Anderson, N., Moscoso, S., Bertua, C. and De Fruyt, F. (2003a) 'International validity generalization of GMA and cognitive abilities: A European community meta-analysis', *Personnel Psychology*, 56: 573–605.

Salgado, J.F., Anderson, N., Moscoso, S., Bertua, C., De Fruyt, F. and Rolland, J.P. (2003b) 'A meta-analytic study of general mental ability validity for different occupations in the European Community', *Journal of Applied Psychology*, 88: 1068–81.

Schmidt, F.L. and Hunter, J.E. (1998) 'The validity and utility of selection methods in personnel psychology: Practical and theoretical implications of 85 years of research findings', *Psychological Bulletin*, 124: 262–74.

Schmit, M.J., Kihm, J.A. and Robie, C. (2000) 'Development of a global measure of personality', *Personnel Psychology*, 53: 153–93.

Schmitt, N. (2002) 'A multi-level perspective on personnel selection: Are we ready?', in F.J. Dansereau and F. Yamarino (eds), *Research in multi-level issues: The many faces of multi-level issues*. Oxford, UK: Elsevier, pp. 155–64.

Schmitt, N. and Chan, D. (1998) *Personnel selection. A theoretical approach*. London: Sage.

Schmitt, N. and Kunce, C. (2002) 'The effects of required elaboration of answers to biodata questions', *Personnel Psychology*, 55: 569–87.

Schmitt, N. and Mills, A.E. (2001) 'Traditional tests and job simulations: Minority and majority performance and test validities', *Journal of Applied Psychology*, 86: 451–54.

Schmitt, N. and Oswald, F.L. (2006) 'The impact of corrections for faking on the validity of noncognitive measures in selection settings', *Journal of Applied Psychology*, 91: 613–21.

Schmitt, N., Oswald, F.L., Kim, B.H., Gillespie, M.A., Ramsay, L.J. and Yoo, T.Y. (2003) 'Impact of elaboration on socially desirable responding and the validity of biodata measures', *Journal of Applied Psychology*, 88: 979–88.

Schneider, B., Smith, D.B. and Sipe, W. (2000) 'Multilevel personnel selection', in K. Klein and S. Kozlowski (eds), *Multilevel theory, research, and methods in organizations*. San Francisco, CA: Jossey–Bass, pp. 91–120.

Schuler, R., Dowling, P. and DeCieri, H. (1993) 'An integrative framework of strategic international human resource management', *Journal of Management*, 19: 419–59.

Sinangil, H.K. and Ones, D.S. (2001) 'Expatriate management', in N. Anderson, D.S. Ones, H.K. Sinangil and C. Viswesvaran (eds), *Handbook of industrial, work and organizational psychology*. London, UK: Sage. pp. 424–43.

Slaughter, J.E., Zickar M.J., Highhouse, S. and Mohr, D.C. (2004) 'Personality trait inferences about organizations: Development of a measure and assessment of construct validity', *Journal of Applied Psychology*, 89: 85–103

Stevens, M.J. and Campion, M.A. (1999) 'Staffing work teams: Development and validation of a selection test for teamwork settings', *Journal of Management*, 25: 207–28.

Terpstra, D.E. and Rozell, E.J. (1993) 'The relationship of staffing practices to organizational level measures of performance', *Personnel Psychology*, 46: 27–48.

Tippins, N.T., Beaty, J., Drasgow, F., Gibson, W.M., Pearlman, K., Segall, D.O. and Shepherd, W. (2006) 'Unproctored internet testing in employment settings', *Personnel Psychology*, 59: 189–225.

Turban, D.B. (2001) 'Organizational attractiveness as an employer on college campuses: An examination of the applicant population', *Journal of Vocational Behavior*, 58: 293–312.

Turban, D.B. and Greening, D.W. (1997) 'Corporate social performance and organizational attractiveness to prospective employees', *Academy of Management Journal*, 40: 658–72.

Turban, D.B. and Cable, D.M. (2003) 'Firm reputation and applicant pool characteristics', *Journal of Organizational Behavior*, 24: 733–51.

Van Rooy, D.L., Viswesvaran, C. and Pluta, P. (2005) 'An evaluation of construct validity: What is this thing called Emotional Intelligence?', *Human Performance*, 18: 445–62.

Von Glinow, M.A., Drost, E.A. and Teagarden, M.B. (2002) 'Converging on IHRM best practices: Lessons learned from a globally distributed consortium on theory and practice', *Human Resource Management*, 41: 123–40.

Williamson, I.O., Lepak D.P. and King, J. (2003) 'The effect of company recruitment web site orientation on individuals' perceptions of organizational attractiveness', *Journal of Vocational Behavior*, 63: 242–63.

Wilk, S.L. and Cappelli, P. (2003) 'Understanding the determinants of employer use of selection methods', *Personnel Psychology*, 56: 103–24.

Witt, L.A. (2002) 'The interactive effects of extraversion and conscientiousness on performance', *Journal of Management*, 28: 835–51.

Witt, L.A., Burke, L.A., Barrick, M.R. and Mount, M.K. (2002) 'The interactive effects of conscientiousness and agreeableness on job performance', *Journal of Applied Psychology*, 87: 164–69.

Witt, L.A. and Ferris, G.R. (2003) 'Social skill as moderator of the conscientiousness-performance relationship: Convergent results across four studies', *Journal of Applied Psychology*, 88: 809–20.

Wright, P.M., Gardner, T.M., Moynihan, L.M. and Allen, M.R. (2005) 'The relationship between HR practices and firm performance: Examining causal order', *Personnel Psychology*, 58: 409–46.

Wright, P.M., Gardner, T.M., Moynihan, L.M., Park, H., Gerhart, B. and Delery, J. (2001) 'Measurement error in research on human resources and firm performance: Additional data and suggestions for future research', *Personnel Psychology*, 54: 875–902.

Zeidner, M., Matthews, G. and Roberts, R.D. (2004) 'Emotional intelligence in the workplace: A critical review', *Applied Psychology: An International Review*, 53: 371–99.

10

Training and Development in Organizations

Phyllis Tharenou

Training and development remains an important human resource (HR) practice of interest to researchers, managers, governments, and employees. Training research is of substantial interest and reviews show its enormous and continued growth (e.g., Aguinis and Kraiger, 2009; Ford and Kraiger, 1995; Goldstein, 1980; Goldstein and Gessner, 1988; Latham, 1988; Salas and Cannon-Bowers, 2001; Sonnentag et al., 2004; Tannenbaum and Yukl, 1992; Wexley, 1984). Training is of major interest to practitioners and managers in order to update employee skills, improve job performance and productivity, and develop the competencies employees need to meet the strategic objectives of their organizations (Sugrue and Rivera, 2005; 2006). Training is of significance to governments who facilitate its use to provide the capabilities a country needs for economic growth and to address skill shortages in a highly competitive global economy (Aguinis and Kraiger, 2009). Lastly, training is important to employees for whom it increases employment duration and continuity, pay, and career advancement (Tharenou, 1997).

However, problematic issues continue to arise in regard to the usefulness of and return on training and development (Bunch, 2007). Managers want to know what the return is on their investment (ROI; Phillips and Phillips, 2007). Yet, the impact of training on performance continues to be rarely evaluated and its ROI rarely calculated (Kraiger et al., 2004; Sugrue and Rivera, 2005). Scholars lament that practitioners do not use the results of research to incorporate the well-developed scientific knowledge about training into needs analysis, design, delivery, transfer, and evaluation (Kraiger, 2003; Salas and Cannon-Bowers, 2001; Salas and Kosarzycki, 2003). Governments are criticized for under investing in the training and development needed by their countries for economic growth (Tharenou, 1997).

This chapter provides an audit of the training and development literature and its issues and developments. Training is defined as the systematic acquisition and development of the knowledge, skills, and attitudes required by employees to adequately perform a task or job or to improve performance in the job environment (Goldstein, 1980; Latham, 1988) and as a planned effort by an organization to facilitate the learning of job-related behavior on the part of its employees (Wexley, 1984). The chapter begins by considering the discipline approaches that underlie research on training. Then it examines the process of training by considering its stages: the pre-training stage (training needs analysis, factors predicting participation in training and development, the antecedent conditions to training effectiveness, training design), the training itself (training delivery); and the post-training stage (transfer of training, evaluation of the effects of training). The chapter closes with consideration of future development and research needs in the area.

APPROACHES UNDERLYING RESEARCH INTO TRAINING AND DEVELOPMENT

Four major approaches underlie research into training and development in organizations: those of human resource management (HRM), industrial/organizational (I/O) psychology, labor economics, and industrial relations.

The earlier field of 'personnel management' considered training as one of several separate HR practices and focused on identifying and implementing training models in a series of steps to improve individuals' job performance. By contrast, in the HRM approach, HR practices, including training and development, are used to improve organizational performance, help implement an organization's business strategy and meet its objectives, and help build a sustainable competitive advantage that creates financial performance (Becker and Huselid, 1998; 2006; Lepak et al., 2006). The approach is strategic in terms of managing human resources to meet the organization's objectives.

The theoretical basis for the strategic HRM approach includes the resource-based view (RBV) of the firm (Barney, 1991; Barney and Wright, 1998). High-performance work systems (HPWS) are integrated systems of HR and other work practices that are internally consistent with each other and externally consistent with organizational strategy. HPWS are designed to help develop valuable, unique employee capacities that assist an organization to develop core competencies (Becker and Huselid, 1998) – firm-specific resources and capabilities that enable an organization to enact a strategy that creates value by not being implemented simultaneously by competitors and which competitors find hard to duplicate (Barney, 1991). Developing employees is an effective way of gaining valuable, rare and perhaps unique capacities, and training and development is a key practice, amongst others, to do so (Lepak and Snell, 1999). Training, in combination with other HR practices (e.g., selective staffing, performance-contingent compensation, developmental and merit-based performance appraisal) and other work practices such as work design (self-managed teams, flexible work assignments, teamwork), open communication, quality improvement, and decentralized decision-making, helps develop core competencies by which the organization can gain a sustained competitive advantage.

A further major theoretical basis used in the HRM approach is social exchange theory. Social exchange can be viewed as favors one party provides to another that create diffuse future obligations which, due to a norm of reciprocity, will result in reciprocation by the receiver (Blau, 1964). General training can be viewed as a resource that an employer provides to help an employee that demonstrates support and caring (Balkin and Richebé, 2007). Employees perceive training as an investment in, and commitment to, them and reciprocate in kind with extra effort, commitment, organizational citizenship behavior, and cooperation. Training may be viewed as a gift when provided on its own or when provided as part of HPWS. Because employees can interpret HPWS as expressing appreciation, investment, and recognition due to the rigorous recruitment, extensive training, empowerment, and rewards central to HPWS, they begin to perceive themselves in a social exchange as opposed to a purely economic relationship (Takeuchi et al., 2007). HPWS are thought to result in generalized norms of reciprocity, shared mental models, role making, and organizational citizenship behaviors that then lead to organizational performance (Evans and Davis, 2005).

In contrast to the strategic approaches that underlie the HRM approach to training, industrial/organizational (I/O) psychology focuses on the science of training – how to design, deliver, implement, transfer and evaluate training so that it is effective (Haccoun and Saks, 1998; Kraiger, 2003; Salas and Cannon-Bowers, 2001). Dramatic progress has been made in how to design, deliver and transfer training to the job and appropriate tools, techniques, and interventions have been developed (Haccoun and Saks, 1998; Salas and Cannon-Bowers, 2001). The approach to training was once predominantly behavioral (Goldstein, 1980; Latham, 1988; Wexley, 1984) but has moved to a cognitive approach based on principles from cognitive and instructional psychology to design and deliver training and assist its transfer to the job (Ford and Kraiger, 1995; Tannenbaum and Yukl, 1992). For example, stages of skill acquisition highlight progression through acquiring declarative knowledge (knowledge of facts, what to do), knowledge integration (integration of facts), procedural knowledge (knowledge about how to do things; knowing how), and finally tacit knowledge (about when and why to do things) (Tannenbaum and Yukl, 1992). Meta-cognition refers to the mental processes involved in acquiring knowledge, interpreting feedback and learning from experience (e.g., mental models), especially affecting how training is designed for tasks involving cognitive processes (Howell and Cooke, 1989; Tannenbaum and Yukl, 1992).

A third approach underlying research into training and development is that of labor economics. Based at macro-levels (country, sector/industry, organizational), labor economics seeks to determine what factors cause participation in government-provided, vocational, and company-provided training

and development; what effect training has on individuals' outcomes, especially pay, employment probability and continuity, and performance (e.g., Green et al., 1996; Upward, 2002); how disadvantaged groups (e.g., the unemployed, ethnic minorities, the poor, women) gain and are affected by training and development (Greenberg et al., 2003, 2004; Jones et al., 2008); and how training affects macro-level country, sector, and organizational productivity (e.g., Bartel, 2000). An underlying theoretical approach continues to be human capital theory (Becker, 1962, 1975). Employees invest in training to learn or improve their skills in order to increase pay and status. Employers train employees to gain improvements in productivity through increased knowledge, skill, and ability (KSAs), training those who are likely to remain with the organization and using general types of training because they are less transportable, in order to gain the maximum return from their investment.

The fourth approach underlying research into training and development is that of industrial relations (IR). Unlike HRM, which focuses on the employer as the main stakeholder and on the firm's performance, IR focuses on the employee and the amount of training employees gain, the work practices and conditions that promote training, and on how collective approaches dealing with power imbalances can help gain employees more training (cf. Colakoglu et al., 2006). Hence, as in labor economics, IR focuses on determining who gets training and development and what conditions increase gaining training and development and on how training affects employee outcomes and does so from an employee perspective but from the point of view of employee gains rather than economic growth. IR approaches focus on employee skill acquisition, including through vocational training systems and through identification and development of job competencies on which to base training. A significant research interest is in the effects of collective action and voice by unions to increase members' training (Boheim and Booth, 2004; Heyes and Stuart, 1998) and in examining effects on employee training caused by conditions of employment (e.g., Arulampalam and Booth, 1998).

The four approaches often deal with common research questions, especially which factors predict participation in training and development (all approaches); whether training increases organizational effectiveness (IO psychology, HRM, labor economics); how to develop competencies through training (IO psychology, HRM, IR); and the place of training as part of HPWS and a strategic approach to organizational performance (especially HRM and IR). However, there are also differences in the questions addressed; for example, IO psychology focuses on how to train; labor economics focuses on macro-level causes of acquiring training and on training's effects on individual's pay; and industrial relations includes an emphasis on vocational training and on union voice in training. The approaches often use different research designs. IO psychology focuses on individuals and groups and often uses experimental laboratory designs to investigate how to train individuals and the effects on psychological and behavioral outcomes. Both HRM (usually field data based on surveys) and IO psychology (often laboratory/experimental data) gather data to answer research questions whereas labor economics uses archival data at country, sector and organizational level, often requiring complex data analytic techniques, including econometric methods to answer their research questions. Of the four disciplines, industrial relations is the most likely to use qualitative research designs and adopt case study approaches because of its interest in examining competency development and approaches to training in individual organizations.

THE STAGES OF TRAINING AND DEVELOPMENT

Traditionally, training and development had been conceived of as a five-stage process: needs analysis, design, delivery, transfer, and evaluation. In effect, three stages exist: what occurs prior to training (training needs

analysis, the organizational, job, and person factors that predict participation, antecedent conditions affecting training effectiveness, training design); what occurs during training (its delivery including the methods of training used); and what occurs after training (its transfer, evaluation of its effects) (cf. Salas and Canon-Bowers, 2001). Events that occur before training have a major impact on how effective training is and whether it transfers to the job (Noe, 1986; Salas and Canon-Bowers, 2001). Events that occur after training, especially with respect to how to ensure training transfers to the job, are critical to whether training improves performance (Ford and Weissbein, 1997; Saks and Belcourt, 2006). Of the stages of training, research had traditionally focused on training design and delivery (Goldstein, 1980; Latham, 1988; Wexley, 1984). The research emphasis has shifted to what happens after training: on whether training transfers to the job (Burke and Hutchins, 2007; Ford and Weissbein, 1997) and on the evaluation of the effects of training including determining how it should be evaluated and whether it improves organizational effectiveness (Tharenou et al., 2007).

Training needs analysis

Training needs analysis determines where training and development needs to be conducted in an organization (organization-level analysis), what is to be trained in terms of identifying the knowledge, skills and abilities needed to perform the tasks in a job (task- or operations-level analysis), and what training particular individuals need (individual- or person-level analysis) (McGehee and Thayer, 1961; Moore and Dutton, 1978). The results are intended to lead to the specification of learning objectives and thus affect the design and delivery of training (Salas and Cannon-Bowers, 2001). However, concern continues to be expressed about the lack of adequate models to guide training need analysis (Clarke, 2003), the accuracy of the needs identified, and the relative lack of research in this area compared to other training stages (Aguinis and Kraiger, 2009).

Advances have mostly occurred in the task or operations analysis component of training need analysis. Cognitive task analysis has been added to the previously behavioral emphasis to help identify the knowledge and skills needed to perform tasks and to identify the cognitive capacities and cues that enable trainees to know when to apply these skills (Salas and Cannon-Bowers, 2001). A trend in task analysis has been to focus on identifying the 'competencies' employees need for their jobs (Gangani et al., 2006) which are based on meeting the objectives of the business and in implementing the business strategy (Kraiger, 2003). Competencies are a cluster of interrelated knowledge, skills, values, attitudes or other characteristics important for successful job performance (Kraiger, 2003). There continues to be ongoing interest in identifying competencies to effectively train managers: the cross-cultural competencies needed by expatriate managers (Leiba-O'Sullivan, 1999), the competencies needed by managers in general (Agut and Grau, 2002), the competencies needed to implement diversity initiatives (Roberson et al., 2003), and the competencies needed for the development of HR professionals (Broom et al., 1998; Walker and Stopper, 2000). Task analysis has also advanced from examining individual jobs to determining the training needs required for team performance (e.g., Bowers et al., 1998).

Person analysis has been the least developed aspect of training need analysis. Difficulties continue to be encountered in the adequacy of methods available to measure the discrepancy between the desired and actual behavior of an employee. It continues to be difficult to determine what managers need training in, which tools to use to identify which managers need training, and how to accurately measure a manager's training needs (Agut and Grau, 2002).

What factors predict participation in training and development?

In contrast to the lesser amount of research conducted into training need analysis has been the greater emphasis on identifying the organizational, job, and person factors that predict participation in training and development. A significant body of knowledge has accumulated from HRM, I/O psychology, labor economics and IR studies as to what causes employees to gain training and development.

At an organizational level, training is more likely to occur when it is aligned with the strategic direction of the organization (e.g., Montesino, 2002), when organization change is occurring (e.g., Leigh and Gifford, 1999), when innovative work practices are being introduced (e.g., total quality management, team approaches, lean management) (Lynch and Black, 1998; Snell et al., 2000), and when high performance work systems are being used (Barnard and Rodgers, 2000; Whitfield, 2000). Large organizations, which thus allow economies of scale, and organizations that have high investment in physical capital, and thus need specialized skills, provide more training than others (Lynch and Black, 1998; Tharenou, 1997) as do those where there is union workplace recognition and union involvement in training decisions (Boheim and Booth, 2004; Heyes and Stuart, 1998), suggesting that a collective voice helps gain training for employees. Participation in training and development is more likely to occur in organizational environments where individuals report supervisor support and a supportive climate for development (Sonnentag et al., 2004; Tharenou, 1997).

At the job level, those working in highly skilled jobs (especially managers) receive more training and development than others, presumably due to need and because the training provides greater returns to the organization (Tharenou, 1997).

At the person level, demographic and psychological factors predict participation in training and development. With respect to demographic factors, employees who receive more training and development are younger, may be more educated, and are usually judged to be less likely to leave the organization (Loewenstein and Spletzer, 1997; Tharenou, 1997). There continues to be a substantial interest in how to increase older workers' lower motivation to learn and participation in formal and voluntary training and development (Sonnentag et al., 2004). Gender is not consistently linked to participation in training. Women may participate in less training and development than men (Royalty, 1996) but at times there are no gender differences when other factors are controlled (Keaveny and Inderrieden, 1998; Royalty, 1996; Wooden and VandenHeuvel, 1997). With respect to psychological factors, those who receive more training and development are more motivated to learn than others (Colquitt et al., 2000). A learning and development orientation is the tendency toward involvement in continuous learning (Maurer, 2002).

Overall, the individual factors leading to gaining training support a selection explanation (Green, 1993), especially according to the returns the organization will gain from developing human capital (Becker, 1962, 1975). Employers select workers who they know will provide the most benefits and return from training through (a) being high in ability and thus able to be trained; (b) having a high probability of remaining with the firm or being younger, thus providing a greater opportunity to recoup the investment in training than for others; and (c) being highly motivated to learn, which is likely to result in training being successful.

Antecedent conditions to successful training and development

Antecedent conditions to training are what trainees bring to the training setting, the work environment factors that engage the trainee to learn and participate in the training, and how the training is prepared to maximize the learning experience (Salas and Canon-Bowers, 2001). What individuals bring to the training and the support they gain in the work situation have received increased interest and are important to whether training is effective or not (Noe, 1986; Noe and Colquitt, 2002).

Personal characteristics have become important in determining whether training will be effective. The evidence supports individuals being selected for training based on suitable psychological attributes for effective training. Employees who have high cognitive ability (a finding already known from the personnel selection literature) and motivation to learn are more effectively trained than others as measured by the declarative knowledge, affective reactions, skill acquisition, and self-efficacy they gain from training (Colquitt et al., 2000; Salgado et al., 2003; Sonnentag et al., 2004). Motivation to learn is the desire on the part of the trainee to learn the training material. Training effectiveness is also increased by other pre-training psychological attributes including a learning goal orientation – which is the desire to increase one's competence by developing new skills and mastery, in contrast to a performance goal orientation which is the desire to demonstrate one's competence and to be positively evaluated by others (Salas and Cannon-Bowers, 2001; Sonnentag et al., 2004).

The characteristics of the trainee's work situation are also important to training being effective. Working in a climate that enables the use of newly learned behaviors and skills from training (e.g., having adequate resources, opportunities to use skills, favorable consequences for using skills) and having supervisor and co-worker support for using new learning help facilitate and enhance learning and result in training being effective (Colquitt et al., 2000). How training is framed within the organization (e.g., through having a positive transfer climate, working in a learning organization) is particularly important for training to be effective, especially for certain kinds of training such as diversity training (Holiday et al., 2003).

An individual's motivation to learn is an important attribute that they bring to training that increases its effectiveness and mediates the impact of other facilitating factors (Colquitt et al., 2000; Ford and Noe, 1992). A motivation to learn arises from both individual and situational characteristics. Meta-analyses show that employees who are motivated to learn accord high value to training, lack anxiety, have an internal locus of control, have high achievement motivation, are conscientious, have high self-efficacy (i.e., believe that they can master the learning material and the training), are committed to their organizations, and plan their careers (Colquitt et al., 2000). Employees with high motivation to learn are also associated with having high supervisor and peer support and a positive work climate.

Individual and situational characteristics that occur prior to training are critical to enable transfer of what was learnt in training to the job. Psychological attributes are important for training to transfer (i.e., to result in behavior change on the job) as are work environment support and climate. Meta-analyses show that greater post-training transfer happens to those who, pre-training, accord high value to training, are motivated to learn, are conscientious, have high self-efficacy, are committed to their organizations, explore their careers, and plan their careers (Colquitt et al., 2000). Skill acquisition and postraining self-efficacy are also important antecedents of transfer. The situational characteristics that help learning transfer from the training situation to the job are a positive work climate, supervisor support, and peer support. Transfer of training predicts performance back on the job (Colquitt et al., 2000).

Designing training

Research on designing training has focused on the learning principles that need to be incorporated for training to be effective (Kraiger, 2003; Noe and Colquitt, 2002; Tannenbaum and Yukl, 1992). It has not examined how to design training to be a part of systems of HR practices (HPWS) or to meet or help implement the needs of the business strategy. There has been a major change to the design of training through the incorporation of principles gained from cognitive psychology on how people learn (Howell and Cooke, 1989; Kraiger, 2003; Tannenbaum and Yukl, 1992).

From the I/O psychology literature, training comprises a series of steps that design a plan of instruction based on well-supported learning principles (cf. Ford and Kraiger, 1995; Kraiger, 2003; Noe and Colquitt, 2002; Tannenbaum and Yukl, 1992). Following from the identification through training needs analysis of the knowledge, skills and attitudes (KSAs) or competencies required, the first step is to specify clear specific instructional objectives based on the KSAs and competencies. The second step is to design the training based on the instructional objectives in step one, which involves specifying a desired sequence of training activities and designing the presentation of the training content to incorporate learning principles and assist transfer. The third step is to select the training method, which may be on or off the job, to maximize learning. The fourth step is to ensure a learning environment that enhances the motivation to learn and optimizes learning through the outcomes that can be expected. The final step is to design measures of training effectiveness that are outcome-focused based on the instructional objectives set in step one.

The incorporation of well-supported learning principles validated over many years is important in the training design stage (Kraiger, 2003; Noe and Colquitt, 2002; Tannenbaum and Yukl, 1992). The principles focus on the training content and the trainee's involvement. The training content needs to be designed to be relevant, preferably having identical elements to the job in order for learning to be able transfer to the job; to have stimulus variability to enable it to be interesting; and to have appropriate task sequencing (e.g., from easy to difficult). The design needs to provide opportunities for practice and the best conditions to gain the benefits of practice, usually to use over learning and consideration of whether to use whole or part learning; to enable the mental conceptualization of training material prior to training; and to allow observation of demonstration of the knowledge, skills and attitudes to be learned. Learning principles are incorporated into the design to allow the trainee to learn actively, for example, by incorporating practice, by recalling information from memory, by applying principles to a task, and by using symbolic mental rehearsal (Tannenbaum and Yukl, 1992). Learning principles also include providing reinforcement, providing feedback or knowledge of results during and after practice, and enabling trainees to seek feedback and self-monitor their learning; and catering for differences in trainee aptitudes and prior knowledge.

A relatively new topic of interest is how much learner control or choice should be allowed in the design of training in e-learning environments (DeRouin et al., 2005a). A meta-analysis shows the impact of learner control is very small (Kraiger and Jerden, 2007); learner control benefits only *some* learners in *some* situations (DeRouin et al., 2005a) and improves only *certain* learning outcomes under *certain* conditions (Kraiger and Jerden, 2007). Trainees do not make good instructional use of the control they are given, which may be assisted by adaptive guidance – that is by some form of advisement (Bell and Kozlowski, 2002). Learner control in e-learning situations was more effective for procedural learning (how to do things) than declarative learning (facts about what to do) and retention; for gaining skill-based outcomes than cognitive outcomes; for work than educational tasks; and over training's pace and navigation more than content (Kraiger and Jerden, 2007).

Research interest has developed in whether the wrong people might be trainers. If unskilled or untrained people conduct training, it likely will affect whether the training is properly designed according to training principles and whether it is properly delivered. Problems arise when using untrained or informal or accidental trainers, including line managers and peers, and when incorporating unwilling mentors and coaches into on-the-job training programs (Heslin et al., 2006). This is in contrast to the effectiveness of training gained through using trained trainers or expert trainers overseen by the HR function (Bartlett, 2003). There is also considerable research interest in the problems that occur through the outsourcing of training and development, in which trust and contractual specificity have become major issues (e.g., Gainey and Klaas, 2003).

The delivery of training

Research has focused on how to deliver training as a separate practice rather than on how to deliver it as part of HPWS or to meet the needs or strategy of the business. There has been little research on the change management principles that are needed to successfully implement well-designed training that can transfer to the job and provide positive outcomes, despite the lack of use by practitioners of scientifically-established principles of training design and delivery.

The delivery of training has traditionally focused on the trainee's learning style, the way the training is delivered, and the methods used for training (Tannenbaum and Yukl, 1992), and to a lesser extent on particular populations to be trained or the specific training content. Individuals have different learning styles that may need to be catered for in the design and delivery of training. The original Kolb (1984) framework presented the four learning styles of diverging, assimilating, converging, and accommodating. Efforts continue to develop learning style questionnaires to assess the several models of trainees' styles that exist with debate continuing about their validity and psychometric properties (Sonnentag et al., 2004).

With respect to the way training is delivered, the experiential learning cycle (Kolb, 1984) is the most well-known model trainers use. The process for delivering training comprises the five stages of trainees experiencing concrete events (concrete experience), reflecting on those experiences from different perspectives (reflective observation), generalizing from those reflections by constructing theories which integrate observations (abstract conceptualization) and planning by actively using theories to make decisions and solve problems (active experimentation). Concrete experience can occur off the job as experiential learning activities or on the job through the beneficial effects of having developmental jobs and challenging job situations (Sonnentag et al., 2004).

With respect to the methods used, training is conducted by a range of standard methods whose validity has been well established (Burke and Day, 1986). They include lectures (surprisingly an effective training method), lectures and group discussion, role plays, behavioral role modeling, simulations and business games, and computer-assisted learning/high technology methods. Research continues to support the validity of these traditional methods of delivery (Callahan et al., 2003).

With respect to specific methods, behavior modeling training (observing a model displaying the behavior to be learned, the trainee then practicing the behavior, and then gaining feedback to adjust behavior) continues to be an effective method. However, there are qualifications. Meta-analysis shows that behavior modeling training improves learning the most (declarative and procedural knowledge-skills) and well; improves job behavior less; and improves results outcomes less still and in a very small way (Taylor et al., 2005). Although effects on declarative knowledge (knowledge about facts) decayed over time, training effects on procedural skills (how to do things) and job behavior remained stable or increased, supporting the utility of behavior modeling training for improving skills and job behavior. Transfer of training to job behavior was greatest when conditions linked to transfer were included in the training: when trainees generated practice scenarios, trainees were instructed to set goals, trainees' managers were also trained, and rewards and sanctions were instituted in trainees' work environments for using the new skills (Taylor et al., 2005).

Simulation-based training and games continue to be shown to work well as training methods, especially for the situations encountered in the military and aviation which need to train complex skills that will transfer to the job (Salas and Cannon-Bowers, 2001).

Substantial research also occurs into newer methods of delivering training. They include new forms of team training, error training,

and 'e-learning.' Team training has had a long history, starting from team-building as an organizational development intervention. Major advances have been made through developing other forms of team training (Tannenbaum and Yukl, 1992). Team training is where members of work teams as a group acquire the knowledge and skills and practice behaviors that are needed to work together. Transactive memory appears to underlie the success of some of these new forms of team training (Sonnentag et al., 2004). Transactive memory is a group memory system that details the expertise possessed by group members along with an awareness of who knows what within the group. For example, cross-training (e.g., positional rotation) aims to develop shared mental models among team members and teaches each team member the roles and responsibilities of the others. It has positive effects on team performance (Marks et al., 2002; Sonnentag et al., 2004).

Other forms of team training also give positive results, including team coordination training, team leadership training, team self-correction, and distributed team training (Kraiger, 2003; Salas and Cannon-Bowers, 2001). Crew resource management training is a form of team coordination training designed to prevent errors in the cockpit. It generally produces positive trainee reactions, but has mixed results for effects on learning and behavior change and an unknown impact on organizational results such as safety (Salas et al., 2006). Team training is also being applied to virtual teams who operate using computer-based technology from geographically dispersed locations (Soderlund and Bredin, 2006). Team training is effective if focused on the required team competencies and designed to give trainees realistic opportunities to practice and to gain feedback (Salas and Cannon-Bowers, 2001).

Error training has become a significant new type of active learner training which demonstrates the beneficial effects of trainees making errors during learning (Joung et al., 2006) rather than only being trained in correct methods. Error training stresses trainees' roles as active participants in the learning process

(Sonnentag et al., 2004). Error and stress exposure training result in less stress and improved performance (Salas and Cannon-Bowers, 2001). Meta-analysis showed that error management training has positive effects (over training methods without errors) which are larger for post-training transfer than within-training performance and for structurally distinct performance tasks than for tasks similar to the training (Keith and Frese, 2007). Both active exploration and error encouragement are effective elements.

The most prolific research interest into the newer methods of training has been in the relatively recent 'e-learning', in order to solve the problem of how to make e-learning as effective as face-to-face training (DeRouin et al., 2005b). E-learning is the learning of knowledge, skills and attitudes through web- and computer-based learning technologies or virtual classrooms and digital collaboration. Meta-analysis found that web-based instruction (WBI) was slightly more effective than classroom instruction (CI) for teaching declarative knowledge; the two delivery media were equally effective for teaching procedural knowledge; and trainees were equally satisfied with web-based instruction and classroom instruction (Sitzmann et al., 2006). However, web-based instruction and classroom instruction were equally effective for teaching declarative knowledge when the same instructional methods were used in both, suggesting WBI is not more effective than CI. WBI was more effective than CI for teaching declarative knowledge when trainees were provided with control, practiced the training material and received feedback during training, and were in long courses.

Compared to research on the methods of delivery of training, there has been less focus on training particular populations/types and kinds of content. Of ongoing interest is how to train managers in the competencies they need (Hernez-Broome and Hughes, 2004). Charismatic leadership in managers can be developed through training (Frese et al., 2003); diversity training is given to managers (i.e., to reduce employment discrimination, to support a diverse workforce, to be more receptive to diversity) (e.g., De Meuse *et al.*, 2007; Sanchez and Medkik, 2004); and training in cross-cultural competencies facilitates managers' success on international assignments (Littrell et al., 2006). Meta-analysis supports the effectiveness of management development (Burke and Day, 1986) and managerial leadership development programs increase managers' knowledge strongly, improve their job behavior/expertise but less, and increase systems results/performance outcomes less so, though moderately (Collins and Holton, 2004). Cross-cultural training of expatriate managers increases their performance and adjustment (e.g., Black and Mendenhall, 1990; Morris and Robie, 2001).

Training is effective for older employees, as shown by meta-analysis. Results continue to find that older adults are able to learn new skills but that they show less mastery of training material and take longer to complete training tasks and programs than younger adults (Kubeck et al., 1996). The three instructional methods of lectures, role modeling, and active participation and the two instructional factors of self-pacing and smaller group size are effective for older learners, resulting in high training performance, especially when older employees can self-pace (Callahan et al., 2003).

Transfer of training to the job

Of the stages of training, transfer had been of relatively late interest (Baldwin and Ford, 1988), although the science and theory of how to transfer training to the job are now well developed (Burke and Hutchins, 2007; Ford and Weissbein, 1997). Transfer of training is the extent to which trainees effectively apply the knowledge, skills, behaviors and attitudes gained in training to their jobs (Tannenbaum and Yukl, 1992). It is the evaluation of whether anticipated gains in knowledge, skills and affect from training have been achieved and whether the changes are then applied to the job to generalize skills and retain long-term skills on the job (Ford and Kraiger, 1995). Without transfer, the benefits of training to behavioral change on the job cannot be realized, and, ultimately, the possible improvement in organizational results.

The primary factors influencing transfer are well-established. Particular learner characteristics increase transfer (cognitive ability, self-efficacy, pretraining motivation, anxiety/negative affectivity, openness to experience, perceived utility, career planning, organizational commitment). Particular kinds of intervention design and delivery increase transfer (learning goals, content relevance, practice and feedback, behavioral modeling, error-based examples), although less evidence is available in this category. Recently examined work environment influences are shown to increase transfer (transfer climate, supervisor support, peer support, opportunity to perform) (Burke and Hutchins, 2007).

Transfer arises especially from what occurs before and after training, and not just during training (Saks and Belcourt, 2006), requiring substantial efforts from supervisors to enable transfer to occur. Before training, transfer is affected by what employees bring to the training; transfer especially increases if trainees have high motivation to learn, a high capacity to transfer, and a supportive work environment for applying learning (Colquitt et al., 2000; Noe, 1986). Transfer is also enhanced by how the training has been designed – if the content is relevant to the job and if training corresponds to what is done on the job (i.e., fidelity), transfer increases. During training, successful transfer is determined by how the training is delivered; for example, by enabling practice and over learning to firmly develop principles and skills and by setting goals during training to achieve back on the job.

After training, transfer is increased when the immediate supervisor provides support and encouragement for trainees to apply on the job what they learnt in the training; when peers provide support for the use of the training; when needed resources are provided; and when trainees return to a work climate that helps transfer rather than provides barriers or constraints to block transfer (Colquitt

et al., 2000; Sonnentag et al., 2004). After training, transfer also occurs when trainees are provided with the opportunity to perform what was learnt during the training and by having a short-time interval between the training and the opportunity to use the learning (Ford and Weissbein, 1997; Sonnentag et al., 2004). Research continues into the development of instruments to measure the extent to which a transfer climate exists in an organization (Holton and Elwood, 1997), demonstrating similar cross-country elements of a positive climate, job utility, and provision of rewards (Holton et al., 2000).

Specific strategies such as relapse prevention (training in self-management to prevent slips back into pre-training behaviors) and goal-setting have been investigated to determine if they assist the transfer of training to the job, though the results for their effectiveness are conflicting and managers are not necessarily keen to apply them to help transfer (Hunt and Saks, 2003; Hutchins and Burke, 2006).

It is not known if vertical transfer of training occurs where individuals' learning outcomes and behavior change translates into organizational results (Salas and Cannon-Bowers, 2001). Research is also lacking on whether training introduced as part of a system of HR practices transfers more to the job than when training is conducted as a single practice. Training might transfer more to the job when it is delivered as part of HPWS, when major workplace interventions are being introduced for which it is needed (e.g., total quality management, lean production, business process re-engineering, teamwork), or when it is implemented to meet organizational objectives and business strategy, than when training is introduced as a standalone practice.

Evaluating the effects of training

Interest in the evaluation of training has substantially increased (Alvarez et al., 2004; Collins, 2002). Within organizations, training evaluation is the systematic collection of descriptive and judgmental information necessary to make effective training decisions related to the selection, adoption, value and modification of various training activities (Goldstein, 1980). It is a set of procedures designed to systematically collect valid descriptive and judgmental information about the ways in which a planned change effort has altered or failed to alter organizational processes (Wexley, 1984). Two major areas are the focus of interest: how should training be evaluated (i.e., the validity of any model of outcomes proposed) and does training have positive outcomes or effects.

There has been continued controversy about how training should be evaluated – what criteria should be used and which underlying model or theory of evaluation is valid (Alliger and Janak, 1989; Alliger et al., 1997). Kirkpatrick's four-level model (1959, 1976) is the most used. In the model, training leads to trainee reactions (i.e., how well trainees like the training), which leads to trainee learning (i.e., what knowledge or skills were learnt), which then leads to trainee behavior on the job (i.e., what were the changes in job behavior), which then leads to organization results (i.e., what were the organizational results from training). Phillips (1996a, b) suggests that organizational results from training should then lead to greater financial returns for the organization, an approach consistent with the perspective used in strategic HRM (Becker and Huselid, 2006).

Evidence from meta-analyses has not supported Kirkpatrick's model, especially trainee reactions being related to trainee learning (Alliger et al., 1997; Colquitt et al., 2000). Trainees' reactions were related only in a small way to learning measured as declarative knowledge and skill acquisition (Colquitt et al., 2000). Utility-type reaction measures, assessing trainees' views of training's usefulness for and applicability to job performance, were more strongly related to learning and on-the-job performance (i.e., transfer) than were affective-type reaction measures (Alliger et al., 1997). Utility-type reaction measures were stronger correlates of transfer (on-the-job performance) than were measures

of immediate or retained learning. Hence, if trainees' reactions are to be used to measure the effectiveness of training, they should be of its utility and not of liking for it. Learning was moderately related to behavior change (i.e., transfer) which, in turn, was related to results, which were measured, however, as individuals' job performance (Colquitt et al., 2000) not as organizational results. Thus, conclusions could not be drawn about the validity of the final sequence proposed in Kirkpatrick's (1959, 1976) model.

In sum, too few studies have examined the causal sequence in Kirkpatrick's (1959; 1976) model to draw strong conclusions, especially whether training's effects on behavior change lead to effects on organizational results. Hence, a supported model for evaluating training and development is still not available. New models continue to be developed (e.g., Alvarez et al., 2004; Holton, 1996). But, valid, less expensive, simpler, and more user-friendly designs have been developed to evaluate the effects of training (Arvey et al., 1996). For example, studies show that the internal referencing strategy, in which effect sizes for trained outcomes are compared to effect sizes for non-trained outcomes, provides a research design for evaluation that does not require control groups (e.g., Frese et al., 2003).

By contrast, the second major area of interest with respect to the evaluation of training has clear results. Training works. Traditionally, training has been evaluated at the level of the individual where there are clear positive effects. Meta-analyses and qualitative reviews show that training improves employees' learning (knowledge, skills, attitudes) and behavior back on the job (job performance, output, quality of work) (Aguinis and Kraiger, 2009; Arthur et al., 2003; Burke and Day, 1986; Collins and Holton, 2004; Guzzo et al., 1985; Katzell and Guzzo, 1983). Meta-analyses show that training has a medium to large effect and that its effects on trainees' learning and behavior are stronger than on results (Arthur et al., 2003; Collins and Holton, 2004), which were mostly measured at the individual and not the organizational level. In addition, the training method used, the skill or task characteristic trained, and the choice of evaluation criteria are related to the effectiveness of training programs (Arthur et al., 2003; Burke and Day, 1986; Collins and Holton, 2004).

Most studies have shown immediate effects of training. The small number that have investigated long-term effects have given positive results (Sonnentag et al., 2004). Training also improves employees' organizational attitudes and not only their immediate reactions at the end of the program; for example, training improves employees' commitment to the organization (Bartlett, 2001).

Interest has recently arisen in determining whether training improves organizational effectiveness (Aguinis and Kraiger, 2009; Tharenou, 2006; Tharenou et al., 2007). Some scholars believe that training should improve organizational performance (Martocchio and Baldwin, 1997), whereas others emphasize that training should only have behavioral effects on the individual (Barrie and Pace, 1997). There have been attempts to estimate the ROI from formal company training (Bartel, 2000). The main conclusion drawn was that the ROI of employee training might be higher than previously believed, perhaps in the range of 100–200 per cent (Bartel, 2000), but it was based on very few studies which measured individual-level outcomes.

By contrast, meta-analysis has shown that organizations that train more have greater organizational performance (including productivity and quality) and more positive collective HR outcomes (including satisfaction, skills and competencies, and retention) – although the effect sizes for objective output measures were small. However, organizations that trained more did not have greater objectively measured financial performance (Tharenou et al., 2007). Longitudinal, multivariate, highly controlled studies showed consistently that training improved objectively-measured organizational performance. Hence, training improves organizational performance and HR outcomes and, unsurprisingly for a distal variable, not the bottom line. Training was more related

to objectively-measured organizational effectiveness when used in conjunction with business direction and strategy than when not (Tharenou, 2006; Tharenou et al., 2007). Training was more strongly related to organizational outcomes when matched with key contextual factors of organizational capital intensity and business strategy – in support of a contingency perspective that, when training is matched with business needs, performance improves. Training more often was related independently to organizational outcomes in support of a universalistic perspective and did not need to be part of a system of HR practices. Only a minority of studies showed support for a configurational perspective, in which, when training was part of HPWS, organizational performance was higher than when training was used an independent practice. There was also support from longitudinal studies that organizations with poorer performance subsequently trained their employees more, resulting in increased performance (Tharenou, 2006; Tharenou et al., 2007). The meta-analysis showed much stronger effects of training on subjectively measured outcomes measures, especially when financial performance was subjectively measured, but these effects appeared inflated.

By contrast, the results of a meta-analysis suggested that systems of high performance work practices have stronger positive effects on organizational performance than individual practices do, including training, which still had a positive effect when used independently (Combs et al., 2006). Research needs to examine when training should be used as a separate practice, when it should follow from business strategy, or when it may be best used as part of HPWS and organizational change efforts. In sum, despite the spate of results, more research is needed to determine how training improves organizational performance.

THE FUTURE

Although there has been dramatic progress in the development of the science and practice of training, issues need resolution. Many of the valid ways found for conducting training and the principles found to enhance transfer to the job are not applied by practitioners or endorsed by management (Kraiger, 2003; Salas and Cannon-Bowers, 2001). There are negative attitudes to what are seen as complex, expensive, and effortful processes to design, deliver and implement training, including the more recent cognitive principles and methods (Hesketh, 1997). Research needs to examine how to change managers' and practitioners' attitudes in order to implement what research has found for designing and delivering effective training and transferring it to the job and organization (cf. Hunt and Saks, 2003). The use of strong change management and organizational development principles facilitate the successful implementation of training (Wong et al., 1997) and of training needs analysis (Reed and Yakola, 2006). The implementation of training using the science of training needs to be addressed as a change management process and as part of organizational development strategies. Moreover, training is only one of many methods for increasing organizational performance (Wright and Geroy, 2001) and research needs to more effectively consider training in interaction with other workplaces practices to understand its effects.

A second issue is the separate training literatures that exist in the disciplines of strategic HRM, I/O psychology, labor economics, and industrial relations. For example, the literatures on training in HRM and I/O psychology remain separate. The training practice that forms part of high performance work systems seems remarkably simple and unspecified compared to the complex training design principles and methods found from I/O psychology. There needs to be a marrying together of the principles underlying the strategic HR approach to training and the conditions found in I/O psychology for effective training to occur. Moreover, for training to increase organizational effectiveness, training needs to be effectively designed and delivered and transfer to the job (I/O psychology), be of strategic importance to the organization (strategic HRM), operate in

organizations whose structures and processes enable training to occur (labor economics), and capitalize on the cooperation of the workforce (industrial relations).

More broadly, despite the different interests of HRM (the management perspective), labor economics (the societal perspective), and industrial relations (the employee perspective), all three use an organizational-level lens whereas I/O psychology uses an individual- or team-level lens. A multi-level approach is needed to bridge these traditions. Organizational-level (macro), team-level (meso), and individual-level (micro) training research, models, and theory need to be integrated. For example, training is known to improve an individual's skills, knowledge, and job performance and to improve organizational productivity. But it is not known if the improvement at individual level translates vertically to an improvement at organizational level, or, if it does, how it may do so; for example does it do so through effects at the work unit-level (Kozlowski et al., 2000). Research needs to integrate the individual, work-unit/team, and organizational levels and investigate how individual performance and transfer lead to improved organizational effectiveness (Chen and Klimoski, 2007; Tharenou et al., 2007).

In conclusion, research into training and development in organizations is thriving, underpinned by the approaches developed from strategic human resource management, industry/organizational psychology, labor economics, and industrial relations. Research on training has extended its interest from training models and the steps involved in training of training needs analysis, design, and delivery to the activities conducted pre-training – especially the psychological processes and environmental factors that lead to participation in training and that enable successful transfer of training to the work environment – and post-training – especially the factors that lead to transfer of what is learnt in training to the job and the evaluation of training's effects on organizational effectiveness.

REFERENCES

Aguinis, H. and Kraiger, K. (2009) 'Benefits of training and development for individuals and teams, organizations and society', *Annual Review of Psychology*, 60: 451–74.

Agut, S. and Grau, R. (2002) 'Managerial competency needs and training requests', *Human Resource Development Quarterly*, 13: 31–51.

Alliger, G.M. and Janak, E.A. (1989) 'Kirkpatrick's level of training criteria', *Personnel Psychology*, 42: 583–96.

Alliger, G., Tannenbaum, S., Bennett, W., Traver, H. and Shotland, A. (1997) 'A meta-analysis of the relations among training criteria', *Personnel Psychology*, 50: 341–58.

Alvarez, K., Salas, E. and Garofano, C.M. (2004) 'An integrated model of training evaluation and effectiveness', *Human Resource Development Review*, 3: 385–416.

Arthur, W., Bennett, W., Edens, P. and Bell, S. (2003) 'Effectiveness of training in organizations', *Journal of Applied Psychology*, 88: 234–45.

Arulampalam, W. and Booth, A. (1998) 'Training and labour market flexibility: Is there a trade-off?', *British Journal of Industrial Relations*, 36: 521–36.

Arvey, R., Hyuckseung, Y. and Sackett, P. (1996) 'Statistical power and cost in training evaluation', *Personnel Psychology*, 49: 651–68.

Baldwin, T.T. and Ford, K.J. (1988) 'Transfer of training', *Personnel Psychology*, 41: 63–106.

Balkin, D.B. and Richebé, N. (2007) 'A gift exchange perspective on organizational training', *Human Resource Management Review*, 17: 52–62.

Barnard, M.E. and Rodgers, R.A. (2000) 'How are internally oriented HRM policies related to high-performance work practices? Evidence from Singapore', *International Journal of Human Resource Management*, 11: 1017–46.

Barney, J.B. (1991) 'Firm resources and sustained competitive advantage', *Journal of Management*, 17: 99–120.

Barney, J.B. and Wright, P.M. (1998) 'On becoming a strategic partner', *Human Resource Management*, 37: 31–46.

Barrie, J. and Pace, W. (1997) 'Competence, efficiency, and organizational learning', *Human Resource Development Quarterly*, 8: 335–42.

Bartel, A.P. (2000) 'Measuring the employer's return on investments in training: Evidence from the literature', *Industrial Relations*, 39: 502–24.

Bartlett, K.R. (2001) 'The relationship between training and organizational commitment', *Human Resource Development Quarterly*, 12: 335–52.

Bartlett, K.R. (2003) 'Accidental trainers versus HRD professionals', *Human Resource Development Quarterly*, 14: 231.

Becker, G.S. (1962) 'Investment in human capital: A theoretical analysis', *Journal of Political Economy*, 70 (5, pt. 2): 9–50.

Becker, G.S. (1975) *Human capital theory*. Chicago: University of Chicago Press.

Becker, B.E. and Huselid, M.A. (1998) 'High performance work systems and firm performance', *Research in Personnel and Human Resources Management*, 16: 53–101.

Becker, B.E. and Huselid, M.A. (2006) 'Strategic human resource management', *Journal of Management*, 32: 898–925.

Bell, B. and Kozlowski, S. (2002) 'Adaptive guidance', *Personnel Psychology*, 57: 267–306.

Black, J.S. and Mendenhall, M.E. (1990) 'Cross-cultural training effectiveness', *Academy of Management Review*, 16: 291–317.

Blau, P.M. (1964) *Exchange and Power In Social Life*. New York: Wiley.

Boheim, R. and Booth, A. (2004) 'Trade union presence and employer-provided training in Great Britain', *Industrial Relations*, 43: 520–45.

Bowers, C., Jentsch, F., Salas, E. and Braun, C. (1998) 'Analyzing communication sequences for team training needs assessment', *Human Factors*, 40: 672.

Broom, J., Coleman, J., Davin, D., Farr, P., Fay, J., O'Brien, T., Webster, A. and Wilensky, R. (1998) 'HRPS educational programming', *Human Resource Planning*, 21: 6–9.

Bunch, K. (2007) 'Training failure as a consequence of organizational culture', *Human Resource Development Review*, 6: 142–63.

Burke, L. and Hutchins, H. (2007) 'Training transfer: An integrative literature review', *Human Resource Development Review*, 6: 263–96.

Burke, M.J. and Day, R.R. (1986) 'A cumulative study of the effectiveness of managerial training', *Journal of Applied Psychology*, 71: 232–45.

Callahan, J., Kiker, D. and Cross, T. (2003) 'Does method matter?', *Journal of Management*, 29: 663–80.

Chen, G. and Klimoski, R.J. (2007) 'Training and development of human resources at work', *Human Resource Management Review*, 17: 180–90.

Clarke, N. (2003) 'The politics of training needs analysis', *Journal of Workplace Learning*, 15: 141–53.

Colakoglu, S., Lepak, D.P. and Hong, Y. (2006) 'Measuring HRM effectiveness', *Human Resource Management Review*, 16: 209–18.

Collins, D.B. and Holton, E.F. (2004) 'The effectiveness of managerial leadership development programs', *Human Resource Development Quarterly*, 15: 217–48.

Collins, D.B. (2002) 'Performance-level evaluation methods used in management development studies from 1986–2000', *Human Resource Development Review*, 1: 91–110.

Colquitt, J., Le Pine, J. and Noe, R. (2000) 'Toward an integrative theory of training motivation', *Journal of Applied Psychology*, 85: 678–707.

Combs, J., Liu, Y., Hall, A. and Ketchen, D. (2006) 'How much do high-performance work practices matter?', *Personnel Psychology*, 59: 501–28.

De Meuse, K.P., Hostager, T.J. and O'Neill, K.S. (2007) 'A longitudinal evaluation of senior managers' perceptions and attitudes of a workplace diversity training program', *Human Resource Planning*, 30 (2): 38–46.

DeRouin, R., Fritzsche, B. and Salas, E. (2005a) 'Learner control and workplace e-learning', *Research in Personnel and Resources Management*, 24: 181–214.

DeRouin, R., Fritzsche, B. and Salas, E. (2005b) 'E-learning in organizations', *Journal of Management*, 31: 920–40.

Evans, W.R. and Davis, W.D. (2005) 'High-performance work systems and organizational performance', *Journal of Management*, 31: 758–75.

Ford, J.K. and Kraiger, K. (1995) 'The application of cognitive constructs and principles to the instructional systems model of training', in C.L. Cooper and I.T. Robinson (eds), *International Review of Industrial and Organizational Psychology*. New York: Wiley, pp. 1–48.

Ford, J.K. and Noe, R.M. (1992) 'Emerging issues and new directions for training research', *Research in Personnel and Human Resources Management*, 10: 345–84.

Ford, J.K. and Weissbein, D.A. (1997) 'Transfer of training: An updated review and analysis', *Performance Improvement Quarterly*, 10 (2): 22–41.

Frese, M., Beimel, S. and Schoenborn, S. (2003) 'Action training for charismatic leadership', *Personnel Psychology*, 56: 671–98.

Gainey, T. and Klaas, B. (2003) 'The outsourcing of training and development: factors impacting client satisfaction', *Journal of Management*, 29: 207–29.

Gangani, N., McLean, G. and Braden, R. (2006) 'A competency based human resource development strategy', *Performance Improvement Quarterly*, 19: 127–40.

Goldstein, I. L. (1980) 'Training in work organizations', *Annual Review of Psychology*, 31: 229–72.

Goldstein, I.L. and Gessner, M.J. (1988) 'Training and development in work organizations', in C.L. Cooper and I. Robertson (eds), *International Review of Industrial and Organizational Psychology*. New York: Wiley, pp. 43–72.

Green, F. (1993) 'The determinants of training of male and female employees in Britain', *Oxford Bulletin of Economics and Statistics*, 55: 103–23.

Green, F., Hoskins, M. and Montgomery, S. (1996) 'The effects of company training, further education and the youth training scheme on the earnings of young employees', *Oxford Bulletin of Economics and Statistics*, 58: 469–88.

Greenberg, D.H., Michalopoulos, C. and Robins, P.K. (2003) 'A meta-analysis of government-sponsored training programs', *Industrial and Labor Relations Review*, 57 (1): 31–53.

Greenberg, D.H., Michalopoulos, C. and Robins, P.K. (2004) 'What happens to the effects of government funded training programs over time?', *Journal of Human Resources*, 39: 277–93.

Guzzo, R.A., Jette, R.D. and Katzell, R.A. (1985) 'The effects of psychologically based intervention programs on worker productivity', *Personnel Psychology*, 38: 275–92.

Haccoun, R.R. and Saks, A.M. (1998) 'Training in the 21st Century: Some lessons from the last one', *Canadian Psychology*, 39 (1–2): 33–51.

Hernez-Broome, G. and Hughes, R. (2004) 'Leadership development: past, present and future', *Human Resource Planning*, 27: 24–32.

Hesketh, B. (1997) 'W(h)ither dilemmas in training for transfer', *Applied Psychology: An International Review*, 46: 380–86.

Heslin, A., Vandewalle, D.and Latham, P. (2006) 'Keen to help?', *Personnel Psychology*, 59: 871–902.

Heyes, J. and Stuart, M. (1998) 'Bargaining for skills: Trade unions and training at the workplace', *British Journal of Industrial Relations*, 36: 459–67.

Holiday, C., Knight, J., Paige, D. and Quinones, M. (2003) 'The influence of framing on attitudes towards diversity training', *Human Resource Development Quarterly*, 14: 245.

Holton, E.F. (1996) 'The flawed four-level evaluation model', *Human Resource Development Quarterly*, 7: 5–21.

Holton, I. and Elwood, F. (1997) 'Toward construct validation of a transfer climate instrument', *Human Resource Development Quarterly*, 8: 95–113.

Holton, I., Elwood, E., Bates, R. and Ruona, W. (2000) 'Development of a generalized learning transfer system inventory', *Human Resource Development Quarterly*, 11: 333–60.

Howell, W.C. and Cooke, N.J. (1989) 'Training the human information processor', in L.L. Goldstein (ed.), *Training and Development in Organizations* (pp. 121–82). San Francisco: Jossey-Bass.

Hunt, P. and Saks, A. (2003) 'Translating training science into practice', *Human Resource Development Quarterly*, 14: 181–98.

Hutchins, H.M. and Burke, L.A. (2006) 'Has relapse prevention received a fair shake?', *Human Resource Development Review*, 5: 8–24.

Jones, M.K., Latreille, P.L. and Sloane, P.J. (2008) 'Crossing the tracks?', *British Journal of Industrial Relations*, 46: 268–82.

Joung, W., Hesketh, B. and Neal, A. (2006) 'Using "war stories" to train for adaptive performance', *Applied Psychology: An International Review*, 55: 282–302.

Katzell, R.A. and Guzzo, R.A. (1983) 'Psychological approaches to productivity improvement', *American Psychologist*, 38: 468–72.

Keaveny, T. and Inderrieden, E. (1998) 'Gender differences in employer-supported training and education', *Journal of Vocational Behavior*, 54: 71–81.

Keith, N. and Frese, M. (2007) 'Effectiveness of error management training: A meta-analysis', *Journal of Applied Psychology*, 93: 59–69.

Kirkpatrick, D.L. (1959) 'Techniques for evaluating training programs', *Journal of ASTD*, 13: 3–9.

Kirkpatrick, D.L. (1976) 'Evaluation of training', in R.L. Craig (ed.), *Training and Development Handbook*. New York: McGraw-Hill, pp. 301–19.

Kolb, D.A. (1984) *Experiential Learning*. Englewood Cliffs, NJ: Prentice-Hall.

Kozlowski, S.W.J., Brown, K.G., Weissbein, D.A., Cannon-Bowers, J.A. and Salas, E. (2000) 'A multi-level perspective on training effectiveness', in K.J. Klein and S.W.J. Kozlowski (eds), *Multilevel Theory, Research, and Methods in Organizations*. San Francisco: Jossey-Bass, pp. 157–210.

Kraiger, K. (2003) 'Perspectives on training and development', in W.C. Borman, D. Ilgen, and R. Klimoski (eds), *Handbook of Psychology*. Hoboken, NJ: John Wiley and Sons, pp. 171–92.

Kraiger, K. and Jerden, E. (2007) 'A new look at learner control: Meta-analytic results and directions for future research, in S.M. Fiore and E. Salas (eds), *Where is the learning in distance learning? Towards a Science of Distributed Learning and Training*. Washington, DC: APA Books, pp. 65–90.

Kraiger, K., McLinden, D. and Casper, W. (2004) 'Collaborative planning for training impact', *Human Resource Management*, 43: 337–51.

Kubeck, J.E., Delp, N.D., Haslett, T.K. and McDaniel, M.A. (1996) 'Does job-related training performance decline with age?', *Psychology and Aging*, 11: 92–107.

Latham, G.P. (1988) 'Human resource training and development', *Annual Review of Psychology*, 39: 545–82.

Leiba-O'Sullivan, S. (1999) 'The distinction between stable and dynamic cross-cultural competencies', *Journal of International Business Studies*, 30: 709–26.

Leigh, D. and Gifford, K. (1999) 'Workplace transformation and worker up-skilling: The perspective of individual workers', *Industrial Relations*, 38: 174–91.

Lepak, D., Liao, H., Chung, Y. and Harden, E. (2006) 'A conceptual review of human resource management systems in strategic human resource management research', *Research in Personnel and Human Resources Management*, 25: 217–71.

Lepak, D.P. and Snell, S.A. (1999) 'The human resource architecture', *Academy of Management Review*, 24: 31–48.

Littrell, L.N., Salas, E., Hess, K.P., Paley, M. and Riedel, S. (2006) 'Expatriate preparation', *Human Resource Development Review*, 5: 355–88.

Loewenstein, M.A. and Spletzer, J.R. (1997) 'Delayed formal on-the-job-training', *Industrial and Labor Relations Review*, 51: 82–99.

Lynch, L.M. and Black, S.E. (1998) 'Beyond the incidence of employer-provided training', *Industrial and Labor Relations Review*, 52 (1): 64–81.

Marks, M., Sabella, M. Burke, S. and Zaccaro, S. (2002) 'The impact of cross-training on team effectiveness', *Journal of Applied Psychology*, 87: 3–13.

Martocchio, J.J. and Baldwin, T.T. (1997) 'The evolution of strategic organizational training', *Research in Personnel and Human Resources Management*, 15: 1–46.

Maurer, T.J. (2002) 'Employee learning and development orientation', *Human Resource Development Review*, 1: 9–44.

McGehee, W. and Thayer, P.W. (1961) *Training in Business and Industry*. New York: Wiley.

Montesino, M. (2002) 'Strategic alignment of training, transfer-enhancing behaviors, and training usage', *Human Resource Development Quarterly*, 13: 89–108.

Moore, M.C. and Dutton, P. (1978) 'Training needs analysis: Review and critique', *Academy of Management Review*, 3: 531–45.

Morris, M. and Robie, C. (2001) 'A meta-analysis of the effects of cross-cultural training on expatriate performance and adjustment', *International Journal of Training and Development*, 5 (2): 112–25.

Noe, R.A. (1986) 'Trainees' attributes and attitudes: Neglected influences on training effectiveness', *Academy of Management Review*, 11: 736–49.

Noe, R.A. and Colquitt, J.A. (2002) 'Planning for training impact', in K. Kraiger (ed.), *Creating, Implementing, and Maintaining Effective Training and Development*. San Francisco: Jossey-Bass, pp. 53–79.

THE SAGE HANDBOOK OF HUMAN RESOURCE MANAGEMENT

Phillips, J.J. (1996a) 'ROI', *Training and Development*, 50 (2): 42–47.

Phillips, J.J. (1996b) 'Was it the training?' *Training and Development*, 50 (3): 28–32.

Phillips, J.J and Phillips, P. (2007) 'Measuring return on investment in leadership development', in K. Hannum, J. Martineau, and C. Reinelt (eds), *The Handbook of Leadership Development*. San Francisco: Jossey-Bass, pp. 137–66.

Reed, J. and Yakola, M. (2006) 'What role can a training needs analysis play in organizational change?', *Journal of Organizational Change Management*, 19: 393–407.

Roberson, L., Kulik, C. and Pepper, M. (2003) 'Using needs assessment to resolve controversies in diversity training design', *Group and Organization Management*, 28: 148–74.

Royalty, A.B. (1996) 'The effects of job turnover on the training of men and women', *Industrial and Labor Relations Review*, 49: 506–21.

Saks, A. and Belcourt, M. (2006) 'An investigation of training activities and transfer of training in organizations', *Human Resource Management*, 45: 629–48.

Salas, E. and Cannon-Bowers, J.A. (2001) 'The science of training: A decade of progress', *Annual Review of Psychology*, 52: 471–99.

Salas, E. and Kosarzycki, M. (2003) 'Why don't organizations pay attention to (and use) findings from the science of training', *Human Resource Development Quarterly*, 14: 487–91.

Salas, E., Wilson, K., Burke, C. and Wightman, D. (2006) 'Does crew resource management training work?', *Human Factors*, 48: 392–23.

Salgado, J., Anderson, N., Moscoso, S., Bertua, C. and de Fruyt, F. (2003) 'International validity generalization of GMA and cognitive abilities: A European community meta-analysis', *Personnel Psychology*, 56: 573–605.

Sanchez, J. and Medkik, N. (2004) 'The effects of diversity awareness training on differential treatment', *Group and Organization Management*, 29: 517–36.

Sitzmann, T., Kraiger, K., Stewart, D. and Wisher, R. (2006) 'The comparative effectiveness of web based and classroom based instruction: A meta-analysis', *Personnel Psychology*, 59: 623–64.

Snell, S., Lepak, D., Dean, J. and Youndt, M. (2000) 'Selection and training for integrated manufacturing', *Journal of Management Studies*, 37: 445–66.

Soderlund, J. and Bredin, K. (2006) 'Training for virtual teams: an investigation of current practices and future needs', *Human Resource Management*, 45: 229–47.

Sonnentag, S., Niessen, C. and Ohly, S. (2004) 'Learning at work: Training and development', in C.L. Cooper and I.T. Robertson (eds), *International Review of Industrial and Organizational Psychology*. New York: Wiley, pp. 249–89.

Sugrue, B. and Rivera, R.J. (2005) *State of the industry*. Alexandria, VA: ASTD.

Sugrue, B. and Rivera, R.J. (2006) *State of the Industry in Leading Enterprises*. Alexandria, VA: ASTD.

Takeuchi, R., Lepak, D.P., Wang, H. and Takuechi, K. (2007) 'An empirical examination of the mechanism mediating between high performance work systems and the performance of Japanese organizations', *Journal of Applied Psychology*, 92: 1069–83.

Tannenbaum, S.I. and Yukl, G. (1992) 'Training and development in work organizations', *Annual Review of Psychology*, 43: 399–41.

Taylor, P.J., Russ-Eft, D.E. and Chan, D.W.L. (2005) 'A meta-analytic review of behavior modeling training', *Journal of Applied Psychology*, 90: 692–709.

Tharenou, P. (1997) 'Determinants of participation in training and development', in C.L. Cooper and D.M. Rousseau (eds), *Trends in Organizational Behavior*. New York: John Wiley and Sons, pp. 15–28.

Tharenou, P. (2006) 'Do organizations get positive results from training?', in P. Holland and H. De Cieri (eds), *Contemporary Issues in Human Resource Development*. Melbourne: McGraw Hill, pp. 153–74.

Tharenou, P., Saks, A.M. and Moore, C. (2007) 'A review and critique of research on training and organizational-level outcomes', *Human Resource Management Review*, 17: 251–73.

Upward, R. (2002) 'Evaluating outcomes from the Youth Training Scheme using matched firm-trainee data', *Oxford Bulletin of Economics and Statistics*, 64: 277–306.

Walker, J. and Stopper, W. (2000) 'Developing human resource leaders', *Human Resource Planning*, 23: 38–44.

Wexley, K. (1984) 'Personnel training', *Annual Review of Psychology*, 35: 519–51.

Whitfield, K. (2000) 'High performance workplaces, training and the distribution of skills', *Industrial Relations*, 39: 1–25.

Wong, C., Marshall, J.N., Alderman, N. and Thwaites, A. (1997) 'Management training in small and medium-sized enterprises: Methodological and conceptual issues', *International Journal of Human Resource Management*, 8: 44–65.

Wooden, M. and VandenHeuvel, A. (1997) 'Gender discrimination in training', *British Journal of Industrial Relations*, 35: 627–33.

Wright, P.C. and Geroy, G.D. (2001) 'Changing the mindset', *International Journal of Human Resource Management*, 12: 586–600.

11

Management and Leadership Development

Christopher Mabey and Tim Finch-Lees

INTRODUCTION

Management and leadership development (MLD) is central to an organization's human resource management (HRM) and a litmus test of the value it places upon its staff. The strategic training and development of managers and leaders is widely regarded as one of four progressive HR policies (Becker and Huselid, 1998). Much of the writing in the arena of MLD is based on a series of causal links which underlie this thinking. The first is that an organization's business and HR strategy will, or at least should, shape the design, style and priority afforded to training and development activities. The second is that these activities, providing they are well delivered and contextualized, will enhance the skills and competencies of managers. The third proposed link is that these skills and competencies, newly acquired by these individuals, will translate into collective capability, which in turn, will lead to that organization performing in a superior way to its competitors. This chain of events, however, is usually more assumed than articulated, more hoped-for than empirically demonstrated.

By way of critically reviewing the current state of MLD we set out to do three things in this chapter. First we assess the evidence for the sequential links in this chain. Second, we note along the way the gaps or shortcomings in these literatures. Many of these are associated with the functionalist stance and methodology which tend to dominate MLD research. Third, in the latter part of the chapter we propose three alternative conceptual approaches, which have the capacity for opening up our understanding of MLD in different ways. We conclude by advocating that the field will benefit from further research which adopts more than one approach, and where possible, facilitates dialogue between them.

LINKING BUSINESS AND MLD STRATEGY

Most organizations have got to the point of recognizing that MLD is more than a tactical or knee-jerk response to a skills gap.

Obviously there is a legitimate place for sending individuals on a course to improve their presentation skills, for example, or sponsoring a cohort of managers on an MBA but, increasingly, organizations are using MLD as part of a wider strategy to achieve their longer term aspirations.

Strategic intent

Propelling most MLD initiatives is strategic intent. And this is not just the case for private companies. Because public and not-for-profit enterprises cannot register success simply in terms of profit and market share, the way their management teams acquire resources and deliver services is increasingly becoming a driver for sustainable 'growth'. Across all sectors then, organizations and agencies turn to MLD to achieve this. Despite the logical appeal of creating and harnessing individual skills and competency around business strategies, this can be problematic for a number of reasons. First, we know that the formulation and implementation of strategy at any level is an uncertain, emergent and iterative process (Stacey, 1996). Even if the strategic intent can be clearly articulated, it may take many months or even years before the first fruits of concerted development begin to appear. The issue of time lag applies to all HR interventions, but is particularly true of MLD. It presents the distinct possibility that the original strategy has now shifted in focus and/or some of the design features have become outmoded. Furthermore, the evolution of corporate strategy, and by implication MLD strategy, is likely to be messy and overtaken by unpredictable events. At best, it gives those responsible for deriving such strategies 'some sense of control and direction in the midst of chaotic and unpredictable reality' (Pattison, 1997: 30–1). Even where organizational objectives are stated, these may bear little resemblance to the actual intentions and values of those initiating and sponsoring the development (Lees, 1992).

More pragmatically, it seems that linking corporate and MLD strategy is an unfulfilled aspiration for most organizations. In only one of Gratton et al.'s (1999) eight case organizations, each one a 'leading edge' corporation, was there a sophisticated attempt to link business strategy to human resource strategy (p. 204). The same appears to apply to management development. In a study of 22 'leading firms' in the US, Siebert and Hall (1995) found that only two companies, 3M and Motorola, conducted their training of managers in an outwardly focused way, in the sense that business priorities were the trigger for development. An investigation into management development in UK organizations was carried out by the Chartered Institute of Personnel and Development (CIPD, 2002). This involved a survey of 433 organizations, as well as consultation groups with senior executives and interviews with HR/D Directors and a leading business school. Integrating management development with the implementation of organizational goals was seen as a top priority by 85 per cent of senior managers, yet only 16 per cent of the survey respondents believe their organizations were very effective at developing business plans that specify the management capabilities required, while 30 per cent of organizations do not even have business plans.

Changing culture

Increasingly, MLD interventions have been conscripted not just to build skills to support strategy but also to change attitudes as part of a wider attempt to shift culture. Given that culture is a central, all-pervasive reality of organizational life, encompassing the spectrum of attitudes, values and norms that make up the distinctive feel of an enterprise, this is indeed a bold aspiration. Bate (1995) elaborates four different strategies adopted by organizations seeking to change their cultures. The so-called 'indoctrinative approach' is one that relies heavily upon training and development. This kind of intervention, with its reliance on democracy and consultation, is softer and more communal than the prescription of the 'aggressive approach' and the subterfuge of the 'corrosive approach'. Nevertheless it is still a socialization programme where the aim is to fit the participating individuals into a pre-formulated definition of the situation. 'They are therefore "taught" courses [...] and do not presuppose the existence of any kind of reciprocal interaction or mutual learning' (1995: 194). With some irony, he refers to the contention that cultural learning can only occur in routine, continuous, experiential and interactive settings, and notes that, almost by definition, indoctrinative programmes are non-routine, discontinuous, non-experiential and conducted in a non-interactive setting.

However, participants in development programmes are not easily duped. Responses to one culture change effort in a leading UK food retailing organization were reported as varying from re-orientation (apparent adoption of new value sets), re-interpretation (partial acceptance), re-invention (recycling of existing values so that they are presented as in alignment with the newly-espoused values) to outright rejection. The researchers (Ogbonna and Harris, 1998) conclude that while managements have become more sophisticated in their attempts to change cultures, participants in associated training have also become shrewder in their tactics of accommodation and/or resistance.

This example illustrates that MLD, as a lever to facilitate change, is too often viewed as a neutral process, where the only resistance trainees have to absorbing new knowledge or acquiring new skills is their individual capacity or learning style. Such a view neglects the nature of learning as a politicized process where new knowledge, systems and techniques are viewed suspiciously, even rejected because they are seen to represent the priorities of others whose interests are distinct and possibly opposed, or to result in a re-allocation of organizational resources, or a weakening of a section's traditional power-base.

For all the appeal of harnessing MLD as a catalyst for strategic change in organizations, it can be seen that this approach is far from straightforward.

THE LINK BETWEEN MLD AND ENHANCED SKILL AND COMPETENCE

The second link concerns employing MLD to make a strategic enterprise-level contribution. Some efforts to develop skills and competence are more successful than others and it is worth asking why. Here we examine four approaches that have become, in a sense, emblematic of progressive MLD in recent years. All show a degree of promise of overcoming some of the systemic problems inherent in training and development initiatives. But, as we shall see, each attracts its own criticism and we await better evidence as to their conclusive contribution to individual and organizational capability.

Competency frameworks

Competency-based development has been a major and growing organizational activity over the past decade and a half. It was reported in the US that businesses spent $100 million per year over recent years implementing competency models (Athey and Orth, 1999). An estimate put the number of UK employees covered by such schemes at over 3.2 million (Rankin, 2001), and a longitudinal study of nearly 100 UK firms found a significant increase in the adoption of competency-based development from 2000 to 2004 (Mabey 2005: 44).

Competency frameworks have the capacity to assist management development in several ways. Arriving at a recognizable competency profile for particular management positions/career paths in a given organization helps provide a common language and observable behaviours for different standards of performance. This removes ambiguity and addresses the often heard complaint of shifting 'corporate goalposts'. Competencies also serve to translate organizational strategies into individual priorities, enabling managers to fine tune their development around a few skill areas which have high salience for their own and the organization's success. Providing sufficient cultural latitude is given to definitions, terminology and local patterns of working;

this can even be achieved across international business units. A further advantage is that a common set of competencies introduces the possibility of horizontal integration across all HRM policies. If the criteria for recruitment, performance management, promotion, reward and recognition are consistent with the goals of management development, there is at least the possibility of tracking their combined impact on the strategic objectives in a way that is far less likely when such HR initiatives are piecemeal and uncoordinated.

Although criticized, among other things, as a device for ensuring compliance with the corporate ethos via self-regulation (Salaman, 2004) and for reinforcing masculine norms (Rees and Garnsey, 2003), the problem is often perceived as being less to do with the concept of competencies than their implementation. Mole (2004) proposes that competency-based leadership development offers three distinct advantages over more traditional approaches: (1) the focus on real jobs and a real organizational context obviates the time and expense of using off-site residential training, (2) the content can be delivered in short bursts of one day or less, possibly spaced out to allow on-the-job practice of new skills and (3) the possibility of meaningful evaluation is enhanced due to the contextually specific nature of leader performance. It would appear then that practitioners remain largely committed to the approach, with any perceived 'failure' being put down to issues of refinement, as opposed to any fundamental questioning of the concept of competency-based development.

360 degree feedback

Effective personal and professional development is usually catalyzed by accurate feedback on work performance. Rather than relying on the performance feedback from a single, usually senior source, 360 degree feedback (or multi-source, multi-rater feedback) solicits the views of several colleagues at senior, peer and junior levels in the workplace, and occasionally customers.

In 2004 it was estimated that over one third of US companies used some type of 360 degree feedback process for managers (Ostroff et al., 2004). The technique is also used widely in UK organizations (Bailey and Fletcher, 2002).

The growing popularity of 360 degree feedback might be attributed to a number of changes in the way organizations operate. It is particularly relevant to areas of job performance where objective outcome criteria are difficult to measure, such as in the development of management and leadership capabilities. The approach is predicated upon a competency framework (which has enjoyed rapid uptake as discussed in the previous section) and also fits those organizations pursuing a culture of work-based learning and continuous improvement. The increased trend toward remote-working, geographically dispersed workforces and matrix management also lends itself to managers in different locations/functions (rather than the line manager alone) giving and receiving quality feedback on fellow team members.

There is modest evidence that 360 degree feedback improves individual competency in the workplace over time (Bailey and Fletcher, 2002; Siefert et al., 2001), but questions remain. Increasing numbers of employers, especially in the US, are using 360 degree feedback as part of a performance management process. This is likely to remove some of the distinctive benefits: namely that it is voluntary and developmental in focus. Related to this is the issue of anonymity. Some organizations insist on anonymous and confidential ratings. This is primarily to reassure participant raters that there will be no repercussions as a result of their feedback, thus encouraging them to be more honest. It may also be less threatening for participants to receive their feedback on an anonymous basis. Other users of 360 degree feedback argue that named feedback is more useful because it allows the feedback to be contextualized and related to specific situations and relationships, and it can reduce the scope for unconstructive personal comments.

Executive coaching

The use of coaching to develop managers, especially senior executives, has become extremely popular in recent years. Some estimate that executive coaching is growing at 40 per cent per year (*The Economist*, 8th March 2002). A further arresting statistic reveals that 60 per cent of coaching clients say they confide in their coach almost as much as they do in their best friend, spouse or therapist (Withers, 2001). After just five years since its inception the International Coaching Federation was estimated to have more than 15,000 full- or part-time coaching practitioners world-wide and boasted 3500 members, working either as independent consultants or for larger training and development agencies (Arnaud, 2004).

How do we account for the executive coaching explosion? One factor may be disappointment with the learning transfer from more conventional approaches to MLD. Another aspect of collective management development activities is that they often expose weakness and highlight unconscious incompetence as a precursor to building new skills, confidence and competence. Not surprisingly perhaps, senior managers tend to shy away from this kind of feedback and exposure in a relatively public arena. To have the services of a personal coach, operating within a contract of confidentiality, is far more acceptable. Feedback from, say, 360 degree questionnaires (and the growth of coaching alongside the rapid uptake 360 degree feedback in organizations is probably no coincidence), is more palatable when mediated via a coach who is then available to help generate personal strategies for addressing weaknesses. Organizations are increasingly conferring coaching interventions on their high-flying senior managers in recognition of the need for individualized support at a time of major change in organizations. This is by way of an acknowledgement that managers are increasingly isolated (Hirsch and Carter, 2002), with increased workloads and staff responsibility. Managers and leaders need to be able to self-develop as HR departments

shrink. Perhaps more cynically, organizations may also use executive coaching as a kind of palliative to overstretched and stressed members of their senior team. After all, few employees would turn down the opportunity of an empathetic ear and the empowering skills of a well-trained coach. The fact that the organization usually pays dearly for these coaching services adds to the sense of reward. As work and people management burdens increase for senior managers due to de-layering, busy schedules mean less and less time for face-to-face interaction with direct reports. Regionalization of activity can exacerbate these problems of distance and unavailability for managers and their direct reports. Line managers are often ill-equipped or unmotivated to take on the development responsibility for their staff. Executive coaches can provide a convenient substitute for hard-pressed line managers.

As yet, there is little empirical research to validate the efficacy of executive coaching other than that using uncontrolled group or case studies (Grant, 2003). Burgoyne and Jackson (2004) highlight the gap in current research and emphasize the need for more longitudinal studies into the impact of this MLD activity. In a comprehensive review of the literature, Kampa-Kokesch and Anderson (2001) call for more rigorous research into the impact and outcomes of executive coaching. They were only able to identify seven empirical studies in the literature, all of which had design flaws which minimized the generalizability of their findings. Some literature suggests that some management practices like executive coaching, which began in the province of the private sector, are actually having a destabilizing effect on the culture of government organizations into which they are introduced (Newman, 2002). There has since been very little critical analysis of these changes in the public sector from an organizational behaviour perspective (Schofield, 2002).

As with other MLD activities, coaching can be regarded as an effective acculturation device. Some theorists, for example, cite this form of development as an instrument of organizational control, as a means to create corporate elites. Such culturally-sanctioned management and leadership development activities can elicit the compliance of managers, especially when intangible incentives (like the vague suggestion of promotion) are promised in return. In contrast, Arnaud's (2004) polemic makes an important point about the value of executive coaching interventions in providing a valuable symbolic locus and space for potentially counter-cultural 'individual utterances' (2004: 1135) and the expression of 'otherness' inside organizations. Certainly, it would seem undeniable that coaches generally find the opportunity to voice their struggles and to explore alternative solutions as emancipatory.

International assignments

The development of the global or trans-national organization requires senior managers who are not only internationally mobile but who are sensitive to the international and cultural implications of their work. How can such competencies best be developed? Many organizations seek to use international assignments for individual and organizational development, often with the assistance of a centralized human resource function which can plan and track the career of staff on a global basis. However inclusion in or exclusion from, networks and participation in international MLD initiatives can 'cut both ways'. It has been found that women in UK organizations are disproportionately unlikely to benefit from personal and professional development afforded by overseas assignments due to gender bias arising from the predominant use of 'closed, informal selection processes' (Harris, 2002). This is despite evidence that European women can be more effective than men as leaders in regions like Asia because they frequently utilize intuitive and empathetic skills that are highly valued in such host cultures (van der Boon, 2003). Many of the international management development activities described above are designed to foster heterogeneity, where individuals can 'retain their dimensions of diversity while at the same time avoiding such

damaging processes as dysfunctional inter-personal conflict, miscommunication, higher levels of stress, slower decision-making and problems with group cohesiveness' (Kyriaki-dou, 2005: 112). However, there is always a danger that international MLD programmes, far from legitimizing, celebrating and bene-fiting from the diversity inherent to effective knowledge diffusion, can have the opposite effect of reinforcing inequality, homogenizing corporate behaviour and perpetuating cultural conformity.

Undeniably, MLD has an important part to play in building individual and organizational capability. However, the means to achieve this is by no means self-evident. Here we have reviewed four very different methods which are widely regarded as leading edge when it comes to creating cadres of highly capable and committed managers/leaders. Competency based approaches have become almost synonymous with progressive devel-opment, yet their introduction and mainte-nance requires care and close attention to context. Often linked to competencies is 360 degree feedback. Research in the field of organizational psychology largely supports this approach to diagnozing development needs and the finely grained feedback can provide a timely springboard for develop-ment. But again, while representing a distinct improvement upon feedback delivered in an unskilled manner or not at all, there is no panacea here; more case studies are needed to identify the enduring benefits of this approach. The same can be said for coaching and international assignments. Each of these methods appears to yield impressive learning opportunities for the individual, but much depends on the way such opportunities are set up and whether wider organizational processes support, ignore or undermine the fruits of the development experience in each instance.

THE LINK BETWEEN ENHANCED COMPETENCE AND PERFORMANCE

The perceived relationship between MLD, enhanced capability and performance is perhaps the most prized of all. Although the logic and plausibility of this skills-performance link is open to question (e.g. Grugulis and Stoyanova, 2006), this does little to diminish the preoccupation of governments, both national and international, with the calibre of their managers and leaders. In Europe for instance, the globalization of business and the emergence of a new knowledge-based economy are seen to be challenging the adaptability of European education and training systems (European Commission, 2000). In emerging economies, there is a rapid game of 'catch-up' taking place, as governments and enterprises across all sectors seek to address their management and leadership deficiencies (e.g. Wang and Wang, 2006; Osman-Gani and Tan, 2000). In this section we review some of the evidence for this link: first between MLD and enhanced individual capability/performance, and second, the degree to which this 'translates' into collective improvement in performance at the level of the organization.

Impact of MLD on individual capability

Studies have focused on different indicators when assessing the impact on individuals of MLD, and often in the context of wider HR initiatives. In-depth case analysis of seven large, UK based companies was designed to examine the linkages between business strategy, intended HR strategy, strategic HR context, realised HR interventions and outcomes (Gratton et al., 1999). Among the outcomes were such measures as organizational commitment ('the ambience of the firm in terms of morale, satisfaction and shared commitment') and competence ('skills needed for new jobs, a positive attitude towards change and learning'). The research team found mixed evidence for the linking of individual performance to business goals; for instance, training that focused on short-term business needs was pursued by all the companies as a way of creating a flexible and multi-skilled workforce but longer term embedding of

people management processes was far less consistent.

Guest et al. (2000) also built into their model of strategic HRM a measure of employee attitudes and behaviour and were able to confirm a relationship between so called high-commitment HR strategies and positive employee responses. This finding supports those of Guest (1999) who also found a strong impact on feelings of fairness, trust and other elements of the psychological contract, as expressed by employees. In their exploration of a quality programme in a retail organisation, which involved extensive training, Rosenthal et al. (1997) discovered positive effects on individuals. Several months after the training associated with this programme, staff remained committed to it and displayed this commitment in their behaviour. In a study of 16 organizations by Winterton and Winterton (1999), the authors separated out the improvements resulting from management development at an individual performance from those at an organizational level. The former clustered in three areas: specific managerial skills and competence (like project and change management, leadership and motivating others, communications and presentation skills and so on); personal confidence and a sense of empowerment; and thirdly, understanding how to develop others. Where management development made: 'an unambiguous contribution to improvements in IP [individual performance], this was frequently associated with the use of Management Standards' (1999: 107).

Such research supports the impact of MLD upon individual attitudes, including such things as trust perceptions, job satisfaction, goal and organizational commitment, discretionary behaviour, ability to cope and so on. These might be viewed as reliable precursors to capability enhancement, and indeed they are integral parts of the 'People and Performance model' (Purcell et al., 2003). This model traces the impact of training, amongst several other HR policies, upon individuals' skill, motivation and opportunity to participate, which in turn links to commitment, satisfaction and discretionary behaviour to help the firm be successful. Based on their research in 12 UK organizations the research team conclude that: 'effective firms have a level of sophistication in their approach to people management which helps induce discretionary behaviour and above-average performance' (2003: 6).

Direct impact of MLD on performance

While much has been written about the organizational benefits of investing in management and leadership development, empirical studies which test this linkage are still few and far between.

In the in-depth analysis of 16 UK organisations referred to above, 4 were found to be comprehensively adopting 'management standards' as part of their HRD systems and processes. A further three had partially adopted such frameworks and nine had not attempted this or had made little progress in this direction (Winterton and Winterton, 1997). Those in the first category shared certain characteristics: management development and other training was competence based, job profiles or job descriptions related to the competencies outlined in the management standards (UK Management Charter Initiative) and appraisal systems were designed to support the attainment of management standards. The researchers report a statistically significant relationship between such competency-based HRD systems and both individual and business performance. Some support for these results was found in a study of 360 British aerospace establishments, where a significant correlation was found between strategic management capability and business performance, as measured by value added per employee (Thompson, 2000). This was in a context of downsizing, flattening structures and outsourcing (on average 66 per cent had downsized recently). More successful businesses, which also tended to be larger in size, differed in their use of management development in two ways: they utilized personal development plans and

succession planning more extensively and were more likely to be investing in leadership skills and developing global managers. It was also found that this investment was strongly and positively correlated with the pursuit of a high commitment HR strategy and philosophy: in other words, there was senior management commitment to raising management skills, encouraging innovation and investing in development.

In an EC-funded research project analyzing management development in six European countries, interviews were conducted with the HRD manager and a line manager in 600 private sector organizations as part of a study by Mabey and Gooderham (2005). Findings indicate that 25 per cent of variance in organizational performance is explained by three factors: a strategic approach to HRM, a long-term, proactive and strategic approach to management development and, on the part of line managers, a belief that their employer takes management development seriously. Interestingly, neither the presence of management development systems/procedures, nor the amount and variety of MLD activities enhance performance to a significant effect. This study used a seven-item measure of performance covering the quality of goods and services, the ability to attract and retain essential staff and the quality of relationships in the firm. This subjective index was benchmarked by sector over the previous three years and a mean score reported by HRD and line managers. Causal path analysis revealed that a favourable strategic fit (between the firm's chosen business and HRM strategies) and organizational fit (in terms of a coherent longer-term approach to MLD) were significant factors in predicting line manager perceptions of the importance given by their employer to MLD. This positive perception distinguished high performers from low performing companies. A further analysis was undertaken on a sub-sample of 180 of these companies where financial data was available (from the Amadeus database). Again, the perception of line managers proved to be crucial: where they reported positively on their employer's management development strategy, this explained a modest but significant amount of variance (7 per cent) in firm productivity (Mabey and Ramirez, 2003). Unsurprisingly, the quality of the relationship between the employee and their employer appears to be an important mediator. This invokes social exchange theory and is corroborated in a study of 593 employees working in 64 Norwegian banks. A more positive relationship between perceptions of developmental HR practices and work performance was found for those also registering high levels of perceived organizational support, procedural justice and interactional justice (Kuvaas, 2008).

Taken together, these findings lend support to the idea that a contingent approach to MLD confers competitive advantage through enhanced organizational performance because of its inimitability. As such, a properly aligned and therefore distinctive and idiosyncratic management development system represents a core capability (Becker and Gerhart, 1996). However, the challenge of fitting MLD both strategically and organizationally should not be underestimated. Indeed one should construe these findings as a warning to managers to eschew off-the-shelf management development 'solutions'.

Furthermore, unlike technical skills training, MLD often takes place over a sustained period of time and addresses competencies which may take months, if not years, to be internalized and harvested by the organization. For this reason, analysis that spans a number of years is necessary but rare. In a study of insurance sales people, Frayne and Geringer (2000) were able to demonstrate that self-management skill training significantly improved job performance. These performance effects were sustained and gradually increased over time. Another relevant study here is that of 61 large French firms by Arcimoles (1997) which tracked impact over a seven-year period. Investment in training was found to lead to both immediate- and time-lagged economic performance at firm level. However, the study does not isolate the effects of MLD in particular, and as the author admits, an index of investment tells us

very little about either the qualitative aspects or the informal costs and benefits of on-the-job training. Some of these shortcomings are overcome in a longitudinal study of 131 UK private sector companies of all sizes (Mabey, 2005). Focusing just on time-lagged relationships, some facets of the way companies designed and implemented their management development in 2000 led to significantly greater employee engagement, a higher organization performance and greater productivity reported in 2004.

Although rarely traced, the psychological mechanism underlying such relationships appears to be as follows. The effect of consistent and prioritized MLD over time is to build motivation among employees which collectively improves the way the organization competes. This will be partly due to the quality of its products and services (because motivated managers will be inventive and want to please customers), partly due to its ability to attract and retain essential staff (because the firm will gain a reputation as being progressive and caring for its staff) and partly due to the quality of its internal relations, as highlighted by social exchange theory (because, over time, mutual trust will develop). This virtuous cycle is supported by the results of other studies in relation to HRM practices generally (Guest et al., 2001; Purcell et al., 2003; Kuvaas, 2008).

ALTERNATIVES TO FUNCTIONALIST ACCOUNTS OF MLD

So far we have explored MLD very much from a performance perspective. The tendency to rely upon such a functionalist stance has been well explored in the related fields of organization behaviour and human resource management (HRM). Indeed, it leads one commentator to characterize HRM as a modernist project:

> Positivism, with its realist ontology, seeks to explain and predict what happens in the social world by searching for regularities and causal relationships

between its constituent elements. ... To a greater or lesser extent this is the logic which reigns in much of the research on HRM, even when it is case-study based (Legge, 1996: 308).

Similarly, in the arena of work and organizational psychology, Symon and Cassell (2006: 310) note that most researchers fail to make a 'conscious (political) choice to adopt positivism but that it is more of a default option'. The authors attribute this to conventional research training which is steeped in the precepts of positivism and neglects other perspectives.

To a large extent, this is also the case in the field of MLD. Functionalist objectives are often taken for granted and research is often restricted to evaluating the extent to which these are met. Such an approach has been criticized for failing to adequately deal with causality (Kamoche, 2000) and for taking a unitarist perspective, where organizational members are assumed to share a single set of motives and interests (Burgoyne and Jackson 1997). Some would go further, casting MLD as a largely one-sided attempt by senior management to impose control or advance ideological power interests rather than a means to 'develop' employees in any kind of holistic or benevolent sense (Ackers and Preston, 1997). MLD has also been portrayed as a bureaucratic and potentially harmful irrelevance, where standardized portrayals of management bear little resemblance to the diverse worlds of 'real' managers (e.g. Grugulis, 2002). In contrast to these broadly negative critiques, other authors have suggested that deeper insight might be gained by trying to look beyond questions of good or evil (Townley, 1998), success or failure (du Gay et al., 1996) and by searching for more multi-faceted ways in which MLD might simultaneously work for and against the interests of any particular agent. As such, in order to achieve a fuller understanding of MLD, alternatives to the dominant perspective of functionalism are required. There is a burgeoning literature which provides a variety of such alternatives and these can be broadly categorized as social constructivist, dialogic and critical approaches (Mabey and Finch-Lees, 2008).

A social constructivist approach

The functionalist approach to MLD sees development as comprising activities which lead to improved skills at an individual level and enhanced capability at an organizational level. It might be equally tenable to turn such causal thinking on its head. For example, starting with the notion of individual and collective learning, we could then explore the conditions which are most likely to bring this about. We might put less emphasis on management positions and more on managerial processes (irrespective of the title-holders involved); less on organizations as instigators of training programmes and more on organizations, teams, project groups as fertile spaces for learning; less on the control, success and predictability inherent in much development thinking and more on the learning that arises from risk, setback and spontaneity; less on training and performance and more on learning and reflective action (Larsen, 2004).

In contrast to the functionalist approach, there is an explicit recognition that underlying values and/or embedded cultures are essential elements of organizations. The constructivist approach does not ignore strategy and structure, but is more concerned to achieve a better integration between the needs of staff and the conditions in which they work. Development activities from a functionalist perspective will usually be highly-planned, systematized and documented. More interesting, from a constructivist perspective, are the cultural repercussions and significance of such programmes: the symbolic meaning they come to have for variously situated corporate players. And apart from the usual training methods, any activity (a challenging experience, a difficult project to manage, an inspiring 'mentor', a non-work support group and so on) might qualify as development. The HRM language is less about return on investment, assessment and payback and more about talent management, building potential and increasing the capability of individuals and teams. The social constructivist view places emphasis on the way activities conducted under the 'banner' of MLD come to be invested with meaning, and how this meaning is jointly arrived at by many parties.

An example of this approach is the account given by Gold and Smith (2003) of winners of the National Training Awards (NTA) in the UK. Each year awards are given to those organizations across all sizes and sectors deemed to be innovative and effective in training employees. Using story-telling technique, Gold and Smith (2003) conducted interviews and collected documentation from 15 winners. The authors make a number of observations about the way individuals and groups sought to mobilize the efforts of indifferent and sceptical colleagues in their respective firms towards a training agenda. First was how actors within such organizations were able to draw rhetorically upon the resources of talk, thought and action provided by the wider 'learning movement'. This movement is described by Gold and Smith as an array of media attention comprising journals, books, websites, conferences which burgeoned in the 1990s to make learning a hot topic (Contu et al., 1998) and depicted it as an obvious and 'good thing'. And, of course, the very participation in the NTA connoted value since this was emblematic of the emergence and progress of the learning movement.

Second, Gold and Smith found managers in all cases claiming that the ostensible impetus for training and development was to respond to change in varying degrees. Yet, behind this public rationale they found more compelling reasons being identified, such as the discourse of personal empowerment: 'giving people a chance that they never had', the opportunity for experienced managers to put something back and the aspiration of improving job satisfaction and job related safety. A longitudinal analysis of the effects of a life-long learning initiative in a Scottish company arrived at a similar conclusion (Martin et al., 1999). Evidence was found linking the life long learning programme and employee perceptions of careers and fairness even when the company reduced its previous commitment to job security. All this indicates that the background orientation of significant actors can be highly influential in building a case for training and development, quite apart from any intrinsic merit. It also suggests a gap between public rhetoric and subjective reality which has been found in other management development research (Antonacopoulou, 2000; Stiles et al., 1997).

So the constructivist approach turns much functionalist thinking on its head. Almost ignoring the status of 'manager' and the discrete activity labelled management development (Watson, 2001), the concern here is to identify activities which result in effective managing and to understand how learning and development arise through experiential re-framing of work by those engaged in it. This approach helpfully re-clothes MLD with its contextual, tacit, non-rational and emergent properties. Most of us can point to examples of training and development activity in an organization becoming invested with multiple-meanings. More difficult, perhaps, is how to use this perspective to improve the learning experience. Interpretative studies, like that of Sandberg (2000) offer some help here, by pointing the way to a more richly textured understanding of competency development, but such accounts have a way of reverting to normative assumptions.

A dialogic approach

In the sense that we use it in this chapter, the term dialogic encompasses the idea that all discourse can only exist both in relation to prior discourse and in anticipation of future discourse (Bakhtin, 1981; Fairclough, 1992). Any text or utterance is therefore inherently 'intertextual' (Kristeva, 1986) in that it forms part of a dialogue that establishes the conditions of and the potential for all meaning (Wehrle, 1982). Whereas functionalism takes the concept of 'management' or even 'the manager/leader' as pre-constituted foundation points for 'development', the dialogic focuses on the socially and historically situated ways in which these foundations have come to be conceived of in the first place. This opens the way for alternative understandings of the activities associated with MLD. For example, as well as *development* being understood as a means to improve personal and organizational effectiveness (as in functionalism), it also becomes a means for the production of identity, subjectivity and thus for social differentiation. An example of this approach comes from a study by Grey (1994) of graduate trainees in a large UK accounting firm. He found that via various processes of organizational socialization (including MLD), graduates came to discipline themselves via the social construct of 'career'. Career provided the discursive lynchpin around which graduates rapidly learnt the importance of appearing: ambitious, committed, presentable, acquiescent, well-networked, enthusiastic (even when doing the most mundane of tasks) and generally compliant to a variety of other social norms of the organization. One such norm was the expectation that family life would serve as an adjunct and support to work life rather than the converse. For example, one participant in the research alluded to anyone of partnership potential being expected to have a 'well packaged wife'. As such, career and all it entailed went well beyond what was needed for efficient work performance. For Grey, career became the basis for a 'moral' and all encompassing project of the self which, whilst not entirely negative, presented anything but a level playing field for all organizational members. For example, whilst Grey by his own acknowledgement only touches on the gender and diversity implications of his analysis, it is not difficult to appreciate how subjectivities other than those which revolve around masculine heterosexuality are at odds with the careerist ideal that appears to reign within the organization he studied. Importantly, it is not that MLD *per se* dictated the importance of things like a 'well packaged wife' within the Grey study. The point is rather that the very notion of 'development' often serves

to inculcate the importance of careerism which, in turn, can serve as a discursive resource for the more informal and often discriminatory socialization that can take place within organizations.

Much of Grey's analysis is supported by a more recent study of management by objectives (MBO) and mentoring practices within 'Big Six' accountancy firms in the US (Covaleski et al., 1998). The authors found such practices to be constructing managerial subjectivity around careerist norms to the extent that one ex-partner of the firm attested to feeling extreme 'grief' at the loss of his tenure within the firm, likening the event to the loss of a child. Like Grey, the authors also drew attention to the gender implications of such dynamics. For a start, women within the firm had fewer opportunities for mentoring, given the dearth of senior females within the organization combined with the sexual innuendo that often surrounds mixed gender mentoring relationships. What was more, however, women tended to be judged according to different standards than men when striving to adopt the mentoring-inspired careerist subjectivities required for 'success' within these organizations. The most flagrant example of this revolved around a lawsuit against one firm for denying promotion to a female employee on the basis that she was 'too macho' and needed to 'walk, talk and dress more femininely'. A further conclusion of the authors was that mentoring in combination with MBO was instrumental in producing 'corporate clones' in the sense that the organizational form was discernibly duplicated within the managerial subjectivity of each individual. The most vivid example of this comes from a manager who talks of having become more identifiable as a "revenue stream" than as a living, breathing individual.

Fournier (1998) takes the notion of corporate cloning a step further in her Foucauldian analysis of graduate development processes within a large UK service sector organization. She explores how career discourse within this organization operated to engender the dominant notion of 'self as enterprise', an enterprise which, just like any other, became an object needing to be 'assessed and evaluated' (typically via appraisal) and then 'invested in' (typically via training and development). This often involved considerable 'sacrifice' on the part of the individual, all with the aim of becoming more 'marketable' thus generating the highest possible 'returns' in terms of the increased status and material wealth that flow from this type of 'career development'. But Fournier also makes the point that any discourse, including the entrepreneurial careering discourse that she identified, can only achieve and maintain dominance in the face of its deviant, pathological, irrational and ultimately negative 'other'. In her case, this 'other' comprised a more militant discourse of resistance and exploitation, emanating from those who perceived themselves as either unable to access the dominant discourse of enterprise due to structural and political factors and/or those who laid claim to what they perceived as being their more authentic, uncorrupted and integral selves. Consequently, wishing for a world where everyone can and should fit in with entrepreneurial/careerist ideals is futile, not least because such a discourse 'can only govern by invoking and constructing its "other" and by delineating the space within which the reprehensible other may legitimately be bound, i.e. the margins' (pp. 72–3). Having said this, Fournier is careful to avoid any condemnation of the discourse of careerist enterprise or indeed it's opposite. She merely makes the point that each needs the other for either to have any meaning, arguing for discursive plurality and warning against the potentially colonizing influence of enterprise discourse to all forms of life. Amongst the implications of this is that any call for MLD to be rendered more democratic, more inclusive and less discriminatory (for example by doing away with 'fast track' or 'high potential' development schemes), whilst well intentioned, may simply lead to elitist social divisions cropping up elsewhere within the organization if, as may be the case, they are integral to the (dominant) discourse

of organizations. This of course does not preclude the consideration of alternative, perhaps as yet unimagined, discourses.

A critical approach

A critical approach to MLD views the organization as composed of multiple, shifting and conflicting coalitions of interest. It seeks to expose how this facet of organization is typically obscured by dominant yet taken for granted managerial ideologies. For the critical scholar, MLD certainly has the potential to be emancipatory by educating organizational members in the identification and critique of managerial ideology. More often than not, however, critical analyses view MLD as serving merely to obscure the ideological nature of managerial knowledge by presenting it as neutral, apolitical, and universally beneficial.

Various authors have sought to investigate the ways in which MLD can either support or disrupt interests of power and control, and how such functioning can provoke responses ranging from outright resistance to unthinking acquiescence. Rusaw (2000) studied a development programme in a US university, designed to bring about higher levels of trust, fairness and openness of communication within all levels of the organization. As a result of the programme, those from more junior grades reported positive results within their own peer groups. This was accompanied, however, by frustration at a perceived absence of behavioural change at more senior levels. The dean of the university took no action to address such concerns and the climate rapidly deteriorated to a point where levels of dissatisfaction were even greater than had existed prior to the programme. The study illustrates how potentially emancipatory forms of learning for those lower down the organization can meet resistance from those further up, since such learning can *disrupt control* within the organization by threatening existing power structures.

Instead of having emancipatory intent, however, it is just as likely that MLD can be aimed at *strengthening control* by reinforcing existing power structures. In such cases, overt resistance (this time from those lower down the organization) is perhaps less likely to be the outcome than acquiescence. Kamoche (2000) conducted a study of management development at 'IP', a large multinational. The development initiative covered international managers on secondment at IP's UK headquarters and involved a programme of education (resembling a mini-MBA) at the company's prestigious training institute. The programme was seen as a means of socialization and enculturation for the managers in the sometimes mysterious social and corporate workings of IP. It was also seen as a crucial rite of passage for any manager seeking to transit from the 'profane' world of middle management to the 'sacred' terrain of the senior ranks. Through the analytical lens of ideology, Kamoche was able to delve into the largely unspoken assumptions about the 'right' way to behave within IP, whose interests were being served by the programme and why participating managers largely acquiesced in the supposedly integrative values it espoused. In his view, embedding such values within a development programme that simultaneously determined career advancement effectively emasculated potentially deviant and non-conformist individual interests.

From the above we can begin to appreciate why accounts of overt participant resistance to MLD are relatively scarce. From the critical perspective, this is considered more likely to be the result of hegemonic processes at play than any authentic meeting of participants' needs. In the light of this, a number of authors have turned to ideology critique in order to gain insight into the less obvious workings of management development. Bell and Taylor (2004) investigated the ideological assumptions underpinning a number of MLD courses that either explicitly or implicitly invoke notions of spirituality. The authors' main conclusion is that, by focusing exclusively on deep personal transformation as the route to development, such courses deflect attention from political and structural barriers

to organizational change. As such, these kinds of programmes need, in the authors' view, to be seen as potentially repressive rather than enlightening. At a more macro-level, Contu et al. (2003) subject the whole discourse of learning (as typically used in the terms organizational learning, lifelong learning, etc.) to provocative critique. In doing so, the authors consciously acknowledge that theirs could be seen as a heretical move given the difficulty of making the case against a concept that has come to be regarded as universally beneficial, benign and apolitical. However, they argue that it is precisely these properties that render the discourse of learning a significant and hegemonic ideology with real practical force. In their view it has achieved this by conjuring up a nebulous but seductive futuristic vision in which 'old' conflicts (such as those between capital and labour) are rendered invisible within the new and supposed knowledge economy. Like Bell and Taylor (2004), they characterize the learning discourse as both individualizing and individualistic inasmuch as it transforms social subjects into 'learners' who become uniquely responsible for their own employability. Historical and structural causes of social exclusion are thus obscured rendering any prospects for their alleviation more remote.

On a more optimistic note, the academic literature periodically throws up an occasional 'success' story from practitioners employing a critically-informed approach to MLD. One such example comes from Meyerson and Fletcher (2000) who recount how they have employed a form of action learning in addressing issues of gender inequity within a range of different organizations. They maintain that this form of learning can be effective in allowing organizational members to discover for themselves previously hidden forms of gender discrimination (often of a subtle, systemic nature) and then taking sometimes small but eminently practical steps to address them. Their argument is that this 'small wins' approach can cumulatively add up to larger scale systemic or societal change. More typically, however, the literature is characterized by ambivalence and sometimes outright pessimism on the part of those attempting to draw upon a critical approach to the practice of MLD. Interestingly, an example of the former comes once again from Meyerson (Meyerson and Kolb, 2000), in which this time the writers acknowledge the various barriers and difficulties they have encountered in bringing about positive change via their action learning approach. One of the main difficulties emanated from their dual-pronged approach of aiming to alleviate gender discrimination whilst simultaneously seeking to improve organizational effectiveness. This resulted in the gender aspect constantly 'getting lost' as the natural tendency within the project teams was for it to be subordinated to performance imperatives. For some, however (e.g. Hearn, 2000; Fournier and Grey, 2000), this is an eminently predictable consequence of attempting to deploy a critical approach without letting go of functionalist performance concerns. For Hearn, it is entirely plausible that modern capitalist organizations actually derive an aggregate financial benefit from gender inequities. If this is indeed the case, it is functionalism itself (along with its economic and instrumental reasoning) that needs to be called into question rather than it being accommodated within attempts to engender a critical form of MLD. A similar argument is made by Litvin (2002) in her critique of the 'business case' for diversity. Furthermore, Hearn makes the important point that many sources of gender discrimination are actually macro-structural in nature and therefore not necessarily amenable to a 'small wins' approach that relies on development interventions at the organizational level of analysis.

CONCLUSION

The concern to attribute organizational benefits to MLD is understandable. Such activities are expensive, time-consuming and often high-profile. All parties concerned want to be able to demonstrate that such investments are worthwhile. It is perhaps for this reason that a good deal of MLD research has been directed toward tracking the impact of policies and practices upon organizational performance. As discussed, there is growing though still modest empirical support for this relationship, either as part of an integrated HRM approach or, less usually, attributable to an individual intervention. However, the analysis of development from this performance-stance is not without its problems and critics.

In this review, we argue that much of the difficulty stems from almost exclusive reliance upon functionalist assumptions and approaches when investigating MLD. This is an approach that employs a predominantly positivist perspective in an attempt to link MLD activities to increased effectiveness and performance at the levels of the individual, the organization, the nation state or indeed society as a whole (enshrined in such terms as cultural or human capital). However, functionalism provides a far from exhaustive understanding of MLD. It tends to ignore a range of issues, including: the multiple meanings that MLD can take on for participants, sponsors and other stakeholders; the ways in which MLD can shape the identities/subjectivities of organizational actors; the ways in which MLD can be implicated in repressive forms of coercion and control. We have provided no more than a glimpse of these alternative understandings of MLD by our brief explorations of the social constructivist, dialogic and critical literatures on the topic. Our contention is that the significance of MLD in organizations would be further illuminated by studies which consciously adopted one or more of these alternative approaches.

REFERENCES

Ackers, P. and Preston, D. (1997) 'Born again? The ethics and efficacy of the conversion experience in contemporary management development', *Journal of Management Studies*, 34 (5): 677–701.

Antonacopoulou, E (2000) 'Employee development through self-development in three retail banks', *Personnel Review*, 29 (4): 491–508.

Arcimoles, C.H. (1997) 'Human resource policies and company performance: A quantitative approach using longitudinal data', *Organization Studies*, 18 (5): 857–74.

Arnaud, G. (2004) 'A coach or a couch? A Lacanian perspective on executive coaching and consulting', *Human Relations*, 56 (9): 1131–154.

Athey, T. and Orth, M. (1999) 'Emerging competency methods for the future', *Human Resource Management*, 38 (3): 215–26.

Bakhtin, M. (1981) *The Dialogic Imagination: Four Essays.* Austin and London: University of Texas Press.

Bailey, C. and Fletcher, C. (2002) 'The impact of multi-source feedback on management development: Findings from a longitudinal study', *Journal of Organizational Behaviour*, 23 (7): 853–67.

Bate, P. (1995) *Strategies for Cultural Change.* Oxford: Butterworth Heinemann.

Becker, B. and Huselid, M. (1998) 'High performance work systems and firm performance: A synthesis of research and managerial implications', in G. Ferris (ed) *Research in Personnel and Human Resource Management*, Vol 16. Greenwich, CT: JAI Press, pp. 53–101.

Becker, B. and Gerhart, B. (1996) 'The impact of human resource management on organizational performance: Progress and prospects', *Academy of Management Journal*, 39 (4): 779–801.

Bell, E. and Taylor, S. (2004) '"From outward bound to inward bound": The prophetic voices and discursive practices of spiritual management development', *Human Relations*, 57 (4): 439–66.

Burgoyne, J. and Jackson, B. (1987) 'The arena thesis: Management development as a pluralistic meeting point', in J. Burgoyne and M. Reynolds (eds) *Management Learning.* London: Sage, pp. 54–70.

CIPD (2002) *Developing Managers for Effective Performance.* London: Chartered Institute of Personnel and Development.

Contu, A., Grey, C. and Ortenblad, A. (2003) 'Against learning', *Human Relations*, 56 (8): 931–52.

Covaleski, M., Dirsmith, M., Heian, J. and Samuel, S. (1998) 'The calculated and the avowed: Techniques of discipline and struggles over identity in big six public accounting firms', *Administrative Science Quarterly*, 43: 293–327.

du Gay, P., Salaman, G. and Rees, B. (1996) 'The conduct of management and the management of conduct: Contemporary managerial discourse and the constitution of the "competent" manager', *Journal of Management Studies*, 33 (3): 263–82.

European Commission (2000) *The Quality of Vocational Training: Proposal for Action.* Brussels: Directorate General for Education and Training.

Fairclough, N. (1992) *Discourse and Social Change.* Cambridge: Polity Press.

Fournier, V. (1998) 'Stories of development and exploitation: Militant voices in enterprise culture', *Organization*, 5 (1): 55–80.

Fournier, V. and Grey, C. (2000) 'At the critical moment: Conditions and prospects for critical management studies', *Human Relations*, 53 (1): 7–32.

Frayne, A. and Geringer, J. (2000) 'Self-management training for improving job performance: A field experiment involving sales people', *Journal of Applied Psychology*, 85: 361–72.

Gold, J. and Smith, V. (2003) 'Advances towards a learning movement: Translations at work', *Human Resource Development International*, 6 (2): 139–52.

Grant, A.M. (2003) 'Keeping up with the cheese! Research as a foundation for professional coaching of the future', in I.F. Stein (ed.) (2004) *Proceedings of the First ICF Coaching Research Symposium.* Mooresville, NC: International Coach Federation.

Gratton, L., Hope-Hailey, V., Stiles, P. and Truss, C. (1999) *Strategic Human Resource Management.* Oxford: Oxford University Press.

Grey, C. (1994) 'Career as a project of the self and labour process discipline', *Sociology*, 28 (2): 479–97.

Grugulis, I. (2002) 'Nothing serious? Candidates' use of humour in management training', *Human Relations*, 55 (4): 387–406.

Guest, D. (1999) 'Human resource management – the worker's verdict', *Human Resource Management Journal*, 9 (3): 5–25.

Guest, D., Michie, J., Conway, N. and Sheehan, M. (2003) 'Human resource management and corporate performance in the UK', *British Journal of Industrial Relations*, 41 (2): 291–314.

Grugulis, I. and Styanova, D. (2006) *Skills and Performance*, SKOPE Issue Paper 9, Economic and Social Research Council, UK

Harris, H. (2002) 'Think international manager, think male: Why are women not selected for international management assignments?', *Thunderbird International Business Review*, 44 (2): 175–203.

Hearn, J. (2000) 'On the complexity of feminist intervention in organizations', *Organization*, 7 (4): 609–24.

Hirsch, W. and Carter, A. (2002) *New Directions in Management Development* (Report 387). Brighton: Institute of Employment Studies.

Kamoche, K. (2000) 'Developing managers: The functional, the symbolic, the sacred and the profane', *Organisation Studies*, 21 (4): 747–77.

Kampa–Kokesch, S. and Anderson, M.Z. (2001) 'Executive coaching: A comprehensive review of the literature', *Consulting Psychology Journal: Practice and Research*, 53 (4): 205–28.

Kristeva, J. (1986) 'Word, dialogue and novel', in T. Moi (ed.) *The Kristeva Reader*. Oxford: Basil Blackwell. pp. 24–33.

Kuvaas, B. (2008) 'An exploration of how the employee-organization relationship affects the linkage between perception of developmental human resource practices and employee outcomes', *Journal of Management Studies*, 45 (1): 1–25.

Kyriakidou, O. (2005) 'Operational aspects of international human Resource Management', in M. Özbilgin (ed.) *International Human Resource Management: Theory and Practice*. Basingstoke: Palgrave.

Larsen, H. (2004) 'Experiential learning as management development: Theoretical perspective and empirical illustrations', *Advances in Developing Human Resources*, 6 (4): 486–503.

Lees, S. (1992) 'Ten faces of management development', *Management Education and Development*, 23 (2): 89–105.

Legge, K (1996) *Human Resource Management*. Basingstoke: Macmillan Business Press.

Litvin, D.R. (2002) 'The business case for diversity and the "Iron Cage"', in B. Czarniawska and H. Hopfl, (eds) *Casting the other: The Production and Maintenance of Inequality in organizations*. London: Routledge, pp. 160–84.

Mabey, C. (2005) *Management Development Works: The Evidence*. London: Chartered Management Institute, Achieving management excellence research series 1996–2005.

Mabey, C. and Finch-Lees, T. (2008) *Management and Leadership Development,* London: Sage.

Mabey, C. and Gooderham, P. (2005) 'The impact of management development on perceptions of organizational performance', *European Management Review*, 2 (2): 131–42.

Mabey, C. and Ramirez, M. (2005) 'Does management development improve organizational productivity? A six-country analysis of European firms', *International Journal of Human Resource Management*, 16 (7): 1067–82.

Martin, G., Pate, J. and McGoldrick, J. (1999) 'Do HRD investment strategies pay? Exploring the relationship between life–long learning and psychological contracts', *International Journal of Training and Development*, 3 (3): 200–14.

Meyerson, D.E. and Fletcher, J. (2000) 'A modest manifesto for shattering the glass ceiling', *Harvard Business Review* (Jan–Feb): 127–36.

Meyerson, D.E. and Kolb, D.M. (2000) 'Moving out of the "armchair": Developing a framework to bridge the gap between feminist theory and practice', *Organization*, 7 (4): 553–71.

Mole, G. (2004) 'Can leadership be taught?', in J. Storey (ed.) *Leadership in Organizations: Current Issues and Key Trends*. London: Routledge, pp. 125–37.

Newman, J. (2002) 'The New Public Management, modernization and institutional change: Disruptions, disjunctures and dilemmas', in K. McLaughlin, S.P. Osborne and N. Nicholson (eds) *Executive Instinct: Managing the Human Animal in the Information Age*. New York: Crown Publications.

Ogbonna, E. and Harris, L. (1998) 'Managing organizational culture: compliance or genuine change?', *British Journal of Management*, 9: 273–88.

Osman-Gani, A. and Tan, W.L. (2000) 'International training briefing: Training and development in Singapore', *International Journal of Training and Development*, 4 (4): 305–23.

Ostroff, C., Atwater, L. and Feinberg, B. (2004) 'Understanding self-other agreement: A look at rater and rate characteristics, context and outcomes', *Personnel Psychology*, 57: 333–75.

Pattison, S. (1997) *The Faith of the Managers*. London: Cassell.

Purcell, J., Kinnie, N., Hutchinson, S., Rayton, B. and Swart, J. (2003) *Understanding the people and performance link: Unlocking the black box*. London: Chartered Institute of People Development

Rankin, N. (2001) *Benchmarking survey of the 8th Competency Survey: Raising performance through people*, Competency and Emotional Intelligence, 2000/2001 Benchmarking Report. London: IRS Eclipse Group Ltd.

Rees, B. and Garnsey, E. (2003) 'Analysing competence: Gender and identity at work', *Gender, Work and Organization*, 10 (5): 551–71.

Rosenthal, P., Hill, S. and Peccei, R. (1997) 'Checking out service: Evaluating excellence, HRM and TQM in retailing', *Work, Employment and Society*, 11 (3): 481–503.

Rusaw, C.A. (2000) 'Uncovering training resistance', *Journal of Organizational Change Management*, 13 (3): 249–63.

Salaman, G. (2004) 'Competences of managers, competences of leaders', in J.Storey (ed.) *Leadership in Organizations*. London: Routledge, pp. 58–78.

Salaman, G. and Butler, J. (1990) 'Why managers won't learn', *Management Education and Development*, 21 (3): 183–91.

Sandberg, J. (2000) 'Understanding human competence at work: An interpretative approach', *Academy of Management Journal*, 43 (1): 9–26.

Schofield, J. (2002) 'The old ways are the best? The durability and usefulness of bureaucracy in public sector management', *Organization*, 8 (1): 77–96.

Seibert, K.W. and Hall, D. (1995) 'Strengthening the weak link in strategic executive development: Integrating individual development and global business strategy', *Human Resource Management*, 34: 549–67.

Siefert, C., Yukl, G. and McDonald, R. (2001) *A field experiment to evaluate the effects of multi-score feedback on managerial behaviour*, Paper presented to the 10th European Congress of Work and Organization Psychology, Prague.

Stacey, R. (1996) *Strategic Management and Organizational Dynamics*. London: Pitman.

Stiles, P., Gratton, L., Truss, C., Hope-Hailey, V. and McGovern, P. (1997) 'Performance management and the psychological contract', *Human Resource Management Journal*, 7 (1): 57–66.

Symon, G. and Cassell, C. (2006) 'Neglected perspectives in work and organizational psychology', *Journal of Occupational and Organizational Psychology*, 79 (3): 307–14.

Thomson, M. (2000) *Changing Management Capabilities in UK Aerospace*. London: The Society of British Aerospace Companies.

Townley, B. (1998) 'Beyond good and evil: Depth and division in the management of human resources', in A. McKinley and K. Starkey (eds) *Foucault, Management And Organization Theory*. London: Sage, pp. 191–210.

van der Boon, M. (2003) 'Women in international management: An international perspective on women's ways of leadership', *Women in Management Review*, 18 (3): 132–46.

Wang, J. and Wang, G. (2006) 'Exploring human resource development: A case of China management development in a transitioning context', *Human Resource Development Review*, 5 (2): 176–201.

Watson, T. (2001) 'The emergent manager and processes of management pre-learning', *Management Learning*, 32 (2): 221–35.

Wehrle, A.J. (1982) 'Review article: The Dialogic Imagination. Four Essays by M. M. Bakhtin', *The Slavic and East European Journal*, 26 (1): 106–7.

Winterton, J. and Winterton, R. (1997) 'Does management development matter?' *British Journal of Management*, 8: S65–S76.

Withers, P. (2001) 'Bigger and Better', *BC Business*, 29 (4): 50–6.

12

Understanding Performance Management and Appraisal: Supervisory and Employee Perspectives

Michelle Brown and Victoria S. Lim

INTRODUCTION

The employment relationship is open ended, meaning that the level of employee effort is neither fixed nor guaranteed. In response, many organizations establish mechanisms to provide clarity of organizational expectations through the evaluation of an employee's performance. The early systems were referred to as performance appraisal (PA) systems. PA usually involves 'evaluating performance based on the judgments and opinions of subordinates, peers, supervisors, other managers and even workers themselves' (Jackson and Schuler, 2003: 455). Fletcher (2001) suggests that the definition of this term has expanded from a narrow focus on the completion of an annual report on an employees' performance to a term that encompasses a variety of activities 'through

which organizations seek to assess employees and develop their competence, enhance performance and distribute rewards' (p. 473). The outcome of performance appraisals are used to provide career counselling, identify training and development opportunities, adjust rates of pay and provide information for discipline and dismissal decisions. PA has been seen as part of a broader approach known as 'performance management'. In this chapter we will use the term PA and focus on the motivations and tactics that supervisors and employees use in the formal evaluation of an employee's performance.

The research on PA falls into three broad themes. The early work focused on the psychometric properties of appraisal (Milkovich and Widgor, 1991). There are a great many studies that examined the different types of rating scales and formats for evaluating performance (for example, see Arvey and Murphy, 1998). Much of this early research regarded PAs as a test, resulting in an emphasis on validity, reliability and freedom from bias. The basic assumption was that rating inaccuracy was due to inadvertent cognitive errors (Tziner, 1999). The response was to provide supervisors with scales impermeable to cognitive rating biases (Tziner, 1999) and training. For example, researchers examined the impact of behaviourally anchored rating scales or graphic rating scales and identified a range of common errors made by supervisors, such as halo (a favourable rating for all job duties based on good performance in just one job duty), central tendency (rating all employees close to the midpoint of a scale irrespective of true performance) and recency effects (placing too much emphasis on recent performance) (Milkovich and Newman, 2002).

The quest for precision was replaced by an emphasis on how PAs could be engaged to further organisational goals (Milkovich and Widgor, 1991 refer to this as the 'applied tradition'). Research on supervisors continued but the emphasis was on their knowledge of the PA and the level of trust employees had in their supervisor. Debate about the use of performance ratings also commenced about this time: ratings used for developmental purposes were seen to be more lenient than ratings intended to determine pay outcomes (Boswell and Boudreau, 2002).

The third and most contemporary approach focuses on employee reactions to appraisal and the social context in which appraisals occur as these are seen as critical in determining the effectiveness of an appraisal system (Keeping and Levy, 2000; Levy and Williams, 2004). The rationale behind this body of research is that the way employees respond to a system is important to understanding whether the appraisal system is ultimately effective (Cardy and Dobbins, 1994).

The focus of this chapter is on how supervisors and employees manage the processes of PA. The impact of various systems has been extensively researched so few practical or theoretical gains are to be made with further research into design issues (see Milkovich

and Widgor, 1991; Keeping and Levy, 2000; Levy and Williams, 2004). We also have a sizeable body of research that examines the outcomes of appraisal. What is less well understood are the motivations and tactics of the participants operating *within* the system of appraisal. Survey evidence (Nankervis and Compton, 2006) demonstrates that the use of performance appraisal is now common among Australian organizations for both supervisors and employees. A supervisor is likely to find the assessment of their performance is partly a function of the way they manage the evaluations of their employees (Curtis et al., 2005) while employees are likely to face a PA system that is likely to impact on their pay, promotion and job security (Nankervis and Compton, 2006). Further, Treadway et al. (2007) argue that performance appraisals are becoming increasingly subjective. In combination, this provides an incentive for both participants to manage the process in order to ensure that it does them no harm or enhances their prospects within the organization. The way the participants manage the process may ultimately impact on the effectiveness of the PA system.

There is a relatively large body of research that has examined the motivations of supervisors in order to ensure that they provide accurate ratings. We review this literature and provide an agenda for future research. We then turn our attentions to employee motivations and tactics in PA. This is a much smaller body of research and represents a particularly fertile line for future research. We devote our attentions towards more contemporary research publications and provide examples from those publications that are representative of key findings and debates.

SUPERVISORY STRATEGIES IN PERFORMANCE MANAGEMENT

Introduction

The supervisor plays a critical role in the PA process. Supervisors are typically responsible for observing performance, rating performance and conducting the performance appraisal interview (PAI). The way in which supervisors put these major PA activities into practice ultimately determines the effectiveness of the organization's PA system (den Hartog et al., 2004). Consequently, there has been a great deal of PA research that has focused on helping supervisors rate employees more accurately, and how supervisors make decisions when rating employees. More recently, research has started concentrating on the contextual factors that influence the way supervisors rate employees. The following section reviews these main research themes in PA.

Motivation

Early research commonly assumed that supervisors aimed to rate employee performance accurately, and that accuracy in performance ratings was a function of the supervisor's cognitive capability. However, Murphy and Cleveland (1995) argue that rather than being incapable of rating accurately, inaccuracies in ratings were likely to be due to the supervisor's motivation to provide accurate ratings. A number of situational and personal factors contribute to a supervisor's motivation (Harris, 1994). Recent studies have found that a number of situational factors, such as organizational commitment, organizational climate, performance appraisal purpose (PAP), trust in the PA system, confidence in the system and accountability impact the supervisor's motivation to rate accurately. In addition to situational factors, there are also several personal variables that influence the supervisor's motivation, including individual differences, self-efficacy, performance appraisal discomfort (PAD), and goals.

Situational determinants

Organizational climate and organizational commitment

A number of studies demonstrate that organizational climate and organizational commitment play an important role in shaping a supervisor's motivation when conducting PA (Tziner and Murphy, 1999; Tziner et al.,

1998, 2001, 2002, 2005). A participative organizational climate was found to impact supervisors' motivation to provide accurate ratings and helpful performance feedback (Tziner et al., 2001). Characteristics of a participative organizational climate include cooperative relationships, individual responsibility, trust and communication. A participative organization is likely to reduce supervisor-subordinate conflict and political distortion of ratings. Similarly, supervisors who had higher levels of attitudinal commitment provided more accurate ratings (Tziner and Murphy, 1999).

Trust and confidence in the PA system

The perceptions supervisors hold about the PA system also have implications for their motivation in putting the system into practice. Harris (1994) argues that low levels of trust in the PA system will adversely affect the supervisor's motivation to rate accurately. Supervisors with trust in the PA system believe that the performance data will be utilized in a fair and objective manner. If a supervisor has low levels of trust in the PA system, he or she is likely to rate leniently rather than accurately due to the likelihood of negative outcomes for the employee. Tziner et al.'s (1998) study found that supervisors who had lower levels of trust in the PA system provided higher ratings compared to supervisors with higher levels of trust.

Similarly, a supervisor's confidence in the organization's PA system can also impact rating behaviour. Supervisors who have confidence in the PA system perceive it to be a credible activity that provides accurate and useful information about individual employee performance (Tziner and Murphy, 1999). Confidence in the PA system is influenced by whether political factors generally play a role in the formulation of ratings. Perceptions that performance ratings are largely used for political purposes in an organization (e.g., Longenecker et al., 1987) will reduce a supervisor's confidence in the PA system. Consequently, if rating inflation or distortion is the norm in the organization, supervisors are also likely to provide inaccurate ratings. Tziner and Murphy's (1999) study found that supervisors with low levels of confidence in the PA system were more likely to give elevated ratings.

Performance appraisal purpose and accountability

An organization's PA system may serve administrative and/or developmental purposes and this has been found to influence the supervisors' motivation in ratings given to employees. When the purpose of PA is administrative or evaluative, ratings of employee performance are used to determine important human resource decisions such as pay and promotion. In contrast, when PA serves a developmental purpose, the focus is on identify the employee's strengths and weaknesses for training needs and feedback (Jawahar and Williams, 1997; Taylor and Wherry, 1951). Research findings clearly indicate that when ratings are used for administrative purposes, supervisors rated employees more leniently than when rating was used for developmental purposes (Curtis et al., 2005; Jawahar and Williams, 1997; Tziner et al., 2001, 2005).

In his model of rater motivation, Harris (1994) proposed that accountability would be a key situational factor influencing motivation. More recently, there have been a number of studies that have examined the relationship between accountability and the supervisor's motivation in rating employee performance. Accountability refers to the amount of social pressure on the supervisor to justify their rating to others (Harris, 1994). According to accountability theory, holding an individual accountable for the decisions he or she makes will impact the individual's motivational state, and consequently highlight the significance of the task at hand, as well as prompting behaviour that leads toward task accomplishment (Mero et al., 2003)

Mero and Motowidlo (1995) found that when supervisors were made to feel accountable by having to justify their ratings, more accurate ratings were provided. Similar accountability pressures also resulted in reduced contrast effects and halo errors (Palmer and Feldman, 2005). When made accountable, Mero et al. (2003) found

that supervisors increased their attentiveness to performance and recorded better notes relating to the performance and this resulted in greater rating accuracy. Overall, these studies highlight the positive aspects of accountability. However, other studies have found that the 'audience' to whom supervisors are accountable to plays an important role in shaping rating behaviour.

When supervisors are accountable to *their* superiors they tended to rate less leniently (Curtis et al., 2005). Curtis et al. (2005) argue that if the supervisor's superiors are likely to check the ratings and could potentially change their ratings, accountability is increased. Supervisors are motivated to appear competent to their superiors and hence rate less leniently. In contrast, research findings suggest that when supervisors are held accountable to their employees, they are more likely to inflate their ratings (Curtis et al., 2005; Klimoski and Inks, 1990; Roch, 2005; Shore and Tashchian, 2002; 2003). This is especially true when supervisors anticipate a face-to-face meeting with employees who are poor performers (Klimoski and Inks, 1990; Yun et al., 2005).

In general, supervisors do not like giving negative feedback (e.g., Tesser and Rosen, 1975) and employees do not welcome negative feedback about their performance (e.g., Geddes and Baron, 1997). When supervisors know that they are answerable to their employees, the anticipation of adverse employee reactions is likely to motivate supervisors to inflate their rating in order to avoid communicating negative feedback (Curtis et al., 2005; Klimoski and Inks, 1990; Shore and Tashchian, 2002). Another explanation for rating inflation in the context of downward accountability is that when supervisors are aware of the employee's views, they are likely to provide ratings that a similar to that of the employee's expectation. Employees often have an unrealistically positive view of their own performance and are likely to rate themselves highly (Meyer, 1980). For supervisors, this approach towards making rating decisions involves the least amount of effort in information processing (Mero and Motowidlo, 1995).

Personal determinants

Individual differences

A supervisor's personality has also been found to be an important determinant of rating behaviour (Costa and McCrae, 1992). Research suggests that a supervisor's tendency to distort ratings is a relatively stable characteristic of the individual. For example, Bernadin et al. (2000) found that high conscientious supervisors tended to give lower ratings, while supervisors high in Agreeableness were more likely to provide elevated ratings (Costa and McCrae, 1992). Other studies have found that a supervisor's personality influences the relationship between situational factors and rating behaviour. For example, Tziner et al. (2002) found that conscientiousness moderated the relationship between situational determinants (e.g., PA purpose and confidence in the PA system) and the supervisor's rating behaviour. Low conscientious supervisors were more likely to provide ratings that were consistent with their perception of contextual factors. In Roch et al.'s (2005) study high conscientious supervisors felt more accountable. When supervisors where accountable to their employees and expected a face-to-face meeting, Yun et al. (2005) found supervisors high in agreeableness provided more elevated ratings compared to those low on agreeableness.

Researchers have also begun to examine another dispositional characteristic of the rater: self-monitoring. In one such study, Jawahar (2001) found that high self-monitors tended to produce more elevated and inaccurate ratings. Self-monitoring is a stable dispositional characteristic that is related to an individual's tendency to consider and to be influenced by situational conditions. High self-monitors are good at interpreting cues in the social environment and are able to adapt their behaviour to fit the social context. While it seems to suggest that supervisors who are high self-monitors tend to inflate ratings, this may not necessarily be problematic. Jawahar

(2005) also found that high self-monitors are better at noticing situational constraints that impede employee performance, and adjust their ratings accordingly.

Self-efficacy

Some studies have found that the level of a supervisor's self-efficacy affects rating choices. Supervisors with high levels of self-efficacy are expected to be motivated to provide more accurate ratings, as they believe that they have the necessary information, tools and skills to perform the task (Bernadin and Villanova, 2005; Tziner et al., 2005). In contrast, supervisors with lower levels of self-efficacy are likely to lack the motivation to undertake the appraisal task and provide accurate ratings that have been carefully documented (Tziner et al., 2005). Bernadin and Villanova (2005) found that training designed to improve self-efficacy to be effective in reducing rating elevation. However, the role of self-efficacy in shaping supervisors' rating behaviour is not clear-cut. For example, Tziner et al. (1998) found that supervisors with higher levels of self-efficacy were less likely to discriminate between different aspects of performance. Other studies have found a positive relationship between self-efficacy and rating leniency (Tziner and Murphy, 1999; Tziner et al., 2002).

Performance appraisal discomfort

Research suggests that supervisors are uncomfortable about monitoring employee performance, rating performance and communicating feedback (Murphy and Cleveland, 1995). Studies indicate that supervisors reporting high levels of discomfort also tended to rate more leniently (Tziner and Murphy, 1999; Tziner et al., 2001; Villanova et al., 1993). Supervisors are likely to provide lenient ratings to avoid unpleasant consequences that are potentially attached to lower ratings. Smith et al. (2000) also found that supervisors who perceive that PA is associated with important outcomes experienced higher levels of discomfort. In contrast with personality, both self-efficacy and performance appraisal discomfort have been found to be personal factors that can be changed via training interventions (Bernadin and Villanova, 2005).

Goals and appraisal politics

The pursuit of certain goals is also likely to influence a supervisor's motivation (Murphy and Cleveland, 1995). Supervisors will tend to assign employees a rating that facilitates the achievement of their goals and not necessarily the most accurate rating (Cleveland and Murphy, 1992). According to Cleveland and Murphy (1992) the goals supervisors pursue generally relate to 1) the employee's task-performance, 2) maintenance of interpersonal relationships, 3) strategic purposes, and 4) the individual's personal values and beliefs. Murphy et al. (2004) found that when supervisors are observing the same performance, different ratings are given that are consistent with the supervisor's goals.

Appraisal politics is an example of goal-directed behaviour (Cleveland and Murphy, 1992). In studies employing open-ended interviews, supervisors reported manipulating performance ratings to achieve a particular end state (Gioia and Longenecker, 1994; Longenecker et al., 1987). For example, supervisors explained that they inflated performance ratings in order to maintain or improve employee performance (Longenecker et al., 1987). Supervisors also recognized that such political behaviour can produce undesired consequences that include undermining organizational goals and exposing the organization to lawsuits when employees are terminated (Gioia and Longenecker, 1994). In addition to these qualitative studies, Tziner et al. (1996) developed the Questionnaire of Political Considerations in Performance Appraisals (QPCPA) to encourage quantitative studies of appraisal politics. The QPCPA has subsequently been used in recent research examining appraisal politics (e.g., Poon, 2004). Poon's (2004) study examined the outcomes of appraisal politics. This study found that appraisal politics resulted in lowered job satisfaction and, in turn, increased turnover intentions, when

political behaviour stemmed from personal bias or was used to punish employees. However, if political behaviour was exercised for the purpose of motivating employees, it had no effect on job satisfaction and turnover intentions.

Future research

PA research should not merely make theoretical contributions, but also facilitate improvements in practice. A criticism of the PA literature is the lack of attention directed towards how research might inform practice (Bretz et al., 1992). The widespread use of laboratory settings and student samples in many studies fosters the gap between research and practice. However, many recent studies of the social and contextual factors have continued to be conducted within laboratory settings (e.g., Curtis et al., 2005; Roch et al., 2005). While researchers have made attempts to simulate real-life organizational conditions in the laboratory, findings of their studies still need to be replicated in field settings.

As researchers continue to examine the social and contextual factors that influence PA, it is important to ensure that attempts are made to bridge the research-practice gap. Studies examining individual differences have been useful in demonstrating that rating behaviour is a function of the supervisor's personality (e.g., Bernadin et al., 2000; Jawahar, 2001). However, personality is a stable disposition with little applicability to organizations (Bernadin and Villanova, 2005). For example, what measures can organizations implement to encourage supervisors high in Agreeableness to rate more accurately? In order to minimize the research-practice gap, researchers should direct their attention towards examining contextual factors that strengthen or weaken the relationship between personality and rating behaviour. For example Yun et al. (2005) found that supervisors high in Agreeableness were more likely to inflate ratings when a face-to-face meeting was expected. On a practical level, organizations can implement interventions relating to the PAI to moderate the rating behaviour of supervisors with certain personality characteristics.

A key concern within PA research is the tendency of supervisors to inflate ratings. Accountability research indicates that when supervisors expect to justify their ratings to employees in a face-to-face context, ratings are likely to be inflated (for example, Klimoski and Ink, 1990). Thus, in organizations where supervisors are required to formally communicate the rating and provide feedback to employees in a face-to-face during the PA interview, rating inflation is expected to be particularly problematic. It appears that one reason for rating inflation is that supervisors are uncomfortable and lack self-efficacy in communicating lower ratings to employees during the PAI (Bernadin and Villanova, 2005; Villanova et al., 1993). Accurate ratings are likely to be below the employee's own assessment of how well he or she has performed and hence perceived by employees as negative feedback. In general negative feedback is not readily accepted and can result in adverse employee reactions such as aggression (Geddes and Baron, 1997; Ilgen et al., 1979; Meyer, 1980).

Thus it seems useful for future research to focus not only on rating behaviour but also examine how supervisors manage the PA interview. For example, what tactics do supervisors employ when communicating negative feedback to employees during the PA interview? Which tactics help supervisors communicate negative feedback in a way that results in performance improvements whilst minimizing adverse employee reactions? On a practical level, these research findings can be applied to the design of training interventions that help equip supervisors to deliver negative feedback effectively. Furthermore, culture may play a role in the feedback process (Shipper et al., 2007). For example, in high power distance cultures (Hofstede, 2001) employees may accept negative feedback from their supervisor more readily compared to employees from low power distance culture. It would also be interesting to examine whether the tactics managers use to communicate negative feedback differs across cultures.

Previous research suggests that the supervisor's experience in conducting PA provided more accurate ratings (Barnes-Farrel et al., 1991; Cardy et al., 1987; Ostroff and Ilgen, 1992). Similarly, we might anticipate that a supervisor with little experience of PA will utilize different tactics to one with many years of experience. For example, an inexperienced supervisor might be more likely to stick more closely to the rules of the system while an experienced supervisor may be more willing to regard the rules as guidelines. Experienced supervisors may also have a wider range of tactics compared to supervisors with less experience.

Aside from ratings, supervisors may also employ a more subtle approach towards achieving their PA goals (Murphy and Cleveland, 1995; Murphy et al., 2004). The blatant distortion of ratings is associated with the risk of sanctions from the organization, if detected. Tziner and Murphy (1999) found that when supervisors perceived a high risk of being caught they were less likely to distort their ratings. The use of influence tactics in managing the PA process is comparatively less obvious (Falbe and Yukl, 1992; Yukl et al., 1996; Yukl and Tracey, 1992). For example, if supervisors are interested in improving employee performance, they may adopt certain tactics to motivate employees to exert extra effort in order to improve their performance during the PA cycle before the rating stage. Improved employee performance will subsequently be reflected in performance ratings. Hence supervisors are able to achieve their goals through the use of influence tactics without rating distortions. Furthermore, we might anticipate different outcomes from these different approaches: rating distortion is a blunt approach and possibly more likely to lead to unintended outcomes. However, little is known about how supervisors manage other stages of the PA process besides rating, and how this may differ as a result of PA experience.

Future researchers should examine the extent to which supervisors vary their ratings of employees over time. As employees become more familiar with a task, it is likely to be completed more efficiently. Changes in motivation over time and the acquisition of job knowledge can also contribute to changes in performance. Performance ratings should reflect changes in employee performance (Sturman et al., 2005). At present we know very little about whether supervisors are sensitive to changes in employee performance, and to what extent they change their ratings of employees. However, supervisors may not always have the opportunity to observe employee performance for full PA cycle. Under these circumstances, supervisors may avoid evaluating the employee's performance altogether (Fried et al., 1992). However, when avoidance is not an option, how do supervisors manage the PA process when they are limited by time?

Finally, PA researchers have typically focused on a single participant in the PA process – either the supervisor or the employee (Levy and Williams, 2004). Examining the interaction between the participants within the PA process can also be useful in understanding the motivations and strategies of supervisors. To what extent do supervisors alter their approach depending on their 'reading' of the employee? For example, the feedback tactic employed may differ depending on whether the supervisor believes the employee prefers 'straight talking' or a more subtle approach. Furthermore, do supervisors attempt to 'read' all of their employees or maintain a consistent approach in order to be seen as fair?

EMPLOYEE STRATEGIES IN PERFORMANCE MANAGEMENT

Under the measurement tradition, employees were often regarded as passive participants in the PA process: employees working under a well-designed system with an appropriately trained supervisor would respond with high levels of performance. Under the applied tradition, employee reactions to appraisal have been extensively researched. This section looks behind employee reactions to employee motivations and tactics in a PA system. We first review the literature on employee motivations and tactics and then outline an agenda for future research.

Motivation

Appraisals have at their core a desire to maximize the performance of employees in order to further organizational performance (Cardy and Dobbins, 1994). The assumption is that employees are motivated by the desire for a high rating in order to access the financial and non financial rewards (for example, merit bonuses, promotional opportunities and access to training and development programmes). A theoretical basis for this assumption derives from expectancy theory (Vroom, 1964), which predicts that job motivation is improved when employees link job performance and organizational rewards. The anticipation of rewards can motivate people to a higher level of performance (Heneman, 1992).

There is a sizeable body of research that has examined the impact of performance ratings on employees. The rating is a valued outcome as it represents an assessment of the employee's worth to the organization and can be important in maintaining self-esteem (Folger, 1987). An employee's self esteem is affected by performance ratings because research has shown that employees usually rate themselves higher than their supervisors do (Meyer and Walker, 1961). Further, self enhancement theory (Schrauger, 1975) suggests that individuals will react more positively to higher ratings than to lower ratings. Positive evaluations are seen as more accurate, are valued more and are better accepted than negative ratings. Positive ratings elicit positive reactions toward the appraisal (Kacmar et al., 1996). This suggests that employees are motivated to pursue higher ratings. Jackman and Strober (2003) suggest that employees are motivated to *avoid* a low rating

Employee reactions to performance appraisal

PA has been associated with a range of outcomes. Mayer and Davis (1999) reported that PA systems can build trust in the organization. Taylor and Pierce (1999) measured organizational commitment and job satisfaction. They report differences based on the rating of the employee. There was an increase in assessments of job satisfaction and co-operation with one's supervisor upon the introduction of the PA system for low performers (particularly following the planning/goal setting phase). This was in contrast to high performers who had a high base line level of these attitudes towards supervision, followed by substantial drops immediately after receiving appraisal and bonus pay distributions. A study by Taylor and Pierce (1999) found that a PA system did not have a significant impact on the subsequent level of employee effort.

We also have a small body of research that has examined adverse employee reactions to appraisal processes. Brown and Benson (2003) report that PA can stimulate employee efforts beyond that which employees regard as manageable. Difficult performance objectives and the pursuit of higher performance ratings were associated with employee reports of work overload. Gabris and Ihrke (2001) find that procedural and distributive injustice in a performance appraisal system was associated with employee reports of burnout, a form of stress.

Participation in performance appraisal

The perceived fairness of a performance appraisal can have an impact on the overall effectiveness of the system (Dobbins et al., 1990). Employees' perception of performance appraisal fairness is determined, in part, by the capacity to participate in its processes: 'individuals view procedures as most fair when control is vested in the participants' (Konovsky, 2000: 493). Two types of participation have been identified:

instrumental and non instrumental (Korsgaard and Roberson, 1995). Instrumental participation is seen to permit some level of control by employees over processes and decisions. Jawahar (2006) suggests that employees value instrumental participation as they 'may believe that they could use the performance appraisal feedback session to highlight their accomplishments in a manner that would result in higher evaluations' (p. 216). Non instrumental participation is valued because it offers the opportunity to express an opinion regardless of its actual impact, as it satisfies the desire to have one's opinions considered (Korsgaard and Roberson, 1995).

After a meta analysis of participation studies, Cawley et al. (1998: 624) concluded the 'analysis has firmly established that participation in performance appraisal is positively associated with a diverse number of favourable subordinate reactions'. The value of participation is further demonstrated by a link between low involvement and employee reports of stress. Michie and Williams (2003) report high levels of distress among student nurses caused by a low level of involvement in PA decision-making. They also report that employees who have learned to participate, and hence control their work, have lower stress hormones. An alternative perspective on participation is provided by Newton and Findlay (1996: 43) who asked 'do employees really want to take responsibility for improving themselves through their "active" participation in appraisal or rather might they view appraisal as a manipulation which places the burden of "development" on the employee and encourages them to see themselves as a resource which they must polish and refine according to their employer's needs'.

Impression management

Impression management (IM)

refers to the process by which individuals try to influence the impressions others have of them. ... a person's overarching goals when engaging in impression management is to create a desired image in the minds of others which can be achieved by using a variety of tactics (Harris et al., 2007: 278).

The tactics of IM fall into two broad categories: supervisor focused and job focused (Wayne and Liden, 1995).

Supervisory focused impression management techniques involve ingratiation behaviours that are intended to make employees more likeable (for example, flattery or favour rendering) (Bolino et al., 2006). There is a body of research supporting the value of supervisory focused IM as demonstrated by a positive impact on performance evaluations (see Gordon, 1996; Vilela et al., 2007; Wayne and Ferris, 1990; Wayne and Liden, 1995). A supervisor who feels liked and admired by a subordinate is more likely to rate the employee favourably (Wayne and Ferris, 1990; Wayne and Liden, 1995). Job focused impression management techniques are designed to make employees appear more competent at their job (for example self promotion and taking credit for positive events at work (Bolino et al., 2006)). Wayne and Ferris (1990) and Ferris et al. (1994) found that job focused techniques were less liked by supervisors and employees who used them received lower performance ratings from their supervisor. There is also some research that suggests that impression management can create adverse consequences for employees. Crant (1996, quoted in Lam et al., 2007) noted that the use of impression management techniques may result in employees being seen as untruthful, unreliable and calculating.

Attention has now turned to how impression management tactics work. Kacmar et al. (2004) reported that dispositional factors (i.e. self esteem, need for power, job involvement and shyness) were significant in explaining the use of ingratiatory tactics (these include flattery, false modesty, and opinion conformity). Harris et al. (2007) found that individuals who use IM tactics and were high in political skill were more likely to be seen as better performers. Individuals low in political skill who engaged in IM tactics were seen as less effective performers. The explanation for

these findings is that those employees with a high level of political skills were able to use the range of IM tactics more effectively as they tailored their use based on their knowledge of their supervisor.

The challenge for supervisors is to be alert to the use of IM tactics in order to be less susceptible to its effects. Supervisors need to be aware that their performance ratings may be contaminated by the IM tactics of their subordinates. This is particularly significant when the outcomes of a performance appraisal are linked to critical HRM decisions such as pay or promotion (Vilela et al., 2007).

Hochwarter et al. (2007) examine the role of employee reputation and its impact on perceived effectiveness. Individuals who have developed a more favourable reputation are seen as 'more legitimate, competent and trustworthy and typically enjoy the benefits of being viewed as possessing a higher level of status' (p. 568). Further 'individuals perceived as reputable are progressively more prone to be afforded the benefit of the doubt'. Hochwarter et al. (2007) found that reputation moderated the relationship between political behaviour and job performance, such that those with a high reputation were more likely to have higher supervisor reported performance.

The nature of the relationship between an employee and their supervisor has been shown to be critical in assessments of employee performance. In the leader-member exchange (LMX) literature, the higher the quality of the relationship, the better subordinates perform. As the quality of the LMX increases, supervisors provide more support and resources to their subordinates in various tasks that aid career development. Such positive contributions create obligations for the subordinates to reciprocate, which they do by performing more effectively (Chen et al., 2007).

At the other end of the spectrum, there is research on 'abusive supervision', which is defined as 'subordinates perception of the extent to which their supervisors engage in the sustained display of hostile verbal and non verbal behaviours, excluding physical contact' (Tepper, 2000: 178). Tepper et al. (2001) investigate employee responses to abusive supervision, suggesting that there are two broad types of employee resistance: functional and dysfunctional responses. Functional responses involve 'constructive efforts designed to open a dialogue with their supervisors (e.g. requesting clarification and negotiation), while dysfunctional responses involve 'passive–aggressive responses (e.g. acting like one is too busy to complete a request, acting like one did not hear the request or acting like one has forgotten to perform the request' (p. 975). This has implications for PA as Tepper et al. (2001) report that employees in their study retaliated against abusive supervisor by resisting downward influence attempts in a dysfunctional manner.

In combination these studies suggest that employees are not always passive agents in the PA process and when they use IM tactics, work on developing a good reputation or a high quality relationship with their supervisor, they will be more likely to be seen as good performers.

Feedback and performance appraisal

Feedback seeking is a proactive employee behaviour typically seen as an 'explicit verbal request for information on work behaviour and work performance' (Lam et al., 2007: 349). For organizations, feedback provides an opportunity to give direction to employee behaviours and stimulate employee effort, while feedback for employees satisfies a need for information about how they are doing at work (Jawahar, 2006). Kluger and DeNisi (1996) found that while feedback typically improved employee performance, in just over a third of the studies feedback lowered performance.

Feedback can be positive or negative, though employees are not typically receptive to negative feedback. This is because negative feedback may be based on unjust interpersonal treatment (Leung et al., 2001), may cause the recipient to lose face or may damage his or her self image (Bernichon et al., 2003). Jackman and Strober (2003) point out that some employees avoid seeking feedback for fear that it will result in 'impossible demands' (p. 101). Information and clarity of expectations will ensure employees realise the full extent of their supervisor's performance expectations. This fear of feedback is partly based on a view that supervisors focus on the negatives in performance, a product of PA scheme design that requires supervisors to identify improvements. This is particularly the case when the performance objectives are numerical as the suggestions for changes are likely to involve doing 'more' (Coens and Jenkins, 2000). Reaction to negative feedback can vary but, as Bourguignon et al. (2005) point out, reactions to negative feedback may depend on the employees' opportunities for external mobility, relative strength, and loyalty to the organization. Employees who are in a weak position may become cynical.

On the other hand, Chen et al. (2007) suggest that seeking negative feedback is a means of obtaining an accurate view of how employees are perceived and determining how they can reciprocate in ways that will satisfy their supervisors' expectations. Chen et al. argue that negative feedback has a higher instrumental value than positive feedback. Negative feedback gives recipients a better idea of inadequate work behaviour and performance and suggests how they can make improvements according to their supervisor's preferences. Chen et al. (2007) found that a better relationship between the employee and supervisor (measured by LMX, 'leader member exchange') encourages subordinates to seek negative feedback from their immediate supervisor more frequently. This is because such an interaction requires a high level of mutual trust such that subordinates feel able to seek potentially embarrassing or difficult information from their immediate boss.

Supervisors may interpret employee feedback seeking as a desire to improve performance ('performance enhancement motive') or to create a positive impression with their supervisor ('impression management motive'). Researchers have found a positive relationship between employee feedback seeking and 'objective work performance when supervisors interpreted the feedback seeking behaviour as being driven more by performance enhancement motives and less by impression management motives' (Lam et al., 2007: 348). When a supervisor views employee feedback seeking driven by a 'performance enhancement motive' they regard the employee as 'achievement focused and intending to meet a high standard in accomplishing work tasks' (Lam et al., 2007: 350). When are employees likely to be proactive in seeking feedback? Barner-Rasmussen (2003) demonstrated that perceived trust and frequent interaction with supervisors were determinants of the feedback seeking behaviour of subordinates.

Lee (1997) distinguishes feedback from help seeking behaviour. Feedback can be used by employees to monitor their performance, even in the absence of any specific problems. In contrast, help seeking is a more proactive behaviour focussed on solving specific problems. It involves the 'search for another to provide assistance and relief' (Lee, 1997: 338). There are many obstacles to help seeking behaviour, acknowledging incompetence and increasing dependence on others, which can negatively impact on an employee's public image. However, employees who are able to seek help tend to have higher performance evaluations (Lee, 1999). Lee (1997) found that individuals were more likely to seek help more from equal status than unequal status helpers.

Employees are not only the recipients of feedback but are often asked to *provide* feedback on their supervisors as part of a 360 degree feedback model of performance appraisal. Kudisch, Fortunanto & Smith (2006) noted that employees are typically reluctant to provide feedback, which is a problem for the effectiveness of an upward appraisal system (which requires the input of many in order to get a clear picture of a supervisor's performance). Kudisch et al. found that providing employees with knowledge of the upward appraisal system (and

its consequences), support from co-workers and top management and confidence to provide ratings, were important in encouraging employees to provide an assessment of their supervisor. Antonioni (1994) examined employee tactics in an upward feedback system. In his study, employees indicated a strong preference for anonymity when providing feedback on their supervisor for 'fear of reprisal' (p. 354). Further, when they were made accountable for their feedback (by including their name with the feedback) employees rated their supervisor more favourably than those able to remain anonymous.

Resistance in performance appraisal

Employees have a choice in their response to the downward influence tactics used by their supervisors through an appraisal system. Yukl (2002) suggested that employees resist managerial influence attempts 'by making excuses about why the request cannot be carried out, try to persuade the agent to withdraw or change the request, ask higher authorities to overrule the agent's request, delay acting in the hope that the agent will forget about the request, make a pretence of complying but try to sabotage the task or refuse to carry out the request' (p. 143).

Does resistance have any impact on an employee rated performance? Tepper et al. (1998) identified two approaches to resistance: refusing negatively and negotiating. They found that negotiating was positively related to performance, demonstrating that employees' choice of resistance tactics can have an impact of their performance rating. In a subsequent study, Tepper et al. (2006) distinguish between two managerial views of resistance. A uniformly dysfunctional perspective (i.e. supervisors who regard all manifestations of resistance as indicators of ineffective influence and rate subordinates unfavourably when they resist) and a multi-functional perspective (i.e. supervisors regard some manifestations of resistance as more constructive than others and rate subordinates more favourably when they employ constructive resistance tactics). They find that supervisors adopt a uniformly dysfunctional perspective when they have a low quality LMX relationship and adopt a multifunctional perspective when they have a higher quality LMX relationship.

Future directions

Researchers need to focus attention on the tactics used by employees in a PA system. The PAI is in many ways equivalent to a job interview in that it provides the employee an opportunity to manage their supervisor in order to make the right impression and maximize the rewards or minimize any anticipated punishments (Ellis et al., 2002). The selection literature tends to regard the job interview as consisting of three broad parts: preparation for the interview, the interview and dealing with the aftermath of the interview (Bardwell, 1991). This provides a useful research framework for understanding the PA interview from an employee's perspective.

How do employees prepare for the PA interview? We might anticipate that the employee will focus on collecting data for their appraisal, for example locating a copy of the goals set in the first stage of the cycle and their indicators. Jackman and Strober (2003) suggest that this stage might also include collecting feedback by others to take into the meeting with the supervisor. The objective in this phase is to catalogue evidence of activities and achievements during the evaluation cycle.

After the preparation of the formal documentation, the emphasis is likely to shift to developing tactics. Tactical considerations might include timing of the PA interview (e.g. early in the day, late in the day), best way to present the documentation, listening versus talking in the PAI, anticipating supervisory reactions and deciding on how to dress for the interview. Jackman and Strober (2003) identify the importance of developing questions to be asked in the meeting. They also suggest that the employee give thought to how these questions are framed, especially when they deal with issues of negative feedback.

How do employees manage the actual exchange with their supervisor? Do employees get anxious? McCarthy and Goffin (2004) have developed a scale to measure anxiety in a selection interview, which might provide the basis for assessments of anxiety in the PA interview. What tactics do employees invoke when the PA interview is not going as they had anticipated in the preparation phase? Employees need to consider their verbal and non-verbal reactions to issues raised in the interview: should they remain 'physically and emotionally neutral' (Jackman and Strober, 2003: 106) or express their reactions in some way? Should employees take notes in the PA interview? It might be an effective tactic for demonstrating an interest in the observations of the supervisor (see Houdek et al., 2002 for a review of research on note taking in an interview). How do employees 'read' and respond to the non-verbal messages provided by the supervisor? What effect does the tenure under a particular supervisor have on the choice of tactics? The tactics employed during the first PA interview with a supervisor might differ from those employed in subsequent PAI as the employee learns how to 'read' their supervisor more effectively. What effect does previous experience with PA interviews impact on the choice of tactics? Employees in their first appraisal interview might access a narrow set of tactics compared with a veteran of PA interviews. Do employees talk about the tactics they used after the PAI? We might anticipate that employees who have their PAI after other colleagues might approach the interview differently based on the experience of those who went before them. For example they will know of any particular issues that the supervisor is emphasizing in the current round of PA interviews and possibly how the supervisor has rated colleagues.

Do employees use different tactics to accomplish their objectives in a performance appraisal system? The communication literature suggests this is the case with other issues. For example, Lim (1990) found that respondents were more verbally aggressive when their task was to persuade someone who resisted in an unfriendly manner as opposed to a friendly manner. Is an employee's reaction to PA a function of their assessment of how well they managed the process and their supervisor? To what extent do the experiences of one PA impact on the choice of tactics in a subsequent cycle?

Researchers should also be alert to the possibility of dysfunctional tactics. Bourguignon et al. (2005) acknowledge that 'people "manage" performance measures in ways that might create dysfunctional outcomes' (p. 689). We also need to think about the role of counter productive employee strategies, for example cheating. Hochwarter et al. (2007) note that 'backstabbing and upmanship is undertaken to secure benefits only for the actor' (p. 567) and is an 'ingrained component of virtually all work settings' (p. 567). As the consequences of performance appraisal escalate we may anticipate greater use of these tactics.

Once we have established the range of employee tactics researchers should turn their attention to understanding what kinds of employees make the best use of these tactics. These individual differences might also be seen as sources of 'illegitimate strength' (Bourguignon et al., 2005) as not all employees will be effective in invoking appraisal tactics. Researchers should consider the following as potential explanators: age, gender, education and personality (for example as identified by the Big Five personality measure [Costa and McCrae, 1992]: openness to experience, conscientiousness, extraversion, agreeableness and neuroticism). The orientation to work might also provide a way of understanding who uses the tactics to what effect: for example, achievement motivation, status aspiration, work ethic, acquisitiveness, dominance and excellence orientation (Cassidy and Lynn, 1989).

We also need research on the limits to the effectiveness of tactics: three of interest are the responsiveness of the supervisor, the structure of the PA and the orientation of the PA system. Implicit person theory suggests that supervisors can be broadly categorized as 'entity theorists' or as 'incremental theorists' (Heslin et al. 2005). The former believe

that personal attributes are largely fixed which leads them to 'quickly form strong impressions of others that they resist revising even in the light of contradictory information' (p. 843). Incremental theorists are more likely to 'appreciate the dynamic personal and situational determinants of behaviour and they reconsider initial impression after receiving new information' (p. 843). This potentially limits the effectiveness of employee tactics with an 'entity theorist' supervisor. It also suggests that the timing of tactics can be crucial as the first assessments tend to become the anchor for subsequent assessments. Employees who report to an 'instrumental theorist' are more likely to find their tactics effective as these supervisors are more receptive to new information framed by a tactically savvy employee.

Does the level of structure in a PA system limit the extent to which any tactics invoked by an employee can be effective? Campion et al. (1997) suggested that structured job interviews limited the scope for IM techniques. This finding was challenged by Ellis et al. (2002) who found that employees are able to invoke the full range of IM tactics in a structured interview, depending on which tactic they thought would be most likely to succeed.

Tsui and Wu (2005) suggest that human resource management (HRM) is currently focused on employee monitoring and under this approach appraisals are adopted as a cost cutting tool. Under a 'headcount management' (p. 115) approach the emphasis is on current job performance, which they see as inferior to a 'mutual investment' approach which emphasizes broad based contributions. A cost cutting approach may set limits to the effectiveness of employee tactics as supervisors may have less discretion and unable to provide the kinds of outcomes that an employee's tactics in PA were intended to generate.

CONCLUSIONS

PA researchers have typically focused their attentions on either the employee or the supervisor (Levy and Williams, 2004), with an emphasis in trying to make PA systems effective. It is now time to move from a focus on PA systems and their consequences to a focus on how the participants operate *within* these systems. Our review has identified a complex set of motives for both participants in PA and these are an important element in the choice of tactics.

Understanding the motives and tactics of supervisors and employees raises many methodological challenges. We will need to invoke qualitative techniques to identify the full set of motives and tactics while quantitative research will help us identify the extent to which they are used and their implications. We also need a dynamic approach to research in PA as the tactics used by one participant will be a function of those used by the other participant and how these actions and reactions of the participants change over time (Bourguignon and Chiapello, 2005).

Performance appraisals are a widely used tool of human resource management and the outcomes of these systems are used to inform many other HR functions. Investigating the tactics used by the participants in a PA process is an exciting new way to understand the role and consequences of this HRM tool.

REFERENCES

Antionioni, D. (1994) 'The effects of feedback accountability on upward appraisal ratings', *Personnel Psychology*, 47: 349–356.

Arvey, R.D. and Murphy, K.R. (1998) 'Performance evaluation in work settings', *Annual Review of Psychology*, 49: 141–168.

Barner-Rasmussen, W. (2003) 'Determinants of feedback seeking behavior of subsidiary top managers in Multinational Corporations', *International Business Review*, 12 (1): 41–52.

Barnes-Farrell, J.L., L'Heureux, T.J. and Conway, J.M. (1991) 'Impact of gender-related job features on the accurate evaluation of performance information', *Organizational Behavior and Human Decision Processes*, 48: 22–35.

Bardwell, C. (1991) 'Preparing for and Excelling at On Campus Interviews', *Black Collegian*, 22 (2): 122–126.

Bernadin, H.J., Cooke, D.K. and Villanova, P. (2000) 'Conscientiousness and agreeableness as predictors of rating leniency', *Journal of Applied Psychology*, 85: 232–234.

Bernadin, H.J. and Villanova, P. (2005) 'Research streams in rater self-efficacy', *Group and Organization Management*, 30: 61–88.

Bernichon,T., Cook, K.E. and Brown, J.D. (2003) 'Seeking Self-Evaluative Feedback: The Interactive Role of Global Self-Esteem and Specific Self-Views', *Journal of Personality and Social Psychology*, 84 (1): 94–204.

Bourguignon, A. and Chiapello, E. (2005) 'The role of criticism in the dynamics of performance evaluation systems', *Critical Perspectives on Accounting*, 16: 665–700.

Bolino, M.C., Varela, J.A., Bande, B. and Turnley, W.H. (2006) 'The impact of impression management tactics on supervisory ratings of organizational citzenship behaviours', *Journal of Organizational Behavior*, 27: 281–297.

Boswell, W.R. and Boudreau, J.W. (2002) 'Separating the developmental and evaluative performance appraisal uses', *Journal of Business and Psychology*, 16 (3): 391–412.

Bretz, R.D., Milkovich, G.T. and Read, W. (1992) 'The current state of performance appraisal research and practice: concerns, directions and implications', *Journal of Management*, 18: 321–352.

Brown, M. and Benson, J. (2005) 'Managing to Overload? Work overload and performance appraisal processes', *Group and Organization Management*, 30 (1): 99.

Campion, M.A., Palmer, D.K. and Campion, J.E. (1997) 'A review of structure in the selection interview', *Personnel Psychology*, 50: 655–702.

Cawley, B.D., Keeping, L.M. and Levy, P.E. (1998) 'Participation in the performance appraisal process and employee reactions: A meta-analytic review of field investigations', *Journal of Applied Psychology*, 83: 615–633.

Cardy, R.L., Bernardin, H.J., Senderak, M.P., Taylor, K. and Abbott, J.G. (1987) 'The effects of individual performance schemata and dimension familiarization on rating accuracy', *Journal of Occupational Psychology*, 60: 197–205.

Cardy, R.L. and Dobbins, G.H. (1994) *Performance appraisal: alternative perspectives.* Cincinnati, Ohio: South Western Publishing Company.

Cassidy, T. and Lynn, R. (1989) 'A multifactorial approach to achievement motivation: The development of a comprehensive measure', *Journal of Occupational Psychology*, 62: 301–312.

Chen, Z., Lam, W. and Zhong, J.A. (2007) 'Leader-Member Exchange and Member Performance: A New

Look at Individual-Level Negative Feedback-Seeking Behavior and Team-Level Empowerment Climate', *Journal of Applied Psychology*, 92 (1): 202–212.

Cleveland, J.N. and Murphy, K.R. (1992) 'Analyzing performance appraisal as goal-directed behavior', *Research in personnel and human resources management*, 10: 121–185.

Coens, T. and Jenkins, M. (2000) *Abolishing performance appraisals.* San Francisco: Berrett-Koehler Publishers Inc.

Costa, P.T. and McCrae, R.R. (1992) *Revised NEO personality inventory and the NEO five-factor inventory.* Odessa, FL: Psychological Assessment Resources.

Curtis, A.B., Harvey, R.D. and Davden, D. (2005) 'Sources of political distortions in performance appraisals', *Group and Organization Management*, 30: 42–60.

den Hartog, D.N., Boselie, P. and Paauwe, J. (2004) 'Performance management: A model and research agenda', *Applied Psychology: An International Review*, 53: 556–569.

Dobbins, G.H., Cardy, R.L. and Platz-Vieon, S.J. (1990) 'A Contingency Approach to Appraisal Satisfaction: An Initial Investigation of the Joint Effects of Organizational Variables and Appraisal Characteristics', *Journal of Management*, 16 (3): 619–633.

Ellis, A.P.J., West, B.J., Ryan, A.M. and DeShon, R.P. (2002) 'The Use of Impression Management Tactics in Structured Interviews: A Function of Question Type?', *Journal of Applied Psychology*, 87 (6): 1200–1208.

Falbe, C.M. and Yukl, G. (1992) 'Consequences for managers of using single influence tactics and combinations of tactics', *Academy of Management Journal*, 35: 638–652.

Ferris, G.R., Judge, T.A., Rowland, K.M. and Fitzgibbons, D.E. (1994) 'Subordinate influence and the performance evaluation process: Test of a model', *Organizational Behavior and Human Decision Processes*, 58: 101–135.

Fletcher, C. (2001) 'Performance appraisal and management: The developing research agenda', *Journal of Occupational and Organizational Psychology*, 74: 473–487.

Folger, R. (1987) 'Distributive and procedural justice in the workplace', *Social Justice Research*, 1: 143–159.

Fried, Y., Tiegs, R.B. and Bellamy, A.R. (1992) 'Personal and interpersonal predictors of supervisors' avoidance of evaluating subordinates', *Journal of Applied Psychology*, 77: 462–468.

Geddes, D. and Baron, R.A. (1997) 'Workplace aggression as a consequence of negative feedback', *Management Communication Quarterly*, 10: 433–454.

Gabris, G.T. and Ihrke, D.M. (2001) 'Does performance appraisal contribute to heightened levels of employee burnout? The results of one study', *Public Personnel Management*, 30 (2): 157–172.

Gioia, D.A. and Longenecker, C.O. (1994) 'Delving into the dark side: the politics of executive appraisal', *Organizational Dynamics*, 22: 47–58.

Gordon, R.A. (1996) 'Impact of ingratiation on judgements and evaluations: a meta-analtyic investigation', *Journal of Personality and Social Psychology*, 17: 54–70.

Harris, M.M. (1994) 'Rater motivation in the performance appraisal context: A theoretical framework', *Journal of Management*, 20: 737–756.

Harris, K.J., Kacmar, K.M., Zivnuska, S. and Shaw, J.D. (2007) 'The impact of Political Skill on Impression management effectiveness', *Journal of Applied Psychology*, 92 (10): 278–285.

Heneman, R.L. (1992) *Merit Pay: Linking Pay Increases to Performance Ratings.* Reading, Massachusetts: Addison Wesley Publishing Company.

Heslin, P.A., Latham, G.P. and VandeWalle, D. (2005) 'The effect of Implicit Person Theory on Performance Appraisals', *Journal of Applied Psychology*, 90 (5): 842–856.

Hochwarter, W.A., Ferris, G.R., Zinko, R., Arnell, B. and James, M. (2007) 'Reputation as a Moderator of Political Behavior-Work Outcomes Relationships: A Two-Study Investigation with Convergent Results', *Journal of Applied Psychology*, 92(2): 567–576.

Hofstede, G. (2001) *Culture's consequences*, (2nd ed) Beverly Hills, CA: Sage.

Houdek, C.M. (2002) 'Note-Taking in the Employment Interview: Effects on Recall and Judgments', *Journal of Applied Psychology*, 87 (2): 293–303.

Ilgen, D.R., Fisher, C.D. and Taylor, M.S. (1979) 'Consequences of individual feedback on behaviour in organizations', *Journal of Applied Psychology*, 64: 349–371.

Jackman, J.M. and Strober, M.H. (2003) 'Fear of Feedback', *Harvard Business Review*, 81 (4): 101–107.

Jackson, S. and Schuler, R.S. (2003) *Managing Human Resources through strategic partnership* (8th edition) Canada: Thompson.

Jawahar, I.M. (2006) 'Correlates of Satisfaction with Performance Appraisal Feedback', *Journal of Labor Research*, XXVII (2): 213–236.

Jawahar, I.M. (2001) 'Attitudes, self-monitoring and appraisal behaviors', *Journal of Applied Psychology*, 86: 875–883.

Jawahar, I.M. (2005) 'Do raters consider the influence of situational factors on observed performance when evaluating performance? Evidence from three experiments', *Group and Organization Management*, 30: 6–41.

Jawahar, I.M. and Williams, C.R. (1997) 'Where all the children are above average: The performance appraisal purpose effect', *Personnel Psychology*, 50: 905–925.

Kacmar, M.K., Wayne, S.J. and Wright, P.M. (1996) 'Subordinate reactions to the use of impression management tactics and feedback by the supervisor', *Journal of Managerial Issues*, 8 (1): 35.

Kacmar, K.M., Carlson, D.S. and Bratton, V.K. (2004) 'Situational and dsipositional factors as antecedents of ingratiatory behaviours in organisational settings', *Journal of Vocational Behavior*, 65: 309–331.

Keeping, L.M. and Levy, P.E. (2000) 'Performance appraisal reactions: measurement, modelling and method bias', *Journal of Applied Psychology*, 85 (5): 708–723.

Klimoski, R. and Inks, L. (1990) 'Accountability forces in performance appraisal', *Organizational Behavior and Human Decision Processes*, 45: 194–208.

Kluger, A.N. and DeNisi, A. (1996) 'The effects of feedback interventions on performance: A historical review, a meta-analysis, and a preliminary feedback intervention theory', *Psychological Bulletin*, 119: 254–284.

Konovsky, M (2000) 'Understanding procedural justice and its impact on business organisations', *Journal of Management*, 26 (3): 489–511.

Korsgaard, M.A. and Roberson, L. (1995) 'Procedural Justice in Performance Evaluation – the Role of Instrumental and Non-Instrumental Voice in Performance Appraisal Discussions', *Journal of Management*, 21: 657–669.

Kudisch, J.D., Fortunato, V.J. and Smith, A.F.R. (2006) 'Contextual and Individual Difference factors Predicting Individuals' Desire to Provide Upward Feedback', *Group and Organisation Management*, 31 (4): 503–529.

Lam, W.,Huang, X and Snape, E. (2007) 'Feedback seeking behaviour and leader member exchange: do supervisor-attributed motives matter?', *Academy of Management Journal*, 50 (2): 348–363.

Lee, F. (1997) 'When the Going Gets Tough, Do the Tough Ask for Help? Help Seeking and Power Motivation in Organizations', *Organizational Behavior and Human Decision Processes*, 72 (3): 336–363.

Lee, F. (1999) 'Verbal Strategies for Seeking Help in Organisations', *Journal of Applied Social Psychology*, 29 (7): 1472–1496.

Levy, P.E. and Williams, J.R. (2004) 'The social context of performance appraisal: A review and framework for the future', *Journal of Management*, 30: 881–905.

Leung, K., Su, S. and Morris, M.W. (2001) 'When is criticism not constructive? The role of fairness perceptions and dispositional attributes in employee acceptance of critical supervisory feedback', *Human Relations*, 54: 1155–1187.

Lim, T. (1990) 'The influences of receivers' resistance on persuaders' verbal aggressiveness', *Communication Quarterly*, 38: 170–188.

Longenecker, C.O., Gioia, D.A. and Sims, H.P. (1987) 'Behind the mask: The politics of employee appraisal', *Academy of Management Executive*, 1: 183–193.

Mayer, R.C. and Davis, J.H. (1999) 'The Effect of the Performance Appraisal System on Trust for Management: A Field Quasi-Experiment', *Journal of Applied Psychology*, 84 (1): 123–136.

McCarthy, J. and Goffin, R. (2004) 'Measuring Job Interview Anxiety: Beyond Weak Knees and Sweaty Palms', *Personnel Psychology*, 57: 607–637.

Mero, N.P. and Motowidlo, S.J. (1995) 'Effects of rater accountability on the accuracy and the favourability of performance ratings', *Journal of Applied Psychology*, 80: 517–524.

Mero, N.P., Motowidlo, S.J. and Anna, A.L. (2003) 'Effects of accountability or rating behaviour and rater accuracy', *Journal of Applied Social Psychology*, 22: 2493–2514.

Meyer, H.H. and Walker, W.B. (1961) 'Need for Achievement and Risk Preferences as they relate to attitudes toward reward systems and performance appraisal in an industrial setting', *Journal of Applied Psychology*, 45 (4): 251–256.

Meyer, H.H. (1980) 'Self-appraisal of job performance', *Personnel Psychology*, (33): 291–295.

Michie, S. and Williams, S. (2003) 'Reducing work related psychological ill health and sickness absence: a systematic literature review', *Occupational and Environmental Medicine*, 60: 3–17

Milkovich, G.T. and Newman, J., M. (2002) *Compensation* (7th Ed.) Boston: McGraw–Hill Irwin.

Milkovich, G.T. and Wigdor, A.K. (1991) *Pay for performance: evaluating performance appraisal and merit pay.* Washington, DC: National Academy Press.

Murphy, K.R. and Cleveland, J.N. (1995) *Understanding performance appraisal: Social, organizational, and goal–based perspectives.* Thousand Oaks: Sage.

Murphy, K.R., Cleveland, J.N., Skattebo, A.L. and Kinney, T.B. (2004) 'Raters who pursue different goals give different ratings', *Journal of Applied Psychology*, 89: 158–164.

Nankervis, A.R. and Compton, R.L. (2006) 'Performance Management: theory in practice?', *Asia Pacific Journal of HRM*, 44 (1): 83–101.

Newton, T. and Findlay, P. (1996) 'Playing God? The performance of appraisal', *Human Resource Management Journal*, 6 (3): 42–58.

Ostroff, C. and Ilgen, D.R. (1992) 'Cognitive categories or raters and rating accuracy', *Journal of Business and Psychology*, 7: 3–26.

Palmer, J.K. and Feldman, J.M. (2005) 'Accountability and need for cognition effects on contrast, halo and accuracy in performance ratings', *The Journal of Psychology*, 136: 119–137.

Poon, J.M.L. (2004) 'Effects of performance appraisal politics on job satisfaction and turnover intention', *Personnel Review*, 33: 322–334.

Roch, S.G. (2005) 'An investigation of motivational factors influencing performance ratings', *Journal of Managerial Psychology*, 20: 695–711.

Roch, S.G., Ayman, R., Newhouse, N. and Harris, M. (2005) 'Effect of identifiably, rating audience and conscientiousness on rating level', *International Journal of Selection and Assessment*, 13: 53–62.

Schrauger, S.J. (1975) 'Responses to evaluation as a function of initial self perceptions', *Psychological Bulletin*, 82: 581–596.

Shipper, F., Hoffman, R.C. and Rotondo, D.M. (2007) 'Does the 360 feedback process create actionable knowledge equally across cultures?', *Academy of Management Learning and Education*, 6: 33–50.

Shore, T.H. and Tashchian, A. (2002) 'Accountability forces in performance appraisal: effects of self-appraisal information, normative information and task performance', *Journal of Business and Psychology*, 17: 261–274.

Shore, T.H. and Tashchian, A. (2003) 'Effects of sex on raters' accountability', *Psychological Reports*, 92: 693–702.

Smith, W.J., Harrington, K.V. and Houghton, J.D. (2000) 'Predictors of performance appraisal discomfort: A preliminary examination', *Public Personnel Management*, 29: 21–32.

Sturman, M.C., Cheramie, R.A. and Cashen, L.H. (2005) 'The impact of job complexity and performance measurement on the temporal consistency, stability, and test-retest reliability of employee job performance ratings', *Journal of Applied Psychology*, 90: 269–283.

Taylor, P.J. and Pierce, J.L. (1999) 'Effects of Introducing a Performance Management System on Employee's Subsequent Attitudes and Effort', *Public Personnel Management*, 28 (3): 423–445.

Taylor, E.K. and Wherry, R.J. (1951) 'A study of leniency in two rating systems', *Personnel Psychology*, 4: 39–47.

Tepper, B.J., Eisenbach, R.J., Kirby, S.L. and Potter, P.W. (1998) 'Test of a justice-based model of subordinates' resistance to downward influence attempts', *Group and Organisation Management*, 23: 144–160.

Tepper, B.J. (2000) 'Consequences of Abusive Super-vision', *Academy of Management Journal*, 43: 178–190.

Tepper, B.J., Duffy, M.K. and Shaw, J.D. (2001) 'Personality Moderators of the Relationship between Abusive Supervision and Subordinates' Resistance', *Journal of Applied Psychology*, 86 (5): 974–983.

Tepper, B.J. Uhl-Bien, M., Kohut, G.F., Rogelberg, S.G., Lockhart, D.E. and Ensley, M.D. (2006) 'Subordinates' Resistance and Managers' Evaluations of Subordi-nates' Performance', *Journal of Management*, 32: 186–209.

Tesser, A. and Rosen, S. (1975) 'The reluctance to transmit bad news', in L. Berkowitz (ed.), *Advances in Experimental Social Psychology* (Vol. 8). New York: Academic Press. pp. 193–232.

Treadway, D.C., Ferris, G.R., Duke, A.B. and Adams, G.L. (2007) 'The Moderating Role of Subordinate Political Skill on Supervisors' Impressions of Subordinate Ingratiation and Ratings of Subordinate Interpersonal Facilitation', *Journal of Applied Psychology*, 92 (3): 848–855.

Tsui, A.S. and Wu, J.B. (2005) 'The New Employment Relationship Versus the Mutual Investment Approach: Implications for Human Resource Management', *Human Resource Management*, 44 (2): 115–121.

Tziner, A., Latham, G.P., Price, B.S. and Haccoun, R. (1996) 'Development and validation of a question-naire for measuring perceived political considerations in performance appraisal', *Journal of Organizational Behavior*, 17: 179–190.

Tziner, A. (1999) 'The relationship between distal and proximal factors in the use of political considerations in performance appraisal', *Journal of Business and Psychology*, 14 (1): 217–231.

Tziner, A. and Murphy, K.R. (1999) 'Additional evidence of attitudinal influences in performance appraisal', *Journal of Business and Psychology*, 13, 407–419.

Tziner, A., Murphy, K.R. and Cleveland, J.N. (2001) 'Relationships between attitudes toward organiza-tional and performance appraisal systems and rating behaviour', *International Journal of Selection and Assessment*, 9: 226–239.

Tziner, A., Murphy, K.R. and Cleveland, J.N. (2002) 'Does conscientiousness moderate the relationship between attitudes and beliefs regarding perfor-mance appraisal and rating behaviour?', *Interna-tional Journal of Selection and Assessment*, 10: 218–224.

Tziner, A., Murphy, K.R. and Cleveland, J.N. (2005) 'Contextual and rater factors affecting rating behaviour', *Group and Organization Management*, 30: 89–98.

Tziner, A., Murphy, K.R., Cleveland, J.N., Beaudin, G. and Marchand, S. (1998) 'Impact of rater beliefs regarding performance appraisal and its organizational context on appraisal quality', *Journal of Business and Psychology*, 12: 457–467.

Vilela, B.B, Gonzalez, J.A.V., Ferrin, P.F. and Araujo, L. (2007) 'Impression management tactics and affective context: influence on sales performance appraisal', *European Journal of Marketing*, 41, (5–6): 624–639.

Villanova, P., Bernadin, H.J., Dahmus, S.E. and Sims, R.L. (1993) 'Rater leniency and performance appraisal discomfort', *Educational and Psychological Measurement*, 54: 789–799.

Vroom, V.H. (1964) *Work and Motivation*. New York: John Wiley and Sons.

Wayne, S.J. and Ferris, G.R. (1990) 'Influence tactics, affect and exchange quality in supervisor–subordinate interactions: A Laboratory Experiment and field study', *Journal of Applied Psychology*, 75: 487–499.

Wayne, S.J. and Liden, R.C. (1995) 'Effects of Impression Management on Performance Ratings: A Longitudinal Study', *Academy of Management Journal*, 38 (1): 232–260.

Yukl, G. (2002) *Leadership In Organisations*. Upper Saddle River, NJ: Prentice Hall.

Yukl, G., Kim, H. and Falbe, C.M. (1996) 'Antecedents of influence outcomes', *Journal of Applied Psychology*, 81, 309–317.

Yukl, G. and Tracey, J.B. (1992) 'Consequences of influence tactics used with subordinates, peers and the boss', *Journal of Applied Psychology*, 77: 525–535.

Yun, G.J., Donahue, L.M., Dudley, N.M. and McFarland, L.A. (2005) 'Rater personality, rating format and social context: Implications for performance appraisal ratings', *International Journal of Selection and Assessment*, 13: 97–107.

13

Compensation

Barry Gerhart

INTRODUCTION

Across organizations, the single largest operating cost, on average, is employee compensation or remuneration (Blinder, 1990; European Parliament, 1999; US Bureau of Labor Statistics, 2001). Thus, for an organization to be successful, it must effectively manage not only what it spends on compensation, but also what it gets in return. Contextual factors serve to place some limits on compensation decisions. Legal, institutional (e.g., labor union), cultural, and market (product and labor) contextual factors vary across countries and often within countries, meaning that the degree of discretion an organization has in managing compensation decisions will also vary. Nevertheless, organizations typically have at least some discretion in compensation design.[1] This choice can have a major impact at every level of the organization on decisions made by individuals (through its incentive effects), as well as who those individuals are (through its sorting or self-selection and selection effects). In other words, compensation can be a major factor in successfully executing an organization's strategy.

Compensation, or remuneration, can be defined and studied in terms of its key decision/design areas, which include (Gerhart and Milkovich, 1992; Milkovich and Newman, 2008) how pay varies across (and sometimes within) organizations according to its level (how much?), form (what share is paid in cash versus benefits?), structure (how pay differentials depend on job content, individual competencies, job level/promotion, and business unit?), basis or mix (what is the share of base pay relative to variable pay and what criteria determine payouts?), and administration (who makes, communicates, and administers pay decisions?).[2]

I focus here primarily on the pay basis/mix and, to a lesser extent, the pay level, dimensions. I will often refer to these two decisions, respectively, as the 'how to pay?' and 'how much to pay?' decisions (Gerhart and Milkovich, 1992; Gerhart and Rynes, 2003). The reason for the greater focus on the 'how to pay' decision is that it may be the more strategic of the two in terms of the degree to which an organization can differentiate itself from others (Gerhart and Milkovich, 1990). Further, in organizations that differentiate their pay levels from competitors and that are successful over time (in competitive markets), it may be that their pay levels are not independent of how they pay. For example, an organization with a strong pay-for-performance plan (PFP) is more likely to have a high pay level when performance is strong.

I begin with a brief review of theoretical perspectives that help in understanding the potential consequences of different PFP and pay level decisions. As part of this, I highlight key intervening processes. Finally, I address potential pitfalls in using PFP and how contextual factors may influence compensation strategy and effectiveness.[3]

EFFECTS OF PAY

Theoretical mechanisms

The role of pay, specifically PFP, and its effect on the level and direction of motivation in the workplace has sometimes been debated and sometimes ignored in the applied psychological literature on motivation. (See Rynes et al., 2005 for a review, including discussion of theories by Deci, Maslow, and Herzberg.) However, the facts are that in developed economies, monetary rewards are (a) ubiquitous, (b) a major cost in most organizations (see above), and (c) as this chapter will help make clear, can have a major impact (positive or negative) on employee attitudes, choices, and behaviors. Accordingly, in some streams of this literature, it has been recognized that 'Money is the crucial incentive' (Locke, et al., 1980: 379) and that 'the one' issue that should be considered by all organization theories is the relationship between pay and performance' (Lawler, 1971: 273).

From a psychological perspective, Campbell and Pritchard (1976) observe that motivation can be defined in terms of its intensity, direction, and persistence. (Together with ability and situational constraints/opportunities, motivation contributes to observed behavior.) Thus, to fully evaluate the impact of pay on motivation, one must look not only at (enduring) effort level, but also the degree to which effort is directed toward desired objectives.

As Lawler (1971) demonstrates, theories such as reinforcement, expectancy, and equity have deep roots in psychology. Although compensation research using these theories (with the possible exception of equity theory) is no longer very active, their core ideas provide much of the basis for how scholars and many practitioners think of the impact of compensation on employees. A brief review of these theories, as well as the more economics-based agency and efficiency wage theories follows below. (See Gerhart and Rynes, 2003 for a more complete review.)

Reinforcement theory (e.g., Skinner, 1953) is based on Thorndike's Law of Effect, which states that a response followed by a reward is more likely to recur in the future. By the same token, a response not followed by a reward is less likely to recur in the future. These two phenomena are reinforcement and extinction, respectively. A notable feature of Skinner's perspective was his adamant avoidance of cognitive processes in explaining motivation. In Skinner's view, cognitions were by-products of the central driver of motivation, reinforcement contingencies in the environment, and so were not necessary or useful in building a science of behavior.

Subsequently, however, the field of psychology went through its 'cognitive revolution,' which departed from reinforcement theory by focusing on cognitions such as self-reports of attitudes, goals, subjective probabilities, and values. Later theories such as goal-setting (e.g., Locke), expectancy (e.g., Vroom, 1964), and equity (Adams, 1963), all give cognitions a central explanatory role. At the same time, they also continue to recognize the importance of reinforcement processes as drivers of those cognitions and later behavior. The potential value of studying cognitions as mediators is that factors other than compensation and incentives may influence goal choice, effort choice, and behaviors. Measuring cognitions and self-reports may be helpful in understanding why compensation and incentives do or do not work in a particular situations.

In expectancy theory (Campbell and Pritchard, 1976; Vroom, 1964), behavior is seen as a function of ability and motivation. In turn, motivation (also referred to as effort or force) is viewed as a function of beliefs regarding expectancy, instrumentality, and valence. Expectancy is the perceived link between effort and performance. Instrumentality is the perceived link between performance and outcomes and valence is the expected value (positive or negative) of those outcomes. There is often a focus on compensation's effect on instrumentality. For example, a strong PFP program is likely to generate stronger beliefs that performance leads to high pay than would a weak PFP program or a seniority-based pay system. However, motivation can be undermined not only by weak instrumentality (e.g., weak PFP), but also by weak expectancy (e.g., because of inadequate selection, training or job design) or valence (outcomes that are negative or not sufficiently positively valued).

The unique contribution of equity theory (Adams, 1963) to motivation is its focus on social comparison processes. In essence, it states that how an employee evaluates his/her outcomes from work depends on an assessment of how his/her ratio or outcomes (e.g., perceived compensation and rewards) to inputs (e.g., perceived effort, qualifications, performance) compares to a comparison standard (e.g., a co-worker or peer in another organization). When the ratios are perceived to be equal, equity is perceived and no action (cognitive or behavioral) is taken to change the situation. However, to the extent the ratios are not perceived as equal, there is perceived inequity, and action (behavioral or cognitive) is hypothesized to be taken to restore equity or balance, especially if the inequity is under reward inequity for the focal person (Lawler, 1971).

One reason for focusing on the role of (in)equity is that so many of its potential behavioral consequences (e.g., effort withholding, turnover, theft, collective action, legal action, renegotiation of terms) are undesirable to many or all employers. As a practical matter, many employers use attitude surveys to monitor employee equity perceptions and attitudes in hopes of finding any problems in compensation or other areas early enough to head off undesired consequences. Not surprisingly, then, leading textbooks in compensation management (e.g., Milkovich and Newman, 2008) give a central role to the various aspects of pay equity in helping managers understand how employees react to compensation decisions.

Agency theory starts from the observation that once an entrepreneur hires their first employee, there is separation of ownership and control (Jensen and Meckling, 1976). The entrepreneur (and/or others having ownership stakes, as in a larger firm) retains ownership, but now must deal with an agency relationship, under which the owner (i.e., principal) contracts with one or more employees (i.e., agents) 'to perform some service on their behalf which involves delegating some decision making authority to the agent' (Jensen and Meckling, 1976: 308). The challenge in an agency relationship is that the agent does not necessarily act in the best interests of the principal, giving rise to agency costs, which specifically arise from goal incongruence (the principal and agent have different goals) and information asymmetry (the principal has less information than the agent regarding the value to the principal of the agent's attributes and behaviors).

To control agency costs, the principal must choose a contracting scheme that is behavior-based (pay based on observation of behaviors) and/or outcome-based (pay based on outcomes/results such as profits, productivity, shareholder return). The choice depends on factors such as the relative cost of monitoring behaviors versus outcomes, their relative incentive effects, and the degree of risk aversion among agents. A key issue is the hypothesized trade-off between incentive intensity and risk. Generally, it is assumed that incentive intensity can be stronger under outcome-based contracts because they are more objective, and thus less subject to measurement error (Milgrom and Roberts, 1992). On the other hand, employees, who generally rely on their job as their predominant source of income, are risk averse. Greater incentive intensity is associated, on average, with greater performance outcome variability (which also may not be entirely under the agent's control) and thus, greater compensation risk. Therefore, a compensating differential to the agent for taking on the greater risk of an outcome-based contract is expected under agency theory. (An implication is that strong incentives increase labor cost, meaning that the incentives must drive higher performance to be cost-effective.)

The question is which contract will maximize the gains from incentives, while controlling the costs of shifting risk to workers (Prendergast, 1999)? Consistent with agency theory, companies having more financial risk tend to have less risk-sharing/incentive intensity in their compensation for managers and executives (Aggarwal and Samwick, 1999; Bloom and Milkovich, 1998; Garen, 1994), with there also being some evidence that risk-sharing is least likely in very low or very high financial risk situations (Miller et al., 2002). Also consistent with agency theory, as information asymmetries increase, outcome-based contracts are more likely to be used (Eisenhardt, 1989; Makri et al., 2006; Milkovich et al., 1991).

Although is has been argued that the trade-off between risk and incentives in designing contracts is the main focus of agency theory (e.g., Aggarwal and Samwick, 1999; Prendergast, 1999), the general focus on contracting in agency theory also suggests an assumption that performance, whether results-based or behavior-based or both, plays a key role in determining compensation. In economics, while recognizing that agency costs can compromise the pay-performance relationship, the existence of substantial pay for performance among executives is generally taken as a given, at least in a country like the US, where stock plans are the source of most executive wealth creation (Murphy, 1999). However, in other fields (e.g., management), there is greater skepticism regarding the degree to which executive compensation and performance are related,

with a greater role for power and politics generally being seen. (For a give-and-take on theses issues, see articles by Bebchuk and Fried, 2006; Conyon et al., 2006. See Devers et al. for a review of recent studies.) A review and empirical study by Nyberg et al. (2007) suggests that the management literature has underestimated the role of performance, and thus the applicability of agency theory, in determining executive compensation.

Efficiency wage theory seeks to provide an economically rational explanation for why firms have different pay levels.[4] The essential argument is that firms pay high wages either because some aspect of their technology and/or human resource system requires higher than average quality workers or because monitoring performance is more difficult due to information asymmetry (Krueger and Summers, 1998; Yellen, 1984). Paying a higher than average wage may discourage shirking because the worker at the high-wage firm does not want to risk losing his/her wage premium (Cappelli and Chauvin, 1991). This effect is expected to be magnified to the degree that the risk of job loss increases. The unemployment rate is one indicator of risk of job loss and Yellen (1984) states that 'Unemployment plays a valuable role in creating work incentives.'[5] Another implication of efficiency wage theory is that supervision and efficiency wages may be substitutes for one another (Groshen and Krueger, 1990; Neal, 1993). In other words, shirking can be controlled either by having many supervisors closely monitoring behaviors or by having fewer supervisors but a higher potential wage penalty if shirking is observed. Lazear (1979: 1266) states that without an appropriate pay system, workers would have an 'incentive to cheat, shirk, and engage in malfeasant behavior.'

Theoretical themes and intervening processes

To greatly simplify, one can say that in the above theories, pay operates on motivation and performance in two general ways (Gerhart and Milkovich, 1992; Gerhart and Rynes,

2003; Lazear, 1986). First, there is the potential for an incentive effect, defined as the impact of pay on current employees' motivational state. The incentive effect is how pay influences individual and aggregate motivation, holding the attributes of the workforce constant and it has been the focus of the great majority of theory and research in compensation, especially outside of economics.

Second, there is the potential for a sorting effect, which we define as the impact of pay on performance via its impact on the attributes of the workforce. Different types of pay systems may cause different types of people to apply to and stay with an organization (self-select) and these different people may have different levels of ability or trait-like motivation, or different levels of attributes (e.g., team skills) that enhance effectiveness more in some organizations than in others. Organizations too may differentially select and retain employees, depending on the nature of their pay level and/or PFP strategies. The self-selection aspect of sorting and its application to the effects of pay is based primarily on work in economics (e.g., Lazear, 1986), but the idea is consistent with Schneider's (1987) attraction-selection-attrition (ASA) idea in the applied psychology literature. Evidence suggests that the magnitude of ASA processes can be substantial (Schneider et al., 1998).

Together, the sorting and incentive ideas provide one broad conceptual framework for thinking about intervening processes in studying the effects of compensation. Another is the ability-motivation-opportunity to contribute (AMO) framework (Appelbaum et al., 2000, Boxall et al., 2007). Compensation seems most likely to influence workforce ability and motivation, less likely to come into play in the 'O' component, which has more to do with job design and participation in decisions. (As noted later, however, the 'O' component and the AMO dimensions in general are quite relevant in addressing horizontal alignment in HR and compensation.) The impact of compensation on workforce ability is expected to operate primarily through its sorting effects, but

some forms of compensation (for example, skill-based or competency-based pay) can also directly influence ability via incentive effects. Management development over time via different job assignments and experiences (especially those involving upward mobility) is also typically supported by compensation systems through promotion incentives (sometimes described as tournament systems). Other incentive effects, such as motivation and effort on the current job, are perhaps more straightforward.

Gerhart and Milkovich (1992) called for compensation research to include intervening variables (and) at 'multiple levels' of analysis in studying compensation and performance, because 'if a link is found ... possible mediating mechanisms can be examined to help establish why the link exists and whether (or which) causal interpretation is warranted' (p. 533). Beyond the general mediating mechanisms discussed above, more detailed intervening variables might include employee attitudes, individual performance and/or competencies, and employee turnover (broken out by performance levels). Other relevant mediators, depending on the particular goals of the unit or organization, would be citizenship behavior, teamwork, climate for innovation, motivation, and engagement. Note that while HR practices such as compensation might be thought of as operating at the level of the organization or work unit, the mediators discussed here are often conceptualized as individual level processes. Therefore, models (e.g., hierarchical linear modeling, Raudenbush and Bryk, 2002) designed to handle multiple levels may prove useful in empirical work addressing this type of mediaton.

A final mediator that is perhaps obvious, but nevertheless sometimes ignored in research (as opposed to practice) is cost. Higher pay levels and/or higher staffing levels drive up labor costs. In addition, according to agency theory, incentive intensity, because it shifts risk to workers, is also expected to drive up pay levels by requiring a compensating differential for risk. We address the cost issue more fully below.

EFFECTS OF PAY LEVEL

Although competitive pressures drive firms to minimize costs and maximize benefits, the cost side means that, in the absence of higher productivity, quality, superior products development, customer responsiveness and so forth, firms must keep total labor costs in line with those of competitors by controlling total compensation per employee and/or by controlling employee headcount. In a global world, cost control includes an ongoing search for the lowest cost location for production, all else being equal (e.g., proximity to customers and suppliers, worker skill levels) which is to varying degrees, depending on the product, technology, and work organization, a partial function of labor costs. As Table 13.1 makes clear, labor costs differ significantly across the world. (What Table 13.1 does not show is that labor costs also vary across companies within many countries.)

As noted previously, efficiency wage theory suggests that higher wages may have positive sorting and incentive effects. More specifically, the observable benefits of higher wages may include (Gerhart and Rynes, 2003): higher pay satisfaction (Currall et al.,

Table 13.1 Average hourly labor costs for manufacturing production workers, by country (US dollars), 2005

United States	24
Canada	24
Germany	33
France	25
United Kingdom	26
Spain	18
Czech Republic	6
Japan	22
Mexico	3
Hong Kong[a]	6
Korea	14
Sri Lanka[b]	0.52
China[c]	0.57

Note: Wage rates rounded to nearest dollar except when rate is less than one dollar.

Sources: US Bureau of Labor Statistics, www.bls.gov; Banister, J. (2005)
[a]Special Administrative Region of China
[b]2004 [c]2002.

2005; Williams et al., 2006; for a review, see Heneman and Judge, 2000), improved attraction and retention of employees (for a review, see Barber and Bretz, 2000), and higher quality, effort, and/or performance (e.g., Yellen, 1984; Klass and McClendon, 1996).

In discussing pay level from a public policy perspective, a distinction is sometimes made between 'low road' (low pay level) versus 'high road' (high pay level) human resource systems (Gerhart, 2007).[6] Using the AMO model, a 'high road' policy typically combines higher ('efficiency') wages with high levels of worker responsibility and autonomy and often team-based work (O), all of which may require a higher quality workforce (A). To the extent that the high road HR system is costly, due to not only high wages but also high investment in AMO areas broadly, it may not align typically as well with a cost leadership business strategy as would a less costly, low road strategy. Historically, this is perhaps most readily seen in the way that firms often move low skill work offshore to locations where it can be done much more cheaply. More recently, there has been a great deal of attention given to the movement of skilled work (e.g., writing computer code; tax preparation) offshore to less expensive locations. We return later to the question of under what circumstances a high road, high pay level strategy is most likely effective.

Cost is an outcome that has been explicitly recognized and quantified in cost-benefit models such as utility analysis (Brogden, 1949; Boudreau, 1991), but the application of utility analysis to compensation, with explicit attention to not only its benefits, but also the costs of pay programs, has been surprisingly rare (Klaas and McCledon, 1996; Sturman et al., 2003; Gerhart and Rynes, 2003). This is ironic because, inside of organizations, it often seems to be cost that gets the lion's share of attention. Cappelli and Neumark (2001) observe this same omission in much of the broader literature on the effectiveness of HR systems. Indeed, they interpret their findings as indicating that high road HR systems 'raise labor costs … but the net effect on overall profitability is unclear' (p. 766).

I conclude the discussion of pay level at this point because the pay level decision is one that is (or should be) made in tandem with the how to pay decision (Gerhart and Rynes, 2003). For example, any organization operating in a competitive market will have difficulty being successful over time with a high pay level that is not paired with high performance at the individual and organizational level. Thus, the how to pay or PFP decision.

EFFECTS OF PAY FOR PERFORMANCE (PFP)

Types of PFP programs include profit sharing, stock plans, gainsharing, individual incentives, sales commissions, and merit pay (Milkovich and Newman, 2008). As Table 13.2 shows, these programs can be classified on two dimensions (Milkovich and Wigdor, 1991): level of measurement of performance (e.g., individual, plant, organization) and type of performance measure (results-oriented or behavior-oriented). It is important to note that, in practice, many employees are covered by hybrid pay programs (e.g., a combination of merit pay and profit sharing).

US companies well-known for their use of PFP include Lincoln Electric, Nucor Steel, Whole Foods, Hewlett-Packard, Southwest Airlines, and General Electric, to name just a few. Each uses a different form of PFP, with varying degrees of relative emphasis on individual, group/unit, and/or organization level performance. Outside the US, in countries with less of a tradition of PFP, there appears to be a movement in some cases (e.g., Japan, Korea) toward greater emphasis

on PFP at all organization levels. In these and many other countries, there has been a clear movement toward greater use of PFP for selected employee groups (e.g., executives), (Towers Perrin, 2006).

Incentive effects

In a meta-analysis of potential productivity-enhancing interventions in actual work settings, Locke et al. (1980) found that the introduction of individual pay incentives increased productivity by an average of 30%.[7] This finding was based on studies that were conducted in real organizations (as opposed to laboratories), used either control groups or before-and-after designs, and measured performance via 'hard' criteria (e.g., physical output) rather than supervisory ratings.

Subsequent research also supports the powerful incentive effects of pay. A meta-analysis by Guzzo et al. (1985) found that financial incentives had a large mean effect on productivity ($d = 2.12$).[8] More recent meta-analyses (Jenkins et al., 1998; Judiesch, 1994; Stajkovic and Luthans, 1997) likewise provide strong support for a significant positive relationship between financial rewards and performance.

There has also been research on plans using collective performance, including gainsharing, profit sharing, and stock plans. (For reviews, see Gerhart and Milkovich, 1992; Gerhart and Rynes, 2003.) Without delving into the specific findings of this literature, a few general observations are in order. First, whereas most of the individual level research follows the same people over time, thus probably yielding what are essentially incentive effects, studies of plans using collective

Table 13.2   Pay for performance (PFP) programs, by level and type of performance measure

Type of performance measure	Level of performance measure			
	Individual	Facility/plant	Organization	Multiple levels
Behavior-based	Merit pay		Merit pay for executives	Hybrid
Results-based	Individual incentives Sales commission	Gainsharing	Profit sharing stock plans	Hybrid
Results-based and behavior-based	Hybrid	Hybrid	Hybrid	Hybrid

performance as the dependent variable do not usually hold the workforce constant as the design often involves between-company and/or longitudinal tracking of companies. Thus, it is difficult to separate incentive and sorting effects. Second, the set of relevant determinants of collective performance (e.g., profitability) is perhaps larger than in the typical study of individual incentive plans. Again, this makes it more of a challenge to isolate the impact of compensation relative to other factors.

In studies of executives, keeping in mind that some of these same challenges apply (given that performance is usually defined as firm-level performance), evidence suggests that PFP plan design may influence a wide range of strategic decisions (Gerhart, 2000), including staffing patterns, diversification, research and development investment, capital investment, and reaction to takeover attempts. Likewise, over time, organizational strategy is more likely to change when (executive) pay strategy changes (Carpenter, 2000). Thus, there is consistent evidence that pay strategy does influence managerial goal choice.

Sorting effects

After reading the studies reviewed above, the reader would be well aware of the incentive mechanism, but quite possibly unaware of the sorting mechanism as a possible explanation for the observed effects. As noted, to the extent the above studies track the same individuals before and after the intervention, they do indeed estimate incentive effects. However, to the degree the individuals making up the workforce changed in response to a PFP intervention, then at least some of the improvement in performance might be due to a sorting effect. Lazear (2000), for example, reported a 44% increase in productivity when a glass installation company switched from salaries to individual incentives. Of this increase, roughly 50% was due to existing workers increasing their productivity, while the other 50% was attributable to less productive workers quitting and being replaced by more productive workers over time.

Cadsby et al. (2007) likewise found that both incentive and sorting effects explained the positive impact of PFP on productivity. Their study, set in the laboratory, was designed so that subjects went through multiple rounds. In some rounds, subjects were assigned to a PFP plan, while in other rounds they were assigned to work under a fixed salary plan. In yet other rounds, they were asked to choose either the fixed salary or the PFP plan to work under (i.e., they were asked to self-select). Cadsby et al. found that by the last rounds in their experiment, the PFP condition generated 38% higher performance than the fixed salary condition and that the sorting effect (less risk averse and more productive subjects being more likely to select the PFP condition) was actually about twice as large as the incentive effect in accounting for this 38% difference. In explaining why they found a sorting effect that was larger than that found by Lazear (which was also substantial), Cadsby et al. observe that in the Lazear study, few employees chose to leave the organization, presumably because there was no downside risk to the PFP plan implemented there. Thus, most of the sorting effect in the Lazear study was probably attributable to new hires being more productive than current employees on average, without much of the sorting effect being due to lower performing employees leaving the organization.

Evidence suggests that PFP is more attractive to higher performers than to lower performers. For example, Trank and her colleagues (2002) found that the highest-achieving college students place considerably more importance on being paid for performance than do their lesser-achieving counterparts. Likewise, persons with higher need for achievement (Bretz et al., 1989; Turban and Keon, 1993), and lower risk aversion (Cadsby et al., 2007; Cable and Judge, 1994) also prefer jobs where pay is linked more closely to performance. Since these are all characteristics that some or most employers desire, such individual differences are important for employers to keep in mind. Other research shows that high performers are most likely to quit and seek other employment if their performance is not sufficiently recognized with financial rewards (Salamin and Hom, 2005; Trevor et al., 1997). Conversely, low performers are more likely to stay with an employer when pay-performance relationships are weaker (Harrison et al., 1996).

Finally, to the degree that sorting effects are important, they may make it appear as though the relationship between pay and performance is weaker than it really is (Gerhart and Rynes, 2003). For example, to the degree that organizations are selective and valid in their decisions regarding who to hire and who to retain, the remaining group of employees will be unrepresentative in that their average performance level should increase as selectivity and validity increase (Boudreau and Berger, 1985). So, even if there is little observed variance in performance and/or pay within this group (i.e., there is range restriction), this selected group of employees may have above market pay and above market performance. Thus, in this example, there is no (observed) relationship between pay and performance within the firm, but there would be a significant relationship between pay and performance between firms. Similarly, on the employee side of the decision, it may be that high performers self-select such that they are more likely to join and remain with organizations that have PFP. In summary, even when there is little observed variance in performance ratings and/or pay within an organization, it may nevertheless be the case that PFP, via sorting effects, have resulted in major differences in performance between organizations.

The challenge of defining and measuring performance

A limitation of the meta-analytic evidence reviewed earlier on the effects of PFP is that in most of the included studies, physical output measures of performance (e.g., number of index cards sorted, number of trees planted) were available, (and related to this) tasks were simple, and individual contributions were usually separable (Gerhart and Rynes, 2003).

In contrast, in many jobs, some or all of these three characteristics do not apply (Lawler, 1971). The widespread use of merit pay and its subjective performance measures, is to an extent, a result of this fact (Milkovich and Wigdor, 1991). While this mismatch is recognized in the applied psychology literature, there remains little work that uses strong research designs to study more widely used individual-oriented PFP plans such as merit pay (Heneman, 1992) or hybrids of different PFP programs (Gerhart and Rynes, 2003). The economics literature is also coming to grips with the performance measurement challenge, acknowledging that there has been a tendency in discussions of incentives to assume that performance can be 'easily measured' (Gibbons, 1998: 118) and that, as a result, 'economists have tended to place excessive focus on the contracts of workers for whom output measures are easily observed' despite the fact that 'most people don't work in jobs like these' (Prendergast, 1999: 57).

Returning to Table 13.2, recall that performance measures vary in at least two respects. First, as emphasized in agency theory, they can be results-oriented (e.g., number of units produced) behavior-oriented (e.g., supervisory evaluations of effort or quality)? Second, performance can focus on individual or collective contributions.

Among the potential advantages of behavior-oriented measures are that they (Gerhart, 2000), can be used for any type of job, permit the rater to factor in variables that are not under the employee's control (but that nevertheless influence performance), thus reducing the risk-sharing concerns identified in agency theory. They also allow a focus on whether results are achieved using acceptable means and behaviors, carry less risk of measurement deficiency, or the possibility that employees will focus only on explicitly measured tasks or results at the expense of other objectives. On the other hand, the subjectivity/measurement error of behavior-oriented measures (for a review, see Viswesvaran et al., 1996) can make it more difficult for organizations to justify differentiating between employees (Milkovich and Wigdor, 1991) using stronger incentive intensity (Milgrom and Roberts, 1992), unless steps are taken to improve reliability and credibility (e.g., using multiple raters, Viswesvaran et al., 1996). Managers may also have disincentives to differentiate (Murphy and Cleveland, 1995).

Results-oriented measures (e.g., productivity, sales volume, shareholder return, profitability), while more objective and thus often more credible to employees as a basis for differentiation, and thus more typically used to provide more powerful incentives, also have potential drawbacks. As noted, relevant objective measures are not available for most jobs, especially at the individual level. Moreover, as also noted, agency theory emphasizes that results-based plans (e.g., individual incentives, gainsharing, profit-sharing) increase risk-bearing among employees (Gibbons, 1998). Poor performance on such measures (and thus decreasing or disappearing payouts), especially if attributed to factors employees see as beyond their own control (e.g., poor decisions by top executives), tend to result in negative employee reactions, often resulting in pressure to either revise the plan in a way that weakens incentives (Gerhart, 2001) or to abandon the plan (e.g., Petty et al., 1992). Finally, narrowly defined results-oriented measures may result in some aspects of performance being ignored and undesirable means used to maximize incentive payouts.

Performance measures also vary according to whether they emphasize individual or group (or collective) performance. Incentive effects (in terms of instrumentality perceptions) are generally stronger under individual performance plans (Schwab, 1973). Also, positive sorting effects may be realized as the most productive and achievement-oriented employees appear to prefer or gravitate to such plans (e.g., Bretz et al., 1989; Lazear, 1986; Trank et al., 2002; Trevor et al., 1997). On the other hand, too much focus on individual performance may undermine cooperation and teamwork, which are widely viewed as increasingly important in gaining competitive advantage through people (Deming, 1986; Pfeffer, 1998).

However, using group-based incentives creates other challenges, not only with respect to sorting effects, but also incentive effects, especially in anything but small groups: 'Unless the number of individuals in a group is quite small, or unless there is coercion or some other special device to make individuals act in their common interest, *rational self-interested individuals will not act to achieve their common or group interests*' (Olson, 1965: 1–2, emphasis in the original). Theory and research across fields (e.g., variously described as the common-resource problem, public-goods problem, free-rider problem, or social loafing problem) has identified a fundamental challenge in using group incentives (Gerhart and Rynes, 2003; Kidwell and Bennett, 1993); when people share the obligation to provide a resource (e.g., effort), it will be undersupplied because the residual returns (e.g., profit sharing payouts) to the effort are often shared relatively equally, rather than distributed in proportion to contributions.

In summary, performance measures must have a meaningful link to what the organization is trying to accomplish, be sufficiently inclusive of key aspects of performance, balance sometimes competing objectives, and be seen as fair and credible by employees. Organizations often attempt to achieve these goals by using multiple measures of performance, aggregate and individual, results and behavior-oriented (e.g., as in a Balanced Scorecard), and adjusting incentive intensity, to an important extent, based on the degree to which valid and credible performance measurement is believed to be achievable. The main constraint on using multiple measures is the complexity introduced and the risk that this will work against employees' understanding of the plan and, thus, their motivation. Indeed, even among executives, understanding and the perceived value of stock options appears to diverge from that provided by standard financial models (Devers et al., 2007).

CAUTIONS AND PITFALLS

Any discussion of PFP 'must consider whether the potential for impressive gains in performance' from such plans is 'likely to outweigh the potential problems, which can be serious' (Gerhart, 2001: 222). Indeed, using such plans, perhaps especially so when combined with strong incentive intensity, has been described as 'a high risk, high reward strategy' (Gerhart et al., 1996: 222).

Of course, there are risks in choosing a high pay level as well, especially if it's not linked to high performance. In a global world, contracts (implicit or explicit) between organizations and employees that were once good for both may no longer be viable for one or both parties. This change may occur over time (e.g., the automobile industry in the US and Europe), leading to either changes in the employment contract (lower wages/benefits and/or more productivity/flexibility in tasks/hours) or a change in the location of production to a lower-cost part of the country or the world. In the absence of either or both changes in response to changing competitive conditions, market share and profitability, and ultimately survival, are put at risk.

Returning to the risks in using PFP, several issues can come into play. First, PFP may not be implemented with sufficient strength. It may exist as a stated policy, but not as a meaningful practice experienced by employees. Even where (e.g., in the United States) most private sector organizations tend to claim that they have PFP policies (or researchers claim that they are studying PFP policies), there is, in fact, sometimes little meaningful empirical relationship between pay and performance (Gerhart and Milkovich, 1992; Gerhart and Rynes, 2003; Trevor et al., 1997). In the case of merit pay, for example, two factors that often weaken its strength are lack of differentiation in performance ratings and lack of differentiation in pay increases even when performance ratings do vary. Not surprisingly then, when employees are asked about how much PFP there is in their own organizations, they tend to say 'not very much.' In a survey of employees in

335 companies conducted by the HayGroup (2002), employees were asked whether they agreed with the statement, 'If my performance improves, I will receive better compensation'. Only 35% agreed, whereas 27% neither agreed nor disagreed, and 38% disagreed with this statement.

A second potential problem, somewhat ironically, is that the implementation of PFP may sometimes 'work' too well. Here, the danger is that a PFP program can act as a blunt instrument that may result in unintended and harmful consequences. Successful organizations must balance multiple objectives (e.g., customer relationships and long-term earnings against short-term opportunistic earnings). In designing an incentive plan to support this balance, it must be kept in mind that people tend to do what is rewarded and objectives not rewarded tend to be ignored. Lawler (1971: 171) warned that 'it is quite difficult to establish criteria that are both measurable quantitatively and inclusive of all the important job behaviors,' and 'if an employee is not evaluated in terms of an activity, he will not be motivated to perform it.' Based on their laboratory study, Wright et al. (1993) concluded that 'When individuals are committed to difficult goals, they may strive to achieve these goals at the expense of the performance of other behaviors that are necessary for organizational effectiveness' (p. 129). Prendergast (1999: 8) likewise argues that 'Contracts offering incentives can give rise to dysfunctional behavioral responses, whereby agents emphasize only those aspects of performance that are rewarded.' Milgrom and Roberts (1992: 228) refer to this as the equal compensation principle: 'If an employee's allocation of time or attention between two different activities cannot be monitored by the employer, then either the marginal rates of return to the employee must be equal, or the activity with the lower marginal rate of return receives no time or attention.'

How long a PFP plan remains in place is sometimes used as a measure of its success. While a short-term gain in performance from a pay plan that does not last long should not be dismissed, it is nevertheless useful to keep in mind that, in a fair number of cases, such plans do not last long (Gerhart et al., 1996). For example, Beer and Cannon's analysis (2004) of 13 PFP 'experiments' conducted at Hewlett-Packard in the mid-1990s found that, in 12 of the 13 cases, the program did not survive.

All else equal, a plan that generates longer-term performance gains is preferred and changing plans too often can result in a counterproductive 'flavor-of-the-month' perception among employees (Beer and Cannon, 2004). Data on survival rates is also important for drawing statistical conclusions (Gerhart et al., 1996). Plans that survive for short periods are more likely to be excluded from studies of pay plan effectiveness, thus resulting in the plans included in the sample looking more effective than they really are in the full population.

While the risks of PFP programs must be acknowledged and understood, the 'high reward' aspect of 'high risk, high reward' means that not making sufficient use of PFP can put an organization at risk in a different way in terms of its competitiveness. Second, PFP programs can be one critical piece in a strategy to change the culture of an organization, especially if there is sufficient hiring and turnover to allow sorting effects to change workforce composition. In the case of a start-up company or location, PFP and other aspects of compensation and HR can be used to set the cultural tone and achieve fit from the beginning.

ALIGNMENT AND CONTEXTUAL FACTORS

In view of the challenges in designing and implementing PFP plans, it is useful to consider how contextual factors might affect whether a PFP plan is likely to be successful. The preceding discussion regarding challenges in measuring performance has begun to take us down that path. A further discussion of contextual factors and alignment follows below.

Alignment

Terms such as alignment, synergy, fit, and complimentarity describe the idea that the effects of two or more factors are non-additive and dependent on contextual factors.[9] According to Milgrom and Roberts (1992: 108): 'Several activities are mutually complementary if doing more of any activity increases (or at least does not decrease) the marginal profitability of any other activity in the group' (p. 108). They then propose a more stringent definition: 'a group of activities is strongly complementary when raising the levels of a subset of activities in the group greatly increases the returns to raising the levels of the other activities' (p. 109). An example given by Gerhart and Rynes (2003) is where a gainsharing program alone results in an average performance increase of 10%, while a suggestion system alone results in an average performance increase of 10%. However, when used in combination, their total effect is not additive (i.e., 20%), but is rather non-additive (e.g., 30%). So, the effect of the gainsharing program is contingent on a contextual factor, in this case, another aspect of HR (Gerhart and Rynes, 2003).

There are two general classes of contingency factors: person and situation. Our earlier discussion of sorting effects highlighted some of the relevant person factors (e.g., risk aversion, need for achievement, academic performance) that predict preference for PFP. In addition, other person characteristics may predict preferences for particular types of PFP. For example, Cable and Judge (1994) found that individual-based PFP was preferred, on average, by those with high self-efficacy, but as might be expected, less preferred, on average, by those scoring high on collectivism.

There are three key aspects of pay strategy alignment or fit that focus on the situation or environmental context (Gerhart, 2000; Gerhart and Rynes, 2003): horizontal alignment (between pay strategy and other dimensions of HR management, as in the gainsharing example above), vertical alignment with organizational strategy (i.e., corporate and business strategy), and internal alignment between different dimensions of pay strategy (e.g., pay level and pay basis). Only a brief review is provided here. (For more detail, see Gerhart, 2000; Gerhart and Rynes, 2003; Gomez-Mejia and Balkin, 1992; Milkovich, 1988).

The primary focus of the pay strategy literature has been on vertical alignment. Aspects of corporate strategy such as the process, degree and type of diversification (Kerr, 1985; Gomez-Mejia, 1992; Pitts, 1976) and the firm's life cycle (e.g., growth, maintenance), (Ellig, 1981) are associated with different compensation strategies (Gomez-Mejia and Balkin, 1992; Kroumova and Sesis, 2006; Yanadori and Marler, 2006). Evidence also suggests performance differences based on fit such that growth firms do perform better with an incentive-based strategy (Balkin and Gomez-Mejia, 1987) and that the effectiveness of an incentive-based strategy depends to a degree on the level of diversification (Gomez-Mejia, 1992). Alignment of pay strategy with business strategy (e.g., Porter, 1985; Miles and Snow, 1978) may also have performance consequences (e.g., Rajagopolan, 1996). Another developing stream of work on non-executives at the business unit level focuses on the alignment between pay strategy and manufacturing strategy (Shaw et al., 2002; Snell and Dean, 1994). Finally, as noted previously, consistent with agency theory, companies having more financial risk tend to have less risk-sharing in their compensation for managers and executives (Aggarwal and Samwick, 1999; Bloom and Milkovich, 1998; Garen, 1994). Thus, both the risk aversion of the individual and risk properties of the situation are relevant (Wiseman et al., 2000).

Turning to the role of pay level in vertical alignment, as noted earlier, the potential benefits of high wages may be more important in some firms than in others. Higher pay levels, either for the organization as a whole or for critical jobs, may be well-suited to particular strategies, such as higher value-added customer segments. The key work recognizing that firms differ in their choice of low road versus high road HR systems,

even within narrow industries, has been conducted by Hunter (2000) in health care and Batt (2001) in telecommunications. Batt, for example, reported that firms having a focus on large-business customers paid 68% higher than firms with no dominant customer focus and that most of this higher pay was due to hiring workers with higher levels of human capital. Similarly, evidence suggests that organizations making greater use of so-called high performance work practices (teams, quality circles, total quality management, job rotation) also pay higher wages (Osterman, 2006).

Boxall and Purcell (2003: 68) provide a nice summary, which only needs to be amended with the important observation that, as we have just seen, the value-added created may differ within sectors according to firm differences in strategy:

> Overall, research suggests that the sort of HR practices that foster high commitment from talented employees are most popular in those sectors where quality is a major competitive factor and where firms need to exploit advanced technology (as in complex manufacturing) or engage in a highly skilled interaction with clients (as in professional services). In these sorts of higher value-added sectors, firms need more competence and loyalty from their employees and are more able to pay for them. In sectors where these conditions are not met—where output per employee is not high—employers adopt more modest employment policies.

In contrast to the work on vertical alignment, horizontal alignment of pay strategy with other employment practices has been studied, mostly using non-executive employees and mostly in the context of work on so-called high-performance work systems and HR systems. The effect of an HR system on effectiveness is thought to operate, as noted earlier, via the intervening variables of ability, motivation, and opportunity, or AMO (Appelbaum et al., 2000; Batt, 2002; Boxall and Purcell, 2003; Gerhart, 2007). One problem with studying horizontal fit, however, is that the hypothesized role of pay and/or PFP, as well as the way these constructs are operationalized, tends to differ across studies, making it difficult to draw robust conclusions about what other HR strategy elements work best with particular pay and PFP approaches (Becker and Gerhart, 1996; Gerhart and Rynes, 2003).

Nevertheless, certain potential areas of fit and mis-fit can be identified (Gerhart and Rynes, 2003; Rynes et al., 2005). For instance, with respect to the 'O' component, it seems likely that group-based incentive plans (e.g., gainsharing, profit sharing, stock options) will be more effective in smaller groups (Kaufman, 1992; Kruse, 1993) than in larger groups or organizations. In addition, in situations where work is more interdependent, it may be that some shift in emphasis from individual performance to group performance will be more effective (e.g., Shaw et al., 2002). Nevertheless, it must be kept in mind that even where tasks are interdependent, if there are individual differences in ability and/or performance that are important, then placing too little weight on individual performance in compensation can lead to undesired sorting effects, such that high performers may not join or remain with the group or organization.

The issue of horizontal alignment can also be approached more broadly. Although compensation is extremely important in motivation and effectiveness, it is important to continue to keep in mind that compensation is part of a broader employment relationship, broader than some of the contract notions we have discussed, which center on the compensation aspect. The literature on HR systems (e.g., the AMO framework) conveys this broader view as does work on psychological contracts (e.g, Rousseau and Ho, 2000; Tsui et al., 1997). Likewise, earlier work by Herbert Simon (1957), for example, viewed employment as a relationship where mutual (longer-term) obligations on the part of the employee and employer could be efficient. The hope is that an organization will obtain the 'consummate cooperation' of employees, 'an affirmative job attitude [that] includes the use of judgment, filling gaps, and taking initiative' (Williamson et al., 1975: 266). Organizations often seek to support this objective through employee ownership. For example, roughly one-half of the publicly traded companies on the 100 Best Companies to Work For list offer stock options to all or nearly all employees (Fortune, 1999: 126).

The third area of fit, internal alignment, has been the least studied. The work of Gomez-Mejia and Balkin (1992) has sought to identify overarching compensation strategies, but more work is needed to document which aspects of pay tend to cluster together in organizations and whether certain clusters are more effective and/or what contingency factors are most important. In any event, the modest evidence that exists concerning the degree of actual alignment between pay and other HR strategy dimensions suggests that there is less alignment than one might wish (Wright et al., 2001).

Although it could be included as a part of vertical alignment, another type of alignment that is important is that between pay strategy and country. Countries differ on a multitude of dimensions that can affect management practice (Dowling et al., forthcoming), including the regulatory environment (e.g., requirements for worker participation in firm governance), institutional environment (e.g., strength of labor unions, accepted HR practices in areas like compensation), and cultural values (e.g., Hofstede's (1980) dimensions of individualism/collectivism, long-term orientation, masculinity-femininity, power distance, and uncertainty avoidance). As such, a good deal of attention has been devoted to the constraints that organizations face when it comes to choosing which HR and pay strategies (a) can be implemented, and (b) if able to be implemented, which will be effective. Thus, organizations must decide how best to balance standardization and localization in designing HR and pay practices.

While practices that are effective in one country are not necessarily going to be effective or even feasible in another country (due, for example, to legal or strong institutionalized traditions) one should be careful not to give too much weight to contingency factors generally, including country. For example, in the case of the five cultural values dimensions made famous by Hofstede (1980, 2001), evidence shows that country actually explains only a small percentage of variance in individual employee cultural values (Gerhart and Fang, 2005). There is good reason to believe that organizations have considerable room to be different from the country norm in many countries in at least some key areas of HR (Gerhart and Fang, 2005) and pay strategy (Bloom and Milkovich, 1999).

Also, country norms as they relate to HR and pay strategy can and do change. As mentioned earlier, one example, is executive compensation. Countries like Germany, South Korea, and Japan changed from essentially no use of long-term incentives (e.g., stock options, stock grants) for top executives in 1998 to substantial use by 2005 (Towers Perrin, 2006). Another example mentioned earlier is the significant change in South Korea (Choi, 2004) and in Japan (Morris et al., 2006; Jung and Cheon, 2006; Robinson and Shimizu, 2006) away from seniority-based pay toward PFP. A third example is the dramatic decline in private sector unionism in the United States, which stands at 7.4% of the workforce in 2006. A fourth example is the decentralization (e.g., from industry to firm or plant level) of collective bargaining in many parts of the world (Katz et al., 2004). Finally, in their multi-country study, Katz and Darbishire (2002) highlight what they call 'converging divergences,' to indicate that there is a set of multiple employment/HR system models shared across countries, with the multiple and different models existing in each country to varying degrees.

Thus, it is important to recognize not only institutional pressures toward conformity in a country, but also that, at least in some respects, depending on the country, the timeframe, and the particular policy, there can be room to be unique and the strategy literature tells us that being the same as everyone else is unlikely to generate anything more than competitive parity, whereas being different, while perhaps being more risk, has the potential to generate sustained competitive advantage (e.g., the resource based view of the firm; Barney, 1991). Some work has been done addressing how the RBV is relevant to HR strategy broadly (Becker and Gerhart, 1996; Colbert, 2004; Barney and Wright, 1998), but beyond Gerhart et al. (1996) there has not been much application to pay strategy.

Turning to methodology, a challenge in studying contextual or contingent effects is that if only firms and units that achieve some minimal level of alignment survive (Hannan and Freeman, 1977), alignment may be so important that it is almost impossible for the researcher to observe substantial departures from alignment (Gerhart et al., 1996; Gerhart and Rynes, 2003). In this case, restricted range in alignment would reduce the statistical power available to observe a relationship between alignment and performance. This may help explain why the idea of fit, while often thought to be critical, has not received as strong support as might be expected in HR research broadly and in the area of compensation, specifically (Gerhart et al., 1996; Gerhart, 2007; Wright and Sherman, 1999).

Finally, although fit is typically seen as an important goal, this should perhaps be tempered by the possibility that fit can be a double-edged sword when it comes to compensation and HR systems. Gerhart et al. (1996) pointed out that the system (and resulting workforce) that fits the current business strategy may quickly become a poor fit if the business strategy changes. A less tightly aligned set of HR practices, where bets were hedged, might make a successful adaptation more likely. As Boxall and Purcell (2003: 56) put it: 'In a changing environment, there is always a strategic tension between performing in the present context and preparing for the future.' Perhaps in recognition of the limitations of static vertical fit, some recent work on HR systems emphasizes the importance of agility in HR systems and strategy (Dyer and Shafer, 1999) and relatedly, of flexibility (Wright and Snell, 1998), or what might be seen as a capability for achieving dynamic fit. As a key part of an HR system, compensation must then be evaluated on an ongoing basis to consider its contribution to flexibility. Some examples of compensation programs that are seen as promoting flexibility are skill-based and competency-based pay, as well as broadbands (in place of more detailed pay grades).

CONCLUSION

Compensation involves decisions in multiple areas. My focus in this chapter has been on PFP and, to a lesser extent, pay level. I provided an overview of some of the most important theoretical approaches in understanding the potential impact of compensation decisions on performance. I have highlighted the potential for well-designed PFP plans to make a substantial contribution to organization performance through effects on intervening mechanisms such as incentive and sorting. I have also noted the potential for PFP plans to cause serious problems, often as a result of unintended consequences. To an important extent, these unintended consequences stem from the difficulty in specifying and measuring performance, a challenge that is perhaps often overlooked and/or underestimated in the literature on PFP.

I suggested that the probability of success of PFP plans might be improved by effective alignment with contextual factors such as organization and human resource strategy. However, no matter how well thought-out and planned, the fact remains that the stronger the incentive intensity, the greater not only their potential positive impact, but also their potential to have a negative impact. At the same time, the risk of having strong incentives must be balanced against the risk that using weaker incentives will miss the opportunity to help drive stronger performance. In closing, I note that firms achieve success by taking different paths, which vary both in terms of how much they pay and how they pay, including how strong incentives they use.

NOTES

1 Even in an environment where there is little discretion in compensation policy and practice (e.g., because of legal and institutional forces within a particular country), an organization can often obtain greater discretion by expanding its business in a different environment (e.g., a different industry, a different country, etc.) that permits greater discretion in policy and practice.

2 Benefits represent a substantial share of compensation cost to employers in the US, for example, given that many (especially larger) companies fund retirement and health care for employees.

3 Compensation can be defined to include non-monetary rewards as well. Both monetary and non-monetary rewards are important in the workplace. For a review of the importance of monetary and non-monetary rewards in the workplace, see Rynes et al. (2004). However, monetary compensation is unique among rewards in the following respects (Gerhart and Rynes, 2003; Lawler, 1971; Rottenberg, 1956). First, compensation is one of the most visible aspects of a job to both current employees and job seekers. Second, unlike some other job characteristics (e.g., job responsibility, working in teams), most people prefer more money to less. Third, money can be instrumental for meeting a wide array of needs, including economic consumption, self-esteem, status, and feedback regarding achievement. Given the central importance of monetary compensation, as well as limits on what can be covered in a single chapter, the main focus here is on pay or monetary rewards.

4 A strict, traditional, neoclassical economics view would find the notion that employers (at least within a particular market) have a choice when it comes to pay level to be misguided, because the forces of supply and demand yield, in the long run, a single going/market wage that all employers must pay to avoid too high costs in the product market on the one hand and the inability to attract and retain a sufficient quantity and quality of workers in the labor market on the other. The only way that an employer could pay higher wages than other employers would be if better quality workers were hired. In that case, the ratio of worker quality to cost would be unchanged, meaning both that the apparent difference in pay levels was not real, disappearing upon appropriate adjustment for worker quality and that employers would not necessarily realize any advantage from using a high wage, high worker quality strategy. However, evidence of persistent and arguably non-illusory differences in compensation levels (see Gerhart and Rynes, 2003 for a review) between companies operating in the same market has resulted in greater attention to why such differences exist and more general acknowledgment, including in economics (Boyer and Smith, 2001), recognition that employers have some discretion in their choice of pay level. In response, efficiency wage theory provides an economics-based rationale for why some firms may benefit from higher (lower) wages.

5 This idea is similar to Karl Marx's concept of the 'reserve army' of unemployed being used by employers to keep their workforces in line.

6 This section draws freely on Gerhart (2007).

7 This section draws freely on Gerhart (2008).

8 The *d* statistic is defined as the difference between the dependent variable mean for Group A versus Group B, divided by the pooled standard deviation of Groups A and B. Thus, it gives the difference between Group A and B in terms of standard deviation units.

9 This section draws freely on Gerhart and Rynes (2003).

REFERENCES

Adams, J.S. (1963) 'Toward an understanding of inequity', *Journal of Abnormal Psychology*, 67: 422–36.

Aggarwal, R.K. and Samwick, A.A. (1999) 'The other side of the trade-off: The impact of risk on executive compensation', *Journal of Political Economy*, 107: 65–105.

Appelbaum, E., Bailey, T., Berg, P. and Kalleberg, A. (2000) *Manufacturing Advantage: Why High Performance Work Systems Pay Off*. Ithaca, NY: Cornell University Press.

Barney, J.B. (1991) 'Firm resources and sustained competitive advantage', *Journal of Management*, 17: 99–120.

Barney, J.B. and Wright, P.M. (1998) 'On becoming a strategic partner: The role of human resources in gaining competitive advantage', *Human Resource Management*, 37: 31–46.

Barber, A.E. and Bretz, R.D. Jr. (2000) Compensation, attraction and retention, in S.L. Rynes and B. Gerhart (eds), *Compensation in Organizations*, pp. 32–60. San Francisco, CA: Jossey-Bass.

Batt, R. (2001) 'Explaining intra-occupational wage inequality in telecommunications services: customer segmentation, human resource practices, and union decline', *Industrial and Labor Relations Review*, 54 (2A): 425–49.

Balkin, D.B. and Gomez-Mejia, L.R. (1987) Matching compensation and organizational strategies, *Strategic Management Journal*, 11, 153–169.

Bebchuk, L.A. and Fried, J.M. (2006) 'Pay without performance: Overview of the issues', *The Academy of Management Perspectives*, 20 (1): 5–24.

Becker, B. and Gerhart, B. (1996) 'The impact of human resource management on organizational performance: Progress and prospects', *Academy of Management Journal*, 39: 779–801.

Beer, M. and Cannon, M.D. (2004) 'Promise and peril in implementing pay-for-performance', *Human Resource Management*, 43: 3–20.

Blinder, A.S. (ed.) *Paying for productivity*. Washington, D.C.: Brookings Institution.

Bloom, M. and Milkovich, G.T. (1998) 'Relationships among risk, incentive pay, and organizational performance', *Academy of Management Journal*, 41: 283–97.

Boyer, G.R. and Smith, R.S. (2001) The development of the neoclassical tradition in labor economics. *Industrial and Labor Relations Review*, 54, 199–223.

Boudreau, J.W. (1991) 'Utility analysis for decisions in human resource management', in M.D. Dunnette and L.M. Hough (eds), *Handbook of Industrial and Organizational Psychology*. Palo Alto, CA: Consulting Psychologists Press, 2nd edn, pp. 621–745.

Boxall, P. and Purcell, J. (2003) *Strategy and Human Resource Management*. Hampshire, England: Palgrave Macmillan.

Boudreau, J.W. and Berger, C.J. (1985) Decision-theoretic utility analysis applied to employee separations and acquisitions. *Journal of Applied Psychology* [monograph], 73, 467–81.

Branch, S. (1999). The 100 best companies to work for in America. *Fortune*, January, 66–80.

Bretz, R.D., Ash, R.A. and Dreher, G.F. (1989) 'Do people make the place? An examination of the attraction-selection-attrition hypothesis', *Personnel Psychology*, 42: 561–81.

Brogden, H.E. (1949) 'When testing pays off', *Personnel Psychology*, 2: 171–85.

Cable, D.M. and Judge, T.A. (1994) 'Pay preferences and job search decisions: A person-organization fit perspective', *Personnel Psychology*, 47: 317–348.

Cadsby, C.B., Song, F., and Tapon, F. (2007) 'Sorting and incentive effects of pay-for-performance: An experimental investigation', *Academy of Management Journal*, 50: 387–405.

Carpenter, M.A. (2000) The price of change: The role of CEO compensation in strategic variation and deviation from industry strategy norms, *Journal of Management*, 26, 1179–98.

Campbell, J.P. and Pritchard, R.D. (1976) 'Motivation theory in industrial and organizational psychology', in M.D. Dunnette (ed.), *Handbook of Industrial and Organizational Psychology*. Chicago, IL: Rand McNally, pp. 63–130.

Capelli, P. and Chauvin, K. (1991) 'An interplant test of the efficiency wage hypothesis', *Quarterly Journal of Economics*, 106 (3): 769–87.

Cappelli, P. and Neumark, D. (2001) 'Do "High-Performance" work practices improve establishment-level outcomes?', *Industrial and Labor Relations Review*, 54 (4): 737–75.

Colbert, B.A. (2004) The complex resource-based view. *Strategic Management Journal*, 29, 341–58.

Conyon, M. J. (2006) 'Executive compensation and incentives', *The Academy of Management Perspectives*, 20 (1): 25–44.

Currall, S.C., Towler, A.J., Judge, T.A. and Kohn, L. (2005) 'Pay satisfaction and organizational outcomes', *Personnel Psychology*, 58: 613–40.

Deming, W.E. (1986) *Out of the crisis*. Cambridge: MIT, Center for Advanced Engineering Study.

Devers, C.E., Cannella, A.A., Reilly, G.P., and Yoder, M.E. 2007. Executive Compensation: A multidisciplinary review of recent developments. *Journal of Management*, 33: 1016–72.

Dowling P.J., Festing, M., and Engle, A.D. Sr. (2008) *International Human Resource Management*. (5th edn) London: Thomson Learning.

Dyer, L. and Shafer, R.A. (1999) 'From human resource strategy to organizational effectiveness: Lessons from research on organizational agility', in P. Wright, L. Dyer, J. Boudreau and G. Milkovich (eds), *Strategic Human Resources Management in the Twenty-First Century*. Supplement to G.R. Ferris (ed.), *Research in Personnel and Human Resources Management*. Stanford, CT: JAI Press. pp. 145–74.

Eisenhardt, K.M. (1989) 'Agency- and institutional-theory explanations: The case of retail sales compensation', *Academy of Management Journal*, 31: 488–511.

Ellig, B.R. (1981) Compensation elements: Market phase determines the mix. *Compensation Review*, (Third Quarter), 30–8.

European Parliament (1999) *Labour Costs and Wage Policy within EMU*. Directorate-General for Research, Economic Affairs Series, ECON 111 EN. Luxembourg.

Garen, J.E. (1994) 'Executive compensation and principal-agent theory', *Journal of Political Economy*, 102: 1175–200.

Gerhart, B. (2000) 'Compensation strategy and organizational performance', in S.L. Rynes and B. Gerhart (eds), *Compensation in Organizations*. San Francicso: Jossey-Bass. pp. 151–194.

Gerhart, B. (2001) 'Balancing results and behaviors in pay for performance plans', in Charles Fay (ed.), *The Executive Handbook of Compensation*. Free Press. pp. 214–37.

Gerhart, B. (2007) 'Horizontal and vertical fit in human resource systems', in C. Ostroff and T. Judge (eds), *Perspectives on Organizational Fit*. SIOP Organizational Frontiers Series. New York: Lawrence Erlbaum Associates, Taylor and Francis Group. pp. 317–48.

Gerhart, B. (2008) Compensation. In John Storey and Patrick Wright (eds), *The Routledge Companion to Strategic Human Resource Management*. London, U.K.: Routledge.

Gerhart, B. and Fang, M. (2005) 'National culture and human resource management: assumptions and evidence', *International Journal of Human Resource Management*, 16: 975–90.

Gerhart, B. and Milkovich, G.T. (1990) 'Organizational differences in managerial compensation and financial performance', *Academy of Management Journal*, 33: 663–91.

Gerhart, B. and Milkovich, G.T. (1992) 'Employee compensation: Research and practice', in M.D. Dunnette and L.M. Hough, (eds), *Handbook of Industrial and Organizational Psychology*, 2nd edn. Palo Alto, CA: Consulting Psychologists Press, Inc. pp 481–570.

Gerhart, B. and Rynes, S.L. (2003) *Compensation: Theory, evidence, and strategic implications*. Thousand Oaks, CA: Sage.

Gerhart, B., Trevor, C. and Graham, M. (1996) 'New Directions in Employee Compensation Research', in G.R. Ferris (ed.), *Research in Personnel and Human Resources Management*. pp. 143–203.

Gibbons, R. (1998) 'Incentives in organizations', *Journal of Economic Perspectives*, 12: 115–32.

Gomez-Mejia, L.R. and Balkin, D.B. (1992) *Compensation, Organizational Strategy, and Firm Performance*. Cincinnati, Ohio: Southwestern Publishing.

Groshen, E. and Krueger, A.B. (1990) 'The structure of supervision and pay in hospitals', *Industrial and Labor Relations Review*, 43: S134–S46.

Guzzo, R.A., Jette, R.D. and Katzell, R.A. (1985) 'The effects of psychologically based intervention programs on worker productivity: A meta-analysis', *Personnel Psychology*, 38: 275–91.

Harrison, D.A, Virick, M. and William, S. (1996) 'Working without a net: Time, performance, and turnover under maximally contingent rewards', *Journal of Applied Psychology*, 81: 331–45.

HayGroup (2002) *Managing Performance: Achieving Outstanding Performance Through a 'Culture of Dialogue.'* Working Paper.

Hannan, M.T., and Freeman, J. 1977. The population ecology of organizations. *American Journal of Sociology*, 82, 929–64.

Heneman, H.G. III and Judge, T.A. (2000) 'Compensation attitudes', in S.L. Rynes and B. Gerhart (eds), *Compensation in Organizations*. San Francicso: Jossey-Bass. pp. 61–103

Hofstede, G. (1980) *Culture's consequences: International differences in work-related values*. Beverly Hills, CA: Sage.

Hofstede, G. (2001) *Culture's consequences: Comparing values, behaviors, institutions, and organizations across nations*. Thousand Oaks, CA: Sage, 2nd Edition.

Hunter, L.W. (2000) 'What determines job quality in nursing homes?', *Industrial and Labor Relations Review*, 53: 463–81.

Jenkins, D.G. Jr., Mitra, A., Gupta, N. and Shaw, J.D. (1998) 'Are financial incentives related to performance? A meta-analytic review of empirical research', *Journal of Applied Psychology*, 83: 777–87.

Jensen, M.C. and Meckling, W.H. (1976) 'Theory of the firm: Managerial behavior, agency costs, and ownership structure', *Journal of Financial Economics*, 3: 305–60.

Judiesch, M.K. (1994) *The effects of incentive compensation systems on productivity, individual differences in output variability and selection utility*. Unpublished doctoral dissertation, University of Iowa.

Jung, E. and Cheon, B. (2006) Economic crisis and changes in employment relations in Japan and Korea. *Asian Survey*, *46*(3), 457–76.

Katz, H.C. and Darbishire. (2002) *Converging Divergences: Worldwide Changes in Employment Systems*. Ithaca, NY: Cornell University Press.

Katz, H.C., Lee, W. and Lee, J. (2004) *The New Structure of Labor Relations: Tripartism and Decentralization*. Ithaca, NY: ILR Press/Cornell University.

Kaufman, R.T. (1992) The effects of Improshare on productivity. *Industrial and Labor Relations Review*, 45, 311–22.

Kruse, D.L. (1993) *Profit sharing: Does it make a difference?* Kalamazoo, MI: Upjohn Institute.

Kerr, J.L. (1985) Diversification strategies and managerial rewards. *Academy of Management Journal*, *28*, 155–79.

Kidwell, R.E. and Bennett, N. (1993) 'Employee propensity to withhold effort: A conceptual model to intersect three avenues of research', *Academy of Management Review*, 18: 429–56.

Klaas, B.S. and McCledon, J.A. (1996) 'To lead, lag, or match: Estimating the financial impact of pay level policies', *Personnel Psychology*, 49: 121–41.

Kroumova, M.K. and Sesis, J.C. (2006) 'Intellectual capital, monitoring, and risk: What predicts the adoption of employee stock options?', *Industrial Relations*, 45: 734–52.

Krueger, A.B. and Summers, L.H. (1988) 'Efficiency wages and the inter-industry wage structure', *Econometrica*, 56: 259–93.

Lawler, E.E. III (1971) *Pay and Organizational Effectiveness*. New York: McGraw-Hill.

Lazear, E.P. (1979) 'Why is there mandatory retirement?', *Journal of Political Economy*, 87: 1261–84.

Lazear, E.P. (1986) 'Salaries and piece rates', *Journal of Business*, 59: 405–32.

Lazear, E.P. (2000) 'Performance pay and productivity', *American Economic Review*, 90: 1346–61.

Locke, E.A., Feren, D.B., McCaleb, V.M., Shaw, K.N. and Denny, A.T. (1980) 'The relative effectiveness of four methods of motivating employee performance', in K.D. Duncan, M.M. Gruenberg and D. Wallis (eds.), *Changes in Working Life*. New York: Wiley. pp. 363–88.

Makri, M., Lane, P.J., and Gomez-Mejia, L. (2006) CEO incentives, innovation, and performance in technology-intensive firms. *Strategic Management Journal*, 27, 1057–80.

Miles, R.E. and Snow, C.C. (1978) *Organizational Strategy, Structure, and Process*. New York: McGraw-Hill.

Miller, J.S., Wiseman, R.M., and Gomez-Mejia, L.R., 2002. The fit between CEO compensation design and firm risk. *Academy of Management Journal*, 45: 745–56.

Milgrom, P. and Roberts, J. (1992) *Economics, Organization, and Management*. Englewood Cliffs, NJ: Prentice-Hall.

Milkovich, G.T. (1988) 'A strategic perspective on compensation management', *Research in Personnel and Human Resources Management*, 6: 263–88.

Milkovich, G.T., Gerhart, B. and Hannon, J. (1991) 'The effects of research and development intensity on managerial compensation in large organizations', *Journal of High Technology Management Research*, 2: 133–50.

Milkovich, G.T. and Newman, J.M. (2008) *Compensation*. Boston: McGraw-Hill/Irwin, 9th edition.

Milkovich, G. and Wigdor, A. (1991) *Pay for Performance: Evaluating Performance Appraisal and Merit Pay*. Washington, DC: National Academy Press.

Morris, J, Hassard, J., and McCann, L. (2006) New organizational forms, human resource management and structural convergence? A study of Japanese organizations. *Organization studies*, *27*, 1485–511.

Murphy, K.J. (1999) 'Executive compensation', in O. Ashenfelter and D. Card (eds), *Handbook of Labor Economics*, Volume 3. Amsterdam: North Holland. pp. 2485–567.

Murphy, K.R. and Cleveland, J.N. (1995) *Understanding Performance Appraisal*. Thousand Oaks, CA: Sage Publications.

Neal, D. (1993) Supervision and wages across industries. *Review of Economics and Statistics*, *75*, 409–17.

Nyberg, A.J., Fulmer, I.S. and Gerhart, B. (2007) *Correcting Misconceptions about CEO Pay for Performance: An Alternative Approach for Evaluating the Alignment Between CEO Return and Shareholder Return*. Unpublished Manuscript, School of Business, University of Wisconsin-Madison.

Olson, M. (1965) *The logic of collective action: Public Goods and the Theory of Groups*. Cambridge, MA: Harvard University Press.

Osterman, P. (2006) The wage effects of high performance work organization in manufacturing. *Industrial and Labor Relations Review*, *59*, 187–204.

Petty, M.M., Singleton, B., and Connell, D.W. (1992) 'An experimental evaluation of an organizational incentive plan in the electric utility industry', *Journal of Applied Psychology*, 77: 427–36.

Pfeffer, J. (1998) *The human equation: Building profits by putting people first*. Boston: Harvard Business School.

Pitts, R.A. (1976) 'Diversification strategies and organizational policies of large diversified firms', *Journal of Economics and Business*, 8: 181–88.

Porter, M. (1985) *Competitive Advantage*. New York: Free Press.

Prendergast, C. (1999) 'The provision of incentives in firms', *Journal of Economic Literature*, 37: 7–63.

Rajagopalan, N. (1996) 'Strategic orientations, incentive plan adoptions, and firm performance: Evidence from electric utility firms', *Strategic Management Journal*, 18: 761–85.

Raudenbush, S.W. and Bryk, A.S. (2002) *Hierarchical linear models*. Thousand Oaks, CA: Sage Publications.

Robinson, P. and Shimizu, N. (2006) Japanese corporate restructuring: CEO priorities as a window on environmental and organizational change. *Academy of Management Perspectives*, *20*(3), 44–75.

Rottenberg, S. (1956) 'On choice in labor markets', *Industrial and Labor Relations Review*, 9: 183–99.

Rousseau, D.M. and Ho, V.T. (2000) Psychological contract issues in compensation. In Rynes and Gerhart (eds). In S.L. Rynes and B. Gerhart (eds), *Compensation in Organizations*, pp. 273–310. San Francisco, CA: Jossey-Bass.

Rynes, S.L., Gerhart, B. and Parks, L. (2004) *Annual Review of Psychology*, Personnel psychology: Performance evaluation and pay for performance. 56: 571–600.

Salamin, A. and Hom, P.W. (2005) 'In search of the elusive U-shaped performance-turnover relationship: are high performing Swiss bankers more liable to quit?', *Journal of Applied Psychology*, 90: 1204–16.

Schneider, B., Hanges, P.J., Smith, B. and Salvaggio, A.N. (2003) 'Which comes first: employee attitudes or organizational financial and market performance', *Journal of Applied Psychology*, 88: 836–51.

Schwab, D.P. (1973) 'Impact of alternative compensation systems on pay valence and instrumentality

perceptions', *Journal of Applied Psychology*, 58: 308–12.

Schneider, B. (1987) 'The people make the place', *Personnel Psychology*, 40: 437–53.

Schneider, B., Smith, D.B., Taylor, S., and Fleenor, J. 1998. Personality and organizations: A test of the homogeneity of personality hypothesis. *Journal of Applied Psychology*, *83*, 462–70.

Shaw J.D., Gupta N. and Delery J.E. (2002) 'Pay dispersion and workforce performance: Moderating effects of incentives and interdependence', *Strategic Management Journal*, 23: 491–512.

Simon, H.A. (1957) *Models of Man*. New York: John Wiley and Sons.

Skinner, B.F. (1953) *Science and Human Behavior*. New York: Macmillan.

Snell, S.A. and Dean, J.W. Jr. (1994) 'Strategic compensation for integrated manufacturing: The moderating effects of jobs and organizational inertia', *Academy of Management Journal*, 37: 1109–40.

Stajkovic, A.D. and Luthans, F. (1997) 'A meta-analysis of the effects of organizational behavior modification on task performance, 1975–1995', *Academy of Management Journal*, 40: 1122–49.

Sturman, M.C., Trevor, C.O., Boudreau, J.W. and Gerhart, B. (2003) 'Is it worth it to win the talent war? Evaluating the utility of performance-based pay', *Personnel Psychology*, 56: 997–1035.

Trank, C.Q., Rynes, S.L. and Bretz, R.D. Jr. (2002) 'Attracting applicants in the war for talent: Differences in work preferences among high achievers', *Journal of Business and Psychology*, 17: 331–45.

Towers Perrin (2006) Worldwide total remuneration, 2005–2006. www.towersperrin.com

Trevor, C.O., Gerhart ,B. and Boudreau, J.W. (1997) 'Voluntary turnover and job performance: Curvilinearity and the moderating influences of salary growth and promotions', *Journal of Applied Psychology*, 82: 44–61.

Tsui, A.S., Pearce, J.L., Porter, L.W. and Tripoli, A.M. (1997) 'Alternative approaches to the employee-organization relationship: Does investment in employees pay off?', *Academy of Management Journal*, 40: 1089–1121.

Turban, D.B. and Keon, T.L. 1993. Organizational attractiveness: An interactionist perspective. *Journal of Applied Psychology*, 78, 184–193.

U.S. Bureau of Labor Statistics. 2001. Productivity and costs. http://www.bls.gov/lpc/peoplebox.htm.

Visweswaran, C., Ones, D.S. and Schmidt, F.L. (1996) 'Comparative analysis of the reliability of job performance ratings', *Journal of Applied Psychology*, 81: 557–74.

Vroom, V.H. (1964) *Work and Motivation*. New York: Wiley.

Weiss, A. (1987) 'Incentives and worker behavior: Some evidence', in H.R. Nalbantian (ed.), *Incentives, Cooperation, and Risk Taking*. Lanham, MD: Rowman and Littlefield. pp. 137–150.

Williams, M.L., McDaniel, M.A. and Nguyen, N. T. (2006) 'A meta-analysis of the antecedents and consequences of pay level satisfaction', *Journal of Applied Psychology*, 91: 392–413.

Wiseman, R.M., Gomez-Mejia, L.R., and Fugate, M. (2000) Rethinking compensation risk, in S.L. Rynes and B. Gerhart (eds), *Compensation in Organizations*, 32–60. San Francisco, CA: Jossey-Bass.

Williamson, O.E., Wachter, M.L. and Harris, J.E. (1975) 'Understanding the employment relation: The analysis of idiosyncratic exchange', *Bell Journal of Economics*, 6: 250–80.

Wright, P.M., George, J.M., Farnsworth, S.R. and McMahan, G.C. (1993) 'Productivity and extra-role behavior: The effects of goals and incentives on spontaneous helping', *Journal of Applied Psychology*, 78: 374–81.

Wright, P.M., McMahan, G., Snell, S. and Gerhart, B. (2001) 'Comparing line and HR executives' perceptions of HR effectiveness: Services, roles, and contributions', *Human Resource Management*, 40: 111–24.

Wright, P.M. and Sherman, W.S. (1999) 'Failing to find fit in strategic human resource management: Theoretical and empirical problems', in P. Wright, L. Dyer, J. Boudreau, and G. Milkovich (eds), *Strategic Human Resources Management in the Twenty-First Century*. Supplement to G.R. Ferris (ed.), *Research in personnel and human resources management*. Stanford, CT: JAI Press, pp. 53–74.

Wright, P.M. and Snell, S.A. (1998) 'Toward a unifying framework for exploring fit and flexibility in strategic human resource management', *Academy of Management Review*, 23: 756–73.

Yanadori, Y. and Marler, J.H. (2006) 'Compensation strategy: Does business strategy influence compensation in high-technology firms?', *Strategic Management Journal*, 27: 559–70.

Yellen, J.L. (1984) 'Efficiency wage models of unemployment', *American Economic Review*, 74: 200–5.

14

HRM and Equal Opportunities

Anne-Marie Greene

INTRODUCTION

This chapter aims to present a summary of research and writing on equality and diversity within the field of human resource management (HRM). It begins by providing some background context in which the central theme of the discussion is the move in thought from liberal approaches to equality based on 'sameness', to diversity approaches founded on 'difference'. The chapter explores the question of what this means for HRM and the HR function, looking at the implications for thinking about diversity management (DM) in organisations. Here the chapter is broadly structured around issues that have been selected because they represent some key themes of current academic and practitioner HRM literature; namely, the gap between the rhetoric and 'reality' of theory and practice and the problems of making a business case; moving towards 'best fit' or contextualised policies and practices; and looking at who should have responsibility for diversity within organisations. Reflecting the nature of academic and practitioner research in the field of equality and diversity, this summary will largely be from an Anglo-American perspective.

A NOTE ON TERMINOLOGY

There is no doubt that there is a huge debate about terminology in the field of equality and diversity. Examining 'diversity' as a concept, Prasad et al. state that the term has 'multiple, overlapping and conflicting meanings' (2006: 1) and with so many stakeholders laying claim to and offering differing interpretations of it, it becomes a 'literal and literary quagmire for scholars and practitioners alike' (Prasad et al., 2006: 4). Looking at the international literature, a variety of terms are in usage (for example, equal opportunities, equal employment opportunity, affirmative action (AA), positive action, equity policies, managing diversity, diversity management to name but a few). The title given to this chapter is 'HRM and Equal Opportunities', but the term 'equal opportunities' (EO) is one that is most common in the UK context and arguably has little relevance elsewhere. For example, Jain et al. (2003), when undertaking a comparative study (involving India, Malaysia, Canada, the US, South Africa and the UK) do not use the term 'EO' at all, distinguishing between 'affirmative action', 'employment equity' and 'diversity management' as terms they consider relevant (despite the fact that the UK is included in their study). Academics and practitioners in New Zealand and Australia are more likely to talk more about 'equity' while in the US, 'affirmative action' and 'managing diversity' are terms commonly invoked. There is also no consensus about what the different terms mean, whether they have relevance in different national contexts, and whether they mean the same kinds of activities and policies in the different contexts or whether each is a distinctly different approach (Foster and Harris, 2005; Kirton, forthcoming). For the sake of brevity, this chapter is not primarily concerned with elucidating the debates around, or the implications of, the particular terms used and will use the terms equality and diversity interchangeably, much as HR practitioners do themselves. However, even those familiar with the term EO may find it somewhat anachronistic in the 2000s, particularly if the term is viewed, as it has often been characterised, as an approach predominantly concerned with compliance with anti-discrimination legislation. To this end, it is worth flagging up a key conceptual development in the field: the increasing rise of the diversity approach (however it may end up being termed) within organisations.

EO TO DIVERSITY MANAGEMENT

What is meant by a diversity approach is a shift in thought in two main areas: a focus on treating people differently; and a focus on the business case. First, a move away from traditional liberal and radical conceptions of equality (Jewson and Mason, 1986), based around treating everyone the same – a 'sameness' approach – towards approaches

based on recognising and valuing people's differences – a 'difference' or 'diversity' approach (Liff, 1997). There is further debate about whether differences should be narrowly conceived as concerned with social groups (e.g. women, black and minority ethnic people etc), or broadened to encompass a greater variety of individual differences (Prasad et al., 2006: 2; Kirton, forthcoming). Second, the rise of the business case as the primary rationale for equality and diversity action is also an important aspect of the diversity approach. Traditional EO or affirmative action approaches, aimed to redress discrimination and historical injustices faced by certain groups in the workforce (e.g. especially women and black and minority ethnic people) underpinned by legislation. However, diversity approaches start from a position that sees human differences as a resource, the utilisation of which is crucial for competitiveness and improving organisational performance.

Diversity policies are introduced specifically in order to meet organisational goals: in this sense the concept or model is business-driven, rather than underpinned by broader notions of social justice (Kaler, 2001). Noon and Ogbonna (2001) argue that this is the key analytical differentiation between EO and 'managing diversity', that they are underpinned by two different rationales: EO by the social justice (or moral) case and 'managing diversity' by the business case. However, arguably this difference is overstated and what has actually occurred is a shift in *emphasis* rather than a fundamental re-conceptualisation (Kirton, forthcoming; Cornelius, 2002). In other words, while EO policies may utilise business rationales, they do so in order to achieve moral or social justice ends. In contrast, diversity policies are generally seen to have a more exclusive focus on the business case (Kaler, 2001: 59).

A major academic preoccupation has been whether diversity management (DM) is simply a name change or an entirely new policy approach, delivering significantly different outcomes. This echoes the older debates about the differences in practice between HRM and personnel management (Purcell, 2001; Hoque and Noon, 2001). As will be discussed later, it is debatable whether or not the move to diversity really means any deep changes in the substantive content of organizational policies (Kirton and Greene, 2005). However, as Kirton (forthcoming) states, it is still useful (for researchers at least) to characterise the two approaches (EO/AA and diversity) as indicating different, and perhaps competing emphases as this provides a conceptual map to locate organizational policies (Noon and Ogbonna 2001).

Litvin (2006; 1997) provides a useful summary of the historical development of the diversity approach, tracing its origins to the US in the late 1980s. This begins with the publication of the Workforce 2000 report (Johnston and Packer, 1987), and its predictions of dramatic demographic changes, leading to an increasingly diverse workforce (increasingly minority ethnic, feminised and ageing). As Litvin states, 'it is difficult to overstate the influence of the demographic predictions attributed to Workforce 2000 in the construction of the business case for diversity' (2006: 81). Thus businesses needed to meet the challenges and threats of the diverse workforce but also needed to capitalise on it. Common benefits cited include: taking advantage of diversity in the labour market; maximising employee potential; managing across borders and cultures; creating business opportunities and enhancing creativity (Cornelius et al. 2001).

Moreover, reflecting the previous discussion of the move in thought away from EO, diversity or 'difference' approaches have definitely become more dominant. While a comparison of the websites of 241 organisations in 8 European countries indicates the wide divergence in the way that dimensions of diversity are described, and the fact that the term 'diversity' is not yet automatically used in many countries in Europe except for the UK (Singh and Point, 2003), it is clear that diversity is a familiar term in many organisations in the UK, mainland Europe, Scandinavia, Australia, New Zealand and Canada (Blommaert and Verschueren

1998; de los Reyes 2000; Humphries and Grice 1995; Jones et al. 2000; Kersten 2000; Lorbiecki and Jack 2000; Sinclair 2000). The terms 'managing diversity', 'diversity management' or simply 'diversity policy' have thus become the new labels in many organisations worldwide, for policies and practices that would once have fallen under the heading of EO/AA, equity or simply 'equality policy'.

In summary, regardless of the contested nature and level of debate around these issues, there are a number of key features relating to the move towards a diversity approach that are worth highlighting as having implications for HRM theory, policy and practice:

(i)   the importance of the business case, rather than legal compulsion or the social justice case;
(ii) a broader range of individual and social group based differences;
(iii) the requirement for a systemic (or cultural) transformation of the organisation, rather than a reliance on legal regulation and bureaucratic procedures;
(iv) that the issues are the responsibility of the whole organisation, not just the HR function (see also Kirton forthcoming; Cox 1994; Kandola and Fullerton 1998; Kersten 2000).

These features will be returned to in the next section.

IMPORTANCE OF EQUALITY AND DIVERSITY FOR HRM

Looking at diversity policy and practice within the field of HRM is important because, first, the HR function is where responsibility for equality and diversity policies normally lies. Whatever terminology is used and despite the various critiques, equality and/or diversity issues have without doubt become increasingly important within the HRM field over the last 15 to 20 years. In contrast to the early to mid 1990s, most quality HRM texts and practitioner guides now have at least one chapter on equality or diversity issues. Scan the websites of practitioner organisations like the Chartered Institute of Personnel and Development (CIPD) in the UK (www.cipd.co.uk), or the Society for HRM (SHRM) in the US (www.shrm.org) and it is clear that diversity has become an essential part of HRM theory and practice, indeed the CIPD proclaims 'Managing diversity is central to good people management in the view of the CIPD' (CIPD, 2004). Many writers agree that there is considerable 'fit' between the development of HRM and diversity approaches to equality. Indeed, Miller states that 'Managing diversity can arguably be classed as the HRM approach to equality initiatives in the workplace' (1996: 206). Thus, moves to diversity approaches to equality match moves in thought about people management. Webb points to the 'fit' between the two, seeing the move towards diversity approaches as capturing 'the wider political shift from collective models of industrial relations, state regulation and associated bureaucratic control procedures to deregulation, free market competition and notions of human resource management based on maximising the contribution of the individual' (1997: 164).

In addition, a cursory glance at any demographic statistics or workforce surveys indicates that, despite years of anti-discrimination legislation and equality action, there is still much work to be done to improve the situation of women, minority ethnic, disabled, lesbian and gay and older and younger people in the workplace (see for example an international summary in Kossek et al., 2006; or in Europe in Kirton and Greene, 2005).

Despite the rhetoric of equality and diversity being central to HRM policy, practice does not always seem to match up. Motivated by frustration at the limited progress, equality and diversity issues have become part of a wider critique of HRM (Kamenou and Fearfull, 2006), with some writers consistently arguing that HRM theory, policy and practice may be at odds with the promotion of EO (Dickens, 1998a; Benschop, 2001; Kirton and Greene, 2005; Zanoni and Janssens, 2005). Such writers point to the fact that

equality and diversity issues are still often absent from mainstream HRM debate, where theory, policy and practice tends to assume the generic universal employee (Dickens, 1998a, 1998b; Benschop, 2001). Indeed, Dickens states that 'most research and writing on HRM ... does not make gender visible unless the primary focus is women or equal opportunities' (1998a: 34). It is interesting for example to consider the place of diversity issues within this handbook on HRM; i.e. is this specific chapter on EO the only place that diversity issues come up?

WHAT DOES DIVERSITY MEAN FOR HRM THEORY, POLICY AND PRACTICE?

In 1998, at the height of the debates about the meaning of HRM, Linda Dickens wrote an article in the *Human Resource Management Journal* addressing the question of 'What HRM means for gender equality' (Dickens, 1998a). In this, she looked at a number of key features of HRM and asserted that the 'soft' model of HRM, usually seen as good for women, may actually be problematic for women and gender equality. Some of her arguments will be drawn on in this chapter; however I intend to ask a slightly different but related question of 'What diversity means for HRM', in other words, what the move to difference or diversity approaches means for practitioners (most commonly in HR) dealing with equality and diversity issues.

It has already been established that a central feature of diversity management is the primacy of the business case. Indeed, Litvin goes so far as to see the business case as the 'mega discourse' of diversity (2006: 85), meaning that the achievement of organisational economic goals becomes the overriding guiding principle and explanatory device for those tasked with equality and diversity policy in organisations. This is arguably in contrast to those working within a traditional EO paradigm, where the emphasis was the social justice case aimed at redressing inequalities, often underpinned by a legislative regulatory imperative. So, for HR practitioners, perhaps the most significant legacy of the move towards diversity approaches is that the pressure is on to demonstrate the DROI 'diversity return on investment' (Hubbard, 1999, cited in Litvin, 2006: 84). This is reminiscent of the preoccupation of the link between HRM and performance: 'the holy grail of the optimum utilisation of human resources in pursuit of organisational goals' (Legge, 1995: xiii). However, just as it is with HRM practice more broadly, the link between diversity and performance outcomes is far from conclusive, and the direct benefits highly contested (Kossek et al., 2006; Kochan et al., 2003; Kirton, forthcoming; Benschop, 2001; Nkomo and Cox, 1996), such that Litvin concludes that 'despite their efforts, researchers have failed to generate solid, unequivocal support for the proposition that engaging in diversity initiatives is a good investment' (2006: 78). For every study that appears to show some positive correlation, there are an equal number that appear to show the opposite.

Many of the explanations for the difficulties in making the DROI link relates to the types of research carried out and their methodologies, or how to separate out the myriad of variables that could affect organisational outcomes from those specific to diversity. These arguments have been rehearsed many times in relation to wider HRM research (for a review see Boxall and Purcell, 2000; Legge 2001). However, there are some explanations that have more specific relevance to the theory and practice of diversity management in particular.

PROBLEMS WITH THE BUSINESS CASE

It would be naive to completely write off the need for organisations to have some business related rationale for equality and diversity policies, particularly given the amounts of money often involved in diversity programmes. In addition, traditional EO approaches have always made some use of the business case, at the very least the imperative to avoid litigation costs (Kirton and Greene, 2005). Some commentators talk about the social justice and business cases coinciding and that increased social justice can lead to organisational benefits, for example the marketing potential and enhanced reputation associated with being an ethical business, or being an 'employer of choice' (Gagnon and Cornelius, 2002; Liff and Dickens, 2000; Dickens, 2000; Dickens, 1999). However, if there is no complementary recourse to a broader social justice or moral case beyond direct and quantifiable organisational benefits, then critics claim that the diversity approach may ignore deep seated societal discrimination and patterns of disadvantage (Kaler, 2001; Webb, 1997; Liff, 1997). Moreover, Kirton (forthcoming) outlines what she terms as the 'dilemma of the business case'. Business case arguments are inevitably 'contingent, variable, selective and partial' (Dickens, 2006: 299) and depend on economic premises, which means that action is only encouraged when diversity and business needs coincide. There is always the danger that a business case can be marshaled as a justification for not taking action on EO (Dickens, 1999) or where a business case can be made for the exploitation of certain employees. Kirton (forthcoming) cites a number of international examples (including WalMart and Coca Cola) illustrating this. Subeliani and Tsogas' (2005) case study in the Netherlands finds that the economic imperative to increase customer service ratings saw diversity initiatives used to increase the number of minority customers, whilst leaving the disadvantaged work situation of ethnic employees within the company untouched. In other words, there is no necessary connection between having a diverse workforce and practicing equality.

LACK OF CONCEPTUAL CLARITY MEANS CONFUSION IN PRACTICE

A further question relates to whether diversity is 'do-able' (Prasad and Mills, 1997), and the difficulties faced by practitioners when they try to develop and implement diversity policies. Part of the 'do-ability', relates to whether practitioners understand what diversity policies are for and how to implement them. The level of academic confusion around diversity terminology was discussed earlier in this chapter, and it is clear that this lack of conceptual clarity extends to those who are tasked with the development and implementation of equality and diversity policy within organisations. An understanding of how different actors in organisations understand equality and diversity helps us to appreciate how and why actual policy and practice are formulated, implemented, resisted and challenged. However research findings indicate that if there are conceptual misunderstandings and lack of clarity by scholars in this area, this is only exacerbated for practitioners within organisations.

An example of how conceptual confusion impacts on policy and practice concerns whether policies should be based on the principles of 'sameness' or 'difference' – that is, is the aim of an equality and diversity policy to treat everyone the same or to respond to people's different needs? In her study of EO policy and practice in the 1980s in the UK, Cockburn (1989) found that people interpreted equality policies in workplaces differently depending on what was expected and desired from them in their various roles. Cockburn identified the interests of the shareholder who has a strong personal commitment to equality, the executive team who see equality as a profit-making policy relating to marketing technique and customer orientation, the lawyers who want equality initiatives to avoid employment tribunal cases of discrimination, the personnel managers who see equality as part of wider management trends, and the line management who are only concerned with equality if it does not conflict with maintaining work discipline and cost budgeting.

More recently, Foster and Harris' (2005) study of diversity management in the UK retail industry, ironically entitled 'Easy to say, difficult to do', identified the 'analytical muddle' faced by line-managers with responsibility for equality and diversity. Different understandings of the rationale for and the way in which policies should be approached, led to significant problems in implementation. Similarly, Nentwich's (2006) study finds EO officers in Switzerland using confusing and contradictory rationales for policy interventions. Qualitative findings from a UK study across a number of industrial sectors uncover real confusion amongst equality and diversity practitioners about what the terms mean and what organizational policies are actually striving to achieve (Kirton et al., 2006a).

The issue is that conceptual confusion can lead to policy confusion. Kirton and Greene (2005: 214) outline a summary of mainstream policy in the UK and find a mixture of sameness and difference approaches. This means the overall policy aim is not always clear: it may be to ensure people are treated equally, achieve equality of outcome, or recognise and value people's difference? For example, the difficulties of coming up with policy that responds to employees' needs and desires to be treated differently and the same as each other simultaneously (for example to be treated the same during recruitment and selection, but having different needs as a parent requiring flexible working also recognised) (Foster and Harris, 2005: 12). This relates directly to what Liff and Wajcman (1996) call 'mobile subjectivities', where people have both multiple differences and similarities. Similarly, Liff (1999: 73) provides a good illustration of this, looking at policies at BT, where she highlights the difficulties of having policy frameworks which simultaneously aim to ignore and respond to differences, because there is little understanding of the basis for deciding when it is appropriate to recognise differences and when to ignore them.

Critics of EO (for example Kandola and Fullerton 1998) argue that an individualised diversity approach that embraces all differences has the advantage of avoiding backlash, resistance and hostility from 'majority' groups (white men). However, linking to the previous section it is questionable whether an individualised business case for diversity can be made effectively and whether effective policies can be devised around individual differences. How are managers, to whom diversity policy implementation is devolved, expected to respond to a myriad of individual differences, especially given the range of possibilities? Woodhams and Danieli (2000) clearly illustrate the difficulty of the business case for diversity in the case of disabled employees. The exact nature of impairment, and the extent to which it is disabling, is particular to each person, and thus disability is perhaps the dimension of diversity where individual differences are most salient. Woodhams and Danieli argue that it would be hard to justify diversity policies in purely business case terms because of this level of individuality, which would inevitably lead to increased costs. Therefore the argument follows that disability equality policy has to have some underpinning collective group focus imperative (probably supported by law). Woodhams and Danieli's analysis is important in touching on the inherent contradiction within the rhetoric of diversity. This is that the business case for recognising diversity is prioritised; however if the approach is conceptualised solely as concerned with individual differences, identified and dealt with on an individual basis, then it becomes very difficult to make a viable business case.

THE NEED FOR CONTEXTUALISED POLICIES: BEST FIT APPROACHES?

Another preoccupation in academic and practitioner research involves the debate over whether organisations should take a best practice or best fit approach to HRM. There is a plethora of academic writing extolling the virtues of both approaches, and a large number of models and typologies (see Boxall and Purcell, 2000 for a useful international review). As is often the case in such polarised debates, a common pathway through is to establish a preference for a middle ground, so for example Boxall and Purcell (2000: 193) talk of 'unique fit' and 'exclusive practice' so that best practices are

situated appropriately in context. A similar situation has evolved within the literature on diversity and the business case. First, rather than seeing diversity as an alternative to equality, a commonly cited position is to ensure that social group based approaches underpin any diversity intervention (Liff, 1999; Kaler, 2001; Miller, 1996) so that diversity management is more of a shift, rather than a departure from EO or AA policies, not least because laws and regulations impose certain requirements on employers (Kirton, forthcoming).

Second, if there is to be a focus on the business case, then better to have a business case specific to the particular organisational context. As Kirton (forthcoming) points out, the most common position taken by organisations is to put forward very generic, 'best practice' business case arguments. This is despite the fact that the dominant view in mainstream HRM writing is that the focus should be on 'best fit'. There are now a number of writers who highlight the importance of contextualised approaches to diversity management (Janssens and Zanoni, 2005; Benschop, 2001; Kamenou and Fearfull, 2006; Dass and Parker, 1999). Those practitioners responsible for equality and diversity issues within organisations need to be aware of how the wider political, legal and economic context affects policy, so that different kinds of difference are likely to have greater salience in some places and certain moments (Prasad et al., 2006: 3). So, for example, implementing individualised policies in the UK, where there is a strong legal framework based around social groups, becomes extremely difficult (Foster and Harris, 2005; Lorbiecki and Jack, 2000: S28). Linehan and Hanappi-Egger (2005) identify the different concerns and targets for policy between different EU countries. In addition, diversity policies should be tailored to the specific organisational context. Thus Dass and Parker (1999) claim that an organisation's diversity approach will depend on the degree of pressure for diversity action, the types of diversity in question and managerial attitudes to diversity. Janssens and Zanoni (2005) identify the role of the customer and profile of customer service as a key determinant on the types of diversity policy and approach that are implemented.

That the approach and policy should be tailored to the specific organisational context seems a very common sense notion which for practitioners should lead to a 'more contextually informed and organisationally realistic view of diversity management than is all too often suggested by the equality literature' (Foster and Harris, 2005: 14).

However, it is worthwhile adding a note of caution. Indeed, linking to the discussion above about the contingent nature of the business case, it is clear that the specific organisational context may also be a convenient way of not dealing with diversity issues. For example, Dass and Parker (1999) provide a typology of four perspectives and four responses to diversity that one could imagine would be very attractive to practitioners struggling with implementing effective diversity practices. However, beyond its function as a descriptive typology of ideal types, Dass and Parker specifically state that their typology can be used by practitioners 'to examine their internal and external environments to adopt an approach to implementation that matches their particular context ... suggest[ing] opportunities for achieving fit, but ... also an argument for purposefully choosing an approach to managing diversity' (1999: 78). While at the one extreme this offers practitioners the 'choice' to adopt a proactive, long term transformative approach to diversity (their 'Learning Perspective'), the problem is that at the other end of the spectrum is the 'Resistance Perspective' where diversity is viewed as a threat and where unfair discriminatory practice appears to be an approach that is seen to 'fit' with a particular type of organisational context.

THE INEQUALITY EMBEDDED IN HRM PRACTICES AND STRUCTURES

Part of the academic critique of HRM also relates to the ways in which HRM

structures and practices can themselves be detrimental to the progress of equality and diversity within organisations. With regard to action on gender, Dickens (1998a) looks at a number of key features of HRM (for example 'commitment', 'flexibility', 'selection appraisal' and 'reward') and asserts that the 'soft' model of HRM may actually be more problematic for women and gender equality than is generally acknowledged. Thus, she argues that the concept of 'commitment' is itself gendered, whilst the requirement within 'flexibility' for numerically and functionally flexible employees may actually reinforce the disadvantage faced by women. Kirton and Greene (2005: chapter 9) extend Dickens' analysis to other aspects of the HRM model and to other aspects of social group disadvantage. Koene and Van Riemsdijk (2005) support Dickens' findings with regard to the treatment of 'non standard' employees in their study of temporary employees in the Netherlands. They highlight the way in which mainstream literature on strategic HRM calls for managers to distinguish between different types of employee in a way which leads to the detrimental treatment of those on temporary employment contracts. Also in the Netherlands, Benschop's (2001) study identifies the way in which HRM strategies and activities mediate the performance effects of diversity, where a very traditional HRM approach means that any potential beneficial effects of diversity were missed out on. Overall, Dickens states: 'those in organisations with a commitment to equality need to develop a sensitivity to the way in which apparently gender neutral HRM techniques may contribute to the gendering process' (1998a: 35).

Overall, given the difficulties in actually managing diversity in practice, it is not so surprising that in most cases there is a large gap between the rhetoric of diversity policy (individualised, valuing differences, transformative approach) and diversity practices which in reality tend to have more continuity with traditional EO approaches (Kossek et al., 2006). A recent CIPD report is a case in point. While the literature review preceding the report states 'legislation is not the main driver for diversity' (CIPD: 2005: 4), the findings indicate the opposite, indeed 68% of respondents put legislative pressure in the top five drivers for diversity action, with 32% stating it as the most important (CIPD, 2007). Given the difficulty of generating policy based around individual differences, it is perhaps to be expected that diversity policies are usually targeted at social groups, namely women, black and minority ethnic people, disabled people (CIPD, 2007: 9) much as EO policies were, even if claims are made that they include everyone (Litvin, 1997). In this case, regarding the question of what diversity means for HRM, it is tempting to answer that it means very little in practice, except for increased confusion for practitioners.

WHO IS RESPONSIBLE FOR DIVERSITY WITHIN ORGANISATIONS?

The quote from Dickens above leads us to another key area to consider in terms of what diversity means for HRM – namely who is or should be responsible for diversity within an organisation. Does the diversity approach mean anything different for practitioners in this area? Within mainstream HRM literature, there are two associated developments that are relevant. First, that HRM should play a much more strategic role in organisations and that there should be devolution of responsibility for HRM beyond the HR function.

Looking at the first, the level to which HRM is integrated within business strategy (Guest, 1987) is one of the key aspects of difference that is identified between HRM and personnel management – that people management issues are brought into the remit of strategic decision making (Hoque and Noon, 2001: 7). However, the effectiveness of integration depends on the role of the human resource function within the organisation, which often does not hold a powerful position in comparison, for example, to marketing, production, finance or sales (Cattaneo et al., 1994). Paradoxically, longitudinal evidence from the UK continues to show a decline in the presence of those with

human resources responsibilities on company boards of directors (Kersley et al., 2005; Cully et al., 1999). Additionally, nearly one third of workplaces in the UK had no strategic plan at all in the human resources area (ibid: 62).

Add diversity into the mix and it seems that it often plays even less of an important role than other aspects of HRM. Gooch and Ledwith (1996) provide a detailed analysis of the way in which equality issues become constrained and controlled when they are anchored within the powerless personnel or HR function. Evidence from research in the UK finds that EO/diversity practitioners are most often at middle management level, only 18% were contracted to work full time on equality and diversity issues, very few organisations have specialist diversity or EO functions and 70% of respondent organisations did not have a designated budget for equality and diversity issues (CIPD, 2007). Given that the people who have to develop and implement policy have such limited access to legitimacy, resources, and power, then it is perhaps not so surprising that highly successful policies are not necessarily forthcoming. If resources are so limited in contexts like the UK, where diversity is seen to have such a central role (at least in rhetoric), the situation may be worse elsewhere. For example, Zanko's (2003) study of HRM in 21 countries in the Asia-Pacific region appeared to find that employers in only four countries (Taipei, Korea, Chile and Canada) mentioned diversity matters in their list of most important HRM issues.

Furthermore, diversity policies can not stand alone but must be supported within the wider HRM portfolio. This has links to the need for horizontal integration of HRM, ensuring that the human resources policies form a coherent entity, for example that payment systems and work organisations complement each other. Hoque and Noon's (2003) analysis of UK data finds that while most companies have formal equality policies in place, these tend to be 'empty shells', with only 50% of workplaces adopting any back-up support policies, and 16% having no support policies at all. This is seen as crucial to effective equality outcomes and, in line with the HRM rhetoric, policies would need to be part of an integrated and coherent system. Kossek et al.'s (2003) research endorses the need for horizontally integrated support policies for diversity initiatives. In their study in the US, they found that the aim of increasing workforce diversity through hiring policy could have negative consequences for group/team cohesion, and could lead to detriment for the 'minority' groups recruited (whether this be women, black and minority ethnic workers, disabled workers, etc.) if the hiring policy is not supported by additional HR policies. Such policies would need to ensure that sufficient numbers of 'minority' individuals were recruited to avoid their isolation and that they were provided with the resources (training, functional, information) to allow them to enter work groups on an equal footing.

The second relevant development in HRM is the view that people management issues should not be the exclusive concern of the HR function. The idea here is that the human resource function should devolve HR responsibilities and activities, such that line-managers are directly empowered to take responsibility for managing people (see summary in Cornelius et al., 2001). A similar argument is made for equality and diversity policies (Kandola and Fullerton, 1998) so that the primary diversity constituency in organisations becomes line-managers (Kirton and Greene, 2006). This can be linked directly to the business case rationale, where it is felt that diversity will become more embedded in everyday organisational practices if it is taken up by those directly involved at the front line of the business.

However, devolution to the line is neither easy nor necessarily advantageous from a diversity point of view. Implicit within the strategic integration or 'mainstreaming' of human resources issues within HRM is the idea that HR/personnel specialists should 'give away' some of their power and responsibility as professionals to other management functions (Gooch and Blackburn, 2002; Cornelius et al., 2001).

Guest (1987: 519) discusses the difficulty that line-managers have in accepting such an abdication of responsibility. Gooch and Blackburn (2002: 145) summarise research suggesting that line-managers are selective about which aspects of human resource management they choose to be involved with and indeed tend to choose those that involve the setting of short-term business targets (Leach, 1995). A short-term approach is unlikely to do much to advance the equality and diversity project. Foster and Harris (2005) clearly indicate how line-managers in their study saw the implementation of diversity initiatives as unattractive when faced with the monitoring of their own performance against operational targets that usually do not include diversity dimensions. Indeed, a recent CIPD report finds that diversity as a performance criteria is only used in 19% of organisations, and is only included in the performance appraisals of managers in 16% of organisations (CIPD, 2006). Dickens (1998a) alerts us to the fact that devolution to line-managers is not necessarily good news where equality and diversity issues are concerned, not only because of the context in which they operate, but also because it represents a shift away from expertise in equality issues within organisations. Thus, despite the rhetoric, equality and diversity issues remain firmly established within the realms of the HR function.

Within the devolution debate it is also argued that responsibility for implementation of diversity policy should move beyond line-management to everyone in the organisation. Kirton et al. (2006) in the UK found that the majority of diversity practitioners believed that 'leadership' of equality and diversity issues had to come from all levels of the organisation. Lack of wider 'buy-in' and ingrained negative attitudes from non-managerial employees were seen as serious barriers to valuing diversity. Despite a widespread rhetorical commitment to wider involvement, in practice only a very small group of organisations had integrated, multi-channel forms of communication and consultation that genuinely seemed to proactively engage employees in the diversity agenda. Most non-managerial employees had little idea about what policies existed, and importantly, did not understand the rationale for these policies or how they were supposed to be involved. Similar findings emerged from a study of 200 companies in four EU countries (EC, 2003) where this 'awareness gap' (p. 7) was identified as a major obstacle limiting the scale of investment in diversity, largely because it led to a 'fear of change'. A report by the CIPD (2007) found that just over one third of organizations do not involve employees in the design and implementation of their diversity policies and practices. As discussed in Konrad et al. (forthcoming), a problem with diversity policy and implementation is the limited extent of stakeholder involvement. In contrast, evidence from Sweden (Dehrenz et al., 2002), and the Netherlands, Denmark and New Zealand (Rasmussen et al., 2004) illustrates the strength and positive outcomes that arise out of policies that are negotiated with wider stakeholders such as trade unions. This suggests that if organisations genuinely want all organisational members to 'own' diversity policy, then they need to open up channels of consultation and communication at an early stage in the development of initiatives.

CONCLUDING COMMENTS

This chapter aimed to consider the question of what diversity means for HRM, in particular tracing moves in thought from sameness to difference approaches. The discussion has identified a large 'rhetoric/reality gap' in that while key tenets of a diversity approach encourage policy based around individual differences, sharing of responsibility amongst a wider group of stakeholders and directly linking diversity to organizational outcomes, the reality is that much policy still looks very much the same as it did under EO approaches. Policy still seems to be based around the key social groups facing disadvantage, whilst legal compliance still seems to be a major motivator for action in this area. In addition,

policy development and implementation still seems firmly situated within the HR function, where the status and resources available to equality and diversity still appear to be extremely limited.

Moreover, while there is no doubt that diversity has significant theoretical advantages over EO, moves to diversity approaches seem to have made policy and practice in this area significantly more complicated. The foregoing discussion has highlighted the conceptual confusion experienced by practitioners, both with regard to what diversity means and the difficulty of making policy based around individual differences or in demonstrating the business case.

The polarisation of the academic debate about EO and DM, often couched in 'either/or' terms, is not particularly helpful for practitioners struggling to develop and implement policy. In thinking about ways that academics and practitioners might move forward, it might be better to look at ways that the two approaches can be better integrated. Part of this is raising awareness and understanding exercise. Reflecting on the conceptual confusion, Foster and Harris state that

> conducting an audit that includes all parties in the employment relationship, and addresses basic questions as 'where are we now?', 'where do we want to be?', and 'what do we need to do get there', is a useful starting point for employers seeking to develop appropriate and achievable diversity practices (2006: 14).

This exercise would be useful for both academics trying to understand how diversity is understood in organisations (but would require sufficiently qualitative research designs) and for practitioners trying to work out what approaches and policies might be most appropriate.

Ensuring that the widest group of organisational stakeholders (importantly including non managerial employees) is informed and involved in the development and implementation of equality and diversity policies is also a priority that must be addressed. With regard to academic research that has the potential to be most useful to practitioners, it is therefore important that research designs involve methodologies that include the widest variety of organisational stakeholders, particularly employees and their representatives. For HR practitioners, Dickens (1997), for example, suggests that collective equality bargaining by trade unions could underpin and generalise employers' diversity initiatives, while the law could generalise and underpin both of these. It is important that in taking up some of the diversity approaches, the support and protection offered by legislation and formalised procedures are not lost and are still fought for. Diversity approaches potentially offer appropriate and much needed challenges to organisational cultures, but doubtless need to be underpinned by more EO policies and legislative protection.

REFERENCES

Benschop, Y. (2001) 'Pride, prejudice and performance: Relations between HRM, diversity and performance', *International Journal of Human Resource Management*, 12: 7, 1166–81.

Blommaert, J. and Verschueren, J. (1998) *Debating Diversity*. London: Routledge.

Boxall, P. and Purcell, J. (2000) 'Strategic human resource management: Where have we come from and where should we be going?', *International Journal of Management Reviews*, 2 (2): 183–203.

Cattaneo, R., Reavley, M. and Templer, A. (1994) 'Women in management as a strategic HR initiative', *Women in Management Review*, 9: 2.

CIPD (2007) *Diversity in Business: A Focus for Progress*. London: Chartered Institute of Personnel and Development. http://www.cipd.co.uk/subjects/dvsequl/general/_dvstybsfcs.htm?IsSrchRes=1 accessed May 2007.

CIPD (2006) *Diversity in Business-How Much Progress have Employers Made? First Findings*. London: Chartered Institute of Personnel and Development. http://www.cipd.co.uk/subjects/dvsequl/general/_dvrstybus.htm?IsSrchRes=1 accessed May 2007.

CIPD (2005) *Managing diversity: Linking Theory and Practice to Business Performance*. London: Chartered Institute of Personnel and Development, London. http://www.cipd.co.uk/subjects/dvsequl/general/mandivlink0405.htm?IsSrchRes=1 accessed May 2007.

CIPD (2004) *Diversity: Stacking up the Evidence*. London: Chartered Institute of Personnel and Development, London. http://www.cipd.co.uk/subjects/dvsequl/general/diversity.htm?IsSrchRes=1 accessed May 2007.

Cockburn, C. (1989) 'Equality: the long and short agenda', *Industrial Relations Journal*, Autumn, 213–25.

Cornelius, N. (2002) 'Introduction and overview', in Cornelius, N. (ed.) *Building Workplace Equality: Ethics, diversity and inclusion*. London: Thomson, pp. 1–5.

Cornelius, N., Gooch, L. and Todd, S. (2001) 'Managing difference fairly: An integrated partnership approach', in M. Noon and E. Ogbonna (eds) *Equality, Diversity and Disadvantage in Employment*. Basingstoke: Palgrave.

Cox, T. (1994) 'A comment on the language of diversity,' *Organization*, 1 (1): 51–8.

Cully, M., Woodland, S., O'Reilly, A. and Dix, G. (1999) *Britain at work*. London: Routledge.

Dass, P. and Parker, B. (1999) 'Strategies for managing human resource diversity: From resistance to learning,' *Academy of Management Executive*, 13 (2): 68–80.

De los Reyes, P (2000) 'Diversity at work: Paradoxes, possibilities and problems in the Swedish discourse on diversity,' *Economic and Industrial Democracy*, 21: 253–66.

Dick, P. and Cassell, C. (2002) 'Barriers to managing diversity in a UK constabulary: The role of discourse,' *Journal of Management Studies*, 39 (7): 953–76.

Dickens, L. (2006) 'Re-regulation for gender equality: From either/or to both', *Industrial Relations Journal*, 37 (4): 299–309.

Dickens, L. (2000) 'Still wasting resources? Equality in employment?', in S. Bach and K. Sisson (eds) *Personnel Management: A Comprehensive Guide to Theory and Practice*, 3rd edition. Blackwell.

Dickens, L. (1999) 'Beyond the business case: a three-pronged approach to equality action', *Human Resource Management Journal*, 9 (1): 9–19.

Dickens, L. (1998a) 'What HRM means for gender equality', *Human Resource Management Journal*, 8 (1): 23–40.

Dickens, L. (1998b) 'Gender, race and employment equality in Britain: inadequate strategies and the role of industrial relations actors', *Industrial Relations Journal*, 28 (4): 282–289.

EC (2003) *The costs and benefits of diversity: A study on methods and indicators to measure the cost effectiveness of diversity policies in enterprises: Executive summary*. Brussels: European Commission.

Foster, C. and Harris, L. (2005) 'Easy to say, difficult to do: diversity management in retail', *Human Resource Management Journal*, 15 (3): 4–17.

Gagnon, S. and Cornelius, N. (2002) 'From equality to managing diversity to capabilities: A new theory of workplace diversity', in N. Cornelius (ed.) *Building Workplace Equality: Ethics, Diversity and Inclusion.* London: Thomson, pp. 13–58.

Gooch, L. and Blackburn, A. (2002) 'Managing people-equality, diversity and human resource management: Issues for line managers', in N. Cornelius (ed.), *Building Workplace Equality: Ethics, Diversity and Inclusion.* London: Thomson.

Gooch, L. and Ledwith, S. (1996) 'Women in personnel management-re-visioning of a handmaiden's role?', in S. Ledwith and F. Colgan (eds) *Women in Organisations.* London: Macmillan.

Greene, A.M., Kirton, G. and Wrench, J. (2005) 'Trade union perspectives on diversity management: A comparison of the UK and Denmark', *European Journal of Industrial Relations*, 11 (2): 179–96.

Guest, D. (1987) 'Human resource management and industrial relations' *Journal of Management Studies*, 24 (5): 503–21.

Hoque, K. and Noon, M. (2001) 'Counting Angels: A comparison of personnel and HR specialists', *Human Resource Management Journal*, 11 (3): 5–22.

Hoque, K. and Noon, M. (2004) 'Equal opportunities policy and practice in Britain: Evaluating the 'empty shell' hypothesis', *Work Employment and Society*, 18 (3): 481–506.

Humphries, M. and Grice, S. (1995) 'Equal employment opportunity and the management of diversity', *Journal of Organizational Change Management*, 8 (5): 17–32.

Jain, H.C., Sloane, P.J. and Horwitz, F.M. (2003) *Employment Equity and Affirmative Action.* Armonk: M.E. Sharpe, Inc.

Janssens, M. and Zanoni, P. (2005) 'Many diversities for many services: Theorizing diversity (management) in service companies', *Human Relations*, 58 (3): 311–340.

Johnston, W. and Packer, A. (1987) *Workforce 2000: Work and workers for the 21st century.* Indianapolis: Hudson Institute.

Jones, D., Pringle, J.K. and Shepherd, D. (2000) ' "Managing diversity" meets Aotearoa/New Zealand', *Personnel Review*, 29 (3): 364–80.

Kaler, J. (2001) 'Diversity, equality, morality', in M. Noon and E. Ogbonna (eds) *Diversity, Equality and Disadvantage in Employment.* Basingstoke: Palgrave, pp. 51–64.

Kamenou, N. and Fearfull, A. (2006) 'Ethnic minority women: A lost voice in HRM', *Human Resource Management Journal*, 16 (2): 154–72.

Kandola, R. and Fullerton, J. (1998) *Managing the Mosaic: Diversity in Action.* London: Chartered Institute of Personnel and Development.

Kelly, E. and Dobbin, F. (1998) 'How affirmative action became diversity management', *The American Behavioral Scientist*, 41 (7): 960–84.

Kersley, B., Alpin, C., Forth, J., Bryson, A., Bewley, H., Dix, G. and Oxenbridge, S. (2005) *First Findings from the 2004 Workplace Employment Relations Survey*, London: Department of Trade and Industry.

Kersten, A. (2000) 'Diversity management: Dialogue, dialectics and diversion', *Journal of Occupational Change Management*, 13 (3): 235–48.

Kirby, E. and Harter, L. (2002) 'Speaking the language of the bottom-line: The metaphor of "managing diversity"', *The Journal of Business Communication*, 40 (1): 28–49.

Kirton, G. (forthcoming) 'Managing multi-culturally in organizations in a diverse society', in S. Clegg and C. Cooper (eds) *Handbook of Macro Organisational Behaviour.* London: Sage.

Kirton G and Greene, A. M. (2005) *The Dynamics of Managing Diversity: A Critical Approach*, 2nd edition. Oxford: Butterworth Heinemann.

Kirton G. and Greene A.M. (2006) 'The discourse of diversity in unionised contexts: Views from trade union equality officers', *Personnel Review*, 34.

Kirton, G., Greene, A.M. and Dean, D. (2006) 'The multi-dimensional nature of work in the 'diversity industry' paper presented at the *EURODIV Conference* on 'Qualitative Diversity Research: Looking ahead', Marie Curie research programme, Leuven, September 18–20.

Kirton, G., Greene, A. M., and Dean., D (2007) 'British diversity professionals as change agents – radicals, tempered radicals or liberal reformers?', *International Journal of Human Resource Management*, 18 (11): 1979–94.

Kirton, G., Greene, A.M., Dean, D. and Creegan, C. (2006) Findings from an ESF funded project 'Involvement of stakeholders in diversity management' http://www2.warwick.ac.uk/fac/soc/wbs/research/irru/research/esfdiversity/professional_perspectives_report_01_06.pdf

Kochan, T., Bezrukova, K. et al. (2003) 'The effects of diversity on business performance: report of the diversity research network', *Human Resource Management*, 42 (1): 3–21.

Koene, B. and van Riemsdijk, M. (2005) 'Managing temporary workers: Work identity, diversity and operational HR choices', *Human Resource Management Journal*, 15 (1): 76–92.

Konrad, A., Prasad, P. and Pringle, J. (2006) (eds) *Handbook of Workplace Diversity.* London: Sage.

Kossek, E, Lobel, S. A. and Brown, J. (2006) 'Human resource strategies to manage workforce diversity: Examining the business case', in A. Konrad, P. Prasad and J. Pringle (2006) (eds), *Handbook of Workplace Diversity*. London: Sage, pp. 53–74.

Kossek, E., Markel, K. et al. (2003) 'Increasing diversity as an HRM change strategy', *Journal of Organizational Change Management*, 16 (3): 328–52.

Leach, J. (1995) 'Letting go or holding on: The devolution of operational personnel activities', *Human Resource Management Journal*, 41–55.

Legge, K. (2001) 'Silver bullet or spent round? Assessing the meaning of the "high commitment management"/performance link', in J. Storey (ed.) *Human Resource Management: A Critical Text*. Thomson Learning.

Legge, K. (1995) *HRM Rhetorics and Realities*. Basingstoke: Macmillan.

Legge, K. (1989) 'Human resource management: A critical analysis', in J. Storey (ed.) *New Perspectives in Human Resource Management*. London: Routledge.

Liff, S. (1999) 'Diversity and Equal opportunities: Room for a constructive compromise?', *Human Resource Management Journal*, 9 (1): 65–75.

Liff, S. (1997) 'Two routes to managing diversity: Individual differences or social group characteristics', *Employee Relations*, 19 (1): 11–26.

Liff, S. and Dickens, L. (2000) 'Ethics and equality: Reconciling false dilemmas', in D. Winstanley and L. Woodall (eds) *Ethical Issues in Contemporary Human Resource Management*. London: Macmillan.

Liff, S. and Wajcman, J. (1996) ' "Sameness" and "difference" revisited: Which way forward for equal opportunity initiatives?', *Journal of Management Studies*, 33 (1): 79–95.

Linehan, M. and Hanappi-Egger, E. (2006) 'Diversity and diversity management: A comparative advantage?', in H. Holt Larsen and W. Mayrhofer (eds) *Managing Human Resources in Europe*. Abingdon: Routledge, pp. 217–34.

Litvin, D. (1997) 'The discourse of diversity: From biology to management', *Organization*, 4 (2): 187–209.

Litvin, D. (2006) 'Diversity: making space for a better case', in P. Prasad, J. Pringle and A. Konrad (eds) *Handbook of Workplace Diversity*. London: Sage, pp. 75–94.

Lorbiecki, A. and Jack, G. (2000) 'Critical turns in the evolution of diversity management', *British Journal of Management*, 11 (Special Issue): S17–S31.

Miller, D. (1996) 'Equality management: towards a materialist approach', *Gender Work and Organisation*, 3 (4): 202–14.

Nentwich, J. (2006) 'Changing gender: The discursive construction of equal opportunities', *Gender, Work and Organization*, 13 (6): 499–521.

Nkomo, S.M. and Cox, T.J. (1996) 'Diverse identities in organizations', in S. R. Clegg, C. Hardy and W.R. Nord (eds) *Handbook of Organization Studies*. London: Sage, pp. 338–56.

Noon, M. and Ogbonna, E. (2001) *Equality, Diversity and Disadvantage in Employment*. Basingstoke: Palgrave.

Point, V. and Singh, V. (2003) 'Defining and dimensionalising diversity: evidence from corporate websites across Europe', *European Management Journal*, 21 (6): 750–61.

Prasad, P. and Mills, A. (1997) 'From showcase to shadow: Understanding the dilemmas of managing workplace diversity', in P. Prasad, A. Mills, E. Elmes and A. Prasad (eds) *Managing the Organizational Melting Pot. Dilemmas of Workplace Diversity*. Thousand Oaks: Sage, pp. 3–30.

Prasad, P., Pringle, J. and Konrad, A. (2006) 'Examining the contours of workplace diversity: Concepts, contexts and challenges', in P. Prasad, J. Pringle and A. Konrad (eds) *The Handbook of Workplace Diversity*. London: Sage, pp. 1–22.

Pringle, J., Konrad, A., and Greene, A.M., (forthcoming) 'Implementing employment equity in gendered organisations for gendered lives', in S. Clegg and C. Cooper (eds) *Handbook of Macro Organisational Behaviour*. London: Sage.

Purcell, J. (2001) 'Personnel and Human Resource Managers: Power, Prestige and Potential', *Human Resource Management Journal*, 11 (3): 3–4.

Ross, R. and Schneider, R. (1992) *From Equality to Diversity*. London: Pitman.

Sinclair, A. (2006) 'Critical diversity management practice in Australia: romanced or co-opted?', in P. Prasad, J. Pringle and A. Konrad (eds) *Handbook of Workplace diversity*. London: Sage, pp. 511–530.

Sinclair, A. (2000) 'Women within diversity: risks and possibilities', *Women in Management Review*, 15 (5/6): 237–245.

Subeliani, D. and Tsogas, G. (2005) 'Managing diversity in the Netherlands: A case study of Rabobank,' *International Journal of Human Resource Management*, 16 (5): 831–51.

Webb, J. (1997) 'The politics of equal opportunity', *Gender, Work and Organisation*, 4 (3): 159–169.

Zanko, M (2003) 'Change and diversity: HRM issues and trends in the Asia Pacific region', *Asia Pacific Journal of Human Resources*, 41 (1): 75–87.

Zanoni, P. and Janssens, M. (2003) 'Deconstructing difference: The rhetoric of human resource managers' diversity discourses', *Organization Studies*, 25 (1): 55–74.

15

Involvement and Participation

Graham Dietz, Adrian Wilkinson
and Tom Redman

The notion of increasing levels of employee engagement in determining or at least influencing work activities and organisational decision-making is not a new idea. In their classic review of the literature, Glew et al. (1995) cite Hugo Munsterberg's *Psychology and Industrial Efficiency* (1913) and the Hawthorne studies from the mid-1930s (Mayo, 1933), while Kaufmann (2003) cites William Basset's *When the Workmen Help You Manage* (1919). Ivancevic (1979: 253–254) acknowledges the work of Argyris, Coch and French, Likert, McGregor and Mulder as later influences on the development of our understanding of 'employee involvement and participation' (hereafter 'EIP'). EIP is a longstanding and enduring issue.

EIP is also a multi-dimensional idea. There are a daunting number of issues to consider. These include the ongoing debate over what constitutes all of the possible manifestations of EIP (e.g. 'involvement', 'participation', 'voice' and 'empowerment'), what distinguishes them from each other and how each should be operationalised. Cotton (1993), Dundon et al. (2004) and Wilkinson et al. (1997) have all addressed the definition debate.

The history of EIP in general terms is also worth considering, as is the history of particular techniques, and analyses of the contemporary context shaping EIP research. Abrahamson (1996, 1997) and Wilkinson (1998) have provided overviews of the history of the idea, while Bartunek and Spreitzer (2006) have accounted for the evolution of 'empowerment'. Strauss (2006) has examined the contemporary context.

Finally, perhaps the ultimate question – the effect of EIP schemes on organisational performance and employee well-being indicators – also demands attention. There have been several meta-analyses and reviews (see Handel and Levine, 2004; Locke and Schweiger, 1979; Miller and Monge, 1986; Wagner, 1994).

Rather less explored are the factors that distinguish effective schemes from ineffective ones. Yet, as Magjuka and Baldwin (1991: 794) highlighted, there is a compelling need for 'empirical research which identifies the relevant design variables [for EIP schemes' effectiveness] and links such variables with programme outcomes'. Fenton-O'Creevy (1998: 68) noted: 'The most significant question to answer is no longer "what are the benefits of employee involvement?" Rather, it is "What makes the difference between effective employee involvement programmes and those that fail to achieve their objectives?"' This is our focus in this chapter. Rather than go over familiar ground on definition, context and outcomes we explore 'the conditions in which policies and practices are introduced [that] can influence outcomes', and 'the processes' of engagement among participants (Kessler and Purcell, 1996: 668). The practical benefits of this have been articulated by Zeitz et al. (1999: 742): 'Knowing the long-term prognosis of a practice can help in making decisions about allocating resources – instrumental and symbolic – to that practice. Practices that are destined to be entrenched may warrant more resources than transitory practices'.

The chapter proceeds as follows. We begin with a short summary of the definition debate over EIP before setting EIP within the wider strategic HRM agenda. Next, we expand upon Glew and colleagues' 1995 framework for understanding the factors impacting upon EIP schemes, to help us order the literature in a coherent fashion. In so doing, we advance the idea that EIP schemes can be studied according to life-cycle effects. Accordingly, the rest of the chapter covers the factors that determine the 'birth', early development, final design, longevity and the ultimate effectiveness of EIP schemes. Throughout we suggest several future research agendas.

DEFINITIONS

The literature remains bedevilled by imprecise definitions of EIP even 30 years on from early attempts at synthesis (see Dachler and Wilpert, 1978; Locke and Schweiger, 1979).

Table 15.1   Possible EIP schemes

Attitude surveys	Quality circles
Continuous improvement groups	Suggestion schemes
European works councils	Self-managing teams
Job enrichment/re-design	T-groups
Joint management-staff committees	Teamworking
Joint working parties	Works councils
'Kaizen'	Team briefings

This is, in part, due to the myriad possible schemes that fall under the broad category of involvement/participation/empowerment (Sashkin, 1976) – see Table 15.1 – and to the 're-branding' of old schemes. Even today, scholars active in research into such schemes might disagree on basic definitions, and fail to recognise a given scheme as falling under the category assigned to it by another scholar,[1] because authors are imposing value judgements and/or using disciplinary conventions not shared by other schools of thought on EIP.

Seeking precise definitions, Vandervelde (1979, cited in Glew et al., 1995: 400) called for schemes to be defined precisely according to their 'who, what, where and how aspects' (see too Bowen and Lawler, 1992). Locke and Schweiger's (1979) widely cited definition presents 'participative decision making' as 'joint decision-making or influence sharing between hierarchical superiors and their subordinates'. Glew and colleagues (1995: 401) also see a hierarchical dimension (people working higher up the organisation bestowing 'opportunities' for input to their subordinates) as definitional to participation schemes. Tjosvold (1987: 739) similarly defines 'participation' as joint decision-making arrangements 'in which *employees are invited* to help solve organisational problems' (emphasis added). Such schemes '*give employees the legitimacy* to discuss organisational issues and problems and provide a setting for decision making' (Tjosvold, 1987: emphasis added). This hierarchical dimension is too restrictive for definitional purposes, however. Some schemes may not feature a hierarchical split and may comprise horizontal relationships instead, such as self-managing teams.[2]

Moreover, the Glew et al. agenda – confined solely to improving organisational performance – is too narrow. What is true, however, of all EIP schemes is that they seek to push influence, and even responsibility for, decisions down the organisational hierarchy (McMahan et al., 1998: 198).

Glew and colleagues' (1995) other criteria for EIP schemes are that they involve more than one person – participation is not an individual endeavour – in a manner that is visible to others. Further, EIP schemes are often seen as 'extra-role' or 'role-expanding' for those involved. But the crucial defining characteristic is the presence of a voice opportunity for participants, where voice refers to 'any vehicle through which an individual has increased impact on some element of the organisation … without voice, there can be no enactment of participation' (Glew et al., 1995: 402; see also Kaufman, 2003: 178). This final distinguishing feature allows us to concentrate in this chapter only on those schemes that provide employees with a credible and active input into decision-making (Strauss, 2006: 779). Accordingly, we do not discuss information sharing devices such as newsletters, team briefings and attitude surveys, though these devices may indirectly provide bottom-up employee voice (Peccei et al., 2005).[3]

We also intend to isolate the EIP component from broader programmes such as 'high performance work systems' (cf. Huselid, 1995) as the content of such systems extends far beyond EIP. That said, in our review we reflect on Ledford's and Lawler argument (1994) that isolating EIP in this manner can lead to a de-contextualised and non-systemic analysis, and that this narrow focus may explain the modest impact of many EIP programmes.

In sum, our working definition of EIP is:

Employer-sanctioned schemes that extend to employee collectivities a 'voice' in organisational decision-making in a manner that allows employees to exercise significant influence over the processes and outcomes of decision making.

This definition incorporates both 'substantive' and 'consultative' forms of participation (cf. Levine and Tyson, 1990), where the former equates to shared decision-making on the job, while the latter resembles a consultation exercise.

Such schemes can be categorised along a variety of dimensions (see Marchington et al., 1992; Marchington and Wilkinson, 2005), including:

- Purpose: why the scheme was initiated, to serve what and whose ends?
- Level: at what level of the organisational hierarchy does the scheme operate: team, workplace, divisional, strategic;
- Scope of the agenda: which subjects, and which decisions, are dealt with by the scheme (e.g. Hespe and Wall's (1976) three categories: 'local' [i.e. workplace and task concerns], 'medium' [i.e. workplace policies] and 'distant' [i.e. organisational strategy matters]; Connor (1992) identified nine different decision agendas;
- Direct or indirect: whether the scheme involves individual employees themselves [direct], or representatives of employees [indirect]
- Depth: the extent of employees' influence over the final decision, ranging from 'hardly any' through serving in an 'advisory' capacity to 'joint decision-making' up to full 'employee control'; alternative categories are 'suggestion involvement', 'job involvement' and 'high-involvement' in employers' strategy and policy (Bowen and Lawler, 1992); 'setting goals', 'decision-making', 'solving problems' and 'designing and implementing change' (Sashkin, 1976).

EIP AND HRM

The necessity for some form of EIP appears in most HRM models, such as Pfeffer's (1998) set of seven universal 'best practices' used in better performing firms. Many authors draw upon human capital theory (Becker, 1964) arguing that harnessing employees' skills and knowledge can add economic value to the firm (see Riordan et al., 2005: 474). EIP schemes enhance decision-making by tapping employees' direct knowledge of possible solutions to organisational problems and their initiative (Hodson, 2001: 208), what Deming (1988) refers to as 'extracting the gold from the (employee) mine'. This links with the claim from the resource-based view of the firm (Barney, 1991) that employees' skills and knowledge are one source of unique sustainable competitive advantage.

EIP is a cornerstone of the 'AMO' model put forward by Appelbaum and colleagues (2000), in which the 'A' stands for enhancing employees' abilities, the 'M' for enhancing their motivation, and the 'O' stands for 'opportunities' for employees to participate, or utilise their abilities and motivation. EIP not only provides these opportunities but in so doing, arguably, increases employee motivation (Gollan et al., 2006: 500; Miller and Monge, 1986) and allows employees to use their abilities more than if no EIP opportunities existed. The theory is that this should increase performance levels.

Another performance-driven rationale for EIP is that employees' participation in them equates to additional, or discretionary, effort expended on behalf of the organisation 'beyond contract' (Fox, 1974). Higher levels of organisational citizenship behaviours [OCB] (Cappelli and Rogovsky, 1998) should improve firm performance (Glew et al., 1995; Spreitzer and Mishra, 1999; Wilkinson, 1998; 2008). Yet such behaviours are sometimes interpreted by unions and academic sceptics as work intensification (Ramsay et al., 2000), especially when participation is expected as an everyday work activity.

EIP schemes can also be used to encourage shared norms and organisational values (Sashkin, 1976). By inducing employee compliance with organisational goals, firms can anticipate extra discretionary effort, and also reduce costly monitoring of employee behaviour (Spreitzer and Mishra, 1999: 162). Yet several critics have equated this purpose with union substitution. EIP schemes may be seen as creating organisational commitment and reducing union commitment, with negative consequences for active union participation as employees' hearts and minds are won over to the organisation's agenda. Critics of EIP have further suggested that it can undermine union militancy, and preserves unfettered management prerogative (Parker and Slaughter, 1988). However, a recent American study found that 'with each additional EIP experience union commitment *increases*', and that disaffection with ineffective EIP drives employees back toward their union (Hoell, 2004: 272 – emphasis added).

In empirical studies of the link between firm HRM practices and firm performance, EIP schemes feature prominently in operationalisations of HRM. In a sample of 104 empirical studies from 1995–2004, Boselie et al. (2005) found that 39 studies included measures of *direct* EIP, including seminal studies from Cooke (1994), Guthrie (2001), Huselid (1995) and MacDuffie (1995) while 11 studies included *indirect* forms, including key work from Batt et al. (2002), Delery and Doty (1996), and Ichiowski et al. (1997).

There is also a 'democratic humanism' (Wilkinson, 1998) or 'affective' (Miller and Monge, 1986), argument in favour of EIP. This views employee engagement in decisions as a good thing in and of itself, regardless of any effect on organisational performance metrics. Cappelli and Rogovsky (1998: 637) cite Adler's (1993) study in the celebrated NUMMI factory in Fremont, California, in which lean production methods ruthlessly constrain work tasks within narrow and de-skilled parameters, and yet NUMMI employees are able and even happy to 'put up with boring, 'unenriched' tasks because they have employee involvement'. In other words, managers may use EIP as a counter-weight to otherwise dispiriting aspects of daily work (see also Freeman and Kleiner, 2000).

In sum, EIP in whatever form is widely believed to improve firm performance and enhance employees' well-being. However, as we shall demonstrate, securing that added value is by no means a straightforward task.

Establishing and running EIP schemes

Glew and colleagues' (1995) holistic framework adapted for this chapter (see Figure 15.1) depicts each component of the process of establishing and running an EIP scheme. Their 'starting point' for any scheme is that managers see the potential to improve

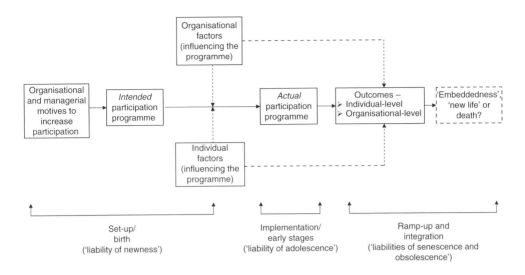

Figure 15.1   Glew and colleagues' (1995) framework of the participation process – adapted.

organisational performance – howsoever defined; managerial motives have 'a direct effect on the programmes that organisations and managers intend to implement' (Glew et al., 1995: 404). Thus, understanding these managerial motives as the catalyst for the scheme is a requirement of any research into such schemes.

Second, managers may design the EIP scheme in most cases (Glew et al., 1995: 397). However, case study evidence attests that the intended design and the actual scheme implemented rarely resemble each other (Kaufman, 2003; Labianca et al., 2000; Marchington et al., 1993; Wilkinson and Ackers 1995; Wilkinson et al. 1992). We discuss possible reasons for this mismatch.

Third, 'an at-present unspecified set of *organisational* and *individual* factors may act as obstacles while other organisational and individual factors may serve as facilitators' (Glew et al., 1995: 397; see also Sashkin, 1976). This corresponds to a contingency model of participation (Heller et al., 1998: 190–219). We discuss the most salient issues on these factors.

Finally, the scheme will have its outcomes, for the participants themselves, for the workplace and/or organisation as a whole, and for trade unions, where present. Here we

extend the 'outcomes' debate to consider the fate of the EIP scheme itself.

Glew et al.'s framework has the merit of including the influence of broader organisational and external contexts, and the impact that the history of setting the scheme up has on process and outcomes. Moreover, it does not restrict attention to the content of practices or to outcomes. Most importantly, it is sensitive to the perceptions and enthusiasm and capacities of managers involved in the design and implementation of the scheme, and employees on its receiving end.

A further theoretical framework which we can use to gather, order and analyse the literature on EIP comes from models of the adoption of work practices (Strauss, 2006). EIP schemes may be thought of as evolving over a typical 'life-cycle' of a new working practice. Lesure et al. (2004) synthesised a selected range of studies on the adoption of 'best practice' to produce a generic model (Figure 15.2).

As can be seen, a variety of issues determines the adoption decision, after which the scheme passes through four more 'overlapping' stages (cf. Tjosvold, 1987: 2, 32): set-up ('the decision to proceed'), implementation ('the mere launch of the programme'), ramp-up (the immediate usage

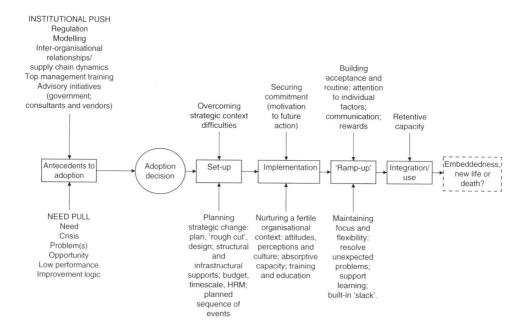

Figure 15.2   Lesure et al. (2004): model for the adoption of innovative work practices – adapted.

phase, during which problems are anticipated and addressed, and initial organisational learning begins), and integration (once the scheme has been routinised and embedded into organisational practice: 'entrenched', to use Zeitz et al.'s term (1999)). Each phase is shaped in part by a variety of factors as shown.

The overlaps between Lesure et al. and Glew et al. are readily apparent: 'managerial motives' equates to 'adoption decision', while 'intended and actual participation programme' equates to 'set-up' and 'implementation'. However, the Lesure model extends the process to depict the scheme's future prospects (the 'integration' stage), which have been hitherto neglected (Zeitz et al., 1999: 742). Recognising the often-truncated lifetime of these schemes (Kaufman, 2003: 188), we therefore extend both frameworks a stage further to include the 'fate' of the scheme: whether it becomes embedded, morphs into something else, or fails to survive and 'dies off'.

Analogies with population ecology models of firm survival are helpful (Hannan and Freeman, 1984; Henderson, 1999; Stinchcombe, 1965). Borrowing from these

models, we see that at each stage of the scheme's life-cycle, it may be threatened by a particular 'liability'. At set-up, the 'liability of newness' militates against new schemes which are often rejected due to preferences for older, 'more reliable' EIP practices: 'it is easier to continue existing routines than to create or borrow new ones' (Henderson, 1999: 282). In this scenario, the scheme never gets initiated (Strauss, 2006: 783). The second liability, 'the liability of adolescence', afflicts the formative 'birth pangs' period of launch and implementation. An analogy here is of a 'honeymoon period' (cf. Heller, 1998) during which EIP schemes may survive for a short period on their initial assets (e.g. participants' enthusiasm, organisational resources in terms of budget, senior management support and training), but should these run out schemes struggle without them. The third and fourth liabilities affect the mature phase of the scheme (i.e. beyond integration): the 'liability of senescence' materialises when schemes become inefficient, unproductive and unresponsive, and no longer fit for purpose, while the 'liability of obsolescence' means that the scheme can be seen as no longer fit for purpose because it is outdated, and cannot be adapted to serve 'new organisational realities'. Support for an ageing process of EIP schemes has come from Kato (2006), while Strauss adopts a life-cycle model when he recounts the demise of the famous NUMMI and Saturn arrangements (2006: 784–787). The main questions are, therefore, why do schemes suffer from particular liabilities over the course of their life-cycle, and what factors can inoculate the scheme against these threats?

The following sections present the findings from selected EIP studies that have looked into each component of Glew and colleagues' framework, drawing for the most part upon work published since their 1995 article (for additional references and research evidence on each variable, readers are urged to consult the original article). We also locate studies within our 'life-cycle' model.

THE 'BIRTH': MANAGERIAL MOTIVES AND RATIONALES FOR EIP

The Glew et al. framework posits a direct effect from managerial motives for having a scheme on the programme that they subsequently design and implement. Yet, surprisingly, they could find little research examining manager's thought-processes when setting up such schemes. Some 14 years on, this gap has not been filled.

For Lesure et al. (2004), there are powerful 'institutional pushes' (such as regulatory requirements and what is deemed professional 'best practice') and 'need pulls' (such as competitive pressures) that urge firms to adopt new practices, including EIP. These push and pull effects interact in complex ways, yet the authors note, 'many surveys confirm that institutional push mechanisms are often the sole driver for adoption' and with limited impact (Lesure et al., 2004: 48). Glew and colleagues also cite Kanter's (1983) claim that most managerial reasoning on EIP schemes is superficial, and 'faddish'.[4]

Second, an alternative thesis is that managers' awareness of, and concerns regarding, a performance gap between what they would like and what they have creates a socio-psychological anxiety or cognitive dissonance (Festinger, 1957) that can be alleviated by adopting the lauded management techniques of their day (such as variants of EIP) – provided that a discourse linking reasons for the performance gap with a ready-made solution has been disseminated, of course.

Third, most managers wish to be seen to be complying with prevailing norms of rationality and progressiveness, and they can do so efficiently by adopting lauded management techniques. Abrahamson and Fairchild (1999) looked specifically at the lifecycle of the fashion for one form of EIP, quality circles, in the US and confirmed a strong co-evolution between the discourse on quality circles and its diffusion.

Fourth, and related, managers follow 'high-fashion' organisations (Marchington et al., 1993). One of the most important managerial motivators for the introduction of EIP is a desire by managers to be noticed internally and to engage in impression management through the creation of new schemes. Equally, the strong influence of a 'star company' with well-developed EIP practices in a geographical region can result in considerable activity in the adoption of EIP in that locality.[5] Thus, adoption of EIP may have much to do with simple 'mimetic isomorphism' (cf. DiMaggio and Powell, 1990), or managers' self-interest, driven by macro-level 'management fashions'.

Strauss (2006: 787) argues that schemes 'are likely to be adopted only if they are perceived to have some sort of payoff in productivity, quality, turnover, satisfaction and the like – and they are dropped because they are perceived not to have such payoffs'. On this 'likely payoff' calculation, Bowen and Lawler (1992) see five purposes for empowering service staff: facilitating quicker responses to customer needs, particularly for dissatisfied customers (through spontaneous 'rule-bending'); employees feeling better about themselves and their jobs (work acquires more meaning and is more challenging); employees interacting with 'warmth and enthusiasm' with customers (passing on managers' concern for employees to customers); the solicitation of great ideas from employees as to improvements to the organisation and, finally, valuable word-of-mouth advertising and customer retention (from people telling their friends about exceptional service). Yet these alleged benefits are weighed against costs: a greater monetary investment in selection and training (to screen out likely poor performers); higher overall labour costs (from higher wages to retaining good, empowered staff), and potentially slower or inconsistent service delivery, violations of 'fair play', 'giveaways' and bad decisions (due to irregular acts of discretion by employees).

This suggests that managerial motivation for initiating an EIP scheme is a multidimensional and often internally contradictory variable. As we shall see in subsequent sections, competing explanations are examined in case study evidence from, among others, Kaufman (2003), Labianca et al. (2000), Timming (2007), Vallas (2003), and Wilkinson et al. (2004).

ORGANISATIONAL FACTORS INFLUENCING THE EIP SCHEME'S DESIGN AND IMPLEMENTATION

Glew et al. (1995: 408) noted how several authors have argued for stronger effects from 'situational variables than from individual [employee] differences'. EIP schemes in a given organisation appear to reflect its particular external and internal circumstances, notably size, task complexity, strategy, workforce profile, and 'participation climate'.

In Connor's (1992) study of Oregon nursing homes, size and task complexity was associated with more use of employee participation schemes, but the results for profit-motive were limited. Addison et al. (1997: 443) found that size, age, and branch plant status [an ownership variable] were strong determinants of the presence of a works council in Germany (where it is mandated by law in firms with more than five employees) but, interestingly, works councils were less common where teamworking (i.e. direct EIP) was practised. This suggests that direct/indirect forms may act as substitutes in Germany. Miller and Monge (1986) found no significant effect from industrial sector on participation use.

With specific regard to service workers, Bowen and Lawler (1992) outlined 'five contingencies that determine which approach to EIP to adopt', which is arrived at by rating each contingency on a scale of 1–5 (see Table 15.2). Their 'rule of thumb'-style propositions are that the higher organisations score their business on each contingency, the more appropriate 'empowerment' becomes, and the higher the cumulative score the more appropriate 'empowerment' becomes. Overall scores of 5–10 point to a production line approach, 11–15 to allowing staff to offer suggestions, 16–20 to providing staff with opportunities to re-design their jobs and work processes, while 21 and above suggests high-level systematic 'empowerment' at all organisational levels.

Table 15.2   Bowen and Lawler: five contingencies for introducing 'empowerment' in service work.

Contingency	'Production line' approach			'Empowerment' approach	
	1	2	3	4	5
Business strategy	Low-cost, high volume			Differentiation, customised, personalised	
Tie to the customer	Transactional, short-term			Relationship-building, long-term	
Technology	Routine, simple			Non-routine, complex	
Business environment	Predictable, few surprises			Unpredictable, many surprises	
Profile of workforce	'Theory X' managers, employees with low growth needs, low social needs and weak interpersonal skills			'Theory Y' managers, employees with high growth needs, high social needs and strong interpersonal skills	

Miller and Monge's (1986) meta-analysis reported that working in a strong participation-oriented climate had a strong positive effect on employee satisfaction. Yet, as Riordan et al. (2005) concede, the planned creation of a climate is formidably difficult. In their study of EI climate's effect on organisational performance, they measured EI climate along four dimensions: *power* (employees have sufficient influence over the final decision), *information* (parties have sufficient information to make effective decisions), *training* (parties are trained in the skills and knowledge necessary to make the scheme work), and *reward* (any performance benefits for the organisation will be shared with participants). They theorised that firms with a stronger EI climate (i.e. high levels of all four attributes) would report higher corporate financial performance and lower employee turnover, and that greater employee morale – through higher employee commitment and job satisfaction – would fully mediate this relationship. Their multi-level study of employees in 92 North American insurance companies confirmed positive effects for EI climate on financial performance and turnover, but only commitment served as a mediator. In a separate study, Vandenberg et al. (1999, cited in Riordan et al., 2005: 484) found that other practices supportive of an EI climate included having a clear vision and direction, incentives linked to EIP behaviours, the promotion of flexible work practices and semi-autonomous job designs, and significant resources dedicated to continuous learning. Bowen and Lawler (1992), in discussing 'empowerment' argued that four 'organizational ingredients' must be shared with frontline employees in order for such schemes to work: *Power* to make decisions that influence organisational [or workplace] direction and performance; *Information* about the organisation and its current circumstances and future intentions; *Rewards* based on the organisation's performance; *Knowledge* that enables employees to understand the 'information' given to them. In three British public health organisations Bach (2004) found

that the overwhelming 'performance targets' climate militated against the effectiveness of both direct and indirect forms of employee voice – despite staff enthusiasm for a greater voice.[6]

All of this suggests that EI climate would be a potentially very interesting line of research for EIP. There is a need to understand the antecedents and consequences of EI climate in more depth. Climate research in organisational behaviour in general is developing rapidly (Hoffman et al., 2003; Lindell and Brandt, 2000; Schneider et al., 2002), and further EI climate studies would be a valuable contribution to a fuller understanding of climate research.

A related variable to 'climate' is the degree of embeddedness, or entrenchment, of EIP schemes in the internal running of the organisation: an effective 'participation climate' is only achievable with embedded schemes. Lawler et al. (1995) argued that wide internal diffusion of EIP determines the success of the programmes (see also Zeitz et al., 1999). For Cox et al. (2006: 252), 'the degree of embeddedness reflects the centrality of EIP to the workplace and will thus affect the strength of its impact'. The latter group of researchers conceptualise embeddedness along two dimensions: *breadth* (how many EIP schemes operate in the workplace), and *depth* (the scope and relevance of the agenda, and the regularity of the meetings). Using nationally representative UK data, Cox et al. found that additive combinations of practices on both dimensions showed consistently positive associations with employee organisational commitment and job satisfaction. Thus, employees' attitudes to EIP are dependent, *inter alia*, upon the prior experiences of EIP and work in general, management approaches to employee relations, and the recent and projected organisation's performance.

Another form of embeddedness is the degree to which EIP schemes suffuse internal social networks within the organisation. Rubinstein and Kochan's (2001) study of the Saturn plant showed that cross-functional social networks contribute to the initial success of EIP. One conclusion from Labianca et al.'s (2000) study of an 'empowerment' programme inside a healthcare company is that both managers' and employees' 'schemas' on the programme must align in order for the programme to be taken seriously. They found that this alignment can be 'massive and sudden, given sufficient disconfirmation' (Labianca et al., 2000: 252) of the old schema 'through enacted behaviour by management *and* employees' (Labianca et al., 2000: 253: emphasis in the original), including the open airing of grievances about the old ways of doing things. Interestingly, they suggest that managers' defensive efforts to override employees' initial scepticism or resistance may only 'reinforce the old schema that employee concerns are insignificant compared to management's' (Labianca et al., 2000), echoing Tjosvold's (1987) support for 'productive controversy'. In sum, embeddedness is only realised when managers and employees come to interpret the EIP scheme *similarly*. Managers may have to take a few hits before this can happen.

Missing from the Glew et al. framework is the influence of national culture. In common with much of the management literature, most published EIP studies have been conducted in North American work settings (see Poutsma and Huijgen, 1999, for a European review). The influence of national culture norms has been explored in several studies, and the evidence casts doubt on the universal applicability of schemes extending to employees' influence over their work. For example, McFarlin et al. (1992) reported hostility among British, Dutch and Spanish managers to their American multi-national parent's attempt to 'export' an American variant of EIP. Welsh et al.'s (1993) study inside a textiles factory in Russia found that a US-made participation programme clashed with Russian norms of solidarity and support for one's leader [which the scheme potentially undermined]. Additionally, the workers had been 'frustrated by a façade of participation' in the past, and so withheld suggestions on improvements and seemed to deliberately reduce their performance levels in order to avoid engagement with

EIP (Welsh et al., 1993: 73–74). While Welsh and colleagues infer that this may be a national cultural phenomenon, similar attitudes and behaviours have also been observed in Western settings (Cox et al., 2006). All this suggests that disentangling national cultural effects from organisational context could be a useful direction for further research.

INDIVIDUAL EMPLOYEE FACTORS INFLUENCING EIP SCHEME DESIGN AND IMPLEMENTATION

Cappelli and Rogovsky (1998: 635) note how, for most studies, the mechanisms through which programmes are believed to contribute to improved work performance 'turn mainly on relationships with psychological needs'. Lam et al. (2002) argue that 'researchers should look beyond situational and methodological moderators and examine psychological pre-dispositions' to learn more about the factors likely to influence EIP schemes' effectiveness. Thus, the *pre-dispositions* and *self-interests* of those involved – supervisors, managers, workers – are pertinent. We take each constituency in turn.

Managers' and supervisors' dispositions, motivators and needs

One of the most widely observed factors hampering EIP is management scepticism or even outright hostility. Managers may not always implement the scheme in the manner intended. Soliciting employees' input into organisational activities that were previously the exclusive domain of supervisors and/or managers shifts the balance of power in the standard employee-manager relationship, however modestly (Batt: 2004; Klein, 1984: 95). Managers and supervisors can perceive this as an unacceptable encroachment on their 'prerogative' (Glew et al., 1995: 410; see also Purcell, 1991). Many managers see redistribution of influence as a 'zero-sum game': 'It can only diminish their own [control and influence]' (Fenton O'Creevy, 1998: 71). Similarly, Wilkinson noted

> ... the removal of expert power [with the intro-duction of an EIP scheme designed to share decision-making responsibility] is often perceived as a significant threat and participative management is seen as a burden to many middle managers, and it is not surprising they do not universally welcome it (1999: 52)

Aside from the loss of status and perceived assault on managerial prerogative and hence on their self-identity, Spreitzer and Mishra (1999: 156) put a different emphasis on the risks involved for managers:

> The very act of involving lower echelon employees requires some risk on the part of managers who make themselves vulnerable by ceding authority to lower echelon employees, authority that was previ-ously restricted to the manager ... a fundamental problem facing managers is how they can give up control through the involvement of employees in decision making without losing control.[7]

Thus, studying the perspective of those most likely to be charged with the design and implementation of the schemes is critical to understanding what determines effectiveness.

The theme of resistance is 'remarkably constant' in the literature (Fenton-O'Creevy, 1998: 69). He described several kinds of middle manager resistance behaviours:

1 rubbishing the scheme;
2 expressing only mild or forced enthusiasm for the scheme – the signal received by employees being equivalent to the first tactic;
3 controlling access to the scheme, whether to favourites (as a reward) or miscreants (as a punishment); using the scheme to confer favours or exert discipline;
4 coercing participants into taking part, and producing the outcomes sought by the manager – regardless of the EIP scheme's remit.

In his study of 155 UK organisations, Fenton-O'Creevy found lack of senior man-agement support to be the strongest con-tributor to middle management resistance, as well as the absence of any incentives

for managers to comply. A 'trickle-down' effect appears to be in operation here with middle managers managing their direct reports in the way they themselves are managed. A perceived threat to job security or promotion opportunities was also influential. The practical implication is that middle management resistance is, unsurprisingly, linked to lower reported benefits from the scheme for the organisation. Thus, if an organisation accepts the rationale behind EIP and anticipates the performance benefits, then planned steps to overcome managerial scepticism is an organisational imperative. Yet Fenton-O'Creevy argued that middle management resistance 'may be a symptom of a wider failure to set up employee involvement initiatives properly' (1998: 80): the variance in middle management resistance and scheme effectiveness may be explained by organisation-level variables, such as reward systems, EI climate and senior management support.

Klein (1984) summarised her research into front-line supervisors' engagement with EIP schemes in eight US manufacturing plants of four multi-nationals. She noted the common refrain of 'what's in it for us?' Supervisors' main concerns were threefold: threat to job security, threat to their established job definition, and the perceived extra burden of time and effort associated with implementing EIP schemes. From her observational study, Klein identified five types of resistant front-line supervisors.

1 'Theory Xers': Managers who are used to, and prefer, command and control styles of management for whom EIP is anathema.
2 'Status seekers': Managers who wish to retain their power and internal status for whom EIP seems to undermines their self-identity.
3 'Sceptics': Managers with no fundamental objec-tions but considerable doubts as to whether the scheme will work, or endure.
4 'Equality seekers': Managers who want EIP for them too.
5 'Deal makers': Managers who have come to rely upon their informal deal-making powers in order to manage, for whom the rules and processes of EIP are a threat.

For Klein (1984), training programmes in running EIP tend to be ineffective. More successful interventions to persuade front-line supervisors to relent and support EIP are: showing it to them in action, giving them their own input into higher-level decision-making (including on the design of the EIP scheme itself), and support networks.

By contrast, Vallas' (2003: 244) study of teamwork and continuous improvement programmes inside four paper mills in the U.S found that middle managers might *embrace* EIP as a means of '*expanding* their authority in ways that they had not previously enjoyed' (emphasis in the original), principally by making EIP participants under their charge feel like 'a band apart' from the rest of the workforce in a manner that bolsters managers' own authority (2003: 237). Vallas concluded, 'the outcome of workplace change [i.e. EIP] initiatives tends to reflect the distribution of control over the implementation of the process itself' (p. 245).

Batt's (2004) research inside a large U.S corporation illustrates what she calls the 'political' dimension of EIP schemes (in her case, self-managed and off-line teams). She looked at the effect of involvement in teams for workers, supervisors and managers on three dependent variables – job satisfaction, discretion, and job security – and found that 'organizational position is significantly related to work-related attitudes [regarding the team programmes] but not in entirely predictable ways' (2004: 205). Batt expected that workers would enjoy the extra discretion and hence report higher levels of satisfaction (though this effect would be much weaker for the much less influential off-line team format); supervisors would be more sanguine and even fearful over possible losses to their discretion and job security, and middle managers would gain if they were rewarded personally for any organisational performance improvements secured, but they might suffer if the team structure led to stressful conflicts among workers and supervisors. Overall, she found minimal impacts on any of the outcomes from off-line teams, reinforcing a recurrent finding

in the literature: cosmetic schemes that do not disturb existing power dynamics in organisational decision-making tend not to be effective for anyone. On self-managed teams, Batt concluded,

> Workers benefited significantly [from more discretion, which primarily mediated their job satisfaction], supervisors lost out [largely from a loss of job security], and middle managers who initiated self-managed teams had higher levels of employment security than their more traditional counterparts [though, overall, the positive outcomes for middle managers were rather modest in magnitude] (p. 200).

Finally, Spreitzer and Mishra explored the impact of managers' trust in their employees (across four factors: employees' reliability, openness, concern and competence) on managers' willingness to allow employees to engage in participation schemes, and the impact of the schemes on three measures of organisational performance (mediated by managers' willingness to support them). They further compared trust against managers' other options for coping with their vulnerability in participation schemes, incentivising employees' cooperation and giving employees' performance feedback. In a survey of 43 firms in the American automotive industry, all three control mechanisms had significant effects on managerial engagement with EIP. In concluding, the authors argued, '… trust, performance information and incentives must be employed in tandem with a willingness of managers to involve lower echelon employees in decision-making to achieve desired performance effects' (Spreitzer and Mishra, 1999: 176).

Employee dispositions, capacities, motivations and needs

Coyle-Shapiro and Morrow (2003: 321) note that 'the consistent emphasis on the role of top management as the key driver for change downplays the role of individual differences' when it comes to whether *employees* adopt a favourable orientation toward EIP schemes. Riordan et al. (2005: 472) echo this point by noting how EIP programmes 'will be meaningless unless employees behave in ways that are supportive of EI'. Thus, while understanding the perspective of the instigators and co-ordinators of EIP schemes is crucial, so too is awareness of the factors that shape the level of engagement of the recipients and enactors of such schemes – the employees themselves. Hespe and Wall (1976) cited Walker (1972: 1183) thus: 'If there is little interest and pressure for workers' participation among workers, little difference is made by their having high capacities and high relative power, or by a high acceptance of workers' participation on the part of management'.

Neumann (1989, cited in Glew et al., 1995) proposed three categories of explanations as to why individuals might choose not to engage in EIP schemes. Each reflects disposition and motivation in different ways.

1 Structural: the awareness that the real decisions are made outside the EIP scheme, so why bother?
2 Relational: whether the organisation's hierarchical arrangements 'promote competition and emphasize rank and status over mastery and competence' (Glew et al., 1995: 410).
3 Societal: the effects of employee socialisation, ideology or history of labour-management relations.

In a similar fashion, Coyle-Shapiro and Morrow (2003: 321) invoke the model of 'person-environment fit' (p. 322), in which 'desirable outcomes are optimised when employee (i.e. person) desires, values and abilities are congruent with job (i.e. environment) characteristics'.

Allen et al. (1997: 118) reasoned that participation rates in such schemes 'depend on employee *self-selection*', and so understanding this process of deliberation – whether to get involved or not – is critical to understanding what might make schemes work or collapse (p. 119). They applied expectancy theory to the issue: taking part is subject to assessments of whether this is feasible, whether the scheme is likely to succeed, and whether the benefits accrued by the employee

are attractive enough. Specifically, willing volunteers will see in well-designed EIP schemes opportunities for personal growth and personal achievement. Additionally, they theorised that powerful social norms in the workplace would also determine employees' self-selection decisions: people surrounded by family and friends who are also positive about the scheme will be more likely to volunteer.

This line of work is suggestive of the value of applying Fishbein and Ajzen's (1975) theory of reasoned action to examine employees' participation in EIP. This approach views attitudes and subjective norms as predicting behavioural intentions, which in turn predict actual behaviour. Subjective norms reflect the extent to which significant others, such as family, friends and co-workers, express support for EIP. In line with the general theoretical approach in reasoned action studies, subjective norms are measured as the product of the perceived normative beliefs of others and the individual's motivation to comply with such beliefs (Kelloway and Barling, 1993). The theory of reasoned action assumes that the behaviour in question is volitional, so that behavioural intention provides a sufficient explanation of actual behaviour. In fact, many types of EIP behaviour are not necessarily under employees' volitional control, but are also affected by such factors as personal skills and capacities, and the availability of sufficient time or opportunity – as we discussed above. This is explicitly recognised in Ajzen's revision to the theory of reasoned action, known as the 'theory of planned behaviour' (Ajzen, 1991). This includes an additional predictor of behavioural intentions and of actual behaviour: 'perceived behavioural control'. Ajzen defines this as the degree to which an individual's ability to perform the behaviour in question is perceived by the individual to be volitional. There has yet to be any published study we can find in which the theory of planned behaviour has been applied to decisions concerning engagement with EIP. This could be a fruitful line of future work.

Allen and colleagues' (1997) study inside a large electric utility company with a programme of weekly team-based problem solving meetings confirmed that people with an 'internal' locus of control and high growth needs will be more favourably disposed to getting involved in EIP voluntarily, and such people might constitute a 'target group' for schemes to be aimed at. Their study endorses a contingent approach derived from expectancy theory. The obvious practical implication is that, given these 'dynamics', 'not all employees will be interested in participating' (p. 137) and 'volunteers and non-volunteers are different before they get involved in the EI process' (p. 138). They offer a salutary note of caution against the universal use of such interventions: 'It is probably unreasonable to expect profound changes in organisational performance and culture given the limited number of individuals likely to be interested in participation over time' (Allen et al., 1997: 138).

From our review of the literature, it is surprising that we have been unable to locate any study examining the relationship between the so-called 'Big Five' personality dimensions and employee participation in EIP. Given literally hundreds of studies of the relationship between the big five personality dimensions and behaviour at work (see Barrick and Mount, 1991), this is an important omission in the EIP literature.

Lam et al. (2002) looked at the moderating effects of another individual disposition on perceived participation in decision-making and employee performance: employees' allocentrism (a predominately collectivist orientation in individuals) or idiocentrism (a fundamentally individualistic orientation). They also looked into employees' perceptions of their self- and group-efficacy as a further moderator, and at the interaction effects between these variables. They hypothesised that group members with highly allocentric beliefs would appreciate EIP opportunities but *only if* they also have confidence in the groups' efficacy, while highly idiocentric employees would only welcome EIP schemes if their self-efficacy beliefs were also high. Employees possessing these complementary combinations of beliefs would be expected to perform better in the schemes. Studies in Hong Kong and the US confirmed that the variables did interact in the manner hypothesised. The authors concluded: 'Participative decision-making interventions will be more successful to the extent that programme developers match them to the values of target recipients and train them in ways that increase their most relevant efficacy cognitions' (Lam et al., 2002: 913).

Coyle-Shapiro and Morrow (2003) reported mixed results from their study of 'TQM orientation', operationalised by scales on teamwork and continuous improvement. They found that individual-level employee factors (such as trust in one's colleagues and continuous improvement behaviours) explained unique variance in teamwork, active involvement in work, allegiance to quality and personal accountability over and above that accounted for by demographic and organisation-level factors (such as top management support). These individual factors 'are better predictors of TQM orientation' (p. 334). They conclude: 'The inherent drive to reduce system variability [in TQM] places an undue emphasis on getting the system right, and in doing so, neglects the potentially significant impact of individual dispositions and the interactions between these individual characteristics and the system within which individuals work' (Coyle-Shapiro and Morrow, 2003: 335). It is to the system of EIP that we now turn.

THE ACTUAL PARTICIPATION PROGRAMME

'In reality, of course, it is the actual participation programme, rather than the intended one, that results in whatever outcomes are realised' (Glew et al., 1995: 399). Sashkin (1976: 80) noted how, even after the careful contingent design of a scheme, 'there remains the issue of changing to that approach from whatever currently exists'. In this section we discuss how EIP schemes come about, and the forms taken, with a particular emphasis on research into the impact of interpersonal dynamics and changing mind-sets and orientations, or 'schemas' (Bartunek, 1984).

Group composition and resources

Magjuka and Baldwin (1991) found that, of seven design variables identified by managers as potentially affecting EIP schemes' effectiveness, three – team heterogeneity, team size and information access – accounted for half the variance in participant and supervisor ratings of teamworking schemes' effectiveness. Of these three, information access proved the most decisive. The authors note how this finding counters some widely shared beliefs, especially among managers, that 'there may be a *disutility* to ensuring an open access structure for EIP teams' (p. 807), arising from the substantial extra costs incurred in providing this extent of information. EIP thrives upon information-sharing and struggles in its absence.

Problem or decision type

As Tjosvold (1987: 745) noted, 'people working together are superior to individuals [e.g., managers] working alone, especially for complex tasks. The flipside of this is that participation may be counterproductive for relatively straightforward organisational decisions' (Tjosvold, 1987). Yet this contradicts a common assumption in the literature that lower-level employees, unfamiliar with the opportunity to influence organisational decision-making, will value it more highly than their organisational superiors for whom such input is expected.

Cappelli and Rogovsky (1998) looked at employee involvement schemes inside eight US public utilities to explore the effects on employees' organisational citizenship behaviours, and whether this is mediated through perceptions of the five dimensions of job enrichment ('variety of tasks', 'perceived job significance', 'degree of employee autonomy', 'feedback from the organisation' and 'identity with the organisation'). They compared results for two decision types: a) organisation of work tasks, and b) employment practices. They hypothesised that the former would be significant for OCB and would lead to positive assessments of all five job enrichment characteristics, but that the latter would have less of an impact on OCB and would only operate through positive effects on 'variety of tasks' and 'perceived job significance'. Importantly, their measure captured employees' perceived *actual influence* over these decisions, rather than whether they thought they had the *opportunity* to do so. The results confirmed their hypotheses, though they also found important *direct* effects of involvement in work organisation decisions that did not operate through the five job enrichment mechanisms (1998: 645). In sum, 'involvement *per se* improves OCB' (p. 647), but this effect is particularly pronounced for decisions relating to work organisation (i.e. to local workplace and immediate task concerns) – echoing earlier studies by Hespe and Wall (1976) and Wall and Lischeron (1977).

Taken together, the findings seem to recommend that EIP initiatives targeted at localised problem-solving will be met with more employee enthusiasm than more distal decisions, as the former decisions fall within employees' capacity to offer *meaningful* input.

Interpersonal dynamics and mind-sets

As well as requiring some degree of enthusiasm for EIP in the first place, the quality of the interpersonal dynamics between the managerial participants and their staff counterparts directly affects the experience of both parties and the outcomes of the participation. It can be seen as the 'crucible' within which EIP schemes thrive or fail. Vallas comments thus:

> … workplace change [i.e. introducing EIP] is not akin to a surgical procedure performed under anaesthesia. Rather, it constitutes a negotiated phenomenon in which the language, rhetoric, and strategies that particular occupational groups employ can either blur or heighten the boundaries that exist within the firm (2003: 227).

Lesure and colleagues found from their review of studies into the adoption of new work practices that, 'The importance of employee commitment at [the implementation] stage receives very mixed support, not to say no support. However, research suggests that training and educating the employees about the new practices is much more important than trying to secure their commitment at this stage' (Lesure et al., 2004: 75).

Tjosvold (1987) has proffered some thoughts on interpersonal dynamics. His model cites 'cooperative goals' (a common purpose and sense of genuine rather than facile interdependence) as one obvious influential factor determining these interactions, yet his other factor, 'productive controversy' (i.e. pitching opposing views against each other *deliberately*) is more counter-intuitive, given that one of the unspoken objectives of participation schemes is often a sense of cohesiveness and unity of purpose among employees and managers. In support of the merits of his controversy dynamic, Tjosvold cites the dangers of groupthink and the avoidance of discussing opposing information as dynamics that stifle effective problem solving. Productive controversy helps participants to subject their own position to doubt, inspires curiosity and the desire to understand the alternative standpoint. These processes, Tjosvold claims, have been found to aid decision-making. Productive controversy is facilitated by the presence of cooperative goals, as participants feel able to disagree in pursuit of a commonly acceptable and valued outcome; a climate of respect in which challenges to others' views do not undermine perceived competence, and the practice of constructive discussion wherein parties seek to influence rather than dominate other participants.

Labianca et al. (2000) conducted an in-depth case study over two years of an 'empowerment' programme in a health care organisation, from which they produced an iterative model of 'schema change': in other words, participants' evolving interpretations of, and hence support for, the scheme. Their findings suggest that, 'change recipients' failure to revise old decision-making schemas and to enact new schemas during a pivotal period in the empowerment effort created resistance to change' (Labianca et al., 2000: 236). Their four stages of schema change are:

1 Motivation to change;
2 'New schema generation' – when managers' perceptions and employees' perceptions and aspirations may clash;
3 'Iterative schema comparison' – when the newly emerging schema is compared to the old way of doing things, and tangible, enduring shifts in approach are either confirmed or refuted by parties' actions and outcomes, and
4 'Stabilisation – depending on stages 2 and 3, either the old schema remains or it is replaced by the new schema.

The authors found that, during the pivotal stage 3, 'employees evaluated all of management's ongoing actions as to whether the actions were more consistent with the original decision-making schema or with their expected new participation schema' (Labianca et al., 2000: 250). They note that employees' resistance to such schemes 'may stem as much from difficulties in revising the well-established, ingrained decision-making schema [in place prior to the EIP scheme] as from intentional self-interested behaviour' (p. 236). They further observe, 'Until the actions of managers and employees consistently match the new schema, employees are likely to be sceptical of the empowerment effort' (p. 251; see also Rosenthal et al, 1997).

Timming's study (2007) of a British multi-national's European works council also illustrates the importance of interpersonal dynamics: in this case, as a negative influence tactic used by management. Timming found evidence of managers' 'proactive fragmentation' of the employee representatives through the 'reification of competitive tendencies between workers' and the creation of 'privileged groupings' (pp. 257–258). Managers in one company used a deliberate 'divide-and-rule-via-the-privileging-of-one-group-over-another' approach (p. 257) which, unsurprisingly, intensified a lack of collaboration among the different workforces, but failed to improve workforce-management relations. Timming suggests that this may be based less upon a 'calculative strategy for enhancing organisational performance, but rather on a historico-cultural attitude' within UK industry of antipathy toward EIP.

OUTCOMES

Previous reviews and meta-analyses of the impact of participation on performance outcomes have reported 'mixed' (Cappelli and Rogovsky, 1998) and somewhat 'equivocal' results (Lam et al., 2002), with even the most positive effects being rather modest (Wagner, 1994). Locke and Schweiger's (1979) original review can be summarised as finding positive effects on job satisfaction but, generally, less of an impact on actual performance levels. The authors did not offer too many firm conclusions, due to what they saw as the likely influence of so many other hidden or latent variables, principally around employees' knowledge and motivation, and various task, group and leadership attributes at the organisational level.

For their meta-analysis of 47 EIP studies, Miller and Monge (1986) looked at participation schemes' effect on productivity and employees' job satisfaction. They presented three theoretical rationales for the anticipated positive effect. The first was the *cognitive* model: EIP schemes enhance information flow, which leads to better decisions and employees' understanding of the final decisions, while increases in satisfaction are derived from employees' observation of tangible positive results and from pride in their specific inputs. The second model was *affective*: EIP schemes satisfy employees' higher-order needs of self-expression, growth and independence, and they contribute to improved productivity through an initial mediating phase characterised by enhanced motivation which, in turn, produces greater satisfaction. It is the *act* of participation that works, not necessarily the outcome. Finally, their *contingent* model sees EIP schemes as subject to moderating variables such as participants' personality, the decision situations,

superior-subordinate relations, job level and organisational values/climate. This latter model challenges the dominant assumption in the affective model that the need for participation is universal. Across the 47 studies, Miller and Monge found no support for various contingency-derived predictions, including for job level or sector (though they could not test personality differences). There was stronger support for participation's effect on satisfaction than on productivity. There was stronger support overall for the cognitive model ('moderately strong') over the affective alternative ('low, but significant'), suggesting that EIP schemes might work best when employees are deploying specific knowledge to problems pertinent to their own work – again, echoing previously cited studies on employees' parochial interest in EIP. Miller and Monge concluded that the cognitive model might better explain observed effects on productivity, while the affective model might better explain effects on satisfaction.

Wagner (1994) reported from his meta-analysis that the overall effect of participative decision-making on job performance was positive but small, especially after omitting single source studies (i.e. the same respondent for both independent and dependent variables).

In another meta-analysis, Doucouliagos (1995) looked at anticipated effects from various EIP schemes, including forms of joint decision-making/influence sharing on organisational commitment, efficiency, productivity, work effort and 'free rider' problems (all presumed to be positive), and managerial power and managerial decision-making (presumed to be negative). He further compared findings from 'labour-managed firms' (i.e. worker cooperatives) with 'participatory capitalist firms'. Overall, the average correlations proved to be small. An interesting finding was that profit-sharing performed worse than participative decision-making in participatory capitalist firms.

Freeman and Kleiner (2000) also report barely any effect on productivity from eight different forms of EIP, but they did find substantial improvements to employee well-being, including 'looking forward to going to work' and employees' trust in their company. They conclude with a rare appeal to the 'welfare capitalism'/'affective' rationale for EIP: 'Since EI[P] has no adverse effects or a slight positive effect on the bottom line, firms will offer it to please their workers' (p. 22).

Handel and Levine's (2004) review of studies conducted in the US looked in-depth into the link between EIP schemes and wage levels, as well as other employee outcomes. Overall, their summary position is that EIP 'can improve organisational outcomes *if the reforms are serious*' (2004: 38 – emphasis added), but the evidence on workers' welfare, including pay, is 'mixed' and most positive effects are modest. They conclude:

> While these findings do not support the most positive views of EI as a 'high-road' solution to the problems of poor wage growth and increased inequality, they do not indicate that management by stress is typical, nor do they suggest that skill-biased organisational change is a significant cause of inequality growth (pp. 39–40).

Charlwood and Terry (2007) analysed nationally representative data on workplace practices in the UK, and found that unionised forms of representative engagement were associated with reduced wage dispersion (their 'equity' outcome), but also with reduced productivity (their 'efficiency' outcome); non-union forums had no effect on either outcome. Intriguingly, the authors reported that 'dual-channel representation [i.e. unionised and non-unionised forums, together] would appear to offer employees the benefits of union representation (flatter wage structures) without the possible employer disadvantages (lower productivity)'. (ibid. 334–335) However, they cautioned against drawing causal inferences.

That an HR policy often hailed as a panacea for all organisational deficiencies and tribulations (see Peters and Waterman, 1982; Pfeffer, 1998) should suffer such disappointing findings might have been expected to dampen advocates' enthusiasm. But this has not been the case, and EIP continues to resurface as a potential solution to organisations' enduring performance and morale challenges.

One reason for EIP's modest impact may be that identified by Ledford and Lawler (1994): it may be that many researchers define EIP so narrowly that 'it cannot have a major impact on organisational performance or employee well-being'. EIP schemes are not seen in the context of other organisational policies and practice:

> It is as though participation researchers are unaware of organisation design theory, especially systems theory... Any intervention that is not reinforced by multiple subsystems is unlikely to have major effects on performance or satisfaction because it is likely to be overwhelmed by organisational subsystems that do *not* reinforce participation (Ledford and Lawler, 1994: 634).

Riordan et al. (2005) also stress the importance of a supportive broader organisational context, without which isolated EIP practice will all too likely struggle and wither away.

Understanding, therefore, how to generate the 'mutual reinforcement' of different subsystems (i.e. the elements of EIP schemes discussed in this chapter) remains a key challenge. Researchers and practitioners alike need to view EIP in the context of the complementarities it enjoys, or lacks, with other HR policies. This, of course, is the configurational approach to HRM (Delery and Doty, 1996), and the argument for 'internal fit' (Wood, 1999).

THE FATE OF THE SCHEME

One gap in the literature concerns the fate of EIP schemes. In their review of the adoption of new work practices, Lesure et al.'s (2004) note the importance of the 'integration' stage but they devote only a page to the scant research. They conclude, '... there is, in academic circles, a general belief that retention of a best practice past the ramp-up stage should not be taken for granted. This remains to be confirmed by research. Research also needs to address how managers can improve "retentive capacity"' (Lesure et al., 2004: 93).

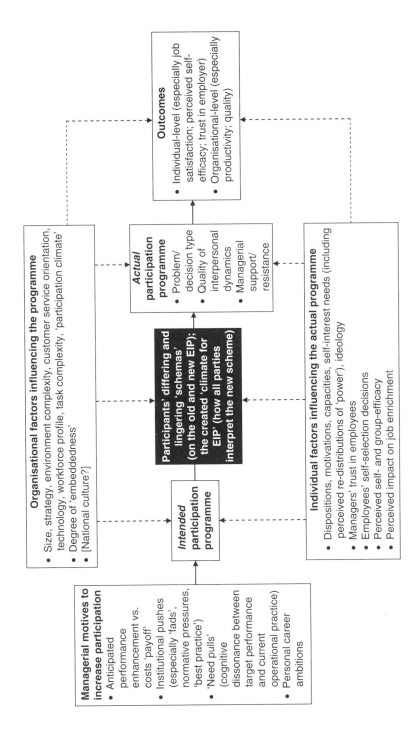

Figure 15.3 Glew and colleagues' framework of the participation process – with identified factors from previous research.

We see three possible 'fates' for EIP (Figure 15.1). The first is that the scheme is considered legitimate and valuable (howsoever defined) and becomes embedded in organisational routine; the second is that it fails to deliver to the satisfaction of one or more parties and is either 'killed off' or allowed to die from lack of care, and the third is that EIP lives on as a principle but its original form is replaced with a new scheme. There is some work which supports this latter notion of reinvention as schemes are worn out but revived under a new guise (Wilkinson et al., 2007).

Chi et al.'s (2007) longitudinal study on the adoption and termination of EIPs sheds some light on their fate. The failure rate of EIPs can be high and firms' use of such programmes is not continuous, with a suggestion from their data is that it can take as long as 20 years for firms to find a steady-state distribution. Chi et al.'s analysis finds firms are less likely to terminate EIPs when they have other advanced HR practices and business strategies supportive of employee autonomy in the workplace. Equally, firms terminate EIPs as bundles, which further implies that the polices are complementary with each other.

CONCLUSION

Figure 15.3 summarises in diagrammatic form some of the most influential variables that we have identified from the literature for each element of Glew and colleagues' original framework.

The allure of EIP's potential is generally made on three counts: its contribution to organisational effectiveness, its contribution to satisfying basic human needs and making good use of employees' skills, and its possible impact on reducing 'political inequalities' inside organisations (see Strauss, 2006: 801). This attraction continues to draw generations of managers into planning, designing and implementing new forms of worker involvement and participation. However, as this chapter has demonstrated, the overwhelming impression from the literature is of a multitude

of factors that can determine success or failure. Moreover, each one of these variables is itself complex and the nature of the interactions among them even more so. George Strauss offered what seems to us a measured and elegant summary position on EIP thus:

> My perspective on participation has always been somewhat ambivalent and sometimes cynical. I have always believed participation as a theory, in part because *when it works* (a key point), it provides a win-win solution to a central organisational problem: how to satisfy workers' needs while simultaneously achieving organisational objectives. Today, my view is that workers' participation can 'work' (by a variety of measures) but making it work is very difficult. My hopes for it are considerably diminished (Strauss, 2006: 778).

NOTES

1 To illustrate, what Labianca et al. (2000) call an 'empowerment' programme in their study conforms to what Kessler and Purcell (1996) called a 'joint working party'; what Tjosvold (1987: 739) calls 'participation' ('a setting in which managers and employees can exchange information and ideas to solve problems') does not comply with a convention in the British literature that 'participation' schemes must be indirect and representative in form. That said, Gollan et al.'s (2006: 499) definition of 'participation' in a special issue of *Industrial Relations* (encompassing 'the range of mechanisms used to involve the workforce in decisions at all levels of the organisation – *whether direct or indirect* – conducted with employees or through their representatives': our emphasis) ignores this distinction. Finally, Bartunek and Spreitzer (2006) examined 17 different meanings of 'empowerment'.

2 There is also a somewhat paternalistic, even patronising whiff implied by the 'gift' of input being bestowed upon grateful employees.

3 This chapter will not look at financial forms of participation, such as share ownership and profit-related pay. This is reserved for the chapter on compensation.

4 Abrahamson's work on management fashions (Abrahamson, 1996, 1997; Abrahamson and Fairchild, 1999) suggests some insights into managerial impetus for EIP. First, EIP would be classed as a 'normative' rather than a 'rational' rhetoric for managing employees as it 'can render employees more productive by shaping their thoughts and capitalising on their emotions' (Abrahamson, 1997: 493) by satisfying their needs [including for a 'voice' in the workplace]. Abrahamson hypothesised, and

found in his studies counting academic and popular business press articles, that discourses advocating normative techniques have tended to emerge at the end of the upswing of a Kondratieff long wave, just before the downswing. Thus, managers' enthusiasm for EIP may be linked to a downturn in macro-economic trends and their disinterest may be shaped by economic upswings.

5 When Nissan set up its plant in the North East of England in the 1980s, Hague (1989) commented on the rapid 'Japanisation' of 'Geordie-land' (a colloquial term for people from Newcastle – even though the plant is technically down the road in Sunderland).

6 A respondent for Harlos' study (2001: 332) of voice systems told of managers analysing the handwriting of submissions to an anonymous suggestion box and checking shift attendance records to identify authors.

7 This last comment echoes, perhaps unwittingly, down the years to the celebrated conclusion in the Donovan enquiry into British industrial relations structures in the late 1960s: to regain control managers may have to share it with workers (Fox and Flanders, 1975).

REFERENCES

Abrahamson, E. (1996) 'Management fashion', *Academy of Management Review*, 21 (1): 254–85.

Abrahamson, E. (1997) 'The emergence and prevalence of employee management rhetorics: the effects of long waves, labor unions and turnover, 1875 to 1992', *Academy of Management Journal*, 40 (3): 491–533.

Abrahamson, E. and Fairchild, G. (1999) 'Management fashion: lifecycles, triggers and collective learning processes', *Administrative Science Quarterly*, 44 (4): 708–40

Ackers, P., Marchington, M., Wilkinson, A. and Dundon, T. (2006) 'Employee participation in Britain: from collective bargaining and industrial democracy to employee involvement and social partnership – Two decades of Manchester/Loughborough Research', *Decision*, 33 (1): 76–88

Addison, J.T., Schnabel, C. and Wagner, J (1997) 'On the determinants of mandatory works councils in Germany', *Industrial Relations*, 36 (4): 419–45.

Ajzen, I (1991) 'The theory of planned behavior', *Organizational Behavior and Human Decision Processes*, 50 (2): 179–211.

Allen, R.E., Lucero, M.A. and van Norman, K.L. (1997) 'An examination of the individual's decision to participate in an employee involvement program', *Group and Organisation Management*, 22 (1): 117–43.

Appelbaum, E., Bailey, T., Berg, P and Kalleberg, A (2000) 'Manufacturing advantage: Why high-performance systems pay off'. Ithaca, NY: Cornell University Press.

Bach, S. (2004) 'Employee participation and union voice in the national health service', *Human Resource Management Journal*, 14 (2): 3–19.

Barrick, M.R. and Mount, M.K. (1991) 'The big five personality dimensions and job performance: A meta-analysis', *Personnel Psychology*, 44 (1): 1–26

Bartunek, J (1984) 'Changing interpretive schemes and organizational restructuring: The example of a religious order'. *Administrative Science Quarterly*, 29, 355–372.

Bartunek, J.M. and Spreitzer, G.M. (2006) 'The interdisciplinary career of a popular construct used in management: Empowerment in the late 21st century', *Journal of Management Inquiry*, 15 (3): 255–73.

Barney, J.B. (1991) 'Firm resources and sustainable competitive advantage', *Journal of Management*, 17, 99–12.

Batt, R (2004) 'Who benefits from teams? Comparing workers, supervisors and managers', *Industrial Relations*, 43 (1): 183–212.

Batt, R., Colvin, A.J.S. and Keefe, J. (2002) 'Employee voice, human resource practices, and quit rates: Evidence from the telecommunications industry', *Industrial and Labor Relations Review*, 55 (4): 573–94.

Becker, G (1964) 'Human capital'. New York: Columbia University Press.

Bowen, D.E. and Lawler III, E.E. (1992) 'The empowerment of service workers: What, why, how and when', *Sloan Management Review*, Spring: 31–9.

Boselie, P., Dietz, G. and Boon, C. (2005) "Commonalities and contradictions in research on human resource management and performance", *Human Resource Management Journal*, 15 (3), 67–94.

Boxall, P. and Purcell, J. (2003) *Strategy and human resource management*. London: Palgrave Macmillan.

Cappelli, P. and Rogovsky, N. (1998) 'Employee involvement and organizational citizenship: Implications for labor law reform and "lean production"', *Industrial and Labor Relations Review*, 51 (4): 633–53.

Chi, W., Freeman, R.B. and Kleiner, M. (2007) 'Adoption and termination of employee involvement programs.' Working paper 12878. Cambridge, MA, National Bureau of Economic Research.

Cohen, S.G. and Bailey, D.E. (1997) 'What makes teams work: Group effectiveness research from the shop floor to the executive suite', *Journal of Management*, 23 (3): 239–90.

Connor, P.E. (1992) 'Decision-making participation patterns: The role of organizational context', *Academy of Management Review*, 35 (1): 218–31.

Cooke, W.N. (1994) 'Employee participation programs, group-based incentives, and company performance: A union-nonunion comparison', *Industrial and Labor Relations Review*, 47 (4): 594–609.

Cox, A., Zagelmeyer, S. and Marchington, M. (2006) 'Embedding employee involvement and participation at work', *Human Resource Management Journal*, 16 (3): 250–67.

Cotton, J. (1993) 'Employee involvement'. Newbury Park, CA: Sage.

Coyle-Shapiro, J.A-M. and Morrow, P.C. (2003) 'The role of individual differences in employee adoption of TQM orientation', *Journal of Vocational Behavior*, 62 (62): 320–40.

Cressey, P., Eldridge, J. and MacInnes, J. (1985) *Just Managing: Authority and Democracy in Industry*. Milton Keynes: Open University Press.

Dachler, H.P. and Wilpert, B. (1978) 'Conceptual dimensions and boundaries of participation in organisations: A critical evaluation'. *Administrative Science Quarterly*, 23 (1), 1–39.

Delery, J.E. and Doty, D.H. (1996) 'Modes of theorizing in strategic human resource management: Tests of universalistic, contingency, and configurational performance predictions', *Academy of Management Journal*, 39 (4): 802–35.

Deming, W.E. (1988) *Out of the Crisis: Quality, Productivity and Competitive Position*. Cambridge: Cambridge University Press.

DiMaggio, P.J. and Powell, W.W. (1983) 'The iron cage revisited: Institutionalisomorphism and collective rationality in organizational fields', *American Sociological Review*, 48 (2), 147–169.

Doucouliagos, C. (1995) 'Worker participation and productivity in labor-managed and participatory capitalist firms: A meta-analysis', *Industrial and Labor Relations Review*, 49 (1): 58–77.

Dundon, T., Wilkinson, A., Marchington, M. and Ackers, P. (2004) 'The meanings and purpose of employee voice', *International Journal of Human Resource Management*, 15 (6): 1149–70.

Fenton-O'Creevy, M. (1998) 'Employee involvement and the middle manager: Evidence from a survey of organizations', *Journal of Organizational Behavior*, 19: 67–84.

Festinger, L. (1957) *A theory of cognitive dissonance*. Evanston, IL: Row, Peterson.

Fishbein, M. and Ajzen, I. (1975) *Belief, Attitude, Intention, and Behavior: An Introduction to Theory and Research*. Reading MA: Addison-Wesley.

Fox, A. and , Flanders A. (1975) 'Collective bargaining: From Donovan to Durkheim', in Flanders, A. (ed.), *Management and Unions: The Theory and Reform of Industrial Relations*. London: Faber and Faber.

Fox, A. (1974) 'Beyond contract: Work, power and trust relations'. London: Faber and Faber.

Freeman, R.B. and Kleiner, M.M. (2000) 'Who benefits most from employee involvement: Firms or workers?', *American Economic Review*, 90 (2): 219–23.

Glew, D.J., O'Leary-Kelly, A.M., Griffin, R.W. and van Fleet, D.D. (1995) 'Participation in organizations: A preview of the issues and proposed framework for future analysis', *Journal of Management*, 21 (3): 395–421.

Gollan, P.J., Poutsma, E. and Veersma, U. (2006) 'Editors' introduction: New roads in organizational participation?', *Industrial Relations*, 45 (4), 499–512.

Guthrie, J.P. (2001) 'High-involvement work practices, turnover, and productivity: Evidence from New Zealand', *Academy of Management Journal*, 44: 180–90.

Hague, R. (1989) 'Japanising Geordie-land?', *Employee Relations*, 11 (2): 3–16.

Hannan, M.T. and Freeman, J. (1984) 'Structural inertia and organizational Change', *American Sociological Review*, 49: 149–164.

Handel, M.J. and Levine, D.I. (2004) 'Editor's introduction: The effects of new work practices on workers', *Industrial Relations*, 43 (1): 1–43.

Harlos, K.P. (2001) 'When organizational voice systems fail: More on the deaf-ear syndrome and frustration effects', *Journal of Applied Behavioural Science*, 37 (3): 324–42.

Heller, F., Pusic, E., Strauss, G. and Wilpert, B. (1998) 'Organisational participation: Myth and reality'. Oxford: Oxford University Press.

Henderson, A.D. (1999) 'Firm strategy and age dependence: A contingent view of the liabilities of newness, adolescence and obsolescence', *Administrative Science Quarterly*, 44 (2): 281–314.

Hespe, G. and Wall, T. (1976) 'The demand for participation among employees', *Human Relations*, 29 (5): 411–28.

Hodson, R. (2001) 'Disorganized, unilateral, and participative organizations: New insights from the ethnographic literature'. *Industrial Relations*, 40 (2), 204–230.

Hofmann, D.A., Morgeson, F.P. and Gerras, S.J. (2003) 'Climate as a moderator of the relationship between leader-member exchange and content specific citizenship: Safety climate as an exemplar', *Journal of Applied Psychology*, 88 (1): 170–78.

Hoell, R.C. (2004) 'How employee involvement affects union commitment', *Journal of Labor Research*, 25 (2), 267–277.

Huselid, M.A. (1995) 'The impact of human resource management practices on turnover, productivity, and corporate financial Performance', *Academy of Management Journal*, 38 (3): 635–72.

Ichniowski, C., Shaw, K. and Prennushi, G. (1997) 'The effects of human resource management practices on productivity: A study of steel finishing lines', *American Economic Review*, 87 (3): 291–313.

Ivancevic, J.M. (1979) 'An Analysis of Participation in Decision Making Among Project Engineers', *Academy of Management Journal*, 22 (2): 253–69.

Kanter, R.M. (1983) 'Dilemmas of managing participation', *Organizational Dynamics*, 11 (1): 5–27.

Kato, T. (2006) 'Determinants of the extent of participatory employment practices: Evidence from Japan', *Industrial Relations*, 45 (4): 579–605.

Kaufman, B. (2003) 'High-level employee involvement at Delta Air Lines', *Human Resource Management*, 42 (2): 175–90.

Kelloway, E.K. and Barling, J. (1993) " 'Members" participation in local union activities: Measurement, prediction and replication', *Journal of Applied Psychology*, 78 (2): 262–79.

Kessler, I. and Purcell, J. (1996) 'The value of joint working parties', *Work, Employment and Society*, 10 (4): 663–82.

Klein, J.A. (1984) 'Why supervisors resist employee involvement', *Harvard Business Review*, 62, Sept/Oct: 87–95.

Labianca, G., Gray, B. and Brass, D.J. (2000) 'A grounded model of organizational schema change during empowerment', *Organization Science*, 11 (2): 235–57.

Lam, S.S., Chen, X-P. and Schaubroek, J. (2002) 'Participative decision-making and employee performance in different cultures: The moderating effects of allocentrism/idiocentrism and efficacy', *Academy of Management Journal*, 45 (5): 905–14.

Ledford, G.E. and Lawler III, E.E. (1994) 'Research on employee participation: Beating a dead horse?', *Academy of Management Review*, 19 (October): 633–6.

Lesure, M., Birdi, K., Bauer, J., Denyer, D. and Neely, A. (2004) 'Adoption of promising practice: A systematic review of the literature', *AIM Research*, February.

Levine, D. and Tyson, L.D. (1990) 'Participation, productivity, and the firm's environment', in A Blinder (ed.), *Paying for productivity*. Washington D.C: Brookings Institution, 183–243.

Lindell, M.K. and Brandt, C.J. (2000) 'Climate quality and climate consensus as mediators of the relationship between organizational antecedents and outcomes', *Journal of Applied Psychology*, 85 (3): 331–48.

Locke, E.A. and Schweiger, D.M. (1979) 'Participation in decision-making: One more look', in B Staw (ed),

'Research in organizational behavior', 1, 265–339. Greenwich, CT: JAI Press.

McMahan, G.C., Bell, M., and Virick, M., (1998) "Strategic human resource management: Employee involvement, diversity, and international issues", *Human Resource Management Review*, 8(3), 193–214.

MacDuffie, J.P. (1995) 'Human resource bundles and manufacturing performance: Flexible production systems in the world auto industry', *Industrial and Labor Relations Review*, 48 (2): 197–221.

McFarlin, D.B., Sweeney, P.D. and Cotton, J.L. (1992) 'Attitudes toward employee participation in decision-making: A comparison of European and American managers in a United States multinational company', *Human Resource Management*, 31 (4): 363–83.

Magjuka, R.J. and Baldwin, T.T. (1991) 'Team-based employee involvement programs: Effects of design and administration', *Personnel Psychology*, 44: 793–812.

Marchington, M., Wilkinson, A., Ackers, P. and Goodman, J. (1993) 'The influence of managerial relations on waves of employment involvement', *British Journal of Industrial Relations*, 31 (4): 543–76.

Marchington, M., Wilkinson, A., Ackers, P. and Goodman, J. (1994) 'Understanding the meaning of participation: Views from the workplace', *Human Relations*, 47 (8): 867–94.

Marchington, M. and Wilkinson, A. (2005) 'Direct participation and involvement', in S. Bach (ed), *Managing Human Resources: Personnel Management in Transition*, 4th edition. Oxford: Blackwell, pp. 398–423.

Mayo, E. (1933) *The Human Problems of an Industrial Civilization*. New York, London: Routledge.

Miller, K.I. and Monge, P.R. (1986) 'Participation, productivity and satisfaction: A meta-analytic review', *Academy of Management Journal*, 29 (4): 727–53.

Neumann, J.E. (1989) 'Why people don't participate in organizational change', in R. Woodman and W. Pasmore (eds), *'Research in organizational change and development'*, Vol. 3. Greenwich, CT: JAI Press, pp. 181–212.

Parker, M. and Slaughter, J. (1988) *Choosing Sides: Unions and the Team Concept*. Boston, MA: South End Press.

Parker, S.K., Wall, T.D. and Jackson, P.R. (1997) " 'That's not my job": Developing flexible employee work orientations', *Academy of Management Journal*, 40 (4): 899–929.

Peccei, R., Bewley, H., Gospel, H. and Willman, P. (2005) 'Is it good to talk? Information disclosure and organisational performance in the UK', *British Journal of Industrial Relations*, 43 (1): 11–39.

Peters, T and Waterman, R (1982). 'In search of excellence'. New York, NY: Harper and Row.

Pfeffer, J (1998). 'The human equation'. Cambridge, MA: Harvard Business Press.

Poutsma, E. and Huijgen, F. (1999) 'European diversity in the use of participation schemes', *Economic and Industrial Democracy*, 20 (2): 197–223.

Ramsay, H., Scholarios, D. and Harley, B. (2000) 'Employees and high-performance work systems: Testing inside the black box', *British Journal of Industrial Relations*, 38 (3), 501–531.

Riordan, C.M., Vandenberg, R.J. and Richardson, H.A. (2005) 'Employee involvement climate and organisational effectiveness', *Human Resource Management*, 44 (4): 471–88.

Rosenthal, P., Hill, S. and Peccei, R. (1997) 'Checking out service: Evaluating excellence, HRM and TQM in retailing', *Work, Employment and Society*, 11 (3): 481–503.

Rubinstein, S. and Kochan, T.A. (2001) 'Learning from Saturn'. Ithaca, NY: IRL Press.

Sashkin, M. (1976) 'Changing toward participative management approaches: A model and methods', *Academy of Management Review*, July: 75–86.

Schneider, B., Salvaggio, A.N., and Subirats, M. (2002) 'Climate strength: A new direction for climate research', *Journal of Applied Psychology*, 87 (2): 220–9.

Spreitzer, G.M. and Mishra, A.K. (1999) 'Giving up without losing control: Trust and its substitutes' effects on managers' involving employees in decision making', *Group and Organization Management*, 24 (2), 155–187.

Stinchcombe, A.L. (1965) 'Social structure and organizations', in J.G. March (ed.), 'Handbook of Organizations', 142–193, Chicago, IL: Rand-McNally.

Strauss, G (2006) 'Worker participation – some underconsidered issues', *Industrial Relations*, 45 (4): 778–803.

Timming, A.R. (2007) 'European works councils and the dark side of managing worker voice', *Human Resource Management Journal*, 17 (3): 248–64.

Tjosvold, D (1987) 'Participation: A close look at its dynamics', *Journal of Management*, 13 (4): 739–50.

Vallas, S.P. (2003) 'Why teamwork fails: Obstacles to workplace change in four manufacturing plants', *American Sociological Review*, 68 (April): 223–50.

Vandenberg, R.J., Richardson, H.A and Eastman, L.J (1999) 'The impact of high involvement work

processes upon organisational effectiveness: A 2nd-order latent variable approach', *Group and Organization Management*, 24: 300–39.

Wall, T.D. and Lischeron, J.A. (1977) *Worker participation: A critique of the literature and some fresh evidence.* Maidenhead: McGraw-Hill.

Wagner, J.A. (1994) 'Participation's effect on performance and satisfaction: A reconsideration of the research evidence'. *Academy of Management Review*, 19 (2), 312–330.

Welsh, D.H., Luthans, F. and Sommer, S.M. (1993) 'Managing Russian factory workers: The impact of U.S-based behavioural and participation techniques', *Academy of Management Journal*, 36 (1): 58–79.

Wilkinson A., Marchington, M., Ackers, P. and Goodman, J. (1992) 'Total quality management and employee involvement'. *Human Resource Management Journal*, 2 (4): 1–20.

Wilkinson, A. (1998) 'Empowerment: Theory and practice', *Personnel Review*, 27 (1): 40–56.

Wilkinson, A. (2008) 'Empowerment', in Clegg, S. and Bailey, J. (eds), *Encyclopaedia of Organisational Studies*. London: Sage.

Wilkinson, A. and Ackers, P. (1995) 'When two cultures meet: New Industrial Relations at Japanco', *International Journal of Human Resource Management*, 6 (4): 849–71.

Wilkinson, A., Godfrey, G. and Marchington, M. (1997) 'Bouquets, brickbats and blinkers: Total Quality Management and Employee Involvement', *Organization Studies*, 18 (5): 799–820.

Wilkinson, A., Dundon, T., Marchington, M. and Ackers, P. (2004) 'Changing patterns of employee voice', *Journal of Industrial Relations*, 46 (3): 298–322.

Wilkinson A., Dundon, T. and Grugulis, I. (2007) 'Information but not Consultation: Exploring employee involvement in SMEs', *International Journal of Human Resource Management*, 18 (7): 1279–97.

Wilkinson, A., Gollan, P., Lewin, D. and Marchington, M. (2009) *Participation in Organisations*. Oxford: Oxford University Press

Wood, S. (1999) 'Human resource management and performance', *International Journal of Management Reviews*, 1 (4): 367–413.

Zeitz, G., Mittal, V. and McAuley, B. (1999) 'Distinguishing adoption and entrenchment of management practices: A framework for analysis'. *Organization Studies*, 20 (5), 741–776.

16

Extending the Reach of Job Design Theory: Going Beyond the Job Characteristics Model

Sharon K. Parker and Sandra Ohly

I get fed up sometimes, you know, but you just have to put up with that, and I just carry on, me, just plod on … You get into work, you get that feeling that you just keep coming everyday, and you think, 'Oh, clock in, do my job, clock out, and that's it like', … that's what I'm paid to do anyway (Production operator; Parker, 1994).

Because you know you work hard for a piece of work, to plan for the work, to carry out the work, and at the end you feel this great sense of achievement that it has been down to you (Portfolio worker cited in Clinton et al., in press: 187)

INTRODUCTION

These quotes show two very different reactions to work. The first employee expressed meaninglessness and lack of intrinsic motivation, whereas the second reported a high level of ownership and a strong sense of achievement. Further analysis shows these feelings largely reflect the quality of work design. For the production operator, employed in a traditionally-organized engineering company, the job allowed little opportunity for using discretion, was highly repetitive, and had no apparent impact on important outcomes (Parker, 1994). In contrast, as a portfolio worker, the second employees' job had considerable autonomy, challenge, and variety, resulting in a strong sense of engagement. These briefs scenarios highlight that the way that jobs are structured and organized, or their work design, can have a profound impact on employees' motivation and behavior. Indeed, the way jobs are designed can also affect organizational success, as shown by the proliferation of popular practices that have work design issues at their core (lean production, empowerment, high performance systems, team work, cellular teams, re-engineering, to name but a few).

Our goal in this chapter is to review where we are at with work design research. To begin, we provide a brief overview of classic work design theories and research, followed by an outline of some alternative theoretical perspectives. We then return to the dominant concern of mainstream work design research – the relationship between work characteristics and outcomes – and we identify several ways this approach has been developed to better meet the needs of the contemporary work place. Finally, we suggest further methodological and theoretical developments to extend the reach of work design.

Classic theory and studies

Derived from Taylorism and scientific management principles (Taylor, 1911), jobs in the early 20th century were broken down into their most simplified elements to reduce training times, with managers closely controlling the work. Not surprisingly, the early work design theories that arose in response to these boring and alienating jobs mainly focused on work characteristics that lead to motivation and favorable job attitudes. Herzberg et al. (1959) proposed that 'motivator' factors such as level of recognition lead to job satisfaction, while an absence of extrinsic 'hygiene' factors, such as salary, lead to job dissatisfaction. Although research has failed to support this model (e.g, Hulin and Smith, 1967), it inspired the practice of job enrichment, or the creation of challenging and responsible jobs to promote motivation and performance (Paul et al., 1969).

The principle of job enrichment was further supported by the job characteristics model (JCM) by Hackman and Oldham (Hackman and Oldham, 1980), which proposed that five job characteristics (task variety, autonomy, feedback, significance and identity) promote individual motivation, job satisfaction, and performance through critical psychological states such as experienced meaningfulness. The beneficial effects of jobs with these

characteristics are expected to be greater for individuals high on growth need strength who have a preference for growth and learning at work. Some studies have demonstrated the proposed moderating role of growth need strength (e.g., Johns et al., 1992); others have not (Tiegs et al., 1992).

Two early meta-analytic studies supported the core proposition of the JCM, showing the five job characteristics collectively relate to attitudinal outcomes such as job satisfaction and motivation, as well as, to a weaker extent, ratings of work effectiveness and absenteeism (Fried and Ferris, 1987; Loher et al., 1985). An expanded meta-analysis supported the importance of work characteristics affecting these outcomes, as well as other outcomes (organizational commitment, role perceptions, turnover intentions), and identified experienced meaning as the most important state mediating the relationship between job characteristics and outcomes (Humphrey et al., in press).

These meta-analytic studies collated findings across multiple studies, but many studies with cross-sectional designs were included. Longitudinal studies are thus an important complement to the above evidence. One classic study is that by Griffin (1991). The jobs of bank tellers were enriched to include a wider range of activities, greater autonomy, enhanced feedback, and increased responsibility for meeting customer needs. The intervention led to a durable change in job characteristics, a short-term increase of job satisfaction and commitment, and a performance increase in the long run. In a study with the opposite intervention, Parker (2003) showed that the job deskilling associated with lean production, particularly the installation of a moving assembly line, reduced employees' commitment, lowered their self-efficacy, and increased their depression. In yet a third example of a longitudinal study, but in this case conducted across multiple organizations, Birdi and colleagues (in press) investigated the productivity of 308 companies over 22 years. Empowerment, defined as passing considerable operational management responsibility to individuals or teams, was associated with performance benefits. Interestingly, there were no performance benefits associated with total quality management, just-in-time, advanced manufacturing technology, or supply-chain partnering. All together, these and other longitudinal studies provide reasonably consistent and strong evidence for the effects of job enrichment on attitudes and affective reactions like job satisfaction, although there is somewhat more mixed evidence for performance (Parker and Wall, 1998) and relatively small associations for absence (Rentsch and Steel, 1998).

While JCM and job enrichment are mainly concerned with individual jobs, the sociotechnical systems approach to work design emphasizes group work (Trist and Bamforth, 1951). An early study showed that a new mechanistic method of coal mining destroyed the social support system that coal miners relied on and fragmented the work, with consequent high absence rates and poor work motivation (Trist and Bamforth, 1951). In a second coal mine, the destructive effects of the new mechanistic method were alleviated because miners found a way to realize a form of group work (Cherns, 1995). This early research led to the idea of autonomous work teams that enable employees to work on complete tasks and that grant employees substantive collective autonomy.

Subsequent research typically shows positive attitudinal effects of autonomous work groups (see Sonnentag, 1996, for a review), with evidence somewhat less consistent for performance. For example, one study showed benefits of autonomous work groups for employee satisfaction, but not for productivity (Wall et al., 1986), whereas another showed increased productivity and a decrease in customer complaints (Antoni, 1997). Nevertheless, the idea that autonomous work groups are always beneficial for employees has also been challenged by studies adopting a more critical approach. In particular, Barker (1993) showed that employees in autonomous teams exercised a high level of control over each other's behavior. The long term effects of such 'concertive control' on team members' well-being and motivation needs further inquiry.

Additional theoretical perspectives on work design

The JCM approach rests on the assumption that individuals have needs that are fulfilled by the characteristics of their jobs, and thus lead to satisfaction, work motivation and performance. However, the social information processing perspective emphasizes the role of the social context as an influence on how individuals interpret events and job characteristics (Salancik and Pfeffer, 1978). For example, an employee who perceives low autonomy in their job might do so because the level compares unfavorably with others who have more complex jobs (Oldham et al., 1982). There is indeed evidence to suggest that social cues do affect perceptions of work characteristics, but overall these studies suggest the effects are weaker than those of objective job features (Taber and Taylor, 1990). Likewise, studies show that social factors have less influence on attitudinal and performance outcomes than objective work design features (Griffin, 1983; Pierce et al., 1979). Thus social cues are important, but they do not usurp the motivating value of work characteristics per se.

An attempt to integrate work design and work stress research is the model by (Karasek, 1979; Karasek and Theorell, 1990). Karasek proposed that high job demands will negatively affect well-being when job control is low, and high demands will promote an active approach to work when job control is high. Empirical support for this interaction between demands and control is mixed (de Lange et al., 2003; Taris and Kompier, 2005), with studies pointing to the importance of additional conditions such as social support (Van Yperen and Hagedoorn, 2003) or proactive personality (Parker and Sprigg, 1999). Nevertheless, Karasek's model has been particularly associated with the idea that high job demands are not necessarily detrimental for performance outcomes.

Psychological empowerment is also relevant to any discussion of work design. Psychological empowerment refers to the motivational state of experiencing meaning, impact, competence (or self-efficacy), and a sense of choice (or self-determination) (Conger and Kanungo, 1988; Spreitzer, 1995; Thomas and Velthouse, 1990). Although often posited as a new area of inquiry, there is a large conceptual overlap between empowerment and the critical psychological states in the JCM, and there is evidence that psychological empowerment mediates the relationship between work characteristics and outcomes (for a review see Parker and Ohly, 2007). Nevertheless, the literature on psychological empowerment differs from the JCM in that it recognizes that the feelings of empowerment can arise from influences other than the traditional job characteristics, for example from social support (Corsun and Enz, 1999) or access to information (Spreitzer, 1996). Models of psychological engagement, defined as feeling responsible for job performance and caring about the outcomes of performance (e.g., Britt et al., 2007), similarly have strong parallels with job characteristics theory. For example, they identify antecedents of engagement such as control over performance (autonomy) and importance of job (task significance), and focus on job performance and well-being as key outcomes.

A quite different perspective on work design is an interdisciplinary one. In this perspective, the JCM and Herzberg's model, are classified as representing a motivational approach to work design (Campion and McClelland, 1991). Three other approaches with different recommendations for the design of jobs are identified: first, the mechanistic approach of designing simplified jobs to reduce training costs and chance for error; second, the biological approach which aims at improving the ergonomic design of work to alleviate physical stress; and third, the perceptual-motor approach which is concerned with ensuring that job demands do not exceed cognitive abilities, to reduce overload, errors and accidents. The classification reminds us that various outcomes of job design are valued in different disciplines. However, it is important to note that the job characteristics typically considered in the motivational approach are also positively associated with outcomes that would be classified under the three other approaches, such as quicker response times (Wall and Jackson, 1995) and efficiency (Campion and McClelland, 1991).

Finally, it is significant to note that most of the work design research and theory described thus far can be considered as coming from a functionalist paradigm. Holman et al. (2002a; see also Torraco, 2005) review how alternative epistemological perspectives can be helpful in understanding work design.

Extensions to the work characteristics approach

In this section, we return to the work characteristics approach, which seeks to understand the relationship between job characteristics and outcomes. Recent models (Morgeson and Campion, 2003; Parker et al., 2001) include expansions over and above the JCM in regard to work characteristics, outcomes, mechanisms, contingencies, and antecedents of work design. We consider each of these extensions next.

EXTENDED WORK CHARACTERISTICS

Frequently, the five work characteristics identified in the JCM have been categorized into one indicator, referred to as job scope, job enrichment, and job complexity (e.g., Stone and Gueutal, 1984). Nevertheless, there are important characteristics of work over and above the big five of the JCM (Edwards et al., 1999; Roberts and Glick, 1981). In their Work Design Questionnaire, Morgensen and Humphrey (2006) distinguished 21 work features within four broad categories of work characteristics: Task motivation (e.g., autonomy, job feedback), knowledge motivation (e.g., problem solving demands), social (e.g., interdependence, feedback from others), and contextual (e.g., work conditions). Social work characteristics have long been of interest (e.g., Karasek and Theorell's (1990] demands-control-support model), and their importance is confirmed by meta-analytic evidence showing that social characteristics explain substantive amounts of variance in job behaviors and job attitudes beyond traditional job characteristics (Humphrey et al., in press).

Changes occurring in the modern work place also highlight new work characteristics that deserve attention (Parker et al., 2001). For example, emotion work (or emotional labor) refers to the requirement to show adequate emotions at work (Zapf, 2002). Evidence suggests that having to display emotions that are not experienced (emotional dissonance) can cause distress (Tschan et al., 2005), although this pressure appears to be alleviated by job control (Grandey et al., 2004). Likewise, electronic performance monitoring, the use of systems to collect, store, analyze and report the actions of individuals or groups (Nebeker and Tatum, 1993), is an attribute of work that is rapidly becoming more prevalent. It too can be associated with negative outcomes, including emotional exhaustion (Holman et al., 2002b) and lower performance on complex tasks (Douthitt and Aiello, 2001). As with emotion work, these negative effects can be buffered by giving employees control over the timing of monitoring and handling of the information. (Alge et al., 2006).

An important issue concerns how to identify the key work characteristics to include in a particular study. Parker et al. (2001) advocated careful consideration of the context. Consider, for example, the issue of portfolio workers, or those self employed workers who work for a number of organizations or clients for fees (Totterdell et al., 2006). Portfolio workers typically report high levels of autonomy and variety (Cohen and Mallon, 1999), but, at the same time, they also often experience inconsistent work flow, social isolation and high levels of uncertainty. In any examination of portfolio workers, therefore, it would certainly be important to extend beyond the five traditional work characteristics.

Finally, it is important to note the debate about the assessment of work characteristics. Using job incumbent's perceptions is most common, but has been criticized because perceptions not only reflect objective characteristics but also the incumbent's mood, personality, meaning, and social cues (e.g., Salancik and Pfeffer, 1978). Nevertheless, despite such concerns, evidence suggests that employee self-ratings can closely match objective job features, as shown by, for example, high convergence between self-ratings and ratings from external observers (Fried and Ferris, 1987). Ideally, one should aim to complement the use of job incumbent's perceptions with other approaches, such as using managers' ratings of work characteristics, using data bases of occupations such as O*NET, or aggregating measures of individual job perceptions to the group or job level. Most important, the measurement strategy should match the type assessment one wants to make. For example, where global perceptions of jobs are needed, self or other reports might be best, whereas if it is emergent job characteristics that one wants to assess, self-reports within specific time frames, such as daily diary methods, might be preferable (see Daniels, 2006).

EXPANDED OUTCOMES

What are the consequences of work design? Influenced by the JCM, a strong focus has been on the effect of work design on employees' job attitudes and affective reactions, particularly motivation and job satisfaction (see Wall et al., 1986). From a behavioral perspective, most attention has been given to absence, turnover, and performance. Over and above these outcomes, health has been an increasingly important focus. In terms of mental health, work characteristics have been linked to burnout. (Bakker et al., 2005), depression, anxiety, and psychological distress (Karasek, 1979; Parker, 2003; Stansfeld et al., 1997). Overall, there is consistent evidence of the negative effects of excess demands on mental health (e.g., Frese, 1985), although more mixed evidence for the positive mental health effect of job control (e.g. Dwyer and Fox, 2000). In terms of physical health, although this research is relatively under-developed, work characteristics affect a diverse array of outcomes, such as cardiovascular disease (van der Doef and Maes, 1998), injury and work safety (Barling et al., 2003), fatigue (Van Yperen and Hagedoorn, 2003), and musculoskeletal pain (Sprigg et al., in press). An interesting development concerns the effects of work design beyond the job. Individuals who have high levels of control in their job, and lower demands, feel less need for recovery in the evening (Sonnentag and Zijlstra, 2006) which, in turn, positively affects their well-being.

One recommendation has been to expand investigation of performance outcomes beyond productivity-oriented indicators to include, for example, customer satisfaction, creativity and innovation, and proactive behavior. In the few studies considering the effect of work design on customers, job control appears to be a key factor. For example, task control was consistently related to various facets of customer satisfaction with kindergarten teachers (Dormann and Kaiser, 2002). Job control and job complexity also show consistent positive relationships with employee creativity (Harrison et al., 2006) and with employee proactivity (Ohly et al., 2006; Parker et al., 2006). The relationship of time pressure and creativity/innovation is more complex, with evidence for positive (Andrews and Farris, 1972; Ohly and Fritz, in prep.), negative (Amabile et al., 1996) and inverted U-shape relationships (Baer and Oldham, 2006; Ohly et al., 2006). How time pressure affects creativity is likely to depend on if it is appraised as challenging or hindering (Amabile et al., 1996), but more work is needed to understand what influences such appraisals.

As well as an expanded set of outcomes, the developments in multi-level techniques have led to more sophisticated explorations of outcomes at different levels. One example concerns research that examines within-person variations in outcomes, such as affect, and how these are affected by work design (Fisher, 2002). For example, within-person research suggests that individuals with high job control are more successful in calming down after a stressful event (Elfering et al., 2005). Another development is to examine how work characteristics at one level (e.g., team work design) affect motivational processes at multiple levels, including team

and individual motivation (e.g., Chen and Kanfer, 2006).

EXTENDED MECHANISMS

As discussed already, experienced meaningfulness is one of the most important mechanisms established in work design research. Thus, enriched job characteristics result in a stronger sense of meaning, which leads to job satisfaction and motivation. Nevertheless, there are other motivational mechanisms. For example, Grant (in press) showed that lifeguards whose task significance was increased reported a stronger sense of social worth and social impact, which in turn increased their job dedication and helping. As a result of interest in proactive behavior, more proactive forms of motivation have also been linked to work characteristics, such as role-breadth self-efficacy, flexible role orientation, and control orientation (for a review see Parker and Ohly, in press). Nevertheless, as Parker and Ohly (in press) have argued, work design theory has yet to fully incorporate advances in motivation theory, for example, with regard to goal generation and goal striving.

As well as motivational pathways, there is also good evidence for a learning mechanism, that is, employees' working 'smarter'. From the perspective of German action regulation theory (Frese and Zapf, 1994), job characteristics like autonomy allow employees to develop, and apply, greater knowledge, more appropriate task strategies and meta-cognitive strategies. The role of such knowledge-based mechanisms is supported in empirical studies. A work design initiative to give machine operators greater opportunity for fault correction, coupled with access to information and technical support, led to an increase in fault-management knowledge (Leach et al., 2003). Likewise, autonomous work group members learn from each other (Pearce and Ravlin, 1987) and, because they assume more responsibility for external coordination with others in other organizations, gain an understanding of the broader work process (Batt, 1999).

As the number of work design outcomes expand, so too do the potential explanatory mechanisms. For example, in regard to safety, job variety might alleviate boredom and increase attentiveness, thereby reducing risks, whereas excess job demands might cause short cuts to be taken, thereby increasing the chance of injury. In the case of health, job enrichment might promote more active coping; and high work load might cause musculoskeletal damage via the mechanism of biomechanical strain. Research on these types of processes is in its infancy (for a review see Parker et al., 2003).

CONTINGENCIES OVER AND ABOVE GROWTH NEED STRENGTH

Contingencies refer to the factors that affect whether and to what extent work design leads to the predicted outcomes. The traditional idea is that individuals with high growth need strength will feel more motivated by enriched work characteristics because this type of work better fits their needs. A wide array of other potential individual differences have been considered as moderators, by and large with inconsistent findings (e.g., see Morgeson and Campion, 2003).

Interestingly, despite its obvious relevance, the person-environment fit literature has not been well integrated into work design research. Three forms of fit can be distinguished (Cable and DeRue, 2002). Person-organization fit describes the perceived match of individual and organizational values, and is linked to organizational identification and low turnover. The research on growth need strength fits within this perspective. Need-supplies fit refers to the perception of rewards a job supplies in return for performance, and is related to job and career satisfaction. Demands-abilities fit, the perceived congruence between demands of a job and a person's abilities, moderates the relationship between job scope and strain such that strain only results when perceived fit is low (Xie and Johns, 1995). Neither the moderating role

of rewards, nor abilities, has had much consideration in work design research.

Once again, as with mechanisms, the relevance of contingencies will depend on both the work characteristics and the outcome being considered. Whereas growth need strength is an appropriate focus when considering enriched jobs as a motivational force, other variables are likely to be important if one is considering different motivational processes, or indeed, non-motivational processes. For example, a study of service workers showed that emotional demands were only negative for employee well-being when individuals lacked emotional competence (Giardini and Frese, 2006). Likewise, focusing on strain outcomes rather than motivation, Parker and Sprigg's (1999) study suggested that when employees are faced with jobs with high autonomy as well as high demands, those with a proactive personality take advantage of the autonomy to reduce demands and avoid strain, whereas less proactive employees felt higher degrees of strain, presumably because they did not act on the greater autonomy afforded them. These studies illustrate that there is little point in seeking global moderators of work characteristics-outcome relationships. Instead, one should look closely at the particular relationship in question.

Although understanding individual contingencies can help to identify whom work redesign will most benefit, practical implications are limited because jobs are most often redesigned for many employees, and it might not be sensible to design jobs separately for each individual, In contrast, if contextual contingencies are ignored, inappropriate work design choices will be made or appropriate choices will be ineffective. Two contextual factors that have had particular attention are interdependence and uncertainty (Cummings and Blumberg, 1987). Evidence is somewhat mixed for interdependence (e.g., Sprigg et al., 2000; Batt, 1999). However, for uncertainty, there is quite consistent evidence from production contexts that job enrichment, especially job autonomy, is most powerful in enhancing performance when uncertainty is high (e.g., Wall et al., 1990; Wright and

Cordery, 1999), probably because autonomy enables the quick responses and the learning needed to be successful in such contexts. Such thinking has parallels with more general organizational theory that proposes mechanistic structures for stable conditions and organic structures for uncertain environments (Burns and Stalker, 1961; Cummings and Blumberg, 1987; Lawrence and Lorsch, 1969; Thompson, 1967).

In a similar vein, but applied to customer service contexts, Batt (1999) suggested that where organizations aim to build long term relationships with customers by providing quality service, employees need high levels of autonomy and skill to meet a wide range of demands at any one time. Consistent with this idea, there are reports of job enrichment and other such work practices being introduced in some call centers, especially those where quality relationships with customers are required (Frenkel et al., 1999).

Beyond uncertainty and interdependence, many other contextual factors are likely to affect whether job redesign leads to the predicted outcomes, such as how well the change process is introduced, the organization's 'readiness' for work redesign, and the level of employee job security (Pearson, 1992). There has been some research considering national cultural influences, but more is needed. Robert and colleagues (Robert et al., 2000) found that empowerment was associated with lower job satisfaction in India, which they attributed the conflict of this form of work with cultural deference to hierarchy and status. Yet such a conclusion contrasts with early studies of successful autonomous work groups in Indian textile companies (Rice, 1958).

Drawing on sociotechnical systems theory, it has often been proposed that broader work organization and human resource systems (e.g. reward, training, information systems) need to align with the work design in order for it to be effective (e.g., Parker and Cordery, 2007). Contrary to this idea of alignment, however, Morgeson et al. (2006) found that work redesign into autonomous work groups only had a positive effect on self-reported performance when reward, feedback, and information systems were poor, suggesting a substituting rather than a synergistic effect.

INFLUENCES ON, AND CAUSES OF, WORK CHARACTERISTICS

Work design does not exist in a vaccuum. Job characteristics derive from, and are embedded within, a larger organizational system. The greater the level of organizational formalization and centralization, for example, the lower the autonomy, variety, and task identity (Pierce and Dunham, 1978; Rousseau, 1978a). At the same time, work characteristics are not only perceived differently by job incumbents, but differentially crafted by them. A final extension, therefore, has been to consider factors that shape, influence, or constrain work characteristics.

An array of contextual factors influence and constrain the choice of work design, including factors internal to the organization (e.g., management style, technology, or nature of the tasks) and factors external to the organization (e.g., the uncertainty of the environment, customer demands, the nature of the labor market). One implication of these broader influences on work design is that it means work can be 'redesigned' in ways over and above direct manipulation of job characteristics, such as by removing demarcation barriers or leaders to delegate greater authority.

In particular, organizational structure influences work design. Indeed, there is evidence that job characteristics mediate the relationship between technological and structural context of the organization and outcomes such as satisfaction (Oldham and Hackman, 1981; Rousseau, 1978b). This mediating idea has been applied to understanding the effects of new organizational practices. Intermediate roles of work design have been reported for lean production (Jackson and Mullarkey, 2000; Parker, 2003), temporary employment contracts (Parker et al., 2002), just-in-time (Jackson and Martin, 1996), performance monitoring (Carayon, 1994), teleworking (Feldman and Gainey, 1997), and team working (Kirkman and Rosen, 1999). From this perspective the effects on outcomes of these practices depends, at least to some degree, on how the practice impinges on work design. An implication, therefore, is that work design can be deliberately changed to bring about better outcomes.

Such positive work design choices, however, might be relatively rare. Dean and Snell (1991) showed that, although integrated manufacturing is likely to be most successful when work designs are also enriched, several sources of organizational inertia (size, performance, etc.) mitigate the effect of integrated manufacturing on work design. Other research suggests that work design is typically neglected when new technologies and practices are introduced, and this is usually to the detriment of their effectiveness (e.g. Waterson et al., 1999). In other words, structures and practices that 'should' result in more enriched work designs will not necessarily do so. The role of organizational inertia, and other such forces, in moderating how new practices affect work design is clearly an important area for further enquiry.

A further important consideration is the role of the job incumbent in influencing his/her work design (Vough and Parker, in press; Wrzesniewski and Dutton, 2001). The idea that individuals mould their work characteristics to fit their individual abilities or personalities is a long standing one (role making, Graen, 1976; task revision, Staw and Boettger, 1990). Recent research has examined how self-efficacy and proactive behavior affect work design and vice versa. Frese and colleagues (Frese et al., in press) showed that job control and job complexity were associated with greater personal initiative, which led, in the longer term, to even higher levels of job control and job complexity. This more dynamic perspective on how work design is affected by individuals holds much promise, especially within the knowledge worker context, as we elaborate shortly.

FURTHER DIRECTIONS

The above extensions better align work characteristics theory to the emerging work context. Over and above these extensions,

additional calls for developing include, for example: a more detailed look at the relational architecture of jobs and their consequences (see Grant, 2007); how work design principles might apply to customers who are expected to co-produce the service (Cordery, 2006); how the blurring of boundaries between work and home brought about by technology necessitates more attention to the home-work interface, as well as consideration of outcomes such as life satisfaction (Rousseau, 1997); how the changing nature of careers suggests it might be fruitful to think about work design over broader time spans than an individual job; how other work systems relate to, and augment or constrain, work design (Cordery and Parker, 2006); how to best redesign work and support its implementation (Parker and Wall, 1998); and the relevance of work design theory to other national cultures (e.g., Kirkman and Shapiro, 1997).

Here, we focus on two important avenues for theoretical development that have been relatively neglected in reviews thus far.

WORK DESIGN AND ORGANIZING

Several theorists have proposed that the meaning of organization is changing, and with it, the need to re-orient theories in our field (Heath and Sitkin, 2001; Rousseau, 1997). In particular, rather than thinking of 'organization' as an entity, the recommended emphasis is on organization as a dynamic process, or 'organizing'. Understanding organizing is particularly important in light of the increasingly fluid, flexible, complex and rapidly changing firms and work roles that characterize today's organizations (Rousseau, 1997). Such contexts, it is argued, require much more attention to 'how people solve the dynamic problems of aligning goals and co-ordinating action' (Heath and Sitkin, 2001: 54).

We propose two implications of an organizing emphasis for work design theory. First, work design might affect processes important for organizing, such as trust, communication, collaboration, group mental models, and group norms. There is some evidence that this is so (e.g. Parker and Axtell, 2001;

Grant, in press). Nevertheless, by far the bulk of work design research has focused on individual-level motivational or well-being mechanisms, with little attention on how work design affects collective processes, or even how it affects individual-level attitudes and behaviors that are especially important for collective action. The same observation is true in the group-level research. Whilst there are exceptions (e.g. Tesluk and Mathieu, 1999), overall there are few studies linking group work design and organizing outcomes. We see great potential in addressing questions such as how the level of self-management of a group affects the level of implicit task co-ordination (Rico et al., 2008), the use and effectiveness of team processes (Marks et al., 2001), the development of 'swift trust', and other such collective attitudes, cognitions, and behaviors.

A second implication of thinking about work design in relation to organizing is that work design *is* a way of organizing. Work design choices are inherently choices about how to organize. For example, a self-managing work group represents a different way of achieving a collective goal than a supervisor-led team. One consequence of thinking about work design in this way is that it suggests a more holistic approach to the study of work design. Rather than looking at individual work characteristics and their relationship with outcomes, which has been the dominant focus of late, one might describe how the tasks, jobs, roles, and projects are organized, focusing on the whole set of work characteristics, along with the consequences of those organizing choices. Such an approach implies methods that enable a detailed and contextualized description of the overall work design and its consequences (cf. Trist and Bamforth, 1951).

WORK DESIGN FOR KNOWLEDGE WORKERS AND PROFESSIONALS

Not surprisingly given its origins, work design research has primarily focused on the value of enriching simplified jobs, typically in contexts such as manufacturing and call centers where jobs are relatively deskilled. This work has extended to nurses, teachers, and other such samples, where enrichment principles also have resonance. However, many professional and knowledge work jobs already possess relatively high levels of autonomy, variety, and challenge, and hence the reduction of work load pressure might be more important in this context. Elsbach and Hargadon (2006) proposed that, to avoid professional work becoming relentlessly mindful and stress inducing (p. 471), each work day should be designed with scheduled bouts of mindless, cognitively undemanding work tasks inserted between more challenging and time pressured work tasks that make up most of the day. Dutton and Ragins (2007) similarly suggested making job demands more manageable by chunking tasks into do-able pieces that employees can do easily and thereby build up their confidence and momentum. Another angle is to change the way that work demands are perceived. Meta-analyses suggest that high job demands can positively relate to performance (LePine et al., 2005) and job attitudes (Podsakoff et al., in press), possibly because they might be seen as challenging and give the opportunity to reach work-related goals. Because high job demands also lead to strain reactions, research is needed to determine the conditions that enable the perception of high demands as challenging. It is also important to identify how to protect employees against long-term health consequences of demands, such as by promoting recovery (e.g. Sonnentag and Zijlstra, 2006).

We also suggest much more attention to interdependence, which is likely to be high and complex within professional/ knowledge work settings. In particular, does the need to help meet others' needs and goals constrain job autonomy? For example, Janz et al. (1997) found that, for knowledge workers, the positive main effect of team autonomy over planning and work processes on levels of team motivation was reduced as levels of task interdependence increased. The presence of regulations in particular professions (e.g., financial regulations, health care protocols) might similarly serve to reduce autonomy, or perhaps even augment it in some circumstances.

A further set of questions relates to the role of the individual in managing, shaping, and proactively influencing, their work design. We propose that professionals and knowledge workers will be particularly active in shaping their work characteristics, in part a consequence of greater latitude in their jobs to do so, but also a result of their high education levels and aspiration for career progression. For example, professional workers might deliberately schedule tasks that are low in cognitive demands for afternoons when they are tired; or do a minimum amount of client contact work per week to preserve their sense of job significance. They might bargain, via ideals, greater autonomy or variety in their work (Rousseau et al., 2006). Porfolio workers might manager their job quality over time and across multiple projects – seeking challenge in some projects, but deliberately counterbalancing these with some more routine projects that allow recuperation. All together, as one extends work design theory to better incorporate the context of higher-level professional and knowledge work, the role of individuals in actively shaping their work design is likely to assume even greater salience.

Finally, focusing on professional and knowledge work also gives rise to a question about outcomes. In particular, one might consider how work design can promote the development of capability necessary for effective performance in these challenging contexts. For example, job enrichment under conditions of managed work load might promote the creativity that is often essential for this type of work (Elsbach and Hargadon, 2006). Likewise, certain combinations of autonomy and feedback might promote the development of more effective self-regulation skills, which are argued to be especially important for performance in novel and complex settings. A further example is that interventions such as job rotation could increase managers' understanding of the bigger picture, as well

as to broaden social networks; both of which are important for successful managerial performance. One might also recognize that for this group, as well as for others such as portfolio workers or contract workers working for multiple organizations, outcomes such as organizational commitment are less relevant than occupational commitment.

A FINAL COMMENT: FROM THEORY TO PRACTICE TO THEORY

Whilst there has undoubtedly been a swing towards the rhetoric of enriched work designs, as reflected by the constant references to empowerment, high performance, and the like, good quality work design is not as widespread as one might expect. National level surveys suggest high demands and low control in many jobs (e.g., the Bristol Stress and Health Survey; Smith, Johal, Wadsworth, Peters, and Davey Smith, 2000) and, as suggested earlier, organizations often do not make good work design choices when introducing new technologies and practices. For these reasons alone, work design deserves continued attention from researchers. We need to become better at translating research findings to practice, such as by developing evidence-based tools, processes, and guidance to analyze work design and facilitate its redesign. In many countries there is a need for more systematic tracking of work characteristics at a national level; identifying the prevalence of key work characteristics as well as how they are influenced by new trends and policies. By actively aiming to influence practice and policy, academics can not only respond to changes in work design, but shape them.

As well as better applying what we know, work design research needs to keep pace with the profound changes that are occurring in the wider work context and amongst the workforce itself. Work design theory has already developed to encompass many of these changes, expanding the work characteristics and outcomes it considers, as well as mechanisms and contingencies.

However, as we have suggested here, there are further important ways that theory can and should develop. We proposed two particularly important avenues – the need to further investigate how work design can promote organizing and how it can help support the effectiveness and well-being of knowledge workers. We believe that by updating theory along these and related lines, work design research will flourish and thereby guide the effective design of contemporary and future jobs.

REFERENCES

Alge, B.J., Ballinger, G.A., Tangirala, S. and Oakley, J.L. (2006) *Information Privacy in Organizations: Empowering Creative and Extrarole Performance, Journal of Applied Psychology*, 91(1), 221.

Amabile, T.M., Conti, R., Coon, H., Lazenby, J. and Herron, M. (1996) 'Assessing the work enviroment for creativity', *Academy of Management Journal*, 39: 1154–84.

Andrews, F. and Farris, G.F. (1972) 'Time pressure and performance of scientist and engineers: A five-year panel study', *Organizational Behavior and Human Decision Processes*, 8: 185–200.

Antoni, C.H. (1997) 'Social and economic effects of introducing semi-autonomous work groups – A quasi experimental longitudinal study', *Zeitschrift fur Arbeits- und Organisationspsychologie*, 41: 131–42.

Baer, M. and Oldham, G.R. (2006) 'The curvilinear relation between experienced creative time pressure and creativity: Moderating effects of support, support for creativity and openness to experience', *Journal of Applied Psychology*, 91: 963–70.

Bakker, A.B., Demerouti, E. and Euwema, M.C. (2005) 'Job resources buffer the impact of job demands on burnout', *Journal of Occupational Health Psychology*, 10: 170–80.

Barker, J.R. (1993) 'Tightening the iron cage: Concertive control in self-managing teams', *Administrative Science Quarterly*, 38: 408–37.

Barling, J., Kelloway, E.K. and Iverson, R.D. (2003) 'High-quality work, job satisfaction, and occupational injuries', *Journal of Applied Psychology*, 88: 276–83.

Batt, R. (1999) 'Work organization, technology, and performance in customer service sales', *Industrial and Labor Relations Review*, 52.

Birdi, K., Clegg, C., Patterson, M., Robinson, A., Stride, C.B., Wall, T.D. et al. (2008) The impact of human resource and operational management practices on company productivity: A longitudinal study. *Personnel Psychology*, 61(3), 467–501.

Britt, T.W., Dickinson, J.M., Moore, D., Castro, C.A. and Adler, A.B. (2007) 'Correlates and Consequences of Morale Versus Depression Under Stressful Conditions', *Journal of Occupational Health Psychology*, 12: 34–47.

Burns, T. and Stalker, G.M. (1961) *The Management of Innovation*. London: Tavistock.

Cable, D.M. and DeRue, D. (2002) 'The convergent and discriminant validity of subjective fit perceptions', *Journal of Applied Psychology*, 87: 875–84.

Campion, M.A. and McClelland, C.L. (1991) 'Interdisciplinary examination of the costs and benefits of enlarged jobs: A job design quasi-experiment', *Journal of Applied Psychology*, 76: 186–98.

Carayon, P. (1994) 'Effects of electronic performance monitoring on job design and worker stress: Results of two studies', *International Journal of Human-Computer Interaction*, 6: 177–90.

Chen, G. and Kanfer, R. (2006) 'Towards a systems theory of motivated behavior in work teams', *Research in Organizational Behavior*, 27: 223–67.

Cherns, A. (1997). Die Tavistock-Untersuchungen und ihre Auswirkungen. In S. Greif, H. Holling and N. Nicholson (eds.), *Arbeits- und Organisationspsychologie: Internationales Handbuch in Schlüsselbegriffen* (pp. 483–488). Weinheim: Beltz.

Clinton, M., Totterdell, P. and Wood, S. (2006). A grounded theory of portfolio working: Experiencing the smallest of small businesses. *International Small Business Journal*, 24(2), 179.

Cohen, L. and Mallon, M. (1999) 'The transition form organisational employment to portfolio working: Perceptions of "Boundarylessness"', *Work, Employment and Society*, 13: 329–52.

Conger, J.A. and Kanungo, R.N. (1988) 'The empowerment process: Integrating theory and practice', *Academy of Management Review*, 13: 471–82.

Cordery, J. (2006, May) *One more time: How do you motivate customers? Applying work design principles to co-production arrangements in service organizations*. Paper presented at the SIOP 21st annual conference, Dallas, TX.

Cordery, J. and Parker, S.K. (2007) Work organisation. In P. Boxall, J. Purcell and P. Wright (Eds.), *The Oxford Handbook of Human Resource Management* (pp. 187–209). Oxford: Oxford university press.

Corsun, D.L., and Enz, C.A. (1999) Prediction psychological empowerment among service workers: The effect of support-based relationships. *Human Relations*, 52, 205–224.

Cummings, T.G. and Blumberg, M. (1987) 'Advanced manufacturing technology and work design', in T.D. Wall, C.W. Clegg and N.J. Kemp (eds), *The Human Side of Advanced Manufacturing Technology*. Chichester, UK: Wiley, pp. 37–60.

Daniels, K. (2006) 'Rethinking job characteristics in work stress research', *Human Relations*, 59: 267–90.

de Lange, A.H., Taris, T.W., Kompier, M.A.J., Houtman, I.L.D. and Bongers, P.M. (2003) '"The very best of the millennium": Longitudinal research and the demand-control-(support) model', *Journal of Occupational Health Psychology*, 8: 282–305.

Dean, J.W. and Snell, S.A. (1991) 'Integrated manufacturing and job design: Moderating effects of organizational inertia', *Academy of Management Journal*, 34: 776–804.

Dormann, C. and Kaiser, D.M. (2002) 'Job conditions and customer satisfaction', *European Journal of Work and Organizational Psychology*, 11: 257–83.

Douthitt, E.A. and Aiello, J.R. (2001) 'The role of participation and control in the effects of computer monitoring on fairness perceptions, task satisfaction, and performance', *Journal of Applied Psychology*, 86: 867–74.

Dutton, J.E. (2003) *Energize Your Workplace: How to Create and Sustain High–Quality Connections at Work*. San Francisco, CA: Jossey-Bass.

Dutton, J.E. and Ragins, B.R. (eds). (2007) Exploring relationships at work: Building a theoretical and research foundation. Routledge.

Dwyer, D.J. and Fox, M.L. (2000) 'The moderating role of hostility in the relationship between enriched jobs and health', *Academy of Management Journal*, 43: 1086–96.

Edwards, J.R., Scully, J.A. and Brtek, M.D. (1999) 'The measurement of work: Hierachical representation of the multimethod job design questionnaire', *Personnel Psychology*, 52: 305–34.

Elfering, A., Grebner, S., Semmer, N.K., Kaiser-Freiburghaus, D., Lauper-Del Ponte, S. and Witschi, I. (2005) 'Chronic job stressors and job control: Effects on event-related coping success and well-being', *Journal of Occupational and Organizational Psychology*, 78: 237–52.

Elsbach, K.D. and Hargadon, A.B. (2006) 'Enhancing creativity through "mindless" work: A framework of workday design', *Organization Science*, 17: 470–83.

Feldman, D.C. and Gainey, T.W. (1997) 'Patterns of telecommuting and their consequences: Framing the research Agenda', *Human Resource Management Review*, 7: 369–88.

Fisher, C.D. (2002) 'Antecedents and consequences of real-time affective reactions at work', *Motivation and Emotion*, 26: 3–30.

Frenkel, S.J., Korczynski, M., Shire, K.A. and Tam, M. (1999) *On the Front Line: Organization of Work in Information Economy*. London: Cornell University Press.

Frese, M. (1985) 'Stress at work and psychosomatic complaints: A causal interpretation', *Journal of Applied Psychology*, 70: 314–28.

Frese, M., Garst, H. and Fay, D. (2007) Making things happen: Reciprocal relationships between work characteristics and personal initiative (PI) in a fourwave longitudinal structural equation mode. *Journal of Applied Psychology*, 92(4), 1084–1102.

Frese, M. and Zapf, D. (1994) 'Action as the core of work psychology: A German approach', in H. C. Triandis, M. D. Dunnette and L. M. Hough (eds), *Handbook of Industrial and Organizational Psychology* (Second ed., Vol. 4). Palo Alto, CA: Consulting Psychologist Press, pp. 271–340.

Fried, Y. and Ferris, G.R. (1987) 'The validity of the Job Characteristics Model: A review and meta-analysis', *Personnel Psychology*, 40: 287–322.

Giardini, A. and Frese, M. (2006) 'Reducing the negative effects of emotion work in service occupations: Emotional competence as a psychological resource', *Journal of Occupational Health Psychology*, 11: 63–75.

Graen, G.B. (1976) 'Role making processes within complex organizations', in M. D. Dunnette (ed.), *Handbook of Industrial and Organizational Psychology*. Stokie, Il: Rand McNally, pp. 1201–45.

Grandey, A.A., Dickter, D.N. and Sin, H.-P. (2004) 'The customer is not always right: Customer aggression and emotion regulation of service employees', *Journal of Organizational Behavior*, 25: 397–418.

Grant, A.M. (2007) 'Relational job design and the motivation to make a prosocial difference', *Academy of Management Review*, 32: 393–417.

Grant, A. M. (2008) The significance of task significance: Job performance effects, relational mechanisms, and boundary conditions. *Journal of Applied Psychology*, 93(1), 108–124.

Griffin, R.W. (1983) 'Objective and social sources of information in task redesign: A field experiment', *Administrative Science Quarterly*, 28: 184–200.

Griffin, R.W. (1991) 'Effects of work redesign on employee perceptions, attitudes, and behaviors: A long-term investigation', *Academy of Management Journal*, 34: 425–35.

Hackman, J.R. and Oldham, G.R. (1980) *Work redesign*. Reading, MA: Addison-Wesley.

Harrison, M.M., Neff, N.L., Schwall, A.R. and Zhao, X. (2006, May) *A meta-analytic investigation of individual creativity and innovation*. Paper presented at the Annual conference of the Society for Industrial and Organizational Psychology, Dallas, TX.

Heath, C. and Sitkin, S.B. (2001) 'Big-B versus Big-O: What is organizational about organizational behavior?', *Journal of Organizational Behavior*, 22: 43–58.

Herzberg, F., Mausner, B. and Snyderman, B. (1959) *The Motivation to Work*. Oxford, England: Wiley.

Holman, D., Clegg, C. and Waterson, P. (2002a) 'Navigating the territory of job design', *Applied Ergonomics*, 33: 197–205.

Holman, D., Chissick, C. and Totterdell, P. (2002b) 'The effects of performance monitoring on emotional labor and well-being in call centers', *Motivation and Emotion*, 26: 57–81.

Hulin, C.L. and Smith, P.A. (1967) 'An empirical investigation of two implications of the two-factor theory of job satisfaction', *Journal of Applied Psychology*, 51: 396–402.

Humphrey, S.E., Nahrgang, J.D., and Morgeson, F.P. (2007) Integrating motivational, social, and contextual work design features: A meta-analytic summary and theoretical extension of the work design literature. *Journal of Applied Psychology*, 92(5), 1332–56.

Jackson, P.R. and Martin, R. (1996) 'Impact of just-in-time on job content, employee attitudes and well-being: A longitudinal study', *Ergonomics*, 39: 1–16.

Jackson, P.R. and Mullarkey, S. (2000) 'Lean production teams and health in garment manufacture', *Journal of Occupational Health Psychology*, 5: 231–45.

Janz, B.D., Colquitt, J.A. and Noe, R.A. (1997) 'Knowledge worker team effectiveness: The role of autonomy, interdependence, team development, and contextual support variables', *Personnel Psychology*, 50: 877–904.

Johns, G., Xie, J.L. and Fang, Y. (1992) 'Mediating and moderating effects in job design', *Journal of Management*, 18: 657–76.

Karasek, R. (1979) 'Job demands, job decision latitude, and mental strain: Implications for job redesign', *Administrative Science Quarterly*, 24: 285–306.

Karasek, R. and Theorell, T. (1990) *Healthy work: Stress, productivity, and the reconstruction of working life*. New York: Basic Books.

Kirkman, B.L. and Rosen, B. (1999) 'Beyond self-management: Antecedents and consequences of team empowerment', *Academy of Management Journal*, 42: 58–74.

Kirkman, B.L. and Shapiro, D.L. (1997) 'The impact of cultural values on employee resistance to teams: Toward a model of globalized self-managing work team effectiveness', *Academy of Management Review*, 22: 730–57.

Lawrence, P.R. and Lorsch, J.W. (1969) *Organization and environment: Managing differentiation and integration*: RD Irwin.

Leach, D.J., Wall, T.D. and Jackson, P.R. (2003) The effect of empowerment on job knowledge: An empirical test involving operators of complex technology. *Journal of Occupational and Organizational Psychology*, 76(1), 27–52.

LePine, J.A., Podsakoff, N.P. and LePine, M.A. (2005) 'A meta-analytic test of the challenge stress-hindrance stress framework: An explanation for inconsistent relationships between stressors and performance', *Academy of Management Journal*, 48: 764–75.

Loher, B.T., Noe, R.A., Moeller, N.L. and Fitzgerald, M.P. (1985) 'A meta-analysis of the relation of job characteristics to job satisfaction', *Journal of Applied Psychology*, 70: 280–89.

Marks, M.A., Mathieu, J.E. and Zaccaro, S.J. (2001) A temporally based framework and taxonomy of team processes. *Academy of Management Review*, 26(3), 356–76.

Morgeson, F.P. and Campion, M.A. (2003) Work design. In W.C. Borman, D.R. Ilgen and R.J. Klimoski (eds.), *Handbook of psychology: Industrial and organizational psychology* (Vol. 12, pp. 423–52). New York, NY: John Wiley and Sons, Inc.

Morgeson, F.P. and Humphrey, S.E. (2006) 'The work design questionnaire (WDQ): Developing and validating a comprehensive measures for assessing job design and the nature of work', *Journal of Applied Psychology*, 91: 1321–39.

Morgeson, F.P., Johnson, M.D., Campion, M.A., Medsker, G.J. and Mumford, T.V. (2006) 'Understanding reactions to job redesign: A quasi–experimental investigation of the moderating effects of organizational context on perceptions of performance behavior', *Personnel Psychology*, 59: 333–63.

Nebeker, D.M. and Tatum, B.C. (1993) 'The effects of computer monitoring, standards, and rewards on work performance, job satisfaction, and stress', *Journal of Applied Social Psychology*, 23: 508–36.

Ohly, S. and Fritz, C. (in prep.) Work characteristics, challenge appraisal, creativity and proactive behavior: A multi-level study.

Ohly, S., Sonnentag, S. and Pluntke, F. (2006) 'Routinization, work characteristics, and their relationships with creative and proactive behaviors', *Journal of Organizational Behavior*, 27: 257–79.

Oldham, G.R. (1996) 'Job design', in C.L. Cooper and I.T. Robertson (eds), *International Review of Industrial and Organizational Psychology*. Chichester, UK: Wiley, pp. 33–60.

Oldham, G.R. and Hackman, J. (1981) 'Relationships between organizational structure and employee reactions: Comparing alternative frameworks', *Administrative Science Quarterly*, 26: 66–83.

Oldham, G.R., Nottenburg, G., Kassner, M.W., Ferris, G.R., Fedor, D. and Masters, M. (1982)

'The selection and consequences of job comparisons', *Organizational Behavior and Human Performance*, 29: 84–111.

Parker, S.K. (1996) An investigation of attitudes amongst production employees. *International Journal of Human Factors in Manufacturing*, 6(3), 281–303.

Parker, S.K. (2003) 'Longitudinal effects of lean production on employee outcomes and the mediating role of work characteristics', *Journal of Applied Psychology*, 88: 620–34.

Parker, S.K. and Axtell, C.M. (2001) 'Seeing another viewpoint: Antecedents and outcomes of employee perspective taking', *Academy of Management Journal*, 44: 1085–1100.

Parker, S.K. and Cordery, J. (2007) 'Work organization', in P. Boxall, J. Purcell and P. Wright (eds), *The Oxford Handbook of Human Resource Management*. Oxford: Oxford University Press.

Parker, S.K., Griffin, M.A., Sprigg, C.A. and Wall, T.D. (2002) 'Effect of temporary contracts on perceived work characteristics and job strain', *Personnel Psychology*, 55: 689–719.

Parker, S.K., and Ohly, S. (2008) Job design and work role demands. In R. Kanfer, G. Chen and R. Pritchard (eds.), *Work motivation: Past, present, and future. SIOP Frontiers Series* (pp. 233–284). Hillsdale, NJ: Laurence Erlbaum Associates.

Parker, S.K. and Sprigg, C.A. (1999) 'Minimizing strain and maximizing learning: The role of job demands, job control, and proactive personality', *Journal of Applied Psychology*, 84: 925–39.

Parker, S.K., Turner, N. and Griffin, M.A. (2003) Designing healthy work. In D.A. Hofmann & L.E. Tetrick (Eds.), *Health and safety in organizations: A multi-level perspective* (pp. 91–130). San Francisco, CA: Jossey-Bass.

Parker, S.K. and Wall, T.D. (1998) *Job and Work Design*. London: Sage.

Parker, S.K., Wall, T.D. and Cordery, J.L. (2001) 'Future work design research and practice: towards an elaborated model of work design', *Journal of Occupational and Organizational Psychology*, 74: 413–40.

Parker, S.K., Williams, E.S. and Turner, N. (2006) 'Modeling the antecedents of proactive behavior at work', *Journal of Applied Psychology*, 91: 636–52.

Paul, J.P., Robertson, K.B. and Herzberg, F. (1969) 'Job enrichment pays off', *Harvard Business Review*, 47: 61–78.

Pearce, J.A. and Ravlin, F.C. (1987) 'The desing and activation of self-regulating work groups', *Human Relations*, 40: 751–82.

Pearson, C.A.L. (1992) 'Autonomous work groups: An evaluation at an industrial site', *Human Relations*, 45: 905–36.

Pierce, J.L. and Dunham, R.B. (1978) 'The measurement of perceived job characteristics: The job diagnostic survey versus the job characteristics inventory', *Academy of Management Journal*, 21: 123–8.

Pierce, J.L., Dunham, R.B. and Blackburn, R.S. (1979) Social systems structure, job design, and growth need strength: A test of a congruency model. *Academy of Management Journal*, 22, 223–240.

Podsakoff, N.P., LePine, J.A. and LePine, M.A. (2007) Differential challenge stressor-hindrance stressor relationships with job attitudes, turnover intentions, turnover, and withdrawal behavior: A meta-analysis. *Journal of Applied Psychology*, 92(2), 438–454.

Rentsch, J.R. and Steel, R.P. (1998) 'Testing the durability of job characteristics as predictors of absenteeism over a six-year period', *Personnel Psychology*, 51: 165–90.

Rice, A. (1958) *Productivity and Social Organization: The Ahmedabad Experiment, Technical Innovation, Work Organization and Management*. Oxford: Tavistock.

Rico, R., Sánchez-Manzanares, M., Gil, F., and Gibson, C. (2008) Team implicit coordination processes: A team knowledge-based approach. *Academy of Management Review*, 33(1), 163–184.

Robert, C., Probst, T.M., Martocchio, J.J., Drasgow, F. and Lawler, J.J. (2000) 'Empowerment and continuous improvement in the United States, Mexico, Poland, and India: Predicting fit on the basis of the dimensions of power distance and individualism', *Journal of Applied Psychology*, 85: 643–58.

Roberts, K.H. and Glick, W. (1981) 'The job characteristics approach to task design: A critical review', *Journal of Applied Psychology*, 66: 193–217.

Rousseau, D.M. (1978a) 'Characteristics of departments, positions, and individuals: Contexts for attitudes and behavior', *Administrative Science Quarterly*, 23: 521–40.

Rousseau, D.M. (1978b) 'Measures of technology as predictors of employee attitude', *Journal of Applied Psychology*, 63: 213–18.

Rousseau, D.M. (1997) 'Organizational behavior in the new organizational era', *Annual Review of Psychology*, 48: 515–46.

Rousseau, D.M., Ho, V.T. and Greenberg, J. (2006) 'I-deals: Idiosyncratic terms in employment relationships', *Academy of Management Review*, 31: 977–94.

Salancik, G.R. and Pfeffer, J. (1978) 'A social information processing approach to job attitudes and task design', *Administrative Science Quarterly*, 23: 224–53.

Smith, A., Johal, S., Wadsworth, E., Peters, T. and Davey Smith, G. (2000) *The scale and impact of occupational stress: The Bristol stress and health at work study*. London, UK: HSE Books.

Sonnentag, S. (1996) 'Work group factors and individual well-being', in M.A. West (ed.), *Handbook of Work Group Psychology*. Chichester: Wiley, pp. 345–67.

Sonnentag, S. and Zijlstra, F.R. (2006) 'Job Characteristics and Off-Job Activities as Predictors of Need for Recovery, Well-Being, and Fatigue', *Journal of Applied Psychology*, 91: 330–50.

Spreitzer, G.M. (1995) 'Psychological empowerment in the workplace: Dimensions, measurement, and validation', *Academy of Management Journal*, 38: 1442–65.

Spreitzer, G.M. (1996) 'Social structural characteristics of psychological empowerment', *Academy of Management Journal*, 39: 483–504.

Sprigg, C.A., Jackson, P.R. and Parker, S.K. (2000) 'Production teamworking: The importance of interdependence and autonomy for employee strain and satisfaction', *Human Relations*, 53: 1519–43.

Sprigg, C.A., Stride, C.B., Wall, T.D., Holman, D.J. and Smith, P.R. (2007) Work characteristics, musculoskeletal disorders, and the mediating role of psychological strain: A study of call center employees. *Journal of applied psychology*, 92(5), 1456.

Stansfeld, S. A., Fuhrer, R., Head, J., Ferrie, J. and Shipley, M. (1997) Work and psychiatric disorder in the Whitehall II Study. *Journal of Psychosomatic Research*, 43(1), 73–81.

Staw, B.M. and Boettger, R.D. (1990) 'Task revision: A neglected form of work performance', *Academy of Management Journal*, 33: 534–59.

Stone, E.F. and Gueutal, H.G. (1984) 'On the premature death of need-satisfaction models: An investigation of Salancik and Pfeffer's views on priming and consistency artifacts', *Journal of Management*, 10: 237–49.

Taber, T.D. and Taylor, E. (1990) 'A review and evaluation of the psychometric properties of the Job Diagnostic Survey', *Personnel Psychology*, 43: 467–500.

Taris, T.W. and Kompier, M.A.J. (2005) 'Job demands, job control, strain and learning behavior: Review and research agenda', in A.-S.G. Antoniou and C.L. Cooper (eds), *Research companion to organizational health psychology* (Vol. 17). Northampton, MA: Edward Elgar Publishing, pp. 132–50.

Taylor, F.W. (1911) *The Principles of Scientific Management*. New York, NY: Harper.

Tesluk, P.E. and Mathieu, J.E. (1999) 'Overcoming roadblocks to effectiveness: Incorporating management of performance barriers into models of work group effectiveness', *Journal of Applied Psychology*, 84: 200–17.

Thompson, J.D. (1967) *Organizations in action*. New York: McGraw-Hill.

Thomas, K.W. and Velthouse, B.A. (1990) 'Cognitive elements of empowerment: An "interpretive" model of intrinsic task motivation', *Academy of Management Review*, 15: 666–81.

Tiegs, R.B., Tetrick, L.E. and Fried, Y. (1992) 'Growth need strength and context satisfactions as moderators of the relations of the job characteristics model', *Journal of Management*, 18: 575–93.

Torraco, R.J. (2005) 'Work design theory: A review and critique with implications for human resource development', *Human Resource Development Quarterly*, 16: 85–109.

Totterdell, P., Wood, S.J. and Wall, T.D. (2006) 'An intra-individual test of the demands-control model: A weekly diary study of job strain in portfolio workers', *Journal of Occupational and Organizational Psychology*, 78: 1–23.

Trist, E.L. and Bamforth, K.W. (1951) 'Some social and psychological consequences of the long-wall method of coal-getting', *Human Relations*, 4: 3–38.

Tschan, F., Rochat, S. and Zapf, D. (2005) 'It's not only clients: Studying emotion work with clients and co-workers with an event-sampling approach', *Journal of Occupational and Organizational Psychology*, 78: 195–220.

van der Doef, M. and Maes, S. (1998) 'The job demand-control(-support) model and physical health outcomes: A review of the strain and buffer hypotheses', *Psychology and Health*, 13: 909–36.

Van Yperen, N.W. and Hagedoorn, M. (2003) 'Do high job demands increase intrinsic motivation or fatigue or both? The role of job control and job social support', *Academy of Management Journal*, 46: 339–48.

Vough, H.C. and Parker, S.K. (2008) Work design research: Still going strong. In C.L. Cooper and J. Barling (eds.), *The SAGE handbook of organizational behavior* (pp. 410–426). London: Sage.

Wall, T.D., Corbett, J., Martin, R., Clegg, C.W. and et al. (1990) 'Advanced manufacturing technology, work design, and performance: A change study', *Journal of Applied Psychology*, 75: 691–7.

Wall, T.D. and Jackson, P.R. (1995) New manufacturing initiatives and shopfloor job design. In A. Howard (ed.), *The changing nature of work* (pp. 139–174). San Francisco, CA: Jossey-Bass.

Wall, T.D., Kemp, N.J., Jackson, P.R. and Clegg, C.W. (1986) 'Outcomes of autonomous workgroups: A long-term field experiment', *Academy of Management Journal*, 29: 280–304.

Waterson, P.E., Clegg, C.W., Bolden, R., Pepper, K., Warr, P.B. and Wall, T.D. (1999) 'The use and effectiveness of modern manufacturing practices: A survey of UK industry', *International Journal of Production Research*, 37: 2271–92.

Wright, B.M. and Cordery, J.L. (1999) 'Production uncertainty as a contextual moderator of employee reactions to job design', *Journal of Applied Psychology*, 84: 456–63.

Wrzensniewski, A. and Dutton, J.E. (2001) 'Crafting a job: Revisioning employees as active crafters of their work', *Academy of Management Review*, 26: 179–201.

Xie, J.L. and Johns, G. (1995) 'Job scope and stress: Can job scope be too high?', *Academy of Management Journal*, 38: 1288–309.

Zapf, D. (2002) 'Emotion work and psychological well-being: A review of the literature and some conceptual considerations', *Human Resource Management Review*, 12: 237–68.

17

Occupational Health and Safety in the Modern World of Work

Rebecca Loudoun and Richard Johnstone

INTRODUCTION OVERVIEW DATA ON HAZARDS, ILLNESS AND INJURY

According to the principles of the United Nations (UN), World Health Organization (WHO) and the International Labor Organisation (ILO), 'every citizen of the world has a right to healthy and safe work and to a work environment that enables him or her to live a socially and economically productive life' (WHO, 1995: 1). Only a few citizens are afforded this right, however, as evidenced by the high numbers of occupational illnesses, diseases and fatalities in most countries.

The ILO estimates that over 2 million people die every year from occupational accidents and diseases, some 270 million people suffer serious non-fatal injuries every year and another 160 million fall ill for shorter or longer periods from work-related causes (Takala, 2005). In economic terms the loss of capital and associated costs caused by accidents, occupational and work-related

diseases as well as stress and lack of motivation is equally worrying. Looking at organisational losses arising from accidents and more especially, chronic ill-health, it is now estimated that between two and ten per cent of the workforce is absent from work every day; the ILO estimates that in total these costs amount to approximately 4–5 per cent of the world's GDP.

Although some industrialised nations have achieved substantial reductions in the number of occupational deaths and injuries (Stout and Linn, 2002), very few (5–10 per cent) workers in developing countries and 20–50 per cent of workers in most industrialised countries have access to occupational health services (WHO, 2003). As a result work related injuries, illnesses and deaths remain at unacceptably high levels and many workers and their families experience significant hardship and suffering. As outlined by WHO (1995) this health burden, suffering and economic loss is unnecessary and largely preventable.

It is important to note that these figures vary by gender, age, industry, country and sector, with, for example, young workers and those in developing countries experiencing higher injury rates than older workers and those in developed countries. Figures also vary over time. In part this is because of changes in employment patterns, technology and production techniques but they are also affected by current understandings about the scope of occupation-related health problems, which depend on many factors, including the definition of health that is employed, the existing state of medical knowledge and the effectiveness of reporting agencies such as workers' compensation schemes. The purpose of this chapter is to consider these intervening factors and their affect on health and safety performance, management strategies and enforcement strategies. The chapter starts by exploring the broadening meaning and focus of workplace health and safety as well as the forces driving this change. Following this, international developments affecting work and production are examined, together with their influence on occupational injury and disease. The chapter finishes by exploring developments in strategies to manage and regulate health and safety along with current and future challenges for policy makers, workers and managers of health and safety.

INTERPRETING OCCUPATIONAL HEALTH AND SAFETY AND WELLBEING AT WORK

A general definition of health and safety at work usually describes it as dealing with illnesses, diseases, accidents and injuries that occur in the workplace, or are attributable to workplace processes (Loyd, 2002). What this means in practice, however is more problematic. At a joint meeting of the WHO and the ILO health was considered as the 'development and promotion of healthy and safe work, work environments and work organizations' and 'an individual's physical, mental and social well-being, general health and personal development' (WHO, 1995: 41).

Although the last two decades have seen countries progressively embracing this broader view, nearly all, except perhaps the Nordic countries, have relied on a more traditional view of health and safety that focuses on the absence of disease and deformity and fails to consider the working environment (Bohle and Quinlan, 2000: 7). The 'working environment' now generally includes hazard specific issues as well as more general issues such as the organisation and conditions of work and an express recognition that things such as the length, scheduling and organisation of working time have an impact on workers' physical and psychological health.

The broadening definition of health and safety at work has been driven by progress in research aimed at understanding the causal links between workplace variables and occupationally related illness. However, along with this understanding comes recognition that relationships between the array of psychological, physical and chemical hazards and occupational ill-health are complex, interrelated and often affected by variables outside the workplace. Bohle and Quinlan (2000: 8) illustrate this point further.

> The simultaneous exposure of workers to excessive heat and noise, to two or more hazardous substances (say lead and diesel fumes) or to excessive hours of work and supervisory pressure or sexual harassment will have health outcomes which cannot be deduced by simply adding those associated with exposures to each hazard individually. Further, physical, chemical and organisational risks like the examples just given all may interact. Indeed it is relatively easy to conceive of a workplace, such as a lead/zinc foundry, where all these factors just mentioned can be found.

Establishing causal links is likely to become more difficult, however, as multiple job holdings are increasingly common and the divide between work and non-work activities is becoming less distinct for many workers (Sullivan and Lewis, 2006). The incursion of work into other areas of an employee's life is illustrated in the recent ILO study of employment in the EU with almost 20 per cent of European workers reporting working at least a quarter of the time from home (Parent-Thirion et al., 2006). Similarly, almost a quarter of all workers reported taking work home in an Australian study; an increase of four per cent since 2000 (CCH, 2006).

Establishing these causal links and estimating the extent of workplace illness and injury is also likely to become more difficult if workers' compensation and other accident and disease recording systems fail to take account of changing employment patterns. As outlined in the following section the last two decades have seen the expansion of employment in areas that are not generally recorded for the purposes of accident and diseases statistics (such as self employees and contractors) or employment that leaves workers with less job security (such as highly casualised, transitory or unlawful employment relationships), which usually results in workers failing to report injuries or hazards or lodge claims for compensation. This mismatch between statistical gathering techniques and employment patterns will result in official statistics becoming progressively less representative of the incidence of occupational injury and disease (Fishback et al., 2000).

It is also important to note that recognition of emergent occupational health and safety (OHS) hazards is influenced by a range of social, economic and political factors (Levenstein and Wooding, 1997). Some accident and disease recoding systems – particularly workers' compensation systems – have been slow to recognise some types of injuries, and especially diseases (which are often only partly the result of work), and as such they can underestimate work-related diseases such as mesothelioma and stress related illnesses.

This is also the case for decisions about health policy such as priorities for reform and intervention. These decisions are rarely neutral, value-free or objective; they are currently governed by two (often) opposing goals, workers' health and economic rationality (Benach et al., 2002). Determining which of these goals takes priority at the workplace, state and national level depends on the political ideology, values and power of key actors involved in the decision making process (Walt, 1998).

Interactions between these actors and resulting strategies to eliminate or minimise

workplace health and safety risks must consider the increasingly rapid rate at which workplaces are changing. Economic integration and the liberalisation of international trade has intensified over recent years and, together with the rapid expansion in information technology, is bringing about radical changes in our workplaces and society more generally. The most influential of these changes for OHS is a significant and widespread change in labour markets and work organisation, which in turn has produced fundamental changes in the nature of work, organisations, work relationships and risk. These and other developments affecting safety and health at work are examined in the next section.

INTERNATIONAL DEVELOPMENTS AFFECTING OHS

Overview

Changes at work affecting health and safety can be grouped into three interrelated strands: changes in employment structures and work arrangements; changes in industry and occupation distribution; and changes in the demographic makeup of the workforce. The impact of work changes on health and safety is usually complex, generating some positive consequences but also major challenges for OHS managers, regulators and those administrating workers' compensation and rehabilitation regimes.

Changes in employment structures and work arrangements

One of the most significant changes affecting work globally over the past 20 years is changes in employment structures which have altered the timing, location, intensity and security of employment. At the broadest level there has been a pronounced expansion in what used to be considered 'nonstandard', 'alternate' or 'atypical' employment, namely self employment, casual/temporary and part-time and fixed term or temporary employment. These work arrangements, typically labelled 'precarious' employment or 'contingent' work are characterised by formally short-term, temporary or insecure work achieved by: decreasing the expected period of the employment, increasing its uncertainty, or weakening the claims that workers and employers can make on one another by virtue of the altered employment relationship (Johnstone et al., 2005). There is some debate in the literature about the inclusion of some work arrangements as precarious work (such as permanent part-time employment and self employment) as they don't share all of these features, but central to all arrangements is a reduction in commitment required in employment. For workers at the disadvantaged or lower end of the spectrum this has resulted in jobs that are highly insecure and lacking in control over work processes and timing. For others, such as highly educated and valued flexible knowledge workers and some teleworkers, changes have resulted in employment practices that leave workers independent and empowered to determine their own working arrangements. These workers are still contingent to the extent that organisations do not make explicit or implicit guarantees of ongoing employment but they generally have a great deal of control over when, how and where to perform their work (Fragoso and Kleemer, 2005)

Reduced security in employment can also be extended to non-contingent work, however, which is why some commentators argue that these jobs have also become more precarious or uncertain in their continuity. In general these commentators argue that widespread layoffs, replacement of full time jobs with part-positions and the increase of temporary work have lead to most workers feeling less secure about their employment (Auer, 2006; Probst, 2000). Looking at precarious employment narrowly defined, there is a rapidly expanding body of research recording the spread of this type of work in most advanced economies, including Europe (De Grip et al., 1997; Brewster et al., 1997), North America (Bureau of Labor Statistics, 1995 and Hipple, 2001) and Australasia (Burgess and de Ruyter, 2000a; Campbell and Burgess, 2001). As an

example Quinlan and Bohle (2004: 83–84) use a combination of unpublished OECD statistics and findings from a study comparing Australia and Europe to show that the proportion of the workforce holding temporary jobs in Australia and 14 EU countries grew by 43.67 per cent between 1983 and 1999. Similar increases can be found for Canada (see Lowe, 2001) and the USA (Hipple, 2001). By 1999 workers holding a casual or temporary job and non-employees (self-employed, subcontractors, etc.) constituted 30 per cent of the workforce in the US (Hipple, 2001) and 48 per cent in Australia (Burgess and de Ruyter, 2000b: 252).

The growth of precarious employment has seen a corresponding decline in permanent/tenured full-time jobs, especially for males (Ferrie, 1999: 59) and a growth in multiple job holdings. For example, in the most recent European Working Conditions Survey nearly five per cent of all EU workers (except those in France, UK, PT and CV) reported having a second paid job, with this figure increasing to nearly 15 per cent for the Scandinavian countries, the Netherlands and Eastern Europe (Parent-Thirion et al., 2006).

The most important provider of new jobs has been small-scale enterprises and self-employment. Indeed most workers in Europe are now employed in small businesses (Parent-Thirion et al., 2006). This trend has been driven by repeated rounds of downsizing by large public and private organisations as well as a greater resort to outsourcing and labour hire (Walters and Lamm, 2004).

There have also been changes to the timing of work, with a growth in shiftwork – including night work and compressed work schedules – and long work hours brought about by the introduction of systems involving flexible scheduling, reduced staffing levels and paid and unpaid overtime (Harrington, 2001). In total, an estimated 22 per cent of the global workforce is working more than 48 hours per week, with this figure being even higher in some countries and industries. For example working hours are particularly high in certain service industries, such as wholesale and retail trade; hotels and restaurants; and transport, storage and communications, all of which also commonly involve shift work and work at night or (Lee et al., 2007).

Implications for health and safety

There is a now a substantial body of international research indicating that employment arrangements involving a high degree of insecurity and limited control over work processes and timing are associated with inferior standards of health and safety performance. In particular, evidence links high job insecurity to poorer mental health outcomes, bullying and other forms of occupational violence, higher injury and illness rates and less knowledge of and compliance with legislative requirements (For a review of these studies see Lewchuk et al., 2003). In a large-scale, metastudy of research on the effects of job insecurity and work, Quinlan et al. (2001) found a clear adverse association between precarious employment and OHS, with almost 90 per cent of studies finding a measurable adverse effect in terms of least one of a range of indices (including higher injury and illness rates, occupational violence, cardiovascular disease and psychological distress/mental illness and less knowledge of and compliance with legislative requirements). Later and more industry specific reviews report similar findings (see Sverke et al., 2002).

Where new forms of employment arrangements have resulted in workers having more capacity to decide on working arrangements – that is, to alter the timing, location or amount of paid work that they do to accommodate personal preferences – arrangements have resulted in reduced work–family conflict (Berry and Rao, 1997) and increased flexibility (e.g. Gillespie et al., 1995). Some research also shows that workers in these types of employment – usually those with skills in high demand areas such as information technology and medical services – report reduced total work hours achieved through greater productivity and reduced commuting (Mirchandani, 1998).

Explanations to explain the adverse effects of precarious employment tend to centre on markedly inferior employment conditions provided to precarious workers compared with permanent workers. For example, in most industrialised countries casual, temporary and part time workers are less likely to be unionised and find it more difficult to access regulatory protection (Campbell and Burgess, 1997). This means that they are less likely to receive training – including training in OHS – and they are more likely to lack job specific knowledge and experience, leading to increased disorganisation in the workplace. There is also likely to be more ambiguity about coverage of workers in some work situations and uncertainty about responsibility for OHS. Furthermore, the competitive pressures on subcontractors and other small business owners mean that concerns to maximise profit and production can be superior to worker health (Walters and Frick, 2000).

Looking at the health and safety effects of work hours, research indicates that shiftworkers experience a broader range of negative health symptoms more frequently and more severely than day workers (Folkard and Lombardi, 2006). There is a large body of evidence indicating that shiftworkers, in general, and nightworkers, in particular, suffer acutely and chronically impaired health and wellbeing, including sleep problems headaches, anxiety, poor concentration, nervousness, mild depression, and mood disturbances, cardiovascular and musculoskeletal problems (Costa, 2003). Shiftwork is also linked with peptic ulcer disease, coronary heart disease and compromised pregnancy outcome (see Knutsson, 2003 for a review of this research).

Changes in industry and occupation distribution

The last three decades have seen marked intersectoral shifts in employment with, for example, a significant decline in the proportion of the workforce employed in traditional, physically demanding sectors such as manufacturing, forestry mining and construction and a growth in the helping profession and service industries such as hospitality, health, education and tourism, finance and information services (Takala, 2005). Using the UK as an example, 1.6 million new jobs were created in business and miscellaneous services in 2001 while 795,000 jobs were lost in primary industries, utilities and manufacturing (Institute for Employment Research, 2001). Primary industries and manufacturing are expected to account for less than 14 per cent of total employment in England by 2010 while business and miscellaneous services are expected to account for over 30 per cent.

Implications for health and safety

The changing nature of work and employment has brought a changing pattern of occupational injury and ill-health. For example, as a result of developments in production and employment patterns, the nature of the hazards faced by workers today has changed. While this has resulted in a reduction in the number of work related health problems in some industries, many problems have migrated to the other sectors, albeit in another form and new risks – such as repetitive strain injuries, exposure to new biological and chemical agents and radiation – have emerged.

Evidence indicates that the last two decades, have seen a favourable decline in fatal accident trends in industrialised countries due, in part, to the change in patterns of employment described above, most notably the shift out of manufacturing. Even within these traditionally hazardous industries, however, changes in production and management techniques have resulted in changes in patterns of occupational injury and disease. Automation in general is a common feature of working life with over two thirds of all workers now using a computer in their daily work (Parent-Thirion et al., 2006). As a result patterns for injury have shifted towards musculoskeletal disorders such as backache, muscular pains in the neck and shoulders. These disorders arise as a result of a combination of interrelated factors, including workstation design, work organisation, job content and working time patterns.

Work in the new areas of employment also differs from work in more traditional industries in that the pace and intensity of work is determined by human demands from clients, passengers, patients and colleagues rather than machinery and production targets (see Parent-Thirion et al., 2006). As a consequence, injury and disease patterns have shifted towards psychosocial or mental health and well-being problems such as occupational stress and anxiety. Violence and harassment at work and its negative impact on psychological well-being is also now recognised as an emerging epidemic in most industrialised countries (Peterson and Mayhew, 2005).

Changes to workforce demographics

Workforce demographics have changed significantly in the last 30 years. Of particular importance for OHS is an ageing of the workforce, a long-term increase in female participation rates and changes to the youth labour market.

In many ways this group of changes is interrelated with changes in work arrangements and industry and occupation distribution as the growth in these areas has depended on increasing participation from groups that have traditionally played only a minor part in the labour force. For example, the growth of temporary and part-time work has depended on increasing female participation in the workforce. Although part-time employment has always been a possibility, it developed in the 1960s as a response to labour shortages and the need to conscript women who had child-care responsibilities. It developed particularly in the new service industries where temporal patterns of demand made part-time employment a cost-effective option for employers. The strategy was very successful with, for example, participation rates for married women increasing from 33 per cent in 1971 to 59 per cent in 2003 (ABS, 1972, 2003a). On average, women now make up about 42 per cent of the estimated global paid working population (WHO, 2004) and are expected to fill over 65 per cent of all newly created jobs over the period to 2010 (Institute of Employment Research, 2003).

Looking at young people, the picture is much the same. The growth in service industries has largely been filled by young workers who are willing to accept casual part-time employment scheduled outside traditional daytime work hours. (Campbell and Burgess 1997: 27; Brooks and Davis, 1996: 153). Looking at the Australian example, labour force participation rates for teenagers have increased by nearly 10 per cent in the last three decades to 61 per cent in 2003 and the rates for males and females have become almost equal (ABS, 2003b). This increase is entirely in the part-time and casual labour force where nonstandard work hours have become the norm. Indeed, the percentage of teenagers with a casual job in Australia has doubled since 1984 (Campbell and Burgess, 2001) and participation rates for 15–19 year-olds in the part-time labour force have increased from 5 per cent in 1971 to 41 per cent, while the full-time participation rate has fallen from 49 per cent to 21 per cent (ABS, 1971; 2003b). A similar pattern can be found in most industrialised countries (see Mayhew, 2005).

The position of older workers in the labour force is somewhat different. Owing to demographic changes, changes in industrial relations policies and advances in health care, these workers are now making up a larger share of the labour force across a wider spread of industries and occupations (Green, 2003). Although some countries have seen an average lowering of retirement age, other countries are increasing the age of retirement and encouraging experienced workers to continue in their employment. Workers aged 60 years or more now comprise over 5 per cent of the labour force; the number of older workers increases threefold if workers aged 50–59 are included (Takala, 2005). This trend is expected to continue in industrialised and developing countries over the coming decade at an increasing rate (WHO, 2004).

Implications for health and safety

Research has identified marked health and injury differences amongst workers based on age and gender. For example, the increased labour force participation of adolescents is coupled with a growing realisation of their vulnerability in the labour market. It is commonly accepted in the literature that young people are an especially high-risk group in terms of occupational injury and disease, with some research indicating that they are at the highest risk of lost time injuries compared to all other workers (Dupre, 2000). There is also evidence that workers over 65 years-old are more at risk of accident and injury, especially males in these age groups (Leigh et al., 2006; Takala, 2005). Furthermore, some groups of older workers, particularly those that work on shifts or at night, have greater ill-health symptoms such as gastrointestinal and sleep problems (Tepas et al., 1993).

Looking at gender differences, women and men generally report different physical and psychological stressors such as repetitive work, heavy lifting and monotony (WHO, 2004). Further, owing to their physical makeup women report gender specific problems such as miscarriages, low birth weight and malformations arising from exposure to pesticides, solvents and organic pollutants, heavy workload, postural factors and shift work (WHO, 2004).

Younger workers and females also report different patterns of occupational injury as a result of the generally narrow industry sub-groups that they work in. For instance, in youths, work with deep fryers resulted in a substantial number of severe burns in the fast food industry. Similarly, a large proportion of workers are employed in services, particularly health care and as such they are disproportionably exposed to risks of infection (including needle-stick injuries), violence, musculoskeletal injuries and burnout (Forastieri, 2000; WHO, 2004). Women also suffer discrimination, mobbing and harassment more often than men, especially if they enter non-traditional occupations (WHO, 2004).

The causes for these different patterns of injury and illness are varied. Explanations for adolescents generally centre on organisational and individual factors related to the physical and psychological development of adolescents and the type of work they perform. Looking at developmental factors, adolescents tend to have higher risk taking behaviour and less job experience than adults and they generally use equipment designed for adult proportions (Knight et al., 1995;

Loughlin and Frone, 2004). The causes for these increases amongst older workers usually involve a combination of psychophysical, psychosocial and stress-related factors, as well as muscular-skeletal and other ageing factors (Takala, 2005). By far the most persuasive explanation for young workers and female workers relates to their precarious position in the labour force. As mentioned, women and youths are concentrated in part time and casual positions and as such they disproportionably suffer from growing competitive pressures, limited possibilities for training and promotion, and inadequate social benefits (e.g. sick leave and holiday leave) (Knight et al., 1995; Takala, 2005).

Summary

This section has outlined global changes affecting the incidence and severity of injuries, diseases and fatalities in modern workplaces. These changes have been brought about by change in labour markets and work organisation driven by globalisation and developments in communication technologies. The employment shifts discussed are expected to increase and become more widespread in the future. Although some positive developments have occurred, particularly in traditionally hazardous industries, there is a large and compelling body of evidence that many modern work arrangements pose a serious threat to the maintenance of existing standards of OHS and present major challenges for OHS management and regulation.

It must be noted, however that the changes discussed have not happened to all groups in the labour market to the same extent and at the same time. As mentioned throughout the section, employment changes vary by country, by gender, by age, by sector and by industry, with particularly adverse consequences for vulnerable groups in the labour force such as women and young people. For example in some countries, such as The US, Australia, France and Spain, there has been a significant increase in temporary employment among young workers brought about by the expansion of work in service industries. Indeed, fast food employs more young people in Australia and the US than any other industry. Looking at male workers, the decline in full-time employment has impacted mostly on this group; their jobs have largely been replaced with temporary and part-time workers which have been filled disproportionately by female workers. At the same time men have traditionally occupied the more hazardous jobs in traditional industries (up to 86 per cent in high income countries) so the shift to more serviced based employment has had a beneficial impact on the instance of occupational deaths amongst this group (Takala, 2005).

Although changes to working and production techniques have occurred on a reasonably global scale, countries have responded to the changes in very different ways. In some instances compliance with international standards, including OHS management (OHSM) standards that are increasingly demanded by supply chain partners and governments alike, have resulted in similar working conditions and outcomes for health and safety management across country borders. In other instances, however, different ideological values of government officials, unions, employers, corporations, scientific experts and agencies and power relationships between them have resulted in very different regulatory frameworks for managing OHS. The rest of this chapter is directed at exploring these frameworks. Traditional models for managing OHS are briefly examined first before moving on to key features of OHS statutes and provisions for worker involvement in the advanced market economies.

REGULATORY DEVELOPMENTS AND RESPONSES TO THE CHANGING WORLD OF WORK

It is generally accepted that the first attempt to regulate health and safety at work is to be found in the early nineteenth century British Factories Acts, beginning with *Health and Morals of Apprentices Act* 1802, *An Act for the Regulation of Cotton Mills and Factories* 1819 (amended in 1825 and 1831), *Factory Regulation Act* 1833 and the *Factories Amendment Act* 1844. While the earlier statutes were principally concerned with regulating the length of the working day for children and young people, the 1844 Act introduced, for the first time, minimum safety standards and the 'traditional model' of OHS regulation. This traditional model relied upon detailed, highly technical specification standards, principally focused on specifying safeguards for dangerous machinery. It was enforced by an independent state inspectorate vested with broad inspection powers, and relying on negotiated compliance utilising informal enforcement methods (advice, education and persuasion), coupled with formal prosecution using the criminal law in the last resort. The great advantage of this traditional specification standard approach was that duty holders knew exactly what to do, and OHS inspectorates found the legislation relatively easy to enforce.

In the second half of the nineteenth century and the beginning of the twentieth, this model of OHS regulation was adopted not only in the various British colonies, but in most of Europe, north America, and in other parts of the world. The weaknesses of this traditional approach are now well known. It frequently resulted in a mass of detailed and technical rules, often difficult to understand, and difficult to keep up to date. Standards were developed *ad hoc* to resolve problems as they arose, and concentrated mainly on factory-based physical hazards, resulting in uneven coverage across workplaces. Specification standards did not encourage or even enable employers to be innovative and to look for cheaper or more cost-efficient solutions. They also ignored the now well accepted view that many hazards do not arise from the static features of the workplace, but from the way work is organised. The traditional factory legislation created a climate of dependence on state regulation, with little involvement in OHS by workers and unions.

By the late 1960s, the weaknesses in this traditional model, based as it was on the British model, coupled with political and economic developments, created a policy environment in which the recommendations of the 1972 British Robens Report appeared attractive. The report proposed a modification of the regulatory model, based on two principal objectives, each of which responded to the criticisms of the traditional model.

The first was the streamlining of the state's role in the traditional regulatory system, through the 'creation of a more unified and integrated system' (Robens Report, para 41). This involved bringing together all of the OHS legislation into one umbrella statute, containing broad 'general duties' covering a range of parties affecting workplace health and safety, including employers, the self-employed, occupiers, manufacturers, suppliers, and designers of plant and substances and employees. The skeleton statutory general duties were to be 'fleshed out' with standards in regulations and codes of practice. A unified OHS inspectorate was to have new administrative sanctions (improvement and prohibition notices) to supplement prosecution. Prosecutions were to be brought against corporate officers, as well as against the corporate employer.

The second objective, recognising the practical limitations of external state regulation, was the creation of 'a more effectively self-regulating system' (Robens Report, para 41). In the Robens vision, self-regulation involves workers and management, at workplace level, working together to achieve, and improve upon, the OHS standards specified by the state. The most important element in the Robens' model of self-regulation was that 'there should be a statutory duty on every employer to consult with … employees or their representatives at the workplace on measures for promoting safety and health at work, and to provide for the participation of employees in the development of such measures' (Robens Report, para 70). The principal vehicle for employee representation was to be the health and safety representative, who was, in the pure Robens model, to be consulted by employers. Employees were also to be represented on health and safety committees. The Robens model also envisaged greater co-operation between the OHS inspectorate and employee representatives, an obligation upon employers to develop OHS policies and rules, and a requirement for Boards of Directors to lodge prescribed OHS information with corporate regulators.

The so-called 'Robens model' and variations on that model were adopted in the UK in 1974, and in other countries, particularly Australia and Canada from the late 1970s and the 1980s. In both Australia and Canada, for constitutional reasons, OHS regulation is principally the concern of the states and territories in Australia (although there is a federal statute covering federal government employees), and the provinces in Canada. In the United States until 1970 OHS was regulated at state level. In 1970 Congress used its powers to regulate interstate trade and commerce to enact the *Occupational Safety and Health Act* 1970. The Act is a form of co-operative federalism, in which standards are largely set by the federal government, and responsibility for administering the standards is delegated to the states. In Sweden, the new style regulatory model was to be found in the *Work Environment Act* 1977 and in Denmark in the *Working Environment Act* 1975.

An important development, particularly on OHS regulation in Europe, has been a series of European Community (EC) directives on OHS since 1989, which are now required to be introduced into the domestic law of community members. Directives bind member states as to the result to be achieved, but leave to each national authority the choice of form and methods. Most important is the 1989 Framework Directive for the *Introduction of Measures to Encourage Improvements in Safety and Health of Workers* which sought to improve and harmonise the conditions of health and safety for European workers, and establishes OHS principles to be followed by employers. The key provisions of the Directive impose a duty on employers: 'to ensure the health and safety of workers in every aspect related to the work' (article 5(1)); and 'to take the measures necessary for the safety and health protection of workers, including prevention of occupational risks and provision of information and training, as well as provision of the necessary organisation and means' (art 6(1)). Article 6 sets out a series of important principles of prevention, which include (art 6(2)) '(a) avoiding risks; (b) evaluating the risks that cannot be avoided; (c) combating the risk at source; (d) adapting the work to the individual …; (g) developing a coherent overall prevention policy which covers technology, organisation of work, working conditions, social relationships and the influence of factors related to the working environment' and '(g) giving collective protective measures priority over individual protective measures.' Article 6(3) requires the employer to 'evaluate the risks to the safety and health of workers inter alia in the choice of work equipment, the chemical substances or preparations used, and the fitting out of workplaces', and then, 'subsequent to this evaluation and as necessary, the preventive measures and the working and production methods implemented by the employer must:

- assure the improvement in the level of protection afforded to workers with regards to safety and health,
- be integrated into all the activities of the undertaking and/or establishment and at all hierarchical levels.'

Further, Article 7 requires the employer to designate one or more workers to carry out these preventive functions, and, if there are no competent personnel, the employer must enlist competent external services or persons. Article 9 requires the employer to be in possession of an assessment of the risks to safety and health at work and to decide on the protective measures to be taken. Article 11 requires employers to consult workers and/or their representatives and to allow them to take part in discussion in relation to all areas of OHS.

As Walters and Jensen (2000, 87) observe, the provisions of the Directive supplement:

> Legislative strategies for the regulation and control of the work environment (i.e. specifications and performance standards) with active intervention of legislative measures in processes which had been previously assumed to be within the prerogative of management (i.e. systems based standards). Also implied in this approach is a relationship between effective prevention strategies on health and safety in enterprises and the wider issue of the control of quality in all aspects of the management of work. It may also imply a closer relationship between health and safety management (traditionally a fairly peripheral issue) and the management of quality – normally central to the concern of management.

Developments in OHS standard setting

The new OHS statutes notably impose broad ranging general duties on employers, covering all workplaces (although there are some exceptions for industries regulated by other statutes, such as aviation, fishing and shipping in Denmark and mining in some Australian states), in contrast to the traditional approach which focused only on designated premises (such as factories), processes or activities.

In the US, the OSH Act 1970 imposes a specific duty on employers to comply with a myriad of detailed occupational safety and health standards promulgated under the Act. In all cases not covered by specific standards, employers must comply with the OSH Act's 'general duty' clause (section 5(a)(1) which requires that each employer 'furnish … a place of employment which [is] free from recognised hazards that are causing or are likely to cause death or serious physical harm to his employees. Self-employed persons (who might be contractors or subcontractors) neither have duties imposed upon them, nor are they protected by the employer's duty. Since 1993 there have been various unsuccessful attempts to introduce a requirement that all employers provide a written safety and health programme, the purpose of which would be to identify and control hazards

before injury or illness occurred. Nevertheless health and safety programs are required in some OSHA standards, most notably the construction industry.

The general duty provisions are better developed in the UK, Scandinavian and Australian OHS statutes. The *Health and Safety at Work Act* 1974 (UK) and the Australian OHS statutes impose broad ranging general duties on employers and employees, and also on a wide range of other parties, such as self-employed persons, persons in control of workplaces, manufacturers, suppliers and importers of plant and substances, and designers, installers and erectors of plant. The duties are usually qualified in that duty holders need only implement reasonably practicable measures. The great benefit of this formulation of the duty is that they cover all sources and types of risks, from physical to psycho-social. Recent judicial interpretations of the general duties emphasise that they require a duty holder to take positive, proactive, comprehensive and systematic steps to search for and eliminate any possible areas of risk to OHS, which some commentators suggest requires a risk management approach (see Bluff and Johnstone, 2005: 212–214). In any event, duties to take proactive risk management approaches are amplified in regulations (see, for example, the *Management of Health and Safety at Work Regulations* 1992 (UK)) and codes of practice under all of these statutes, most of which contain general requirements for risk management; and all have hazard specific provisions.

The Swedish *Work Environment Act* 1977, amended in the early 1990s in response to the EU framework directive, states OHS standards very broadly and with considerable sophistication, and is essentially 'framework' legislation in that it sets goals and outlines systems and techniques and allocates responsibilities in general terms for the working environment. It is notable for its focus on the broader working environment, and the emphasis on systematic OHS management. It also illustrates a common Scandinavian regulatory provision: that of requiring an employer to engage an occupational health service. Chapter 2 of the Act, for example, specifies in section 1 that:

> The working environment shall be satisfactory with regard to the nature of the work and social and technical progress in the community. ... Working conditions shall be adapted to people's differing physical and mental aptitudes. The employee shall be given the opportunity of participating in the design of his own working situation and in processes of change and development affecting his own work. Technology, work organisation and job content shall be designed in such a way that the employee is not subjected to physical or mental strains which can lead to ill-health or accidents. Forms of remuneration and the distribution of working hours shall also be taken into account in this connection. Closely controlled or restricted work shall be avoided or limited. Efforts shall be made to ensure that work provides opportunities of variety, social contact and co-operation, as well as coherence between different tasks. Furthermore, efforts shall be made to ensure that working conditions provide opportunities for personal and vocational development, as well as for self-determination and professional responsibility.

Part 3 of the Act sets out general obligations, which include requiring the employer and employee to 'co-operate to establish a good working environment'. Further (sections 2 and 2a):

> The employer shall take all the precautions necessary to prevent the employee from being exposed to health hazards or accident risks. One basic principle in this connection shall be for everything capable of leading to ill-health or accidents to be altered or replaced in such a way that the risk of ill-health or accidents is eliminated.
>
> The employer shall systematically plan, direct and control activities in a manner which leads to the working environment meeting the requirements for a good work environment. ...
>
> To the extent which the activity requires, the employer shall document the working environment and measures to improve the same. Action plans shall be drawn up in this connection. ...

Regulations (ordinances) may be promulgated to specify in more detail what is required of employers or others under the Act.

The 1977 Act (Part 3 section 2b) requires employers to 'be responsible for the availability of the occupational health services which the working conditions require'. An occupational health service is 'an independent expert resource' in relation to the 'working environment and rehabilitation', which works 'for the prevention and elimination of health risks at workplaces', and has 'the competence to identify and describe connections between the working environment, organisation, productivity and health'. The cost of the occupational health service is born by employers.

The Danish *Working Environment Act* 1975 imposes broad duties on employers to ensure safe and healthy working conditions, and to ensure that work is performed safely and without risks to health. Since 1997 the Act has institutionalised systematic OHS management in the form of workplace assessments – as required by the EU Directive. Section 15a of the Act now provides that:

> (1) The employer shall ensure the preparation of a written workplace assessment of the safety and health conditions at the workplace, taking due regard to the nature of the work, the work methods and work processes which are applied, as well as the size and organisation of the enterprise. The workplace assessment shall remain at the enterprise and be available to the management and employees at the enterprise, as well as the Danish Working Environment Authority. A workplace assessment shall be revised when there are changes in work, work methods, work processes, etc., and these changes are significant for safety and health at work. The workplace assessment shall be revised at least every three years.

The 1975 Act also obliges employers engaged in hazardous work and in other specified industries to participate in occupational health services, a local and private system which operates at three levels to provide individual company services, industry-wide services and services for local centres.

The UK and Australian statutes are also notable in extending the duty of the employer and self-employed person to cover persons who are not employees. Many of these provisions (including the those in the UK, Victoria and Queensland) are so broadly drafted that they afford protection to all kinds of workers (including contractors, sub-contractors, labour hire workers and outworkers), howsoever engaged (see Johnstone, 1999, 2006). These provisions have the potential to protect contractors and their employees, temporary workers, workers in supply chain arrangements, and other kinds of contingent and precarious workers (see, for example, James et al., 2007)

As workers bear the brunt of failure to manage OHS, and because they are likely to have first hand knowledge of hazards, and ways of abating them, there are ethical and practical reasons to ensure that workers are engaged in participatory mechanisms. Most statutes have provisions to ensure this participation at varying levels. These provisions are considered in the following section.

Worker participation in OHS

A growing body of evidence demonstrates the positive benefits of worker participation in OHS (for a summary see Walters and Frick, 2000; Nichols et al., 2004), including a relationship between objective indicators of OHS performance (such as injury rates or hazard exposures) in workplaces where structures of worker representation are in place (union presence, joint safety committees or worker/union safety representatives). This evidence comes from many countries, including those where participatory mechanisms are not mandated by legislation. Further, evidence suggests participatory mechanisms with higher levels of worker involvement are superior to those where involvement is more circumscribed. The OHS statutes in most countries recognise that workers, as the group most affected by workplace hazards, have an important contribution to make to systematic OHS management by identifying workplace hazards, being consulted over workplace changes affecting OHS, receiving OHS information, working with employers and regulators to implement OHS programs, and, when necessary, to take direct action to protect themselves from danger.

As noted above, the UK Robens Report emphasised the importance of worker involvement in dispelling workplace apathy.

The UK *Health and Safety at Work Act* 1974 provides for the participation of employees in OHS through the institutions of health and safety representatives and health and safety committees. Regulations made under the Act give health and safety representatives the right to investigate dangerous hazards and occurrences, to investigate worker complaints, to make representations to employers, to represent employers in consultations with inspectors, to receive information from inspectors, to attend meetings of safety committees, and to receive paid time off for training and to perform other functions. Employers are required to establish a health and safety committee within three months of being requested to do so.

The Australian provisions for workplace participation are based on the UK provisions, but in some of the states, the powers given to health and safety representatives are much stronger than those vested in the UK, and resemble the powers given to Swedish safety delegates (see below). In all jurisdictions but the Northern Territory, the OHS statutes make provision for worker elected health and safety representatives. In Victoria, South Australia, the Commonwealth and the Australian Capital Territory, the powers given to representatives are quite broad, and include rights to training inspection, consultation information and similar issues. They include the power to issue a provisional improvement notice (a default notice in South Australia), and the right to direct that direct work cease (though the provisions vary between the jurisdictions). Western Australia, Queensland and Tasmania give much weaker consultative powers to representatives. The Tasmanian and Northern Territory statutes codify the common law right of a worker to refuse to perform dangerous work. Each of the statutes provides for health and safety committees, comprised of employer and employee representatives.

The Scandinavian countries have gone further in involving workers directly in decision-making processes. The 1977 *Swedish Work Environment Act* provides that worker control is a critical aspect of a healthy working environment. Employee safety delegates are elected for a period of three years by local unions (and in non-union workplaces, by employees) at workplaces with five or more employees. Larger workplaces have a number of safety delegates, one of whom is elected as a chief safety delegate. Unlike UK safety representatives, Swedish safety delegates have the right to stop dangerous work process pending an investigation by an inspector. They also have the right to participate in the planning of new premises, devices, work processes, work methods and the use of substances liable to cause ill health or injuries. Employers must inform delegates of any changes which will have a significant impact on conditions in the areas they represent. Employers must respond to representations by delegates without delay, and if matters are not resolved satisfactorily, they can be referred to an inspector or joint employer-employee health and safety committee. The local trade union may appoint a regional safety representative (RSR) in firms with less than 50 workers where there is at least one trade union member. The RSRs have rights of access to such workplaces and similar rights to investigation and inspection to those held by ordinary safety delegates in Sweden. The mandated RSRs tasks include acting as itinerant representatives who inspect and investigate OHS conditions in small enterprises, and request changes they consider necessary to achieve improvements in the working environment; promoting employee participation in OHS, including the recruitment, training and support of in-house HSRs; and activating local OHS work, within the overall framework for systematic management of the working environment in small enterprises. The situation in Denmark is substantially similar to the Swedish position (see Gunningham and Johnstone, 1999: 355–8).

In the US there is little scope under the occupational safety and health legislation for workers to be involved at workplace level, although there is nothing to prevent workers raising OHS issues in the broader context of collective bargaining.

Ensuring that workers are afforded the protection offered by the statutes described above, as well as the opportunity to participate in decisions that affect their health and safety at work, requires inspection and enforcement. The varying approaches taken to workplace inspections and enforcement of OHS statutes are examined in the following section.

OHS inspection and enforcement

In most countries, the OHS statute establishes an OHS inspectorate, and vests that inspectorate with broad powers to enter workplaces and to inspect workplaces, plant, equipment and substances. Historically, inspection has focused mainly on the examination of plant and other physical artefacts in the workplace. In recent years, however, with OHS standards increasingly requiring duty holders to take a systematic approach to OHS management, inspectors in some jurisdictions have attempted to examine how employers manage OHS instead of, or in addition to, the inspection of the physical workplace. As Von Richthofen (2002: 205) notes, the 'traditional approach whereby inspectors aimed simply to identify legal irregularities and then give advice or impose sanctions, depending on the seriousness of the offence, is increasingly discredited'. The challenge for contemporary OHS inspectorates is to change their inspection and enforcement approaches to inspect systematic OHS management. In this approach, the traditional focus on hazardous conditions and work practices is not abandoned but provides signals of weaknesses in OHS management to be uncovered, and is part of the 'evidence' of the effectiveness of OHS management. Further, the inspectorates not only have to inspect workplaces but also to develop strategies to motivate duty holders to develop their approaches to systematic OHSM, using not only threats of sanctions, but also the commercial self-interest of management, and by demonstrating the efficiency and effectiveness of the OHSM approach (Von Richthofen, 2002: 208).

This has raised at least two issues for OHS inspectorates. How should an OHS inspector go about inspecting the quality of an organisation's systematic OHS management? How can inspectors use diagnoses of the quality of a firm's OHSM to ensure that 'good' firms with sound OHSM systems are left to self-regulate, and 'poor' performers receive greater attention from the regulator?

The answer to the first question is that OHS inspectorates will need to learn how to conduct effective 'systems audits'. The literature (see, for example, Waring, 1996: 178–182; Parker, 2003: 13; Bluff, 2003) suggests that 'an effective auditor' would do more than look at the 'paper systems' developed by an organisation. The auditor should adopt a triangulated approach to data collection (Waring, 1996: 178–182; Parker, 2003: 13; Bluff, 2003) which involves (Bluff, 2003):

> Interviews with a representative sample of managers, supervisors and workers, observation of conditions and activities, and examination of supporting documentation, including key procedures and records of developmental and preventive action (for example, training needs analysis, plans and records of competencies achieved, action plans, design and procurement standards, committee minutes, work procedures, and so on).

There is evidence that such approaches are being taken in some European countries and North America to adapt OHS inspection programs to accommodate and encourage duty holders to implement systematic OHSM (see Larsson, 1996; Gunningham and Johnstone, 1999: 107–111, 149–51, 378–82; Karageorgiou et al., 2000: 274–80; Hedegaard Riis and Jensen, 2002; Jensen, 2003; Popma et al., 2002; Frick, 2002; Von Richthofen, 2002: 189–208).

The answer to the second question begins by conceiving of the inspectorate as the 'overseer of the company's own efforts to regulate' (Hutter, 2001: 305). To do this, the inspector needs to identify the firm's level of compliance and self-regulation, and then adjust its enforcement response to the level of effective self-regulation, so that the inspector has a high degree of involvement in the early stages of compliance, and

gradually reduces, and changes, her role. Such approaches have been used in many countries, most notably the Swedish Work Environment Management (SWEM) inspection approach (see Brun, 2006), the Danish model of Adapted Inspection (see Jensen and Jensen, 2004), and US OSHA's 'Focused Inspection' in the construction industry (see Gunningham and Johnstone, 1999; Needleman, 2000).

In the UK, Australia, Sweden and Denmark, OHS inspectorates have powers to impose administrative sanctions. In the UK and Australia inspectors can issue improvement notices (requiring a hazard to be remedied within a specified time) and prohibition notices (requiring work to cease until the hazard is removed)) and can prosecute offenders for contraventions of the OHS statute. In some Australian jurisdictions (for example New South Wales, Queensland, Tasmania, the ACT and the Northern Territory) inspectors can also issue infringement notices ('on-the-spot' fines). Some of the Australian OHS statutes offer defendants the possibility of negotiating an enforceable undertaking with the prosecuting authority. Enforceable undertakings have been included in the OHS statutes in Victoria, Queensland, Tasmania, the ACT and the Commonwealth statute. Essentially these provisions empower the inspectorate to accept from a person a written undertaking about remedial measures in connection with a contravention of the OHS Act. If the inspectorate can prove that the person has contravened any of the terms of the undertaking, a court may make appropriate orders, which might include directing the person to comply with the terms of the undertaking; and/or ordering the person to compensate any other person who has suffered loss or damage as a result of the contravention. Prosecution is available in most OHS statutes for serious contraventions. The level of penalties that can be imposed for a successful prosecution vary considerably from country to country, with maximum fines being relatively low in Scandinavia and the rest of continental Europe, and higher in some of the Australian states. Some Australian jurisdictions are exploring sanctions beyond the fine. New sanctions include:

- adverse publicity court orders, in which the court orders the convicted defendant to publicise the offence, conviction and penalty (New South Wales, Victoria, South Australia, and the ACT);
- a court order that the offender participate in an OHS-related project (New South Wales, Victoria and South Australia);
- an order requiring the defendant to take remedial measures (New South Wales and the ACT) or to undertake training (South Australia);
- upon proof of the offences, the court adjourning the case with or without conviction and requiring the defendant to give an undertaking not to re-offend within two years and to engage a consultant, develop systematic OHS management, and have the OHS management approach monitored by a third party (Victoria). The Western Australian Act offers defendants the option of substituting an undertaking for a fine, when convicted of specific relatively minor offences. The undertaking might include undertaking to take steps to improve OHS at the workplace or other parts of the defendant's business; publicising the offence; remedying the offence; or undertaking an OHS project.

Inspectors in Europe and Australia have a broad discretion as to the enforcement action they will take when contraventions are detected. There has been a longstanding debate regarding the role of the inspectorate in maximising compliance with OHS statutory standards: is the best way to *advise* and *persuade* employers to comply with standards or to *punish* them for not doing so (the 'deterrence strategy') (see, for example, Hutter 1997; Hawkins 2002)? The 'advise and persuade' model is centrally concerned with achieving the goals of the regulatory system and to prevent rather than to punish contraventions. It essentially relies on persuasion to achieve compliance, and emphasises cooperation rather than confrontation, and conciliation and negotiation rather than coercion. The threat of enforcement remains in the background, to be used where all other strategies fail. There is, however, little, if any, empirical evidence showing that the 'advise and persuade' model on its own does indeed reduce workplace injury and disease.

The argument for punishment relies on the classical deterrence model, which argues that regulated organisations are profit-driven rational actors which will comply with a regulatory provision when they judge that the benefits of compliance (including avoiding fines or other sanctions) exceed the costs of compliance. The punish or deterrence strategy emphasises a confrontational style of enforcement and the sanctioning of rule-breaking behaviour. Future compliance with the rule may be a by-product of enforcement action, but it is not its central purpose. Critics argue that a punishment orientated approach is essentially reactive (Sparrow, 2000: 182–5). With most crimes, this means that prosecution takes place once the damage has been done (although this is not necessarily so for 'inchoate' OHS offences, which require safe systems of work). Further, it is often argued that punishment-based approaches can trigger a culture of regulatory resistance amongst some employers, and rely too heavily on the state to enforce the law, rather than helping people to comply.

The dominance of the advice and persuasion approach, at least in relation to OHS, was established in the mid-nineteenth century in Great Britain and in Australia from the 1870s. Recently, in Australia, there is evidence that OHS regulators in some states have taken a stronger approach to prosecution, but it is still the case that most enforcement action involves informal advice and persuasion, and, to a lesser extent, the use of administrative sanctions.

The approach to enforcement in the United States differs significantly from the European and Australian approach. Whereas inspectors in Europe and Australia have discretion as to the enforcement measures they may take, Occupational Safety and Health Administration inspectors (called 'compliance officers') have little discretion, and in most cases are required to take some formal action when non-compliance is detected. Inspectors must report violations to the Area Director, who decides whether to issue a citation. Citations describe the specific nature of the violation and lay down a specified time for abatement of the condition specified in the citation. Within a reasonable time after the citation, the Secretary of Labor must notify the employer of proposed penalties for the violation. If the employer does not contest the violation or penalty, it becomes final. The OSH Act provides for a range of penalties for different sorts of violation, although the level of penalties is low (averaging under $1,000) when compared to penalties in Australia and the UK. Criminal prosecutions for violations are relatively rare.

OHS regulation in developing countries

The description above of developments in OHS regulation in Europe, North America and Australia focuses on issues at the forefront of debates about OHS regulation in industrialised countries. While much progress has been made in OHS regulation in industrialised countries, those countries face challenges rarely found in the developed countries, and obstacles which have impeded progress on improving OHS in Africa, South America and parts of Asia (World Health Organization Regional Office for Africa, 2005). OHS in these countries are often competing with other priorities – such as poverty alleviation, HIV/AIDS and water and sanitation issues (see Gutierrez 2000). OHS regulatory measures are sometimes undermined by inadequate levels of education and the consequences of globalisation – social and gender inequality, persistent poverty, threats to peace and security, deregulation and reduced state intervention in the economy, and shifting dangerous machinery, substances and work from industrialised to developing countries (World Health Organization Regional Office for Africa, 2005). One consequence is that OHS regulatory regimes in developing countries are often focused on fundamental hazards like dangerous machinery and hazardous substances, so that issues arising from work organisation, such as stress and other psychosocial hazards receive little, if any, attention (GOHNET Newsletter, 2007).

A further complexity for OHS regulation in developing countries is the rapid expansion of the informal economy, where economic activity is not recognised or protected by state authorities. Current estimates suggest that the informal economy both in South America and in India represent 60 per cent of national income, and in some parts of Africa it is as high as 95 per cent; and of the 88 million women workers in India, only 4.5 million work in the organised sector (GOHNET Newsletter, 2007: 5). Workers in the informal economy are generally not protected by OHS standards and social protection programs such as unemployment benefits or health insurance coverage (Gutierrez 2000) – even though these informal sector workers are often the outsourced workers of large internal and local enterprises (GOHNET Newsletter, 2007: 5).

Globalisation has also spawned new industries in developing countries, some of which are difficult to regulate. One example is the 'export-processing zones' (or 'maliquiladora') representing the assembly industry in Central America (Guttierrez, 2000; Lowenson, 1999; GOHNET Newsletter, 2007: 4). Approximately 90 per cent of workers in this industry are women or children. Work conditions include job instability, temporary contracts and subcontracting, long working hours, unrealistic production quotas and incentives, inadequate restrictions on overtime, low wages and a high incidence of sexual harassment. These conditions lead to excessive injuries to workers from dangerous machinery, and ill-health from dust, noise, inadequate ventilation, exposure to dangerous chemicals and very intense and stressful work (GOHNET Newsletter, 2007: 4).

In recent years various international and regional programs have been initiated in order to address OHS in developing countries. Examples include the World Health Organization (WHO)/International Labor Organization Joint Effort on Occupational Health and Safety in Africa, the WHO Global Strategy for Occupational Health for All, the WHO Global Plan of Action on Occupational Health

2008–2017, and the Global Network of WHO Collaborating Centres in Occupational Health.

CONCLUSION

The broad developments in the labour market, and in approaches to systematic OHS management canvassed earlier in this chapter, raise significant issues for OHS regulators, which have, to date, not been satisfactorily addressed. OHS regulatory models have tended to focus on requiring 'employers' to ensure the safety of employees. While it is true that the post-Robens reforms, particularly in the UK, Australia and Canada, have cast duties on the self-employed as well as employers, and brought 'persons who are not employees' under the umbrella of protection, regulators have been slow to develop regulations, codes of practice and inspection and enforcement strategies to ensure that the regulatory model covers all forms of business organisation (Johnstone and Wilson, 2006) and all types of workers (Johnstone, 2006). At the same time, provisions for worker participation tend to be crafted to enable 'employees' to elect health and safety representatives, so that workers who are not employees of the employer at the particular workplace are unable to be part of the process (Johnstone et al., 2005). If OHS regulation is to respond adequately to changing forms of business organisation and working relationships, the OHS statutes will need to be recast to regulate all persons involved in a business undertaking in relation to all workers involved in the undertaking, to ensure that all kinds of workers can be involved in participatory structures, and that inspectorates develop inspection programs to reach all forms of work, and all forms of work organisation, including home-based workers.

While, as this chapter shows, there has been a clear trend for regulators to require duty holders to take systematic approaches to OHS management at the workplace, the research evidence (see, for example, Jensen 2002; Saksvik et al., 2003) suggests that business organisations have difficulty engaging with the risk management process and producing good quality OHS outcomes. When faced with the requirement to undertake systematic OHSM, firms, particularly small and medium sized firms (SMEs), tend to focus on already well known problems; take superficial approaches to analysing the issues, generate paperwork rather than preventative action, fail to eliminate or control risks at the source, and are not good at involving workers in all aspects of risk assessment. The research suggests a need for organisational learning and development of a local understanding about work environment risks amongst people at the workplace to equip firms to re-examine established norms and old routines, take a more expansive approach to recognising hazards and risks, and develop and implement higher-order OHS improvements (Jensen 2002; Saksvik et al., 2003). It also suggests that regulators, peak employer organisations and other OHS organisations need to do more to develop the OHS risk management skills of business organisations. There is also little evidence that inspectorates have learned how to inspect the quality of systematic OHS management, as opposed to the OHS of the 'physical' dimensions of the workplace. If these difficulties in fully implementing the regulatory model which institutionalises systematic OHS management are not adequately addressed in the next decade, it may suggest that regulators will need to rethink the regulatory model and abandon the contemporary fascination with systematic OHS management for regulatory standards that SMEs find easier to respond to.

From a human resource management perspective, of course, there is more to OHS than reactive management efforts to ensure minimal compliance with OHS standards (Reason et al., 1998). Recent research has begun to investigate the degree to which job characteristics associated with high performance work systems influence OHS outcomes (Barling et al., 2003). While there is little consistency in the literature as to what constitutes a high performance system, Barling et al. (2003: 277) observe that the literature suggests that there:

> are several factors supporting a link between high-quality work and occupational safety. First, autonomy is a critical aspect of high quality work. But for autonomy to be used successfully, employees must have the required skills, pointing to the importance of higher training. ... Moreover, safety training has been considered an important element of total quality management. ... Second, greater autonomy is also associated with increased participation in decision making, which may lead to better decisions about safety. Third, and perhaps most important, greater job autonomy and control allow individuals over time to focus not just on fault remediation, but also on prevention, which would have a significant impact on safety in the long term.

Barling et al.'s own research (2003) suggests that high quality jobs can affect workplace injury levels directly, because when employees have access to jobs that provide them with autonomy, over time they become more proactive and involved in preventive action. Involvement in high quality work can also have indirect effects on injury levels, because such work results in higher job satisfaction, and 'employees who experience greater levels of job satisfaction work more safely and enjoy greater safety orientation' (Barling et al., 2003: 280). Further research is needed to refine our understanding of which other aspects of high quality work have a significant impact on OHS.

Further, while organisational OHS issues have tended not to be mainstream issues in the management research, one exception is the growing body of research on safety climate – although the literature in this area is still bedevilled by conceptual ambiguity' (Zohar, 2002: 75). There is some research indicating that leadership approaches 'associated with greater concern for group-members' welfare, arising from closer, individualised relationships, promote supervisory safety practices creating higher safety climates, and hence, safer behaviour' (Zohar, 2002: 88) – suggesting that these issues should be further addressed in safety research. These human resource management issues, in turn, pose

challenges to regulators, who will need to develop regulatory approaches which encourage OHS management responses that aspire to achieve far more than 'minimal compliance'.

REFERENCES

Auer, P. (2006) 'Protected mobility for employment and decent work: Labour market security in a globalized world', *Journal of Industrial Relations*, 48 (1): 21–40.

Australian Bureau of Statistics (1972) *1971 Census of Population and Housing: The Labour Force, Australia* (Bulletin 5, Part 9), Canberra (Ref. No. 2.87.9).

Australian Bureau of Statistics (2003a) *Marriages and Divorces, 2003*, Canberra (Cat. No. 3310.0)

Australian Bureau of Statistics (2003b) *The Labour Force, February 2003*, Canberra (Cat. No. 6203.0)

Barling, J., Kelloway, E.K. and Iverson, R.D. (2003) 'High quality work, job satisfaction and occupational injuries', *Journal of Applied Psychology*, 88: 276–83.

Benach, J., Muntaner, C., Benavides, F.G., Amable1, M. and Jodar, P. (2002) 'A new occupational health agenda for a new work environment', *Scandinavian Journal of Work Environment and Health*, 28 (3): 191–6.

Berry, J.O. and Rao, J.M. (1997) 'Balancing employment and fatherhood', *Journal of Family Issues*, 18 (4): 386–402.

Bluff, E. and Johnstone, R. (2005) 'The relationship between reasonably practicable and risk management', *Australian Journal of Labour Law*, 18 (3): 197–239.

Bluff, E. (2003), *Systematic Management of Occupational Health and Safety*, Working Paper 20, National Research Centre for Occupational Health and Safety Regulation, The Australian National University, Canberra.

Bohle, P. and Quinlan, M. (2000) *Managing Occupational Health and Safety: A Multidisciplinary Approach*, Macmillan, Melbourne, 2nd edition, Bolton.

Brewster, C., Mayne, L. and Tregaskis, O. (1997) 'Flexible working in Europe', *Journal of World Business*, 32 (2): 133–51.

Brooks, D.R. and Davis, L.K. (1996) 'Work-related injuries to Massachusetts teens 1987–1990', *Am J Ind Med*, 29 (2): 153–60.

Brun, A. (2006) The inspector's dilemma under regulated self-regulation, Policy and Practice in Health and Safety, vol 4(2), pp. 3–23

Bureau of Labor Statistics (1995) *New Data on Contingent and Alternate Employment, Report 900*, US Department of Labor, Washington DC.

Burgess, J. and de Ruyter, A. (2000a) 'Declining job quality: another cost of unemployment', *Economic and Labour Relations Review*, 11 (2): 246–69.

Burgess, J. and de Ruyter, A. (2000b) 'Job security in Australia: Broadening the analysis', *Australian Journal of Social Issues*, 35 (3): 215–34.

Campbell, I. and Burgess, J. (2001) 'Casual employment in Australia and temporary employment in Europe: Developing a cross national comparison', *Work, Employment and Society*, 15 (1): 171–84.

Campbell, I. and Burgess, J. (1997) *National Patterns of Temporary Employment: The Distinctive Case of Casual Employment in Australia*, NKCIR Working Paper No. 53, Melbourne, NKCIR, Monash University.

CCH OHS Alert 28 and 29 May 2002; 18 February 2004; 29 May 2006.

Costa, G. (2003) 'Shiftwork and occupational medicine: An overview', *Occupational Medicine*, 53 (2): 83–8.

De Grip, A., Hoevenberg, J. and Williams, E. (1997) 'Atypical employment in the European Union', *International Labour Review*, 136 (1): 49–71.

Dupre, D. (2000) 'Accidents at work in the EU' Statistics in Focus: Population and Social Conditions (Catalogue Number: CA–NK–00–004–EN–I), Luxembourg: Eurostat.

Ferrie, J. (1999) 'Health consequences of job insecurity', in Marmot, M., Ferrie, J. and Zilgilo, E. (eds), *Labour Market Changes and Job Insecurity: A Challenge for Social Welfare and Health Promotion*. Copenhagen: World Health Organisation. pp. 59–101.

Fishback, P.V. and Kantor, S.E. (eds) (2000) *A Prelude to the Welfare State: The Origins of Workers' Compensation*. Chicago: University of Chicago Press, pp. xiii, 316.

Folkard, S., and Lombardi, D.A. (2006) 'Modelling the impact of the components of long work hours on injuries and "accidents"', *American Journal of Industrial Medicine*, 49 (11): 953–63.

Forastieri, V. (2000) *Women Workers and Gender Issues on Occupational Safety and Health*. International Labor Office, Geneva. Available from; http://www.ilo.org/public/english/protection/safework/gender/womenwk.htm.

Fragoso, J.L. and Kleemer, B.H. (2005) 'How to distinguish between independent contractors and employees', *Management Research News*, 28 (2/3): 136–49.

Frick, K. (2002) 'Sweden: Occupational Health and Safety Management Strategies from 1970–2001', in Walters, D. (ed.), *Regulating Health and Safety Management in the European Union: A Study of the Dynamics of Change.* Brussels: Peter Lang. pp.211–34.

Gillespie, A., Richardson, R. and Cornford, J. (1995) 'Review of Telework in Britain: Implications for Public Policy'. Report prepared for the Parliamentary Office of Science and Technology, Centre for Urban and Regional Development Studies, University of Newcastle upon Tyne.

GOHNET (2007) Newsletter, Special Issues, The Global Occupational Health Network.

Green, A. (2003) 'Labour market trends, Skill needs and the ageing of the workforce: A challenge for employability?', *Local Economy*, 18 (4): 306–21.

Gunningham, N. and Johnstone, R. (1999) *Regulating Workplace Safety: Systems and Sanctions*, Oxford Socio-legal Series. Oxford: Oxford University Press.

Guttierrez, E. (2000) 'Workers' Health in Latin America and the Caribbean: Looking to the Future', *Perspectives in Health*, 5 (2) (http://www.paho.org/English/DPI/Number10_article1.htm).

Harrington, J.M. (2001) 'Health effects of shift work and extended hours of work', *Journal of Occupational and Environmental Medicine*, 58: 68–72.

Hawkins, K. (2002) *Law as a Last Resort: Prosecution Decision-Making in a Regulatory Agency*. Oxford: Oxford University Press.

Hedegaard Riis, A. and Jensen, P. (2002) 'Denmark: Transforming Risk Assessment to Workplace Assessment', in Walters, D (ed.), *Regulating Health and Safety Management in the European Union: A study of the Dynamics of Change*. Brussels: Peter Lang. pp. 59–80.

Hipple, S. (2001) 'Contingent work in the late-1990s', *Monthly Labor Review*, 124 (3): 3–27.

Hutter, B. (1997) *Compliance: Regulation and Enforcement*. Oxford: OUP.

Hutter, B.M. (2001) *Regulation and Risk: Occupational Health and Safety on the Railways*. Oxford: OUP.

Institute for Employment Research (2001) Projections for qualifications and qualifications: 2000/2001 – regional results, Coventry: DfES/IER, University of Warwick, Coventry.

Institute of Employment Research (2003) *Skills in England*. Coventry: LCS.

James, P. Johnstone, R. Quinlan, M. and Walters, D. (2007) 'Regulating supply chains to improve health and safety', *Industrial law Journal*, 36: 163–87.

Jensen, P. (2002) 'Assessing assessment: the Danish experience of worker participation in risk assessment', *Economic and Industrial Democracy*, 23 (2): 201.

Jensen, P.L. (2003) 'Carrots and Sticks – Inspection Strategies in Denmark', paper prepared for Australian OHS Regulation for the 21st Century Conference, Gold Coast, July, 2003.

Jensen, P.L. and Jensen, J. (2004) Adapted Inspection: An Example of Responsive Enforcement. in Bluff, L., Gunningham, N. and Johnstone, R. (eds), *OHS Regulation for a Changing World of Work*, The Federation Press, Sydney, pp. 179–184.

Johnstone, R. (1999) 'Paradigm crossed? the statutory occupational health and safety obligations of the business undertaking', *Australian Journal of Labour Law*, 12: 73–112.

Johnstone, R. (2006) 'Regulating Occupational Health and Safety in a Changing Labour Market', in Arup, C., Gahan P., Howe J., Johnstone, R., Mitchell, R. and O'Donnell, A. (eds), *Labour Law and Labour Market Regulation*. Sydney: Federation Press, pp. 617–636.

Johnstone, R. Quinlan, M. and Walters, D. (2005) 'Statutory occupational health and safety workplace arrangements for the modern labour market', *Journal of Industrial Relations*, 47: 93–116.

Johnstone, R. and Wilson, T. (2006) 'Take me to your employer: The organisational reach of occupational health and safety regulation', *Australian Journal of Labour Law*, 19: 59–80.

Knight, E., Castillo, D. and Layne, L. (1995) 'A detailed analysis of work related injury among youth treated in emergency departments', *American Journal of Independent Medicine*, 27: 793–805.

Karageorgiou, A., Jensen, P.L., Walters, D.R. and Wilthagen, T. (2000) 'Risk Assessment in Four Members States in the European Union', in Frick, K., Jensen, P., Quinlan, M. and Wilthagen, T. (eds), *Systematic Occupational Health and Safety Management: Perspectives on an International Development*. Amsterdam: Pergamon. pp. 251–84

Knutsson, A. (2003) 'Health disorders of shiftworkers', *Occupational Medicine*, 53 (2): 103–8.

Larsson, T. (1996) *Systems Control Development in Sweden*. A paper presented at the Workshop on Integrated Control/Systems Control, Dublin.

Lee, S., McCann, D. and Messenger, J.C. (2007) Working Time Around the World: Trends in working hours, laws, and policies in a global comparative perspective. London and Geneva: Routledge and ILO.

Leigh, J.P., Waehrer, G., Miller, T.R. and McCurdy, S.A. (2006) 'Costs differences across demographic groups and types of occupational injuries and illnesses', *American Journal of Industrial Medicine*, 49: 845–53.

Levenstein, C. and Wooding, J. (eds) (1997) *Work, Health and Environment. Old Problems, New Solutions*. New York. Guilford press.

Lewchuk, W., de Wolff, A., King, A. and Polanyi, M. (2003) 'From job strain to employment strain: health effects of precarious work', *Just Labour*, 3: 23–35.

Loughlin, C. and Frone, M.R. (2004) 'Young Workers Occupational Safety' in Barling, J. and Frone, M.R. (eds) *The Psychology of Workplace Safety*, Washington: American Psychological Association, pp. 107–27.

Lowe, G. (2001) *The quality of work: A people centred agenda*. Don Mills, Ontario Canada: Oxford University Press.

Lowenson, R. (1999) 'Women's occupational health in globalization and development', *American Journal of industrial Medicine*, 36: 34–42.

Loyd, M. (ed.) (2002) *Occupational health and safety in New Zealand: Contemporary Social research*. Palmerston North: Dunmore Press Limited.

Mayhew, C. (2005) 'Work-related injuries among adolescent and child workers: The non-reported OHS epidemic', in Peterson, C.L. and Mayhew, C. (eds), *Occupational Health and Safety: International influences and the 'new epidemics'*. New York: Baywood Publishing Company, pp. 97–117.

Mirchandani, K. (1998) 'No Longer a Struggle? Teleworkers' Reconstruction of the Work- Non-Work Boundary', in Jackson, P.J. and van der Wielen, J.M. (eds), *Teleworking: International Perspectives, from Telecommuting to the Virtual Organisation*. London: Routledge, pp. 118–35.

Needleman, C. (2000) OSHA at the crossroads: Conflicting frameworks for regulating OHS in the United States. In: Frick K.J.P., Quinlan, M., Wilthagen, T., editors. *Systematic OHS Management: Perspectives on an international development*. Amsterdam, The Netherlands: Elsevier. pp. 67–85.

Nichols, T., Walters, D. and Tasiran, A.C. (2004) 'The Relation between Arrangements for Health and Safety and Injury Rates – The Evidence-Based Case Revisited', School of Social Sciences, Cardiff University, Working Paper Series 48, June 2004.

Parent-Thirion, Agnès, Fernández Macías, Enrique, Hurley, John and Vermeylen, G. (2006), Fourth European survey on working conditions 2005, European Foundation for the Improvement of Living and Working Conditions, Dublin.

Parker, C. (2003) ' "Arm Twisting, Auditing and Accountability": What Regulators and Compliance Professionals should know about the Use of Enforceable Undertaking to Promote Compliance', presentation to the Australian Compliance Institute, Melbourne, 28 May, 2003.

Peterson, C. and Mayhew, C. (eds) (2005) *Occupational Health and Safety: International influences and the 'new epidemics'*. New York: Baywood Publishing Company.

Popma, J., Schaapman, M. and Wilthagen, T. (2002) 'The Netherlands: Implementation within wider regulatory reform', in Walters, D. (ed.), *Regulation Health* and Safety Management in the European Union: A Study of Dynamic Change. Brussells: Peter Lang. pp. 177–209.

Probst, T. (2000) 'Wedded to the job: Moderating effects of job involvement on the consequences of job insecurity', Journal of Occupational Health Psychology, 5 (1): 63–73.

Quinlan, M. and Bohle, P. (2004) 'Contingent work and occupational safety', in Barling, J. and Frone, M.R. (eds.), The Psychology of Workplace Safety. Washington: APA Books, pp. 81–106.

Quinlan, M., Mayhew, C. and Bohle, P. (2001) 'The global expansion of precarious employment, work disorganisation, and consequences for occupational health: A review of recent research', International Journal of Health Services, 31 (2): 335–414.

Reason, J., Parker, D. and Lawton, R. (1998) 'Organizational controls and safety: The varieties of rule-related behaviour', Journal of Occupational and Organizational Psychology, 71: 289–304.

Saksvik, P., Torvatn, H. and Nytrø, K. (2003) 'Systematic occupational health and safety work in Norway: A decade of implementation', Safety Science, 41 (9): 721.

Sparrow, M. (2000) The Regulatory Craft – Controlling Risks, Solving Problems and Managing Compliance. Washington: The Brookings Institutions.

Stout, N.A. and Linn, H.I. (2002) 'Occupational injury prevention research: Progress and priorities', Injury Prevention, 8: 9–14.

Sullivan, C. and Lewis, S. (2006) 'Work at home and the work-family interface', in Jones, F., Burke, R.J. and Westman, M. (eds), Managing the work-home interface: A psychological perspective. London: Psychology Press, pp. 143–62.

Takala, J. (2005) Introductory Report: Decent Work – Safe Work. International Labour Organization. Available from http://www.ilo.org/public/english/protection/safework/wdcongrs17/intrep.pd.

Tepas, D.I., Duchon, J.C. and Gersten, A.H. (1993) 'Shiftwork and the older worker', Experimental Ageing Research, 19: 295–320.

Sverke, M., Hellgren, J. and Naswall, K. (2002) 'No security: A meta-analysis and review of job insecurity and its consequences', Journal of Occupational Health Psychology, 7: 242–64.

Von Richthofen, W. (2002) Labour Inspection: A Guide to the Profession. Geneva: ILO.

Walt, G. (1998) Health Policy. An introduction to process and power. London: Zed Books.

Walters, D. and Frick, K. (2000) 'Worker Participation and the Management of Occupational Health and Safety: Reinforcing or Conflicting Strategies', in Frick, K., Jensen, P.L., Quinlan, M. and Wilthagen, T. (eds), Systematic Occupational Health and Safety Management: Perspectives on an International Development. Amsterdam: Pergamon. pp. 43–65.

Walters, D. and Jensen, P.L. (2000) 'The Discourse and Purpose Behind the Development of the EU Framework Directive', pp. 87–98 in K. Frick et al. (eds) Systematic Occupational Health and Safety Management: Perspectives on an International Development. Oxford: Elsevier.

Walters, D.R. and Lamm, F. (2004) 'OHS in Small Organisations: Some Challenges and Ways Forward', in Bluff, E., Gunningham, N. and Johnstone, R. (eds), OHS Regulation for a Changing World of Work. Australia: Federation Press, pp. 94–120.

Waring, A. (1996) Safety Management Systems. London: Chapman and Hall.

World Health Organization (1995) Global strategy on occupational health for all: The way to health at work. Available from http://www.who.int/occupational_health/publications/globstrategy/en/index.html

World Health Organization (2003) Factsheet no. 84, revised 2003. Occupational Health – Ethically correct, Economically sound.

World Health Organization (2004) Gender, Health and Work. World Health Organization. Available from http://www.who.int/gender/other_health/Gender,HealthandWorklast.pdf

World Health Organization Regional Office for Africa (2005) Implementation of the Resolution of Occupational Health and Safety in the African Region, Meeting Report, World Health Organization Regional Office for Africa.

Zohar, D. (2002) 'The effects of leadership dimensions, safety climate, and assigned priorities on major injuries in work groups', Journal of Organizational Behaviour, 23: 75–92

18

Industrial Relations and Collective Bargaining

Thomas A. Kochan and Greg J. Bamber

What are industrial relations (IR)? The pioneers of the field tended to use the term in a broad and interdisciplinary sense. Then, the term covered the practice and study of all aspects of work and employment. The field has been developed from the work of Fabians Sydney and Beatrice Webb (1894, 1897) in Britain and institutional economists such as John R. Commons (1909, 1934) in the USA. On both sides of the Atlantic these public intellectuals and their associates were searching for ways to understand *and* influence IR in ways that distinguished their normative, theoretical, and methodological approaches from Marx (1849) on the one hand and classical or neo-classical economics (Marshall, 1920) on the other.

Since those early days, others have developed the field considerably to incorporate concepts and methods from other disciplines such as: accounting, history, law, management, politics, psychology and sociology. We see IR in a broad sense as dealing with all aspects of the employment relationship, including

human resource management (HRM), work and employment. However, many other broader aspects of IR are discussed in separate chapters of this Handbook. Therefore, this particular chapter focuses more specifically on the *institutions* and *processes* associated with collective bargaining, negotiations and job regulation, including unions, and other forms of collective employee representation.

There have been many attempts to develop theory in this field although IR is often descriptive in nature and relatively lacking in theory for several reasons. These include the practitioner and policy-orientation of the field. There has also been a tendency to focus on the formal institutional and legal structures, rather than on the more complex informal practices and processes. Nonetheless, there are influential theoretical and intellectual foundations, to which we now turn. First, we will discuss industrial relations and then we will focus more specifically on collective bargaining.

FOUNDATIONS OF INDUSTRIAL RELATIONS

Marx provided an intellectual rationale and stimulus to the IR field. He argued that labour was more than just a commodity or factor of production subject to deterministic laws of supply and demand. Instead, the free will of human beings make labour much more than an inanimate object. This insight is an enduring normative premise in IR and has motivated much of the research in the field. That is, while affected by market forces similar to other factors, labour deserves and requires special treatment in theory and practice, because workers can take individual or collective actions to influence market outcomes, and work and employment relationships are value-laden activities with important social as well as economic consequences. For these reasons, IR research, public policies, and practices may be as concerned about equity as efficiency at work (Barbash, 1984; Meltz, 1989). Moreover, freedom of association at work is recognized as a fundamental human right in democratic societies and, therefore, the ability of workers to have a *voice* in or be engaged in determining their conditions of work is an important aspect of IR (see: Dundon et al., 2004; Bamber, 2005; Bamber et al., 2009 and the chapter by Budd in this book).

Although Marx provided a point of departure, many scholars in the field have challenged other elements of Marxist analysis. Marx saw conflict at work as inevitable and all-encompassing, arising from the class conflict in the capitalist system of production. Conflict could be eliminated only by the revolutionary overthrow of that system. This became a major point of differentiation between Marxist and labour process schools of IR on the one hand (Braverman, 1974; Hyman, 1975) and the more pluralist model which has been influential in research in the IR field in English-speaking countries (Fox, 1971; Kochan, 1980).

For the Webbs, unions were necessary to provide increased social support and bargaining power. In due course, however, they expected unions to develop into institutions promoting state regulation and working for the common benefit of all workers and for the wider community. Thus, rather than through the revolution predicted by Marx, societies would develop gradually to balance better the interests of workers, employers and the wider communities.

While the Webbs studied IR in Britain in the late 19th and early 20th century (they have been described as historians, sociologists and historical economists – see Kaufman, 2004: 164), there was a change in the economics field in the US. Certain economists were frustrated with the mathematical analysis of late 19th century economic research. Consequently, in 1886, Robert Ely tried to bring a more empirical, and institutional form of economics to bear on current issues. Under the leadership of Ely's protégé, Commons, the emerging IR field focused on the study of labour and working conditions using inductive methods and focused particularly on the collective institutions and organizations of workers and employers governing work and employment.

Such institutionalists also saw labour as more than a commodity. But, unlike Marx, Commons and those who followed saw the conflicts of interests between employers and employees as a legitimate aspect of differences in economic interests, rather than as a product of the capitalist system. Employees have the right to pursue their own interests collectively, to improve their economic rewards and other aspects of their working lives. These conflicting interests are not, however, absolute. Employers and employees also have common interests that link them in interdependent relationships. Both parties usually want to generate value from their relationships so that there is more value to share. Thus IR involves an inevitable mix of separate, perhaps conflicting goals, as well as common or shared goals. The challenge of IR theory, therefore, focuses on finding equitable and efficient settlement of differences, and ways to support value-creating solutions where interests overlap (Walton and McKersie, 1965; Fox, 1970).

The early institutionalists were strong proponents of research and involvement in policy-making and institution building. They studied labour markets and IR through field work more than through deductive model building. Their research and personal involvement provided a foundation for the policy proposals in the labour legislation of the US New Deal and the UK welfare state, including: unemployment insurance, workers' compensation, child and women's labour protections, minimum wages, and social security. Building on these foundations, Bruce Kaufman (2007) sees IR as 'the study and practice of finding a balance between market forces and institutions and the social objectives of efficiency, fairness and human self-development in the employment relationship'.

LINKS BETWEEN IR AND OTHER DISCIPLINES

Kuhn (1970) argues that a new paradigm for the study of a phenomenon must be judged by whether it is better able to solve problems than its alternatives. So let us briefly consider IR against this criterion at various stages of its development.

Scientific management

Scientific management dominated the study of US management and the design of work systems in the early 20th century. The objective was to use engineering principles to find the optimal, most efficient methods for carrying out tasks and controlling labour through appropriate economic incentives and supervision. It was assumed that following such scientific principles would eliminate conflicts of interests at work (Taylor, 1895). This view of management and IR saw no rationale for worker voice, representation, or practices that might try to balance power between workers and managers. Because efficient work would be rewarded, it would

in turn generate worker satisfaction. This virtuous cycle would prevent conflict in employment relationships. Thus, scientific management theory contrasted with the normative assumptions of IR.

Industrial psychology

Almost simultaneously, industrial psychology was being developed as another field of study in parallel to scientific management. By contrast with institutional economics, individuals, not collective groups or organizations, were the central unit of analysis. It was assumed that enterprises were closed systems where management controlled workplace decisions.

Human relations

In the 1920s the field of Human Relations was developed in the USA. This offered another paradigm for the study of IR. The human relations school focused on work groups as the key unit of analysis and the social dynamics that shaped worker attitudes and behaviour. Human relations theorists countered scientific-management arguments by proposing that worker satisfaction drove efficiency at work, rather than the other way around (Rothlisberger and Dickson, 1939). These ideas fostered the development of welfare capitalism in the 1920s. Large US firms sought to provide a set of benefits and positive working conditions to achieve efficiency, and in the process of doing so, eliminate the incentives of workers to join unions (Jacoby, 1991).

The study of personnel management was built on human relations and industrial psychology (or occupational psychology in the UK). The development of personnel management was fostered by the management of the armed forces as well as the paternalist legacies from pioneers of such Quaker firms in the UK like Cadbury, Rowntree and Lever Brothers (Child, 1969).

In the first part of the 20th century, then, there were alternative paradigms competing for influence with an IR paradigm.

The depression of the 1930s and the two world wars increased the prominence of IR practices and research in intellectual and policy debates about work and management. Industrial relations solutions were sought to address increases in the number of strikes and high levels of unemployment. There was also a growing appreciation of the need to establish a set of minimum labour standards and methods to improve workers' bargaining power in relation to their employers to improve on such minimum conditions. In many contexts, such floors were constructed by collective bargaining.

COLLECTIVE BARGAINING

What is collective bargaining? For the International Labour Organization (ILO), collective bargaining is the activity or process leading up to the conclusion of a collective agreement. In ILO Recommendation 91, collective agreements are defined as:

> all agreements in *writing* (our emphasis) regarding working conditions and terms of employment concluded between an employer, a group of employers or one or more employers' organizations, on the one hand, and one or more representative workers' organizations, or, in the absence of such organizations, the representatives of the workers duly elected and authorized by them in accordance with national laws and regulations, on the other. (Gernigon et al., 2000)

Our approach to collective bargaining is broader than that of the ILO. In our view, collective bargaining may take place even though it may not lead to the conclusion of a collective agreement *in writing*. On occasion, collective bargaining may take place even though the parties do not conclude a collective agreement and might reach an impasse. On other occasions, UK shop stewards, for example, may conclude an informal collective agreement that becomes an accepted custom or practice, but is not necessarily *in writing*.

There is usually some conflict of interest between the IR parties, but they choose to negotiate since they see bargaining as preferable to other means of deciding the issues at stake – such as litigation, open conflict without communication, walking away from the relationship entirely or just conceding. Because they accept the idea of give and take, both bargaining parties expect that they can make gains (or at least stem losses) through bargaining. These processes can also offer more than just conflict management. They can be the mechanism through which two parties can 'create something new that neither could do on its own' (Lewicki et al., 2005).

In the early stages of industrialization, the IR parties began collective bargaining in many countries as a means of regulating pay and a few other conditions of employment. Groups of employees and left-wing political groups saw it as a way of replacing unilateral decision-making by employers and of overcoming the weak bargaining position of *individual* employees. Usually occurring at enterprise and craft level, but occasionally at industry level – as in the British cotton industry – it also suited the sociological features of manufacturing industries which concentrated sizeable groups of wage earners doing similar tasks into workplaces that were relatively large. Moreover, it gave practical expression to the nascent feelings of solidarity among employees. Union organization channelled such feelings, perhaps earlier directed in a sporadic fashion, towards strikes or other forms of dispute, in a more systematic manner towards the establishment of a *common rule* in a given craft, district, enterprise, or industry.

In the mid-19th century in the UK, as governments and employers did not recognize unions, collective bargaining rarely played an important role, apart from among select groups of craftsmen. Many negotiations took place in an atmosphere of crisis under the pressure of sanctions (e.g. strikes or lockouts) and collective agreements had only a *de facto* validity. Many of them were the creations of temporary coalitions of employees that subsequently disbanded. When unions grew in strength and were able to obtain recognition (around the end of the 19th century in some European countries and Australasia, but a few decades later in the USA and most other developed market economies (DMEs)), the parties developed collective bargaining, which became a key element of nearly all IR systems of DMEs, albeit with different styles, patterns and traditions in different contexts. Collective bargaining was not always instigated by workers' interests. In many cases employers sought to use it to get workers and their unions to agree to a given set of terms and conditions for a specific period. Some early workers' collectivities would simply make demands and strike if the employer did not concede. Such collectivities did not want the delays of negotiations.

The UK tradition emphasized the voluntary character of negotiations and autonomy for the bargaining parties, with little legal intervention and often a high degree of informality. In a divergence from their UK heritage, following a wave of industrial strife in the 1890s, Australia and New Zealand experimented with the notion of compulsory and legally binding arbitration, which its advocates saw as an effective method of preventing and settling industrial disputes (Niland, 1978). Although it is often assumed there is a clear distinction between collective bargaining and arbitration, many such arbitration awards follow on from collective bargaining.

In continental Europe, the growth of collective bargaining was facilitated by the incorporation of collective agreements in the legal system of various countries as a new source of IR rules. This process started with the Dutch Civil Code (1907) and the Swiss Code of Obligations (1911) and was followed by legislation in Norway (1915), Germany (1918), France (1919), Finland (1924), and (again) the Netherlands (1927). Such laws acknowledged that collective agreements were a valid way of determining conditions of employment for a group of employees.

Not only have such influences helped to shape other national models, they have also been reflected in the conventions and recommendations adopted by the ILO. The Continental European approaches induced most of the provisions on effects, interpretation and extension of agreements included

in ILO Recommendation 92 on Collective Agreements, 1951. The British influence inspired the reference to 'machinery for voluntary negotiations' in one of the key provisions of Convention 98 on the Right to Organize and to Bargain Collectively, 1949. Elements of the American penchant for regulating collective bargaining procedures (see below) appear in Recommendation 163 concerning the Promotion of Collective Bargaining, 1981.

Despite these international influences, national contexts for collective bargaining vary widely. In some European countries, collective agreements bind only affiliated members of the signatory union. In the UK and a few other countries, a collective agreement is not legally binding unless specifically requested by the parties (which they rarely do); if such a request is not made, the enforcement of the 'voluntary agreement' hinges on the goodwill or relative strength of the parties. Such countries have tended not to regulate negotiations; this reflected the wish of the parties to preserve the autonomy of collective bargaining and avoid government intervention. Nevertheless, the notion of a voluntary agreement is increasingly being challenged and, in practice, agreements apply to the generality of employees, even in countries where they are supposed to bind only union affiliates. In the absence of legislative provisions, rules dealing with the negotiations develop as part of a specialized jurisprudence, custom and practice or by an explicit decision of the parties.

THE US NEW DEAL ERA, WWII AND THE WAR LABOR BOARD

In the USA, from 1932 to 1945 IR scholars and practitioners had an unprecedented impact on national policy and private practices of IR. Major developments in this period included the 1935 National Labor Relations (Wagner) Act introducing the novel New Deal principles governing the orderly conduct of negotiations. The War Labor Board (1941–45) that was charged with controlling wages and mediating collective bargaining negotiations played a key role in legitimating and starting the long-term diffusion of many modern personnel practices and benefits, including collective bargaining, arbitration, cost of living pay increases, paid time off for vacations and sick leave, health insurance, pensions and other benefits.

In the two decades after 1945 practically-oriented scholars from institutional economics, sociology, political science, law, history, and psychology strived to understand and helped to regulate IR. Two sets of questions featured prominently in IR research then: (1) how does collective bargaining work? and (2) what are the effects of unions and collective bargaining on management, the workforce, and the economy?

The growing presence and pressure of unions and collective bargaining exerted a shock effect on management. Personnel practices had become more professionalized and applied in more uniform fashion and managers had to search for ways to improve productivity to recoup the higher labour costs resulting from collective bargaining (Slichter et al., 1960). Much IR research examined the dynamics of labour-management relations and the causes of strikes and/or industrial peace (Golden and Parker, 1955). Apart from in the USA, much of this work was carried out using case studies of specific unions or of IR in particular workplaces or industries (e.g. Batstone et al., 1977).

Dunlop (1958) criticized post-war IR research for being characterized by too many facts chasing too little theory. He sought to correct this by proposing a general systems theory of IR. He argued that the central task for IR theory was to explain variations in the rules regulating jobs. These rules were set in interactions among three key actors – unions, management, and government. These interactions were conditioned by external market, technological, and societal forces. The system was bound together by what Dunlop argued was a shared ideology valuing democracy, respect for market forces, and worker rights. Although Dunlop's framework was not accepted as a general theory of IR, it became the starting

point for much subsequent research on IR and collective bargaining.

ANALYZING COLLECTIVE BARGAINING

Hugh Clegg (1976) uses six 'dimensions' of collective bargaining structures to explain the comparative historical experience of union behaviour. He defines union behaviour as: density of membership, external structure, internal government, workplace organization, strikes, attitudes, industrial democracy, and political action. These dimensions are: the 'level' at which bargaining takes place; the 'extent' or inclusiveness of coverage of the process and outcome relative to the potential population of employers and employees; the 'scope' or range of issues bargained; the 'depth' or the degree of involvement of local or plant level union officials in bargaining; 'union security' or support from employers for union recruitment and retention of members; and the 'degree of control', which refers to the extent to which a collective agreement includes obligatory standards and effective grievance procedures. To these can be added the 'form' or type of bargaining structure related to the degree of institutionalization or state involvement in collective bargaining. Focusing on changes to at least some of these dimensions is an effective method for analyzing comparative changes to collective bargaining structures over time and space (see Thornthwaite and Sheldon, 1996).

Clegg (1976) argues that his dimensions of collective bargaining are themselves mainly determined by the structures of management and of employers' organizations; 'but where the law has intervened in the early stages, it may have played an equally important part, or an even more important part, in shaping collective bargaining'. In contrast to the widespread failure to appreciate how the role of employers in collective bargaining varies from country to country, Adams and Sisson seek to examine employer behaviour within the development of collective bargaining cross-nationally.

Adams points out that western European employers' behaviour towards unions differs significantly from those in North America (Adams, 1981). In the former, typically, employers are organized into strong associations that engage in collective bargaining with unions (and with the state). By contrast, in North America, employers have generally not formed strong associations. Even where they have, it is much less usual for those associations to engage in collective bargaining. Adams holds that these differences are attributable to the different early political, economic, and organizational strategies of the various labour movements and how these induced differing degrees of state intervention and employer compromise.

Sisson compares the role of employers and their organizations in the development of collective bargaining in seven countries (Sisson, 1987). He also concludes that differences between the countries were rooted in their historical experiences, particularly flowing from the impact of industrialization. In Western Europe and Australasia, multi-employer bargaining emerged as the predominant pattern, largely because employers in the metal working industries were confronted with the challenge of national unions organized along occupational or industrial lines. In contrast, single-employer bargaining developed in the USA and Japan because the relatively large employers that had emerged at an early stage of industrialization in both countries were able to exert pressure on unions to bargain at the enterprise level.

Thelen (1999) also contributes to debates about such institutions as collective bargaining by explaining the historical origins of important cross-national differences in institutions in particular countries (Germany, Britain, the US and Japan). She also provides a theory of institutional change over time and proposes a way of thinking about institutional development and path dependency.

To understand collective bargaining, it is useful to look first at bargaining more generally, including the added complexities that team bargaining and representation bring.

We then consider the implications of bargaining in an IR context. Bargaining and negotiation are essentially the same process (and we use both terms interchangeably).

There are two main approaches to bargaining: distributive and integrative (Walton and McKersie, 1991). Of course they differ fundamentally on what is at stake. An assumption under *distributive bargaining* is that what one side wins, the other side loses. It is essentially competitive and assumes a zero-sum game or fixed size 'pie'. Success means getting as much as possible of something contested at the expense of the other side. Much IR bargaining could be characterized as distributive. On central issues such as pay, there is usually a conflict over the share available for wages relative to profits. Moreover, in collective bargaining about pay, management typically frames the issue as a fixed-sized 'pie'.

By contrast, *integrative bargaining* is a cooperative approach that emphasizes the quality of the relationship between the parties as well as the substantive issues at stake. An assumption under *integrative bargaining* is that constructive negotiators can enlarge 'the pie' by, for example, identifying areas of common interest that may not have been obvious before the negotiations. In IR, although distributive bargaining approaches may dominate (e.g. pay issues), the parties may also use more integrative approaches when negotiating on other issues (such as work organization and training described below). Power (or the perception of relative power) is fundamental to bargaining processes and outcomes. This is particularly so for distributive bargaining. Thus, most bargaining processes involve parties 'framing' issues, as each side attempts to influence the perceptions and attitudes of the other.

Collective bargaining adds extra layers of complexity to other types of bargaining. Collective bargaining means that one party is a group of employees or representative of the group. Usually, the other party is an employer or agent representing employers. Representatives of government may form a third party.

Constituency bargaining creates the need for intra-organizational bargaining before, during and even after the main bargaining process. For example, union negotiators may need to get the approval of their members to a set of bargaining demands and then, again, at the completion of the main negotiations, for any agreement reached with the employer or employers' association.

The IR context, its history, its ramifications and its effects can also make collective bargaining a complex and even emotional process. Through collective bargaining, the parties aim to reach an agreement that will regulate terms and conditions of employment. These agreements have different titles in different countries; e.g. 'collective agreements' (UK), 'labor contracts' (USA) and enterprise bargaining agreements (Australia). Historically, employees and their unions have developed *collective* bargaining because, as individuals, employees suffer an enormous power imbalance compared with their employers.

Individual bargaining, to the extent that employers bargain with individual employees, can leave most employees vulnerable to exploitation. Collective bargaining, therefore, concerns conflicts over many of the most important aspects of people's lives. It shapes people's lives at work, their life chances as a reflection of their income gained through employment, employment security and careers, the balance between their work and non-work lives, health and safety, post-employment security and a range of other issues, which, in some countries, are related to broader social security provisions.

The Webbs (1897) were the first to analyze collective bargaining. They saw it as an alternative to 'individual bargaining' and 'autonomous regulation' and one of three union strategies to regulate protectively and improve their members' employment conditions; the others being 'mutual insurance' and 'legal enactment'. Research and thinking about the concept developed in various countries. For example, in the USA, Commons (1934) investigated negotiations and compromise among the divergent interests of

unions, employers and the public. Slichter et al. (1960) saw it as a system of industrial jurisprudence, while Chamberlain and Kuhn (1986) analyzed collective bargaining in terms of three theories: a marketing theory (a means of contracting for the sale of labour); a governmental theory (a form of industrial government); and a managerial theory (a method of management).

There was much debate about whether political (i.e. pressures from union members and the need for union leaders to match settlements achieved in other industries or occupations) (Ross, 1948) or economic forces (Dunlop, 1944) were the primary drivers of pay determination. Of course both are important – political forces are influential within a range, but are usually exercised in a context of markets. A reformulation of the debate suggested that bargaining power includes a mixture of political, economic and 'pure power' forces and that these should be incorporated into a more complete theory of pay determination under collective bargaining (Levinson, 1968).

In the UK, Flanders pointed out that it was misleading to contrast collective bargaining with individual bargaining. Each employee starting a new job has an individual contract, not a collective one. But a collective agreement can provide a minimum-rights framework for individuals in employment. Flanders (1975: 213ff) saw collective bargaining as a political process, involving joint rule-making and power relationships which could enhance the dignity of employees. Others examined collective bargaining as an institutionalization of industrial conflict (e.g. Dubin, 1954: 37–47; Fox, 1971: 135ff). Subsequent scholars have applied analytical insights into collective bargaining from the fields of law, economics, organizational behaviour, and human resource management (HRM) whereas earlier analyses had a more descriptive 'historical-institutional' approach (Katz et al., 2007).

There is a wide variety of views on collective bargaining. In its broad sense, collective bargaining is a process of accommodating different or opposing interests. It includes all sorts of bipartite or tripartite discussions relating to employment and IR that may affect a group of employees directly or indirectly. The notion of bargaining implies that the parties are aiming to reach agreement, if necessary, by competitive negotiation.

Consultation can be a less competitive process through which the parties may exchange views without necessarily engaging in the give-and-take which is usually part of reaching agreement. For example, before making a decision, employers may listen to employees' views. Nevertheless, consultation processes can be phases of the collective bargaining process and so can also be included within a broad view of collective bargaining.

A narrower but more precise meaning of collective bargaining implies only bipartite negotiations, with an intention to reach agreement. In addition to the more specific negotiations between employers and unions (the two main 'parties'), a broad view of collective bargaining also includes *the state* as a third party, which may be involved in political bargaining and tripartite negotiations at the centralized national (economy-wide) level.

The broad and narrow senses of collective bargaining come together in the *coordination* of collective bargaining processes. Through coordination, bargaining parties on either side attempt to achieve common outcomes. Coordination within the one side (employer, union or even the state) can involve one or more of: information exchange, consultation, target setting and even joint strategizing. Sometimes, these processes may also involve the bargaining counterpart (the other 'side'). Such coordination can occur among union delegates or local managers across work units in one workplace or among union or managerial negotiators responsible for workplace-level bargaining within a multi-workplace employing organization. At more centralized levels, it involves union or employer representatives within a particular industry or industry representatives on each side, coordinating approaches at national or even international levels.

Coordination can include *procedural* and *substantive* issues with the intention that these will shape a number of separate but interdependent collective bargaining rounds. As part of a feedback and review process, coordination may continue throughout the life of these bargaining processes. Coordination is most important in *decentralized* bargaining environments. For example, Japanese unions have long used their annual national *Shunto* (spring bargaining offensive) to coordinate and advocate claims that enterprise unions will then bargain at company level. In the USA, unions have long used a more 'horizontal' form of coordination (pattern bargaining) to spread industry norms and expectations company-by-company throughout particular sectors. In Europe, there has been a recent growth in vertical and horizontal coordination processes to deal with the challenges of the European Union (EU) and multi-national corporations (MNCs) (Sisson and Marginson, 2002; Traxler, 2003). Unions in other parts of the world (e.g. South Korea and Australia) also used pattern bargaining within decentralized bargaining systems.

THE 1980s AND BEYOND: A PERIOD OF TRANSFORMATION

The 1980s was a watershed decade for the study and practice of IR. There was debate in the USA about whether reductions in real and nominal pay and other changes observed in collective bargaining were simply temporary adjustments to the recession of 1981–83 or signalled a more permanent structural shift in the wage determination process and in IR more generally. Wage determination and IR practices changed fundamentally in the 1980s as there was a decline in the power of strike threats, and a weakening of unions in general. Strike rates have declined precipitously to the point that US government agencies devote much less attention to them than in the past.

The combined influence of the recession, increased international competition, and a shift to a conservative government under

President Ronald Reagan, led a set of changes that created anomalies for much of post war IR theory and empirical research. US Management became more openly hostile and aggressive in avoiding new union organizing, moving operations from union to non-union workplaces, often in the South. Management replaced unions as the driving force in shaping the process and outcomes of collective bargaining. Nominal wage reductions were negotiated in many employment contracts. New employer approaches to work organization and employee participation challenged traditional job structures and labour management relations. These developments led to an expanded model of IR that emphasized how employment relationships and outcomes are shaped by decisions on the part of management (but also by unions and government) regarding collective bargaining, workplace relations, and personnel policies, as well as by a new focus on the part of management on high-level business/competitive strategies (Kochan et al., 1986).

In the UK, Margaret Thatcher led a Conservative government throughout the 1980s. This government sought to change the 'balance of power' between employers and workers (and their unions). The IR and employment laws were re-written to weaken the rights of workers and unions. Further, this government intervened in major strikes that were aimed to curb the power and role of unions, particularly the miners' union, which formerly had been seen as one of the most powerful and militant (Marchington et al., 2004).

By contrast with the USA and UK, Australia had a federal government from 1983, which had close links with and was sympathetic to the unions. This government agreed on a series of 'accords' with the central council of unions. These accords followed from a form of national-level collective bargaining. Nevertheless, as in the USA and UK, there was a dramatic decline in the density of unionization. This situation was compounded by the 1996–2007 Conservative government introducing tough anti-worker and anti-union laws. These included the outlawing of pattern bargaining (Lansbury and Wailes, 2004).

Such changes to the dynamics of collective IR in the US, UK, Australia and other countries gave more scope to current managers than to their predecessors, to choose forms of IR arrangements which might not involve unions. Analysis of how these choices played out and affected outcomes has been a focus of IR research since the 1980s. Researchers have been assessing, for instance, the effects of different combinations of employment practices on firm performance, reflecting various contrasting systems' perspectives on IR and the emerging emphasis on complementary practices in personnel economics (Milgrom and Roberts, 1992).

By the end of the 20th century flexible work systems and employee involvement in production and workplace decisions were increasingly serving as positive complements to investments in technology and training. This produced significant improvements in productivity and service quality (Ichniowski et al., 1996; Appelbaum et al., 2000). The theory and evidence suggested that a high wage-high productivity equilibrium was possible in sectors as diverse as manufacturing, airlines, health care and financial services. Yet such 'high performance' work systems (HPWS) did not diffuse widely across the economy, in part because of the costs and other challenges of transitioning from more traditional practices, and in part because they competed with a low wage-low cost paradigm. These two competing models of IR practice compete with each other across most industries and occupations in the US and other countries. A central theoretical and policy question in the IR field focuses on whether a high wage-high productivity equilibrium can be sustained in the face of low wage-low cost competition in labour and product markets and, if so, how to best encourage adoption of these strategies.

In most of the US cases where HPWS have been examined, managers have aimed to introduce variants of HPWS which did not include an apparent role for collective bargaining. In this sense, perhaps there are fewer links between HPWS and collective bargaining than between HPWS and earlier 'unitarist' approaches such as scientific management and human relations.

PUBLIC POLICY DEBATES

A proposition driving policy debates in the last decade was that the changes in the workforce, nature of work, and the economy had outpaced adaptations in public policies, institutions, and practices in employment relations and that this gap was imposing costs on workers and the economy (Osterman et al., 2001). Efforts to build consensus on changes needed in labour and employment policies have failed since the late 1970s (Kochan, 1995). One result is that, in another sense, the US field of IR has returned approximately to where it began in the early years of the 20th century when Commons (1909) documented the mismatch between policies and institutions and workplace relations as the US economy changed from an agrarian base to a manufacturing base.

Similarly, in the UK, there have been further recent echoes of the early 20th century. The post-1997 UK New Labour government's National Minimum Wage Act 1998 reflected a failure of collective bargaining to eradicate low pay. This is why, in the early 20th century, the UK government had established wages boards (which later became wages councils).

CONCLUSIONS: FROM INDUSTRIAL RELATIONS AND COLLECTIVE BARGAINING TO EMPLOYMENT RELATIONS AND VOICE AT WORK

In many countries, the 20th century saw the rise and fall of IR and collective bargaining. By the early 21st century, there had been a significant decline in the percentage of people covered by collective bargaining and other formal IR institutions (e.g. unions) in comparison with the high watermarks of coverage at various stages in the 20th century. This change reflects at least three factors: first, the changing structure of employment with a dramatic growth of the service sector; second,

the changing approach by managers towards shifting their rhetoric and practice towards more 'individualized' and less collective relations with employees; third, governments have changed their rhetoric and legislation in a similar direction.

In recent years even the terms IR and collective bargaining have increasingly been questioned as the labels for the study of people at work. Many scholars have changed the labels used to describe their field of inquiry and/or teaching from IR to work and employment relations, human resource management, voice, work and organizational studies, and a variety of other terms. A fresh wave of scholars from such disciplines as sociology, political science, economics, history, geography and social psychology have taken up the study of work and employment issues, leading to some re-orientations of the field and to renewed competition among such disciplines for influence in shaping the future study and practice of IR and collective bargaining.

The research questions that are most central to this field reflect two interrelated realities: (1) globalization of economic activity, and (2) the importance of knowledge and innovation in structuring work and shaping economic outcomes. Globalization and changes in technology have increased the mobility of capital, work, and workers, thereby weakening the influence of national laws, institutions, and norms in shaping employment relationships and outcomes. Again, as in the early 20th century, labour costs are under intense competition, but in the early 21st century more labour markets are international. This reflects not so much the international mobility of labour, but rather an increasingly clear international division of labour, including more 'off shoring' from the DMEs of manufacturing (e.g. to China) and services (e.g. to India).

The increased ease of locating work and expansion of trade across national borders affects a wide range of work and employment issues and outcomes. Globalization has been associated with, among other things, changes in the distribution of wages and profits, growth in income inequality, and greater and more widely distributed job insecurity. Within firms, globalization of production and supply chains diffuses responsibility for employment decisions and policies blurring the traditional definition of employers and employees. There is further blurring by the increased use of sub-contracting and so-called atypical forms of work. Such effects are being subjected to analysis, measurement of the direction and magnitude of their effects, and debate over how to adapt policies and institutions to cope with them. These international and organizational developments also make it more difficult to regulate IR and collective bargaining with national laws and firm-centred rules and policies.

The outcome of such debates could have important consequences for the design of institutions of worker voice in employment relationships. For much of the 20th century, labour law in the USA, UK and elsewhere was based on a premise that employees should be allowed to bargain over wages, hours and working conditions, but that enterprise owners and their managers should have the preroga-tive to make strategic business decisions. If, by investing their human capital, employees become a residual risk bearer similar to financial investors, then there is no logical basis for excluding workers from a voice in strategic decisions and corporate governance. Thus, some scholars have extended the study of IR and collective bargaining to include issues of corporate strategy and governance and theories of the firm (e.g. Gospel and Pendleton, 2003).

The field has also expanded in response to changes in the relationships between work and family/personal life. Work and family life were tightly linked in the pre-industrial agrarian economy because they were co-located (e.g. families lived and worked on the farm) while men, women and children all contributed to the production process. With the growth of the industrial economy, there was a clearer division of labour and physical separation in work and family life. The male breadwinner emerged as the prototypical worker, with the assumption that he had a wife at home attending to family responsibilities.

With the growth in the labour force participation of women and the slowdown in the growth of real wages, there have been moves to spread working hours between men and women, and between mothers and fathers. This again increases the interdependence of work and family life and calls for changes in workplace and HRM practices to provide flexibility in hours and career options for women and men. Thus, work and family issues have become an important topic of research and policy analysis within the field of work and employment relations (Lansbury and Baird, 2004; Bailyn, 2006; Kossak, 2006; Drago, 2007).

The study of work and employment rela-tions in countries around the world parallels most of the trends observed in the US, UK and Australia. Throughout much of the 20th century, studies of unions and industrial con-flict dominated country-specific research and international comparisons of IR and collective bargaining. In the 1960s a debate arose over whether technological changes and increasing economic interdependencies would lead to a convergence in employment systems and practices or whether differences observed across countries would endure because of the influence of national culture and other institu-tional forces (Kerr et al., 1960). This debate has waxed and waned, though researchers have shifted to more micro level (industry, occupational, and regional) comparisons to try to clarify the forces leading to convergence and divergence in employment relationships (Katz and Darbishire, 2000; Bamber et al., 2004). Moreover, researchers in the field of international IR (e.g. Kaufman, 2004) are analyzing and debating most of the issues and developments discussed here in many other countries.

In a sense, the field of work and employ-ment relations has returned to its IR origins in the US and UK. Like the first two decades of the 20th century, many contem-porary researchers are focusing on a broad proposition that the type of economy, work-force, the nature of work and its relationship to other institutions such as family life have all changed dramatically, while public policies and institutions still reflect the legacy of a declining industrial-based economy. The gap between policies and institutions and contemporary realities of work and family life lie at the heart of the tensions and pressures building in workplaces. A central task of those investigating contemporary work and employment issues, like their IR forerunners, is to conduct research and policy analysis that prepares for when the political forces align to make it possible to improve policy and practice. This task is all the more important following the post-2007 global financial crisis.

REFERENCES

Adams, R. (1981) 'A theory of employer attitudes and behaviour towards trade unions in Western Europe and North America', in G. Dlugos and K. Weiermair (eds), in collaboration with W. Dorow, *Management Under Differing Value Systems*. Berlin: de Gruyer, pp. 277–93.

Appelbaum, E., Bailey, T., Berg, P. and Kalleberg, A. (2000) *Manufacturing Advantage*. Ithaca, NY: Cornell University/ILR Press.

Bailyn, L. (2006) *Breaking the Mold*, 2nd edition. Ithaca, NY: Cornell/ILR Press.

Bamber, G.J. (2005) 'The geometry of comparative industrial relations: Efficiency, equity and voice', *Employee Responsibilities and Rights Journal*, 17 (2): 119–22.

Bamber, G.J., Hoffer Gittell, J., Kochan, T.A. and von Nordenflytch, A. (2009) *Up in the Air: How Airlines Can Improve Performance by Engaging their Employees*. Ithaca, NY: Cornell University Press.

Bamber, G.J., Lansbury, R. and Wailes, N. (2004) *International and Comparative Employment Relations*. London: Sage.

Barbash, J. (1984) *The Elements of Industrial Relations*. Madison: University of Wisconsin Press.

Batstone, E., Boraston, I. and Frenkel, S. (1977) *Shop Stewards in Action: The Organization of Workplace conflict and Accommodation*. Oxford: Blackwell.

Braverman, H. (1974) Labor and monopoly capital: The degradation of work in the twentieth century. New York: Monthly Review Press.

Budd, J. (2004) *Employment Relations with a Human Face*. Ithaca, NY: Cornell University/ILR Press.

Chamberlain, N. W. and Kuhn, J. W. (1986), *Collective Bargaining*, New York: McGraw-Hill.

Child, J. (1969) *British Management Thought: A Critical Analysis*. London: Allen and Unwin.

Clegg, H. (1970) *The System of Industrial Relations in Great Britain*. London: Blackwell.

Clegg, H.A. (1976) *Trade Unionism Under Collective Bargaining: A Theory Based on Comparisons of Six Countries*. Oxford: Blackwell.

Commons, J. (1909) 'American shoemakers, 1648–1895', *Quarterly Journal of Economics*, 24 (November): 39–98.

Commons, J. (1934) *Institutional Economics: Its Place in the Political Economy*. New York: Macmillan.

Drago, R. (2007) *Striking a Balance*. Boston, MA.: Dollars and Sense.

Dubin, R. (1954) 'Constructive Aspects of Industrial Conflict', in *Industrial Conflict*, A Kornhauser, R. Dubin and A.M. Ross (eds), New York: McGraw-Hill.

Dundon, T., Wilkinson, A., Marchington, M. and Ackers, P. (2004) 'The meanings and purpose of employee voice,' *International Journal of Human Resource Management*, 15 (6): 1149–70.

Dunlop, J. (1944) *Wage Determination under Trade Unions*. New York: MacMillan.

Dunlop, J.T. (1958) *Industrial Relations Systems*. New York: McGraw-Hill.

Flanders, A. (ed.) (1975) 'Collective Bargaining: A Theoretical Analysis' in *Management and Unions: The Theory and Reform of Industrial Relations*, London: Faber.

Fox, A. (1971) *A Sociology of Work and Industry*. London: Collier MacMillan.

Gernigon, B., Odero, A. and Guido, H. (2000) 'ILO principles concerning collective bargaining', *International Labour Review*, 33–55.

Golden, C. and Parker, V. (1955) *Causes of Industrial Peace*. New York: Harper and Row.

Gospel, H. and Pendleton, A. (2003) 'Finance, corporate governance and the management of labour: A conceptual and comparative analysis', *British Journal of Industrial Relations*, 41 (3): 557–82.

Hyman, R. (1975) *Industrial Relations: A Marxist Introduction*. London: MacMillan.

Ichniowski, C., Kochan, T., Levine, D., Olson, C. and Strauss, G. (1996) 'What works at work: Overview and assessment?', *Industrial Relations*, 35: 299–333.

Jacoby, S. (1991) *Masters to Managers*. New York: Columbia University Press.

Katz, H. and Darbashire, O. (2000) *Converging Divergences*. Ithaca, NY: Cornell/ILR Press.

Katz, H.C., Kochan, T.A. and Colvin, A.J.S. (2007) *An Introduction to Collective Bargaining and Industrial Relations*, 2nd ed. New York: McGraw-Hill/Irwin.

Kaufman, B. (2004) *The Global Evolution of Industrial Relations: Events, Ideas and the IIRA*. Geneva: International Labour Office, International Industrial Relations Association.

Kaufman, B. (2007) 'The core principle and fundamental theorem of industrial relations', Working Paper 07–01, Andrew Young School of Policy Studies Research Paper Series, Georgia State University.

Kerr, C., Dunlop, J., Harbison, F. and Myers, C. (1960) *Industrialism and Industrial Man*. Cambridge: Harvard University Press.

Kochan, T. (1980) *Industrial Relations: From Theory to Policy and Practice*. Homewood, IL: Irwin.

Kochan, T. (1995) 'Using the Dunlop report for mutual gain', *Industrial Relations*, 34: 350–66.

Kochan, T., Katz, H. and McKersie, R. (1986) *The Transformation of American Industrial Relations*. New York: McGraw-Hill.

Kossak, E. (2006) 'Work and family in America: growing tensions between employment policy and a transformed workforce', in E. Lawler and J. O'Toole (eds), *America at Work*. New York: Palgrave MacMillan, pp. 53–72.

Kuhn, T. (1970) *The Structure of Scientific Revolutions*, Chicago: University of Chicago Press.

Lansbury, R.D. and Baird, M. (2004) 'Broadening the horizons of HRM: Lessons for Australia from the US experience', *Asia Pacific Journal of Human Resources*, 42 (2): 147–55.

Lansbury, R.D. and Wailes, N. (2004) 'Employment relations in Australia', in G.J. Bamber, R.D. Lansbury and N. Wailes (eds), *International and Comparative Employment Relations: Globalisation and the Developed Market Economies*. London: Sage, pp. 119–45.

Lester, R. (1952) 'A range theory of wage differentials', *Industrial and Labor Relations Review*, 5: 433–50.

Levinson, H. (1968) 'Wage determination under collective bargaining', in A. Flanders (ed.), *Collective Bargaining*. London: Palgrave Books, pp. 86–117.

Lewicki, R.J., Barry, B. and Saunders, D.M. (2005) *Negotiation*, 5th ed. Boston: McGraw-Hill/Irwin.

Marchington, M., Goodman, J. and Berridge, J. (2004) 'Employment relations in Britain', in G.J. Bamber, R.D. Lansbury and N. Wailes (eds), *International and Comparative Employment Relations: Globalisation and the Developed Market Economies*. London: Sage, pp. 36–66.

Marshall, A. (1920) *Principles of Economics*, 8th ed. London: MacMillan.

Marx, K. (1849) 'Wages, labor and capital', reprinted in Tucker, R., *The Marx-Engels Reader*. New York: Norton.

Milgrom, P. and Roberts, J. (1992) *Economics, Organizations, and Management*. Upper Saddle River, NJ: Prentice Hall.

Meltz, N. (1989) 'Industrial relations: Balancing efficiency and equity', in J. Barbash, and K. Barbash (eds), *Theories and Concepts of Comparative Industrial Relations*. Columbia, SC: University of South Carolina Press, pp. 109–13.

Niland, J. (1978) *Collective Bargaining and Compulsory Arbitration in Australia*. Sydney: New South Wales University Press.

Osterman, P., Kochan, T., Locke, R. and Piore, M. (2001) *Working in America: A Blueprint for the New Labor Market*. Cambridge: MIT Press.

Roethlisberger, F. and Dickson, W. (1939) *Management and the Worker*. Cambridge: Harvard University Press.

Ross, A. (1948) *Trade Union Wage Policy*. Berkeley: University of California Press.

Selznick, P. (1984) *Leadership in Administration*. Berkeley: University of California Press.

Sisson, K. (1987) *The Management of Collective Bargaining: An International Comparison*. Oxford: Blackwell.

Sisson, K. and Marginson, P. (2002) 'Co-ordinated bargaining: A process for our times?', *British Journal of Industrial Relations*: 197–220.

Slichter, S.H., Healy, J.J. and Livernash, E.R. (1960) *The Impact of Collective Bargaining on Management*, Washington DC: Brookings Institution.

Slichter, S., Livernash, R. and Healy, J. (1960) *The Impact of Collective Bargaining on Management*. Washington, DC: The Brookings Institution.

Taylor, F. (1895) 'A piece rate system, being a step toward partial solution of the labor problem', *Transactions*, 16: 856–83.

Thelen, K. (1999) 'Historical institutionalism in comparative politics', *Annual Review of Political Science*, 2: 369–404.

Traxler, F. (2003) 'Co-ordinated bargaining: A stocktaking of its preconditions, practices and performance', *Industrial Relations Journal*, 194–209.

Thornthwaite, L. and Sheldon, P. (1996) 'The metal trades industry association, bargaining structures and the accord', *Journal of Industrial Relations*, 171–95.

Walton, R. and McKersie, R. (1965) *A Behavioral Theory of Labor Negotiations*. New York: McGraw-Hill.

Webb, S. and Webb, B. (1894) *The History of Trade Unions*. London: Longmans, Green.

Webb, S. and Webb, B. (1897) *Industrial Democracy*. London: Longmans, Green.

19

Discipline and Grievances

Brian S. Klaas

INTRODUCTION

At first glance, the topic of discipline and grievances may seem narrow and, perhaps, far removed from the pressing issues facing senior HR executives. Further, interest in disciplinary and grievance procedures has historically been greatest within traditional industries with a significant union presence (Colvin, 2003). Our topic for this chapter often suggests images of progressive discipline and active representation of employees by union officials. And such images seem far removed from life within many knowledge-based or more entrepreneurial organizations. For many such firms, greater emphasis is placed on developing processes that encourage commitment to organizational goals, flexibility, and the development of valued competencies – processes that both allow for competitive advantage and minimize the need for discipline and grievances (Cappelli, 1999; Abraham and McKersie, 1990).

Why then focus on discipline and grievances? While changes in industry structure may well have affected how we

think about employee discipline, problematic employee behavior is still a regular feature of organizational life (Butterfield et al., 2005). While high performance work systems may well be effective in reducing the incidence of problematic behavior, elimination of such behavior is not a realistic goal. Senior managers from many different sectors of the economy report having to confront an extensive list of problem behavior – regardless of high involvement work practices. This list includes such issues as chemical dependency among employees, employees with weak ethical standards, managers that are personally abusive, employees whose performance is spiraling downward for no obvious reason, and employees who are unwilling to change their behavior in response to changing conditions (Wheeler et al., 2004). And sadly, problem behavior is a feature of organizational life that rarely lends itself to easy solutions. Managers frequently struggle with questions about whether they should just look the other way, whether they are obligated to give a problem employee a chance to improve, and whether treating a problem employee fairly puts the organization at undue risk (Butterfield et al., 1996).

Further, some of the changes occurring in the structure of the employment relationship make these questions more difficult for managers to address. Much conventional wisdom about how disciplinary matters should be addressed is based on settings where there is a long-term employee-employer relationship, with some level of investment by the employer in workforce human capital (Cappelli, 1999; Althauser, 1989). Questions exist, however, about appropriate models for discipline when the employment relationship involves less in the way of a commitment between the employee and the employer.

Similarly, while traditional grievance procedures may be featured less prominently within organizations, firms are still confronted with questions about what rights to grant employees regarding the ability to challenge disciplinary action (Colvin, 2002; Colvin et al., 2006). Prompted both by a desire to build a committed workforce and by a desire to manage litigation risks, firms continue to experiment with different mechanisms to allow employees to challenge disciplinary action (Cooper et al., 2000; Feuille and Delaney, 1992). But for firms and for employees, what are the consequences of these different systems of workplace justice? How should such systems be designed to both meet the needs of the employer and protect employee rights? And does the appropriate design of such systems vary with the structure of the employment relationship within a given organization?

In this chapter, we will first examine what research tells us about the appropriate use of discipline by managers and about the appropriate design of disciplinary systems. Our goal is to both identify what is known and to identify key questions that need to be addressed in future research. Following this, we will then review research examining different approaches to systems of workplace justice – again with the goal of identifying what is known and what key questions need to be addressed in future research.

EMPLOYEE DISCIPLINE AND THE DISCIPLINARY SYSTEM

Alternative models for the disciplinary system

Before examining the empirical research literature, it is appropriate to first discuss different models for employee discipline that have emerged. Traditional models for managing employee discipline can be characterized by the following goals: a) ensuring consistent treatment of employees by clearly specifying standards for employee conduct; b) ensuring that employees are aware of organizational expectations and the consequences of problem behavior; c) ensuring employees have the opportunity to modify their behavior (except under conditions where doing so would create undue risk for the organization); and d) ensuring that managers can take progressively more severe action to obtain compliance with organizational expectations. Traditional models are designed to provide managers with the tools necessary to address problem behavior, to help the employee see the consequences of failing to comply with organizational expectations, and to help the employee see managerial actions as being driven by standards of justice (Wheeler et al., 2004).

This traditional model is, in many ways, based on the assumption that there is a long-term employment relationship and that the firm invests in the human capital of its workforce. Where there are expectations of long-term relationship, employees often are assumed to have some 'ownership rights' with regard to their job. A shared belief is thought to exist among employees that the employer is obligated to show justification for dismissing an employee. Where there are expectations of a long-term relationship, the traditional model of discipline might well be viewed as useful to ensuring that severe action will be taken when it is justified and that employees will be protected from unjustified action (Feuille and Delaney, 1992). It ensures that employees were fully informed of expectations and, if appropriate, given the opportunity to modify their behavior. Similarly, by giving employees the opportunity to improve, such systems are designed to ensure that managers make reasonable efforts to retain experienced and trained employees. Executed properly, such a system has the potential to contribute to the development of a committed and motivated workforce – one that perceives its employer as both maintaining high expectations and being fair in its application of standards (Klaas and Dell'omo, 1997).

Other models of discipline also exist. Within other models, much less formality exists with regard to actions taken prior to termination. Because formality is minimized, managerial discretion is enhanced. While employees may well be provided with feedback regarding the need to improve, management is not obligated to be explicit about the conditions under which termination will occur (Klaas et al., 1998). These more flexible systems are designed to ensure that managers have the discretion to respond to changing conditions by using dismissal if they feel it is justified (Klaas and Dell'omo, 1997). They are based on the assumption that employees may feel less ownership regarding their job, that there is sufficient fluidity in the labor market to minimize the consequences of termination for the employee, and that it in some settings it is difficult to specify in advance what is required to maintain employment (Cappelli, 1999). In addition, these more flexible models are based on the idea that providing formal documented warnings can result in costly employee reactions. These more flexible models are also based on the idea that formal systems often require managers to invest too much time in attempting to rehabilitate a problem employee. As a result, the goal of these more flexible models is to allow managers to more quickly and efficiently address problem behavior within the workplace. While this efficiency comes at the expense of employee rights, these models are also premised on the notion of fluid labor markets and interchangeable jobs (Colvin, 2003).

Theory and research on punishment and discipline

While research on the effects of alternative disciplinary systems is relatively limited, there is a substantial body of work examining the impact of using discipline and also examining managerial decision-making regarding discipline. Both of these literatures have substantial implications for our understanding of how managers should use discipline and how organizations should structure disciplinary systems.

The impact of discipline on the sanctioned employee

Traditional disciplinary systems are premised on the idea that discipline can improve workplace performance by changing the behavior of the disciplined employee – and, failing that, by removing the problem employee from the organization (Arvey and Jones, 1985). A number of studies have examined the impact of punishment on the recipient of the punishment – with the findings being mixed in terms of the direction and nature of the effect. Because the use of discipline is punitive in nature, negative responses to the disciplinary action could well be the result. Researchers have also found that the magnitude of the negative reaction varies with the severity of the punishment and also whether the disciplinary action followed the violation of a formal disciplinary rule (Atwater et al., 2001; Ball et al., 1994; Podsakoff et al., 1982).

Negative affective reactions on the part of the recipient are, perhaps, to be expected (Podsakoff et al., 1984; Arvey and Jones, 1985). When a manager takes formal disciplinary action, they are moving beyond constructive feedback. When efforts to change employee behavior are focused on constructive communication, the manager is demonstrating respect for the employee and is signaling that the parties can develop a satisfactory employer-employee relationship via collaborative means. From a social exchange framework, demonstrating respect for the employee has the potential to elicit efforts to reciprocate from the employee – making cooperation and positive affective reactions more likely. By contrast, when formal disciplinary action is taken, the manager is signaling that the employee cannot be trusted to respond in a cooperative fashion (O'Reilly and Weitz, 1989). For example, when formal warnings are used, the manager is indicating that they believe that the threat of termination is needed in order to achieve the desired change in behavior. Further, by taking formal action, the manager is signaling that the resources necessary to resolve the problems at hand reside outside of the supervisor-employee relationship (Atwater et al., 2001).

From the standpoint of the recipient of disciplinary action, many scholars argue that negative affective reactions are likely (Atwater et al., 2001). What is less clear is whether these negative affective reactions would prevent improved employee behavior. Because disciplinary action implies a threat of more severe action, employees might well be expected to change their behavior to avoid more severe sanctions (such as termination). Motivated by a desire to avoid more severe sanctions that likely include the loss of income and career opportunities, employees may well be expected to change the behavior addressed in the disciplinary action (Arvey and Jones, 1984). While negative affect may impact organizational commitment and turnover intentions – at least in the short-term – the sanctioned behavior is likely to improve (Trevino, 1992; Ball et al., 1994). Indeed, there is some evidence to support this within the literature (Arvey et al., 1984; Baum and Youngblood, 1975; Podsakoff and Todor, 1985).

However, it is important to note that this positive effect appears to depend on a few key contingencies. For example, severity of sanction appears to be a critical variable, with positive effects less likely to be observed when the sanction (and the threatened sanction) is less harsh (Greer and Labig, 1987; Trevino and Ball, 1992). From a motivational standpoint, the utility of changing behavior is likely to be greater when it is clear that failure to comply with organizational norms would be costly for the individual. This raises questions,

therefore, about the likely impact of using discipline in settings where managers must gradually increase the severity of sanctions prior to being able to take severe action. If negative affect results from the use of formal sanctions and those same sanctions do not yield significant change in the specific behavior addressed until the sanctions finally reach a high level of severity, the benefit to the organization of using formal discipline may well be more limited.

In addition to severity of the sanction, the perceived fairness of the sanction may also be relevant. Where the application of the sanction is seen by the employee as being unfair or unjustified, the employee may not fully understand how to avoid being sanctioned in the future. To the extent that the sanction is seen as random or a function of bias, the employee may be less likely to believe that their behavior determines whether sanctions will be applied. In sum, then, existing empirical research suggests that use of disciplinary sanctions is often likely to result in both negative affective reactions and improved employee behavior (Atwater et al., 2001; Podsakoff et al., 1982). But whether such improved behavior is actually observed depends on factors likely to affect employee perceptions regarding the utility of efforts to change behavior.

Discipline and the impact on the work group

As Trevino (1992) suggests, discipline affects not only the attitudes and behavior of the sanctioned employee, it also affects observers within the work unit. Once again, however, discipline can affect co-workers in complex ways. To the extent that disciplinary action is seen as justified by co-workers, it has the potential to enhance equity perceptions within the work unit. Further, sanctioning employee behavior that deviates from organizational standards can reinforce important norms and, in doing so, help establish a productive culture within the work unit. And, of course, action taken against one employee can function to deter disciplinary violations among observers (Niehoff et al., 1998; O'Reilly and Puffer, 1989).

Here, too, important contingencies exist. In particular, justice perceptions among co-workers regarding disciplinary action are likely to be critical in determining the impact of that action on performance and outcomes in the overall work unit. Trevino (1992) emphasizes the importance of retributive justice perceptions among co-workers. She theorizes that where there is agreement among co-workers regarding the importance of a rule or norm that is violated, co-workers are likely to believe that retribution is necessary in order to maintain justice. Under such circumstances, the use of disciplinary sanctions is likely to enhance perceptions of equity. Ignoring the violation is likely to adversely affect justice perceptions and, potentially, affect the willingness of co-workers to contribute to the organization (Schnake, 1987).

Theory also suggests that attributions made by co-workers are likely to moderate the effects observed. The positive effect on co-workers of sanctioning an employee is likely to be stronger when the employee is seen as responsible for the violation, where harm occurred because of the violation, and where the employee had previously disregarded important norms (Niehoff et al., 1998). Further, use of disciplinary sanctions in response to norm violations is likely to affect co-worker perceptions regarding the likely consequences should they violate that same norm (O'Reilly and Puffer, 1989; O'Reilly and Weitz, 1980). Theory suggests that these deterrence effects are likely to be stronger when the sanction is more severe and when the supervisor is seen as having substantial credibility prior to the administration of the sanction (Trevino, 1992).

In sum, with regard to observers of disciplinary action, when disciplinary sanctions are applied in response to clear violations of valued norms, justice perceptions are likely to be enhanced. Further, the potential exists for behavioral outcomes to improve as well. When norms regarding appropriate behavior are more clearly established, observer behavior that deviates from these norms is less likely.

The overall impact of discipline on work unit behavior and performance will be determined both by the attitudes and behavior of the recipient of discipline and the behavior of co-workers. Further, the potential exists for sanctions to affect the disciplined employee and co-workers differently. While desirable to fully understand the conditions under which positive and negative effects are observed for both the disciplined employee and co-workers, from an applied standpoint, it may be necessary to examine the effects of discipline on the work group as a whole. In one study, O'Reilly and Weitz (1980) examined the impact of discipline and terminations on work unit performance and found that increased use of discipline and termination was associated with higher levels of work unit performance (within a retail store context). Unfortunately, an extensive empirical literature did not develop following this interesting and provocative study. In particular, little empirical attention has been given to how critical contextual factors are likely to moderate the relationship between discipline and work unit outcomes.

Managerial decision-making regarding discipline

An extensive body of literature has examined how managers make decisions about whether and how severely to discipline an employee (Judge and Martocchio, 1996). Research has shown that managerial decisions about sanctions are strongly affected by attributions made about the cause of the problem behavior. Where factors lead to an internal attribution (with blame being assigned to the employee), managers are more willing to take severe action against the employee. By contrast, factors leading to an external attribution are associated with a reduced willingness to take action (Mitchell and Wood, 1980).

Managers have also been found to be influenced by characteristics of the disciplinary system (Klaas and Feldman, 1993; Klaas et al., 1998). Before taking action, managers are likely to assess the utility of sanctioning the employee. Further, disciplinary systems vary in terms of the burden the manager must meet before significant action can be taken. They also vary in terms of the features that are likely to affect whether the employee will be able to successfully challenge disciplinary action. Findings show that in instances where disciplinary action is clearly not justified and also in instances where action is clearly justified, characteristics of the disciplinary system have little impact on the willingness of managers to take disciplinary action. However, where there is some ambiguity regarding the merits of the case, characteristics of the disciplinary system have a more significant impact. Systems that place a greater burden on the manager in terms of justifying severe action and that grant employees significant latitude in challenging disciplinary action resulted in less willingness to take disciplinary action when the case involves some ambiguity (Klaas and Dell'omo, 1997). From a motivational standpoint, taking disciplinary action has the potential to produce improved work unit performance for the manager. However, if a manager can take severe action only if they engage in a substantial amount of preliminary activity, the benefits may well be offset by the costs. Along the same lines, the expected benefit of taking action is likely to be lower when there is significant uncertainty regarding whether a sanction will be upheld upon review.

Implications for practice and for future research

Organizations are faced with significant questions about how disciplinary systems should be structured and also about how aggressive managers should be in using discipline to address problematic behavior. What does research tell us? Some evidence exists to suggest that the willingness to use formal discipline (up to and including termination) can produce benefits that outweigh the costs. However, quite clearly, this suggestion is based on many contingencies that relate to the organizational setting and

the disciplinary system. For example, in the study showing a positive relationship between discipline and work unit performance (O'Reilly and Weitz, 1980), substantial use was made of both less severe formal action and termination. What happens in settings there is limited reliance on the traditional model of discipline? What happens where mangers provide feedback via informal cues and communication and then use termination when employees do not respond as needed? Terminating employees without formal warning raises key questions. Does such an approach deprive the problem employee of a sufficient opportunity to improve? Does the use of more subtle communication of displeasure with performance reduce the negative affective reactions thought to be associated with punitive sanctions? Also, do you risk creating questions among co-workers about the legitimacy of any terminations that do occur? Does providing formal warnings or suspensions (with the associated negative reaction by the sanctioned employee) create an awareness within the work unit of both the behavior being sanctioned and efforts by the management to correct the behavior? This awareness may well play a critical role in terms of affecting justice perceptions among co-workers when more severe disciplinary action is taken. It is possible, then, that justice perceptions among co-workers will be negatively affected when a termination occurs that is preceded only by informal cues and communication. This then raises the possibility that – in settings where informal cues and communication are used to initially address problem behavior – increased use of termination will negatively affect co-worker justice perceptions and, in turn, work unit outcomes. With regard to the problem employee, using more informal means at early stages of the disciplinary process would be less likely to create negative affective reactions, simply because sanctions are not formally applied. However, affective reactions at the point of termination may be greater if the informal cues and communication were not appropriately processed. While reactance at this stage would be unlikely to affect work group performance, potentially, it could lead to negative outcomes in the form of litigation (Goldman, 2003).

An important issue both for future research and for organizations is how work unit outcomes are affected by the use of termination when little formal action is required prior to termination. This issue has implications both for the behavior of managers in addressing problematic behavior and it has implications for questions regarding the desirability of more flexible versus more traditional disciplinary systems.

Another contingency that may affect the relationship between the use of discipline and work unit outcomes relates to how difficult it is for the manager to move from less severe disciplinary action to termination. In those systems where termination is made more difficult, much time may transpire between initiating disciplinary action and termination (Klaas and Dell'omo, 1997). In such settings, how will the use of discipline affect work unit outcomes? Because the severity of the typical disciplinary sanction is likely to be more minimal, less social learning is likely to occur within the work group when a manager sanctions an employee (Trevino, 1992). Further, as noted earlier, sanctions can lead to reactance by the disciplined employee (Arvey and Jones, 1998). Whether a sanction is ultimately effective in changing behavior despite this reactance depends on the employee recognizing that it is in their interest to change their behavior.

If the employee doesn't expect the initial sanction to be quickly followed by much harsher action, behavioral change may be more minimal. Given there are costs to managers with taking disciplinary action, this raises questions about the relationship between discipline and work unit outcomes in settings where there are substantial limits on a manager's ability to move from less severe formal sanctions to termination. This suggestion, again, highlights the importance of understanding how the context as it relates to the disciplinary system might affect the relationship between the use of discipline and work unit outcomes.

Still another contingency relating to the broader context involves expectations regarding long-term employment with the firm. Many of the arguments made above assume that employees view termination as severe punishment. However, where there is little commitment between employer and employee, where the firm makes little investment in the human capital of its workforce, and where jobs are seen by employees as largely interchangeable with positions in similar firms (Cappelli, 1999), termination may be viewed differently. If true, these changes in the structure of our labor market may limit the degree to which the employee feels compelled to respond to warnings in order to avoid termination (Cappelli and Chauvin, 1991). It would also affect what sort of preliminary action management must take in order to ensure that co-workers see termination as a just response to problematic behavior. Where termination is seen as a less severe event, co-workers may be less likely to expect that managers provide formal warning to employees prior to termination. Once again, the suggestion being made here is that organizational context is likely to play an important role in determining how both the recipient of discipline and co-workers will react to the use of sanctions. This suggestion further argues for the idea that the appropriate use of discipline and the appropriate design of disciplinary systems will vary with these contextual variables.

Still another contextual variable likely to be important (and one suggested by existing theory) relates to the credibility of the manager (Trevino, 1992). Where supervisor credibility is high, there is likely to be less negative reactance from an employee that is disciplined and, as a result, less in the way of negative behavioral consequences. Similarly, where supervisor credibility is high, managerial decisions regarding discipline are more likely to be seen by co-workers as justified. Thus, discipline is more likely to be seen as just, making it more likely that co-workers will learn from observing the disciplinary action taken by the manager. But how far should we take this argument? Does this mean that where supervisors have less credibility with their subordinates they should avoid disciplinary action? While empirical evidence here is lacking, one proposition to consider is that appropriate behavior for managers lacking credibility involves limiting their use of discipline to situations where the offense is severe and where the need for action is obvious to all or can be made obvious to all.

While theory and research suggests that there is likely to be a positive relationship between the willingness to take disciplinary action and work unit outcomes, the strength and direction of this relationship is likely to be highly dependent on the moderators identified above. It should be noted that while there is a strong basis for expecting these contextual moderators to play a role, research is relatively limited. From the standpoint of drawing implications for research, this would suggest a need for research that examines how these contextual factors moderate the relationship between the willingness to use discipline and work unit outcomes.

One additional issue relating to the use of discipline by managers that may deserve attention is the form of the relationship between the use of discipline and work unit outcomes. While some use of discipline may be critical to establishing workplace norms and enhancing justice perceptions, at some point the potential exists for managers to create a punitive workplace culture. At some point, then, the use of discipline could negatively affect justice perceptions and also could create ambiguity about the conditions under which employees will be terminated. As such, particularly in settings where managers have more discretion with regard to utilizing more severe sanctions, some consideration might well be given to the possibility of a curvilinear relationship between the use of discipline and work unit outcomes.

It is also important to address the implications of existing research for the design of disciplinary systems. From an applied standpoint, questions exist regarding how much discretion managers should have in making disciplinary decisions. As noted above, research suggests that where there are significant constraints and limitations on managers, they are often unwilling to take action against the employee unless there is no ambiguity regarding the case (Klaas and Dell'omo, 1997). What is less clear are the implications of using a disciplinary system that imposes few restrictions on managers. What are the implications of such a system for employee justice perceptions, for managerial use of discipline and dismissal, and for litigation risks? And are such systems most effective when there are limited expectations regarding long-term employment prospects. Because the loss of employment is viewed as a less significant event, protection from the unfair dismissal may be less relevant in determining how employees view their employer. While much research has been done on discipline and punishment, from an applied standpoint, many important questions remain.

GRIEVANCES OVER DISCIPLINARY ACTION: WORKPLACE JUSTICE SYSTEMS

Workplace justice systems are very much linked to questions about how organizations should manage discipline. It is through systems of workplace justice that organizations allow employees to challenge disciplinary action taken against them by their manager. It should be noted that systems of workplace justice are very much affected by the industrial relations institutions within the country where a firm is operating (Wheeler et al., 2003). Within some countries, systems of workplace justice are determined largely by statute, in others employers have substantial discretion. Because it is beyond the scope of this paper to address the wide array of institutional requirements relating to systems of workplace justice across different countries, we will discuss systems within settings where firms have some discretion regarding whether and how to use systems of workplace justice.

Employer motivation to use workplace justice systems

Why do employers provide employees with the right to challenge disciplinary action even when not required to do so by statute? Evidence from non-union firms in the US suggest a number of different motives (Colvin, 2004). In some cases, employers are motivated by a desire to more effectively manage litigation risks. Over the last decade, increased use of employment arbitration has been observed (Bingham, 1996). Where used, employees are typically required to agree to submit all legal disputes (including claims regarding wrongful discharge) to employment arbitration. Arbitrator rulings are final and arbitrators are authorized to provide damages consistent with legal statute (Bingham, 1995; Cooper et al., 2000). Further, evidence suggests that use of employment arbitration is greatest among employers with the greatest litigation risks (Colvin, 2003). In other cases, employers appear to be influenced by a union-avoidance motive. By providing employees with an effective voice mechanism, employers are able to reduce the appeal of unionization. Use of procedures such as peer review has been found to be more likely in firms thought to be facing a greater threat of unionization (Colvin, 2004). In addition to these external pressures, firms are also likely to be motivated by internal factors as well. Providing employees with voice to challenge management decisions regarding discipline and other matters is generally viewed as consistent with high involvement work practices (Bemmels, 1997; Batt et al., 2002). Providing employees with the right to challenge management decisions is thought to enhance procedural justice perceptions among employees which, in turn, is likely to positively affect other practices designed to affect employee motivation and commitment (Folger and Cropanzano, 1998; Greenberg, 2006; Dundon et al., 2004; Lind and Tyler, 1998).

The impact of workplace justice systems

Clearly, the use of workplace justice systems may be influenced by different motives. Regardless of the motive behind the use of such systems by employers, questions still exist about how such systems affect how disciplinary action impacts work unit outcomes and also the willingness of managers to make use of discipline. How does providing employees with the opportunity to challenge disciplinary action before a peer review committee or an employment arbitrator affect how a disciplined employee perceives the disciplinary action? Similarly, how does providing this opportunity affect how co-workers react to observing disciplinary action?

With regard to the disciplined employee, in theory, providing employees with voice opportunities should reduce negative affective reactions to discipline (Boroff and Lewin, 1997). Negative affective reactions in response to discipline are thought to be least likely when that action is seen as justified or legitimate. If disciplinary action is challenged by an employee and then affirmed by a review process, the action is more likely to be seen as legitimate (Bemmels, 1997; Lewin and Peterson, 1999). Arguably, even making voice opportunities available to employees may affect perceptions regarding the legitimacy of disciplinary action. Where such voice opportunities exist, the disciplined employee is likely to perceive disciplinary action as action taken that management believes would withstand scrutiny by the review process (Dundon et al., 2004; Batt et al., 2002). To the extent that voice systems reduce reactance to discipline, they may strengthen the relationship between the use of discipline and work unit outcomes. However, it should be noted that, in the extreme, such systems could also affect assessments by the employee regarding the need to change behavior in response to disciplinary action. If the review process is seen as increasing the burden of proof upon the manager to the point that disciplinary action is hard to defend

(Klaas and Dell'omo, 1997), employees may increasingly see themselves as having some level of protection from severe disciplinary action.

Such systems could also affect how co-workers respond to observing disciplinary action. As noted earlier, disciplinary action has the potential to positively affect work unit outcomes – but only if that action is seen as justified (Niehoff et al., 1998). While co-workers have some information regarding the events leading up to disciplinary action, often they must rely on signals or cues regarding the merits of disciplinary action. For example, if the employee has a history of disciplinary problems, co-workers are thought to be more likely to see action as being justified. Where the supervisor has credibility, disciplinary action is also likely to be seen by co-workers as justified (Trevino, 1992). Workplace justice systems can serve as a mechanism by which to help co-workers interpret the legitimacy of disciplinary action. Where an employee's challenge to disciplinary action is rejected upon review, it is more likely that co-workers will perceive the disciplinary action as legitimate, thus enhancing justice perceptions within the work group. Moreover, even where employees don't actually appeal their disciplinary action, the presence of a viable system of workplace justice is likely to enhance perceptions regarding the legitimacy of the disciplinary action. The failure to appeal disciplinary action where a viable grievance system exists may well be seen as a cue that the sanction was justified.

Of course, systems of workplace justice also have the potential to negatively affect how the use of discipline affects workplace outcomes and, more generally, the operation of disciplinary systems. The above argument assumes that systems of workplace justice will allow employees to appeal action which they think is unfair and that the process will reject cases where sanctions were ill-advised and affirm cases where sanctions were justified. Just as systems of workplace justice can be found that actually do little to protect employee rights, there are also systems that offer very substantial protections – perhaps to

the point that it is difficult for managers to justify taking severe disciplinary action (Wheeler et al., 2004). To the extent that protections offered employees are excessive, systems of workplace justice have the potential to raise questions within the work group about whether managerial sanctions ultimately will be enforced.

As noted above, the degree of protection offered by the system of workplace justice is likely to have implications for how disciplinary action and disciplinary systems will impact work unit outcomes. It should also be noted that significant differences have been observed across different systems of workplace justice in the willingness to rule in favor of the employee. Such differences are expected given variation in how systems of workplace justice are structured and designed. For example, in some systems built around employment arbitration, employees are required to submit all legal disputes to arbitration rather than to the court system. Arbitrators are authorized to review whether legal statute has been violated. However, unless specifically authorized, employment arbitrators are not authorized to review whether there was just cause for termination (Bingham and Besch, 2000; Bingham, 1995). This alone could create significant differences with other types of workplace justice systems. But differences might well be expected, even where employment arbitrators are authorized to review disciplinary action using 'for cause' standards. Consider the contrast to decisions made by peer review panels. Given differences in background characteristics, peer review panelists may be expected to be more likely than employment arbitrators to identify with the needs and interests of the employee. Further, employment arbitrators have a financial interest in being selected for arbitration cases in the future and employers are thought to play a dominant role in the selection process (Bingham, 1996).

Research has compared decisions made by employment arbitrators, peer review panelists, and HR managers to each other and also to jurors and to labor arbitrators operating with a collective bargaining system (Bingham and

Mesch, 2000). In a policy capturing study, decision-makers were required to respond to disciplinary cases that varied in terms of factors such as strength of the evidence against the employee, employee characteristics, procedural compliance by management, and evidence of employer wrong doing. Comparisons were made across the following decision-maker roles: employment arbitrators instructed to find for the employee if the employer violated legal statute in disciplining the employer, employment arbitrators instructed to evaluate both whether there was a violation of legal statute and whether the termination met for-cause requirements, peer review panelists instructed to determine whether termination was consistent with company policy, HR managers instructed to determine if they would approve the termination, former jurors in employment-related cases, and labor arbitrators instructed to review the case using just-cause standards typical in settings where there is collective bargaining. Significant differences were observed across these different workplace justice systems in the likelihood of the employee receiving a favorable ruling. Overall, the employee's appeal was least likely to be granted when it was heard by employment arbitrators reviewing whether there was a statutory violation, followed by employment arbitrators reviewing cases both from the standpoint of statutory violations and for-cause standards. This was followed by peer review panelists, HR managers, jurors, and, finally, labor arbitrators. It should be noted as well that differences were also observed in the weight given to different case characteristics within these different systems of workplace justice (Klaas et al., 2005).

Much variation exists in the structure and design of systems of workplace justice and research shows that these differences have substantial implications for an employee's prospects of winning should they challenge discipline or termination. From an empirical standpoint, what is not known is how these differences affect the impact of disciplinary action on work unit outcomes. Systems such as peer review appear to offer broader protection from unfair disciplinary action than systems that focus more on the enforcement of legal statute. Does this broader protection help or hinder the operation of the disciplinary system? Is the impact of disciplinary sanctions on work unit outcomes more positive when employees have access to a system of workplace justice that offers greater protection from unfair dismissal? As noted above, the potential exists for there to be a positive impact. Disciplinary decisions that are upheld by processes that offer broader rights to employees are more likely to be seen as legitimate by workers and, thus, more likely to enhance behavioral outcomes among observers of disciplinary action. Further, it is likely that even providing access to such review processes is likely to affect how disciplinary action is viewed – even if it is not appealed.

Such questions need to be addressed because they have implications for how organizations should design grievance systems for employees. Currently, firms have little in the way of empirical evidence to guide them in determining how much protection to offer to employees through the appeal system. A common concern raised about appeal processes is that they interfere with the manager's ability to make effective use of discipline. To the extent that employees are granted protection through appeal processes, there is likely to be greater uncertainty regarding whether disciplinary decisions will be upheld. Such uncertainty may make managers reluctant to use disciplinary action and, thus, may interfere with the degree to which discipline is used to change employee behavior and otherwise establish clear norms. While this remains a possible outcome, as discussed above, another viable scenario is that strong appeal processes will enhance the degree to which disciplinary action is seen as legitimate, which will allow for disciplinary action to establish work norms.

In making the above arguments, we are assuming that workplace justice systems would be seen by employees as having some value. Evidence suggests that among professional and managerial employees, sufficient weight is placed upon how workplace justices systems are structured to affect job choice decisions (Mahony, Klaas et al., 2005). While it is unlikely that applicants would anticipate having to make use of these systems, they are likely to be treated as a proxy for overall treatment of employees within the organization. However, it is less clear whether significant weight would be given to systems of workplace justice by employees with less attachment to their employer. Under such conditions, workplace justice systems may play a less important role in determining how observers of disciplinary action and also recipients of discipline react to disciplinary sanctions.

More generally, as we continue to observe changes in the structure of our labor markets (Cappelli, 1999), it is important to recognize that these changes may have implications for employee expectations regarding justice systems. Within the workplace justice literature, much attention has been given to the EVLN (exit, voice, loyalty, and neglect) model (Rusbult et al., 1988; Boroff and Lewin, 1997; Olson-Buchanan and Boswell, 2002). It is argued that where viable voice models are provided to employees, they are likely to respond to concerns within the workplace by using voice systems rather than using the exit or neglect responses. However, questions remain about the role of voice within labor markets where jobs are viewed as short-term and generally interchangeable with positions in other firms. In such settings, the cost of exist are more minimal, making the voice option less salient. And where the voice option is less salient, management efforts to provide voice may do less to affect how disciplinary action is perceived by observers or the recipient of disciplinary action.

It should be noted that while the issues addressed above are important, other issues may also impact how organizations should proceed with regard to workplace justice systems. For example, independent of the impact on work unit outcomes, workplace justice systems might well be justified based on the impact on the willingness of employees to use litigation in response to employment disputes.

Moreover, normative questions surround the issue of workplace justice. Within our current labor market model, what rights and protections do employees deserve within the workplace? In settings where the employee-employer relationship is characterized by long-term relationships and investment by both sides in that relationship, some level of voice might well be justified purely on normative grounds.

SUMMARY

While the use of discipline and reactions to discipline has been the subject of much study, significant questions remain about how discipline should be used within organizations and how both disciplinary systems and systems of workplace justice should be structured. Drawing on the existing literature, we have attempted to highlight the processes by which discipline and both disciplinary and workplace justice systems might impact work unit outcomes. We have also attempted to show how factors associated with the organizational context are likely to affect how these processes actually affect outcomes. We further argued that understanding the moderating role of these contextual factors is likely to be critical to understanding how managers should use discipline and how firms should structure systems and processes relating to employee discipline.

REFERENCES

Abraham, K.G. and McKersie, R.B. (1990) *New Developments in the Labor Market: Toward a New Institutional Paradigm.* Cambridge, Mass: The MIT Press.
Althauser, R.P. (1989) 'Internal labor markets', *Annual Review of Sociology*, 15: 143–61.
Arvey, R.D. and Jones, A.P. (1985) 'The use of discipline in organizational settings: A framework for future research', *Research in Organizational Behavior*, 7: 367–408.
Arvey, R.D., Davis, G.A. and Nelson, S.M. (1984) 'Use of discipline in an organization: A field study', *Journal of Applied Psychology*, 69: 448–60.

Atwater, L.E., Waldman, D.A., Carey, J.A. and Cartier, P. (2001) 'Recipient and observer reactions to discipline: Are managers experiencing wishful thinking?', *Journal of Organizational Behavior*, 22: 249–70.

Ball, G.A., Trevino, L.K. and Sims, H.P. (1994) 'Just and unjust punishment: Influence on subordinate performance and citizenship', *Academy of Management Journal*, 37: 299–322.

Batt, R. Colvin, A.J.S. and Keefe, J. (2002) 'Employee voice, human resource practices, and quit rates: Evidence from the telecommunications industry', *Industrial and Labor Relations Review*, 55: 573–94.

Baum, J.F. and Youngblood, S.A. (1975) 'Impact of an organizational control policy on absenteeism, performance, and satisfaction', *Journal of Applied Psychology*, 60: 688–94.

Bemmels, B. (1997) 'Exit voice, and loyalty in employment relationships', in D. Lewin, D.J.B. Mitchell and M.A. Zaidi (eds), *The Human Resource Management Handbook*. Greenwich, Conn.: JAI Press, pp. 245–59.

Bingham, L.B. (1995) 'Is there a bias in arbitration of non-union employment. Disputes?', *International Journal of Conflict Management*, 6: 369–97.

Bingham, L.B. (1996) 'Emerging due process concerns in employment arbitration: A look at actual cases', *Labor Law Journal*, 47: 108–26.

Bingham, L.B. and Mesch, D.J. (2000) 'Decision making in employment and arbitration', *Industrial Relations*, 39: 671–94.

Boroff, K.E. and Lewin, D. (1997) 'Loyalty, voice, and intent to exit a union firm: A conceptual and empirical analysis', *Industrial and Labor Relations Review*, 51: 50–63.

Butterfield, K.D., Trevino, L.K., Wade, K.J. and Bail, G.A. (2005) 'Organizational punishment from the manager's perspective: An exploratory study', *Journal of Managerial Issues*, 17: 362–82.

Butterfield, K.D., Trevino, L.K. and Ball, G.A. (1996) 'Punishment from the manager's perspective: A grounded investigation and inductive model', *Academy of Management Journal*, 39: 1479–512.

Cappelli, P. (1999) *The new deal at work: Managing the market driven workforce*. Boston, MA : Harvard Business School Press.

Cappelli, P. and Chauvin, K. (1991) 'A test of an efficiency model of grievance activity', *Industrial and Labor Relations Review*, 45: 3–14.

Colvin, A.J.S. (2003) 'Institutional pressures, human resource strategies, and the rise of nonunion dispute resolution procedures', *Industrial and Labor Relations Review*, 56: 375–92.

Colvin, A.J.S. (2004) 'Adoption and use of dispute resolution procedures in the nonunion workplace', in D. Lewin and B.E. Kaufman (eds), *Advances in Industrial and Labor Relations*, 13: 69–95.

Colvin, A.J.S., Klaas, B.S. and Mahony, D. (2006) 'Research on alternative dispute resolution', in D. Lewin (ed.), *Contemporary Issues in Employment Relations*, pp. 103–47.

Cooper, L.J., Nolan, D.R. and Bales, R.A. (2000) *ADR in the workplace*. St. Paul, MN:

Dundon, T., Wilkinson, A., Marchington, M. and Ackers, M. (2004) 'The meaning and purpose of employee voice', *International Journal of Human Resource Management*, 15: 1149–70.

Feuille, P. and Delaney, J.T. (1992) 'The individual pursuit of organizational justice: Grievance procedures in nonunion workplaces', in G.R. Ferris and K.M. Rowland (eds), *Research in Personnel and Human Resource Management*. Stamford, CT: JAI Press, pp. 187–232.

Folger, R. and Cropanzano, R. (1998) *Organizational Justice and Human Resource Management*. Thousand Oaks, CA: Sage.

Goldman, B. (2003) 'An application of referent cognitions theory to legal-claiming by terminated workers: The role of organizational justice and anger', *Journal of Management*, 29: 705–28.

Greenberg, J. (2006) 'Losing sleep over organizational injustice: Attenuating insomniac reactions to underpayment inequity with supervisory training in interactional injustice', *Journal of Applied Psychology*, 91: 58–69.

Greer, C.R. and Labig, C.E. (1987) 'Employee reactions to disciplinary action', *Human Relations*, 40: 507–24.

Judge, T.A. and Martocchio, J.J. (1996) 'Dispositional Influences on Attributions Concerning Absenteeism', *Journal of Management*, 22: 837–68.

Klaas, B.S., Brown, M. and Heneman, H.G. III. (1998) 'The determinants of organizations' usage of employee dismissal', *Journal of Labor Research*, 19: 149–64.

Klaas, B.S. and Feldman, D.C. (1993) 'The evaluation of disciplinary appeals', *Human Resource Management Review*, 3: 49–81.

Klaas, B.S., Mahony, D. and Wheeler, H.N. (2006) 'Decision-making about workplace disputes: A policy-capturing study of employment arbitrators, labor arbitrators, and jurors', *Industrial Relations*, 45: 68–95.

Klaas, B.S. and Dell'omo, G.G. (1997) 'Managerial use of dismissal: Organizational-level determinants', *Personnel Psychology*, 50: 927–54.

Lewin, D. and Peterson, R.B. (1999) 'Behavioral outcomes of grievance activity', *Industrial Relations*, 38: 554–76.

Lind, E.A. and Tyler, T.R. (1988) *The social psychology of procedural justice*. New York: Plenum Press.

Mahoney, D., Klaas, B.S., McClendon, J.A. and Varma, A. (2005) 'The effects of employment arbitration and employee rights on organizational attraction', *Human Resource Management*, 44: 449–70.

Mitchell, T. and Wood, R. (1980) 'Supervisors' response to poor performance: A test of an attributional model', *Organizational Behavior and Human Decision Processes*, 25: 125–28.

Niehoff, B.P., Paul, R.J. and Bunch, J.F.S. (1998) 'The social effects of punishment events: The influence of the performance record and the severity of the punishment on observers' justice perceptions', *Journal of Organizational Behavior*, 19: 589–602.

Olson-Buchanan, J.B. and Boswell, W.R. (2002) 'The role of employee loyalty and formality in voicing discontent', *Journal of Applied Psychology*, 87: 1167–74.

O'Reilly, C.A. III and Weitz, B. (1980) 'Managing marginal employees: The use of warnings and dismissal', *Administrative Science Quarterly*, 25: 476–88.

O'Reilly, C.A. III and Puffer, S.M. (1989) 'The impact of rewards and punishments in a social context: A laboratory and field experiment', *Journal of Occupational Psychology*, 61: 41–53.

Podsakoff, P. and Todor, W. (1985) 'Relationship between leader reward and punishment behavior and group productivity', *Journal of Management*, 11: 55–73.

Podsakoff, P. Todor, W. and Skov, R. (1982) 'Effects of leader contingent and non–contingent reward and punishment behaviors on subordinate performance and satisfaction', *Academy of Management Journal*, 25: 810–21.

Podsakoff, P. Todor, W., Grover, R. and Huber, V. (1984) 'Situational moderators of leader reward and punishment behavior: Fact or fiction?', *Organizational Behavior and Human Performance*, 34: 21–63.

Rusbult, C.E., Farrell, D., Rogers, G. and Mainous, A.G. (1988) 'Impact of exchange variables on exit, voice, loyalty, and neglect: An integrative model of responses to declining job status satisfaction', *Academy of Management Journal*, 31: 599–627.

Schnake, M.E. (1987) 'Vicarious punishment in a work setting: a failure to replicate', *Psychological Reports*, 61: 379–86.

Trevino, L.K. (1992) 'The social effects of punishment in organizations: A justice perspective', *Academy of Management Review*, 17: 647–76.

Trevino, L.K. and Ball, G.A. (1992) 'The social implications of punishing unethical behavior: Observers' cognitive and affective reactions', *Journal of Management*, 18: 751–68.

Wheeler, H.N., Klaas, B.S. and Mahony, D.M. (2004) *Workplace Justice Without Unions*. Kalamazoo, MI: Upjohn Institute.

20

Downsizing and Redundancy

Wayne F. Cascio

INTRODUCTION

There is a large and growing literature on the subject of downsizing and redundancy. At the same time, however, there is much about their effects that we simply do not know. This chapter will begin by providing some definitions and important distinctions in terms, followed by a description of the economic rationale that drives layoffs. Then we will consider the extent of downsizing in the United States, Western Europe, Asia, and Australia, followed by a discussion of methods used to execute downsizing and redundancy strategies. We also will examine alternatives to downsizing, and survey research in that area. The chapter concludes with a discussion of the effects of downsizing and redundancy at multiple levels – individuals who stay, those who leave, local communities, and on firms, particularly knowledge-based organizations. As we shall see, there are many unanswered questions about the full range of effects of downsizing and redundancy. This poses an ongoing challenge for social science research.

SOME DEFINITIONS AND IMPORTANT DISTINCTIONS

Downsizing and redundancy are forms of organizational restructuring. Organizational restructuring refers to planned changes in organizational structure that affect the use of people. Organizational restructuring often results in workforce reductions that may be accomplished through mechanisms such as attrition, early retirements, voluntary severance agreements ('buy-outs'), or layoffs. The term 'layoffs' is used sometimes as if it were synonymous with 'downsizing,' but downsizing is a broad term that can include any number of combinations of reductions in a firm's use of assets – financial (stock or cash), physical (plants and other infrastructure), human, or informational (databases). Layoffs are the same as employment downsizing and redundancy.

Employment downsizing, in turn, is not the same thing as organizational decline (Cascio, 2007). Downsizing is an intentional, proactive management strategy, whereas decline is an environmental or organizational phenomenon that occurs involuntarily and results in erosion of an organization's resource base. As an example, the advent of digital photography, disposable cameras, and other imaging products signaled a steep decline in the demand for the kind of instant photographic cameras and films that Polaroid had pioneered in the 1940s. On October 12, 2001 Polaroid was forced to declare bankruptcy.

WHY ARE LAYOFFS ATTRACTIVE?

Layoffs began as a strategy exclusively for cost-cutting, but they have also become part of a management strategy for adjusting workforce competencies (McKinley et al., 2000; Osterman, 2000). Layoffs increase a firm's flexibility over the transition process. That is, organizations quickly and efficiently can remove employees whose skills no longer fit their strategies or add to their market values (Zatzick and Iverson, 2006).

There are at least two important differences, however, between layoffs and other workforce-reduction strategies such as attrition and early retirement offers (Zatzick and Iverson, 2006). One, layoffs allow organizations to control downsizing strategically. Management can target specific employees or groups of employees and determine the depth of the cuts. Such control is essential for adjusting the skills and capabilities of a workforce. Two, layoffs increase workplace responsiveness to environmental change by facilitating quick removal of employees who lack appropriate skills.

As an example, consider the strategy at Progress Energy Corporation (Lublin and Thurm, 2006). After launching an early-retirement program to help reduce annual operating costs by $100 million, Progress managers identified 450 specific jobs they wanted to eliminate and shared the list with employees to help the workers in affected departments make their decisions. They told employees they would consider layoffs if not enough people applied. To avoid a brain drain in some areas, they limited the number of people who could leave, as in engineering.

In the end, 1,450 employees agreed to take the buy-out – far more than Progress expected. As a result, Progress went on a hiring binge, adding roughly 1,000 new employees with the kinds of skills the company needed, with 600 openings still pending. Even with the buy-outs, the company still had to lay off about 65 employees because in some departments not enough workers accepted the buy-outs.

THE ECONOMIC RATIONALE THAT DRIVES LAYOFFS

What makes downsizing and redundancy strategies so compelling to firms worldwide? Firms undertake downsizing with the expectation that they will achieve financial and organizational benefits (Bruton et al., 1996; Cascio, 1993; Kets de Vries and Balazs, 1997; Surowiecki, 2007). The economic rationale is straightforward. It begins with the premise that there really are only two ways to make money in business: either cut costs or increase revenues. Which are more predictable, future costs or future revenues? Anyone who makes monthly mortgage payments knows that future costs are far more predictable than future revenues. Payroll expenses represent fixed costs, so by cutting payroll, other things remaining equal, firms should reduce expenses. Reduced expenses translate into increased earnings, and earnings drive stock prices. Higher stock prices make investors and analysts happy.

The key phrase is 'other things remaining equal.' As we shall see, other things often do not remain equal, and that is why many of the anticipated benefits of employment downsizing or redundancy strategies do not always materialize (Cascio, 2002a). A former executive at AT&T and Lucent Technologies bemoaned the formula that top managers at those companies seemed to rely on in order to navigate any crisis: 'Cut headcount, cut budgets, reduce senior management (especially those who were threats or outspoken), and always reorganize' (Franks, 2007: A15).

The result? 'Anyone can lay off personnel, cut budgets, and change an organization chart. It takes true genius and creativity to grow a business. Without that genius, executives at any level are just managers' (Franks, 2007: A15).

Certainly there is nothing wrong with cutting costs, and in any dynamic economy layoffs will be necessary (Surowiecki, 2007). The problem is that too many companies define workers solely in terms of how much they cost, rather than how much value they create. As an example, consider Circuit City, which laid off 3,400 of its most experienced sales associates because they earned 51 cents per hour too much. After downsizing it is certainly easier to measure a lower wage bill than it is to see the business a company is not getting because it has too few sales people, or the new products it is not inventing because its R&D staff is too small. These lost opportunities may be hard to measure, but over time they can have a huge impact on corporate performance (Surowiecki, 2007). As we noted above, however, downsizing by whatever strategy is not always wrong.

WHEN DOWNSIZING MAKES SENSE

There are at least two circumstances where employment downsizing may be warranted. The first occurs in companies that find them-selves saddled with non-performing assets or consistently unprofitable subsidiaries. They should consider selling them to buyers who can make better use of those assets. Employees associated with those assets or subsidiaries often go with them to the new buyers. The second instance occurs when jobs rely on old technology that is no longer commercially viable. This was the case in the newspaper industry following the advent of computer-based typesetting. There simply was no longer a need for compositors, a trade that had been handed down from generation to generation. However, indiscriminate 'slash-and-burn' tactics, such as across-the-board downsizing of employees, seldom lead to long-term gains in productivity, profits, or

stock prices, as we shall see. First, however, let us consider the global reach of downsizing.

Extent of downsizing

Downsizing is often associated with the fluid labor markets and limited legal protections for workers in the United States (Baumol et al., 2003; Cascio et al., 1999; Uchitelle, 2006). While it is true that downsizing occurs on a large scale in the United States, the phenomenon is global in scope. In the United States at least, there is a difference between the numbers of layoffs announced versus the number actually recorded by the Bureau of Labor Statistics of the US Department of Labor. The BLS records 'mass layoff events' as those involving 50 or more workers. As a result, its numbers underestimate the actual numbers of layoffs (Guthrie and Datta, 2008). With that in mind, Figure 20.1 below shows the numbers of mass layoff events involving at least 50 employees from the same employer, from 1996 through the end of 2008, as reported by the Bureau of Labor Statistics.

As the results of Table 20.1 show, the number of mass layoffs peaked in 2008 (21,137) reached its highest level since 2001. More than 5.5 million jobs were lost from December, 2007 (the beginning of the latest economic recession) through April, 2009. In 2006, for example, 35,000 workers at General Motors accepted checks ranging from $35,000 to $140,000 to retire early (GM, 2006). Another 38,000 took similar buy-outs at Ford Motor Company (Gustafson, 2006).

In the United Kingdom, Worrall et al. (2000) reported that there were more than 200,000 notified redundancies in the UK each year. Layoffs also occur often in Asia, Australia, India, China and throughout Europe as well (Thornton, 2009). Thus Japan's chip and electronics conglomerates shed tens of thousands of jobs in the first few years of the 21st century as the worldwide information-technology slump and fierce competition from foreign rivals battered their bottom lines. From 2001 to 2004, for example, Matsushita Electric Industrial Company (whose brand names include Panasonic and Technics)

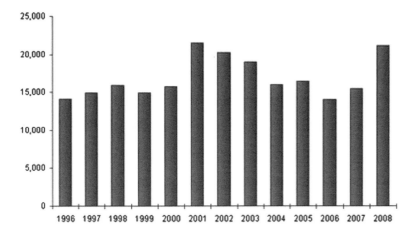

Figure 20.1   Number of mass layoff events involving at least 50 employees from a single employer, 1996–2008.
Source: U.S. Department of Labor, Bureau of Labor Statistics.

slashed its domestic workforce by 19 per cent, to 112,000, as it closed 30 factories (Rowley and Tashiro, 2005). In mainland China, more than 25.5 million people were laid-off from state-owned firms between 1998 and 2001. Another 20 million were expected to be laid off from traditional state-owned firms by 2006 (China Warns, 2002).

The incidence of layoffs varies among countries in Western Europe. Labor laws in countries such as Italy, France, Germany, and Spain make it difficult and expensive to dismiss workers. In Germany, for example, all 'redundancies' must by law be negotiated in detail by a workers' council, which is a compulsory part of any big German company, and often has a say in which workers can be fired. Moreover, setting the terms of severance is tricky, because the law is vague and German courts often award compensation if workers claim they received inadequate settlements. In France, layoffs are rare. Even if companies offer generous severance settlements to French workers, as both Michelin and Marks and Spencer did, the very announcement of layoffs triggers a political firestorm (Winestock, 2002).

Denmark is an exception to the European approach described above. Its government allows liberal hiring and firing, as in the US, and it has imposed limits on the duration of its high unemployment benefits. How does it pay for such extensive retraining? it also invests more than any other country, as a percentage of its gross domestic product (4.4 per cent) in retraining those who have lost jobs. It calls its approach 'flexicurity.' How does it pay for such extensive retraining? Its tax revenues account for 50 per cent of GDP, second only to Sweden.

Every three months the government polls employers in the Copenhagen area to identify what jobs they will need in the coming years, and it uses the feedback to identify the next labor shortages. It then offers training programs for those occupations. Denmark's different regions use that policy with some variations, constantly experimenting, as officials learn what works. Nation-wide, about two-thirds of Danes who are laid off have a new job within a year. In the aggregate, the unusual mix of the free market and big government helped Denmark cut its unemployment rate in half, from about 10 per cent in the early 1990s to under five per cent in 2006 (Walker, 2006).

DOWNSIZING METHODS

Generally speaking, an organization that decides to eliminate redundant employees does so by using one or more of four broad methods (Redman and Wilkinson, 2006). The simplest is natural attrition, in which firms do not replace a person who leaves. With this approach employees have the opportunity to exercise free choice in deciding whether to stay or leave, and thus the potential for conflict and feelings of powerlessness is minimized. At the same time, however, it may pose serious problems for management, because it is unplanned and uncontrollable.

Voluntary redundancy, including buy-out offers, is a second approach to downsizing the workforce. The buy-out plans offered by Ford Motor Company are typical. Offers ranged from $35,000 for workers with 30 or more years of service who could leave and keep their full retiree benefits, to a flat payment of $100,000 to younger workers who agreed to leave the automaker and to give up retiree healthcare and Ford pensions. For workers who chose to go to college or vocational school for four years, Ford provided half their usual pay, about $27,000 on average, while they received full medical coverage and their tuition was paid. Workers who chose this plan could keep any accumulated pension but had to leave behind any retiree health benefits (McCracken, 2006).

A key research question is who tends to leave? While organizations would like to see low performers who are easy to replace walk out the door, it is entirely possible that those with the largest number of options in the external labor market are most likely to leave – high performers who are difficult to replace. A third possibility is that members of both high- and low-performing groups will tend to leave out of fear that they could be dismissed without any financial cushion at a later date. In one of the very few studies to examine this question, Savery et al. (1998) found that high absenteeism and low commitment are associated with those expressing interest in voluntary redundancy. This issue has both theoretical and practical implications, and more research on it is sorely needed.

A third strategy for downsizing is compulsory redundancy – termination – with no choice by the departing employees. This strategy is characteristic of plant closures or the wholesale elimination of departments or business units. Although it is distinctly unpalatable to employees, the managers who make the decisions about which plants or jobs to eliminate have the opportunity to design and implement criteria based on the needs of the business (Redman and Wilkinson, 2006). Furthermore, eliminating jobs (and all of the positions that comprise them) or entire business units makes it less likely that individual employees would prevail with lawsuits alleging unfair discrimination.

A final strategy for downsizing is early retirement offers. As the Ford Motor Company example illustrated, these are often part of a broader buy-out scheme in which a company offers more generous retirement benefits in return for an employee's promise to leave at a time certain in the future. Sometimes the offers are staggered to prevent a mass exodus. Retention bonuses with different quit dates may be used to ensure an orderly exit.

From an organizational view, early retirement has the advantage of opening up promotion opportunities for younger workers (Lublin and Thurm, 2006; McGoldrick and Cooper, 1989). Research indicates that both personal and situational factors affect retirement decisions. Personally, individuals with Type A behavior patterns (hard-driving, aggressive, impatient) are less likely to prefer to retire, while those with obsolete job skills, chronic health problems, and sufficient financial resources are more likely to retire. In terms of one's personal situation, employees are more likely to retire to the extent that they have reached their occupational goals, that their jobs have undesirable characteristics, that home life is seen as preferable to work life, and that there are attractive alternative (leisure) activities (Greene, 1992; Kim and Feldman, 1998). Regardless of the reason for accepting an early-retirement offer, one advantage is that it carries less of a stigma than does the other 'R' word – redundancy.

There are also two important downside risks associated with early-retirement programs, and they should be noted. One, perceptions of overly generous benefits to early retirees tends to be associated with *higher* intentions to quit on the part of ineligible employees who remain (Mollica and DeWitt, 2000). Two, as we noted earlier, open-ended, non-targeted, early-retirement programs may lead to the loss of highly skilled employees and managers (Hymowitz, 2001). Unfortunately there is a large gap in the research literature on the relative merits of alternative strategies for implementing early-retirement programs. Deepening our understanding of this issue will have both theoretical as well as practical payoffs.

ALTERNATIVES TO DOWNSIZING

While a considerable body of research continues to focus on downsizing, its implementation, and its effects, there is much less effort devoted to understanding the impacts of alternatives to downsizing. Two surveys that each included more than 110 different companies in the US found that the most common alternatives included the following: lower incentive payouts, delayed salary increases, salary freezes, freezes on promotions, delays in new-hire start dates, reducing perquisites, revoking job offers, and offering unpaid vacations (Lavelle, 2001; White, 2001). These are all relatively short-term fixes.

Far less common within firms are long-term solutions such as the three R's: redeployment, relocation, and retraining (Cascio, 2002a; 2002b). At a broader level, both Japan and the Scandinavian countries have the most developed forms of employment protection, with graded steps for reductions in costs (Redman and Wilkinson, 2006). In the case of Japan, this includes redeployment, relocation, retraining, transfer, and even the suspending of dividends and cutting the salaries of senior managers.

There is a very limited body of research that examines the relative financial effects of these alternatives on firms, and the psychological effects (attitudinal and behavioral) on individual employees (e.g., see Cascio and Wynn, 2004). This is not surprising, since the number of firms, at least in the US, that have implemented such long-term solutions is limited. Why? I believe that it is often a matter of the mental models that senior managers have about human resources.

In 1995 I wrote a publication for the US Department of Labor entitled *Guide to Responsible Restructuring* (US Department of Labor, 1995). As I investigated the approaches that various companies, large and small, public and private, adopted in their efforts to restructure, what became obvious was that companies differed in terms of how they viewed their employees. Indeed, they almost seemed to separate themselves logically into two groups. One group of firms, by far the larger of the two, saw employees as *costs to be cut*. The other, much smaller group of firms, saw employees as *assets to be developed*. Therein lay a major difference in the approaches they took to restructure their organizations.

- Employees as costs to be cut – these are the downsizers. They constantly ask themselves, what is the minimum number of employees we need to run this company? What is the irreducible core number of employees the business requires?
- Employees as assets to be developed – these are the responsible restructurers. They constantly ask themselves, 'How can we change the way we do business, so that we can use the people we currently have more effectively?

The downsizers see employees as commodities – like paper clips or light bulbs – interchangeable and substitutable – one for another. This is a 'plug-in' mentality: plug them in when you need them, pull the plug when you no longer need them. In contrast, responsible restructurers see employees as sources of innovation and renewal. They see in employees the potential to grow their businesses.

Pfeffer (2005) characterized 'changing the mental models' of managers as the most important responsibility of human resource professionals. Changing a mental model from one based on the view of employees as costs to be cut to one based on employees as assets to be developed is no easy task, since most models of business and behavior are unconscious and implicit (Pfeffer, 2005). Often such models are implied by an organization's practices (e.g., repetitive downsizing), and they get transferred because organizations often copy (benchmark) what others do. On top of that, belief and ideology play a large part in management decisions, yet all too infrequently we fail to examine the evidence for and the assumptions that underlie those beliefs (Pfeffer and Sutton, 2006). Because what we do comes from what and how we think, interventions designed to uncover and change the mental models of decision-makers, particularly those that affect their philosophies about the people in their organizations, may have very high leverage. Unfortunately, there is almost no systematic research on this issue, but the need is great to deepen our understanding of it.

THE EFFECTS OF DOWNSIZING AND REDUNDANCY

Downsizing is often motivated by a desire to reduce labor expenses in order to stem eroding profitability and/or to increase future profitability (Guthrie and Datta, 2008). In increasingly competitive markets, 'downsizing has turned into one of the inevitable outcomes of living in a global world where continual adjustments to products, services, and the price of labor are needed to remain competitive' (Kets de Vries and Balazs, 1997: 12). At the same time, Cameron (1994) described downsizing as the 'most pervasive, yet under-studied, phenomenon in the business world' (p. 183). Many studies have been conducted since that statement was written, yet, relative to the frequency

with which downsizing occurs, the actual number of published studies remains rather limited.

Direct and indirect costs

Research exists at the individual and at the firm level, even at the level of individual communities (Feldman, 2003; Pelley, 2009; Zaslow, 2006), on the effects of downsizing and redundancy. In short, the effects of downsizing extend beyond those who lose their jobs. Downsizing also alters the work environment of those employees and managers who remain in the organization, known as survivors (Westman, 2007). Let us begin our treatment by examining some of the direct and indirect costs that firms incur when they downsize (Buono, 2003; Cascio, 2004; Uchitelle, 2006). These are shown in Table 20.1.

Because institutional infrastructures vary so much across countries, some of the costs shown in Table 20.1 may apply quite differently (e.g., unemployment taxes, supplemental unemployment benefits, pension and benefit payouts). There also may be other costs that are not shown in Table 20.1 that may apply in specific circumstances.

One of the biggest costs is in employee morale and associated attitudinal effects. In fact it has often been said that employee morale is the first casualty in a downsizing. Study after study has found that morale and trust declined after a downsizing (Appelbaum et al., 1999; Kets de Vries and Balazs, 1997; Mirvis, 1997). So also does organizational commitment (Brockner et al., 1987; Knudsen et al., 2003), job satisfaction (Armstrong-Stassen, 2002;

Table 20.1   Direct and indirect costs of employment downsizing

Direct costs	Indirect costs
Severance pay, in lieu of notice	Recruiting and employment costs of new hires
Accrued vacation and sick pay	Low morale, risk-averse survivors
Supplemental unemployment benefits	Increase in unemployment tax rate
Outplacement	Lack of staff when economy rebounds, training and retraining
Pension and benefit payouts	Potential lawsuits from aggrieved employees
Administrative processing costs	Heightened insecurity, reduced productivity
Costs of rehiring former employees	Loss of institutional memory and trust in management

Luthans and Sommer, 1999); and job involvement (Brockner et al., 1988). At the same time, stress levels increase (Buono, 2003; Cascio, 1993; O'Neil and Lenn, 1995), due, at least in part, to the loss of a sense of personal control over important events in one's life (Devine et al., 2003). This constellation of symptoms is known as survivor syndrome. Two concepts are central to understanding it: the psychological contract and organizational justice (distributive and procedural) (Westman, 2007).

The psychological contract and organizational justice

A psychological contract refers to an individual's expectations concerning obligations that exist between an employee and an organization. These expectations are not necessarily derived from specific promises, but rather are inferred from the employer's actions (Rousseau, 2001). One of the expectations that employees have is for fair treatment. Layoffs are often interpreted by employees as a breach of the psychological contract, and surviving employees may respond psychologically, by withholding effort and involvement, or physically, through absences and/or quitting (De Meuse et al., 2004; De Meuse Marks, & Dai, in press; Mishra and Spreitzer, 1998). For example, high-performing employees often take jobs elsewhere in order to avoid the uncertainties and ambiguities in a downsizing environment (Iverson and Pullman, 2000; Rosenblatt and Sheaffer, 2001).

In the wake of decisions that affect them, such as those involving pay, promotions, or layoffs, employees often ask, 'Was that fair?' Judgments about the fairness or equity of procedures used to make decisions, that is, procedural justice, are rooted in the perceptions of employees. Strong research evidence indicates that such perceptions lead to important consequences, such as employee behavior and attitudes (Colquitt et al., 2001; Kanovsky, 2000). When employees feel that they have not been treated fairly, they may retaliate in the form of theft, sabotage, and even violence (Greenberg, 1997).

Conversely, procedurally fair treatment has been demonstrated to result in reduced stress (Elovainio et al., 2001) and increased performance, job satisfaction, commitment to an organization, and trust. It also encourages organizational citizenship behaviors (OCBs) – discretionary behaviors performed outside of one's formal role that help other employees perform their jobs or that show support for and conscientiousness toward the organization (Colquitt et al., 2001). OCBs include behaviors such as the following (Borman and Motowidlo, 1993):

- volunteering to carry out activities that are not formally a part of one's job;
- persisting with extra enthusiasm or effort when necessary to complete one's own tasks successfully;
- helping and cooperating with others;
- following organizational rules and procedures, even when they are personally inconvenient;
- endorsing, supporting, and defending organizational objectives.

Effect of downsizing on knowledge-based organizations and social networks

Knowledge-based organizations, from high-technology firms to the financial-services industry, depend heavily on their employees – their stock of human capital – to innovate and grow. Knowledge-based organizations are collections of networks in which interrelationships among individuals, that is, social networks, generate learning and knowledge. This knowledge base constitutes a firm's 'memory.' Because a single individual has multiple relationships in such an organization, indiscriminate, non-selective downsizing has the potential to inflict considerable damage on the learning and memory capacity of organizations. Such a loss damages ongoing processes and operations, forfeits current contacts, and may lead to foregone business opportunities.

Empirical evidence indicates that the damage is far greater than might be implied by a simple tally of individuals

(Fisher and White, 2000; Gittins, 2001; Littler and Innes, 2003; Priti, 2000). Organizations at greatest risk include those that operate in rapidly evolving industries, such as biotechnology, pharmaceuticals, and software, where survival depends on a firm's ability to innovate constantly.

Recognizing that upset employees are less productive and more averse to risk, a growing number of companies are retaining consultants to host 'venting' sessions, and they are using retention bonuses and restricted stock to ensure that high-priority employees stick around (Lublin and Thurm, 2006). Not surprisingly, many of the same consultants are also being asked to counsel the very managers who did the firing, managers who report elevated levels of exhaustion and stress from doing so (Firing line, 2007).

Effects of downsizing on firm performance

An issue that naturally arises, at the level of the firm, is the long-term impact on employee productivity, company profitability, and stock prices. At a general level, one can find studies that downsizing has positive effects (Wayhan and Werner, 2000), negative effects (Cascio et al., 1997; Uchitelle, 2006), or no effects (Cameron et al., 1991) on firm performance. Two more recent studies used large data sets to examine the impact of downsizing on accounting measures of firm performance as well as on stock-market performance (Cascio and Young, 2003; De Meuse et al., 2004). Both found that companies that conducted large-scale layoffs significantly underperformed, as compared to those who conducted fewer or no layoffs, with respect to profit margin, return on investment, return on equity, market-to-book ratio, and industry-adjusted total return on common stock.

In terms of employee productivity, Baumol et al. (2003) found that while productivity (output per worker) declined following downsizing, the decline was offset by savings in unit labor costs, with market value being unaffected . Similarly, Cappelli (2000) found that while labor productivity decreases following downsizing, there are also reductions in labor costs.

Effects on those laid off and on communities

Not surprisingly, laid-off employees are often stressed out, particularly as their buy-out packages dwindle. Uchitelle (2006) marshals a considerable body of evidence to argue that a layoff-happy business culture in the United States is creating a society of downwardly mobile, insecure workers. As an example, consider the 47-year-old executive who, after 25 years with Procter & Gamble, loses her $150,000-per-year job in a buyout. When one of the cheaper, young staffers hired to replace her falters, she is rehired as a 'consultant' – at $75 per hour for three to five hours a week. There is also the laid-off sixty-something who strenuously works his alumni network only to net zero job offers, despite his degrees from Harvard and Wharton. His depressing conclusion? His education paradoxically hurt him because it created a set of expectations that he can never fulfill.

What about the impact on communities? Broomfield Hills, Michigan, a wealthy suburb of Detroit whose residents include large numbers of executives from General Motors and Ford, is typical of communities that depend heavily on just one or two employers or on a single industry. Mirroring the woes in the auto industry, foreclosures were way up, while charitable giving was way down in 2006. A local country club even had a waiting list – for members who want to quit. Many residents changed their lifestyles, in ways both large and small, as they worried about the economy or their jobs. When they did not spend money, local merchants like Sidney Krandall and Sons, Jewelers, founded in 1911, had to shut their doors. At weddings and bar- and bat-mitzvahs, more hosts served chicken instead of steak, and decorations were less extravagant. Bar bills, however, rose sharply. Physicians were affected as patients lost health-insurance coverage and postponed medical care. As these few examples illustrate, the effects of fear and uncertainty rippled through the entire fabric of the local economy (Zaslow, 2006).

The news is not all bad, however. While research has revealed a variety of negative health consequences associated with lay-off victims (Leana and Feldman, 1992; Leana et al., 1998), this is not necessarily true for those who accept voluntary buyout packages. In an Australian study, 71 individuals who had accepted voluntary buyout packages (after 7–44 years of service, with an average of 25 years) were contacted 2–7 years after leaving their firms. Almost 90 per cent were married, and about half had dependent children. Surprisingly, 61% considered their health to be about the same, and 29% considered it to be 'better' or 'much better' (Clarke and Patrickson, 2001).

What about those who stay? Following a 20-month restructuring process that included 10,500 job cuts, Intel administered an Organizational Health Survey (Frauenheim, 2008). Results were not encouraging to the company. Just 55 per cent of Intel employees reported that they were satisfied with their career-development opportunities at the firm, while 44 per cent of the employees would leave the company for a job elsewhere with similar pay and benefits. Asked to respond to the statement, 'At Intel, informed risk-taking is valued regardless of the outcome, only 50 per cent agreed. Consistent with these findings, just 48 per cent of Intel employees agreed or strongly agreed with the statement, 'I believe that action will be taken based on the results of this survey.' In a company whose business strategy is to harness the power of innovation to stay ahead of its rivals by making its own products obsolete, risk-averse employees, many of whom distrust management, could undermine that strategy in the long term.

Contextual influences on the effects of downsizing

With a few exceptions (e.g., Chadwick et al., 2004; Nixon et al., 2004; Zatzick and Iverson, 2006), research to date has not systematically examined organizational practices or contextual conditions that may influence the effectiveness of employee downsizing. The following two studies show how that is beginning to change. In the first, Zatzick and Iverson (2006) examined how layoffs moderate the relationship between high-involvement work practices and productivity, and how continued investments in high-involvement work practices through the period of layoffs maintain workforce productivity.

High-involvement work practices are those that create firm-specific employee capabilities that are difficult for other firms to imitate or transfer (Lepak and Snell, 1999). They cover a wide range of systems and routines, from team-based production and semi-autonomous work groups, to gainsharing and flexible work design, to information-sharing and training and development opportunities.

Using a large sample of Canadian firms that responded to a Workplace and Employee Survey conducted by Statistics Canada over a 4-year period, Zatznick and Iverson (2006) found a negative relationship between high-involvement work practices and productivity in workplaces with higher layoff rates. Workplaces that continued to invest in high-involvement work practices, however, were able to avoid productivity losses, as compared to workplaces that discontinued such investments. These findings have four important implications for future research.

One, how do employees view downsizing within the context of a high-involvement workplace, particularly in terms of trading off job security for the opportunity to develop skills through training? Two, it is entirely possible that firms that institute high-involvement work practices do not maintain them. In other words, it is possible that such practices vary from year to year. We know almost nothing about the effects of such fluctuations on employee attitudes, capabilities, and workplace productivity. Three, countries with generous 'safety nets' for laid-off employees, such as required severance pay, healthcare coverage, and retraining opportunities, may make it possible for high-involvement work places to 'justify' the decision to lay off employees. We saw that earlier in our example of the Danish system. To what extent do findings in the research literature on high-involvement work practices, or, more generally, on the effects of downsizing, conducted in countries with generous safety nets generalize to those with more limited safety nets?

CONCLUSIONS

While considerable research has been done on some aspects of employment downsizing, such as the extent of downsizing in developed countries, the methods used to execute that strategy, and some of the direct effects on firms and survivors, the broad landscape of downsizing remains largely unexplored. We know little about the long-term effects of alternatives to downsizing, and much of the literature that currently exists about the effects on the physical and mental health of individuals and communities is anecdotal in nature. We also know little about the long-term impact of downsizing on innovation and individual or work-group productivity. Finally, with few exceptions, the effects of organizational practices or contextual conditions that may influence the overall effectiveness of employee downsizing are yet to be discovered. Of one thing we can be sure, however: pressures to cut costs and increase productivity will not abate. Social science research has great potential to inform the debate about the full range of the effects of downsizing.

REFERENCES

Appelbaum, S.H., Everard, A. and Hung, L.T.S. (1999) 'Strategic downsizing: Critical success factors', *Management Decisions*, 37 (7): 535–52.

Armstrong-Stassen, M. (2002) 'Designated redundant but escaping layoff: A special group of layoff survivors', *Journal of Occupational and Organizational Psychology*, 75: 1–13.

Baumol, J.W., Blinder, S.A. and Wolff, N.E. (2003) *Downsizing in America: Reality, causes, and consequences*. NY: Russell Sage Foundation Press.

Borman, W.C. and Motowidlo, S.J. (1993) 'Expanding the criterion domain to include elements of contextual performance', in N. Schmitt and W.C. Borman (eds), *Personnel Selection in Organizations*. San Francisco: Jossey-Bass, pp. 71–98.

Brockner, J., Grover, S., Reed, T., De Witt, R. and O'Malley, M. (1987) 'Survivors' reactions to layoffs: We get by with a little help for our friends', *Administrative Science Quarterly*, 32: 526–41.

Brockner, J., Grover, S. and Blonder, M.D. (1988) 'Predictors of survivors' job involvement following layoffs: A field study', *Journal of Applied Psychology*, 73: 436–42.

Bruton, G., Keels, J. and Shook, C. (1996) 'Downsizing the firm: Answering the strategic questions', *Academy of Management Executive*, 10: 38–45.

Buono, A.F. (2003) 'The hidden costs and benefits of organizational resizing activities', in K.P. De Meuse and M.L. Marks (eds), *Resizing the Organization*. San Francisco: Jossey-Bass, pp. 306–46.

Cameron, K.S. (1994) 'Investigating organizational downsizing: Fundamental issues', *Human Resource Management*, 33: 183–88.

Cameron, K.S., Freeman, S.J. and Mishra, A.K. (1991) 'Best practices in white collar downsizing: Managing contradictions', *Academy of Management Executive*, 5: 57–73.

Cappelli, P. (2000) *Examining the incidence of downsizing and its effect on establishment performance*. Washington, D.C.: National Bureau of Economic Research, NBER Working Paper 7742.

Cascio, W.F. (2007) 'Downsizing', in S.G. Rogelberg (ed.), *Encyclopedia of Industrial and Organizational Psychology* (Vol. 1). Thousand Oaks, CA: Sage, pp. 163–66.

Cascio, W.F. (2004) 'Downsizing and outplacement', in S. Zedeck (vol. ed.), *Encyclopedia of Applied Psychology*. NY: Academic Press. Vol. 1, pp. 621–26.

Cascio, W.F. (2002a) *Responsible Restructuring: Creative and Profitable Alternatives to Layoffs*. San Francisco: Berrett-Kohler.

Cascio, W.F. (2002b) 'Strategies for responsible restructuring', *Academy of Management Executive*, 16 (3): 80–91.

Cascio, W.F. (1993) 'Downsizing: what do we know? What have we learned?', *Academy of Management Executive*, 7: 95–103.

Cascio, W.F. and Wynn, P. (2004) 'Managing a downsizing process', *Human Resource Management Journal*, 43 (4): 425–36.

Cascio, W.F., Morris, J. and Young, C. (1999) 'Downsizing after all these years: Questions and answers about who did it, how many did it, and who benefited from it', *Organizational Dynamics*, 1 (3): 78–87.

Cascio, W.F. and Young, C.E. (2003) 'Financial consequences of employment–change decisions in major U.S. corporations, 1982–2000', in K.P. De Meuse and M.L. Marks (eds), *Resizing the Organization*. San Francisco: Jossey-Bass, pp. 131–56.

Cascio, W., Young, C.E. and Morris, J.R. (1997) 'Financial consequences of employment-change decisions in major U.S. corporations', *Academy of Management Journal*, 40: 1175–89.

Chadwick, C., Hunter, L.W. and Walston, S.L. (2004) 'Effects of downsizing practices on the performance of hospitals', *Strategic Management Journal*, 25: 405–27.

China warns of 20 million urban jobless, *South China Morning Post*, 30 April 2002, p. 1.

Clarke, M. and Patrickson, M. (2001) 'Does downsized mean down and out?', *Asia Pacific Journal of Human Resources*, 39 (1): 63–78.

Colquitt, J.A., Conlon, D.E., Wesson, M.J., Porter, C.O.L.H. and Ng, K.Y. (2001) 'Justice at the millennium: A meta-analytic review of 25 years of organizational justice research', *Journal of Applied Psychology*, 86: 425–45.

De Meuse, K.P., Bergmann, T.J., Vanderheiden, P.A. and Roraff, C.E. (2004) 'New evidence regarding organizational downsizing and a firm's financial performance: A long-term analysis', *Journal of Management Issues*, 16: 155–77.

De Meuse, K.P., Marks, M.L., and Dai, G. (In press). Organizational downsizing, mergers and acquisitions, and strategic alliances: Using theory and research to enhance practice. In S. Zedeck (ed.), Handbook of industrial and organizational psychology. Washington, D. C.: APA Books.

Devine, K., Reay, T., Stainton, L. and Collins-Nakai, R. (2003) 'Downsizing outcomes: Better a victim than a survivor?', *Human Resource Management*, 42 (2): 109–24.

Elovainio, M., Kivimaki, M. and Helkama, K. (2001) 'Organizational justice evaluations, job control, and occupational strain', *Journal of Applied Psychology*, 86: 418–24.

Feldman, D.C. (2003) 'The impact of layoffs on family, friendship, and community networks', in K.P. De Meuse and M.L. Marks (eds), *Resizing the Organization*. San Francisco: Jossey-Bass, pp. 188–219.

Firing line: I dodged the ax. Now I'm in agony. (2007, Oct. 22) *Business Week*, p. 94.

Fisher, S.R. and White, M.A. (2000) 'Downsizing in a learning organization: Are there hidden costs?', *Academy of Management Review*, 25: 244–51.

Franks, G.F. III. (2007, Nov. 14). Executives vs. managers. *The Wall Street Journal*, p. A15.

Frauenhaeim, E. (2008) 'Culture crash', *Workforce Management*, 1: 12–17.

Gittins, R. (2001, Aug. 1). Survivors of downsizing count the cost, *Sydney Morning Herald*, p. 12.

GM: A rush to the exits (2006, July 10). *Business Week*, p. 24.

Greenberg, J. (1997) *The quest for justice on the job*. Thousand Oaks, CA: Sage.

Greene, M.S. (1992) *Retirement: A new beginning*. St. John's, Newfoundland, Canada: Jesperson Press.

Gustafson, S. (2006, December 15). 38,000 take Ford buyouts. *The Denver Post*, p. 6C.

Guthrie, J.P. and Datta, D.K. (2008) 'Dumb and dumber: The impact of downsizing on firm performance as moderated by industry conditions', *Organization Science*, 19 (1): 108–23.

Hymowitz, C. (2001, July 24). Using layoffs to battle downturns often costs more than it saves, *The Wall Street Journal*, p. B1.

Iverson, R.D, and Pullman, J.A. (2000) 'Determinants of voluntary turnover and layoffs in an environment of repeated downsizing following a merger: An event history analysis', *Journal of Management*, 26: 977–1003.

Kanovsky, M. (2000) 'Understanding procedural justice and its impact on business organizations', *Journal of Management*, 26: 489–511.

Kets deVries, M.F.R. and Balazs, K. (1997) 'The downside of downsizing', *Human Relations*, 50 (1): 11–50.

Kim, S. and Feldman, D.C. (1998) 'Healthy, wealthy, or wise: Predicting actual acceptances of early retirement incentives at three points in time', *Personnel Psychology*, 51 : 623–42.

Knudsen, H.K., Johnson, J.A., Martin, J.K. and Roman, P.M. (2003) 'Downsizing survival: The experience of work and organizational commitment', *Sociological Inquiry*, 73: 265–83.

Lavelle, L. (2001, Dec. 3). Thinking beyond the one-size-fits-all pay cut, *Business Week*, p. 45.

Leana, C.R. and Feldman, D.C. (1992) *Coping with job loss: How individuals, organizations, and communities respond to lay-offs*. New York: Macmillan/Lexington Books.

Leana, C.R., Feldman, D.C. and Tan, G.Y. (1998) 'Predictors of coping behavior after a lay-off', *Journal of Organizational Behavior*, 19 (1): 85–97.

Lepak, D.P. and Snell, S.A. (1999) 'The human resource architecture: Toward a theory of human capital allocation and development', *Academy of Management Review*, 24: 31–48.

Littler, C. and Innes, P. (2003) 'Downsizing and deknowledging the firm', *Work, Employment, and Society*, 17 (1): 73–100.

Lublin, J.S., and Thurm, S. (2006, March 27). How companies calculate odds in buyout offers, *The Wall Street Journal*, pp. B1, B3.

Luthans, B.C. and Sommer, S.M. (1999) 'The impact of downsizing on workplace attitudes', *Group and Organization Management*, 24: 46–70.

McCracken, J. (2006) Ford aims to cut union workforce through buyouts, *The Wall Street Journal*, pp. A1, A10.

McGoldrick, A.E. and Cooper, C.L. (1988). Early retirement. Brookfield, VT: Gower.

McKinley, W., Zhao, J. and Rust, K.G. (2000) 'A socio-cognitive interpretation of organizational downsizing', *Academy of Management Review*, 25: 227–43.

Mirvis, P.H. (1997) 'Human resource management: Leaders, laggards, and followers', *The Academy of Management Executive*, 11 (2): 43–56.

Mishra, A.K. and Spreitzer, G.M. (1998) 'Explaining how survivors respond to downsizing: The roles of trust, empowerment, justice, and work redesign', *Academy of Management Review*, 23: 567–89.

Mollica, K.A. and DeWitt, R.L. (2000) 'When others retire early: What about me?', *Academy of Management Journal*, 43: 1068–75.

Nixon, R.D., Hitt, M.A., Lee, H. and Jeong, E. (2004) 'Market reactions to announcements of corporate downsizing actions and implementation strategies', *Strategic Management Journal*, 25: 1121–29.

O'Neil, H.M. and Lenn, D.J. (1995) 'Voices of survivors: Words that downsizing CEOs should hear', *Academy of Management Executive*, 9 (4): 23–34.

Osterman, P. (2000) 'Work reorganization in an era of restructuring: Trends in diffusion and effects on employee welfare', *Industrial and Labor Relations Review*, 53: 179–96.

Pelley, S. (2009, Jan. 27). The winter of our hardship. 60 Minutes Newsmagazine, Produced by S. Granatstein and N. Young.

Pfeffer, J. (2005) 'Changing mental models: HR's most important task', in M. Losey, S. Meisinger and D. Ulrich (eds), *The Future of Human Resource Management*. Hoboken, NJ: Wiley, pp. 163–71.

Pfeffer, J. and Sutton, R.I. (2006) *Hard facts, dangerous half-truths and total nonsense*. Boston, MA: Harvard Business School Press.

Priti, P.S. (2000) 'Network destruction: The structural implications of downsizing', *Academy of Management Journal*, 43: 101–12.

Redman, T. and Wilkinson, A. (2006) 'Downsizing', in T. Redman and A. Wilkinson (eds), *Contemporary Human Resource Management* (2nd ed.). London: FT/Prentice Hall, pp. 356–81.

Rosenblatt, Z. and Sheaffer, Z. (2001) 'Brain drain in declining organizations: Toward a research agenda', *Journal of Organizational Behavior*, 22: 409–24.

Rousseau, D.M. (2001) 'Schema, promise, and mutuality: The building blocs of the psychological contract', *Journal of Occupational and Organizational Psychology*, 74: 511–41.

Rowley, I. and Toshiro, H. (2005, March 21). Lessons from Matsushita's playbook, *Business Week*, p. 32.

Savery, L.K., Travaglione, A. and Firns, I.G.J. (1998) 'The links between absenteeism and commitment during downsizing', *Personnel Review*, 27 (4): 312–24.

Surowiecki, J. (2007, April 30) It's the workforce, stupid! *The New Yorker*. Downloaded from www.newyorker.com/talk/financial on May 2, 2007.

Thornton, E. (2009, March 2). Around the world, employees are fighting layoffs. BusinessWeek, pp. 52, 53.

Uchitelle, L. (2006) *The disposable American: Layoffs and their consequences*. NY: Vintage Books.

U.S. Department of Labor (1995) *Guide to responsible restructuring*. Washington, D.C.: U.S. Government Printing Office.

Walker, M. (2006, March 21) Soft landing: For the Danish, a job loss can be learning experience, *The Wall Street Journal*, pp. A1, A11.

Wayhan, V.B. and Werner, S. (2000) 'The impact of workface reductions on financial performance: A longitudinal perspective', *Journal of Management*, 26: 341–63.

Westman, M. (2007) 'Survivors' syndrome', in S. G. Rogelberg (ed.), *Encyclopedia of Industrial and Organizational Psychology* (Vol. 2). Thousand Oaks, CA: Sage, pp. 782–84.

White, R.D. (2001, Dec. 17). Firms find ways to avoid staff cuts, *The Los Angeles Times*, pp. C1, C4.

Winestock, G. (2002, June 21). A reticent European right balks on labor, *The Wall Street Journal*, pp. A6, A7.

Worrall, L., Cooper, C. and Campbell, F. (2000) 'The impact of organizational change on UK managers' perceptions of their working lives', in R. Burke and C. Cooper (eds), *The organization in crisis*. Oxford: Blackwell, pp. 20–43.

Zaslow, J. (2006, April 1–2). Down and out in Bloomfield Hills, Michigan, *The Wall Street Journal*, pp. A1, A8.

Zatzick, C.D. and Iverson, R.D. (2006) 'High-involvement management and workforce reduction: Competitive advantage or disadvantage?', *Academy of Management Journal*, 49: 999–1015.

PART III

Contemporary Issues

21

Strategic Human Resources Management: Where Do We Go From Here?[1]

Brian E. Becker and Mark A. Huselid

INTRODUCTION

The field of Strategic Human Resources Management (SHRM) has enjoyed a remarkable ascendancy over the last two decades, as both an academic literature and focus of management practice. The parallel growth in both the research literature and interest among practicing managers is a notable departure from the more common experience, where managers are either unaware or simply uninterested in scholarly developments in our field. As the field of HR strategy begins to mature, we believe that it is time to take stock of where it stands as both a field of inquiry and management practice. While drawing on nearly two decades of solid academic progress, this exercise is explicitly prospective. This paper is not intended as an encyclopedic analysis of prior work (see Becker and Huselid, 1998, for an earlier review), but instead will emphasize what we believe should be the future direction of the field over the next decade.

We begin with the most pressing theoretical challenge facing SHRM, a useful articulation of the 'black box' that describes the strategic logic between a firm's HR architecture and its subsequent performance. How does the logic of this 'black box' explain HR's contribution to a firm's sustained competitive advantage? Following recent work in the strategy literature, we call for a new emphasis on strategy implementation as the focal mediating construct in SHRM. Specifically, we argue that it is the fit between the HR architecture and the strategic capabilities and business processes that implement strategy that is the basis of HR's contribution to competitive advantage. This will require an increasing level of differentiation of the HR architecture (Lepak and Snell, 1999), both within the firm and between firms.

Next we address the challenges facing future empirical work. That discussion is divided into two broad sections. First we consider the empirical implications of the proposed emphasis on strategy implementation. We highlight the need for new measures of intermediate outcomes and the importance of estimating HR's impact in managerially significant terms. Secondly, we examine recent challenges to the magnitude of HR's estimated effect on firm performance in prior work. While we agree that questions of measurement error, omitted variable bias and mutual causation should be explored, recent studies that have examined these issues tend to raise more questions than they answer.

This theoretical and empirical foundation highlights several new directions in SHRM research. In the next section, we extend this discussion of a future research agenda to several related questions. This agenda is organized around four broad research questions and considers both the theoretical and empirical implications of our analysis. In several cases, the questions and the methods mark a significant departure from past work in SHRM. Finally, we will assess the state of SHRM practice, both the remarkable progress and the significant hurdles facing HR managers looking to implement these ideas.

SHRM THEORY – A NEW EMPHASIS

The field of HR strategy differs from traditional HR management research in two important ways. First, SHRM focuses on organizational performance rather than individual performance. Second, it also emphasizes the role of HR management *systems* as solutions to business problems (including positive and negative complementarities) rather than individual HR management practices in isolation. But strategic means more than a systems focus or even financial performance. Strategy is about building sustainable competitive advantage that in turn creates above average financial performance. The simplest depiction of the SHRM model is a relationship between a firm's HR Architecture and firm performance. The HR Architecture is comprised of the systems, practices, competencies, and

employee performance behaviors that reflect the development and management of the firm's strategic human capital. Above average firm performance associated with the HR Architecture reflects the quasi rents associated with that strategic resource.

For the most part prior SHRM theory has focused on the nature of the HR Architecture. What is the nature of the appropriate HR system (i.e. single practices or systems)? What are they key mediating variables (i.e. commitment) within the HR Architecture? The architectural metaphor (Becker and Gerhart, 1996; Becker and Huselid, 1998, Lepak and Snell, 1999; Wright et al., 2001) is important because it highlights the locus of value creation in SHRM. While strategic human capital is reflected in the 'human' assets in the organization, it is created and managed through the organizational system reflected in the HR architecture.

The notion of the HR architecture as a value-creating system raises the question of the appropriate locus of strategic value creation. Emphasis in the SHRM literature ranges from the HR system, the resulting workforce skills and competencies, employee commitment and engagement, to employee performance. Within this architectural framework, we would emphasize the importance of the HR system as the most important strategic asset. First, it is the source of value creation in the subsequent outcomes in the HR architecture. Second, it has the potential for greater inimitability based on how it aligned with the firm's strategy. Finally, unlike human capital, it is immobile.

With a few exceptions (Becker and Huselid, 1998; Huselid et al., 2005a, 2005b; Wright et al., 2001) there has been little effort to extend SHRM theory in a way that formally integrates the mechanism through which the HR architecture actually influences firm performance. Gerhart (2005), for example, has recently suggested that SHRM move closer to the individual level by emphasizing HR's impact on employee relations and attitudes. The heavy focus on the character of the HR Architecture is the natural comfort zone of HR scholars. Going forward, however, we need more theoretical work on the 'black box' *between* the HR Architecture and firm performance, and less emphasis on the 'black box' *within* the HR Architecture. The theoretical literature is out of balance. SHRM is an intermediate or meso theory, and as such it draws as much on the strategy literature as the HR literature. Recent developments in the strategy literature, however, suggest a particularly valuable direction for theoretical work in SHRM.

A new emphasis on strategy implementation

The resource-based view (RBV) of the firm has long provided a core theoretical rationale for HR's potential role as a strategic asset in the firm (Wright and McMahan, 1992). The notion that organizations can build competitive advantage, and as a result above average financial performance, based on valuable and inimitable internal resources, offers an appealing rationale for HR's strategic importance. This integration tends to focus on human capital, or employee level attributes, and the RBV's emphasis on recognizing existing strategic resources rather than the development of those strategic assets. However, there is little evidence of the impact of this theoretical work on the empirical SHRM literature. Instead the most we can say is that we have a set of empirical results that are consistent with the theoretical implications of the strategy literature, but do not follow from an SHRM theory that directly integrates that theoretical literature. As Barney (2001) has observed more broadly about the influence of RBV theory, the strategy literature simply provides a theoretical context for examining the implications of HR for firm performance.

Priem and Butler's (2001) concern about the 'level of abstraction' in RBV theory applies to SHRM theory as well. The link between the HR Architecture and most RBV concepts remains too abstract and too indirect to guide either empirical work on the 'black box' in SHRM or management practice. However, recent attention to the independent influence of 'implementation' in the strategy

literature offers an opportunity to make the theoretical HR-firm performance link more concrete. As Barney (2001) has noted, implementation was originally omitted from the RBV as a 'theoretical convenience,' under the assumption that 'implementation follows, almost automatically' (p. 53). Implementation has played a similar role in SHRM theory. Rather than considering implementation as an independent theoretical construct, SHRM theory has relied on the implication that an appropriate match between the HR Architecture and strategic choice (e.g. Porter's positioning strategies like differentiation or cost leadership) results in effective implementation.

RBV theorists now recognize that 'the ability to implement strategies is, by itself, a resource that can be a source of competitive advantage' (Barney, 2001: 54). Implementation should be given similar prominence in SHRM theory. The HR system – firm performance link is not as direct as suggested by the prior SHRM literature. It has long been recognized that intermediate outcomes, as part of an indirect link, are central to a more complete understanding of how the HR architecture drives firm performance (Becker and Gerhart, 1996). The question is: What are the most important intermediate outcomes?

A new emphasis on strategy implementation in SHRM theory implies a new set of intermediate outcomes, and a new locus of fit for the HR architecture. While the SHRM literature has always acknowledged the importance of an HR-strategy fit (Schuler and Jackson, 1987; Wright and Snell, 1998), the nature of that fit implies a generic relationship between the HR architecture and the larger competitive strategy. Irrespective of the strategic framework being used (Miles and Snow, 1994; Porter, 1985) prior work typically posits three or four competitive strategies available to the firm, and an appropriate HR architecture for each of these competitive strategies. For example, an HR focus on rewarding outcomes rather than procedures is suggested as an appropriate fit with a Prospector (innovation) strategy (Miles and Snow, 1994). Similarly, role behaviors that emphasized risk-taking were deemed an appropriate fit with an innovation strategy (Jackson and Schuler, 1995). Since there are only a limited number of competitive strategy types, it follows that there are a limited number of appropriate HR architectures. This notion of fit obviously limits the uniqueness of HR architectures across firms, makes them easier to imitate, and reduces their value as sources sustainable of competitive advantage. The empirical evidence seems to bear this out. Despite a general consensus that fit ought to play a central role in SHRM theory, empirical tests of this generic HR-competitive strategy contingency have provided little support for a fit hypothesis (Becker and Huselid, 1998; Delery and Doty, 1996; Huselid, 1995).

Despite the lack of empirical support, we agree that contingencies should continue to play a central role in SHRM theory. But those contingencies should not focus on the ultimate positioning strategy or at the level of Miles and Snow typologies. The point of alignment should be closer to the HR architecture. The challenge is to operationalize the process of strategy implementation within SHRM theory so that it can provide a useful guide to empirical work. Here we need to rely on the strategy literature, but recognize that it too continues to struggle with these issues. We would echo Priem and Butler's (2001: 34) observation that a more careful delineation of 'the specific mechanisms purported to generate competitive advantage' is required, as are more 'actionable prescriptions' (p. 31). Thomas and Tymon (1982) more generally refer to this latter characteristic as operational validity and emphasize the need to construct theories with independent variables that managers can control. The RBV literature's reliance on constructs that are difficult to operationalize in practice limits the prescriptive value of the theory for managers (Priem and Butler, 2001), and extends to efforts to integrate RBV into SHRM theory.

With that caveat in mind, the most general answer to the question of how to operationalize strategy implementation as a key intermediate variable within SHRM theory is to focus on a firm's strategic capabilities.

In the RBV literature terms like resources and capabilities 'are used interchangeably and refer to the tangible and intangible assets firms use to develop and implement their strategies' (Ray et al., 2004: 24). Makadok (2001), however, makes the distinction that capabilities are firm-specific and embedded in the organization. More importantly their purpose is to enhance the productivity of other resources and as such serve as 'intermediate goods' (Amit and Shoemaker, 1993). This intermediate role fits well within the black box between the HR architecture and firm performance.

The notion of an intermediate good also highlights the importance of 'connectedness' and location of strategic capabilities within a strategy implementation system (Siggelkow, 2002). It builds on what Ray et al. (2004: 25) describe as 'important common ground' between Porter's emphasis on 'activities' and the RBV focus on resources and capabilities. Porter's (1996) concept of the strategy-activity system and Siggelkow's (2002) notion of core and elaborating organizational elements both represent a system of capabilities that implement strategy. While the SHRM literature tends to focus on Porter's notion of market positioning, emphasizing a mix of differentiation or cost-leadership, Porter argues that the underlying strategic activities that drive that position are in fact the essence of strategy. 'Competitive strategy ... means deliberately choosing a different set of activities to deliver a unique mix of value' (Porter, 1996: 64). For example, at Wal-Mart an integrated combination of distribution, logistics, just-in-time order fulfillment, considerable focus on stocking stores differentially to meet customer needs in each area, and very close relationships with suppliers helped to create an organizational capability and first-mover advantage that is difficult for competitors to imitate. The important point is not simply that a system of internal organizational activities might have strategic value in any organization, but rather that this strategic activity system has value in large part because it will differ across competitors. In other words, simply choosing a generic positioning strategy does not imply a particular strategic activity system. Similarly, choosing a generic positioning strategy does not imply a particular HR Architecture.

We are not the first to argue that strategic capabilities should play a role in a more fully articulated SHRM framework. Wright et al. (2001) propose a more comprehensive integration of RBV concepts like dynamic capabilities into SHRM theory, though the ultimate links to firm performance are not discussed. In our view, strategic capabilities can more usefully be integrated into SHRM theory if they are linked directly to strategy implementation. This will increase their operational validity and provide much clearer implications for contingencies and fit.

So how is our proposed use of the term strategic capability more concrete and operationally valid? The strategy literature has not agreed on a common terminology, but several recent efforts have attempted to operationalize the notion of capabilities by their relationship to concrete business processes. We think this is a productive direction for extending SHRM theory. Eisenhardt and Martin (2000), for example, note that capabilities 'are neither vague nor tautologically defined abstractions' (p. 1106). Instead they are a 'set of specific and identifiable processes, such as product development, strategic decision making, and alliancing.' Similarly, according to Ray et al. (2004) business processes 'are the way that the competitive potential of a firm's resources and capabilities are realized and deserve study in their own right' (p. 26). They go on to argue that RBV hypotheses are often more directly, and appropriately, tested using business process effectiveness as the dependent variable rather than overall firm performance. Returning to our question posed above, namely which intermediate outcomes should we use to reflect strategy implementation; the answer is strategic business processes.

A new emphasis on differentiation

Following emerging trends in the strategy literature, we argue that SHRM theory should be extended to focus on effective strategy implementation as the key mediating variable between the HR architecture and firm performance. That focus on strategy implementation is operationalized and made concrete by a focus on strategic capabilities and activity systems reflected in strategic business processes. We say strategic because not all business processes will have equal value. Strategic value requires that these business processes are a source, perhaps *the* source, of the value customers derive from the firm's products or services. Whether this value proposition can rise to the level of sustainable competitive advantage will depend on the ease and cost of imitation by competitors. In our framework the strategic impact of the HR architecture is directly related to the strategic value created by these business processes.

A new locus of fit goes directly to the familiar debate about best practices vs. configurations or contingencies. Structurally this discussion focuses on whether there is one 'best' HR architecture that creates value for all firms, whether there are two or three appropriate architectures (configurations), or whether there are two or three with returns that vary with the larger strategic positioning strategy (contingency theories). While we have examined these issues in our own work, this entire line of inquiry seems more driven by empirical convenience than theoretical logic. None of these perspectives is consistent with a strategic logic based on firm specific and inimitable resources. Given the small number of potential architectures and limited number of strategic contingencies (Porter positioning strategies), these approaches are all largely variations on the best practice story. The issue is not whether contingencies should play a role in SHRM theory, but rather the locus of fit and the nature of that contingency. Nevertheless, we do not believe that it is an either/or story. There is consistent empirical support (discussed in the next section) for even the simplest of these explanations. The market for these ideas is not very efficient and may reflect what Pfeffer and Sutton (2000) describe as the 'knowing-doing' gap. As a result, adoption apparently provides competitive advantage, even if it is not sustainable. What is missing is a more theoretically appropriate test of the contingency story.

This current approach to theorizing about and measuring fit implies very little variation or differentiation of the HR architecture, either between firms or within firms. By contrast, our theoretical focus on the capabilities and activity systems that are the foundation of strategic business processes implies a great deal more differentiation between firms. For example, two firms with the same positioning strategy may well be in different industries and rely on dramatically different capabilities to create value for their customers (e.g. alliancing, Gulati, 1998; forecasting, Makadok and Walker, 2000; client services, Ethiraj et al., 2005). The cross-sectional variation here is not a question of 'high performance' vs. 'low performance' HR systems, but rather a question of which 'high performance' system is appropriate. Unique and firm specific HR architectures that contribute to unique and inimitable strategic capabilities will contribute to sustainable competitive advantage. But even HR architectures that are fitted to strategic business processes common among all close competitors should create more near term competitive advantage than more generic best practice architectures, or two or three variations fitted to the larger positioning strategy.

If the HR architecture is fitted to the strategic business process, rather than the more generic positioning strategy, it also follows that there will be a need for greater differentiation of HR architecture(s) within the firm. Lepak and Snell (1999, 2002) have led the call for greater theoretical and empirical attention to differentiating the HR architecture, a direction we strongly endorse. They note that the SHRM literature has tended to emphasize a 'holistic' view of human capital and 'the extent to which a set of practices is used across employees of a firm as well as the consistency of these practices across the firm' (p. 32). Their key insight is that not all employees, or employee skills,

are inherently strategic and employees with different roles in the value creation process ought to be managed differently.

For Lepak and Snell the basis for differentiating a firm's HR architecture is the value and uniqueness of an employee's skill. In effect they develop four separate HR architectures that vary by HR system, employment relationship and employment mode. Depending on their mix of skill value and uniqueness, employee groups would be managed with one of four appropriate architectures (quadrants). It is a heavily bottom up story. In describing their logic for including certain employees in their Quadrant 1 (knowledge-based employment), Lepak and Snell (2002) argue that '[b]ecause of their value, these employees are able to contribute to a firm's strategic objectives' (p. 520). For us, the relationship is more top down. We would say 'when employees are able to contribute to a firm's strategic objectives, they have (strategic) value.' In other words, human capital is only strategically important if it directly implements the firm's strategy. Presumably not all strategic processes will be highly dependent on human capital. As that dependency increases, employee performance behaviors in that business process are increasingly a complement to effective strategy implementation. As the elements of the HR architecture within the domain of that business process are uniquely fitted (differentiated) to produce those behaviors, the HR architecture itself increasingly becomes a strategic asset.

We also believe that the point of fit, and therefore the locus of differentiation, is the job, not the employee. A focus on jobs is an effort to consider both the supply and demand side of human capital. In other words, the value of employee skills within a firm is not just a supply side phenomenon. It is a function of how those skills are used and where they are used. The value of a strategic job is derived from the value of a strategic business process and could easily extend to hourly workers and manual trades (Teece et al., 1997). Just as in real estate, what is important about the job is location, location, location. Jobs located in strategic business processes have more value than jobs located in other areas of the business, even if they have the same job title. A computer programming job located in a strategic software development process has more value than the same job in a support function. The uniqueness of the skills required for that job is a secondary issue. The HR architecture should focus on the jobs in a strategic business process. The hiring and development practices may well vary across jobs in a strategic business process depending on how firm specific the skill requirements might be.

It is not, however, just a question of identifying strategic and non-strategic jobs. It is equally important to recognize that the HR architecture might have to be differentiated across different strategic capabilities within the same firm. Porter observes (1996: 62) that 'strategic positioning means performing different activities from rivals or performing similar activities in different ways.' This puts considerable emphasis on the strategic value of differentiation rather than best practices and universalistic approaches to HR strategy. As a corollary, it puts a different emphasis on the nature of HR's contingency with strategy. Zajac et al. (2000: 450), in their review of the role of contingency theories in the strategy literature, conclude that more attention should be given to the 'uniqueness of strategic fit for a particular organization at a particular point in time.' We believe that future theoretical work in SHRM should follow a similar direction.

This new direction reflects an evolution in our own thinking over the last decade. While our earlier work (Becker and Huselid, 1998; Huselid, 1995) tested for the firm-level impact of internal and external fit, the empirical results were much more consistent with a 'best practice' story. Despite our call here for increasing levels of focus and differentiation in workforce investments, we continue to believe that many firms will benefit from the adoption of high performance work system 'best practices.' How is this possible? In both our survey data and fieldwork we have consistently found that that the degree

to which firms effectively manage even the 'HR basics' varies substantially across organizations. As a result the variance in workforce management 'quality' across firms is quite large. Indeed, we would hypothesize that the existence of this variance is part of the reason why we see such robust HR-firm performance effects. The economic returns to product quality have dissipated over time as they have been factor price equalized. Similarly, if most firms did an excellent job managing their workforces, the impact on firm performance would likely be much smaller. Strategic HR gains will be much harder to capture when (or if) the HRM market approaches equilibrium. Whether this market failure is due to a lack of knowledge, a lack of managerial competence, or an inability to execute (or more likely some combination) is open for conjecture, and hopefully future research. However, our main conclusion is that the real strategic opportunity for most firms over the next decade requires a greater emphasis on contingencies and differentiation. Again, it is not a question of either/or, but a question of the appropriate balance.

This perspective is summarized in Figure 21.1. The framework begins with a common set of positioning strategies, but implements those strategies with a system of interrelated business process that have a significant firm-specific dimension. The core elements in a set of strategic business processes (e.g., process A, process B) have both a core and differentiated fit to the HR architecture. The core or best practice fit is that part of the HR architecture that has equal value in all strategic business processes. The differentiated fit is that part of the overall HR architecture that is structured to provide the unique human requirements of a specific business process. For example, HR architecture A is fit to strategic process A and differs significantly from HR architecture B. In each case, these unique architectures provide the human capital attributes (competencies, commitment or motivation) and employee performance behaviors required in the strategic jobs in a

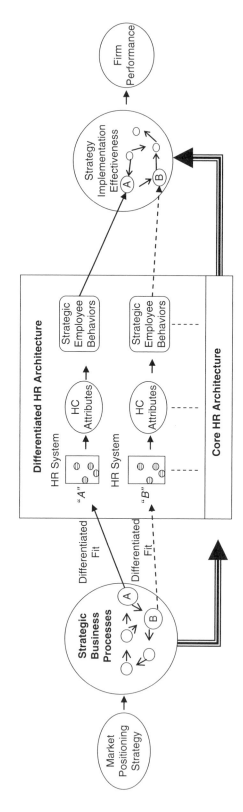

Figure 21.1   Differentiating the HR architecture contingent on strategic business practices

particular business practice. Effective strategy implementation is then a function of both core and differentiated fit.

EMPIRICAL WORK GOING FORWARD

The focus on 'managerial significance'

Before turning to a more focused discussion of several empirical issues, it is important to highlight an important feature of SHRM research. Unlike much of organizational research, the dependent variables in SHRM typically have obvious and direct managerial relevance (e.g. shareholder value, return on assets, labor productivity). SHRM effects can be expressed in units that are managerially significant and this has a direct bearing on the influence of this literature.

Ferraro et al. (2005) and Bazerman (2005) have recently debated why economic research is more influential than the work of other social scientists. We agree with Bazerman that non-economists are influential when they too make 'novel prescriptions that are relevant to the marketplace' by focusing their research on 'economic outcome variables' (p. 27). This observation is particularly applicable to SHRM research. For example, based on the results of five national surveys between 1991 and 2000 and data collected from more than 3,200 firms, we have estimated that 'the effect of a one standard deviation change in the HR system is 10–20% of a firm's market value' (Huselid and Becker, 2000: 851). More broadly in a meta-analysis of 92 recent studies on the HR-firm performance relationship, Combs et al. (2006) find that a one standard deviation increase in the use of high performance work systems is associated with 4.6 percent increase in ROA. The interest in SHRM, particularly among managers, is at least as much about the dependent variable as the independent variable. HR has become an answer to a very important question, how can we improve a firm's financial performance?

Focusing on managerial significance in SHRM empirical work also serves to strengthen the validity of those results. First, financial effects such as an *x* percent change in shareholder value or *y* percent change in return on assets provide a compelling external validation to results that otherwise are simply 'statistically significant.' The larger business and strategy literature offers reasonable boundaries for the effects of a wide range of managerial innovations. The validity of SHRM empirical results should be interpreted within this context. Studies that imply 70–80% increases in firm financial performance metrics based on reasonable changes in one or two HR practices can be questioned as theoretically and empirically implausible. Second, an empirical literature that focuses on managerially relevant effects provides an important point of comparison for future work. Going forward, empirical work should be located within a cumulative body of effect sizes. This will not only serve to validate these new results but also clearly highlight their contribution well.

Specific empirical issues

Empirical SHRM research has been an exciting line of inquiry for more than a decade, and it is not our purpose to provide a comprehensive review of that literature. Instead this section will focus on two objectives. First, we will examine several of the empirical challenges that would follow from a theoretical emphasis on strategy implementation and differentiation of the HR architecture. Second, we revisit several methodological challenges that continue to confront this literature and suggest where further work is required.

A new focus on intermediate outcomes and strategy implementation

The strategy literature focuses on sustained competitive advantage as the basis for above average firm performance. This requires an equivalent emphasis on higher order measures of firm performance in SHRM research. Nevertheless, one of the implications of our proposed theoretical focus on strategy implementation is that empirical

SHRM research can be refocused on key intermediate outcomes. By locating effective strategy implementation as an explicit intervening variable in SHRM theory, strategically focused empirical research does not necessarily require firm financial performance as the dependent variable. Empirical work in SHRM should be extended to include a focus on measures of effective strategy implementation. Particular attention should be given to those strategic business processes that have high human capital content. But it is essential that these measures have a theoretically clear line of sight to the ultimate strategic (financial) outcomes. In order for SHRM 'effects' to be strategically significant, the dependent variable must have a clear strategic significance.

A new focus on intermediate outcomes poses several challenges. Most importantly it means that intermediate outcome measures will have to be 'strategically validated,' demonstrating their importance to effective strategy implementation in a particular sample of firms. The challenge will be to develop research designs that reflect the firm specific and idiosyncratic character of these intermediate outcomes. The elements of a firm's strategic business processes with the most strategic value are likely to vary across firms and across strategies, making large scale multi-industry studies more difficult. While there may be a 'best practice' dimension to some of these business practices (Eisenhardt and Martin, 2000), particularly among close competitors, SHRM researchers need to be equally attentive to their firm specific characteristics. In either case the design of empirical work that focuses on strategic business processes must carefully establish that the particular process is indeed strategically significant to the organizations in the sample. Even such processes like customer service which have widespread appeal may not always be strategically important. Porter (1996), for example, describes strategic activity systems from three disparate industries (airlines, retail furniture and financial services) and 'limited' customer service is a dimension of effective strategy implementation in two of the three companies.

Our call for increased focus on intermediate outcomes should not be interpreted as encouraging a greater use of unit level and plant level financial performance as the solution. Intermediate financial measures do not measure the strategy implementation process or illuminate the 'black box' in SHRM. Intermediate financial outcomes would only be appropriate dependent measures when testing an empirical model in which the strategic business process or another element of strategy implementation mediates the relation between HR and the financial outcome (e.g. Skaggs and Youndt, 2004).

Indeed, future SHRM empirical work may benefit from a return to more narrowly drawn industry studies like MacDuffie (1995). However, instead of focusing on production units and operational performance, the focus should be on strategic business processes. A good example of research that moves us in this direction is the recent work by Collins and Smith (2006). Here the authors limit their analysis to high tech firms, and focus on the impact of the HR architecture on knowledge exchange capabilities. There is a well developed theoretical rationale for HR's influence on knowledge exchange as well as a clear rationale for the strategic importance of knowledge exchange in a high tech firm. Similarly, Skaggs and Youndt (2004) develop a theoretical rationale for differentiating the service production process and the appropriate HR architecture within a narrow industry sector as the basis for their empirical hypotheses. Likewise, the strategy literature has routinely relied on in depth 'context specific' analyses (Ethiraj et al., 2005; Makadok and Walker, 2000, Raff, 2000) to study the evolution and impact of strategic capabilities.

A new focus on fit and contingencies

Our proposal to refocus SHRM theory on strategy implementation, and by implication strategic business processes, also suggests both a new emphasis and a new focus for fit in the empirical SHRM literature. If these strategic business processes or their underlying activity systems are differentiated across firms and within firms, then HR architectures should be equally differentiated. The nature and appropriate level of this HR differentiation is an empirical question, and one that bears directly on the role of contingencies and fit in SHRM. Incorporating an increased level of differentiation into SHRM will require new direct measures of fit and much less reliance on the more familiar moderator variable approach. The moderator variable approach has an appeal if one is testing whether the effect of a 'best practice' HR system varies over a small set of strategic positioning strategies. By contrast we argue that the value of the HR architecture is in large part determined by the fit between the HR architecture and a largely idiosyncratic business process. In a broad cross sectional sample there is neither a 'best' HR architecture nor a small set of strategic moderators.

Locating strategy implementation as the locus of fit has direct implications for notions of external and internal fit. Internal or horizontal fit (among the elements of the HR architecture) and external fit or vertical fit (between the HR architecture and a strategic business process) are no longer independent constructs. First, internal fit should have no value in the absence of external fit. A highly integrated, mutual reinforcing system of HR practices, all of which do little to improve strategy execution, will have little strategic value. Second, if the HR architecture, and by definition this means the elements within that architecture, is focused on executing strategic business process, the architecture will necessarily have internal fit.

An emphasis on principles?

Colbert (2004: 345) has recently revisited the distinction between principles, policies and practices in SHRM (Becker and Gerhart 1996; Schuler, 1992) and argues that from a systems perspective it is the principles of the HR system that are the central points of managerial leverage. He gives as an example, 'employee participation in all aspects of the business is critical in our success.' Once the principles are established, policies and

practices 'will self organize, which can mean that they flow in concert with the particular idiosyncratic context of the firm ... ' (p. 351).

Empirical work focusing on strategy implementation and the necessary fit between the HR architecture and strategy business processes, might also benefit from an emphasis on SHRM's organizing principles as an initial point of departure. An example of several principles that might be explored empirically include the following:

- the HR architecture should focus on strategy implementation rather than strategic positioning;
- differentiate the HR architecture as required by key business processes;
- disproportionately invest in employee performance in strategic jobs.

It is important to point out that while these principles represent an increase in the level of abstraction above policies and practices, they should not devolve into the conceptual murkiness for which RBV theory has been criticized. They need to retain their operational validity. Ericksen and Dyer's (2004) work on strategic HR in 'high reliability' organizations is a good example. To the extent that SHRM empirical work focuses on principles, the hypotheses necessarily move in the direction of 'best practices.' This in turn will allow for more conventional fit analysis, using moderators rather than the direct measures of fit described above.

The prescriptive challenge

Finally we should highlight an important caveat to a more prominent role for contingencies in empirical SHRM research. Zajac et al. (2000: 429) note that while fit 'is one of the most widely shared and enduring assumptions' in the strategy literature, there has been very little research on the subject, either empirically or theoretically, in recent years. Among the reasons they give for this declining attention to fit is the nature of the concept. It is inherently multidimensional and not easily captured by simple bivariate statements. Introducing increasingly differentiated HR architectures and strategic business process in SHRM, as we have proposed, reflects that multidimensional challenge. Zajac et al. (2000), however, make a more fundamental point that bears directly on the nature of SHRM research. They also observe that fit requires scholars to make normative statements about what organizations should do rather than descriptive statements about what they did do (p. 430). Indeed, to the extent that SHRM theory emphasizes organizational relationships (like fit and alignment) linking HR to other organizational processes within the HR-firm performance 'black box,' HR scholars have likely moved beyond the current experience of most organizations.

We are prescribing how firms ought to structure their HR architecture, not necessarily describing how they currently structure their HR architecture. Typical cross sectional studies implicitly assume that some firms will structure their HR architectures more 'appropriately' than other firms and that those differences will be reflected in improved firm performance, other things being equal. Perhaps those firms with high values on the HR measure have knowingly chosen such policies, or maybe they just got lucky, but the empirical analysis will reveal what may be a heretofore unrealized effect. Estimating these effects and testing these hypotheses is much more difficult when most firms have yet to implement the more prescriptive recommendations. For some hypotheses this may require a move away from large sample survey research and more emphasis on case studies and small 'experiments' with cutting edge organizations.

Considering alternative explanations

Finally, any analysis of a literature based largely on field research raises the question of how well that literature has ruled out alternative explanations. The SHRM empirical literature has mushroomed in recent years and there is consistent evidence that 'high performance' HR systems, broadly defined, have positive effects on firm performance

that are both statistically and managerially significant (Combs et al., forthcoming). These results are increasingly refined as studies report results with effects on financial performance expressed in financial magnitudes with clear managerial implications. Despite this progress, it is appropriate to assess how well this literature has addressed three key methodological challenges that would call these results into question: omitted variable bias, measurement error, and mutual causation or simultaneity.

Before considering these issues, however, it is important to make an observation about the point of comparison. In other words, alternative compared to what?[2] The most common alternative explanation in the managerial literature tends to be 'no effect.' The question is whether we are observing an effect, in the case of the SHRM literature a positive relationship between HR and firm performance, when in fact there is no true relationship. This, however, is a relatively blunt standard. Literatures like economics, for example, are much more likely to focus on degrees of estimation bias. Empirical labor economics might focus on whether the rate of return on education is $x\%$ or $y\%$, or whether the union effect on wages is overstated or understated in prior work. Those literatures have evolved to the point where the empirical interest is not so much in demonstrating that there is a non-zero effect, but rather carefully estimating the magnitude of that effect. One reason for this is that effects matter because they are expressed in economically meaningful units. This of course highlights our earlier point about the significance of the dependent variable in SHRM research. We are in a position to develop a meaningful conversation about the size of HR's effect, and the magnitude of potential biases in those estimates, rather than simply focusing on whether the effects exist at all.

Omitted variable bias
Empirical relationships in the SHRM literature typically take the form of regression models, with a measure of organizational performance modeled as a function of the

HR architecture and various control variables. Omitted variable bias occurs if an omitted variable is correlated with both the HR variable and the dependent variable. The direction and magnitude of that bias will depend on the direction and magnitude of those correlations. There are two ways in which commonly used estimation models in the empirical SHRM literature might raise questions about omitted variables. The first follows from our earlier discussion of the importance of the dependent variable as the source of SHRM's influence. Dependent variables like productivity (revenue per employee), return on assets or a shareholder value measure all have enormous theoretical and empirical literatures associated with them. There are well developed estimation models in those literatures that typically extend beyond one or two independent variables. It is important that empirical SHRM research reflects the richness of these models. Otherwise our literature is open to questions about whether the effects of the HR variables are also reflecting the effects of variables that have been omitted from the conventional estimation model for that particular dependent variable. At a minimum, if those additional variables have been omitted from the model authors ought to explain why this omission is not a significant threat to the validity of their results.

A more fully specified estimation model based on the prior empirical literature for a particular dependent variable is a reasonably tractable problem. The measures are generally available in the same data sets as the dependent variable. A more challenging problem involves omitted variables that reflect other management policies that also influence firm performance. For example, are firms that have outstanding marketing strategies, or excel at supply chain management, also more likely to have high performance HR systems? We examined this alternative explanation in an earlier analysis (Huselid and Becker, 1997). Using a simple rating of the quality of 'other' management functions in the firm relative to close competitors as our measure, the effect of the HPWS system measure was virtually unchanged when the 'other management'

variable was included in the model. Of course if such value creating policies do coexist with the presence of a HPWS, it may well mean that those effects are overstated in their respective literatures, and it is HR that deserves more credit. The success of these other policies, like marketing or supply chain management, may in large part be due to the employee performance in those functions, which is the result of the firm's high-performance HR system.

In addition there are a wide range of 'people' oriented practices, like leadership, that we would normally consider as positive influences on firm performance, yet may also be positively correlated with the presence of a high performance work system (HPWS). One approach to the problem is to argue that control variables capture these other effects, but we would have to believe the mechanism by which these other variables affect performance is considerably different than the way in which HR affects performance. Otherwise, we would be 'controlling' for the HR effects as well. The value of such controls seems more plausible for the non-people oriented policies.

While this issue continues to be a challenge for the empirical SHRM literature, particularly the multi-industry cross-sectional studies, there is no easy solution. Certainly we recommend that future work at least attempts to address this issue with some additional measures of these other policies. Again, we do not expect these studies to find that HR has no effect, but rather continue to provide a greater precision to the growing body of point estimates. Future research may benefit from more attention to small quasi experimental studies that follow the introduction of SHRM changes, particularly if they focus on the type of differentiated fit we discussed above. This approach would have the potential to control for other policies that might be held constant over the introduction of the HR changes.

Measurement error bias

In recent years, the role of measurement error in the HR measures has been a subject of some interest in the empirical SHRM literature. Gerhart et al. (2000) contended that SHRM effects based on single respondent surveys were significantly undermined by the presence of measurement error in the SHRM measures. We have argued (Huselid and Becker, 2000) that where single respondents were key informants and HR practice measures focused on more objective attributes (like hours of training), the effects reported in large scale multi-industry samples such as our own work were not significantly influenced by the issues raised by Gerhart et al. (2000). Furthermore, it was our view that if this issue was to be considered a serious challenge to the growing empirical literature, the magnitude of the problem could only be evaluated within the context of samples similar to our own work rather than in the small sample of very large organizations used in Gerhart et al. (2000). Absent this kind of compelling evidence, a general expectation of a multi-respondent design for work in SHRM would essentially render large scale studies infeasible.

Over the last five years there have indeed been a number of SHRM studies using multi-respondent designs in national multi-industry samples. Notably, several have been conducted by the co-authors (Wright and Snell) of the Gerhart et al. (2000) paper. Each of these studies reveals a similar pattern. Beginning with a large national sampling frame, the authors attempt to collect data from multiple respondents, the response rate is trivial, and the inter-rater reliability using the very small sample of firms with multiple respondents is quite high. Finally, the analysis is ultimately based on the only feasible sample – single respondent measures.

In an early effort to collect multi-rater measures, Lepak and Snell (2002) surveyed 2375 firms, but were forced to rely on just '23 firms in which identical surveys were completed' (p. 529) as the basis for their reliability calculations. Not surprisingly, the study's analysis was not based on the multi-respondent sample. Later, Youndt and Snell (2004) surveyed 919 firms and attempted to collect responses from both the CEO and VP

for HR. The response rate was somewhat higher than in Lepak and Snell (2002), but still yielded just 71 observations. While Youndt and Snell ultimately merged both single and multiple respondent firms, their analysis of the multi-respondent reliabilities indicated that because 'multiple top level executives from the same firm provided very similar responses, there is evidence to suggest that whether we had responses from one or numerous executives from each firm our results would be similar.' Most recently, a paper co-authored by Pat Wright (Datta et al., 2005) reports a multi-respondent sample of just 33 firms (p. 143) out of a sampling frame of 971 manufacturing firms. The authors conclude with some understatement that, indeed, when it comes to multiple respondent surveys 'a high response rate in multi-industry research designs may prove challenging' (p. 143). More to the issue of whether prior empirical results should be called into question, the results of this study, which relied in part on the HR index measures developed in Huselid (1995) reported effects on labor productivity (the only dependent variable) well within the same range reported previously in Huselid (1995) and Becker and Huselid (1998).

So where does this leave us? It is important that these and other studies have explored the implications of single rater surveys using multi-industry samples similar to those that had been called into question by Gerhart et al. (2000). However, even as the work of several of the original authors of the Gerhart et al. (2000) paper has demonstrated, there is nothing in these subsequent studies that casts significant doubt on the earlier single respondent based results. With the challenges of large scale survey research in this area increasingly daunting, we believe that the wisest use of scarce research resources should be devoted to increasing overall response rates among well crafted single respondent surveys. There seems to be little incremental contribution to continuing to divert those resources to largely futile (and apparently unnecessary) efforts to develop multi-respondent samples.

Mutual causation and simultaneity

A common concern expressed in the empirical literature is the caveat that the positive cross-sectional HR-firm performance relationship is in part influenced by mutual causation, or simultaneity bias. Unfortunately, this issue tends to typically receive a perfunctory mention in the 'Limitations' section of most empirical papers and is rarely addressed directly. Notable exceptions are recent papers by Guest et al. (2003) and Wright et al. (2005).

On this issue, it is probably useful to recall Fisher's dictum. R.A. Fisher, the eminent statistician, was reportedly once asked for his advice about how to move from association to causation, and his recommendation was simple: 'make your theories more elaborate' (Cox, 1992: 292). Indeed, the saliency of this issue in the SHRM literature is directly related to the 'black box' between the HR architecture and firm performance. Going forward, focusing on the link between the HR architecture and strategy implementation provides a clearer strategic rationale for HR's ultimate impact on firm performance. More importantly, it suggests little theoretical rationale for reverse causation.

Unfortunately the prior SHRM literature lacks the kind of well developed theoretical framework that would inform a well specified empirical model on this issue. The initial logic tends to posit mutual positive effects, or at least a positive effect from firm performance to the HR system. But why do we necessarily assume that high performance HR systems require significantly more financial resources? SHRM is more about how the firm's resources are spent and the focus of the HR system than about the level of spending on HR. The positive firm performance-HR story also seems to suggest that the discipline and acumen that otherwise produced outstanding financial results are missing as these companies throw money at an HR fad. It may be the case that the same business acumen and discipline that creates success in the rest of the business is also more likely to recognize the wisdom of an SHRM approach. This explanation, however, is closer to the 'other management' bias described earlier.

Indeed, one could just as easily argue that in fact it is not the more successful firms that adopt these systems, but instead it is the struggling firms who turn to their HR systems as an opportunity to improve performance. This of course would still be reflected in mutual causation in a cross-sectional sample, though a single equation model with HR as the independent variable would tend to understate HR's true effect.

Assume that we develop a theoretical logic that firm financial performance affects the HR system. How should these expectations be incorporated into empirical work? One approach might be to locate natural experiments where HR changes are measured and subsequent changes in financial performance observed for otherwise similar organizations or even organizational units. This type of result would give us some evidence that HR's effect on financial performance could be 'real.' Once a series of such studies accumulated they would in the aggregate provide a compelling test of this alternative hypothesis.

An alternative approach is to improve our estimation models when analyzing the more common large scale cross-sectional data sets. The problem is any mechanism that gives rise to HR and firm performance being jointly determined will be very difficult to model. We are not likely to know when an HR change was implemented, or how much time is required before any effects will have been realized (Guest et al., 2003). Recent work by both Wright et al. (2005) and Guest et al. (2003) rely on analyses of HR measures at time T, and measures of firm performance at time $T+1$ and $T-1$. They argue that the absence of an HR effect on Performance at T+1, controlling for Performance at $T-1$, calls into question any interpretation that HR's effect in prior cross sectional research is a causal relationship. Guest et al. (2003), however, correctly observes that this approach is really a 'test for the impact of HR practices on change in performance' (p.297). This of course is a very conservative test of HR's effect on performance. There is no reason to believe that in any sample of

HR and firm performance at time T that HR's unrealized effect is all that significant. Indeed the strategy literature focuses on cross sectional heterogeneity in firm performance, and strategies will be successful when they result in sustainable competitive advantage. HR's contribution to competitive advantage is much more likely to be reflected in differences in the levels of profitability than in rates of change.

Wright et al. (2005) recognize this issue and point out that a 'dual causation' model might well explain their results. We agree. Unfortunately, Wright et al.'s (2005) observation that 'the observed payoff [of HR practices] may be far less than the estimates provided in past research' (p. 433) is simply not informed by their analysis. The single equation results could be overstated, or understated, by a lot or little. The dual causation hypothesis requires empirical testing and we are aware of only one paper (Huselid, 1995) that tested these effects in a simultaneous equation system. In that study, the HR effects were slightly more positive in the multiple equation estimates (p. 666).

Where does this leave us? We agree with both Guest et al. (2003) and Wright et al. (2005) that the issue of simultaneity bias should be more systematically considered in the empirical SHRM literature, though it does not strike us as the most compelling alternative explanation to the extant literature. Having said that, the literature would benefit from a comprehensive treatment of the dual causation thesis, where the estimates are based on a simultaneous equation system and drawn from the kinds of multi-industry samples that have been called into question. Guest et al. (2003) and Wright et al. (2005) raise the right question, but the empirical tests do not correspond to the complexity of the problem. Aside from the reliance on pre and post performance measures to capture dual causation, Wright et al. (2005) limit their analysis to simple and partial correlations. While their reliance on data from a single firm arguably should reduce the variance in the firm performance measures, the simple correlation between HR practices

and profitability never explains more than 10 percent of the variance in their profitability measure (Table 4, p. 429). Surely this residual variance is attributable to something other than measurement error in the dependent variable. The most likely explanation is the systematic influence of other differences among these units, differences that may also be correlated with the level of HR practices. Once again, this is a literature where the effects matter and those effects presume a reasonable set of control variables to rule out the most basic alternative explanations.[3]

We would also make what is perhaps a philosophical observation about how these types of methodological issues are best examined. Guest et al. (2003), for example, examines the causality question within a large scale multi-industry analysis of UK data. The sample and context are equivalent to the types of prior US studies where causality has been called into question. We have adopted a similar approach in our own work (Becker and Huselid, 1998; Huselid, 1995; Huselid and Becker, 1996). Wright et al. (2005) distinguish between studies that examine methodological as opposed to theoretical issues, which follows the approach in Gerhart et al. (2000). We have argued that such narrowly drawn methodological papers, typically based on just a handful of firms, or even multiple units in the same firm, simply raise more questions than they answer (Huselid and Becker, 2000). Moreover, it seems unnecessary. Just as the authors in Gerhart et al. (2000) could have reanalyzed their own data to examine these questions, Wright recently co-authored a paper (Datta et al. 2005) that could have easily included pre and post performance measures as part of the analysis. Instead, there is simply the acknowledgement that 'it is also possible that firms experiencing higher productivity are better positioned to invest in high performance practices.' (p. 143). Unfortunately, there is no indication of when these productivity measures were collected so the reader can only speculate how the results fit into the kinds of criticisms raised in Wright et al. (2005).

AN AGENDA FOR FUTURE RESEARCH

A clearer articulation of the 'black box' between HR and firm performance is the most pressing theoretical and empirical challenge in the SHRM literature. This requires a new emphasis on integrating strategy implementation as the central mediating variable in the HR-firm performance relationship. It goes to the core of what makes SHRM *strategic*, and not simply a traditional HR perspective with a new set of dependent variables. There are also direct implications for the nature of fit and contingencies in SHRM. It highlights the significance of a *differentiated* HR architecture not just across firms, but also within firms.

Moving the literature in this new direction suggests a rich and varied research agenda, both theoretically and empirically. Several of these new directions were discussed above. However, there are a number of related questions that also need to be considered.

Measuring the workforce differentiation construct

We believe that an important priority for future research is the development of reliable and valid instrumentation for the differentiation construct. Based on the theoretical model we have presented (see Figure 20.1), our empirical work, and our experiences in a wide variety of organizations, we have developed a taxonomy of four stages of workforce differentiation (Becker et al., 2009). We believe these stages to be mutually exclusive, exhaustive, and cumulative in their differentiation complexity. However, as the stage each firm adopts is essentially a 'choice' variable, firms do not necessarily have to move though them in stages, and can move from Stage 1 to 4 (and presumably back again).

Stage 1

In the first (and most common) stage, firms do not have an explicit workforce differentiation strategy. Instead, they, to a greater or lesser degree attempt to adopt HR management 'best practices.' Several factors are key indicators of this stage. First, the choice of HR management practices is largely independent of firm strategy, and is instead driven by an effort to mimic global or industry based best practices. As we described above, given the substantial variance in HR management 'quality' across firms, there exists the potential for economic returns due to an 'early mover' advantage for firms adopting these best practices, and one that may endure for several years. Thus, for the most advanced firms in Stage 1, adopting HR best practices (or *high performance work systems*) should have a positive impact on firm performance, but the magnitude of this impact should diminish as more firms adopt these practices (Becker and Huselid, 1998; Huselid, 1995).

Stage 2

We believe that that the second stage of workforce differentiation complexity occurs when firms begin to align their generic business strategies with their overall HR function strategies. For example, firms following a *low cost* positioning strategy (in Porter's framework) might seek to orient all of their HR management practices around cost reduction, while firms following a *differentiation* strategy might attempt to adopt HR practices leading to innovation (Beatty and Schneier, 1997). While this approach has the advantage of beginning to create a greater alignment between business, workforce and HR function strategies, in reality it is just a refinement of the 'best practices' strategy we described in Stage 1. Thus the fundamental distinction between Stages 1 and 2 is that in the former one overarching 'best' HR architecture is believed to exist, whereas in the latter there are three 'best' architectures – one for each of the key positioning strategies (e.g., cost leadership, differentiation, and focus). While this approach is likely to be an improvement over Stage 1 in most firms, it suffers from similar challenges associated with the ease of inimitability and subsequent loss of competitive position as more firms attempt to adopt this approach. Creating the potential for long term rents from workforce management strategies requires the additional levels of differentiation we describe in Stages 3 and 4.

Stage 3

The key difference between Stage 3 and the preceding stages is that the adoption of differentiated workforce management practices is based on strategic capability, and not on overall firm positioning strategy. Philosophically, managers in Stage 3 firms have made the decision to invest disproportionately in the workforce in the areas of the business providing the greatest economic returns. This implies a movement away from a 'best practice' or 'employer of choice' workforce strategy. For example, a pharmaceutical business may have a positioning strategy focused on introducing new medicines, perhaps in the area of oncology. A Stage 1 firm would adopt HR 'best practices' independent of these business goals, whereas a Stage 2 firm would structure an overarching HR architecture based on innovation. In Stage 3, managers recognize that effective execution of the firm's business strategies relies on several strategic capabilities, perhaps including R&D acumen, world class manufacturing expertise, and sales and marketing. Stage 3 firms recognize that even though the positioning strategy might be one of 'focus' the strategic capabilities needed to deliver the strategy are quite different and need to be managed accordingly. So, Stage 3 firms differentiate by strategic capability, not positioning strategy, and as a consequence, would be likely to have different HR architectures in R&D, manufacturing, and sales.

Stage 4

In Stage 4 the locus of workforce differentiation moves from the strategic capability to the strategic job (or A Position) that is nested within that capability (we further elaborate on the specific research needs associated with A positions below). For example, in the pharmaceutical company example described above, managers would begin with an understanding that R&D acumen was a key driver of their business success. But even within the R&D function,

some jobs are more critical to strategic success than others, and that disproportionate investments must be made to ensure that the very best employees were placed in the firm's critical jobs, serving the corporations most important customers. Strategic or A positions are important, not only because of their key role in driving the strategic capability, but also because the employees holding those jobs tend to exhibit wide ranges in performance (Huselid et al., 2005). In short, the impact of A jobs on the firm's strategic capabilities provides the *context* for an improvement in strategy execution, while the variability in employee performance provides the specific *opportunity* for managers to act (by increasing mean employee performance and reducing the variance). Stage 4 firms differentially focus their managerial efforts on these jobs because they provide a clear and unambiguous path to strategy execution, and offer the highest yield investment for scarce managerial time and resources. As a consequence, the HR architectures in these firms are likewise differentiated by positioning strategy, by strategic capability within positioning strategy, and finally, by job within strategic capability.

Articulating the limits of HR's strategic impact

Given SHRM's strategic focus, a core question is always how HR influences firm performance. Porter (1996), however, distinguishes between managerial decisions that create competitive advantage and those that simply improve operational excellence. Going forward we need more work delineating the theoretical and empirical limits of HR's strategic impact. For example, does slow and imperfect diffusion of SHRM ideas among HR professionals result in significant financial gains from HR's improved operational excellence? How does this market failure explanation square with the highly successful 'diffusion industry' of conferences and workshops that purport to share 'best practices'?

Given a new focus on strategy implementation, under what conditions will the impact of the HR architecture move along the continuum from operational efficiency to sustained competitive advantage? Will that effect vary with product market dynamism and product life cycles? Are there some capabilities and perhaps some industry segments where HR's strategic impact is likely to be inconsequential? Empirical work that examines the relationship between several easily copied or 'best' HR practices and measures of financial performance needs to consider why those practices are strategic and not simply better HR.

Our own work (Becker and Huselid, 1998; Huselid, 1995) emphasizes HR systems that are not so easily imitated, and we can demonstrate meaningful effects on multiple measures of firm performance over multiple national samples. Nevertheless we cannot rule out the possibility that much of those effects represent improved operational excellence rather than a sustainable competitive advantage. This distinction continues to challenge empirical work in the strategy literature as well. The difference between the two literatures is largely one of recognition. Strategy researchers are more aware of the problem.

The limits of differentiation

We have argued for a much greater focus on differentiation in the HR Architecture, both between firms and within firms. But this should not be interpreted as another variation of the debate over universal versus contingent HR systems. That distinction is too narrow, emphasizing the contingency with a small set of positioning strategies. When contingencies are instead focused on the processes that implement a strategy, the appropriate question is not best practice vs. contingencies. The interesting question will focus on the appropriate mix between core and differentiated HR practices, and whether certain practices are more easily differentiated. What features of the strategic or organizational environment will determine the appropriate mix of differentiation and best practices for a particular firm? Likewise, are there particular functions within the

HR architecture that are more appropriately offered as a best practice, while others are more likely candidates for differentiation?

A greater emphasis on differentiation within the firm means that fit will play a much more central role in SHRM theory. Does this approach necessarily create a tension between the benefits of fit, and the constraints on flexibility (Wright and Snell, 1998)? In particular, what are the limits imposed by dynamic market environments, and would those apply to all strategic business processes in the organization? It is not just that greater fit might come at some cost in terms of flexibility. What is the relative magnitude of those costs and benefits, both theoretically and empirically?

Perhaps more important is the issue of differentiation among firms. The extant SHRM literature suggests very little differentiation. If strategy implementation is the core value creation mechanism for SHRM, what is the optimal mix of differentiation among HR architectures of close competitors? Building competitive advantage around strategic capabilities requires a degree of differentiation in those capabilities across close competitors. Eisenhardt and Martin (2000) find that strategic business processes often approach best practices among close competitors, though they may be executed differently. SHRM empirical work would benefit from a similar analysis of HR architectures within the context of close competitors. Specifically, do HR architectures that are differentiated across similar business processes provide significant improvements in the execution of those strategic business processes among close competitors? Do HR architectures that appear to be best practices in large multi-industry studies in fact reveal meaningful differentiation when analyzed within the impact on strategic business processes among close competitors?

A new emphasis on strategic jobs

We argue that HR's strategic impact is contingent on its contribution to the effectiveness of strategic business processes. The value of this impact increases as the HR architecture is differentiated by strategic business processes. We posit that this impact works disproportionately through 'A' or strategic jobs in those business processes (Huselid et al., 2005). This implies that some jobs are strategic (and more valuable) and others are not. The construct of the strategic job needs to be more fully articulated. Why are some jobs in a strategic business process disproportionately valuable? What determines that difference in value? In particular, what are the boundary conditions for this construct? How do we reconcile the notion of strategic jobs with potential interdependencies among jobs? There seems to be a particularly interesting opportunity to explore the concept of the strategic job from a network perspective. Strategic jobs are consistent with a hub and spoke network. But are some strategies more effectively implemented with decentralized networks, where there is no obvious strategic job?

Introducing strategic jobs as a key construct in SHRM will require a wide range of new empirical work as well. There are at least two fundamental questions that need to be explored. The first is whether in fact strategic jobs exist in practice? What is the evidence that a small number of jobs in an organization create a disproportionate share of the firm's strategic value? What is the magnitude of any value differential? The second question would examine the strategic impact of disproportionately investing in strategic jobs. We would expect a significantly higher return from investments in strategic jobs than from investments in non-strategic jobs. By what mechanism and by what degree does the firm's HR architecture affect that value differential?

What is the likely impact on employees of strategic differentiation?

The impact of SHRM on employees, as opposed to firm performance, has been a recurring question in the literature (Osterman, 2006). A strategy of disproportionate investments in strategic jobs is more about a reallocation of resources within the labor force than a redistribution between the labor force and shareholders. Nevertheless, Pfeffer (2005) argues strongly in favor of HR systems that minimize status differences among employees. It is clear that a new emphasis on strategic and non-strategic jobs would not only result in significant differences in how some employees interact with the HR architecture, but also the level of investment directed to the employees in those jobs categories would be considerably different (Huselid et al., 2005). These are important theoretical and empirical questions for SHRM. What is the impact on employees in non-strategic jobs from disproportionate investments in strategic jobs? Where is the greater cost, among employees in strategic jobs who are currently underperforming in an undifferentiated system, or among employees in non-strategic jobs whose performance might be affected by a differentiated system?

SHRM IN PRACTICE

Any discussion of the future of SHRM needs to acknowledge the central role of management practice, both as a basis for the widespread interest in the field as well as validity check on our research agenda. If the prescriptions from the HR strategy literature prove to be either inaccessible or irrelevant to practicing managers, the vitality and prominence of the field will surely suffer. This section highlights what we consider to be the most important challenges facing organizations as they attempt to turn SHRM concepts into practice.[4] Beyond providing some useful insight for practice, we hope these observations will also inform SHRM scholarship more generally as well.

Workforce strategy rather than HR architecture

The most general implementation challenge facing HR professionals reflects an interesting conundrum. We find wide-spread acceptance among senior HR and line managers of the notion that an appropriately designed and implemented HR strategy can make a managerially significant contribution to their firm's financial performance. Any skepticism they express generally reflects the extent to which they believe the managers in their own firms are capable of the transition. Most HR professionals, and certainly all senior HR professionals, want to play a strategic role in their organizations, if for no other reason than senior line managers increasingly demand it. Unfortunately, while SHRM theory focuses on inimitable HR systems aligned to strategic goals, HR professionals too often focus on cost control and efficiency gains in an effort to demonstrate their bottom line success. New measures with names like 'human capital value added' are sometimes used to justify traditional practices and approaches to workforce measurement (e.g., cost per employee or benefits expense as a proportion of revenue). This approach merely reinforces the view that the HR function is a cost center, and does very little to improve the firm's strategy implementation.

Even in a firm where HR professionals (and line managers) understand SHRM concepts, the HR function's legacy reputation is often a significant hurdle to overcome. As one line manager put it, 'I'm absolutely convinced that doing a better job managing the workforce would create considerable wealth in our business. I'm just not convinced that anyone in the HR department can help us get there.' This quote highlights an important distinction between managing the workforce and managing the HR function. The notion of workforce strategy is understood by managers in much the same way as academics speak of the HR architecture, with one important difference. It highlights a shared responsibility for strategic workforce performance between line managers and HR professionals that is not as central in the HR Architecture construct.

This is not just a case of putting a new title on the same story. There is a lesson here for both managers and academics. The notion of workforce strategy appears to be a much more effective organizing principle for SHRM concepts in practice because the involvement

of line managers provides a much clearer line of sight to an emphasis on strategy execution. The concepts of fit and alignment in SHRM theory are more easily implemented when line managers and HR professionals focus on strategic business processes, and not individual HR practices. It helps to mitigate the all too common situation where HR professionals find the organization's strategic goals either unclear or inconsistent, making it all but impossible to determine the human capital dimension of those goals.

The challenge of differentiation

A related issue that poses a major departure from past practice is the increased emphasis on differentiation. There are really two dimensions of differentiation that have to be considered here. The first is more structural in terms of differentially focusing the workforce strategy on strategic versus non-strategic jobs. HR professionals tend to associate 'strategic' with practices that are firm wide and cover a broad range of employees, along the lines of a core behavioral competency. We find that the acceptance of more differentiation to be directly related to the adoption of the broader approach to workforce strategy described above. It provides a clear and legitimate basis for identifying the differential value of jobs, and is typically endorsed by line managers. Disproportionate investments in strategic jobs appear more compelling when the *status quo* is a strategy that tends to under-invest in the strategic jobs and over-invest in the non-strategic jobs (Huselid et al., 2005). Once the strategic rationale for this differentiation is explained to managers they often react as if a burden has been lifted. The mantra that 'employees are our most important asset' often permeates organizations, but in reality managers often interpret this to mean that they need to invest in everyone in equal measure. The notion of differential investment based on a strategic logic provides an actionable solution.

The second implication of differentiation is at the level of employee performance. This means making meaningful performance distinctions among employees, particularly in strategic jobs. These distinctions will mean greater, not less, variation in rewards and greater efforts to exit those employees who do not meet the organization's performance standards. Implementing this increased differentiation again reflects the increased role of line managers. Designing an HR system with greater differentiation is not the problem. The challenge is motivating line managers to implement these systems. Not surprisingly, motivating the line managers requires that they be held accountable for the results of the workforce strategy and the extent to which they manage talent effectively. Again, this suggests that future SHRM research should incorporate a wider notion of the HR architecture, and in particular the role of line managers in implementing a workforce strategy.

The measurement challenge

HR professionals face an additional challenge, or what some may call a motivation, when attempting to adopt differentiated workforce strategies. We alluded earlier to the pressure to measure HR's performance in a way that demonstrates its strategic contribution. Citing the broad academic evidence of HR's strategic impact only goes so far. Too often senior HR leaders are reduced to presenting results from the latest employee survey, or trends for various turnover rates. When the CEO asks 'why is this important?,' they have no good answer. A solution to this problem requires a distinction between the human capital dimension of strategy implementation (SHRM's focus) and the HR function. Traditional HR measures (like cost per hire) focus on the performance of the HR function and tend to rely on external benchmarks. This not only limits consideration of HR's performance in terms of administrative efficiency, but implicitly treats strategies as commodities with appropriate market benchmarks. A key point that we made in *The Workforce Scorecard* was that most organizations have much better accountability and control systems for raw materials (roughly

15 percent of total expenses) than they do the workforce (65% of total expenses). As a result, a hospital can pinpoint the source of a defective bandage or a manufacturing firm can identify the supplier of a bad bearing with a high degree of accuracy and speed. However, most firms have no clue as to the source or reason for their defective (or high quality) managers, if in fact they even know who they are. For firms to effectively execute business strategy, they must develop a much better understanding of the causes and consequences of workforce performance. They must also do a much better job of holding line managers accountable for the most expensive resource that has been assigned to them.

Measures are answers to questions, and most benchmarking measures do not answer a strategic HR question for an organization. By contrast the intermediate measures implied by our emphasis on strategy implementation put more emphasis on results that appropriately capture HR's strategic contribution (Becker et al., 2001; Huselid et al., 2005). While not traditionally part of HR's measurement system, HR professionals recognize the value of such measures because line managers value them as well. The measurement of intangibles is a developing area in management, and one that is particularly applicable to the field of SHRM (Ittner and Larker, 2003).

New competencies in workforce management

What it means for HR leaders to play a strategic role in their firms role has changed considerably, especially over the last five years. Senior managers continue to struggle with how to redesign and expand the role of the HR function and the system of workforce management practices in an attempt to capture the value described in the empirical HR strategy literature. Following the earlier logic in the paper, we believe that the HR function's strategic role needs to focus more heavily on the workforce component of the firm's strategic capabilities. This will have important implications for how HR is managed and how it is evaluated in the organization. A focus on strategic capabilities will mean for HR professionals a much greater emphasis on *differentiation*. This will take the form not only of differentiation relative to competitors but also more differentiation within their own organizations. We believe that managers need to focus on how to align the HR systems and workforce investments at the level of the strategic business process. Such a focus requires disproportionate investments in 'strategic' jobs and the need to increasingly differentiate employee performance within those jobs.

We believe that despite the substantial discussion in the academic and popular press about the importance of HR playing the role of 'strategic partner' to line management, there remains a considerable amount of variance in the capabilities of HR managers. In fact, in our own research we have found HR managers to be much more effective at the technical or operational aspects of HR's role than they were at strategy execution (Huselid et al., 1997), although the strategy execution had a much larger impact on firm performance. Addressing this issue effectively will require new research focused on clearly articulating the common body of knowledge, skills, competencies, and behaviors needed to be effective workforce strategy managers, for both those in HR as well as line roles.

Many authors have noted that the role of HR manager is a complex one, necessarily focused on meeting the needs of multiple constituencies (Ulrich and Brockbank, 2005). These multiple roles and constituencies are likely to require multiple competencies from HR leaders as well. Unlike their colleagues in finance, accounting, and marketing, however, the vast majority of HR professionals do not have professional degrees or any type of certification in HR. As a consequence, it is perhaps unsurprising that they do not possess such broad competencies. While the literature on general managerial competencies has a long history, the literature on the specific competencies needed for HR managers is much more limited. We believe that a useful line of research would blend the literatures on general manager and HR managers competencies,

with a specific focus on those competencies and behaviors directly related to strategy execution.

CONCLUDING REMARKS

In the last 15 years the field of HR strategy has had a remarkable influence on both the academic literature and management practice.[5] One of the purposes for writing this paper is to highlight this important relationship between SHRM scholarship and management practice. In our view, it's what makes this line of inquiry both interesting (Bartunek et al. 2006) and influential (Bazerman, 2005). By comparison, consider earlier efforts to link HR decisions and firm financial performance, such as utility analysis that have largely disappeared from the literature. Despite this remarkable progress, the field of SHRM may be at a crossroads. The empirical literature demonstrating that HR could influence meaningful financial outcomes was once a novel and exciting result for managers. But that time has passed. To a substantial degree, managers now 'get it' and do not have to be persuaded that the quality with which they manage the workforce has strategic impact. What they now need is help in understanding how to generate and sustain those potential returns.

While academic research continues to replicate and refine these empirical results, the practice of HR strategy has moved beyond whether or not there is a significant return to better workforce management. Managers are asking questions like 'What are the key strategic positions in our organization and how should they be managed?' and 'How can we design and implement a workforce management system that helps us to execute strategy and create wealth?' This signals an evolution in the research problems confronting SHRM, as well as the foundation for an equally exciting 15 years going forward. While the directions for future theoretical and empirical work discussed previously are rooted in an evolving academic literature, they are fundamentally influenced by the experience of managers who are attempting to implement these ideas. The most fundamental lesson from that experience is that while SHRM was initially an HR-centric paradigm, it is rapidly moving out of the hands of HR professionals into the hands of line managers and senior executives. HR professionals will play a role, but they may not be taking the lead.

The role of strategy implementation in the 'black box' between the HR architecture and firm performance reflects this centrality of the line manager and the associated broader focus on workforce management. This shift in the SHRM axis within the firm needs to be reflected in SHRM research as well. Recent calls for evidenced-based management (Pfeffer and Sutton, 2006) have emphasized the importance of incorporating the *logic* of academic research into managerial decision-making as much as the empirical results. In our view the logic of the HR-firm performance relationship has evolved over the last 15 years and both scholarship and practice need to reflect that shift.

ACKNOWLEDGEMENTS

We are grateful to Steve Frenkel, Dave Lepak, and seminar participants at Monash University for comments on an earlier version of this manuscript.

NOTES

1 This paper is a slightly revised version of our paper with the same title which appeared in the December 2006 issue of the *Journal of Management*, 32 (6): 898–925.

2 Several of the issues raised in this section were also discussed in Becker and Huselid (1998).

3 As an example of where this reliance on correlations yields misleading results, Wright et al. describe the effects of controlling for an alternative explanation in one our studies (Huselid and Becker, 1997). Using our correlation matrix they calculate a partial correlation between HR and firm performance that 'reduces the observed correlation from .25 to .18' (p. 434). However they fail to note that the regression coefficient for the HR index, which of course provides a much more complete control for alternative explanations, actually increased slightly when the additional control was included (Huselid

and Becker, 1997; Table 1, cols 3 and 6, p. 147). Wright et al.'s observation that this partial correlation provides 'at least some evidence for the possibility of a spurious correlation' (p. 434) is a considerable misinterpretation of our actual results.

4 These judgments, though admittedly subjective, are based on our experience in scores of organizations, both domestically and internationally, over the last twenty years.

5 One indication of SHRM's academic impact is that among all of the articles published in the *Academy of Management Journal* since 1990, three of the ten most highly cited papers are in the field of HR strategy.

REFERENCES

Amit, R. and Shoemaker, P.J.H. (1993) 'Strategic assets and organizational rent', *Strategic Management Journal*, 14 (1): 33–46.

Bartunek, J.M., Rynes, S.L. and Ireland, R.D. (2006) 'What makes management research interesting, and why does it matter?', *Academy of Management Journal*, 49 (1): 9–15.

Bazerman, M.H. (2005) 'Conducting influential research: The need for prescriptive implications', *Academy of Management Review*, 30 (1): 25–31.

Barney, J.B. (2001) 'Is the resource-based 'view' a useful perspective for strategic management research? Yes,' *Academy of Management Review*, 26 (1): 41–56.

Beatty, R.W. and Schneier, C.E. (1997) 'New HR roles to impact organizational performance: From partners to players', *Human Resource Management*, 36 (1): 29–37.

Becker, B.E., Huselid, M.A. and Beatty, R.W. (2009) *The Differentiated Workforce: Translating Talent Intro Strategic Action*. Boston: Harvard Business Press.

Becker, B.E., Huselid, M.A. and Ulrich, D. (2001) *The HR Scorecard: Linking People, Strategy and Performance.* Boston: Harvard Business School Press.

Becker, B.E. and Gerhart, B. (1996) 'Human resources and organizational performance: progress and prospects', *Academy of Management Journal (Special Issue: Human Resources and Organizational Performance)*, 39 (4): 779–801.

Becker, B.E. and Huselid, M.A. (1998) 'High performance work systems and firm performance: A synthesis of research and managerial implications,' *Research in Personnel and Human Resource Management*, 16: 53–101.

Colbert, B.A. (2004) 'The complex resource-based view: Implications for theory and practice in strategic human resource management,' *Academy of Management Review*, 28 (3): 341–58.

Collins, C.J. and Smith, K.G. (2006) 'Knowledge exchange and combination: The role of human resource practices in the performance of high technology firms,' *Academy of Management Journal*, 49: 544–60.

Combs, J.G., Ketchen Jr., D.J, Hall, A.T. and Yongmei, L. (forthcoming) 'Do high performance work practices matter?: A meta-analysis of their effects on organizational performance,' *Personnel Psychology*.

Combs, J. G., Ketchen, D. J., Jr., Hall, A. T. and Liu, Y. (2006) Do high performance work practices matter? A metaanalysis of their effects on organizational performance. Personnel Psychology, 59: 501–528.

Cox, D.R. (1992) 'Causality: Some statistical aspects,' *Journal of the Royal Statistical Society*, series A, 155, part 2: 291–301.

Datta, D.K., Guthrie, J.P. and Wright, P.M. (2005) 'Human resource management and labor productivity: Does industry matter?', *Academy of Management Journal*, 48 (1): 135–45.

Delery, J.E. and Doty, D.H. (1996) 'Modes of theorizing in strategic human resource management: Tests of universalistic, contingent and configurational performance predictions', *Academy of Management Journal*, 39 (4): 802–35.

Eisenhardt, K.M. and Martin, J.A. (2000) 'Dynamic capabilities: What are they?', *Strategic Management Journal*, 21: 1105–21.

Ericksen, J. and Dyer, L. (2004) 'Toward a strategic human resource management model of high reliability organization performance,' working paper, (CAHRS: Ithaca), 1–36.

Ethiraj, S.K., Kale P., Krishnan, M.S. and Singh, J.V. (2005) 'Where do capabilities come from and how do they matter? a study in the software services industry', *Strategic Management Journal*, 26: 25–45.

Ferraro, F., Pfeffer, J. and Sutton, R.I. (2005) 'Economics language and assumptions: How theories can become self-fulfilling', *Academy of Management Review*, 31 (1): 8–24.

Gerhart, B. (2005) 'Human resources and business performance: Findings, unanswered questions, and an alternative approach,' *Management Revue*, 16 (2): 174–85.

Gerhart, B., Wright P.M., McMahan, G.C. and Snell, S.A. (2000) 'Measurement error in research on human resources and firm performance: How much error is there and how does it influence effect size estimates?', *Personnel Psychology*, 53 (4): 803–34.

Guest, D.E., Michie, J., Conway, N. and Sheehan, M. (2003) 'Human resource management and corporate performance in the UK,' *British Journal of Industrial Relations*, 41 (2): 291–314.

Gulati, R. (1998) 'Alliances and networks,' *Strategic Management Journal*, (19): 293–317.

Huselid, M.A. (1995) 'The impact of human resource management practices on turnover, productivity and corporate financial performance,' *Academy of Management Journal*, 38 (3): 635–72.

Huselid, M.A. and Becker, B.E. (1997) 'The impact of high performance work systems, implementation effectiveness, and alignment with strategy on shareholder wealth', *Academy of Management Best Papers Proceedings*, 144–8.

Huselid, M.A. and Becker, B.E. (2000) 'Comment on measurement error in research on human resources and firm performance: How much error is there and how does it influence effect size estimates?', by Gerhart, Wright, McMahan, and Snell,' *Personnel Psychology*, 53 (4): 835–54.

Huselid, M.A., Beatty, R.W. and Becker, B.E. (2005a) "A players' or 'A positions'? the strategic logic of workforce management,' *Harvard Business Review*, December: 110–7.

Huselid, M.A., Becker, B.E. and Beatty, R.W. (2005b) *The Workforce Scorecard*: Managing Human Capital to Execute Strategy. Boston: Harvard Business School Press.

Ittner, C.D. and Larker, D.F. (2003) 'Coming up short on nonfinancial performance,' *Harvard Business Review*, 81: 88–95.

Jackson, S.E. and Schuler, R.S. (1995) 'Understanding human resource management in the context of organizations and their environments,' *Annual Review of Psychology*, 46: 237–64.

Lepak, D.P. and Snell, S.A. (2002) 'Examining the human resources architecture: The relationships among human capital, employment and resource configurations,' *Journal of Management*, 28 (4): 517–43.

Lepak, D.P. and Snell, S.A. (1999) 'The human resource architecture: toward a theory of human capital allocation and development,' *Academy of Management Review*, 24 (1): 31–48.

MacDuffie, J.P. (1995) 'Human resource bundles and manufacturing performance – organizational logic and flexible productions systems in the world auto industry,' *Academy of Management Journal*, 48 (2): 197–221.

Makdadok, R. (2001) 'Toward a synthesis of the resource-based and dynamic-capability views of rent creation,' *Strategic Management Journal*, 22: 397–401.

Makadok, R. and Walker, G. (2000) 'Identifying a distinctive competence: Forecasting ability in the money fund industry,' *Strategic Management Journal*, 21: 853–64.

Miles, R.E. and Snow, C.C. (1994) *Fit, Failure and the Hall of Fame*. New York: The Free Press.

Osterman, P. (2006) 'The wage effects of high performance work organizations in manufacturing,' *Industrial and Labor Relations Review*, 59 (2): 187–204.

Pfeffer, J. (2005) 'Producing sustainable competitive advantage through the effective management of people,' *Academy of Management Executive*, 19 (4): 95–106.

Pfeffer, J. and Sutton, R.I. (2000) *The Knowing-Ding Gap: How Smart Companies Turn Knowledge Into Action*. Boston: Harvard Business School Press.

Pfeffer, J. and Sutton, R.I. (2006) *Hard facts, dangerous half-truths, and total nonsense: Profiting from evidence based management*. Boston: Harvard Business School Press.

Porter, M. (1996) 'What is strategy?', *Harvard Business Review*, November–December: 61–78.

Porter, M. (1985) *Competitive Advantage: Creating and Sustaining Superior Performance*. New York: Free Press.

Priem, R.L. and Butler, J.E. (2001) 'Is the resource-based "view" a useful perspective for strategic management research?,' *Academy of Management Review*, 26 (1): 22–40.

Raff, D.G. (2000) 'Superstores and the evolution of firm capabilities in American bookselling', *Strategic Management Journal*, 21 (10/11): 1043–60.

Ray, G, Barney, J.B. and Muhanna W.A. (2004) 'Capabilities, business processes, and competitive advantage: Choosing the dependent variable in empirical tests of the resource-based view', *Strategic Management Journal*, 25: 23–37.

Schuler, R.S. (1992) 'Strategic human resource management: Linking people with the needs of the business,' *Organizational Dynamics*, 22: 19–32.

Schuler, R.S. and Jackson, S.E. (1987) 'Linking competitive strategies with human resources prac-

tices,' *Academy of Management Executive*, 1 (3): 207–20.

Skaggs, B.C. and Youndt, M. (2004) 'Strategic positioning, human capital and performance in service organizations,' *Strategic Management Journal*, 25: 85–99.

Siggelkow, N. (2002) 'Evolution toward fit', *Administrative Science Quarterly*, 47: 125–59.

Thomas, K.W. and Tymon, W.G. Jr. (1982) ' Necessary properties of relevant research: Lessons from recent criticisms of the organizational sciences,' *Academy of Management Review*, 7: 345–52.

Teece, D.J., Pisano, G. and Shuen, A. (1997) 'Dynamic capabilities and strategic management,' *Strategic Management Journal*, 18 (7): 509–33.

Ulrich, D. and Brockbank, W. (2005) *The HR Value Proposition*. Boston: Harvard Business School Press.

Wright, P.M., Gardner, T.M., Moynihan, L.M. and Allen, M.R. (2005) 'The relationship between HR practices and firm performance: Examining causal order,' *Personnel Psychology*, 58: 409–46.

Wright, P.M., Dunford, B.B. and Snell, S.A. (2001) 'Human resources and the resource based view of the firm,' *Journal of Management*, 27 (6): 701–21.

Wright, P.M. and Snell, S.A. (1998) 'Toward a unifying framework for exploring fit and flexibility in strategic human resources management,' *Academy of Management Review*, 23 (4): 756–72.

Wright, P.M and McMahan, G. (1992) 'Theoretical perspectives for strategic human resources management,' *Journal of Management*, 18 (2): 295–320.

Youndt, M.A. and Snell, S.A. (2004) 'Human resource configurations, intellectual capital, and organizational performance,' *Journal of Managerial Issues*, 16 (3): 337–60.

Zajac, E.J., Kraatz, M.S. and Bresser, R.K.F. (2000) 'Modeling the dynamics of strategic fit: A normative approach to strategic change,' *Strategic Management Journal*, 21: 429–53.

22

The Employee Experience of Work

Francis Green, Katy Huxley and
Keith Whitfield

INTRODUCTION

Recent years have witnessed substantial economic growth throughout the industrialised world, and whilst many workers have become financially better-off, there is increasing evidence that the more non-material aspects of the employees' experience of work may not have improved commensurately. They may have even become worse in certain key respects, particularly in relation to the intensity of work and the associated job stress. This inevitably raises fundamental questions as to whether the increase in employee financial well-being has been bought at the expense of other aspects of well-being, and whether this cost has been particularly high for some workers. Other pertinent questions include: Is increased material affluence a good indicator of well-being in the modern society? Have the key changes in the employee experience been evenly distributed or concentrated in particular areas, or on particular groups of workers? In addition to these questions, there

are issues about the causes of these changes, and whether policy changes can invoke positive improvements in what workers take from their jobs. There are also questions about the role of the human resource management and work organisation in mediating and moderating these relationships.

The broader origins of the changing worker experience over the last quarter century lie in the complex interactions between the evolution of the increasingly competitive business environment and the politically-driven changes in the regulatory regime surrounding work. In this period, the economy has become more open, and many establishments have had to face increasingly competitive product markets. Multinational ownership has burgeoned, potentially spreading new ideas about the management of labour. The deregulation and liberalisation of financial markets has increased the exposure to external pressures faced by workers across a range of industries. Meanwhile, protection for labour has been lessened by the decline in union presence throughout the world. The workforce has become increasingly feminised, which has brought with it many changes in how work is both done and experienced. In addition, an 'HRM Revolution' has been purportedly taking place, with some organisations said to be striving to obtain greater competitive advantage in their product markets by the better recruitment, deployment, development and utilisation of their human resources, with 'better' increasingly being defined in terms of bottom-line performance rather than employee well-being, or some broader definition of societal welfare.

In this chapter, we consider what is known about a number of the central aspects of the employee experience, and then bring to bear evidence about the links between worker, job and employer characteristics and some of the key elements in that experience, including the impact of HRM. The chapter focuses predominantly on information relating to Great Britain, and especially to information that has been gathered for that country from a wide range of social surveys that have examined various aspects of the employee experience. Particular emphasis is placed upon the British Workplace Employment Relations Surveys, which represent extremely powerful bases on which to conduct research on the worker experience. This strong focus on Britain is therefore partly due to the comprehensive information-set that exists for this country, which thereby allows a deeper analysis of the issues therein than in other countries, and partly because of the location in that country of this chapter's authors. However, the international evidence suggests that Britain has not been unique in this area, and that workers throughout the industrialised world have fared much the same as their British counterparts. Where there are differences we attempt to outline them.

The story that is told is complex, just like the employee experience of work. Not all of the indicators of employee well-being have gone in the same direction, and not all have reacted to changes in the external environment in a similar fashion, or in ways that are readily explicable. Moreover, the employee experience has seemingly varied widely for differing groups of worker. Above all, there is a compelling story to be told about how life in the world of work has evolved in the recent past, and why this might have occurred.

THE EMPLOYEE EXPERIENCE OF WORK

The employee's experience of work is multidimensional. While the principal reason to work for many people is to gain economic security, there is far more to a good work experience than simply high pay. In particular, recent years have brought to the fore the need of workers to balance their work-life commitments against their non-work (principally family) commitments, and to ensure that the satisfaction gained from a high wage is not earned at too high a cost in other aspects of their lives. Moreover, recent years have seen increasing emphasis on the need for workers to ensure that they do not impose pressures on themselves in their working environment that lower their personal well-being, such that their working-lives enrich rather than enfeeble them as people. All work-roles contain a complex mixture of elements that enhance or detract from the employee experience and, furthermore, each worker has his or her own particular relationship to these elements. What enhances the well-being of some workers impoverishes others.

In general, HRM researchers have been much less inclined to examine the employee experience of work than the performance of the employing organisations to which they belong, but there is a growing literature that is redressing this imbalance. Such studies have emanated from a wide range of subject-areas and research interests, and have focused on a number of different aspects of the experience of work. Prime among the researchers examining such issues have been organisational psychologists and industrial sociologists, but recent years have seen a growing interest by economists in the area. The motivations of such researchers have ranged from an interest in changes in psychological well-being on society in general, to a concern for the development of policies to improve the effectiveness of organisations in increasingly complex operating environments.

By and large, researchers have tended to concentrate their attention on a limited range of proxies to represent the employees' experience of work – material well-being (especially take-home pay), job satisfaction, employee well-being, job security, and employee influence over how work is done. These are among the more measurable phenomena that contribute to a better or worse experience of work.

It is frequently argued that wages are, on their own and in themselves, a very good proxy for the overall work experience. The evidence cited in support of this view is that those earning high wages tend also to enjoy good working conditions, more autonomy and less work insecurity. However, there are strong grounds for looking beyond wages to gauge changes in the employee work experience. For example, the correlation between wages and workplace autonomy is far from perfect, with many workers in lower-status occupations enjoying considerable task autonomy. Moreover, even if wages are, overall, positively associated with beneficial working conditions, it does not follow that changes over time in the one imply changes in the other in the same direction or to the same degree, since the association can easily strengthen or weaken over time.

The subjective evidence also indicates that workers often see factors other than wages as at least as important. When British respondents to the International Social Survey Programme survey of 2005 were asked to say which factors were important to them personally in a job, 74 per cent responded that high pay was important or very important, suggesting that pay is an essential aspect of job quality. However, the equivalent figures for job security, or a job that is 'useful to society' were 96 per cent and 68 per cent respectively. Other aspects of job quality were also highly rated, suggesting that high pay is only one among several constituents of the employee experience, and by no means the single most important.

An understanding of changing job quality therefore necessitates a multi-faceted perspective, going beyond the material rewards of employment. Key non-material *extrinsic* aspects of the workers' experience include security and risk, work hours and work intensity, and the fit between work-life and the other areas of a worker's life ('work-life balance'). The notion of work-life balance, the ability of an individual to pursue personal goals as well as professional goals, has become of increasing importance throughout the industrialised world. Just as important as the extrinsic aspects of work-life (both material and non-material) are the *intrinsic* features of jobs, among which autonomy and skill-use are central. These have been changing markedly and in complex ways in recent years.

Research to date has indicated that there is a complicated set of relationships to explain, as the measurable indicators of the employee experience often point in different directions. Differing trends and differing correlates reveal both positive and negative patterns in employee experiences of work. It is therefore not possible to say whether the overall work experience is getting better or worse over time, or whether one group of workers has a better or worse overall experience. At most, we can make more conditional statements that highlight particular aspects of the work experience which are getting better or worse for particular groups of workers.

Job satisfaction is often viewed as a form of overall measure of the employees' experience, though the approach of differing social scientists to it is extremely variable. Rose (2007) notes that economists view job satisfaction as a proxy for worker utility and human happiness, whereas sociologists have tended to look at the influence of preferences, tastes, gender and work orientations upon it among differing social groups. Policy-makers are also interested in trends in its level, both within and across nation-states.

Job satisfaction has achieved such a wide usage mainly because it has proved to be such a good predictor of objective behaviour such as job-quitting and absenteeism, and many employers make use of job satisfaction questionnaires as part of their overall human resource strategy. However, important though it is for a whole host of workplace behaviours, it is widely recognised that job satisfaction is only one part of the sub-set of subjective feelings that constitute even employee well-being, let alone the whole employee experience. Moreover, the extent to which workers are satisfied depends to a considerable extent on what they are expecting from their job rather than vis à vis some universal baseline. Interpreting variations and trends in satisfaction is thus not straightforward.

Recent years have seen the development of a variety of new indicators of workers' well-being. Wood (2008) notes that, in many such studies, well-being is typically associated with happiness, even though happiness is only one element of well-being, '… which also includes feelings of self-esteem or self-worth (self-validation), as well as overall mental health' (p. 155) He notes that many of these empirical studies have used the Warr framework or something similar, which identifies three axes for measuring well-being:

1) feeling good to feeling bad;
2) anxiety to contentment;
3) depression to enthusiasm.

The first is associated with job satisfaction, the latter two with psychological well-being. Research evidence suggests that the last two tend to vary with the degree of discretion that workers have to undertake their jobs, and the level of the demands placed upon them.

One of the key factors that enhance the employee experience is job security. This tends to vary markedly through time as the economy prospers and suffers. It also varies across space, as some jobs are associated with higher levels of job security than others. This is partly a function of the nature of the activity undertaken by the employing organisation and the degree of stability in the external environment in which it operates, and partly due to strategic choices made by its

policy-formers that are intended to develop greater levels of commitment of workers towards the organisation and its goals and values, such as the pursuit of high commitment or high involvement management philosophies.

The influence that workers have over their work-roles has also been identified as a key factor in affecting the employee experience – the greater the influence, the better the reported experience. Such influence is, however, multi-dimensional. It can vary according to the factor concerned. Some work-roles involve varying degrees of influence over, for example, pay, how work is done and how hard workers work. Correspondingly, workers differ in the degree to which they value such influence and differing components thereof. Again, interpretation of how workers value work influence is far from straightforward.

To try and capture all of these aspects of the employee experience by simple measures, let alone a single measure, is impossible. However, the research evidence is beginning to build up a larger and more clearly-defined picture of the employee work experience, and how it varies across both time and space. The objective of this chapter is to try and summarise some of the key elements within that research literature.

TRENDS IN THE EMPLOYEE EXPERIENCE OF WORK IN RECENT TIMES

Wages

Beginning with the material side of work, there is no doubt that average wages have increased substantially in many nations since 1970. There is a sharp contrast, however, between European nations and those elsewhere. In the larger European nations, real wages rose steadily after 1970, though the increase only really began in the Scandinavian countries in the mid-1980s. Outside Europe, wages have remained fairly stable, and among non-European nations, Japan is the only country in which wages increased significantly. Overall, and to a not inconsiderable extent, there has been something of a convergence in world-wide average pay, with the increase in low pay countries greater than in high pay countries (Green, 2006: 117).

For most countries, there has also been increased wage inequality during this period. For example, the ratio of the wages of those at the ninetieth percentile in the pay rankings to that at the tenth percentile more than doubled in New Zealand in the 1980s and 1990s, and increased by more than fifty per cent in the USA, Italy, the UK, Ireland, the Netherlands, Australia and Sweden. Only a small number of countries (notably Norway, Switzerland, France, Finland and Japan) experienced significant falls in this index. The three main causal factors popularly said to be underpinning this change are the rapid growth of manufacturing in low-wage nations, the widespread diffusion of information and communication technologies and (for the US) a deceleration in the growth of college-educated labour. However, researchers are increasingly questioning such explanations and are typically according a more important causal role in generating this higher inequality to changes in labour market institutions and the implementation of deregulatory labour market policies, rather than to changes in the supply and demand for particular types of labour (Green, 2006: 122).

In Britain, workers in all categories of work are substantially better off for wages than they have ever been. Between 1985 and 2002, real wages rose by 37 per cent in private businesses (Green, 2006: 117). The advance has been sustained and even increased in the last decade, with real private and public sector wages rising by an average of 2¾ per cent and 2¼ per cent respectively per year 1995–2005 (Fitzner, 2006: 10). Thus, taken on average, workers in Britain have been gaining a portion of the increased material affluence generated by rising productivity.

The wage rises were not, however, uniform across all workers. Changes in wage inequality have meant that different groups experienced differential improvements. For some,

increased inequality may have been manifested as a reduction in the fairness of rewards. For most of the 1980s and 1990s, those on higher wages were also the relative gainers (Goos and Manning, 2007; Atkinson, 2007a, 2007b). Indeed, a continual theme of this period is the 'fanning-out' of top earnings. Among those in the top half of the distribution, the higher the wages, the greater the wage growth. In the latter part of the 1990s, the pattern in Britain was altered in the lower half of the distribution. Between 1996 and 2003, wages for those at the lowest tenth percentile of the wage distribution were growing faster than median wages (Atkinson, 2007a; Fitzner, 2006). This reversal is linked to, but not entirely explained by, the introduction of the National Minimum Wage in 1999, which was increased in real terms every October, especially in 2001, 2003 and 2004.

Another significant feature of the changing distribution of the material employee experience in Britain has been the increasing proportion of low paid jobs, such as care work and hospital ward assistance. Between 1976 and 1995, although the incidence of highly-skilled and better-paid jobs increased the most, substantial positive employment growth also occurred for those in the lowest-wage (and arguably lowest-skilled) jobs, while middle-wage jobs declined in importance. There was therefore a process of job polarisation, hypothesised to be a consequence of high productivity improvements in middle-level routine jobs derived from automation, while low-skilled non-routine jobs continued to resist transformation by computers (Goos and Manning, 2007; Autor et al., 2003). However, job polarisation in Britain appears to have reached a plateau by the mid-1990s. Since then, the pattern of jobs growth has become more complex. The very lowest paid jobs have gone into decline, while those in the second poorest decile and in the richest decile have grown rapidly; there has been no further indication of a declining middle (Fitzner, 2006: 15).

Changing wages and job growth in Britain have interlinked to generate a pattern of, at first, substantially increasing wage inequality during the 1980s, followed by a mixed picture of either stable or slowly rising wage inequality during the 1990s. According to data from the Family Expenditure Survey, the Gini coefficient for men's wage inequality rose from 0.262 in 1980 to 0.324 in 1990, and more slowly to 0.350 by 1998. For women, the Gini coefficient also rose in the 1980s (from 0.359 in 1980 to 0.401 in 1990), but was virtually unchanged at 0.403 in 1998 (Machin, 2003). Since its introduction, the National Minimum Wage, by raising the wages of low paid workers, has kept inequality in check, but has been counter-balanced by continued increases at the top end of the pay scale. The ratio of the top decile to median earnings increased steadily between 1980 and 2004 (Atkinson, 2007b). In recent years, high-level managers and performers, in the UK as in the US, have appeared to reap especially large rises in earnings.

Job (in)security

The problem of job insecurity – the risk of job loss or of other uncertainties within the job – is a perennial issue which could hardly be removed altogether in a modern society. Nevertheless, over the last quarter century, progress on wages has to some extent been matched by very significant improvements in workers' security, albeit after enduring a period of sustained mass unemployment. This is despite a major increase in the last decade of the twentieth century in the perception of job insecurity in some areas, as evidenced by press references thereof (Green, 2006: 127).

In Britain, the aggregate unemployment rate, which at its peak reached nearly twelve per cent in 1984 and which topped ten per cent for six consecutive years in the 1980s, hovered at around five per cent in the first five years of the 21st century. The proportion of employment separations that were involuntary fell from 37 per cent in 1995 to 28 per cent in 2005, and the annual rate of redundancy fell from 8 per cent to under 6 per cent in the same period (Fitzner, 2006).

The reduction in these objective indicators of insecurity was followed eventually by reductions in the subjective indicators. Such perceptions of insecurity can be measured by workers' expectations of job loss. In 1986, some 15 per cent of British workers reported that there was at least an even chance that they would lose their job involuntarily within a year. Approximately the same proportion took this view in 1997, reflecting the persistence of the climate of fear that had been induced by mass redundancies in manufacturing during the 1980s, and in important service sectors during the early 1990s. However, by the end of the decade, the fear of unemployment was unsurprisingly wearing off. The proportion expecting at least an even chance of job loss fell to 12 per cent by 2001 (Green, 2006). Moreover, should they in fact lose their jobs, employees became increasingly confident of finding equally good ones elsewhere. In short, despite a less regulated employment system than that found in many European countries, the success of macro-economic management, at least up until the middle of the first decade of the twenty-first century, resulted in a more secure external work environment for many millions of British workers. Whether the declining economic circumstances following the so-called credit crunch in the latter part of the twenty-first century's first decade will re-ignite these insecurity fears is a key question.

A similar picture is obtained from US information on the perceived risk of job loss. Looking at those who responded that they were fairly or highly likely to lose their jobs (the highly insecure), the proportion peaked at around 15 per cent in 1982, and then declined to 8 per cent in 1989, before fluctuating between these points in the 1990s. Generally, this perception tracked changes in the unemployment rate. The same is true in Germany, though the unification of that country inevitably caused a significant rise in perceived insecurity in the 1990s, particularly in the former East Germany (Green, 2006: 132–6).

An important change has been a re-distribution of the risk of job loss from blue collar to white collar workers.

In Britain, professional workers were the most secure group in 1986, but the least secure in 1997. In the US, white-collar occupations reported greater insecurity in the 1990s than in the 1980s, while blue collar workers recorded a decline. Perhaps this explains the increased press reporting of job insecurity at a time of increasing security – it could be that the reporting of anecdotal evidence is dominated by the experiences of the upper and middle occupational groups (Green, 2006: 136–8). The evidence also shows that workers in foreign-owned establishments felt the increase in insecurity most, suggesting that intensified global competition may be the key source of job insecurity.

Work-based accidents

Improvement has also been seen in respect of another aspect of risk: the chances of being involved in work-based accidents. The indices of both fatal and serious accidents fell significantly in the European Union and the United States in the last decade of the twentieth century. This would seem to be the continuation of a long-term trend. In Britain, for example, the Health and Safety Executive reported that the rate of fatal injuries was cut by a factor of two-thirds between 1981 and the present decade. To some extent, this improvement is attributable to the decline in manufacturing industries over this period, but there were also big declines in injury rates *within* each industry. In Sweden, the numbers dying each year from accidents at work fell from over 400 in the mid-1950s to less than 50 at the turn of the century.

The main health and safety domain, however, in which there is no consistent picture of improvement is self-reported stress. Though self-reports are not always reliable in this sphere, both these and other data indicate that stress became more of a problem in Britain through the 1990s; though the incidence of stress since 2000 has fluctuated, with no clear upward or downward trend. In 2006–7, 13.5 million working days were reported lost owing to stress, depression or anxiety, about 0.60 work days per worker year.

Work effort

Stress and anxiety may be the overt symptoms of excess work effort, and increasing work pressure. Increasing work effort in the last quarter century has accompanied increasing affluence (Green, 2006; Fagan and Burchell, 2006). Up to the late 1970s, Britain's workplaces had been steadily reducing working time requirements for workers, which is interpretable as part of a very long term fall in work time, allowing more leisure and family time. The decline was halted, however, and followed by a small rise in average working time up to the middle of the 1990s. Extra pressure on time followed from an increasing concentration of work within households, while other households found themselves with no work at all for any member. Two-adult households added six hours to their joint weekly work-load between 1981 and 1998. There was also a palpable increase in work intensity over this period, with workers being required to work harder during the hours they were at work. New technologies and associated forms of work organisation were facilitating the closing of the gaps in the working day, and hence this process is referred to as 'effort-biased technological change'. The increased work intensity, while hard to confirm and measure objectively, shows up in successive surveys which recount the proportions of workers perceiving that their job 'requires (them) to work very hard' and other similar questions. The responses show distinctive increases, on average, for Britain between 1992 and 1997; and there are strong reasons to suspect that this intensification began some time earlier during the 1980s.

After 1997, however, the average work effort of British workers has seemingly remained on its already-high plane, but without showing signs of growing still more (Green, 2006; Green, 2008; Fagan and Burchell, 2006; Gallie, 2006). Employee working hours also peaked in the middle part of the 1990s at 33.5 hours per week (39.3 hours for full-timers), thereafter tracking downwards to around 32 (37.3) hours in

2004. There was a concomitant decline in the number of employees working especially long hours; for example, the proportion working over 45 hours fell by nearly 8 per cent between 1997 and 2003.

Evidence of work intensification can also be found in other industrialised countries. According to the work effort index of the European Foundation for the Improvement of Living and Working Conditions, work intensification was a widespread, though not ubiquitous, phenomenon in Europe in the 1990s. It rose particularly strongly in Italy, Ireland, France, Luxembourg, the Netherlands and Belgium. At the end of the twentieth century, it was highest in Sweden and Finland and lowest in Portugal and Spain. In Australia, the 1994 Bargaining Survey found that more than three-fifths of workers reported that they were working harder than a year before. This is further supported in analyses of large-scale surveys of Australia and New Zealand (Allan et al., 1999). Perceptions of work intensification were most highly found among managers and professional workers. US analyses also found increases in the level of non-discretionary work effort, and in workers suffering from the effects of work overload (Cappelli et al., 1997).

Skills

An important aspect of job-quality lies in the skills used in jobs, and there is robust evidence that, on average, British workers are being called on to exercise higher levels of skill in several domains. Jobs are requiring higher entry-level qualifications and longer training times, and are taking longer to learn. Computer skills requirements have risen steadily since the mid 1980s, and the needs for other generic skills, such as problem-solving skills and communications skills, have been increasing in the last decade (Felstead et al., 2007). Educational achievement levels have been increasing rapidly over this period with, for example, increasing proportions of graduates in the workforce. Despite some evidence of increasing over-qualification, the levels of

perceived over-skilling in the workforce did not substantially increase between 1992 and 2006 (Green and Zhu, 2008). Thus, modest though some of the increases are, as far as skill use is concerned, the worker experience generally improved over the period. This story of up-skilling is common across the whole industrialised world. For example, skill requirements data for the US, Germany and Britain all reveal a substantial increase in the proportion of jobs requiring college-educated labour in the latter part of the twentieth century (Green, 2006).

Autonomy

Against this improvement in skill-level must be set a decline in workplace autonomy (Gallie et al. 2004). In Britain, surveys have indicated that task discretion, the ability to determine aspects of the tasks that individuals do in their jobs, fell steadily between 1992 and 2001 (Green, 2006). Perceived choice over tasks appear to have declined since at least 1986. The declines in discretion were found in all sectors of the economy, but were most pronounced among professional workers, many of whom found that their traditional presumptions of autonomy were being eroded. The decline was most for females in part-time jobs and professional workers, and least for managers. A similar survey in Finland, however, found some increases in task discretion (Lehto and Sutela, 1999). However, a European-wide study by the European Foundation for Living and Working Conditions, comparing 1996 and 2000, also suggested declines in Belgium, Denmark, Italy, Ireland, and Portugal. The reverse was the case in Austria and Germany.

Employee well-being

While higher wages, the greater use of skill, and reduced insecurity and accident risks all point in the direction of a better experience for workers, these plusses have been balanced by intensifications of work effort and declines in worker autonomy, as well as increasing stress levels. One searches in vain for any single index of the employee experience, and so the normative verdict about the change in the experience of employees during our period of investigation must be summed up as 'mixed'. One can, however, make use of psychological constructs to gauge the overall well-being of people that is associated with their work. Instruments have been devised and tested, usually in small-scale settings, for measuring well-being at work. One indication of change in well-being is shown in responses to Warr's three-item index of work strain. In Britain, this shows a rise in average work strain between 1992 and 2001 (Green, 2006). Unfortunately, more comprehensive instruments for worker well-being are not available on a consistent, population-wide basis over time, making it hard to measure change over a long time period.

Looking at how jobs have changed over time, using individual-based surveys, it is found that the average job satisfaction of nations is either stationary or falling (Green, 2006). In Germany, there was a major slump in job satisfaction from 1984 to 1997, after which there was a slight recovery. In the US, there was an extremely slight decline from 1973 onwards, which ceased in the early 1990s. There was a more substantial recorded fall in job satisfaction in Norway between 1989 and 1997 (Green, 2006: 157–8). Between 1994 and 2000, there were slight declines in average satisfaction in France, Spain, Austria, Belgium, Denmark, Finland, Italy, Portugal and Greece.

British workers in 2001 were somewhat less satisfied overall than their counterparts in 1992 (Green and Tsitsianis, 2004). The decline in satisfaction was most evident with respect to the intrinsic domains of work. Thus, workers became less satisfied with 'the work itself'. Intrinsic domains often tend to dominate extrinsic domains in the determination of overall job satisfaction. Satisfaction with extrinsic domains, especially with pay and security, increased somewhat, especially at the turn of the millennium. Green and Tsitsianis (2004) show that the decline in overall job satisfaction can be attributed mainly to increasing work effort and declining autonomy.

CORRELATES OF WORKER DISCONTENT

Part of the problem facing policy-makers is that there remains much that is unknown about the determinants or even the associates of good and bad worker experiences. One issue is that most studies of the worker experience are focused on the small scale – on particular firms or jobs, or on tightly defined industries. The objective of this section, therefore, is to report on a study of the correlates of poor employee experiences using the most recent survey of the British Workplace Employment Relations Survey series – WERS2004 (Green and Whitfield, 2009). We used measures of job insecurity, stress, work intensity, low job influence, and dissatisfaction as dependent variables in multivariate analyses that included a wide variety of proxies for relevant organisational, establishment and individual factors. Given the cross-sectional nature of the data-set, it was not possible to make precise causal inferences, though some such suggestions can tentatively be made. Rather, the idea was to see which factors are most strongly associated with the employees' experience of work, as a potential basis for further research and/or policy-related work that can attempt to disentangle the underlying causal relationships.

What are the features of workers and of working life that appear to influence employees' perceptions of their experience of work? Starting with gender, studies have generally found that women have higher job satisfaction than men. Sloane and Williams (2000) suggested that this represents their self-selection into jobs with highly valued attributes rather than any innate gender differences. Bender and Heywood (2006), in a study of PhD-level scientists, found that the lower level of job satisfaction of female academics was due to the lower value that they placed on pay and tenure. Our analysis of WERS2004 suggested that working women tend to perceive a greater degree of stress and work intensity than men (see Green and Whitfield, 2009). Whether this reflects differences in the type of work that they do, or in greater difficulties in balancing work and other life pressures is debatable. A similar finding has been obtained in the US and for an earlier British study (Gorman and Kmec, 2007). The explanation advanced there was that the gender difference is an implicit form of discrimination in that women are subject to more exacting demands. In contrast, Gaunt and Benjamin (2007) suggested that men are generally more vulnerable to job-related stress, and that gender ideology has a crucial role in moderating this relationship. They also suggested that men experience greater job insecurity. Our analysis also showed that men report greater job insecurity, though the difference is not statistically significant. Men are much more dissatisfied with the level of their pay than women, despite a continuing and significant gender pay gap (Green and Whitfield, 2009). A possible explanation is that men have higher expectations for their pay than women. On all of the other proxies for the experience of work, there was very little difference between men and women.

There were strong findings for workers with disability and health problems. Workers who report these have a much more negative experience of work. In every analysis, the coefficient on this variable was positive and significant. This is hardly surprising, as poor health and/or a disability typically has a detrimental impact on experiences in all walks of life.

What about the effect of working long hours? There has been very little work on the relationship between long working hours and the employee experience of work, though Bacon et al. (2005) have indicated that workers moving from an 8-hour to a 12-hour shift system expressed an increase in satisfaction. Our analysis indicated that those who work long hours are less likely to feel insecure, or to report a lack of influence over their work. They are less likely to feel dissatisfied about the achievement that they

get from their work, or the influence that they have over their job. However, long-hours workers are more likely to feel stress and high work intensity. These associations should not be seen as indicating a particular direction of causation. It might, for example, be that some workers choose to work long hours precisely because they are satisfied with their work.

The experience of work is not associated with the life-cycle in a simple way. Younger workers tend to feel less insecure and less stressed, but they are more likely to report a lack of influence over their jobs. Moreover, there is no clear relationship between age and the amount of dissatisfaction that is expressed in relation to any of the aspects of dissatisfaction that we examined.

Educational qualifications appear to play a part in the employee experience. Workers with degrees are more likely to feel insecure and to experience a high level of work intensity. But they are less likely to report a lack of influence at work. They are also less likely to be dissatisfied with the amount of pay that they receive. But they are more likely to be dissatisfied with the sense of achievement that they gain from their work and the amount of influence that they have over their jobs. This finding supports the conclusion reached by Belfield and Harris (2002) that job satisfaction is neutral across different education grades.

The size of firm also appears to matter for the employee experience. Workers in larger organisations report higher levels of insecurity, more stress and work intensity, higher levels of lack of influence and more dissatisfaction than those in smaller and medium-sized organisations. The implication appears to be that the employee experience in smaller workplaces is significantly better than in larger workplaces and organisations. It supports those who assert that 'small is beautiful', relative to those who see smaller workplaces as 'bleak houses' (Dundon et al., 2001). Nevertheless, it should be remembered that workers in larger organisations also tend to be paid a wage premium for otherwise similar jobs. It is possible that this premium is in part a compensation for an inferior experience of work.

There are two competing views of the impact of 'high performance' work organisation practices on employee experience. The more positive suggests that such practices typically lead to increased levels of discretion, improved job security and enhanced job satisfaction (for example, Kalmi and Kauhanen, 2008). By contrast, the more critical view suggests that these practices are more commonly associated with increased job intensity and reduced security (for example, Delbridge et al., 1992; Brenner et al., 2004). Harley (2001), however, using the WERS98, found no statistically significant relationship between team membership and measures of employee well-being. Using WERS2004, Wood (2008) concluded that employee well-being is negatively related to job demands and positively related to the control that a worker has over his/her job. Deploying WERS98, Cox et al. (2006) found that the greater the breadth and depth of employee involvement and participation practices, the higher the levels of organisational commitment and job satisfaction of workers.

Our analysis of the WERS2004 data indicated that the experience of workers in workplaces with employee involvement practices varies. For example, quality circles are associated with less negative experiences, but that the reverse applies to the use of briefing committees. Why this is the case is a matter for conjecture. It is notable that workers in workplaces with briefing committees and quality circles do not feel that they have less sense of influence at work than those without. While the latter is compatible with the findings of Delbridge and Whitfield (2001), using WERS98 data, the former stands in stark contrast to results in this study. The impact of joint consultative committees and team-working on the employee experience does not seem to be strong. By contrast, using the earlier WERS data set, Delbridge and Whitfield (2001) found strong negative associations between influence and team responsibility for a product or service, but strong positive associations in relation to

influence when a team appoints their own leader.

Analysis of WERS98 indicated that union members are generally less satisfied than non-members (Guest and Conway, 1999, 2004). The authors ascribe this to the lack of strong employee voice in workplaces where employers are anti-union. Bryson et al. (2004) found that allowing for endogenous selection processes in the sorting of workers into unionised jobs eliminated the job satisfaction difference between unionised and non-unionised workers, implying that the lower job satisfaction of the former is due to selection rather than causal processes. Our analysis indicated that workers in workplaces with recognised unions tend to have a more negative experience of work than elsewhere. In particular, they are more likely to state that they have no time to get their work done, to express a lack of influence over their pace of work, and be dissatisfied about various aspects of their jobs. Well might trade unions have been described by C. Wright Mills as 'managers of discontent'.

HRM AND THE EMPLOYEE EXPERIENCE OF WORK

The last decades of the twentieth century and the beginning of the 21st century are said by some to have witnessed an 'HRM Revolution', in which the management of people at work has been transformed from the reactive, non-strategic Personnel Management to the more pro-active, strategic Human Resource Management (Redman and Wilkinson, 2006: chapter 1) Indeed, it has been suggested that the change has been even more dramatic than just a change in the people function; it has also involved a fundamental shift in how the whole production process is conceived and developed. Some researchers have gone so far as to suggest that there has been the widespread development of a range of so-called high performance work systems that aim to put in place holistic arrangements for the achievement of sustainable competitive advantage, the most notable being the high commitment and high involvement approaches to the management of employees at work (Appelbaum and Batt, 1994).

A key issue concerns how these have impacted on the employee experience of work. On the one hand, it has been suggested that the advent of such approaches to people management would benefit both employers and employees, as part of the development of a 'mutual gains enterprise' (Kochan and Osterman, 1994). Others have asserted that the process will involve both winners and losers (e.g. Zuboff, 1988), and still others have suggested that the main impact will be the intensification of the work process, to the detriment of the employee experience (e.g. Graham 1993).

An overview of work on the impact of employee involvement and related practices on wages (Handel and Levine, 2004) concluded that, '… many programs have no effect on wages, while on average, the effect is a small increase in wages after companies introduce new work systems with higher employee involvement.' (p.1). The study also found that there is no evidence that involvement consistently increases employment security, and that when it is, '… not used as a form of speedup, it gives workers more autonomy, recognizes the value of their contributions, improves job satisfaction and feelings of voice, and often lowers quit rates' (p. 39). The review also indicates that there is no evidence that management-by-stress is typical, or that skill-biased organisational change is a major cause of growing inequality.

Black et al. (2004) also presented a mixed picture in this area. Using a US data-set, they found that firms do seem to reward some of their employees for engaging in high-performance work practices and that this leads towards increased wage inequality. Some such practices, such as self-managed teams, were seen to be associated with greater employment reductions, and others, such as job rotation, with the reverse. Similarly, Forth and Millward (2004), using the 1998 WERS survey, found that British private sector workplaces adopting a high-involvement management approach paid

higher wages, and that the wage premium is little affected by the choice of employee involvement practices, but does appear to occur only when such practices are supported by job security guarantees. In contrast, Handel and Gittleman (2004), using a US data-set, found little evidence that practices associated with high-performance work systems are associated with higher wages. In a study of British workplaces, Whitfield (2000) found that workplaces exhibiting high performance work practices had higher levels of employee training than those that did not, and that those with a more comprehensive set of these (or bundle) exhibited much higher levels than those that did not. This mainly reflected a greater intensity of training for those undertaking it, than a greater breadth of training across the workforce. There was, however, little evidence that the presence of these practices at a workplace was promoting a polarisation in the distribution of skills, in the sense that those workplaces with more high performance practices were no more likely to concentrate training on those in the higher occupational groupings.

A study of 1,200 workers, supervisors and middle managers in a large unionised US telecommunications company (Batt, 2004) showed that participation in self-managed teams is associated with higher levels of perceived discretion, employment security, and satisfaction for workers and the opposite for supervisors. Middle managers who initiate team innovation reported higher levels of employment security, but were otherwise similar to those not involved in innovations.

The associated issue of the impact on employees of the use of flexible work practices has also been studied in some depth. Using a US data-set, Brenner et al. (2004) found a large and positive statistically-significant relationship between cumulative trauma disorders and the use of quality circles and just-in-time production techniques. Cappelli and Neumark (2004), using US establishment-level data, found that functional flexibility was related to both lower involuntary and voluntary turnover. However, contrary to the core-periphery hypothesis, they also discovered that contingent work and the involuntary turnover of the permanent workforce were positively related in all sectors.

A key element of some high performance work systems is employee share-ownership. The evidence is that the presence of such a plan typically has a positive impact upon organisational performance (Renaud et al., 2004; Sengupta et al., 2007). The impact on employees is, however, much less well-researched and less certain. Renaud et al.'s (2004) study of a large Canadian financial services institution with operations across Canada and the United States indicated that participation in a stock purchase plan can yield both improved individual performance and compensation, but that this could derive from the nature of those joining the plan rather than any impact of the plan *per se*. Sengupta et al. (2007), using British establishment data showed that, contrary to much assertion in the underlying literature, the levels of commitment of workers in establishments with share-ownership schemes was no higher than elsewhere, and may even have been slightly lower. However, they also found that employee turnover was much lower in share-ownership workplaces, suggesting that there might be some sort of 'golden handcuff' mechanism at work. This is said to reduce the propensity of workers to leave share-ownership workplaces, thereby decreasing their hiring and training costs.

Two recent studies using the British WIRS/WERS surveys cast some new light on these issues. The first is by David Guest and Alex Bryson (2009) and looks at the evolution of the people management function within British workplaces from 1980 to 2004 and its relationship to the employee experience, and the second is by Stephen Wood and Alex Bryson (2009) and examines the impact of High Involvement Management practices on employees.

Guest and Bryson find that a growing proportion of British workplaces had a personnel/HRM specialist in place during the 1980 to 2004 period, and that an increasing proportion of these specialists had relevant qualifications.

However, they find that such specialists are more likely to be associated with traditional approaches to people management than the more modern forms of HRM. Moreover, they find that, where personnel specialists are present, including qualified specialists, performance tends to be poorer. In short, the evidence is not one of a revolution led by the HRM community, but a world in which this community has rather constrained workplace change.

Wood and Bryson show that there has been an increase in the incidence of High Involvement Management (HIM) at the British workplace during this period, and that it seems to have been developed in a systematic manner. However, even in 2004, only a minority of workplaces seemed to have a strong high involvement orientation, and furthermore its introduction was strongly associated with Total Quality Management and other lean production methods. There was no evidence that HIM improved worker well-being. If anything, it would seem to be associated with higher levels of worker anxiety.

Overall, the evidence is that the advent of the more pro-active HRM approach and related approaches involving high involvement and high commitment work practices have not had a strong impact on the employee experience of work. The suggestion is that such changes have helped improve the employee experience a little, though the impact would seem to have been far from universal. There is also evidence that the rolling-out of such innovations might not have been as strong as some commentators might have implied.

CONCLUSION

The employee experience of work has changed substantially in recent times. Taken as a whole, workers have been using higher skill levels and experienced higher wages, less insecurity and a lower risk of accident. But they have experienced the intensification of work effort and a decline in autonomy, as well as fluctuating stress levels. Moreover, the improvements in insecurity have been nullified by the rises in unemployment following the 2008 economic crisis. Indeed, the analyses in this chapter all pre-date this crisis. In hard times, issues of job quality tend to take second place to the quantitative side of the labour market.

The employee experience is disproportionately associated, according to our analysis, with particular characteristics of workers and of workplaces. Workplace and organisational size have a persistent association with adverse employee experience. Workers in smaller workplaces generally report better experience of work. Those with health problems are worse off. Bearing in mind that poor working conditions often contribute to health problems, they experience greater work stress and are more insecure. With the exception that women are more likely than men to report greater stress and work intensity, a third notable finding is that the experiences of men and women differ relatively little. Whether these differences in stress levels are due to types of work or work-life balance is debatable. Before the 2008 crisis, insecurity came down for both men and women, whilst dissatisfaction with pay has changed little. Policies to address poor work conditions can therefore be gender neutral. Finally, while those working long hours feel relatively high stress and work intensity, this appears to be counter-balanced by perceptions of their having more influence over their jobs. In general, their levels of dissatisfaction are lower than those working shorter hours. There is little evidence that the advent of new management practices associated with HRM have had a strong positive impact on the employee's experience. In some notable cases, the reverse may well be the case, and such innovations have, in some places, raised levels of worker anxiety.

There is considerable variation across the economy in employees' experience of the quality of their working lives. There are no simple answers to questions as to whether the experience of work is getting better or worse. What is clear, however, is that the current high levels of work intensity that evolved during the 1990s are a potent source of worker strain. Policies to enable smarter, more efficient, but less intensive working are needed if there is to be an improvement in this dimension of workers' experience. Also of concern is the lower level of worker autonomy that appears to have evolved in recent times, not least because highly intensive work combined with low autonomy is known to be especially detrimental to health. One of the pressing issues for contemporary research is whether the sorts of practices being advocated in managerial and government circles to generate 'high performance' in companies are also conducive to generating better jobs for workers. This is far from being a given.

REFERENCES

Allan, C., Brosnan, P. and Walsh, P. (1999) 'Human resource strategies, workplace reform and industrial restructuring in Australia and New Zealand', *International Journal of Human Resource Management*, 10 (5): 828–41.

Applebaum, E. and Batt, R. (1994) *The New American Workplace*. Ithaca, NY: ILR Press.

Atkinson, A.B. (2007a) 'The distribution of earnings in OECD countries,' *International Labour Review*, 146 (1–2): 41–60.

Atkinson, A.B. (2007b) 'The long run earnings distribution in five countries: "remarkable stability," U, V or W?', *Review of Income and Wealth*, 53: 1–24.

Autor, D.H., F. Levy and Murnane, R.J. (2003) 'The skill content of recent technological change: An empirical exploration', *Quarterly Journal of Economics*, 118 (4): 1279–1333.

Bacon, N., Blyton, P. and Dastmalchian, A. (2005) 'The significance of working time arrangements accompanying the introduction of teamworking evidence from employees', *British Journal of Industrial Relations*, 43: 681–701.

Batt, R. (2004) 'Who Benefits from teams? Comparing workers, supervisors, and managers', *Industrial Relations*, 43 (1): 183–212.

Belfield, C.R. and Harris, R.D.F. (2002) 'How well do theories of job matching explain variations in job satisfaction across education levels? Evidence for UK graduates', *Applied Economics*, 34: 535–48.

Bender, K.A and Heywood, J.S. (2006) 'Job satisfaction of the highly educated: The role of gender, academic tenure, and earnings', *Scottish Journal of Political Economy*, 52 (2): 253–79.

Black, S.E, Lynch, L.M. and Krivelyova, A. (2004) 'How workers fare when employers innovate', *Industrial Relations*, 43 (1): 44–66.

Brenner, M.D, Fairris, D., Ruser, J. (2004) "Flexible' work practices and occupational safety and health: Exploring the relationship between cumulative trauma disorders and workplace transformation', *Industrial Relations*, 43 (1): 242–66.

Bryson, A., Cappellari, L. and Lucifora, C. (2004) 'Does union membership really reduce job satisfaction?', *British Journal of Industrial Relations*, 42 (3): 439–59.

Cappelli, P., Bassi, L., Katz, H., Knoke, D., Osterman, P. and Useem, M. (1997) *Change at Work*. Oxford, England: Oxford University Press.

Cappelli, P. and Neumark, D. (2004) 'External churning and internal flexibility: Evidence on the functional flexibility and core-periphery hypotheses', *Industrial Relations*, 43 (1): 148–82.

Cox, A., Zagelmeyer, S. and Marchington, M. (2006) 'Embedding employee involvement and participation at work', *Human Resource Management Journal*, 16 (3): 250–67.

Delbridge, R., Turnbull, P. and Wilkinson, B. (1992) 'Pushing back the frontiers: management control and work intensification under JIT/TQM factory regimes', *New Technology, Work and Employment*, 7 (2): 97–106.

Delbridge, R. and Whitfield, K. (2001) 'Employee perceptions of job influence and organizational participation', *Industrial Relations*, 40 (3): 472–89.

Dundon, T., Grugulis, I. and Wilkinson, A. (2001) 'New management techniques in small and medium-sized enterprises,' in T. Redman and A. Wilkinson (eds), *Contemporary Human Resource Management: Text and Cases*. London: FT/Prentice Hall, pp. 432–63.

Fagan, C. and Burchell, B. (2006) L'intensification du travail et les différences hommes/femmes: conclusions des enquetes européennes sur les conditions de travail, *Organisation et intensité du travail*. P. Askenazy, D. Cartron, F.d. Coninck, et al. Toulouse: OCTARÈS Éditions, pp. 161–80.

Felstead, A., Gallie, D., Green, F. and Zhou, Y. (2007) *Skills At Work, 1986 to 2006*. University of Oxford, SKOPE.

Fitzner, G. (2006) *How have employees fared? Recent UK Trends*, Department for Trade and Industry, Employment Relations Research Series No. 56.

Forth, J. and Millward, N. (2004) 'High involvement management and pay in Britain', *Industrial Relations*, 43 (1): 98–119.

Gallie, D. (2006) L'intensification du travail en Europe 1996–2001?, *Organisation et intensité du travail*. P. Askenazy, D. Cartron, F.d. Coninck et al. Toulouse: OCTARÈS Éditions, pp. 239–60.

Gallie, D., Felstead, A. and Green, F. (2004) 'Changing patterns of task discretion in Britain,' *Work, Employment and Society*, 18 (2): 243–66.

Gaunt, R. and Benjamin, O. (2007) 'Job insecurity, stress and gender', *Community, Work and Family*, 10 (3): 341–55.

Goos, M. and Manning, A. (2007) 'Lousy and lovely jobs: The rising polarization of work in Britain,' *Review of Economics and Statistics*, 89 (1): 118–33.

Gorman, E.H. and Kmec, J.A. (2007) 'We (have to) try harder. Gender and required work effort in Britain and the United States,' *Gender and Society*, 21 (6): 828–56.

Graham, L. (1993) 'Inside a Japanese transplant: A critical perspective', *Work and Occupations*, 20: 147–73.

Green, F. (2006) *Demanding Work. The Paradox of Job Quality in the Affluent Economy*. Woodstock: Princeton University Press.

Green, F. (2008) 'Work effort and worker well-being in the age of affluence', in C. Cooper and R. Burke (eds), *The Long Work Hours Culture: Causes, Consquences and Choices*. Oxford: Emerald Group Publishing Limited.

Green, F. and Tsitsianis, N. (2005) 'An investigation of national trends in job satisfaction in Britain and Germany', *British Journal of Industrial Relations*, 43 (3): 401–29.

Green, F. and Whitfield, K. (2009) 'Employees' experiences of work', in W. Brown, A. Bryson, J. Forth and K. Whitfield (eds), *The Evolution of the Modern Workplace*. Cambridge: Cambridge University Press.

Green, F. and Zhu, Y. (2008) *Overqualification, Job Dissatisfaction, and Increasing Dispersion in the Returns to Graduate Education*, University of Kent, Discussion Papers in Economics, 0803.

Guest, D. and Bryson, A. (2009) 'From industrial relations to human resource management: The changing role of the personnel function', in W. Brown, A. Bryson, J. Forth and K. Whitfield (eds.), *The Evolution of the Modern Workplace*. Cambridge: Cambridge University Press.

Guest, D. and Conway, N. (1999) *How Dissatisfied Are British Workers? A Survey of Surveys*. London: IPD.

Guest, D. and Conway, N. (2004) 'Exploring the paradox of unionised worker dissatisfaction', *Industrial Relations Journal*, 35 (2): 102–21.

Handel, M.J. and Gittleman, M. (2004) 'Is there a wage payoff to innovative work practices', *Industrial Relations*, 43 (1): 67–97.

Handel, M.J. and Levine, D.I. (2004) 'Editors' introduction: The effects of new work practices on workers', *Industrial Relations*, 43 (1): 1–43.

Harley, B. (2001) 'Team membership and the experience of work in Britain: An analysis of the WERS98 data.' *Work, Employment and Society*, 15 (4): 721–42.

Kalmi, P. and Kauhanen, A. (2008) 'Workplace innovations and employee outcomes: Evidence from Finland', *Industrial Relations*, 47 (3): 430–59.

Kochan, T.A. and Osterman, P. (1994) *The Mutual Gains Enterprise*. Cambridge, Mass.: Harvard Business School Press.

Lehto, A.-M. and Sutela, H. (1999) *Efficient, More Efficient, Exhausted*. Helsinki: Statistics Finland.

Machin, S. (2003) 'Wage inequality since 1975', in R. Dickens, P. Gregg and J. Wadsworth, *The Labour Market Under New Labour*. Basingstoke: Palgrave Macmillan, pp. 191–213.

Redman, T. and Wilkinson, A. (2006) *Contemporary human resource management: text and cases*, London: Prentice Hall/FT.

Renaud, S., St-onge, S. and Magnan, M. (2004) 'The impact of stock purchase plan participation on workers' Individual Cash Compensation', *Industrial Relations*, 43 (1): 120–47.

Rose, M. (2007) 'Why so fed-up and footloose in IT? Spelling out the associations between occupation and overall job satisfaction shown by WERS2004,' *Industrial Relations Journal*, 38 (4): 356–84.

Sengupta, S., Whitfield, K. and McNabb, R. (2007) 'Employee share ownership and performance: Golden path or golden handcuffs?', *International Journal of Human Resource Management*, 18 (8): 1507–38.

Sloane, P.J. and Williams, H. (2000) 'Job satisfaction, comparison earnings, and gender', *Labour*, 14 (3): 473–502.

Whitfield, K. (2000) 'High-performance workplaces, training, and the distribution of skills', *Industrial Relations*, 39 (1): 1–25.

Wood, S. (2008) 'Job Characteristics, employee voice and well-being in Britain,' *Industrial Relations Journal*, 39 (2): 153–68.

Wood, S. and Bryson, A. (2009) 'High involvement management,' in W. Brown, A. Bryson, J. Forth and K. Whitfield (eds), *The Evolution of the Modern Workplace*. Cambridge: Cambridge University Press.

Zuboff, S. (1988) *In the Age of the Smart Machine: The Future of Work and Power*. New York: Basic Books.

23

Human Resource Management in Developing Countries

Pawan S. Budhwar and Yaw A. Debrah

INTRODUCTION

Until recent years, the study of human resource management (HRM) in developing countries was overshadowed by that of international human resource management. Implicit in the dominance of international human resource management was the conception that only aspects of HRM in multinational firms (MNCs) in developing countries were worthy of the attention of researchers. In parallel, this view downplayed the existence and importance of HRM practices in local (indigenous) firms in developing countries. This was due to the fact that most local firms were generally small and micro enterprises often managed by family members and employing relatives or friends. In such organisations, people management was mainly informal rather than formal and as such meaningful HRM practices were conspicuous by their absence (Nguyen and Bryant, 2004). However, with increasing economic

globalisation and its associated international competitiveness, as well as the privatisation of public enterprises in developing countries, the importance of local firms in competing in the global economy has come to the fore. With this has come the realisation of the importance of local firms developing their HRM functions to give them a competitive edge (Steel, 1992). Moreover, with the emergence of developing countries such as China and India as important economic powers, it is now very timely to understand the nature of HRM in developing countries.

In view of these developments, this chapter does three things. First, it explains the concept of developing countries and highlights the need, in the globalised era, to understand HRM in these countries. Second, it assesses the conceptual models that have been employed to explain the dynamics of HRM in developing countries. This draws on examples from different parts of the world to enlighten us on the main factors influencing HRM in developing countries. Finally, it highlights the key challenges facing HRM in developing countries and presents propositions along which future research that can be conducted to enhance our understanding of the role and nature of HRM in developing countries.

DEVELOPING COUNTRIES AND HRM

There is less consensus on the definition of the term 'developing country'. Many authors use terms such as 'less developed countries', 'newly industrialised countries', 'third world countries', 'emerging nations', 'emerging markets', and 'transitional economies' interchangeably for developing countries (for details see Budhwar and Debrah, 2004, 2005). For the purposes of this chapter, 'developing countries' are the ones which are in their early growth stages of economic development and are in the process of industrialising (see Budhwar and Debrah, 2004; Napier and Vu, 1998). This is an 'ideal' type description as all developing countries are at different stages of economic development. The term developing countries in this chapter is, thus, used in a broad generic sense to represent all countries other then advanced industrialised societies which we refer to as developed countries. We also define HRM in a broad sense as issues concerned with the management of all employees and employment relationships in a firm.

In the last two decades or so, scholars (see for example, Jaeger and Kanungo, 1990; Budhwar and Debrah, 2001a, 2004) have highlighted the dearth of HRM research on developing countries and have repeatedly called for more research in the area. A survey of the literature shows that until recent years, only a handful of studies had been conducted (see, for example, Austin, 1990; Sparrow and Budhwar, 1997; Budhwar and Debrah, 2001a; Kiggundu et al., 1983; Kanungo, 1995; Warner, 2000), on HRM in developing countries. This can probably be explained in terms of the lack of interest of researchers to study HRM issues in poor countries with mainly small firms having less formal and structured HR systems. Presently, due a number of major reasons such as the rapidly increasing levels of foreign direct investment (FDI) by MNCs in developing countries, the increasing numbers of subsidiaries of MNCs in the developing world, the projection of significant increase in the number of people to be employed by MNCs in developing countries, the emerging trends of self-initiated repatriates to developing countries (e.g. to both China and India), the prediction that many global businesses will be from emerging markets (Deresky, 2008), and the strong projection that BRIC countries (Brazil, Russia, China and India) would emerge as the new world economic powers, are all major factors that are likely to lead to interest in HRM in developing countries. In view of the above, there is now a strong interest on the part of researchers to understand the pattern of and relevant management systems for developing countries (see Kiriazov et al., 2000; Budhwar and Debrah, 2001, 2004; Das, 2002; Klingner and Campos, 2002; Murphy, 2002; Zhu and Nyland, 2004; Gomez-Samper and Monteferrante, 2005; Debrah and Ofori, 2006; Hasler et al., 2006; Lynham and Cunningham, 2006).

In response to the increasing interest in developing countries a number of major journals have devoted special issues to the area (see, for example, Special Issues of *Journal of International Business Studies*, 2001, 32 (1); *Academy of Management Journal*, 2000, 43, (3); *Academy of Management Executive,* May 2001). Also, some dedicated volumes under the 'Global HRM Series' have been developed which analyse various aspects of HRM in different developing countries around the globe. For example, Budhwar's (2004a) volume focuses on the HR in the Asia-Pacific region, Budhwar and Mellahi (2006) cover people management issues in the Middle-East region, Kamoche et al. (2004) examine HRM in the African context, and Elvira and Davila (2005) reveal the diverse nature of HRM in Latin America. More recently, some journals (e.g., *International*

Journal of HRM, 2005, 2007 and *Employee Relations,* 2007) have devoted special issues to the analysis of HRM in specific regions in the developing world. Similarly, some academic journals have organised special issues for specific countries such as China and India (e.g., *International Journal of HRM,* 2002; *Human Resource Management,* 2009).

Another reason for the interest in HRM in developing countries is the fact that the majority of the world's population live in developing countries and the projection is that, amongst the top ten nations which will have greatest population increase in the next five decades, nine are developing countries (US being the only developed country) (DNA, 2006). Also, developing countries act as: 1) significant *'buyers'*; 2) important *'suppliers'* of different resources (both natural and human) to industrialised nations; 3) *'competitors'* to developed countries with lower labour costs; 4) *'strategic regional centres'* for expansion of MNCs; 5) *'production sites'* for MNCs; and 6) *'capital users'*, i.e. from private creditors such as international banks, FDI, and foreign aid (for more details see Budhwar and Debrah, 2004a; Kanungo, 2000; Napier and Vu, 1998).

Due to globalisation and related factors, the movement of people around the globe has increased significantly. In 2006 alone, close to 200 million people lived outside the country of their origin (BBC, 2006). This and the above mentioned facts highlight the great extent to which both developed and developing countries have now become interdependent on each other. This is also evident from the creation of various economic international trading blocs and *'growth triangles'* (Debrah et al., 2000). Growth triangle is a type of regional or sub-regional economic cooperation and integration which makes it possible for complementarities in factor endowments of three or more countries to be tapped for trade and investment purposes. It is essentially a form of strategic alliance which relies on the exploitation of the principles of comparative advantage to attract FDI for the production of exports (Waldron, 1997). The expansion

of the European Union has allowed the free movement of people from the less developed member states to developed countries like the UK. This, however, has created new challenges regarding how to manage such culturally diverse people. In such circumstances it is important to realise that the 'state-of-the-art' management practices and techniques which are dictated by unique configurations of different cultural and institutional factors, evolved in the context of Western cultural values, cannot be uncritically adopted in developing countries or to manage efficiently people moving from them to developed nations (Mendonca, 2000). Therefore, there is now a more pressing need to research and highlight what kind of HR policies and practices are relevant for developing countries.

From a theoretical perspective, the field of HRM has reached a stage where we now have reliable information about the nature of HRM systems in developed nations. However, we are still looking for answers to a number of big questions regarding the field of HRM in the context of developing countries. Some of the primary questions in this regard are: to what extent are HRM systems of developed and developing nations converging or diverging? What is unique about HRM in developing countries? To what extent can MNCs successfully transfer best practice HRM systems to their subsidiaries in these contexts? What are the main factors and variables which significantly determine HRM policies and practices of firms operating in developing countries? What are the appropriate frameworks, methodologies and approaches for conducting HRM research in developing countries? Answers to such questions will contribute to the development of HRM theories and relevant policies and practices in developing countries (Budhwar and Debrah, 2004). This is particularly imperative in view of the fact that most developing countries have liberalised their economies and opened their doors to foreign investors. Moreover, focusing on developing nations would add a new impetus to HRM research and allow researchers to go beyond the current predominant emphasis on research in countries in the European Union and North America.

In the absence of established and tried research frameworks, the critical issue before researchers is how to conduct meaningful research in developing countries. Lately scholars in the field (see Schuler et al., 2002; Budhwar and Sparrow, 2002) have reemphasized the need to conduct research that can help to highlight the context specific aspects of HRM. In this regard Budhwar and associates (see Budhwar and Debrah, 2001b; Budhwar and Sparrow, 1998, 2002) have developed a contextual model which helps to analyse the context specific nature of HRM in a cross-national setting. These authors have identified three levels of factors and variables, which are known to influence HRM policies and practices, and worth considering for cross-national investigations. These are: national factors (involving national culture, national institutions, business sectors and dynamic business environment); contingent variables (such as age, size, nature, ownership, life cycle stage of organization); and organizational strategies (such as the ones proposed by Miles and Snow and Porter) and policies related to primary HR functions and internal labour markets (for details of the main aspects of these factors and variables see Budhwar and Sparrow, 2002).

Perhaps, very large projects, spanning a long period of time can effectively examine the influence of all the three sets of factors and variables on HRM systems of a particular nation at a given period of time. However, considering the infancy stage of HRM in many developing countries and the argument that HRM in a cross-national context can be best analysed by examining the influence of national factors (Brewster et al., 1996; Budhwar and Sparrow, 1998), it would be sensible to initially examine the impact of the main national factors on HRM in different developing countries. This will help to draw useful cross-national comparisons regarding the scenario of HRM in such countries. The national factors such as culture and institutions form the macro environment of organisations in a national context.

This approach has been recently adopted by Budhwar and Debrah (2004), Budhwar (2004) and Budhwar and Mellahi (2006) to examine the HRM systems in developing countries and to highlight the context-specific nature of HRM, developing in Asia, the Middle-East and Africa. The next section provides examples from these analyses in the form of nature of HRM functions and the key factors influencing the HRM in different national contexts.

FACTORS DETERMINING HRM IN DEVELOPING COUNTRIES

In a review of the impact of the main issues affecting HRM in thirteen developing countries, Debrah and Budhwar (2004b) identified three major influences. These are: a) religious influences (Islam, Hinduism, Buddhism, and traditional beliefs in spirits, fetishes and gods); b) traditional cultural beliefs (e.g., Confucianism, African traditional practices and institutions, caste in India, etc); and c) western colonial and modern influences.

Along similar lines, Mellahi and Budhwar (2006) analysed HR related studies in the Middle-East and suggested that despite the accelerating globalisation of business, people in the region have retained their work-related cultural values and as a result have different attitudes towards employment and work. This is mainly due to the fact that influences of traditional cultural values on work processes is deeply rooted, especially in the absence of formal, structured and rationalised systems and do not change in short to medium term. For example countries like Kuwait, Egypt, Iran, Saudi Arabia, Turkey and Morocco show a degree of homogeneity around high power distance, collectivism, Islamic values and Arab traditions. Further, the high power distance exhibited in some Middle Eastern countries (such as Kuwait, Saudi Arabia, Morocco and Egypt) has an impact on managers' perception towards the delegation of authority to lower levels in the organisation and ways of interaction with employees. It also tends to produce centralised decision making processes, unwillingness to delegate responsibility, and rigidly designed and expected to be followed HRM policies (also see Benson and Al Arkoubi, 2006; Ali and Al-Kazemi, 2006; Hatem, 2006). Such influences are an outcome of a given socio-cultural, political and economic context (apart from other factors) which take a long time to change, especially in the case of developing countries. However, as countries and regions of the world develop economically, politically and technologically, we can see such impacts to diminish and taken over by a more professional and rationalised approach to HRM. Hence, such influences are less visible in developed nations.

Further, Mellahi (2006) and Abdalla (2006) highlight the strong prevalence of collectivism and Arab (and Turkish and Persian) traditions in Saudi Arabia and Qatar, where loyalty to one's family and friends is expected to override loyalty to organisational procedures and as such has resulted in the use of inequitable criteria in recruitment, promotion and compensation. The influence of Islamic values and principles of *Shura* i.e., consultation, social harmony and respect are manifested in consensus decision making styles. Equally, respect for authority and age and concern for the well being of employees and society at large are also evident in HRM policies and practices in organisations in the Middle-East (see Mellahi and Budhwar, 2006).

Debrah and Budhwar (2004) highlight the influence of Islamic religion on HR management in countries like Iran, Pakistan, Saudi Arabia and Algeria. Arguably, of all the factors influencing HRM in these countries, the Islamic influence is probably the dominant one. Their further analysis of HRM in the Sub-Saharan African countries reveals that traditional African culture exerts strong influence on HRM. In Ghana, Nigeria, Kenya and elsewhere in Africa, people in organisations still place a lot of emphasis on traditional beliefs such as spirits, witchcraft, fetishes, and gods (see Gardiner, 1996), traditions and institutions, customs

and socio-cultural issues (Debrah, 2000). In Kiggundu's (1989) view these traditional practices tend to have negative effects on organisational performance. In particular, they compromise the integrity and efficiency of formal bureaucratic system, injecting an element of subjectivity in HR functions such as recruitment and selection, performance appraisal, promotion, demotion and compensation. Such practices remove fairness from the treatment of employees and HR decision making in organisations (Beugre and Offodile, 2001).

Similar to other developing countries, HRM in both India and Nepal is significantly influenced both by national culture and national institutions. Hinduism, as the dominant religion in both these countries, exerts pressures on HRM. Budhwar (2004b) and Adhikari and Muller (2004) suggest that HRM practices in these two countries is governed largely by social contacts, based on one's caste, religion, economic status and political affiliation. Similarly, in both China and Taiwan, just as in Korea, Confucian values have found their way into management, for example, *'Guanxi', face* and *'renqing'* are some of the means of regulating interpersonal relationships in Chinese organisations. Although it is evident that there are some differences in the management practices in the three East Asian countries some traditional cultures have similar, if not the same, impacts on management in all three countries.

There is also still a strong influence of British colonial traditions in India and Nepal in the form of numerous legislation and red-tape ridden bureaucratic system. Again, in common with other African countries the provisions of labour laws are not seriously implemented and, moreover, the uncooperative and disruptive nature of unions reduces the efficiency of organisations. However, all this is now challenged and is slowly changing due to the pressures created by the liberalisation of the economy and increased global competition.

Apart from the above, other institutions (for example, trade unions, legal systems and employers' associations) are important aspects of national factors (in Budhwar and associates context model) which are known to significantly influence HRM in different cross-national contexts. With the changes in the economic systems of developing countries and changes in the role of the government we are witnessing changes in HRM policies and practices in different national settings. In most cases, the scanty available evidence suggests that the role of governments has shifted from an interventionist (where it used to develop centralised HR framework for organisations to follow), to an abstentionist role, giving organisations a free hand over HRM matters, albeit within a legal framework in many developing countries such as in Egypt, Algeria, Turkey, Morocco, Saudi Arabia and Iran. For example, in Algeria, HRM departments have been asked by the government to change from being a purely administrative function to developing effective HRM systems to help firms compete at home and abroad. As a result, HRM departments are asked to undergo radical changes to grapple with the new challenges of the market driven economy. However, given the lack of HRM skills in most developing countries HR managers have been muddling through, often relying on 'trial and error' to cope with the impact of market liberalisation and severe international competition (see Mellahi and Budhwar, 2006).

Many developing countries whose human resources do not possess key skills and capabilities (mainly due to less developed educational and vocational institutions) are experiencing difficulties in the employment of qualified locals (for example in many Middle-East countries such as Kuwait, Saudi Arabia, Qatar, UAE and Oman). But governments in such countries are putting pressure on private sector firms to employ more locals (Mellahi, 2006). In particular, a trend is emerging in the UAE (*Emiratisation*) and in Oman (*Omanisation*) where a strong emphasis is placed on recruiting locals (see Rees et al., 2007; Al-Hamadi et al., 2007). Given the top down nature of these policies, private

firms view government policies to employ locals as unrealistic and that they undermine their ability to compete. Further, while past HRM practices in the private sector in these countries, such as free hand to 'hire and fire', and compensation based purely on financial rewards, were designed to manage a foreign workforce with minimum rights (for example in Qatar and Saudi Arabia), these practices are not attuned to the needs of local workers who are protected by government legislation and have high demands and expectations from their employers (for more details see Mellahi and Budhwar, 2006).

At another level, both political and legal framework in different developing countries influence HRM policies and practices in their own unique way. For example, China allows the existence of only one national union which functions strictly according to the wishes of the communist party. But, in India there are many local, regional and national unions which generally function in an adversarial way (see Saini and Budhwar, 2004).

Apart from the above-mentioned national culture and national institutions, the dynamic business environment is also known to influence HRM in developing countries. For example, Debrah and Budhwar (2004) argue that in many developing countries, to enhance international competitiveness in the globalised era has become a national priority. As a result, economic liberalisation, deregulation and privatisation feature prominently in many developing countries' restructuring programmes. The economic liberalisation and restructuring in developing countries brought on by globalisation have in turn initiated changes in HRM policies and practices (as is the case in most sub-Saharan African countries). For example, there is clear evidence of the near 'demise' of permanent employment in both public and private sectors in many developing countries. In particular, we are witnessing the rise of the 'insecure workforce' and the disappearance of the standard forms of employment (see, for example, Mbaku, 1999).

Research undertaken by Mellahi and Budhwar (2006) also reveals the significant role of a country's historical context in the developments of specific HRM models. For example, in the case of Iran, the Islamic revolution has contributed significantly in shaping its HRM practices by moving from merit and competence based criteria in selecting and rewarding employees to putting more emphasis on ideological orientation and personal trust and loyalty (also see Namazie and Tayeb, 2006). Similarly, in North African countries (such as Morocco, Algeria and Tunisia), the impact of the French colonialism on HRM policies is clearly evident, in particular the predominance of French language as a criterion for entry to professional jobs and for career advancement. In addition to the above factors, national wealth, composition of workforce, trade unions, employment legislations (as discussed above), all combine together to create a unique country or region specific HRM model. For instance, the Middle-East has some of the richest countries in the world (such as the UAE and Qatar) and some of the poorest countries in the world (for example, Yemen).

These various factors in different countries, understandably, result in different approaches to HRM. On this issue, Benson and Al Arkoubi (2006) report that in Morocco it is rare for small and medium size organisations to invest in formal training. While this is partly due to the fact that managers are not convinced or perhaps do not value the possible impact of HRM on improving organisational performance, there is some evidence that organisation can hardly afford the cost of conducting such training. This is not the case in other countries in the region, such as the UAE, where training and development of locals is extensive.

In addition to the issue of varying impact of wealth disparity on HRD, the structure and composition of the labour market also yield different HRM systems. For instance, because of the small size of indigenous population, GCC countries (Gulf Co-operation Council) require an extensive use of foreign labour to develop their infrastructure and manage their economies. As a result, the structure of the labour market in GCC countries is markedly different from the rest of the Middle-East. While unemployment is high in both GCC countries and other Middle Eastern countries, the causes underpinning unemployment are different in GCC countries from those causing unemployment in other Middle Eastern countries. In Algeria, Egypt, Morocco, and Tunisia unemployment is caused by lack of jobs in the labour market to absorb the high number of young people entering the job market. In GCC countries, however, unemployment is caused by local people shunning socially undesirable jobs (see, for example, Mellahi, 2006). Finally, while most Middle Eastern countries provide workers with the right to form and join trade unions, in GCCs countries trade unions are not allowed (this is probably due to GCCs high dependence on foreign workers from Asia), although a new form of work associations emerged in the early 2000s. However, the role of these associations is often limited to dealing with abuse of foreign workers such as delay in payments of salaries and arbitrary deportation (for more details see Mellahi and Budhwar, 2006).

The above discussion highlights the impact of a number of factors and variables on HRM in developing countries. However, the main challenge facing HRM scholars in developing countries is how to delineate the impact of different factors and variables on HRM in each country. In order to take the field further and guide researchers to conduct meaningful research in future, in the next section we identify some of the key challenges facing HRM in developing countries and put forward some future research directions for HRM researchers in developing countries. Dealing with the same should result in the development of both appropriate HRM theory and practice suitable for developing countries.

DEVELOPING HRM RESEARCH IN DEVELOPING COUNTRIES

By far the most important challenge for HRM researchers is the development of theoretical/conceptual models that facilitate the conduct of research which can highlight the context specific nature of HRM functions in general. Schuler et al. (2002: 41), who highlighting the importance of context-specific nature of HRM and the strong need to pursue research in the area, say that 'HRM research in contextual isolation is not only misleading, but it strongly hinders the understanding of core aspects of the phenomenon in any significant way'. Considering such pressing demands, we have proposed below a number of future research directions.

Future research direction 1

Researchers need to focus on illuminating our understanding about the context-specific nature of personnel functions and relevant HRM system(s) in developing countries. We argue that the contents of the contextual model by Budhwar and colleagues (see Figure 23.1) of factors and variables affecting HRM in cross-national settings can significantly help to reveal the context specific nature of HRM in developing countries. Perhaps the key challenge in the successful adoption of this model for research in developing countries is the adoption of appropriate methodologies as the proposed constructs and measures might not be equally valid in each developing country due to the differences in them.

Nevertheless, future research in developing countries should aim to:

Future research direction 2

Throw light on the main factors and variables which determine HRM systems applicable to specific developing countries.

With the pressures for change facing HR managers in developing countries as a result of globalisation and international competitiveness, one would have thought that organisations would develop HR strategic responses. But, with the exception of some countries such as Taiwan, South Korea and to some extent in India, where HR departments are involved in the formulation of business strategies and HR is closely linked to business strategy, one does not get the impression that there is a movement towards HRM (as understood in Western academic sense) in most of the developing countries (see Debrah and Budhwar, 2004).

Perhaps these countries have not fully embraced a strategic integrated and focused approach to HRM. Perhaps most firms operating (indeed the exception can be the MNCs) in many developing countries are not aware of the benefits of such an integrated approach. Or, even if they have an idea about it they are perhaps not sure about how they can pursue this in practice. The existing

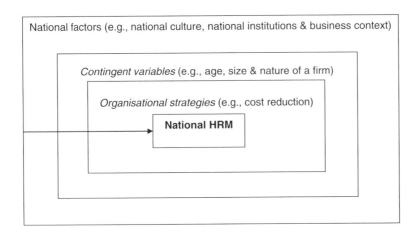

Figure 23.1   Factors influencing cross-national HRM

literature (for example, Brewster and Larsen, 1992; Budhwar and Sparrow, 1997, 2002) provides details of both benefits of strategic integration of HRM into the corporate strategy and also scales which organisations can adopt in practice. In this regard, future research should:

Future research direction 3

Aim to highlight the extent to which strategic HRM is practised by firms in developing countries and its related benefits and also the obstacles in the practise of HRM.

This is necessary because commentators (such as Kanungo and Jaeger, 1990) caution against the attempts by both researchers and practitioners to try to blindly adopt the western HRM models, approaches, measures or scales in the developing countries context. As a result of possible differences due to a combination of factors between developed and developing nations and issues related to concept equivalence (amongst others), adoption of western HRM constructs to developing countries will not be sensible. To get a real picture of HRM scenario in developing countries there is then a need to:

Future research direction 4

Highlight the unique aspects of indigenous HRM policies and practices. Also, research should examine which western/global standardized HR policies and practices can be successfully implemented in the developing countries context and why and/or why not.

This is related to a re-emergent debate in the field of western HRM relating to the convergence-divergence thesis (Katz and Darbishire, 2001; McGaughey and De Cerie, 1999). To what extent HRM systems of developing countries are converging or diverging is then worthy of examination by future researchers. Budhwar (2004a) summarises the convergence-divergence debate examined by scholars in the Asia-Pacific developing countries. Though, over the last few years,

research evidence has helped to supplant the convergence view with the knowledge that managerial attitudes, values, behaviours, and efficacy differs across national cultures (see McGaughey and De Cerie, 1999), recent investigations in the Asia-Pacific region (see for example, Warner, 2002) emphasise the notion of 'soft convergence' (partial impact) as an outcome of globalisation. From the MNCs' perspective, the implementation of global standardised HRM practices and policies (with local adjustments) is also an indication of soft convergence (see Bjorkman and Budhwar, 2007). Globalisation and international trade and finance place pressures on firms to standardise practices and policies. Considering the sheer variations (such as population, geography, economies, economic development phase, labour markets, sociocultural, legal and political set-up, and HRM systems) in the developing countries around the world, it will not be sensible to talk about significant or 'hard convergence'. Possibly, a thorough cross-national analysis of the key factors which form the basis of national HRM systems and the level (both depth and acceptance) at which a given HR practice is adopted in different developing countries, can help to examine the convergence-divergence thesis in a more meaningful manner. Hence, researchers should:

Future research direction 5

Examine the 'convergence-divergence' thesis for HRM in developing countries and highlight the main factors contributing to either of these.

As discussed above, there is emerging evidence suggesting that globalisation, liberalisation and structural adjustment affect HRM systems in developing Asian countries. Also, the impact of both legislation and unions on reemployment relations is highlighted in the literature on developing countries. However, due to the scarcity of research evidence and the transition phase of things, it is not clear what new pattern(s) of employment relations are emerging in developing countries. Hence, future research should endeavour to:

Future research direction 6

Reveal the emerging patterns of employment relations in developing countries and highlight the main factors contributing to the development of these patterns.

The existing research highlights distinction in patterns of HRM systems based on industrial sectors (see Budhwar and Sparrow, 2002). At the moment, specific sectors are appearing to be dominant in certain national contexts. For example, in the Chinese context, manufacturing is the dominant industrial sector. Similarly, in the Indian set-up, information technology related services, along with R&D, are dominating. In the Arab context, it is the oil sector which leads the way. In this regard, there is then a need to examine and highlight:

Future research direction 7

The kinds of HRM systems suitable for specific industrial sectors that are dominant in specific developing countries.

During the transition phase of economies (for example from developing to developed) a key challenge for HRM in developing countries can be the effects of the transition from an established HRM systems to a new one (for example from collectivist to individualised HRM practices or from experience based to performance related compensation system). How to achieve an effective and successful change at a macro level is then a critical challenge for all managers in developing countries. Future research should attempt to:

Future research direction 8

Achieve a balance between the traditional management customs which are strongly dictated by socio-cultural aspects of a given society and the changing emphasis of HRM functions. Key steps which can help in this regard should also be highlighted.

We assert that globalisation and its associated international competitive pressures have precipitated the introduction of flexibility of operations, contingent reward systems, lean production methodologies in a process of ongoing change to underpin efficiency, thereby leading to new challenges to HRM at organisational level, particularly with regard to industrial relations policy and practice (Debrah and Budhwar, 2004). Still, it will not be sensible to generalise such developments to all the developing countries. However, this kind of information is useful to both researchers and practitioners in the field of HRM as it indicates the direction in which things are moving in developing countries.

Future research direction 9

We propose that future research should highlight the emerging nature of industrial relations policy and practice in developing countries.

We stress that employee relations practices within present day organisations, including internal labour market (ILM) structures in most developing countries, are dictated by factors such as social and cultural values, religious beliefs, caste/ethnic based stratification, political affiliation and economic power (for example, in the Indian context, see Saini and Budhwar, 2004). Such types of ILMs result in the decrease in organisational performance and breed corruption and red-tapism. In the context of the changes taking place in most developing countries in terms of privatisation and structural adjustment programmes, there is now a strong need for HRM systems in these countries to be consistent with rationalised, objective and systematic employment systems. This is already happening in some of the countries, such as India. However, there is a dearth of information available from most developing countries in this regard. This forms an important agenda for future research.

Future research direction 10

It is our view that future research should highlight the emerging nature and constituents of ILMs in firms operating in developing countries. In addition, it should explore the main factors which determine ILMs in the changing business environment in developing countries.

It is apparent that most developing nations have established legal structures in the form of relevant labour laws to safeguard the interests of employees. However, in many cases the provisions of the labour laws are not at all seriously implemented, which results in the exploitation of employees. Child labour and minimum wage laws are typical examples. Relevant law enforcing agencies in developing countries need to ensure serious implementation and enforcement of such provisions. Moreover, many developing countries do not actively promote equal opportunities, hence the existence of disadvantage on the grounds of ethnicity, gender and age. This is another important challenge facing HRM in developing countries and HRM managers need to develop policies accordingly to tackle these problems. In this regard the following proposition is proposed.

Future research direction 11

We assert that future research needs to draw attention to the nature and kind of legislation suitable to safeguard the present workforce in developing countries. It should reveal which existing laws are now obsolete and badly need amending.

It is believed that, once the above mentioned research issues are investigated and their useful results are adopted by HR practitioners in developing nations, then it should help to improve firms' performance. This, then, leads to the latest and on-going debate in the field, i.e. the extent to which HRM helps in organisational performance (see Katou and Budhwar, 2007). The literature also reveals that most research investigations in this regard have been conducted in western developed nations and there is a strong scarcity of such studies in the developing nations' context.

Future research direction 12

Finally, future research needs to examine the extent to which HRM practices in firms operating in developing countries are contributing to improving organisational performance. Also, future research should accentuate the dominant perspective (i.e., best practice, contingency or configurational) within this field in the developing countries context.

CONCLUSION

We have made an attempt in this chapter to provide an overview of the scenario of HRM in developing countries and developed a number of propositions for future research. We believe that findings derived from research carried out with these propositions should help to take the field further. Nevertheless, in the absence of research culture, conducting research in the developing countries is more challenging in getting access, getting quality data (because many people are reluctant to participate in questionnaire surveys), adopting valid and reliable measures and scales, getting funding from Western funding bodies to conduct research in developing countries, publishing such research in top tier management journals and so on. However, considering the rapid pace with which MNCs are entering these countries and the growing economic power of some developing countries, it has now become an imperative for scholars to research and reveal to the world the relevant HRM systems for firms operating in these nations. We hope that the information provided in this chapter will be useful to both researchers and practitioners who have an interest in developing countries.

REFERENCES

Abdalla, I.A. (2006) 'Human resource management in Qatar', in P. Budhwar and K. Mellahi (eds) *Managing Human Resources in the Middle-East*. London: Routledge, pp. 121–44.
Academy of Management Executive (2001) May.

Academy of Management Journal (2000) Special Research Forum on Emerging Economies, 43 (3).

Adhikari, D. and Muller, M. (2004) 'Human resource management in Nepal', in P. Budhwar and Y.A. Debrah (eds), *Human Resource Management in Developing Countries.* London: Routledge, pp. 91–101.

Al-Hamadi, A.B., Budhwar, P. and Shipton, H. (2007) 'Managing human resources in the Sultanate of Oman', *International Journal of Human Resource Management*, 18(1): 100–13

Ali, A.J. and Al-Kazemi, A. (2006) 'Human resource management in Kuwait', in P. Budhwar and K. Mellahi (eds), *Managing Human Resources in the Middle-East.* London: Routledge, pp. 79–96.

Austin, J.E. (1990) *Managing in Developing Countries.* New York: The Free Press.

BBC (2006) Global Migrants Reach 191 Million. http://news.bbc.co.uk/2/hi/americas/5054214.stm? headline=Global~migrants~reach~

Benson, P. and Al Arkoubi, K. (2006) 'Human resource management in Morocco', in P. Budhwar and K. Mellahi, (eds), *Managing Human Resources in the Middle-East.* London: Routledge, pp. 273–90.

Beugre, D. and Offodile, F. (2001) Managing for organizational effectiveness in sub-Saharan Africa: a culture-fit model, *International Journal of HRM*, 12(4): 535–50.

Bjorkman, I. and Budhwar, P. (2007) 'When in Rome …? human resource management and performance of foreign firms operating in India', *Employee Relations*, 29(6): 595–610.

Brewster, C., Tregaskis, O., Hegewisch, A. and Mayne, L. (1996) 'Comparative research in human resource management: A review and an example', *The International Journal of Human Resource Management*, 7(3): 586–604.

Brewster, C. and Larsen, H.H. (1992) 'Human resource management in Europe: Evidence from ten countries', *The International Journal of Human Resource Management*, 3(3): 409–33.

Budhwar, P. (2004a) 'Human Resource Management in India', in. P. Budhwar and Y.A. Debrah (eds), *Human Resource Management in Developing Countries.* London: Routledge, pp. 75–90.

Budhwar, P. (2004b) (ed.) *Managing Human Resources in Asia-Pacific.* Routledge: London.

Budhwar, P. and Debrah, Y.A. (2004) (eds) *Human Resource Management in Developing Countries.* London: Routledge.

Budhwar, P. and Debrah, Y.A. (2005) 'International HRM in developing countries', in H. Scullion and M. Linehan (eds), *International Human Resource Management.* London: Palgrave, pp. 259–80.

Budhwar, P. and Debrah, Y.A. (2001a) (eds) *Human Resource Management in Developing Countries.* London: Routledge.

Budhwar, P. and Debrah, Y.A. (2001b) 'Rethinking comparative and cross national human resource management research', *The International Journal of Human Resource Management*, 12(3): 497–515.

Budhwar, P. and Mellahi, K. (eds) (2006) *Managing Human Resources in the Middle East.* London: Routledge.

Budhwar, P. and Sparrow, P. (1997) 'Evaluating levels of strategic integration and devolvement of human resource management in India', *The International Journal of Human Resource Management*, 8(4): 476–94.

Budhwar, P. and Sparrow, P. (1998) 'National factors determining Indian and British HRM practices: An empirical study', *Management International Review*, 38 (Special Issue 2): 105–21.

Budhwar, P. and Sparrow, P. (2002) 'An integrative framework for determining cross national human resource management practices', *Human Resource Management Review*, 12(3): 377–403.

Charmes, J. (1999) 'Micro-enterprises in West Africa', in K. King and S. McGrath (eds), *Enterprise in Africa: Between Poverty and Growth.* London: Intermediate Technology.

Daily News & Analysis (2007) World Population to Reach 9.2 Billion in 2050: United Nations Research. *http://www.dnaindia.com/dnaPrint.asp? NewsID=1084760&CatID=9*

Das, S.P. (2002) 'Foreign Direct investment and the relative wage in a developing economy', *Journal of Development Economics*, 67(1): 55–77.

Debrah, Y.A. (2000) 'Management in Ghana', in M. Warner (ed.), *Management in Emerging Countries.* London: Thomson Learning, pp. 189–97.

Debrah, Y.A. and Budhwar, P. (2004) 'Conclusion: International competitive pressures and the challenges for HRM in developing countries', in P. Budhwar and Debrah, Y.A. (eds), *Human Resource Management in Developing Countries.* London: Routledge, pp. 75–90.

Debrah, Y.A., McGovern, I. and Budhwar, P. (2000) 'Complementarity or competition: The development of human resources in a growth triangle', *The International Journal of Human Resource Management*, 11(2): 314–35.

Debrah, Y.A. and Ofori, G. (2006) 'HRD of professionals in an emerging economy: The case of the Tanzanian construction industry', *The International Journal of Human Resource Management*, 17(3): 440.

Deresky, H. (2008) *International Management: Managing Across Borders and Cultures.* Singapore: Pearson Education.

Elvira, M.M. and Davila, A. (2005) *Managing Human Resources in the Latin America.* London: Routledge.

Employee Relations (2007) People Management in India and the Sub Continent. (Guest Editor, P. Budhwar).

Gardiner, K. (1996) 'Managing in different cultures: The case of Ghana', in B. Towers (ed.), *The Handbook of Human Resource Management.* Oxford: Blackwell, pp. 488–510.

Gomez-Samper, H. and Monteferrante, P. (2005) 'Managing people in Venezuela: Where are we headed?', *The International Journal of Human Resource Management*, 16(12): 2255–67.

Hasler, M.G., Thompson, M.D. and Schuler, M. (2006) 'National HRD in transitional societies in the developing world: Brazil', *Advances in Developing Human Resources*, 8(1): 99–116.

Hatem, T. (2006) 'Human resource management in Egypt', in P. Budhwar and K. Mellahi (eds), *Managing Human Resources in the Middle-East.* London: Routledge, pp. 199–218.

Human Resource Management (2009) Emerging Patterns of HRM in the New Indian Economic Environment (Guest Editors, P. Budhwar and A. Varma).

International Journal of Human Resource Management (2002) HRM in China Revisited, 13 (Guest Editor, M. Warner).

International Journal of Human Resource Management (2005) HRM in Latin America, 16 (12) (Guest Editors, M.M. Elvira and A. Davila).

International Journal of Human Resource Management (2007) Managing HRs in the Middle–East, 18(1) (Guest Editors, P. Budhwar and K. Mellahi).

Jaeger, A.M. and Kanungo, R.N. (1990) (eds) *Management in Developing Countries.* New York: Routledge.

Journal of International Business Studies (2001) Symposium: The Impact of Developing Economies and Economies in Transition on the Future of International Business, 32 (1).

Kamoche, K., Debrah, Y.A., Horwitz, F. and G.M. Murlia (2005) *Managing Human Resources in Africa.* London: Routledge.

Kanungo, R.N. (1995) (ed.) *Employee Management in Developing Countries.* Greenwich, London: JAI Press Inc.

Kanungo, R.N. (2000) 'Business culture, the emerging countries', in M. Warner (ed.), *Regional Encyclopaedia of Business and Management: Management in the Emerging Countries.* London: Thomson Learning Business Press, pp. 60–7.

Kanungo, R.N. and Jaeger, A.M. (1990) 'Introduction: The need for indigenous management in developing countries', in A.M. Jaeger and R.N. Kanungo, (eds), *Management in Developing Countries*, London: Routledge, pp. 1–19.

Katou, A. and Budhwar, P. (2007) 'The effect of human resource management policies on organizational performance in Greek manufacturing firms', *Thunderbird International Business Review*, 49(1): 1–36.

Katz, H.C. and Darbishire, O. (2001) 'Converging divergences: World changes in employment systems', *Industrial and Labour Relations Review*, 54(3): 681–716.

Kiggundu, M.N. (1989) *Managing Organizations in Developing Countries.* Connecticut: Kumarian Press.

Kiggundu, M.N., Jorgensen, J.J. and Hafsi, T. (1983) 'Administrative theory and practice in developing countries: A synthesis', *Administrative Science Quarterly*, 28: 66–84.

Kiriazov, D., Sullivan, S.E. and Tu, H.S (2000) 'Business success in Eastern Europe: Understanding and customizing HRM', *Business Horizon*, 43 (1): 39–48.

Klingner, D.E. and Campos, V.P. (2002) 'Building public HRM capacity in Latin America and the Caribbean: What works and what doesn't', *Public Organization Review*, 2(4): 349–58.

Lynham, S.A. and Cunningham, P.W. (2006) 'National HRD in transitional societies in the developing world: Concept and challenges', *Advances in Developing Human Resources*, 8(1): 116–36.

Mbaku, J.M. (1999) 'A balance sheet of structural adjustment in Africa: Towards a sustainable development agenda', in J.M. Mbaku (ed.), *Preparing Africa for the Twenty–First Century: Strategies for Peaceful Coexistence and Sustainable Development.* Aldershot: Ashgate, pp. 119–49.

McGaughey, S.L. and De Cerie, H. (1999) 'Reassessment of convergence and divergence dynamics: Implications for international HRM', *The International Journal of Human Resource Management*, 10(2), 235–50.

Mellahi, K. (2006) 'Human resource Management in Saudi Arabia', in P. Budhwar and K. Mellahi (eds) *Managing Human Resources in the Middle-East.* London: Routledge, pp. 97–120.

Mellahi, K. and Budhwar, P. (2006) 'HRM challenges in the Middle–East: Agenda for future research and policy', in P. Budhwar and K. Mellahi (eds), *Managing Human Resources in the Middle-East.* London: Routledge, pp. 291–301.

Mendonca, M. (2000) 'Human resource management in the emerging countries', in M. Warner (ed.) *Regional Encyclopaedia of Business and Management: Management in the Emerging Countries.* London: Thomson Learning Business Press, pp. 86–94.

Murphy, T.E. (2002) 'Market forces and the Middle East's new interest in HRM', *Business Horizons*, 45 (5): 63–70.

Namazie, P. and Tayeb, M. (2006) 'Human resource management in Iran', in P. Budhwar and K. Mellahi (eds), *Managing Human Resources in the Middle-East*. London: Routledge, pp. 20–39.

Napier, N.K. and Vu, V.T. (1998) 'International human resource management in developing and transitional economy countries: A breed apart?', *Human Resource Management Review*, 8(1): 39–77.

Nguyen, T.V. and Bryant, S.E. (2004) 'A study of the formality of human resource management practices in small and medium-sized enterprises in Vietnam', *International Small Business Journal*, 22 (6): 595–618.

Rees, C.J., Mamman, A. and Braik, A.B. (2007) 'Emiratization as a strategic HRM change initiative: Case study evidence from a UAE petroleum company', *The International Journal of HRM*, 18(1): 33–53.

Saini, D. and Budhwar, P. (2004) 'Human resource management in India', in P. Budhwar (ed.), *Managing Human Resources in Asia-Pacific*. London: Routledge, pp. 113–39.

Schuler, R.S., Budhwar, P. and Florkowski, G.W. (2002) 'International human resource management: Review and critique', *International Journal of Management Reviews*, 4(1): 41–70.

Sparrow, P. and Budhwar, P. (1997) 'Competition and change: Mapping the Indian HRM recipe against world-wide patterns', *Journal of World Business*, 32(3): 224–42.

Steel, W.F. (1992) 'How small enterprises in Ghana have responded to adjustment', *The World Bank Economic Review*, 6(3): 423–38.

Warner, M. (2000) (ed.) *Regional Encyclopaedia of Business and Management: Management in the Emerging Countries*. London: Thomson Learning Business Press.

Warner, M. (2002) 'Globalization, labour markets and human resources in Asia-Pacific economies: An overview', *International Journal of Human Resource Management*, 13(3): 384–98.

Waldron, D.G. (1997) 'Growth triangles: A strategic assessment', *Multinational Business Review*, 5(1): 53–67.

Zhu, C.J. amd Nyland, C. (2004) 'Marketization and social protection reform: Emerging HRM issues in China', *The International Journal of Human Resource Management*, 15(5): 853–64.

24

HRM and National Economic Performance

Jonathan Michie

INTRODUCTION

The management of labour has been recognised as a crucial determinant of national economic performance for as long as national economic performance has been analysed. The first analysis of the relative wealth of nations identified the division of labour as being fundamental to labour productivity and hence to the economic prosperity of the firm in question and of the economy in aggregate (Smith, 1776). Adam Smith's *Wealth of Nations* was presented as five 'Books', and the title of the first one opens with 'Of the Causes of Improvement in the Productive Powers of Labour ...'. Chapter One is 'Of the Division of Labour'. The opening sentence of the Wealth of Nations is: 'The greatest improvement in the productive powers of labour, and the greater part of the skill, dexterity, and judgement with which it is any where directed, or applied, seem to have been the effects of the division of labour' (Smith, 1776: 7).

Thus, the management of labour – or human resources – was put centre stage from the start. Of course, Adam Smith recognised that other factors were crucial, most obviously machinery. But, as he pointed out when discussing machinery: 'the invention of which the same division of labour has probably given occasion' (Smith, 1776: 8). Thus, machinery is not a 'given' that can be added to other exogenous variables such as 'labour', from which a predetermined output will derive. On the contrary, the productivity of machinery will itself tend to be enhanced over time, in part caused by the very growth process to which it is contributing. As was pointed out much later, growth is endogenous.

The role and importance of workforce skills has remained central to the economic analysis of labour and to the field of Human Resource Management (HRM).

Clearly this argument should not be pushed too far. The literature and field has developed since 1776. But it is interesting to at least reflect on the degree to which many of the fundamental issues have been long recognised. Thus, it is argued today that the productivity of labour depends on a range of factors, to all of which HRM can contribute either directly or indirectly, and it would certainly be possible to present the current literature as identifying three key areas: first, skills and hence training; secondly, work organisation, to the design of which employees can have an important input; and thirdly the state of technology, where again HRM can play a role through facilitating innovation from employees.

Note that Adam Smith argued that this labour productivity is determined by:

> ...three different circumstances; first to the increase of dexterity in every particular workman; secondly, to the saving of the time which is commonly lost in passing from one species of work to another; and lastly, to the invention of a great number of machines which facilitate and abridge labour, and enable one man to do the work of many. (Smith, 1776: 11)

The parallels should be clear. Now, many of today's HRM scholars would certainly not consider themselves as economists. Some might be surprised to find such clear echoes of themes within today's HRM literature being present in the writings of Adam Smith, generally regarded as the founder of modern economics. But then Adam Smith and the 'classical' economists had a rather different and broader view of the subject than do today's mainstream 'neoclassical' economists. Not much – if any – of the *Wealth of Nations* would be accepted for publication in any of today's leading economics journals.

Perhaps even more central to today's HRM literature is Marx's distinction between the value of labour power on the one hand, and the value created by that labour power on the other. This he saw as the fundamental source of surplus value and hence the economic dynamism of both individual firms and capitalist economies. The money form of the 'value of labour power' was for Marx the wage. The money form of the value created by labour was the price at which the goods and services created by that labour was sold, less the cost of inputs. The key point is that these two sums are not necessarily equivalent.

Indeed, unless the latter is – or can be made to be – greater than the wage, there will be no economic incentive to hire the worker. The determinants of the two quantities are quite distinct, separated not only logically but also by time and place. While there can be attempts to bring the two together, this does not alter the basic conceptual point. With the proviso about payment by results, the wage can be seen as having been largely agreed before the work commences. The quantity of goods and services that this labour produces is the result of quite different factors – which Marx viewed as class struggle at the point of production, but which today might be seen as HRM.

This is not to imply that HRM is necessarily focussed on increasing work intensity (to use a term common to both the current literature and Marx's analysis of the process). Quite the contrary, HRM may consist of 'progressive' practices aimed at creating a 'high commitment work system' that will enhance the motivation of employees and thus make them more innovative and productive. Such an effect may work through all three routes identified by Adam Smith above, with increased training leading to enhanced dexterity, employee involvement leading to improved work organisation, and participation leading to successful innovations being proposed by the workforce. The point is that this will boost labour productivity and thus the quantity of goods and services produced by that labour, and the monetary value at which these will be sold. This may lead to a rise in the wage or it may not. That is a separate question, albeit a related one, since a rise in the wage may play a role in motivating the employees.

INSIDE THE BLACK BOX

So, the importance of the management of labour to national economic performance has long been recognised. For much of the 20th century this took the form of analysing industrial relations and other management practices at a macroeconomic level.

Economists tended to ignore what went on within the 'black box' of the firm, where outputs were a function of the labour and other inputs. This neoclassical analysis tended to forget or eliminate the insights from Adam Smith, Marx and others that actually this is not the case at all – the outputs will depend on the success with which the labour process is designed, organised and managed.

The shift from industrial relations to Human Resource Management from the 1970s onwards reflected what was happening within the leading industrialised economies at the time, where national bargaining was breaking down, trade union coverage was shrinking, and there was a growing recognition that the interesting economic questions were indeed within the 'black box' of the firm that the economics profession had deliberately avoided – indeed, had assumed away.

In the UK, the 1940s and 1950s had witnessed various attempts to learn from American management practices. One outcome of this was the establishment and growth of business schools in the UK, which had long been a feature in the US. In the early 1960s the National Economic Development Office was established by the then Conservative Government, which brought together Government, business and labour at national and industry-sector level to analyse how to improve national economic performance. It was taken for granted that labour-employer co-operation was key to this, over wage bargaining, productivity agreements and so forth. The National Economic Development Office was eventually abolished in the early 1990s.

The Human Resource Management literature has focussed instead on how management practices within the company or workplace can improve organisational outcomes and corporate performance. These will include reducing labour turnover and absenteeism, and enhancing productivity, innovation and ultimately profitability and the share price. In aggregate this contributes to national economic performance.

HRM AND CORPORATE PERFORMANCE

HRM and other related management practices can be seen to have a positive impact, potentially at least, through a number of avenues. These may be self-reinforcing. Indeed, some may be necessary for others to operate.

Firstly, training and other policies can improve the skill levels of the workforce. At an individual company level, skill levels can also be influenced by recruitment and selection policies. But having a skilled workforce may not be sufficient if employees are not prepared to apply those skills to boost productivity. In order to encourage or otherwise extract that application may require an additional set of HRM practices. This may be achieved by closer monitoring and performance management – insisting on the necessary effort being applied on pain of disciplinary action, loss of pay or other benefits, and ultimately dismissal. On the other hand, the desired level of effort might be achieved from employees if they were appropriately motivated and committed to the success of the organisation. Policies to share information and involve the employees might for example have such an effect. These alternative approaches are sometimes behind the different uses of the terms 'high performance work systems' – where the emphasis is on achieving the performance by whatever means – and 'high commitment work systems' where the result is achieved by creating the necessary degree of motivation and commitment from the workforce.

Secondly, then, HRM needs to ensure that there is the necessary degree of commitment and motivation for employees to apply their skills and aptitudes appropriately, or other practices involving monitoring and enforcement may be pursued to the same ends. But again, there is nothing to be gained by upskilling and motivating the workforce if the production line keeps moving along at 40 units an hour. Work organisation is thus an important third element, to allow the skills and motivation to actually make a difference to outcomes and hence to productivity.

This may involve working harder or it may just involve working smarter. Improved job design and work organisation could reduce work intensity and stress while at the same time delivering improved performance.

So thirdly, HRM needs to be aligned with appropriate work organisation. But more than this, HRM practices of participation and involvement may create a more innovative workforce that generates ideas for better job design and work organisation (Ciavarella, 2003).

THE LITERATURE

An excellent brief guide to the Human Resource Management literature is provided by Geare (2001), on which this section draws heavily. Geare argues that 'a useful starting point for a study of Human Resource Management' is the 1987 edition of Schuler's *Personnel and Human Resource Management*, '...as it illustrates how, in the 1980s, the term began to gain domination in the United States over the term "personnel management" – without any real change in substance' (Geare, 2001: 752).

HRM and corporate performance

Any link from HRM to national economic performance has to operate at a corporate level. This is also, of course, the ultimate motivation for companies to invest in HRM – to see a return on that investment. The Holy Grail of the HRM literature is thus in many ways the HRM-performance issue: does the introduction and implementation of human resource management and associated practices improve organisational outcomes (such as reduced absenteeism and labour turnover) and boost corporate performance (via improved productivity leading to increased profits)?

There is a large literature on this fundamental issue. As always in social science, it is extremely difficult to prove any specific causal links or processes, since all the factors tend to be inter-related, with causation running in both directions, and a plethora of outside factors – some of which are unknown and still others unknowable – impacting on the variables in question. Put most simply, when companies that have invested in HRM are found to enjoy higher profits, is it the HRM that has caused the profit levels, or is it the other way round, with higher profits allowing the firm to invest in more expensive HRM practices? Or perhaps both are caused by some third factor, such as enlightened and innovative management?

One route of enquiry can be through the use of time series data, to find out whether the rise in profits was previous or subsequent to the investment in HRM. But, even here, Lord Kaldor warned more than 25 years ago of the danger of inferring causation from historical time in the context of monetarism (Kaldor, 1982). Milton Friedman had argued that inflation was caused by the growth of the money supply, whereas Kaldor and Keynesians generally saw both phenomena as the result of other factors in the 'real' economy, with increased production causing both upward pressure on prices and the money supply. Friedman's answer was that it was the growth in the money supply that rose first, with inflation following only after a lag (Friedman and Schwartz, 1982). Kaldor responded by referring to the high growth in the money supply that is generally observed around the beginning of December, as companies pay wages earlier, sometimes accompanied by annual bonuses, and consumers may spend more than normal. Kaldor argued that just because it was the growth in the money supply that occurred first, in early December, with Christmas not occurring until December 25th, did not mean that the growth in the money supply had caused Christmas. Quite the contrary, in fact.

The HRM-performance relation has therefore been analysed in the academic literature using a combination of quantitative and qualitative methods. Where possible behaviour has been tracked over time. The findings from the literature have generally been that there is indeed a statistically significant correlation between the adoption and implementation of HRM practices on the one hand, and corporate performance on the other, with a causal relation generally being argued to have been identified from the HRM practices to the corporate outcomes. On the US evidence and literature, see for example Appelbaum et al., 2000; Becker and Gerhart, 1996; Becker and Huselid, 1998; Huselid and Becker, 1996; Huselid, 1995; Ichniowski et al., 1994, 1997; Kochan and Osterman, 1994; MacDuffie, 1995; Osterman, 1994, 1999.

On the UK evidence and literature, see for example Guest et al., 2000, 2003; Hoque, 1999; Wood and Albanese, 1995; Wood and de Menezes, 1998; Wood, 1999; Michie and Sheehan, 1999a, 2001.

Strategic human resource management

Linking HRM to organisational strategy has created a large literature on 'strategic human resource management'. An early review of the strategic human resource management literature is provided by Lengnick-Hall and Lengnick-Hall (1988), who also provide their own 'growth readiness' matrix to capture the basic features of their typology for the strategic management of human resources.

Michie and Sheehan (2005) consider the extent to which any HRM-performance link – as for example found in their 2001 study – might be contingent upon the strategy being pursued by the firm. Michie and Sheehan (2005) therefore repeated the analysis conducted and reported in Michie and Sheehan (2001), but this time running the tests separately depending on the corporate strategy being pursued by the firms. The previously reported statistically significant correlation between HRM on the one hand and corporate performance on the other, as detailed in Michie and Sheehan (2001), was found to lose its statistical significance when the tests were repeated, looking only at those firms that were pursuing a cost-cutting strategy. Thus, if the firm was pursuing a cost-cutting strategy, it should not after all expect to find a statistically significant effect from investing in HRM on its subsequent corporate performance, as might have been expected had they been guided by the results from the literature that

failed to distinguish between firms according to the different corporate strategies being pursued. For those firms that were pursuing a quality enhancing or innovative strategy, the previous findings of a statistically significant link between HRM and performance were confirmed.

Liu et al. (2007) draw on data from more than 19,000 organisations, concluding that human resource management adds significant value for organisations, and in line with the above findings, that this value added is strongest when human resource systems are emphasised rather than individual practices, and when human resource management decisions are tied to strategy.

International human resource management

Welch (1994) provides an early review of the then-emerging literature on international human resource management. Welch (1994) examines how four Australian companies managed expatriates with regard to selection, pre-departure training, compensation and repatriation. On selection, no consideration was given to the international aspect. Some pre-departure training took place, but this was said to be as a result of hindsight in some cases rather than forethought.

Today the international context of human resource management clearly impinges to some degree at least on most companies and other organisations wherever in the world they are operating, since at least the more skilled employees will have a choice of employers, including most likely multinational companies, and may also be geographically flexible. Where companies are actually operating across borders, or outsourcing work offshore, the international aspect to HRM become unavoidable. For example, for a multinational company based in an industrialised economy, there is the issue of pay rates abroad, where employees from the home country would not be prepared to work for the wages paid in the developing economy in which the multinational company may be operating. In general this will be dealt with by paying different salaries to 'ex patriots', but this raises HRM issues rather than solves them.

Moore and Jennings (1995) report on the practice of HRM in eleven Pacific Rim countries, namely Australia, Canada, Hong Kong, Japan, New Zealand, China, South Korea, Singapore, Taiwan and Thailand, as well as the US.

THE ISSUES

An important issue that is raised by the literature referred to above, that generally finds a positive relation between HRM and corporate performance, is why HRM practices are not more commonly adopted.

One answer is that suggested by Michie and Sheehan (2005) referred to above, namely that these benefits will not follow automatically, and in particular may be contingent on corporate strategy. Thus, firms that are pursuing a cost-cutting strategy may be well advised to ignore the suggestion that they invest in HRM.

In terms of national economic performance, the implication of this might be that the economy needs to decide on its strategy nationally, and encourage behaviour accordingly. Just as companies can decide what market niche to go for, perhaps nations need to do similarly within the global marketplace. For a country that thinks it can prosper through cost-cutting and beating rivals on price, such strategies should perhaps be encouraged. For those that think they cannot compete on that agenda and need instead to move up the value chain and compete on the basis of higher quality and innovation, then investing in HRM might be consistent with such a choice of strategy. Of course such generalisations can be pushed too far. Even an economy that is very competitive on price will also have some areas of high quality and concomitantly high cost. Likewise a high quality and innovative economy will also have some sectors and firms for whom price will remain the key competitive factor. But broadly, national economies can and do seek to play to their competitive advantages. And the key development from Ricardo to Porter (1980, 1985) is that economies

do not have to rely on endowment-given comparative advantages, but rather can create their own competitive advantages. And in this, investment in HRM may be key. Just as there are varieties of capitalism (Hall and Soskice, 2001), so there are varieties of HRM systems, and these can be explicitly developed and enhanced.

Small and medium sized enterprises

Even for economies such as Europe and the US, where the consensus is clearly that national economic performance depends on competing on the basis of product innovation and high quality goods, the implication that investment in HRM is necessary to underpin a quality enhancing and innovative strategy may not translate easily to the small and medium sized enterprise (SME) sector (on which, see Bacon et al., 1996; Cassell et al., 2002; Chandler and McEvoy, 2000; Deshpande and Golhar, 1994; deKok and Uhlaner, 2001; Duberley and Walley, 1995; Hayton, 2003; Heneman et al., 2000; Hornby and Kuratko, 1990; Marlow, 2002).

In many cases these firms will be too small for some of the HR practices and policies to make much sense. Nevertheless, the broad findings of a positive link between HRM and outcomes has been found empirically (see, for example, Michie and Sheehan, 2008a). And here too the outcomes are contingent on the firm's strategy, even though strategy might have been thought to be another area that would not necessarily apply to the SME sector (see Michie and Sheehan, 2008b).

Objective and subjective data

HRM researchers are fortunate in having several large datasets that can be utilised. In the UK there has been a series of major surveys every five years or so, with the titles evolving over time, starting as the Workplace Industrial Relations Survey (WIRS), then Workplace Employee Relations Survey, and most recently the Workplace Employment Relations Survey (WERS). And in the EU there has been the introduction of some relevant questions into the European 'Community Innovation Surveys'. But to really 'get inside the black box' of the firm requires detailed qualitative work, interviewing the managers and employees concerned. One issue is therefore whether the resulting 'subjective' data can be trusted for drawing unbiased conclusions.

This question was investigated in depth by Wall et al. (2004). This included repeating previous studies but introducing 'objective' data in place of the 'subjective' data that had been used in the original studies. The outcome suggested that the subjective data was just as reliable. However, this should not give rise to complacency. The Wall et al. (2004) study showed that the degree to which this was true – that results were unchanged whether subjective or objective data were used – did depend from study to study. And this was in the context of them being confident that in all the studies looked at proper care had been taken to avoid bias or other problems with the 'subjective' data.

The conclusion is thus twofold. Firstly, properly collected, subjective data can indeed be used to generate statistically significant results in which we can have just as much confidence as we would have had if 'objective data' had been used – for example from audited company accounts. But secondly, in collecting such 'subjective' data it is vital that researchers take care to avoid the various pitfalls that otherwise can lead to bias in such data, which would indeed invalidate any subsequent findings from the analysis of such data.

Innovation

National economic performance will be influenced by the economy's ability to innovate over time. This includes both product innovation, to develop new and more attractive goods and services that will gain market share globally, and process innovation that will allow such goods and services to be produced and supplied more efficiently or effectively. Most governments and other public bodies

acknowledge the importance of fostering innovation.

The implication of much of the HRM literature referred to above would be that investing in HRM, including training but also employee involvement and participation, might enhance the national economy's capacity and dynamic capabilities to innovate and improve both the product offering and work organisation over time. Functional flexibility may play an important role here, enabling employees to adapt to new work organisation and job designs as appropriate.

But, in the hands of politicians, the term 'flexibility' has proved to be a dangerous and little-understood concept. The obvious appeal of flexibility just referred to has led to generalised calls for 'labour flexibility' with inadequate conceptualisation of what is being called for or why, let alone any acknowledgement that the single concept – and policy proposal – may contain mutually contradictory elements. Thus, the sort of flexibility referred to above that might be expected to help facilitate higher levels of innovation and hence boost national economic performance can be termed functional flexibility. Translating the general concept of flexibility into national economic policy terms has led some to push the quite different outcome of numerical flexibility, encouraging a 'hire and fire' mentality. The contrast and contradiction can be seen quite starkly by analysing HRM in practice.

High commitment work systems that attempt to foster improved economic performance through enhanced functional flexibility often explicitly include job security guarantees – the precise opposite of numerical flexibility. The reason is not hard to see. The aim is to encourage employees to suggest ways of making the production process more efficient. Put starkly, this means identifying ways of making their own jobs redundant. In the context of a company that is seeking to improve its performance in order to expand market share, then the more efficient it can be made, the more successful this is likely to be, with more jobs and better paid jobs being created within the company. For the firm, offering a 'no redundancy' assurance in such a process does not constrain their intended actions at all. And if it encourages the process then it represents a costless benefit to the firm.

Trying to entice firms down a high innovation road by encouraging a hire and fire model of flexibility may therefore be at best encouraging them down a cul de sac. Yet this was in part at least the rationale behind the labour market reforms in the UK of the 1980s, designed to 'free up' the labour market, restore 'management's right to manage', and thus foster a dynamic and innovative economy.

Using the UK's 1990 Workplace Industrial Relations Survey (WIRS), Michie and Sheehan (1999b) found that firms that had taken advantage of these labour market reforms tended to be less innovative than those firms that had ignored them. Following up with their own survey of companies, Michie and Sheehan (2003) found the same result. Innovation was fostered by investment in high commitment work systems – which tended to include employment guarantees – rather than the 'low road' conception of labour flexibility as 'hire and fire' numerical flexibility. A similar link between HRM on the one hand and innovation on the other was found by Michie et al. (2004) using data from French firms.

Absorptive capacity

National economic performance will also depend on the strength of the science base and on the ability to transfer knowledge from the science base to commercially successful goods and services. The ability of firms to identify, transfer and take advantage of new knowledge has been referred to as 'absorptive capacity'. There has been some criticism of the 'absorptive capacity' literature for having used this term without really testing or developing it. But the importance of the substantive point remains clear. Equally clear is the important role that HRM can play, not only in underpinning the success of a nation's science base, but, perhaps more importantly, in creating the conditions for

a country's firms to successfully identify the new knowledge that will be relevant to emerging market opportunities, and to transfer that knowledge to the firm and utilise it successfully in the development of new products and services, producing these in the most efficient and effective way, including through the use of innovative new work processes as appropriate. In all this, HRM may play a key enabling role. Firstly, to ensure that the firm's employees have the technical and other competence to identify the relevant new knowledge. Secondly to allow them to make proper and full use of that new knowledge for the firm's product development and work organisation processes.

One of the points of this absorptive capacity literature is that university-corporate links move centre stage. And of course such links should in any case be included in any analysis of the impact of HRM on national economic performance. Because the quality of the employees being taken on by firms will depend in part on the quality of the nation's university education, and on the ability of firms and universities to match the right graduates to the right companies. This is not a simple process. Universities and firms spend considerable resources to try to get this right. It can include not just the University Careers Office and the company attending careers events, but also firms taking on students for project placements, providing guest lecturers to universities, and so on. Firms are sometimes explicit that their motive for participating in such schemes is precisely so they can identify the right graduates to hire. But also to allow the graduates to determine whether the firm is right for the student, since if not it is in everyone's best interest for this to be realised sooner rather than later – and preferably before the hire.

Corporate-university links also include Executive Education courses and Continuing Professional Development, and commissioning research and consultancy from universities, all of which again is relevant to the firm's and the economy's HRM, and to national economic competitiveness. Such activities also enhance the firm's absorptive capacity and thus may boost national economic performance by making more effective the transfer of knowledge from the science base to the corporate sector that can commercialise that new knowledge and translate it into an increased global market share for goods and services produced within that country. And hence to national economic performance.

The links from HRM to national economic performance are thus many and varied. They are generally not simple. But they are certainly important. If they are not clearly understood then not only may firms miss out on potentially profitable opportunities, but national economic policy may inadvertently prove counter-productive, for example by promoting 'management's right to manage badly', by encouraging a hire and fire approach to flexibility when what is needed is enhanced functional flexibility in order to boost innovation.

THE THEORY

The theory as to why HRM might affect national economic performance should be fairly clear. Neoclassical economics suggests that outputs are a function of inputs, so there is no need to look inside the 'black box' of the firm. Within this paradigm one might struggle to find a theoretical basis for HRM. And perhaps this is part of the reason why the HRM community has appeared to be so obsessed with the need for 'theory'. Expectancy theory from psychology fits well enough, suggesting that employees will make greater effort if they expect that to result in a reward. But that is hardly rocket science. Once it is accepted that outputs are not predetermined by a given production function, and that in fact employees can provide discretionary effort, the need for HRM becomes clear – to encourage and make best use of this discretionary effort. Encouragement involves creating a motivated and committed workforce, which can be facilitated through information sharing, involvement and participation. Making best use of such effort will require appropriate job design and work organisation, which again

will benefit from HR policies of consultation, involvement and participation.

This all makes perfect sense looked at through the eyes of a modern-day Adam Smith, who saw employee dexterity and work organisation as key to labour productivity and national economic performance – or to the wealth of nations.

Much of the economic profession has taken a rather wide detour since. But with the growth of economics within management and business schools internationally, the focus has inevitably returned more on the real world. Unrealistic assumptions tend to get shorter shrift than within more mainstream economics departments. The HRM literature has also benefited from industrial sociologists, organisational psychologists and others with an interest in discovering what actually happens within the workplace. This has allowed the analysis of national economic performance to break free from aggregate production functions. Instead it is acknowledged that with given inputs, outputs are not given but will depend on a range of factors, most notably the degree of discretionary effort that employees will make and the innovations that they may propose to both products and processes. HRM can also enhance the economy's science base, and boost companies' absorptive capacity for new ideas to be translated into profitable growth of market shares globally. National economic prosperity will thus continue to depend importantly on the success or otherwise with which HRM and related management practices are adopted and implemented across the economy. This will therefore remain a rich research agenda for the foreseeable future.

THE EVIDENCE

Some of the evidence has been referred to above. However, there is a wealth of additional work, for example demonstrating that HR policies that are consistent with the firm's strategy – strategic human resource management (SHRM) – are more effective than would otherwise be the case (Miles and

Snow, 1984; Schuler and Jackson, 1987; Truss and Gratton, 1994; Delery and Doty, 1996; Khatri, 2000; Guthrie et al., 2002).

A growing body of research has examined the relationships between firms' use of flexible employment contracts and HR practices, on the one hand, and corporate performance on the other (Storey et al., 2002; Kleinknecht, 1998; Kleinknecht et al., 1997; Michie and Sheehan-Quinn, 2001). The sort of labour market deregulation pursued in Britain over the 1980s may risk being detrimental to long-run economic performance by leading to neglect or undervaluing of assets and processes such as training which are vital to long-term development and economic progress (Michie and Wilkinson, 1995; Kitson and Michie, 1996). Research using the British Household Panel Survey 1991–5 that investigated the link between skill acquisition and labour market flexibility (proxied by employment status, contract type, and lack of union coverage) found that workers:

> ...on short-term employment contracts, who are working part-time, or are not covered by a union collective agreement, are significantly less likely to be involved in any work-related training to improve or increase their skills. These findings suggest that there is a trade-off between expanding the more marginal forms of employment, and expanding the proportion of the workforce getting work-related training (Arulampalam and Booth, 1998: 521).

In addition, if the time horizons of firms become shortened, the pursuit of what economists would characterise as 'efficiency gains' may come to dominate other sorts of gains to be had from innovation and technological progress. This becomes problematic if the pursuit of short-term efficiency gains reduces the potential of the system for economic progress (Michie and Prendergast, 1998).

In the UK, a major programme of research was commissioned by the Economic and Social Research Council (ESRC) into the 'Future of Work' at the very end of the last century and the first few years of this. Broadly, the findings were consistent with those reported elsewhere in this chapter (see, for example, Guest et al., 2001, 2003). In particular, this programme of work taken as a whole gave a far more realistic picture of current realities and future scenarios than had gained currency amongst opinion formers sold on popular writers depicting a 'weightless economy' or other variants on the 'end of work' projections that have re-emerged in different guises at various times over the past thirty years or more.

In developing countries the emphasis may have been more on 'human capital enhancement' rather than HRM, but the issues are just as important. Other than the level of industrialisation and economic development, a major difference for these economies has been the different relation that multinational corporations and foreign direct investment play. The issue of foreign direct investment and whether this will enhance human capital in developing economies has certain parallels with the issue of absorptive capacity referred to above. The extent to which benefit is gained from such FDI will depend in part on the nature of that FDI, but it will depend also on the absorptive capacity of the economy in question. HRM can, then, play a positive role here if it enhances the absorptive capacity of companies within the economies that are recipients of that FDI. (See Michie, 2002, where this is argued in detail.)

CONCLUSIONS

Wall and Wood (2005) provide a convincing critique of much of the existing HRM-performance literature. The difficulty of establishing causation within social science lies at the heart of this, with existing studies not having been able to gather sufficient cross-sectional data from enough organisations and enough individuals within each organisation to be able to really establish causality. They therefore argue for a 'big science' approach that would enable this research agenda to be taken forward.

In the meantime, some progress may be made by testing across different countries, sectors and time periods. It is also important to test whether the resulting outcomes are contingent, say, on the size of firms, or on the strategy pursued by the firm. As reported above, existing research suggests that similar results are found for small and medium firms as for large firms. But these results do indeed appear to be contingent on the corporate strategy being pursued. Governments might therefore be able to influence their national economic performance, both by enhancing the quality of human resource management practices adopted and pursued, and by encouraging firms to adopt quality enhancing and innovative strategies that are consistent with and supportive of such HRM strategies.

This chapter has considered the link between HRM and national economic performance in terms of how human resource management practices might enhance that performance in terms of productivity and competitiveness. However, there are other economic outcomes that might be considered to constitute aspects of 'performance' such as the degree of income, wealth and social inequality within a country. It may be that for any given level of national income per head, or measure of relative economic competitiveness, nations may differ in the degree of inequality, and that human resource management practices might influence these outcomes. Thus, for example, human resource management practices include pay and conditions, including for example employee share ownership. The focus of both the academic research and public and corporate policy agenda tends to be on the performance outcomes that such policies might deliver in terms of employee motivation, commitment, work effort and productivity. But another outcome may be a different distribution of income and wealth within a nation with a widespread adoption of such human resource practices, as against a nation where they are not.

Whether, for example, employee share ownership would be expected to impact on employee motivation and organisational outcomes is considered by Michie and Oughton (2003). While such an outcome is clearly the intention of governments that provide

tax incentives for such schemes, the actual impact on corporate performance is likely to depend on a number of intermediary factors. However, governments may also be aware of the possible impact that such policies might have on the distribution of income and wealth. To the extent that such policies reduce this – or in today's context, perhaps more relevant would be if they limited the increase in inequality that might otherwise have occurred – then this might be seen as a desirable policy outcome in its own right. This could be on social and welfare grounds alone. But note that increased inequality is likely to involve various social and economic costs, and conversely such inequality will certainly be costly for governments to try to tackle after the event. So there would still be a link with economic performance. Finally, increased social inequality might militate against the sort of high commitment work systems that involve high levels of skills, participation and co-operation. Thus, such inequality may undermine the sort of HRM agenda necessary for a knowledge intensive economy seeking to compete on the basis of innovation and quality enhancement.

In addition to the effects that HRM may have on national economic performance by directly impacting on corporate performance, there may be a further effect through influencing the degree and success of co-operation that occurs between companies in the economy. There is evidence that firms that co-operate are more likely to innovate (Kitson et al., 2003). The ability of a firm to successfully co-operate may be dependent on the human resource management practices and processes within that company. Thus, a company that pursues successful human resource policies of participation and involvement is likely to have a workforce better able and more capable of co-operating with others and of gaining from such co-operation. There are clear parallels here with the discussion above regarding absorptive capacity, which again is likely to be enhanced by such policies and outcomes. There are also links to the above discussion of flexibility – a functionally flexible workforce is likely to be better placed to co-operate with another company or organisation. Thus, HRM policies that enhance functional flexibility may impact beneficially on national economic performance through three different routes. Firstly, via boosting the productivity of the firm directly, as the employee is able to move more quickly and effectively onto a new task than would otherwise be the case. Secondly, by enhancing the absorptive capacity of the firm, increasing the likelihood that new knowledge can be profitably utilised by the firm to deliver new products or services, quite probably via new processes. And thirdly, by facilitating productive co-operation between companies, which is likely to boost the innovative performance of the national economy over time.

REFERENCES

Appelbaum, E., Bailey, T., Berg, P. and Kalleberg, A.L. (2000) *Manufacturing Advantage: Why High-Performance Work Systems Pay Off.* Ithaca, NY: Cornell University Press.

Arulampalam, W. and Booth, A. (1998) 'Training and labour market flexibility: Is there a trade-off?', *British Journal of Industrial Relations*, 36 (1): 521–36.

Bacon, N., Ackers, P., Storey, J. and Coates, D. (1996) 'It's a small world: managing human resource management in small businesses', *International Journal of Human Resource Management*, 1 (1): 82–98.

Becker, B. and Gerhart, D (1996) 'The impact of human resource management on organizational performance: progress and prospects', *Academy of Management Journal*, 39 (4): 779–801.

Becker, B.E. and Huselid, M.A. (1998) 'High performance work systems and firm performance: A synthesis of research and managerial implications', in G.R. Feffis (ed.), *Research in Personnel and Human Resources*, Vol. 16. Stanford, CT: JAI Press, pp. 53–101.

Cassell, C., Nadin, S., Gray, M. and Clegg, C. (2002) 'Exploring human resource management practices in small and medium sized enterprises', *Personnel Review*, 31 (5/6): 671–92.

Chandler, G.N. and McEvoy, G.M. (2000) 'Human resource management, TQM, and firm performance in small and medium-size enterprises', *Entrepreneurship: Theory and Practice*, 25 (1): 43–57.

Ciavarella, M. (2003) 'The adoption of high-involvement practices and processes in emergent developing firms: A descriptive and prescriptive approach', *Human Resource Management*, 42 (4): 337–56.

Delery, J. and Doty, D.H. (1996) 'Models of theorizing in strategic human resource management: Tests of universalistic, contingency, and configurational performance predictions', *Academy of Management Journal*, 39 (4): 802–35.

Deshpande, S.P. and D.Y. Golhar (1994) 'HRM practices in large and small manufacturing firms: A comparative study', *Journal of Small Business Management*, 32 (2): 49–56.

deKok, J. and L.M. Uhlaner (2001) 'Organization context and human resource management in the small firms', *Small Business Economics*, 17 (4): 273–91.

Duberley, J.P. and Walley, P. (1995) 'Assessing the adoption of HRM by small and medium-sized manufacturing organizations', *International Journal of Human Resource Management*, 4 (4): 891–909.

Friedman, M. and Schwartz, A.J. (1982) *Monetary Trends in the United States and the United Kingdom: Their Relation to Income, Prices, and Interest Rates, 1867–1975*, National Bureau of Economic Research, Chicago: The University of Chicago Press.

Geare, Alan James (2001) 'Human resource management', in J. Michie (ed.), *Reader's Guide to the Social Sciences.* London and Chicago: Fitzroy Dearborn and Routledge, pp. 752–3.

Guest, D., Michie, J., Sheehan, M. and Conway, N. (2000) *Employee Relations, HRM and Business Performance: An Analysis of the 1998 Workplace Employee Relations Survey*, London: Chartered Institute of Personnel and Development.

Guest, D., King, Z., Conway, N., Michie, J. and Sheehan-Quinn, M. (2001) *Voices from the Boardroom.* London: Chartered Institute of Personnel and Development.

Guest, D. Michie, J., Conway, N. and Sheehan, M. (2003) 'A study of human resource management and corporate performance in the UK', *British Journal of Industrial Relations*, 41 (2): 291–314.

Guthrie, J., Spell, C. and Nyamori, O. (2002) 'Correlated and consequences of high involvement work practice: The role of competitive strategy', *International Journal of Human Resource Management*, 13 (1): 183–97.

Hall, P.A. and Soskice, D.W. (2001) *Varieties of Capitalism*, Oxford: Oxford University Press.

Hayton, J. (2003) 'Strategic human capital management in SMEs: Am empirical study of entrepreneurial performance', *Human Resource Management*, 42 (2): 375–91.

Heneman, R.L., Tansky, J.W. and Camp, S.M. (2000) 'Human resource management practices in small and medium-sized enterprises: Unanswered questions and future research perspectives', *Entrepreneurship: Theory and Practice*, 25 (1): 11–26.

Hoque, K. (1999) 'Human resource management and performance in the UK hotel industry', *British Journal of Industrial Relations*, 37 (3): 419–43.

Hornby, J.S. and Kuratko, D.F. (1990) 'Human resource management in small business: Critical issues for the 1990s', *Journal of Small Business Management*, 28 (2): 9–18.

Huselid, M. (1995) 'The impact of human resource management on turnover, productivity and corporate financial performance', *Academy of Management Journal*, 38 (3): 635–72.

Huselid, M. and Becker, B. (1996) 'Methodological issues in cross-sectional and panel estimates of the human resource-firm performance link', *Industrial Relations*, 35 (3): 400–22.

Ichniowski, C., Shaw, K. and Prennushi, G. (1997) 'The effects of human resource management on productivity: a study of steel finishing line', *American Economic Review*, 87 (3): 291–313.

Ichniowski, C., Shaw, K. and Prennushi, G. (1994) *The Effects of Human Resource Management Practices on Productivity*. New York: Columbia University Press.

Kaldor, N. (1982) *The Scourge of Monetarism*, Oxford: Oxford University Press.

Khatri, N. (2000) 'Managing human resource for competitive advantage: A study of companies in singapore', *International Journal of Human Resource Management*, 11 (2): 336–65.

Kitson, M. and Michie, J. (1996) 'Britain's industrial performance since 1960: Underinvestment and relative decline', *The Economic Journal*, 106 (434): 196–212.

Kitson, M., Michie, J. and Sheehan, M. (2003) 'Markets, competition, cooperation and innovation', in D. Coffey and C. Thornley (eds), *Industrial and Labour Market Policy and Performance*. London: Routledge, Chapter 3, pp. 29–44

Kleinknecht, A. (1998) 'Is labour market flexibility harmful to innovation?', *Cambridge Journal of Economics*, 22(3): 387–96.

Kleinknecht, A., Oostendorp, R. and Pradhan, M. (1997) 'Flexible labour, firm growth and employment: An exploration of micro data in the Netherlands', mimeo, 2 December.

Kochan, T. and Osterman, P. (1994) *Mutual Gains*. Bostson, MA: Harvard Business School.

Liu, Y., Combs, J.G., Ketchen, D.J. and Duane Ireland, R. (2007) 'The value of human resource management for organisational performance', *Business Horizons*, 50 (6): 503–11.

Llengnick-Hall, Cynthia A. and Lengnick-Hall, Mark L. (1988) 'Strategic human resources management: A review of the literature and a proposed typology', *Academy of Management Review*, 13 (3): 454–70

MacDuffie, J. (1995) 'Human resource bundles and manufacturing performance: Organizational logic and flexible production systems in the world auto industry', *Industrial and Labour Relations Review*, 48 (2): 197–221.

Marlow, S. (2002) 'Regulating labour management in smaller firms', *Human Resource Management Journal*, 12 (3): 5–25.

Michie, J. (2002) 'Foreign direct investment and human capital enhancement in developing countries', *Competition and Change*, 6 (4): 363–72.

Michie, J., Lorenz, E. and Wilkinson, F. (2004) 'HRM complementarities and innovative performance in French and British industry', in J. Christensen and B.-Å. Lundvall (eds), *Product Innovation, Interactive Learning and Economic Performance*. London: Elsevier, pp. 181–210.

Michie, J. and Prendergast, R. (1998) 'Government intervention in a dynamic economy', *New Political Economy*, 3 (3): 391–406.

Michie, J. and Oughton, C. (2003) 'HRM, employee share ownership and corporate performance', *Research and Practice in HRM*, 11 (1): 15–36.

Michie, J. and Sheehan, M. (1999a) 'HRM practices, R&D expenditure and innovative investment: Evidence from the UK's 1990 Workplace Industrial Relations Survey (WIRS)', *Industrial and Corporate Change*, 8 (2): 211–33.

Michie, J. and Sheehan, M. (1999b) 'No innovation without representation? An analysis of participation, representation, R&D and innovation', *Economic Analysis*, 2 (2): 85–97.

Michie J. and Sheehan, M (2003) 'Labour market deregulation, flexibility and innovation', *Cambridge Journal of Economics*, 27 (1): 123–43.

Michie, J. and Sheehan, M. (2005) 'Business strategy, human resources, labour market flexibility and competitive advantage', *International Journal of Human Resource Management*, 15 (3): 445–64.

Michie, J. and Sheehan, M. (2008a) Human resource management and corporate performance: evidence from UK and US small firms, in R. Bassett and S. Mayson (eds), *International Handbook of Entrepreneurship and HRM*, Edward Elgar.

Michie, J. and Sheehan, M. (2008b) Business strategy and corporate performance in small firms, in C. van Beers, A. Kleinknecht, R. Ortt and R. Verburg (eds), *Innovation Systems and Firm Performance*, Palgrave Macmillan.

Michie, J. and Sheehan-Quinn, M. (2001) 'Labour market flexibility, human resource management and corporate performance', *British Journal of Management*, 12 (4): 287–306.

Michie, J. and Wilkinson, F. (1995) 'Wages, government policy and unemployment', *Review of Political Economy*, 7 (2): 133–49.

Miles, R. and Snow, C. (1984) 'Designing strategic human resource systems', *Organizational Dynamics*, 13 (1): 35–52.

Moore, Larry F. and Devereaux Jennings, P. (eds) (1995) *Human Resource Management on the Pacific Rim*, Berlin and New York: de Gruyter.

Osterman, P. (1994) 'How common is workplace transformation and who adopts it?', *Industrial and Labor Relations Review*, 47: 173–88.

Osterman, P. (1999) *Securing Prosperity*. Princeton: Princeton University Press.

Porter, M. (1980) *Competitive Strategy: Techniques for Analysing Industries and Competitors*. New York: The Free Press.

Porter, M. (1985) *Competitive Advantage: Creating and Sustaining Superior Performance*. New York: Free Press.

Ricardo, David (1817) *On the Principles of Political Economy and Taxation*. London: John Murray.

Schuler, Randall S. (1987) *Personnel and Human Resource Management*, 3rd edition. St Paul: West Publishing.

Schuler, R. and Jackson, S. (1987) 'Linking competitive strategies with human resource management practices', *Academy of Management Executive*, 1 (3): 207–19.

Smith, Adam (1776) *An Inquiry into the Nature and Causes of the Wealth of Nations*, The University of Chicago Press (1976).

Storey, D.J. and Westhead, P. (1997) Managing training in small firms – a case of market failure?, *Human Resource Management Journal*, 7 (2): 61–71.

Storey, J., Quintas, P., Taylor, P. and Fowle, W. (2002) 'Flexible employment contracts and their implications for product and process innovation', *International Journal of Human Resource Management*, 13(1): 1–18

Truss, C. and Gratton, L. (1994) 'Strategic human resource management: A conceptual approach', *International Journal of Human Resource Management*, 5 (3): 663–86.

Wall, T.D., Michie, J., Patterson, M., Wood, S.J., Sheehan, M., Clegg, C.W. and West M.A. (2004) 'On the validity of subjective measures of company financial performance', *Personnel Psychology*, 57: 95–118.

Wall, T.D. and Wood, S.J. (2005) 'The romance of HRM and business performance, and the case for big science', *Human Relations*, April.

Welch, Denice (1994) 'Determinants of international human resource management approaches and activities: A suggested framework', *Journal of Management Studies*, 31(2): 139–64.

Wood, S. (1999) 'Getting the measure of the transformed high-performance organization', *British Journal of Industrial Relations*, 37 (3): 4391–417.

Wood, S. and Albanese, M. (1995) 'Can we speak of high commitment management on the shop floor?', *Journal of Management Studies*, 32: 215–47.

Wood, S. and de Menezes, L. (1998) 'High commitment management in the UK: Evidence from the workplace industrial relations survey, and employers' manpower and skills practices survey', *Human Relations*, 51: 485–515.

25

Human Resource Management and the Resource Based View

Paul Boselie and Jaap Paauwe

INTRODUCTION

According to Delery and Shaw (2001), there is general agreement that (1) human capital can be a source of competitive advantage, (2) that HR practices have the most direct influence on the human capital of a firm, and (3) that the complex nature of HR systems of practice can enhance the inimitability of the system. This view is supported by recent books on strategic HRM (Boxall and Purcell, 2008; Paauwe, 2004). Human resources belong to a firm's most valuable assets. Since the late 1990s there is a growing body of literature focusing on creating (sustained) competitive advantage for organizations through the development of core competences, tacit knowledge and dynamic capabilities (Paauwe, 2004). Reflecting on the past decade we conclude that the resource-based view (RBV) (Barney, 1991) has become one of the dominant theories in the debate on strategic HRM and on how human resources

and related HR practices can have an effect on firm performance. In fact, RBV was found in 30 per cent of the empirical studies on HRM and performance between 1994 and 2003, ranked in third place after strategic contingency approaches and Abilities-Motivation-Opportunity theory (AMO theory), present in 41 and 40 per cent of studies, respectively (Boselie et al., 2005). However, RBV is often merely named[1] in HR research and not really tested or applied with the exception of a few articles (Wright and Barney, 1998; Boxall and Steeneveld, 1999). In this chapter we will give an overview of the RBV and its impact on human resource management.

This chapter aims to extend the 'classic' RBV approach in HRM with new institutionalism (DiMaggio and Powell, 1983) on context and with strategic balance approaches (Oliver, 1997; Deephouse, 1999; Paauwe, 2004). Our main reason for doing this is that in this way we correct the RBV for an overly narrow focus on the importance of internal resources. New institutionalism and the balanced approaches provide insights in the search for unique (balanced) combinations of strategy, practices, structures and systems, taking into account both the different external environments (market and institutional mechanisms) and the internal resources, capabilities and administrative heritage of an organization.

The chapter starts with an overview of general RBV theory (section 2). Next, we take a closer look at RBV in HR research itself using illustrations of empirical studies that apply RBV or at least claim to apply RBV (section 3). In section 4, we summarize the general critiques of the RBV, for example whether the RBV is tautological, difficulties in measuring and testing RBV, the static nature of RBV, and the over emphasis on the internal organizational environment. This motivates us to search for alternative approaches and new institutionalism and the strategic balance theory are considered (section 5). Finally, in section 6, we discuss the value of these alternative approaches on RBV in future HR research, including the implications for methods and techniques.

RBV THEORY

Resource-based theory led to a change in strategic management thinking from an 'outside-in' approach – with an emphasis on external, industry-based competitive issues (Porter, 1980) – to an 'inside-out' approach (Baden-Fuller and Stopford, 1994), in which internal resources constitute the starting point for understanding organizational success (Paauwe and Boselie, 2003). The shift from external oriented Porter-like frameworks towards the internal oriented resource-based view is reflected in the following statement by Wright and McMahan (1992):

> This RBV of competitive advantage differs from the traditional strategy paradigm in that the emphasis of the resource-based view of competitive advantage is on the link between strategy and internal resources of the firm. The RBV is firm-focused whereas the traditional strategic analysis

paradigm has had an industry-environment focus (Wright and McMahan, 1992).

The RBV roots go back to the book of Penrose (1959). She was one of the first to acknowledge the value and quality of human resources in terms of (unique) knowledge and experience. According to Boxall and Purcell (2003: 72) her analysis 'proceeded from what has become a fundamental premise in the theory of business strategy: firms are heterogeneous.' Even in a situation of perfect competition there are fundamental differences between organizations operating in the same business environment. It took 25 years before Penrose's (1959) ideas were picked up in strategic management by Wernerfelt (1984). In essence RBV also offers a critique of the dominant models of the 1980s, in particular the model of Porter (1980, 1985). Boxall (1996), for example, argues that Porter-like approaches make fairly (implicit) heroic assumptions about the cleverness of the leadership team and their ability to make efficient and effective choices, the convenience of actual HR interventions such as hiring and training a capable workforce, and the relative naïveté of cultural changes within an organization. Porter's framework of industry analysis and resulting competitive strategies focuses on the relevance of the external environment, which we also encounter in the early strategic HR models (e.g. Beer et al., 1984). The outside-in approaches (Porter, 1980) put a lot of emphasis on the external analysis in terms of opportunities and threats, while the inside-out RBV approach (Barney, 1991) focuses on the internal analysis and the strengths and weaknesses of organizations. This shift in strategic management has had major implications on the field of HRM.

Barney (1991) argues that sustained competitive advantage is determined by resources that are valuable, rare, inimitable, and non-substitutable. Boxall and Purcell (2003: 75) call these four conditions 'the qualities of desirable resources.' Resources which can be distinguished in financial resources in terms of equity, debt and retained earnings, physical resources like machines and factories, human resources in terms of experience, intelligence and wisdom associated with the firm, and organizational resources such as teamwork, trust, systems, organizational design, management information systems and budgeting techniques. Firm resources can be imperfectly imitable for one or a combination of three reasons (Dierickx and Cool, 1989): the ability of a firm to obtain a resource is dependent on unique historical conditions (path dependency), the link between the resources possessed by a firm and a firm's sustained competitive advantage is causally ambiguous (causal ambiguity), and the resources generating a firm's advantage is socially complex (social complexity). Path dependency captures the idea that valuable resources are developed over time and the fact that their competitive success does not simply come from making choices in the present but have their origin and starting point in a chain of events, incidents and choices in the past (Barney, 1991). This chain of events and managerial choices over time, in combination with the complexity of social interactions of actors involved, form the basis of the second barrier to imitation according to RBV: social complexity. Unique networks of internal and external connections are natural barriers for imitation by rivals (Boxall and Purcell, 2003: 77). The third type of barrier

in RBV is causal ambiguity; it is difficult for people who have not been involved in the decision making process to assess the specific cause/effect relationships in organizations.

RBV IN HR RESEARCH

Authors such as Paauwe (1994), Wright et al. (1994), Boxall (1996), Kamoche (1996), Delery and Shaw (2001), Wright et al. (2001) and Boxall and Purcell (2008) have specifically applied this theory to the field of HRM, positing that it is people who encompass the properties of value (they contribute to firm efficiency or effectiveness), rarity (they are not widely available, at least not in the kind of quality organizations prefer), inimitability (they cannot easily be replicated by competitors), and non-substitutability (other resources cannot fulfill the same function) which, according to Barney (1991), are the necessary conditions for organizational success. Reasoning from an HR perspective, the condition of 'not easy to imitate' is one of the most important.

According to Delery and Shaw (2001), the resource-based view offers the researcher several advantages in investigating the strategic nature of HRM. The RBV focuses on competitive advantage from the perspective of inimitable (human) resources that are

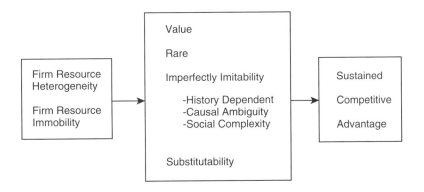

Figure 25.1   The relationship between resource heterogeneity and immobility, value, rareness, imperfect imitability, and substitutability, and sustained competitive advantage.
Source: Figure Two. Page 112. Barney, J. (1991) Firm resources and sustained competitive advantage. *Journal of Management.*17(1): 99–120.

less visible or transparent, in contrast with, for example, technological and physical resources. And the RBV emphasizes the complexity of organizational systems in determining competitive advantage, related to the bundles and systems approach to HRM research. Furthermore, the RBV is concerned with sustained competitive advantage or profitability at firm level, whereas other theoretical frameworks focus on behavioral outcomes (e.g. the behavioral perspective) or internal efficiency issues (e.g. transaction cost and agency theories). Finally, the RBV's breadth can be applied to a variety of research issues.

To illustrate the application of RBV in HR research we selected ten empirical studies, starting with an article by Huselid (1995). These ten HR studies were published in international academic journals such as the *Academy of Management Journal, Human Resource Management* (USA), the *Human Resource Management Journal* (UK), the *Journal of Management*, the *Journal of Management Studies, Organization Studies* and the *Strategic Management Journal* in the period 1995–2003. These publications stem from multiple countries all over the world, including data from Korea, New Zealand, the Netherlands, Spain, the United Kingdom and the USA, representing a diversity of researchers in the HR field. We argue that these studies are a good representation of the RBV application in HR research over the last decade, reflecting about 25 per cent of all empirical studies on HRM and performance in the period 1994–2003, as studied by Boselie et al. (2005).

Huselid (1995) looks at the impact of HR systems on employee turnover, productivity, Tobin's q and GRATE[2] within 968 US firms using survey data from HR managers. This is an excellent study and one of the first to empirically test the added value of HRM. The article is highly cited, although often criticized on methods and techniques as well (see, for example, Gerhart, 2005 on systems approaches). Huselid (1995: 637) refers to Barney's (1991) RBV, stating that 'human resources can be a source of sustained competitive advantage.' Next he explains how the four RBV criteria – resources need to be valuable, rare, inimitable, and non-substitutable – can be applied to HRM and the HR-performance link in particular. He then uses the high performance work systems thesis, advocated by Bailey (1993) and nowadays known as the AMO theory, to suggest that certain HRM practices increase employees' discretionary effort and that this type of behavior will lead to superior firm performance. Huselid (1995) shows significant statistical relationships between HRM and outcome variables. However, the author does not fully explain how the added value by HRM will contribute to sustained competitive advantage of an organization. In other words, some HR practices or bundles of practices can increase performance, but this does not automatically result in superior firm performance or long term competitive advantage.

The second article we would like to discuss is the one by Koch and McGrath (1996). Their study focuses on the impact of HR policies on labor productivity in 319 US business units. The business units in their study were defined as a subunit of a company having 10 percent or more of total sales and assets of the organization. Koch and McGrath (1996: 342) argue that 'using business units as the unit of analysis allows for more exact classification by industry, given the high degree of diversification among US companies.' The data were collected using surveys filled in by HR executives of these business units in multiple industries. The authors explicitly build on RBV theory suggesting 'that a central objective of the human resource function of a firm is to enhance the firm's competitive position by creating superior "human capital" resources, in parallel with the product/market strategy the firm pursues at any given time' (Koch and McGrath, 1996: 336). The authors blend the RBV theory with the human capital perspective, something picked up later by several other researchers (e.g. Wright et al., 2001). According to Koch and McGrath (1996) HR investments are the key to superior firm performance reflected in other outcome variables like labor productivity. More specifically the authors study the link between what they call a system of HR sophistication and productivity. Overall HR sophistication includes (1) investments in HR planning, (2) investments in hiring, and (3) investments in employee development. Again, positive relationships between HRM and performance are found in this study.

The third article is by Barney and Wright (1998) building on Barney's (1991) original piece and translating it to the HR field. Barney and Wright (1998) present the VRIO framework[3] based on prior literature (Barney, 1997), consultancy activities of both authors and input from participants in executive training. The VRIO framework presents a hierarchical model asking four basic questions (Barney, 1997, Table 5.2: 163):

1. Is a resource valuable?
2. Is a resource rare?
3. Is a resource difficult to imitate?
4. Is a resource supported by the organization?

The strength of this model is the hierarchical element in it. If a resource is not valuable there is competitive disadvantage and firm performance is below normal. And if a resource is valuable the VRIO framework directs the user to go to the question whether that resource is rare. If the resource is not rare there is competitive parity and firm performance is normal. If that resource is rare the next question on whether the resource is difficult to imitate becomes relevant. If that resource is not difficult to imitate there is temporary competitive advantage and firm performance is above normal. If the resource is difficult the fourth question on whether that resource is supported by the organization becomes relevant in the framework. If the resource is supported by the organization (for example through culture management or specific work design and systems) there is sustained competitive advantage and firm performance is above normal. The VRIO framework helps us to understand that there are several routes towards organizational survival. Some organizations simply survive

on the second or third level, creating normal or above normal performance, doing some things right, while probably only few organizations achieve the highest level of creating superior performance through HRM (Mirvis, 1997). Most of the existing empirical studies do not make a distinction between normal, above normal and superior performance, although RBV is mainly focused on the highest level.

Boxall and Steeneveld (1999) were one of the first to focus research on industry-based, longitudinal investigations into the relationship between human resource strategy and competitive advantage using data from engineering consultancies in New Zealand. Peter Boxall was one of the first non-US scholars to apply RBV in the HR field (see Boxall, 1996). Other early non-US scholars that focused on RBV in HRM are Kamoche (1996), Mueller (1996) and Paauwe (1994). Boxall and Steeneveld (1999) provide an extensive overview of RBV literature and its implications for HRM. Their study is unique for three reasons. First, the authors used a longitudinal design creating opportunities for analyzing causal relationships. Second, the study is focused on one single industry paying extra attention to the specific context of that sector and therefore controlling for a substantial number of environmental factors that are difficult to control for in a multiple industry research design. Third, Boxall and Steeneveld (1999: 448) apply a case study method presenting 'the opportunity to uncover competing versions of organizational reality, and allowance to explore the historical context, all within a rich vein of contextual data,' as suggested by Pettigrew (1990). The authors argue that longitudinal case study research can identify the RBV's key elements of 'causal ambiguity,' 'path dependency' and 'social complexity' in relationship to unique HRM patterns in organizations, in contrast to 'the statistical study of large populations' (Boxall and Steeneveld, 1999: 449). The results in this study suggest that industry leadership can be achieved through superior HRM, although there was insufficient evidence to conclude that any of the consultancy firms in this study had established that position.

Bae and Lawler (2000) examine the effects of organizational and HRM strategies on firm performance in South Korea. Survey data from 138 firms were used for analysis. An important RBV argument in this study builds on the notion that an organization with management that strongly values HRM and people as a source of competitive advantage is more likely to use high-involvement HRM strategies. In other words, Bae and Lawler (2000) focus on whether management perceives the potential value of employees in an organization. Their high-involvement HRM construct consists of extensive training, empowerment, highly selective staffing, performance-based pay, and broad job design. Strong support is found for the positive link between values of HRM/people and the use of high-involvement HRM, suggesting management's view on HRM and people matter. There is also support for the added value of HRM reflected in significant relationships between high-involvement HRM and firm performance.

Doorewaard and Meihuizen (2000) apply the RBV to study the added value of human resource management to the performance of professional service organizations in the Netherlands using a qualitative research strategy. The authors themselves claim to build on Boxall and Steeneveld's (1999) approach discussed above. Doorewaard and Meihuizen (2000) make use of 64 interviews conducted with consultants from different firms. Key elements in their approach include the notion of organizational context, sector specific performance outcomes that may indicate superior performance for that specific population of firms, high involvement HR practices (for example selective recruitment and selection), work design (hierarchical layers, staff/line relations, job design and information technology), and organizational culture (processes of meaning formulation, changing sets of values). The Doorewaard and Meihuizen (2000) approach presents a rich model incorporating key RBV elements and the potential to study critical success factors. However, their model is rather complicated because of the inclusion of so many

different variables. The diagnostic framework presented can be used to get a better understanding of how HRM is embedded in the organizational context and how the nature of this embeddedness (the alignment between HRM and the organization) can contribute to superior performance. One of their key findings in their search for drivers of organizational success is the concept of the organization's strategic options. These strategic options (or strategic choices) are steering devices for HRM. In other words, given a rather homogeneous organizational environment in a certain population of firms there is still room for strategic choice for each of the members of that population.

Hutchinson et al. (2000) present research on high commitment management in the British RAC call centre making explicit use of the RBV stating that '… the weakness of survey data is that it is difficult to capture the essential processes that occur in the micro-politics of the organization to explain why things happen, the order in which they occur and the complex interplay of action and reaction' (Hutchinson et al., 2000: 63). The authors stress the importance of the concept of *idiosyncratic contingency*, reflecting the notion that successful firms develop an approach which is linked and integrated to their own circumstances. The researchers applied a longitudinal case study method focused on a single organization. The case study involved twenty interviews in 1997 and two focus group meetings six months later, including both line mangers and HR managers. 18 months after the start of the project another research meeting was organized to study further developments and the impact of prior HR interventions. The HR interventions were all part of a larger organizational change program, including team working and new team manager roles, new compensation and performance related pay, new recruitment and selection techniques, training and development, communication, and employee involvement in quality improvements. The performance outcomes at the RAC, including number of calls, abandoned call rate, labor turnover, absenteeism, customer satisfaction and employee satisfaction, all improved between 1997 and 1998 at the time of the research, suggesting that the changes in the HRM might have had positive effects on firm performance. However, caution is required because of the nature of the research method (a case study technique applied to one single organization). The richness of this analysis is in the longitudinal approach using organization specific in-depth information from the interviews and focus group meetings. The approach offers opportunities to unwrap and understand the so-called *emerging patterns of action* in HRM in an organization (Purcell, 1999). These patterns are emphasized in the RBV through the notion of 'path dependency.' Their findings suggest that managing successful change is much more than copying best practices in HRM. Instead, long term success depends more on company specific high performance work processes, because so-called best HR-practices are essentially easily copied.

Way (2002) studies high performance work systems within the US small business sector using data from 446 firms that employ at least 20 but fewer than 100 employees. The author builds on the notion that human resources can be a source of sustained competitive advantage, according to the RBV (Barney, 1991). Way (2002) acknowledges the relevance of the external environmental factors that impact a firm in the process of determining if human resources meet the RBV criteria of value, rareness, inimitability, and non-substitutability. HRM practices that contribute to superior firm performance are defined in this study according to the high performance work systems (HPWS) thesis, including the following practices: staffing (selective), compensation, flexible job assignments, teamwork, training and communication (Way, 2002: 767). The author finds support for the negative impact of HPWS on employee turnover. Way's (2002) research is interesting and valuable to the HR field because of its focus on small firms, an area often forgotten in HR research that tends to focus on large multinational – mainly Fortune 500 – companies (Keegan and Boselie, 2006).

De La Cruz-Deniz and De Saa-Perez (2003) apply a resource-based view using data from the Spanish savings bank sector. The authors argue that HRM based on a set of social responsibility principles will encourage employees' collaboration, this way creating unique competitive advantage. Blending the institutional component of social responsibility in order to respond to their employees' interests with high-commitment HRM is thought to enable unique combinations that create excellent performance. Wood (1999) and Paauwe (2004) label this phenomenon: Environmental fit (the alignment of HRM and the external institutional context). The data were collected from 30 firms using questionnaires. They find some support for the hypothesis that companies establishing a corporate responsiveness toward employees will have greater profitability. These companies adopted some form of high-commitment HR practices that allow the creation and development of their human capital base. From a RBV perspective this study is interesting and relevant because of its implicit notion of the environmental fit and the possibility of unique combinations of HR practices and environmental factors.

Finally, Marchington et al. (2003) explored HRM in the British road haulage industry applying the RBV and drawing on longitudinal data from seven small firms. The authors make use of a modified version of the resource based view, acknowledging that a minimum set of HR practices ('table stakes') is necessary for the continued survival of firms within an industry (continued viability in an industry) and the potential of HR investments that create industry leadership. The authors also emphasize the distinction between *human capital advantage* (the value of the human capital pool in an organization at a certain point in time, for example embedded in exceptional human talent) and *organizational process advantage* ('causally ambiguous, social complex, historically evolved processes – such as learning and cooperation – that emerge and are difficult to imitate,' Marchington et al., 2003: 9). This distinction was originally pinpointed by Boxall (1996, 1998).

Marchington et al. (2003) argue that case studies probably offer the best way forward to study how HRM contributes to viability ('table stakes'), competitive advantage (for example through human capital advantage) and sustained competitive advantage (industry leadership through organizational process advantage). Recruitment of road haulage drivers and their retention are the two main HR issues for this type of organization at the time of the research, and were therefore investigated in detail. Their empirical research is based on interviews with owner-managers, the managers or directors responsible for the recruitment of staff and drivers in the first phase of the study (1998) and on repeat discussions in the second phase of the study (2000). The researchers consider the longitudinal method to be essential for exploring path dependency in HR interventions and outcomes. The findings suggest that the nature of the road haulage industry being a high labor-turnover industry with serious labor shortages (available drivers) make drivers valuable and rare according to RBV standards. Next Marchington et al. (2003) argue that value and rareness are easily demonstrated. In principle all drivers are substitutable if they have the appropriate licenses and diplomas. However, to be different from competitors in terms of imitability the results show that the road haulage firms in the sample use different approaches, including providing good working conditions, quality vehicles, employment security, some training, a friendly atmosphere and good relationships between management and staff. Networking in both product and labor markets, strengthened by good leadership and longstanding commercial connections, create unique reputations and positions of the firms towards potential and current employees. These networks, in combination with the corporate image of an organization, are difficult to imitate by competitors or newcomers and therefore a source for sustained competitive advantage according to the RBV.

Overall, these empirical studies share some common limitations. First, five out of ten of the studies presented here are cross-sectional reflecting one point in time. This causes serious problems with respect to potential causality between the independent and dependent variables. Second, some of the studies, including Huselid (1995) and Koch and McGrath (1996), use research units from multiple industries. The focus on multiple industries does not fully take into account the fundamental differences in environmental settings between branches of industry. These differences can be the results of trade union influence, employers' associations, labor legislation, collective bargaining agreements, the nature of the business (for example services versus manufacturing) and professional bodies linked to different sectors. In technical terms we argue that most authors do not fully take into account the RBV's notion of firm heterogeneity linked to the external environment of the organization (like to the branch of industry) and the unique administrative heritage of each organization. Third, the survey based studies mostly use single source data (one respondent per organization) and these respondents are often HR professionals. The research by Gerhart et al. (2000) shows the backside of single source research in HRM and suggests a minimum of four raters per organization when measuring HRM concepts and a minimum of three raters per organization when measuring some kind of performance indicator. Fourth, the longitudinal case studies presented here experience the problem of generalizability. In other words, to what extent are the results from one call center study or seven road haulage firms representative for other organizations in other industries? Finally, most researchers pay little attention to how the mechanism of creating superior performance through HR investments actually works. The Marchington et al. (2003) study and the work by Barney and Wright (1998) are exceptions to this, although the Barney and Wright paper is not fully empirical with its VRIO framework.

In summary, the ten empirical HR studies using the resource based view presented here illustrate the following interesting lessons. First, the majority of these studies build on the high performance work systems (HPWS) thesis and the AMO-theory, as presented by Bailey (1993) in order to explain the potential contribution of HR practices to superior firm performance. Huselid (1995), for example, argues that HR practices that stimulate employees' abilities (through development), motivation (through the right set of incentives) and opportunity to participate (through empowerment, involvement and autonomy) results in discretionary effort (organizational citizenship behavior) and excellent firm performance. We argue that RBV and AMO-theory are complementary and can be used simultaneously in HR research, as suggested by Boselie et al. (2005). However, the results of most of the empirical studies are confusing and undermine the RBV notions. In finding statistically significant results on the impact of certain best practices in HRM on performance without fully taking into account path dependency, causal ambiguity and social complexity embedded in the individual organization's blueprint (or unique history), suggests that organizations can be successful simply by applying these HR practices. In so doing these organizations may be able to create temporary competitive advantage. It is, however, unclear if the empirical results in the studies also indicate sustained competitive advantage as suggested by the RBV. We therefore argue that, although the RBV is often used to frame HR studies, most best practices findings provide no explicit support for the RBV other than noting HR practices are important. It is therefore important to make a clear distinction between competitive advantage and sustained competitive advantage. Barney and Wright's (1998) VRIO framework suggests that the difference between 'regular' competitive advantage and sustained competitive advantage is made through the support of the resource by organization. This issue is also stressed in a slightly different way by Marchington et al. (2003) in their distinction between a necessary minimum of HRM ('table stakes'), HRM aimed at creating viability in an industry and HRM that drives industry leadership. In line with this framework Barney and Wright (1998) examine RBV from an HR perspective,

suggesting different ways of organizational survival. Not all organizations survive on the basis of superior performance as suggested by the RBV; some firms simply survive by above average performance and in this way avoid becoming a laggard. This idea is also suggested by Mirvis (1997) who makes a distinction between leaders, fast followers, slow followers and laggards in HRM. Existing HR research applying RBV does not fully acknowledge this distinction highlighted by Mirvis (1997) and Barney and Wright (1998).

Second, several studies emphasize the relevance of context, but only four actually incorporate organizational context explicitly in the research design and analysis (Boxall and Steeneveld, 1999; Doorewaard and Meihuizen, 2000; Hutchinson et al., 2000; Marchington et al., 2003). This point is related to the nature of the methods used. Only four studies apply a qualitative research technique and, given the nature of the RBV claims, we even seriously doubt whether using quantitative techniques through surveys exclusively will ever fully capture the potential contribution of RBV theorizing with respect to HR's contribution to sustained competitive advantage of the firm.

Third, the human capital perspective is explicitly linked to RBV in two studies (Koch and McGrath, 1996; Barney and Wright, 1998) stressing the relevance of HR investment in, for example planning, hiring and employee development. We argue that, as with the AMO-theory, RBV and human capital theory are complementary and can be used simultaneously to study the contribution of HRM to sustained firm performance.

Fourth, Boxall and Steenveld (1999) and Doorewaard and Meihuizen (2000) make a strong plea for industry-based research, preferably using longitudinal data to avoid misinterpreting fundamental differences between branches of industry and the impact on HRM.

Finally, De La Cruz-Deniz and De Saa-Perez (2003) introduce the notion of social responsibility and its potential alignment with HRM, leading to superior performance.

This institutional component is important for the search of unique linkages between the external organizational environment (environmental fit) and HRM.

CRITIQUES ON RBV

The popularity of the RBV in the 1990s also resulted in theoretical critiques. Priem and Butler (2001) argue that the RBV framework is either paraphrased or simply cited by conceptual and empirical researchers, without augmented definition. They question whether the RBV should be regarded as a theory. There appears to be an underlying problem in the statement that value and rarity of resources lead to competitive advantage, because both the independent (valuable and rare organizational resources) and dependent variables (competitive advantage) are defined in terms of value and rarity (Priem and Butler, 2001). Other potential problems relate to: the lack of clarity with respect to the relationship between the independent variables (characteristics of organizational resources) and the dependent variable (competitive advantage), also known as the black box dilemma; the static nature of RBV statements; and the simplified strategic analysis of the RBV with respect to the organizational environment.

The tautological issue raised by Priem and Butler (2001) relates to Guest's (1997) earlier notions that there is still a lack of theory with respect to (1) what is HRM, (2) what is performance, and (3) what is the link between HRM and performance. AMO-theory (or the HPWS thesis) and human capital theory represent good candidates for theory on the content of human resource management (*what is HRM?*). AMO-theory and the HPWS thesis provide a framework focused on valuable and potentially unique HR practices. The human capital perspective in RBV perspective is much more focused on employees. The distinction between employees (human resources) and HR practices as potential sources for sustained competitive advantage is also made by Wright et al. (1994). Wright et al. (2001) go one step further in the blending

of these three theories (RBV, AMO and human capital) by making a distinction between (a) human capital (employees' value in terms of their knowledge, skills and abilities), (b) social capital (employees' social networks and unique relationships) and (c) organizational capital (including unique practices, systems and structures). HR practices are assumed to be the basis for human, social and organizational capital. This partly solves the tautological problem with respect to the independent variable in the RBV analysis, whether it is the human capital component or the HR practices component. However, we are still puzzled by what is performance. How do we measure and identify sustained competitive advantage? The classic analysis by Peters and Waterman (1982) in the end failed to identify firms with sustained competitive advantage based on past financial performance. A more balanced perspective, taking into account a multi-dimensional performance construct, as suggested by Oliver (1997), Deephouse (1999), Boxall and Purcell (2008) and Paauwe (2004) might be the solution for solving the tautological issue with respect to *what is performance*. These balanced perspectives take into account multiple stakeholders (shareholders, managers, trade unions, works councils) and their long term interests, represented in a wide range of outcome variables, both financial (sales, profits, growth and market value) and non-financial (corporate image, employee satisfaction, employee commitment, absence due to illness, stress levels, fairness, legitimacy). We will get back to this issue in describing and discussing strategic balance theories in section five of this chapter.

The second issue raised by Priem and Butler (2001) refers to the lack of clarity with respect to the HRM and performance link, an issue also raised by Guest (1997) mentioned earlier in this chapter: *What is the nature of the link between HRM and performance?* This dilemma is also known as the 'black box' problem (Wright and Gardner, 2003). Part of this problem is related to the multi-level nature of it (Paauwe and Boselie, 2005). The potential for unique HR value chain includes strategic alignment between the business strategy and the HR strategy, HR design and policy development, HR implementation by both HR-managers and front line managers, the perception of HRM interventions by employees, employees' reactions in terms of attitudes, behaviors and cognitive elements to the HR practices, firm performance (for example in terms of productivity, flexibility and social legitimacy), and finally (superior) firm performance. This value chain involves multiple actors (top managers, HR professionals, front line managers and employees) on different organizational levels. Recent work by Wright and Nishii (2006), who make a distinction between intended, actual and perceived HR practices and the study by Bowen and Ostroff (2004) on HR system strength are very useful and helpful in getting a better understanding of the relationship between independent variables (HRM related) and dependent variables (performance related). Progress is made on this problem raised by Priem and Butler (2001), although more empirical research on this matter is required.

The third issue pointed out by Priem and Butler (2001) is focused on the static nature of RBV statements not fully taking into account the organizational dynamics and notions on change. In their analysis on strategic fit and internal fit Boon et al. (2007) add an additional third type of fit closely related and relevant to both strategic fit (alignment between business strategy and HRM) and internal fit (alignment of individual HR practices towards a coherent and consistent HR system): *Adaptation* fit. This type of fit is focused on the organizational capability of the organization to adapt to changes in the environment and the extent to which HR practices enact or support this adaptation process in a timely or even pro-active way. In strategic management theorizing this kind of fit is known as 'dynamic capability.'

The fourth problem raised by Priem and Butler (2001) emphasizes the lack of attention to the external environment in most RBV approaches, with the few exceptions of Oliver (1997), Boxall and Steeneveld

(1999), Doorewaard and Meihuizen (2000) and Paauwe and Boselie (2003). The RBV in research is often overly and and exclusively focused on the internal environment of the organization in the search for unique combinations of resources and (internal) organizational factors, not fully taking into account (1) the impact of the external environment in terms of both market and institutional mechanisms (Oliver, 1997; Paauwe, 2004) and (2) the potential for unique combinations between internal resources and external mechanisms. An example of the latter is the concept of institutional entrepreneurship. This concept reflects the opportunities organizations have, even in a highly institutionalized context, to be the fastest and best in the process of adapting to new rules, agreements and new legislation. This notion of institutional entrepreneurship as a potential RBV source for competitive advantage is closely related to the notion of strategic option (Doorewaard and Meihuizen, 2000) or strategic choice (Child, 1997; Paauwe, 2004) made earlier in this chapter. We fully agree with Priem and Butler (2001) that it is important to take into account the external environment of an organization.

Next to Priem and Butler's (2001) four main critiques on contemporary RBV – the tautological problem, the lack of clarity of the HRM and performance link, the static nature and the lack of attention to the external environment – we would like to add two other general critiques on the RBV that also affect RBV applications in HRM. First, RBV implicitly builds on the assumption of economic rationality of the actors (dominant coalition) involved. That is a typical economic but rather naïve and unrealistic assumption. Other rationalities are involved whenever decisions are being made, for example, normative rationalities ('taken for granted' decisions) that are closely related to institutional mechanisms as presented by DiMaggio and Powell (1983). Strategic decision making can be affected by institutional mechanisms and their related rationalities (Paauwe and Boselie, 2003, based on Dimaggio and Powell, 1983): coercive mechanisms that stem from legislation and the influence of social partners (trade unions, employer's associations and works councils), normative mechanisms that stem from professional bodies, and mimetic mechanisms that are the response to uncertainty or the result of hypes and trends in management. Second, we would like to emphasize the underestimation of critical incidents in RBV research till now. For example, a large scale accountancy scandal (Enron, Parmalat, WorldOnline, Ahold, Shell) affects the whole company, potentially damaging the corporate image, employees' trust in top management, customer relationships and shareholders' trust in the continuity of the firm. Job insecurity, employee dissatisfaction and higher levels of intention to leave the firm can lead to the destruction of the firm's human capital (employee turnover), social capital (substantial less efforts for cooperation and building or maintaining network relationships) and organizational capital (no new recruitment and reducing training expenditure). Some of these recent critical incidents have a much larger impact on the firm's long term performance than the common reorganizations and acquisitions every organization faces once in a while. Therefore it is important to acknowledge the potential impact of these dramatic incidents in RBV and HR research. In the next section we will focus on three alternative approaches for RBV applications in future HR research.

AN ALTERNATIVE RBV APPROACH

The resource based view provides a powerful model for analyzing the potential contribution of human resource management to sustained competitive advantage of an organization. It has rightly served to counteract the misbalance of taking only into account external (market) conditions, as put forward and promoted by Porter (1980) and in this way focusing on the importance of investing in and cultivating internal resources. Yet, context can't be overlooked and RBV runs the risk of being overly focused on an inside-out view. This is actually one of

the main criticisms of RBV (Priem and Butler, 2001). New institutionalism provides an alternative theoretical framework for incorporating the context in RBV-HR research (DiMaggio and Powell, 1983; Marchington et al., 2003; Paauwe and Boselie, 2003). Secondly, institutional mechanisms (coercive, normative and mimetic) can also provide the basis for creating unique combinations between internal (human) resources and the organizational context. The strategic balance theory (Oliver, 1997; Deephouse, 1999; Paauwe, 2004; Paauwe and Boselie, 2007) is an alternative theory for extending the RBV approaches in HRM in the search for long term success. The strategic balance theory acknowledges two types of often conflicting external mechanisms that affect an organization and it's HRM:

1. Market mechanisms (products, markets and technology);
2. Institutional mechanisms (legislation, professional norms and values).

Long term success or sustained competitive advantage can only be achieved when organizations meet the criteria or standards set by the market mechanisms (for example being efficient, effective, reliable and profitable) and the criteria or rules set by the institutional mechanisms (for example, being fair towards your employees, avoiding job losses, taking care of employee well-being and adapting to new labor legislation). Deephouse's (1999) analysis in the banking industry suggests that organizations are better off in the long run when taking into account both economic criteria like sales, growth, profits and market value and social criteria like relationships with trade unions, corporate reputation and employee satisfaction (Paauwe, 2004). Oliver (1997) is one of the first researchers who blended the resource based view and new institutionalism in search for a broader contextual framework for explaining long term organizational success. Paauwe and Boselie (2003) were one of the first to do so for the field of human resource management.

Until now institutional notions have mainly been considered to be constraints for an organization. New labor laws on contingent work or diversity in the workplace are often seen as limitations on the organization's room to maneuver. The majority of organizations will probably deal with these new issues in a reactive way mainly ticking the box in order to avoid law suits or negative publicity that might affect the organization's financial performance and reputation. Extending both Barney and Wright's (1998) VRIO framework and Mirvis's (1997) leaders and laggards model with the institutional perspective provides a new way of analyzing organizational success. Leaders (Mirvis, 1997) are doing much better on the adoption of best practices in HRM than Laggards (Mirvis, 1997) not only on the best practices that enhance financial performance (for example those increasing labor productivity), but also best practices that enhance social legitimacy and fairness towards individual employees (for example work life balance practices in HRM). Paauwe (2004) makes a distinction between HRM's role in delivering 'economic value' and 'moral value'. From an Institutional–RBV perspective (strategic balance theory) Paauwe (2004) argues that organizations can create unique approaches in HRM for sustainable competitive advantage through balancing added value notions (efficiency, effectiveness, flexibility, innovativeness and quality) and moral value notions (individual fairness, social legitimacy, participation, solidarity and trust), in this way blending both notions of economic rationality and relational rationality.

CONCLUSION

The RBV analysis in this chapter has both theoretical and methodological implications that can be used in future research in the field of HRM. These implications should not be seen as a normative guideline for HR research. The theoretical and methodological implications presented here hopefully give some food for thought when developing new

research in this area. We are aware of the fact that the nature of HR research (an applied field of research heavily depending on input from practice) almost always results in methodological and technical limitations (for example maximum number of respondents per unit of analysis and response rates). We encourage HR researchers to pursue the search for the holy grail in HRM with at least taking into account some of the issues summarized below.

Theoretical implications

First, the resource based view can easily be extended with the *Abilities-Motivation-Opportunity theory* on HR practices. The HR practices in AMO are also known as high performance work practices (HPWPs) and are ideally aligned into a consistent and coherent human resource system (a high performance work system). These practices can be a first step in the creation of organizational success. This does not automatically imply that the non-HPWPs such as salary administration and salary payment are not important for an organization. The AMO-theory linked to the RBV does shed light on what HR practices can contribute to success.

Second, the RBV and *human capital theory* go hand in hand and can be useful in the analysis of the HR value proposition as suggested by Wright et al. (2001). Their study emphasizes the different components of capital linked to employees that potentially contribute to the firm's success.

1. Human capital represents the value of the workforce's (unique) knowledge, skills and abilities.
2. Social capital is embedded in the unique value of social relationships between employees within the organization, but also between employees (for example account managers) and their customers outside the organization.
3. Organizational capital includes all hardware and software of the organizational systems. HR practices themselves are part of organizational capital and the unique combinations of these HR practices into consistent and coherent HR systems (internal or horizontal fit) can increase firm value.

Unique combinations between these three – human, social and organizational – can be a source of sustained competitive advantage on itself. Boxall's (1996) distinction between *human capital advantage* and *organizational process advantage* is highly relevant in this context. Organizations can possess competitive advantage based on a talented workforce, but this might just not be good enough for achieving long term success. Creating industry leadership highly depends on the organization's capabilities to enact organizational process advantage in which human capital is integrated with social capital (for example unique networks with customers) and organizational capital (for example a unique organizational climate supported by information and communication systems).

Third, in order to fully understand an organizational context it is important to link the RBV to *new institutionalism*, as suggested by Oliver (1997). This way one of Priem and Butler's (2001) fundamental issues with respect to RBV's contextual limitations might be solved. The 'traditional' RBV approach is too much inside-out focused with little or no attention paid to an organization's institutional environment. With contemporary debates on corporate governance and compliance the HR function itself is more and more involved in strategic decision making, not only aimed at increasing financial performance to please the shareholders, but also in decision making aimed at monitoring employee behavior and creating an organizational climate in which risks of corporate scandals are minimized.

Finally, the new institutional approach in combination with the RBV is the foundation for the *strategic balance theory* (Deephouse, 1999; Paauwe, 2004). This balanced perspective goes one step further than just incorporating an institutional model for the sake of institutional mechanisms that affect organizations on a daily basis like labor legislation and trade unions. This strategic balance theory focuses on creating long term success through smart and entrepreneurial designs that meet both market and institutional criteria. A US company in the USA

employing a substantial number of employees with an ethnic background from a Middle American country came up with the idea to use the knowledge and experiences of this specific group of employees in order to target their country of origin. This way the company created a unique diversity management program that contributed to the firm's market penetration strategy, the employee involvement and commitment of the employees and positive publicity on their diversity management program. It might be interesting to try and identify leading firms from a strategic balance perspective in order to learn about drivers for long term success.

Overall, we conclude that the RBV has a lot of potential for further research in HRM, in particular in combination with other theories (AMO, human capital, new institutionalism and strategic balance).

Methodological implications

First, the empirical HR research conducted to date is dominated by quantitative analyses, mainly focused on the effects of HRM on performance and potential moderating and mediating effects. If we read and interpret the resource based view in detail we might start to wonder whether quantitative techniques will ever prove HRM's contribution to sustained competitive advantage. The RBV itself is much closer linked to a configurational approach – leaving room for equifinality principles on the basis of the uniqueness of every organization – than to a contingency approach in which predetermined combinations of practices with each other and combinations of a system of practices with other organizational factors (for example the strategy and the production system) are central. In order to fully understand an organization's context, in particular its administrative heritage, other research techniques than survey methods (historical analysis, interviews and archival data analysis) are required (see, for example, the study by Boxall and Steeneveld 1999). However, qualitative research itself is time consuming, very difficult in terms of reliability and validity, and not sufficient enough to answer the added value question. Therefore we propose a combination of both qualitative and quantitative research techniques, taking into account the feasibility of these techniques when applied in practice.

Second, we propose a multi-actor and multi-rater design in which multiple stakeholders are represented (for example employees, front line managers, HR professionals, controllers, top managers, members of the works council, trade union offices and shareholders) and multiple respondents per unit of analysis are used to optimize both validity and reliability of the data. Again we are aware of the fact that applied research has its limitations and sometimes we should be very happy with just one or two respondents per organization because of potential difficulties in getting access to certain organizations.

Third, making a strong plea for more longitudinal research designs is almost a cliché. Almost all empirical HR studies end with the suggestion of more longitudinal research. However, longitudinal research is often time consuming and very expensive. And in addition to that the current dynamics and flexibility of respondents moving from one job to another and from one firm to the other makes it even more difficult to track former respondents for a second measurement. Longitudinal research can only be performed in close corporation with one or a limited number of firms (for example within one multinational company) being part of the organization's regular employee survey. Another possibility for longitudinal research is in cooperation with other academics in Big Science projects such as the Workplace Employment Relations Survey (WERS) in the UK (Wall and Wood, 2005; Delbridge and Whitfield, 2007).

Fourth, from an institutional perspective it is clear that both countries and sectors have a huge impact on organizations. Within industry analysis at least partly controls for some of these institutional mechanisms that can be significant between different branches of industry. Arthur's (1994) steel mill analysis is an example of such an approach. This way the organizations involved more or less share the same institutional environment. Linked to the notion of within industry analysis is the notion of business unit analysis in cases including large multinational companies (MNCs). These MNCs are often conglomerates with divisions operating in different markets. Research at MNC corporate level is often less valid because of the firm's internal heterogeneity in activities and markets. The validity of research data can be increased by focusing on the divisions or business units within MNCs.

Finally, a strategic balance approach implies the incorporation of a multi-dimensional performance construct taking into account economic and other outcomes. From a balanced perspective long term success is determined by the organization's efficiency, quality, innovativeness, flexibility and profitability, but also its social legitimacy, corporate reputation (corporate branding towards potential employees and reputation in the media), relationship with trade unions and fairness towards employees, taking into account employment security, fair payment and employee well-being.

NOTES

1 The classic RBV article by Barney (1991) in *Journal of Management* was cited more than 5600 times according to Google Scholar and a substantial number of citations stem from the HR field. Citations in the text of a study do not automatically mean that the specific theory is actually being used and applied in that research (Sutton and Staw, 1995).

2 Both Tobin's q and GRATE (gross return on assets) are financial performance indicators often used in HRM and performance research (Boselie et al., 2005).

3 VRIO is an abbreviation of value, rareness, imitability and organization.

REFERENCES

Arthur, J.B. (1994) 'Effect of human resource systems on manufactoring performance and turnover', *Academy of Management Journal*, 37 (3): 670–87.

Bae, J. and Lawler, J.J. (2000) 'Organizational performance and HRM strategies in Korea: Impact on firm performance in an emerging economy', *Academy of Management Journal*, 43 (3): 502–17.

Bailey, T. (1993) 'Organizational innovation in the apparel industry', *Industrial Relations*, 32 (1): 30–48.

Barney, J.B. (1991) 'Firm resources and sustained competitive advantage', *Journal of Management*, 17 (1): 99–120.

Barney, J.B. (1997) *Gaining and sustaining competitive advantages*. Reading, MA: Addison-Wesley.

Barney, J.B. and Wright, P.M. (1998) On becoming a strategic partner: The roles of human resources in gaining competitive advantage, *Human Resource Management*, 37: 31–46.

Beer, M., Spector, B., Lawrence, P., Mills, D.Q. and Walton, R. (1984) *Human Resource Management: A General Manager's Perspective*. New York: Free Press.

Boon, C., Boselie, P., Paauwe, J. and Den Hartog, D.N. (2007) *Measuring strategic and internal fit in HRM: An alternative approach*. Proceedings of The Academy of Management Annual Meeting, Philadelphia, PA.

Boselie, P., Dietz, G. and Boon, C. (2005) 'Commonalities and contradictions in HRM and performance research', *Human Resource Management Journal*, 15 (3): 67–94.

Bowen, D.E. and Ostroff, C. (2004) 'Understanding HRM–firm performance linkages: The role of the "strength" of the HRM system', *Academy of Management Review*, 29 (2): 203–21.

Boxall, P. (1996) 'The strategic HRM debate and the resource-based view of the firm', *Human Resource Management Journal*, 6 (3): 59–75.

Boxall, P. (1998) 'Achieving competitive advantage through human resource strategy: Towards a theory of industry dynamics', *Human Resource Management Review*, 8 (3): 265–88.

Boxall, P. and Steeneveld, M. (1999) 'Human resource strategy and competitive advantage: A longitudinal study of engineering consultancies', *Journal of Management Studies*, 36 (4): 443–63.

Boxall, P. and Purcell, J. (2003) *Strategy and human resource management*. New York: Palgrave MacMillan.

Boxall, P. and Purcell, J. (2008) *Strategy and human resource management*. New York: Palgrave MacMillan, second edition.

Child, J. (1997) 'Strategic choice in the analysis of action, structure, organizations and environment: Retrospect and prospect', *Organization Studies*, 18 (1): 43–76.

Deephouse, D.L. (1999) 'To be different, or to be the same? It's a question (and theory) of strategic balance', *Strategic Management Journal*, 20 (2): 147–66.

De la Cruz Deniz-Deniz, M. and De Saa-Perez, P. (2003) 'A resource-based view of corporate responsibility toward employees', *Organization Studies*, 24 (2): 299–319.

Delbridge, R. and Whitfield, K. (2007) 'More than mere fragments? The use of the Workplace Employment Relations Survey data in HRM research', *The International Journal of Human Resource Management*, 18 (12): 2166–81.

Delery, J.E. and Shaw, J.D. (2001) 'The strategic management of people in work organizations: Review, synthesis, and extension', in G.R. Ferris (ed.), *Research in personnel and human resource management*, Vol. 20. Stamford, CT: JAI Press, pp. 167–97.

Dierickx, I. and Cool, K. (1989) 'Asset stock accumulation and sustainability of competitive advantage', *Management Science*, 35 (12): 1504–11.

DiMaggio, P.J. and Powell, W.W. (1983) 'The iron cage revisited: Institutional isomorphism and collective rationality in organizational fields', *American Sociological Review*, 48 (2): 147–69.

Doorewaard, H. and Meihuizen, H. (2000) 'Strategic performance options in professional service organisations', *Human Resource Management Journal*, 10 (2): 39–57.

Gerhart, B. (2005) 'Human resources and business performance: Findings, unanswered quaestions, and an alternative approach', *Management Review*, 16 (2): 174–85.

Gerhart, B., Wright, P.M., McMahan, G.C. and Snell, S.A. (2000) 'Measurement error in research on human resources and firm performance: How much error is there and how does it influence effect size estimates', *Personnel Psychology*, 53 (4): 803–34.

Guest, D.E. (1997) 'Human resource management and performance: A review and research agenda', *International Journal of Human Resource Management*, 8 (3): 263–76.

Huselid, M.A. (1995) 'The impact of human resource management practices on turnover, productivity, and corporate financial performance', *Academy of Management Journal*, 38 (3): 635–72.

Hutchinson, S., Purcell, J. and Kinnie, N. (2000) 'Evolving high commitment management and the experience of the RAC call centre', *Human Resource Management Journal*, 10 (1): 63–78.

Kamoche, K. (1996) 'The integration-differentiation puzzle: a resource-capability perspective in international human resource management', *The International Journal of Human Resource Management*, 7 (1): 230–44.

Keegan, A. and Boselie, P. (2006) 'The lack of impact of dissensus inspired analysis on developments in the field of human resource management', *Journal of Management Studies*, 43 (7): 1491–11.

Koch, M.J. and McGrath, R.G. (1996) 'Improving labor productivity: Human resource management policies do matter', *Strategic Management Journal*, 17 (5): 335–54.

Marchington, M., Carroll, M. and Boxall, P. (2003) 'Labour scarcity and the survival of small firms: A resource-based view of the road haulage industry', *Human Resource Management Journal*, 13 (4): 5–22.

Mirvis, P.H. (1997) 'Human resource management: Leaders, laggards, and followers', *Academy of Management Executive*, 11 (2): 43–56.

Mueller, F. (1996) 'Human resources as strategic assets: An evolutionary resource-based theory', *Journal of Management Studies*, 33 (6): 757–85.

Oliver, C. (1997) 'Sustainable competitive advantage: combining institutional and resource-based views', *Strategic Management Journal*, 18 (9): 697–713.

Paauwe, J. (1994) *Organiseren: Een grensoverschrijdende passie*. Oratie, Alphen aan den Rijn: Samson Bedrijfsinformatie.

Paauwe, J. (2004) *HRM and performance: Achieving long-term viability*. Oxford: Oxford University Press.

Paauwe, J. and Boselie, P. (2003) 'Challenging "strategic HRM" and the relevance of the institutional setting', *Human Resource Management Journal*, 13 (3): 56–70.

Paauwe, J. and Boselie, P. (2005) "'Best practices. in spite of performance": Just a matter of imitation?', *International Journal of Human Resource Management*, 16 (6): 987–1003.

Paauwe, J. and Boselie, P. (2007) 'HRM and societal embeddedness', in P. Boxall, J. Purcell, and P.M. Wright (eds), *The Oxford Handbook of Human Resource Management*. New York, NY: Oxford University Press, 166–84.

Penrose, E.T.(1959) *The theory of the growth of the firm*. Oxford, Oxford University Press.

Peters, T. and Waterman, R. (1982) *In Search of Excellence: Lessons from America's Best–Run Companies*. New York: Harper and Row.

Pettigrew, A.M. (1990) 'Longitudinal field research on change: Theory and practice', *Organization Science*, 1 (3): 267–92.

Porter, M.E. (1980) *Competitive strategy*. New York: Free Press.

Porter, M.E. (1985) *Competitive advantage: Creating and sustaining superior performance*. New York: Free Press.

Priem, R.L. and Butler, J.E. (2001) 'Is the resource-based "view" a useful perspective for strategic management research?', *The Academy of Management Review*, 26 (1): 22–40.

Purcell, J. (1999) 'Best practice and best fit: Chimera or cul-de-sac?', *Human Resource Management Journal*, 9 (3): 26–41.

Stopford, J.M. and Baden-Fuller, C.W.F. (1994) 'Creating corporate entrepreneurship', *Strategic Management Journal*, 15 (7): 521–36.

Sutton, R.I. and Staw, B.M. (1995) 'ASQ forum: What theory is NOT', *Administrative Science Quarterly*, 40 (3): 371–84.

Wall, T.D. and Wood, S.J. (2005) 'The romance of human resource management and business performance, and the case for big science', *Human Relations*, 58 (4): 29–62.

Way, S.A. (2002) 'High performance work systems and intermediate indicators of firm performance within the US small business sector', *Journal of Management*, 28 (6): 765–85.

Wernerfelt, B. (1984) 'A resource-based view of the firm', *Strategic Management Journal*, 5 (2): 171–80.

Wood, S. (1999) 'Human resource management and performance', *International Journal of Management Reviews*, 1 (4): 367–413.

Wright, P.M. and McMahan, G.C. (1992) 'Theoretical perspectives for strategic human resource management', *Journal of Management*, 18 (2): 295–320.

Wright, P.M., McMahan, G.C. and McWilliams, A. (1994) 'Human resources and sustained competitive advantage: A resource-based perspective', *International Journal of Human Resource Management*, 5 (2): 301–26.

Wright, P.M. and Barney, J.B. (1998) 'On becoming a strategic partner: The role of human resources in gaining competitive advantage', *Human Resource Management*, 37 (1): 31–46.

Wright, P.M., Dunford, B.B. and Snell, S.A. (2001) 'Human resources and the resource based view of the firm', *Journal of Management*, 27 (6): 701–21.

Wright, P.M. and Gardner, T.M. (2003) 'The human resource-firm performance relationship: Methodological and theoretical challenges', in D. Holman, T.D. Wall, C.W. Clegg, P. Sparrow and A. Howard (eds), *The New Workplace: A Guide to the Human Impact of Modern Working Practices*, London: John Wiley and Sons.

Wright, P.M. and Nishii, L.H. (2006) *Strategic HRM and organizational behavior: Integrating multiple levels of analysis*. Working Paper 26. Ithaca, NY: CAHRS at Cornell University.

26

Complexity-Based Agile Enterprises: Putting Self-Organizing Emergence to Work

Lee Dyer and Jeff Ericksen

You are unlikely to see the future if you're standing in the mainstream.

Gary Hamel

Pathbreaking is a lot more rewarding than benchmarking

Gary Hamel and C.K. Prahalad

We live in turbulent times. Many organizations currently operate, either by choice or chance, in a maelstrom of fickle customers, shifting markets, rapid-fire technological change, and obsolescing business models. Traditional notions of strategizing, organizing, and resource management, including human resource management, that have served so well for so long are increasingly being challenged. Accordingly, some firms that compete in dynamic marketplaces characterized by turmoil and frequent upheavals are on the lookout for new and more appropriate ways of doing business (e.g., Hamel and Valikangas, 2003; Hamel 2007). In general, their quests take one of two paths (as shown in Figure 26.1).

By far the most common (the left side of Figure 26.1) takes the bureaucratic model and its emphasis on sustained competitive advantage, hierarchy, continuity, stability, and discipline as given. And then from this base the approach explores ways to make the model more innovative (Christensen, 1997), dynamic (Peterson and Mannix, 2003), adaptive (Haeckel, 1999), kinetic (Fradette and Michaud, 1998), resilient (Hamel and Valikangas, 2003), and so forth. The second path, far less-traveled (and illustrated by the right side of Figure 26.1), emanates from a different paradigm. It postulates that under conditions of hypercompetition and creative destruction, the best firms can hope for is

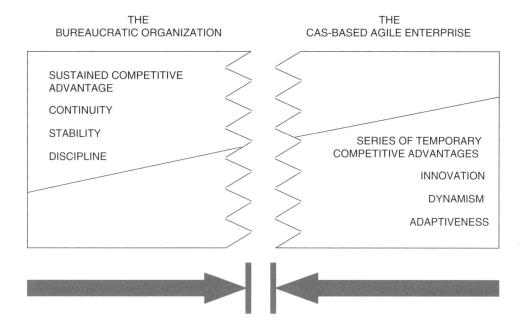

Figure 26.1   Bureaucracy vs. CAS-based agile enterprises

to attain a series of temporary competitive advantages that, with luck, add up to long-term survival. It suggests, in turn, that temporary competitive advantages stem from continuous streams of leading edge products, services, and solutions which emanate from organizational milieus that emphasize innovation, dynamism, and adaptiveness, blended with just enough stability and discipline to keep them from spinning out of control.

It might be thought that these two paths constitute a difference without a distinction and that eventually they would naturally converge. Given their fundamental differences, however, we are inclined to think otherwise, as the gap in the middle of Figure 26.1 indicates and our subsequent discussion illustrates.

We approach the analysis from the right-hand side of Figure 26.1 using concepts derived from complexity science (some say complexity sciences, since as Axelrod and Cohen (1999: 15) note, '... there is little convergence among [complexity science] theorists ... it is not a field in which a crisp and unified theory has already been developed, nor is ...expected in the next few years'). Complexity science eased into the

management and organization literatures in the US during the 1990s. A few researchers and writers began viewing marketplaces and organizations as, or at least as analogous to, the complex adaptive systems (CASs) studied by biologists, chemists, and so on and thus conceptualizing and studying them as such (Anderson, 1999). Over time, this notion gained a fair amount of traction in some circles. It has its own journal: *E:CO* (formerly *Emergence, Complexity and Organization*), now in its eighth year. At least 30 books of this genre had been published by the late 1990s (Maguire and McKelvey, 1999), and many more have appeared since (e.g., Bennet and Bennet, 2004; Fulmer, 2000; Hazy et al., 2007; Lewin and Regine, 2000; and Pascale et al., 2000). (For a comprehensive review of this literature, see Holbrook [2003])

Interestingly, much of this literature implicitly or explicitly accepts the fundamental precepts of the bureaucratic model – managerial control, hierarchy, and so forth – and, as a result, many of its prescriptions and exemplar organizations differ very little from those found in more conventional analyses. Thus, it offers very little that is new or thought-provoking for serious students of human resource management. Pascale et al. (2000: 13) in their book *Surfing the Edge of Chaos* are particularly up front about this: 'What we are advocating is appropriate use of tools of the old paradigm, incorporated in a new management repertoire.' Some suggest that this amounts to little more than using CAS-based concepts to serve up old wine in old bottles using new labels (e.g., Stacey et al., 2000).

So we take a different, more radical tack by exploring an approach to 'harnessing complexity' (Axelrod and Cohen, 1999) that we call Complexity-based Agile Enterprises (C-bAEs). This approach, we believe, has the potential to take full advantage of the insights that complexity science has to offer and to open up new avenues with respect to unleashing human initiative and creativity in organizations. Richardson (2005: 394) reminds us, however, that 'Complexity "thinking" is the art of maintaining the tension between pretending we know something and knowing that we know nothing for sure.' Thus, our analysis is admittedly speculative. We lay no claim to having all the answers, or even to knowing all of the right questions. In the pages that follow, we initially explore a few key complexity science concepts and weave

them into a framework that is then used to guide the remainder of our analysis, which focuses on three key organizational processes: strategizing, organizing, and mobilizing.

SOME KEY CONCEPTS FROM THE CAS LITERATURE

Although the CAS-based literature is eclectic, from it we can extract six key concepts that are particularly relevant for our purposes: CASs, agents, interactions, self-organizing, edge of chaos, emergence, and emergent properties.

CASs are commonly conceptualized as holistic structures composed of hierarchically nested levels, such as those shown in Figure 26.2. In biology, the structures might consist of subcomponents such as organisms, species, and ecosystems; in the business realm, participants, contexts, and marketplaces. The usual practice is to refer to a focal subcomponent as the CAS and the key actors as agents. When an ecosystem is the CAS, for example, species are the agents; when a species is the CAS, organisms are the agents; and so on. In general, whether in biology or business, the central issues include, first, how CASs of interest fit (or do not fit) within their larger structures and thus survive

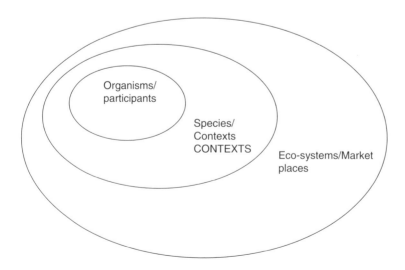

Figure 26.2   Complex adaptive systems – hierarchically nested levels

(or die) and, second, how this fit (or lack of fit) is enhanced (or diminished) by the agents' ongoing interactions with one another and with various artifacts (objects used by agents).

CASs co-evolve by means of self orga- nizing. This is not the customary '… view of the autonomous [agent] first thinking and then choosing an action, but of [agents] in relationship[s] continuously evoking and provoking responses in each other, responses that each paradoxically selects and chooses' (Stacey et al., 2000: 172). Here is how the process works (Prigogine, 1997). Constant interactions among agents regularly amplify into bifurcations (essentially Y's in the road) where the agents are forced to make conscious or unconscious 'choices.' Feedback from these 'choices' then sets off more interactions which create additional bifurcations and more 'choices,' and so forth and so on ad infinitum. And thus CASs evolve, or more precisely are co-evolved by self-organizing agents, over time. The process is akin to an un-choreographed, spontaneous dance '… that proceeds through a subtle interplay of competition and cooperation, creation and mutual adaptation' (Holbrook, 2003: 83). When it comes to self-organizing, as the term suggests, no one is in control and there is no grand plan or design. Whatever happens, happens.

Self-organizing works when CASs exist in a certain state, commonly and somewhat provocatively referred to as the edge of chaos, where the defining property is an ongoing dialectic between dynamism and stability, freedom and control. To grasp the essence of the edge of chaos, imagine a continuum with three states (Holbrook, 2003: 15). At the left is State 1 where stability or equilibrium reigns. In the middle is State II characterized by punctuated equilibrium. At the right is State III where chaos or disequilibrium reigns. Now, between States II and III, but edging over toward State III, insert State IV – the edge of chaos – where elements of disequilibrium and equilibrium are in constant interaction. This state (which despite the name is a state, not a precipice) is where self-organizing thrives.

And fortunately, it is the state that self- organizing naturally tends to favor. Research in many realms (although alas not in work organizations) has shown that CASs drift towards State IV in the interest of survival (see Holbrook, 2003: 15–20). In States I or II, stability drives out dynamism, innovation is throttled, and momentum is lost to other, more adaptable CASs. In State III, the opposite occurs and CASs essentially spin out of control and self-destruct. In State IV, however, they capitalize on the forces of yin and yang, a flow of opposite, yet complementary energies and continue to co-evolve.

Self-organizing at the edge of chaos engenders emergence, which can involve two types of outcomes – new forms of CASs and outputs. The beauty of emergence is that it tends to consist of outcomes imbued with two critical emergent properties: novelty (in the sense of being truly unique) and coherence. At one level, as CASs co-evolve they constantly emerge in new forms of dynamic processes and patterns. Often emergent forms are the outcomes of interest. But for firms, forms tell only part, albeit an important part, of the story. System outputs are also critical. Self-organizing at the edge of chaos tends to engender a stream of innovative, but also potentially viable, products, services and solutions (for explanations of how and why this occurs see Holbrook, 2003: 39–46 and Storey et al., 2000: Chapter 6). And it is this ability that tends to separate winners from losers in dynamic marketplaces. This, then, is why we believe the CAS-based approach has so much potential vis-à-vis flattened, decentralized, and streamlined bureaucracies.

But, of course, there are a couple of catches. CASs' outcomes typically display two additional and related emergent proper- ties: unpredictability and uncertainty (Cilliers, 2005; Gershenson and Heylighen, 2005). This is so for three interrelated reasons. First, CASs are very sensitive to what are (somewhat erro- neously) called initial conditions; that is, they have histories that are constantly unfolding and, thus, the nature of any emergent outcome, which is fleeting and hard to pin down, has a major impact on the nature of the next emergent outcome, and so forth and so on ad infinitum. A slight twitch here and there and everything might well be different. Second, in CASs interactions among agents and the resulting feedback patterns are voluminous, rich, and non-linear and so can lead just about anywhere. Third, small perturbations in CASs sometimes reverberate into major changes (it is said, for example, that the fluttering of butterflies in Brazil can potentially unleash windstorms in Texas), while large ones are sometimes absorbed with barely a ripple.

Given this combination of circumstances – uncertain 'initial conditions', tangled webs of untraceable interactions and feedback loops, and unknown perturbation patterns – it is hardly surprising that CASs reveal no simple cause and effect relationships. This, in turn, means that at any given time actual emergent outcomes – forms and outputs – are only a few of the many that could have occurred (Kurtz and Snowden, 2003). Further, there is no guarantee that they will be valuable. As noted earlier (refer back to Figure 26.2), CASs are also agents embedded in larger CASs which, of course, are also self-organizing, so no particular outcome is assured a positive fate. In brief, self-organizing at the edge of chaos is capable of engendering all manner of outcomes and no one knows for sure what will emerge until the emergence occurs. And even then it is far from certain that anyone will like it (Storey et al., 2000: 152–154). This, of course, can be unnerving.

CASs AT WORK

Consider the tower-building termites of Africa and Australia (this account is adapted from Wheatley and Kellner-Rogers, 1996: 68). Within their CASs, these agents instinctively form groups that are constantly in motion acting and reacting to what is going on around them, moving dirt around sometimes cooperatively and sometimes competitively in seemingly random fashion, conducting what in essence is a plethora of unplanned experiments. All on their own; as far as anyone knows there are no termite architects,

designers, or straw bosses. No question, the termites go down plenty of blind alleys and make a fair share of mistakes, but when things come together the results are immense towers (the largest in the world relative to the size of their builders) that are engineering marvels filled with specialized chambers, perfectly formed arches and tunnels, and even air-conditioning systems. This is self-organizing emergence at work.

Or consider the case of Linux (Axelrod and Cohen, 1999: 52–58; Iannacci, 2005). This well-known computer operating system is the product of ongoing interactions among a constantly evolving cadre of volunteers (agents) located around the globe. No one actively recruits these techies or does anything special to keep them in the fold; they come and go as they please. No one tells them what to do or how to do it either. They collaborate with whom they choose, for as long as they choose, and how they choose. Virtual teams form and re-form all the time. This turmoil engenders some useless code, but also a fair amount that is truly innovative and even elegant (a group of senior engineers, called 'system maintainers', ultimately determines what code does and does not make it into official Linux releases, but this group has no direct control over the process). So far, somewhat against the odds, Linux's approach to so-called open source software development has been immensely successful, churning out versions of an operating system that have become increasingly formidable challengers to the hegemony of Microsoft's Windows, as well as other proprietary systems. This is also self-organizing emergence at work.

As these examples suggest, in CASs and by extension C-bAEs, self-organizing emergence is a two-edged sword. On the one hand, it has the power to engender emergent outcomes that are on the cutting edge of imagination and innovation. On the other hand, it forces an explicit recognition of the fact that creativity and uncertainty are opposite sides of the same coin. To potentially reap the benefits it is essential to learn to live with life at the edge of chaos, with constant change, and with inherent unpredictability. CASs eschew the familiar trappings of traditional organizations in hopes of unleashing the full range of their distributed intelligence. They are heterarchies with no *a priori* pecking orders. No one gets to stand aloof or aside and decide. If any agents or groups of agents (executives, say, or human resource managers) presume to provide blueprints to guide self-organizing, then it is not self organizing. And if they attempt to dictate what should emerge, then it is not emergence (Stacey et al., 2000: 145).

STRATEGIZING AND ORGANIZING

The termite and Linux examples suggest that in C-bAEs self-organizing is likely to focus, in part, on two highly interconnected processes and their emergent outcomes. One is strategizing, which engenders (sometimes novel, coherent, and salient) outputs such as products, services, and solutions. The other is organizing, by which participants unfold ongoing variations in their organizational forms and dynamics – evolving patchworks of connections, collaborations, and work arrangements. A discussion of these processes and potential outcomes follows.

STRATEGIZING: CO-EVOLVING EMERGENT OUTPUTS

In the CAS-based literature, analogies are often drawn between biological eco-systems and marketplaces, only in the former instance species are the agents, while in the latter case products, services, and solutions are (Peltoniemi, 2006). The fitness landscape is a commonly used metaphor in both analyses (Kaufmann, 1995). Fitness landscapes consist of many constantly evolving peaks and valleys. Peaks represent points of fitness with high potential payoffs, while valleys represent depths of unfitness with no potential payoffs. Since fitness landscapes are CASs, they are self-organizing – that is, it is ongoing interactions among agents (e.g., competing products) that engender the endless ebbing and flowing of peaks and valleys. In this view, then, marketplaces are treated not as external entities with known or estimable opportunities and threats, but rather as encapsulating places in which agents are enveloped by unknown and unpredictable patterns of opportunities and threats that come and go. To be sure, products, services, and solutions are in pursuit of their own advantages, but they do not determine their own fates. In the end, success or failure depends on the cumulative effects of the many interactions that occur, over which there may be some leverage but certainly no control.

Fitness landscapes take many forms. Some are quite smooth (characterized by periodic change) and some are tumultuous (characterized by constant change). Between these extremes are so-called rugged landscapes (characterized by considerable, but not constant change). Landscapes are considered rugged if they sometimes contain fairly high peaks that last a while before they collapse. In marketplaces, fairly high peaks are created by products, services, or solutions that find willing customers or clients and sell well for a while. Sometimes products, services, and solutions create high peaks virtually unmolested. More often, though, when they head up what appear to be potentially high peaks, competitors or government agencies, or some other agents counter and if they are successful the peaks cap out at relatively low levels or even evaporate. If these counter-moves are weak, however, the peaks continue to grow and achieve some measure of stability, allowing the extraction of revenues. Eventually, jousting among agents (e.g., tough negotiations with customers or clients) puts peaks on shaky ground. Counter-moves may create temporary sanctuaries, but sooner or later these efforts become futile and peaks are abandoned so that resources are freed for other, more promising pursuits. Overall, then, rugged landscapes are dynamic equilibriums consisting of inherent and ubiquitous tensions that drive constant change coupled with occasional stability.

C-bAEs engender rugged landscapes. Ongoing, real-time interactions among organizational participants form strategies – choices about where, with what, and how to compete on rugged landscapes. Products, services, or solutions emerge as participants, muck about in marketplaces searching for or trying to sustain or abandoning peaks, while trying to avoid languishing in valleys. Rather than dwelling on things as they would like them to be (i.e., ideal states), participants start with things the way they are and then move forward. They create and experiment with options to see what works, and adapt quickly to capitalize on emerging opportunities and avert impending disasters, and in the process incrementally co-create (with other agents) uncertain futures (Kawai, 2005; Snowden, 2006). This mucking about on rugged landscapes is in lieu of conducting formal strategic planning processes which, of course, are pointless exercises in marketplaces fraught with multiple plausible paths and players all destined for indeterminate places (Chelariu et al., 2002 [cited in Holbrook, 2003]; Carlisle and McMillan, 2006).

Thus, in C-bAEs, every venture is in perpetual beta mode (McGrath and Keil, 2007; Tapscott and Williams, 2006: 256–257). Stewart (2007) puts it this way:

> The voyage is unclear. Success comes to those who read the unobvious but critical complications of wind and current, who exploit every puff in the doldrums, who seize the chance for a long run downwind, who tack tirelessly in the fact of adversity, and who abandon the sail when conditions are not right.

More formally, in C-bAEs, participants are called upon to nurture endless streams of ventures – potential and actual products, services, or solutions – through strategic cycles consisting of as many as four phases: exploration, exploitation, adaptation, and exit (see Figure 26.3).

In exploration, participants conduct low-cost, discovery-driven probes into marketplaces to test ideas and develop prototypes, capture and analyze signs of potential, and quickly make educated guesses about which ventures are and are not worthy of pursuit (Brown and Eisenhardt, 1997; McGrath and Boisot, 2005; Pisano, 1994). They then move promising ventures on to exploitation, where they do their best to capitalize on competitive advantages and thus generate revenues. Since stuff happens on rugged landscapes, participants also exercise an instinctive, almost automatic ability to sense potential complications early, assess their significance swiftly and accurately, and adapt accordingly (Lewin and Volberda, 1999). Notwithstanding, they also know that on rugged landscapes no peaks last forever, so exit is inevitable. When the time seems right, they do not hesitate to abandon marginal ideas or even to cannibalize existing marketplace offerings when they have run their courses (Foster and Kaplan, 2001; Horn et al., 2006).

How do we know that this type of strategizing will generate enough sufficiently novel and yet coherent outputs to provide firms with at least reasonable chances of attaining periodic advantages on rugged landscapes? The short answer is: We don't for sure. But the CAS-based perspective suggests that it may. The well-spring here is creativity – the constant generation of new, novel, and potentially useful ideas – and this is what ongoing interactions among savvy participants tend to do. Bennet and Bennet (2004: 115) explain it this way:

> Teams and communities … facilitate … creativity. Ideas are probed through the dialogues of teams and the virtual interactions of communities, placed in incubation as knowledge workers intermingle these exchanges with actions. Illumination occurs in many forms, possibly by several members of the team or community, and as it is shared offers the potential for quick verification and validation, as well as the opportunity for additional probing leading to additional new ideas. These ideas are the mental implements used to gain competitive advantage. Since ideas build upon ideas, the more these implements are used, the more ideas available for use, and the more opportunity for the organization to develop and fulfill its own unique competitive advantage.

From the well-spring of creativity springs innovation – the process of transforming a wealth of potentially useful ideas into streams

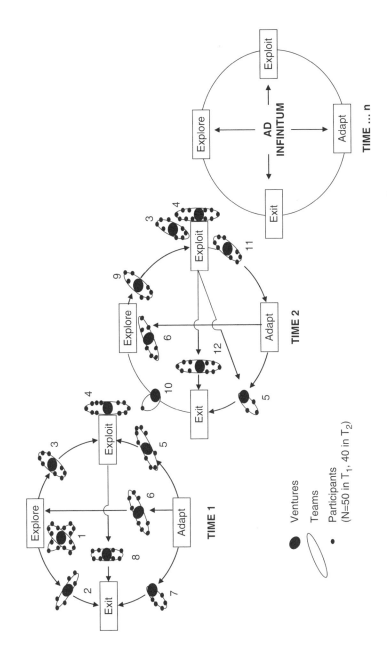

Figure 26.3   Strategizing-organizing ventures and teams

of unique and coherent outputs (products, services, and solutions). The type of strategizing we describe has the potential to do this for a number of reasons. First, C-bAE participants are perpetually close to the action, which makes them particularly knowledgeable about marketplace dynamics and enhances both the efficacy and timeliness of the strategic moves they initiate. Experiments at Hewlett-Packard and Eli Lilly, for example, have shown that participants on the ground are superior to highly trained professionals when it comes to discerning dynamic market movements (Surowiecki, 2004: 221). Second, participants process marketplace intelligence and make choices about resource allocations on the spot and rapidly, free of the organizational labyrinths and layers that bind more traditional firms (Christensen, 1997), thus facilitating transitions among the four phases of the strategic cycle (exploration, exploitation, adaptation, and exit). Third, participants become used to constant change, thus reducing the trauma and resulting friction that otherwise might result from ongoing rounds of creation and destruction.

Theoretically, at least as noted, there are no assurances that things will work out this way. There is always the chance that marketplace dynamics and/or internal self-organizing will degenerate into stasis, thus engendering insufficient creativity and innovation to locate, climb, and temporarily sustain high peaks on rugged landscapes. Or that one or both will spin totally out of control and into chaos. Whether or not these things occur depends, in part, on what happens when C-bAE participants co-evolve emergent forms – a process we call organizing.

ORGANIZING: CO-EVOLVING EMERGENT FORMS

Clearly, C-bAEs have no predetermined or permanent organizational structures – no a priori or fixed hierarchies, or departments, or line and staff differentiations (which of course includes human resource functions). Rather, self-organizing at the edge of chaos engenders

a variety of organizational forms over time depending on the many 'choices' participants make at various bifurcation points. In other words, organizing is analogous to and in fact constantly interacts with strategizing. So, the rugged landscape metaphor applies here as well. In organizing, interactions among participants create various organizational arrangements that those involved hope will scale fitness peaks (i.e., have the capacity to nurture ventures into more advantageous positions). When this appears to be happening, the arrangements are pursued; when not, they are altered or abandoned. This means that organizational forms, like ventures, are in perpetual beta mode and also constantly traversing cycles of exploration, exploitation, adaptation, and exit. While prediction is impossible, we can speculate that, in general, the prevailing organizational arrangements in C-bAEs will consist of numerous, continuously evolving teams.

Figure 26.3 illustrates the process. A snapshot at Time 1 shows that this fictitious C-bAE was pursuing eight ventures through various points on the strategic cycle. To this end, its 50 participants had formed nine teams involving some 70 roles (some participants were on multiple teams). By Time 2, the firm was again pursuing eight ventures, although four of the originals were gone and four new ones had formed – and three of the four originals had moved to different points on the strategic cycle. At this point there were 40 participants who had organized themselves into nine teams involving 61 roles (10 of the original 50 participants had removed themselves from the strategic cycle, although not necessarily from the firm). Snapshots taken at Times 3, 4, and so on would, of course, show quite different patterns of ventures, teams, and participants. Further, a more finely-grained look at the team level would reveal participants maneuvering to meet new challenges by incessantly altering team structures and processes as well as their own activities and roles.

These are ongoing dynamics. Nonetheless, as teams coalesce around ventures, especially during exploitation, they usually settle down (i.e., toggle back toward the stability end of the edge of chaos zone) at least temporarily. Participants consensually establish semi-permanent working relationships, which can involve temporary hierarchies consisting of coordinators (such as the 'system maintainers' at Linux), team leaders, sub-team leaders, and the like, as well as boundary conditions, goals, priorities, deadlines, and rules of engagement. But – and this is the important point – these relationships, roles, boundary conditions, and so forth are not chiseled in stone and are usually subject to revocation when teams disband (Kawai, 2005).

Not uncommonly, C-bAE participants form organizational infrastructures consisting of artifacts through which work is done. Examples might be core business processes, work-place designs, and information technologies (Axelrod and Cohen, 1999). These tend to be relatively permanent, so it is important that they be designed in ways that promote rather than restrict participant interactions and facilitate rather than restrict self-organizing. Obviously, this is an important issue, but since it is also largely unexplored at this point we offer just a few preliminary thoughts on the way things may go.

Consider core business processes, which govern recurring patterns of interactions among participants, are essential features of organizational life. They are both broad-based (e.g., budgeting) and more focused (e.g., procedures for conducting experiments during exploration or guidelines for service delivery during exploitation (Axelrod and Cohen, 1999: 113–114). Fortunately, as researchers have come to realize, both types are inherent dualities that, when properly designed, serve as much to liberate behavior as to restrict it (Feldman and Pentland, 2003). Generally, then, for C-bAEs the guiding principle is to favor protocols over standard operating procedures. Protocols leave ample space for participants to toggle between innovative and routine behaviors as situations require, while standard operating procedures impose hard-and-fast constraints and thus are best confined to circumstances where they cannot be avoided (e.g., to assure legal compliance).

The same general principle applies when participants are designing workplaces. First, units should be kept small. When they have more than 150–200 people, the evidence suggests, meaningful interactions among participants tend to decline precipitously (Gladwell, 2000: 175–192). Second, within facilities, fixed gives way to flexible. Becker and Sims (2001), for example, advocate an 'integrated portfolio strategy' that incorporates modular buildings, open spaces with easily movable panels in place of walls, nomadic plug-and-play work stations, and easily assembled and thus transportable furniture. This eliminates artificial barriers and makes it easy for C-bAE participants to co-create their own temporary work spaces on an as-needed basis (see also Conlin, 2006; Joroff and Bell, 2001). This may well become less of an issue over time, though, as C-bAE participants increasingly work virtually. Beyond some tipping point, it may be that physical locations become little more than pared down, often leased drop-in centers. Or perhaps even passé. Socialtext, a small quasi-C-bAE, for instance, operates entirely with no physical facilities at all (Tapscott and Williams, 2006: 251–253).

C-bAEs inevitably employ cutting-edge technologies. Irrespective of specific applications, however, systems should be designed to unfailingly foster participant interactions and self-organizing. In C-bAEs it is critical that what one participant knows, all have easy access to on a real-time basis. This, in turn, implies the adoption of distributed and open information systems where the input, manipulation, and retrieval of information is a snap and only minimally restricted (e.g., for legal reasons). It also implies the widespread use of what Tapscott and Williams (2006: 11) call 'weapons of mass collaboration.' These include Internet– and intranet–based wikis, blogs, and the like that facilitate hookups between projects and potential contributors and, once the two are connected, make it easy for participants to share knowledge and engage with each other on a peer-to-peer basis wherever they may be, just as participants in open source ecosystems do. Wikis, in particular, facilitate self-organizing.

As Ross Mayfield, founder of Socialtext puts it, 'Wikis hand control over to users to create their own way of organizing knowledge, workplaces, processes, and perhaps even their own applications in ways they've not been able to do before.' (quoted in Tapscott and Williams, 2006: 255).

In sum, then, C-bAEs begin their organizational lives *tabulae rasae*. Complexity science suggest that ongoing interactions among self-organizing participants, if the system sustains the edge of chaos, will engender an ongoing series of truly novel and yet coherent organizational configurations – forms and infrastructures. The precise nature of these, of course, remains to be seen, although we can be quite sure that at various times the forms will incorporate elements of stability – hierarchies, goals, priorities, and the like – as well as semi-permanent artifacts such as protocols, maneuverable work spaces, and cutting-edge technologies to facilitate the flow of work. Naturally, the hope and indeed the expectation is that the unfurling patterns will more often facilitate than hamper the strategizing process and, thus promote firm survival. But, as always, there are no guarantees.

MOBILIZING

In nature, the strategizing-organizing nexus is pretty much the whole story. Tower-building termites, as far as we know, work with whatever resources nature provides. C-bAEs could do pretty much the same, although when it comes to 'harnessing complexity' there are good reasons to believe that this might not be the best way to go (Axelrod and Cohen, 1999: Chapter 2). Unlike termites, human beings are prone to making conscious choices about resources. And obviously people differ when it comes to the attributes that make them more or less suited to thriving in hyperactive social communities where they are constantly called upon to co-create their own futures. It is likely, then, that C-bAE participants not only will, but also should, constantly strive to create conditions that might enhance their organizing and strategizing activities.

We call this process mobilizing. Once again, it involves participants self-organizing at the edge of chaos – this time in efforts to emerge novel, coherent, and salient combinations of participant attributes (which means, in effect, turning the process back onto themselves). Again, the rugged landscape metaphor applies. Sometimes participants pursue configurations that co-create fitness peaks (i.e., that enhance organizing and strategizing) and thus are retained for a while. Other times they run into obstacles and their efforts are adapted or discontinued. In other words, in C-bAEs participant configurations, like organizational configurations and ventures, are in perpetual beta mode, once again constantly traversing cycles of exploration, exploitation, adaptation, and exit.

Mobilizing is in large part analogous to human resource strategizing. It is aimed at getting the right numbers of the right types of participants in the right places at the right times doing the right things right – where right is defined as contributing to successful organizing and strategizing. Students of human resource strategy will recognize this concept as vertical fit or alignment (Dyer and Ericksen, 2007). But there is a unique twist here. In traditional firms, business strategies and structures are expected to endure for some time so vertical alignment is viewed as a relatively static state. In C-bAEs, however, organizing and strategizing are dynamic processes that center on ventures, which means that vertical alignments (plural) are constantly emerging moving targets. In these firms, then, thoughts of creating enduring vertical alignments give way to efforts aimed at enhancing the likelihood of attaining an ongoing series of temporary vertical alignments. And this, we postulate, requires participant scalability (Dyer and Ericksen, 2007).

Participant scalability emanates from two factors: calibrations and fluidity. The former refers to participants' collective capacity to ascertain what needs to be done to promote effective organizing and strategizing. The latter refers to participants' collective capacity to move themselves from where they are to where they need to be and/or to shift from less important and less effective behaviors to more important and more effective behaviors – and to do efficaciously and in timely, rapid, and cost effective ways (Dyer and Ericksen, 2007; Hamel and Valikangas, 2003). Participants who have mastered calibrations sniff out potential opportunities with recurring fidelity, while those who exhibit fluidity pounce on the most promising of these opportunities with alacrity. Calibrations without fluidity mean many lost chances, while fluidity without calibrations means a lot of wasted motion. So we suspect that C-bAEs need both. But it cannot be said that these are necessarily sufficient conditions for success, given the inherent uncertainties involved.

So, how do C-bAE participants go about enhancing their own scalability? Here we speculate on a few things that might help, dividing them into two categories: shared mindsets and participant attributes.

COEVOLVING SHARED MINDSETS

For C-bAEs, shared mindsets – configurations of visions, values, and the like – serve as relatively stable navigational beacons. Long staples in the traditional management literature (e.g., Ulrich and Lake, 1990), shared mindsets are, we believe, even more essential for firms embroiled in constant change. Not everyone agrees, though. Stacey (1996: 15), for example, flatly states that any attempt by C-bAEs to '… inspire [participants] to follow some common vision, share the same culture, and pull together is to remove the mess that is the very raw material of creativity.' In his view, however, shared mindsets are constraints imposed by managers (or others). We, on the other hand, assume that they can just as easily be liberating factors developed by the participants themselves.

Recall Linux's far-flung, ever-shifting cadre of volunteers. They embrace a shared mindset that incorporates both ends and means. There is a common purpose – 'To best the beast from Redmond' – as well as a few generally accepted operating norms –

e.g., openness, irreversibility, and visibility (Axelrod and Cohen, 1999: 52-58; Iannacci, 2005). None of these were mandated. They were adopted and are accepted because the Linux volunteers perceive that on balance they do more to foster than inhibit '… the mess that is the very raw material of creativity.' We see no reason why other C-bAE's participants would see things differently.

Shared purposes articulate the collective hopes of participants. Stated in fairly general and aspirational terms, they actually encourage the exercise of discretion. 'To best the beast from Redmond' and Google's 'To organize the world's information' are attractive ideas to many folks. They rally the troops in ways that expand horizons by reflecting lofty ambitions and ever-rising bars (the beast and the world's information keep moving on). But they also serve to keep expanded horizons from becoming infinite, especially if they refrain from dictating what participants should do and instead help to clarify what they probably ought not pursue (Linux and Google's participants are surely not working on the next big thing in, say, barbeques). Further, as participants deploy and perform they need some way to use the feedback that is constantly rolling in. Do their efforts and outputs seem to be more or less directionally correct? Are they mobilizing efficaciously and in timely, rapid, and cost-effective ways? To decide, it obviously helps to have a pretty good idea of where they are trying to go.

Shared operating norms define how participants behave with one another. In C-bAEs they essentially replace bureaucratic webs of rules and controls as guides to decision-making. While we cannot specify what any particular C-bAE's norms should be – that is up to the participants themselves – we can say for sure that it takes more than simply stating them to make them real. Ultimately, what counts is what is lived and reinforced by each and every participant each and every day. This is true in all organizations, but especially so in C-bAEs where prevailing norms are likely to be quite different from those participants have previously internalized from their experiences in traditional firms. We see this frequently in classroom simulations. Students usually put considerable time and effort into deriving and communicating a set of seemingly appropriate operating norms. Yet they typically find that it takes several weeks and often some (sometimes painful) violations before they truly begin to embrace the new ways (e.g., by openly sharing information), while shucking behavior derived from pre-conceived notions of how classrooms 'really' work (e.g., the hoarding of information). And a few never quite get there.

In sum, co-evolving shared mindsets around a novel paradigm is certainly a difficult process that has to be done with care to avoid becoming the fool's errand that Stacey makes it out to be. But we know from the research of Argyris and Schon (1978) and others that mental models drive a lot of behavior. Absent appropriate shared purposes and operating norms, we believe, C-bAE participants lack navigational beacons on which to base their calibrations and the behavioral consistencies that foster the high level of trust on which fluidity ultimately depends.

CO-EVOLVING PARTICIPANT POPULATIONS

In C-bAEs, participants collectively decide who joins and, to some extent, who stays and goes, while also exerting influence over what is done by whom when. That is, they are the arbiters of their firm's human and social capital (Nahapiet and Ghoshal (1998)). And it takes rich stocks of both to sustain quality calibrations and fluidity on an ongoing basis. (These days, we realize, relevant stocks of human and social capital extend well beyond organizational boundaries – see, for example, Tapscott and Williams [2006] – but that issue requires a fuller exposition than is possible here.)

Again, some might contend that C-bAEs' participants need not pay particular attention to enhancing stocks of human and social capital since both will automatically improve with experience. In the CAS-based literature,

this is known as crossover, the process by which species are regularly improved as genetic contributions from parents are constantly recombined (Axelrod and Cohen, 1999: 41–42). Generally, it seems reasonable to expect that the more participants interact the better they get at it – up to the point of saturation anyway (McFadyen and Cannella, 2004). We contend, however, that while crossover is inevitable and essential, it is also insufficient and thus, once again, there is no good reason for C-bAEs simply to let nature take its course. Instead, there are a number of things participants might do to develop human capital without damaging social capital, to enhance social capital without diminishing human capital, or preferably to enrich both in one fell swoop. We consider these possibilities in four categories: staffing, development, rewards, and work load (note that this takes us into realms that in more traditional organizations would be considered the bailiwick of human resource organizations and professionals).

Staffing

A major way that CASs evolve is through the creation, transformation, and destruction of agents (Axelrod and Cohen, 1999: 38–61). This suggests the need for C-bAE participants to give careful consideration to the ways in which they collectively flow in, through, and out of their firms.

Participant inflows

Initially, C-bAEs need to generate qualified applicants. This is no slam-dunk. Given the pervasiveness of the bureaucratic paradigm, it is unlikely that a large number of qualified applicants even exists. Not everyone, as Lebaron (1999) reminds us, is particularly eager to live at the edge of chaos. Research (as well as our classroom simulation experiences) bears him out. In a recent survey of 2,000 knowledge workers in 32 countries, for example, only about 25 percent of the respondents could reasonably be classified as 'agile performers' (DiRomualdo and Winter, 2005). One partial solution here might lie with the increasingly popular on-demand recruiting services (ODRSs) (Frase-Blunt, 2003). On the demand side, ODRSs, unlike contingency search firms, contract with clients for extended periods of time and come to know their needs well. On the supply side, they specialize by industry or competencies so they should be able to find and reliably ferret out potential agile performers quickly and easily.

Of course, C-bAEs' participants still retain responsibility for making final hiring decisions. They are looking for applicants who will likely enhance both human and social capital. One set of essential competencies pertains to technical knowledge and skills in areas such the dynamics of marketplaces and technologies under-girding potential and current products, services, and solutions. Here the emphasis would be on divergence; that is, on finding applicants who collectively possess strong foundational aptitudes and/or a breadth of well-developed competencies and thus have the potential not only to see the full range of potential calibrations, but also to demonstrate fluidity by deploying and contributing across a wide range of assignments and tasks (Wright and Snell, 1998). But as much as divergence, or variation, is emphasized in the CAS-based literature (e.g., Axelrod and Coher, 1999: 32–58), convergence is essential with respect to other competencies and attributes. That is, C-bAEs are likely to seek participants who individually top the scales and collectively display minimum variance on competencies such as creativity, interpersonal capabilities, and teaming skills (Morgeson et al., 2005) and attributes such as a tolerance for ambiguity and a predisposition toward and comfort with constant change, which research suggests emanate from inherent personality traits such as proactivity, adaptivity, and resilience (Baterman and Crant, 1993; Sherehiy et al., 2007). Consider Google's vaunted hiring process. It '… values nonconformity nearly as highly as genius [and gives] preference … to candidates who have weird avocations and out-of-the-ordinary experiences' (Hamel, 2006: A16). According to the company's Web site (www.Google.com), 'Googlers range

from former neurosurgeons, CEOs, and U.S. puzzle champions to alligator wrestlers and former marines … '. While this seems to work for Google, obviously a great deal of research remains to be done before we know whether hiring for divergence on the technical side and convergence on the cultural side really serves to enhance calibrations and fluidity in C-bAEs.

Participant throughflows

When it comes to throughflows, C-bAEs encounter a dilemma. Fostering divergence encourages the use of throughflows to enhance participant development by broadening exposure to a variety of ventures. Godin (2000), for example, urges organizations in rapidly changing situations to embrace the notion of serial incompetence – a willing, even eager acceptance of the risks associated with bouts of temporary incompetence as the inevitable price of ongoing development. What firms need, he contends, are '… folks who are quick enough to master a task and restless enough to try something new [as soon as they have]' (Godin, 2000: 234). But obviously this can be overdone. Carried to its logical extreme, it would require C-bAEs to modify the pursuit of temporary vertical alignments, which require that participants take on assignments and tasks for which they are already well-equipped (Wright and Snell, 1998). Clearly, there is no one right answer here so a lot of experimentation (including perhaps some computer modeling) will be necessary to uncover even conditional accommodations to this apparent conundrum.

Participant outflows

It might be thought that to preserve human and social capital, C-bAEs participants should encourage long-term employment relationships, absent of course any thoughts of guarantees. But in non-growth situations, it may be necessary (even with the advent of serial incompetence) to encourage some involuntary turnover to open the door for new blood. Further, there will always be selection errors that have to be rectified. And finally,

C-bAEs are at least as vulnerable as other organizations to tectonic shifts that lead to over-staffing and/or competency misalignments that do not yield to timely, rapid, and cost effective internal corrections. The danger here is that these essential adaptations will be excessively delayed and/or handled badly once they are addressed. How, then, to make them happen in real time? And well?

In C-bAEs, true incompetents, as well as malingerers and free-riders really stand out. But this does not mean they are easy to deal with. In classroom simulations, for example, we have found that while rare, such cases usually remain unaddressed unless and until they become flagrant and problematic. Absent a strong sharing of the C-bAEs' common purpose, student participants tend to favor congeniality and harmony over confrontation. When serious cases are allowed to fester, the generalized negative effects on human capital (motivation) and social capital (cooperation and trust) are palpable. When such situations are confronted, improvements tend to be almost immediate and equally apparent – and especially so when it is perceived that justice was done. In our view, C-bAEs can benefit from these experiences. First, in problem cases, procrastination probably can be precluded if there is a strong sense of shared purpose, as well as a generalized norm of constructive confrontation. Second, and not surprisingly, the fairer the processes

and outcomes, the better the results for all concerned. This suggests that it might be wise for C-bAE participants to form and invest resources in training standing teams (preferably with rotating memberships) that have authority to investigate problems, implement corrective measures, and, when warranted, mete out sanctions.

In the event of tectonic shifts, an applicable model might be a variant of AES Corporation's compensation process (described in Table 26.1 and discussed below). As warning signs accumulate, participants would form small teams of respected colleagues to look at the facts, recommend courses of action, and widely disseminate all relevant information. If the teams decide that the best solution (or only feasible option) is layoffs, they would set goals and solicit self-nominations. These would then circulate for a period of open discussion (redundant non-volunteers would be encouraged to pony up, while valuable non-redundant volunteers would be encouraged to stay). Ultimately, the original teams would decide who would be granted packages to leave (the process could be repeated as necessary until the goal was reached). Undoubtedly, this would work only if severance pay and perks were generous and quality outplacement assistance was part of the package. If a process of this sort were successful in rebalancing human capital, it should also go a long way toward

Table 26.1 Self-managing pay at AES Corporation

First, … a group put together a plant budget that was consistent with [the] business plan. The budget had a line item for the total compensation expense … They decided that the total compensation paid to everyone in the plant could not exceed the budgeted number. A task force … had already researched comparable levels in the area … That information was shared with everyone at the plant. Each individual was asked to propose his or her own salary for the year ahead and then to send the proposal to every other person in the plant for comment. After a week long comment period, each person made a decision about his or her own compensation. When the amounts were tallied, the sum exceeded the budget, but not by much. As it turned out, only one person had settled on a pay level substantially higher than others of comparable responsibility, skill level, and experience had. He was also one of the few who had not followed the advice of colleagues to adjust his pay. After he was given this information, he agreed to reduce his proposed salary, and the revised compensation total allowed the plant to meet its original budget.

The individuals who participated in this approach were changed by the process. They had a much better understanding of how compensation affected the overall economics of the organization. They learned the value of seeking advice when they had to balance competing interests. They put the interests of other stakeholders on a par with or even ahead of their own. The process pulled team members together and helped some make the transition from workers to business people… This method of setting compensation was stressful, successful, and fun.

Source: Bakke, D.W. (2005). *Joy at Work*. Seattle, WA: PVG, pp. 125–6.

sustaining social capital since research has consistently shown that the morale of layoff survivors is enhanced if they perceive that their departing colleagues got a good deal (Brockner et al., 1994; Naumann, Bies and Martin, 1995). When all is said and done, however, it is our guess is that the challenge of dealing with involuntary participant outflows on a timely, rapid, and cost-effective basis will be a major stumbling block for many C-bAEs.

The preceding discussion assumes C-bAEs should be staffed at least in large part with regular rather than temporary participants. But is this the best way to go? Rousseau and Arthur (1999: 9) say no, 'In highly dynamic business environments, ... maximum flexibility through free agency is the employment strategy of choice.' There is no question that their approach enhances external fluidity by making it relatively easy for participants to join and leave on a timely basis, usually rapidly and sometimes relatively cheaply (Matusik and Hill, 1998). And it is the way that open source systems such as Linux operate. We wonder, however, if it doesn't also incur a high price with respect to both human and social capital. It means that many, if not most, participants may be new to the enterprise and thus lacking in firm-specific knowledge and also that they are essentially strangers who lack any meaningful interactive experiences with one another (Leanna and van Buren, 1999). To what extent, if at all, do these factors inhibit the quality of both calibrations and internal fluidity to the point where the benefits of external fluidity are neutralized? Once again, the answer to this question is likely situational. So it falls to C-bAE participants to experiment with various mixes of regular and temporary participants over time in search of blends that appear to work under various sets of circumstances.

Development

Assuming quality staffing, the concept of serial incompetence presupposes continuous participant development. To some extent, as noted earlier, this occurs naturally. But the hectic pace of C-bAEs could easily discourage participants from taking the time needed to reflect on and really absorb the lessons inherent in their day-to-day experiences. In this context, it might help if they set learning goals. Seijts and Latham (2005), for example, found that in rapidly changing and ambiguous settings, participants who set specific and challenging learning goals consistently outperformed those who set equally specific and challenging output goals, primarily because they took the time to seek out, process, and incrementally apply (i.e., experiment with) accumulating feedback. Another possible approach, popular with agile combat units in the US Army, involves so-called 'after-action reviews' (AARs) (Darling et al., 2005). This process, notwithstanding its moniker, involves far more than venture postmortems. It encourages teams to use performance – calibrations and fluidity – to enhance learning by routinely allocating time at major transition points (e.g., when ventures move from exploration to exploitation, undergo key adaptations, and end) to hold no-holds-barred, what went right/what went wrong feedback sessions to capture key individual and collective learning (naturally avoiding finger-pointing and recriminations). AARs provide a double-whammy, enhancing both human and social capital simultaneously.

It seems unlikely, however, that C-bAE participants can rely exclusively on developmental experiences that occur in the thick of things. One danger lies in the potential dilution of essential expertise in the form of core knowledge and skills as participants take on increasingly diverse assignments and challenges. To combat this, participants may choose to form communities of practice wherein those with common specialties and interests congregate (physically or virtually) to help each other stay on the leading edge (Cohen and Prusak, 2001: 53–80). Also, in the final analysis participants undoubtedly would find it essential to engage in a fair amount of individual learning on their own time, no doubt using Web-based or other forms of self-study programs.

Rewards

The CAS-based literature generally assumes that self-organizing is intrinsically motivating (Wheatley and Kellner-Rogers, 1996). And indeed, self-organizing does provide C-bAE participants with all three of the core elements traditionally thought to enhance intrinsic motivation: (1) autonomy; (2) expansive, challenging, and meaningful work; and (3) plenty of feedback (Hackman and Oldham, 1976). But, then, there is the unavoidable, although seldom addressed issue of pay. A pretty good case can be made that intrinsic motivation is potentially at risk if participants put too much emphasis on pay and especially on pay as an incentive (Kohn, 1993; Pfeffer, 1998). Perhaps, however, there are things that C-bAEs can do to minimize this risk.

One key issue pertains to process. No question, C-bAE participants decide how and how much they are paid, as well as issues having to do with policy and program designs. But this is pretty much wide open territory with few precedents. Table 26.1 illustrates one possibility. It describes an interesting experiment that occurred in one of AES Corporation's plants (Bakke, 2005: 125–6). Although employee participation, not self-organizing, was the norm here, pay plan participants still made the two most difficult decisions – how much money would be available for distribution and who got what. This kind of process has a number of important implications for C-bAEs. First, the inherent analyses, communication, and discussions help to embed knowledge about organizational realities, thus enhancing calibration. Second, the process helps to build social capital as everyone involved is required to consider the greater good over and above his or her own interests. And third, in the end the process provides a workable solution to one of the most vexing challenges C-bAEs are likely to face.

But what about broader policy and program decisions? Here we know of no precedents. C-bAEs probably have to offer high pay relative to prevailing market rates to compete for the kinds of talent they need. Certainly, this must be person-based pay since there are no fixed hierarchical levels or jobs. As indicated above, it is difficult to say whether or not incentives or merit pay should be offered. If the answer is yes, they probably should be based at least partly on firm performance using metrics that reinforce progress toward attaining shared purposes, as well as partly on individual contributions to venture or team performance (although attributions of credit are especially difficult when participants are frequently moving around – see Axelrod and Cohen [1999: 135–144]). Then there is the question of how much differentiation is too much. Too little may lead major contributors to feel underpaid and to withhold or withdraw their human capital, while too much could eat away at solidarity and reciprocity and thus destroy the social capital on which C-bAEs depend (Bottom et al., 2006).

Work load

In C-bAEs, the potential for overwork looms large. Participants control what they do and the allure of the work (i.e., the very same factors that enhance intrinsic motivation) can be highly seductive (Holwerda, 2006). It is easy for time poverty to become a status symbol, a signaling device to others that one is carrying her or his own weight, and then some. C-bAEs need hard-driving participants, of course. But too much of a good thing is not necessarily a good thing. It can lead to burnout, high levels of dysfunctional stress, and emotional exhaustion (Dollard et al., 2000; Xie and Johns, 1995), as well as to the loss of non-work identity (Rousseau and Arthur, 1999). How, then, do C-bAEs' participants keep from becoming their own worst enemies? This is another tough nut to crack. For one thing, there are great individual differences involved; workloads that are fine for some may be way over the top for others. Further, formal programs of the types tried in traditional organizations (on site child care, concierges, hair salons, and such, as well as part-time work, flex-time, and work at home) often simply serve as enablers of overwork or are rendered impotent by countervailing social pressures (Cohen and Single, 2001). Perhaps the answer lies in a conscious attempt to instill some discipline on this score. Participants, for example, might establish shared operating norms that set limits on the appropriation of their human capital and attempt to reinforce them through extant social capital. Admittedly, though, this may be akin to hiring alcoholics to guard a liquor store.

CONCLUSION

Clearly, the vast majority of firms competing in dynamic marketplaces are content to do so with spruced-up bureaucracies. This is understandable, even rational. But it is not the only possibility. Risk-takers looking to take a quantum leap ahead by adopting the next big thing in organizational paradigms might want to give the CAS-based approach a try. There are reasons to believe that C-bAEs may, in hypercompetitive situations, be better than traditional organizations at attaining series of temporary competitive advantages and thus at surviving over time. But, of course, at this juncture we cannot be sure of this. Despite a fair amount of research in natural settings and with computer simulations, we know very little about how the CAS-based approach is best operationalized within actual firms. So pioneers would have to make some giant leaps of faith.

Human resource researchers can help. The challenge, in a nutshell, is to ascertain whether and in what ways our traditional theories, concepts, and nostrums do and do not apply in C-bAEs – and where they are lacking, to propose new ones that might. Caution is in order though. Communities of scholars are CASs – interactive agents who by and large self-organize at the edge of chaos (i.e., under few, but some restraints) to form collaborations and engender novel and often coherent (and sometimes even salient) outcomes – new knowledge, lectures, articles, books, and such. Efforts to constrain the dynamics of this process or to pre-ordain its

outcomes, especially in the present context, would constitute inappropriate attempts to undermine self-organizing and stifle emergence. Thus, all we dare do is offer a few tentative thoughts for human resource scholars to consider.

Potential data sources are scarce. One, of course, is previous research. Scholars of various stripes are applying complexity science concepts to organizational settings and, although few focus directly on human resource issues, their work is often tangentially suggestive (as we have tried to show here). Insights can also be gleaned from the experiences of quasi-C-bAE (i.e., firms exploring alternatives to traditional management approaches) such as Whole Foods, Gore-Tex, and Google (see Hamel, 2007: Chapters 4–6), always keeping in mind that these observations are at best suggestive since, by definition, none of these firms has fully embraced the key tenets of complexity science (especially self-organizing). Scholars can also learn from experiments of their own making. Classroom simulations have provided us with useful insights, as the foregoing suggests and Langfred (2007) has recently demonstrated (using a sample of self-managed in teams in an MBA program). The analogy of detective work comes to mind; at this point, it seems, the research task is more a matter of piecing together clues obtained from various sources than of hoping to find the one killer app where everything falls into place. This, in turn, suggests the use of exploratory field studies and ad hoc and computer-based simulations over attempts to test predetermined hypotheses using tightly designed experiments or surveys. (Cause and effect hypotheses would seem to be incongruent with C-bAEs' holistic dynamics and inherent unpredictably anyway.)

So, what are we looking for? For starters, evidence of vertical alignments, keeping in mind that in C-bAEs this is a kinetic not static concept. Participants organize and strategize. Alignments occur when participants congregate and perform in ways that engender novel and coherent organizational forms and strategies (products, services, or solutions) that become competitive in their marketplaces. One potentially fruitful avenue of research, then, would be to identify or create situations where C-bAE participants succeed (or just as usefully do not succeed) in fostering vertical alignments and then attempting to uncover the factors that help (or hinder) their scalability (i.e., their abilities to assemble in and effectively utilize salutary self-configurations in timely, rapid, and reasonably uneventful ways) (Dyer and Ericksen, 2007). Specifically, what are the factors that appear to facilitate (or inhibit) their calibrations – i.e., lines of sight – and/or their fluidity – i.e., flows and behavioral adjustments? Initially the analysis would focus on the patterns and dynamics of interactions among the participants involved, with particular attention being given to the ways in which these patterns and dynamics appear to be influenced by extant contextual conditions (e.g., the presence [or absence] of clearly shared purposes and social capital) and/or the collective characteristics of the participants themselves (e.g., high [or not so high] divergence on technical competencies and/or high [or not so high] convergence on cultural attributes). Further analysis might uncover how previous decisions by participants or by the simulation designers had fostered (or inhibited) the formation of shared purposes, social capital, mixes of competencies and attributes, and so forth and so on.

The purpose here is not to suggest how research ventures should flow, but rather to illustrate how they might unfurl. The aim is to entice a few human resource scholars into the realm of C-bAEs and thus incite useful discourses and interactions among them and with other complexity science scholars to the mutual benefit of both. As van Uden (2005: 64–65) points out:

> On an ongoing basis, students of organization explore other disciplines, borrow ideas and concepts they believe can make a contribution of some kind, and try to fit these newly adopted ideas and concepts into existing research programmes. Concepts that prove successful in making a contribution ... become part of normal organizational

discourse ... There is no reason to expect that students of organization will approach the science of complexity in a way that is fundamentally different ...does complexity science help us build competitively advanced firms or does it not?

ACKNOWLEDGEMENTS

Financial support for the preparation of this chapter was provided by the Center for Advanced Human Resource Studies (CAHRS), ILR School, Cornell University and by a grant accompanying The Michael R. Losey Human Resource Research Award accorded to the first author by the Society for Human Resource Management (SHRM).

REFERENCES

Anderson, P. (1999) 'Complexity theory and organization science', *Organization Science*, 10 (3): 216–32.

Argyris, C. and Schon (1978) *Organizational Learning: A Theory of Action Perspective*. Reading, MA: Addison-Wesley.

Axelrod, R. and Cohen, M. (1999) *Harnessing Complexity*. New York: The Free Press.

Bakke, D. (2005) *Joy at Work*. Seattle, WA: PVG.

Bateman, T. and Crant, J. (1993) 'The proactive component of organizational behaviour: A measure and correlates', *Journal of Organizational Behaviour*, 14: 103–18.

Becker, F. and Sims, W. (2001) *Offices that Work: Balancing Communications, Flexibility, and Cost*. Ithaca, NY: Cornell University's International Workplace Studies Program.

Bennet, A. and Bennet, D. (2004) *Organizational Survival in the New World: The Intelligent Complex Adaptive System*. New York, NY: Elsevier.

Bottom, W., Holloway, J., Miller, G., Mislin, A. and Whitford, A. (2006) 'Building a pathway to cooperation: Negotiation and social exchange between principal and agent', *Administrative Science Quarterly*, 51 (1): 29–58.

Brockner, J., Konovsky, M., Cooper–Schneider, R., Folger, R., Martin, C. and Bies, R. (1994) 'Interactive Effects of Procedural Justice and Outcome Negativity on Victims and Survivors of Job Loss', *Academy of Management Journal*, 37 (2): 398–409.

Brown, S. and Eisehnardt, K. (1997) 'The art of continuous change: Linking complexity theory and time-paced evolution in relentlessly shifting organizations', *Administrative Science Quarterly*, 42 (1): 1–35.

Carlisle, Y. and McMillan, E. (2006) 'Guest Editors' Introduction', *E:CO*, 8 (1): vi–ix.

Chelariu, C., Johnston, W, and Young (2002) 'Learning to improvise, improvising to learn: a process of responding to complex environments', *Journal of Business Research*, 55: 141–47.

Christensen, C. (1997) *The Innovator's Dilemma*. Boston, MA: Harvard Business School Press.

Cilliers, P. (2005) 'Knowing Complex Systems', in K. Richardson (ed.) *Managing Organizational Complexity: Philosophy, Theory, Application*. Greenwich, CT: Information Age Publishing, pp. 7–20.

Cohen, D. and Prusak, L. (2001) *In Good Company*. Boston, MA: Harvard Business School Press.

Cohen, J. and Single, L. (2001) 'An examination of the perceived impact of flexible work arrangements on professional opportunities in public accounting', *Journal of Business Ethics*, 32: 317–28.

Conlin, M. (2006) 'Square Feet: Oh, How Square!', *Business Week*, July 3: 100–1.

Darling, M., Parry, C., and Moore, J. (2005) 'Learning in the thick of it', *Harvard Business Review*, July–August: 84–92.

DiRomualdo, T. and Winter, J. (2005) *Manifesto for the New Agile Workplace*. Oxford, UK: Career Innovation Company.

Dollard, M., Winefield, H., Winfield, A. and Jonge, J. (2000) 'Psychosocial job strain and productivity in human service workers: A test of the demand-control-support model', *Journal of Occupational and Organizational Psychology*, 73: 501–10.

Dyer, L. and Ericksen, J. (2007) 'Dynamic organizations: Achieving marketplace agility through workforce scalability', in J. Storey (ed.) *Human Resource Management: A Critical Text* (3rd Edition). London: Thomson Learning.

Feldman, M. and Pentland, B. (2003) 'Reconceptualizing organizational routines as a source of flexibility and change', *Administrative Science Quarterly*, 48 (1): 94–118.

Foster, R. and Kaplan, S. (2001) *Creative Destruction: Why Companies that are Built to Last Underperform the Market and How to Transform Them*. New York, NY: Currency.

Fradette, M. and Michaud, S. (1998) *Corporate Kinetics*. New York: NY: Simon and Schuster.

Frase-Blunt, M. (2003) 'A recruiting spigot', *HR Magazine*, 48 (4): 70–9.

Fulmer, W. (2000) *Shaping the Adaptive Organization*. New York, NY: AMACOM.

Gershenson, C. and Heylighen, F. (2005) 'How can we think complex?', in K. Richardson (ed.) *Managing Organizational Complexity: Philosophy, Theory, Application*. Greenwich, CT: Information Age Publishing, pp. 47–62.

Gladwell, M. (2000) *The Tipping Point*. Boston, MA: Little, Brown and Company.

Godin, S. (2000) 'In the face of change, the competent are helpless', *Fast Company*, January–February: 230–34.

Hackman, J. and Oldham, G. (1976) 'Motivation through the design of work', *Organizational Behavior and Human Performance*, 16: 250–79.

Haeckel, S. (1999) *Adaptive Enterprises: Creating and Leading Sense-and-Respond Organizations*. Boston, MA: Harvard Business School Press.

Hamel, G. (2006) 'Management a la google', *Wall Street Journal*, August 26: A16.

Hamel, G. (2007) *The Future of Management*. Boston: Harvard Business School Press.

Hamel, G. and Valikangas, L. (2003) 'The quest for resilience', *Harvard Business Review*, September: 52–63.

Hazy, J., Goldstein, J. and Lichtensteim, B. (2007) *Complex System Leadership Theory*. Mansfield, MA: ISCE Publishing.

Holbrook, M. (2003) 'Adventures in complexity: An essay on dynamic open complex adaptive systems, butterfly effects, self-organizing order, coevolution, the ecological perspective, fitness landscapes, market spaces, emergent beauty at the edge of chaos, and all that jazz', *Academy of Marketing Science Review*, 6: 1–181.

Holwerda, J. (2006) 'Professional work in the agile environment: Effects on employees, the organization, and work structures', Ithaca, NY: Unpublished manuscript (36 pages)

Horn, J., Lovallo, D. and Viguerie, S. (2006) 'Learning to let go; making better exit decisions', *The McKinsey Quarterly*, 2: 2–8.

Hoyt, D. and Rao, H. (2006) *Rite-Solutions: Mavericks Unleashing the Quiet Genius of Employees*. Stanford, CA: Stanford Graduate School of Business Case HR-27.

Iannacci, F. (2005) 'Coordination processes in open source software development: The linux case study', *E:CO*, 7 (2): 21–31.

Joroff, M. and Bell, M. (2001) *The Agile Workplace: Supporting People and their Work*. Boston, MA: Gartner.

Kao, J. (1996) *Oticon(A)*. Boston, MA: Harvard Business School Case 9–395–155.

Kauffman, S. (1995) *At Home in the Universe: The Search for Laws of Self-Organization and Complexity.* New York, NY: Oxford University Press.

Kawai, T. (2005) 'The improvised-orchestration model of organizational evolution', in K. Richardson (ed.) *Managing Organizational Complexity: Philosophy, Theory, Application.* Greenwich, CT: Information Age Publishing, pp. 313–30.

Kohn, A. (1993) 'Why incentive plans cannot work', *Harvard Business Review*, September–October: 54–63.

Kurtz, C. and Snowden, D. (2003) 'The new dynamics of strategy: Sensemaking in a complex and complicated world', *IBM Systems Journal*, 42 (3): 462–83.

Langfred, C. (2007) 'The downside of self-management: A longitudinal study of the effects of conflict on trust, autonomy, and task interdependence in self-managing teams', *Academy of Management Journal*, 50 (4): 885–900.

Leanna, C. and van Buren, H. (1999) 'Organizational social capital and employment practices', *Academy of Management Review*, 24 (3): 538–55.

Lebaron, D. (1999) 'The gurus speak: Complexity and organizations', *Emergence*, 1 (1): 73–91.

Lewin, A. and Volberda (1999) 'Prolegomena on co-evolution: A framework for research on strategy and new organizational forms', *Organization Science*, 10: 519–34.

Lewin, R. and Regine, B. (2000) *Weaving Complexity and Business: Engaging the Soul at Work.* New York, NY: Texere.

Maguire, S. and McKelvey, B (1999) 'Complexity and management: moving from fad to firm foundations', *Emergence*, 1 (2): 19–61.

Matusik, S. and Hill, C. (1998) 'The utilization of contingent work, knowledge creation, and competitive advantage', *Academy of Management Review*, 23 (4): 680–97.

McFadyen, M. and Cannella, A. (2004) 'Social capital and knowledge creation: Diminishing returns of the number and strength of exchange relationships', *Academy of Management Journal*, 47 (5): 735–46.

McGrath, R. and Boisot, M. (2005) 'Options complexes: Going beyond real options reasoning', *E:CO*, 7 (2): 2–13.

McGrath, R. and Keil, T. (2007) 'The value captor's process: Getting the most out of new business ventures', *Harvard Business Review*, May: 128–36.

Morgeson, F., Reider, M. and Campion, M. (2005) 'Selecting individuals in team settings: The importance of social skills, personality characteristics, and teamwork knowledge', *Personnel Psychology*, 58 (3): 583–611.

Nahapiet, J. and Ghoshal, S. (1998) 'Social capital, intellectual capital, and the organizational advantage', *Academy of Management Review*, 23 (2): 242–66.

Naumann, S., Bies, R. and Martin, C. (1995) 'The roles of organizational support and justice during layoffs', *Academy of Management Journal*, 38 (1): 89–109.

Pascale, R., Millemann, M. and Gioja, L. (2000) *Surfing at the Edge of Chaos.* New York, NY: Crown Business.

Peltoniemi, M. (2006) 'Preliminary theoretical framework for the study of business ecosystems', *E:CO*, 8 (1): 10–19.

Peterson, R. and Mannix, E. (2003) *Leading and Managing People in the Dynamic Organization.* Mahwah, NJ: Lawrence Erlbaum Associates.

Pfeffer, J. (1998) 'Six dangerous myths about pay', *Harvard Business Review*, May–June: 109–19.

Pisano, G. (1994) 'Knowledge, integration, and the locus of learning: an empirical analysis of process development', *Strategic Management Journal*, Winter Special Issue 15: 85–100.

Prigogine, I. (1997) *The End of Certainty: Time, Chaos and the New Laws of Nature.* New York, NY: The Free Press.

Richardson, K. (2005) 'To be or not to be? that is not the question: Complexity theory and the need for critical thinking', in K. Richardson (ed.) *Managing Organizational Complexity: Philosophy, Theory, Application.* Greenwich, CT: Information Age Press, pp. 21–46.

Rousseau, D. and Arthur, M. (1999) 'The boundaryless human resource function: Building agency and community in the new economic era', *Organizational Dynamics*, Spring: 7–18.

Seijts, G. and Latham, G. (2005) 'Learning versus performance goals: when should each be used?', *Academy of Management Executive*, 19 (1): 124–31.

Sherehiy, B., Karwowski, W. and Layer, J. (2007) 'A review of enterprise agility: Concepts, frameworks, and attributes', *International Journal of Industrial Ergonomics*, 37: 445–60.

Snowden, D. (2006) 'Stories from the Frontier', *E:CO*, 8 (1): 85–8.

Stacey, R. (1996) *Complexity and Creativity in Organizations.* San Francisco: Berrett-Koehler Publishers.

Stacey, R., Griffin, D. and Shaw, P. (2000) *Complexity and Management: Fad or Radical Challenge to Systems Thinking?* London, UK: Routledge.

Stewart, T. (2007) 'Making a difference', *Harvard Business Review*, March: 14.

Surowiecki, J. (2004) *The Wisdom of Crowds.* New York, NY: Doubleday.

Tapscott, D. and Williams, A. (2006) *Wikinomics: How Mass Collaboration Changes Everything.* New York, NY: Penguin Group.

Ulrich, D. and Lake, D. (1990) *Organizational Capability: Competing from the Inside Out.* New York, NY: Wiley.

Van Uden, J. (2005) 'Using complexity science in organization studies: A case for loose application', *E:CO*, 7 (1): 60–6.

Wheatley, M. and Kellner-Rogers (1996). *A Simpler Way.* San Francisco, CA: Berrett-Koehler Publishers.

Wright, P. and Snell, S. (1998) 'Toward a unifying framework for exploring fit and flexibility in strategic human resource management', *Academy of Management Review*, 23 (4): 756–72.

Xie, J. and Johns, G. (1995) 'Job scope and stress: Can job scope be too high?', *Academy of Management Journal*, 38 (5): 1288–1309.

27

Human Resource Management across Organizational Boundaries

Mick Marchington, Fang Lee Cooke
and Gail Hebson

INTRODUCTION

Most studies of human resource management
tend to assume, albeit implicitly, that workers
are employed under the umbrella of a single
firm. This is hardly surprising given the
way employment law defines the contract
as derived from the relationship between a
single employer and its employees, and the
fact that decisions in dismissal or other cases
are made with the notion of 'control' over
the employment contract as a central tenet
(Rubery et al., 2002). It may also have been
a reasonably accurate characterization of how
employment was structured in the so-called
'golden age' of the post-war period in most
western democracies, when workers could
expect to be on the receiving end of a standard
contract which implied long-term, permanent
employment at a particular workplace. This
was the ground on which versions of high
commitment HRM blossomed and against

which, despite substantial critiques of its
universal application (see Marchington and
Grugulis, 2000; Godard, 2004 for examples),
employers are urged to benchmark their
activities. In addition, many of the principal
metrics used to evaluate the HR contribution –
such as high levels of job satisfaction and
organizational commitment and low levels
of labour turnover and grievance activity –
implicitly assume a stable and continuing
workforce that expects to remain with their
existing employers and show some allegiance
to them.

However, it is now rare for all those
working at a single establishment to be
employed by the host organization, the
employer that owns and/or operates the site.
Growth in contracting has meant that many
jobs, both in the private and public sector, have
been outsourced to other firms that provide
services, ranging from catering, cleaning and
security on the one hand, through to HR, IT

and other professional services on the other. Despite some attempts to categorize these jobs as peripheral or low skill in general, it is clear that some are actually core to the organization's operations, either in terms of their centrality to its vision and mission or located in customer-facing operations which are arguably the key to commercial success (Lepak and Snell, 1999; Marchington et al., 2005; 2009; Nesheim et al., 2007). The concept of the single organization with clear and explicit boundaries to its operation, if this ever were true, no longer represents the dominant paradigm in practice. There is little doubt that research and theory are struggling to keep up with this new reality, and the majority of publications focus on issues *within* the organization, tending to neglect that some people – in some cases a majority – are actually legally employed by another organization. They do not even constitute a forgotten workforce; they just remain invisible or are referenced solely in the introductory context to the main research topic.

This sets the scene for the remainder of the chapter. In the next section, we briefly develop the notion of HRM across organizational boundaries, demonstrating the range of different forms this may take in practice. Then there is a review of material analyzing whether or not it is possible to have commitment to more

than one employing organization. Following this, we then turn to a brief review of three HR practices that contribute to commitment and which are rendered complex in a multi-employer environment; these are pay and rewards, skills and career development, voice and communications. Finally, a number of implications are drawn for the study and practice of HRM in the context of multi-employer networks.

INTO THE REALM OF THE MULTI-EMPLOYER NETWORK

Fortunately there is a growing recognition that this group of workers exists and plays a part in the production of goods and services delivered by the host employer. Yet this takes many different forms, from the relatively simple case of links between employers and HRM up and down the supply chain through to networks that comprise several different employers operating at the same workplace, where staff on varying contracts work alongside one another. In this latter case there is a myriad of influences on the HR practices used by any of these employers. This is illustrated in Table 27.1 below.

In the supply chain literature, for example, it has long been established that, in general, people working for suppliers tend to have

Table 27.1   Contrasting forms of contracts across organizational boundaries

Features of contract/Nature of contract	Location of employers	Parties to contract	Labour process	Employment conditions
Link up and down supply chain	Employers operate at different places of work	Series of one-to-one relationships	Staff work at different places of work	Separate employers, but some attempt to influence HR at supplier
Agency workers at host organization	Employers operate at different places of work	Series of one-to-one relationships	Staff work alongside each other at same place of work	Separate employers but obvious client influence over HRM
Partnership between two employers	Employers operate at same place of work	One-to-one relationship	Staff work alongside each other at same place of work	Joint initiatives to manage HR through single appointments process for managers
Multi-employer workplaces	Employers operate at same place of work	Multiple and interlocking relationships	Range of staff work alongside each other from different contracts	Separate and joint initiatives to manage HR depending on contract

worse terms and conditions than their clients and customers, and that clients can have a major influence over HR practices such as training and pay systems (Hunter et al., 1996; Benson, 1998; Swart and Kinnie, 2003; Truss, 2004) as well as wage levels (Locke et al., 2007). But these workers are at arms-length from those working for the client, typically employed at another site and indeed in another country (Coyle-Shapiro et al., 2006; Walsh and Deery, 2006). Whilst it may be reasonable to ignore the HR practices that govern the conditions of these workers when studying the client firm in this situation, this is not the case if people employed by more than one organization work on the same site/department – as happens with agency workers. The latter have a different employer from those they typically work alongside in the office, the hospital or the school, and their wages are paid by the agency rather than by the host employer. Moreover they are subject to different disciplinary rules than those with whom they share a workplace. At the same time, however, the agency is not able to see how they perform their duties in the workplace nor have much influence over the groups to which they are allocated or the projects on which they work. It is clear that this situation is already considerably more complex, and subject to competing and possibly countervailing influences, than the standard, single employer-employee relationship (Marchington et al., 2005).

Yet further down the line, away from the simple contract, is the joint venture, alliance or partnership, in which staff work alongside each other in multi-project teams for an organization that has been set up specifically for the purpose of meeting some customer need. Alliances may be tight or loose. In the former case, where a new organization is born, we then revert to the traditional model, albeit one that has suffered turbulence as staff transfer to different employers or workplaces, and have to get used to a new environment. Even here things are not so simple because, in the UK public sector, for example, over the past decade or so, people who used to work for a local authority have

been transferred to a private sector firm, and continue to do the same work as they used to – but now with a new employer and quite different terms and conditions (Cooke et al., 2004). Moreover they still pass work to colleagues who continue to be employed by the local authority and they share the same buildings, canteens and parking spaces. In the latter case, where people remain employed by the original employer despite the setting-up of a partnership, line management responsibility may be shared between the different organizations – as in the case where a team comprising social workers and community nurses are managed by someone from the local authority, even though they work on NHS premises (Boaden et al., 2008).

Thus far, this discussion of HRM across organizational boundaries has moved us away from a focus on the single employer-employee relationship to the idea that two employers might operate alongside each other. Yet, this still over-simplifies the situation as there are many workplaces where the staff working alongside each other are employed by a number of different organizations (e.g., client, host firm, agency) as part of a wider network of collaborating employers. The passenger handing in their ticket at the railway station or the airport might not be able to tell who the guard or the check-in agent works for, and maybe that does not matter until a problem arises. Similarly, the patient might not be able to tell the difference between staff employed by the NHS from those who work for an agency or a private sector firm as they wear the same uniform. But the fact these staff can be employed on quite different contracts does matter because in some cases there are hugely different rates of pay, access to training or career development, or opportunities to be involved in workplace discussions. Indeed, if the HR outcomes received by one group are substantially better than their colleagues, this can result in worker discontent and frustration, and even high levels of job mobility between organizations. This is not just a UK phenomenon of course as research from Australia (Benson, 1998), New Zealand

(Peel and Boxall, 2005), Hong Kong (Chan et al., 2006), Norway (Nesheim et al., 2007) and the USA (Lepak et al., 2007) shows.

This is not just an HR issue of course, and it is critical that we look beyond HRM for the source of some of these complexities. Commercial contracts between suppliers and customers, or between different agencies operating together in a partnership, shape the nature of HRM in the respective organizations. As we see in subsequent sections of the chapter, if an organization has chosen to outsource some of its work to a small firm or use an agency to provide labour because it is looking for cost reduction, it should come as no surprise that terms and conditions of employment will reflect that. On the other hand, a decision to pay above the going rate, to ensure that staff are continually re-trained and they are provided with a voice, then the HR and organizational outcomes are likely – all other things being equal – to be more beneficial. Other factors that influence HRM relate to the size and length of the commercial contract, the degree to which the parties agree to share risk, and the mechanisms in place to ensure that decisions are made in an open and constructive manner (Coyle-Shapiro et al., 2006; Marchington and Vincent, 2004). More generally, levels of trust and power differentials both within and between the collaborating organizations, and within wider institutional networks, also shape future patterns of HRM in significantly different ways (De Wever et al., 2005).

COMMITMENT ACROSS ORGANIZATIONAL BOUNDARIES

A major argument in HRM theory is that workers need to show commitment to organizational goals, particularly when employers are facing heightened competitive pressures. According to Guest and Dewe (1991: 78), the core of the concept of commitment is 'the acceptance of the goals and values of the organization, or what might be termed identity with the organization'. It is argued

that committed workers will produce better organizational performance (Gittell et al., 2008; Walton, 1985). HRM literature has also emphasized the importance of developing a strong organizational culture that encompasses shared beliefs and values as the key to developing employee commitment. As Gallie et al. (1998) note, employers may seek to influence worker commitment to organizational goals through HR practices and through the culture or values which they communicate to employees.

However, the notion of organizational commitment, identity and loyalty becomes problematic in situations where the notion of the single employer is open to question (Rubery et al., 2002). This is particularly pertinent in the case of multiple employers on a single site or where workers working for a service supplier firm have to adopt the identity of their non-employer client firm. It is also the case in public-private partnerships, where workers who are transferred from the public to the private sector may retain public sector values which diverge from those of their new employer. It is therefore often difficult for any individual organization (be it the legal employer or the client firm receiving the services) operating in a multi-employer environment to impose its own organizational values and culture on workers without simultaneously having to juggle with that of other organizations in the commercial relationship.

Our study of multi-employer sites (Marchington et al., 2005) found that employers use a variety of methods to amplify the visual image of their organization to workers employed by suppliers on one of their contracts. In so doing the intention is to increase workers' psychological commitment to the client rather than to their own employer. For example, in a multi-client call centre, customer service representatives (CSRs) are required to greet telephone callers in a way which aims to give these (potential) customers the impression they are speaking to an employee of the client company. In addition, premium client companies are encouraged to get involved in training and monitoring the CSRs from the call centre, and provide them with the client firms' T-shirts and stationery in order to help them identify with the client and differentiate themselves from colleagues providing services to other clients. In some cases, non-employer client organizations are even more proactive, often doing more than the worker's own employer, to develop commitment, identity and loyalty. This direct involvement in people management is undertaken to ensure that quality of service delivery matches their requirements. For instance, in order to increase 'bonding' between airlines and handling agents, prestigious airlines use the incentive of free flights, plus team-building activities, as part of a management strategy to secure the commitment of sub-contracted workers who are temporarily working for them (Rubery et al., 2003).

Though more complex than the 'simple' employer-employee relationship, the above situation is relatively straightforward in so far as there are only two employers in the picture – a supplier and a client. However, where a contractor provides services to multiple clients at the same workplace, workers may be required to display commitment to several organizations. For example, passenger handling agents employed by a firm which provides services to airlines can be required to put on several different uniforms in a single shift when they provide check-in and boarding services for different airlines. These workers may be simultaneously subject to HR interventions from a number of firms who compete for their loyalty and commitment. Yet more complex is the situation where a service supplier firm – such as a multi-client call centre – offers various types of employment contract (e.g., permanent, temporary and agency) to a workforce that delivers services to a number of client firms. While some of these firms are willing to accept HR interventions from their clients, others tend to resist the attempt by client firms to compete for the commitment of their own staff and instead reinforce their own HR policies, company culture and values (Marchington et al., 2005).

This discussion illustrates that it is difficult to conceptualize organizational commitment in a multi-employer environment, largely because it reduces the potential for employers to create a stable internal, high trust environment within a fragmented network. However, existing studies have found it is possible for workers to have multiple commitments, for example to trade union and employer (e.g. Angle and Perry, 1986; Guest and Dewe, 1991), to the organization, supervisors, co-workers and customers (Chan et al., 2006; Cooper-Hakim and Viswesvaran, 2005; Redman and Snape, 2005), to both the public and private sector ethos (Hebson et al., 2003; Pratchett and Wingfield, 1996), and to different organizations in a multi-employer environment (Rubery et al., 2003). There have also been some studies examining the commitment of contingent or agency workers to their client firm as well as to their employer, largely following on from work by Gallagher and McLean Parks (2001); it is interesting to note they made use of the term 'worker' rather than employee in order to examine commitment across organizational boundaries. They clarify that, although the legal employer pays the wages of agency staff, for example, most of the day-to-day experience of work is under the control and influence of the client. Moreover, they raise doubts about the efficacy of trying to develop commitment amongst non-employees as their time with the client may be 'rather "transitory" as they move from one client organization to another' (2001: 193). Of course, agency workers can also be listed with more than one agency at a time, and spread their work not just between clients but also between agencies, depending on where work is available or they can get the best deals.

Two recent studies have examined organizational commitment amongst groups of contracted-out or contingent workers, and despite both relying on relatively small samples they do show it is possible for dual commitment to occur. For example, Liden et al. (2003) found that contingent workers in a US manufacturing setting showed commitment to the client firm and to their employer provided they felt the client was concerned about fairness and that perceived organizational support was high. The reverse was also true; treating contingent workers as second class citizens led to lower levels of commitment. Coyle-Shapiro et al. (2006) reported similar findings from their study of contracts between four private sector firms and a local authority in the UK, noting that reciprocity gave rise to felt obligation.

This may be due to the client providing more favourable employment opportunities such as the prospect of a longer-term job, higher levels of pay, a career path or the chance to have their voice heard at work. For example, temporary workers may be committed to the client firm they currently work for in the hope of gaining longer-term employment (Saxenian, 1996) or because it sounds more glamorous and has better fringe benefits than working for their legal employer (Rubery et al., 2003). As Bartel (2001) observes, people working across organizational boundaries are more committed to their own employer only if they feel that this organization enjoys high external prestige. Nevertheless, we should not be over-optimistic about the ability of client organizations to secure agency or sub-contract workers' commitment to their goals unless there are serious attempts to provide better working conditions. Apart from those professional staff that are able to extract superior conditions because they are in short supply, evidence shows that most workers employed across organizational boundaries suffer from reduced job security, low pay and increased work intensification as a consequence of the commercial contracts that govern relations between clients and suppliers (Burchell et al., 1999; Marchington et al., 2005).

COMPLEXITIES IN DETERMINING PAY AND REWARD

The determination of pay involves a host of stakeholders and is influenced by a range of factors both internal and external to the employing organization. These include, for example, legislation, government policies, trade unions and employers associations, sectoral performance, product market position, and labour market conditions. Writers on pay systems (e.g. Kessler, 2000; Poole and Jenkins, 1998) highlight the dynamic tension that managements encounter in devising an appropriate reward structure and level of pay for their workforce. On the one hand, they need to maintain a level of consistency, fairness and equity within and across groups of employees in the internal labour market. On the other, they need to take advantage of the external labour market to source workers at a lower price and provide employers with higher levels of operational flexibility (e.g. Bone, 2006).

Inter-organizational business contracting relationships represent not only a further dimension that intensifies this internal/external tension (Marchington et al., 2005), but also provide opportunities for management to restructure its workforce and introduce new reward packages to keep down costs. More specifically, these pressures and opportunities arise through a number of scenarios. First, client firms may influence the terms and conditions of people employed by suppliers of labour, whether these are agencies, partners or other firms in the supply chain. This can occur through demands for contract staff or those who work for suppliers to be paid specific amounts and to follow the principles of work organization set down by clients. Consider the case of a handling firm at an airport that acts as a temping agency for a large number of airlines and seconds its passenger handling agents to them. Some of the more prestigious airlines demand their seconded agents are paid a wage premium above the normal level the handling firm offers to its passenger handling agents in order to elicit higher levels of commitment and motivation from these agents to provide better service. Another source of influence is the cost model adopted for each business contract between clients and suppliers at the same workplace. While some clients choose not to go for the lowest tender price and consequently either allow for some management discretion, or require suppliers, to offer better wages and conditions, others operate according to a cost reduction model of HRM and result in lower wage levels. Since many outsourced contracts tend to be relatively short term, sometimes with opportunities to renew, this means that the influence of client firms can open up wide variations in pay packages amongst workers who perform broadly similar tasks. This sort of flexibility makes harmonization of terms and conditions difficult, if not impossible, and it also constrains the flexible deployment of workers across different business contracts.

Second, rather than being seen as a constraint, the intervention of client firms may actually provide supplier firms with opportunities to offer less favourable pay packages to new workers as a way of reducing employment costs, particularly in cases where trade unions were influential. An example of this was found in Rubery et al. (2003), where the existing workforce employed by a handling firm at an airport had been paid up to 30 per cent above the market rate, and had in place a non-redundancy policy and restricted shift patterns. In preparation for bids for new commercial contracts with the airport, the firm set up subsidiaries and newly-recruited workers received much less generous conditions than those that were already in employment – including fixed-term contracts. In this situation, the contractor played an active role in exploiting the business and labour market conditions and by-passing the trade union, so that workers employed by the firm were paid at least three separate rates of pay according to whether they were existing employees, new workers on fixed-term contracts or agency staff who supplemented the workforce over the summer period. In the UK over the last decade, two and three-tier workforces have become more common, certainly as public sector organizations have been subject to privatization. However, whilst paying lower rates may be attractive to a client seeking reduced costs via contracting-out, it can also cause problems with labour retention and product quality, as well as being a major source of tension between workers

who are on different terms and conditions yet need to cooperate with each other to achieve targets. In the housing benefits case studied by Marchington et al. (2003), some individuals chose to hop from one form of contract to another – for instance from private firm to agency – in order to maximize their short-term earnings. This short-term opportunistic behaviour caused resentment from in-house staff, leading to frictions at work.

Finally, the outsourcing of service provision may result in the transfer of the business, as well as the staff, from the client to the supplier firms. In the UK, staff transferred under these circumstances may be protected by the Transfer of Undertakings (Protection of Employment) (TUPE) Regulations, which in principle should ensure that their contracts are preserved intact. However, where workers have been transferred from a number of firms into the same organization, a range of different terms and conditions may apply to workers performing broadly similar tasks, and this diversity creates additional barriers for management attempts to adopt a coherent and consistent HR policy. Nevertheless, research evidence suggests that the impact of TUPE has been limited in part due to the complexity of the issue, legislative loopholes and the impossibility to provide a comprehensive coverage of all aspects of employment terms and conditions, especially informal customs and practice (Cooke et al., 2004; Domberger, 1998). More worryingly, given that a larger proportion of women than men work in the service sector, where many of these changes are taking place, it is likely that their pay and conditions continue to lag behind those of men in multi-employer networks.

CHANGING SKILLS AND CAREERS IN NEW ORGANIZATIONAL FORMS

Many of the changes identified in the nature of skills and careers have been linked to changes in organizational forms. Specifically, explanations have centred upon the degree to which there has been a shift away from internalized employment arrangements that foster skill and career development through internal labour markets to one based on externalized employment arrangements characterized by networks of contractors, suppliers and clients. Internal labour markets ensure a link between skills and careers as individuals take sequential steps up the organization in what constitutes a 'natural skills progression'. (Doeringer and Piore, 1971). Processes of externalization undermine this by challenging the model that connects firm-specific skills with career advancement within the context of a singular, long term employment relationship between employee and employer (Cappelli, 1999). Whether processes of externalization have been exaggerated is an ongoing debate and the evidence, related to job tenure and steady rather than rising levels of contingent work, suggests the shift is not as pronounced as was depicted in the late 1990s (McGovern et al., 2007). However, it is certainly the case that changing organizational forms do bring about significant changes in the nature of skills and careers because of the shift away from the employing organization making the key decisions that shape employment.

Research shows that the nature of these changes are uneven and contradictory. In relation to skills, one of the key advantages of network forms is to facilitate learning across organizational boundaries, which should in theory encourage skill development. However, the evidence is mixed; in knowledge intensive firms, skilled and professional workers – such as IT specialists – benefit through experience of different workplaces, friendships and collaborations (Grugulis et al., 2003), but for less skilled workers the outlook is much more pessimistic. This is particularly apparent in relation to outsourcing, which in general has been shown to have a detrimental effect on skills. Walsh and Deery (2006) show a decline in opportunities for training and promotion for outsourced customer service workers compared with those employees retained in-house; this was due to the provider's limited resources to develop skills rather than a conscious decision not to develop them.

Even where motives for contracting are not solely related to cost-cutting, it is impossible to guarantee an environment conducive to practising and promoting skilled work. This happened with housing benefit workers who were transferred to a private sector firm, where the rationale for outsourcing was a combination of the need to acquire specialist expertise and technology and government pressures to improve performance. These skilled and professional workers experienced a decline in their skills, particularly in the capacity to use discretion, because of increased forms of monitoring. This was due to unequal power relations between the client and the contractor that led to the use of more direct contractual systems of control, including the stringent application of key performance indicators (Marchington et al., 2003).

Key trends identified in survey research on skills are the rise of 'social skills' (in the UK, see Felstead et al., 2002) and the rise of 'general' skills (in the United States, see Gould, 2002). Such trends can be linked to changing organizational forms, although this connection remains relatively unexplored. For example, boundary spanning employees in network forms are required to manage the multiple relationships that arise between clients, contractors and customers in order to achieve success (Marchington et al., 2005). Yet the processes that hinder or promote skill development in these situations are directly related to commercial contracts that impact on the employment relationship. These often create unforeseen tensions and unintended consequences. As Rubery et al. (2002: 669) argue, despite the best intentions of employers, 'it may be impossible for employers to make use of more direct contractual systems of control while at the same time increasing the autonomy of employees to take charge and manage complex relationships'.

The skills needed to develop careers in changing organizations are held to be more 'general' rather than firm-specific. However, in reality those working within changing organizational forms often need both general and firm-specific skills to build careers. If we take the example of the boundary-spanners mentioned above, Marchington et al. (2005) identify this as a new career route for those who manage inter-organizational relationships. These managers build sustainable relationships between the partners through a mixture of persuasion, influence, negotiation and power but central to their legitimacy is also their past firm-specific knowledge. Thus, while much of the literature assumes that firm-specific knowledge is redundant, this example shows how the value of context-specific knowledge continues. Yet, only when this is combined with more transferable 'entrepreneurial qualities' can it provide the avenue for career success. Here, individual responsibility for careers becomes ever more important in changing organizational forms. Martin (2005) found this to be the case in a study of Australian managers who in the context of organizational restructuring were reliant less on 'organizational' assets to build careers and more on social capital in the form of networking and marketing reputations. Others have argued that those managers too rooted in past forms of firm-specific skills and knowledge merely 'survive' new organizational forms, while the newer, and often younger, employees who display more 'entrepreneurial qualities' are more likely to progress in the firm despite their lack of technical grounding (Mulholland, 1998).

The new focus on individual responsibility for careers is most apparent in debates that outline a shift from organizational to boundaryless careers (Arthur and Rousseau, 1996). The boundaryless career involves individuals taking personal responsibility for their careers and moving between organizations in order to develop their employability and is seen to be a pattern particularly applicable to knowledge workers. The concept has been criticized on the grounds that the image of constant movement is over-exaggerated and such a thesis is applicable to only a few specific workers and industries (White et al., 2004). Even recent research in Silicon Valley, where many arguments for a shift to boundarylessness are at their most persuasive, has found variation in employment strategies and the use of varying incentives to generate commitment to the firms (Baron et al., 2001). Other studies show the importance of societal context in determining degrees of boundarylessness. For example, Donnelly (2008) uses case study evidence of consultancy work in the UK and the Netherlands to show how careers are shaped by societal context. For example, in the Netherlands Donnelly found elongated career structures linked to the education system in operation and the temporal flexibility utilized was also influenced by societal norms.

However, if career management by the firm is predicated on a long term view of both individual and employer needs (Schein, 1978), then the shorter contractual relationships that are often central to new organizational forms can serve to undermine this. It is important to note that this is not always the case. Contractual relationships that extend the employment relationship beyond the confines of the single organization can bring new career opportunities. For example, Colling (2005) shows how outsourced catering staff were able to utilize opportunities in different contract sites. However, a change that does appear to be significant, and can be related to less stable organizational contexts, is a discernible shift towards individuals taking responsibility for developing their own careers (Guest and King 2005), a trend that is bound to be reinforced by the fragmentation of large employment units and their replacement by smaller firms or individuals operating across networks (Storey et al., 2005). Rubery et al. (2002) highlight the dangers of promoting such instrumental behaviour towards careers and skills as an individual's main concern will be to develop their own employability rather than sharing knowledge and learning to benefit the network as a whole. This would certainly seem to be the case in the context of those industries that are experiencing skills shortages, such as television-programme making in the UK (Currie et al., 2006). Currie et al. show how employees have responded to organizational change by developing their careers through the use of occupational communities and a key research question is whether the blurring of organizational boundaries, and the associated unravelling of the ties between the single organization and the individual, has perpetuated this.

A shift to new organizational networks also has gendered implications, particularly as women's careers have been disadvantaged by traditional organizational forms. Research by Smith-Doer (2004) found the careers of women scientists developed better within network rather than hierarchical firms. However, other research evidence is less optimistic. Flatter hierarchies can mean an erosion of middle management positions where women have fared well in the past. There are some instances of women gaining from the creation of middle management roles in new organizational forms, particularly team leader roles that are needed to smooth over inter-organizational tensions between clients and contractors. However, these are premised on the display of gendered typical 'soft skills' that are rarely accompanied by substantial pay increases and fail to provide the experience and skills necessary to progress further (Hebson and Grugulis, 2005). Thus, there is no simple connection between the development of new organizational forms and how these impact on skills and careers. Consequences for skills and careers depend on the specific contractual relationships between employers and how these shape HRM, and because such relationships are unstable and shifting it becomes difficult for organizations and individuals to put in place a long term skills and career strategy.

SEARCHING FOR WORKER VOICE IN MULTI-EMPLOYER NETWORKS

Voice is a complex and multi-faceted phenomenon, comprising both indirect (collective) and direct (individual) forms. It is widely acknowledged that the former has declined substantially throughout most developed economies since the early 1980s, especially voice through trade unions. There are two sets of inter-connected explanations for this. First, it is argued that workers are keen to join unions but prevented from doing

so, either by management actions to prevent them gaining access, or by union failures to organize at workplaces where there are small numbers of potential members; this suggests an unfulfilled desire on the part of workers. The second argument is that there has been a withering away of support and workers no longer display much interest in collective voice, preferring instead to listen to their supervisors or go straight to management if they have queries. In the UK, this has led to an almost doubling (to nearly 50 per cent of the workforce) in what has been termed the 'never generation' (Bryson and Gomez, 2003) – that is people who have never been a member of a trade union during their working lives. Questions are then raised about what fills the gap if collective voice declines, and again in most developed economies, direct voice has grown significantly in terms of its presence if not its influence (Cox et al., 2006).

Opportunities for either indirect or direct voice are particularly fragmented at workplaces that are subject to inter-organizational contracting. This is inevitable because workers are confronted with increased difficulties collaborating with their colleagues in other organizations, partly due to logistical problems but also due to the fact they are often seen as competitors. Compared with the relatively 'simple' situation of a single employer-employee relationship, any move to contracting – whether down a supply chain, through a partnership or sub-contracting relationship at the same workplace or at a multi-employer site – increases the barriers to effective voice. As Erickson et al. (2002) note, union organizing is very difficult where the ultimate employer is 'elusive' due to layers of sub-contracting which diffuse responsibility across multiple actors.

The most straightforward situation is where workers are deployed on a temporary basis at the site of another employer. They can find it hard to develop strong ties with colleagues on 'permanent' contracts because they may only be working with them for the odd day at a time. Even when agency workers are on longer-term placements, say as a teacher at one school for a term, they are often resented by permanent staff, seen either as a threat to continued employment or as inadequately trained and insufficiently committed to student needs. At the same time, agency workers are likely to have different concerns from other staff at the school, thus making it more difficult to identify shared grievances or provide opportunities to unify their voice under a common cause. Moreover, a further problem arises for staff based at the workplace of another employer because their own employer is not immediately available if they wish to raise a grievance. Yet, more seriously, they tend to miss out on management communications because they are located elsewhere. This has clear gender implications as women often turn to agency working in order to combine work and family (Albert and Bradley, 1998); accordingly they are particularly vulnerable to loss of voice. However, even if mechanisms were available, it is understandable that agency workers would be reticent to raise concerns, either with their own employer or with the host employer, for fear it will reduce their opportunities for work in the future if they are identified as someone prepared to argue for their rights (Marchington et al., 2005). In short, such workers can find they are effectively disenfranchised from voice, both of a collective and an individual nature, and lack of access to information or consultation can have a major impact on their commitment to organizational (and union) goals.

A slightly different situation arises when staff from different employers work alongside one another on a semi-permanent basis, either in a partnership or in a multi-employer workplace, serving the same customers or patients. We have already shown how HRM can become fragmented in these situations because employers offer a range of different terms and conditions, including voice. Some may be represented by a trade union because that fits with overall employer strategy, time may be allowed for union members to meet during working hours, and management might be keen to enhance communications with all their staff. At the opposite extreme, those working for another employer at the

same site may find they are denied access to a union and any communications they receive from management are brief, out-of-date and irrelevant. The potential for friction between staff is therefore considerable, with far-reaching, negative implications, both for customer service and product quality (Marchington et al., 2005). Even in situations where there are attempts to unify structures – such as in health and social care – problems are not necessarily overcome by the appointment of a single manager to oversee the work of people from different employers; tensions and contradictions still remain between them due to differences in employment conditions and work organization. A common complaint by staff working for a manager from a different employer or at a site away from the rest of their original colleagues is that they feel isolated from regular communication loops and lack voice (Boaden et al., 2008).

It is typical to view loss of voice merely as an outcome of the shift to new organizational forms, something that arises directly as a *consequence* of contracting. Whilst this is accurate to some extent, it fails to acknowledge that the *rationale* for contracting in the first place might be because employers were keen to use agency workers or private sector firms purely in order to lower operating costs. Similarly, a key factor in the client's decision to outsource in the first place might have been to reduce the power and influence of trade unions or break up problematic groups of workers, and any subsequent loss of voice cannot therefore be seen as an unfortunate outcome of restructuring (Marchington et al., 2005). Once again, this has gender implications because many of the jobs that are contracted-out are low paid and held by women working in catering, cleaning and domestic work. While such jobs are generally difficult to organize in the private sector, public sector unions have been much more successful in unionizing these female-dominated groups of workers with high profile campaigns, for example around equal pay for work of equal value. Of course employers that play this game can also generate risks because their staff, being directly exposed to the superior conditions enjoyed by other people working next to them, may decide to quit and join one of the other employers at the same workplace.

There is some evidence that trade unions and governments are thinking beyond conventional responses which rely on the concept of the single employer and seeking to shape the conditions under which sub-contracting can take place. For example, in the UK, there have been attempts through the law (TUPE) and there are now requirements for contractors bidding for work with NHS Trusts to pay Agenda for Change pay rates. Associated with this seem to be added expectations that private sector firms should also recognize other issues to do with fair treatment (Marchington et al., 2009). In the USA, some trade unions have instigated novel ways of organizing to work with community groups to strengthen the position of poorly-paid workers at the bottom of the hierarchy (Osterman, 2006). For example, social movement unionism has identified two ways in which unions might counteract fragmented capital – new methods of recruiting, and targeting multi-employers or those that have influence over them. Other ways forward to protect workers in firms down the supply chain have been assessed by Locke et al. (2007).

CONCLUSIONS AND IMPLICATIONS

The purpose of this chapter has been to analyze HRM in an environment characterized by contracting between organizations, something which – though increasingly prevalent in most developed countries – remains undertheorized in the literature. In a short chapter it is impossible to cover the entire range of HR issues, so we made the choice to focus on the role of worker commitment and three aspects of HRM that can affect this: namely, pay determination, skill and careers, and voice.

The main conclusion is that HR policies and practices become more fragmented, disjointed and blurred as decisions are made by clients (or suppliers) that ultimately shape the conditions of workers employed by supplier (or client) organizations. At one level, this could be seen as problematic as it reduces consistency in decision-making and creates additional uncertainties for workers. Pay, for example, may be lower at a contractor than it was at the original employer or clients may seek to intervene in decisions about which workers should receive higher pay or get promoted. Similarly, career structures that may have appeared clear and unambiguous are rendered complex and disordered following a decision to sub-contract work (and workers) from one organization to another. Moreover, voice structures and processes become confused, and in some cases workers suffer by not being able to join recognized trade unions as well as missing out on communications from their own managers when they are employed at another site, for example when employed as an agency worker.

Yet, rather than seeing this merely as a consequence of contracting relations that is beyond the control of the client, an alternative perspective would see fragmentation, blurring and disorder as part of the rationale for contracting in the first place. In their attempt to increase flexibility and achieve restructuring, employers have taken advantage of greater opportunities to outsource work in order to reduce pay levels, make workers more responsible for their own careers, and deny them an independent voice at the workplace. As with other studies of HRM, it appears that women tend to bear the brunt of these consequences, largely because they are employed in greater numbers in (already low-paid) jobs that are most susceptible to sub-contracting across the network, and their career prospects are further limited.

Of course not all employers take this line, and some prefer to develop close, trusting relations with other organizations in order to ensure that customers receive reliable service and first class product quality. Much depends on the initial reasons that employers choose to use alternative suppliers rather than keep work internal to the organization, and HRM is inevitably shaped by these sorts of decisions. For example, in an environment where clients sell on the basis of high quality, it is more likely they will seek to persuade or require their suppliers to adopt a 'high road' approach to HRM. Conversely, where clients are more interested in reducing costs to the absolute minimum, then workers are likely to suffer the consequences of this strategy through 'low road' HRM. Whilst workers are more likely to be losers rather than winners in this process, such a scenario is not inevitable. Broadly, in order to establish which forms HRM takes in multi-employer networks, it is necessary to assess the balance of power between employers, the degree to which they seek to develop trust and the extent to which risk is passed from clients to supplier firms, and ultimately on to their staff. This requires an analytical mindset that links broader organizational and HR decisions together.

REFERENCES

Albert, S. and Bradley, K. (1998) 'Professional temporary agencies, women and professional discretion: Implications for organizations and management', *British Journal of Management*, 9: 261–72.

Angle, H. and Perry, J. (1986) 'Dual commitment labour-management relationship climate', *Academy of Management Journal*, 29 (1): 31–50.

Arthur, M.B. and Rousseau, D.M. (1996) *The Boundaryless Career: A New Employment Principle for a New Organisational Era.* Oxford: Oxford University Press.

Baron, J.N., Hannan, M., and Burton, M.D. (2001) 'Labor pains: Change in the organizational models and employee turnover in young high-tech firms', *American Journal of Sociology*, 106 (4): 960–1012.

Bartel, C. (2001) 'Social comparison in boundary-spanning work: Effects of community outreach on members' organizational identity and identification', *Administrative Science Quarterly*, 46 (3): 379–413.

Benson, J. (1998) 'Dual commitment: Contract workers in Australian manufacturing enterprises', *Journal of Management Studies*, 35 (3): 355–75.

Boaden, R., Marchington, M., Hyde, P., Harris, C., Sparrow, P., Pass, S., Carroll, M. and Cortvriend, P. (2008) *Improving Health through Human Resource Management: The process of engagement and alignment.* London: Chartered Institute of Personnel and Development.

Bone, J. (2006) ' "The longest day": "flexible contracts, performance-related pay and risk shifting in the UK direct selling sector', *Work, Employment and Society*, 20 (1): 109–27.

Bryson, A., and Gomez, R. (2003) 'Buying into union membership', in Gospel, H. and Wood, S. (eds) *Representing workers: union recognition and membership in Britain.* London: Routledge. pp. 72–91.

Burchell, B., Day, D., Hudson, M., Ladipo, D., Mankelow, R., Nolan, J., Reed, H. Wichert, I. and Wilkinson, F. (1999) *Job Insecurity and Work Intensification: flexibility and the changing boundaries of work*, Joseph Rowntree Foundation. York

Cappelli, P. (1999) 'Career jobs are dead', *California Management Review*, 42 (1): 146–67.

Chan, A., Feng, T.Q., Redman, T. and Snape, E. (2006) 'Evaluating the multi-dimensional view of employee commitment: A comparative UK-Chinese study', *International Journal of Human Resource Management*, 17 (11): 1873–87.

Colling, T. (2005) 'Managing human resources in the networked organisation', in S. Bach (ed.) *Managing Human Resources.* Oxford: Blackwell, pp. 90–112.

Cooke, F.L., Earnshaw, J., Marchington, M. and Rubery, J. (2004) 'For better and for worse? Transfer of undertakings and the reshaping of employment relations', *International Journal of Human Resource Management*, 15 (2): 276–94.

Cooper-Hakim, A. and Viswesvaran, C. (2005) 'The construct of work commitment: Testing and integrative framework', *Psychology Bulletin*, 131 (2): 241–59.

Cox, A., Zagelmeyer, S. and Marchington, M., (2006) 'Embedding employee involvement and participation at work', *Human Resource Management Journal*, 16 (3): 250–267.

Coyle-Shapiro, J., Morrow, P. and Kessler, I. (2006) 'Serving two organizations: Exploring the employment relationship of contracted employees', *Human Resource Management*, 45 (4): 561–83.

Currie, G., Tempest, S. and Starkey, K. (2006) 'New careers for old? Organizational and individual responses to changing boundaries', *International Journal of Human Resource Management*, 17 (4): 755–74.

De Wever, S. Martens, R. and Vandenbempt, K. (2005) 'The impact of trust on strategic resource acquisition through interorganizational networks: Towards a conceptual model', *Human Relations*, 58 (12): 1523–43.

Doeringer, P.B. and Piore, M.J. (1971) *Internal Labour Markets and Manpower Analysis.* Lexington: Heath.

Domberger, S. (1998) *The Contracting Organization: A Strategic Guide to Outsourcing.* Oxford: Oxford University Press.

Donnelly, R. (2008) 'Careers and temporal flexibility in the new economy: An Anglo-Dutch comparison of the organization of consultancy work', *Human Resource Management Journal*, 18 (3): 197–215.

Erickson, C. L., Fisk, C.L., Milkman, R., Mitchell, D.J.B. and Wong, K. (2002) 'Justice for janitors in Los Angeles: Lessons from three rounds of negotiations', *British Journal of Industrial Relations*, 40 (3): 543–68.

Felstead, A., Gallie, D., and Green, F. (2002) *Work Skills in Britain 1985–2002*, Nottingham: DfES Publications.

Gallagher, D. and McLean Parks, J. (2001) 'I pledge thee my troth … contingently: Commitment and the contingent work relationship', *Human Resource Management Review*, 11 (3): 181–208.

Gallie, D., White, M., Cheng, Y. and Tomlinson, M. (1998) *Restructuring the Employment Relationship.* Oxford: Oxford University Press.

Gittell, J., Weinberg, D., Pfefferle, S. and Bishop, C. (2008) 'Impact of relational coordination on job satisfaction and quality outcomes: A study of nursing homes', *Human Resource Management Journal*, 18 (2): 154–70.

Godard, J. (2004) 'A critical assessment of the high performance paradigm', *British Journal of Industrial Relations*, 42 (2): 349–78.

Gould, E. (2002) 'Rising wage inequality, comparative advantage and the growing importance of general skills in the United States' *Journal of Labor Economics,* 20 (1): 105–47.

Grugulis, I. Vincent, S. and Hebson, G. (2003) 'The future of professional work? The rise of the "network form" and the decline of discretion', *Human Resource Management Journal*, 13 (2): 49–59.

Guest, D. and Dewe, P. (1991) 'Company or trade union: Which wins workers' allegiance? A study of commitment in the UK electronics industry', *British Journal of Industry Relations*, 29 (1): 75–96.

Guest, D. and King, Z. (2005) 'Management development and career development', in S. Bach (ed.) *Managing Human Resources*, Oxford: Blackwell, pp. 237–65.

Hebson, G., Grimshaw, D. and Marchington, M. (2003) 'PPPs and the changing public sector ethos: Case-study evidence from the health and local authority sectors' *Work, Employment and Society*, 17 (3): 481–501.

Hebson, G. and Grugulis, I. (2005) 'Gender and new organizational forms', in Marchington, M., Grimshaw, D., Rubery, J. and Willmott, H. (2005): *Fragmenting Work:Blurring Organizational Boundaries and Disordering Hierarchies*, Oxford: Oxford University Press. 217–238

Hunter, L., Beaumont, P. and Sinclair, D. (1996) 'A "partnership" route to HRM', *Journal of Management Studies*, 33 (2): 235–57.

Kessler, I. (2000) 'Remuneration systems', in S. Bach and K. Sisson (eds) *Personnel Management*, Oxford: Blackwell, pp. 264–86.

Lepak, D. and Snell, S. (1999) 'The strategic management of human capital: Determinants and implications of different relationships', *Academy of Management Review*, 24 (1): 1–18.

Lepak, D., Taylor, S., Tekleab, A., Marrone, J. and Cohen, D. (2007), 'An examination of the use of high-investment human resource systems for core and support employees', *Human Resource Management*, 46 (2): 223–46.

Liden, R., Wayne, S., Kraimer, M. and Sparrowe, R. (2003) 'The dual commitment of contingent workers: An examination of contingents' commitment to the agency and the organization', *Journal of Organizational Behaviour*, 24 (5): 609–25.

Locke, R., Qin, F. and Brause, A. (2007), 'Does monitoring improve labour standards? Lessons from Nike', *Industrial and Labour Relations Review*, 61 (1): 1–31.

McGovern, P., Hill, Stephen, Mills, C., White, Michael (2007) *Market, Class and Employment.* Oxford: Oxford University Press.

Marchington, M. and Grugulis, I. (2000) "'Best Practice" HRM: Perfect opportunity or dangerous illusion?', *International Journal of Human Resource Management*, 11 (16): 1104–24.

Marchington, M., Cooke, F.L. and Hebson, G. (2003) 'Performing for the "customer": Managing housing benefit operations across organizational boundaries', *Local Government Studies*, 29 (1): 51–74.

Marchington, M. and Vincent, S. (2004) 'Analysing the influence of institutional, organizational and interpersonal forces in shaping inter-organizational relations', *Journal of Management Studies*, 41 (6): 1029–56.

Marchington, M., Grimshaw, D., Rubery, J. and Willmott, H. (2005) *Fragmenting Work: Blurring Organizational Boundaries and Disordering Hierarchies*, Oxford: Oxford University Press.

Marchington, M., Carroll, M., Grimshaw, D., Pass, S. and Rubery, J. (2009), *Managing People in Networked Organizations*, London, Chartered Institute of Personnel and Development.

Martin, B. (2005) 'Managers after the era of organizational restructuring: Towards a second managerial revolution', *Work, Employment and Society*, 19 (4): 747–60.

Mulholland, K. (1998) 'Survivors versus "movers and shakers": The reconstitution of management and careers in the privatized utilities', in P. Thompson and C. Warhurst (eds) *Workplaces of the Future*, London: Macmillan. pp. 184–203.

Nesheim, T., Olson, K.M. and Kalleberg, A.L. (2007) 'Externalizing the core: firms' use of employment intermediaries in the information and communication technology industries', *Human Resource Management*, 46 (2): 247–64.

Osterman, P. (2006) 'Community organizing and employee representation', *British Journal of Industrial Relations*, 44 (4): 629–49.

Peel, S. and Boxall, P. (2005) 'When is contracting preferable to employment? An exploration of management *and* worker perspectives', *Journal of Management Studies*, 42 (8): 1675–97.

Pratchett, L. and Wingfield, M. (1996) 'Petty bureaucracy and woolly minded liberalism? The changing ethos of local government officers', *Public Administration,* 74: 639–56.

Poole, M. and Jenkins, G. (1998) 'Human resource management and the theory of rewards: Evidence from a national survey', *British Journal of Industrial Relations* 36 (2): 227–47.

Redman, T. and Snape, E., (2005) 'Unpacking commitment: Multiple loyalties and employee behaviour', *Journal of Management Studies*, 42 (2): 301–28.

Rubery, J., Earnshaw, J., Marchington, M., Cooke, F.L. and Vincent, S. (2002) 'Changing organizational forms and the employment relationship', *Journal of Management Studies*, 39 (5): 645–72.

Rubery, J., Cooke, F.L., Marchington, M. and Earnshaw, J. (2003) 'Inter-organizational relations and employment in a multi-employer environment', *British Journal of Industrial Relations*, 41 (2): 265–89.

Saxenian, A. (1996) 'Beyond boundaries: Open labour markets and learning in Silicon Valley', in M.B. Arthur and D.M. Rousseau (eds) *The Boundaryless Career: A New Employment Principle for a New Organizational Era.* Oxford: Oxford University Press, pp. 23–39.

Schein, E.H. (1978) *Career Dynamics: Matching Individual and Organisational Needs.* Reading, MA: Addison Wesley.

Smith-Doerr, L. (2004) *Women's Work: Gender Equality vs. Hierarchy in the Life Sciences*, Boulder: Lynne Rienner Publishers.

Storey, J., Salaman, G. and Platman, K. (2005) 'Living with enterprise in an enterprise economy: Freelance and contract workers in the media', *Human Relations*, 58(8): 1033–54

Swart, J. and Kinnie, N. (2003) 'Knowledge-intensive firms: The influence of the client on HR systems', *Human Resource Management Journal*, 13 (3): 37–55.

Truss, C. (2004) 'Who's in the driving seat? Managing human resources in a franchise firm', *Human Resource Management Journal*, 14 (4): 57–75.

Walsh, J. and Deery, S. (2006) 'Refashioning organizational boundaries: Outsourcing customer service work', *Journal of Management Studies*, 43 (3): 557–82.

Walton, R. (1985) 'From control to commitment in the workplace', *Harvard Business Review*, March–April: 77–84.

White, M., Hill, S., Mills, C. and Smeaton, D. (2004) *Managing to change? British Workplaces and the Future of Work.* Hampshire: Palgrave Macmillan.

28

Ethics and HRM

Chris Provis

INTRODUCTION

This chapter identifies some ways in which established ethical theory can be applied to issues of HRM, and some theoretical issues which are especially salient in HRM.

Modern literature on ethical theory contains a number of prominent approaches that are relevant to HRM (see, for example, Solomon, 1992; Winstanley and Woodall, 2000; Claydon, 2000). Some have ancient roots, like virtue ethics, an approach to ethics which suggests that a criterion for judging behaviour can be found in the extent to which the behaviour manifests good character. Such a view can be found both in Aristotle and Confucius. Other well-known approaches include consequentialism, the view that actions can always be assessed in ethical terms just by considering their consequences, and deontology, the view that not only actions' consequences are relevant but also their intrinsic nature or the extent to which they conform with fundamental moral rules. Common deontological considerations are honesty, justice and fairness. After identifying ethical issues in HRM and the implications that the different approaches to ethics have for

those issues, towards the end of the chapter we shall say more about the different approaches themselves. To begin with, though, we ought to notice the general types of questions they aim to deal with.

A primary question for ethics is what actions ought to be done, that is which actions are right and which are wrong. Should I work back late to complete this important project, or leave early because my son expects me to take him to soccer practice? Another primary question is about value, that is which things are good and which are bad. Working hard can be good, but is it better than spending time at home with my family? Consequentialism offers a link between those two sorts of questions: an action is right if, and only if, it results in as much good or as little bad as any other available action. For human resource management, there is likely to be some emphasis on questions of rightness, but both sorts of questions are relevant. For example, some of the questions we touch on below revolve around the extent to which human resource policies and practices can be justified by the role they play in achievement of good organisational outcomes. That sort of view raises both the question whether such policies and practices can indeed be justified by outcomes, and also the question to what extent the organisational outcomes are genuinely good.

All those questions are normative, or pre-scriptive questions. That is, they are questions about what actually is right, or good. It is questions of that type that we shall mainly be concerned with here. Literature about ethics also includes descriptive material, such as survey studies about people's attitudes toward pay issues, or about what organisational processes are perceived as fair, and so on. These are essentially studies in psychology and sociology, and do not necessarily have direct implications about normative issues. However, such studies allow use of empir-ical methodologies which are common in other parts of human resource management literature, and may occasionally replace nor-mative analysis because of scepticism about possibilities of reaching conclusions about normative issues, sometimes associated with ethical relativism, the view that the truth of ethical claims is relative to individuals or communities who hold them.

It is beyond the scope of our present discussion to address general issues of ethical scepticism or relativism. However, both are difficult positions to defend consistently, since the sceptic or relativist typically seeks to argue that others ought to agree with sceptical or relativist conclusions, and that the requirement to agree is not in itself relative or subject to sceptical doubt. For that reason, general sceptical or relativist views are more likely to intrude covertly than to be argued explicitly, and we shall put them aside. It will be assumed here that it is possible to address normative issues through processes of discussion and analysis.

Nevertheless, it is worth noticing that a limited form of relativism has some direct relevance to human resource management in our increasingly globalised economy. It is at least true that different communities accept different norms and ethical views about a variety of issues, from the status of women to the importance of personal ties in staff selection (see for example, Sue-Chan and

Dasborough, 2006) and the use of child labour (Kolk and Van Tulder, 2004). It will be a question of ethics how to deal with disagreement about such issues (De George, 1999). However, the question how to deal with such disagreement seems to be one to address through analysis and discussion, and not simply put aside on grounds of relativism or sceptical doubt.

Our discussion therefore is about normative questions, and they revolve mainly around issues of rightness, rather than goodness: issues about what actions are right or wrong. Empirical studies of beliefs and attitudes do not address those issues directly, although we shall note several areas where empirical points are relevant to normative claims.

In the context of human resource man-agement, there are two normative areas to consider. On the one hand, we have to con-sider actions by human resource managers, whether individual actions or systematic human resource practices. Thus, for example, there are ethical questions to be considered about how human resource managers ought to treat applicants for employment, or about the policies they ought to put in place regarding pay and conditions. On the other hand, we have to consider ethical issues about actions by all organisational members, to the extent that these may be affected by human resource practices and policies. Kolodinsky notes that 'HR increasingly has become the focus of responsibility for compliance and ethics initiatives and resolution of such problems in organisations' (Kolodinsky, 2006: 48). Thus, for example, human resource policies may address issues of harassment or bullying, or of whistleblowing. Such policies may even include explicit 'ethics policies', perhaps embodying an organisational code of ethics and some supporting processes.

It is not necessarily straightforward to establish policies and processes that encour-age right action. It is well known that incentive systems can encourage one form of action, even when official organisational statements seek something different (Kerr, 1991). Codes of ethics or codes of conduct can identify right action, but may not be effective in bringing it about (Cassell et al., 1997). Human resource managers may act well insofar as their individual actions are concerned, and in policies on such matters as pay and conditions, but it is a step beyond that for human resource policies and practices to encourage and support ethical action by all organisational members.

It might seem that this would be a task for an area closely related to HRM, the area of human resource development, and indeed it is surprising that 'the relationship between Human Resource Development (HRD) and ethics has been largely ignored' (Hatcher, 2006: 87). However, it would be an error to assume that ethics is just a matter of individual development. Some business ethics literature focuses especially on questions about how to encourage and support ethical behaviour. Summarising some of the implications, Treviño and Nelson say that:

> Although ... internal factors such as individual moral development are important, we know that for most people ethical conduct depends, to a large extent, on external factors such as the rules of the work context, the reward system, what peers are doing, what authority figures expect, the roles people are asked to play, and more (Treviño and Nelson, 2007: 179).

One implication of this work is that it should not actually be human resource managers alone who have responsibility for supporting and fostering right action within organisations, even if Kolodinsky is correct that HR is increasingly the focus for ethics initiatives. As Weaver says, 'ethics must be integrated across, and have the support of, routine organizational functions' (Weaver, 2004: 123). Nevertheless, our focus here is on matters where human resource managers are likely to face distinctive expectations and responsibilities.

In summary, there are a number of different approaches to theoretical ethics, and different approaches may have different implications for human resource management. Although the literature includes a significant proportion of descriptive ethics about people's perceptions and attitudes, the crucial questions are

normative ones, about what human resource managers ought to do in their own actions and in policies and practices that encourage or inhibit various types of actions by organisational members. In the next section, we survey some issues that have raised specific ethical questions. We then conclude with comment on different approaches to ethical analysis and discussion, and their implications.

ETHICAL ISSUES IN HRM

We may divide issues of ethical significance into two categories: traditional HRM concerns, and new concerns that result from rapid and widespread change to organisational arrangements.

Traditional concerns

Traditional areas of HRM include recruitment and selection of staff, management of pay and conditions of work, training and development, and grievance handling. Known earlier as personnel management, the term 'human resource management' came into vogue in the 1980s. Explanations include the increased salience of personnel issues in a more competitive environment, and diminishing union strength, which led to a reduced salience for collective bargaining in many organisations (Kochan et al., 1986; Beaumont, 1993; Legge, 2007). It has often been associated with changed approaches and attitudes (Storey, 1994: 272), as well as an extended range of tasks. Nevertheless, in retaining past responsibilities of personnel management, it has retained some important ethical issues from the past, as well as creating new ones.

In particular, of course, in administration of pay and conditions, issues arise about how much employees ought to be paid, and what other conditions they ought to be afforded. Pay is often the most salient issue. Here, deontological concerns about justice, fairness and desert have been prominent. For example, issues of discrimination have been a focus for ethical discussion, in particular where there have been explicit differences in rates payable to men and to women. While it has become widely accepted that such differences cannot be justified in moral terms, there continues to be debate about the extent to which overall income differentials reflect continuing discrimination against specific groups, not resulting from explicit wage differentials, but from discrimination in hiring, promotion, or absence of conditions like appropriate child care (Burton, 1991). Apart from such questions about discrimination against some groups, ethical issues also arise about the extent to which it is possible to justify payment at different levels to workers in different countries, especially as multinational companies and global capital flows lead to relocation of industries in countries where wages and other conditions are lower than they have been in prior locations.

In recent years some particular attention has also been given to ethical questions about the very high pay often received by CEOs and other senior officials of major companies (Moriarty, 2005). This question clearly raises similar ethical considerations to questions about the pay of other workers. However, there are also a number of issues that are specific to this case, such as the effect of stock options (Angel and McCabe, 2007), and the question of CEO pay is more often considered in discussions about corporate governance than human resource management.

Apart from the impact of hiring practices on pay levels, there are general concerns about fairness and justice as significant ethical considerations in hiring decisions (Alder and Gilbert, 2006). However, it is not necessarily clear what fairness requires in these areas, whether in matters like hiring or in remuneration practices. Justice can either be seen to require some degree of equality – say, between entitlements of members of different groups or communities – or to recognise people's desert (Sadurski, 1985). In hiring, there might be several considerations relevant to desert. It might be considered that people with higher qualifications are more deserving of hire, or it might be suggested that preference ought to be given to people who are members of groups who have been disadvantaged by discrimination in the past, or it might be argued that how much a person actually needs the job is crucial in deciding who deserves to be employed (Cohen et al., 1977). Those sorts of considerations may sometimes reinforce one another, but in other cases they may point in different directions.

Similarly, in remuneration practice, qualifications might again be a factor relevant to desert, but so might be the effort or skill people bring to the job, the amount of time they work, or their seniority. There can be tension between prescriptions of justice, and what is seen to promote general well-being, especially because it may be argued that free labour markets promote efficiency and thereby improved economic output, with improved well-being for people in general, even if some injustices may be done to individuals to achieve that. For example, it may be argued that higher income differentials promote skill acquisition, even if that involves some degree of unfairness to individuals who are unable to acquire and exercise such skills.

The argument depends at least in part on empirical claims about effects of higher or lower skill differentials. Do they or do they not promote skill acquisition? If so, to what extent? More generally, ethical discussion can be affected by empirical questions about the effects of legislation regarding wages, the effects of collective bargaining, and of anti-discrimination laws. In matters like those, ethical discussion becomes mingled with political debate about free markets, and the extent to which labour markets ought to be regulated. For example, Frank has argued that market mechanisms will result in a lower than optimum provision of health and safety arrangements in firms (Frank, 1985: 125–131, 220–223). As a result, quite apart from considerations of justice, there are moral reasons directly related to people's well-being to ensure such arrangements are in place.

More generally, there is a long-standing argument that individual employees are at a disadvantage in market-based negotiations with employers, and so ought to be allowed to bargain collectively with employers (Córdova, 1990: 152). One ethical question which therefore has to be confronted by human resource management policies is whether unionisation of employers ought to be encouraged or discouraged (Legge, 2007). Ackers has said with some justification that 'the big debate in employment ethics concerns how far the state and social agencies, like trade unions, should be allowed to regulate the free market in order to protect workers' wages and conditions' (Ackers, 2001: 382). Even if it is accepted as ethically proper to discourage unionism, it is possible to raise ethical questions about the means of discouragement used, and there has been substantial criticism of the ethics of some methods of 'union-busting' (McClendon, 2006).

Another area in which justice and respect for persons seem to be important is grievance handling and dismissal. Where individuals are employed by large organisations, it may be asked to what extent they ought to be afforded similar rights to due process and natural justice as we may expect them to be afforded as citizens within a nation-state. The same general question arises in literature about employee participation, 'empowerment' or 'voice': To what extent should employees be afforded the same democratic rights as they might expect as citizens (Blumberg, 1973; Budd, 2004)?

One way of approaching such questions is by reference to a contractual relationship between employees and employers. This might be considered as analogous to the 'social contract' which political theorists have referred to, but there is a significant difference in that the 'social contract' is generally acknowledged to be purely hypothetical, and used to consider what reasonable political arrangements citizens might agree to as part of such a contract, or what obligations can reasonably be attributed to them (Simmons, 1979). This contrasts with employment situations, which usually embody some actual contract, even if it is not documented. Contractual employment arrangements often include some obligations of obedience on

the part of employees, and may be argued to override any obligations on employers to afford voice and due process to employees.

That argument may be countered by the retort that it only moves back the ethical issue to the question what are ethical terms for a contract of employment (Radin and Werhane, 2003). In general, it seems clear that not all practices allowed by law are ethically proper (see e.g. Wasserstrom, 1971), and ethical requirements may go beyond legal requirements. Thus, for example, in matters of training and human resource development, it may be appropriate for the needs of employees to be considered, as well as the needs of the organisation, even if there is no legal requirement for such consideration (Van Buren, 2003). An ethical case could be made in consequentialist terms referring to the benefits for employees, and it could also be made in terms of virtue ethics, by reference to developing human potential, and in terms of justice: what employees deserve.

However it is made, that case may certainly be contested, and is especially likely to be contested in the highly competitive environment that many organisations have found themselves in over recent years. As noted above, such changes have seen the emergence of a range of new ethical issues for human resource management. Indeed, a good deal of recent writing about ethical issues of human resource management focuses primarily on these newly emerging issues rather than on those that have been mentioned so far.

The new environment

The idea 'human resource management' replaced 'personnel management' partly because of the perception that more competitive environments required management of employees to be more fully integrated into overall organisational strategies, and the new approach has raised a variety of new ethical issues (Legge, 2000). Many organisations have had to meet changed conditions by increasing their flexibility, enabling them to adjust production or output to changes in demand and other environmental factors, and a natural part of integrating human resource management into business strategy has been to increase flexibility in the deployment of labour. This especially has raised new issues (Stanworth, 2000; Boxall and Purcell, 2007). For example, one well-known tactic used to achieve this has been a distinction between 'core' and 'peripheral' employees, where the latter may have employment arrangements which afford them substantially lower job security and predictability of employment than earlier arrangements. These or other arrangements can be imposed in the face of union opposition in some cases because increased mobility of capital offers employers opportunities for moving operations to alternative locations where wage standards are lower. They inevitably pose questions about fairness.

A number of other areas within human resource management have also seen developments which result from closer integration of human resource practices into overall business strategy. One is performance management. Winstanley notes that 'performance management is one of the most frequently criticised human resource management practices, usually in terms of technical effectiveness and motivational aspects' (Winstanley, 2000: 191), and that endeavours to meet such criticisms have tended to take the form of closer integration of performance management with organisational objectives, to ensure that individuals' performance chimes with those objectives as closely as possible. The result can be forms of behaviour control by management which raise concerns about employee autonomy, and renewed concern about the extent to which organisational objectives can properly be taken for granted, without room for employee 'voice' (Budd, 2004). Fox's earlier distinction between unitarist and pluralist frameworks has been drawn on to articulate ethical concerns in the new environment (Ackers, 2002).

In addressing such questions we may need to consider what options employers have open to them. It is an empirical question to what extent competitive pressures do require organisations to impose such arrangements on

employees, in the sense that it is an empirical question whether a particular organisation can continue to operate effectively without doing so. In the private sector, the question may revolve around profitability; in the public sector, around issues of public debt and economic management, or around the urgency and importance of the organisation's tasks. The question cannot be answered by ethical analysis alone, but ethical analysis can do two things. One, it can identify what empirical points it is crucial to address if human resource policies are to be morally defensible. Two, it can draw attention to the fact that if the socio-economic environment embodies conditions that make such policies inevitable, then there is an ethical requirement on us to consider ways in which the socio-economic environment may be modified to ameliorate the need for such policies.

This last point is a significant one throughout the ethics of human resource management. It was noted above that within organisations we need to consider how far human resource policies support or inhibit ethical action by all organisation members, as well as considering directly the ethics of human resource policies and the actions of human resource managers. At a higher level, it seems important to consider to what extent the overall socio-economic environment affects the extent to which human resource policies can satisfy reasonable ethical requirements. The general point is that often our regard for ethics should take into account the extent to which actions support or inhibit ethical action by others, and not only the direct ethical assessment of our own actions.

The establishment of competitive situations is an example of creation of contexts which may possibly inhibit ethical action, if they discourage mutual assistance and cooperation (Ackers, 2003: 9). That can occur within organisations, for example by payment schemes which give employees incentives to compete with one another, as well as being a facet of a wider socio-economic environment which increases competition amongst organisations. Both within organisations and amongst them, such competition is sometimes referred to as a means of stimulating efficiency. If it does so then the resulting improved delivery of goods and services is an ethical consideration in its favour. However, another outcome to be considered in conjunction with that improved output might be some discouragement of cooperative and mutually supportive relationships amongst individuals. For example, in their account of 'human resource maximisation' in 'just-in-time' work systems, Delbridge and Turnbull noted that the systems 'harness the peer pressure of fellow team members to ensure compliance with company objectives' (Delbridge and Turnbull, 1992: 63), and commented that within just-in-time quality control systems, 'the basis of quality control is therefore *management through blame*' (Delbridge and Turnbull, 1992: 65, italics in original).

Within organisations, there are other structural arrangements as well as competition amongst employees that can lead to ethical problems. One is simply the pressure to complete certain tasks within a limited amount of time. Van den Broek studied a call centre staffed by professional social workers who received and evaluated reports of child abuse. These employees found themselves caught between the obligations placed on them as employees to complete a certain quantity of work within a set time, and the obligations they felt as part of their professional role responsibilities. One of van den Broek's interviewees went so far as to say that their supervisor had 'no understanding or respect for the fact that there are humans and human lives involved, children's lives' (van den Broek, 2003: 245). In that case, employees felt themselves caught between conflicting obligations. That is a concern partly because of the stress it imposes, which may affect employees' well-being, and partly because it means that one way or another employees must fail to satisfy obligations they have.

Although that problem arose in van den Broek's study because of the employees' specific professional role, the same kind of ethical problem arises much more widely in the context where employees

are striving to attain 'work-life balance'. This has become a major item of discussion in recent HRM literature (see, for example, Albrecht, 2003; Houston, 2005) as a result of the pressure which work increasingly seems to place on people's other commitments, notably commitments to family members. The idea of 'family-friendly' work practices and workplaces is partly a response to competitive pressures which demand longer and less convenient hours of work from employees. To the extent that such issues impact especially on women (Simpson, 2000), they raise ethical questions of fairness and justice, but they are not confined to women, and wherever they occur they raise the same general issues about conflicts of obligations which are problematic in themselves and a source of psychological stress.

Employees and managers who find themselves in such situations confront what is sometimes referred to by ethics writers as the 'dirty hands' problem. This was originally conceived as a problem of politics, the idea that 'the vocation of politics somehow rightly requires its practitioners to violate important moral standards which prevail outside politics' (Coady, 1991: 373). However, the problem can be conceived as a more general one: as any situation which leads us into 'a violation and a betrayal of a person, value, or principle', where this is a sacrifice made for some moral or ethical demand that has a more pressing call on us (Stocker, 1990: 18).

Very often the pressures that create such dilemmas arise from cost pressures on organisations, imposed by a highly competitive socio-economic environment. To the extent that this environment means that managers and others confront such moral dilemmas on a regular basis, then we have the problem referred to above, that the environment itself seems to be ethically problematic. The ethics of human resource management therefore requires attention to institutional structures and arrangements from two different points of view. On the one hand, human resource policies and decisions construct situations in which other individuals have to make choices, and it seems morally problematic to construct situations in which others regularly confront such dilemmas. On the other hand, human resource policies and decisions are themselves arrived at under environmental constraints, and if these constraints limit the room for ethical action, then it may be that ethics requires more attention to the socio-economic environment than to the decisions themselves.

Other emerging ethical issues do not seem so directly to result from competitive pressures. For example, there have been concerns about worker privacy in the context of such issues as workplace surveillance and drug testing. Techniques of surveillance have emerged in conjunction with developments in the technology of work, and include monitoring of employee telephone calls, e-mail messages or internet usage.

Issues of privacy raise a new type of ethical consideration. While other issues discussed so far can be considered in terms of deontological considerations like justice or consequentialist attention to outcomes and their effects on people's well-being, matters of privacy seem to be most amenable to consideration in terms of rights: employee rights to decide for themselves how they act in certain areas, and rights to be free from certain forms of surveillance. Acceptance that there are such rights seems natural if we respect individuals as autonomous agents whose sense of self is morally important (Nye, 2002). However, claims to such rights may be met by counter-claims from employers and managers: rights to manage the business as they see fit, or rights to monitor certain aspects of employee behaviour which are argued to be relevant to work outcomes (Loch et al., 1998; Nye, 2002).

Here, once more, ethical discussion needs to be conducted in close alliance with empirical investigation. In some cases, for example, employee internet usage could involve organisations in legal liability (for example, through downloading and promulgating copyright material). It may be an issue once again to what extent employers have different, less intrusive options available to them. However, basic ethical issues may also be contested. For example, on the one hand, it may be contended that employers have absolute rights to monitor usage of equipment they provide. On the other hand, it may be argued to the contrary that employees have rights to free expression of thoughts and ideas inherent in their status as citizens in a democratic society (assuming that the social setting is a democratic one), and that unduly intrusive monitoring contravenes such rights.

Drug testing of employees raises similar questions, albeit with some differences (Cranford, 1998; Greenwood et al., 2006). Once again, it seems important to attend to factual matters. Different ethical considerations may apply in regard to testing employees for drugs which can threaten the safety of employees or others, compared with pre-employment testing to determine whether prospective employees use recreational drugs which may have only dubious relevance to their employment. In either case, it will be important to what extent the testing process is reliable, and other factors may also be ethically relevant, such as the extent to which it is voluntary to undergo testing. That sort of consideration will be relevant to ethical discussion whether it is conducted in consequentialist terms (when the reliability of testing will be a major concern), or in deontological terms or in terms of human rights (when issues like consent and due process may loom large).

Workplace surveillance and drug testing are associated with concerns about management intrusion into areas which are properly considered private to employees. Similar concerns have also been expressed about 'emotional labour', a term coined by Arlie Hochschild in *The Managed Heart* (1983). Emotional labour consists of managing one's emotional display, often so as to present an appearance which is appealing or acceptable to a customer: in Hochschild's phrase, being 'nicer than natural' (or, in some cases, like debt collectors, being 'nastier than natural'). It is not new for employees to manage and to be expected to manage their emotional display (see e.g., Bigus, 1972), but Hochschild's work began a new era of research and analysis which has included debate over the ethical implications of emotional labour. Some ethical issues about emotional labour revolve around the issue of 'authenticity', because emotions are related to an individual's 'self' with special intimacy (Ashforth and Humphrey, 1993; Erickson and Wharton, 1997), but another more tangible set of concerns is about the extent to which demands for certain types of emotional labour may encourage deceptive behaviour by employees (Provis, 2001). Issues of deception and honesty are themselves a wide concern in areas of human resource management, both in the context of communication within organisations, and in the context of labour relations bargaining (Provis, 2000), but many of the issues are not unique to this area, and similarly the ethical issues that arise in regard to emotional labour seem likely to be instances of wider ethical concerns to do with honesty or authenticity.

On the other hand, another area where ethical concerns have been receiving more and more attention does seem specific to human resource management. These concerns are about the extent to which employees have or ought to have rights to protection if they publicly identify legal or moral shortcomings in employer activities: so-called 'whistleblower' protection. As with emotional labour, discussion of whistleblowing can be found in past literature, but it has recently become more of a focus within human resource management. Lewis notes that 'the conventional but simplistic view of whistleblowers is that they are troublemakers who deserve to be punished for disloyalty' (Lewis, 2000: 268). However, it is not hard to find accounts which emphasise the extent to which whistleblowers tend to be 'conservative people devoted to their work and their organizations' (Glazer and Glazer, 1989: 5). While accusations of disloyalty have sometimes been made against whistleblowers, it seems hard to understand how such accusations can be supported morally in those many cases where whistleblowers have identified illegal activities by their employing organisations. It is possible that there may

be more room for argument in cases where activities are unethical but not illegal. Often, what is unethical is a matter of vigorous contestation. However, many documented cases suggest that cases where whistleblowers have identified activities that are unethical but not illegal are nevertheless ones where widely accepted community norms are being violated, and it is once again difficult to see what basis there can be for ethical criticism of employees who refuse to support such activities by their organisations. In such cases, it seems as though criticisms of whistleblowers can only reflect uncritical unitarist acceptance of management authority and organisational aims.

The case where difficulty arises is when an employee considers an activity to be legally or morally problematic but there is a sound case to be made for the opposite view (Miceli and Near, 1997). To what extent should dissent be accepted in such cases? For human resource management, the answer seems to be to ensure that mechanisms are in place that allow genuine consideration of dissenting points of view. Standard accounts of the ethics of whistleblowing refer to the extent to which the whistleblower has exhausted other options before blowing the whistle (Davis, 2003: 545–6), and it seems to be an implication that organisations are well advised to have in place realistic options for people to appeal to who have concerns about organisational policies or actions. The practical difficulty is to ensure that such mechanisms allow such genuine consideration without being unduly cumbersome and costly, and without imperilling organisational effectiveness (Lewis, 2002).

Those sorts of practical points arise in a number of HRM's ethical issues. Another is in management of workforce diversity. Earlier issues to do with discrimination have increasingly been caught up under this wider heading, as many communities include more and more groups with different ethnic backgrounds, religious commitments and cultural norms, and organisations hire more employees who have widely different characteristics in those respects, adding complexity to existing concerns about discrimination on grounds such as gender and race. While workforce diversity is sometimes commended as beneficial for organisations as well as desirable in itself, there is also evidence that it can sometimes impair organisational performance (Ogbonna and Harris, 2006: 382–3). Management difficulties can include the need to deal with religious conflict tied to cultural and ethnic diversity (Ogbonna and Harris, 2006: 394–5), and the fact that such diversity can also be tied to differences in linguistic ability (Ogbonna and Harris, 2006: 400). The problems can be exacerbated to the extent that they pose risks to safety. Managing them can be costly, and difficult also to the extent that they require dealing with issues of toleration that are intricate and emotive.

Here, we find raised in acute form two general points that we have already touched on. One is the fact that issues of ethics are often contested. Diversity management can involve dealing with clashes of culture and religion which are intimately tied to conflicting ethical views, but we have seen a variety of other cases where contestation is likely, from the relevance of different factors in determining pay, to clashes over organisational authority and rights to due process. Another is the difficulty of encouraging and supporting ethical action, a difficulty made all the greater by contestation about what is actually ethical. These two points lead us into some more general considerations about approaches to ethics in human resource management.

APPROACHES TO ETHICS

Lafer has written tellingly that 'while there is much debate over the correct philosophical approach to HR ethics, the one thing that most scholars share is the knowledge that their work is largely ignored by business managers' (Lafer, 2005: 275). Why should that be so?

One reason could be inherent in the nature of human resource management itself. A few years ago, the title of Karen Legge's article posed the questions 'Is HRM Ethical? Can HRM be Ethical?' (Legge, 1998). While noting differences between 'hard' and 'soft' models of human resource management, she noted that very many human resource arrangements start with a disadvantage if they are attempting to be ethical, in that most employment arrangements emerge from bargains between employers and employees which the latter are constrained to accept, imperilling any claim that the arrangements are freely consented to, and so violating at the outset one fundamental condition that would be widely considered as a pre-requisite for ethical status. Along similar lines, Greenwood has said that 'On the face of it, HRM violates any number of ethical proscriptions against using people. To call a person a resource is already to tread dangerously close to placing that human in the same category with office furniture and computers' (2002: 261). If it is true that human resource management contains ethical problems in its very conception, then it is hard to see what can be said about its ethics that will be useful to practising managers, and it is not surprising that they ignore academic writing about human resource ethics.

That in itself would not mean that such writing is pointless and irrelevant. Practising managers are not the only possible audience it may have. Anyone who has a hand in developing socio-economic policy – employees and ordinary citizens not least of all – might find it worth considering. It was noted above that if the environmental constraints on organisations create circumstances where people are constantly confronted by ethical dilemmas, then there seems to be a need for us to do what we can to change the environment. If the competitive pressures on managers force them into human resource policies which are ethically problematic, then the pressures are problematic, and everyone who can do so ought to take a hand in lessening them.

However, it may be possible to go beyond that. The fact that managers are subject to multiple practical constraints is something to be aware of whenever we give advice to them, ethical or otherwise. It is important to bear in mind those multiple demands and constraints that create moral dilemmas. Nevertheless, lessening those conflicts may not be the only thing to be done. As Coady has commented, we sometimes find ourselves in situations where 'you are damned if you do and damned if you don't, but one route can still make more moral sense than the other' (Coady, 1990: 272). The question is how to provide advice that helps managers make moral sense of such complex situations.

We then come to a further reason why human resource managers tend not to be greatly influenced by academic ethics writing. There are a variety of ethical positions to be found in the literature, and it is not always easy for readers to see a practicable road through them. Even if we believe that it is possible to take account of ethical considerations in difficult circumstances, we still have to deal with the fact that there seem to be a plethora of different approaches to ethical decision-making, which tend to prescribe different courses of action. At the outset, we mentioned virtue ethics, consequentialism and deontology, and we have seen some places where these approaches are relevant to human resource management. But which approach do we choose? Virtue ethics is the approach which suggests that actions ought to be evaluated by the extent to which they show moral virtue. Consequentialism is the view that only consequences matter in determining what is right. It is opposed by deontology, which is sometimes taken to comprise any non-consequentialist approach, or sometimes just those non-consequentialist views which emphasise the importance of justice and moral rules (for some discussion of terminology, see e.g. Pettit, 1991: 230; Davis, 1991; Cohen, 2004: 40–1). Prominent variants include the modern work of John Rawls, noted for its emphasis on the idea of fairness (Rawls, 1972).

In many cases, it is difficult enough to choose an ethical direction on the basis of those often conflicting approaches, but they do not exhaust the field. Other approaches revolve around ideas about human rights. The latter views may be forms of deontology, and have sometimes attracted forceful

opposition from consequentialists, starting with Bentham's well-known reference to rights as 'nonsense on stilts' (Bentham, 1843). As well as these, there are nowadays a number of other substantial approaches to be found, both in general ethics literature and in literature pertaining specifically to human resource management. One set of views revolves around the idea that we have obligations to particular other people, in contrast to the idea common both to Kantian and utilitarian views that our ethical statements must be 'universalisable': independent of the specific identity of any of the individuals involved (see e.g. Blum, 1980). Depending on how they are interpreted in practice, such views could have notable implications for human resource management, since they might contradict common views about the wrongness of nepotism and personal allegiance in organisational life. They are related to views based on the idea of 'care' which have emerged notably from work by Carol Gilligan, who argued that women's ethical decision-making tends to be different from men's by having greater regard for concrete relationships, in contrast to abstract principles (Gilligan, 1982).

Such approaches may also have some affinity with the 'stakeholder' approach which has come to prominence in business ethics since the work of Edward Freeman (e.g. Freeman, 1984), especially because of its opposition to the claim that business corporations have obligations only to their shareholders. Stakeholders may comprise a number of parties, including employees, and stakeholder theory can be used in analysis of ethical issues of human resource management (Greenwood and De Cieri, 2006). To the extent that such theories identify obligations as arising from relationships with specific individuals, groups or organisations, they, too, may run in a direction contrary to views which identify obligations as emerging from abstract, general considerations, whether of utility, justice or otherwise.

Here, it is easy to enter deep water, and in theoretical ethics there can be debate about the extent to which obligations based on specific relationships to particular parties can be taken account of in theories which revolve around abstract, universal considerations (see e.g. Pettit, 1988). That fact in itself highlights part of our difficulty. If we enter closely into such matters, it is unlikely that practising managers will be inclined to follow us there, and it will be no surprise that our work is ignored. If we do not, however, we run the risk of over-simplifying or distorting ethical views, and creating an appearance that choice of an ethical view is a matter of personal preference more than of thought and logic. The number of views we have just alluded to is daunting enough, and that brief summary does not purport to exhaust the field.

The variety of different views should not disguise the fact that on many issues there is broad agreement about what is ethical and what is not. Nevertheless, the points we have touched on above include many where there is scope for real ethical conflict over issues that constantly recur. How much should people be paid? How do we balance demands of efficiency and due process? How do we reconcile opposed claims by different individuals in an organisation? What rights do employees have, in the face of management authority and management demands? If there are different ethical theories which give contrary answers to such questions, what practical guidance can they offer?

Unfortunately for practical managers, the guidance which they provide is not straightforward, but that is not a failing of ethical theorists; it is inherent in the nature of ethics itself. It is misguided to hope for simple criteria which give unequivocal answers. Ghoshal (2005) has argued forcefully that bad theories promulgated by business academics have had multiple ill effects on business practice. We may be tempted toward such theories for various reasons. One reason, noted by Ghoshal and by others, is to imitate natural science, ignoring differences between the natural world and the human, social world. Another reason, equally relevant here, may be the desire to offer simple, easily usable methods to practising managers, taking attention away from the true complexities and subtleties that those managers confront. Ethics revolves around dimensions of human experience and intention and effort and perception which escape clear-cut remedies and answers. It can be the absence of such clarity and simplicity which encourages subjectivism and relativism. Modern management often seeks measurement and computation, and if it fails to find it in some area, then it may look on the area with scepticism and suspicion. We may face that response when ethical theories do not offer a generally acceptable set of criteria or standards that can be applied in a routine way. However, what ethical theories may do is identify the sorts of general considerations that are relevant to ethical conversation and discussion, and identify the errors we fall into when we proffer over-simple answers to hard questions. For human resource management, what ethical theories can do is not lay out a set of answers, but assist in considering and discussing issues, highlighting some of the things that are relevant to that consideration and discussion.

ACKNOWLEDGMENTS

The author is grateful to the editors and to Marilyn Clarke for comments on earlier versions of this chapter, and to Michelle Greenwood for several stimulating and useful discussions about ethics and HRM.

REFERENCES

Ackers, P. (2001) 'Employment ethics', in T. Redman and A. Wilkinson (eds)., *Contemporary Human Resource Management.* London: Pearson, pp. 377–403.

Ackers, P. (2002) 'Reframing employment relations: The case for neo-pluralism', *Industrial Relations Journal*, 33 (1): 2–19.

Ackers, P. (2003) 'The work-life balance from the perspective of economic policy actors', *Social Policy & Society*, 2 (3): 221–29.

Albrecht, G.H. (2003) 'How friendly are family friendly policies?' *Business Ethics Quarterly*, 13 (2): 177–92.

Alder, G.S. and Gilbert, J. (2006) 'Achieving ethics and fairness in hiring: Going beyond the law', *Journal of Business Ethics*, 68 (4): 449–64.

Angel, J.J. and McCabe, D.M. (2007) 'The ethics of managerial compensation: The case of executive stock options', *Journal of Business Ethics*, 78 (1–2): 225–35 (DOI 10.1007/s10551-006-9326-8).

Arlie Hochschild, A.R. (1983) *The Managed Heart*. Berkeley: University of California Press.

Ashforth, B.E. and Humphrey, R.H. (1993) 'Emotional labor in service roles: The influence of identity', *Academy of Management Review*, 18 (1): 88–115.

Beaumont, P.B. (1993) *Human Resource Management: Key Concepts and Skills*. London: Sage.

Bentham, J. (1843) *Anarchical Fallacies*. Edinburgh.

Bigus, O.E. (1972) 'The milkman and his customer', *Urban Life and Culture*, 1 (2): 131–65.

Blum, L.A. (1980) *Friendship, Altruism and Morality*. London: Routledge and Kegan Paul.

Blumberg, P.I. (1973) 'Corporate responsibility and the employee's duty of loyalty and obedience: A preliminary enquiry', in D. Votaw and S.P. Sethi (eds), *The Corporate Dilemma*. Englewood Cliffs, N.J.: Prentice-Hall, pp. 82–113.

Boxall, P. and Purcell, J. (2007) 'Strategic management and human resources: The pursuit of productivity, flexibility, and legitimacy', in A. Pinnington, R. Macklin and T. Campbell (eds), *Human Resource Management Ethics and Employment*. Oxford: Oxford University Press, pp. 66–80.

Budd, J.W. (2004) *Employment with a Human Face*. Ithaca: Cornell University Press.

Burton, C. (1991) *The Promise and the Price: The Struggle for Equal Opportunity in Women's Employment*. Sydney: Allen & Unwin.

Cassell, C., Johnson, P. and Smith, K. (1997) 'Opening the black box: Corporate codes of ethics in their organizational context', *Journal of Business Ethics*, 16 (10): 1077–93.

Claydon, T. (2000) 'Employee participation and involvement', in D. Winstanley and J. Woodall (eds), *Ethical Issues in Contemporary Human Resource Management*. London: Palgrave Macmillan, pp. 208–23.

Coady, C.A.J. (1990) 'Messy morality and the art of the possible', *Proceedings of the Aristotelian Society*, Supp. Vol. 64: 259–79.

Coady, C.A.J. (1991) 'Politics and the problem of dirty hands', in P. Singer (ed.), *A Companion to Ethics*. Oxford: Blackwell, pp. 373–83.

Cohen, M., Nagel, T. and Scanlon, T. (eds) (1977) *Equality and Preferential Treatment*. Princeton, NJ: Princeton University Press.

Cohen, S. (2004) *The Nature of Moral Reasoning*. Melbourne: Oxford University Press.

Córdova, E. (1990) 'Collective bargaining', in R. Blanpain (ed.), *Comparative Labour Law and Industrial Relations in Industrialised Market Economies*, 4th edition, Vol. 2. Deventer, The Netherlands: Kluwer Law and Taxation Publishers, pp. 151–177.

Cranford, M. (1998) 'Drug testing and the right to privacy: Arguing the ethics of workplace drug testing', *Journal of Business Ethics*, 17 (16): 1805–15.

Davis, M. (2003) 'Whistleblowing', in H. LaFollette (ed.), *The Oxford Handbook of Practical Ethics*. Oxford: Oxford University Press, pp. 539–63.

Davis, N. (1991) 'Contemporary deontology', in P. Singer (ed.), *A Companion to Ethics*. Oxford: Blackwell, pp. 205–18.

De George, R.T. (1999) 'International business ethics', in R.E. Frederick (ed.), *A Companion to Business Ethics*. Oxford: Blackwell, pp. 233–42.

Delbridge, R. and Turnbull, P. (1992) 'Human resource maximization: The management of labour under just-in-time manufacturing systems', in P. Blyton and P. Turnbull (eds), *Reassessing Human Resource Management*. London: Sage, pp. 56–73.

Erickson, R.J. and Wharton, A.S. (1997) 'Inauthenticity and depression', *Work and Occupations*, 24 (2): 188–213.

Frank, R.H. (1985) *Choosing the Right Pond*. New York: Oxford University Press.

Freeman, R.E. (1984) *Strategic Management: A Stakeholder Approach*. Boston: Pitman.

Ghoshal, S. (2005) 'Bad management theories are destroying good management practices', *Academy of Management Learning & Education*, 4 (1): 75–91.

Gilligan, C. (1982) *In a Different Voice*. Cambridge, Mass: Harvard University Press.

Glazer, M.P. and Glazer, P.M. (1989) *The Whistleblowers*. New York: Basic Books.

Greenwood, M. and De Cieri, H. (2006) 'Stakeholder theory and the ethics of HRM', in A. Pinnington, R. Macklin and T. Campbell (eds), *Human Resource Management Ethics and Employment*. Oxford: Oxford University Press, pp. 119–36.

Greenwood, M.R. (2002) 'Ethics and HRM: A review and conceptual analysis', *Journal of Business Ethics*, 36 (3): 261–78.

Greenwood, M.R., Holland, P. and Choong, K. (2006) 'Reevaluating drug testing: Questions of moral and symbolic control', in J.R. Deckop (ed.), *Human Resource Management Ethics*. Greenwich, Conn.: Information Age Publishing, pp. 161–180.

Hatcher, T. (2006) 'An examination of the potential of human resource development (HRD) to improve organizational ethics', in J.R. Deckop (ed.), *Human Resource Management Ethics*. Greenwich, Conn.: Information Age Publishing, 87–110.

Hochschild, A.R. (1983) *The Managed Heart*, University of California Press, Berkeley.

Houston, D. (ed.) (2005) *Work-Life Balance in the 21st Century*. New York: Palgrave Macmillan.

Kerr, S. (1991) 'On the folly of rewarding A, while hoping for B', in R.M. Steers and L.W. Porter (eds), *Motivation and Work Behavior*, 5th edition. New York: McGraw-Hill, pp. 485–98. Originally published in *Academy of Management Journal*, 18 (3) (1975), 769–83.

Kochan, T.A., Katz, H.C. and McKersie, R.B. (1986) *The Transformation of American Industrial Relations*. New York: Basic Books.

Kolk, A. and Van Tulder, R. (2004) 'Ethics in international business: Multinational approaches to child labor', *Journal of World Business*, 39 (1): 49–60.

Kolodinsky, R.W. (2006) 'Wisdom, ethics, and human resources management', in J.R. Deckop (ed.), *Human Resource Management Ethics*. Greenwich, Conn.: Information Age Publishing, pp. 47–69.

Lafer, G. (2005) 'The critical failure of workplace ethics', in J.W. Budd and J.G. Scoville (eds), *The Ethics of Human Resources and Industrial Relations*. Champaign, Ill.: Labor and Employment Relations Association, pp. 273–97.

Legge, K. (1998) 'Is HRM ethical? can HRM be ethical?' in M. Parker (ed.), *Ethics & Organizations*. London: Sage, pp. 150–172.

Legge, K. (2000) 'The ethical context of HRM: The ethical organisation in the boundaryless world', in D. Winstanley and J. Woodall (eds), *Ethical Issues in Contemporary Human Resource Management*. London: Palgrave Macmillan, pp. 23–40.

Legge, K. (2007) 'The ethics of HRM in dealing with individual employees without collective representation', in A. Pinnington, R. Macklin and T. Campbell (eds), *Human Resource Management Ethics and Employment*. Oxford: Oxford University Press, pp. 35–51.

Lewis, D. (2000) 'Whistleblowing', in D. Winstanley and J. Woodall (eds), *Ethical Issues in Contemporary Human Resource Management*. London: Palgrave Macmillan, pp. 267–77.

Lewis, D. (2002) 'Whistleblowing procedures at work: What are the implications for human resource practitioners?' *Business Ethics: A European Review*, 11 (3): 202–09.

Loch, K.D., S. Conger and E. Oz. (1998) 'Ownership, privacy and monitoring in the workplace: A debate on technology and ethics', *Journal of Business Ethics*, 17 (6): 653–63.

McClendon, J. (2006) 'The Consequences and Challenges of Union Decline', in J.R. Deckop (ed.), *Human Resource Management Ethics*. Greenwich, Conn.: Information Age Publishing, pp. 261–281.

Miceli, M.P. and Near, J.P. (1997) 'Whistle-blowing as antisocial behavior', in R.A. Giacalone and J. Greenberg (eds), *Antisocial Behavior in Organizations*. Thousand Oaks, Calif.: Sage, pp. 130–49.

Moriarty, J. (2005) 'Do CEOs get paid too much?', *Business Ethics Quarterly*, 15 (2): 257–81.

Nye, D. (2002) 'The "Privacy in employment" critique: A consideration of some of the arguments for "Ethical" HRM professional practice', *Business Ethics: A European Review*, 11 (3): 224–32.

Ogbonna, E. and Harris, L.C. (2006) 'The dynamics of employee relationships in an ethnically diverse workforce', *Human Relations*, 59 (3): 379–407.

Pettit, P. (1988) 'The paradox of loyalty', *American Philosophical Quarterly*, 25 (2): 163–71.

Pettit, P. (1991) 'Consequentialism', in P. Singer (ed.), *A Companion to Ethics*. Oxford: Blackwell, pp. 230–40.

Provis, C. (2000) 'Ethics, deception and labor negotiation', *Journal of Business Ethics*, 28 (2): 145–58.

Provis, C. (2001) 'The ethics of emotional labour', *Australian Journal of Professional and Applied Ethics*, 3 (2): 1–15.

Radin, T.J. and Werhane, P.H. (2003) 'Employment-at-will, employee rights, and future directions for employment', *Business Ethics Quarterly*, 13 (2): 113–30.

Rawls, J. (1972) *A Theory of Justice*. Oxford: Clarendon Press.

Sadurski, W. (1985) *Giving Desert Its Due*. Dordrecht: Reidel.

Simmons, A.J. (1979) *Moral Principles and Political Obligation*. Princeton: Princeton University Press.

Simpson, R. (2000) 'Presenteeism and the impact of long hours on managers', in D. Winstanley and J. Woodall (eds), *Ethical Issues in Contemporary Human Resource Management*. London: Palgrave Macmillan, pp. 156–71.

Solomon, R.C. (1992) *Ethics and Excellence*. New York: Oxford University Press.

Solomon, R.C. (1999) 'Business ethics and virtue', in R.E. Frederick (ed.) *A Companion to Business Ethics*. Oxford: Blackwell, pp. 30–37.

Stanworth, C. (2000) 'Flexible working patterns', in D. Winstanley and J. Woodall, (eds), *Ethical Issues in Contemporary Human Resource Management*. London: Palgrave Macmillan, pp. 137–155.

Stocker, M. (1990) *Plural and Conflicting Values*. Oxford: Clarendon Press.

Storey, J. (1994) 'The take-up of human resource management by mainstream companies: Key lessons from research', in J.R. Niland, R.D. Lansbury and C. Verevis (eds), *The Future of Industrial Relations*. Thousand Oaks: Sage, pp. 270–92.

Sue-Chan, C. and Dasborough, M.T. (2006) 'The influence of relation-based and rule-based regulations on hiring decisions in the Australian and Hong Kong Chinese cultural contexts', *International Journal of Human Resource Management*, 17 (7): 1267–92.

Treviño, L.K. and Nelson, K.A. (2007) *Managing Business Ethics: Straight Talk About How To Do It Right,* 4th. edition. New York: John Wiley & Sons.

Van Buren, H.J., III. (2003) 'Boundaryless careers and employability obligations', *Business Ethics Quarterly,* 13 (2): 131–49.

van den Broek, D. (2003) 'Selling human services: Public sector rationalisation and the call centre labour process', *Australian Bulletin of Labour*, 29 (3): 236–52.

Wasserstrom, R.A. (ed.) (1971) *Morality and the Law*. Belmont, Calif: Wadsworth.

Weaver, G.R. (2004) 'Ethics and employees: Making the connection', *Academy of Management Executive*, 18 (2): 121–25.

Winstanley, D. (2000) 'Conditions of worth and the performance management paradox', in D. Winstanley and J. Woodall, (eds), *Ethical Issues in Contemporary Human Resource Management*. London: Palgrave Macmillan, pp. 189–207.

Winstanley, D. and Woodall, J. (2000) 'Introduction', in D. Winstanley and J. Woodall, (eds), *Ethical Issues in Contemporary Human Resource Management*. London: Palgrave Macmillan, pp. 3–22.

29

Working Time and Work-Life Balance

Janet Walsh

INTRODUCTION

In the United States and Britain, as well as in other advanced economies, there has been intense debate about the time demands and pressures of work and their impact on employees' ability to coordinate their work and non-work commitments. Such concerns have surfaced in the argument that employees are experiencing a 'time squeeze' (Hochschild, 1997), with some commentators pronouncing that people are indeed 'fighting for time' (Epstein and Kalleberg, 2004). An important consequence of this debate is that governments and employers have become increasingly more involved in formulating and implementing policies designed to enhance the ability of employees to manage their work and family/life demands.

Within this context, the chapter discusses key developments in working time and work-life balance, examining in particular human resource policy making in this area. In the first section we examine trends in working time, the debate about the 'time squeeze' and the effects of work-life conflict on

employees and their organisations. Following this, evidence on work-life/family policy making is considered, including the ways in which work-life/family initiatives can assist employees in coordinating their work and nonwork activities. Finally, the implementation and future development of human resource initiatives in the work-family/life policy area are examined.

TRENDS IN WORKING TIME: THE TIME SQUEEZE?

There is a widely held view that the time demands and pressures of paid employment have escalated, with serious negative consequences for employees' family and social lives (Bunting, 2004). A number of factors underscore contemporary concerns about the issues of overwork and work-life balance. Perceptions of an intensification of work activity have occurred in part because of the employment reductions that have accompanied successive waves of corporate restructuring. For those employees who have retained their jobs, greater job insecurity and higher workloads have often been the consequence (Cappelli, 1995). New information technologies have also placed increasing demands on employees due to the fact that employers can more intensively monitor the time employees spend at work. In addition, employers can now communicate with employees outside of conventional work hours thus leading to the phenomenon of '24/7' access (Spector et al., 2004).

The 'time squeeze' is not necessarily a uniform trend, however, with important international variations in the extent to which employees work long hours. Employees in the US, the UK, Australia and Japan have been more likely to work longer hours (48 hours plus) than employees in continental Europe and Scandinavia (see Table 29.1). Indeed, in contrast to other European Union countries, the UK has shown high levels of long hours working, particularly among full-time male employees (Kodz et al., 2003: 87).

Furthermore, in the US, the UK, Australia and Japan, long hours working is not only evident among professional and managerial employees, as it is in many economies, but also lower level workers. In 1999, for instance, a significantly higher proportion of full-time male *manual* employees worked over 48 hours in the UK than in any other European Union country and in Japan it has been commonplace for employees in manufacturing to work large amounts of unscheduled overtime in order to fulfil production targets (Graham, 1995). According to Kodz et al. (2003: 15) two factors contribute to inter-country variations in working hours. Firstly, (paid) long hours, especially among manual workers, are more prevalent in countries that have higher levels of income inequality, mainly because overtime work is used to supplement relatively low hourly wage rates. Secondly, countries that have not sought to regulate working time, through either legislation or collective contractual agreements, have significantly higher proportions of employees working long hours.

Perceptions of a 'time squeeze' are also fuelled by changes in the nature of people's

Table 29.1   International variations in long hours working (48 hours plus)

	% employees working long hours	
	Men	Women
Group 1		
Japan	36	14
Australia	33	15
USA	25	11
UK	22	9
Group 2		
Germany	14	6
France	13	7
Sweden	12	6
Finland	11	4
Denmark	11	3
Italy	7	2
Netherlands	5	1

Note: All 1999 except the USA (1997) and Japan and Australia (both 1994). All 'actual' hours except Japan, Australia and USA ('usual'). Long hours threshold is over 48 for all countries except the USA (over 49 hours).

Source: Kodz et al. (2003: table 6.14)

domestic obligations. Drawing on American evidence, Jacobs and Gerson (2001; 2004) contend that the shift from male-breadwinner families to dual-income and single-parent households, rather than increases in the length of the working week, are critical to understanding why employees feel overworked. They contend that while average working time in the US has remained relatively stable, this masks a large increase in the combined working time of married couples – from 52.5 hours per week in 1970 to 63.1 per week in 2000. From this perspective it is the growth of dual-earner households that underpins people's perceptions of a 'time squeeze', with women's employment activity providing the main increase in couples' working time.

Nevertheless, the growth in women's paid employment does not appear to have transformed men's and women's domestic obligations. Although there is some indication that working fathers are now more willing to share child-care and household work, the gender division of tasks in many households is far from equal. Maume's (2006) analysis of

American data suggests that full-time married women are much more likely than full-time married men to restrict their work efforts (i.e. work fewer hours, refuse to travel, turn down a promotion, etc.) because of family responsibilities. Indeed this appears to be the case even when men and women both work full-time in professional and managerial jobs. Not surprisingly, women's work restrictions increase when they have children, particularly younger children, while parenthood has a negligible effect on men's work activity. As Maume (2006: 859) concludes 'gender traditionalism' rather than egalitarianism appears to characterise the contemporary household, even for full-time managerial and professional couples.

WORKING HOURS AND 'FACE TIME'

Despite international variations in working hours, the tendency for managerial and professional employees to work long hours is endemic in most developed economies. Not only do male managers work the longest hours in Britain but also the EU member states as a whole (Kodz et al., 2003:14). Why might this be the case? Working hours appear to be long among managerial employees because of their tendency to engage in 'competitive presenteeism' (Simpson, 1998). According to Simpson (1998) many managers who have experienced corporate restructuring feel they can only retain their positions by working long hours as a way of displaying commitment to the job.

More generally, in 'knowledge based' occupations, such as technical, professional and managerial work, the output of individuals may be difficult to ascertain so managers use 'face time' or an employee's physical presence at work as evidence of their productivity and effort.

Perlow's (1998) study of the work patterns of American software engineers demonstrates that managers actively shaped employees' expectations about working time by imposing work demands, such as meetings, deadlines and extra work; monitoring employees, for

Table 29.2   Reasons for working overtime in the UK's third work-life balance employee survey (N = 1,088 employees)

Reason for working overtime	% employees
Too much work to finish in normal hours	44
To make more money	19
Employer expects it	8
Staff shortages	5
The nature of the job	4
Meet deadlines/finish job	4
Like job	3
Meetings/training/events	2
Organisation encourages it	1
Do not want to let colleagues down	1
Pressure from work	1
Business travel	1

Source: Adapted from Hooker et al. (2007: table 2.4)

instance checking work and observing individuals in the execution of tasks and, finally, by managers displaying or 'modelling' the work activities and behaviours they sought from their subordinates.

The behaviour of co-workers, too, can be a contributory factor. An examination of law firms (Landers et al., 1996) suggests that junior lawyers were inclined to work longer hours if co-workers increased their hours. Such 'positional competition' compels individuals to work progressively longer hours thus leading to an outcome that is less optimal than one in which fewer hours are worked. This vicious cycle of escalating work hours has been aptly described as a prisoner's dilemma (Eastman, 1998).

In respect of people's reasons for working overtime, it appears that work overload ('too much work to finish in normal hours') is a critical factor (see Table 29.2). Similarly, lawyers who experienced intense work pressure, as well as those who were strongly committed to their work, were more inclined to work longer hours (Wallace, 1997). Psychological factors may also influence the tendency of people to work long hours. Brett and Stroh (2003) found that male managers who worked the longest hours (61 or more hours a week) not only benefited financially, but also experienced a heightened sense of self-esteem and accomplishment. In general, individuals are most likely to work long hours if they have:

- strong career identities;
- experience of work overload;
- supervisors who expect them to work long hours;
- fewer nonwork responsibilities;
- relatively greater financial needs (Major et al., 2002: 433).

Gender role expectations and childcare responsibilities may also influence people's hours of work. Analysis of the 1998 British Workplace Employee Relations Survey (WERS 98) demonstrates that full-time male employees were significantly more likely to work long hours than their female counterparts (Kodz et al., 2003: 42). Lengthy working hours were especially prevalent among men who were 25 to 50 years old, highly educated and in managerial occupations. It is arguable that male managers are able to work long hours because many are married to full-time homemakers who facilitate such intense work activity (Brett and Stroh, 2003).

Some commentators, however, dispute the notion that long work hours can be equated with 'overwork'. The female finance executives in Blair-Loy's (2004) study did not perceive long hours as 'overwork' because many of them were strongly committed to their work activity, occasionally to the extent that they experienced 'a heightened sense of purpose and meaning' (p. 306). Nevertheless, long work hours may not necessarily indicate that working time is being used efficiently. When the work schedules of a group of software engineers were altered, not only were the majority of engineers able to spend less time at work but they also believed they were more productive (Perlow, 1999). Moreover, while long hours may not be perceived as uniformly burdensome, there is evidence that such work patterns can damage people's health and psychological well-being. An analysis of 21 studies concluded that people who worked longer hours experienced poorer physical and psychological health (Sparks et al., 1997). Indeed, it is the potentially negative impact of work hours on people's health and well-being that has precipitated the legal regulation of working time, particularly in Europe.

Recent evidence from Britain suggests that legislation can affect, at least partially, people's working time habits. Since the introduction of the (European) Working Time Regulations there has been a slight reduction in the proportion of employees who usually work more than 48 hours a week (from 13 per cent in 1998 to 11 per cent in 2004) (Kersley et al., 2006: 266), as well as a significant fall in the incidence of overtime (from 67 per cent of employees in 2003 to 52 per cent in 2006) (Hooker et al., 2007). However, a significant proportion of British employees still work more than 48 hours a week, especially male employees, and long hours working remains widespread among managers. The British 2004 Workplace Employment Relations Survey (WERS 2004) reveals that managers were more likely to work long hours than non-managerial employees and they were less likely to be able to work flexitime or reduce their hours[1] (Kersley et al., 2006).

Thus, even when working time is regulated, as is the case in European countries, long working hours remain a pervasive characteristic of many managerial and professional jobs. In this context legislation has not precipitated major shifts in working time norms, at least for these occupational groups. It is against this backdrop that public concern about employees' work-life balance has grown, particularly regarding the impact of long work hours on employees' work and social lives.

WORKING HOURS AND WORK-LIFE CONFLICT

Much of the debate about employees' work-life balance presumes that excessively long working hours precipitate conflict between an individual's work and family roles. A person's involvement in multiple roles, however, may not necessarily have deleterious consequences. Indeed, multiple roles can have a positive impact on employees' well-being, particularly when the roles are fulfilling and rewarding (Greenhaus and Powell, 2006: 73). Nearly one in four female managers in Ruderman et al.'s (2002) study perceived that their personal lives provided psychological benefits, including feelings of confidence and self-esteem, which served to enhance their work performance. Indeed, an individual's commitment to multiple roles, such as parent, spouse and employee, was significantly associated with life satisfaction and a positive sense of self-worth and self-esteem.

Nevertheless, although participation in work and family roles can be beneficial, it is generally acknowledged that there is a point beyond which such commitments can become 'burdensome' and 'stressful' (Ruderman et al. 2002: 73). Within this context long work hours can be an important catalyst for work-family conflict, commonly defined as 'a form of interrole conflict in which the role pressures from the work and family domains are mutually incompatible in some respect' (Greenhaus and Beutell, 1985: 77; White et al., 2003). Moreover, long work hours not only lead to work to family conflict but are also indirectly associated with increased depression and other stress-related health problems (Major et al., 2002). For many employees, therefore, the more hours worked, the more likely it is that they will experience work to family/home conflict. Excessive work-family conflict however does not necessarily mean that employees prefer to spend less time at work. Employees may only be inclined to seek shorter work schedules when they are well off financially (Reynolds, 2003). Moreover, there is a tendency for professional and female employees to prefer shorter hours than manual and male employees.

Alongside long work hours, other features of the work context are significant predictors of work-family conflict, including variable and inflexible work schedules, weekend and shift work. Moreover, the nature of people's jobs and work regimes is an influential factor. Employees who face excessive work demands, as well as those who have limited job autonomy and discretion, are more inclined to report work-family conflict (Eby et al., 2005). In this case low job autonomy appears to constrain the ability of employees to control the timing of work and thus to coordinate their work and family activities.

A rather more controversial issue is whether particular types of employees are more prone to work-family/life conflict than others. Certainly the evidence indicates that dual earner couples and individuals with caring responsibilities, such as young children, large families and dependent elders, are more likely to experience work-family/life conflict (Roehling et al., 2003; Eby et al., 2005). It is also plausible that disparities in work and family role pressures might lead to gender differences in perceptions of work-family/life conflict. In some studies women report more work to family conflict than men, particularly when working longer hours (c.f. Gutek et al., 1991; Batt and Valcour, 2003).

A particular focus of the debate on the 'overwork culture' has been the effects of work-family/life conflict on people's health and well-being. Generally, studies suggest that greater levels of work-family conflict are associated with stress at work and increased burnout (Allen et al., 2000). Work-to-family conflict also appears to promote lower levels of life satisfaction, as well as physical and mental health complaints, including fatigue, nervous tension and depression (Allen et al., 2002: 293). Furthermore, work-family conflict has serious organisational consequences. People with high levels of work-family conflict tend to be less satisfied with their careers (Martins et al., 2002) and jobs in general (Allen et al., 2000). There is also a tendency for individuals experiencing work to family conflict to display less organisational commitment and higher turnover (Allen et al., 2000). Similarly, employees who report higher levels of family to work conflict are more likely to be absent from work (Anderson et al., 2002).

Evidence of the negative outcomes associated with work-life conflict has led to the development of programmes and policies that might alleviate such role pressures.

The focus of human resource policy making has thus shifted in recent years to measures that are designed to facilitate better work-life integration. It is the nature of these organisational work-life policies and practices that will be explored in the next section.

WORK-LIFE BALANCE POLICIES

Work-life balance policies encompass a variety of organisational initiatives that were initially designed to assist employees with the integration of paid work with family obligations and commitments. Generally, three types of measures are prominent (cf. Glass and Estes, 1997).

- Policies that seek to reduce employees' working hours so that they are able to fulfil their parental and caring obligations, for instance, part-time, term-time work and the provision of leave for vacation, illness, childbearing and family care.
- Policies that enhance employees' flexibility or control over the scheduling of work hours and the location of work, including flexi-time, compressed workweeks, job sharing and working at home.
- Policies that provide financial support and assistance to employees in respect of childcare, eldercare and the provision of support for sick children, as well as on- or off-site day care centres for children.

Extent of provision

Although there have been increases in employee entitlements to maternity and childcare leave in almost all OECD countries, there are large variations between countries in the provision of work-family benefits. Clearly, the availability of programmes and policies depends on the degree to which governments have sought to regulate employees' entitlements to work-family arrangements. In Northern Europe, especially the Nordic countries, there have been strong state policies on family welfare and benefits. By contrast, in the United States, the United Kingdom, Australia and Japan, employers have traditionally played a much more important role in the provision of family friendly arrangements, although they have generally not compensated for low levels of state provision (OECD 2001: 133). In the United States, for example, despite the unpaid parental leave provisions of the 1993 Family and Medical Leave Act, national governments have played a comparatively weak role in the regulation of family benefits. Minimal state entitlements and low levels of trade union membership have meant that employers have had a greater role in the development of family responsive policies in the United States than elsewhere (Glass and Fujimoto, 1995).

The case of Britain

Britain has occupied something of a midpoint between the United States and Western European countries in respect of family benefit entitlements. Despite a welfare state, governments have been generally reluctant to intervene in work-family policy making, even in the context of European Union Directives on working time and parental leave. Nevertheless, in the light of mounting concern about employees' work and family responsibilities, successive Labour Governments have sought to strengthen employees' entitlements to work-family policies over the past decade. New regulations on parental leave, part-time work and working time have been implemented, while the *Employment Act 2002* introduced paid paternity leave, improved maternity leave and pay, and offered parents and carers a new right to request flexible working. Furthermore, the *Work and Families Act 2006* has extended the right to request flexible working to carers of adults and strengthened further employees' entitlements to paid maternity and paternity leave.

As might be expected in the light of recent legislation, employers in Britain appear to have enhanced their family-friendly work practices. In WERS 2004 managers reported an increase in the actual provision of work-life balance arrangements, especially flexible working and paid leave. The ability to reduce

Table 29.3   Flexible-working and leave arrangements for non-managerial employees in continuing workplaces, 1998 and 2004

	% of continuing workplaces	
	1998	*2004*
Flexible working arrangement		
Switching from full-time to part-time hours	46	64
Flexi-time	19	26
Job-sharing	31	41
Homeworking	16	28
Term-time only	14	28
Annualised hours	8	13
Zero hours contracts	3	5
Leave arrangements		
Parental leave	38	73
Paid paternity/discretionary leave for fathers	48	92
Special paid leave in emergencies	24	31

Base: All continuing workplaces with 10 or more employees in 1998 and 2004. Figures are weighted and based on responses from at least 847 managers.

Source: Kersley et al. (2005: table 9).

working hours (70 per cent of workplaces) and to increase working hours (57 per cent of workplaces) were the most common flexible working arrangements, while flexitime (where an employee has no set start or finish time) was available in just over a third of workplaces (35 per cent) (Kersley et al., 2006: 250). In addition, there appear to have been substantial increases in the availability of paid paternity leave, parental leave and emergency paid leave (see Table 29.3) (Kersley et al., 2005: 30). Nevertheless, the provision of leave and financial assistance for the care of older adults appears to be rare (6 per cent and less than 1 per cent of workplaces respectively), and employers still remain reluctant to provide direct forms of child care assistance, such as workplace nurseries (Kersley et al., 2006: 254).

Of course, employees' perceptions of the availability of family friendly provisions might not necessarily be congruent with managers' reports. In this respect, while WERS 2004 indicates that employees perceived an

overall increase in the availability of flexible work arrangements, they believed certain types of provision to be far less widespread than others. In general, job sharing and working from home were considered by employees to be much less widely available than flexitime and reduced hours working. Moreover, a striking finding is the extent of uncertainty among employees about the availability of work-life benefits. Between 16 and 37 per cent of employees were unaware whether such benefits were available to them, arguably reflecting poor communication by organisations (Kersley et al., 2006: 252). Interestingly, Budd and Mumford's (2006: 38) analysis of WERS 98 indicated that those employees most likely to require work-family benefits, for instance single mothers in low-paying jobs, were less likely to perceive that they were available, while those least likely to need such benefits (e.g. well-paid, older-aged males) had the highest perceived access. This is believed to reflect the tendency of employers to use family-friendly policies as a recruitment tool for employees in higher-level jobs.

Finally, a critical question is the degree to which employees in Britain are actually using (as opposed to reporting the availability of) work-life balance practices. The 2006 Work-Life Balance Employee Survey (Hooker et al., 2007) shows that the practices most commonly taken up by employees were flexitime (49 per cent), working from home (44 per cent) and part-time work (38 per cent), although there had been little change in the overall proportions of employees working flexibly. Similarly, 17 per cent of employees had made use of their legal right to request flexible working (the same proportion as in 2003), with most employers agreeing to these requests. Importantly, however, the survey found a high level of flexible working that had been agreed informally with employers, with over half the workforce stating that they had worked flexibly in the past year. At the same time, the degree of unmet demand from employees for almost all flexible working arrangements had fallen. Overall, then, the evidence from Britain indicates that legislation on work-life benefits has stimulated increases in the availability of family leave provisions and certain types of flexible working. Employees perceive an overall increase in their access to flexible working arrangements, with flexitime, part-time work and working from home most commonly utilised if available.

Characteristics of the 'family-friendly' employer

While certain types of 'family-friendly' benefits may have become more prevalent in Britain and elsewhere, it is apparent that these are not uniformly distributed among workplaces. Some organisations and workplaces are more likely than others to adopt work-family/life policies. What factors might influence an organisation's responsiveness to work and family/life issues? An 'organisational adaptation' perspective suggests that the characteristics of a workforce influence the degree to which management perceives employment issues such as work-life balance to be significant (Wood et al., 2003). Hence, it might be anticipated that organisations with greater proportions of women and highly educated professional and technical staff will experience strong demand for work-family benefits, thus increasing employer responsiveness.

Alternatively, it has been suggested that organisational adoption of family friendly management practices is affected by a variety of institutional pressures and demands enshrined in regulations, laws and societal norms. Due to their size and visibility, it might be expected that large employers and public organisations would have a strong incentive to be responsive to institutional pressures for employer involvement in work-family issues (Goodstein, 1994). At the same time, large organisations are prone to have human resource specialists for whom work-life balance is likely to be a salient employment issue (Milliken et al., 1998). Similarly, the strong diffusion of work-family practices within an organisation's sector is likely to encourage non-adopters to implement such benefits.

Research indicates that the adoption of work-family/life policies is indeed strongly associated with workplace and organisational size. In general, larger organisations in both the US and Britain appear more likely to adopt work-family benefits (Goodstein, 1994; Glass and Fujimoto, 1995; Wood et al., 2003). Not surprisingly, such benefits are also more common in organisations with human resource departments and equal opportunities provision (Osterman, 1995; Wood et al., 2003). There is also some evidence that the more widely diffused a work-family practice within an organisation's sector or industry, the more likely that an organisation will adopt it (Goodstein, 1994). Similarly, the predominance of women in a workplace, as well as technical and professional staff are associated with employer involvement in work-family issues (Goodstein, 1994; Osterman, 1995).

An analysis of 'family friendly flexible management' in Britain (*viz.* part-time work, job sharing, working from home, parental leave, etc.) showed that in the late 1990s such practices were significantly more prevalent in public sector workplaces, the health industry and the financial services sector (Wood et al., 2003). By 2004, however, family friendly provisions, such as childcare support/assistance, leave arrangements and flexible working, were no longer significantly less available in private sector workplaces. This indicates that the government's work-life balance legislation may have precipitated a 'catch-up' in provision with the public sector. At the same time, larger workplaces, those with more female and technical employees and the financial services industry still had a higher incidence of practices (Whitehouse et al., 2007).

Interestingly, senior human resource managers appear to affect the responsiveness of an organisation is to work-family issues. Milliken et al. (1998) found that work-family benefits were more likely in organisations where senior human resource staff viewed work and family concerns as important and perceived that such matters would negatively affect employee productivity if they were not acted upon. Organisations that collected data on demographic and work-family matters, including employee surveys, exit interviews, were also more responsive to work-family issues.

Unions too may positively influence the adoption of work-family practices. Not only may unions articulate employee demands for certain types of benefits, but they may also provide information about policies and assist workers in using them (Budd and Mumford, 2004). Glass and Fujimoto (1995) found that American unions significantly improved the availability of leave arrangements, although they were not particularly conducive to the provision of child care assistance. Similarly, an analysis of WERS 98 showed that union presence significantly reduced the availability of some types of work-life balance practices, for example homeworking and flexible hours arrangements, but was positively associated with others, such as job sharing, parental leave and special paid leave (Budd and Mumford, 2004). Hence, unions appear to have mixed effects on work-family benefit provision.

Finally, a strand of research has emphasised the importance of high commitment management practices (*viz.* quality circles, employee participation and discretion) as a determinant of work-family benefit provision. According to Osterman (1995: 685) 'these new or transformed work systems are potentially related to work-family benefits because, for the new work systems to function, they require high levels of employee commitment to the enterprise and depend on employee initiative and employee ideas'. Although US evidence (Berg et al., 2003; Osterman, 1995) suggests that high commitment management practices enhance both the availability of work-family benefits and people's perceptions of their work-life balance, other studies have failed to confirm such findings. Indeed, in Britain certain high commitment practices, such as appraisal systems, appear to heighten levels of work-life conflict for both men and women (White et al., 2003).

Organisational benefits of work-family/life policies

Although most employers do not attempt to quantify the costs of work-family/life programmes, the business case benefits, such as reduced turnover and absenteeism, increased recruitment and retention, are widely cited rationales for their introduction in both small and larger organisations (Dex and Scheibl, 2001). However, some commentators remain unconvinced of the business case, arguing that work-life policies do not necessarily enhance organisational effectiveness, with few demonstrable positive effects on employee recruitment, retention, well-being or productivity (Sutton and Noe, 2005).

Certainly organisations may benefit from some types of work-family/life policies more than others. For instance, there appear to be many organisational benefits associated with flexible work schedules, including positive effects on employees' job satisfaction, productivity and absenteeism (Baltes et al., 1999; Dalton and Mesch, 1990). Indeed, it has been shown that employees who have access to flexible scheduling tend to have significantly greater organisational commitment regardless of the extent to which they have used such arrangements (Grover and Crooker, 1995; Scandura and Lankau, 1997). Furthermore, flexible schedules appear to be beneficial for employee well-being. Thomas and Ganster (1995) found that, of a number of work-life policies, only flexible schedules reduced work-family conflict, enhanced job satisfaction and improved people's psychological and physical health (*viz.* depression, cholesterol levels).

The evidence is rather more mixed in respect of childcare support. Certainly employees who have access to maternity leave and information about available child care do appear to be more inclined to remain with their employer (Grover and Crooker, 1995). However, while there is some evidence that workplace nurseries can reduce absenteeism and turnover (Milkovich and Gomez, 1976), other studies have failed to confirm such findings (e.g. Goff et al., 1990). Nevertheless,

Kossek and Nichol (1992) did find that users of workplace nurseries held more positive attitudes about their work and family responsibilities and were less likely to experience child care problems. Such provision may therefore create an environment in which employees are freed of anxieties about child care and are able to concentrate more effectively on their jobs. A critical factor here, however, may be the quality of the child care, rather than whether it is provided by an employer. Employees who are satisfied with their child care arrangements appear to experience less work-family conflict and, in turn, are less likely to be absent from work (Goff et al., 1990).

In general, then, work-family/life policies can have beneficial effects on individuals and their organisations. Employees whose organisations provide more work-family benefits appear to hold more positive work attitudes, including greater organisational commitment and less intention to leave their organisations (Thompson et al., 1999). Indeed, people appear to be more attached to organisations that offer family-friendly policies whether or not they have actually used those policies. According to Grover and Crooker (1995: 274) family-friendly policies have this effect because they symbolise a 'wider corporate concern' for employees. Furthermore, work-life policies may engender among employees a 'generalised sense of obligation to the workplace', with people more likely to engage in organisational citizenship behaviour, such as assisting co-workers and supervisors with their job duties and suggesting improvements, the more useful they perceive the work-life benefits available to them (Lambert, 2000: 811).

Of course, there is a view that the most effective organisational approach towards work-family conflict is one that seeks to combine work-life policies with complementary work systems and human resource practices (Batt and Valcour, 2003). Work design appears to be especially important in this regard. Employees who enjoy greater autonomy and discretion at work experience more control over managing their work and family demands and less work-family conflict.

Hence, employees with genuine flexibility and control over their work arrangements are not only more satisfied at work, but are also more content with their family lives (Clark, 2001).

Fewer studies have sought to investigate the impact of work-family policies on organisational performance. There is some evidence however that organisations with a greater range or 'bundle' of work-family policies, including childcare provision and assistance, flexible scheduling, parental leave, eldercare support, experience higher perceived organisational performance (Perry-Smith and Blum, 2000). However, work-life programmes do appear to positively affect the actual productivity of firms, particularly when there are larger numbers of women and professionals in the workforce (Konrad and Mangel, 2000). Finally, work-life programmes can enhance shareholder return. An examination of Fortune 500 companies showed that announcements of work-family initiatives led to increases in share prices, thereby indicating that investors view such programmes positively (Arthur and Cooke, 2004).

In summary, there is evidence to suggest that work-family policies can have positive consequences for both employee well-being and organisational effectiveness. Nevertheless, it is also apparent that employees may be reluctant to use such initiatives. The next section moves on to explore the factors that influence the utilisation of work-family policies and the barriers to the implementation of programmes.

MANAGING WORK-FAMILY/LIFE INITIATIVES

Barriers to utilisation

Although organisations can offer a range of family-friendly provisions, employees may not take advantage of these benefits. Many employees are reluctant to utilise work-life programmes, such as part-time or flexible work schedules, because they fear it will hinder their career advancement. Moreover, such beliefs may be especially pronounced in organisations which value 'face time' as an indicator of an employees' productivity or commitment. Another reason for the low utilisation rates of family friendly programmes is what Hochschild (1997) terms the 'impermeable "clay layer" of middle management'. (p. 31) Her investigation of a Fortune 500 company indicated that while most employees perceived considerable support for work-life policies from senior management, they were far more sceptical of the stance of middle management. As Hochschild (1997: 32) rightly notes, much depends on whether middle managers view work-life policies as either an employee 'privilege' or 'right'. Work-family/life programmes may therefore be underutilised because managers are reluctant to allow their employees to participate or apply the policies inconsistently.

The social context of the workplace appears to play a critical role in influencing employees' decisions to use work-life/family programmes. As Grover and Crooker (1995: 285) state 'even the most family friendly workplace policies are at best useless, or worse, counterproductive, if the work climate does not support them'. Not surprisingly, supportive work-family cultures, defined as 'the extent to which an organisation supports and values the integration of employees' work and family lives', are associated with greater utilisation rates of work-family benefits (Thompson et al., 1999). Furthermore, employees who perceive a supportive work-family culture report lower levels of work to family conflict and greater attachment to their organisations (Thompson et al., 1999: 409).

People's interpersonal relationships within workplaces also affect the ability of employees to manage their work and family demands. Social support from managers and co-workers appears to reduce the likelihood of employees experiencing work-family conflict, as do mentoring relationships (Anderson et al., 2002; Nielson et al., 2001). Furthermore, supportive supervisors and co-workers improve the retention rates of female employees, particularly following childbirth. According to Glass and Riley (1998: 1427) 'organisations that want to minimize turnover among childbearing women need to attend to the interpersonal treatment of these workers, communicating their value to the workplace and making reasonable accommodations to the temporary disabilities of pregnancy'. Hence, a family-friendly work climate, as well as supportive managers and co-workers, positively influence people's decisions to utilise work-life programmes, as well as their general work attitudes and behaviour.

'Family-friendly' backlash

Not surprisingly, the traditional focus of work-life policies has been on employees with children or other caregiving responsibilities. Hence, employees without family responsibilities can feel 'excluded' and thus inequitably treated. This can often occur as a consequence of the informal actions of managers, notably in the allocation of tasks and workloads. Nord et al. (2002) document, for instance, that 'employees with children were able to choose their flexible schedules first, forcing single/non-parent employees to work around those schedules'. Inevitably this often meant that employees without children were scheduled to work the later shifts, regardless of their own activities outside of work. As a consequence users of work-life policies may experience a 'backlash' due to the perception that they are receiving, in some way, unfair advantages at the expense of their co-workers. Poor communication, particularly about the effectiveness of work-life programmes, can also lead to the stigmatisation of users of work-life policies, reflected in cynical comments about those who use flextime and telecommuting (cf. Nord et al., 2002: 229).

It is difficult to ascertain the magnitude of 'family friendly' backlash. The 2006 British Work-Life Balance Survey asked employees whose co-workers had worked one or more flexible arrangements if there had been any negative consequences to them of their co-workers' arrangements (Hooker et al. 2007: 82, 192). Around one third of respondents reported negative consequences, with 15 per cent citing work-related outcomes, such as 'having to cover colleagues' workload', 'increased workload', 'staff shortages', etc. Communication problems, such as 'colleagues not being available for meetings' and 'lack of interaction', were perceived to be the most negative effect of colleagues' working from home. Other research suggests that male employees and parents of older children are most likely to view work-family policies unfavourably, primarily because such programmes are less relevant to their needs (Parker and Allen, 2001).

Organisational responses to the 'backlash' phenomenon vary. Some organisations have sought to broaden the scope of work-life policies to embrace a range of nonwork commitments, including employees' leisure interests and voluntary work activities. According to Lobel and Kossek (1996: 241), 'broader definitions of family are not enough; we need to change our focus from work/family to work/personal life. Every individual needs to manage the relationship between personal life and work life'. Moreover, it is recommended that organisations integrate their work-life programmes into general diversity initiatives in order to meet the needs of employees with different work and personal life profiles. Inevitably such a focus involves organisations assessing the needs and preferences of their employees and thus designing programmes that take into consideration the individual requirements of employees. For instance, employees at an international consulting firm wanted new programmes, including paid sabbatical leave and improved technical support for telecommuters, in addition to existing work-life initiatives (Nord et al., 2002: 230). Involving employees in the planning and implementation of work-life initiatives may therefore widen the scope and relevance of programmes and improve their effectiveness (Sutton and Noe, 2005).

In order to overcome 'backlash' problems, an organisation's human resource practices may require considerable adjustment (Nord et al., 2002: 236). Firstly, formal procedures governing the allocation of work assignments may be required to ensure that all employees are equitably treated, and

in particular to inhibit employees without children being overloaded. Secondly, alternative work arrangements, such as flexitime and telecommuting, are likely to warrant changes in training, performance evaluation and compensation systems so that employees are appropriately developed and recognised for their organisational inputs. According to Nord et al. (2002: 236) it is important that organisations 'overcome tendencies to underutilise telecommuters or devalue the contributions or commitment of flextime employees'. Thirdly, career development and promotion systems may need to be reformulated in accordance with the goals of work-life programmes, especially if employees take leave for personal development or family care, and are deployed on work assignments that are less demanding in terms of travel and client contact. Finally, it is recommended that human resource practitioners manage communication flows between the users of work-life initiatives and senior management, notably by providing information about the experiences of employees on such programmes.

In summary, co-worker resentments, sometimes referred to as 'family friendly backlash', have in some cases precipitated changes in the character of work-life policies, as well as a refashioning of the human resource practices that accompany such policies. Developments include a widening of the scope of policies to embrace a more varied range of work/personal life commitments, and the integration of work-life programmes into organisational diversity and 'cultural change' initiatives.

CONCLUSION

Employees' struggle to reconcile their work and lifestyle commitments has been the focus of considerable attention from both academics and policy makers in recent years. This reflects intense concern over the time demands and pressures of paid employment, precipitated in part by the imperatives of corporate restructuring and new information and communication technologies. Perceptions of a 'time squeeze' (Hochschild, 1997) are more acute in some countries than others, however. In the United States, Australia and Britain long hours working is evident not only among professional and managerial employees (as it is elsewhere), but also among employees in lower-level occupations. It is uncertain, however, whether long work hours are the main cause of the problems of overwork and work-life imbalance. The increasing prominence of dual-income and single-parent households rather than increases in the length of the working week *per se* may well underpin people's perceptions of a 'time famine'.

Clearly, people's inclination to work long hours is driven by a number of factors. All too often 'face time', notably people's physical presence at work, is taken as a sign of employees' productivity and commitment. Managers communicate their expectations about working hours through processes of monitoring and target-setting, while co-workers often increase their working hours in order to enhance their status and position relative to others. Aside from these social and organisational factors, however, individual employees appear to work very long hours for the financial and psychological rewards they derive from doing so. Although rewards might be forthcoming, it is also clear that long working hours can precipitate perceptions of work-life conflict and damage people's physical and psychological health. Indeed, excessive work-life conflict appears to have serious negative consequences for both employees and their organisations, leading to job and career dissatisfaction, lower organisational commitment and higher turnover.

It is against this backdrop that work-family/life policies have been developed in order to assist employees with the integration of paid employment with their family and leisure activities. The role played by employers in the provision of such initiatives, however, is very much dependent on the extent of governmental regulation of employees' work-family entitlements. As discussed above, the state has intervened considerably less in the United States than in European countries. The UK provides an interesting focus of analysis, as government mandated benefits have increased over the past decade due to the Labour Government's commitment to improving employees' work-life balance. This has led to a marked expansion of 'family friendly' arrangements, especially flexible working and paid leave.

Aside from government provision, the research indicates that some types of organisations are more likely to implement work-family/life policies than others, most notably large organisations, public sector workplaces and firms with human resource departments and female-oriented workforces. Senior human resource managers also play an important role in the diffusion of work-family benefits, particularly if they perceive work and family matters to be important for an organisation's bottom-line performance. In addition, US research has highlighted a positive relationship between high commitment management practices and work-family benefit provision, while other studies suggest that it is the combination of work-life policies with jobs that allow autonomy and discretion that is most likely to improve people's work-life balance.

What, then, are the business benefits of work-life policies? Certainly, work-life benefits appear to enhance people's commitment to, and willingness to remain, with their organisations. Given that positive work attitudes occur whether or not individuals actually use work-life policies, it is plausible that employees view such initiatives as an expression of corporate concern for their welfare (Grover and Crooker, 1995). In general, moreover, organisations that have a more extensive range or bundle of work-family policies have superior organisational performance. The potential business benefits of work-life policies, therefore, deserve to be highlighted with positive implications for firm-level productivity and shareholder value.

Despite organisational benefits, however, work-family/life practices are not necessarily easy or straightforward to administer. In order to maximise the utilisation of work-life benefits, organisations need to foster a supportive work climate, such that managers and co-workers are sensitive to employees' non-work commitments. At the same time, such programmes need to be administered in an 'inclusive' fashion so that employees without dependent children or care giving responsibilities are not excluded from the scope of work-life programmes or unfairly burdened due to co-workers working flexibly or taking leave entitlements. Human resource practitioners have a vital role to play in the implementation of work-life programmes, particularly in ensuring that training, appraisal, promotion and reward systems are aligned with policy goals and that users and non-users experience fair treatment.

Such observations are suggestive of a number of future research issues. The identification of work practices and human resource management policies that might reduce the propensity of individuals to work long hours in high pressure work cultures, particularly among professionals and managers, is a vital issue that requires further investigation. In addition, research on the actual implementation of work-family policies and programmes in a variety of different occupational and industrial contexts is merited, including the introduction of flexible work and reduced hours arrangements in work contexts where 'presenteeism' has been pervasive. At the same time it is apparent that much of the academic research on the impact of work-life/family programmes underlines the need for supportive supervisor and managerial behaviours if employee utilisation is to be maximised. To date, however, it has been unclear exactly what such social support should entail. Research being conducted in the US by Kossek and Hammer (2008) is seeking to shed light on this issue by identifying the type of supervisor behaviours that are most family supportive and to examine the consequences of such behaviours for the work, family and health outcomes of subordinates. Similarly, given the popularity of the 'business case' for work-family/life interventions, research on the effects of specific policies and practices on a range of indicators of job and organisational performance would serve to shed light on the 'bottom line' implications of such programmes.

Finally, it is important to investigate how work-life policies are evolving. It is apparent that the focus of work-life policy making is shifting to cater for the needs and requirements of a wider range of employees, rather than simply parents (mothers) of young children. Such developments are a response, in part, to the growing diversity of employees' personal lifestyles, as well as a pragmatic attempt to deal with the threat of 'backlash' from employees that have been considered ineligible for traditional work-family/life programmes. Nevertheless, there are some risks involved in such moves (cf. Lewis, 1996), notably that employees' struggle to coordinate work and family care responsibilities, including parental and elder care obligations, is underplayed and thus obscured by an increasingly broad and disparate work-life policy agenda.

NOTE

1 In the 2004 British Workplace Employment Relations Survey only 27 per cent of managers reported that they had *never* worked more than 48 hours a week over the previous year, compared with 41 per cent of supervisors and 63 per cent of other non-managerial employees. Moreover, in nearly two thirds of workplaces (61 per cent) managerial employees were not able to reduce their working hours and in just over a quarter (28 per cent) they were not able to work flexitime (Kersley et al., 2006: 267, 251).

REFERENCES

Allen, T.D., Herst, D.E.L., Bruck, C.S. and Sutton, M. (2000) 'Consequences Associated With Work-to-Family Conflict: A Review and Agenda for Future Research', *Journal of Occupational Health Psychology*, 5 (2):278–308.

Anderson, S.E., Coffey, B.S. and Byerly, R.T. (2002) 'Formal Organizational Initiatives and Informal Workplace Practices: Links to Work-Family Conflict and Job-Related Outcomes', *Journal of Management*, 28 (6):787–810.

Arthur, M.M. and Cook, A. (2004) 'Taking Stock of Work-Family Initiatives: How Announcements of

"Family-Friendly" Human Resource Decisions Affect Shareholder Value', *Industrial and Labor Relations Review*, 57 (4):599–613.

Baltes, B.B., Briggs, T.E., Huff, J.W., Wright, J.A. and Neuman, G.A. (1999) 'Flexible and Compressed Workweek Schedules: A Meta-Analysis of Their Effects on Work-Related Criteria', *Journal of Applied Psychology*, 84 (4):496–513.

Batt, R. and Valcour, Monique P. (2003) 'Human Resources Practices as Predictors of Work-Family Outcomes and Employee Turnover', *Industrial Relations*, 42 (3):189–220.

Berg, P., Kalleberg, A.L. and Appelbaum, E. (2003) 'Balancing Work and Family: The Role of High Commitment Environments', *Industrial Relations*, 42 (3):168–188.

Blair-Loy, M. (2004) Work Devotion and Work Time. In C.F. Epstein and A.L. Kalleberg (eds) *Fighting for Time*. New York: Russell Sage Foundation, 282–316.

Brett, J.M. and Stroh, L.K. (2003) 'Working 61 Plus Hours a Week: Why Do Managers Do It?', *Journal of Applied Psychology*, 88 (1):67–78.

Budd, J.W. and Mumford, K.A. (2004) 'Trade Unions and Family-Friendly Policies in Britain', *Industrial and Labor Relations Review*, 57 (2): 204–220.

Budd, J.W. and Mumford, K.A. (2006) 'Family-Friendly Work Practices in Britain: Availability and Perceived Accessibility', *Human Resource Management*, 45 (1):23–42.

Bunting, M. (2004) *Willing Slaves: How the Overwork Culture is Ruling Our Lives*. London: HarperCollins.

Cappelli, P. (1995) 'Rethinking Employment', *British Journal of Industrial Relations*, 33 (4):563–602.

Clark, S.C. (2001) 'Work Cultures and Work/Family Balance', *Journal of Vocational Behavior*, 58 (3): 348–365.

Dalton, D.R. and Mesch, D. (1990) 'The Impact of Flexible Scheduling on Employee Attendance and Turnover', *Administrative Science Quarterly*, 35 (2):370–387.

Dex, S. and Scheibl, F. (2001) 'Flexible and Family-friendly Working Arrangements in UK-Based SMEs: Business cases', *British Journal of Industrial Relations*, 39 (3): 411–432.

Eastman, W. (1998) 'Working for Position: Women, Men, and Managerial Work Hours', *Industrial Relations*, 37 (1):51–66.

Eby, L.T., Casper, W.J., Lockwood, A., Bordeaux, C. and Brinley, A. (2005) 'Work and Family Research in IO/OB: Content Analysis and Review of the Literature (1980–2002)', *Journal of Vocational Behavior*, 66 (1):124–197.

Epstein, C.F. and Kalleberg, A.L. (2004) Time and Work: Changes and Challenges. In C.F. Epstein and A.L. Kalleberg (eds) *Fighting for Time*. New York: Russell Sage Foundation, 1–21.

Glass, J.L. and Estes, S.B. (1997) 'The Family Responsive Workplace', *Annual Review of Sociology*, 23:289–313.

Glass, J.L. and Fujimoto, T. (1995) 'Employer Characteristics and the Provision of Family Responsive Policies', *Work and Occupations*, 22 (4):380–411.

Glass, J.L. and Riley, L. (1998) 'Family Responsive Policies and Employee Retention Following Childbirth', *Social Forces*, 76 (4): 1401–1435.

Goff, S.J., Mount, M.K. and Jamison, R.L. (1990) 'Employer Supported Child Care, Work-Family Conflict, and Absenteeism: A Field Study', *Personnel Psychology*, 43 (4):793–809.

Goodstein, J.D. (1994) 'Institutional Pressures and Strategic Responsiveness: Employer Involvement in Work-Family Issues', *Academy of Management Journal*, 37 (2):350–82.

Graham, L. (1995) *On the Line at Subaru-Isuzu*. Ithaca, Cornell University: ILR Press.

Greenhaus, J.H. and Beutell, N.J. (1985) 'Sources of Conflict between Work and Family Roles', *Academy of Management Journal*, 10 (1):76–88.

Greenhaus, J.H. and Powell, G.N. (2006) 'When Work and Family are Allies: A Theory of Work-Family Enrichment', *Academy of Management Review*, 31 (1):72–92.

Grover, S.L. and Crooker, K.J. (1995) 'Who Appreciates Family-Responsive Human Resource Policies: the Impact of Family-Friendly Policies on the Organizational Attachment of Parents and Non-Parents', *Personnel Psychology*, 48 (2):271–88.

Gutek, B.A., Searle, S. and Klepa, L. (1991) 'Rational versus Gender Role Explanations for Work-Family Conflict', *Journal of Applied Psychology*, 76 (4):560–8.

Hochschild, A.R. (1997) *The Time Bind*. New York: Henry Holt & Company.

Hooker, H., Neathey, F., Casebourne, J., Munro, M. (2007) The Third Work-Life Balance Employee Survey. DTI Employment Relations Research Series No. 58. London: DTI.

Jacobs, J.A. and Gerson, K. (2001) 'Overworked Individuals or Overworked Families?', *Work and Occupations*, 28 (1):40–63.

Jacobs, J.A. and Gerson, K. (2004) Understanding Changes in American Working Time: A Synthesis. In C.F. Epstein and A.L. Kalleberg (eds) *Fighting for Time*. New York: Russell Sage Foundation, 25–45.

Kersley, B., Alpin, C., Forth, J., Bryson, A., Bewley, H., Dix, G. and Oxenbridge, S. (2005) *Inside the Workplace: First Findings from the 2004*

Workplace Employment Relations Survey (WERS 2004). London: DTI.

Kersley, B., Alpin, C., Forth, J., Bryson, A., Bewley, H., Dix, G. and Oxenbridge, S. (2006) *Inside the Workplace: Findings from the 2004 Workplace Employment Relations Survey*. London: Routledge.

Kodz, J., Davis, S., Lain, D., Strebler, M., Rick, J., Bates, P., Cummings, J., Meager, N., Trinczek, R. and Palmer, S. (2003) *Working Long Hours: A Review of the Evidence. Volume 1 – Main Report*. Department of Trade and Industry, Employment Relations Research Series No. 16. London: DTI.

Konrad, A.M. and Mangel, R. (2000) 'The Impact of Work-Life Programs on Firm Productivity', *Strategic Management Journal*, 21 (12): 1225–1237.

Kossek, E.E. and Hammer, L. (2008) *Survey of Work and Nonwork Demands: A Feedback Report*. Based on the National Work, Family and Health Network Pilot Study for U.S. Grocery Industry Store. US: Work, Family and Health Network.

Kossek, E.E. and Nichol, V. (1992) 'The Effects of On-Site Child Care on Employee Attitudes and Performance', *Personnel Psychology*, 45 (2):485–509.

Lambert, S.J. (2000) 'Added Benefits: The Link Between Work-Life Benefits and Organizational Citizenship Behavior', *Academy of Management Journal*, 43 (5):801–15.

Landers, R.M., Rebitzer, R.B. and Taylor, L.J. (1996) Human Resources Practices and the Demographic Transformation of Professional Labor Markets. In P. Osterman (ed) Broken Ladders: Managerial Careers in the New Economy. New York: Oxford University Press, 215–246.

Lewis, S. (1996) Rethinking Employment: An Organizational Culture Change Framework. In S. Lewis and J. Lewis (eds) *The Work-Family Challenge*. London: Sage, 1–19.

Lobel, S. and Kossek, E.E. (1996) Human Resource Strategies to Support Diversity in Work and Personal Lifestyles: Beyond the "Family Friendly" Organization. In E.E. Kossek and S.A. Lobel (eds) *Managing Diversity*. Oxford: Blackwell, 221–244.

Major, V.S., Klein, K.J. and Ehrhart, M.G. (2002) 'Work Time, Work Interference with Family, and Psychological Distress', *Journal of Applied Psychology*, 87 (3):427–436.

Martins, L.L., Eddleston, K.A. and Veiga, J.F. (2002) 'Moderators of the Relationship between Work-Family Conflict and Career Satisfaction', *Academy of Management Journal*, 45 (2):399–409.

Maume, D.J. (2006) 'Gender Differences in Restricting Work Efforts because of Family Responsibilities', *Journal of Marriage and Family*, 68 (4), November: 859–869.

Milkovich, G. and Gomez, L.R. (1976) 'Child Care and Selected Work Behaviours', *Academy of Management Journal*, 19 (1):111–115.

Milliken, F.J., Martins, L.L. and Morgan, H. (1998) 'Explaining Organizational Responsiveness to Work-Family Issues: The Role of Human Resource Executives as Issue Interpreters', *Academy of Management Journal*, 41 (5):580–592.

Nielson, T.R., Carlson, D.S. and Lankau, M.J. (2001) 'The Supportive Mentor as a Means of Reducing Work-Family Conflict', *Journal of Vocational Behavior*, 59 (3):364–381.

Nord, W.R., Fox, S., Phoenix, A. and Viano, K. (2002) 'Real-World Reactions to Work-Life Balance Programs: Lessons for Effective Implementation', *Organizational Dynamics*, 30 (3):223–238.

Organisation for Economic Co-operation and Development (OECD) (2001) *Employment Outlook*. Paris: OECD.

Osterman, P. (1995) 'Work/family Programs and the Employment Relationship', *Administrative Science Quarterly*, 40 (4):681–700.

Parker, L. and Allen, T.D. (2001) 'Work/Family Benefits: Variables Related to Employees' Fairness Perceptions', *Journal of Vocational Behavior*, 58 (3): 453–468.

Perlow, L.A. (1998) 'Boundary Control: The Social Ordering of Work and Family Time in a High-tech Corporation', *Administrative Science Quarterly*, 43 (2):328–357.

Perlow, L.A. (1999) *Finding Time: How Corporations, Individuals, and Families Can Benefit from New Work Practices*. CUP: ILR Press.

Perry-Smith, J.E. and Blum, T.C. (2000) 'Work-Family Human Resource Bundles and Perceived Organizational Performance', *Academy of Management Journal*, 43 (6):1107–1117.

Reynolds, J. (2003) 'You Can't Always Get the Hours You Want: Mismatches between Actual and Preferred Work Hours in the U.S.', *Social Forces* 81 (4):1171–1199.

Roehling, P.V., Moen, P. and Batt, R. (2003) Spillover. In P. Moen (ed) *It's About Time: Couples and Careers*. ILR/Cornell University Press, 101–121.

Ruderman, M.N., Ohlott, P.J., Panzer, K. and King, S.N. (2002) 'Benefits of Multiple Roles for Managerial Women', *Academy of Management Journal*, 45 (2): 315–330.

Scandura, T.A. and Lankau, M.J. (1997) 'Relationships of Gender, Family Responsibility and Flexible Work Hours to Organizational Commitment and Job Satisfaction', *Journal of Organizational Behavior*, 18 (4):377–91.

Simpson, R. (1998) 'Presenteeism, Power and Organisational Change: Long Hours as a Career Barrier and the Impact on the Working Lives of Women Managers', *British Journal of Management*, 9 (s1): 37–50.

Sparks, K., Cooper, C., Fried, Y. and Shirom, A. (1997) 'The Effects of Hours of Work on Health: A Meta-Analytic Review', *Journal of Occupational and Organizational Psychology*, 70: 391–408.

Spector, P., Cooper, C.L., Poelmans, S., Allen, T.D., O'Driscoll, M., Sanchez, J.I., Siu Ling, O., Dewe, P., Hart, P. and Lu, L. (2004) 'A Cross-National Comparative study of Work-Family Stressors, Working Hours, and Well-being: China and Latin America Versus The Anglo World', *Personnel Psychology*, 57 (1):119–142.

Sutton, K.L. and Noe, R.A. (2005) Family Friendly Programs and Work-Life Integration: More Myth than Magic? In E.E. Kossek and S.J. Lambert (eds) *Work and Life Integration: Organizational, Cultural and Individual Perspectives*. Mahwah, NJ: Erbaum, 151–170.

Thomas, L.T. and Ganster, D.C. (1995) 'Impact of Family-Supportive Work Variables on Work-Family Conflict and Strain: A Control Perspective', *Journal of Applied Psychology*, 80 (1): 6–15.

Thompson, C.A., Beauvais, L.L. and Lyness, K.S. (1999) 'When Work-Family Benefits are not Enough: The Influence of Work-Family Culture on Benefit Utilization, Organizational Attachment, and Work-Family Conflict', *Journal of Vocational Behavior*, 54 (3):392–415.

Wallace, J. (1997) 'It's About time: A Study of Hours Worked and Work Spillover Among Law Firm Lawyers', *Journal of Vocational Behavior*, 50 (2): 227–248.

White, M., Hill, S., McGovern, P., Mills, C. and Smeaton, D. (2003) ' "high-Performance" Management Practices, Working Hours and Work-Life Balance'. *British Journal of Industrial Relations*, 41 (2):175–195.

Whitehouse, G., Haynes, M., MacDonald, F. and Arts, D. (2007) *Reassessing the 'Family-friendly Workplace': Trends and Influences in Britain, 1998–2004*. DTI Employment Relations Research Series, No. 76. London: DTI.

Wood, S.J., De Menezes, L.M. and Lasaosa, A. (2003) 'Family-Friendly Management in Great Britain: Testing Various Perspectives', *Industrial Relations*, 42 (3):221–250.

PART IV

Sectoral Perspectives

30

Human Resource Management in the Service Sector

Jody Hoffer Gittell and Rob Seidner

INTRODUCTION

The service sector now accounts for over 70% of employment in the industrialized economies of the world, with Norway and the United States out front at over 75% of employment (OECD, 2005). Telecommunications, transportation, wholesale/retail, finance, insurance and business services account for about 60% of all employment created in the industrialized economies over the past decade, while community, social and personal services, including health and education, account for the remaining 40%. Looking ahead, this growth is expected to continue, with nearly 20% employment growth expected in services in the next decade in the US, with no change expected in manufacturing employment (US Bureau of Labor Statistics, 2006). Given that many existing human resource management practices were developed in the context of

manufacturing, these data suggest a need to consider seriously a human resource management (HRM) perspective on service work .

Our starting point is that service work differs from work in the manufacturing sector and, moreover, that it differs in ways that are relevant for HRM. The most obvious and perhaps important difference lies in the degree of contact between employees and customers. As we know from both the Schneider and Bowen (1985) service mirroring model and the Schlesinger and Heskett (1992) service profit chain model, front-line employees matter in services in part because they develop relationships with customers, directly influencing organizational performance. Organizational scholars have focused on the customer interface as a distinctive feature of service delivery, examining customer/provider dynamics in the context of air travel (Hochschild, 1983), fast food restaurants (Leidner, 1991), retail stores (e.g. Rafaeli, 1989; Sutton and Rafaeli, 1988), nursing homes (e.g. Eaton, 2000; Dodson and Zincavage, forthcoming), restaurants and hotels (Salanova et al., 2005), hair salons (Liao and Chuang, 2007), and hospitals (e.g. Wrzesniewski and Dutton, 2001). This literature describes vividly the interpersonal dynamics between individual providers and individual customers that shape the service delivery experience.

Relative to manufacturing work, service work is characterized by the simultaneity of production and consumption, by high levels of uncertainty and task interdependence, and by the role that customers play as potential co-producers in the service delivery process. Together, these features of service work pose a dilemma for HRM. On the one hand, employee behavior is potentially more influential due to the direct customer/provider interface, but at the same time it is more difficult to control due to the greater difficulty of measuring performance, supervising work, pre-programming work and coordinating work, between service workers and with the customer. Together, these conditions suggest the importance of investments in HRM. But at the same time, another feature of service work is that it is labor intensive relative to manufacturing and as a result, cost competition in this sector tends to focus on the reduction of labor costs, which may discourage investments in HRM.

Drawing upon an extensive research literature on HRM in the service sector, this chapter addresses two fundamental questions. First, we ask whether HRM is important for achieving performance outcomes in the service sector. We contrast the argument that HRM is more important in the service sector due to the direct customer/provider interface, with the argument that HRM may be less important in this sector due to the labor intensive nature of the work process and the resulting tendency to compete through the reduction of labor costs at the low end of the product market. Second, we ask how HRM influences performance outcomes in the

service sector. We consider three alternative mechanisms – 1) motivation and commitment, 2) human capital and skills, and 3) social capital or relationships – through which HRM may influence service performance.

RELATIVE IMPORTANCE OF HRM IN THE SERVICE SECTOR

There are two competing arguments regarding the importance of human resource management in the service sector relative to manufacturing. The first argument suggests that HRM is more important for achieving performance outcomes in the service sector than elsewhere due to the direct customer/provider interface, while the second argument suggests that HRM may be less important for achieving performance outcomes in the service sector, or at least in large segments of it, due to the labor intensive nature of the work and the resultant tendency to compete on labor costs at the lower end of the product market.

HRM matters more in service sector

Schneider and Bowen (1993) argue that service work is distinctive: first, in services there is a permeable boundary between customers and employees such that the behavior of one directly influences behavior and outcomes for the other. Due to direct contact between customers and employees in the process of service delivery, a process of psychological mirroring occurs such that the satisfaction of one affects the satisfaction of the other. Secondly, services are produced and consumed simultaneously so that there is a need to achieve quality throughout the organization, even by employees who do not have direct customer contact, due to the inability to do a quality control check after production to ensure quality. According to Schneider and Bowen, these characteristics of service work increase the importance of human resource management for achieving desired performance outcomes in the service sector. More specifically:

Managers, in their pursuit of service quality, need to create two related, but different, climates: a climate for service and a climate for employee well-being. The first requires practices such as systems and logistics support – anything that creates an organization setting in which customers feel their needs are being met. The second focuses on meeting the needs of employees through quality HRM practices (Schneider and Bowen, 1993: 43)

Building on this argument Schlesinger and Heskett (1991; 1992) developed a theoretical model called the service profit chain, arguing that customer satisfaction is a critical driver of profitability in the service sector, and that service employees in turn are a critical driver of customer satisfaction. By extension, companies that seek to be profitable in the service sector should invest heavily in the management of their human resources. This literature documents the prevalence and cost of employee turnover in the service sector, and the potential for a so-called 'cycle of failure' to develop, in which poor working conditions lead to employee turnover, which increases employee workload and customer dissatisfaction, which further decreases employee satisfaction, further contributing to employee turnover.

Ulrich and colleagues (1991) argued similarly for the importance of HRM in the service sector based on the fact that service employees have direct contact with customers and therefore a direct influence on their satisfaction. If managers can build something positive with employees, they argued, then they should be able to see results with their customers because customers will bond with employees and respond to good service. Managers should therefore develop HRM practices with the goal of building both employee attachment and customer attachment. But to do this, managers need to be familiar with customer expectations and requirements as well as with employee expectations and requirements.

Consistent with these arguments, studies have demonstrated links between human resource management and service outcomes. Chase and Bowen (1991) found evidence that employee selection and training impact service quality and customer satisfaction. In a study of customers and employees in 28 bank branches, Schneider and Bowen (1993) found that climates of service and employee well being are correlated with overall customer perceptions of service quality. HRM positively influences quality outcomes such as patient mortality (West et al., 2002) and patient satisfaction with the quality of care (Gittell et al., 2009), while also explaining performance differences among call centers (Batt, 1999), airlines (Gittell, 2001), nursing homes (Bishop, et al., 2008) and banks (Richard and Johnson, 2004; Hunter, 2000; Bartel, 2004). A recent test of the service profit chain model, based on a sample of 291 service organizations, demonstrated that progressive HRM practices led to employee satisfaction, which in turn impacted both service quality and customer satisfaction (Voss et al., 2005). Together this stream of work supports the argument that HRM plays an important role in achieving desired outcomes in the service sector, implying that investments in HRM pay off in this sector.

HRM matters less in service sector

Other theorists have argued that there are attributes of the service sector that may discourage substantial investments in HRM. Legge (1995: 67) pointed out that an organization 'that chooses to compete in a labour intensive, high volume, low cost industry generating profits through increasing market share' is likely to adopt human resource practices that treat 'employees as a variable input and a cost to be minimised.' In manufacturing, by comparison, firms can more readily gain from investments in progressive HRM regardless of whether they choose to compete on costs or on quality. Due to relatively high capital intensity of manufacturing firms, even firms that choose to compete on costs can do so by increasing the productivity of their capital assets rather than by reducing labor costs.

Manufacturing firms can therefore benefit from investments in HRM, whether their strategy is to engage employees in increasing quality, or in reducing costs. Consistent with Legge's argument, Keltner and Finegold (1996: 57) report that:

> Most service-sector firms have been slow to redesign work practices. From hotels to banks to retail outlets, service-sector managers continue to rely on an 'industrial model' of service delivery. They have organized work so as to tolerate low skills and short employment tenures and continue to concentrate on cutting costs rather than adding value (Schlesinger and Heskett, 1991). By thinking mainly about price competition, most service managers have invested minimally in their employees. Downward pressure on wages, minimal training expenditures, and heavy use of part-time workers have reduced personnel costs and maintained managers' flexibility to cut the work-force when demand slackens.

Likewise, Batt (2000) argued, because service industries are labor intensive with relatively few barriers to entry, service firms that compete on costs tend to compete through the reduction of labor costs, leaving little room for achieving payoffs from investments in HRM. In other higher value-added segments of the service sector, firms can earn rents and compete on dimensions other than cost, thus giving them greater potential to invest in HRM and earn a return on their investment. As Batt (2000: 547) explained:

> In service operations, labour still comprises 60 per cent of costs, and labour productivity continues to grow at less than 1 per cent annually. Despite the vision of high involvement and quality service, therefore, reducing labour costs continues to be a major priority in services, particularly in price-conscious mass markets. Put simply, for low margin customers, the costs of high involvement work systems are likely to be prohibitive but for high value-added customers, relationship management via high involvement work systems has a high pay-off. The logic of customer segmentation in services, therefore, suggests a fairly straightforward relationship between the choice of work system and the potential revenue stream of the customer.

Similarly, Boxall (2003: 15) argued: 'Cost-based low margin competition in services tends to drive out possibilities for HR advantage, except where firms can fund greater HR investment out of premium branding.' In support of these arguments, a recent study of the hotel industry in Australia found that while hotel workplaces in general continue to be associated with high levels of numerical and temporal flexibility and greater informality of HR policies, larger luxury hotels were adopting more systematic employee management techniques and strengthening their internal labor markets through functional flexibility initiatives, moving toward a more progressive, value-added approach to HRM (Knox and Walsh, 2005).

This segmentation argument is not completely contradictory to that of Schneider and Bowen; indeed the implication of this argument is that the Schneider and Bowen argument can hold true in high-value added segments of services. But in low-value added segments of services, where costs are the primary determinant of competitive success, the segmentation argument implies that neither the permeable boundary between employee and customer nor the simultaneity of production and consumption may be sufficient to encourage significant investments in HRM. Even though gains in service quality could certainly be achieved through HRM in these firms, consistent with Schneider and Bowen, these gains in service quality might not command a sufficient premium to make an investment in them worthwhile and sustainable.

Others have argued that the impact of HRM on service performance is contingent not on a firm's focus on high versus low value added segments of the market, but rather on other competitive factors such as the need for strategic flexibility (Roca-Puig et al., 2005), or strategic positioning more generally (Skaggs and Youndt, 2005). Hunter (2000) argues for yet a different kind of contingency, namely that service firms are more likely to use HRM to achieve flexibility in deployment across time rather than function, therefore adopting human resource innovations that allow employees the ability to match their work to idiosyncratic schedules or demands of customers.

Relevance of HRM for firms engaged in low cost competition?

Given the rise of the service sector as a proportion of developed economies, and given the spread of low cost competition across broad segments of the service sector, the segmentation argument made by Legge (1995) and others has important ramifications for the future viability of high performance HRM. From the airline industry to the healthcare industry, service industries that were once relatively protected from competition and which once served as sources of high wage middle class jobs are now subject to the onslaught of low cost competition. There is pressure for even high-end providers, including professional service firms, to provide cost-effective solutions and services, particularly when the client is another business that is facing cost competition in their own product market, and particularly as the potential for off-shoring some elements of professional services is realized. If the segmentation argument is correct, then by implication the relevance of high performance HRM may soon be confined to a relatively small segment of developed economies, i.e. capital intensive manufacturing, and services that are protected from low cost competition.

But although the segmentation argument may accurately describes the competitive strategies of many firms that operate in low cost segments of service industries, it does not necessarily suggest that firms do not have other viable choices. Even when labor costs are the focus of a firm's competitive strategy, those costs can be reduced not only through cutting wages and benefits but also through increasing labor productivity. To the extent that investing in HRM is a viable strategy for increasing labor productivity as well as service quality, investments in HRM should pay off quite well in segments of the service sector where low costs are essential for competitive success.

Interestingly, this argument has surfaced from time to time as a possibility, but is then largely ignored by those who raise it, as though it is a logical possibility but one

that does not deserve serious consideration. For example, Boxall's (2003) analysis of potential competitive strategies is based on a two by two matrix between service differentiation and business outcomes, in which one quadrant includes firms with low service differentiation but nevertheless the ability to achieve sustained competitive advantage through 'unique cost-reduction skills in mass markets' (2003: 11). However, in the detailed analysis that accompanies this matrix, this particular type of firm is not discussed.

Secondly, even in low cost markets, there are basic quality standards that customers continue to demand. In the airline industry, these basic quality standards no longer include 'frills' such as meals and business class seating, but they do include safe, reliable, on-time travel along with decent treatment by service providers. In healthcare, which has also been hit by pressures to reduce costs, the quality standards expected by customers and managed care payers still include basics such as patient safety, desired healthcare outcomes and decent treatment by care providers.

There is little doubt that HRM investments are relevant for achieving this challenging set of goals. In other words, low cost competition is not just about moving down the cost/quality curve to a lower cost segment, sacrificing quality in the effort to achieve low costs. Rather the most successful low cost competitors in the service industry, just as in manufacturing, are those who find ways to push out the production possibilities frontier, achieving the basic quality standards demanded by customers without the 'frills' while increasing productivity to achieve lower costs at the same time. Put simply, successful lower cost competition requires companies to meet both productivity and quality goals, and investments in HRM contribute significantly to their ability to do so. Womack et al. (1990) made this argument based on the concept of lean manufacturing, while Heskett and colleagues (1990) made this argument based on the concept of breakthrough service. Batt (1999; 2002) demonstrated that companies pursuing low cost competition can indeed benefit from investments in HRM, showing that HR strategies can help firms to achieve both quality and productivity outcomes in low cost segments. In airlines a service industry that has been re-defined by low cost competition, Gittell (2003) showed that HRM enables firms to achieve both higher quality and productivity by building relational coordination across front-line workers in different functions.

HOW HRM IMPACTS PERFORMANCE IN SERVICES: COMMITMENT, SKILL AND RELATIONSHIPS

In addition to the fundamental question of *whether* HRM matters for performance in the service sector, there is a secondary argument regarding *how* HRM impacts performance in this sector. What are the mechanisms through which HRM is expected to make a difference in the service sector, and are those mechanisms expected to be any different in services than in manufacturing? In this section, we evaluate three alternative mechanisms – motivation and commitment; human capital and skill; and social capital and relationships – and their ability to explain how HRM affects performance in the service sector. We do not see these mechanisms as mutually exclusive but rather as a set of mechanisms that together can help to explain the impact of HRM on service performance.

Motivation and commitment in the service sector

The most common argument for how HRM affects performance in the service sector, often implicit but sometimes tested explicitly, is that HRM increases employee commitment and that committed employees in turn deliver higher quality services to customers due to higher levels of effort (Ulrich et al., 1991; Worsfold, 1999). Commitment is considered to be particularly important in service settings due to the challenges of monitoring and measuring employee behavior. Investments in HRM are believed to increase commitment, involvement and empowerment, transforming

employees from mere employees into partners for achieving organizational goals (Caspersz, 2006). Commitment-based HRM practices create an organizational climate that motivates employees to act in the best interest of the organization, thus enhancing performance (Osterman, 1988; Lawler, 1988; Mahoney and Watson, 1993; Tsui, Pearce, Porter and Hite, 1995; Bishop et al., 2008).

Consistent with this view, studies have found that particular work practices are associated with increased employee control over work, increased employee involvement and higher levels of commitment (e.g. Tsui et al., 1997; Whitener, 2001), and that these behaviors in turn are positively associated with performance (e.g. Rosenberg and Rosenstein, 1980; Estrin et al., Ichniowski et al., 1996, 1987; Tomer, 2001). Findings from a recent study suggests that different HRM practices may matter for commitment depending on the type of service employee – professional, manager or front-line worker (Kinnie et al., 2005), but supports the argument that HRM builds commitment, thus supporting performance goals.

Bartel's (2004) finding of a positive relationship between bank branch performance and employees' satisfaction with the quality of performance evaluation, feedback, and recognition suggests the importance of the motivational dimension of a high performance work system. Her findings suggest that these HRM practices positively affect performance due to their impact on employee motivation and commitment, even though the intermediate variables are not measured. In a study of South African service organizations, organizational commitment was measured explicitly and was found to play a mediating role in the relationship between frontline employees' perceptions of HRM and their service behavior (Browning, 2006).

HRM practices that inspire employee commitment are believed to include involvement, discretion and empowerment and are often contrasted to HRM practices that aim to establish control. The argument has typically been that commitment-based HRM is more effective than control-based HRM in the service sector, but some argue this is only true when there is some degree of customization to be carried out by service employees, and enough job autonomy that discretionary effort can make a difference for performance outcomes (Frenkel et al., 1998). Frenkel et al. (1998) found further that customer service call centers tend to use a hybrid form of human resource management based on both commitment and control, due to the organization of work that allows some degree of employee autonomy along with fairly standardized work processes. They label this hybrid form 'mass customized bureaucracy.' In a review of frontline service work, Korcynski (2005) notes that there has been an increase in discretion given to service workers in recent years, but that this discretion tends to be narrowly confined, particularly to the service recovery aspects of the job rather than to the original service delivery.

Interestingly, Rees (1995) found that service firms that engage in quality management tend to use a mixed form of HRM, including some elements of control and other elements of commitment. On the one hand, these firms tend to use forms of employee 'empowerment' such as a flattening of the hierarchy and the reduction of direct supervision, but on the other hand, this empowerment is coupled with closer monitoring and tighter controls over work. Other findings also question the dichotomy between commitment and control forms of human resource management. Gittell (2001) found that airlines that reduced supervision as part of a move toward 'empowerment' also increased the intensity of performance measurement, while airlines with higher levels of supervision used more informal forms of performance measurement, which was more conducive to teamwork and to achieving desired service quality outcomes, as well as efficiency performance. Boselie et al. (2003) found that control forms of human resource management based on direct supervision and direct forms of quality control were associated with certain desirable outcomes, such as the reduction of employee absenteeism and the reduced length of employee absences.

Human capital or skill in the service sector

HRM is often presumed to affect service outcomes by increasing the human capital or skills of frontline service providers. According to human capital theory, HRM practices can improve organizational performance by increasing the knowledge or skills of employees (Becker, 1975). To be successful, firms must invest in and maintain the workforce just as they invest in and maintain the capital infrastructure. Progressive HRM can foster the development of human capital in the form of firm-specific idiosyncratic skills (Gibbert, 2006), creating a performance advantage for organizations (e.g., Freid and Hisrich, 1994; MacMillan et al., 1987; Tyebjee and Bruno, 1984) through processes such as improved problem-solving and improved customization by employees (Batt, 2002).

Skaggs and Youndt (2004) test a model in which human capital is the mediating variable between HRM and performance outcomes. Sometimes human capital is interpreted as the mediating variable between HRM and outcomes, even when human capital is not measured. For example, Pérez, and Falcón (2004) found that savings banks with HR policies aimed at the creation and development of their staff achieved higher productivity than those without such policies, and interpreted this as evidence that HRM influences productivity outcomes through its impact on the development of human capital.

An alternative interpretation of the association between high performance HRM and human capital is offered by Bacon and Hoque (2005). Their analysis found that the strongest overall predictor of the extent of adoption of HRM practices in small to medium sized enterprises was the skill-mix of the workforce. Firms with a higher proportion of low-skilled workers were less likely to have adopted five of the eight practices asked about, suggesting the possibility that human capital is a predictor of the adoption of HRM practices, rather than an outcome of these practices. More likely, the selection of skilled employees, investment in their training and design of jobs to make use of those skills, are complementary HRM factors that together result in higher levels of human capital and higher service performance.

Social capital and relationships in the service sector

Relationships are another potential mediator between progressive human resource management and service outcomes. While relationships are recognized as an important driver of outcomes in the service workplace, much of the focus has been on the employee/customer relationship. As argued by both the Schneider and Bowen (1985) service mirroring model and the Schlesinger and Heskett (1992) service profit chain model, front-line employees matter in services in part because they develop relationships with customers, thereby directly influencing organizational performance. As noted in the introduction to this chapter, organizational scholars have focused on the customer interface as a distinctive feature of service delivery, examining customer/provider dynamics in many service contexts, vividly describing the interpersonal dynamics between individual providers and individual customers that shape the service delivery experience and the outcomes experienced by customers.

Other scholars have argued that organizations can go beyond customer/provider relationships to achieve customer/organization relationships with the result of improving customer satisfaction and customer loyalty (Siehl et al., 1992; Peppers and Rogers, 1993; Bitner, 1995; Cross and Smith, 1995). Gutek and her colleagues argue that while only individual providers can establish real relationships with customers, due to the importance of interpersonal dynamics in building a relationship, organizations can establish pseudo-relationships with customers that offer many of the same benefits (Gutek, 1995; Gutek et al., 1999; Gutek, 1999). HRM can play an important role in supporting employee/customer relationships, according to Remy and Kopel (2002), if HRM is explicitly tailored for that purpose. When

building customer/provider relationships is the goal:

> The aim [of HRM] is to establish a certain flexibility in the customer relationship while remaining faithful to the interests of the companies. The tools and practices of HRM facilitate the adaptation of the staff to meet the needs of the customer. HRM becomes less standardized and is rather geared to the control of work behavior consistent with 'the new relational objectives of the company' (Remy and Kopel, 2002: 50).

This argument is highly consistent with the commitment model of HRM presented above, not surprisingly, since the focus of the HRM literature in the service sector has been on the customer/provider relationship and the need for a commitment rather than control approach to managing this relationship.

However, there is another type of relationship beyond the customer/provider relationship that plays a critical but relatively overlooked role in the service delivery process: the relationships that exist *among service providers* who are engaged in jointly providing a service to a given customer. The importance of coordination is already well established in the organizational literature (Fayol, 1925; Coase, 1937; Kogut and Zander, 1996). Service and production processes involve interdependent tasks that must be integrated effectively in order to achieve high quality, efficient outcomes. Often coordination occurs through routines, scheduling, preplanning or standardization, with minimal need for interaction among service providers (Galbraith, 1977). However, because these programmed means of coordination have limited bandwidth (Daft and Lengel, 1986), they are expected to be most effective in settings with pooled or sequential interdependence rather than reciprocal interdependence (Thompson, 1967), with low levels of uncertainty (Argote, 1982; Van de Ven et al., 1976), and without severe time constraints (Adler, 1995).

Service operations typically have coordination requirements that cannot be met by programmed forms of coordination alone (Gittell, 2002). Service operations typically are characterized by reciprocal interdependence, requiring iterative inter actions among service providers rather than the sequential hand-offs performed by workers on a production line. Many service operations also have high levels of uncertainty relative to manufacturing due to the difficulty of buffering service operations from the external environment. Finally, most service settings are highly time-constrained; they are designed to provide a service to customers, real time, simultaneous with the demand, without imposing excessive waiting times on customers. Under these conditions, effective coordination has been argued to depend on the nature of the relationships that exist among those engaged in providing the service. Relational coordination, 'a mutually reinforcing process of interaction between communication and relationships carried out for the purpose of task integration,' is expected to increase performance in settings that require improvization rather than simple reliance on pre-programmed modes of action (Gittell, 2002: 301).

Though the human capital perspective recognizes that skills and knowledge must be shared among employees to be useful, and though the commitment-based perspective recognizes the importance of manager/worker relationships in achieving motivation and commitment, neither of these perspectives explicitly conceptualizes *relationships between employees* as the desired intermediate outcome of high performance human resource management in the service sector. Relatively little is known about how organizations influence the development of relationships among their employees though some progress has been made. Leana and Van Buren (1999) argued that stable employment relationships and reciprocity norms can facilitate the formation of social capital among employees, though this argument was not made specifically with respect to service organizations. Gittell (2000) argued that human resource practices can be re-designed to foster relational coordination among employees who are engaged in a common work process. When carried out consistently across work practices, this form

of redesign is argued to result in a high performance work system that is amenable to the development of working relationships. These re-designed work practices, including selection, conflict resolution, performance measurement, supervision and boundary spanner roles, predicted significantly higher levels of relational coordination among airline employees.

Lopez et al. (2005) argued that high performance work practices encourage employees to engage in collective learning, resulting in increased multi-disciplinary knowledge and thereby contributing to firm performance. They showed that hiring, training, incentive pay and participation in decision-making contribute to organizational learning, which in turn contributes to firm performance. Vogus (2006) argued that that high performance work practices such as selection, training, performance appraisal, empowerment and job security contribute to high quality interactions and mindfulness by signaling to employees the importance of relationships, and that these high quality interactions contribute to higher quality outcomes for patients, particularly patient safety. Vogus demonstrated that the impact of these high performance practices on patient safety outcomes is mediated by the quality of interactions and mindfulness among the nursing staff on hospital units. Gittell et al. (2009) further developed this argument by focusing on the development of relational coordination across multiple workgroups engaged in delivering patient care. They identified the work practices that increased levels of relational coordination among doctors, nurses, physical therapists, social workers and case managers, in turn improving quality and efficiency outcomes for patients.

Though the forms of social capital explored in the above empirical studies are varied, including relational coordination (Gittell, 2000), collective learning (Lopez et al., 2005) and mindful organizing (Vogus, 2006), together these studies suggest an alternative model of HRM in the service sector in which work practices influence organizational outcomes by helping to build relationships between employees, thus increasing the ability of employees to provide high quality service to their customers, and to do so efficiently.

CONCLUSION

This chapter has considered two questions regarding HRM in the service sector. First, we asked whether HRM is important for achieving performance outcomes in the service sector, relative to the manufacturing sector. We contrasted the argument that HRM is more important in the service sector due to the direct customer/provider interface with the argument that HRM may be less important in this sector due to the labor intensive nature of the work process, and the resultant tendency to compete through the reduction of labor costs at the low end of the product market. Due to the increasing importance of low cost competition in the service sector, the stakes behind this particular argument are high. We found that the segmentation argument tends to overlook the importance of HRM for increasing productivity and efficiency, and thus for achieving low costs. It also seems to overlook the importance of achieving quality even in a 'no frills' environment, given the continued importance of basic good treatment and reliability of outcomes even in a no frills environment. Once we consider these issues, the potential for HRM investments to pay off, even in low cost segments of the market, becomes clear. For example, organizations like Southwest in the airline industry and Costco in the retail industry stand out as examples of a viable approach to low cost competition in which progressive HRM plays a central role. Still, it is useful to recognize the pressures for firms that engage in low cost competition to under-invest in HRM, and to consider potential ways to counteract these pressures.

One potential way to counteract the incentives to under-invest in HRM is through a vibrant union movement, and in particular through unions that are willing to engage employers in joint efforts to invest in the workforce. Much of the employment growth expected in the service sector in industrialized countries in the coming decade is expected to be in low wage service occupations due to the increasing exodus of highly skilled jobs overseas to less developed countries (AFL-CIO, 2006), suggesting additional potential for the growth of service sector unionization. Many segments of service workers are now more highly unionized than production workers in the United States with 13% of manufacturing workers represented by unions, relative to 23% of transportation workers, 27% of utilities workers, 21% of telecommunications workers, 14% of information workers, and 37% of public sector workers (US Bureau of Labor Statistics, 2006). But some segments of the service industry have very low levels of representation, such as financial services at 2%, business services at 3%, and leisure/hospitality at 3%.

Unions that are devoted to the service sector, like SEIU and UNITE HERE, are among the most active unions in the United States from an organizing standpoint, with SEIU also seeking to expand its reach by partnering with unions in other countries (Bai, 2005). Similarly, in Canada, service sector unionization is on the rise. The late 1990s saw an increase in service sector unionization after the nation's labor unions made a concerted effort to focus on the growing part of the Canadian economy that had been viewed as 'the labour movement's Achilles heel' (Yates, 2003: 21). Service sector union activism is evident in Europe as well. In Belgium, service sector employees staged a 10-day strike in 2005 before receiving a five-year contract (EIRR, 2005: 1), while in Switzerland service unions negotiated to establish minimum wages in addition to increased pay (EIRR, 2005: 2). Many countries are still dominated by their manufacturing unions, however (Zientara, 2006), and unionization overall is on the decline. Although previous studies suggest little to no difference in the adoption of HRM by union and non-union firms (Osterman, 1994; Verma, 2005), it remains to be seen whether these new service sector union movements will have a more significant positive impact than traditional manufacturing unions did on the adoption of progressive HRM.

Second, we asked how HRM influences performance outcomes in the service sector. We considered three alternative mechanisms – 1) motivation and commitment, 2) human capital and skills, and 3) social capital or relationships – through which HRM may influence service performance. Each of these arguments has a compelling rationale behind it related to the nature of service work, and a solid set of research findings to support it. We conclude that HRM impacts service performance in a multi-dimensional way, by producing commitment, skills and relationships. How HRM practices can be shaped to meet these three objectives simultaneously is a question for further exploration. Starting in this direction, Leana and Pil (2006) have explored the contribution of both human capital and social capital to performance outcomes in public schools, though the human resource practices that are needed to develop high levels of both human and social capital have not yet been identified. In principle, there is no reason why human resource practices cannot be designed to serve these multiple purposes – employees can be selected for their commitment to organizational goals, for the appropriateness of their individual knowledge and skills, and at the same time for their ability to connect with others to coordinate the work process. Similar arguments could be made with respect to the design of hiring, training, performance measurement, job design and so on.

In conclusion, service work is distinct from manufacturing work due to the direct interface between customers and employees, the simultaneity of production and consumption, the relatively high levels of uncertainty and task interdependence, and the role that customers play as potential co-producers in the service delivery process. Given the importance of these differences, the attention given in the past fifteen years to HRM in service settings has been well placed. But there are also increasing similarities between services and manufacturing. Some service work is being made to follow more of a standardized production model, particularly in back office operations, perhaps decreasing the distinctiveness of service work. At the same time, some manufacturing processes are taking on more of the characteristics of service work, as inventories are reduced to enable goods to be produced 'just in time' in response to customized demand (Womack et al., 1990; Abernathy et al., 1999; Holweg and Pil, 2004), thus moving toward the simultaneity of production and consumption and toward the higher levels of uncertainty and task interdependence that have traditionally made service work distinctive. In addition, manufacturing companies are moving down the value chain to play a growing role in service delivery, as after-sales service support becomes an increasingly important dimension of the product value proposition.

Looking forward, we offer several recommendations for further research. First, as the boundaries between services and manufacturing become more blurred over time, HRM scholars would be well advised to focus less on the sector and more on the characteristics of the work itself when drawing implications for human resource management. Second, we recommend continued efforts to identify the work practices that build relationships in the workplace, particularly among frontline service personnel who are engaged in direct service provision. These work practices are likely to include traditional human resource practices that have been redesigned to encourage shared goals, shared knowledge and mutual respect across functions – for example hiring and training for relational competence as well as functional expertise, and performance measurement systems that encourage workers to look beyond their immediate jobs to the larger work process that they are engaged in. Third, our research needs to look beyond organizational boundaries given that service delivery across multiple organizations is increasingly common as organizations reduce vertical integration and outsource non-core services in order to achieve strategic focus. The relational model of high performance work systems discussed in this chapter can be extended to address cross-organizational service delivery, but work systems have to be designed to encourage the development of relationships with external as well as internal service workers.

REFERENCES

Abernathy, F., Dunlop, J., Hammond, J. and Weil, D. (1999) *A Stitch in Time: Lean Retailing and the Transformation of Manufacturing.* London: Oxford University Press.

Adler, P. (1995) 'Interdepartmental interdependence and coordination: The case of the design/manufacturing interface', *Organization Science*, 6 (2): 147–67.

AFL–CIO (2006) *Fact Sheet 2006: The Service Sector: Productions and Current Stats.* http://www.dpeaflcio.org/programs/factsheets/fs_2006_service_sector.htm.

Argote, L. (1982) 'Input uncertainty and organizational coordination in hospital emergency units', *Administrative Science Quarterly*, 27 (3): 420–34.

Bacon, N. and Hoque, K. (2005) 'HRM in the SME sector: Valuable employees and coercive networks', *International Journal of Human Resource Management*, 16 (11): 1976–99.

Bai, M. (2005) 'The new boss,' *The New York Times Magazine*, Jan. 30.

Bartel, A. (2004) 'Human resource management and organizational performance: Evidence from retail banking', *Industrial and Labor Relations Review*, 57 (2): 181–203.

Batt, R. (2002) 'Managing customer services: Human resource practices, quit rates, and sales growth', *Academy of Management Journal*, 45 (3): 587–97.

Batt, R. (2000) 'Strategic segmentation in front-line services: Matching customers, employees and human resource systems', *International Journal of Human Resource Management*, 11 (3): 540–61.

Batt, R. (1999) 'Work organization, technology, and performance in customer service and sales', *Industrial and Labor Relations Review*, 52 (4): 539–64.

Becker, G.S. (1975) *Human Capital.* New York: Columbia University Press.

Bishop, C.E., Weinberg, D.B., Leutz, W., Dossa, A., Pfefferle, S. and Zincavage, R. (2008) 'Nursing assistants' job commitment: Effect of nursing home organizational factors and impact on resident well-being,' *The Gerontologist*, 48 (Special 1): 36–45.

Bitner, M.J. (1995) 'Building service relationships: It's all about promises', *Journal of the Academy of Marketing Science*, 23 (4): 246–51.

Boselie, P., Paauwe, J. and Richardson, R. (2003) 'Human resource management, institutionalization and organizational performance: A comparison of hospitals, hotels and local government', *International Journal of Human Resource Management*, 14 (8): 1407–29.

Boxall, P. (2003) 'HR strategy and competitive advantage in the service sector', *Human Resource Management Journal*, 13 (3): 5–20.

Browning, V. (2006) 'The relationship between HRM practices and service behaviour in South African service organizations', *International Journal of Human Resource Management*, 17 (7): 1321–38.

Caspersz, D. (2006) 'The "talk" verses the "walk": High performance work systems, labour market flexibility and lessons from Asian employees', *Asia Pacific Business Review*, 12 (2): 149–61.

Chase, R.B. and Bowen, D.E. (1991) 'Service quality and the service delivery system: A diagnostic framework', in S.W. Brown, E. Gummesson, B. Edvardsson and B. Gustavsson (eds), *Service Quality: Multidisciplinary and Multinational Perspectives.* New York: Lexington Books, pp. 157–78.

Coase, R.H. (1937) 'The nature of the firm', *Economica*, 16 (4): 386–405.

Cross, R. and Smith, J. (1995) *Customer Bonding.* Chicago: NTC Business Books.

Daft, R.L. and Lengel, R.H. (1986) 'Organizational information requirements, media richness and structural design', *Management Science*, 32 (5): 554–71.

Dodson, L. and Zincavage, R. (2008) 'It's like a family: Caring labor, exploitation and race in nursing homes', *Gender and Society.* 21 (6): 905–28.

Eaton, S. (2000) 'Beyond unloving care: Linking human resource management and patient care quality in nursing homes', *International Journal of Human Resource Management*, 11 (3): 591–616.

European Industrial Relations Review (2005) 'A health and service sector agreement', 375: 4.

European Industrial Relations Review (2005) 'Trade union demands', 380: 16.

Estrin, S., Jones, D.C. and Svejnar, J. (1987) 'The productivity effects of worker participation: Producer cooperatives in Western economies', *Journal of Comparative Economics*, 11 (1): 40–61.

Fayol, H. (1925) *Industrial and General Administration.* Paris: Dunod.

Freid, V.H. and Hisrich, R.D. (1994) 'Toward a model of venture capital investment decision-making', *Financial Management*, 23 (3): 28–37.

Frenkel, S., Tam, M., Korczynski, M. and Shire, K. (1998) 'Beyond bureaucracy? Work organization in call centres', *International Journal of Human Resource Management*, 9 (6): 957–79.

Galbraith, J. (1977) *Organization Design*. Reading: MA: Addison-Wesley.

Gibbert, M. (2006) 'Generalizing about uniqueness: An essay on an apparent paradox in the resource-based view', *Journal of Management Inquiry*, 15 (2): 124–34.

Gittell, J.H., Seidner, R. and Wimbush, J. (2009) 'A relational model of how high performance work systems work', *Organization Science*, forthcoming.

Gittell, J.H. (2003) *The Southwest Airlines Way: Using the Power of Relationships to Achieve High Performance*. New York: McGraw-Hill.

Gittell, J.H. (2002) 'Relationships between service providers and their impact on customers', *Journal of Service Research*, 4 (4): 299–311.

Gittell, J.H. (2001) 'Supervisory span, relational coordination and flight departure performance: A reassessment of post-bureaucracy theory', *Organization Science*, 12 (4): 467–82.

Gittell, J.H. (2000) 'Organizing work to support relational coordination', *International Journal of Human Resource Management*, 11 (3): 517–39.

Gutek, B.A. (1995) *The Dynamics of Service: Reflections on the Changing Nature of Customer/Provider Interactions*. San Francisco: Jossey-Bass.

Gutek, B.A., Bhappu, A., Liao-Troth, M. and Cherry, B. (1999) 'Distinguishing between service relationships and encounters', *Journal of Applied Psychology*, 84 (2): 218–33.

Gutek, B.A. (1999) 'Service relationships, pseudo-relationships and encounters', in D. Iacobucci and T. Swartz (eds), *Handbook of Services Marketing and Management*. Newbury Park, CA: Sage Publishers, pp. 371–79.

Heskett, J., Sasser, W.E. and Hart, C.W.L. (1990) *Service Breakthroughs*. New York: The Free Press.

Hochschild, A. (1983) *The Managed Heart: Commercialization of Human Feeling*. Berkeley, CA: University of California Press.

Holweg, M. and Pil, F. (2004) *The Second Century: Reconnecting Customer and Value Chain through Build to Order*. Cambridge, MA: MIT Press.

Hunter, L. (2000) 'The adoption of innovative work practices in service establishments', *International Journal of Human Resource Management*, 11 (3): 477–96.

Ichniowski, C., Kochan, T., Levine, D., Olsen, C. and Strauss, G. (1996) 'What works at work: Overview and assessment', *Industrial Relations*, 35 (3): 299–333.

Keltner, B. and Finegold, D. (1996) 'Adding value in banking: Human resource innovations for service firms', *Sloan Management Review*, 38 (1): 57–68.

Kinnie, N., Hutchinson, S., Purcell, J., Rayton, B. and Swart, J. (2005) 'Satisfaction with HR practices and commitment to the organization: Why one size does not fit all', *Human Resource Management Journal*, 15 (4): 9–29.

Knox, A. and Walsh, J. (2005) 'Organisational flexibility and HRM in the hotel industry: Evidence from Australia', *Human Resource Management Journal*, 15 (1): 57–75.

Kogut, B. and Zander, U. (1996) 'What firms do? Coordination, identity, and learning', *Organization Science*, 7 (5): 502–18.

Korczynski, M. (2005) 'Skills in service work: an overview', *Human Resource Management Journal*, 15 (2): 3–14.

Lawler, E.E., III (1988) 'Choosing an involvement strategy', *Acad. Mgt. Exec.*, 2 (3): 197–204.

Leana, C. and Pil, F. (2006) 'Social capital and organizational performance: Evidence from the urban public schools', *Organization Science*, 17 (3): 353–66.

Leana, C. and Van Buren, H.J., III (1999) 'Organizational social capital and employment practices', *Academy of Management Review*, 24: 538–55.

Legge, K. (1995) *Human Resource Management: Rhetorics and Realities*. Basingstoke: Macmillan Press.

Leidner, R. (1991) *Fast Food, Fast Talk: Service Work and the Routinization of Everyday Life*. Berkeley, CA: University of California Press.

Liao, H. and Chuang, A. (2007) 'Transforming service employees and climate: A multilevel, multisource examination of transformational leadership in building long-term service relationships', *Journal of Applied Psychology*, 92 (4): 1006–19.

Lopez, S.P., Peon, M.M.M. and Ordas, C.J.V. (2005) 'Human resource practices, organizational learning and business performance', *Human Resource Development International*, 8 (2): 147–64.

MacMillan, I.C., Zemann, L. and Subbanarasimha, P.N. (1987) 'Criteria distinguishing successful from unsuccessful ventures in the venture screening process', *Journal of Business Venturing*, 2 (2): 123–38.

Mahoney, T.A. and Watson, M.R. (1993) 'Evolving modes of workforce governance: An evaluation', in B.E. Kaufman and M.M. Kleiner (eds), *Employee Representation: Alternatives and Future Directions*. Madison, WI: Industrial Relations Research Association, University of Wisconsin, pp. 135–68.

OECD (2005) *Enhancing the Performance of the Services Sector*. Paris: OECD Publishing.

Osterman, P. (1988) *Employment Futures: Reorganization, Dislocation and Public Policy*. New York: Oxford University Press.

Osterman, P. (1994) 'How common is workplace transformation and who adopts it?' *Industrial and Labor Relations Review*, 47 (2): 173–88.

Peppers, D. and Rogers, M. (1993) *One-to-One Future: Building Relationships One Customer at a Time*. New York: Currency/Doubleday.

Pérez, P. and Falcón, J. (2004) 'The influence of human resource management in savings bank performance', *Service Industries Journal*, 24 (2): 51–66.

Rafaeli, A. (1989) 'When cashiers meet customers: An analysis of the role of supermarket cashiers', *Academy of Management Journal*, 32 (2): 245–73.

Rees, C. (1995) 'Quality management and HRM in the service industry: Some case study evidence', *Employee Relations*, 17 (3): 99–109.

Remy, E. and Kopel, S. (2002) 'Social linking and human resources management in the service sector', *Service Industries Journal*, 22 (1): 35–56.

Richard, O.C. and Johnson, N.B. (2004) 'High performance work practices and human resource management effectiveness: Substitutes or complements?' *Journal of Business Strategy*, 21 (2): 133–48.

Roca-Puig, V., Beltrin-Martin, I., Escrig-Tena, A. and Bou-Llusar, J. (2005) 'Strategic flexibility as a moderator of the relationship between commitment to employees and performance in service firms', *International Journal of Human Resource Management*, 16 (11): 2075–93.

Rosenberg, R.D. and Rosenstein, E. (1980) 'Participation and productivity: An empirical study', *Industrial and Labor Relations Review*, 33 (3): 355–67.

Salanova, M., Agut, S., and Peiro, J.M. (2005) 'Linking organizational resources and work engagement to employee performance and customer loyalty: The mediation of service climate', *Journal of Applied Psychology*, 90 (6): 1217–27.

Schlesinger, L.A. and Heskett, J.L. (1992) 'De-industrialising the service sector: A new model for service firms', in T. Swartz, D. Bowen and S. Brown (eds), *Advances in Services Marketing and Management: Research and Practice*. Greenwich, CT: JAI Press, pp. 159–76.

Schlesinger, L.A. and Heskett, J.L. (1991) 'The service-driven service company', *Harvard Business Review*, 69: 71–81.

Schneider, B. and Bowen, D. (1993) 'The service organization: Human resources management is crucial', *Organizational Dynamics*, 21 (4): 39–52.

Schneider, B. and Bowen, D. (1985) 'Employee and customer perceptions of service in banks: Replication and extension', *Journal of Applied Psychology*, 70 (3): 423–33.

Siehl, C., Bowen, D.E. and Pearson, C.M. (1992) 'Service encounters as rites of integration: An information processing model', *Organization Science*, 3 (4): 537–55.

Skaggs, B. and Youndt, M. (2004) 'Strategic positioning, human capital and performance in service organizations: a customer interaction approach', *Strategic Management Journal*, 25 (1): 85–99.

Sutton, R. and Rafaeli, A. (1988) 'Untangling the relationship between displayed emotions and organizational sales: The case of convenience stores', *Academy of Management Journal*, 31 (3): 461–87.

Thompson, J. (1967) *Organizations in Action: Social Science Bases of Administration Theory*. New York: McGraw-Hill.

Tomer, J.F. (2001) 'Understanding high-performance work systems: The joint contribution of economics and human resource management', *Journal of Socio-Economics*, 30 (1): 63–73.

Tsui, A.S., Pearce, J.L., Porter, L.V. and Tripoli, A.M. (1997) 'Alternative approaches to the employee–organization relationship: Does investment in employees pay off?' *Academy of Management Journal*, 40 (5): 1089–121.

Tsui, A.S., Pearce, J.L., Porter, L.V. and Hite, J.P. (1995) 'Choice of employee-organization relationship: Influence of external and internal organizational factors', in G.R. Ferris (ed.), *Research in Personnel and Human Resource Management*, 13. Greenwich, CT: JAI Press, pp. 117–51.

Tyebjee, T.T. and Bruno, A.V. (1984) 'A model of venture capitalist investment activity', *Management Science*, 30 (9): 1051–66.

Ulrich, D., Halbrook, R., Meder, D., Stuchlik, M. and Thorpe, S. (1991) 'Employee and customer attachment: Synergies for competitive advantage', *Human Resources Planning*, 14 (3): 89–103.

US Bureau of Labor Statistics (2006) *Union Affiliation of Employed Wage and Salary Workers by Occupation and Industry*. http://www.bls.gov/new.release/union2.t03.htm.

Van De Ven, A.H., Delbecq, A.L. and Koenig, A.L., Jr. (1976) 'Determinants of coordination modes within organizations', *American Sociological Review*, 41 (2): 322–38.

Verma, A. (2005) 'What do unions do to the workplace? Union effects on management and HRM policies', *Journal of Labor Research*, 26 (3): 415–49.

Vogus, T. (2006) 'What is it about relationships? A behavioral theory of social capital and performance', *Labor and Employment Relations Proceedings*, pp. 164–73.

Voss, C., Tsikriktsis, N., Funk, B., Yarrow, D. and Owen, J. (2005) 'Managerial choice and performance in service management: A comparison of private sector organizations with further education colleges', *Journal of Operations Management*, 23 (2): 179–95.

West, M., Borrill, C., Dawson, J., Scully, J., Carter, M., Anelay, S., Patterson, M. and Waring, J. (2002) 'The link between the management of employees and patient mortality in acute hospitals', *International Journal of Human Resource Management*, 13: 1299–311.

Whitener, E.M. (2001) 'Do "high commitment" human resource practices affect employee commitment? A cross-level analysis using hierarchical linear modeling', *J. Mgt.* 27(5): 515–35.

Womack, J.P., Jones, D.T. and Roos, D. (1990) *The Machine That Changed the World: The Story of Lean Production*. New York: MacMillan.

Worsfold, P. (1999) 'HRM, performance, commitment and service quality in the hotel industry', *International Journal of Contemporary Hospitality Industry*, 11 (7): 340–48.

Wrzesniewski, A. and Dutton, J.E. (2001) 'Crafting a job: Revisioning employees as active crafters of their work', *Academy of Management Review*, 26 (2): 179–201.

Yates, C. (2003) 'Unions going after private service sector', *Canadian HR Reporter*, 16 (17): 21.

Zientara, P. (2006) 'Employment protection legislation and the growth of the service sector in the European Union', *Economic Affairs*, 26 (4): 46–52.

31

HRM in Small Firms: Respecting and Regulating Informality

Paul Edwards and Monder Ram

INTRODUCTION

Writing an account of HRM in small and medium sized firms (SMEs) is either an easy or a virtually impossible task. It is easy in so far as it is possible to list a series of ways in which SMEs differ from large firms. They are less likely to employ HR specialists, much less likely to negotiate with trade unions, more likely to rely on informal recruitment and appraisal practices, and so on. There is also evidence that such facts are common across many countries. Large firms are strongly shaped by their national environments so that, for example, formal employee representation is taken for granted in Germany and Scandinavia in ways which American managers may find it hard to understand (Wever, 1995). In small firms, such formal institutional effects are weaker, and 'informality' is much more common (Ram, 1994; Cooke, 2005).

The task becomes difficult once one moves beyond such facts to take account of some complexities in relation to what they mean.

- Throughout the industrialized economies, about 97 per cent of firms are 'small' (that is, employ fewer than 50 people), and a spot estimate of how on average they differ from large organizations will conceal a wide range of variation. How can this variation be captured? Studies continue to eschew explanation. To take one example, a study of research on management development treats 'small firms' as a homogeneous category; though it notes that development needs differ, it offers no way of grasping in just what respects firms differ and with what consequences (Fuller-Love, 2006).
- Facts need explanations and, as we will see, once one moves beyond straightforward facts such as the absence of HR specialists the significance of facts can become controversial. Thus one clear fact is that strikes are rare in small firms. This famously led some observers in the past to equate the absence of strikes with a lack of conflict and to

search for an explanation of presumed harmony before the existence of such harmony had been demonstrated (for example, Ingham, 1970).

- Following on from this point, the fact that small firms differ from large ones does not establish whether the difference is due to size or to some other feature; and if size is a causal factor we then need some explanation of this effect.
- Underlying these issues is a deeper one of research evidence. A great deal is written on small firms, and there are several academic journals focused on them. But, first, attention to HRM specifically is sporadic, as illustrated by the fact that some journals have felt the need for special issues on the topic. Second, the literature reflected in these issues tends towards the generation of basic facts on the lines listed above. Third, and most important, is the analytical starting point. Much small-firms research has not adopted a perspective – now common in mainstream HRM (especially Boxall and Purcell, 2003) – in which the firm is seen as an organization comprising groups with differing interests in which power and conflict are central. Employee interests continue to be relatively neglected. In 1990, Curran complained of a lack of attention to 'real people in real enterprises' and the 'complex ways in which the small scale sector is integrated into the economy' (1990: 139). This complaint still has force.

It is true that an important strand of writing has taken a critical view of the nature of the employment relationship in small firms, clearly exploding the myth of harmony and shared purpose (Goss, 1988; Rainnie, 1989).[1] Yet this can simply invert the received wisdom. Two experienced writers state that the reality

> can be very different [from harmony].... [E]mployment relations in SMEs [are] more akin to a 'black hole' or 'bleak house', characterised by poor conditions of employment, low pay, the absence of good (or any) personnel practices...and enforced compliance rather than active employee commitment (Blyton and Turnbull, 2004: 288, emphasis added).

Apart from the get-out clause of 'can be', this statement paints a very bleak picture. The present discussion shares with the critical view an effort to dig beneath the surface so as to understand practice and the meanings

of work. But an application of this view means grasping the complexities of compliance and consent, rather than replacing one simple image with another. That said, it is true that the black hole image applies to *some* small firms, namely, those in low value-added and extremely intensive sectors of the economy – though even here the situation is far more complex than the idea of 'enforced compliance' can grasp (Edwards and Ram, 2006). Note also that this idea has at least as much application to large firms as to small ones, for example in relation to intensive control in call centres and 'cultural control' which can generate intense expectations on employees and dissolve work-home boundaries (Taylor et al., 2002). Indeed, large firms are probably more systematic and calculated in such forms of control than are small ones, and to that extent small firms may leave employees with greater room for discretion.

As to what is 'small', some studies include organizations with as many as 500 employees. Others flag the importance of small firms, but in fact say little about them; Ackroyd (2002), for example, identifies them in a chapter title but devotes only two pages to relevant issues, which in any event cover mainly firms with up to 300 employees. Firms with as many as 300 employees are likely to have many standard HR practices in place, and our focus is thus on the more specifically 'small' firm. A rough indication of the importance of small firms comes from official UK and US statistics which give the distribution of *private sector employment* in 2005, as in Table 31.1 (SBS, 2006; BLS, 2005).

These two countries are among those where SMEs account for the smallest proportion of total employment. Estimates in countries such as Greece and Spain put SME employment

Table 31.1 The distribution of private sector employment in 2005

	UK	USA
Small firms (0–49 employees)	47%	30%
Medium-sized firms (50–249 employees)	12%	19%
Large firms (250 employees or more)	41%	51%

(that is, within firms with 1–249 employees) at about 80 per cent of the total; and given the very large and often poorly measured informal sectors in these countries the true figure may be higher (EIRO, 2006).

Our focus is mainly on 'small' firms, which, as the figures in Table 31.1 show, account for the bulk of SME employment; we would see a firm with up to 100 employees as tending to be small in the more substantive sense of lacking formal hierarchies and procedures. Note also that accounts like Ackroyd's, which focus on medium-sized firms, in fact cover only a minority of employees. We use evidence that does not always follow our restrictions, and we note where relevant the category of firms studied.

What is regarded as a small firm in a specific industrial sector depends on the relative size of other firms in the same sector. Official figures show that small firms account for 75 per cent of private sector employment in construction but only 15 per cent in 'financial intermediation' (banking and the like). A manufacturing firm with 80 employees would be considered small, whereas in large parts of the service sector such as consultancy, software and the media and creative industries, a firm with this many employees would be considered large. There is no ready resolution of this issue. We touch on it below, for example in commenting on how HR practices change as a firm grows. Otherwise, our approach is to address firms that lack formal HR practice – a condition that will affect those that might in fact be 'large' within their own sectors.

A final opening comment is that we approach the issue through the eyes of the HR professional. That is, one could write generally about HR issues in small firms: how do their pay and conditions differ from the situation in large firms, are they as harmonious as is often claimed, and so on? We draw on such writing, but our central question is: how can the HR professional, armed with the toolkit of formal procedures, grasp HR practice in the small firm, and what if anything might be the distinct HR contribution in such a firm?

EXTENT AND MEANING OF HR PRACTICES

We used above the shorthand that small firms lack formal HR systems. A more accurate statement is that such systems are rare compared to the situation in large firms but far from absent, and also that they vary in their extent.

The UK is a good place to establish this statement, since it has a series of Workplace Employment Relations Surveys (WERS) that measure employment practice, the most recent of which in 2004 embraced workplaces with as few as five employees. The 1998 Survey looked at what it called small businesses, defined as workplaces that had 10–99 employees and were not part of larger companies. It found a degree of formality; for example, 70 per cent had a formal disciplinary and dismissals procedure (Cully et al., 1999: 263). European evidence offers a similar picture. A study of management development across seven countries found that, though formal written policies were rare they were not absent, being reported by 29 per cent of 'small' (20–100 employees) firms; moreover, around half of small firms had a training budget. It also makes the point, echoing a long tradition of workplace studies (Terry, 1977), that informality is not the sole preserve of the small firm, and that large ones can often slip from their own rules. We comment on this theme in the conclusion.

The evidence was taken further by the 2004 WERS, which looked specifically at contrasts between small and large companies (Forth et al., 2006). A summary of indices of formal HR processes and strategies is given in Table 31.2.

Several points stand out from the table.

- Family ownership is an important characteristic of small firms; this is addressed below.
- Workplaces owned by small firms are indeed relatively non-formalized. The table has several indicators of formality. The respondent to the survey was the manager with primary responsibility for HR matters; spending a significant amount

Table 31.2   HR processes and strategy by firm size: % of workplaces with given characteristic

	SMEs			
	Small	Medium	Large firms	All private sector
Family owned	81	67	22	43
More than 25% of respondent's time on employment relations	26	51	55	
Respondent has formal HR qualifications	14	20	28	20
Investor in People[a]	12	25	57	31
Any strategic plan	36	64	88	60
Performance appraisal for non-managers	45	63	82	
Any employee representation	12	39	71	39
Any face-to-face communication[b]	78	88	93	85
Any written two-way communication[b]	35	58	81	57
Written EO policy	36	69	93	
% employees covered by collective bargaining	2	9	35	24

Note: Figures relate to private sector workplaces. 'Small' workplaces are those with 5–49 employees; medium-sized workplaces have 50–249 employees; large workplaces have 250 or more employees; Blanks indicate that this specific item is not indicated in the source. Though, as explained in the text, we have conducted our own analysis of WERS 2004 this is on a different basis from that deployed in the source used here, and we have not mixed the two.

[a] Investors in People is the UK body charged with identifying standards for skills and people development and encouraging adoption on these standards. See www.investorsinpeople.co.uk.

[b] Face-to-face communication includes meetings between managers and the work force and team briefings; written two-way communication includes suggestion schemes and employee surveys.

Source: Forth et al. (2006).

of time on HR and having a formal qualification were both associated with size. Other indices of formality are positively associated with size, such as having some kind of formal strategic plan (which need not necessarily embrace *HR* plans). This seems to be a cross-national fact, as studies in the US (Kaman et al., 2001), Australia (Kotey and Slade, 2005), and Canada (Golhar and Deshpande, 1997) suggest.

- Some practices, such as communication with staff, as well as existence of discipline procedures, are widely established in small firms. And a third have formal equal opportunities policies. Formality is far from absent.

- Traditional 'industrial relations' are very rare in small workplaces. Collective bargaining coverage is virtually zero, and other figures show low trade union membership. Related to this, pay setting is a workplace responsibility; not only is there little reliance on collective bargaining but there is also by definition no higher level of management to take on the responsibility. Unlike in large firms, where national or industry agreements operate, or a company has a formal pay structure that is then implemented at workplace level, in small firms pay setting takes place at the workplace with hardly any direct external rules as to how it should be conducted.

Further research by the writers has addressed this point (Storey et al., 2009). It produced an overall formality index, and found that it varied by both workplace and company size. That is, small independent workplaces are the most informal. But larger independent workplaces retain a considerable degree of informality. Small workplaces owned by large companies often have considerable formality.

What lies behind this picture? At one extreme, some writers see small firms as behaving in much the same way as large ones. Way (2002) reports a US survey of 'high performance work systems', embracing such things as self-directed teams and job rotation, group-based performance pay, and formal training. He finds that the *extent* of these systems did not differ between small and large firms. He also argued that their *role* was similar in that they were correlated with measures of performance in much the same way as was the case in studies of large firms (such as Huselid, 1995). A survey of US service sector firms also finds more extensive use of 'high commitment' than of 'bureaucratic' practices, and reports that the former were common across all sizes of firm: 'small firms can no longer be considered unsophisticated practitioners of human resource management' (Kaman et al., 2001: 43).

The data used by Way (2002) and Kaman et al. (2001) come, however, from self reports by managers to telephone surveys, and there was no space to assess what the respondents meant. Some items are almost bound to be high in small organizations. Job rotation, that is the sharing of tasks, is most likely where there is no formal structure of jobs and where, as in small organizations, employees need to take on a range of duties.[2] Similarly, any small organization may be a 'team' in the sense that workers work together. It will not be a team in the sense of the (large firm) literature on teams, which speaks of the ability of teams to allocate tasks among themselves and the election of team leaders. This is the image of an organization with a developed division of labour, in which team work as a mode of work organization replaces some more Taylorized system (Edwards et al., 2002). In small firms, such a division of labour does not exist, and a 'team' has a different meaning. As Bacon et al. (1998: 262) note – ironically in a study stressing the extent of formal practices in small firms – teamworking is 'not about creating formal work groups but maintaining the notion of "all working together"'.[3]

Other items, too, will mean different things. 'Formal' training can mean almost any kind of training, including very basic induction. The UK WERS, which specified that formal meant *off the job* training, reports relatively low levels in small firms. This does not mean that training is absent, and some surveys have attempted to measure informal training in SMEs – albeit with the risk of inviting overestimation by including minor on-going activities (Kitching, 1997). In short, a practice as measured by a survey means different things in small and large organizations.

It is useful to enlarge on this point in relation to some areas of HR practice. Consider first recruitment and selection. One image of small firms is that they rely heavily on informal

means such as personal contacts and referrals from existing employees. WERS 2004 in fact found that informal recruitment methods were used equally by small and large firms (Forth et al., 2006: 33). We would, however, add three points. First, this fact says nothing about the weight placed on particular methods. Second, actual practice may differ from what is reported in a survey. Thus Taylor (2005) reports from four firms that, though managers claimed to use formal methods, employees stressed 'being known' personally and the role of kinship links. Third, practice may vary according to the type of small firm. In relatively unsophisticated firms in sectors such as clothing manufacture and hotels and catering, there is heavy reliance on word of mouth methods. Though formal methods may also be reported, these tend to be used to screen applicants, or when all else fails. What is important is an applicant who is known to the owner and is believed to have the necessary commitment. Technical skills may be less important than harder to define attributes such as attitude and commitment. These tendencies are heightened where firms are run by people from ethnic minorities, who tend to recruit from particular parts of the labour market and for whom kinship ties are often important. Note that this is not a fixed 'ethnic characteristic': minority businesses operating in, say, business services will be much less constrained by kinship ties; white family owned firms in traditional sectors often rely on family and friends; and it is the combination of location in a particular market segment and background that leads to particular emphasis on informal recruitment channels. All that said, we suspect that all small firms tend to place a relatively large emphasis on informal methods of recruitment and even more so when they are selecting employees – who, after all, will have to work closely with existing staff and who indeed need to 'fit in'.

A second key area is performance appraisal. Ongoing research in three sectors – food manufacturing, ICT, and the media and creative industries – is useful here in that it covers traditional and more modern parts of the economy.[4] The extent of use of appraisal was on a par with what would be expected from Table 31.2. Employees also reported the presence of appraisal (with 68 per cent reporting that their performance was appraised) and that the practice was not mere window-dressing: of those reporting the use of appraisal the great majority reported a strong or very strong link between how effectively they worked and their appraisal rating. Yet there was also evidence of a lack of structure in the process. In some firms, workers were unsure whether appraisal had in fact taken place. In most, the process was much less formalized than one would expect in large firms, with rather little documentation or training of appraisers. Perhaps most significantly, evaluations depended on the judgement of managers, who may also be owners of the firm. Taylor (2005) similarly reports for four firms that appraisal targets and associated rewards reflected close personal interaction and were ultimately in the hands of managers. This is not to say that the process is necessarily simply subjective or biased, and little discontent among employees over the issue was recorded in these studies. The key point is that the process is more personalized and informal than the term 'appraisal scheme' tends to convey.

A third issue is payment systems. As noted above, these are important in that it is firm-level decisions that affect pay while formal pay structures seem to be rare. A great deal is thus left to choice. Small firms appear to deal with this choice through rules of thumb, which turn on what seems to be the going rate together with some idea of what is fair. At this point, we need to be clear as to what is in the pay package. Some observers present the small firm as a site of shared benefits between owners and workers, as might be indexed by profit-sharing schemes or bonus arrangements. Yet the research just mentioned found remarkably few systems of this kind, as did earlier research on mainly low value-added firms (Arrowsmith et al., 2003). Cox (2005) reports – from a study of four relatively large (120–450 employees) firms that did use variable pay schemes – that managing both the procedural and distributive aspects of variable pay proved very difficult. In short, formality and informality interact.

UNDERSTANDING MANAGEMENT PROCESSES

The case for an 'integrated' approach has been advanced by Wright and Boswell (2002) in their review of mainstream HRM research, and recently by Harney and Dundon (2006), who focus specifically on small firms. To arrest the prevailing tendency to 'desegregate' HRM, Wright and Boswell (2002) advocate the linking of organizational and individual levels of analysis; and stress the importance of viewing HR practices as part of an HR system rather than discrete entities. Harney and Dundon (2006) suggest that an 'open systems' perspective is best placed to capture the complexity of HR practices in small firms. These authors stress the intersection of external influences such as the product market and internal strategic choice in explaining the complexity of small firm practice. Yet there is one key element absent from their list: the familial context (Edwards and Ram, 2006; Edwards et al., 2006).

We have seen that most small firms are family owned. And many that are not family firms are likely to bear the imprint of their founders, for example the many firms in sectors such as bioscience that were founded as spin-offs from large firms. This was evident in Hannan et al.'s (1995: 513) study of 100 young high technology firms; the authors found 'startling diversity in founders' employment models even among start-up companies within the very same industry, competing directly against one another'. Four types of employment relations were identified:

- a 'factory' model, which emphasized pecuniary attachment and managerial control;
- a 'commitment' model based upon peer and 'cultural' control;
- a professional model that stressed attachment to work; and

- an 'engineering' model that exhibited a more instrumental approach to work relations.

The 'blueprints' of company founders were key to explaining the variety and durability of these approaches.

Hence, management processes will be strongly shaped by the preferences and assumptions of the owning group. This is not to say that there will be one common view. In one firm that we studied there was a long-standing dispute between one member of the owning family and another over the nature and extent of formality, with one arguing for a more systematic approach, including the employment of an HR professional, and the other preferring traditional family ways. The point is that purely personal preferences, which are not necessarily right or wrong, will play a larger role than in large firms. Gilman (2006) reports a firm that used psychometric testing because its founder thought that the method was a good idea.

The longer term development of a firm is also likely to reflect personal choices. Some family firms consciously choose to remain small because they like the family atmosphere and because there is no personal ambition to develop the business. Other rationales for remaining small include the fear that, once a firm becomes significant, it will be the target of a take-over by a large firm. Much will depend on the personal ambitions of owners and whether or not they wish to develop the business for the next generation. Such ambitions, and their implications for human resource practices, rarely attract the importance they merit in standard accounts of human resource management in small firms. Yet they are central to an appreciation of the dynamics of business development in small firms. Wheelock and Baines (1998a: 200), for example, maintain that the survival, maintenance, and growth of the microbusiness cannot be fully appreciated without developing 'an understanding of the relationship within the household … in which the business person is based'. Aldrich and Cliff's (2003) 'family embeddedness perspective', echoes this approach in its explication of the variety

of ways in which developments in the family can influence the trajectory of the enterprise.

In detailed case studies of restaurants, Ram et al. (2001a) found that the development of the business owed much to the dynamics of relations within the household. Many households worked towards the survival of the family enterprise (although there were differences between family members). Such an imperative militated against the substantive 'growth' of the business. However, this did not mean that the business remained static; the key factor appeared to be the priorities of household members at any one particular point in time. The presence of second-generation family members in many of the restaurants suggested a degree of continuity. However, there were many tensions in these firms, which meant that an uncomplicated transition from one generation to another, and smooth employment relations between family members, could not be taken for granted. The 'life-course' of different family members will influence the shape and form of the small business household. Developments in their domestic life circumstances, disenchantment with the often-onerous nature of restaurant work, and inter-family tension militated against unproblematic continuity of the family business.

UNDERSTANDING EMPLOYEE EXPECTATIONS AND RESPONSES

A further piece of the jigsaw concerns what employees expect. Do they want formal procedures, in which case an HR manager may well find formalization to be a sensible strategy, or do they prefer informality?

A brief excursion into debates on employee attitudes will help here. Early research worked from the facts of low strike rates and the like to argue that there was an inherent harmony in small firms. A later reaction reversed the picture, stressing low wages and autocracy which were attributed to the intense market positions faced by small firms (Rainnie, 1989). The latter approach, though more realistic, shared with the former a remarkably small evidence base in terms of employee views. A third approach shared with the first a rather optimistic view but with the difference that employees were not seen as inherently satisfied; instead, small-firm workers tended to stress intrinsic aspects of the job, and satisfaction here meant that low pay was not a major source of discontent (Ingham, 1970). A fourth view said that small-firm workers were not inherently different from others and that size of firm was important only in combination with other factors, so that the age of the worker and the sector in which he or she worked was more important than size in determining attitudes (Curran and Stanworth, 1981). The most recent evidence, from WERS 2004, returns to the influence of size as such, in showing that on a very wide range of indicators small-firm workers are more satisfied than their large-firm counterparts (Forth et al., 2006). More detailed research has shown that this result holds true even when a number of factors, including sector and workers' personal characteristics, are held constant.

Research (see note 1) has also gone further. It has shown that on average formality reduces employee satisfaction in small firms but also that elements of formality have the opposite effect. Most notably performance appraisal and equal opportunities policies were associated with a high level of satisfaction.

Such results suggest that small-firm workers do not seek informality in any overall sense. Moreover, a large body of research has shown that conscious self-selection, whereby workers choose small firms for the intrinsic interest of the work, is likely to be very unusual (Curran and Stanworth, 1979): workers generally lack the information to make such choices, and job choice is a less rational activity than self-selection implies. It is none the less the case that workers find benefits in informality.

Workers' expectations and responses will also be conditioned by the prevailing pattern of social relations in the workplace. Kitching's (1997) study of three contrasting sectors: computer services, employment and secretarial services, and free houses and restaurants identified different kinds of 'culture'. These cultures gave meaning to employment and to the relationship between owner-managers and employees. In computer services, there was a 'work' culture: job satisfaction acquired through the content of work roles was an important feature of employment relations. This contrasted with the more instrumentally-oriented (that is, 'money') culture of employment services firms, and the predominant culture of 'sociability' in free houses and restaurants.

Ram's (1999) intensive case study of a small consultancy firm further illustrates this point. Employees joined the firm because there was an opportunity to be associated with an organisation that had a good 'reputation'; yet there was also the scope to develop their own particular specialisms. One consultant commented that a particular attraction of joining the firms was that it 'had the advantages of shelter and cover but none of the disadvantages of a bureaucracy' (Ram, 1999: 882). In this sense, the employing organization serves as a 'resource that can be used for delivering services to the client and for enhancing personal reputation' (Goffee and Scase, 1995). Others spoke of the prospect of working with a 'team of peers'; the 'exciting' nature of the work; and the 'choices' that the firm offered. However, it is important to note that these features redolent of 'collegiality' 'autonomy' and 'trust' were not the only inducements for joining the company. Competitive financial packages, a directorship, or the prospect of becoming a full partner were also significant.

Or consider a striking finding from studies of relatively low-wage firms (Ram, 1994; Moule, 1998; Holliday, 1995). One might expect that in such low-wage firms in highly competitive industries managerial control would be very tight. In fact, a repeated result is that time-keeping can be lax and that workers come and go with considerable freedom. The reason for this result is that managers in small firms are likely to know the demands of production and to be relaxed if workers go absent at times of slack demand. The *quid pro quo* is that workers are often expected to work overtime at very short notice, commonly without any overtime bonus. There is thus an implicit bargain about work effort, and attempts to formalize the bargain could run into difficulty.

The implications for HR are two-fold. First, workers in small firms develop shared expectations that will shape responses to HR practice. The ways in which, say, performance appraisal would work in Kitching's three cultures are very different. Second, however, cultures have contradictory elements. Thus Ram found that, though consultants enjoyed the informality of the small firm, there were also concerns about the vagueness and secrecy of pay determination. It is moreover possible to change cultures as firms evolve (Ram et al., 2001a). The approach to HR needs to be sensitive to the space for change and the interests that may promote and retard it.

INFLUENCES ON HR PRACTICE

We stressed at the outset that small firms display enormous diversity. We have presented elsewhere a formal framework that models different types of firm and indicates how open they may be to HR practices (Edwards et al., 2006). For example, a very small firm with strong family ownership and control may be resistant to formal HR techniques. For present purposes, we draw on the ideas of the framework by addressing some of the key ways in which small firms vary.

Sector

The importance of sector was underlined by the research of Curran and Stanworth (1981), which demonstrated that workers in two sectors – electronics and printing – often had more in common with large-firm workers from the same sector than with employees of similarly sized firms in different sectors. Scott et al. (1989) developed this approach by identifying four broad sectoral groups: traditional manufacturing, hi-tech manufacturing, traditional services (e.g. hotels) and hi-tech services. Further refinement is necessary if

one wishes to understand the context of a particular firm. In the hotels and catering sector, for example, many firms comply with employment legislation such as the UK National Minimum Wage (Arrowsmith et al., 2003). But it is also true that there are parts of the sector where not only is legal compliance weak but also where there is substantial use of illegal labour (Jones et al., 2006). The reasons for this reflect pressure and opportunity: competitive pressure leads firms to minimize on wage costs, while kinship and communal ties allow employers to recruit co-ethnic workers who are willing to work for illegally low wages. This opportunity structure is itself the product of wider forces in society, including the regime governing immigration and ethnic disadvantage. The result is a labour force with no choice but to work for low wages; firm owners are also pressed to operate in marginal conditions, suffer insecurity, long hours and low incomes, thus sharing the misery of their employees.

HR practices will vary according to sectoral conditions. In the extreme cases just discussed, there are few if any formal HR systems. Recruitment is done through word of mouth and written procedures are largely absent. Mainstream traditional firms are more likely to have in place the basics of written procedures. What is striking about them, however, is the rarity of pay structures: clear schemes that define what a 'job' is and the rewards structure attached to it (Gilman et al., 2002; Tsai et al., 2007). Indeed, the practice of leaving pay very much at the discretion of managers has also been observed in more advanced sectors such as the creative and media industries (Sen Gupta et al., 2006) and also, as we will see below, software consultancies – both qualifying as 'high end' or specifically 'hi-tech' services. Now, the meaning of this informality differs. In professional jobs, regardless of the size of the firm, broad job boundaries and individual responsibility are taken for granted. In the media sector, moreover, freelance employment is widespread and freelancers will be paid in much the same way if they work for a major media company or a small firm – though of course the amounts that they earn will differ (Blair et al., 2003). In traditional firms, the lack of a pay structure does mark out jobs from those in larger firms.

Supply chain relationships between small firms and their larger customers can also affect the nature of HR practices. Power-dependency perspectives (Rainnie, 1989) suggest that the domination by larger customers is such that any scope for enlightened HR practices in small firms is severely limited. However, more optimistic assessments tend to view this relationship as mechanism of 'supplier development', where the large firm facilitates the transfer of knowledge and new work practices to the small enterprise (Hunter et al., 1996). Bacon and Hoque (2005) offer some support for this thesis in their finding that larger customers are associated with a higher likelihood that the small firm will adopt a training strategy and achieve accreditation for HR practices. But this was not accompanied by the adoption of a more widespread set of HR measures, leading the authors to endorse Ram's (2000) finding that HR accreditation may be little more than a procedural measure with no subsequent impact on wider employment practices.

Family ownership and personal control

A regular finding in small business research is that the primary reason for starting a business is personal independence. This means that a substantial number of small firms will prefer small-scale informality and will lack explicit HR policies. Kotey and Slade (2005) report that 36 per cent of 'micro' (defined here as fewer than 5 employees) and 49 per cent of 'small' (5–19 employees) firms had been in existence at least ten years. These are likely to be mature businesses not seeking further growth, and HR practice would need to reflect a desire for continued informality based on personal relationships. Family-owned firms use fewer formal HR practices than similarly-sized non-family firms (de Kok et al., 2006; Reid and Adams, 2001).

Family ownership is likely to exercise some clear effects, of which the most obvious is that non-family employees may be unable to climb to the top of the firm, with implications for career development. In some cases – usually in the more traditional and low-wage sectors – the firm may be used to find jobs for members of the family, which can close off opportunities for other employees as well as having clear implications in that family members may lack relevant business skills and experience.

Mullholland's (1997) study of well-established family businesses in a variety of sectors suggests that such processes are not necessarily confined to 'low value added firms'. Mulholland examined entrepreneurial, managerial and preservation strategies characterizing successful (middle-class) family businesses, drawn from majority white and minority ethnic communities. In one of these cases, owned by an ethnic minority family, the expansion of the business coincided with the incorporation of the founder's five siblings. Mulholland (1997: 695) argues that the employment of male siblings is consistent with the management practices characteristic of industrial family capitalism, providing career paths, while also safeguarding against labour market discrimination that ethnic minorities potentially face. Such opportunities are rarely available to non-family members and are also strongly gendered.

It should be noted that issues of 'insider-outsider' tensions are not limited to small firms. It is a commonplace that large Japanese MNCs tend to favour insiders (Japanese nationals) over outsiders in fields such as promotion. The issue for an HR manager is not so much whether or not a firm is family-owned but the importance placed within a firm's traditions on ascriptive characteristics (membership of a particular in-group) as opposed to achievement and merit.

A regular finding in small business research is a tension between personal control and formal HR practices. A firm may, for example, have reached a size at which it formalizes its procedures, but if the owner maintains detailed engagement these practices may in effect be overridden. Gilman (2006) reports this tendency – significantly in a study not of traditional firms but of successful hi-tech companies. Pay and promotion are important areas in which this happens, with the owner wanting to make decisions as has always been done, often expressing impatience with procedures.

Personal control also has wider and more subtle effects. At one extreme, it can generate a pattern importantly identified as 'fraternalism' by Scase and Goffee (1982) in their study of the construction industry. In this pattern, owners and employees work alongside each other as equals and there is a strong sense of shared identity based not only on the firm but also the traditions of a whole occupation. To the extent that firms here have a formal HR presence, HR practice will need to recognize egalitarianism and possibly avoid or adapt systems such as appraisal.

At the other extreme, personal control can imply autocracy. Evidence of extreme autocracy is in fact limited to certain sectors where sweatshop conditions are most evident (Hoel, 1982). We saw above that in general small-firm workers report high levels of job satisfaction. Moreover, even in sweatshop conditions – that is, where wages are low and market competition is intense – autocracy is commonly moderated to produce 'negotiated paternalism' (Ram, 1994). The key reason is that employers need a degree of worker co-operation. Moreover, family and kin connections mean that there are mutual obligations other than the purely economic, so that straight autocracy is limited.

Between these two extremes lie situations in which personal control is one feature of a complex pattern of relationships. The evidence here is far from clear, not least because it is often presented to attack a stereotype. A standard image of the family firm is that of 'cultural unity [and] integration' (Ainsworth and Cox, 2003: 1463). It is then possible to undermine the image, as in the study just cited: evidence from two Australian family-owned firms shows that unity and integration co-existed with the expendability of employees, and there were also subtle divisions between the immediate family and more distant kin. The danger, as noted at the start of the chapter, lies in inverting the image of unity to stress 'control' in the twin senses of dominance by owners and the successful pursuit of the owners' goals. Such a simple reading of the evidence should be avoided. Ainsworth and Cox (2003: 1476, 1480) in fact offer a more subtle view of culture in small firms. First, employees had a sense of commitment; in the words of one, 'they're a small business trying to make a living so you are a bit more responsible'. Second, the culture was not imposed but was enacted and constituted actively by various groups.

This point can be taken further through a study of a larger firm, a software consultancy with 150 employees (Grugulis et al., 2000). Training and development of staff was stressed, and the firm even had a 'culture manager' (apparently in preference to the HR designation). In selecting new staff, character and attitude were stressed over technical skills. The culture was one of working hard and playing hard, and employees were well-paid and enjoyed satisfying jobs. Control did not mean domination. At the same time, however, there was a strong expectation to fit into the demands of the firm, and employees found it hard to maintain a line between work and home. Control was subtle and it was part of a system producing benefits, but it was none the less real.

Several HR implications stand out. Grugulis et al. (2000: 101) stress that practices in the firm were efforts to 'institutionalise … simple, personal control' and that the firm deployed 'sophisticated HR practices'. The task would then be to design combinations of practices that maintained a culture while also establishing formal mechanisms consistent with it. There might also be tensions to assess. Thus it is reported that there was a pay structure of a kind, but that this was kept very secret and that employees believed that they were paid purely as individuals. As the firm developed, the relevant tensions may well have grown, and balancing a clear pay structure with the freedom to reward individuals as managers saw fit might become a central issue.

Size and growth orientation

A US study reports that, at the start-up of businesses, HR is among the majority of management functions that remain in the hands of the owners (Ardichvili et al., 1998). As firms grow, sets of key functions tend to be delegated at the same time, and delegation of HR tends to be associated with that of many other functions. The implication drawn is that, at this point, an HR role will become important and that a key part of the role will be the training and development of the new cadre of managers. The turning point stated is $1 million in sales, which, with allowance for inflation, might act as some kind of benchmark, though the point is likely to differ widely according to business sector and possibly also country.

A UK study of management development found that small firms with a strong orientation towards growth were the most likely to stress management development (Thomson et al., 1997; also Patton and Marlow, 2002). A US study, using an objective measure of growth (rate of increase of sales), found that high-growth firms put more emphasis on HR practices than did low-growth ones (Carlson et al., 2006). Looking at US firms that had reached the stage of making an Initial Public Offering on the stock market, Welbourne and Andrews (1996) report that firms stressing HR had relatively high survival rates.

However, it is important to note that increased formality is not an inevitable consequence of small firm growth. It is not uncommon for business owners to set up other small ventures to pursue growth objectives. The establishment of 'satellite' enterprises was a noticeable feature of Lazerson's (1988) study of small manufacturing firms in the Italian region of Emilia Romagna. This growth strategy enabled owners to maintain control, secure labour market flexibility, and achieve organizational efficiencies. Importantly, a key factor was the continued existence of extended families, which provided a foundation for economic relations based on cooperation and trust, 'The importance of such non-market relations for economic success ... explains the heavy reliance ex-worker owners place on turning to friends and former colleagues in their search for employees' (Lazerson, 1988: 31). Ackroyd's (1995) account of small 'dynamic' UK based information technology firms offers further support for this *modus operandi*. 'Informal strategic affiliations' and 'temporary alliances' between individuals and organizations of a similar size were integral features of these firms; growth was achieved by 'replication'. Such practices were crucial to the firms' ability to change and diversify the scale of their operations.

An orientation towards growth is not necessarily restricted to the relatively sophisticated firms. We have studied a small bakery, which had been in existence for over 30 years. It was run by two members of one family and in many respects was highly traditional and averse to formal HR systems. Yet it had grown, and two key developments were to employ a production manager from outside the family and to bring in a new director whose role was specifically to challenge the existing directors and to encourage new ways of thinking. Ram et al.'s (2005) study of ethnic minority businesses in the highly competitive restaurant sector further highlights the potential for growth in seeming 'low value added' firms. The popularity of ethnic cuisine has resulted in ethnic restaurants taking an increasing share of rapidly increasing consumer expenditure. Yet, as the study demonstrates, the perceived attractiveness of the restaurant trade has caused the supply of Asian entrepreneurs to out-run even a vigorously expanding demand, resulting in market saturation. Even so, simply because the city-wide and regional markets are expansive, entrepreneurs are granted some scope to shape the trajectory of the business. Ram et al. documented instances of business owners developing new markets, adapting existing niches, and re-oriented working practices. Firms that had sufficient resources expanded by opening more outlets; they had relatively 'open' practices to recruitment and management; complied with employment regulations; and adopted more innovative approaches to new product development. Other firms grew by concentrating on product differentiation rather than multiple business ownership. Hence, rather than investing in new premises, these firms concentrated their efforts on refining their products and developing relationships with key staff that would nurture 'authenticity'.

It is of course an open question as to what determines a growth orientation. To some extent, it is constrained by sectoral location. Firms in declining sectors such as parts of manufacturing, and those that are dominated by very small firms, such as restaurants, will find it hard to grow. It is also strongly shaped by family ownership. To the extent that the owning family uses the business to secure a satisfactory level of income, growth will not be pursued. Growth also brings challenges of managing expansion that may be avoided. A more positive view may be developed consciously by owners with different characteristics, or emerge as a new generation takes over, or develop even more by chance if a particular market niche opens up and allows the firm to fill it.

Change management

In terms of the HR role in growth and change management, there are more opportunities than might appear at first sight. Yet these need to be addressed in a particular way. As Bacon et al. (1998: 260) put it, based on several cases, the challenge was 'managing the introduction of the formalization necessary to retain management control while not destroying the informality and the culture of the small business'. It was not a matter of ending informality but changing its nature and making it more professional.

A detailed case study of a food manufacturing firm is relevant here, not least because it was in a 'traditional manufacturing' sector in Scott et al.'s categorization and yet was able to carry out the processes described by Bacon et al. (see Ram et al., 2001b). The result, as one manager in the firm put it, was that they had 'gone from being very

laid back to being laid back'. A personnel manager was recruited, and formal processes, not only in HR but also in the control of operations, were introduced. These developments reflected but also reinforced the firm's move towards more high value-added products, and also reflected the personal style and ambition of its owner. The implications of not attending to the altered dynamics of informality that arise from business growth are evident in Ram's (1999) ethnography of a small management consultancy firm. During the course of the study, there was much talk of 'growing the business', particularly amongst the directorate. To this end, the owner introduced a formal business plan to the rest of the organization in which he outlined his views on how the firm should develop. The underlying motivation for the business plan, which was the first formal one that the company had introduced since its inception, was bound up with the owner's personal circumstances. In essence, he wanted to retire in five to seven years; and as he approached that time, he did not want to be burdened with working the 50–60 hours per week that he currently had to tolerate. Since the company was still in his name, the owner pointed out that it was necessary to consider the issue of 'succession', and ways in which the company could be re-configured. One of the options was growing the company sufficiently so that it could be sold to a larger concern. Moving towards this kind of 'exit strategy' would, according to the owner, require a more *transparently managed* organization that had approved quality standards across a range of areas. Some nine months after the introduction of the business plan there was little if any talk of growth. There had been little if any attention accorded to actively managing the process of change, with one consultant bemoaning the lack of 'management'. Towards the end of the fieldwork, there was talk of 'redundancies', and the owner declared himself content to become a 'freelancer' and hence *not having to pay the mortgages of six or seven staff*'. It seemed that his aspirations for retirement would have to be achieved by working as a freelancer himself in the future rather than selling a substantial business.

CONCLUSION

We have discussed formality and informality, and argued that the view that small firms are informal, and that this is a weakness, is incorrect: informality is not total, and it brings benefits not least in terms of employee responses. Moreover, much of the focus in large firms in the last ten or twenty years can be analysed in terms of a search for informality: consider delayering and decentralization at strategic levels and team work and empowerment in HR. There are practices that can be learnt from small firms. As Bacon et al. (1998: 267) conclude, communication is direct, and links between employee behaviour and firm performance relatively clear and immediate, while change programmes are more 'organic' and 'authentic'.

This does not mean that informality switches from being a sin to a virtue. As Gray and Mabey (2005: 480) remark, informality can 'co-exist with confusion and uncertainty'. Small firms always face the danger that a decision will be made out of personal preference or in haste. This is particularly the case when they come into contact with the formalities of state regulation in such matters as health and safety and individual employment rights. Informality needs to be kept in check, just as too much formality in large firms can lead to inaction. Informality and formality are enacted and negotiated; they are not eternal unchanging characteristics.

As for models of HRM, Welbourne and Andrews (1996) make the interesting remark that HRM, particularly in its Strategic form, implies a complex, and indeed virtually impossible, task of continually fitting the components of the HR system together and ensuring a 'fit' with business strategy. In our view, this is one of the general problems of the SHRM paradigm. It is particularly salient in small firms, which not only lack the resources the engineer 'fit' but which

are also likely to endanger their informality and flexibility if they try to do so. It makes more sense to think of HR practices as being broadly tied together. The *principles* of SHRM are relevant in encouraging firms to think actively about their HR practice and where it might connect to business strategy. A rapidly growing software firm, for example, might be advised to ensure that it has a payments system that goes beyond the merely *ad hoc*. But more complexity could be counter-productive. The generic recognition that firms have 'idiosyncratic competencies', and wider interest in the resource-based view of the firm, imply that any firm needs to generate its own models (Boxall and Purcell, 2003). This is particularly true of small firms, where personal relationships and the absence of standard approaches, are central. HR in such firms needs to recognize the constraints that arise, but also the possibilities of engaging flexibly in the development of the firm.

NOTES

1 This strand appears to be largely European in its origins, with US research being surprisingly innocent of it (Ram and Edwards, 2003). Our discussion necessarily follows this fact in drawing heavily on European, particularly UK, evidence.

2 We looked at this in WERS 2004, which has data on the proportion of employees trained to do jobs other than their own and the proportion actually performing such jobs. The data show that there is in fact *less* of this cross-job activity in small firms than in large ones; this is also true when we compared very small workplaces (5–9 employees) that were free-standing with workplaces of the same size owned by large (100+ employees) firms. Our interpretation of this turns on the meaning of a 'job'. In large firms, jobs are clearly defined, often through formal job descriptions, and very small workplaces will be, for example, the local branches of financial institutions. In independent establishments, staff will be expected as a matter of course to take on a wider set of duties. One indicator from WERS is that formal job evaluation schemes are rare in small firms. We also found that managers' reports of employee job variety and control pointed to higher levels of autonomy in small than in large workplaces, which is consistent with the view that small-firm jobs are relatively flexible.

3 Note also that Kaman et al. (2001) follow the HPWS literature in including formal grievance

procedures as part of a 'high commitment' model (Huselid, 1995). Such procedures are surely fundamental to traditional personnel management, and including them inflates the extent of 'commitment' practices.

4 This study, by Paul Edwards, Sukanya Sengupta and Chin-Ju Tsai, embraced 89 firms in the 3 sectors, and included management interviews and, in 32 of the firms, data from employees. Some results are reported in Tsai et al., 2007.

REFERENCES

Ackroyd, S. (1995) 'On the structure and dynamics of some small, UK-based information technology firms', *Journal of Management Studies*, 32 (2): 142–61.

Ackroyd, S. (2002) *The Organization of Business.* Oxford: OUP.

Ainsworth, S. and Cox, J. W. (2003) 'Families divided: Culture and control in small family business', *Organization Studies*, 24 (9): 1463–95.

Aldrich, H. E. and Cliff, J. E. (2003) 'The pervasive effects of family on entrepreneurship: Toward a family embeddedness perspective', *Journal of Business Venturing*, 18 (3): 573–96.

Ardichvili, A., Harman, B., Cardozo, R. N. and Reynolds, P. D. (1998) 'The new venture growth', *Human Resource Development Quarterly*, 9 (1): 55–70.

Arrowsmith, J., Gilman, M., Edwards, P. and Ram, M. (2003) 'The impact of the national minimum wage in small firms', *British Journal of Industrial Relations*, 41 (3): 435–56.

Bacon, N., Ackers, P., Storey, J. and Coates, D. (1998) 'It's a small world: Human resources in small businesses', in C. Mabey, G. Salaman and J. Storey (eds), *Strategic Human Resource Management.* London: Sage, pp. 251–68.

Bacon, N. and Hoque, K. (2005) 'HRM in the SME sector: Valuable employees and coercive networks', *International Journal of Human Resource Management*, 16 (11): 1976–99.

Blair, H., Culkin, N. and Randle, K. (2003) 'From London to Los Angeles', *International Journal of Human Resource Management*, 14 (4): 619–33.

BLS (Bureau of Labor Statistics) (2005) *New Quarterly Data From BLS on Business Employment Dynamics By Size of Firm Summary.* www.bls.gov/news.release/cewfs.nr0.

Blyton, P. and Turnbull, P. (2004) *The Dynamics of Employee Relations.* 3rd edn. Basingstoke: Palgrave.

Boxall, P. and Purcell, J. (2003) *Strategy and Human Resource Management.* Basingstoke: Palgrave.

Carlson, D. S., Upton, N. and Seaman, S. (2006) 'The impact of HR practices and compensation design on performance', *Journal of Small Business Management*, 44 (4): 531–43.

Cooke, F. L (2005) 'Employment relations in small commercial businesses in China', *Industrial Relations Journal*, 36 (1): 19–37.

Cox, A. (2005) 'Managing variable pay in smaller workplaces', in S. Marlow, D. Patton. and M. Ram (eds), *Labour Management in Small Firms,* London: Routledge, pp. 26–48.

Cully, M., Woodland, S., O'Reilly, A. and Dix, G. (1999) *Britain at Work.* London: Routledge.

Curran, J. (1990) 'Rethinking economic structure: Exploring the role of the small firm and self-employment in the British economy', *Work, Employment and Society*, 4 (special issue): 125–46.

Curran, J. and Stanworth, J. (1979) 'Self-selection and the small firm worker', *Sociology*, 13 (3): 427–44.

Curran, J. and Stanworth, J. (1981) 'A new look at job satisfaction in the small firm', *Human Relations*, 34 (5): 343–65.

De Kok, J., Uhlaner, L. and Thurik, A. R. (2006) 'Professional HRM practices in family owned-managed enterprises', *Journal of Small Business Management*, 44 (3): 441–60.

Edwards, P and Ram, M. (2006) 'Still living on the edge: Marginal small firms, negotiated orders and the dynamics of the modern economy' *Journal of Management Studies*, 43 (4): 895–916.

Edwards, P., Geary, J. and Sisson, K. (2002) 'New forms of work organization in the workplace', in G. Murray, J. Bélanger, A. Giles and P-A Lapointe (eds), *Work and Employment Relations in the High–performance Workplace.* London: Continuum, pp. 72–119.

Edwards, P., Ram, M., Sen Gupta, S. and Tsai, C. (2006) 'Institutionalized action without institutions: Negotiated meanings in small firms', *Organization*, 13 (5): 701–24.

EIRO (European Industrial Relations Observatory) (2006) 'Employment relations in SMEs'. www.eiro.eurofound.eu.int/2006/02/study/tn060201s.

Forth, J., Bewley, H. and Bryson, A. (2006) *Small and medium-sized enterprises: Findings from the 2004 Workplace Employment Relations Survey.* London: Routledge.

Fuller-Love, N. (2006) 'Management development in small firms', *International Journal of Management Reviews*, 8 (1): 175–98.

Gilman, M. (2006) 'Testing a framework of the organization of small firms', paper to 24th International Labour Process Conference, London.

Gilman, M., Edwards, P., Ram, M., and Arrowsmith, J. (2002) 'Pay determination in small firms in the UK', *Industrial Relations Journal*, 33 (1): 52–67.

Goffee, R. and Scase, R. (1995) *Corporate Realities: The Dynamics of Large and Small Organisations,* London: Routledge.

Golhar, D. Y. and Deshpande, S. (1997) 'HRM practices in large and small canadian manufacturing firms', *Journal of Small Business Management,* 35 (4): 413–29.

Goss, D. (1988) 'Social harmony and the small firm', *Sociological Review,* 36 (1): 114–32.

Gray, C. and Mabey, C. (2005) 'Management development: Key differences between small and large businesses in Europe', *International Small Business Journal,* 23 (4): 467–85.

Grugulis, I., Dundon, T. and Wilkinson, A. (2000) 'Cultural control and the "Culture manager" ', *Work, Employment and Society,* 14 (1): 97–116.

Hannan, M. T., Burton, M. D. and Baron, J. N. (1996) 'Inertia and change in the early years: Employment relations in young, high technology firms', *Industrial and Corporate Change,* 5 (2): 503–56.

Harney, B. and Dundon, T. (2006) 'Capturing complexity: Developing an integrated approach to analysing HRM in SMEs', *Human Resource Management Journal,* 16 (1), 48–73.

Hoel, B. (1982) 'Contemporary clothing sweatshops', in J. West (ed.), *Work, Women and the Labour Market.* London: RKP, pp. 174–186

Holliday, R. (1995) *Investigating Small Firms.* London: Routledge.

Hunter, L., Beaumont, P. and Sinclair, D. (1996) 'A "partnership" route to human resource management', *Journal of Management Studies,* 33 (2): 235–57.

Huselid, M. (1995) 'The impact of human resource management practices on turnover, productivity and corporate financial performance', *Academy of Management Journal,* 38 (4): 635–72.

Ingham, G. K. (1970) *Size of Industrial Organization and Worker Behaviour.* Cambridge: CUP.

Jones, T., Ram, M. and Edwards, P. (2006) 'Shades of grey in the informal economy', *International Journal of Sociology and Social Policy,* 26 (9/10): 357–73.

Kaman, V., McCarthy, A. M., Gulbro, R. D. and Tucker, M. L. (2001) 'Bureaucratic and high commitment hr practices in small service firms', *Human Resource Planning,* 1 (1): 33–44.

Kitching, J. (1997) 'Labour regulation in the small service sector enterprise', PhD thesis, Kingston University.

Kitching, J. (1997) 'Regulating employment relations through workplace learning: A study of small employers, *Human Resource Management Journal,* 17 (1): 42–57.

Kotey, B. and Slade, P. (2005) 'Formal HRM practices in small growing firms', *Journal of Small Business Management,* 43 (1): 16–40.

Lazerson, M. (1988) 'Organizational Growth of Small Firms: An Outcome of Markets and Hierarchies', *American Sociological Review,* 53 (3): 330–41.

Moule, M. (1998) 'Regulation of work in small firms: A view from the inside' *Work, Employment and Society,* 12 (4): 635–53.

Mulholland, K. (1997) 'The family enterprise and business strategies', *Work, Employment and Society,* 11 (4): 685–711.

Patton, D. and Marlow, S. (2002) 'The determinants of management training within smaller firms in the UK', *Journal of Small Business and Enterprise Development,* 9 (2): 260–70.

Rainnie, A. (1989) *Industrial Relations in Small Firms.* London: Routledge.

Ram, M. (1994) *Managing to Survive – Working Lives in Small Firms.* Oxford: Blackwell.

Ram, M. (1999) 'Managing consultants in a small firm – a case study', *Journal of Management Studies,* 36 (6): 875–97.

Ram, M. (2000) 'Investors in people in small firms: Case study evidence from the business services sector', *Personnel Review,* 29 (1): 69–91.

Ram, M., Abbas, T., Sanghera, B., Barlow, G. and Jones, T. (2001) ' "Apprentice entrepreneurs"? Ethnic minority workers in the independent restaurant sector', *Work, Employment and Society,* 15 (2): 353–72.

Ram, M and Edwards, P. (2003) 'Praising Caesar not burying him – what we know about employment relations in small firms', *Work, Employment and Society* 17 (4): 719–30.

Ram, M., Abbas, T., Sanghera, B., Barlow, G. and Jones, T. (2001) 'Making the link: Households and small business activity in a multi-ethnic context', *Community, Work and Family,* 4 (3): 327–48.

Ram, M., Edwards, P., Gilman, M. and Arrowsmith, J. (2001) 'The dynamics of informality', *Work, Employment and Society,* 15 (4): 845–61.

Ram, M., Jones, T., Abbas, T. and Carter, S. (2005) 'Breaking out of survival businesses: The management of growth and development in the South Asian restaurant trade', in S. Marlow, D. Patton and M. Ram (eds), *Labour Management in Small Firms,* London: Routledge, pp. 109–32.

Reid, R. S., Adams, J. S. (2001) 'Human resource management: A survey of practices within family and non-family firms', *Journal of European Industrial Training,* 26 (6): 310–20.

SBS (Small Business Service (2006) 'Small business statistics, 2005'. Available at www.sbs.gov.uk/sbsgov/action.

Scase, R., Goffee, R. (1982) *The Entrepreneurial Middle Class,* London: Croom Helm.

Scott, M., Roberts, I., Holroyd, G. and Sawbridge, D. (1989) *Management and Industrial Relations in Small Firms*. Research Paper 70. London: Department of Employment.

Sengupta, S., Edwards, P. and Tsai, C-J. (2009) 'The good, the bad and the ordinary: work identities in "good" and "bad" jobs in the UK', *Work and Occupations*, 36 (1): 26–55.

Storey, D.J., Saridakis, G., Sengupta, S., Edwards, P. and Blackburn, R. (2009) 'Management formality, size of firm and self-reported job quality (SRJQ) in Great Britain'. Unpublished paper, Centre for Small and Medium-sized Enterprise, University of Warwick.

Taylor, P., Hyman, J., Mulvey, G. and Bain, P. (2002) 'Work organisation, control and the experience of work in call centres', *Work, Employment and Society*, 17 (3): 435–58.

Taylor, S. (2005) 'The Hunting of the Snark', in S. Marlow, D. Patton and M. Ram (eds), *Labour Management in Small Firms*. London: Routledge, pp. 122–41.

Terry, M. (1977) 'The inevitable growth of informality', *British Journal of Industrial Relations*, 15 (1): 75–90.

Thomson, A., Storey, J., Mabey, C., Gray, C., Farmer, E. and Thomson, R. (1997) *A Portrait of Management Development*. London: Institute of Management.

Tsai, C-J., Sen Gupta, S. and Edwards, P. (2007) 'When and why is small beautiful? employment relations in the small firm', *Human Relations*, 60 (12): 1779–808.

Way, S. A. (2002) 'High performance work systems and intermediate indicators of firm performance within the us small business sector', *Journal of Management*, 26 (6): 765–85.

Welbourne, T. M. and Andrews, A. O. (1996) 'Predicting the performance of initial public offerings', *Academy of Management Journal*, 39 (4): 891–919.

Wever, K. (1995) *Negotiating Competitiveness*. Cambridge, Mass.: Harvard Business School Press.

Wheelock, J. and Baines, S. (1998) 'Creating your own job: The behaviour of micro-business households in the risk society', ed. Michie, J. and Reati, A., *Employment, Technology and Economic Needs*. Cheltenham: Edward Elgar.

Wright, P. and Boswell, W. (2002) 'Desegregating HRM: A review and synthesis of micro and macro HRM research', *Journal of Management Studies*, 28 (3): 247–76.

32

HRM in Multinational Companies

Anthony Ferner

INTRODUCTION

This chapter considers the management of human resources across borders within multinational companies (MNCs). This will be referred to as 'international human resource management' (IHRM). The term has been used in a variety of ways in the literature, and one of the tasks of the chapter will be to clarify the terrain to which it refers. The chapter first assesses the meaning of IHRM and its evolution as a field of study. Second, it summarises the conceptual, substantive and methodological preoccupations of work in this area. Among the issues reviewed is one of the defining questions of IHRM, the 'travel' of policies and practices between countries: the conditions under which such diffusion takes place, the nature of the diffusion process, and the impact of host environments on transferred practices. Also examined is the nature of IHRM as a management function: how it is structured, how it is evolving, and the characteristics that distinguish it from HRM in a domestic setting. Finally, the chapter considers areas where the understanding of IHRM is underdeveloped and suggests some directions for the evolution of IHRM research in the future.

CHARACTERISING IHRM AS A FIELD OF STUDY

The definition of IHRM is a vexed question since, as argued below, the focus of the area has been excessively narrow. A relatively broad perspective on IHRM is captured in the following definition from Taylor et al. (1996: 960). An MNC's IHRM system is: 'The set of distinct activities, functions and processes that are directed at attracting, developing and maintaining an MNC's human resources. It is thus the aggregate of the various HRM systems used to manage people in the MNC, both at home and overseas'.

The essence of IHRM, which distinguishes it from HRM in domestic companies, is that it deals with the management of employees *across countries*, and hence across different systems for organising business in general and human resources in particular.[1]

For this reason, there is a strong overlap between IRHM and the field of *comparative HRM* (see chapters 9 and 28 in this volume). Taylor et al.'s definition points to a crucial question: what is the relationship between HRM systems within different national operations of an MNC, and HRM systems within the MNC that transcend national borders? The fact of operating across borders would not matter if national systems were highly convergent. But, despite debates about convergence stemming from 'globalisation', significant differences remain (and indeed new ones emerge) in how countries organise business activity and, more specifically, the management of employees (e.g. Brewster et al., 2004).

A key question for IHRM is how to conceptualise such cross-national differences. Until recently the dominant paradigm has been based on 'cultural values', largely drawing on the work of Hofstede (1980). This perspective suggests that persistent differences in cross-national behaviour derive from fundamental divergences in deep-seated, long-lasting values. Explanatory models, drawing on Hofstede's dimensions, have been used, for example, in pay practice (e.g. Newman and Nollen, 1996; Roth and O'Donnell, 1996; Schuler and Rogovsky, 1998); in employment discrimination (Lawler and Bae, 1998); in upward appraisal (Adsit et al., 1997); and more generally in assessing the transfer of HR practices (e.g. Ngo et al., 1998).

The cultural values perspective has had an important role in drawing attention to the difficulties of 'one-best-way' models of IHRM. The underlying questions (cf. Clark et al., 1999: 520) are: how can 'multicultural' organisations be managed, and to what extent are modifications necessary to parent-country culture in an MNC's operations abroad? Despite its contribution, it is difficult to discern quite why this particular, essentially 'idealist', approach to national difference has had such a pervasive impact. One explanation may lie in the ease with which value dimensions can be reduced to aggregate scores that allow simple, if less than enlightening, cross-country comparisons. The

methodological basis and explanatory value of the approach have been questioned, both from within and outside a culturalist perspective (see e.g. Gerhart and Fang, 2005; McSweeney, 2002). And, as Clark et al. (1999: 521) note, 'cultural variables are commonly introduced ex post as explanatory variables without an a priori explanation of their content and origins'. Despite such concerns, the influence of the 'culturalist' approach is still strong, reflected in the formation of a new journal in 2000, the *International Journal of Cross-cultural Management*, underpinned by concerns with cross-cultural differences in values.

In recent years, writers on IHRM have increasingly adopted a more 'institutionalist' perspective to understanding cross-national differences (e.g. Edward and Rees, 2006; Kostova, 1999). The essence of a comparative institutionalist approach (e.g. Campbell, 2004; Crouch, 2005; Hall and Soskice, 2001) is to seek explanations for differences in behaviour in the way in which economic activity is structured within 'national business systems'. This involves the careful analysis of the formal and informal institutions that have evolved over time to govern business activity. For example, the way in which firms relate to each other in markets, how economies generate the skills they need, the division of labour and the definition of tasks within productive activity, the governance of firms, the legislative framework set by national states, and systems for the management of firm–employee relations all suppose distinctive institutional arrangements that cannot be deduced from differences in a handful of cultural values 'dimensions'.

This is not to say that cultural value differences are irrelevant, merely that by themselves they are inadequate forms of explanation; they do not capture real differences in the ways in which economic activity is organised in different countries, and throw little light on processes of change and evolution within business systems. The real question is how values and norms inform and in turn are shaped by the evolving institutions that govern economic life as actors with real power and distinctive interests construct institutional arrangements, modify them and are in turn constrained and shaped by them.

From this perspective, the core of IHRM as a field may be characterised as how MNCs manage workforces spread over multiple national-institutional 'domains', often with very different ways of organising business activity. Variations between such institutional domains are generally more significant than those found within any single domain. This is not to say that national institutional arrangements are homogeneous. But the national level, coordinated by the actions of an overarching national state, is key to understanding variations in institutional context faced by MNCs in different host environments. Many national institutional 'sub-systems', such as industrial relations machineries, vocational education and training, or the legal framework of employee or union rights, have a very direct influence on how MNCs operate in the terrain of HRM. Other sub-systems – e.g. financial markets or firm governance structures – may have more indirect (though still powerful) influence on how employees are managed.

There is relatively little work on comparative HRM *per se*. Yeung and Wong (1990) devised a matrix capturing two dimensions of variation: an emphasis on performance versus an emphasis on individual welfare; and a reliance on internal versus a reliance on external labour markets. However, as Schuler et al. (2002: 57) note, the utility of the model is limited by the failure to consider the role of the state, or to incorporate macro-level relations between employers, the state and organised labour. More sophisticated, comparative-historical approaches (e.g. Jacoby, 2004) appear to offer a fruitful way forward for generating an understanding of the critical variables. Jacoby's study of the evolution of the HRM function in US and Japanese firms highlights such factors as state intervention and regulation, the nature of corporate governance, the degree of labour unrest and the tightness of labour markets as drivers of the HR function's role.

The existence of institutional differences between countries would not matter if MNCs were merely collections of quasi-autonomous national subsidiaries orientated to their respective local markets. Increasingly, however, such a model of multinational organisation is the exception as firms try to exploit economies of scale or of the scope for international organisational learning by coordinating their activity across countries (Bartlett and Ghoshal, 1998; Dicken, 2003). Such coordination may involve, for example, the international standardisation of processes and products. This may have profound implications for HRM: in order to provide a standardised product to customers globally, firms may seek to standardise skills and training across countries. On this model, local pressures are constraints on the global coordination of MNCs' activities. However, as Edwards and Kuruvilla (2005) point out, local institutional variation is also an opportunity for coordinating activity in a 'segmented' way through an international division of labour or global 'value chain' (e.g. Wilkinson et al., 2001). In segmented coordination, corporate decision-makers exploit national institutional differences in order to configure global value chains in the most effective manner, e.g. by locating low skill operations in countries whose labour markets are poorly regulated and where labour costs are low.

Some writers have criticised the focus on national difference as a key explanatory variable. Colling and Clark (2002), for example, stress the importance of sector, and writers such as Katz and Darbishire (2000) argue that international competition leads to increasing convergence between firms within global sectors (with similar markets, technologies, skills requirements, and so forth), and growing divergence between firms in different sectors within the same country. Nonetheless, the importance of sector does not undermine a comparative institutional perspective. Sectoral governance structures are, for instance, often nationally specific (e.g. Hollingsworth et al. 1994), while MNCs of different nationality tend, for reasons

Porter (1990) would ascribe to competitive advantages rooted in national economies, to concentrate activities in particular sectors. Competition in the world economy takes place on the basis of skills, resources and competitive advantages that are located within specific institutional configurations in different host countries. The question, therefore, is how national-institutional factors *interact* with sector, and how such interaction influences IHRM.

THE EVOLUTION OF HRM IN MULTINATIONALS AS A FOCUS OF STUDY

As Briscoe and Schuler (2004: chapter 1) have claimed, IHRM is of very recent development as an area of practice and research; it was only from the 1990s, for example, that the 'Global Forum' of the US Society for Human Resource Management (SHRM) became 'more than a fairly small group of senior IHR managers from the large US MNEs' concerned primarily with expatriates and the establishment of local subsidiaries (p. 27). Practitioner concern grew in the 1980s and 1990s, in step with the growth in the number of 'transnational corporations', and in their 'transnationality index', a measure of the extent of their operations outside their domestic base (UNCTAD *World Investment Report*, various years).

Academically, the period was marked by the foundation of the *International Journal of Human Resource Management* in 1990. In their valuable review, Clark et al. (1999) identified 118 articles on IHRM from 29 journals (and 200 more on comparative HRM) published between 1977 and 1997. Growth subsequently accelerated: over the following nine years (1998–2006), the *International Journal of Human Resource Management* alone published more than 160 articles primarily concerned with IHRM (author's categorisation); in 2001 the journal moved from six to eight issues a year, and in 2005 to 12 issues a year.

THE SUBSTANTIVE FOCUS OF IHRM

The substantive range of IHRM research has been rather narrow. The single most significant focus of attention, driven by policy and practice concerns, has been the theme of expatriates. Nearly 30 per cent of IHRM articles in the *International Journal of Human Resource Management* are primarily concerned with expatriates (author's classification). Questions concerning the selection, training, adjustment, compensation, repatriation, and failure of expatriates continue to be the standard fare of this strand of research. Latterly, women expatriates have provided an additional focus (e.g. Adler, 2002). Sometimes, expatriates have been considered in the broader context of global staffing issues (e.g. Harvey et al., 2001). A much smaller, and theoretically more resonant, element concerns the functions performed by expatriates, going back to the classic work of Edström and Galbraith (1977); more recent work looks at the role of expatriates in knowledge diffusion (e.g. Delios and Björkman, 2000; Novicevic and Harvey, 2001) and in systems of corporate control (Harzing, 1999). Expatriates have also been the focus of IHRM teaching, dominating graduate IHRM textbooks (e.g. Dowling et al., 1999; Briscoe and Schuler, 2004); discussion of substantive HR issues such as planning, selection, remuneration, and training and development concentrates on expatriate employees. Even the text by Scullion and Linehan (2005), which claims to go beyond expatriates, ends up focusing strongly on the issue. The preoccupation with this group of employees is seen by Schuler et al. (2002) as reflecting the ethnocentric bias of North American scholars: it is consistent with efforts by US MNCs to manage foreign operations through parent-country nationals. In recent years, the balance of the literature has shifted somewhat to examine what might be termed functional alternatives to expatriates – international task forces, short-term assignments, virtual teams and the like (e.g. Harvey et al., 2005; Snell et al., 1998; Tregaskis et al., 2005).

While expatriate concerns have dominated the agenda, HR issues such as pay have received significant attention in their own right. In pay and performance management there has been concern with the development of 'culturally sensitive' global remuneration policies (e.g. Schuler and Rogovsky, 1998); Lindholm et al. (1999) found that performance appraisal systems of European MNCs' Chinese subsidiaries had to be significantly adapted to local culture. Liberman and Torbiörn (2000) looked at an MNC's supposedly standardised regional performance assessment programme in eight European countries and found wide variations in implementation across countries, 'from total adherence to complete absence of quantitative performance assessment of individuals among non-managerial staff' (p. 47). Much of this work sees national difference primarily in terms of cultural values (e.g. Newman and Nollen, 1996; Schuler and Rogovsky, 1998), but other work is more concerned with institutional differences and their impact on MNCs' pay and performance systems (e.g. Almond et al., 2006).

Other individual aspects of HRM have less often been the subject of attention, though there is work on management development (e.g. Evans et al., 1989; Butler et al., 2006); training (e.g. McPherson and Roche, 1997); recruitment (e.g. Gump, 2006); and workforce 'diversity' or equal opportunity policy (Cole and Deskins, 1988; Ferner et al., 2005; McGauran, 2001). In the 1960s and 1970s, there was considerable debate, largely in IR rather than in the personnel management literature, concerning MNCs' impact on national IR systems, particularly collective bargaining and workforce representation (e.g. Kujawa, 1979; Roberts, 1972). Considerable attention was paid to the implications of MNCs' strategic advantages for union power (e.g. ILO, 1976). However, there was little on these aspects of IR from a managerial perspective, as Clark et al. (1999) note.

The impact of MNCs on IR has continued to be a major strand of research, although not in mainstream HR literature. In recent years, the IR literature has engaged with supranational developments, such as the impact of the European Union on employment relations in MNCs – for example, the workings of European works councils (e.g. Marginson and Hall, 2004), and the emergence of cross-national bargaining (e.g. Sisson, 2006).[2] A further strand relates to employee voice, notably the balance between direct forms of management–employee communication and indirect forms through employee representatives and unions (e.g. Tüselmann et al., 2003; Wood and Fenton-O'Creevy, 2005). IR scholars have also continued to examine how work organisation in MNCs varies between different host institutional settings (e.g. Edwards et al., 1999; Kristensen and Zeitlin, 2005; Meardi and Tóth, 2006), again a topic largely ignored in HRM (cf. Clark et al., 1999). Of particular interest has been the international dissemination of lean production and other work organisation techniques by Japanese MNCs (e.g. Dedoussis, 1995; Delbridge, 1998; Doeringer et al., 2003; Elger and Smith, 2005). Finally, the influence of labour costs, national IR systems and employment regulation on locational decision-making by MNCs is an important theme (e.g. Bognanno et al., 2005; Traxler and Woitech, 2000); it also crops up occasionally in the mainstream HRM literature (e.g. Cooke, 2001). An important strand of argument concerns 'regime-shopping' (Streeck, 1997): the extent to which MNCs are able to exploit low labour standards in host locations to force concessions from more protected systems, a process characterised as the 'race to the bottom'.

THEMATIC AND CONCEPTUAL CONCERNS

Strategic contingencies and IHRM strategies

Work on IHRM has tended to exhibit a series of unifying thematic and conceptual concerns. One of the most pervasive, frequently drawing on the work of Bartlett and Ghoshal (1998 (1989)), explores the tension between the opposing needs for global coordination of activities within the MNC and for local responsiveness to the particularities of host 'cultures', markets and institutions (e.g. Bloom et al., 2003; De Cieri and Dowling, 1999; Kostova, 1999; Rosenzweig and Nohria, 1994; Schuler et al., 1993). This is sometimes expressed as the balance between 'integration' through inter-unit linkages, and 'differentiation' to allow operating units to react to local environments (Schuler et al., 1993). HR systems – staff selection, 'acculturation', training, international career management, etc. – are seen as cross-national integration mechanisms, particularly in less traditional MNCs that rely more on integrated networks than traditional, hierarchical command-and-control structures.

Relatedly, many scholars have modelled the contingencies facing IHRM decision-makers, often using frameworks based on the 'integration'–'differentiation' dichotomy (e.g. Schuler et al., 1993; Tayeb, 2005). Writers have typically drawn on Lawrence and Lorsch's (1967) notions of strategic contingency. Factors as diverse as firm size, mode of entry, the nature of markets, technology, employee characteristics and stage of internationalisation have been seen as impacting on strategic IHRM decision-making (cf. Budhwar and Debrah, 2003). Such work emphasises the need for 'fit' between IHRM strategy and the internal and external environments of the MNC.

An example of a prescriptive model based on a strategic contingency approach is that of Bird and Beechler (1995), in their study of Japanese subsidiaries in the USA. They classify the external environment according to the degree to which competition is local or global. Competitive strategies can be based on cost leadership or product differentiation. They argue, for example, that cost leaders with high international integration should adopt a 'utiliser' HRM strategy, in which HR resources are deployed throughout the firm as efficiently as possible, with a lean workforce. However, this strategy is less effective where the firm has to adapt to local

markets. Among the most widely cited models is that of Dowling and de Cieri (1999; see also Schuler et al., 1993). They outline a series of 'exogenous' factors, such as industry characteristics and national culture, and of 'endogenous' factors, such as organisational life cycle, structure, strategy and entry mode. These shape the strategic role of IHRM in determining which HR functions should be devolved and which centralised, the level of resources devoted to IHRM, and the overall HRM approach.

While such models usefully draw attention to the range of factors impinging on IHRM, they may be criticised for a rather abstract and static approach, the proliferation of contextual variables, and the concern with the management of senior and international managers rather than the workforce as a whole. They also tend to be prescriptive in nature, and the evidential basis for their prescriptions is not always clear.

The 'travel of ideas'

The most widely examined of the factors generating 'differentiation' and local responsiveness is national difference. A fundamental question, widely addressed in the literature, is the nature of cross-national transfer of HR policies and practices within MNCs, or to use Czarniawska and Joerges'(1996) resonant phrase, 'the travel of ideas'. Under what conditions and with what rationale does transfer take place? What kinds of HR tend to be transferred (and which do not)? What are the mechanisms through which HR practices are disseminated from parent to foreign affiliates (or vice versa)? What happens to such practices on implementation in different national-institutional contexts?

The conditions under which practices are transferred can be said to rest on two fundamental factors: the value that corporate policy-makers perceive in transfer; and the feasibility of transfer – or to put it simply, motive and opportunity. Taylor et al. (1996) draw on the 'resource-based view of the firm' to delineate 'motive' in terms of the desire to attain competitive advantage through the deployment of resources that are rare, valuable and difficult to imitate. They establish a typology of IHRM strategies according to whether firms have an 'exportive', 'adaptive' or 'integrative' HR orientation. The first seeks to export parent-country practices to foreign affiliates, the second to let local operations adapt to their environment, and the third to take the 'best' approaches and use them to create integrated world-wide systems. In exportive and integrative strategies, senior policy-makers see the cross-national dissemination of HR practices as a source of international competitive advantage. Other things being equal, one may predict, as Edwards and Rees (2006: chapter 5) argue, that MNCs whose global coordination is based on 'standardisation' of operations are likely to see a competitive advantage in diffusion. Conversely, in MNCs with an internationally segmented division of labour (e.g. Dedoussis, 1995), there may be little perceived advantage in disseminating standard global HR practices to operations whose function, skills and resources are quite different from those of other parts of the MNC.

In terms of 'opportunity', Taylor et al. (1996) refer to the 'context-generalisability' of HR practices, that is to say, the degree to which they are capable of operating effectively outside their original context. Such conditions may vary according to the role of the subsidiary within the wider MNC, and to the employee group involved – the parent's desire to exert cross-national control over an employee group will, for example, depend on the extent of company-specific specialist skills and knowledge within the group. Factors such as mode of entry may also affect context-generalisability: 'greenfield' sites may favour transfer because there is no entrenched 'heritage' of practices capable of resisting the importation of novel practices; the reverse is true of acquired 'brownfield' operations (e.g.Guest and Hoque, 1996).

There is extensive literature examining the specific factors that underlie these two conditions (e.g. Doeringer et al., 2003;

Edwards and Ferner, 2003; Edwards and Rees, 2006: chapter 5; Kostova, 1999). National-institutional factors play an important role. MNCs are likely to draw competitive advantage, not merely from company-specific factors, but from the specific institutions of their parent-country business system (cf. Hall and Soskice, 2001; Porter, 1990). They are likely to seek to be innovators abroad in such areas. In the field of HR, US MNCs have traditionally sought to innovate in such areas as payment systems (performance-related pay, performance appraisal, equity-based pay, productivity bargaining, etc.) (e.g. Bloom et al., 2003; Buckley and Enderwick, 1985).

A central element in the international competitive advantage – and context-generalisability – of practices has been the status of the originating business system in the 'hierarchy' of economies within the global economic system. The strength of dominant economies, such as the USA, creates a belief in the efficacy of its HR practices and a dynamic of emulation that Smith and Meiksins (1995) refer to as 'dominance effects', facilitating transfer. Thus there is considerable evidence that US MNCs propagate standardised international HR practices and exert control over subsidiary HR to a greater extent than do MNCs of other nationalities (e.g. Edwards et al., 2007).

However, context-generalisability depends on the extent to which national innovations – for example, in skills systems – can be detached from their domestic context. If practices rely on dense inter-relationships between a range of stakeholders and specific institutions, their ability to function outside these settings is questionable. Such arguments have been made about the German 'dual system' of vocational education (e.g. Dickmann, 2003) and about the Japanese system of 'lifetime employment' (Gill and Wong, 1998). Transferability likewise depends on the host's receptivity, which is influenced by the degree of regulation of HR and employment issues, the existence of appropriate institutional supports for transferred practices, and so on. There have been attempts to assess the 'distance' between different national settings as a prime explanatory factor in the transfer of HR practices. Writers have used the notion of 'cultural distance' (e.g. Kim and Gray, 2005) to explain the presence or absence of transfer, normally based on differences in aggregate scores on Hofstede's value dimensions (Kogut and Singh, 1988). More recently, writers have tried to incorporate a wider range of national differences through the concept of 'institutional distance' (e.g. Kostova, 1999; Xu and Shenkar, 2002). Kostova has operationalised the 'country institutional profile' to capture elements of regulatory, cognitive, and normative institutions within the country of origin and the host country respectively. This has been applied in relation to the use of expatriates (e.g. Gaur et al., 2007), and to expatriate adjustment (e.g. Ramsey, 2005). One problem with such measures is that the implications of distance are ambiguous, as Kim and Gray (2005) point out: some speculate that greater distance reduces transfer of HR practice, while others argue that parent companies' desire to control for uncertainty in culturally or institutionally distant locations leads to greater transfer in such cases.

There is an abundance of literature detailing the obstacles to transfer of HR practices between countries. Tung and Worm (2001), for instance, point to the problems of centralised control of foreign subsidiaries in China: such control impedes attempts to link into the personalised networks ('guanxi') that typify Chinese business relations. Similarly, Lindholm et al. (1999) found that performance appraisal systems transferred to Chinese subsidiaries could not function as they did in the global company: goals had to be 'achievable' because of the risk of loss of face; there was little joint agreeing of objectives, reflecting the strength of hierarchical relations; and it was difficult to make direct criticism of appraisees.

HR practices have been assessed in relation to their susceptibility to local institutional (or cultural) influences. For example, an international consortium of scholars (Geringer et al., 2002) investigated whether there were distinctive categories of 'context free' HR practice, that is, 'practices ... [that] may generally be applicable and effective across different nations, regardless of the societal and organizational contextual conditions' (p. 6). In general, for a given host location, Rosenzweig and Nohria (1994) suggest that practices for non-managerial staff are more likely to be subject to local regulatory and other constraints. Other areas of HR, such as management development and payment systems, are seen as less constrained and hence more likely to be subject to the influence of the MNC's global policy frameworks. Similarly, Morton and Siebert (2001) found that 'local managers possess quite wide freedom concerning recruitment/retention outcomes' in matched UK and continental European plants of MNCs (p. 524). Rosenzweig and Nohria's argument may have been shaped by the fact that the USA was the host location, and its generalisability to other contexts may be questionable. Nevertheless there does seem to be significant support for the notion that some HR/ER practices are more susceptible than others to cross-national transfer. Large-scale survey-based research on MNCs in the UK (Edwards et al., 2007) suggests that higher organisational levels are less likely to influence the content of subsidiary policy on employment representation than on pay and performance or management development; issues of employee involvement are in an intermediate position.

While most studies focus on HR transfers by the parent to foreign subsidiaries, the rise in interest in MNCs as sites of cross-national organisational learning (e.g. Bartlett and Ghoshal, 1998), has generated investigation of the direction of transfer. In MNCs that are increasingly integrated networks rather than top-down hierarchies, it is argued that flows of knowledge – including HR practices – may proceed in any direction, including from subsidiary to headquarters. Edwards (1998; Edwards et al., 2005) has argued that such 'reverse diffusion' depends on a variety of conditions internal and external to the firm, such as the degree of international integration of the MNC and the power relations between its constituent parts.

An innovative approach to transfer is taken by Schmitt and Sadowski (2003), who examine transfer by US and UK MNCs to their subsidiaries in Germany in terms of a model of 'fiscal federalism' borrowed from public policy debates. Transfer takes place where net benefits of transferring policy to the subsidiary outweigh net costs of transfer. The costs of centrally diffusing policy include costs of monitoring, overcoming resistance in the subsidiary, and infringing local custom and practice, if not legal regulation. The costs of decentralisation include the loss of economies of scale, equity issues arising from treating similar groups of employees differently in different countries, and a loss of control and influence over the subsidiary. Schmitt and Sadowski (2003) suggest that in the areas of collective bargaining and employee representation, the German system imposes costs of centralization for MNCs that outweigh costs of decentralization; MNCs therefore adapt to local practice.

The approach provides a flexible and powerful overall model that can accommodate factors such as institutional differences as well as power relations within the MNC (see below). However, it is limited in that it assumes that transfer is an 'either-or' process. In fact, there is considerable research showing that HR practices may be transferred in a modified form, or undergo 'translation' to the new context (cf. Czarniawska and Joerges, 1996). As mentioned above, Lindholm et al. (1999) found evidence that nominally standardised performance appraisal systems functioned distinctively in Chinese subsidiaries. Similarly, examining innovative working practices in the car industry, Scarbrough and Terry (1998) reported an 'adaptation' model of transfer in which the practice is adapted creatively to local circumstances through the interactions of local unions and management. More radically, Boyer et al. (1998) argue, on the basis of a study of work organisation in the automotive industry, that transfer inevitably involves 'creative' hybridisation, whereby an original practice undergoes dynamic modification in order

to work within a new institutional setting. Kostova's work has thrown useful light on such modification processes. Working from a 'new institutionalist' perspective she distinguishes the implementation of a transferred practice from its 'internalisation'. The latter refers to the full assimilation of the practice to the recipient employees' cognitive and normative frames of reference (see also Saka's (2002) study of the internalisation of new working practices in Japanese subsidiaries in the UK).

Underpinning concepts of HR 'hybridisation' and similar notions are often implicit perspectives on power. In reaction to the models of the corporation implicit in much of the international business literature, writers have been concerned to characterise the MNC as the site of intense 'micropolitics' (e.g. Ferner and Edwards, 1995; Geppert and Williams, 2006; Kristensen and Zeitlin, 2005). A key argument here is that subsidiary actors are often able to derive power resources from their knowledge of and embeddedness within the local institutional culture. Actors may influence whether 'imported' policies are adopted wholesale, paid lip service to, adapted, hybridised, or even resisted and rejected by the subsidiary. It should be noted that local actors can use their power resources to facilitate policy adoption rather than to block it. Local knowledge allows MNCs to explore the 'gaps' in the institutional context in order to evade constraints; for example, MNCs operating in the highly regulated German IR context have been observed to shift from one bargaining unit to another in order to win more pay flexibility (e.g. Almond et al., 2006). As Bloom et al. (2003: 1363) observe in relation to international compensation policies, 'Managers in our focal organizations acted as pragmatic experimentalists: they conformed when necessary [to local constraints], resisted when feasible and crafted strategic responses whenever possible'. The transfer of HR policies is seen, in short, as an essentially *political* process.

The implications of the foregoing arguments for practice within MNCs are profound: implementation involves far more than the propagation of a standard international policy. One question concerns the mechanisms for ensuring the transfer and implementation of policy. A commonly observed mechanism is the supplementation of formal policy with 'person-based' transfer, relying on the presence of expatriate managers to disseminate practice and to oversee and monitor compliance. Another mechanism involves the cooption of subsidiary managers into the policy-formulation process, so that they feel they have a stake in the ensuing policy (e.g. Tregaskis et al., 2005). Finally, MNC headquarters generally have sources of power at their disposal with which to invite or compel compliance. International benchmarking and 'coercive comparisons', with their explicit or implicit threat of sanctions, have been widely used to propagate standard working practices in the face of local resistance (e.g. Coller, 1996; Mueller and Purcell, 1992). Moreover, personal rewards and promotion opportunities of senior local managers are in the hands of higher-level decision-makers.

THE ROLE OF THE HR FUNCTION IN MULTINATIONALS

The organisational challenges of managing cross-national workforces in evolving circumstances and across varied national contexts are central to both practitioner and academic concerns. As noted above, the link between IHRM and business strategy has been a preoccupation of prescriptive model-building in the field (e.g. Adler and Ghadar, 1990; Perlmutter, 1969). Scullion and Starkey's study (2000) of 30 UK MNCs identified an emerging corporate HR agenda focusing on senior management development, succession planning, and developing a cadre of international managers. Others have pointed to a role in setting strategic performance and reward frameworks (e.g. Evans and Lorange, 1989). More recently, writers have been concerned about the role of the HR function in the development of unique firm resources as a source of competitive

advantage (e.g. Taylor et al. 1996). This has led to exploration of HR's contribution to knowledge networking (Tregaskis et al., 2005) and the building of social capital (Taylor, 2006).

But, curiously perhaps, the structural form of the IHRM function has been somewhat neglected by researchers (Scullion and Starkey, 2000). Relatively little work has been conducted on the structural evolution of the HRM function in response to such changes in MNC structure as: the development of discrete international businesses with considerable business autonomy within the global MNC; the evolution of supranational regional structures, partly reflecting the consolidation of regional markets such as the EU and NAFTA; and the importance of matrix forms, usually combining business-division and geographical structures (Marginson et al., 1995).

Evidence suggests that the mode of organising the HR function varies considerably between MNCs of different national origin (Edwards et al., 2007; Ferner and Varul, 2000; Wächter et al., 2006). A large-scale representative survey of MNCs in the UK (Edwards et al., 2007) found that the degree of centralisation of HR policy-making, the extent of higher-level scrutiny of subsidiary HR metrics, and the use of 'technologies' of IHRM such as global electronic information management systems for HR (HRIS), all varied. For example, though subsidiaries generally have a relatively high degree of discretion over the formulation of their HR policies, subsidiaries of American MNCs have systematically less discretion on a range of HR issues than firms of other nationalities. They are far more likely than others to have international HRIS, suggesting that the availability of the 'technology' may be a factor in centralised control.

There appear to be a number of trends in how the function is evolving. First, the locus of HR capability above subsidiary level is changing with the increasing use of regional- and business-based international organisational structures. Second, more fluid, informal mechanisms of HR coordination appear to be growing in importance. This can be related to the rise in the 'integrated network' model of MNCs in which expertise is disseminated throughout the firm's operations rather than being monopolised by headquarters. As a result, the identification and diffusion of knowledge and practice in the HR field has become of increasing importance for competitive advantage (e.g. Taylor, 2006). Third, new technologies have enabled a variety of developments that are used to drive cost efficiencies and enhance central oversight of HR across global operations (Sparrow et al., 2004: chapter 4). These include HRIS based on standard software programmes allowing MNCs to monitor and deploy personnel for competitive advantage (Hannon et al., 1996). A related development is increasing use of corporate intranets to deliver global HR services to internal 'customers' (e.g. Ruta, 2005).

Technology has also driven the 'taylorisation' of HRM operations at regional or global level by allowing the separation of routine, repetitive and procedural work from the more strategic work of HR executives. Routine work may be delegated to HR 'shared service centres', often working remotely through call centre operations serving a range of subsidiary operations in different countries. A significant proportion of MNCs – up to half of large MNCs – appear to make use of such international HR service centres (Edwards et al., 2007). An example is IBM's location of its international shared services centre, including HR activity, in Budapest in the early 2000s. Moreover, such 'off-shoring' of HR activities has sometimes been accompanied by outsourcing as specialist 'BPO' (business process outsourcing) firms take over responsibility for off-shored HR and other business functions (e.g. Hoffmann, 2005). This evolution reflects the challenge involved in maintaining specialist shared service centre skills, and the high technological infrastructure costs incurred (Kidman, 2005). However, such emerging trends have not yet been subject to sustained academic analysis.

METHODOLOGICAL APPROACHES TO THE STUDY OF IHRM

Ironically, in view of the dominance of the 'cultural values' paradigm from the 1980s, much work on IHRM is 'US-centric' (see Brewster and Harris, 1999), carried out 'from an American perspective, performed by American (or American-trained) researchers, and mostly done in the top industrialized or developed countries' (Briscoe and Schuler, 2004: 131). Clark et al. (1999: 526) categorise around three-quarters of the IHRM research outputs they examined as being 'ethnocentric' in nature, that is to say, designed by researchers in one culture and subsequently replicated in another culture. The remaining studies used more locally rooted frameworks of interpretation and explanation; or were comparative in the sense of trying to identify both universalist and culturally specific elements. The significance of this lies in doubts as to whether researchers have been careful enough to identify 'functional equivalence' in translating concepts developed within one national business context to other countries (p. 521).

Surveys and case studies have been the predominant methods in IHRM research. Clark et al. (1999: 526–7) found that 41 per cent of IHRM articles identified used surveys, and 27 per cent case studies. Surveys have been used in a wide range of geographical settings. However, drawing up a representative sample of MNCs on the basis of an accurate population listing is beset with difficulties of definition and data accuracy (e.g. Edwards, T. et al., 2007; Rugman, 2005).

Less commonly, existing data from published, notably governmental, sources have been used; an example is the work of Bognanno et al. (2005) examining the influence of wages and IR environments on the investment decisions of US MNCs, using surveys of US direct investment abroad conducted by the US Bureau of Economic Analysis. Survey work has also drawn on existing academic datasets, as in studies based on company-level and workplace employment relations surveys in the UK (e.g. Marginsons et al., 1995), Ireland (e.g. Geary and Roche, 2001), and Australia (Walsh, 2001). Other work (e.g. Fenton-O'Creevy et al., 2008) draws on the Cranet cross-national survey of HRM in a range of companies. Such work has tended to be limited by the fact that the original surveys were not designed as studies of MNCs.

Particularly problematic are attempts to compare populations of MNCs operating in different hosts. Issues of functional equivalence loom large, compounding difficulties of studying single-country MNC populations, and data collection methods appropriate for research in one national context may not work in another. Postal surveys are well accepted as a mode of data collection in the USA or Canada, but poorly accepted in countries such as Mexico where personal contacts are more significant (Geringer et al., 2002). The study by Geringer et al., reported in a special issue of *Human Resource Management*, purports to be about the identification of 'best' international HRM practices, but is in fact a cross-national comparative analysis of HR practices using widely differing data collection methods and, crucially, units of analysis in the different countries surveyed. For example, the sample of managerial respondents in Japan came from a mere three organisations. National surveys varied in the inclusion or exclusion of public sector organisations, sectoral coverage, and firm size. It is hard to see what kind of comparative sense may be made of such heterogeneous datasets, particularly in research on comparative behaviour of populations of MNCs in different countries. For such reasons, there appear to be few comparative surveys of populations of MNCs in different countries.[3]

Partly as a result of the bias towards surveys, most work is cross-sectional: only 6 per cent of the works studied by Clark et al. (1999) used longitudinal methods. Case studies have varied widely in ambition and focus. While many restrict themselves to one host environment, others compare MNCs across two or more hosts (e.g. Almond et al., 2005; Geppert et al., 2003; Meardi and Tóth, 2006; Quintanilla, 2002). In some instances, richly

detailed case studies of single enterprises conducted over a period of years have captured the evolution of IHRM. Two prominent examples, whose concerns range far wider than HRM, are Bélanger et al.'s (1999) study of ABB across several countries in Asia, Europe and North America; and Kristensen and Zeitlin's (2005) dissection of the UK multinational, APV, in Britain, Denmark and the USA. What is notable about these studies, and rather exceptional in the literature, is that they explore multiple organisational levels, rather than restricting themselves either to a subsidiary or an HQ perspective.

Geographical concentration of studies

Observers have commented on the concentration of studies on relatively few countries. Clark et al. (1999: 526) found that 'the UK, US, Japan, France and Germany were the most frequently studied countries, accounting for 48 per cent of all cases'. Beyond these, a relatively small group of countries featured strongly, including Australia, Singapore and Malaysia in Asia, Sweden, the Netherlands and Spain in Europe, and Canada and Mexico in North America. It was not uncommon for studies to lump together companies from a disparate range of European countries into one 'European' category (e.g. Kopp, 1994).

More recent work has shown signs of a shift in geographical emphasis: China's economic development has stimulated a rapidly increasing volume of research on HRM in the subsidiaries of foreign firms and in joint ventures (e.g. Björkman and Lu, 2001; Gamble, 2003; Goodall and Warner, 1997; Tung and Worm, 2001); China also figures prominently in recent IHRM texts and pedagogic case studies (e.g. Björkman and Galunic, 2004; Zhang et al., 2006). The collapse of the Soviet bloc has also provided impetus to studies of MNCs' subsidiaries in eastern Europe and (to a lesser extent) in Russia. Themes have included firm relocation and regime-shopping, particularly by German MNCs, and the transferability of HR practices to the institutional contexts of these emerging states (e.g. Bluhm, 2001; Kahancová and van der Meer, 2006; Meardi and Tóth, 2006). Major gaps remain, however. Despite India's emerging status, relatively little research has been conducted on MNCs operating there.

Given the concentration of MNCs in the developed world, it is unsurprising that the focus is still on a narrow range of *parent* countries: the USA, Germany, Japan, and the UK. MNCs based in other European countries, including France, Finland, Sweden and the Netherlands, have been the subject of occasional study, as have firms from emerging countries such as China (e.g. Shen, 2006).

CONCLUSIONS: FUTURE DIRECTIONS IN INTERNATIONAL HUMAN RESOURCE MANAGEMENT

Developments in the field of IHRM over the past two to three decades may be summarised as follows. First, for much of the period, the conceptual emphasis has been on understanding 'cultural' differences between the host and parent locations of the MNC, and the barriers and opportunities these present for the cross-national transfer of HR policies. Cultural difference has been conceived in terms of cultural values, although more recently a more sophisticated comparative institutionalist perspective has enriched the field.

Second, there has been a preoccupation with modelling the external environmental and internal organisational determinants of IHRM strategy and practice, and with the relationship between IHRM and broader business strategy as the latter has evolved in response to new technologies and the intensification of international competition.

Third, the substantive focus has been rather narrow. Expatriates and their international assignments have absorbed much of the energy of researchers. The staple issues of HR have been studied, notably pay and performance management, and – often from an 'industrial relations' analytical perspective – employee involvement, workforce representation, and work organisation. On the whole, the emphasis has been on managerial rather than 'rank-and-file' employees. The changing structure and role of the IHRM function has received rather less attention than might have been expected.

Fourth, methodology has used both case study and survey methods extensively, but the latter have predominated, as has a cross-sectional approach. Only rarely have studies given equal weight to both the subsidiary level and to corporate headquarters within a firm; rarer still have studies investigated intermediate structures such as global business divisions, geographical regions, or global business functions from an HR perspective (cf. Clark et al., 1999: 531). Geographically, the range of studies has been limited, with disproportionate concentration on a small group of countries, both as parents and as hosts.

This brief summary of the main features of work in the area suggests a number of avenues for future research. *Conceptually*, researchers need to develop increasingly sophisticated understandings of the variables that differentiate one host country from another in terms of HR practice and constraints. Such factors are likely to vary with the HR issue and with the employee group being considered. Much recent work in comparative institutional theory (e.g. Djelic and Quack, 2003) is concerned with how MNCs as institutional actors shape their institutional environment, rather than being passively shaped by it. This is a particularly important concern for researchers, and practitioners, in countries where MNCs dominate the economy; a vigorous debate in Ireland, for example, has examined the extent to which MNCs have influenced the Irish employment relations agenda rather than being constrained to adapt to it (Geary and Roche, 2001; Gunnigle et al., 2006). Similarly, work has looked at the impact of MNCs on the German institutional framework (e.g. Schmitt, 2003; Williams and Geppert, 2006).

Partly as a result of the actions of MNCs, national-institutional environments for HR policy and practice are dynamic and evolving. Moreover, the national level of regulation is not the only one that impacts on MNCs. To what extent is the cross-border management of HR shaped by engagement with institutions and institutional actors below national level – e.g. at the level of the sub-national region or locality in which an MNC's operations are located, in relation to such issues as skills supply or employee representation? How far, too, is IHRM shaped by MNCs' engagement with institutions at supra-national, e.g. EU, level?

Related to the conceptualisation of MNCs as actors within institutions is the question of power. How may issues of organisational power be taken into account in the analysis of IHRM? Power and a 'political' perspective – both at macro- and micro-levels – are often curiously absent from discussion of corporations that are among the most powerful actors in the global economy. Despite a growth of interest in recent years, there is relatively little on the way in which the corporation deploys power resources to shape its HR institutional environment at the macro level – for example, by influencing the framework of labour regulation or the terms on which it is applied. Nor is much known about how the cross-national transfer of HR practices is constrained by the power and interests of a range of actors at different levels within the MNC. Bringing power and politics into the analysis may also provide an opportunity to reintegrate cultural 'values' – not as some idealist, disembodied cultural emanation, but as part of the contested institutional terrain that MNCs inhabit.

The *substance* of IHRM research could be expanded in a number of ways. First and foremost, the focus on managerial staff could be widened to include non-managerial employees. As Marginson et al. (1995: 702) report from their survey, it is striking to observe the extent to which 'MNCs are actively engaged in the management of non-managerial employees at international level'. MNCs routinely collect information internationally on the pay, productivity, training, ethnic diversity, and work attitudes of these employees (Edwards et al., 2007). One aspect of the issue is how employees respond to IHRM initiatives. With few exceptions, this is a neglected topic in the literature, despite its increasing importance in relation to the 'travel of ideas', and to the 'internalisation' of internationally diffused practices (Kostova, 1999; Saka, 2003). How, in short, are employees affected by the policies to which they are subject, and how do they perceive them?

A second substantive area of investigation is, as mentioned above, the evolving nature of the IHRM function itself. This seems potentially fruitful, both for its practical ramifications and for the light it can shed on the relationship between structure and strategy of the function. The ongoing search for a strategic role is intimately bound up with the 'internationalisation' of the pursuit of organisational efficiencies within the function, notably through the increasing, and internationally structured, separation of routine from 'higher-level' HR processes in MNCs.

Third, while IHRM has taken on board the importance of international joint ventures as an organisational form, and has considered issues of off-shoring and outsourcing, it has been less prompt to reflect in such work the theoretical developments of the global value chain literature (cf. Clark et al., 1999: 531) that, implicitly, questions the relevance of organisational boundaries for understanding the cross-national structuring of human resources. Some work already exists in this area and shows the potential for development. For example, Lane and Probert (2006) have investigated the national differentiation of labour management and the structuring of skills within global supply chains in the clothing industry (see also Bair and Ramsay, 2003; Frenkel, 2001). With the continuing evolution of forms of cross-national production networks, such research seems likely to become of increasing importance.

Finally, *methodologically*, there are a number of challenges. First, good, detailed longitudinal studies are rare. In a field evolving so rapidly and dynamically as

IHRM, such studies of key cases are needed to map the evolution, and to trace the linkages between contextual driving forces and IHRM processes and practices. Case studies remain a key method of accessing the subtle and complex processes underlying the management of IHRM. There are particular problems in researching categories of cases of considerable practical and theoretical interest – for example, 'low road' firms whose IHRM is premised on low-skill and low-cost strategies. Second, surveys have been the dominant method in the field, but there are considerable difficulties in identifying robust populations from which to draw reliable representative samples. Moreover, surveys have tended not to generate large comparative datasets, allowing the systematic analysis of the IHRM practices of MNCs in different sorts of host environments. Third, the variety of methods deployed in the field of IHRM has been relatively restricted. A range of innovative methods might prove fruitful. For example, formal network analysis (e.g. Gould, 2003) might be used to track career moves of international managers, power and influence flows within the international HR function, or cross-national learning networks. Such methods could well reach aspects of IHRM unobservable through more conventional means. Finally, the range of geographies covered by research has been limited, and could usefully be expanded. More sophisticated understanding of the institutional dynamics of a wider range of MNC hosts is required, both among developed and developing countries. The latter are also increasingly the source of emerging MNCs that merit study in their own right.

NOTES

1 It should be noted that the broader study of IHRM goes beyond the multinational companies with which this chapter is primarily concerned: it includes, for example, bodies such as the United Nations, or international charities.

2 The establishment of the *European Journal of Industrial Relations* in 1995 provided another outlet for such work.

3 An exception, currently in progress, is work by a consortium of researchers in the UK, Canada, Ireland, Spain, Mexico and Australia using a common core instrument to research HR in populations of MNCs in the respective countries (Edwards et al., 2007; Murray et al., 2006).

REFERENCES

Adler, N.J. (2002) *International Dimensions of Organizational Behavior*, 4th edition. Cincinnati, Ohio: South-Western Publishing.

Adler, N.J. and Ghadar, F. (1990) 'Strategic human resource management: A global perspective', in Pieper, R. (ed.), *Human Resource Management: An International Comparison*. Berlin: De Gruyter, pp. 235–60.

Adsit, D., London, M., Crom, S. and Jones, D. (1997) 'Cross-cultural differences in upward ratings in a multinational company', *International Journal of Human Resource Management*, 8, 4, 385–401.

Almond, P., Edwards, T., Colling, T., Ferner, A., Gunnigle, P., Muller-Camen, M., Quintanilla, J. and Wächter, H. (2005) 'Unraveling home and host country effects: An investigation of the HR policies of an American multinational in four European countries', *Industrial Relations*, 44 (2): 276–306.

Almond, P., Muller-Camen, M., Collings, D. and Quintanilla, J. (2006) 'Pay and performance', in Almond, P. and Ferner, A. (eds), *American Multinationals in Europe: Managing Employment Relations Across National Borders*. Oxford: Oxford University Press, pp. 119–45.

Bair, J. and Ramsay, H. (2003) 'MNCs and global commodity chains: implications for labour strategies', in Cooke, W.N. (ed.), *Multinational companies and global human resource strategies*. Westport, CT: Quorum Books, 43–64.

Bartlett, C. and Ghoshal, S. (1998) *Managing Across Borders*, 2nd edition. London: Hutchinson.

Bélanger, J., Berggren, C., Björkman, T. and Köhler, C. (1999) *Being Local Worldwide: ABB and the Challenge of Global Management*. Ithaca: ILR Press.

Bird, A. and Beechler, S. (1995) 'Links between business strategy and human resource management strategy in U.S.-based Japanese subsidiaries: An empirical investigation', *Journal of International Business Studies*, 26 (1): 23–46.

Bjorkman, I. and Lu, Y. (2001) 'Institutionalisation and bargaining power explanations of human resource management practices in Chinese-Western Joint ventures', *Organization Studies*, 22 (3): 491–512.

Björkman, I. and Galunic, C. (2004) 'Integrative case study: Lincoln electric in China', in Briscoe, D.R. and Schuler, R. (eds), *International Human Resource Management*, Second Edition. London/New York: Routledge, pp. 420–35.

Bloom, M., Milkovich, G.T. and Mitra, A. (2003) 'International compensation: Learning from how managers respond to variations in local host contexts', *International Journal of Human Resource Management*, 14 (8): 1350–67.

Bluhm, K. (2001) 'Exporting or Abandoning the "German Model"?: Labour Policies of German Manufacturing Firms in Central Europe", *European Journal of Industrial Relations*, 7, 2, 157–173.

Bognanno, M.F., Keane, M.P. and Yang, D. (2005) 'The influence of wages and industrial relations environments on the production location decisions of US multinational corporations', *Industrial and Labor Relations Review*, 58 (2): 171–200.

Boyer, R., Charron, E., Jürgens, U. and Tolliday, S. (1998) *Between Imitation and Innovation. The transfer and hybridization of productive models in the international automobile industry*. Oxford: Oxford University Press.

Brewster, C. and Harris, H. (1999) *International HRM: Contemporary Issues in Europe*. London: Routledge.

Brewster, C., W. Mayrhofer, et al., Eds. (2004). *European Human Resource Management - evidence of convergence?* London, Butterworth-Heinemann.

Buckley, P. and Enderwick, P. (1985) *The Industrial Relations Practices of Foreign-Owned Firms in Britain*. London: Macmillan.

Briscoe, D.R. and Schuler, R. (2004) *International Human Resource Management*, Second Edition. London/New York: Routledge.

Budhwar, P. and Debrah, Y. (2001) 'Rethinking comparative and cross–national human resource management research', *International Journal of Human Resource Management*, 12 (3): 497–515.

Butler, P., Collinson, D., Peters, R. and Quintanilla, J. (2006) 'The management of managerial Careers', in Almond, P. and Ferner, A. (eds), *American Multinationals in Europe*. Oxford: Oxford University Press, pp. 172–94.

Campbell, J.L. (2004) *Institutional Change and Globalization*. Princeton, N.J.: Princeton University Press.

Clark, T., Gospel, H. and Montgomery, J. (1999) 'Running on the spot? A review of twenty years of research on the management of human resources in comparative and international perspective', *International Journal of Human Resource Management*, 10 (3): 520–44.

Cole, R.E. and Deskins, D.R. (1988) 'Racial factors in site location and employment patterns of Japanese auto firms in America', *California Management Review*, 31 (1): 9–21.

Coller, X. (1996) 'Managing flexibility in the food industry: A cross-national comparative case study in European multinational companies', *European Journal of industrial Relations*, 2 (2): 153–72.

Colling, T. and Clark, I. (2002) 'Looking for "Americanness": home-country, sector and firm effects on employment systems in an engineering services company', *European Journal of Industrial Relations*, 8 (3): 301–24.

Cooke, W.N. (2001) 'The effects of labour costs and workplace constraints on foreign direct investment among highly industrialized countries', *International Journal of Human Resource Management*, 12 (5): 697–716.

Crouch, C. (2005) *Capitalist Diversity and Change: Recombinant Governance and Institutional Entrepreneurs*. Oxford: Oxford University Press.

Czarniawska, B. and Joerges, B. (1996) 'Travel of ideas', in Czarniawska, B. and Sevon, G. (eds), *Translating Organizational Change*. Berlin: De Gruyter, pp. 13–48.

De Cieri, H. and Dowling, P.J. (1999) 'Strategic human resource management in multinational enterprises: Theoretical and empirical developments', in Wright, P.M., Dyer, L.D., Boudreau, J.W. and Milkovich, G.T. (eds), *Research in Personnel and Human Resources Management: Strategic Human Resources Management in the Twenty-first Century*. Stamford Connecticut: JAI Press, pp. 305–27.

Dedoussis, V. (1995) 'Simply a question of cultural barriers? The search for new perspectives in the transfer of Japanese management practices', *Journal of Management Studies*, 32 (6): 731–45.

Delbridge, R. 1998. *Life on the Line in Contemporary Manufacturing*. Oxford: OUP.

Delios, A. and Bjorkman, I. (2000) 'Expatriate staffing in foreign subsidiaries of Japanese multinational corporations in the PRC and the United States', *International Journal of Human Resource Management*, 11 (2): 278–93.

Dicken, P. (2003) *Global Shift: Reshaping the Global Economic Map in the 21st Century*, 4th edition. London: Sage.

Dickmann, M. (2003) 'Implementing German HRM abroad: Desired, feasible, successful?' *International Journal of Human Resource Management*, 14 (2): 265–83.

Djelic, M.-L. and Quack, S. (2003) *Globalization and Institutions – Redefining the rules of the economic game*. London: Edward Elgar.

Doeringer, P.B., Lorenz, E. and Terkla, D. (2003) 'The adoption and diffusion of high–performance management: Lessons from Japanese multinationals in the West', *Cambridge Journal of Economics*, 27 (2): 265–86

Dowling, P., Welch, D. and Schuler, R. (1999) 'Completing the puzzle: Issues in the development of the field of international human resource management', *Management International Review*. 39 (3): 27–43.

Edström, A. and Galbraith, J. (1977) 'Transfer of manager as a coordination and control strategy in multinational organizations', *Administrative Science Quarterly*, 22 (2): 248–63.

Edwards, T. (1998) 'Multinationals, employment practices and the process of diffusion', *International Journal of Human Resource Management*, 9 (4): 696–709.

Edwards, T. and Rees, C. (2006) *International Human Resource Management: Globalization, National Systems and Multinational Companies*. Harlow: Pearson Education.

Edwards, T. and Kuruvilla, S. (2005) 'International HRM: National business systems, organizational politics and the international division of labour in MNCs', *International Journal of Human Resource Management*, 16 (1): 1–21.

Edwards, T., Almond, P., Clark, I. and Ferner, A. (2005) 'Reverse diffusion in US multinationals: Barriers from the American business system', *Journal of Management Studies*, 42 (6): 1261–86.

Edwards, T., Edwards, P., Ferner, A., Marginson, P. and Tregaskis, O. (2007) 'Charting the contours of multinationals in Britain'. Project report available online at http://www2.warwick.ac.uk/fac/soc/wbs/projects/mncemployment/conference_papers/

Elger, T. and Smith, C. (2005) *Assembling Work: Remaking Factory Regimes in Japanese Multinationals in Britain*. Oxford: Oxford University Press.

Evans, P. and Lorange, P. (1989) 'The two logics behind human resource management', in Evans, P., Doz, Y. and Laurent, A. (eds), *Human Resource Management in International Firms. Change, Globalization, Innovation*. Basingstoke: Macmillan, pp. 144–61.

Evans, P., Lank, E. and Farquhar, A. (1989) 'Managing human resources in the international firm: Lessons from practice', in Evans, P., Doz, Y. and Laurent, A. (eds), *Human Resource Management in International Firms*. London: Macmillan. pp. 367–87.

Fenton-O'Creevy, M., Gooderham, P. and Nordhaug, O. (2008) 'HRM in US subsidiaries in Europe and Australia: Centralization or autonomy?', *Journal of International Business Studies*, 39 (1): 151–66.

Ferner, A. and Edwards, P. (1995) 'Power and the diffusion of organizational change within multinational enterprises', *European Journal of Industrial Relations*, 1 (2): 229–57.

Ferner, A., Almond, P. and Colling, T. (2005) 'Institutional theory and the cross-national transfer of employment policy: The case of 'workforce diversity' in US multinationals', *Journal of International Business Studies*, 36 (3): 304–21.

Ferner, A. and Varul, M.Z. (2000) 'Internationalisation and the personnel function in German multinationals', *Human Resource Management Journal*, 10 (3): 79–96.

Frenkel, S. (2001) 'Globalization, athletic footwear commodity chains and employment relations in China', *Organization Studies*, 22 (4): 531–62.

Gamble, J. (2003) 'Transferring human resource practices from the United Kingdom to China: The limits and potential for convergence', *International Journal of Human Resource Management*, 14 (3).

Gaur, A., Delios, A. and Singh, K. 2007 'Institutional environments, staffing strategies, and subsidiary performance', *Journal of Management*, 33, 4, 611–36.

Geary, J. and Roche, W.K. (2001) 'Multinationals and human resource practices in Ireland: A rejection of the "new conformance thesis"', *International Journal of Human Resource Management*, 12 (1): 109–27.

Geppert, M. and Williams, K. (2006) 'Global, national and local practices in multinational corporations: Towards a sociopolitical framework', *International Journal of Human Resource Management*, 17 (1): 49–69.

Geppert, M., Matten, D. and Williams, K. (2003) 'Change management in MNCs: How global convergence intertwines with national diversities', *Human Relations*, 56 (7): 807–38.

Gerhart, B. and Fang, M. (2005) 'National culture and human resource management: Assumptions and evidence', International Journal of Human Resource Management', 16 (6): 971–86.

Geringer, J.M., Frayne, C.A. and Milliman, J. (2002) 'In search of "best practices" in international human resource management: Research design and methodology', *Human Resource Management*, 41 (1): 5–30.

Gill R. and Wong A. 1998 'The cross-cultural transfer of management practices: The case of Japanese human resource management practices in Singapore', *International Journal of Human Resource Management*, 9, 1, 116–135.

Goodall and Warner, M. (1997) 'Human resources in Sino-foreign joint ventures', *International Journal of Human Resource Management*, 8 (5): 569–94.

Gould, R. (2003) 'Uses of network tools in comparative historical research', in Mahoney, J. and Rueschemeyer, D. (eds), *Comparative Historical Analysis in the Social Sciences*. Cambridge: Cambridge University Press, pp. 241–69.

Guest, D. and Hoque, K. (1996) 'National ownership and HR practices in UK greenfield Sites', *Human Resource Management Journal*, 6 (4): 50–74.

Gump, S.E. (2006) 'Who gets the job? Recruitment and selection at a "second-generation" Japanese automotive components transplant in the US,' *International Journal of Human Resource Management*, 17 (5): 842–59.

Gunnigle, P., Collings, D. and Morley, M. (2006) 'Accommodating global capitalism? State policy and industrial relations in American MNCs in Ireland', in Ferner, A., Quintanilla, J. and Sánchez-Runde, C. (eds), *Multinationals, Institutions and the Construction of Transnational Practices*. Basingstoke: Palgrave, pp. 86–108.

Hall, P. and Soskice, D. (2001) *Varieties of Capitalism*. Oxford: OUP.

Hannon, John, Jelf, Gregory and Brandes, Deborah (1996) 'Human resource information systems: Operational issues and strategic considerations in a global environment', *International Journal of Human Resource Management*, 7 (1): 245–69.

Harvey M., Speier C. and Novecevic M.M. (2001) 'A theory-based framework for strategic global human resource staffing policies and practices', *International Journal of Human Resource Management*, 12 (6): 898–915.

Harvey, Michael, Novicevic, Milorad M. and Garrison, Garry (2005) 'Global virtual teams: A human resource capital architecture', *International Journal of Human Resource Management*, 16 (9): 1583–99.

Harzing, A.-W. (1999) *Managing the Multinationals. An international study of control mechanisms*. Cheltenham: Edward Elgar.

Hoffman, L. (2005) 'Going global: Outsourcing HR offshore', *Human Resources Magazine*, July. (http://www.humanresourcesmagazine.com.au/articles/21/0C032921.asp?Type=60&Category=1287)

Hofstede, G. (1980) *Culture's Consequences*. London: Sage.

Hollingsworth, J.R., Schmitter, P. and Streeck, W. (1994) *Governing Capitalist Economies. Performance and control of economic sectors*. New York/Oxford: Oxford University Press.

ILO (1976) *Multinationals in Western Europe: The Industrial Relations Experience*. Geneva: Intenational Labour Office.

Jacoby, S. (2004) *The Embedded Corporation: Corporate Governance and Employment Relations in Japan and the United States*. Princeton, N.J.: Princeton University Press.

Kahancová, Marta and Meer, Marc van der (2006) 'Coordination, employment flexibility, and industrial relations in Western European multinationals:

Evidence from Poland', *International Journal of Human Resource Management*, 17 (7): 1379–95.

Katz, H. and Darbishire, O. (2000) *Converging Divergences: Worldwide Changes in Employment Systems*. Ithaca: Cornell University Press.

Kidman, A. (2005) 'Negotiating the shared services minefield', *Human Resources Magazine*, September, http://www.sharedservicesbpo.com/file/3262/negotiating–the–shared–services–minefield.html.

Kim, Youngok and Gray, Sidney J. (2005) 'Strategic factors influencing international human resource management practices: An empirical study of Australian multinational corporations', *International Journal of Human Resource Management*, 16 (5): 809–30.

Kogut, B. and Singh, H. (1988) 'The effect of national culture on the choice of entry mode.' *Journal of International Business Studies*, 19 (3): 411–32.

Kopp, R. (1994) 'International human resource policies and practices in Japanese, European, and United States multinationals', *Human Resource Management Journal*, 33 (4): 581–99.

Kostova, T. (1999) 'Transnational transfer of strategic organizational practices: A contextual perspective', *Academy of Management Review*, 24 (2): 308–24.

Kujawa, D. (1979) 'The labour relations of United States multinationals abroad: Comparative and prospective views', *Labour and Society*, 4 (1): 3–25.

Kristensen, P.H. and Zeitlin, J. (2005) *Local Players in Global Games: The strategic constitution of a multinational corporation*. Oxford: Oxford University Press.

Lane, C. and Probert, J. (2006) 'Globalization and labour market segmentation: The impact of global production networks on employment patterns of German and UK clothing firms', in Ferner, A., Quintanilla, J. and Sánchez-Runde, C. (eds), *Multinationals, Institutions and the Construction of Transnational Practices*. Basingstoke: Palgrave, pp. 184–212.

Lawler, John and Bae, Johngseok (1998) 'Overt employment discrimination by multinational firms: Cultural and economic influences in a developing country industrial relations', *Industrial Relations*, 37 (2): 126–52.

Lawrence, P., and Lorsch, J. (1967) *Organization and Environment*. Boston: Harvard Business School Press.

Liberman, L. and Torbiorn, I. (2000) 'Variances in staff-related management practices at eight European country subsidiaries of a global firm', *International Journal of Human Resource Management*, 11 (1): 37–59.

Lindholm, N., Tahvanainen, M. and Björkman, I. (1999) 'Performance appraisal of host country employees:

Western MNEs in China', in Brewster, C. and Harris, H. (eds), *International HRM: Contemporary issues in Europe*. London: Routledge, pp. 143–59.

Marginson, P. and Hall, M. (2004) 'The impact of European works councils on management decision-making in UK- and US-based multinationals: A case study comparison', *British Journal of Industrial Relations*, 42 (2): 209–33.

Marginson, P., Armstrong, P., Edwards, P. and Purcell, J. (1995) 'Managing labour in the global corporation: A survey-based analysis of multinationals operating in the UK', *International Journal of Human Resource Management*, 6 (3): 702–19.

McGauran, A.-M. (2001) 'Masculine, feminine or neutral? In-company equal opportunities policies in Irish and French MNC retailing', *International Journal of Human Resource Management*, 12 (5): 754–71.

McPherson A. H., Roche W. K. (1997) 'Peripheral location equals localized labour? Multinationals and the internationalization of training and development in Ireland', *International Journal of Human Resource Management*, 8 (4): 369–84.

McSweeney, B. (2002) 'Hofstede's model of national cultural differences and their consequences: A triumph of faith – a failure of analysis', *Human Relations*, 55 (1): 89–118.

Meardi, G. and Tóth, A. (2006) 'Who is hybridizing what? Insights on MNCs' employment practices in central Europe', in Ferner, A., Quintanilla, J. and Sánchez-Runde, C. (eds), *Multinationals, Institutions, and the Construction of Transnational Practices*. Basingstoke: Palgrave, pp. 155–83.

Mueller, F. and Purcell, J. (1992) 'The Europeanisation of manufacturing and the decentralisation of bargaining: Multinational management strategies in the European automobile industry', *International Journal of Human Resource Management*, 3 (1): 15–34.

Morton, Jane, Siebert, W.S. (2001) 'Labour market regimes and worker recruitment and retention in the European union: Plant comparisons', *British Journal of Industrial Relations*, 39 (4): 505–28.

Murray, G., Bélanger, J., Harvey, A., Jalette, P. and Levesque, C. (2006) *Employment practices in multinational companies in Canada: Building organizational capabilities and institutions for innovation*. Montreal: CRIMT.

Newman, K. and Nollen, S. (1996) 'Culture and congruence: The fit between management practices and national culture', *Journal of International Business Studies*, 27 (4): 753–78.

Ngo, H., Turban, D., Lau, C. and Lui, S. (1998) 'Human resource practices and firm performance of multinational corporations: Influences of country

Origin', *International Journal of Human Resource Management*, 9 (4): 632–52.

Novicevic, M. and Harvey, M. (2001) 'The emergence of the pluralism construct and the inpatriation process', *International Journal of Human Resource Management*, 12 (3): 333–56.

Perlmutter, H. (1969) 'The tortuous evolution of the multinational firm', *Columbia Journal of World Business*, 4 (1): 9–18.

Porter, M. (1990) *The Competitive Advantage of Nations (with a new introduction)*. Basingstoke: Macmillan.

Quintanilla, J. (2002) *Dirección de Recursos Humanos en Empresas Multinacionales. Las subsidiarias al descubierto*. Madrid: Prentice Hall.

Ramsey, J.R. (2005) 'The role of other orientation on the relationship between institutional distance and expatriate adjustment', *Journal of International Management*, 11 (3): 377–96.

Roberts, B. (1972) 'Factors influencing the organization and style of management and their effect on the pattern of industrial relations in multi-national corporations', in Günter, H. (ed.), *Transnational Industrial Relations*. London: Macmillan, pp. 109–32.

Rosenzweig, P. and Nohria, N. (1994) 'Influences on human resource management practices in multinational corporations', *Journal of International Business Studies*, 25 (2): 229–51.

Roth, K. and O'Donnell, S. (1996) 'Foreign subsidiary compensation strategy: An agency theory perspective', *Academy of Management Journal*, 39 (3): 678–703.

Rugman, A. (2005) *The Regional Multinationals*. Cambridge: Cambridge University Press.

Ruta, C. D. (2005) 'The application of change management theory to HR portal implementation in subsidiaries of multinational corporations', *Human Resource Management*, 44, 1, 35–53.

Saka, A. (2002) 'Institutional limits to the internalization of work systems: A comparative study of three Japanese MNCs in the UK', *European Journal of Industrial Relations*, 8 (3): 251–75.

Scarborough, H. and Terry, M. (1998) 'Forget Japan: The very British response to lean production', *Employee Relations*, 20 (3): 224–36.

Schmitt, M. (2003) 'Deregulation of the German industrial relations system via foreign direct investment: Are the subsidiaries of Anglo-Saxon MNCs a threat for the institutions of industrial democracy in Germany?' *Economic and Industrial Democracy*, 24 (3): 349–77.

Schmitt, M. and Sadowski, D. (2003) 'A rationalistic cost-minimization approach to the international transfer of HRM/IR practices: Anglo-Saxon multinationals in the Federal Republic of Germany', *International Journal of Human Resource Management*. 14 (3): 409–30.

Schuler, R., Budhwar, P. and Florkowski, G. (2002) 'International human resource management: Review and critique', *International Journal of Management Reviews*, 4 (1): 41–70.

Schuler, R. and Rogovsky, N. (1998) 'Understanding compensation practice variations across firms: The impact of national culture', *Journal of International Business Studies*, 29 (1): 159–77.

Schuler, R.S., Dowling, P.J. and De Cieri, H. (1993) 'An integrative framework of strategic international human resource management', *International Journal of Human Resource Management*, 4 (4): 717–64.

Scullion, H. and Linehan, M. (2005) *International Human Resource Management: A Critical Text*. Basingstoke: Palgrave.

Scullion, H. and Starkey, K. (2000) 'The changing role of the corporate human resource function in the international firm', *International Journal of Human Resource Management*, 11 (6): 1061–81.

Shen, Jie (2006) 'Factors affecting international staffing in Chinese multinationals (MNEs)', *International Journal of Human Resource Management*, 17 (2): 295–315

Sisson, Keith (2006) 'International employee representation – a case of industrial relations systems following the market?', in Edwards, T. and Rees, C. (eds), *International Human Resource Management*. Harlow: Prentice Hall, pp. 242–61.

Snell, S.A., Snow, C.C., Davison, S.C. and Hambrick, D.C. (1998) 'Designing and supporting transnational teams: The human resource agenda', *Human Resource Management*, 37 (2): 147–58.

Smith, C. and Meiksins, P. (1995) 'System, society and dominance effects in cross-national organisational analysis', *Work, Employment and Society*, 9 (2): 241–67.

Sparrow, P., Brewster, C. and Harris, H. (2004) *Globalizing Human Resource Management*. London/New York: Routledge.

Tayeb, M. (2005) *International Human Resource Management: A Multinational Company Perspective*. Oxford: OUP.

Taylor, S., Beechler, S. and Napier, N. (1996) 'Toward an integrative model of strategic international human resource management', *Academy of Management Review*, 21 (4): 959–85.

Taylor, S. (2006) 'Emerging Motivations for Global HRM Integration', in Ferner, A., Quintanilla, J. and Sánchez-Runde, C. (eds), *Multinationals, Institutions and the Construction of Transnational Practices*. Basingstoke: Palgrave, pp. 109–30.

Traxler, F. and Woitech, B. (2000) 'Transnational investment and national labour market regimes: A case of 'regime shopping?', *European Journal of Industrial Relations*, 6 (2): 141–59.

Tregaskis, O., Glover, L. and Ferner, A. (2005) *International HR Networks in Multinational Companies*. London: CIPD.

Tung R. L. and Worm V. (2001) 'Network capitalism: The role of human resources in penetrating the China market', *International Journal of Human Resource Management*, 12 (4): 517–34.

Tüselmann, H.-J., Frank, M. and Arne, H. (2003) 'Employee relations in german multinationals in an Anglo-Saxon setting: Toward a Germanic Version of the Anglo-Saxon Approach?,' *European Journal of Industrial Relations*, 9 (3): 327–49.

Wächter, H., Peters, R., Ferner, A., Gunnigle, P. and Quintanilla, J. (2006) 'The role of the international personnel function', in Almond, P. and Ferner, A. (eds), *American Multinationals in Europe: Managing Employment Relations Across National Borders*. Oxford: Oxford University Press, pp. 248–71.

Walsh, J. (2001) 'Human resource management in foreign owned workplaces: Evidence from Australia', *International Journal of Human Resource Management*, 12 (3): 425–44.

Wilkinson, B., Gamble, J., Humphrey, J., Morris, J. and Anthony, D. (2001) 'The new international division of labour in Asian electronics: Work organization and human resources in Japan and Malaysia', *Journal of Management Studies*, 38 (5): 675–95.

Williams, K. and Geppert, M. (2006) 'The German model of employee relations on trial: Negotiated and unilaterally imposed change in multi-national companies', *Industrial Relations Journal*, 37 (1): 48–63.

Wood, Stephen J., Fenton-O'Creevy, Mark P. (2005) 'Direct involvement, representation and employee voice in UK multinationals in Europe', *European Journal of Industrial Relations*, 11 (1): 27–50.

Xu, D. and Shenkar, O. (2002) 'Institutional distance and the multinational enterprise', *Academy of Management Review*, 27 (4): 608–18.

Yeung, A.K.O. and Wong, G.X.Y. (1990) 'A comparative analysis of the practices and performance of human resource management systems in Japan and the PRC', in *Research in Personnel and Human Resources Management*, Suppl. 2. Greenwich, CT: JAI Press.

Zhang, M., Edwards, T. and Edwards, C. (2006) 'Internationalization and developing countries: The case of China', in Edwards, T. and Rees, C. (eds), *International Human Resource Management*. Harlow: Prentice Hall, pp. 129–47.

33

Human Resource Management in the Public Sector

Stephen Bach

INTRODUCTION

Until recently the dominant debates within human resource management (HRM) have paid little attention to HR practice in the public sector. The concern with the degree to which HRM represented a distinctive style of people management had little resonance for public services, widely viewed as subscribing to traditional patterns of personnel management. The emphasis on establishing the links between HRM and corporate performance was of limited relevance to services answerable to a wide range of stakeholders and with contested performance outcomes; and public service organizations rarely figured as exemplars of leading edge HR practice. Curiously, even developments that might have been viewed as highly relevant to HR practice in the public services, such as customer-employee relations and the changing shape of the HR function, paid scant attention

to the public sector (Heskett et al., 2003; Ulrich, 2001).

These perspectives, which assume that there is little noteworthy in HR practice in the public sector have been challenged. Over the last two decades, with varying degrees of intensity, reforms of the public sector, have been adopted across most countries with significant consequences for HR practice (Pollitt and Boukaert, 2004). Many of these reforms stemmed from the new public management (NPM) movement, based on an assumption that management practice in the private sector was equally applicable to developments in the public sector. This development encouraged some convergence of HR practice between the public and private sector and more attention being directed towards HR issues. There has been increased recognition that structural reforms of public services have paid insufficient attention to HR issues: workforce motivation; staff responses to reform; and the degree to which organizations have the HR capacity and competencies to manage change effectively. The World Health Organization (WHO) amongst others, have therefore suggested that effective HR practice is *the* key challenge confronting reform of health systems (WHO, 2006).

Less well documented is an emerging trend that reverses the dominant orthodoxy that the public sector can benefit from the transfer of HR practices that derive from the commercial sector and suggests that the private sector may have things to learn from the prevailing HR ethos in the public sector. In part driven by concerns about 'capitalism unleashed' (Glyn, 2007) and in the wake of corporate scandals at Enron and elsewhere, there is a grudging acknowledgement that core values associated with public service, trust, impartiality and integrity, need to be preserved and reinforced in the public sector. HR policies and organizational cultures that foster such values have relevance for contemporary corporations, exemplified by the surge of interest in corporate social responsibility. Private sector companies' operating environment resembles more closely long-standing features of the public domain: accountability to multiple stakeholders, relatively open scrutiny of performance; and the need to maintain public trust. Consequently, diffusion of HR practice is becoming more two-way, in contrast to the orthodox assumption that the public sector can benefit from the adoption of private sector 'best practice'. This chapter examines the context for HR in the public sector before examining the new public management reforms and the consequences for HR practice.

CONTEXT

The significance of state employment arises from the size and scope of government activity. General government expenditure in industrialized (OECD) countries varies between 36 per cent of GDP in Korea to 57 per cent in Sweden, reflecting the growth of the welfare state since the 1950s with major expansion of employment in health, social services and education (Ketelaar et al., 2007: 11). Even in countries with a small public sector workforce, including Austria, Germany and the Netherlands, state employees still constitute 10–12 per cent of the workforce. At the other end of the spectrum, in the Nordic countries, its share of employment exceeds 25 per cent (Bordogna, 2007: 10). There are a number of difficulties in comparing the size of the public sector workforce. The first relates to ownership and this has become more uncertain as the boundaries of the sector have blurred as a result of privatization and outsourcing. A second complication arises from the distinct historical evolution of public services in individual countries. Although, in virtually all countries the core civil service, military, police and emergency services are state employees, in health, education and social care, usually regarded as public services, this is not invariably the case. Finally, although the definition of public employment is often relatively broad, much scholarship focuses more narrowly on the civil service, so it is often difficult to gauge whether trends apply across a whole country or are confined to the core civil service.

Despite these variations, many of the characteristics of public sector employment which differentiate it from the private sector, derive from the state's unique role as an employer. The 'political contingency' (Ferner, 1988) – the need for governments to be sensitive to their electoral constituency – are prominent in the government's role as employer. Its approach to public sector employment is invariably imbued with a political dimension, especially in sensitive areas of public policy such as crime and national security. This can be illustrated by the establishment of the Department of Homeland Security (DHS) in the US, in the wake of September 11th 2001. In a controversial decision, President Bush determined that employees of the new department should not have the right to join unions or bargain because of the need to maximize managerial flexibility (Masters and Albright, 2003: 171).

State employment decisions are therefore subject to levels of public accountability and transparency that arise from the government's role as custodian of public funds. Decisions, particularly in relation to selection, promotion and rewards, are open to public scrutiny and this has encouraged standardized forms of HR practice. An important aspect of this accountability concerns the pay and conditions of public sector employees; the state has to reconcile the expectation that it should be a fair employer with its duty to taxpayers as the guardian of the public purse. Establishing 'fair' pay has been difficult for those public sector occupations that have no equivalents in the private sector. For many years unilateral pay determination by the state was more prevalent than joint regulation via collective bargaining, using indexation or other forms of comparison with prevailing pay rates in the private sector (Bordogna, 2007).

The gradual extension of collective bargaining rights to civil servants did not preclude trade unions having an important role and in many ways they continue to enjoy considerable organizational advantages compared to their private sector counterparts. They face little hostility from employers in recruiting members and their own managers are often highly unionized. There are few organizational constraints as their potential membership is often concentrated in large employer units and unions recognize that governments are sensitive to the electoral consequences of public service industrial action. Finally, although the public sector has been the target of outsourcing, unions are less threatened by the process of globalization; many public services are less amenable to transfer overseas. Union density is over 75 per cent in countries such as Denmark and Norway and the gap with the private sector is often sizeable. In the UK public sector union density is almost 60 per cent compared to less than 20 per cent in the private sector (Grainger and Crowther, 2007) and even more marked in the US with figures of 38 and 9 per cent respectively (Thomason and Burton, 2003: 72). The main exception to high public sector union density is amongst the former communist countries of central and eastern Europe, where union density in countries such as the Czech Republic and Poland is less than five per cent (Bordogna, 2007: 22).

These contextual features affect the character of the public service workforce. Employment in the public services reflects a complex pattern of gender segregation, rooted in traditional – if changing – assumptions about appropriate employment for men and women. Education, health and social services employ far more women than men and, consequently, in countries such as the UK 65 per cent of employees are women compared to 41 per cent in the private sector. These gender characteristics also contribute to high levels of part-time working in the sector, almost a third work part-time compared to just under a quarter in the private sector (Heap, 2005). One consequence for HR practice is that public sector employers have been more receptive to equal employment policies than sectors such as manufacturing that employ fewer women.

A further distinguishing feature relates to the occupational composition of the public sector workforce and the dominance of professions reflected in high levels of educational attainment amongst its employees. This characteristic is closely associated with the employment of professions including doctors, nurses, teachers and social workers. The HR challenges of managing professions, often characterized as resistant to change, has been one of the key drivers of reform. Finally, the public sector workforce is ageing rapidly and, whereas in 2004 72 per cent of UK public sector workers were 35 and over, the corresponding figure for the private sector was 62 per cent (Heap, 2005). Across the OECD, countries confront a looming retirement wave and this will not only lead to a loss of experienced staff but will also exacerbate workforce shortages (OECD, 2007). Pension policy has become a more prominent HR concern and most countries are attempting to revise upwards the age at which public sector workers can retire with a full pension, which has provoked strong trade union opposition. Overall, the public sector remains a distinctive, very large, labour intensive sector in which the services provided are often inseparable from the employees delivering the service. Consequently, the nature and outcome of any HR reforms depends on the response of the workforce, which is itself shaped by their experience of the existing HR practices.

TRADITIONAL PUBLIC ADMINISTRATION

This approach is associated with a Weberian model of hierarchical authority, underpinned by rule-governed behaviour and functional specialization. It is exemplified by traditional civil service systems that embodied systems of rules about merit-based recruitment and promotion, which usually involved competitive examinations. Rules were established for security of tenure, enabling civil servants to pursue careers, progressing through internal labour markets, often on the basis of seniority. Remuneration was frequently established unilaterally by the state and was based on job-related criteria with little recourse to market value. These rules resulted in uniform employment conditions and they were often formalized in statutes and regulations overseen by a separate central personnel authority (Bach and Della Rocca, 2000).

The main purpose of this model was to clarify the degree of political involvement in staffing decisions and to remove political patronage. The role of the civil service has been to administer state policy in an impartial and neutral manner according to agreed procedures, providing institutional and political stability. The UK has traditionally had the most marked separation of the political and administrative spheres with no formal political involvement in appointment, promotion or dismissal of top civil servants. The continental European tradition grants civil servants a unique legal status exemplifying their role as custodians of the public interest. The strongest version of this governance structure is the special legal status of *Beamte* in Germany, whose position in society is enshrined by

a precisely defined set of legal rights and obligations (Keller, 1999). The USA has a more overtly political staffing system in which top officials are political appointments and can expect to be replaced when the administration changes. When there is more overt political involvement in staffing decisions, there is more external oversight of the recruitment process (e.g. senate confirmation hearings in the US) and greater restrictions on civil servants' ability to act in a party political manner (Ketelaar et al., 2007: 15).

These systems are underpinned by assumptions about the values and motivation of the workforce. The traditional perspective, which has been vigorously contested over recent decades, is that public sector workers are intrinsically motivated. This stems from their sense of vocation and a strong commitment to what the Audit Commission (2002) termed 'making a difference'. This encouraged professional self-regulation and limited state intervention to measure and monitor performance. By contrast, public choice critics that emphasize 'producer capture' suggest that public servants are self-interested and attempt to maximize their utility. They engage in bureau-maximizing behaviour to increase their status and remuneration, facilitated by the absence of competitive pressures or systems of performance management (Niskanen, 1971). These contrasting perspectives have been categorized as 'knightly' and 'knavely' behaviour by Le Grand (2003) who argues that public servants frequently exhibit both forms of behaviour, but that appropriate incentive structures can foster knightly behaviour. This more critical scrutiny of the motives that animate public servants has underpinned the proliferation of systems of performance management in the public services. Nonetheless, although there is some conflicting evidence, many studies continue to highlight the distinctive and altruistic disposition of public sector employees, for example in their greater willingness to volunteer and donate blood (Houston, 2006).

From the 1970s onwards the traditional approach came under increased scrutiny. In the same way that advocates of HRM were disparaging about personnel management so the proponents of the new public management dismissed public administration and its association with Weber's definition of bureaucracy (for example, Osborne and Gaebler, 1992). Bureaucracy was invariably viewed negatively and associated with inflexibility, rigid job demarcations and a preoccupation with inputs rather than outputs. According to the OECD such an approach represented a major impediment to improved performance because 'highly centralised, rule-bound, and inflexible organisations that emphasise process rather than results impede good performance' (OECD, 1995: 7). These criticisms signalled an altered political climate in which the ideas of the new right were in the ascendancy. This reform agenda was characterized by a desire to reduce the size of the public sector, introduce competition and other market principles into the state sector and wrest control of public services from the providers of services. These changes indicated a less benign view of public service professionals in particular and the workforce in general. These ideological shifts were underpinned by a much less favourable economic context with concern that increases in public expenditure were unsustainable and that much greater attention had to be directed at raising public sector efficiency and controlling costs. It was this shift in political and economic context that heralded the emergence of the New Public Management, with significant HR implications.

THE NEW PUBLIC MANAGEMENT

New Public Management has been the dominant reform agenda for the last twenty years. In one sense the ubiquitous nature of NPM reform bears out suggestions that NPM is a global phenomenon and that policy learning is being diffused not only by influential organisations such as the Organization for Economic Co-operation and Development (OECD) but also by global management consultancy firms (Kettl, 2000). Countries as economically and politically diverse as Mongolia, Nepal,

Singapore, as well as high-profile cases such as New Zealand and the UK, have adopted NPM practices, although not always with the intended outcomes (McCourt, 2001; UN, 2005). These developments highlight the need for precision, because loose labelling of all reforms as NPM risks the term being drained of meaning with distinct practices being grouped together. It also signals the importance of differentiating between the presence of NPM practices and the outcomes of such reforms. Debate has shifted in this regard from a focus on the degree to which NPM practices have been diffused across countries towards a much greater focus on interpreting the significance of these reforms, identifying their limitations, and assessing the circumstances under which the intended outcomes are likely to result.

In contrast to traditional public administration which reflects the macro concerns of political science and is orientated to institutions and the role of state actors in the administrative process, NPM originates in economics and is much more focused on micro level questions of incentives, markets and individual behaviour within organizations. The first strand of NPM is based on public choice theory, principal-agent theory and transactions cost economics which share an assumption that all individuals are self-interested and try to maximize their own preferences. The principal enters into a series of contracts with the agent, who undertakes tasks on his behalf, but because of the assumptions about individual utility maximization, it is assumed that the interests of the principal and agent inevitably conflict. NPM therefore is concerned to design contracts and other incentive structures that minimize 'gaming' (also termed 'opportunistic behaviour') by agents. The unflattering assumptions about the behaviour of agents, the public sector workforce and its managers, has provoked considerable hostility from NPM critics (see Boston et al., 1996: 16–40). The second strand of NPM reflects the growth of business schools and management as a discipline and mirrors management practices associated with the 'best practice' school of HRM (Boxall and

Purcell, 2003: 61–64). There is frequently an emphasis on empowering the workforce by ensuring good systems of communication and participation and flexible work roles. These policies are underpinned by robust systems of selection, training and appraisal. These practices seem uncontroversial but when blended with the assumptions about self-serving behaviour of the first strand of NPM, the implementation of performance management in particular has provoked opposition. Employees have expressed concerns that the main goal of NPM is to monitor and control their behaviour. The overall thrust of NPM has therefore been to suggest that the assumptions and practices prevailing in the private sector are applicable to the public sector (for a review see Lynn, 2006). NPM has been colonized by numerous scholars after Hood (1991) first used the term to compare public sector reforms in Australia, Canada, New Zealand, the UK and the United States. The main reforms associated with NPM include:

- promoting increased managerial freedom to manage which strengthens their powers and enables them to adopt private sector corporate practice;
- organizational restructuring that shifts away from traditional bureaucracy towards loosely coupled semi-independent organizational units with devolved managerial responsibility, intended to make them more responsive to citizen demands and more accountable for results;
- greater competition in service provision by the introduction of market-type incentives into the financing and provision of public services. Examples include the outsourcing of services, internal markets and other contractual mechanisms;
- a movement away from an emphasis on policy towards a focus on measurable standards of performance and individual accountability for outputs;
- a shift away from an emphasis on development and investment towards cost-cutting and more efficient use of resources.

This reform agenda has not been implemented in a uniform manner and the UK and New Zealand have frequently been marked out as in the vanguard of reform.

Many continental European countries have experimented with NPM measures but have tried to go with the grain of their legal, political and institutional traditions (Pollitt and Boukaert, 2004). It is also noteworthy that HR practice is an implicit rather than an explicit element of these policy prescriptions and HR initiatives have tended to follow in the wake of structural and financial reforms. It is only as NPM reforms have matured that the consequences for the workforce have been explicitly considered with increasing acknowledgment that poor alignment between structural reforms and HR policy has resulted in dysfunctional outcomes.

The main thrust of NPM has been to erode the distinctive features of HR in the public domain and to encourage convergence in HR practice between the public and private sectors *within* individual nation states. These trends have been facilitated by the privatization of energy, transport and telecommunications sectors and the outsourcing of functions to the private sector. The outcome has been the extension of standard employment law arrangements to public sector employees and the weakening of the special legal or procedural norms that distinguished employment in the state sector. This has frequently led to a reduction in the number of employees covered by specific administrative law and a harmonization of recruitment, promotion and dismissal processes towards prevailing practice in the private sector. In Ireland, the *2004 Public Service Management (Recruitment and Appointments) Act* reformed the recruitment process to facilitate more open and flexible recruitment practices without recourse to a central process. Rules on dismissal and recruitment for many civil servants were relaxed, but this was accompanied by new rights to access unfair dismissal legislation. The picture is not straightforward, however, especially amongst civil servants, because existing employees often retain their special status following privatization with ordinary contracts being applied to newly recruited staff. Thus, in France and Germany former postal and railway staff retained their former employment status (Bordogna, 2007: 19–20).

This highlights the point that without changes in management behaviour, embedded institutional patterns of personnel practice may be hard to alter. It also signals that the new public management's focus on the opportunism of agents may lead to the neglect of the degree to which principals are willing and able to act as principals or may indulge in opportunistic behaviour themselves.

CONSEQUENCES OF HRM REFORM

Apart from these specific changes to the employment status of public sector workers the consequences of NPM for HR practice can be grouped under three main themes: decentralization and devolution, performance management, and flexible service delivery.

Decentralization and devolution

A central element of the reforms has been the fragmentation of organizational units into their constituent business units. These administrative units have been ceded greater responsibility for performance, financial resources and in many cases HR practice. Increased discretion is often devolved to these administrative units for the recruitment, deployment and pay of their staff. The underlying purpose of these reforms has been to move away from monolithic public sector structures, incorporating local priorities, to ensure services are more responsive to the citizens they serve. A prominent rationale for the creation of executive agencies in the UK and elsewhere was that the separation of policy work, from the operational delivery of services in agencies, would ensure that the importance of effective service provision would no longer be subservient to policy. The UK government established around 200 executive agencies in the late 1980s. Similar arrangements have been adopted in civil services across a number of other countries including Australia, Denmark, Ireland, the Netherlands and Sweden (OECD, 2004). In the US Performance Based Organizations (PBOs) were established, but without the

same degree of HR flexibility because PBO HR flexibility and performance agreements could have jeopardized the separation of powers that constitutes an integral feature of the US constitution and union opposition also limited HR flexibilities (Moynihan, 2003).

These new service units typically took on the employer role, along with a notional responsibility for many of the policies and practices required to manage employees. This shift in the level of responsibility for human resource management had a significant impact on a range of institutions, practices and stakeholders. But it is equally apparent that the use made of these HR discretions and the scope to develop distinctive HR policies and practices has often remained constrained. This stems from finance authorities' reluctance to loosen control of the paybill, limited HR capacity and capability to manage more devolved HR systems, and awareness that devolution can lead to the duplication of effort and significantly increase transaction costs. These reforms have not only challenged HR but have also created difficulties for trade unions that are more used to dealing with central negotiations. Pollitt (2006) is more sanguine in his study of executive agencies in Finland, the Netherlands, Sweden and the UK. He reported that performance measurement was becoming more prominent within executive agencies, but he notes also that UK respondents expressed concerns that the policy/operations gap had become too wide with departments becoming increasingly divorced from where policy is applied.

Devolution has also had significant consequences for the HR function. Taking its cue from broader HRM developments, HR has sought to shift to a more strategic, business orientated perspective and to delegate more responsibility to line managers. It is generally recognized that HR issues have a higher profile within public sector organizations than in the past but the degree to which this has been translated into a higher profile and more strategic role for the HR function is more uncertain. In the UK context, where HR devolution has been vigorously promoted, it has frequently been the repository of a range of disparate central government requirements and been subject to short-term pressures. Line managers are not opposed to devolution in principle but because of increased workload pressures are reluctant to take on further responsibilities (Bach, 2004). Devolution has been used to justify abolition or significant downsizing of corporate HR functions, as the 50 per cent cut in staff at the US Office of Personnel Management (OPM) testifies (Gowling and Lindholm, 2002).The uncertainties surrounding the HR function was captured by a comment from a young French civil servant educated at elite *Ecole National d'administration* (ENA) who suggested that 'the best way to make a mess of your career is to be involved in human resource management or this kind of stuff' (cited in Rouban, 2007: 495).

Performance management

The emphasis on performance which combines a focus on outputs with incentives for individuals and organizations that achieve their targets has been the most widespread aspect of NPM reforms. The concept, however, can be applied in different ways and there is a degree of cynicism about the performance mantra espoused by governments alongside some resentment amongst staff at the implication that in the past the workforce was disinterested in performance (Ketelaar et al., 2007), a point contested by Lynn (2006: 8) in relation to the UK and US. The drive towards performance incorporates a variety of practices from individual performance appraisal which may be linked to higher organizational or government level performance targets and there has also been the development of performance indicators and league tables to inform users about the performance of public services. The consequences for the workforce can be linked to a number of themes.

First, performance management has often been viewed as part of a reform agenda to increase the influence of managers and to reduce the autonomy of professional staff directing them towards government defined targets. Power (1997) memorably termed this

the rise of the Audit Society, signifying the increased number of individuals and institutions subject to more intensive audit requirements and it was widely assumed in the 1980s that professional staff would be losers and managers winners. This characterization has been modified and a more nuanced position has emerged in which it is recognized that individual professional groups (nurses, doctors, teachers, social workers) have fared differently. Occupational control of services remains strong with professional staff sometimes developing hybrid roles in which they can be beneficiaries of NPM reforms, despite resenting the imposition of targets that they had not devised and the workload involved in documenting outcomes (Bach, 2004; Farrell and Morris, 2003; Kirkpatrick et al., 2005). The broader point is that performance management arrangements can either be introduced in a relatively low trust manner focused on the *control* of staff or can be more orientated to *dialogue* and development. Pollitt (2006) reported that performance measurement was used in a more consensual 'dialogue' style approach in Finland and Sweden and to a lesser extent the Netherlands, compared to the harder edged 'control' arrangements in the UK.

Second, there is continuing debate about what type of performance is being measured. An important development is the increased emphasis on responsiveness to the needs of the customer and associated efforts to incorporate service quality indicators into performance measures. Some of the workforce implications mirror broader debates in the service sector about the role of the customer as 'a second boss', with government organizations using mystery shoppers to evaluate the quality of service and the performance of employees. As Rosenthal and Peccei point out, in their study of the UK government employment agency Jobcentre Plus, the idea of the 'customer' has a particular meaning in a public service context. Personal Advisors are charged with facilitating customer choices, but at the same time are under pressure to meet their key target of getting people back into work, involving a degree of compulsion

(Rosenthal and Peccei, 2007). As well as illustrating the increased pressure on public sector staff in a target culture, it also indicates the altered behaviour expected of staff. In hospitals, staff have been required to develop new softer competencies such as communication skills, which emphasized a more explicit managerially-defined customer orientation (Bach, 2004: 192). Finally, these developments are encouraging the search for more rounded forms of performance assessment with increased use of balanced scorecards which incorporate employee and customer feedback as part of the assessment process, an approach adopted by the US Federal Office of Personnel Management (Gowling and Lindholm, 2002).

Most controversial has been the adoption of individual performance-related pay (PRP). This practice can be seen to have several attractive features for public sector organizations. Traditional pay systems, characterized by standard pay rates and service related increments, were perceived as weak tools for the management of employee performance because of their limited ability to motivate and incentivize individuals compared to PRP. More practically, it has been viewed as a means of establishing tighter control of the pay bill. Pay systems which generally paid across the board increases and guaranteed annual increments, could be replaced by an approach which rewarded on a much more selective basis, at the same time signalling that public sector workers are accountable and only receive pay increases linked to performance. PRP has spread across many countries from Canada, the Netherlands, New Zealand, the UK and the USA to Denmark, France, Germany, Ireland and Italy, which have often been viewed as reluctant to introduce performance pay (OECD, 2005). Two points, however, need to be kept in mind. First, the numbers covered by PRP are often very small and confined to senior civil servants. In the French case, it was only in 2004 that an element of performance-pay was piloted for 44 directors of central administration in six ministries and although in 2006 it was extended to other senior civil

servants in these departments, the experiment remains limited to a tiny proportion of civil servants (Ketelaar et al., 2007: 43). Second, although there are a few exceptions, in general the performance component comprises a very small proportion of overall pay – often 1–3 per cent – which raises questions about the degree to which the intended incentive effects can operate.

In the UK, there was considerable resistance to performance-related pay because it was viewed as divisive, an objection also raised by Finnish and Swedish managers (Pollitt, 2006: 33). While the UK government was able to introduce PRP into the civil service where it remained the direct employer, its application in other public services was extremely limited. Indeed, even in the civil service it is questionable whether PRP was effective. In terms of pay bill control, there was such a strong assumption amongst employees of an across the board cost of living increase that any attempt to use PRP to motivate staff required additional pay funding in addition to the existing pay bill. In terms of its value as a management tool, research in the UK Inland Revenue Department cast major doubts on the motivational effects of such schemes for public servants (Marsden and Richardson, 1994). Adopting the tenets of expectancy theory the authors found PRP was unlikely to motivate public servants. The setting of tangible performance objectives for public servants is difficult given the range of stakeholders they have to serve and the nature of their work; the clarity of the link between such objectives and pay is likely to be unclear and weak given various pay constraints; and typically public servants place less weight on pay relative to other rewards, especially where the amounts of performance pay available are small. In the absence of an effective performance appraisal system PRP is invariably ineffective.

These findings have been accepted by the OECD, formerly a leading advocate of performance pay, and they conclude that 'PRP is unlikely to motivate a substantial majority of staff, irrespective of the design' (OECD 2005: 6). Nonetheless, following Marsden

(2004) they suggest that PRP has an important role to play in encouraging goal-setting and appraisal, in stimulating managerial change and in renegotiating effort norms upwards. These developments, however, illustrate a wider point that commentators have become much less assertive about the utility of NPM style reforms. In a recent study the OECD endorses some very traditional drivers of performance stating that: 'the single largest driver of performance is easily overlooked. That regards the retention of skilled and competent staff. A continuing loss of good staff will more than cancel out any gains from performance management' (Ketelaar et al., 2007: 17).

Flexible service delivery

The strengthening of management prerogatives was intended to enable labour to be utilized more flexibly. One of the most well known trends has been the increased contracting out (outsourcing) of public services, with the main appeal being a belief that contracting out or at least making a service subject to competitive tendering would reduce the cost and improve the quality of service provision. These measures were initially promoted by governments of the New Right, for example the UK Conservative government of Mrs Thatcher in the 1980s, that made it mandatory to market-test services such as street cleaning and hospital catering. Trade unions have been concerned about contracting out because of job losses and widening gender pay inequalities and they have experienced difficulties in maintaining and representing their membership. These concerns have become more muted as contracting out is being utilized more as a technical tool of governance, that transcends ideological differences, with more attention paid to safeguarding staff terms and conditions of employment. There is also greater scepticism about claims for cost savings generated with some studies pointing to higher costs arising from poorly specified services, higher monitoring costs and the absence of sufficient competition to encourage

competitive bids. Moreover, there has been a shift of emphasis from a preoccupation with the consequences for the workforce to an emphasis on the impact for users. One concern has been a lack of clarity about governance arrangements, making it difficult for users to complain and hold service providers accountable for poor performance (Local Government Ombudsmen, 2007). Public sector managers have become more discerning purchasers of services and are seeking to engage users more in service provision. For these reasons, although there is some new contracting out, evidence from the US notes an increased trend towards contracting back-in as managers balance technical and political concerns to secure public value (see Brudney et al., 2005; Hefetz et al., 2004).

Attempts to make the public sector more permeable to outside talent, facilitate work-life balance, and ensure the workforce is more representative of the citizens it serves has encouraged the growth of more diverse employment arrangements. In contrast to the tradition of secure lifetime employment there has been more recourse to the use of temporary and fixed-term contracts. The proportion of part-time workers has also increased. In the Netherlands nearly 20 per cent of civil servants work on a part time basis with slightly lower proportions in the UK and Norway. In Australia only 4 per cent of public sector staff worked on a part-time basis in 1995, but this increased to 11 per cent by 2005 (OECD, 2006: 65). Many of these measures impact on women, ethnic minorities and people with disabilities who have been under-represented at senior management level. Although there is a long tradition of gender equality legislation amongst some OECD countries, in others, including Japan and Korea, it is a much more recent concern. Strategic plans and quotas are the main HR instruments being used to raise the proportion (currently under 5 per cent) of women in senior management positions.

In a broad sense these initiatives are attempting to widen career paths as organizations try to grow their own workforce and diversify their staff mix. In the UK, amongst shortage occupations such as social work, municipalities are drawing on local labour markets to develop non-professionally qualified social work assistants to progress into social work (Kessler *et al.*, 2006a) with similar developments occurring in relation to teaching and nursing assistants. The paradox here is that, whereas many flexibility practices such as outsourcing are making more recourse to external labour markets, these type of 'grow your own' strategies are contributing to a reinvigoration of internal labour markets and the type of 'bureaucratic' career structures criticized by the proponents of new public management. The challenge is that it can be very difficult for organizations to blend effectively forms of internal and external labour flexibility and there are some signs that employer enthusiasm for externalization has waned.

Employers have also sought greater flexibility in the manner in which they communicate and involve their workforce. Although public sector unions remain important actors there is some unease amongst public sector unions that they may be on the same trajectory of decline as their private sector counterparts, although there are important variations between countries. In the UK, for more than two decades public sector employers have been relatively indifferent to the role of trade unions and have fostered forms of direct involvement that have made trade unions a less important source of employee voice (Bach, 2004). Martinez-Lucio (2007) highlights the degree to which public sector trade unions have broadened their agenda beyond the defence of collective systems of employment regulation. There has been increased engagement with political campaigns seeking to defend public services and the development of alliances with service users that challenge managerial definitions of customer interests. In Spain and Sweden trade unions have negotiated pacts with government to implement programmes of change, such as total quality management. These developments signal that trade unions are slowly moving beyond a traditional 'producer' agenda to one that seeks alliances with users to shape the reform agenda.

Overall, although greater concern for diversity and related measures to increase the representation of ethnic minorities and persons with disabilities in the public sector are to be welcomed, flexibility is often a euphemism for forms of work intensification. Although HR reforms often seek to emphasize the empowerment of staff and increased participation in decision making, the workforce often experience these reforms in terms of increased customer aggression, more surveillance of their work and associated paperwork to demonstrate their contribution, alongside elements of the Taylorization of work.

TOWARDS RESPONSIVE GOVERNANCE?

The adoption of NPM practices has been very widespread and some countries that were previously resistant to this reform agenda are now more open to it (parts of continental Europe, Japan, India). Nonetheless, there is a growing sense that after two decades, the influence of NPM ideas is waning and some commentators have gone further, suggesting that NPM is dead (Dunleavy et al., 2006). It has been recognized for some time that reforms have been adopted and implemented in an uneven manner because of the degree to which some institutional contexts are more open to embedding NPM reforms than other nation states with more consensual, incremental traditions of change (Pollitt and Bouckaert, 2004; Lynn, 2006). More fundamentally, however, is a realization that only in the last few years have the limitations and unintended consequences of NPM been acknowledged by policy makers. Changes in the reform menu are starting to be implemented, altering the type of HR practices adopted in the public sector. These trends have been accompanied by more forceful criticism of NPM and attempts to rehabilitate bureaucracy, highlighting its resilience and frequently unacknowledged benefits (du Gay, 2005).

Two main limitations of NPM have been noted. The first relates to the consequences of disaggregation and the fragmentation of the public sector with the proliferation of semi-autonomous agencies focused on delivery. This has led to significant transactions costs as nominally independent units have duplicated HR and other functions and in the process there has been a substantial loss of central capacity and institutional learning. These shortcomings can be illustrated by experience of the UK executive agencies who were allowed to develop their own agency based pay and grading structures which led to the break-up of national pay determination. The emphasis on delegated pay and grading structures within individual agencies has led to a loss of coherence; there are considerable inconsistencies in pay rates for similar posts and concerns about the absence of gender proofing in pay systems. The break up of a unified civil service has made 'joined-up' government more difficult, inhibiting movement within and between departments which was possible under a unified civil service (Kessler et al., 2006b). In an influential analysis Rhodes (1997; 2007) pointed to the hollowing out of the state from above (by ceding competencies to the European Union), from below (by outsourcing) and sideways (from the spread of executive agencies). He suggested that this led to fragmented service delivery, more networks, operating in a more complex environment, and further constrained the ability of politicians to steer the system, which encouraged further regulation and audit of nominally independent agencies.

The second shortcoming relates to the impact on managerial and workforce behaviour of the incentive structures and targets that are becoming a defining feature of the public sector context. Although directing more attention at enhanced performance has gained wide support, there is considerable unease about the narrow and short-term orientation this has encouraged. The development of a competitive ethos has frequently discouraged co-operation and this has led to detrimental effects as collective, system-wide needs have been neglected. A highly critical report on workforce planning in the NHS concluded that the devolution of workforce planning to individual NHS hospitals led managers to neglect this function and underestimate their requirements, resulting in catastrophic shortages of health sector personnel (Health Committee, 2007). A similar failure of collective action arises can be seen in the increases in hospital acquired infections in the UK which has been associated with increase in outsourcing. These examples raise broader issues of accountability, which were widely debated in the Cave Creek tragedy in New Zealand in which fourteen people were killed in a national park. There was controversy over whether the chief executive of the agency should have resigned or if blame lay with the politicians that established the fiscal and performance environment in which the tragedy occurred (Chapman and Duncan, 2007). There have also been concerns that under NPM an imprecise but nonetheless powerful public sector ethos has been eroded by the disempowerment of professional staff and the establishment of a low-trust managerial culture; this is certainly a widely-voiced grievance amongst professional staff in the UK (Audit Commission, 2002; Bach, 2004).

These developments signal that NPM has lost some of its potency and given way to a new discourse and set of practices associated with governance and networks. The emphasis has shifted from 'government' to 'governance' which focuses on the interdependence between actors, which include the public, private and voluntary sector. These networks may be steered by the state, but they have a degree of autonomy from the state and signal the attempts to overcome the fragmentation of the state under NPM (Rhodes, 2007). The trajectory of public management reforms is represented in stylized fashion in Table 33.1.

For countries such as the UK and New Zealand, which embraced the NPM agenda wholeheartedly, such an approach sets new managerial challenges which revolve around dealing with a diverse array of

Table 33.1 Three models of public administration

	Public administration	Public management	Responsive governance
Citizen-state relationship	Obedience	Entitlement	Empowerment
Accountability of senior officials	Politicians	Customers	Citizens and stakeholders
Guiding principles	Compliance with rules and regulations	Efficiency and results	Accountability, transparency and participation
Key attribute	Impartiality	Performance	Responsiveness
Organizational structure	Hierarchy	Markets	Networks
HR Policy	Distinctive: Specific public sector HR framework	Convergence: HR policy emulates private sector norms	Differentiated: Private sector policies adapted to values of the public domain
Labour-management relations	Traditional: formal institutional mechanisms for voice	Unilateral: managerial discretion and top-down communications	Partnership: a mixture of direct and indirect (via unions) employee involvement

Source: Adapted from UN DESA 2005: 7 © United Nations 2005. Reproduced with permission.

agencies and stakeholders to ensure the delivery of more effective public services.

Organizational reintegration

The reintegration theme seeks to join up and coordinate government activity to reverse the fragmentation of the state into individual corporate entities (Christensen et al., 2007). Mergers of formerly separate agencies to improve co-ordination and effectiveness have occurred in the UK and in New Zealand specialist organizations such as the Special Education Services have been reabsorbed into their parent departments (Dunleavy et al., 2006; Chapman and Duncan, 2007). In Finland 'horizontal governance' has been a key priority for civil service reform with four overarching policy programmes. This approach requires different competencies of senior civil servants, who are assessed on their ability to share knowledge and establish partnerships (Lodge and Kalitowski, 2007). These developments signal a shift away from the idea of the minimalist state towards one in which the state re-engages with its responsibility for its citizens. One outcome has been that since 2000 state employment has started to grow across the OECD as, contrary to the prevailing view of the 1980s, citizens with a heightened sensitivity to risk seem to expect more state intervention to deal with the challenges of modern life. In the case of outsourced airport security, because of concerns about accountability and performance, after the 9/11 terrorist attacks these functions were returned to federal employment. In the UK and New Zealand the government has effectively re-nationalized the rail network and these measures have been accompanied by the ending of sub-contracting of railway maintenance, following a number of high-profile track failures which resulted in fatalities or serious injury in England.

This reintegration theme has also seen a rebalancing of the HR freedoms assigned to individual organizational units and a greater emphasis on managerial discretion being exercised within national framework agreements. This reaffirmation of national employment relations institutions is evident in recent National Health Service pay reforms. There has been a move away from a philosophy of individual trust hospital autonomy and renewed emphasis on NHS trusts implementing core standards, which include a national job evaluation scheme and an NHS wide knowledge and skills framework. These developments also signify some dilution of the drive towards a competitive and commercial ethos with Crown Health Enterprises in New Zealand reverting to being called 'public hospitals' and no longer being guided by commercial principles (Chapman and Duncan, 2007).

Citizen-centred services

A second element concerns citizen involvement and attempts to re-engineer services in a way that focuses on particular client groups and ensures more integrated service delivery. Traditionally, children's services have been divided between health, education and social services departments, but local authorities have established Directors of Children's services and the UK government has set up a central government Ministry for children and families. Similarly 'One Stop Shops' provide service users with a single gateway to a range of services, often accessible by telephone or online. Such a service has not only required multi-skilling, with employees now having to deal with a wide range of queries, but it has often been provided by call centres and therefore in a new type of working environment. These types of reform raise difficult issues about the harmonization of formerly separate HR systems and practices. For example, how are differences in management style addressed in multi-disciplinary community mental healthcare teams where local authority social workers, used to an inclusive and supportive managerial approach, come together with health service staff familiar with a more hierarchical medical-management culture?

Perhaps more profoundly, a citizen-centred approach has begun to challenge traditional work practices. There has been a generalized shift towards the delegation of work from professionals to semi-professionals or assistants, for example the increased authority of nurses to prescribe drugs and manage their own clinics. These developments can ensure more citizen-centred services as often assistants are perceived as more approachable than professionals and these changes can also lead to substantial shifts in the composition of employment with the growth of intermediate occupations. Professions within public services are not only relinquishing some authority to lower-level occupations, but also

adjusting to increased citizen involvement in policy and decision-making making. These initiatives include the use of opinion surveys, focus groups, citizen juries and e-democracy initiatives. In British Columbia, Canada, a Citizens Assembly, comprising 160 ordinary citizens, were tasked with determining the future of the state's electoral systems. These changes not only shift civil servants from policy advisor roles to policy coordination roles, but also indicate that professionals working in more networked and open contexts require different competencies and development (Lodge and Kalitowski, 2007).

Partnership with the workforce

A final element concerns a greater focus on HR issues, which moves beyond a narrow focus on individual performance under NPM towards an agenda focused on employee engagement, leadership development and partnership with the workforce. There is increased awareness that as employment in the public sector is deprivileged and some long-standing assumptions (e.g. more secure employment) are challenged, there is a requirement to engage the workforce to ensure retention and high-quality services. In Australia, Luxembourg and Denmark, retention of public employees is an explicit priority for the government. A commission was set up in Australia during 2003 to establish good practice and suggest practical measures to retain employees, whilst Luxembourg uses pension supplements to achieve the same goal (OECD, 2007).

Governments are trying to re-engage professionals that often felt persecuted by NPM reforms. The UK government has sought to ally itself with professionals by stressing its concern to try to improve their working lives. It has sought to do this by re-structuring the workforce in ways which allow professionals to focus on their core activities. It has used this rationale to justify its pursuit of more flexible work practices. This is illustrated in the case of education in the UK. A workforce re-modelling agreement has attempted to challenge professional job boundaries by giving whole class responsibilities to a new teaching assistant role but at the very same time it has guaranteed that certain administrative 'burdens' will be removed from teachers. Similarly, in the health service the government explicitly implemented an 'Improving Working Lives' standard and this was part of an attempt to demonstrate that the state is an 'employer of choice'. Significant steps have been taken to improve the pay position of public sector employees and, in terms of the greater direct employee involvement mentioned, survey evidence suggests that public sector employees are much more likely than those in the private sector to be communicated with and informed than those in the private sector (Kersley et al., 2005). For example, two thirds of public sector workers are covered by a staff survey, while the figure is barely a third in the private sector.

The term partnership has also emerged in government attempts to change its relationship with the trade unions, although in the UK case there has been a degree of ambiguity about this involvement. Trade unions have continued to express concerns about their inability to prevent increased private sector involvement in service provision and at the workplace level there is considerable evidence to suggest that partnership working is often based on a restricted form of union involvement (Bach, 2004). Similar attempts to promote partnership working with trade unions occurred in the USA in the early 1990s, but also ran into difficulties in terms of the degree of management commitment and uncertainties about the degree of union representativeness (Masters and Albright, 2003).

Overall these three elements indicate a partial reinstatement of the distinctive values and beliefs of the public domain. Against a backdrop of corporate scandals and increased awareness of the degree to which commercial values and narrow self-interest can jeopardize the aspiration to deliver effective services to *all* citizens on equal basis, there have been renewed efforts to identify the core values of public service and in many countries these type of values are being incorporated into codes of conduct, selection criteria and leadership competencies. There is also a growing expectation that staff from the private sector will be attracted into the public sector, not because it is seeking to emulate the private sector, but because of its distinctive ethos, better quality of working life and more rewarding work, a trend noted by Roubon (2007: 479) in his discussion of France.

CONCLUSION

In recent years, the public sector in most countries has been caught up in a continuous process of reform that has major consequences for HR practice. The rise of the NPM movement signified a rejection of traditional models of HRM in the public sector. The establishment of a more assertive managerialism, in conjunction with tighter control of resources, forms of marketization, and changes in organizational structures, ensured that the burden of adjustment was placed squarely on the workforce. Although in many countries the public sector became more efficient, for the workforce this efficiency drive was mainly associated with more intensive working practices, downsizing, tighter control of performance and the dilution of union influence. In terms of HR practice, there have been attempts to 'deprivilege' the employment conditions of public sector workers and there has been a degree of convergence between employment practices in the public and private sector.

In recent years, some of the unexpected consequences of the NPM have increasingly been acknowledged. These difficulties often stemmed from a failure of the NPM reforms to recognize that HR practice has to facilitate both the efficient delivery of public services and also enshrine deeper constitutional values that make up an irreducible political core at the heart of the public sector. Ironically, some of the much derided features of the traditional 'bureaucratic' model of HR practice are being reinvented as the limitations of a fragmented and narrowly-focused target approach are recognized. More emphasis is being placed on valuing the workforce and modernization often explicitly seeks to shift from a cost minimization approach to one modelled on the 'high performance workplace'. There still remains doubt, however, about the capacity of public sector employers to move in this direction at the same time as pressure to demonstrate enhanced efficiency and quality of service intensify.

What is clear is that the public sector will continue to experience organizational reform. The HR agenda will have to take account of a wider variety of providers delivering public services, encompassing public, private and third sector providers and a more diverse workforce, less dominated by the traditional professions, will need to respond to increasingly vocal and demanding citizens.

REFERENCES

Audit Commission (2002) *Recruitment and Retention*. London: Audit Commission.

Bach, S. (2004) *Employment Relations and the Health Service: The Management of Reforms*. London: Routledge.

Bach, S. and Della Rocca, G. (2000) 'The management strategies of public service employers in Europe', *Industrial Relations Journal*, 31 (2): 82–97.

Bordogna, L. (2007) *Industrial Relations in the Public Sector*. Dublin: European Foundation for the Improvement of Living and Working Conditions. www.eurofound.europa.eu/eiro/comparative_index.html

Boston, J., Martin, J., Pallot, J. and Walsh, P. (1996) *Public Management: The New Zealand Model*. Oxford: Oxford University Press.

Boxall, P. Purcell, J. (2003) *Strategy and Human Resource Management*. Basingstoke: Palgrave Macmillan.

Brudney, J., Fernandez, S., Ryu, J. and Wright, D. (2005) 'Exploring and explaining contracting out: Patterns among the American states', *Journal of Public Administration Research and Theory*, 15 (3): 393–419.

Chapman, J. and Duncan, G. (2007) 'Is there now a new "New Zealand model",' *Public Management Review*, 9 (1): 1–25.

Christensen, T., Lie, A. and Laegreid, P. (2007) 'Still fragmented government or reassertion of the centre?', in Christensen, T. and Laegreid, P. (eds) *Transcending New Public Management*. Aldershot: Ashgate. 17–41.

Du Gay, P. (ed) (2005) *The Values of Bureaucracy*. Oxford: Oxford University Press.

Dunleavy, P., Margetts, H., Bastow, S. and Tinkler, J. (2006) 'New public management is dead – long live digital era governance', *Journal of Public Administration Research and Theory*, 16 (3): 467–94.

Farrell, C. and Morris, J. (2003) 'The "Neo-Bureaucratic" state: Professionals, managers and professional managers in schools, general practices and social work', *Organization*, 10 (1): 129–56.

Ferner, A. (1988) *Government, Managers and Industrial Relations*. Oxford: Blackwell.

Glyn, A. (2007) *Capitalism Unleashed: Finance Globalisation and Welfare*. Oxford: Oxford University Press.

Gowling, M. and Lindholm, M-L. (2002) 'Human resources management in the public sector', *Human Resource Management*, 41 (3): 283–95.

Grainger, H. and Crowther, P. (2007) *Trade Union Membership 2006*. London: BERR. http://www.berr.gov.uk/files/file39006.pdf

Health Committee (2007) *Workforce Planning: Fourth Report of Session 2006–07*. London: The Stationery Office.

Heap, D. (2005) 'Characteristics of people employed in the public sector', *Labour Market Trends*, 13 (12): 489–500.

Hefetz, A. and Warner, M. (2004) 'Privatization and its reverse: Explaining the dynamics of the government contracting process', *Journal of Public Administrative Research and Theory*, 14 (2): 171–90.

Heskett, J., Sasser, E. and Schlesinger, L. (2003) *The Value Profit Chain*. Harvard: Harvard Business Press.

Hood, C. (1991) 'A public management for all seasons', *Public Administration*, 69 (1): 3–19.

Houston, D. (2006) 'Walking the walk of public service motivation: public employees and charitable gifts of time blood and money', *Journal of Public Administration Research and Theory*, 16 (1): 67–86.

Keller, B. (1999) 'Germany: Negotiated change, modernization and the challenge of unification', in Bach, S., Bordogna, L., Della Rocca, G. and Winchester, D. (eds) *Public Service Employment Relations in Europe*. London: Routledge, 56–93.

Kessler, I., Bach, S. and Heron, P. (2006a) 'Occupational boundaries in the public services: Assistant roles in social care', *Work, Employment and Society*, 20 (4): 667–85.

Kessler, I. Heron, P. and Ganyon, S. (2006b) 'The fragmentation of pay determination in the civil services: A union member perspective', *Personnel Review*, 35 (1): 6–28.

Ketelaar, A., Manning, N. and Turkisch, E. (2007) *Performance-based Arrangements for Senior Civil Servants. OECD and Other Country Experiences*. Paris: OECD.

Kettl, D. (2000) *The Global Public Management Revolution: A Report on the Transformation of Governance.* Washington: Brookings Institution.

Kirkpatrick, I., Ackroyd, S. and Walker, R. (2005) *The New Managerialism and Public Service Professions,* Palgrave: Basingstoke.

Le Grand, J. (2003) *Motivation, Agency and Public Policy,* Oxford: Oxford University Press.

Local Government Ombudsmen (2007) *Local Partnerships and Citizen Redress.* London: Commission for Local Administration in England.

Lodge, G. and Kalitowski, S. (2007) *Innovations in Government.* London: Institute for Public Policy Research.

Lynn, L. (2006) *Public Management: Old and New.* Abingdon: Routledge.

Marsden, D. and Richardson, R. (1994) 'Performance pay: The effects of merit pay on motivation in the public services', *British Journal of Industrial Relations,* 32 (2): 243–61.

Marsden, D. (2004) 'The role of performance-related pay in renegotiating the "effort-bargain": The case of the British public sector', *Industrial and Labor Relations Review,* 57 (3): 350–70.

Martinez-Lucio, M. (2007) 'Trade unions and employment relations in the context of public sector change', *International Journal of Public Sector Management,* 20 (1): 5–15.

Masters, M. and Albright, R. (2003) 'Federal labor management partnerships: Perspectives, performance, and possibilities', in Brock, J. and Lipsky, D. (eds) *Going Public.* Champagne: IIRA, pp. 171–210.

McCourt, W. (2001) 'The new public selection? anticorruption, psychometric selection and the new public management in Nepal', *Public Management Review,* 3 (3): 325–43.

Moynihan, D. (2003) 'Public management policy in the United States during the Clinton era', *International Public Management Journal,* 6 (3): 371–94.

Niskanen, W. (1971) *Bureaucracy and Representative Government,* Chicago: Aldine-Atherton.

OECD (1995) *Governance in Transition: Public Management Reforms in OECD Countries.* Paris: OECD.

OECD (2004) *Policy Brief: Public Sector Modernisation Changing Organizational Structures.* Paris: OECD.

OECD (2005) *Policy Brief: Paying for Performance: Policies for Government Employees.* Paris: OECD.

OECD (2007) *Public Sector Pensions and the Challenge of an Ageing Workforce.* OECD Working Papers on Public Governance, 2007/2. OECD: Paris.

Osborne, D. and Gaebler, T. (1992) *Reinventing Government.* Reading, Mass: Addisson Wensley.

Power, M. (1997) *The Audit Society.* Oxford: Oxford University Press.

Pollitt, C. (2006) 'Performance management in practice: A comparative study of study executive agencies', *Journal of Public Administrative Research and Theory,* 16 (1): 25–44.

Pollitt, C. and Boukaert, G. (2004) *Public Management Reform,* Oxford: Oxford University Press.

Rhodes, R. (1997) *Understanding Governance.* Buckingham: Open University Press.

Rhodes, R. (2007) 'Understanding governance – Ten years on', *Organization Studies,* 28 (8): 1243–64.

Rosenthal, P. and Peccei, R. (2007) 'The work you want, the help you need': Constructing the customer in jobcentre plus', *Organization,* 14 (2): 201–23.

Rouban, L. (2007) 'Public management and politics: Senior bureaucrats in France', *Public Administration,* 85 (2): 473–501.

Thomason, T. and Burton, J. (2003) 'Unionization trends and labor–management cooperation in the public sector' in Brock, J. and Lipsky, D. (eds) *Going Public.* Champagne: IIRA, pp. 171–210.

Ulrich, D. (2001) *Human Resource Champions: The Next Agenda for Adding Value and Delivering Results.* Harvard: Harvard University Press.

United Nations (2005) *World Public Sector Report 2005.*

World Health Organisation (2006) *Working Together for Health.* Geneva: WHO.

Index

Supporting researchers for more than forty years

Research methods have always been at the core of SAGE's publishing. Sara Miller McCune founded SAGE in 1965 and soon after, she published SAGE's first methods book, Public Policy Evaluation. A few years later, she launched the Quantitative Applications in the Social Sciences series – affectionately known as the "little green books".

Always at the forefront of developing and supporting new approaches in methods, SAGE published early groundbreaking texts and journals in the fields of qualitative methods and evaluation.

Today, more than forty years and two million little green books later, SAGE continues to push the boundaries with a growing list of more than 1,200 research methods books, journals, and reference works across the social, behavioral, and health sciences.

From qualitative, quantitative, mixed methods to evaluation, SAGE is the essential resource for academics and practitioners looking for the latest methods by leading scholars.

www.sagepublications.com

The Qualitative Research Kit

Edited by Uwe Flick

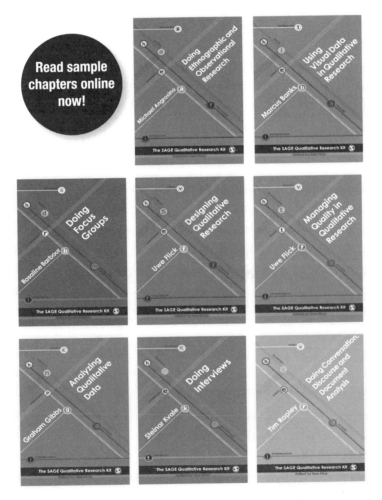

Read sample chapters online now!

Doing Ethnographic and Observational Research — Michael Angrosino — The SAGE Qualitative Research Kit

Using Visual Data in Qualitative Research — Marcus Banks — The SAGE Qualitative Research Kit

Doing Focus Groups — Rosaline Barbour — The SAGE Qualitative Research Kit

Designing Qualitative Research — Uwe Flick — The SAGE Qualitative Research Kit

Managing Quality in Qualitative Research — Uwe Flick — The SAGE Qualitative Research Kit

Analyzing Qualitative Data — Graham Gibbs — The SAGE Qualitative Research Kit

Doing Interviews — Steinar Kvale — The SAGE Qualitative Research Kit

Doing Conversation, Discourse and Document Analysis — Tim Rapley — The SAGE Qualitative Research Kit

www.sagepub.co.uk

Research Methods Books from SAGE

www.sagepub.co.uk